EXAMPLES & EXPLANATIONS

Contracts

EXAMPLES & EXPLANATIONS

Contracts

Ninth Edition

Brian A. Blum
Lewis & Clark Distinguished Professor of Law
Lewis & Clark Law School

ASPEN
PUBLISHING

To contact Customer Service, e-mail customer.service@aspenpublishing.com, call 1-800-950-5259, or mail correspondence to:

Aspen Publishing
Attn: Order Department
1 Wall Street
Burlington, MA 01803

Printed in the United States of America.

1 2 3 4 5 6 7 8 9 0

ISBN 979-8-8890-6812-9

Library of Congress Cataloging-in-Publication Data application is in process.

SUSTAINABLE FORESTRY INITIATIVE Certified Sourcing
www.forests.org
SFI-00756

About Aspen Publishing

Aspen Publishing is a leading provider of legal educational content and digital learning solutions in the U.S. and around the world. Aspen provides best-in-class solutions through authoritative textbooks, written by renowned authors, and breakthrough products such as Connected eBooks, Connected Quizzing, PracticePerfect, and JD-Next.

The Aspen Casebook Series (famously known among law faculty and students as the "red and black" casebooks) encompasses hundreds of highly regarded textbooks in more than eighty disciplines, from large enrollment courses, such as Torts and Contracts, to emerging electives, like Sustainability and the Law of Policing. Study aids such as *Examples & Explanations* help law students master complex subject matter. Aspen's Paralegal, Criminal Justice, and Business Law series bring our hallmark publishing standards to undergraduate students. JD-Next is an innovative online law school prep course and admissions test that offers a realistic preview of law school, teaches underlying skills for academic success, and assesses applicants' academic readiness for law school.

Aspen Publishing is proud to be a UWorld company

Since 2003, UWorld has been a global leader in developing high-quality learning tools for students preparing for high-stakes exams. With a commitment to excellence, UWorld has helped millions of students in undergraduate, graduate, and professional programs in fields such as medicine, nursing, finance, and law achieve their academic and career goals.

Founded by Chandra S. Pemmasani, M.D., during his medical residency, UWorld began focusing on medical education and has since expanded into various academic fields, including law. In 2020, UWorld launched its Legal vertical, starting with its comprehensive Multistate Bar Exam (MBE®) Question Bank, followed by the acquisition of Themis Bar Review, which integrated resources to provide a complete bar exam preparation experience. In 2024, UWorld expanded its offerings by acquiring Aspen Publishing, enhancing its suite of legal education products.

Today, UWorld offers an unparalleled range of study materials that blend active learning methods with expert content, ensuring students and educators can access the most effective resources. From bar preparation to law school success, UWorld is committed to supporting the next generation of legal professionals. Learn more at uworld.com.

To Bryce, Kylie, William,

Lexie, and Katherine with love

Summary of Contents

Contents

Preface

This book aims at helping law students to learn and understand the law of contracts. Most students will use it as a supplementary text in preparing for class, clarifying and supplementing readings assigned for class, reviewing class discussion, and preparing for exams. In deciding on the scope, depth, and approach of the book's coverage I have drawn on my many years of teaching contract law and my perception of which issues and questions students find most difficult. I have focused on what is likely to be most appropriate and helpful to a person who approaches contract law for the first time. This book's goal is to provide clear explanation of the doctrines of contract law, to identify the policies that underlie them, and to show how these doctrines tie in with each other to form the overall law of contracts. I believe that it is important to present legal discussion in concrete form, so I use factual illustrations throughout the book, some hypothetical and some in court opinions, to aid in the explanation of legal rules and principles and to show how they are applied in a factual context.

Changes in the Ninth Edition

In revising this book for the ninth edition, I have retained the scope, approach, and coverage of the eighth edition, including the expanded treatment of standard contracts and contracts formed through electronic media, and notes on the transnational perspective of contract law. I have not changed the overall organization of the book, but have made small changes in the internal reorganization of some chapters to improve clarity. In my revisions for the ninth edition, I have continued my efforts to provide an accessible treatment of the law of contracts, altering text and diagrams to the extent necessary to update and clarify the discussion, adding new cases, and refining the Examples and Explanations by adding new ones and changing or eliminating some of the older ones.

The ninth edition continues to have a glossary at the end of the book, followed by tables of cases and statutes and a comprehensive index.

The Treatment of the Sale of Goods in the Ninth Edition

The ninth edition continues to cover contracts for the sale of goods, governed by Article 2 of the Uniform Commercial Code (UCC Article 2). The extent to which UCC Article 2 is part of the syllabus in contracts courses varies. Some contracts courses omit coverage of UCC Article 2, leaving sales of goods to an elective upper-class course. Others include it to a greater or lesser extent. This book covers sales of goods to the extent that a student may need it in a contracts course that includes the study of UCC Article 2. It discusses applicable provisions of UCC Article 2 with regard to each topic in which sales of goods are subject to rules that differ from those applicable to other contracts. Discussions of UCC Article 2 are clearly demarcated in the text to allow students to identify them.

The Style, Approach, and Purpose of This Book

Materials assigned for reading in preparation for class and the discussion of those materials in class can leave students with uncertainty and questions. Supplementary reading is very helpful to understanding and digesting what is covered in class. To be most useful, such a supplementary text should be written with an awareness of the coverage, depth, and scope of most contracts courses, and with a sense of what students are likely to need by way of additional reading. In writing this book, I have tried to keep that goal in mind. Relying on my own experience as a teacher of contract law, and on the content of casebooks, I have tried to maintain the discussion in this book at the level of sophistication that may be expected in a typical contracts class.

To achieve this purpose, it is not enough to outline legal rules or to state doctrine. Although it is surely one of the aims of a contracts class to teach the current rules of law governing contracts, a knowledge of current legal rules is only one of the components of an adequate understanding of contract law. Students are also expected to comprehend the derivation and development of the rules, their historical and contemporary rationale, the public policies that they are meant to serve, and the way in which they coalesce to form a coherent body of law. Rules and their underlying policies are not static. They develop and change over time, they are often unsettled or formulated differently in different states, and some are the subject of controversy. Therefore, students must also be exposed to the uncertainties of the law and must learn to develop the ability to evaluate critically, to form judgments, and to articulate arguments for or against a legal proposition. In addition, like so many other courses in law school, a contracts course serves the goal of exposing students to broader issues of legal process, legal analysis, dispute resolution, and lawyering skills such as drafting, advising, and evaluating the strength of a case. This book attempts to encompass this range of learning. Its principal aim is the clear and accessible explanation of the fundamentals of the law, with a particular concentration on what information is likely to be helpful to a student who approaches the subject for the first time.

As part of the effort to clarify legal principles and the relationships between contracting parties, I have used diagrams where I believe that visual representations are helpful in clarifying and reinforcing verbal exposition.

The Use of Examples and Explanations

Concrete examples place doctrine and abstract principles in context and show how they operate to affect behavior and resolve disputes. I therefore use factual illustrations extensively, some hypothetical and some drawn from decided cases, in the text itself to illustrate concepts under discussion. In addition, a distinctive feature of this book is the Examples and Explanations at the end of each chapter. Their purpose is not only to provide further illustration and discussion of the subject matter of the text but also to give students a means of self-testing on the topics covered. The Examples pose questions based on hypothetical facts, and the Explanations analyze and offer a resolution to the problems. As a general rule, the Examples and Explanations do more than simply provide a means of reviewing what has been stated in the text. To resolve them adequately, a student must use reasoned argument and must thoughtfully apply the principles set out in the text. You will therefore benefit the most from them if you do not merely read through them but rather take the time to formulate your own answer to an Example before reading its Explanation. This will allow you to test your knowledge and understanding of the material, to practice identifying issues, and to develop skills in composing and organizing answers to the kind of questions commonly found in exams.

The Organization of This Book in Relation to Your Contracts Course

There are a number of different ways to organize a contracts course, and the casebooks reflect quite a diverse approach to the sequence in which material may be covered in class. It is therefore quite possible that a particular contracts course will not follow the same sequence as the chapters in this book. (For example, some courses begin with remedies for breach of contract, which is not covered here until Chapter 18.) I have written this book with an eye on the divergent ways in which the topics of contract law are presented in different classes, so a student should have no trouble reading chapters out of order. To use this book in the same sequence as your contracts course, simply refer to the table of contents to find the part of the book that deals with the subject under discussion in class. You can also use the index, table of cases, and table of statutes to find those sections of the book and those Examples and Explanations that correspond to what you are studying in class.

One of the goals of this book is to help students to see the interconnection between the various doctrines that are covered in the contracts course.

To this end, I have included numerous cross-references in each chapter to direct you to topics covered elsewhere in the book, which have a relationship to the topic discussed in that chapter.

A Recommendation to Read Chapters 1 Through 3 at the Start of Your Contracts Course

Irrespective of the organization of your class, I recommend that you read Chapters 1, 2, and 3 as soon as possible. These short chapters are intended as an introduction to some of the root principles of contract law and legal analysis. They contain basic information and guidance on core concepts, terminology, and case analysis that may not be expressly articulated in your class materials or discussion. By taking the time to work through these chapters at the beginning of the semester, you can avoid the confusion and uncertainty that could arise from unfamiliarity with these basic principles.

The Glossary

A glossary at the end of the book contains succinct definitions of terms that you are likely to encounter in the contracts course. Some of these terms relate specifically to contract law, and others are legal terms that are used more widely. Most of these terms are explained in the body of the book, but the glossary is a means of finding a quick explanation of their meaning.

The Use and Citation of Authority in This Book

To make this book as readable and accessible as possible, I have kept citation of authority to a minimum. You will not find detailed footnotes and citations that you would expect in a treatise or law review article. However, some sources of authority are an integral part of the process of learning contract law and are referred to constantly throughout the book. They are:

1. The Restatement (Second) of Contracts (referred to in the book in abbreviated form as Restatement, Second), a compendious and highly influential formulation of the rules of contract law. The Restatement, Second is introduced and described in Chapter 1.
2. Articles 1 and 2 of the Uniform Commercial Code (UCC). Article 2, governing contracts for the sale of goods, is the principal focus of the book's discussion of the UCC. Article 1 is supplementary to Article 2. It has general provisions applicable to all Articles of the UCC, including Article 2. The scope and operation of these Articles of the UCC are introduced and explained in Chapter 2 and specific provisions are covered throughout the book.

3. Caselaw. Court opinions are a vital source of law in our system. I discuss many cases in the text and in some of the Explanations. I do not use cases merely as authority for legal rules but as factual illustrations and as a means of highlighting legal principles, argument, and reasoning. I selected many of the cases in this book because of their interesting or even entertaining facts. I have tried to use recent cases wherever possible to reflect the law in its contemporary state. However, there are many important or well-known older cases that are commonly taught in contracts courses, and I have included many of those, too. You should therefore find that at least some of the cases discussed here are also included in your class materials.

Brian A. Blum
February 2025

Acknowledgments

I owe thanks to many people who have helped me with successive editions of this book. I have had able research assistance from a number of Lewis and Clark students for each edition. I have also benefited from the guidance and careful editorial work of several members of the staff of Aspen Publishing. Finally, I am grateful to the many students and professors who have used this book and who have offered comments and suggestions.

Contracts

CHAPTER 1

The Meaning of "Contract" and the Basic Attributes of the Contractual Relationship

§1.1 INTRODUCTION

The first three chapters of this book introduce and articulate basic concepts about contract law and the American[1] legal system. Many of the principles and concepts introduced in these three initial chapters appear frequently throughout the book. The purpose of including them here is to form a grounding for legal analysis and to identify themes that run through contract law. This discussion emphasizes that learning the law is more than learning rules. Rules do not exist in a vacuum but must be understood in light of historical perspective, public policy, legal theory, and the legal process.

This chapter begins the introductory survey by defining what is meant by a contract, providing a brief overview of a number of the central themes of contract law, and broadly sketching the contractual relationship. Chapter 2 describes some of the fundamental concepts and distinctions that are essential to a comprehension of contract law in the context of the American legal system as a whole. It explains the importance of historical perspective and

1. Contract law in the United States is commonly referred to as "American" contract law. This is a handy but imprecise label for two reasons. First, the United States is only one of many American countries. Second, as section 2.6 explains, there is no single, unified body of contract law in the United States because contract law is state, not federal law. Therefore, there are over 50 bodies of contract law in the United States, including all the states, U.S. territories, and the District of Columbia. However, there are general principles of contract law that are recognized in all these jurisdictions.

legal theory, describes the nature of the common law system, and introduces the crucial distinction between judge-made law and statutory law, with particular reference to the statute that pervades contract law, Article 2 of the Uniform Commercial Code (UCC), governing contracts for the sale of goods. Chapter 3 concentrates on the nature and composition of judicial opinions and on the method of analyzing and gleaning legal rules from them. Its primary purpose is to explain the doctrine of precedent as it applies in contract law and in the legal system as a whole. The Examples in Chapter 3 are based on a specimen opinion, constructed to provide an exercise in reading, understanding, and applying the precedent of a judicial decision. Contract law is commonly taught through the study of court decisions, so Chapter 3's exercise in the principles and methodology of analyzing a court opinion provides an early opportunity to understand how to approach caselaw and case analysis.

§1.2 THE LEGAL MEANING OF "CONTRACT"

In simple terms, a contract is an exchange relationship created by oral or written agreement between two or more persons, containing at least one promise, and recognized in law as enforceable. This definition reflects several essential elements:

1. An agreement between two or more persons
2. An exchange relationship
3. At least one promise
4. Enforceability

The central concept of each of these elements is introduced below and is discussed in greater detail later in the book.

§1.2.1 An Agreement Between Two or More Persons

a. A Voluntary, Consensual Relationship, Objectively Determined

A contract is a voluntary, consensual relationship between two or more parties. A contract is created by agreement between the parties on the essential terms of their relationship. The element of agreement distinguishes contractual obligation from many other kinds of legal duty (such as the obligation to compensate for negligent injury or to pay taxes) that arise by operation of law from some act or event, without the need for assent.

Although voluntary agreement between the parties is essential to the creation of contract, "agreement" in the legal sense is subject to an important qualification. The law does not require that the parties reach true agreement, in a subjective sense—that their minds are in accord. It is enough that the words and conduct of a party, evaluated on an objective standard, would lead the other party reasonably to understand that agreement was reached. (The reason for using this objective standard is explained in sections 1.4.3 and 4.1.) The requirement that assent must be voluntary means that a party must have sufficient volition to satisfy the legal standard of assent. A court will not likely enforce a contract against a party whose apparent assent falls below this standard because, for example, it was extorted or induced by deceit. (Chapters 13 and 14 focus on several doctrines under which courts evaluate the quality of apparent consent.)

Many, if not most, contracts are not actually negotiated, but are entered into on standard terms, drafted in advance by one of the parties and presented to the other as nonnegotiable. Contract law recognizes the reality and validity of standard contracting and generally treats the nondrafting party's assent to nonnegotiable standard terms as sufficient. Standard contracting is discussed in many parts of this book, but is the particular focus of section 4.1, Chapters 5 and 6, and section 13.12.

b. Most Agreements Do Not Need to Be Recorded to Be Valid

Unless the contract is of a type that is required by statute (called a "statute of frauds") to be recorded[2] and signed, it does not have to be recorded to be a binding and enforceable legal obligation. Most contracts are not covered by a statute of frauds, so that they become binding as soon as oral agreement has been reached. Of course, it may be harder to prove an oral contract than one that has been recorded and signed, but problems of proof should not be confused with the more fundamental question of enforceability.

c. Contracts Distinguished from Nonbinding Agreements

Although contract requires a voluntary agreement between the parties, this does not mean that all voluntary agreements are contracts. People make all kinds of agreements that do not rise to the level of contract. For example, social agreements (the acceptance of a dinner invitation or a commitment

2. The term "recorded" is used throughout this book to mean that the contract is either written in a tangible paper document or is otherwise in a retrievable record in electronic or other form. Before the advent of electronic or other means of recording a document, the common law distinguished written from oral contracts. Today, recording by means other than in a tangible form is recognized as legally effective. Chapter 11 on the statute of frauds fully explains when and to what extent a contract must be recorded in some form, rather than merely agreed to orally, to be legally enforceable.

to go together to see a movie), a politician's campaign promises, and a spouse's promise to clean out the attic next weekend are not contracts. Courts sometimes describe promises of this kind as moral or ethical obligations, rather than legal ones. The distinction between a legally binding contractual obligation and moral obligation is not always easy to draw, but often this question is settled by determining the intent of the parties (measured objectively). In some cases, there may be other indications that the agreement creates only a moral obligation. For example, the requirement of exchange, discussed in section 1.2.2, may be missing. For this reason (as explained in Chapter 7), a promise to give a gift or to contribute to charity may create a moral obligation, but it usually does not qualify as a legally binding contractual obligation.

§1.2.2 An Exchange Relationship

A contract is a relationship. By entering into the agreement, the parties bind themselves to each other for the common purpose of the contract. Some contractual relationships last only a short time and require minimal interaction. For example, a contract for a haircut involves a fairly quick performance by the hairdresser, followed by the fulfillment of the customer's payment obligation. Other contractual relationships, such as leases, construction contracts, or long-term employment contracts, could span many years and require constant dealings between the parties, regulated by detailed provisions in the agreement.

The essential purpose of the contractual relationship is exchange. The trade in property, services, and intangible rights is fundamental to an economy and society, and the primary function of contract is to facilitate and regulate these exchanges. The concept of exchange (discussed more fully in Chapter 7) means that the very essence of contract is a reciprocal relationship in which each party gives up something to get something. These "somethings" are as varied as one could imagine: The owner of a car could sell it for cash or barter it for other goods; a celebrity's personal assistant may promise to reveal the celebrity's dark secrets to a tabloid for cold hard cash; an inventor may trade the rights to an invention for a promise by a manufacturer to develop the idea for mutual profit; a donor may promise a college money in exchange for the college's agreeing to confer an honorary degree on the donor. These situations vary greatly. Some involve tangible things, others intangible rights. Some of the promises have economic value, others do not. Yet their basic format is the same—the parties have reached a bargain leading to a reciprocal exchange of the benefits desired by each of the parties. Chapters 7, 8, and 9 cover the complexities of this exchange relationship. For the present, the important point to note is that exchange is the principal motivation for contracting and the guiding rationale for the rules of contract law.

§1.2.3 Promise

A contractual relationship can be enforced by legal process. Therefore, if the parties simply enter into an instantaneous exchange (say, an exchange of goods for cash, without any warranty relating to the goods) neither makes any commitment, so there is no need for legal enforcement of the exchange. For legal enforcement to be in issue, at least one of the parties must have made a promise to perform something in the future. It is therefore usually said an exchange that involves no promises does not qualify as a contract.

A promise (sometimes called a "covenant") is an undertaking to act or refrain from acting in a specified way at some future time. This promise may be made in clear and express words, or it could be implied—that is, inferred from conduct or from the circumstances of the transaction. The definition of "contract" requires that only one promise needs to be made for an enforceable contract to come into existence. Most contracts involve reciprocal promises—the parties exchange promises so that each promises something to the other. However, there are situations in which one of the parties makes a promise of future action in exchange for an instantaneous performance by the other.[3] Therefore, as long as there is one promise outstanding at the time of reaching agreement, the agreement falls within the definition of a contract.

The following illustration shows the distinction between an instantaneous exchange (also called an executed exchange) and a contractual obligation: Rocky Rapids decided to sell his kayak. He placed it on the sidewalk in front of his house with a sign that read "For sale, $400. This kayak is sold as is, without any warranties as to its condition, quality, or title."[4] Eddy Undertow saw the sign and decided to buy the kayak. He handed over $400 in cash to Rocky and took the kayak away. This is an instantaneous exchange and therefore not a contract. Eddy paid cash and made no promise to do anything else. Rocky's legal obligation was completely performed as soon as he let Eddy take the kayak. He also made no promises.

---

3. Where at the instance of contracting, promises remain outstanding on both sides, the contract is called bilateral. If one of the parties performs its full obligation at the instant of contracting, and all that remains is a promise by the other, the contract is called unilateral. This distinction is explored in section 4.12.

4. A warranty is a promise that the goods sold will conform to some standard, so for the exchange to be purely instantaneous, it must be clear that the seller makes no promises as to the quality or attributes of the goods. The words "as is" are understood to disclaim warranties, and Rocky has emphasized this by adding further language of disclaimer. Assume that the language used by Rocky completely excludes all warranties relating to the kayak.

However, the transaction would have been a contract either if Eddy had not paid cash for the kayak, but had promised to bring the cash to Rocky later that day, or if Rocky had not sold the kayak "as is," but had instead assured Eddy that it was in good condition and watertight. In each of these situations, at least one of the parties would have made a promise—Eddy's promise to pay later and Rocky's warranty are future commitments relating to the exchange of the kayak for money.

§1.2.4 Legal Recognition of Enforceability

a. The Legal Right to Enforcement

Once the parties have entered into an exchange relationship that qualifies as a contract, they commit themselves to perform the promises that they have made in the contract. They have created a set of binding rules that govern their transaction. It is a hallmark of a contractual promise that if it is broken, the party to whom the promise was made can enforce it by initiating suit in court, or by some other legally binding process, such as arbitration.[5]

This does not mean that every breach of contract will end up in litigation or arbitration. In most cases the parties have strong incentives to avoid legal proceedings, which are expensive and time-consuming, and might damage the parties' long-term commercial relationship as well as tarnish the reputation of one or both of them. Therefore, if there is a reasonable prospect of persuading the breaching party to perform or of otherwise settling the contractual dispute informally, the parties are likely to pursue that avenue before resorting to enforcement proceedings. Although a contractual claim may not reach the stage of formal resolution by a court or arbitrator, the power to use a binding legal process to enforce the contract gives the parties confidence in their contractual relationship, provides a deterrence to breach, and assures a means of compelling performance or recovering compensation for failure of performance.

b. The Process of Contractual Enforcement in Court

Although a detailed discussion of the process of judicial enforcement of a contract is beyond the scope of this book, it is helpful to outline the procedure that a party must follow to assert a contractual claim in court

5. Many contracts contain arbitration provisions that prohibit the parties from suing on the contract in court and require them to adjudicate any disputes or claims under the contract by arbitration. Arbitration is explained briefly below. Although the arbitrator is a private person, not a government official, the arbitrator's decision binds the parties and can be enforced by legal process, much like a court judgment.

and to enforce that claim following judgment. The party alleging breach (usually referred to as the "aggrieved party" in this book) institutes action in court by filing a summons and a complaint. If the other party defends the suit, it will file an answer. Various other pleadings and processes follow as the parties prepare for trial. It often happens that the case is settled or disposed of by a summary process before it reaches trial. If not, the case proceeds to trial. Unless the parties have elected a trial by judge alone, factual questions are decided by a jury, and legal issues are decided by the judge. In the first instance, the role of the court is to adjudicate any questions concerning the existence of a valid contract and to resolve any disputes over its terms and their breach. Once it is established that a contract was entered into and breached, the court will enforce it by giving a remedy for the breach.

The most obvious form of remedy may seem to be for the court to force the breaching party to do what was promised. For example, say that Rocky and Eddy entered into a contract under which Rocky agreed to sell the kayak to Eddy for $400. The contract provided that Rocky would deliver the kayak to Eddy the next day in exchange for $400 in cash.[6] The next day, when Eddy arrived with the $400 in hand, Rocky said he had changed his mind and refused to go through with the sale. This is a breach of the contract. If Eddy sued Rocky, one might assume that the primary mode of legal enforcement of the contract would be a court order compelling Rocky to hand over the kayak against payment of the $400.

However, it is a firm principle of contract law (for reasons explained in section 18.10) that the primary remedy for breach of contract is not specific enforcement of the promise. An order compelling performance is available in only exceptional situations. Rather, the primary remedy is a judgment awarding compensatory damages to the party who has established the breach. That is, the aggrieved party must prove that the breach caused financial loss, and the court will award judgment against the breaching party to compensate for that financial loss. Thus, Eddy would have to show that he had lost money or suffered some other kind of quantifiable economic harm as a result of the breach. For example, he may testify that following Rocky's refusal to deliver, he sought to buy another kayak of a similar type and condition, and could not find one of equivalent quality for less than $450. Eddy's damages are $50. The court will award him a money judgment in this amount. If Rocky fails to pay the judgment voluntarily, Eddy will attempt to recover the debt through a process called execution. Under this procedure, the court

6. Distinguish this from the illustration of an instantaneous exchange in section 1.2.3. Here, the kayak is not immediately exchanged for the money. Instead, at the time of entering the contract, both parties promised to perform their obligations on the following day.

issues a writ commanding a court official (usually called a sheriff) to try to seize some of Rocky's property and to sell it at public auction to raise the money needed to satisfy the judgment. If the sheriff is unable to find any property, the judgment debt remains unsatisfied. There is little further that can be done unless Rocky subsequently acquires executable property.

The purpose of sketching this enforcement process here is to make the point that legal enforcement seldom entails judicial compulsion of performance. In most cases, the plaintiff's victory in court is nothing more than a determination that the defendant owes the plaintiff a stated amount of money. This does not end the matter because the plaintiff now has to collect the debt. If the defendant has no means of paying the judgment, the process of trying to enforce the contract could involve additional cost and inconvenience and still end in frustration. This is an important perspective to bear in mind in thinking about the practicality of enforcing a judgment.

c. The Widespread Use of Arbitration as a Means of Enforcing Contracts

As noted earlier, many contracts provide that any disputes arising out of the contract must be resolved by arbitration or by some other process of extra-judicial dispute resolution. Arbitration provisions in contracts, especially in standard contracts, have become very common and are generally enforceable unless a party can show some clear basis in contract law for invalidating the provision. There is a general public policy in favor of arbitration, which is perceived as a speedier and less formal means of resolving disputes than litigation. While this is generally true, it is not always so, and arbitration does have its own shortcomings that call into question whether it is always the best means of resolving disputes. The negative aspects of arbitration are apparent in cases cited in many parts of this book in which one of the parties challenges an arbitration provision, particularly one contained in a standard agreement.

If the parties have validly agreed to arbitration, the case is heard and disposed of by an arbitrator (or panel of arbitrators), a private person (or persons) selected by the process specified in the contract. Although an arbitrator's decision may be appealable to a court on narrow grounds, the arbitrator's determination is usually final and binding on the parties and may be enforced in the same way as a judgment of a court. If a party who entered into an arbitration agreement commences suit in court, the other party will likely move to dismiss or stay the suit and compel arbitration. If the court finds the arbitration agreement to be valid, it will grant the motion.

§1.3 CONTRACT AS A GENERAL BODY OF LAW APPLICABLE TO DIVERSE TRANSACTIONS

Contract law covers a wide range of very different transactions—leases and sales of real and personal property, employment, credit and finance, insurance, construction, and so on. These many and diverse types of contract each have their own attributes and concerns, so it stands to reason that there cannot be a single and uniform body of legal rules that applies to all of them. With each type of contract, special rules have been developed to respond to distinct features of the transaction or particular needs or issues in the commercial context. For example, a whole body of law has developed to protect consumers who purchase goods or seek credit and is not applicable when the purchaser or borrower is a commercial entity; employment contracts are subject to rules designed to regulate the employment relationship, and many of them focus on the protection of employees; a construction or procurement contract with the government is subject to regulations not found elsewhere; insurance and banking contracts are also controlled by specific regulations. This recital could continue at some length. Although each of these categories of contract has its specialized rules, they all share common ground and are based on similar general principles that are encompassed within a general law of contracts.

The law of contracts is the common core of rules and principles applicable to all contracts and it governs except to the extent that it has been varied by laws specific to the transaction. This specific law may have been created by statute or by judicial decision, or both. All kinds of different contracts are considered in this book and in contracts courses. The focus of this book is on this common core of rules and principles, rather than on special rules that may regulate particular kinds of contract, so the emphasis is not on the type of contract, but on general principles commonly applied to contracts of all types.

§1.4 THE FUNDAMENTAL POLICIES AND VALUES OF CONTRACT LAW

The rules of contract law are based on well-established values and public policies. An understanding of the law's basic goals and assumptions is essential to a full appreciation of legal rules. It is therefore useful to identify and articulate significant policy themes from the outset. This section introduces them briefly.

§1.4.1 Freedom of Contract

a. Individual Autonomy

Section 1.3 identified the consensual and voluntary nature of contract. The power to enter contracts and to formulate the terms of the contractual relationship is an exercise of individual autonomy—an integral part of personal liberty. The converse is also true: Because contracting is an exercise of personal liberty, no one may be bound in contract in the absence of that person's assent. In the United States, the power of contracting has been elevated to a status higher than that accorded it under English common law because it is guaranteed by the Constitution. (The due process clause, U.S. Const. amends. V and XIV, and the contracts clause, U.S. Const. art. 1 §10, provide the constitutional safeguards of liberty of contract.)

Liberty of contract is augmented by another right protected by the due process clause—the right to hold and deal with property. Contracts involve the exchange of economic values, whether in the form of tangible property, services, or intangible rights. These are property rights and the power to use or dispose of them or to choose not to do so necessarily brings into play their constitutional protection. Furthermore, where the contract involves the rendition of personal services by an individual, that person's right to dispose of or to withhold those services is protected by the prohibition of involuntary servitude in the Thirteenth Amendment. The ideological basis of contract freedom is reinforced by the pragmatic consideration that economic intercourse is most efficient when its participants desire it and are free to bargain with each other to reach mutually desirable terms.

Although freedom of contract is an important value, it is not the only value that courts seek to uphold in adjudicating contract disputes. Where other public policies are implicated in the contract dispute, the court takes them into account and balances them against the policy of protecting freedom of contract. For example, policies prohibiting criminal enterprise, protecting the environment, or forbidding anticompetitive behavior may restrict the right to make certain contracts, or may prohibit certain terms in a contract. These issues are discussed in detail later. For the present it is enough to note that while contract liberty is an important value, it is subject to a variety of limitations that are justified either by the protection of corresponding rights in other persons or by the demands of other public interests.

b. Imbalance of Bargaining Power and Adhesion

While freedom of contract is a fundamental value, the exercise of this freedom by one person cannot be untrammeled. Like other liberties, it is delimited by corresponding rights held by other persons, and by the state's legitimate interest in appropriate regulation. In an ideal situation, a contractual relationship involves an equal exercise of autonomy by both parties. Each enters the transaction voluntarily and has the knowledge and ability to negotiate its terms. However, in many transactions, this equality does not exist. One of the parties has greater sophistication and bargaining power than the other. In some cases, this imbalance of bargaining power is so great that the stronger party is able to insist that it will only contract on its own terms. If the other party wants the contract, it has no choice but to accept the terms, even if they are one-sided and drafted to favor the interests of the dominant party. For example, a consumer who buys an insurance policy, an airline ticket, or a software program may have some limited ability to select among alternative terms but is otherwise unable to negotiate much of the content of the standard contract used by the dominant party; a small business that buys inventory from a large supplier may have insufficient market power to insist on a change to terms that the supplier has chosen to include in its standard contract.

Contracts of this kind, proffered on a "take-it-or-leave-it" basis, are known as contracts of adhesion because the less powerful party has no choice but to adhere to the proffered terms. (Contracts of adhesion are discussed in several parts of this book, but are focused on particularly in sections 13.11 and 13.12.) Although significant imbalance in bargaining power does diminish the contractual autonomy of the weaker party, the general approach of the law is to recognize that such an imbalance is an inevitable feature of a market economy in many transactions and that it diminishes the complete exercise of freedom of contract by one of the parties. The general policy of contract law is therefore not to interfere with contracts merely because one party had the power to formulate and impose its terms on the other. However, to prevent the abuse of this power, contract law contains many doctrines, some developed by courts and others enacted by legislation, that regulate it and allow judicial intervention when the dominant party's conduct exceeds the bounds of hard bargaining and becomes unfair bargaining or improper imposition. These doctrines are referred to in many parts of this book, but are addressed particularly in Chapter 13.

§1.4.2 The Morality of Promise—*Pacta Sunt Servanda*

The Latin maxim *pacta sunt servanda* (agreements must be kept) comes from Canon law.[7] It reflects a longstanding moral dimension of contract law—that there is an ethical as well as a legal obligation to keep contractual promises.

7. Canon law is a system of ecclesiastical law developed from Roman law by the medieval Catholic Church. Although it is not part of the English common law, it existed as a parallel system in England, governing matters within the Church's jurisdiction, until the English Church broke away from Rome. As a result of their long period of coexistence, many principles of Canon law influenced the common law.

Contracts should be honored not only because reliability is necessary to foster economic interaction, as discussed in section 1.4.3, but simply because it is morally wrong to break them. The role that this basic moral value plays in contract law is subtle. Courts and scholars often underplay the moral aspect of keeping promises and deal with breach of contract in purely economic terms. It is often suggested, for example, that breach of contract is an acceptable economic choice, provided that the breaching party pays monetary compensation. Nevertheless, it would be a mistake to assume that society or courts are indifferent to the ethical implications of dishonoring contracts. Where a party has breached a contract deliberately, unethically, or in bad faith, this may have an impact on the disposition of the case or the remedy. In some cases, the court expresses its disapproval of the conduct and its adverse consequences. However, even where moral condemnation is not articulated, the choice of applicable rules sometimes reflects disapprobation of wrongful conduct. Outside the realm of litigation, social pressure and business relationships frequently provide disincentives to treat contractual undertakings in a cavalier fashion.

§1.4.3 Accountability for Conduct and Reliance

The objective test of assent was introduced in section 1.2 and is discussed more fully in section 4.1. In determining whether or not a person agreed to a contract or to specific contractual terms, the person's manifested conduct by words or action has more weight than testimony about the party's actual intentions. An emphasis on the objective appearance of assent is important not only because of evidentiary considerations (that is, it is easier to prove because it is observable) but also because one of the fundamental values of contract law is that a person should be held accountable for words or acts reasonably manifesting intent to contract, and that the other party, acting reasonably, should be entitled to rely on that manifestation of assent. (Note that the perception of the conduct by the other party is also subject to an objective test of reasonableness. Contract law does not seek to protect the unreasonable reliance of a party who places an idiosyncratic or irrational interpretation on conduct.) Thus, the principles of accountability and reliance qualify the value of voluntariness—volition is not measured by the true and actual state of mind of a party, but by that state of mind as made apparent to the other contracting party. Evidence of a party's subjective desire not to enter a contract cannot overcome the party's signification of assent to the contract by word or conduct unless the party's manifestation of assent was induced by trickery, coercion, or other illegitimate means, as discussed in section 4.1 and Chapter 13.

The value of protecting reasonable reliance is pervasive in contract law. It has both a specific and a general aspect. It is specific in that a person who has entered a contract has the right to rely on the other party's undertakings. If they are breached, the law must enforce them. It is general because when parties in numerous specific situations feel secure in relying on promises, the expectation arises in society as a whole that contracts can be relied on, and that legal recourse is available for breach. This general sense of reliance, sometimes called "security of contracts" or "security of transactions," is indispensable to economic interaction. If it did not exist, there would be little incentive to make contracts.

In summary, accountability for conduct that induces reasonable reliance is a vital goal of contract law. This is tempered by the consideration that in some cases manifested conduct is induced by illegitimate means, and one who uses such means cannot truly be regarded as having relied on the apparent assent.

§1.4.4 Commercial and Societal Considerations

Because most contracts are concerned with economic exchanges, contract law is quintessentially economic in its purpose. Its goal is to facilitate trade and commerce, to regulate the manner in which people deal with each other in the marketplace, and to enforce commercial obligations. Contract law is therefore oriented toward a market economy. A strong focus on the economic role of contract law sees its principal goal as facilitating transactions on a free market in the most efficient way — the rules of contract law should aim to encourage commercial interaction that creates the greatest economic value for the parties and society. However, many scholars and judges recognize that contract law should also advance other values such as fairness in contract terms, doing justice between the parties, avoiding undue hardship to one of the parties, or furthering the public interest.[8]

Examples

EXAMPLES

1. Liquidators, Inc., held a liquidation sale of the inventory of a furniture store that had gone out of business.[9] Employees of Liquidators, Inc., placed price tags on all the items offered for sale and posted a large sign on the premises that stated "Liquidation sale! All sales are final. All items sold without any warranty." The sign was prominent and was undisputedly seen and understood by all buyers before they made their purchases. At the sale, a customer bought a sofa priced at $400. The customer gave Liquidators, Inc., $400 in cash, loaded the sofa onto a pickup, and drove away. Did Liquidators, Inc., enter a contract with the customer?

8. Philosophical views of the role of contract law are briefly identified in section 2.3.
9. This transaction involves a sale of goods. It would therefore be subject to Article 2 of the Uniform Commercial Code. This statute is introduced in section 2.7 and is referred to frequently throughout the book. However, Article 2 is not needed to answer this Example or any others in this set that involve a sale of goods.

2. Would the answer to Example 1 change if all the facts are the same, except that the customer had paid Liquidators, Inc., an additional $25 as a fee for Liquidators delivering the sofa later in the day?

3. Another customer at the liquidation sale selected a table for $300. The customer had no means of transporting the table, and so agreed with Liquidators, Inc., that it would deliver the table the next day and would collect payment on delivery. Do the parties have a contract?

4. Maggie Zine owns a newsstand. She needed to visit the dentist one morning. On the night before, she asked her brother if he would take care of the stand during the morning. Her brother agreed to do it if Maggie paid him $50 in advance. She agreed and gave him $50 in cash. Did Maggie and her brother enter into a contract that evening?

5. In March Harry asked Tom, his oldest friend, to be his best man at his wedding on June 1. Harry told Tom that if he would agree to be his best man, Harry would buy him a new suit to wear at the wedding. Tom agreed. On May 25, Tom told Harry that he had decided to leave on a two-week vacation the next day, so he would not be able to attend Harry's wedding or to be his best man. Is Tom's commitment to Harry contractual? If it is, can Harry obtain an order of specific performance, compelling Tom to be his best man?

6. May was browsing through an antique store. Prominent signs were posted in several places throughout the store: "Please be careful in handling the merchandise. If you damage merchandise, you will be responsible to pay for it." May picked up a porcelain figurine to examine it. The figurine slipped out of her fingers and smashed into pieces on the floor. It bore a price tag of $1,500. Does May have a contract with the store under which she is committed to pay it $1,500?

Explanations

1. Both the customer and Liquidators, Inc., have performed instantaneously—delivery of the goods was exchanged for payment of the cash. Because there are no outstanding obligations at the time of agreement, there is nothing to enforce as a contract. Liquidators, Inc., would have assumed an obligation if it had warranted the sofa or had given any other undertaking. However, the sign on the premises made it clear that Liquidators, Inc., did not undertake any such future commitment.[10]

10. The possibility of a warranty and its disclaimer was also raised in the illustration in section 1.2.3 involving Rocky's sale of his kayak to Eddy. Assume that the disclaimer effectively excluded any warranty.

2. The answer would change if the customer paid an additional $25 as a delivery fee, because this is not an instantaneous exchange of performances and therefore qualifies as a contract. Liquidator's performance is not complete at the time of the sale because it has made a promise to deliver the sofa, which it must perform later that day.[11]

3. Liquidators, Inc., entered into an agreement with the customer for the sale of the table. Under the agreement, both parties have made promises that will be performed in the future, so this agreement does qualify as a contract.

4. Maggie's agreement with her brother satisfies all the attributes of a contract: They agreed to enter into a commercial relationship under which Maggie exchanged money for her brother's promise to provide services the next day. It does not matter that they are family members; nor is it necessary that the arrangement comply with any formalities. Although Maggie's performance appears complete, her brother has a promise outstanding at the time of the agreement.

5. When Tom accepted Harry's invitation to be his best man, they made an agreement under which they exchanged promises—Tom promised to perform the duties of best man, and Harry promised him a new suit. (These are the principal promises. There were probably others implied in the relationship as well.) This may therefore appear to have the hallmarks of a contract. However, where the commitments are social in nature, a court may find that they are not contractual because the parties did not reasonably intend them to be so. This distinction does not mean that a contract must necessarily have a commercial purpose. It is possible for parties to make a contract that does not have a commercial goal. However, the lack of a commercial purpose, the presence of apparent noncommercial motives for the agreement, and the general societal expectation that promises of this kind do not create legal relationships suggest that the parties did not intend to enter into a legally enforceable relationship. If so, this is not a contract and Harry has no legal basis for enforcing Tom's promise. Even if this had been a breach of contract, a court would not have issued an order of specific performance, compelling Tom to perform his duties as best man. As mentioned in section 1.2.4.b and explained more fully in section 18.10.1, the remedy of specific performance is not readily granted, especially where the performance would involve the rendition of personal services by an individual.

---

11. This Example and Example 3 involve sales of goods. As explained in Chapter 11, a sale of goods for over $500 must be evidenced by a record to be enforceable (that is, it is subject to a statute of frauds). The sales in these Examples were for under $500, there is no need for a record of the transaction and an oral agreement is sufficient.

6. This Example introduces two principles. First, it shows that a contract can arise by implication from conduct, and it need not be spelled out in express terms. Second, it shows that terms of a contract do not necessarily have to be contained in a document or spoken. A contract could include terms that are posted or otherwise made conspicuously part of the contract at the time that the contract is entered. (A similar situation occurs in Example 1, where the sign stating that the goods were sold without any warrantees was effective, thereby excluding any warranties and making the transaction an instantaneous exchange.) It is therefore possible that a contract was created under which the store allowed May to handle the merchandise in exchange for her promise to pay for anything that she broke. (Note that even if the store cannot establish a contract here, it may be able to claim damages from May in tort because her negligence resulted in damage to the store's property.)

CHAPTER 2

Facets of the Law of Contract and the Source of Its Rules, Processes, and Traditions

§2.1 THE PURPOSE OF THIS CHAPTER

Chapter 1 introduces the legal concept of contract and outlines the policies and values of contract law. This chapter covers some more fundamentals by introducing and explaining some basic principles that are useful to know in advance of studying substantive principles of contract law in later chapters. Sections 2.2 and 2.3 provide a brief historical and theoretical perspective. Sections 2.4, 2.5, and 2.6 outline the source of contract law and some of the structural and conceptual aspects of the legal system of which it forms a part. Section 2.7 introduces Article 2 of the Uniform Commercial Code (UCC), a statute that governs contracts for the sale of goods. Sales of goods are very common contracts, so Article 2 comes up constantly in the rest of this book. Section 2.8 introduces and explains the role of the Restatement, Second, of Contracts, an influential compilation of the rules of contract law that have been generally applied by courts. Section 2.9 introduces a transnational perspective on contract law. Although the focus of the contracts course and this book is on domestic (that is, American) contract law, these brief notes on the transnational perspective are included in most chapters and have the modest aim of providing some insight into how the concepts and principles of the American law of contracts comport with or differ from those that might be found in other legal systems.

§2.2 THE HISTORICAL PERSPECTIVE OF CONTRACT LAW

The primary purpose of the contracts course is to teach the contemporary law of contract. However, some sense of the history of contract law is useful to a full appreciation of current law. Indeed, the very process by which the law is decided involves some degree of historical analysis, as the discussion of precedent in Chapter 3 shows. Most of the rules and principles of contract law were developed in the past. Some of them have remained relatively unchanged while others have been adapted or overruled as they have become superannuated. These changes tend to be evolutionary and incremental, built on a traditional framework that is still apparent.

Therefore, although the contracts course is not a course in legal history, the historical progression of the law, largely through court opinions,[1] is at the very heart of the common law system of jurisprudence. Historical perspective permits a fuller understanding, not only of the substantive principles of current law, but also of the process of legal evolution. Lawyers must often try to predict how a court may decide an issue that could arise in the transaction, so an awareness of how and why the law changes over time enhances the ability to predict the direction that the law may or should take in the future.

§2.3 CLASSICAL AND CONTEMPORARY CONTRACT LAW

§2.3.1 Classical Contract Law

Although the common law of contracts is many centuries old, it did not become a systematic, interwoven body of doctrine until relatively recently. Prior to the eighteenth century the law of contracts was not a cohesive system of rules, linked by general principles, but a collection of discrete rules, each specifically applicable to various particular types of transactions. From the eighteenth century, English legal scholars began to think of contract law in more systematic terms. They began to recognize that the specific rules reflected a general approach to contracts that could be identified and formulated as broader doctrine. This trend developed further in both England and America during the nineteenth century, at a time when economic and industrial expansion called for a more sophisticated and comprehensive system of contract law. It reached its zenith in what is referred to as the classical

1. Chapter 3 examines the judicial development of the common law through the doctrine of precedent.

period, which spanned the last decades of the nineteenth century and the beginning of the twentieth. The Restatement of Contracts, published in the 1930s (introduced in section 2.8) reflects the mature thinking of the classical school, but by that stage the classical conception had already begun the process of change that leads into the contemporary period.

To find a general doctrine of contract, the classicists examined decided cases, extracting from them a set of coherent and well-defined rules, which they then used as the basis for constructing more abstract general principles. The general principles formed a framework for organizing and linking the rules into a body of doctrine. Some classicists went so far as to conceive of law as analogous to a science in which certain and consistent results could be achieved in the resolution of cases by the rather mechanical process of selecting the right rule from the body of doctrine and applying it to the facts.

The classical school reflects the priorities of its age, which greatly valued free enterprise, private autonomy, and a laissez-faire approach to economic activity. Classical theory therefore stressed the facilitation of contractual relationships and favored a strictly objective approach, in which assent to a contract was based on the parties' manifested intent, rather than on the subjective agreement of each of the parties. The classical approach was also heavily influenced by the legal philosophy of positivism, which stressed the primacy of legal rules and considered the court's principal role to be finding and applying those rules to the facts of individual cases. Because of its emphasis on clear rules that could be applied rather mechanically in deciding cases, classicism tends to be relatively formalistic and rigid, which has led to an alternative label for the approach—formalism.

§2.3.2 Contemporary Contract Law

By the late nineteenth century, some legal scholars began to challenge the formalism and rule orientation of the classical approach. It was perceived as too rigid, inadequately aligned with social policy and judicial decision-making, and biased in favor of dominant contracting parties. Succeeding schools of legal philosophy turned away from heavy reliance on rules that may create the illusion of certainty, but do not in fact adequately reflect what really occurs in the resolution of cases. Instead, law came to be studied in a multidisciplinary way, taking into account its social context and the actual workings of the legal system. While many different approaches to contract law can be identified during the twentieth century, the two most influential schools were the sociological jurisprudents, who studied the relationship between law and society, and the legal realists, who stressed the dynamics of the legal process, challenged the preeminence of rules, and advocated a looser, more flexible approach to legal analysis. Many of the once-radical ideas of the legal realist movement have become widely accepted and commonplace today. For example, it is now regarded as self-evident that law should reflect social policy, it should evolve as society evolves, and it should be grounded on the factual investigation of practices in the marketplace.

Today, legal realism (also called neoclassicism) is the prevalent legal philosophy. In fact, it is conventional enough that it is sometimes labeled as traditionalist. Lawyers and judges have become used to thinking about law in a broader context and to considering not merely what the doctrine says, but also how it actually works in light of such factors as the makeup and philosophy of the judiciary, the use of legal tactics, and the social goals to be achieved. In this respect, the legal realists forever changed the way of thinking about law. Although legal realism permeates the current approach to the law, other schools of thought continue to evolve as scholars and judges build on or challenge the realist tradition. It is not possible, in this short introduction, to identify and describe all the strains of modern contract theory. However, it is at least worth mentioning some of the jurisprudential writing that has made an impact on the way in which contract law is perceived.

The promissory theory of contracts emphasizes the morality of keeping promises and argues that the sanctity of promise is the core justification of contract law. The consent theory of contract focuses on the assent of the parties as the primary value to be served and protected by the rules of contract law. The relational theory criticizes traditional contract theory for not sufficiently taking into account that many contracts involve ongoing relationships between the parties, which affect their contractual behavior and expectations. The critical legal studies movement explores the doctrines of contract law from the perspective of groups that have historically been excluded from power, and criticizes traditional contract rules as instruments of the dominant economic class. This movement argues, in essence, that although rules may appear to be neutral, they have come about as a result of political choices, made by persons who hold political power to serve the interests of their class. Critical race theory examines how the apparently neutral principles of law impact and discriminate against people who have historically been excluded from the economic mainstream, such as people of color.

The Law and Economics movement has had a significant impact on contemporary law. Although the movement consists of scholars who have differing views, the common thread of the scholarship is to examine law from the perspective of economic principles, and to be concerned with the economic efficiency of legal rules. Commonly, those who advocate the economic analysis of law urge that laws should be primarily concerned with the facilitation of exchanges on the free market, and should not seek to regulate conduct as a means of social engineering. As a reaction to the economic modeling of the law and economics movement, a number of scholars have applied principles of behavioral economics to the study of contract law. These scholars examine the psychological reaction to legal rules and the interaction between the law and the behavior and perceptions of the persons affected by it.

Finally, some scholars and judges adopt an approach that has been described as neoformalist. They believe that the law has drifted too far away from the rule-orientation of the classical period, so that judges have too much discretion and the law has become too uncertain and unpredictable. They advocate a stronger emphasis on rules and at least a partial return to a more formalistic approach to the application of legal rules.

In sum, contemporary contract law is a mix of doctrine, policy, and process, at a stage of sophistication that goes beyond that of the classicists. Nevertheless, the classical period was an important stage in the development of contract law. The classicists' quest for a comprehensive body of clear and certain rules provided an organizing principle that has been crucial in the evolution of contract law. Many of the current rules and principles of contract law were formulated during the classical period and modern developments have proceeded from that base. The law of contracts still reflects the tension between the classicists' desire for certainty and formality (an orientation toward clear rules) and the need to understand the legal process and to develop flexible rules that accommodate and correctly describe that process.

§2.4 THE MEANING OF "COMMON LAW"

The meaning of the term "common law" varies depending on the context in which it is used. It could refer to the system of law developed in England and subsequently adopted by other countries, such as the United States, that were formerly British colonies; or it could refer to the judge-made component of a common law system; or it could refer to a process of legal analysis used in a common law system. Each of these meanings is explained below.

§2.4.1 "Common Law" Used to Designate a Legal System Based on English Law

In early times, much of English law was based on local custom, applied in local courts. As the centralized Royal Courts began to increase in importance, their decisions formed the basis of a national law that gradually overshadowed local law. This national law, common to all of England,[2] came to

2. The text refers to English, not British, common law because Britain does not have a unitary legal system. English common law applies in England and Wales. Northern Ireland's law is based on English law, but has its own variants. Scots law is quite distinct from English law. It draws its legal tradition from both English and civil law.

be called the "common law." When Britain established colonies around the world the settlers transplanted English law into these foreign territories. In most of the ex-colonies, including those that became the United States, the common law of England has remained the basic legal system.[3] Therefore, the term "common law" used in the broadest international sense, designates a country whose legal system is based on the common law of England. These countries share a legal heritage and an approach to legal analysis even though they may have widely different political, economic, and social structures and may have diverged in their rules of substantive law.

Most other countries in the world have legal systems derived from Roman law, as developed in continental Europe. Because the source of Roman law was the *Corpus Juris Civilis* of the emperor Justinian, these systems are called civilian. Cross-pollination and the unifying pressure of international commerce have reduced the differences between the civil law and the common law, but each system continues to have a distinctive approach to legal analysis. In the present context, probably the most striking difference is that civilian systems have a long tradition of comprehensive codification and tend to focus on their codes and scholarly commentary as a source of law. By contrast, common law systems tend to emphasize more strongly the role of the judge in the development of the law.

§2.4.2 "Common Law" Used to Denote the Judge-Made Component of a Common Law System

When the focus moves from the international (i.e., characterizing the legal system as a whole) to the domestic (i.e., examining the components of the system), "common law" takes on a different meaning. It refers to those portions of the law based on decisions of the courts, as distinct from those created by legislation. Contracts is described as a common law subject because most of its rules have been developed over the years by judges rather than by legislators. (This process of development is described in Chapter 3.)

This does not mean that there is no statute law governing contracts. Even in early times, the English parliament enacted some laws concerning contracts which formed part of the received common law system in the American colonies. In the modern period, legislative action has increased considerably, and there are many areas of contract law that have been subjected to statutory rules. Some of these statutes codify common law rules. That is, they take rules and principles already developed by judges and put

3. Louisiana is the only state whose legal heritage is not common law because it adopted the civilian system, in the form of the French Code Napoleon, during the short period that it was a French possession. The basic framework of Louisiana law is therefore civilian, even though subsequent developments in its law have been influenced by other states.

them into statutory form. The purpose of this may be to reinforce or clarify the law or to make it more accessible. A statute may do more than codify, though. It may reform, alter, or modernize common law rules; it may intervene to hasten or mold the development of doctrine; it may be enacted with the express purpose of changing legal rules developed by courts; or it may create new rules designed to deal with a problem not yet addressed by courts. As noted in section 1.3, some statutes are confined to particular contracts while others are of general application. Contracts are governed by state law, as explained in section 2.6, so some states have more extensive statutory treatment of contract than others. Although legislatures have, over the years, enacted many laws that relate to contracts, the field is still regarded as part of the common law, because judge-made rules continue to predominate, not only in developing nonstatutory law, but also in the interpretation of the meaning and scope of statutory enactments.

§2.4.3 "Common Law" Used to Denote a Process or Approach to Legal Analysis

The prior two meanings of "common law" are relatively easy to spot, but the term is also used in a more subtle sense. It is sometimes used to describe the mode of legal thinking and the process of judicial development inherent in a common law system.

As mentioned before, the common law develops through the decisions of judges in actual cases. Whether a rule's origin is the common law or statute, it will ultimately be applied by a judge in a specific case. In deciding the case, the judge interprets and may embellish the rule. Over time, as courts apply the rule in more and more cases, it acquires a judicial gloss that becomes part of the law. Therefore, in using patterns of thinking and modes of analysis molded by the common law tradition, judges continue to develop the law, even if the source of law is statutory. This process is as much part of the common law as the judicial creation of rules. In a civilian jurisdiction, by contrast, the judicial application of statutory rules tends to be more confined to the case under decision, and is less likely to be influential in the development of legal doctrine.

§2.5 THE DISTINCTION BETWEEN LAW AND EQUITY

The distinction between law and equity permeates the common law system, and is discussed in several sections of this book. In everyday usage, "equity" simply means fairness. In law, it is sometimes used this way as well. However, it also has a more technical meaning.

Sections 2.4.1 and 3.2 briefly discuss the way in which the Royal Courts developed the common law. As practiced in the Royal Courts during its formative period, the common law was a rigid system based on forms of action that were established by commands of the Crown, called writs. The forms of action established by the writs were narrow, specific, and formalistic. The courts had some power to expand a writ to include causes of action that bore a relationship to those covered by the writ, and new writs were granted from time to time, enlarging the range of cases that the Royal Courts could adjudicate. However, in some situations a person who merited relief could not fit the case into a recognized writ, and could therefore not obtain any remedy at law. Where the Royal Courts did not have the power to grant a remedy because the case did not fall within a recognized writ, the Crown had the prerogative to intervene if fairness and justice (equity) so demanded. The chancellor, the highest royal officer, exercised this prerogative on behalf of the Crown.

Over time, the volume of cases submitted to the chancellor for equitable relief grew to the extent that it became necessary to establish judicial body to deal with them. This led to the creation of a new court, called the Court of Chancery with jurisdiction to adjudicate claims for equitable relief. The Court of Chancery developed as a court parallel to courts of law, with its own rules and principles.

This dual system of jurisdiction lasted for many centuries. Over time, it became a matter of established practice that certain claims and remedies were legal in nature and others were equitable. For example, a claim for damages for breach of contract was within the jurisdiction of the law courts, but law courts had no power to order a party to perform the contract. Therefore, a claim for specific performance of a contract (that is, an order compelling a party to perform its contractual undertakings) could only be granted by the equity court. Furthermore, the equity court would not assume jurisdiction unless the plaintiff could show that the legal remedy of damages was not an adequate remedy under all the circumstances of the case. Thus, the common law system, in its broad sense, incorporated a jurisdictional division between the courts of common law (used here in a narrower sense) and equity. This dual system was part of the common law of England adopted by American jurisdictions, and it thereby became part of the American system. The distinction between law and equity is even reflected in the U.S. Constitution. For example, Article III §2 extends the judicial power of the United States to all cases in law and equity arising under the Constitution or the laws of the United States. Amendment VII preserves the right to a jury trial in suits at common law but does not do so with regard to equitable suits because courts of equity did not have juries.

Since the nineteenth century the distinction between law and equity has been eroding both in England and in the United States. Separate courts of equity have been abolished in the federal system and in most states. Courts of general jurisdiction now hear both legal and equitable suits. Also, the substantive distinction between law and equity is fading as many principles of equity gradually become incorporated into the law as legal principles. However, the distinction is not entirely dead, and it has an impact in many areas. For example, the availability of remedies is still influenced by the rule that a party who claims equitable relief must show that the legal remedy is inadequate; the right to a jury trial is commonly associated only with actions at law and is generally not available in equity suits; an appellate court has a much wider scope of review in an equity suit; and some courts still confine some equitable defenses and doctrines to suits in equity and do not recognize them in actions at law. Again, it must be stressed that none of these distinctions are applied with the same rigor as they used to be, and there are many cases in which courts have moved away from them. Nevertheless, the tradition is strong and its breakdown is gradual and uneven, so it must be taken into account even in modern cases. The law-equity distinction emerges periodically in later chapters of this book where the distinction is relevant to rights and remedies.

§2.6 STATE LAW GOVERNS CONTRACTS

The common law of contract (as well as much of the statutory law governing contracts) is state law. Although there is some federal law applicable to contracts, it is limited to federal concerns such as the regulation of interstate commerce or to contracts entered into by the federal government. Because contracts are within the realm of state law, most contracts cases are decided by state courts. However, federal courts often have jurisdiction over cases that involve issues of state contract law (for example, because there is diversity of citizenship, or because the contract dispute arises in a bankruptcy case under federal law), so it is common to find a federal court deciding a state law contracts issue. Where a federal court hears a state law contracts case, it applies the law of the state whose law governs the transaction, and is bound by state law precedents. (*See* section 3.2.2.)

Contract law in this country is commonly referred to as "American" contract law, which may suggest that there is a single body of contract law in the United States. This is a convenient shorthand way to describe general principles of contract law that are widely recognized in the many state jurisdictions within the United States. However, there are in fact 50 different bodies of state contract law in this country, as well as those in U.S. territories and the District of Columbia. Although this means that there are differences in the law from one jurisdiction to another, the shared common law heritage as well as ongoing influences between states results in a significant degree of similarity in the laws of the states. This makes it possible to study a generalized law of contract in law schools, and to select cases based not on the state from which they emanate, but on the quality of their facts and legal exposition. Therefore, while a particular rule of law may not be followed in every state, or there may be variations in doctrine from state to state, contracts courses and this book focus on rules and principles that are broadly accepted and are a fair representation of the law in most states.

§2.7 THE UNIFORM COMMERCIAL CODE (UCC)

§2.7.1 The UCC as a Uniform Model Statute and State Legislation

a. The Creation and Purpose of the UCC

As mentioned in section 2.4.2, contracts are generally governed by common law except to the extent that legislation has been enacted to codify, change, or add to it. The UCC is such a statute. Although most of contract law is, in a sense, commercial, the UCC is not applicable to all contracts. It covers only certain specific types of commercial transactions. Each type of transaction is provided for in a separate article of the UCC. The most pervasive type of transaction covered by the UCC is the sale of goods, governed by UCC Article 2. Sales of goods are very commonplace types of contract, and there is a close relationship between Article 2 and the development of the common law of contracts. Therefore, this book covers the relevant provisions of UCC Article 2 alongside the corresponding common law rules.[4] This coverage is basic, leaving more in-depth study of Article 2 to specialized classes. In addition to Article 2, this book refers periodically to provisions of UCC Article 1, which is a general article containing definitions and general principles applicable throughout the UCC.

The UCC was promulgated in the mid-twentieth century. Some of its provisions were innovative, but others were based on earlier statutes or on principles and rules that were already established in common law. That is, the purpose of the UCC was in part to modernize the law and to bring it into accord with contemporary commercial practice, and in part to codify and clarify existing legal doctrine. Apart from codifying and reforming commercial law, the other goal of the UCC is to unify it throughout the

4. Some contracts courses include basic coverage of Article 2, while others do not handle Article 2, which is offered in an upper-class course on sales of goods.

country. Like the law of contracts generally, commercial law is state law. It is therefore not appropriate for the United States Congress to create a unified commercial law by federal legislation.[5] However, considerable unity of law among the states can be achieved by creating a model commercial code, which is then made available for state legislatures to enact. The UCC is such a model code. It was drafted jointly by two very influential national law reform organizations: the Uniform Law Commission (ULC)[6] and the American Law Institute (ALI). Their work resulted in the completion of a model code (called the "Official Text") during the 1950s. The aim of having this model code adopted by state legislatures was fully successful, and it has been enacted in every state.[7] The enactments are substantially, but not entirely, uniform because some states have made legislative variations from the standard model provisions. In addition, identically-worded provisions in each state may be interpreted differently by the courts of different states.

b. Revisions of the UCC

The process of reform and updating did not end with the enactment of the original draft of the Code. Shortly after the completion of the model code, a Permanent Editorial Board was set up to review the Code and propose amendments. The process of amendment is slow because the drafters take many years to develop recommendations for change, and after the proposed changes are promulgated by ULC and ALI, they still have to be adopted by state legislatures. Nevertheless, since the enactment of the UCC, changes have been proposed by ULC and ALI to various Articles of the UCC, and, with some exceptions, those revisions have generally been adopted by state legislatures.

Articles 1 and 2 have been reviewed periodically since their original enactment. A 2001 revision of Article 1 by ULC and ALI has been widely adopted by the states. ULC and ALI also proposed an extensive revision of Article 2 in 2003, but this attempt to update Article 2 was unsuccessful and was withdrawn after states declined to enact it. A limited amendment to Article 2 was promulgated by ULC and ALI in 2022 and has already been enacted by several states.

---

5. This does not mean that the United States Congress is completely uninvolved in enacting legislation relating to contract and commercial law. The commerce clause (U.S. Const. art. 1 §8 cl. 3) gives Congress considerable power to pass laws that regulate interstate commerce. However, the power to enact general commercial law is reserved to the states under the Constitution.

6. The ULC was originally called the National Conference of Commissioners on Uniform State Laws (NCCUSL). It is referred to in this book by its current name, ULC.

7. Louisiana did not enact the UCC as a whole because its underlying legal system is civilian, as explained in footnote 3 above. It has enacted some portions of the UCC.

c. Citations to the UCC

When the UCC is cited in this book and in other texts, the citation is to the model code—that is, to the Official Text as promulgated by ULC and ALI. For example, section 102 of Article 2 is cited as §2.102. However, when a UCC section is cited in a case, the court usually cites the state statute in which the Code was enacted in the court's jurisdiction. For example, a Connecticut court would cite section 102 of Article 2 as Conn. Gen. Stat. §42a-2-102, and an Oregon court would cite it as Or. Rev. Stat. §72-1020. As these citations show, it is usually not that difficult to identify the model code section because it is typically incorporated into the statutory citation. As noted before, most sections of the UCC have been enacted by states in exactly the same form as they appear in the Official Text. However, it occasionally happens that a state deviates from the Official Text in enacting a particular provision. Nevertheless, for the most part the Official Text reliably represents the actual law as enacted by the states. Of course, a practitioner in a state that has made a nonuniform change must be aware of that change because the language enacted by the state legislature, not the Official Text, is the law in that state.

d. The Official Comments to the UCC

When ULC and ALI drafted the original Code and its revisions they included a commentary after each section to explain and expand on the provisions of the section. This commentary, called the Official Comments, is not part of the statute and therefore not binding law, as the text of the actual enacted section is. However, the commentary is very important because it reflects the intentions of the drafters. Courts treat the Official Comments as highly influential and often rely on them in interpreting the Code.

§2.7.2 The Use and Application of UCC Article 2

As mentioned already, the UCC covers a variety of different types of commercial transactions, and each type of transaction is contained in a separate, self-contained article. The only articles covered in this book are Article 2, governing the sale of goods, and Article 1, which has general provisions applicable in all articles, including Article 2.

a. The Scope of Article 2: The Transactions to Which It Applies

UCC §2.102 states that Article 2 applies to "transactions in goods." Although the word "transaction" is broader than the word "sale," the transactions to which Article 2 applies are in fact sales of goods. If the contract in issue is a sale of goods, Article 2 governs and must be applied. Conversely, if the contract in issue is not a sale of goods, Article 2 does not apply to it, and it is governed by other law. In many cases, this other law is the common law of contracts. Therefore, the first thing to determine when dealing with a contracts case is whether or not the transaction is a sale of goods.

Although Article 2 must be applied to a sale of goods, Article 2 does not contain every rule of law that may be applicable to the transaction. There are many issues that could arise in a sale of goods that are not covered by the provisions of Article 2. Where those issues arise, UCC §1.103(b) states that unless the Code displaces them, principles of law and equity supplement the provisions of the Code. The Code was drafted with the intention that common law principles complement the Code provisions and are to be used in conjunction with them to cover any areas that are not provided for in the Code. There are many areas of contract law in which Article 2 does not have specific provisions, so that UCC §1.103(b) incorporates common law rules (including equitable principles) and makes them applicable to the sale of goods.

b. The Meaning of "Sale"

UCC §2.106(1) states that "a sale consists in the passing of title from the seller to the buyer for a price." As this definition indicates, there are two essential characteristics of a sale. One is that title (ownership of the goods) must pass from the seller to the buyer, and the other is that the buyer must pay for them. The price paid for the goods is usually money, but it need not be. UCC §2.304 states that the price may be payable in money or otherwise.

Because the passage of title is an element of a sale, Article 2 does not apply to a transaction in which the owner of property merely leases it for a period of time. In a lease, the owner retains title of the leased goods, which must be returned at the end of the lease period. (Leases of goods are dealt with separately in the UCC, by Article 2A. Article 2A is not covered in the typical contracts course and is not mentioned again in this book.) Likewise, if the owner of property donates it to another person, the gift is not a sale of the goods, so it is governed by common law, not Article 2.

c. The Meaning of "Goods"

Goods are defined in UCC §2.105(1) as movable things. The definition expressly includes goods that are specially manufactured for the buyer, livestock, and growing crops and expressly excludes money and various intangible rights. Although the definition does not say that an item must be tangible to qualify as goods, this is implicit in the word "things," which connotes objects with material existence. In many cases, it is relatively easy to tell whether a contract involves a sale of goods. For example, a customer's purchase of clothing from a department store is obviously a sale of goods. In a few cases, the nature and physical attributes of the commodity must be examined more closely to decide if it is movable and tangible. For example, in *In re Escalera Resources Co.*, 563 B.R. 336 (Bankr. D. Colo. 2017), the court had to decide whether electricity was goods. Noting that courts are divided on that question, it analyzed the nature and properties of electricity and classified it as goods because it does have a tangible existence and is sold and transmitted in measurable quantities. (Any doubt about the tangible existence of electricity can be resolved by grabbing a live wire.)

The requirement that the object of the sale must be movable distinguishes goods from real property. Therefore, the purchase of land, including any structure built into the land, such as a house, is not a sale of goods. Movable goods are also distinguished from services and intangible rights. For example, a contract with a laundry to clean clothes, while relating to goods, is for the provision of a service, not a sale of goods. Similarly, the purchase of shares in a corporation or of coverage under a life insurance policy is a sale of intangible rights, not goods.

d. The Classification of Intellectual Property

The proper classification of the transfer of rights to hold and use intellectual property (such as software, music, books, and video games) can be difficult. It is neither clear whether the object of the sale qualifies as goods nor if the grant of the right to use the intellectual property is a sale. The copyright in intellectual property is held by its creator, and when the creator permits a user to use that intellectual property, the transaction is not a transfer of title to the property. The holder keeps the copyright and merely conveys to the user a license to use the intellectual property.

If the intellectual property is embodied in a physical object, it is possible to distinguish the object itself from the rights to the underlying intellectual property. For example, if a novel is embodied in a printed book, it is easy to separate the physical object—the book—from its content—the copyrighted text. The purchase of the book transfers the ownership of that tangible object for a price, even if the rights to the underlying intellectual property are not also transferred. Therefore, it is clear that a sale of goods has occurred. The buyer, as owner of the book, has full rights to possess, use, or dispose of it. However, the buyer does not have the right to reproduce or transfer the intellectual content of the book in violation of the author's copyright. This is an easy case because books are regarded as having inherent value as objects.

However, matters become more complicated where the physical object containing the intellectual property has little or no real inherent value, but is simply a means of transferring the intellectual property to the purchaser for purposes of its use under the license. For example, valuable software transferred to the purchaser by means of a cheap disk is less of a sale of the disk than a transfer of a license. Courts have struggled with the ambiguous nature of these transactions. Where copyrighted creative work is embodied in a physical form, there is some likelihood that a court will classify the transaction as a sale of goods, even though the real value of the object is in its content and the creator's copyright may restrict the use of the object.

Nevertheless, there is less likelihood that a court will find a sale of goods where this very same intellectual property is delivered electronically, without any physical object changing hands. Where intellectual property, whether software or written or recorded matter, is downloaded directly by the seller to the buyer's computer or other device, this is more logically treated, not as a sale of goods, but as a sale of intangible rights—a license to use the intellectual property. It elevates form over substance to treat the transfer of a license electronically from that accomplished by a physical object used merely as a conduit for the transfer. The court drew attention to this incongruity in *Conwell v. Gray Loon Outdoor Marketing Group, Inc.*, 906 N.E.2d 805 (Ind. 2009), in which it noted that it would be a mistake to treat software as goods merely because it is contained in a tangible medium rather than delivered electronically. In *Conwell*, the court noted that even where intellectual property is transferred electronically, some courts have distinguished between standard, out-of-the-box software, which they classify as goods, and custom-designed software, which they hold not to be goods. In *Pain Center of SE Indiana, LLC v. Origin Healthcare Solutions, LLC*, 893 F.3d 454 (7th Cir. 2018), the court applied this distinction, holding that standard, preexisting billing software qualified as goods, even though it had been made available electronically to the customer.

e. The Law Applicable to Hybrid Transactions

A hybrid transaction is a contract in which a sale of goods is combined with the sale of other property or services. Hybrid transactions are common. For example, a contract to repair a car usually includes both the supply of parts (a sale of goods) and the provision of labor. Where parties have entered into a hybrid transaction, it must be determined whether and to what extent Article 2 applies to the contract. Prior to 2022, Article 2 did not prescribe any test for deciding this question, so courts had to decide it. In 2022, ALI and ULC amended the Official Text of UCC §§2.102 and 2.106 to tackle the issue of what law applies to a hybrid transaction. These amendments have been enacted by several states, and govern the handling of hybrid transactions in those states. In states that have not enacted the amendments, the treatment of hybrid transactions continues to be determined by case law.

i. The Court-Created Predominant Purpose Test

The most widely accepted judicially-created test for deciding whether Article 2 applies to a hybrid transaction is the "predominant purpose" or "predominant factor" test. If the sale of goods is the more significant aspect of the transaction, and the other part of the seller's performance is incidental to the sale, Article 2 applies. However, if the sale of goods is ancillary to the other performance, Article 2 does not apply and the transaction is governed by other law. In many transactions this other law is the common law of contracts. The determination of the predominant purpose of the contract is based on several factors, including the language of the contract, the allocation of the contract price between the goods and the other performance, the reason for entering the contract, and the nature of the seller's business.

The predominant purpose test creates an all-or-nothing result — the entire transaction is either governed by Article 2 or by other law. A minority of courts do not apply the predominant purpose test, but use a "gravamen" or "bifurcation" test instead. Under these roughly equivalent tests, the court does not classify the contract as a whole one way or the other, but applies Article 2 to the sale-of-goods aspect of the transaction and applies other law to those aspects of the transaction that are not related to the sale of goods.

ii. The 2022 Amendments to UCC §§2.102 and 2.106

The 2022 amendments to the Official Text of Article 2 provide a basis for deciding on the law to be applied to hybrid transactions. The amendments add a definition of "hybrid transaction" in UCC §2.106(5), which identifies a hybrid transaction as a single transaction involving the sale of goods combined with either the provision of services, or the lease of other goods, or the sale, lease, or license of property other than goods. UCC §2.102(2) prescribes the manner in which these transactions are to be treated. It does not use the term "predominant purpose," used in prior cases, but refers merely to whether the sale-of-goods aspects of the transaction "predominate." Official Comment 3 indicates that the reason for this is to focus simply on which aspect of the transaction is predominant without having to make a finding as to the purpose of the parties.

Official Comment 2 to UCC §2.102 describes UCC §2.102(2) as establishing a two-tiered test that combines aspects of the predominant purpose test and the bifurcation approach. Article 2 applies if the sale-of-goods aspects of the transaction predominate, but there is some possibility that other law may apply to aspects of the transaction unrelated to the sale of goods. However, if other aspects of the transaction predominate, only the provisions of Article 2 that relate primarily to the sale of goods apply, and other law governs aspects of the transaction that are not directly pertinent to the sale of goods.

If the sale-of-goods aspects of the transaction do not predominate, UCC §2.102(2)(a) applies the provisions of Article 2 only to that part of the contract that relates primarily to the sales aspect of the transaction. Provisions of Article 2 that relate primarily to the transaction as a whole do not apply. That is, other law applies to the transaction as a whole, but Article 2 provisions do apply to the sale-of-goods aspect of the contract. Official Comments 2 and 5 indicate that even if the sale-of-goods aspects of the transaction do not predominate, Article 2 provisions, such as the warranties applicable to goods sold, would apply to that portion of the contract that relates to the sale of goods. However, more general provisions, such as the rules relating to contract formation or the need for a signed record under the statute of frauds, would not apply.

If the sale-of-goods aspects predominate, UCC §2.102(2)(b) applies Article 2 to the transaction as a whole. However, the section qualifies this by stating that in appropriate circumstances, other law could apply to those aspects of the transaction that do not relate to the sale of goods. Examples in Official Comment 4 illustrate circumstances in which this qualification might apply. A contract for the replacement of a roof includes the installation of new shingles and the removal of the existing shingles. This is a hybrid transaction because the supply of the new shingles is a sale of goods, but the removal of the old shingles and the installation of the new ones is a service. Even if the sale-of-goods aspect of the transaction predominates, other law, such as a law requiring the roofer to be licensed, or a law that implies a warranty on the quality of the work, would apply to the labor aspects of the transaction.

Official Comment 3 addresses the question of how to determine which aspect of a hybrid transaction predominates, and states that this is left to the court's evaluation on a case-by-case basis. It lists factors that have been identified by courts under the judicially-created predominant purpose test, including the language of the contract, the portion of the contract price attributable, respectively, to the sale of goods and the other aspect of the transaction, the purpose of the parties in entering the contract, and the nature of the business of the parties.

f. The Importance of Deciding the Question of Scope Correctly

In some cases, the determination of scope has no effect on the outcome of the case because it would be resolved the same way under UCC Article 2 and common law. There are two reasons why this would occur. First, there are many provisions in Article 2 that are based on common law principles, so there is no difference between Article 2 and the common law on the question in issue. Second, Article 2 is not a comprehensive codification of all the rules governing the sale of goods, so there are many issues that are not covered at all in Article 2. UCC §1.103(b) provides that the general principles of law and equity supplement UCC provisions unless inconsistent with them. As a result, if the question to be resolved in relation to a sale of goods is not provided for in Article 2, it is resolved by applying the common law. However, where Article 2 and common law diverge, deciding whether and to what extent Article 2 applies is crucial. For example, if the transaction is a sale of goods, the statute of frauds under Article 2 requires most such contracts to be recorded and signed,[8] but there may be no statute of frauds applicable to the transaction if it is not predominantly a sale of goods, and the statute of limitations (the period within which a party must commence suit) may differ depending on whether the transaction is a sale of goods.

g. Special Rules of Article 2 That Apply Only to Merchants

If a contract is a sale of goods, Article 2 applies, irrespective of who the parties to the contract may be. It is the nature of the transaction, not the attributes or occupation of the parties, that is determinative. However, some sections of Article 2 distinguish parties who qualify as merchants from those who do not, and have special rules that apply to the sale where one or both parties are merchants.

"Merchant" is defined in UCC §2.104(1) to include a person who deals in goods of the kind involved in the transaction, or who, "otherwise by his occupation, holds himself out as having knowledge or skill peculiar to the practices or goods involved in the transaction." As this definition indicates, two categories of persons qualify as merchants. The first is those who are in the business of dealing in the goods of that kind, such as a wholesaler or retailer of such goods. The second is a broader category that includes persons who may not actually deal in such goods, but who, by who virtue of their business, reasonably appear to have expertise in the goods or in practices involved in transactions of the type involved. Courts differ on the exact scope of this second category of merchant. Official Comment 1 to UCC §2.104 indicates that the definition is intended to apply to professionals in the field, as distinct from a casual or inexperienced seller or buyer. Clearly, it would not apply to an ordinary consumer who buys goods for personal use or who sells a personal item in a casual sale.

Although a casual buyer or seller does not qualify as a merchant, the alternative definition of "merchant" (having expertise relating to goods or transactions of that type) could apply to a business that buys goods, not for resale, but for its own use. For example, a bank does not buy computers to resell them to its customers, so it presumably does not "deal in" computers. However, if it regularly buys computers for use in its operations, it could qualify it as a merchant with regard to those transactions, either because it

8. The statute of frauds relating to the sale of goods is discussed in Chapter 11.

has knowledge or skill relating to computers, or because it has knowledge or skill relating to transactions for the acquisition of office equipment. In *Vanguard Energy Services, LLC v. Shihadeh*, 82 N.E.3d 1284 (Ill. App. 2017), the contract involved the sale of natural gas, which, like electricity, is a movable, tangible object and hence goods. The buyer bought the gas simply to heat its building. It had no knowledge or skill relating to natural gas, and was simply the end user of the seller's product. The court held that the mere fact that the buyer was in business and procured goods for use in the business was not enough to establish that the buyer had knowledge or skill in relation to the practices involved in transaction of the type involved in this sale.

An example involving warranties illustrates the significance that merchant status could have in the resolution of a dispute. A warranty is an undertaking by the seller of goods that the goods meet specified standards, perform in a particular way, or are free of defects. UCC §2.313 recognizes that any seller (whether or not a merchant) could provide an express warranty relating to the goods, thereby undertaking by words or conduct that the goods will conform to a particular standard, description, or sample. In addition, Article 2 provides for various implied warranties that a seller is deemed to have given as a matter of law unless the contract specifically disclaims them. One of these implied warranties is the warranty of merchantability under UCC §2.314, which promises, in essence, that the goods would be acceptable in the trade and are fit for the ordinary purposes for which they are used. The implied warranty of merchantability is confined to sellers who qualify as merchants. The significance of this is demonstrated by a small claims case, *Petti v. Deridder*, 186 N.Y.S.3d 897 (N.Y. Just. Ct. 2023). The seller sold a washer and dryer to the buyer on Facebook Marketplace, an e-commerce platform that allows a Facebook subscriber to list goods for sale, and to negotiate the sale with a person that responds to the listing. At the time of the sale, the seller assured the buyer that the appliances "worked great." After taking delivery of the appliances, the buyer discovered that the washer was defective and needed expensive repair, so the buyer sued the seller in small claims court for a refund of the price of the washer. One of the bases for the claim was the implied warranty of merchantability. However, this seller was not a merchant, but merely a casual seller, who did not deal in goods of that kind or have knowledge or skill peculiar to the practices or goods involved in the transaction. The buyer therefore had no claim based on the implied warranty of merchantability, which applies only to merchant sellers. (However, because the seller had misguidedly assured the buyer that the washer "worked great" the court held him liable on the basis of that express warranty.)

There is further discussion of the merchant status in Article 2 in several parts of this book, for example, in sections 4.13.4, 6.3.2, and 11.3.3. For the present, just take note that Article 2 applies to everyone who enters into a contract for the sale of goods. It is only in those specific situations in which Article 2 expressly provides different rules where one or both parties to the sale are merchants that the question of whether a party meets the definition of merchant is relevant.

§2.7.3 The Influence of Article 2 in Cases Involving Contracts Other Than Sales of Goods

After Article 2 was enacted in the mid-twentieth century, it had a significant impact on the development of the common law, beyond transactions involving the sale of goods. Although it is not directly applicable to transactions that are not sales of goods, courts have been influenced by its provisions in the development of the general common law of contract. The result of this trend is that in many areas, differences between Article 2 and the common law have diminished over the years. The Restatement (Second) of Contracts, drafted after the enactment of the UCC, reflects this trend by reformulating a number of common law rules to bring them more closely in accord with Article 2.

§2.8 THE RESTATEMENT (SECOND) OF CONTRACTS

Contract texts and court opinions frequently cite the Restatement (Second) of Contracts (referred to from now on as Restatement, Second). The Restatement, Second, looks like a statute. It has numbered sections that set out rules in statutory style, followed by comments and illustrations. However, unlike the UCC, the Restatement, Second, is not a statute. It is a secondary authority[9]—a textbook formulated by the American Law Institute,[10] articulating the rules of the common law of contract, largely based on the drafters' analysis of court decisions.

As its title suggests, the Restatement, Second, is the second edition of the Restatement of Contracts to be published. The First Restatement, produced in the 1930s, was the first thorough systematization of American contract law and the first comprehensive attempt to give coherent form to American contract doctrine. As such, it was immensely important in the development of the modern common law of contracts. As mentioned in sections 2.3.1 and

9. The term "secondary authority" refers to legal writings like textbooks, law review articles, and commentaries that lack the binding force of official sources of law—such as statutes and court decisions (called "primary authority"). To the extent that a secondary authority is reliable and persuasive, it could be influential, but it never binds a court.

10. The American Law Institute (ALI) is identified in section 2.7.1 as the organization that collaborated with the ULC in drafting the UCC.

2.3.2, it combines elements of the classical approach and legal realism. The Restatement, Second, published in final form in 1981, extensively revised and updated the original Restatement. The Restatement, Second, reflects the post-classicist thinking described in section 2.3.2, and is also heavily influenced by the UCC, which had been widely enacted by states by the time that work was begun on the Restatement, Second. The rules in the Restatement, Second, are largely extracted from cases that had been decided at the time that it was drafted, but this does not mean that they actually represent what the majority of courts had held. Despite its name, the Restatement, Second, does not necessarily "restate" the settled law. Indeed, given the number of jurisdictions involved, it is often not possible to find a settled law. Also, because it seeks to offer guidance on the direction that its drafters believed the law should take, it sometimes favors a legal rule that had only minimal acceptance in decided cases. The Restatement, Second, is now over 40 years old, so there have been many cases decided since its publication. Courts have embraced many of the rules as articulated in the Restatement, Second, thereby reinforcing the drafter's exposition of the law. However, there are some rules set out in the Restatement, Second, that have not gained widespread judicial recognition, so that its account of those rules is not a reliable indicator of the law. Therefore, the best approach to the Restatement, Second, is to recognize that it is a very important and influential account of the law, frequently relied on by courts, but not binding on courts and not necessarily a reflection of what courts in a particular jurisdiction may have decided. Divergence between the Restatement, Second, and court opinions is noted periodically in other chapters of this book.

§2.9 A TRANSNATIONAL PERSPECTIVE ON CONTRACT LAW

The contracts course focuses on domestic contract law (that is, the law applicable within the United States to contracts entered into in the United States). However, many contracts are entered into between parties in the United States and parties in foreign countries. Transnational contracts are beyond the scope of this book, but it is useful for students to have some sense of what may lie beyond the borders of domestic law. To that end, most chapters of this book include a brief transnational perspective. The purpose of these notes is not to present detailed or comprehensive information on foreign or transnational contract law but merely to take note that other legal systems may sometimes have rules that are similar to those of American domestic law, but may sometimes approach issues quite differently.

Commonly, the law applicable to contracts across national boundaries is the domestic law of one of the countries whose citizen or resident is a party to the contract or the domestic law of the place where the contract was formed. This is because the parties may select the law of that jurisdiction as the law governing their contract or because international rules of choice of law determine that it is the applicable law. It is therefore possible that one would find, for example, that in one case New York law governs a contract entered into between a U.S. company and a German company, and in another case that German law is applicable.

Where the law of a foreign country governs the transaction, that law will likely have some similarities to American domestic law of contracts because many basic principles of contract law are universal. However, there could be notable differences. Just to give one example: The distinction between law and equity, described in section 2.5, is a creation of English law and is not found in countries that have a civilian legal system. As a result, the preference for damages over specific performance, described in section 1.2.4, which is based on the law-equity distinction, is not typically found in civilian systems.

The term comparative law is used to describe a comparative study of the law of two nations (for example, a study of American and French law relating to the formation of contract). Comparative law is distinct from international law, which is the law governing the relationship between nations and, in some situations, applicable to citizens of nations in the international sphere. For the most part, comparative law—the comparison of our system to that of other countries—is of greatest interest and relevance in the field of contracts. However, the examination of the laws of multiple nations would be difficult and exhausting. Therefore, the transnational perspectives in this book are based on two documents that provide a reasonable insight into principles of transnational law. One is the UNIDROIT Principles of International Commercial Contracts (UNIDROIT Principles), and the other is the United Nations Convention on Contracts for the International Sale of Goods (CISG).

The UNIDROIT Principles are a set of principles first promulgated in 1994 and updated periodically since then. This document is not a treaty but a compilation of general rules that are recommended as applicable to transnational commercial transactions. The status of this document is similar to that of the Restatement, Second: It is not binding law but is an influential scholarly publication. The authors studied the law of many countries and sought to distill them into a set of broadly accepted common principles. Although the UNIDROIT Principles are not binding rules, parties can adopt them in a contract, or they could have persuasive force in the adjudication of transnational contracts.

The CISG is a treaty. It has been ratified by the United States (as well as about 70 other countries), so it is binding law in transactions that fall within its scope. As its title indicates, it applies to sales of goods, so it is a kind of international version of Article 2. Like Article 2, its scope is confined to sales of goods, but its applicability is more restricted than Article

2. Under CISG Article 1, it applies only if both parties' places of business are in signatory states, the transaction is not a consumer sale, and the parties have not excluded its application in their contract.

EXAMPLES

Examples

1. As mentioned in section 2.7, UCC Article 2 is directly applicable only to sales of goods, even though it may have persuasive influence in cases involving other contracts. Students studying contract law often overlook this and become muddled, forgetting about Article 2 when the contract is a sale of goods or citing it as the governing law when the contract does not involve a sale of goods. These simple questions on the scope of Article 2 emphasize the distinction between sales of goods and other contracts. Which of the following contracts would be governed by Article 2?
   a. The sale of a condominium
   b. A contract to employ someone as a sales clerk in a clothing store
   c. The sale of a cow
   d. The sale of a meal in a restaurant
   e. The sale of a cake by a bakery

2. Buyer bought a mePhone by going to the manufacturer's website and ordering it online. The mePhone performs multiple functions such as phone, text, email, Internet browser, and camera. Its electronic innards are encased in a small rectangular box with a screen in the front. The mePhone sells for $800. The physical product costs $100 to make, and the value of the instrument lies in its electronic functioning. Is the purchase of the mePhone a sale of goods?

3. Mark Marchand is a wealthy merchant. He recently discovered that St. Francis of Assisi is the patron saint of merchants, so he decided to honor the saint by placing a large sculpture of him in the lobby of his building. He entered into a contract with Chip Chisel, a sculptor, under which Chip agreed to carve a 15-foot-high marble sculpture of St. Francis for a price of $100,000. (The piece of marble cost Chip $15,000. The rest of the price for the sculpture represents his labor in executing the sculpture.) Is this a sale of goods? Would your answer change if Mark, not Chip, supplied the piece of marble?

4. Sally bought a new car, so she advertised her old car for sale. Ben responded to the advertisement, and on May 1, Sally and Ben made an oral agreement that Ben would buy the car for $6,000. The parties arranged that delivery and payment would take place on May 5. On May 3, Sally called Ben and canceled the sale. This is a breach of contract. It would cost Ben $6,500 to buy an equivalent used car, so Ben has suffered damages of $500 — the difference between the contract price and

the cost of buying an equivalent car on the market.[11] If Article 2 applies, Ben cannot sue Sally because an oral contract is unenforceable under the Article 2 statute of frauds (UCC §2.201), which requires a contract for the sale of goods for a price of $500 or more to be recorded and signed. However, if Article 2 does not apply, Ben can enforce the contract, because the common law does not have a statute of frauds applicable under these circumstances.[12] Ben argues that Article 2 does not apply because neither he nor Sally is a merchant. Is he right? Would he be right if Sally had been a used car dealer?

5. A contract between Business, Inc. and Tech Solutions, Inc. provided that Tech would supply billing and account management software to Business and would also provide services in relation to the use of the software, such as technical training and support. Some time after the contract was entered, Business discovered that defects in the software had caused it significant losses. Business therefore sued Tech for damages. Tech raised the defense that Business had waited too long to bring the suit, which was barred by the statute of limitations. The limitation period under UCC Article 2 is much shorter than that for common law contracts. Business filed its complaint after the UCC limitation period had run, but before the end of the longer common law limitation period. Therefore, Tech's statute of limitations defense would succeed if the contract was predominantly a sale of goods, but would fail if it was not. For this reason, it is crucial to decide whether the sale of goods or the service predominates.
   a. Is there any sale of goods in this transaction?
   b. If there is, what information is relevant to decide whether or not the sale of goods is the predominant aspect of the transaction?

Explanations

1. a. Although this is a sale, a condominium is not goods but real property, so UCC Article 2 does not govern the transaction. Under UCC §2-105(1), goods must be movable, tangible things. The building materials that went into building the condominium were once goods, before they became incorporated into the structure. But once they were so incorporated, they became united with the land and became real property.
   b. Although the clerk will be selling clothing (goods) in the course of employment, the contract to employ the clerk is not a sale of goods but a contract for labor (services).

11. Damages based on the difference between the contract price and the cost of a reasonable substitute is a common form of damages for breach of contract. Damages issues are raised regularly throughout this book and are focused on in Chapter 18.

12. The statute of frauds relating to the sale of goods and common law transactions is discussed in Chapter 11.

c. The cow is a living animal, not an inanimate object, but it still qualifies as goods. Livestock and crops (including unborn animals and growing crops) are specifically included within the definition of goods in UCC §2.105.

d. A restaurant meal involves both the sale of the food and the provision of services associated with it, such as serving it and providing a table at which to eat it as well as crockery and silverware. It is therefore a hybrid transaction. The initial decision is to determine whether the sale of goods or the provision of services predominates. The court must make this determination based on all the circumstances of the transaction, including the relative value of the goods and the services provided under the contract, any relevant contract language used by the parties, and their reasonable expectations based on the commercial context, including the nature of the transaction and the restaurant's business.

   Once it is established whether the sale of goods or the service predominates, the appropriate governing law must be selected. Under the judicially-created predominant purpose test, which still applies in states that have not enacted the 2022 amendments to UCC §2.102 and 2.106, if the predominant purpose of the contract is the sale of goods, with incidental services, Article 2 applies to the transaction as a whole, but if services are predominant and the goods are supplied incidentally to the service, other law applies to the entire transaction.

   In states that have enacted the 2022 amendments to UCC §§2.102 and 2.106, the approach is more nuanced than the judicially created predominant purpose test. If the sale-of-goods aspects of the transaction do not predominate, UCC §2.102(2)(a) applies the provisions of Article 2 only to that part of the contract that relates primarily to the sales aspect of the transaction (that is, to the supply of the food). For example, Article 2 would supply an implied warranty that the food is fit to be eaten. Article 2 provisions that relate primarily to the transaction as a whole, such as the Article 2 rules governing formation of the contract, are inapplicable, and are subject to common law principles.

   If the sale-of-goods aspects predominate, UCC §2.102(2)(b) applies Article 2 to the transaction as a whole. However, the section recognizes that in appropriate circumstances, other law could apply to those aspects of the transaction that do not relate to the sale of goods. For example, health laws regulating the conduct of a restaurant business would apply.

e. The bakery provided labor to bake the cake, so it may seem that this is also a hybrid transaction, but it is not. It is just a sale of goods. Almost all goods go through some manufacturing or preparation process before they are sold, but pre-sale labor in making the goods and preparing them for sale does not make this into a hybrid transaction. If the buyer simply buys the end product of a manufacturing process, and no labor or services are provided in conjunction with the sale, the transaction is purely a sale of goods. In *Marisco, Ltd. v. GL Engineering & Construction, Pte., Ltd.*, 2020 WL 556393 (D. Haw. 2020), the manufacturer of a floating dry dock sought to dismiss a claim for breach of implied warranty under UCC Article 2 on the basis that Article 2 did not apply to the transaction because the labor and services involved in building the dock predominated over the materials used in its fabrication. The court denied the motion, noting that a dry dock fits the definition of "goods" because it is a moveable thing, and that the contract appeared to be the sale of the finished dock, rather than a hybrid transaction involving both goods and services.

2. The purchase of the mePhone is a sale of goods. The device is a movable, physical object. It does not matter that the ability to use it is dependent on software that itself may not be goods. The phone is not simply a conduit for the delivery of the software. It is a movable, tangible item (very much like a modern car or fridge) that requires software to make it function. It is not relevant to the phone's classification as goods that the cost of making it is small in relation to its price, or that it was bought online.

3. Although the sculpture is large and probably needs heavy machinery to move it, it is tangible, movable property, and therefore goods. Like the cake in Example 2e, the sculpture is the end product of a manufacturing process, and Mark is just buying the end product without any services relating to it. Therefore, this is not a hybrid transaction, so it is not necessary to decide whether the sale of goods or the labor predominates. It does not matter that the skill and work in making the sculpture is significantly more valuable than the marble. This is true of many manufactured goods. A sale involves transfer of title from the seller to the buyer, so the correct approach is to ask whether the end product, on which the presale labor has been expended, is the object of the transfer of title. If it is, the transaction is a sale of goods, even though the process of manufacture involves labor as well as materials, and even if the value of the labor greatly exceeds that of the materials. Therefore, if the seller's labor is entirely employed in the creation of the tangible, movable end-product that is sold, the transaction is properly treated as a sale of goods.

   The answer would change if Mark supplied the marble because Chip would then be supplying no goods at all and there is no transfer of title to the physical object, which was owned by Mark at all times. Chip would therefore be performing labor on Mark's chunk of marble. The transaction would not be governed by Article 2.

4. Ben would be wrong in both cases. This Example emphasizes what was said in section 2.7.2(f): Article 2 applies if the transaction qualifies as a

sale of goods, which this does. It applies to all sales of goods irrespective of whether one or both parties are merchants. Although there are some provisions of Article 2 that are expressly stated to be applicable only if one or both parties are merchants, the absence or presence of this status makes no difference in the rest of Article 2. Ben cannot enforce the oral contract against Sally because it is subject to Article 2 and the statute of frauds applies.

5. This Example is based on *Pain Center of SE Indiana, LLC v. Origin Healthcare Solutions, LLC*, cited in section 2.7.2d. That case involved a dispute between Pain Center, a medical clinic, and Origin Healthcare Solutions, the provider of billing and account management software.
   a. As noted in section 2.7.2d, in *Pain Center* the court held that even though the software was not provided to the clinic in a tangible medium, it was nevertheless goods under UCC Article 2 because it was standard, preexisting non-customized software. A court that adopts this approach would classify the software as goods. Another court may focus on the intangible nature of the software and disagree with the conclusion that it should be classified as goods.
   b. If there is a sale of goods component in the contract, it must be determined if it is the predominant aspect of the transaction. In addition to access to the software, the contract in *Pain Center* provided for various related services to be performed by Origin, such as training and support and the submission of claims for payment to medical insurers. The contract was therefore a hybrid transaction, including a sale of both goods and services. After the contract had been performed for some years, the clinic discovered that defects in the software had caused it significant losses and it sued Origin, which raised the defense that the claim was barred by the statute of limitations. This defense would succeed if the sale-of-goods aspect predominated, but would fail if the services aspect of the contract predominated. This was because the suit was brought after the shorter Article 2 statute of limitations had run, but before the end of the longer common law limitation period.

      Courts have identified several factors that should be considered in deciding which aspect of the transaction predominates: The language of the contract, the relative cost of the goods and the services, the nature of the seller's business, and the reason for entering the contract. In *Pain Center*, the court did not find much guidance in the language of the contract. However, the portion of the price allocated to the service component of the contract was higher than that for the goods. The court also found that the principal goal of the contract was to give Pain Center access to Origin's services in collecting payments, and that the software was just a vehicle for Pain Center to communicate claims information to Origin to enable it to render that service. As a result, the court found that the sale of services was the predominant aspect of the transaction, with the sale of goods ancillary to that purpose. Therefore, the shorter UCC statute of limitations did not apply. The longer common law limitation period had not ended by the time that suit was brought, so Pain Center's claim was not barred.

CHAPTER 3

The Doctrine of Precedent and a Contract Case Analysis

§3.1 STUDYING CONTRACT LAW THROUGH APPELLATE CASES

This chapter is primarily concerned with case analysis and the doctrine of precedent. In a common law system, the decisions of appellate courts are an important source of law because the legal rules established by an appellate court become precedents that must be followed in subsequent cases. In a field of law like contracts, in which legal rules are primarily created by courts rather than by the legislature, court decisions are the principal source of legal doctrine. This is why so many law school courses are taught predominantly through the study of court opinions and why the analysis of cases is such an important legal skill. This chapter focuses on the method of reading and analyzing cases—a crucial competence in a common law system. The text of this chapter explains the creation and comprehension of judicial precedent and the Examples and Explanations at the end of the chapter focus on the skill of understanding how to read a court opinion and to garner the legal rules and principles that it enunciates.

Determining the law from a judicial opinion can be trickier than reading a statutory provision, because the opinion includes an outline of the facts of the particular case and often also contains some legal discussion that is not part of the court's binding pronouncement of the law. It is important to take note of the particular facts and procedural context of the case because these qualify and confine the scope of the legal rules that the court enunciates. The facts of the case play another role too—they provide a story that gives the legal discussion a context and makes it less abstract.

In focusing on cases, course materials may overemphasize litigation by presenting transactions that have gone so irreconcilably wrong that the parties have felt it necessary to litigate rather than resolve their dispute by negotiation and compromise. However, only a fraction of contracts end up in litigation and fewer still reach the highest courts without being settled along the way. In addition, many lawyers who work in the field of contract law do not litigate at all, but spend their time on counseling clients, assisting clients in negotiation, and drafting the agreement. Therefore, even though there is an unavoidable emphasis on litigation when law is studied through cases, issues of client counseling, negotiation, and contract formation often emerge from the facts of a case.

State court cases in casebooks are mostly decisions of appellate courts. In fact, trial court opinions are not binding precedent, and only a few states publish them.[1] States typically have at least two levels of appellate courts. In some states there may be multiple avenues of appeal before a case reaches the point where an appellant may petition the state's supreme court to hear the appeal. For the sake of simplicity, this description uses a two-level appeal structure in which the decision of a trial court may first be appealed to an intermediate court of appeals, with the possibility thereafter for an appeal to the state's supreme court. Unlike trial courts, which consist of a single judge (with or without a jury), an appellate court sits in panels consisting of several judges. The exact size of the panel varies from one jurisdiction to another. If all the judges on the panel agree on the result and its rationale, the court is able to render a unanimous decision. However, it is common for members of an appellate panel to disagree on the proper disposition of the case. When that happens, the decision of the court is that adopted by the majority of judges on the panel. The majority opinion is written by one of the judges and is joined by the other judges who support it. A judge who disagrees with the reasoning of the majority but agrees with the result writes a concurring opinion and a judge who disagrees with the resolution reached by the majority writes a dissenting opinion. If there is more than one concurring or dissenting judge, they may join in the concurring or dissenting opinion or may write separate concurring or dissenting opinions. Sometimes a panel is so badly divided that no majority of its judges sign onto any opinion. In that case, the opinion with the most votes becomes the plurality opinion of the court.

1. As noted in section 2.6, federal courts regularly deal with contracts cases as well. In the federal system, trial court decisions are published and are often included in casebooks. However, they also do not have binding precedential force.

§3.2 HOW JUDGES MAKE CONTRACT LAW: JUDICIAL PRECEDENT

§3.2.1 What Is Precedent?

As mentioned in section 2.4.1, the common law developed in the Royal Courts of England in which judges, acting on royal authority, decided disputes between subjects. As these judges decided cases over time, they recognized the value of deciding similar cases in the same way. This allows for efficiency in the administration of justice, it enables people to predict case outcomes more accurately, and it serves a fundamental conception of justice: the equal treatment of people in like situations. As the common law developed, it became established practice for court decisions to be recorded so that they could be used as the basis of resolving later cases. This meant that a decision no longer only settled the dispute between the immediate parties. It formed a rule to be followed in the next case involving similar facts. As the number of recorded decisions grew to cover a greater variety of cases, the collection of legal rules expanded to create a compendious body of law. The principle that a judicial decision creates a rule of law, binding on later cases involving similar facts and legal issues, is known as the doctrine of precedent or, in Latin, *stare decisis* (roughly translated "the decision stands").

§3.2.2 Who Is Bound by Precedent?

Obviously, the parties to a case are bound by the judicial determination of their suit. However, the doctrine of precedent deals with the binding effect of the decision beyond the parties, on later like cases between other litigants. The facts of the earlier and later cases play a significant role in the determination of whether the earlier decision is a binding precedent. If there are significant differences in the facts of the cases, the later court may decline to follow the precedent of the earlier case on the grounds that the facts of the cases are distinguishable—that the earlier decision must be confined to its particular facts and is not applicable to the different facts of the later case. This does not mean that the two cases must have exactly the same facts. The issue is whether the crucial factual elements are sufficiently similar that the second case comes within the rule of the first. Even when there are notable factual differences, the later court may find the circumstances of the cases to be analogous, so that the rule may be treated as governing the second case as well.

The factual similarity of the cases is not the only issue to consider in deciding the precedential relevance of the prior case, which may also be affected by other factors, such as the procedural context in which the earlier court rendered its decision or the scope and purpose of the court's decision. In addition, the previous court opinion may be unclear or ambiguous, so that its scope and meaning may have to be interpreted by the later court. This may allow the later court to decline to follow the decision of a prior court by finding that it is distinguishable, or by interpreting it as consistent with the later court's holding.

Precedents are not universally binding on every court. The binding force of a precedent depends on the seniority of the court and the jurisdiction in which it sits. The court that decided the case should follow its own precedents. This is true even where the membership of the court changes, so that different judges hear the later case. Therefore, for example, a state supreme court usually considers itself bound by a precedent that it set in an earlier case. However, a court cannot be absolutely bound by its own precedents, and may depart from them where the court concludes that the precedent is wrong or no longer tenable. A court's decision to overrule its own precedent is not taken lightly. The court weighs the need for flexibility and development in the law against the policies of predictability and fairness that motivate the doctrine of precedent.

A precedent is absolutely binding on courts of inferior rank in the same judicial hierarchy. Unlike the court that decided the prior case, a lower court cannot simply refuse to follow a precedent because it considers it to be wrong. (However, as noted above, the lower court may find a basis for holding that the precedent is not on point, either as a matter of interpretation, or by distinguishing the prior case.) As explained in section 2.6, the judicial hierarchy that usually deals with contract cases is the state court system. Therefore, if the state supreme court decides a case, the rule of that case binds every other court in that state. If a case is not appealed to the state supreme court, the intermediate appellate court makes the final decision in the case. Its decision binds all courts in the state except for the supreme court, which is senior in the judicial hierarchy.[2] If, later on, a different case involving the same legal issue reaches the supreme court, the court may find the earlier decision of the intermediate appellate court persuasive, and may decide to adopt it. However, it is not bound to do so. A case decided, even by the highest court, in one judicial hierarchy (that is, the supreme court of one state) does not bind any court in another judicial hierarchy (another state). Again, however, it could be of persuasive weight because courts often look to the cases decided in other states for guidance in resolving issues of first impression in their own jurisdictions.

2. With the proviso, stated above, that the appellate court itself may decide to overrule its own precedent.

The relationship between state and federal courts is too complex for discussion in any depth here. As a broad rule, when a federal court decides a matter of state law, it must follow precedents established by the courts of that state. If the superior courts of the state have not yet had occasion to decide the particular legal issue, the federal court must try to determine from analogous or related caselaw how the state's supreme court would be likely to decide the matter if presented with it. Because a federal court is outside the state's judicial hierarchy, its decision on a matter of state law does not absolutely bind the courts of the state, but it is persuasive authority.

Finally, it is important to recognize the relationship between judge-made law and legislation. Unless the court has pronounced on a matter of constitutional interpretation that cannot be overturned by legislation, the legislature may enact a statute that overrides a judicial precedent, even by the state's highest court.

§3.2.3 The Drawbacks of the System of Precedent

The system of precedent aims at predictability, stability, and fairness by promoting consistency in the legal rules applied to successive cases. The system also has some drawbacks. First, there is inertia inherent in the system which can allow an unsound or outdated rule to persist for some time either because the state supreme court declines to overturn it or because there has not been an occasion for the court to reevaluate it.

Second, rulemaking through court decisions tends to be sporadic and disorganized. When a legislature decides to enact a law, it can proceed in an orderly way to address the problem comprehensively. It can hold hearings, order staff research, and engage in debate. A statute can then be fashioned that is designed to deal with all the issues involved and to set out all the applicable rules. Caselaw develops more spasmodically. Courts have no control over the order in which cases arise, and they can respond only to the immediate issues involved in each case. They cannot legislate broadly but must confine themselves to resolving the dispute at hand, based on the facts of that specific case. As a result, judicial development of doctrine is haphazard. Some areas of law may be covered thoroughly because they are litigated frequently, while others may languish for decades. Some areas of the law may thus be regularly refined and updated while others are neglected. It sometimes happens that a major issue remains unresolved for years, because no party has wished to pursue it to the point of a definitive appellate pronouncement. These gaps may be filled by legislative action, but they often are not.

Third, it is often harder to find the legal rule in a judicial opinion than in a statute. Statutes directly state the rules enacted by the legislature. Judge-made rules are contained in opinions, which can be dense, detailed, and lengthy pieces of writing. An opinion sets out the facts of the case, identifies and articulates the applicable legal principles, and finally reaches a decision or judgment resolving the issues between the parties. Somewhere in this body of writing, there are legal rules that serve as precedent. It is not always obvious what these rules are. To find them, the lawyer must study and interpret the case. If the case has been decided by a divided appellate court, concurring or dissenting opinions can call into question the scope, force, and durability of the majority or plurality opinion.

§3.3 THE ANATOMY OF A JUDICIAL OPINION

§3.3.1 *Ratio Decidendi* (Rule or Holding) and *Obiter Dictum*

Court opinions state the facts of the case, as determined by the factfinder (the jury, or in non-jury cases, the judge) after weighing the evidence and resolving conflicts in testimony. The factual conclusions reached at trial are not disturbed on appeal unless they are so unreasonable that no support can be found for them in the evidence. Therefore, the recital of facts in an appellate opinion is based on the findings at trial. The factual basis of the opinion is very important because the rule of the case must be determined with reference to it.

Having laid the factual foundation for its decision, the court proceeds to resolve the legal issues. The judge could simply state the rule to be applied and give judgment. However, in most cases that involve significant legal issues, the judge justifies and articulates the rationale for the rule and its application in the case. The statement of the rule and its reasoning are the portion of the case that constitutes the precedent. This part of the opinion is called the rule or the holding or, in Latin, the *ratio decidendi* (roughly translated as "reasoning for the decision").

Frequently, the opinion does not confine itself to matter that is directly related to the resolution of the dispute before the court, but ranges beyond this to deal with ancillary or collateral matters on which the judge considers it necessary to express a view. These collateral discussions may be included, for example, to further explain and qualify the holding or to give guidance in future cases on how this court will view variations of the factual circumstances. This collateral matter is called *obiter dictum* ("said in passing") or simply dictum (dicta, in the plural form). Because a dictum is not necessary to the disposition of the case, it is not binding precedent and has only persuasive value. Its persuasive value depends on the seniority of the court that issued the opinion. For example, a dictum in a unanimous supreme court opinion strongly signals how the court will likely decide that question, so it is highly influential to a lower court. The Examples provide a simple exercise in identifying the rule of a case and distinguishing it from dictum.

§3.3.2 The Process of Inductive and Deductive Reasoning in the Creation and Application of Legal Rules

When a general rule is applied to a particular case, a process of deductive reasoning is followed. The general rule, accepted as true, serves as the major premise. The particular facts to which it will be applied are the minor premise. Provided that there is a necessary connection between these two premises, a conclusion is produced that must also be true. For example:

Major premise (the generally applicable rule of law): To form a contract, the recipient of an offer (the offeree) must communicate acceptance of it to the party making the offer (the offeror) within the time stipulated in the offer.

Minor premise (the particular facts): The offeree in this case communicated acceptance of the offer to the offeror on the day after the time stipulated in the offer.

Conclusion: The offeree's attempt at acceptance was too late and did not form a contract.

Deductive reasoning therefore, allows a rule of law to be applied in a particular case. But where did this major premise, the rule of law, come from? In the common law, most such rules have been created by precedent through a process opposite from deductive reasoning: The ruling in a particular case is generalized to create a rule of law applicable beyond the case. This is called inductive reasoning. In an earlier case the offer stated that, to accept the offer, the offeree must communicate acceptance to the offeror by not later than three days after the date of the offer. The offeree decided to accept the offer, but did not communicate acceptance of it to the offeror until five days after the date of the offer. In that case, the state supreme court ruled that the offer had lapsed at the end of the three-day acceptance period specified in in offer, and that the offeree's attempted acceptance five days after the offer was ineffective and did not create a contract. The doctrine of precedent thereafter generalizes the decision of the supreme court in that case, creating a rule that not just the offeree in that case, but all offerees, must accept the offer before its lapse date to create a contract. In the next case, involving an attempt to accept an offer after its lapse date, this rule is applied by deductive reasoning to resolve the question of whether the late response is an effective acceptance.

As this example indicates, there must be a connection between the major premise (the general rule of law derived from the earlier case) and the minor premise (the facts of the current case) for the precedent to be on point and binding. This usually means that there must be a sufficient factual similarity between the cases to make the precedent applicable. If that connection is weak, so that there are notable factual difference between the cases, the earlier precedent may be persuasive and applied by analogy, but it would not be binding. For example, the later case involves a contract under which a customer booked a seven-day cruise. The contract stated that the customer could cancel the booking without any penalty by giving notice to the cruise line within two days of booking the cruise. The customer gave the notice three days after booking the cruise. The question of whether the late notice was effective to terminate the contract is different from the question of whether the late acceptance of an offer creates a contract, so the precedent of the earlier case is not directly on point. However, there is an analogy between the situations and the rationale for requiring a timely response is similar, so the earlier case is a helpful persuasive precedent

When a court's decision is based on a prior case that serves as precedent, the earlier case is cited as authority for the rule applied in the later decision. In some cases, this citation of authority may be the only justification advanced by the court for the rule. That is, in deciding in a particular way, the court may rely solely on an established rule and advance no explanation of its own. However, many court opinions do not just rely on precedential authority to support the disposition of the case. The opinion may explain why a precedent is or is not on point, evaluate the arguments made by the parties, offer its own analysis of the law, and articulate policy concerns that focus on such questions as the public interest or the equities between the parties. As a result, many court opinions are complex and nuanced and need to be studied carefully and critically.

§3.4 A TRANSNATIONAL PERSPECTIVE ON THE DOCTRINE OF PRECEDENT

The doctrine of precedent is a central feature of the common law system, but court decisions do not carry the same weight in civilian systems. Although civilian systems accord some weight to judicial precedent, they rely primarily on comprehensive codes and scholarly commentary as the source of legal rules. Civilians typically see the role of courts as dispute resolution, not lawmaking—the court's job is to apply the law to the facts of the case for the purpose of settling the immediate dispute between the parties, and not to establish legal rules that will be applicable to later cases. With the exception of certain high courts and constitutional tribunals, court decisions in civilian countries are short, not very analytical, and fact-based.

§3.5 A FICTITIOUS OPINION ON AN EXCULPATORY AGREEMENT EXECUTED BY A PARENT ON BEHALF OF A MINOR

The Examples following this section are all concerned with the doctrine of precedent and are based on the following opinion of a fictitious state supreme court. (Although the opinion is fictitious, the issues discussed and the cases cited are real.) The opinion deals with the question of whether the plaintiff, a minor, is bound by a contract executed by his father on his behalf. The contract in issue is an agreement releasing the operator of a ski area from liability for any injury that the minor may suffer while skiing.[3] Such agreements are widely used by providers of services and are commonly called exculpatory agreements, liability releases, or waivers. The fictional state supreme court consists of nine justices. Seven joined the majority opinion, one concurred, and one dissented. The Examples follow the opinion.

De CISIS, Justice, delivered the opinion of the court.

Last year, the plaintiff, a 16-year-old boy, was severely injured while skiing on a ski slope owned and operated by the defendant ski resort. Before the plaintiff was admitted to the ski slope, his father, who had taken him to the ski area, signed a standard document which the defendant required of all users of the ski slope. It released the defendant from all liability for injury suffered by the plaintiff in the ski area, including claims based on the negligence of the defendant or its employees. As a result of his injuries, the plaintiff incurred significant medical expenses and suffered intense pain and discomfort for many months. The plaintiff, represented by his guardian ad litem,[4] commenced this suit against the defendant for damages for his medical expenses and pain and suffering, alleging that his injury was caused by the defendant's negligent maintenance of the ski slopes. The defendant moved to dismiss the complaint on the grounds that the exculpatory agreement, signed by the plaintiff's father, waived his right to sue. The plaintiff opposed the motion for dismissal, asserting that any contract entered into by a minor is avoidable by the minor and cannot be enforced against him, whether the minor entered into the contract on his own or represented by a parent. The plaintiff argued that this rule is particularly applicable to an exculpatory agreement because, as a matter of public policy, a parent does

3. The issues discussed by the fictional court in this opinion are covered in sections 13.13, and 14.2. It is not necessary to read those sections to deal with these Examples, which focus on the doctrine of precedent. All the relevant rules and principles of substantive law that are needed to answer the questions here are set out in the opinion.

4. A guardian ad litem is a person appointed by the court to appear in the lawsuit on behalf of a minor or a person who lacks mental capacity.

not have the legal power to waive a child's right to claim damages for personal injury. The trial court granted the defendant's motion to dismiss, holding that a parent does have the legal power to waive liability for personal injury on behalf of a child and that such a waiver is not contrary to public policy. The court of appeals affirmed.

It is well established, and conceded by the defendant, that a minor lacks contractual capacity and therefore has the right to disaffirm any contract that he entered into prior to reaching the age of majority, which is 18 years old in this state. Therefore, it is beyond doubt that the plaintiff would not have been bound by the exculpatory agreement had he executed it himself. This rule is intended to protect minors from exploitation, improvidence, and bad judgment. *See, e.g., Douglass v. Pflueger Hawai'i, Inc.*, 135 P.3d 129 (Haw. 2006). However, the defendant seeks to persuade us that this concern is not present where the minor's parent enters the agreement on his behalf.

We have not previously had occasion to rule on whether a parent can bind a minor child to a waiver of liability, but this question has been addressed by several other courts. Some courts have held that the broad parental authority to contract on behalf of a minor child encompasses the power to bind the child to an exculpatory agreement. *See, e.g., Justice v. Marvel LLC*, 965 N.W.2d 335 (Min. Ct. App. 2021), *rev'd on other grounds*, 979 N.W.2d 894 (Minn. 2022). However, many courts have held that a parent does not have the power to deprive a minor of the right to sue for personal injury damages by executing a pre-injury exculpatory agreement on behalf of the minor, and have permitted the minor to disaffirm such waivers. *See, e.g., Woodman v. Kera, LLC*, 785 N.W.2d 1 (Mich. 2010) (noting that under the state's common law, firmly established for over a century, a minor cannot be bound to a pre-injury exculpatory agreement executed by a parent or guardian); *Hojnowski v. Vans Skate Park*, 901 A.2d 381 (N.J. 2006) (stressing the importance of protecting children from parental improvidence); *Cooper v. Aspen Skiing Co.*, 48 P.3d 1229 (Colo. 2002) (holding that to allow a parent to release a child's future claims for negligent injury would leave the minor in an unacceptably precarious position, with no recourse against the tortfeasor).

Some courts have confined this rule to cases in which the defendant was a commercial enterprise, and have upheld an exculpatory agreement executed by the parent in favor of schools, municipalities, or volunteer-run or nonprofit organizations. *See, e.g., Zivich v. Mentor Soccer Club, Inc.*, 696 N.E.2d 201 (Ohio 1998) (reasoning that where the defendant is a nonprofit or volunteer organization, a parent's pre-injury exculpatory agreement binds the minor because the inability to control liability and the cost of insuring against it would preclude such organizations from operating). *But see Galloway v. State*, 790 N.W.2d 252 (Iowa 2010) (prioritizing the protection of children over the speculative harm to school and other nonprofit activities); *BJ's Wholesale Club v. Rosen*, 80 A.3d 345 (Md. 2013) (refusing to distinguish between commercial and noncommercial defendants). It is a legitimate concern that community activity offered by volunteer and nonprofit organizations could not be sustained if these organizations could not insulate themselves from liability. However, this concern cannot overturn the more compelling argument that upholding an exculpatory agreement by a parent is a disincentive to care and leaves the minor unprotected from negligence.

The defendant argues that parents are empowered to make decisions for their minor children in the most important aspects of life, including such vital matters as health, safety, and education. A parent should therefore also have the power to execute an exculpatory agreement to enable the child to engage in a chosen activity. However, the policy of protecting children from negligent injury must be the predominant concern. To uphold a parent's agreement to waive negligence liability on behalf of a child creates a disincentive to the exercise of care by the service provider and leaves the child unprotected from the parent's careless or thoughtless release of the important right of recourse for personal injury. We therefore follow those cases in which courts have held that the power to bind a minor to an exculpatory agreement is not within the proper scope of parental authority.

We do not decide today if a parent can ever bind a minor to a contract. However, exculpatory agreements, even those entered into by an adult of full contractual capacity, raise the particular question of whether it is good public policy to allow a service provider to demand its customer's advance absolution from negligence. We have not yet pronounced on this question, but courts in other states have indicated discomfort in enforcing such agreements, even where executed by an adult, because they allow the purveyor of services to shift the burden of injury to the other party and to escape responsibility for negligence. *See, e.g., Gershon v. Regency Driving Center*, 845 A.2d 720 (N.J. Super. Ct. App. Div. 2004) (noting that exculpatory agreements are generally disfavored for this reason). Courts have not necessarily found such agreements to be invalid per se, but have scrutinized them closely and have not been inclined to enforce them if they were unilaterally imposed without genuine bargaining. *See, e.g., Hawkins v. Peart*, 37 P.3d 1062 (Utah 2001) (noting the unacceptable shifting of the risk of injury by a unilaterally imposed exculpatory clause); *Chadwick v. Colt Ross Outfitters*, 100 P.3d 465 (Colo. 2004) (holding that an exculpatory agreement violates public policy if the signatory is put at the mercy of the other party's negligence as a result of an obvious disadvantage in bargaining power); *Bagley v. Mt. Bachelor*, 340 P.3d 27 (Or. 2014) (holding a release of liability to be avoidable as unconscionable); *Brigance v. Vail Summit Resorts, Inc.*, 883 F.3d 1243 (10th Cir. 2018) (articulating four factors to be considered in deciding whether an exculpatory agreement is enforceable). These decisions strike an appropriate balance between the public interest in holding a party accountable for negligent conduct and the countervailing public interest in freedom of contract, which allows purveyors of recreational activity to use the device of contract to protect themselves from the risk of crippling liability. However, in light of our decision that the exculpatory agreement in this case is avoidable on grounds of the plaintiff's minority, we do not have to address the issue of the general enforceability of these agreements today.

The courts below erred in dismissing the suit. We reverse and remand this matter for trial.

QUIBBLE, Justice, concurring.

I agree with the conclusion that this case must go to trial. However, I disagree with the majority's narrow basis for refusing to enforce the waiver. Even had the plaintiff not been a minor, the waiver should be invalidated on the grounds that it is contrary to the fundamental public policy of holding an actor accountable for negligent conduct. The provider of a service, whether essential or recreational, should not be able to evade responsibility for negligent conduct causing injury, merely by requiring a customer to sign a standard, nonnegotiable form that is directly against the customer's interests.

CONTRA, Justice, dissenting.

In allowing the plaintiff to avoid this contract, the majority adopts an absurdly rigid approach. While it is true that minors need protection from improvident action and exploitation by adults, and from ill-considered or badly-motivated parental decisions, there is no evidence in this case to suggest that any such factors were present. By refusing to permit a parent to waive liability on behalf of a child, the majority creates an untenable situation in which children will find it increasingly difficult to participate in recreational activity because it will become too risky and costly for a business to allow them access to those activities. The law allows parents to make numerous significant and life-changing decisions for their children, so it seems absurd to single out this one for proscription. In the absence of evidence of a parent's bad motives or the other party's improper or deceptive conduct, this liability waiver should be upheld and the decisions below affirmed.

EXAMPLES

Examples

1. Consider the following questions based on this opinion:
   a. What is the holding of the case?
   b. What nonbinding dicta can you find in the majority opinion?
   c. What is the precedential effect of the dissenting opinion?
   d. It is easy to see why a judge who disagrees with the majority's disposition would be motivated to write a dissenting opinion. But why would a judge who agrees with the majority's conclusion feel the need to write a concurring opinion? What purpose does the concurring opinion serve in this case?

e. What is the impact and authority of the cases cited in the majority opinion? Do any bind the court? Is the majority opinion simply based on the authority of these cases? If not, what rationales does the majority use to support its resolution of the case?
f. In addition to deciding the dispute between the particular parties in this case, the effect of the court's decision under the doctrine of precedent is to render all future agreements of this kind unenforceable. The court is therefore setting public policy for the state and creating a legal rule that becomes universally binding in the state. This is close to a legislative function. The doctrine of precedent confers this lawmaking power on the court, but are there, or should there be, any restraints on the court's exercise of this lawmaking task, which normally falls within the legislative realm?

2. Subsequent to this case, the supreme court of another state must resolve a case with substantially similar facts. There is no judicial precedent on this issue in this other jurisdiction. What impact will this decision have on the resolution of the subsequent case?

3. Subsequent to this case, trial courts in the same state must decide whether the contracts in the following cases are avoidable. Are the trial courts bound to find the contract avoidable on the authority of this supreme court opinion? If not, does the opinion offer any guidance to the trial courts on whether the contract should be avoidable?
   a. A pre-injury exculpatory agreement, signed by the minor's parent on the minor's behalf, was executed in favor of a volunteer-organized basketball club.
   b. Parents settled their minor child's personal injury claim after suit had been brought. No exculpatory agreement was entered into before the minor was admitted to a commercial trampoline park. The minor was injured while jumping on one of the trampolines and sued the trampoline park for personal injury damages. After the suit was commenced, the minor's parents accepted the defendant's offer to settle the case. In exchange for a cash payment, the settlement agreement waived any claims that the minor may have against the defendant.
   c. The exculpatory agreement was in a standard contract entered into by an adult before the adult used a commercial wall-climbing facility. After the adult was injured in a fall, allegedly caused by the negligence of the operator of the facility, the adult sued for damages.
   d. A minor bought a car, assisted by a parent. The minor signed the contract and the parent signed a statement immediately below the minor's signature, expressly giving the minor permission to enter into the contract. The minor no longer wishes to keep the car and seeks to avoid the contract.

Explanations

1. a. The holding of the case is the legal rule of the case that becomes binding precedent. It is narrowly confined to those pronouncements of law necessary to resolve the factual issues in the case and is considerably narrower than the court's discourse on the law. The rule in this case is that a parent is not empowered to bind a minor child, aged under 18 years, to a pre-injury exculpatory agreement.

   b. There are two dicta in the majority opinion. A dictum is a statement on the law that is not necessary for the resolution of the case but is nevertheless pronounced on by the court. A dictum is not binding precedent, but it has persuasive value. By including dicta in its opinion, the court expounds on legal doctrine and policy and provides guidance on how it would be likely to deal with a later case that presents the issue covered by the dictum. The majority opinion contains the following two dicta:

      i. A minor lacks contractual capacity and therefore has the right to disaffirm any contract, including but not limited to an exculpatory agreement, that the minor entered into prior to reaching the age of majority, which is 18 years old. (This is only dictum case because the minor in this case did not enter the agreement himself.)

      ii. The rule announced in this opinion applies, not only to an exculpatory agreement executed in favor of a commercial enterprise, but also to one in favor of a volunteer-run or nonprofit organization. (This is a dictum because the defendant in this case was neither a volunteer-run nor a nonprofit organization. Therefore, although the court clearly states that no exception should be made for these organizations, this pronouncement was not necessary to the disposition of this case.)

      The court also alludes to other possible issues that may arise in a case with different facts—whether a parent can bind a minor to a contract other than an exculpatory agreement, whether a parent can bind a minor to a post-injury waiver of liability, and whether an adult's exculpatory agreement is enforceable as against the adult. However, the court's reference to these issues is noncommittal and does not rise to the level of a pronouncement on the law. They are discussed in Examples 3b, c, and d.

   c. The dissenting opinion is merely the view of this individual judge. No part of it, whether directly related to the facts or not, is the holding of the case. It is not binding precedent. However, a dissent can be influential, particularly when it is the well-reasoned opinion of a respected jurist. When a court in another jurisdiction seeks persuasive authority, a dissenting opinion may be preferred to the majority approach. Even in this jurisdiction, the majority of the court may move in the direction of the dissent over time, so that the precedent of this case could be overturned in a future case.

d. Most commonly, a judge is motivated to write a concurring opinion when the judge agrees with the judgment of the court (so the judge does not dissent from the judgment) but reaches the conclusion on a different basis. In this case, the concurring judge agrees with the majority that the disclaimer is invalid, but bases this conclusion on the much broader and more sweeping ground that all standard exculpatory agreements should be voidable as contrary to public policy. A concurring opinion may not be as starkly contrary to the majority opinion as it is in this case, but may just express a qualification or limitation that the majority declined to articulate.

e. The majority opinion is not based on binding precedent because the court has not addressed this issue before. The cases that it cites are merely an account of how courts have resolved the issues in other states, so they are just persuasive. Where courts of other jurisdictions have disagreed on an issue, the court will follow the cases it finds more compelling. The court does that in this opinion and explains why it favors those cases that held the agreement to be avoidable: The overarching policy of protecting minors from their own and their parent's improvidence outweighs the right of parents to make this decision for their minor children and the service provider's interest in ameliorating the risk of liability. As the dissent shows, not all members of the court agree on this balance, which the dissent feels should tilt the opposite way.

f. One of the perpetual issues confronting courts is the relationship between the judicial and the legislative role. While judges clearly do make law through the common law process, this function is circumscribed by the predominant lawmaking authority of the legislature. Therefore, if the state legislature has set the public policy relating to an issue by enacting a statute, the court must defer to the legislature and must apply the statute. However, where, as in this case, no statute exists, the judge often has to examine and articulate public policy to justify the outcome of the case. The legal rule formulated by the court in resolving the case becomes binding law by virtue of the doctrine of precedent. Courts often express wariness about overstepping the judicial function and intruding into the legislative realm, and tailor their opinions as narrowly as possible to minimize the lawmaking extent of the opinion. The legislature's dominant lawmaking authority also means that it has the power to enact a statute after the case has been decided to overturn the precedent set by the court.

2. This decision is not binding precedent in another judicial hierarchy. When a court deals with an issue of first impression in its jurisdiction, it is likely to seek guidance by consulting the decisions in other jurisdictions. Because the court of another state is not bound by the majority

opinion, it could find the different approaches in either the concurring or dissenting opinion to be more persuasive.

3. a. As stated in Explanation 1(b)(ii), the court does indicate in a dictum that its decision should apply to a volunteer-run or nonprofit organization. This does not bind the trial court in the later case, because it is not the rule of the supreme court case, which involved a commercial enterprise. However, the dictum is very powerful because it signals that if the trial court's decision is to the contrary, that decision will likely be reversed on appeal.
   b. The supreme court opinion deals with an exculpatory agreement entered into before the injury occurred and the whole emphasis of the case is on the impropriety of allowing a parent to execute a pre-injury waiver of the minor's right to claim any damages that the minor may suffer thereafter as a result of the defendant's negligence. The court does not indicate whether it would apply the same rule to a post-injury claim waiver, tied to the settlement of the minor's claim. A court could find that the same concerns about protecting the minor from parental improvidence continue to apply after injury, and apply the same rule. However, the situations are quite different in that the minor was not deprived of the right to litigate the claim and will receive compensation under the settlement agreement. This could lead the court to a different conclusion.
   c. The supreme court discusses exculpatory agreements entered into by an adult of full contractual capacity and raises the question of whether it is good public policy to enforce any agreement that absolves a service provider from negligence. However, the court makes it clear that this is an issue for another time. In its overview of decisions from other jurisdictions, the opinion does suggest how the court may approach an exculpatory agreement entered into by an adult. It notes that exculpatory agreements are generally disfavored because they allow the service provider to shift the burden of injury to the other party and avoid responsibility for negligence. The court's choice of cited cases indicates that it is particularly concerned about agreements that are unilaterally imposed on a party who lacks bargaining power, thereby suggesting that a focus on circumstances under which the agreement was entered may be the best way to balance the public interest in holding a party accountable for negligence against freedom of contract and the interest in allowing a purveyor of services to manage risk.
   d. The supreme court expressly states that it does not decide whether a parent can ever bind a minor to a contract and it offers no hint of how it might resolve the question of whether parental consent or permission could bind a minor. All that it makes clear in its brief comment on this question is that its decision in this case is to be confined to exculpatory agreements.

CHAPTER 4

The Objective Test and Basic Principles of Offer and Acceptance

§4.1 THE OBJECTIVE TEST OF ASSENT

§4.1.1 The Concept of Intent, Evaluated Objectively

For a contract to be formed, the parties must intend to enter a contractual relationship. The terms of the contract are those on which they have mutually agreed. The formation of this relationship necessarily requires that the parties communicate their intentions to each other by words, conduct, or both. Each of the parties must signal intent to enter into the contract through words and actions that are observed and given meaning—that is, interpreted—by the other. If the communications accurately reflect the intentions of both parties and are clearly understood, this interaction creates true subjective assent by both parties, so it can be said that there is a "meeting of the minds" on the creation of the contract and its terms—perceived intent corresponds to what each party had in mind. But this is not always so. The communication of intent can be fouled by so many different causes such as the use of language that does not accurately convey its intended meaning, misapprehension by the party to whom the communication is addressed, unexpressed assumptions that are not shared, or unarticulated circumstances or goals.

Where it turns out that the minds of the parties were not actually in accord, a dispute may arise over whether the parties entered a contract at all, or over the terms on which they agreed. Their communications must be interpreted to resolve this dispute. Interpretation of the parties' words and actions is therefore a pervasive theme in the area of contract formation, as it is throughout contract law. One of the fundamental principles of modern contract law is that where a court seeks to ascertain the intent of the parties, it does not focus on what each party may have thought or believed it was agreeing to (that is, the party's subjective intent) but on the reasonable perception of that intent, as conveyed by the party's words or actions (the party's objective intent).

§4.1.2 The Rationale for Using an Objective Test of Assent

When imperfect communication leads to a dispute about the existence or terms of a contract, two fundamental contract policies must be accommodated. The consensual nature of contract pulls in the direction of not holding a person to a contract in the absence of actual agreement to be bound. However, too strong an emphasis on true assent undermines the reliance interest of the other party. The protection of reliance is an important goal of contract law. If no one could rely on words or conduct that indicate assent, it would be difficult for anyone to have confidence in the system of commercial exchange. This requires that a person must generally be held accountable for behavior that signifies assent, and must not be able to escape the manifestation of a contractual commitment merely by claiming that assent was not intended. To allow this would permit one party to disappoint the reasonable expectations of the other by the self-serving and unverifiable assertion that manifested intent did not actually represent what the party intended.

Courts have not always stressed the importance of the reliance interest. Court opinions prior to the late nineteenth century suggest that early courts did require a real "meeting of the minds," in the sense that there could be no contract unless the parties' subjective intent coincided on the creation and terms of the relationship. However, even if this was the prevailing attitude in earlier law, it changed around the classical period,[1] during which the importance of protecting the reliance interest was heavily emphasized. Classical contract law moved away firmly and sharply from any recognition of subjective agreement and favored a strict application of the objective test of assent.[2] If agreement was apparent from the manifestations of assent, reasonably interpreted, a contract had been formed on the terms reflected

1. The classical period, which ran from the end of the nineteenth century to the early twentieth century, is described in section 2.3.1.

2. The strict application of the objective test is summed up by a famous passage from the opinion of Judge Learned Hand in *Hotchkiss v. National City Bank of New York*, 200 F. 287, 293 (S.D.N.Y. 1911): "A contract has, strictly speaking, nothing to do with the personal or individual intent of the parties. A contract is an obligation attached by mere force of law to certain acts of the parties, usually words, which ordinarily accompany and represent a known intent. If, however, it were proved by twenty bishops that either party, when he used the words, intended something else than the usual meaning which the law imposes upon them, he would still be held."

in the manifestation. It was neither necessary nor permissible to receive testimony on what either party actually thought or believed. (As explained in section 4.1.3, modern courts are no longer that hostile to evidence of subjective intent where it could have some relevance in explaining an objective manifestation of assent.)

The objective test is now firmly established as the basis for determining contractual assent. Although it is common to find passages in modern court opinions that describe contractual assent as a "meeting of the minds," this is intended figuratively and does not mean that the court is suggesting a requirement of true subjective agreement. The parties' minds are deemed to have met if their objective manifestations lead to that conclusion. This contemporary approach is reflected in several sections of the Restatement, Second. In defining a promise, §2 speaks of a manifestation of intent by the promisor that justifies the promisee in understanding that a commitment has been made; §3 describes "agreement" as a manifestation of mutual assent; and §§19 and 20 stress the accountability principle by holding a party liable for deliberate manifestations by words or conduct, made with reason to know that they will create a reasonable impression of assent.[3]

§4.1.3 The Operation of the Objective Test

a. The Evaluation of Objective Evidence

The objective test requires that manifestations of assent must be interpreted, not in light of what the utterer actually meant or the other party actually understood, but from the standpoint of what that utterance reasonably meant in the entire context of the transaction. That is, the focus is not on what the words or actions actually meant to either party but on their rational meaning—what they reasonably would mean if interpreted by a reasonable person in the position of the parties in the context of the transaction. The reasonable person is simply a construct whose reasonable apprehension of the meaning of manifestations is based on a community standard, as identified by the trier of fact, often the jury.

The following example illustrates the way in which the reasonable person construct focuses the inquiry: Lender lent Borrower $10,000. Under the loan agreement, Borrower promised to repay the loan "with interest at the market rate within one year of the date of receiving the advance." At the time that the contract was executed, the market interest rate was 4 percent.

3. Uniform Commercial Code (UCC) Article 2 does not specifically address the objective test, which is therefore governed by the general principles of common law by virtue of §1.103(b), which adopts the general principles of common law to the extent that they are not displaced by the particular provisions of the UCC. (*See* section 2.7.2.)

At the time of the repayment date, the market interest rate was 5 percent. This led to a dispute between Lender and Borrower about the meaning of "interest at the market rate." Lender contends that it meant that the market rate must be measured at the time of repayment of the loan and interest, while Borrower contends that it meant that the rate must be fixed at the rate prevailing at the time the loan was made. The meaning of "market rate" is not determined by what either Lender or Borrower thought it meant, but is based on what reasonable people in the parties' position would have understood the term to mean under all the circumstances of the transaction. This determination is made by focusing on objective evidence—that is, observable significations of intent—to establish contractual intent. This evidence consists of the language used by the parties in the agreement, as well as any other communications between them or any other overt behavior. It also covers any custom or usage in the marketplace, as well as any generally accepted meaning of the language used in the parties' communications.

b. The Relevance of Evidence of Subjective Intent Under the Objective Test

An objective manifestation of intent may not be clear and unambiguous, and may be susceptible of different meanings. Therefore, while contemporary courts uniformly apply the objective test, they recognize that subjective evidence of what a party thought or intended could be relevant to explain the meaning of a party's overt expression of intent. However, because the focus is on the objective meaning of words or conduct, evidence of subjective intent is only relevant and persuasive to the extent that it is credible and compatible with the overt behavior. Therefore, in the above example, evidence of each of the parties' actual understanding of "interest at the market rate" should be admissible as relevant to explain the meaning of that ambiguous term. The parties are contending for two possible alternative meanings—either that the rate at the date of contracting or the rate at the date of payment. Both are plausible and are not in conflict with the parties' objective manifestation. However, if the subjective evidence cannot be reconciled with the objective manifestation, it is implausible and has no probative value. For example, testimony by the Borrower that it believed that the loan was interest-free cannot be squared with parties' manifestation of intent that the borrower must pay interest at the market rate.

SR International Business Insurance Co. v. World Trade Center Properties, LLC, 467 F.3d 107 (2d Cir. 2006), demonstrates a modern court's approach to the admission of subjective evidence under the objective test. Various insurance companies had issued binders (commitments to insure pending the execution of a final insurance policy) on the World Trade Center in New York. The binders provided for coverage of $3.5 billion "per occurrence." After the terrorist attack on the twin towers on September 11, 2001, the parties disputed the meaning of the term "per occurrence." The insured (the lessee of the buildings) argued that each of the two attacks on the towers by separate planes was a separate occurrence. The insurers argued that because the planes were flown in a concerted attack, the two crashes should be treated as a single occurrence. On the insured's interpretation the maximum coverage amount would be $7 billion, double the amount under the insurer's interpretation. The trial court admitted testimony of the insurers' witnesses about what they thought the policies meant. On appeal, the insured parties argued that the trial court should have excluded this subjective evidence. The court of appeals found no error in the admission of the evidence. It expressed the established principle that a contract must be interpreted objectively, based on the parties' manifested intent, rather than their actual intent. However, even though uncommunicated subjective intent is not in itself determinative of the intended meaning of a contract, the court held that it could be relevant and admissible to cast light on the meaning of the objective manifestations.

c. Softening the Objective Test to Protect a Party from Improper Bargaining

Although the objective test holds a party to apparent assent, as demonstrated by the party's words and conduct, it is appropriate to question a party's manifestation of assent if it was induced by the other party's improper and unfair conduct. The requirement of reasonable notice of terms, discussed below, and the doctrines of fraud, duress, and unconscionability, discussed in Chapter 13, all recognize that if a party's apparent consent was the product of the other party's failure to present the terms conspicuously, or its deception, its improper threat, or its unfair abuse of superior bargaining power, the party whose manifestation of assent was induced by that conduct may be able to establish grounds to avoid the contract notwithstanding apparent consent to it. In addition, the doctrine of mistake, discussed in Chapter 15, allows a party to avoid a contract notwithstanding apparent consent where the party's manifestation was induced by a factual error that merits relief. The doctrines in Chapters 13 and 15 are just noted here to acknowledge their potential application, and are explored in detail in those later chapters.

§4.1.4 The Duty to Read

The objective test binds a party to manifested assent, so a party who communicates assent to a contract without reading and understanding its terms cannot claim a lack of consent on the grounds that the party never actually knew or subjectively agreed to its terms. Courts often express this principle by saying that a party has a duty to read a document (whether that document is written on paper in tangible form or is presented electronically, such as on a website) before signifying assent to it.

A party's failure to read or understand terms commonly occurs with standard contracts drafted by the other party. Standard contracts are pervasive and are surely the most common type of contracts. A business that enters into repetitive transactions will have devised a set of terms in advance, which it presents to each contracting partner for agreement at the time of the transaction. People often do not bother to read standard contracts before indicating assent to them, which they may do by signing a paper document, clicking an "I agree" button on a website, or just by submitting an order on a website that contains the terms or a link to them. Provided that the standard terms were adequately brought to the attention of the nondrafting party, that party's objective communication of assent will usually bind it, even if that party did not bother to read the terms and was subjectively ignorant of them when manifesting assent to them.[4]

A few cases involving standard contracts illustrate the duty to read. In *Kibler v. Blue Knob Recreation, Inc.*, 184 A.3d 974 (Pa. Super. Ct. 2018), Kibler signed a standard exculpatory agreement when he applied for a season pass at a ski resort. There was no evidence that he read the agreement before he signed it. The agreement released the resort from liability for any injury Kibler may suffer while skiing at the resort. He was subsequently injured while skiing and sued the resort to recover damages for his injuries. The court granted the resort's motion for summary judgment, holding that the release bound Kibler. It was clear, unambiguous, and conspicuous and because he had a duty to read it, he could not evade it by claiming that he had not read it and was subjectively unaware of its contents. In *Kendall Imports, LLC v. Diaz*, 215 So. 3d 95 (Fla. Dist. Ct. App. 2017), the buyers bought a car from a dealer. The buyers signed a purchase order and financing agreement that included an arbitration clause. They signed it even though they did not know what it said because they could not read or speak English, the language in which it was written. When a dispute later arose in relation to the transaction, the buyers commenced suit against the dealer, which answered by filing a motion to compel arbitration. The trial court denied the motion. The court of appeals reversed, holding that the arbitration agreement bound the buyers. There was no evidence that the dealer had rushed, pressured, or coerced the buyers into signing the agreement, and the buyers had the duty to ensure that they knew and understood what they were signing, even if that required getting someone to translate it for them.

---

4. Chapter 5 focuses on standard contracting and includes a more detailed discussion of adequate notice of standard terms and the duty to read standard contracts.

These cases involved standard agreements printed on paper, but much standard contracting is conducted on the Internet. The same principle applies to electronic significations of assent. In *Starke v. SquareTrade, Inc.*, 913 F.3d 279 (2d Cir. 2019), Starke made an online purchase of a service contract and protection plan for a CD player. He subsequently sued SquareTrade, alleging that its marketing of the plan was deceptive. SquareTrade moved to stay the suit and compel arbitration on the strength of an arbitration provision in its standard terms. Starke could have read the standard terms by clicking on a link on the website or in an email confirming the sale, but he did not do so. The court noted that even though Starke did not actually know about the arbitration provision, he would be bound by it under the duty to read had he been given adequate notice of the standard terms. However, on the facts of this case, the court concluded that he did not have a duty to read the terms because the website was not set up in a way that made the standard terms conspicuous and accessible. In addition to illustrating the duty to read in an electronic transaction, this case highlights an important qualification to the duty to read standard terms: A person will not be held to unread standard terms unless they are presented in a way that would alert a reasonable person to their existence and would allow for ready access to them. Starke likely would have been bound by the arbitration provision had the website been organized in a way that highlighted the existence of standard terms in a conspicuous manner and allowed immediate access to them, either on the page itself or via a link. Better still, Stark would not have been able to claim ignorance of unread terms if the website required him to click a button or check a box that acknowledged that he had read and accepted the terms. (The question of reasonable notice of standard terms is discussed further in Chapter 5.)

§4.1.5 Lack of Serious Intent: Jokes, Bluffs, and Hyperbole

Miscommunication of intent can result from many different causes. Most commonly, the problem is inadvertent failure to express intent clearly. However, there are some cases in which a party who claims lack of contractual intent alleges that the manifestation of intent was not serious, but was a joke, a bluff, or hyperbole, and that the other party should have realized it.

In *Lucy v. Zehmer*, 84 S.E.2d 516 (Va. 1954), Zehmer, the owner of a farm, contended that his offer to sell it to Lucy was a bluff. The alleged contract was made while the parties sat drinking one evening in a restaurant operated by Zehmer. The memorial of the alleged contract was written in very sketchy terms on the reverse side of a restaurant guest check. When Lucy sought to enforce the sale, Zehmer claimed that it was not intended seriously. He testified that he and Lucy had been drinking too much, and he was just calling Lucy's bluff because he did not believe that

Lucy had the money to buy the property. Whatever Zehmer's actual intent may have been, the court found that Lucy was in earnest and under the objective test, had no reason to believe that Zehmer was not. (The court also declined to allow Zehmer to avoid the contract on grounds of mental disability caused by intoxication because it did not believe that Zehmer was drunk enough.)

In *Leonard v. PepsiCo, Inc.*, 88 F. Supp. 2d 116 (S.D.N.Y. 1999), *aff'd* 210 F.3d 88 (2d Cir. 2000), the court found that an alleged offer should have been reasonably understood as a joke. Pepsi conducted a promotional campaign in which buyers of Pepsi products could earn "Pepsi points" that could be redeemed for prizes listed in a catalog. The points did not all have to be earned by consuming soft drinks. As long as 15 actual points were submitted with the redemption form, the remaining points required for the prize could be purchased for ten cents a point. Pepsi aired a television commercial to promote the campaign. The commercial centered on a teenager flying to school in a Harrier jet. Although the commercial showed various prizes that could be won (such as T-shirts and sunglasses) and the number of points needed to win them, it also suggested that the jet might be a prize. This is because as the commercial ended with the teenager landing the jet on the grounds of his high school, the words "Harrier fighter, 7,000,000 points" appeared on the screen. Leonard submitted a redemption form claiming the jet. He included the 15 original Pepsi points and a check for just under $700,000 to buy the balance of the 7 million points needed. Pepsi refused to award the jet to him on a number of theories. One of them was that the jet was used in the commercial merely for humor and entertainment, and could not reasonably have been understood as a real prize. (The other theories are discussed in Example 10.) The court agreed. It found that no reasonable person could have understood the commercial to be a serious offer of a jet, but would have realized that the jet was used just to add an absurd comic touch and to exaggerate the excitement of the drink. Furthermore, the fact that a Harrier is a fierce war machine unsuitable for consumer use and costing some $23 million would alert the reasonable viewer that it could not possibly be offered in exchange for about $700,000.

In *Kolodziej v. Mason*, 774 F.3d 736 (11th Cir. 2014), Mason, a lawyer defending a client in a murder trial, gave a television interview in which he challenged the prosecution's case. He asserted that his client could not have committed the murder because he had arrived at the airport only 28 minutes before the murder and it would have been impossible for him to get to the scene of the murder in 28 minutes. Mason stated that he challenged anybody to show him that it was possible to get from the airport to the murder scene within 28 minutes, and if anyone could show that, he would pay them a million dollars. Kolodziej, an enterprising law student, decided to accept the challenge and recorded himself traveling from the airport to the murder scene in under 28 minutes. When Mason refused to pay him the one million dollars, he sued. The court granted Mason's motion for summary judgment on several grounds. One of them was that a reasonable person would not have understood Mason's statement to be an invitation to contract. Contrasting the case to *Lucy v. Zehmer*, the court said that it would be apparent to a reasonable person that the exaggerated amount of one million dollars was just hyperbole—a rhetorical expression made not as a serious offer for any commercial purpose, but just as a means of emphasizing a weakness in the prosecutor's theory of the case. The court said that reference to the million dollars was really just equivalent to some other idiom, such as "I'll eat my hat."

§4.2 THE PURPOSE AND APPLICATION OF THE RULES OF OFFER AND ACCEPTANCE

§4.2.1 Introduction

The formation of the contract is the beginning of the parties' legal relationship, but it is also the culmination of a process of bargaining. This does not mean that the parties always get together and negotiate the terms of the contract. In many cases, there is no bargaining in this sense at all—one of the parties proposes a contract on stated terms that the other accepts without qualification. In other cases, the path to contract formation may be long and arduous. Initial proposals may lead to counterproposals, negotiations, and compromise. If the transaction is complex, each step in the process may require consultation with different corporate departments, technical experts, and attorneys. In either event, where this interaction is successful, there comes a time when the parties reach agreement and bind themselves to the relationship—a contract comes into being.

Sometimes the creation of a contract is marked by the signing of a written or electronically recorded memorial of the agreement.[5] When this happens, it is relatively easy to fix the time of formation and the exact terms of the contract. However, this helpful indicator of formation is not always present because the parties may have formed a contract without recording it in a formal comprehensive writing. A contract could be entirely oral,[6]

5. In colloquial speech, people often talk of "signing a contract." Strictly speaking, this is inaccurate terminology. The contract is the legal relationship between the parties, and the document that is signed is actually the record or memorial of that contract.

6. Under the statute of frauds (*see* Chapter 11), certain types of contracts are not enforceable unless their essential terms are recorded either in a signed writing or in some other form (such as an electronic document). However, many contracts are not subject to this rule and are fully valid and enforceable in oral form. Even where the law does not require it for enforceability, the lack of a recorded memorial of the contract could result in problems of proof if a dispute arises as to the existence or the terms of an oral contract.

without any written record of it; it could be contained in a series of correspondence or in some other collection of interrelated documents; it could have been made orally with the intention of later drafting and signing a written memorial or it may be partly written and partly oral. Such circumstances may create uncertainty and disputes over the question of whether a contract was formed at all, and if so, whether certain terms became part of it. The rules of offer and acceptance provide a framework for resolving these questions.

The offer and acceptance model conceives of a process of bargaining between the parties that leads to the formation of a contract. It developed in the context of an interaction in which the parties dicker over the terms of their relationship. It is sometimes said that this model is too old-fashioned and rudimentary to be helpful in an age in which such a large amount of contracting is done on standard terms, much of it through electronic media. However, the model has proved to be remarkably durable, and courts continue to apply the well-established rules, sometimes with an adjustment or modification, to transactions that were not conceived of when the rules were first developed. (Chapter 5 deals specifically with standard contracts and contracting via electronic media.)

§4.2.2 When Are Offer and Acceptance Issues Presented?

Not every contract dispute raises formation issues because the parties may not disagree on questions of formation. For example, they may concede that a contract was formed on stated terms, but may have a dispute about whether the performance of one of them conformed to what was promised, or a dispute about whether events arising after contract formation justify one of the parties in refusing to perform. The rules of offer and acceptance tend to be relevant in three types of dispute: First, the rules of offer and acceptance may be used to determine if a contract came into existence at all where the parties dispute whether their communications resulted in the formation of a contract. Second, even if it is settled that a contract was formed, a determination of which communication constituted the offer, and which was the acceptance, can resolve a dispute about the content of the contract. Third, the rules of offer and acceptance can be relevant to the determination of which state's law governs the contract or which state's courts have jurisdiction to hear a dispute over the contract. This issue may arise where the parties are located in different jurisdictions and communicate across state lines, so that the point of contract formation becomes relevant to choice of law and jurisdiction. This third situation is merely noted here and is not discussed further. The remainder of this chapter is confined to the application of offer and acceptance rules to resolve questions about the existence and terms of the contract.

§4.2.3 The Basic Offer and Acceptance Model at Common Law

The rules of offer and acceptance are based on a particular conception of how contracts are formed. In the simplest terms, they envisage that one person[7] (called the offeror) makes an offer to another person (the offeree) to enter into a contract on specified terms. The offer creates a power of acceptance in the offeree, who can bring the contract into existence by signifying acceptance of the transaction on the proposed terms. If the offeree rejects the offer either expressly or simply by not accepting it within a particular time, the offer lapses and no contract arises. If the offeree is interested in forming a contract, but not on the exact terms proposed, the offeree may respond by making a counteroffer, which has the effect of terminating the original offer and reversing the process: The original offeror now becomes the offeree with the power of acceptance. This could go on several more times until the parties reach accord or tire of trying. There are some variations and complications that could arise, as the following sections show. The basic offer and acceptance model is represented in Diagram 4A.

Diagram 4A

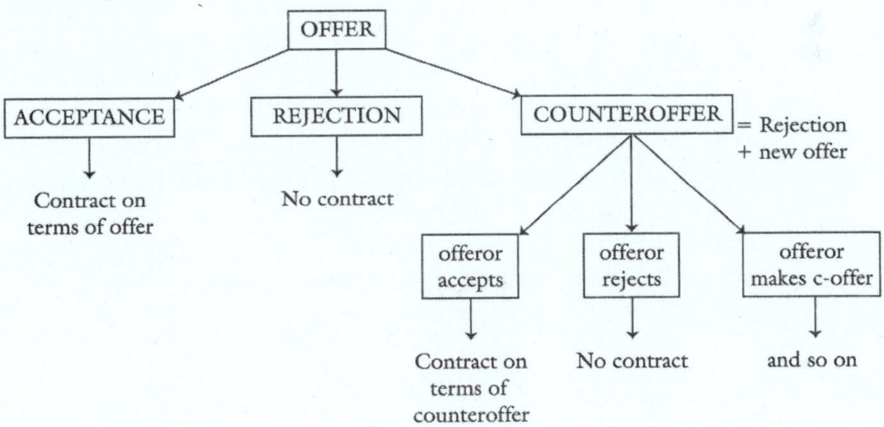

7. The legal meaning of the word "person" includes not only individuals but also incorporated organizations such as corporations, partnerships, associations, and government bodies. When an organization contracts, it is represented by an authorized officer who acts as its agent.

The rules of offer and acceptance, as represented in Diagram 4A, merely indicate a framework for analyzing the process of offer and acceptance and may suggest that the rules are technical and can be applied mechanically. However, the application of the rules to the facts of the case can be complex and nuanced because the communications between the parties often require interpretation in context, taking into account the language used by the parties, the factual circumstances of their interactions, commercial practice, and standards of reasonableness and good faith. Modern courts generally disfavor a rigid and technical approach to offer and acceptance and try to give effect to the reasonable intent of the parties.

§4.3 THE RULES OF OFFER AND ACCEPTANCE APPLICABLE IN SALES OF GOODS UNDER UCC ARTICLE 2

Where a transaction is a sale of goods, UCC Article 2 governs and must be applied. Goods are defined in §2.105(1) to include movable things other than money and various intangible rights. A sale of goods is defined in §2.106(1) as the passing of title from the seller to the buyer for a price, which §2.304, states may be payable in money or otherwise.[8] If Article 2 contains a provision relating to the issue in question, that provision displaces the equivalent rule of common law. However, Article 2 does not deal comprehensively with all the issues that could arise in a sale of goods. Therefore, if Article 2 has no provision on an issue, §1.103(b) provides that the general principles of common law apply to the sale.

In the area of offer and acceptance, there are some questions that Article 2 resolves differently from common law,[9] so a correct determination of the nature of the transaction could have significant consequences. However, Article 2 has only a few sections that deal with offer and acceptance, so common law rules apply extensively in this area of the law. Except where the discussion in this chapter identifies variant rules in Article 2, the common law rules of offer and acceptance apply to sales of goods.

---

8. *See* section 2.7.2 for a fuller explanation of these provisions and a discussion of when Article 2 governs a transaction.

9. For example, Article 2 differs from the common law in its treatment of irrevocable offers, as discussed in section 4.13.4, and it diverges from the common law in its approach to resolving disparities between documents exchanged by the parties in the course of contract formation, as discussed in Chapter 6. Also, a sale of goods for a price of $500 or more must be sufficiently recorded and signed to comply with Article 2's statute of frauds, discussed in Chapter 11.

The two Code sections that most directly address general formation issues are §§2.204 and 2.206. The fundamental point made by §2.204 is that the court should focus on the existence of agreement between the parties, whether shown by words or conduct, and if agreement is apparent, the court should not be concerned about technicalities but should do what it can to uphold and enforce the contract. Section 2.206 eschews technical rules on the manner and medium of acceptance and emphasizes that an offer should be interpreted as inviting acceptance by any reasonable mode unless the offer or circumstances make it clear that the mode is restricted. When Article 2 was promulgated in the 1950s, the flexibility reflected in §§2.204 and 2.206 contrasted with a more rigid approach apparent in common law cases. However, modern cases apply the principles reflected in §§2.204 and 2.206 in common law cases as well.

§4.4 THE NATURE OF AN OFFER, AS DISTINCT FROM A PRELIMINARY PROPOSAL

§4.4.1 Distinguishing an Offer from a Solicitation

Restatement, Second, §24 describes an offer as a "manifestation of willingness to enter into a bargain, so made as to justify another person in understanding that his assent to that bargain is invited and will conclude it." This definition identifies the hallmarks of an offer. The offer must contain these elements either expressly or by implication:

1. Because an offer must be manifested, it must necessarily be communicated to the person to whom it is addressed.
2. The offer must indicate a desire to enter into a contract. To do this it has to specify the performances to be exchanged and the terms that will govern the relationship. A communication that omits essential terms of the proposed transaction is not likely to be an offer. Therefore, the comprehensiveness and specificity of the terms in the communication are an important indication of whether it is reasonably interpreted as an offer, rather than just a preliminary proposal that opens negotiations.
3. The offer must expressly or impliedly invite acceptance. To be an offer, the communication must convey the reasonable understanding (determined by an objective standard) that the offeror intends a contract to arise and expects to be committed upon acceptance. That is, to be an offer, the communication must confer on the offeree the power to decide whether or not a contract will come into being.

4. Although the power to bring the contract into existence by acceptance belongs to the offeree, the offeror has the power to specify its terms. To qualify as a valid acceptance, the offeree's response must signify agreement to the terms that are set out in the offer. If the response proposes terms different from those offered, it does not qualify as a valid acceptance. (This is discussed in sections 4.7 and 4.8.)
5. The offer must be directed at some person or group of persons. Although an offer is usually addressed to a specific person, it is legally possible to make an offer to a defined or undefined group. Where this happens, the offer must be interpreted to determine if it contemplates multiple acceptances or may be accepted only by the first person to reply.
6. As long as the offer sets out the terms of the proposed contract with adequate specificity, it does not have to prescribe the manner and time for effective acceptance. If it does not do so, acceptance must be communicated by a reasonable mode within a reasonable time. If the offer does prescribe a manner and time for effective acceptance, the offeree must comply with those instructions for the acceptance to be effective.

The requirement that an offer must be reasonably understood as inviting an acceptance that will create the contract distinguishes an offer from a proposal intended as nothing more than an overture—that is, a tentative expression of interest in transacting, an invitation to make an offer, or a request for information that may lead to an offer. A proposal that reserves to the proponent the final say on whether to be bound cannot be an offer. The person initiating contractual negotiations must therefore be careful to choose language that makes it clear whether the communication is an offer or merely a preliminary nonbinding proposal. If that intent is not clearly expressed, the nature of the communication is determined under the objective test by asking whether the language used within the context of the communication would cause a reasonable addressee to understand that the proponent intended to be bound on acceptance

For example, an owner of property is clearly making an offer to sell the property to a prospective buyer by writing, "I offer to sell you block 2 of lot 10, Madison County for $2 million cash. If you wish to buy this property, you must deliver your written acceptance to me by midnight on Wednesday, September 30, 2024." The strong wording (including the use of the terms "offer" and "acceptance") leave little doubt that an offer is intended. On the other hand, the owner is clearly not making an offer by writing, "I wish to sell block 2 of lot 10, Madison County and will consider an offer of not less than $2 million. I invite you to make an offer if you are interested in purchasing it." Between these two poles, the owner's communication may be ambiguous or unclear, creating uncertainty about its legal effect. For example, the property owner's letter would fall short of expressing clear intent if it states, "I am willing to sell block 2 of lot 10, Madison County to you for $2 million cash. If you are interested, please let me know as soon as possible." This flabby language obfuscates the owner's intention and could lead the addressee to understand the communication to be an offer, whether or not the owner meant it as such. The ambiguity could result in a dispute, and possibly litigation, over its meaning and legal effect.

The above examples provide no information apart from the language of the owner's communication, so the meaning of the communication must be resolved purely on an interpretation of the plain and ordinary meaning of that language. The words used in a communication are the primary indicators of what was intended, but where the language is unclear, there may be information beyond the text of the communication (contextual evidence) that is relevant to determining its reasonable meaning. This contextual evidence may include information about the relationship of the parties, any previous dealings between them, and any prior communications relating to this transaction that may cast light on how the recipient reasonably should have understood the communication. If the parties are members of the same community or trade, common practices or trade usages may also be relevant to determining the reasonable understanding of a communication.

§4.4.2 Offers or Solicitations to Multiple Parties and Advertisements

In most transactions, a proposal to make a contract is directed to a specific, identified person, as happened in the above examples of communications relating to the potential sale of a piece of real property. However, an offeror could communicate a desire to enter a contract with multiple persons. The addressees could be a defined group or the public at large. Most commonly, this occurs where a person places an advertisement (including any communication in which goods or services are proffered for sale) in a newspaper, catalog, website, or other medium of mass communication. The question of whether an advertisement is an offer or merely an invitation to make an offer must be resolved by the usual process of interpreting its apparent reasonable intent in light of its language in context. If it is an offer, the advertiser is bound to a recipient of the communication as soon as that recipient signifies assent to its terms. If it is not an offer, but merely a solicitation, a recipient makes an offer by responding and the advertiser has the discretion to accept or reject that offer. Therefore, the question of whether or not an advertisement is an offer can have serious consequences if the advertiser did not expect to be committed to contracts with all persons who respond to the advertisement. An advertiser who does not intend to make an offer in the advertisement can avoid uncertainty about its legal effect by making it clear in the advertisement that it is not an offer. However, if an advertisement does not do that, the uncertainty has to be resolved by a close examination of the language used in the advertisement as well as common practices or expectations in the marketplace that might lead to a reasonable understanding that the advertisement is or is not an offer.

Lefkowitz v. Great Minneapolis Surplus Store, 86 N.W.2d 689 (Minn. 1957), is a frequently cited case that found an advertisement to be an offer. The store published newspaper advertisements in two successive weeks advertising a fur coat and a fur stole. Each of the advertisements stated that these valuable garments would be sold for $1 on the next Saturday at exactly 9 A.M., "First Come First Served." Although the plaintiff was the first person at the store on both Saturday mornings and he tendered the $1, the store refused to sell a coat to him on the grounds that the offer was intended for women only. The plaintiff sued for damages for breach of contract based on the difference between the value of the garments and the $1 price. The store contended that the advertisements were not offers but merely invitations to the public to make offers to the store. The plaintiff made an offer, which it declined. The court said that while this is the usual presumption, the legal effect of the advertisement depends on its apparent intent as reasonably understood by the plaintiff. The terms of the advertisements were clear, definite, explicit, and left nothing open for negotiation. They therefore qualified as offers.

Consumer expectations are an important factor in determining if an advertisement should be reasonably understood as an offer or just a solicitation. However, many courts apply the presumption, expressed in *Lefkowitz* and numerous other cases, that an advertisement is no more than a solicitation unless it has language that indicates the apparent intent to make an offer. (*Leonard v. PepsiCo*, discussed in section 4.1.5, adopted the same approach.)

Lefkowitz involved a communication in a newspaper, but today a public communication can be accomplished in so many different ways. The proffering of goods and services on a website is the most common. In *Schultz v. American Airlines, Inc.*, 2018 WL 7287194 (S.D. Fla. 2018), *aff'd on other grounds*, 855 F. App'x 656 (11th Cir. 2021), Schultz visited American Airlines', website to book an airline ticket. She saw a flight listed for $197 and proceeded to book it. When she reached the stage of paying for it, she entered her credit card information and clicked a "pay now" button on the screen. She received the immediate response that American could not issue the ticket for $197 because the price had risen to $297. Schultz sued American for breach of contract, but the court held that she had failed to establish a contract because the listing of the booking and price on the website was not an offer. Citing several cases, including *Lefkowitz* and *Leonard*, it applied the presumption that an advertisement is not an offer unless there are sufficient facts to overcome that presumption. The court found that the facts did not overcome the presumption because the website allowed the customer to customize the booking by selecting seats and other options, reasonably indicating that the booking process was a form of negotiation which would be completed by the customer ultimately making the offer after completing the selections.

In *Script Transform, LLC v. Motorola Mobility, LLC*, 522 F. Supp. 3d 414 (N.D. Ill. 2021), Script sued Motorola for patent infringement on the basis that Motorola had offered to sell Script's patented products on its website. The website included a "buy now" button, which Script argued constituted an offer to sell the products. However, the court found that the website was not an offer. It contained no pricing information and it stated that Motorola was not the seller of the product. Furthermore, the customer could not actually buy the product by clicking the "buy now" button, which merely directed the customer to the website of another company that manufactured the product.

In addition to websites, other electronic communications to the public could be reasonably understood as offers. *Kolodziej*, discussed in section 4.1.5, found that a statement by a lawyer in a television interview could not reasonably have been understood as an offer because the statement was just rhetorical. However, had it not been rhetorical, it could have qualified as an offer for a unilateral contract,[10] which could have been accepted by performance of the act called for. In *Augstein v. Leslie*, 2012 WL 4928914 (S.D.N.Y 2012), the court found that a YouTube video was an offer. Leslie, a singer-songwriter, posted a video on YouTube in which he advertised a reward of $1 million for the return of his laptop (containing valuable intellectual property, such as his music). Augstein found the laptop and returned it. The court held that the YouTube video was clearly intended to induce performance—the return of the laptop—and it was therefore an offer for a unilateral contract, which Augstein accepted by performance. The court dismissed the argument that a YouTube video could not constitute an offer, pointing out that it is the reasonable meaning of the communication that is crucial, not the medium in which it is conveyed.

§4.5 THE EXPIRY OF THE OFFER BY PASSAGE OF TIME

§4.5.1 The Specified or Reasonable Duration of the Offer

An offer does not last forever. It has a limited duration and lapses if not accepted in time. As the creator of the offer, the offeror is entitled to specify

10. Unilateral contracts are explained in section 4.12.

the time within which the acceptance must be made. If the offeror does not state the duration of the offer, it must be accepted within a reasonable time. The offeror takes a risk by not specifying a time for acceptance because the question of what period is reasonable for acceptance may be unclear until settled by litigation. To decide what time is reasonable, the factfinder must ask what amount of time would be needed to receive, consider, and reply to the offer under all the circumstances of the transaction. Where the parties are in each other's presence, the reasonable time for acceptance might conclude as soon as they part company, but if they communicate at a distance by mail or similar noninstantaneous means, the time for transmission must be taken into account. Other factors relevant to this question include the nature of the transaction; the relationship of the parties; any course of dealing, custom, or trade usage; the means of communication used; and the stability of the market.

An offeror who uses very precise and clear language in specifying the lapse date of the offer can eliminate the risk of uncertainty. However, an offeror who is less precise may find that ambiguity in the lapse date leads to a dispute. For example, if the offer required acceptance by 5 P.M. Pacific Daylight Time on Friday, June 5, 2024, there can be no doubt as to the exact time that the power of acceptance ended. However, an acceptance required "within five days" is ambiguous because it does not indicate if the five-day period runs from the date of the writing or receipt of the offer, or what time the offer will lapse on that final day.

§4.5.2 The Effect of a Late Attempt to Accept

If the offeree attempts to accept the offer after the period for acceptance has expired, the legal effect of this late communication may be difficult to decide and depends on the circumstances and the content of the late acceptance. It could simply be a futile act of no legal consequence, or it could be a new offer by the former offeree, creating a power of acceptance in the original offeror.

§4.6 TERMINATION OF THE OFFER FOR REASONS OTHER THAN EXPIRY BY LAPSE OF TIME

The stated or reasonable duration should be thought of as the longest period that an offer could remain open. It may terminate even before that under the following four circumstances identified in Restatement, Second, §36.

§4.6.1 Rejection

The offeree does not have to take positive action to reject an offer. Except in unusual circumstances (discussed in section 4.10.2), an offeror cannot set up an offer so that the offeree is deemed to accept it by failing to respond. That is, in most situations, silence or inaction cannot constitute acceptance. Therefore, rejection occurs as a matter of course simply if the offeree fails to respond to the offer before it expires. However, an offeree may choose to communicate rejection of the offer before it expires by lapse of time, and if that happens, the offer lapses immediately on communication. Once rejection has been communicated, the offeree cannot recant the rejection and accept, because the offer has come to an end. A purported acceptance after rejection could qualify as a new offer by the former offeree.

§4.6.2 Counteroffer

An offeree may wish to enter the transaction proposed by the offeror, but on terms different from those set out in the offer. To qualify as an acceptance, the response to an offer must agree to the offeror's terms. If it expresses agreement to the transaction, subject to some change in the terms, it is not an acceptance, but a counteroffer. A counteroffer is defined in Restatement, Second, §39 as an offer by the offeree to the offeror, relating to the same matter as the original offer and proposing a different substitute bargain. The counteroffer is therefore both a rejection of the offer and a new offer by the former offeree for a contract on different terms. It thus terminates the original offer and gives the original offeror the power to accept the counteroffer. Because the counteroffer is a rejection of the original offer, the offeree cannot accept the original offer if the offeror rejects the counteroffer. For example, in *Jameson v. Still*, 643 S.W.3d 306 (Mo. 2022), Jameson, who was injured in a collision with a vehicle driven by Still, made an offer to Still's insurer to settle the matter. The insurer responded with a counteroffer to settle for a lower amount. After Jameson rejected the counteroffer and commenced suit, the insurer attempted to accept Jameson's initial offer, arguing that a statute had changed the common law rule that a counteroffer is a rejection of the offer. The court rejected the insurer's interpretation of the statute and held that the common law rule applied — the counteroffer was a rejection of the offer, which was no longer open for acceptance by the insurer.

In some cases, it is obvious that a response is a counteroffer, but in others, the meaning of language used by the offeree in response to an offer may be less clear and harder to determine. This is discussed in section 4.8.

§4.6.3 The Offeror's Death or Mental Disability

The traditional rule, included in Restatement, Second, §36, is that the offer lapses automatically if the offeror dies or becomes mentally incapacitated before the offer is accepted. Death of the offeror terminates the offer only if it occurs before acceptance. If the offeror dies after acceptance, the contract remains in force and becomes an asset and obligation of the offeror's estate.

Similarly, if the offeror becomes mentally incompetent between the time of making the offer and the time of acceptance, the offer lapses. But if the mental disability arises after acceptance, it does not affect the formation of the contract.

§4.6.4 Revocation

Unless the offer qualifies as an option or as a firm offer under UCC Article 2 (discussed in section 4.13), an undertaking to keep it open for a particular period is not binding on the offeror. The offeror therefore has the power to revoke the offer at any time before its acceptance, whether or not the offer states that it will be held open for a stated time.

Revocation only becomes effective when it is communicated to the offeree. This usually means either that the offeree has received notice of revocation from the offeror (direct revocation) or that the offeree has learned from some other reliable source that the offer has been withdrawn (indirect revocation). It is therefore possible that an offeree could have accepted the offer before it has been effectively revoked by the offeree's receipt or knowledge of the revocation. For direct revocation to be effective, the notice of revocation must clearly indicate on a reasonable interpretation that the offeror is no longer willing to enter the contract. The requirement that the offeree must receive the notice means that the revocation becomes effective as soon as notice of it is delivered to the offeree at the appropriate place through the appropriate medium, whether or not the offeree actually reads it. If the offer was made to the public in an advertisement, it is effectively revoked by publishing the notice of revocation in the same way as the offer, whether or not a particular offeree actually read it.

Even if the offeror failed to give direct notice of revocation, the offer could be revoked indirectly if the offeror takes action clearly inconsistent with the continued intent to enter a contract, and the offeree obtains reliable information of this action. The principle of indirect revocation was enunciated by the nineteenth-century English case, *Dickinson v. Dodds*, 2 Ch. D. 463 (1876). The offeror did not notify the offeree that he revoked his offer to sell a piece of real property, but before the offeree had accepted the offer, he heard from another source that the property had been sold to someone else.

The court held that this indirectly-learned information was sufficient notice of revocation and it terminated the offer.

§4.7 THE NATURE AND EFFECT OF ACCEPTANCE

Acceptance is the offeree's manifestation of assent to the offer. It is the event that brings the contract into existence because, as noted before, the offer necessarily contemplates that the parties will become bound immediately upon the offeree's exercise of the power of acceptance.

Acceptance must be a volitional act, performed deliberately with the intent to enter a contract on the terms of the offer. Like the intent to make an offer, intent to accept is determined objectively. The question is not whether the offeree actually intended to accept, but whether a reasonable person in the offeror's position would have understood the manifestation as an acceptance.[11] Only the offeree may accept the offer. The offeree is, of course, the person whose acceptance is invited by the offer. This is most commonly a single specific person, but an offer could be made to several identified persons or even to a broad or unidentified group. Unless the offer indicates otherwise, or is clearly open to anyone who sees it, it is personal to, and can only be accepted by, the person or persons to whom it is addressed. An identified offeree cannot transfer the power of acceptance.[12]

The offeror, as the proponent of the transaction, has the power to set out not only the terms of the proposed contract itself but also the requirements for an effective acceptance. For the offeree's communication of acceptance be valid, it must acquiesce in the offeror's terms and must manifest this agreement in the manner and within the time prescribed. If the offer does not prescribe a manner or time for acceptance, a reasonableness standard applies.

§4.8 THE EFFECT OF INCONSISTENCY BETWEEN THE OFFER AND THE RESPONSE: COUNTEROFFER

To be an acceptance, the response to the offer must indicate unqualified acceptance of the terms proposed by the offer. If it indicates an interest in

11. As noted in section 4.1.3c, if the manifestation of acceptance is induced by fraud, duress, or other improper bargaining, a court may hold that the offeree is not bound by the manifestation of acceptance.

12. This rule only applies to offers. Once a contract has been formed, a party has the right to transfer rights and duties under the contract. Chapter 19 discusses the assignment of contract rights and the delegation of contract duties.

entering into the transaction, but on different terms, it likely qualifies as a counteroffer. The legal effect of a counteroffer is to reject the original offer, which thereby lapses, and to make a new offer by the offeree for a contract on different terms, which the original offeror may accept, creating a contract on the counteroffer's terms.

The strictest test for deciding if a nonconforming response is a counteroffer is called the "mirror image" or "ribbon matching" rule. It requires that response to the offer must correspond exactly with the offer to constitute an acceptance. Any variation of terms in the response, no matter how small, disqualifies it as an acceptance. Many courts have softened this test, and treat a response as an acceptance if it indicates intent to enter the contract, but makes only immaterial changes to the terms set out in the offer. This approach allows for greater flexibility in finding a contract where the response to the offer substantially agrees with it, but makes only a trivial or technical change to it. A variation from the offer is material if it goes to the very essence of the contract, significantly changing the basis of the bargain proposed by the original offeror. Materiality is determined by interpreting the language of the offer and the acceptance in the context of the transaction. If the court finds that a response with immaterial changes is an acceptance, this does not mean that the offeree's changes become part of the contract. The response is treated as an unqualified acceptance of the offeror's terms, and the variations in the acceptance are treated as proposals to amend the contract, which will only become part of the contract if the offeror agrees to them.[13]

Not all equivocal or qualified responses to an offer are counteroffers. If the manifested intent of the communication is unclear, its purpose and effect must be determined by interpretation. For example, the owner of block 2 of lot 10, Madison County offers to sell it to the offeree for $2 million. The offeree clearly makes a counteroffer by responding, "Thanks for your offer. I am interested in buying block 2 of lot 10, Madison County, but your asking price is too high. I offer to pay you $1.8 million for the property." This language makes it clear that a counteroffer is intended because it indicates interest in the transaction but not at the price proposed by the offeror. It then explicitly states that it "offers" to pay a different price (surely a material variation from the offer) and signifies intent to enter the contract if the original offeror agrees to that price. The response therefore rejects the original offer and substitutes a new offer to the former offeror. However, say that the response stated, "Thanks for your offer. Although I am interested in buying block 2 of lot 10, Madison County, I cannot accept your offer because your asking price is too high." This cannot be a counteroffer because it does not propose a new price. However, it also indicates that the

13. UCC §2.207 has a special rule for handling discrepancies between the offer and the response where the parties exchange writings. This is discussed in Chapter 6.

offeree does not intend to enter the transaction on the terms proposed by the offeror. It must therefore be reasonably understood as rejection with an explanation. Its legal effect is simply to terminate the offer. The offeree's response is even more ambiguous if it says, "Thanks for your offer. Would you accept $1.9 million?" This is not an acceptance, but it may not be a counteroffer either, which would terminate the buyer's power of acceptance. It may be merely a request for modification of terms, intended to keep alive the buyer's opportunity to accept the offer if the offeror sticks to the asking price.

In some cases, a response may seem to be a counteroffer, but the terms of the offer and response must be interpreted to ascertain whether it really is. For example, the response may seem to add terms that are not expressed in the offer but are implicit in the offer or would be incorporated into the offer by law or usage. If so, the response may appear superficially to be a counteroffer, but it is in fact an unqualified acceptance, because it merely articulates what was inherent in the offer. For example, the owner of block 2 of lot 10, Madison County offers to sell the property to a prospective buyer for $2 million. The offeree responds, "I accept your offer, subject to your proof of clear title, payment to be placed in escrow and made to you against transfer of the deed." The offer is silent on these points. It did not warrant good title and said nothing about payment being concurrent with transfer of the deed. However, these terms are implied into a contract for the sale of real property by common usage and accepted legal practice, so they can be interpreted as an implicit part of the offer in the absence of language clearly excluding them. Therefore, articulating them in the acceptance does not harm its effectiveness.

§4.9 THE MODE OF ACCEPTANCE

An acceptance must be manifested and communicated. The offeror has control over the manner of acceptance, and, in addition to stipulating the terms of the proposed contract, the offeror may specify what the offeree must do to accept. To be an effective acceptance, the offeree's response must be in conformity with these instructions. However, if the offer does not require acceptance to take a particular form, no special formalities are required for effective acceptance.[14] It may be signified in any manner reasonable under the circumstances, including spoken or written words or conduct, and conveyed by any reasonable means of communication. In most contracts, acceptance is by words or conduct that create a promise to perform at some point

14. However, if the statute of frauds applies, its requirements of recording and signature must be satisfied, as discussed in Chapter 11.

in the future. However, some contracts (called "unilateral contracts" and discussed in section 4.12) allow for the offeree to accept by rendering the contractual performance called for in the offer.

The instructions concerning acceptance (that is, the procedure that must be followed by the offeree to accept) can be characterized as the procedural content of the offer, as opposed to its substantive content—the terms of the proposed contract itself. The substantive terms are central—they go to the very heart of the relationship and are the offeror's dominant concern. The instructions for acceptance are ancillary to the offeror's principal purpose of securing a contract. They are concerned only with the way in which the offeree communicates assent and are aimed at a communication process that the offeror considers most convenient and efficacious. The manner of acceptance is ancillary to the goal of making a contract. Some offerors may not care about prescribing a procedure for acceptance, but others may wish to control it. An offeror who desires firm control over the mode of acceptance can achieve this by stipulating that the stated mode of acceptance is exclusive (that is, it the only way in which the offer may be accepted). If the offeror prescribes a mode of acceptance but does not clearly make it exclusive, an acceptance is likely effective if it is communicated by a means that is reasonably equivalent and affords the offeror the same protection as the prescribed mode. An offeror who is concerned about knowing of the acceptance as soon as it takes effect and of having recorded proof of it should prescribe an exclusive mode of acceptance that ensures acceptance only takes effect upon the offeror's personal receipt of a recorded acceptance (such as a letter or an email).

In summary, the rules governing mode of acceptance are:

1. *Exclusive mode.* When the offer clearly manifests the intention that a prescribed mode of acceptance is mandatory and exclusive, the offeree must obey those instructions and comply with them exactly. Unless the language of the offer makes it clear that the offer can be accepted only by use of the specified mode, courts generally assume that the specified mode of acceptance is permissive, rather than exclusive.
2. *Permissive mode.* If the offer specifies a manner of acceptance, but it does not reasonably appear intended as exclusive, any reasonable method of acceptance is effective provided that it is consistent with the specified mode and provides protection to the offeror equal to that of the stated mode. The question of whether the mode used is reasonably consistent with that specified in the offer is resolved by comparing the attributes of the specified mode to the mode used. For example, the offer states, "Please signify your acceptance by mailing your written and signed acceptance by certified mail." The offer does not make it clear that certified mail is the only acceptable medium, so a written, signed acceptance by private courier is

probably a reasonable substitute because it provides written proof of acceptance and a means of proving delivery. An email acceptance may also be permissible. Although the medium is different, it does achieve the same purpose of creating a record of acceptance and verifiable delivery.

3. *Unspecified mode.* If the offer does not specify any mode of acceptance, the test for the appropriateness of the communication is even less stringent. The offeree may use the same mode as used by the offeror, or any other method of communication that is customary for transactions of that kind or is reasonable under the circumstances. For example, in *Ellefson v. Megadeth, Inc.*, 2005 WL 82022 (S.D.N.Y. 2005), the parties (a heavy metal rock band and one of its original members) entered into lengthy negotiations to settle various disputes. Much of the negotiation was by email, culminating in a final version of the offered contract sent by fax. The offeree accepted by signing the offer and returning it by mail. The question in the case was whether mail was a reasonable mode of acceptance. The court held that it was. The use of email and fax during the negotiations and leading up to the offer did not preclude acceptance by mail, because there were no express restrictions on the mode of acceptance and regular mail was a reasonable method of communication under the circumstances.

§4.10 INADVERTENT ACCEPTANCE, SILENCE OR INACTION AS ACCEPTANCE, AND ACCEPTANCE BY CONDUCT

§4.10.1 Inadvertent Acceptance

Although the objective test is used to determine intent to accept, the offeree must at least know about the offer to accept it. To this narrow extent, the offeree's subjective state of mind could take precedence over the offeree's apparent intention. It does not happen too often that an offeree inadvertently manifests intent to accept an offer without knowing of its existence. However, this has come up in cases in which the offeree has not been aware of the offer, but acts in a way that creates the impression of acceptance. *Glover v. Jewish War Veterans of the U.S.*, 68 A.2d 233 (D.C. 1949), is a well-known case involving such a situation. The Jewish War Veterans published an offer of reward for information leading to the arrest and conviction of the murderer of one of its members. On being questioned by the police, Glover furnished information that led to the murderer's apprehension and ultimate conviction. The act of providing the information would have been the acceptance of the offer of reward.[15] However, when Glover gave the information to the police, she did not know of the reward and only found out about it afterward. The court held that she was not entitled to the reward. She could not have intended to accept an offer of which she was unaware. The result of this case could be justified on the basis that because Glover did not know about the offer, it did not induce her to give the information, and she had no reliance interest that required protection. However, a more compelling argument is that the result is unfair. The principal purpose of the rule is to prevent a person from being trapped into an inadvertent manifestation of acceptance, so the rule should not apply when, on discovering that an offer existed, the offeree desires the acceptance to be effective.

Anderson v. Douglas Lomason Co., 540 N.W.2d 277 (Iowa 1995), deals with inadvertent manifestation of acceptance in a different context. The court had to decide whether an employee was protected by a provision in the employees' handbook that required progressive discipline and precluded summary dismissal. When an employer adds a provision to a handbook, this is treated as an offer which the employee accepts by continuing in employment. However, the employee in this case had not read the handbook and did not know of the provision. Therefore, if knowledge of the offer is required for an effective acceptance, this employee would not have been protected by the provision in the handbook barring summary dismissal. The court refused to follow the rule requiring knowledge of the offer for effective acceptance. It reasoned that a strong policy of treating employees evenhandedly would be defeated by distinguishing employees who had read the handbook from those who had not. Note the relationship between this case and the duty to read, discussed in section 4.1.4. Had the term been unfavorable to the employee, he would not have been able to avoid being bound by it by arguing that he had failed to read it. It is consistent with this principle that the employer should not be able to claim that the term is not binding on the ground that the employee's manifestation of acceptance was inadvertent.

§4.10.2 Silence or Inaction as Acceptance

Except in the particular circumstances noted below, the offeror cannot impose a duty on the offeree to take some affirmative step to reject the offer, making failure to act an acceptance. For example, the offer cannot impose a duty on the offeree to speak by stating, "If you do not wish to accept this

15. As explained in section 4.12, the offer in this case was for a unilateral contract, which can be accepted only by rendering the performance under the contract. That is, the act of providing the information is simultaneously the acceptance of the offer and the rendition of the performance called for by the contract in exchange for the reward.

offer, you must deliver notice of rejection to me by Friday, failing which you are deemed to have accepted." *Pride v. Lewis*, 179 S.W.3d 375 (Mo. Ct. App. 2005), applies this principle. A potential buyer of real property made a written offer to purchase it from the owner, accompanied by a payment of earnest money.[16] The owner responded by making a counteroffer. The buyer did not respond to the counteroffer, did not attend the closing, and never requested the return of his earnest money. The seller sued the buyer for damages for breach of contract, claiming that the buyer had accepted the counteroffer by failing to object to it and demand return of his earnest money. The court rejected this argument on the ground that the buyer's silence and inaction could not be treated as an acceptance.

The rule that silence does not constitute acceptance is intended to protect the offeree from imposition. It therefore does not apply if the offeree receives an offer specifying that it will be accepted by silence, and the offeree does not respond, intending to accept the offer by not rejecting it. An offeror who creates the reasonable understanding that no action need be taken to accept the offer cannot later seek to deny a contract by invoking the rule that silence is not acceptance. As a result, an offeror who provides for acceptance by silence will not be able to tell whether or not a contract arose out of the silence.

There are two narrow exceptions to the general rule that silence cannot be acceptance. First, silence operates as acceptance if the offeror proffers property or services with the offer, and the offeree, having a reasonable opportunity to return or refuse them, exercises ownership rights over the property or accepts the benefit of the service. Second, prior dealings between the parties or other circumstances may make it reasonable for the offeror to expect the offeree to give notice of rejection, so that silence constitutes acceptance.

§4.10.3 Distinguishing Acceptance by Silence from Acceptance by Conduct

Acceptance need not always be explicit, so there are some situations in which an offeree does not respond to an offer, but ongoing conduct is enough to signify acceptance. It can be difficult to know when conduct alone, without any expression of assent, constitutes acceptance. For example, in *Morvant v. P. F. Chang's China Bistro, Inc.*, 870 F. Supp. 2d 831 (N.D. Cal. 2012), P. F. Chang (the employer) implemented an arbitration policy in 2006, after Morvant had already started working for it. P. F. Chang gave

16. Earnest money is a deposit on the price of the property, paid by a buyer to indicate the serious intention of proceeding with the transaction.

copies of the agreement to its employees with a cover letter setting out the effective date of the policy and stating that "this policy applies to you." Morvant received but did not sign the agreement or otherwise indicate assent to it but continued working for P. F. Chang for a few months. When Morvant later sued P. F. Chang over alleged breaches of the conditions of employment, P. F. Chang moved to compel arbitration. The court denied the motion on the grounds that Morvant had never signified assent to the agreement. The court characterized the new arbitration policy as an offer, which Morvant did not accept merely by continuing to work for P. F. Chang. However, the court noted (distinguishing other cases) that it would have reached the opposite result if the arbitration agreement or cover letter had specified that continued employment would constitute acceptance of the terms of the arbitration policy.

§4.11 THE EFFECTIVE DATE OF ACCEPTANCE AND THE "MAILBOX" RULE

§4.11.1 The Traditional Rule

The question of when acceptance takes effect is linked to but distinct from the method of acceptance. Where the parties are negotiating face to face or are otherwise in instantaneous communication and are able to hear or observe each other's manifestations immediately, there is no temporal separation between the offeree's expression of acceptance and its communication to the offeror, so there is no need to decide whether acceptance takes effect when it is uttered or when it is heard. Acceptance occurs as soon as it is manifested.

However, where the parties are at a distance and the means of communication entail a delay between the manifestation and the offeror's knowledge of it, there are two possible points at which acceptance could become effective. It could take effect immediately upon its being dispatched or only upon its being received by the offeror. As with the mode of acceptance, the offeror has the right to specify when acceptance becomes effective. In many situations if a mode of acceptance is prescribed, this also implicitly establishes the effective point of the acceptance. For example, if the offer states that acceptance will only take effect upon the personal delivery of a signed, written acceptance, this covers both the mode of acceptance and the event (delivery) that brings it into effect. However, the offeror may not have specified a mode of acceptance or, even having done so, may not have fixed the point at which the acceptance takes effect. For example, the offer may state that acceptance must be by mail but may not make it clear if a contract comes into being upon the acceptance being mailed or only upon its being received by the offeror.

In the absence of specification in the offer, a noninstantaneous acceptance takes effect as soon as it is put out of the offeree's possession and control, provided that the acceptance is made in a manner and via a medium expressly or impliedly authorized by the offer. Therefore, if acceptance by mail is permissible, acceptance occurs as soon as the offeree deposits a properly stamped and addressed acceptance in the mailbox. This is known as the "mailbox" rule or "deposited acceptance" rule. Because acceptance takes effect on depositing the acceptance in the mail, it does not matter if it was received after the offer terminated or was never received at all. The burden is on the offeree to prove proper dispatch, so the offeree should make a good record of the mailing to avoid evidentiary problems. The offeree must also ensure that the letter is correctly addressed, stamped, and otherwise properly prepared for delivery. This requirement is illustrated by *Casto v. State Farm Mutual Automobile Insurance Co.*, 594 N.E.2d 1004 (Ohio App. 1991), in which an insurance company mailed an offer to the insured to renew a car insurance policy. The insured sought to accept the offer by mailing a check for the premium but forgot to put a stamp on the envelope. The post office therefore did not deliver the letter and the premium payment was never received. The insured did not discover this problem until the unstamped letter was returned by the post office. In the interim, the car had been damaged in an accident. The court found that although acceptance by mail was authorized, so that the mailbox rule would have applied to make acceptance effective on mailing the check, the mailbox rule cannot be applied where the offeree cannot show proper mailing.

There have been a number of rationales advanced for the mailbox rule. The most convincing is that the offeror could have allocated the risk of uncertainty, delay, or nonreceipt to the offeree. If an offeror does not take advantage of the right to specify that acceptance is only effective on receipt, the offeror assumes these risks, and the offeree gains the benefit of a reliable basis for establishing the time of effective acceptance.

The mailbox rule does not apply if the offeree initially mails a rejection (including a counteroffer) and then has a change of mind and mails an acceptance. To protect the offeror, who might receive the rejection before the acceptance, the acceptance only takes effect on receipt. Therefore, if it arrives before the rejection, the offer is accepted, and if it arrives afterward, it is ineffective.[17]

If the mailbox rule does not apply, acceptance takes effect only on receipt—the notification of acceptance must come into the possession of

---

17. Some courts hold that the mailbox rule does not apply to options (irrevocable offers), so that the acceptance of an option is effective only on receipt unless the option specifies otherwise. This is discussed in section 4.13.

the addressee or its authorized representative, or must be deposited in an authorized place. Provided this has happened, the addressee does not actually have to read it.

§4.11.2 Application of the Rule to Electronic Media

The mailbox rule is so called because it was established to deal with acceptance through the medium of the mail. However, today, offer and acceptance are commonly conducted via electronic media such as text messages, email, or various Internet-based communications. Some forms of electronic communication are clearly instantaneous, so that even though the parties are not physically in each other's presence, there is no delay between the expression and receipt of acceptance. Where this is so, the general rule, articulated in Restatement, Second, §64, is that acceptance by substantially instantaneous two-way communication, such as by telephone, is treated the same as if the parties are physically in each other's presence. Section 64 was drafted well before the general use of electronic media of communication, but the principle clearly applies to all contemporary means of live communication.

Electronic communications are capable of being substantially instantaneous, but may not be in a particular case because of some disruption or delay, or because the parties are not using them for real-time interaction. Where that is so, the exchange of offer and acceptance may be more analogous to mail than to the telephone—the parties' messages are transmitted through a third party and there is a lag between the time that the acceptance is placed under the control of the transmission service and the time that it is ultimately received by the offeror. Where the parties are not communicating instantaneously, it may be appropriate to apply the mailbox rule, making the acceptance effective immediately upon sending.

§4.12 ACCEPTANCE BY PROMISE OR PERFORMANCE: BILATERAL AND UNILATERAL CONTRACTS

§4.12.1 The Offer for a Bilateral Contract

A bilateral contract is one in which, at the moment of acceptance, both parties to the contract have made promises to perform their contractual obligations at some time in the future. This is true of most contracts, so bilateral contracts are the norm. The less common unilateral contract is one in which the offeree accepts the offer by rendering the very performance that is required under the contract, so that the offeree's act of acceptance also completes the offeree's contractual duties. As a result, at the moment of acceptance, the offeree has no further obligations under the contract, and the offeror is the only party who still has a commitment to perform an outstanding promise. This is why the contract is described as unilateral—because one of the parties (the offeree) has completed performance at the time of forming the contract, so only one of the parties (the offeror) still has a promise of future performance outstanding when the contract is formed. Because most contracts are clearly bilateral, the distinction between bilateral and unilateral contracts is not an issue in most cases.

In most contracts, the offeree manifests acceptance by oral or written words that express assent. When words are used to accept, the acceptance invariably constitutes a promise of future performance. For example, if the owner of block 2 of lot 10, Madison County offers to sell it for $2 million and the offeree replies by expressing acceptance, a contract is created under which both the parties make promises of future performance: The offeror promises to convey the property and the offeree promises to pay the price. Because, at the point of contract formation, both parties have outstanding promises to be performed in the future, the contract is bilateral. This is represented in Diagram 4B.

Diagram 4B

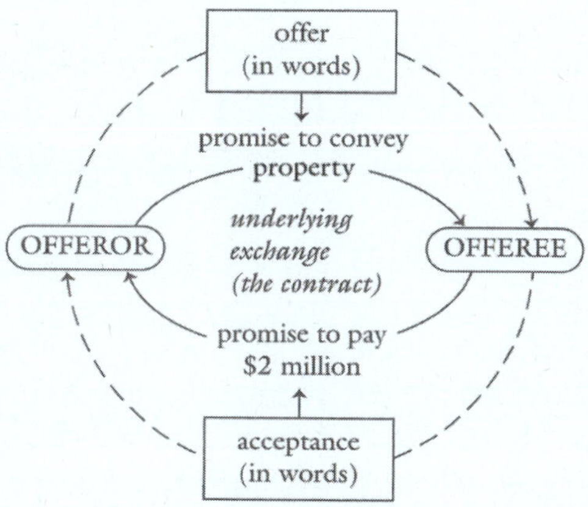

Although most offers are accepted by words, an offeror could call for the acceptance to be conveyed by some act. This is unusual, but it is within the offeror's power to prescribe the mode of acceptance. Therefore, instead of prescribing an acceptance by communicating verbally (for example, by stating that a written acceptance must be received by the offeror by a stated date), the seller of the property (the offeror) could require that the offeree signify acceptance by raising a red flag on the offeree's flagpole by the stated date. This nonverbal signification of acceptance has the same legal effect as the acceptance by words and leads to the identical bilateral contract under which the offeror promises to convey the property and the offeree promises to pay $2 million. Although this offer required the offeree's assent to be signified by conduct instead of words, this is still a bilateral contract. The prescribed act of acceptance is not the offeree's performance under the contract, which is the payment of the price of $2 million. The raising of the flag is just a symbolic act signifying acceptance, no different legally from the act of delivering a communication recording the words "I accept." This is represented in Diagram 4C.

Diagram 4C

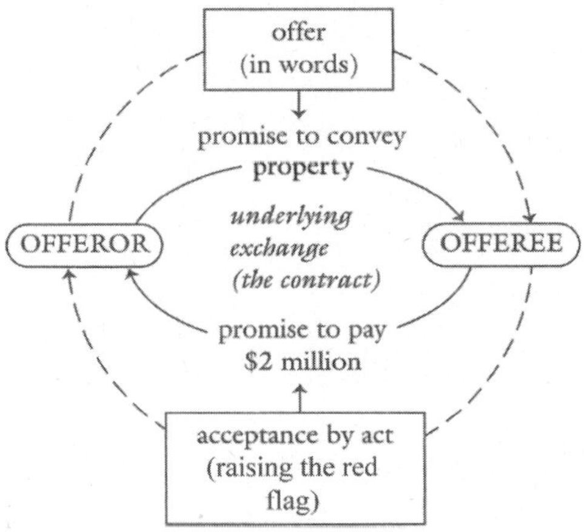

§4.12.2 The Offer for a Unilateral Contract

In the last example, the prescribed act of acceptance was merely intended to symbolize assent to the offer. It is nothing more than a mode of acceptance and has nothing to do with the actual performance—the exchange of detriments—called for by the contract. However, the offeror could have structured the offer so that the act of acceptance is not merely symbolical, but is at the same time also the performance of the offeree's side of the contract. For example, the offer could have stated, "I offer to sell you block 2 of lot 10, Madison County for $2 million. To accept this offer you must come to my office today at 2 P.M. and pay me $2 million in cash. This is the only way that you may accept this offer." The act of acceptance is also the complete act of performance. The offeree's consideration under the contract is furnished in full immediately upon acceptance, and the offeree has no further duty under the contract. All that remains is for the offeror to perform the promise in the offer and to transfer title and possession of the property. The contract qualifies as unilateral because, at the moment of formation, only one of the parties has a promise outstanding. This is represented in Diagram 4D.

Diagram 4D

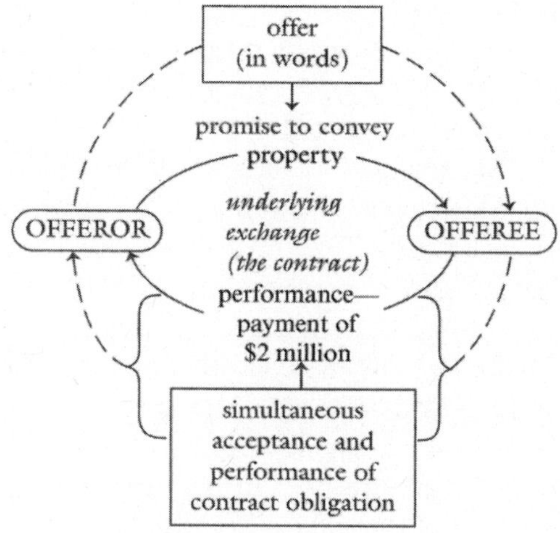

Note, therefore, that "unilateral" does not mean one-sided, in the sense that only one party has given or done something. As explained in Chapter 7, a transaction in which one of the parties has made a promise and the other has given or promised nothing in return lacks consideration and is not a valid and enforceable contract. Rather, the word "unilateral" signifies that although both parties have given consideration, only one of them has made a promise as consideration. The other has furnished consideration by rendering the required exchange performance at the very point of contract formation.

§4.12.3 When the Offer Does Not Clearly Prescribe Promise or Performance as the Exclusive Mode of Acceptance

In the last example, the offeror made it clear that acceptance could only be made by performance of the offeree's consideration, so there is no doubt that a unilateral contract was called for. Similarly, the offer could use clear language that makes promise the only permissible means of acceptance. An offeror who really cares about prescribing either a promise or performance as the exclusive mode of acceptance should use clear language to this effect in the offer to remove any doubt as to that intent. However, even in the absence of such clear language, the nature of the contract itself may lead to the conclusion that acceptance has to be only by promise, or only by performance. In most contracts, the performance is to take place some time after acceptance, so acceptance by promise is the only permissible mode. For example, an offer of employment, made on May 1, calls for the employee to begin work on June 1, but requires acceptance by May 7. In other cases, even in the absence of express language limiting acceptance to performance, the nature of the transaction makes it clear that the offer may be accepted only by performance. For example, a sign posted on a fence around a construction site reads, "$1,000 reward to anyone who reports theft of equipment or materials from this site." It is obvious that this offer does not contemplate formation of a contract by a promise to report theft but may be accepted only by the actual performance of reporting a theft.

However, there are situations in which neither the language of the offer nor its nature and circumstances clearly require either promise or performance to be the exclusive mode of acceptance. If the offer appears to be ambivalent on this question and acceptance by either promise or performance is feasible, the general approach, as reflected in Restatement, Second, §32 and UCC §2.206 (and discussed in section 4.9) applies: The preferred interpretation of the offer is that the offeree may choose to accept either by promise or by performance.

For example, the offeror delivers an offer to the offeree on Monday stating, "I offer to sell you block 2 of lot 10, Madison County for $2 million. If you wish to buy it, you must pay me $2 million in cash at my office on Friday at 2 P.M." Clearly, it is a term of the proposed contract that the buyer's performance—the delivery of the buyer's consideration under the contract—must take place on Friday at 2 P.M. at the seller's office. However, although the offer is clear on the due date of the cash payment, it does not actually say that the only way that the offeree can accept is by making the cash payment on Friday at 2 P.M. The absence of clear language to this effect would likely be interpreted as giving the offeree the choice of accepting either by payment on Friday at 2 P.M. (creating a unilateral contract) or by making a promise of payment at some time before Friday at 2 P.M. (creating a bilateral contract in which the acceptance is by promise to pay the $2 million by Friday at 2 P.M.). Therefore, the offeree is able to close the deal immediately and to bind the offeror before Friday at 2 P.M., by writing to the offeror on Monday, stating, "I accept." A contract immediately comes into existence on dispatch of the letter. The offeree has accepted by making a promise on Monday to perform as required on Friday, and the offeror's offer immediately becomes a promise to convey the property at some future (unspecified but reasonable) time. The early acceptance by promise creates a bilateral contract that binds both parties. The importance of this is that the offer has now become a contract, so the offeror is bound and has lost the right to revoke the offer. Alternatively, the offeree has the option of not accepting by promise before Friday at 2 P.M., but accepting by showing up at that time with the money and accepting by performance. Diagrams 4E and 4F represent these alternative choices of acceptance. Diagram 4E represents the offeree's election to accept by promise on Monday, and Diagram 4F shows the election to accept by performance on Friday.

Diagram 4E. Acceptance by Promise on Monday

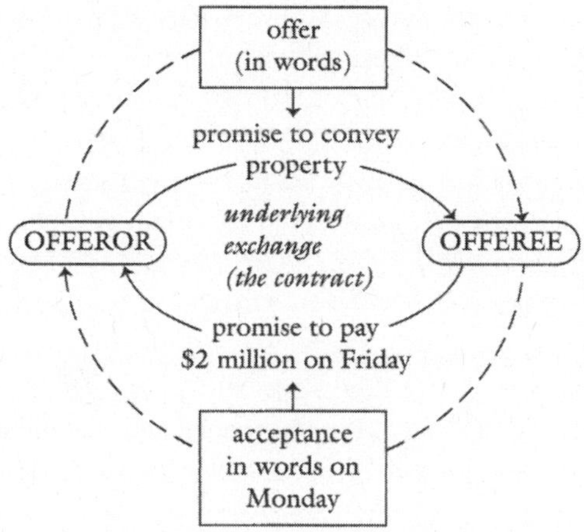

Diagram 4F. Acceptance by Performance on Friday

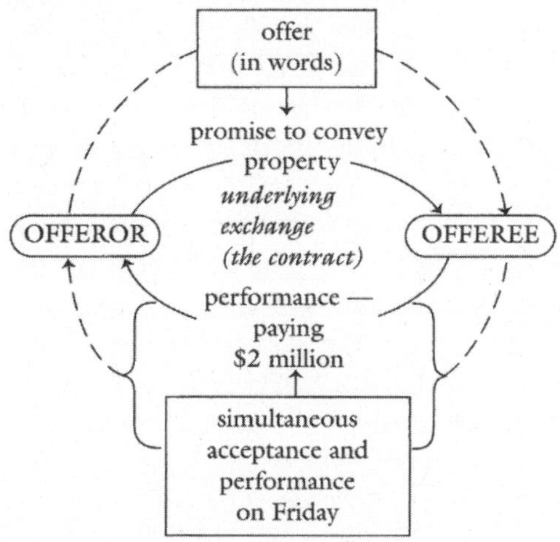

§4.12.4 Acceptance by a Performance That Cannot Be Accomplished Instantly

In the examples concerning the offer to sell block 2 of lot 10, Madison County the offeree's contractual performance was cash payment, a single, relatively instantaneous act. However, some performances take time to complete and cannot be accomplished in one stroke. For example, on Monday, the owner of a house wrote to an arborist offering to pay the arborist $1,000 for cutting down and removing a dead tree next to the house. The offer specified that the arborist must begin the tree removal at 10:00 A.M.

on the Friday of that week and must complete it by not later than 3:00 P.M. The offer stated that it could be accepted at any time up to Friday at 10:00 A.M. It contained no instructions on the manner of acceptance. Based on the general approach that an offer is not interpreted as requiring an exclusive manner of acceptance unless that is clear from its language or nature, this offer would be interpreted as permitting either acceptance by promise at some time up to 10:00 A.M. on Friday, or acceptance by commencing performance on Friday at 10:00 A.M. Therefore, if the arborist accepted by promise at any time up to 10:00 A.M. on Friday, a bilateral contract would come into being.

However, if the arborist did not accept by promise, but began work at 10:00 A.M. on Friday, the starting of work would be the manifestation of intent to accept, but the contractual performance would not be complete at that point because the arborist needs some time to finish the job. If acceptance only takes place on completion of performance, the arborist risks revocation during the process of performing. The offeree is protected from this risk by principles articulated in Restatement, Second, §§62 and 45.

Section 62 applies where (as in this example) the offer does not mandate acceptance by performance, so that it can be accepted either by performance or promise. The offeree's beginning of performance is treated as an implied promise by the offeree to complete the performance within the time required by the offer. Therefore, the commencement of the performance is, in effect, an acceptance by promise creating a bilateral contract. In the present example, as soon as the arborist began work, a bilateral contract came into being under which the arborist committed to complete the work by 3:00 P.M. on Friday, and the owner committed to pay the $1,000 on completion of the work. The creation of an implied promise by beginning performance is represented in Diagram 4G.

Diagram 4G

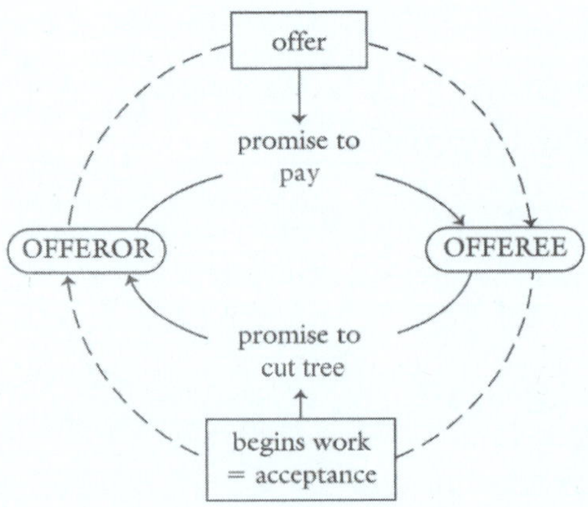

Restatement, Second, §45 applies where the offer calls for performance as the exclusive mode of acceptance (that is, it is clearly an offer only for a unilateral contract). For example, instead of stating that it could be accepted at any time up to Friday at 10:00 A.M., the owner's offer in the above example stated that the work must be begun on Friday at 10 A.M., and the offer can be accepted only by the arborist completing work on that day at 3:00 P.M. This language makes it clear that acceptance by promise is not authorized, so that completion of performance is the exclusive means of acceptance. Restatement, Second, §45 treats the beginning or tender of performance (at 10:00 A.M.) as creating an option in favor of the offeree, so that the offeror loses the right to revoke once performance has been tendered or begun. The offer is finally accepted when the offeree completes the performance by the stipulated time of 3:00 P.M. If the offeree fails to do so, the option is not taken up and the offer lapses. This means that no contract was entered into so that the offeror has no claim against the offeree for breach of contract. The offeror also has no contractual duty to pay the offeree for work that was done before the option lapsed, but the offeree may have an unjust enrichment claim against the offeror to recover the market value of the work done.[18] The creation of an option by beginning performance is represented by Diagram 4H.

Diagram 4H

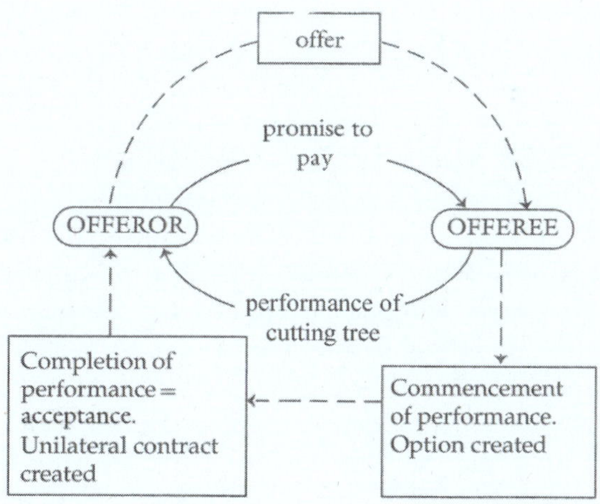

18. Unjust enrichment is discussed in Chapter 9. This cause of action is based on the principle that although no contract arose, the offeror would be unjustly enriched by receiving the benefit of the offeree's work for free.

The option provided for in §45 is more advantageous to the offeree than the implied promise under §62 because treating the beginning of performance as creating a bilateral contract binds the offeree to complete performance, but the option does not. Therefore, the offeree's failure to complete performance would be a breach of contract under §62, but not under §45.

§4.12.5 Notice When an Offer Is Accepted by Performance

As sections 4.9 and 4.11 emphasize, the acceptance of an offer by a promise does not take effect until properly communicated to the offeror. This rule does not apply to a unilateral contract accepted by performance. It is the performance itself, not communication of the intent to accept, that constitutes the effective acceptance. In many cases in which an offer is accepted by performance, the offeror knows that the performance has been rendered, so there is no need for the offeree to inform the offeror of acceptance. However, there are two situations in which the offeree is required to notify the offeror that the acceptance by performance has been accomplished. The first is where the offer requires notice of performance. The second is where the performance is not rendered directly to or in the presence of the offeror and the offeror has no reasonably prompt and reliable means of learning of it. (Say, for example, that the owner of the house does not live in it and resides in a distant state, so would not know if the arborist accepted the offer by removing the tree.) This notice is not itself the acceptance, which occurred upon performance, but the notice must be given within a reasonable time after acceptance, otherwise the acceptance becomes ineffective and the offeror's contractual duty is discharged.

§4.12.6 Reverse Unilateral Contracts

This entire discussion of unilateral contracts is based on the offeree's act of acceptance by performance, leading to a unilateral contract in which the offeree has no promise outstanding at the instant of acceptance, and leaving only the offeror with a remaining promise. This is the usual situation, but it is possible to have a unilateral contract in which the roles of the parties are reversed—the offeror completes performance at the instant of contract formation and the offeree is the party with the outstanding promise. This is called a reverse unilateral contract and is recognized by Restatement, Second, §55, which states that an acceptance by promise could create a unilateral contract where the offeror's performance is completed immediately upon the offeree accepting the offer by promise. In this situation, the offeror tenders complete performance upon making the offer and the offeree accepts the performance and promises to pay for it at a later date.

This qualifies as a unilateral contract because only one party, the offeree, has a promise outstanding at the instant of contract formation. An illustration in the comments to §55 offers the example of an offeror who offers to lend money to the offeree on specified terms and tenders the money in cash. The offeree accepts the cash, thereby promising to repay the loan on the terms specified by the offeror.

§4.13 IRREVOCABLE OFFERS: OPTIONS AND FIRM OFFERS

§4.13.1 The Nature of Options and Firm Offers

An option (called a "firm offer" in UCC Article 2) is a promise to keep an offer open for a stated period of time. By granting a valid option, the offeror makes a binding commitment not to revoke the offer for a specified period, so that the offeree is assured of a set time to consider and respond to the proposal without the risk of its being withdrawn before the expiry date. As noted in section 4.6.4, the offeror's promise to keep an offer open for acceptance for a stated term does not bind the offeror unless it meets the legal requirements for an option under common law or a firm offer under UCC Article 2. At common law, one of these requirements is that the promise to keep the offer open must be supported by consideration separate from the consideration to be exchanged under the proposed contract. (Consideration is covered fully in Chapter 7, but section 4.13.2 provides a brief explanation of consideration doctrine, sufficient for an understanding of options.) As discussed in section 4.13.4, the requirement of consideration, applicable to options under common law, does not apply to most options (called "firm offers" in UCC §2.205) relating to sales of goods.

§4.13.2 Options and Consideration

In *Dickinson v. Dodds*, cited in section 4.6.4 to illustrate indirect revocation of an offer, the court held that the offeror was legally entitled to revoke his offer before its expiry date because the offeree had not given consideration for the offeror's promise to keep the offer open. The complexities of what constitutes consideration are left for Chapter 7. For present purposes, it is enough to understand that in exchange for the grant of an option (the offeror's promise to keep the offer open and not revoke it for a designated period of time), the offeree must give something to the offeror.

The most obvious "something" would be a cash payment or a promise to pay a specific sum of money for the option. But consideration for the option need not be in money. It could also be property or the relinquishment of some legal right. Whatever form the consideration takes, the basic legal requirement is that the grantee must "pay" for the option by transferring or promising money or other property or by sacrificing a legal right in exchange for the promise to keep the option open. The consideration that would be given by the offeree under the contract if the offer was accepted (for example, in a sale of property, the offeree buyer's payment of the price) cannot serve as consideration for the promise not to revoke the offer for the stated period of time. To be valid, the option must have its own separate consideration—the offeree must, in effect, purchase the option by providing an additional consideration, tied to the promise not to revoke. For example, the offeror writes to the offeree offering to sell real property to the offeree for $2 million, and giving the offeree five days to accept. The consideration in the proposed contract is the offeree's promise to pay $2 million in exchange for the offeror's promise to transfer the property to the offeree. These promises will come into effect upon acceptance of the offer. However, the offeree's promise to pay the $2 million under the contract is consideration only for the transfer of the property, and is not consideration for the offeror's promise not to revoke the offer for five days. The offeree would have to give or promise something in addition to bind the offeror to the promise not to revoke, such as a separate payment of, say $100, to "buy" that promise.[19] Diagram 4I represents the distinction between the consideration for the option and the consideration under the underlying contract.

As explained more fully in Chapter 7, one of the principal aims of consideration doctrine is to confine legal enforcement to those transactions in which the parties have actually exchanged promises or performances. It refuses legal enforcement of a gratuitous promise—one that is given as a gift without any return benefit. Options are not usually motivated by gratuitous intent. Their common purpose is commercial—by committing to give the offeree an irrevocable opportunity to accept, the offeror hopes to facilitate a desired economic exchange. For this reason, a court is likely to uphold an option if there is any basis for finding consideration for it, provided that the option has been obtained by fair means, the length of the

19. The rule requiring separate consideration for an option applies only where the promise not to revoke the offer is made in relation to a new contract. If the option is granted within an existing contract, it is part of the bundle of rights exchanged in the contract and is supported by the grantee's contractual consideration. For example, if a five-year lease gives the lessee an option to renew the lease for an additional five-year period, that option is simply one of the rights purchased by the lessee under the lease and is supported by the consideration (such as the payment of rent) given by the lessee under the lease.

Diagram 41

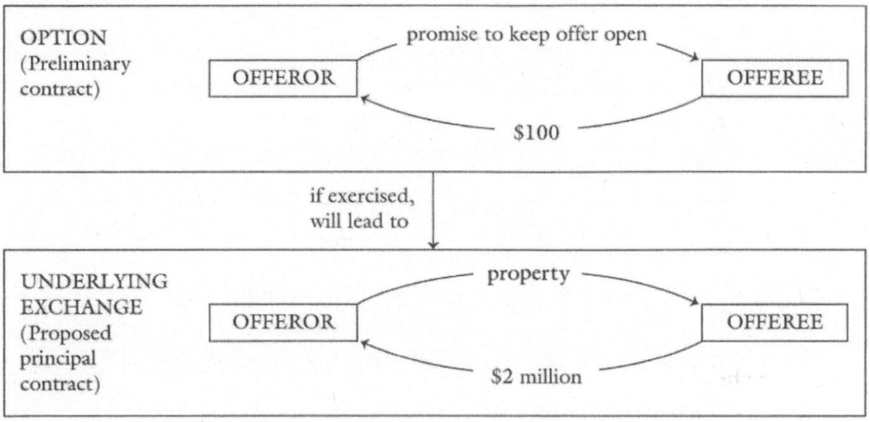

period for acceptance is not unduly long, and the parties have taken the trouble to formalize the grant in a writing that recites that consideration was given. Therefore, courts often accept nominal consideration (a small payment or minimal performance that is patently not equivalent to the actual commercial value of the option) or sham consideration (consideration that is recited in the grant of the option purely for the sake of formality, but not actually given). This approach is reflected in Restatement, Second, §87(1)(a), which says that the grant of an option is valid if it is in writing, is signed by the grantor, recites a purported consideration for the offer, and proposes an exchange on fair terms within a reasonable time.

§4.13.3 The Effect of an Option

As stated already, the principal effect of a valid option is to bind the offeror to keep the offer open for the stated period. The offeree's power of acceptance does not expire until the end of that period and the offeror cannot lawfully revoke the option prior to its expiration. To exercise the option (accept the irrevocable offer), the offeree must communicate acceptance to the offeror within the option period. This usually requires that the offeror actually receives the acceptance. Restatement, Second, §63(b) says that the mailbox rule does not apply to acceptance of a valid option, so that acceptance is effective only on receipt. Comment f to §63 justifies this distinction on the basis that irrevocability sufficiently protects the offeree, so the mailbox rule is not needed to safeguard the offeree's interests or to provide a dependable basis for knowing that the acceptance has occurred. Some courts are unconvinced by this reasoning and see greater merit in having a standard, predictable rule for all acceptances.

§4.13.4 Firm Offers Under UCC §2.205

In a sale of goods, §2.205 dispenses with the need for consideration to validate an option (called a "firm offer" in the section) provided that all of its prerequisites are satisfied—namely:

1. The offer to buy or sell goods must be made by a merchant. A merchant is defined in §2.104(1) as a person who deals in goods of the kind involved in the transaction or who otherwise, by trade or profession, represents having skill or knowledge in regard to the goods or the transaction. In essence, a merchant, as distinct from one whose dealings in the goods is casual or inexpert, is a person who trades professionally in goods of that kind, either as seller or buyer, or is otherwise a professional in business who may reasonably be regarded as possessing skill or knowledge either with regard to the goods themselves, or with regard to transactions of the type in issue.[20]
2. The offer must be in a signed record — either a tangible document or an electronic record.[21]
3. The offer must give an assurance to the offeree that it will be held open. The offer will usually state the time during which it is held open. If it does not, §2.205 provides that it will remain open for a reasonable time.
4. If the assurance is contained on a form supplied by the offeree, the offeror must sign the assurance separately. The purpose of this is to ensure that the offeror was aware of the term and is not bound by an assurance of irrevocability hidden in the offeree's standard terms.
5. The period during which the offer is held open does not exceed three months. Section 2.205 limits the period of irrevocability for a firm offer without consideration to a maximum of three months. If the period during which the offer is open exceeds three months, the offeree must give consideration to validate it.

---

20. The merchant status under Article 2 was introduced in section 2.7.2. As explained there, Article 2 does not generally provide different rules for merchants and casual buyers and sellers, but there are some sections—§2.205 being one of them—that are applicable only to merchants or have stricter standards for them. Some of these sections are applicable only in transactions "between merchants"—that is, if both parties to the transaction are merchants—but others apply if only one of them is. Section 2.205 fits into the latter category, so only the offeror needs to be a merchant for the rule validating firm offers to apply.

21. The Official Text of §2.205 was amended in 2022 to reflect this by substituting "record" for "writing" in the section. The previous version of the Official Text of §2.205 states that the offer must be in a signed "writing." However, even in states that have not enacted the amendment, "writing" is interpreted to include an electronic record.

§4.14 A TRANSNATIONAL PERSPECTIVE ON OFFER AND ACCEPTANCE

This brief note on perspective is not comprehensive. Its purpose is just to sketch how the formation of a contract might be approached in a transnational contract. It merely identifies some of the similarities in general approach and some of the differences between domestic American law and general principles of transnational law, as reflected in the UNIDROIT Principles and the CISG. (*See* section 2.9 for an explanation of the scope and purpose of the UNIDROIT Principles and the CISG.)

Broad general principles of offer and acceptance are expressed in both the UNIDROIT Principles and the CISG in a manner that would sound familiar to an American lawyer. (As explained in section 2.9, the UNIDROIT Principles are not binding law in any country, but rather set out widely accepted general principles applicable to international contracts. In contrast, the CISG is a treaty, and is hence binding law in international sales of goods that fall within its scope, provided that the parties have not excluded its application.) Both the UNIDROIT Principles and the CISG provide for the fundamentals of offer and acceptance in general terms and contain few specific or detailed rules.

Both the CISG and the UNIDROIT Principles adopt the flexible, nontechnical approach to offer and acceptance reflected in UCC §§2.204 and 2.206: To constitute an offer, a proposal must be sufficiently definite and must indicate the offeror's intent to be bound upon acceptance. Acceptance is a statement or conduct indicating intent to assent to the offer. There are some differences from common law principles as well. For example, neither the CISG nor the UNIDROIT Principles recognize the mailbox rule, so acceptance is effective only on receipt unless the offer provides otherwise. Because consideration doctrine is confined to the common law (as explained in Chapter 7), it is not a prerequisite for the validity of an option in either the CISG or the UNIDROIT Principles. Instead, they recognize the validity of a promise not to revoke an offer if it expresses the offeror's intent to make it irrevocable.

Examples

1. To update its rooms, Plush Plaza Hotel, Inc., decided to replace the carpeting throughout the building. It asked Fuzzy Flooring Co. to come to the hotel and give it an estimate of what the recarpeting would cost. A Fuzzy Flooring sales representative came to Plush Plaza with carpet samples and the hotel's manager selected one. The Fuzzy Flooring representative then spent some time taking measurements and making calculations. After this, the representative left a document with the hotel manager headed "Estimate." It included details of the carpet selected, the

quantity of carpet needed, a price for the supply and installation, an estimate of when the job could be started and completed, and a statement that payment was due on completion of the installation. At the end of the estimate there was a sentence that read, "This estimate is good for ten days." Is this an offer or a solicitation?

2. Professor Ivor E. Tower has spent the last three years working on his book titled *Foolproof Contracting: A Lay Person's Guide to Effective Dealmaking*. On completing the book, Ivor set about getting it published. On July 1, he mailed an identical letter and a copy of the manuscript to several publishers. The letter read, "I submit the enclosed manuscript for your consideration. If you would like to publish it, let me know by July 30. I want the book published as soon as possible, at least within this year. If you are willing to commit to this, I would be willing to give it to you on the customary terms and expect the usual royalty of 15 percent of sales."

   One of the publishers to whom he sent the book was Pro Se Prose, Inc. The editors at Pro Se read the book, which was a real page-turner. They decided that they would like to publish it. On July 24, Pro Se mailed a letter to Ivor, in which it accepted the book for publication, committed to have it published within the year, and enclosed its standard contract for Ivor to sign. The terms in the standard contract are those generally found in publishing contracts and included a royalty of 15 percent of sales. On July 25, before receiving Pro Se's letter, Ivor signed a contract with one of its competitors for the book's publication, and he immediately sent an email to Pro Se telling it that the book had been given to another publisher and was no longer available for publication by Pro Se. Ivor received Pro Se's letter later that day. Is Ivor now in the uncomfortable position of having made two contracts for the same book?

3. Ann Teek is an antique dealer. Art Deco collects tableware from the 1920s and 1930s. He visited Ann's store and saw a richly decorated platter made in 1935. It was marked with a $450 price tag. Art told Ann that he was interested in buying it but would like to take it home to see how it would look as part of his collection. Ann agreed to let him take it home for a day on the understanding that if he did not want it, he would return it the next day. Ann took Art's credit card information so that if he decided to keep the platter, he could just call her and she would charge the price of the platter to his card.

   After making this arrangement, Ann had misgivings about selling the platter because she also collected tableware from that period, and it was a very attractive piece. She therefore decided, later that day, to call Art and to tell him that she had changed her mind and wanted the platter back. Ann called, and Art answered the phone. As soon as he heard that it was Ann calling, and before Ann could tell him that she wanted him to return the platter, Art said, "Hi, Ann. I have decided to take the platter. Debit my card." Has Ann sold the platter to Art?

4. Kay Nine had a very demanding job and never had time to wash her dog, who was getting smelly. Kay's friend recommended a mobile dog-grooming service operated by Doug Washer, who had charged the friend $100 to wash and groom her dog at home. On Monday, Kay sent Doug an email stating, "My friend recommended you to me. If you are available, I would like you to come to my house to wash and groom my dog on this Saturday at 9:00 A.M. I understand that your charge is $100, which I will pay to you after you have completed the job." The email included Kay's street address. Kay had not received a reply from Doug by Thursday, so she assumed that he was not interested in doing the job and she had the dog washed and groomed by someone else on Friday. Doug showed up at Kay's house on Saturday morning at 9:00 A.M. with his mobile dog salon, ready to wash and groom Kay's dog. Kay told him that she did not need him anymore because she already had the dog washed by someone else. Doug claims that he and Kay have a contract. Is he correct?

5. Change the facts of Example 4: On Tuesday morning, Doug sent an email response to Kay, saying, "I would be delighted to bath and groom your dog. I will be at your house on Saturday at 9:00 P.M. Thanks for your business." The "P.M." in the email was a typographical error. Doug had meant to type "9:00 A.M." Kay read Doug's email a short while after he sent it and noticed the difference in the time. She did not want Doug to come to her house at 9:00 P.M. because she was going out. She therefore found someone else to groom her dog. Kay did not respond to Doug's email. Unaware of the error, Doug went to Kay's house on Saturday morning at 9:00 A.M. with his mobile dog salon, ready to wash and groom Kay's dog. Kay pointed out to Doug that his email response had said that he would do the work at 9:00 P.M., which was not what she had asked for, so she found someone else to wash the dog. Doug is upset. He feels that they did make a contract on Tuesday and it should have been obvious to Kay from the context that the "P.M." in his email was an error and meant "A.M." If she had any doubt about this, she could easily have cleared it up by sending another email to him. Is Doug correct?

6. Art Walls owns a building whose exterior has been spraypainted by vandals with infuriating regularity. In an attempt to put an end to this expensive nuisance, he placed an advertisement in the newspaper on January 15, offering a reward of $1,000 to "anyone who furnishes information leading to the conviction of those guilty of defacing the walls" of his building. On January 16, the police arrested Fresco Furtive, a young man who was caught in the act of spraypainting another building in the neighborhood. During his interrogation by the police, Fresco confessed

to spraying Art's building as well. Fresco was tried for all these acts of vandalism, convicted, and placed on probation.

Although Fresco was not aware of the reward offer at the time of his confession, he found out about it the next day and immediately claimed the reward. Art rejected his claim, arguing that he never intended to extend the reward offer to the culprit himself. Is Fresco entitled to the reward?

7. Change the facts of Example 6: The police did not arrest and obtain a confession from Fresco Furtive on January 16. However, Fresco's nocturnal artistry had been observed by two witnesses who read Art's reward offer on January 15. Both witnesses independently contacted Art to tell him that Fresco had vandalized his building. One of the witnesses gave the information to Art on January 16, the other gave him the information on January 17. Art reported this information to the police and Fresco was later arrested and tried. Both witnesses testified at Fresco's trial and he was convicted on the strength of their testimony. Both witnesses claim the $1,000 reward. What contractual obligation, if any, does Art have to each of the witnesses?

8. Efficient Enterprises, Inc. felt that its workers needed an incentive to be more productive, so in January it established a program under which all nonmanagerial workers would be evaluated annually on the basis of a set of stated criteria, and those who had satisfied those criteria over the year would receive a bonus of 5 percent of their salary for that year. The incentive program was widely publicized to the employees through posters in the workplace, announcements, and flyers given to each employee, so all the workers knew about it. The management was to conduct the evaluation of workers in November. However, an economic recession occurred in August, which resulted in a dramatic drop in Efficient's revenue. The management decided that the company could no longer afford the incentive program and announced to its workers that it was terminating it. Did Efficient have the right to do this?

9. On April 10, Professor Penny Pincher sent an email to her class, stating that she was looking for a research assistant for the summer. The email stated that she would need 40 hours of work per week from June 1 through August 1 and would pay $16 per hour. The email ended with the sentence, "If you are interested in applying for this position, please send me an email with your resume attached. I plan to make a decision in a week." Maggie Cumlaude, a bright and enterprising student in Penny's class, replied by email on the same day, attaching her resume

and stating, "I am interested in being your research assistant this summer, but $16 per hour is too low. I am willing to work for you for $20 per hour. Penny replied immediately, "Would you consider $18 per hour?"

Penny had not heard from Maggie by April 15 and she had not received any other responses to the email that she sent to her class, so she sent an email to Maggie saying, "O.K. I will pay you $20 per hour." In the interim, on April 13, Maggie had accepted an offer of a summer clerkship at a law firm, and could not do research for Penny as well. She therefore replied immediately to Penny's email of April 15, stating that she was no longer available work for her as a research assistant. Did Maggie breach a contract with Penny by declining to work as her research assistant?

10. Flaky Cereal Co. manufactures "Flaky's Frosties" sugar-coated cornflakes. The logo for this product is a cute cartoon leopard named "Frosty Fangs." To promote the sale of its cornflakes, Flaky ran a competition, which it announced on the back of the cereal boxes. The competition was initiated in January 2024. It enabled people to win various prizes by sending in the tops of cereal boxes accompanied by a form printed on the back of the box. The more tops that were collected, the bigger the prize. The box listed four categories of prizes: Four box tops earned a plastic "Frosty Fangs" pin, 10 earned a cuddly "Frosty Fangs" stuffed toy, 20 earned a "Frosty Fangs" watch, and 1,000 earned a real leopard cub. Each of the prizes was illustrated by a color photograph. The back of the cereal box proclaimed: "Collect your box tops now and send them in by April 1, 2024, to claim your prizes! (Prizes limited to quantities on hand, so don't delay.)"

Flaky's Frosties are Manny Eater's favorite cereal. He saw the promotion on his cereal box and decided that he would really enjoy having a pet leopard. Manny went from one supermarket to another until he had bought 1,000 boxes of Flaky's Frosties. He mailed the box tops to Flakey in February 2024 with a properly completed form and claimed his prize of a leopard cub. (Flaky's Frosties sell for $4 a box, so 1,000 boxes of the cereal cost Mannie $4,000, which is considerably below the value of a leopard cub, which can cost up to $500,000.)

Flaky refused to deliver a leopard club to Manny on several grounds. Consider each of these grounds and decide if any of them justify Flaky's refusal to award the prize to Manny:

a. Flaky denied that it had any legal obligation to Manny because the back of the cereal box was merely an invitation to consumers to claim prizes and not an offer. Therefore, by submitting the box tops and form Manny made the offer, which Flaky rejected.

b. The leopard cub obviously was not intended as a prize but was just a bit of hyperbole to attract attention to the competition. This would be self-evident to any reasonable person because leopards do not make good pets, no consumer could reasonably be expected to consume 1,000 boxes of cereal in the few months before the expiry date of the competition, and no reasonable person would believe that an expensive animal could be won for the cost of 1,000 boxes of cereal.

c. Even if Flaky did make an offer, it expressly stated that prizes were limited to quantities on hand. Flaky never had any leopard cubs, so it had no quantity of cubs on hand.

11. On March 1, 2024, the owner of a plot of land made an offer to sell it to a prospective buyer for $500,000. The offer gave the buyer until 5:00 P.M. on March 7, 2024 to accept it. The final sentence of the offer stated, "In consideration for $10.00 received, the seller undertakes not to withdraw this offer before it expires at 5:00 P.M. on March 7, 2024." On March 4, before the buyer had accepted the offer, the seller delivered a letter to the buyer revoking the offer. Did the seller have the legal right to revoke the offer?

12. On March 1, 2024, a jeweler made a signed, written offer to sell a diamond-encrusted necklace to a prospective buyer for $500,000. The offer gave the buyer until 5:00 P.M. on March 7, 2024 to accept it. The final sentence of the offer stated, "The seller undertakes not to withdraw this offer before it expires at 5:00 P.M. on March 7, 2024." On March 4, before the buyer had accepted the offer, the seller delivered a letter to the buyer revoking the offer. Did the seller have the legal right to revoke the offer?

13. Bogey Bunker, a professional golfer, participated in a charity golf tournament. When he reached the tee for the eighth hole, he saw a brand-new Caddie Lack golf cart parked next to the tee box. A sign attached to the cart read, "Caddie Lack is a proud sponsor of this charity tournament. Hit a hole-in-one at this hole and win this fabulous luxury golf cart." The tournament materials had not mentioned this prize, so Bogey was not aware of it until he saw the display. Bogey hit a hole-in-one and claimed the golf cart from Caddy Lack. However, Caddy Lack refused to award the prize to him on the ground that the prize was restricted to amateurs and he was not eligible for it as a professional golfer. Bogey pointed out that the sign attached to the cart did not mention any such restriction, to which Caddy Lack responded, "The sign didn't need to say it because everyone knows that's the rule." Bogey had never heard of such a rule. Is he entitled to the golf cart?

Explanations

1. Fuzzy Flooring's estimate includes both the sale of the carpet and its installation, so it is a hybrid transaction. As explained in section 2.7.2e, the transaction would be treated as a sale of goods subject to Article 2, if the sale aspect predominates and the labor is incidental, but other law (the common law of contract) would largely apply to it if the service aspect predominates. There are not enough facts to decide this question, but it does not matter because the question of whether Fuzzy Flooring made an offer would be resolved the same way under Article 2 and the common law.

   Where a party uses the heading "estimate" or "price quotation," this creates the initial assumption that the document is a solicitation rather than an offer. However, this initial assumption can be overturned if the language in the document, read in light of any relevant circumstances and usage, indicates a reasonable intent to make an offer. The example does not provide any information about circumstances and usage, so the only basis for determining intent is the language used in the estimate. It does set out all the relevant terms of the contract and appears to leave nothing open to be negotiated. In addition, it concludes with language stating that the estimate is good for ten days. The purpose of this language seems to be to protect Fuzzy Flooring from being contractually bound if Plush Plaza waited too long to reply, and the sentence would not have much point if the estimate was merely soliciting an offer. This language therefore adds force to the argument that this is an offer, open for acceptance within ten days.

   Bourque v. Federal Deposit Insurance Corp., 42 F.3d 704 (5th Cir. 1994), illustrates another situation in which the court had to decide whether an inappositely headed communication was an offer. The FDIC was liquidating a failed savings bank and selling its assets, including a piece of real property that Bourque wanted to buy. Bourque made the original offer to buy the property for $105,500, which the FDIC rejected in a letter stating, "FDIC's counteroffer is $130,000. All offers are subject to approval by the appropriate FDIC delegated authority. FDIC has the right to accept or reject any and all offers." Bourque replied, agreeing to buy the property at this price, but the FDIC sold it to someone else. Bourque claimed that the FDIC made a counteroffer, which he accepted. However, the court found that FDIC's letter was not a counteroffer. Even though it used the word "counteroffer" and specified clear terms, it was qualified by the language that made it clear that the FDIC retained the final say in deciding whether to form the contract.

2. If Ivor's letter of July 1 was an offer, Pro Se Prose's reply of July 24 could constitute an effective acceptance, as discussed below. If it was not an

offer but merely an invitation to deal, Pro Se's letter of July 24 was itself an offer, which Ivor never accepted. A communication is an offer if it manifests the drafter's intent to invite acceptance and conveys the reasonable understanding to the addressee that, upon acceptance, the drafter expects to be committed to a contract without any opportunity for further approval. The test of intent is objective, focusing on what Ivor apparently intended, as perceived by a reasonable person in Pro Se's position. The language of the offer is the most important indication of apparent intent, but the context of the transaction—including any prior dealings between the parties, usages that are or should be familiar to them, or other circumstances relevant to the transaction—can cast light on what must reasonably have been intended. No such contextual evidence is set out in the facts of this Example. (Ivor's reference to customary terms suggests that there are probably usages regarding the content of book publication contracts, but no usage is revealed relating to contract formation.)

The language of Ivor's letter does not solidly convey his intent one way or the other. There are aspects of it that quite strongly suggest an offer: He provides for a specific date for response, he states that he "would be willing" to give the book to Pro Se in exchange for the publication commitment, and he does set out the essential terms on which he would like to contract. The rather vague reference to "customary" terms may suggest that further negotiation is contemplated, but if publication contracts tend to follow a common and well-accepted format, even these terms may be sufficiently certain to be ascertainable. Had the letter indicated that the manuscript had been sent to several publishers, this would have given some indication to Pro Se that it may not have been intended as an offer. However, the letter gives no hint that it has been sent to multiple parties. Where a communication is phrased in the unclear way that Ivor has chosen, it is quite hard to predict how a court will decide what was intended. A person who does not clearly express intent in negotiations runs the risk of being held to an offer when none may actually have been intended.

If Ivor did make an offer, Pro Se's response likely qualifies as an acceptance. By leaving it to Pro Se to formulate terms in accordance with custom, Ivor implies into his offer an intent to contract on terms that are standard and usual in the trade. Provided that the terms in Pro Se's standard contract are indeed customary, they would not conflict with or add to his offer. The response is entirely in accord with Ivor's proposal with regard to the publication date and royalties. Ivor did not stipulate a mode of acceptance and transmitted his offer by mail. Pro Se's response by mail was therefore authorized, and the mailbox rule would apply, making the acceptance effective upon mailing. As a result, the revocation of July 25 was too late.

3. This is clearly a sale of goods, so UCC Article 2 applies. Article 2 has very few specific offer and acceptance rules, and except to the extent that they are displaced by provisions of the Code, general principles of common law are applicable. UCC §2.204(1) and (3) provide a flexible test for deciding whether a contract was formed: It may be made in any manner sufficient to show agreement, including conduct. If the parties intended to contract, missing terms do not cause it to fail for indefiniteness if the court can find a reasonably certain basis for giving a remedy.

   The issue is whether Ann has made an oral contract with Art under which she has committed to sell the platter to him.[22] Ann's conduct in allowing Art to take the platter home is ambiguous. It could be an offer or merely an invitation to Art to make an offer. It is an offer if Art would be justified in understanding that his assent would conclude the bargain, without any need for further assent by Ann. It has sufficiently definite terms to qualify as an offer. The subject matter of the sale and the price are clear: Delivery is to be accomplished by Art retaining the plate, and payment is to occur upon delivery through a credit card debit. If Ann made an offer, §2.206 dispenses with technicality in the mode of acceptance. It presumes that unless a particular manner and medium of acceptance is clearly required, acceptance may be by any means reasonable in the circumstances, and may be either by promise or performance. The parties did contemplate acceptance by telephone as a permissive (although not exclusive mode), and this is how it occurred.

   Although Ann called Art with the intent of revoking, revocation only takes effect when that intent is manifested to the offeree. Art accepted before Ann could express the revocation. Therefore, if Ann's conduct constituted an offer (which it probably does), Art accepted it and Ann is committed to the sale. If Ann's conduct is not an offer, Art's words on the phone would be the offer, and Ann did not accept it, so no contract was created.

4. Doug may or may not be correct. Kay's email to Doug appears to satisfy the elements of an offer. It communicates her willingness to enter into a contract with him, sets out the essential terms of the proposed contract, does not indicate that anything is left for negotiation, and conveys the reasonable understanding that a contract will come into being upon Doug's assent to her terms. The email does not prescribe a method and time of acceptance, but a communication does not need to specify this

22. If the parties made a contract, it would be valid and enforceable, even though it was oral. Article 2 requires an agreement for the sale of goods to be recorded and signed where the price of the goods is $500 or more. This is known as a statute of frauds and is provided for in §2.201, discussed in Chapter 11. However, as the price of the platter is under $500, the statute of frauds does not apply and will not preclude enforcement of the transaction merely on the grounds that there was no signed record of it.

to qualify as an offer. In the absence of instructions on the method and time of acceptance, the offer may be accepted in any manner reasonable under the circumstances and within a reasonable time.

For Kay's offer to result in a contract, Doug must have accepted it. His only communication of assent to the offer is his appearance at Kay's house on Saturday morning at 9:00 A.M., ready and willing to wash and groom the dog. There is no dissonance between the offer and Doug's response because he does not propose any change to the terms that Kay proposed. Therefore, the only questions to be resolved are whether his manner of acceptance was reasonable and timely. The offer does not prescribe acceptance by words as the exclusive method of acceptance, so Doug's acceptance by conduct is permissible. This would not create a unilateral contract because his performance is not instantaneous, but would take a period of time. Therefore, his tender of performance constitutes an implied promise to complete performance in exchange for Kay's promise to pay him, creating a bilateral contract. This is expressed in Restatement, Second, §62, which provides that where an offer permits acceptance either by promise or by performance, the commencement or tender of performance constitutes a promise to complete performance as required by the contract.

The offer does not specify a time for acceptance, so Doug must have accepted within a reasonable time, which is determined under all the circumstances of the transaction. The only circumstances revealed by the facts are that his response was five days after the offer and that Kate apparently considered that the offer had lapsed the day before that, when she hired someone else. Kate's subjective assumption about the duration of the offer is not controlling. The question is how long a reasonable offeree would understand the offer to be open for acceptance. While the answer is not certain, it is arguable that Doug's attempt at acceptance was too late. The offer was made by email and could have been accepted by quick return email, the date proposed for the service was just a few days away, and it could be general practice in the marketplace for a provider of services to indicate assent to a request for services before the date on which they are to be rendered. If Doug's signification of assent came after the offer had lapsed it is not an acceptance and did not form a contract.

5. Doug is wrong. As in Example 4, Kay made an offer that did not specify a required manner of acceptance, so Doug could accept it by promise. His email on Tuesday is surely within a reasonable time, so it does not raise the question of timeliness discussed in Example 4. The problem with his response is that it varies the terms proposed by the offer and it appears to be a counteroffer, not an acceptance. It does not matter that Doug did not intend the change. His objective manifestation of intent, not

his subjective intention, controls. Doug complains that Kay should have realized the error. It may be that a careful recipient would have sensed the error because the text of the email sounds like an unequivocal acceptance. Nevertheless, Doug is accountable for the reasonable meaning of the language that he used and cannot expect Kate to try to divine that he must have meant something different from what he wrote. Maybe it would have been sensible for Kay to send a clarifying email to Doug, but she had no obligation to do that, or to respond in any way to Doug's counteroffer. Her failure to respond is simply a rejection, so no contract was created.

6. The advertisement clearly manifests Art's intention to make an offer. In the absence of language indicating the contrary intent, the reasonable interpretation of a public offer of reward is that the offeror does not seek acceptance by a promise to provide the information, but by the actual furnishing of the information. This is the very act of performance called for by the contract, so acceptance and performance take place at the same time. This creates a unilateral contract under which the informant completes performance at the same time as acceptance, and the only outstanding promise is Art's commitment to pay $1,000. As no time for acceptance was stated, the offer had to be accepted within a reasonable time. The amount of time reasonable for acceptance is a factual question, to be decided under all the circumstances of the case, but acceptance about two days after the offer is probably within a reasonable time, given the nature of the offer and the absence of circumstances indicating greater urgency. By confessing, Fresco did furnish information that led to his conviction for defacing Art's walls. However, there are two arguments against treating the confession as a valid acceptance of Art's offer.

   First, Fresco was not aware of the offer when he provided the information. Even under the objective test, apparent acceptance cannot be treated as acceptance unless deliberate and made with knowledge of the offer. In this respect, Fresco's situation is similar to that of the plaintiff in *Glover v. Jewish War Veterans of the U.S.* discussed in section 4.10. As noted in section 4.10, the rule requiring knowledge of the offer is intended to protect the offeree from being held to an inadvertent manifestation of assent. This rationale does not apply here because, like the plaintiff in *Glover*, Fresco desires the acceptance to be effective. Nevertheless, a court may still apply the rule because Fresco's ignorance of the offer means that he has no reliance interest to protect.

   Second, even if Fresco made the confession with knowledge of the offer and intent to accept it, he has no power of acceptance unless the offer was addressed to him. The offer is addressed to "anyone" and is apparently aimed at the public at large, so on its face it is open for acceptance by any person who reads it and performs the requested act of furnishing the information. However, even though the offer expresses no restriction excluding the culprit as a possible offeree, the context of the offer may lead to the reasonable construction that this restriction was implied. This argument might be bolstered by the public policy of not permitting a criminal to gain from his crime. (But it could be argued that considerations of public interest point in the opposite direction. The reward is for the information, not the crime, and it may encourage a confession.)

7. As in Example 6, Art has made an offer of a unilateral contract which must be accepted by the act of performance called for in the offer. Both witnesses knew of the offer when they furnished the information, so both claim that they are entitled to the reward. A person could make an offer in a way that permits multiple acceptances and thus many contracts. Art could have ensured that he was protected from multiple claims of reward by including language in the offer that made it clear that the offer would no longer be open for acceptance once the information had been provided. However, he failed to do that, so he could be liable for the payment of two rewards unless he immediately published a notice of revocation in the newspaper as soon as he received the information from the first witness on January 16, which he did not do. Art could make the plausible argument that he is not obliged to pay the witness who furnished the information on January 17 because the offer implicitly included this restriction, even in the absence of an express proviso in the offer. Such a restriction could be inherent in the nature of the transaction. It is clear from the offer that a single performance is all that Art needs, so it could be reasonable to infer that the offer is open only to the first person who accepts by rendering the performance requested. Once that performance is given, the object of identifying and prosecuting the criminal has been achieved, and Art gets no benefit from duplicate information. If the condition of expiry is implicit in the offer Art would not have to publish notice of revocation. Therefore, Art would have to pay the $1,000 to the first informant and would have no obligation to pay the second informant because the offer would have lapsed before the second informant accepted. It does not matter that the testimony of both witnesses led to Fresco's conviction. The reward was for the information, not for the testimony.

8. This Example is based on *Storti v. University of Washington*, 330 P.3d 159 (Wash. 2014). The university established an incentive program for its faculty and then suspended the program when it had to reduce expenses for budgetary reasons. In that case, the court held that the announcement of the incentive program was an offer of a unilateral contract, which could be accepted not by promises of faculty members to perform meritoriously but by actual meritorious performance. The

acceptance by performance could not occur instantaneously but would take a full year to complete. However, as soon as the faculty began to work under the program, an option was created under Restatement, Second, §45, which precluded the university from revoking its offer. The resolution in *Storti* seems entirely correct. Once an employer creates an incentive program to encourage its workers to make efforts beyond those called for in the underlying employment contract, the employer should not be able to yank those benefits away after the employees have worked in reliance on the program.

9. Penny's email to the class is not an offer. Although it sets out the terms on which she proposes to contract, she is clearly just calling for applications, reserving to herself the power to decide on which of the applicants, will receive an offer from her. Maggie's email reply is reasonably interpreted as an offer. It impliedly incorporates the terms set out in Penny's announcement, except for the hourly rate, which it increases and it manifests the intent to allow Penny to conclude the contract by accepting its terms.

   Penny's response to Maggie's offer could be a counteroffer. If it is, it operates as a rejection of Maggie's offer, which falls away and is no longer open for acceptance. However, the wording used by Penny is ambiguous. It does not unequivocally reject Maggie's terms, but instead merely asks if Maggie would be amenable to a rate of $18 per hour. A response to an offer that just explores the possibility of a different term could be reasonably interpreted as a negotiation for a change, while holding open the possibility of acceptance if the offeror refuses to budge on her initial demands. If that is so, Penny's email of April 15 could be an acceptance. Maggie's offer did not specify a lapse date, so provided that five days is a reasonable time for acceptance, a contract could have been formed on April 15.

   If Penny's initial response to Maggie was not a counteroffer and Penny's email of April 15 is an acceptance, a contract came into being on April 15. Maggie's decision on April 13 to take the clerking position is not a revocation of her offer because she never communicated revocation of the offer before Penny accepted it (no direct revocation) and Penny had no knowledge of the fact that Maggie had accepted the clerkship (no indirect revocation). If this is so, Maggie's refusal to perform the research work would be a breach of the contract.

10. This transaction could qualify as a sale of goods even though no money was exchanged for the prize. The prizes offered (including the leopard cub) qualify as goods, and the exchange of the box tops could constitute a price. Regardless of whether this is a sale of goods, the issues in this Example would be resolved under principles of common law, which are not displaced by any Code provisions. Flaky's arguments should be resolved as follows:

a. *The argument that the cereal box was a solicitation, not an offer.* The traditional common law assumption is that advertisements (including competitions designed to promote products) cannot usually be interpreted to give members of the public the power to bind the advertiser simply by responding to the advertisement. Advertisements are therefore not usually offers but merely solicitations for offers from the public, so that the initial offer is made by the member of the public who responds to the advertisement. This assumption is still commonly expressed in modern cases, but an advertisement could qualify as an offer if its language in context (including the reasonable expectations in the marketplace) would lead a reasonable person to understand it to be an offer. *Lefkowitz v. Great Minneapolis Surplus Store,* discussed in section 4.4, stated a test that is still widely used: An advertisement could qualify as an offer if it is clear, definite, and explicit; leaves nothing open for negotiation; and makes it apparent to a reasonable person that a commitment is intended without further action by the advertiser. (Restatement, Second, §26, Comment *b* is to similar effect.)

   Flaky's promotion is fully set out on the backs of its cereal boxes, which seem to describe the prizes with particularity (including an illustration) and to set out in detail the mode of responding and the performance required in exchange for the prizes. The boxes also specify an expiry date for responses and contain a limitation to protect Flaky from having to award more prizes than it has on hand. There seems to be nothing left for future resolution, so all that is called for is a response in the proper form. This may indeed be a case in which a court could find that Flaky's choice of language and format belies the normal expectation of a solicitation and creates an offer.

b. *A reasonable person would understand that the leopard cub was not a real prize but just a bit of hyperbole.* This argument is based on several grounds: the unsuitability of leopards as pets, the high number of box tops needed, and the huge discrepancy between the value of the cub and the cost of 1,000 boxes of cereal. These rationales are similar to those advanced by the court in *Leonard v. PepsiCo* (discussed in section 4.1.5 in relation to the objective test) to support the conclusion that the TV commercial could not reasonably have been understood as serious.

   Flaky's joke is not as clearly tongue-in-cheek as PepsiCo's Harrier jet commercial. It could be that a reasonable cereal box reader would have understood that the leopard cub was not seriously intended as a prize, but Flaky took a risk in using deadpan humor that did not make its joke glaringly obvious. (Of course, even if Flaky is held to have made a serious offer, which Manny accepted, it would not necessarily have to deliver the cub to him.[23] However, it would be liable to him for damages measured as the difference between the value of the cub and the contract price.)

c. *Even if Flaky made an offer, prizes were limited to quantities on hand, and Flaky never had a leopard cub.* This interpretation of the qualification gives it an evasive meaning that the advertiser should not be allowed to advance. A more reasonable understanding of the qualification is that Flaky has stocks of all prizes, based on a fair expectation of responses, but that it will be released from supplying prizes once demand for an item exceeds these expectations. To allow Flaky to claim that the language permits it to begin with no prizes of a particular kind would be to condone deceptive advertising.

11. The seller's offer contains an unequivocal promise that it will not be revoked before its stated lapse date. An offeror is not bound by a promise not to revoke an offer unless that promise qualifies as a valid option, which requires that the offeree gives consideration to the offeror separate and distinct from the consideration that would be exchanged in the proposed contract. That is, the $500,000 that would be the buyer's consideration for the property if the contract is concluded cannot also be consideration for the grant of the option to the buyer.

The offer recited a separate consideration of $10 from the buyer in exchange for the seller's promise not to revoke. The facts do not state the actual economic value of an option to buy property worth $500,000, but $10 may be well below that value. If so, the purpose of providing for consideration is not to exchange something of real economic value for the option, but to use nominal consideration purely as a formality to validate the option. Courts generally do not inquire too closely into the question of whether the consideration is equivalent or adequate. (This is explained in section 7.7.) This principle applies particularly strongly to options, for which courts more readily accept the validity of clearly nominal consideration.

The offer states that the $10 consideration was received by the seller. It may be true that the buyer did pay $10 to the seller in exchange for the grant of the option. However, options sometimes recite consideration that was not given, purely for the purpose of validating the option. Even in such a case, a court may hold the option to be binding by refusing to go behind the recital.

23. As explained briefly in sections 1.2.4 and 2.5, and more fully in section 18.10, the common remedy for breach of contract is damages, and a plaintiff has to make a special showing to obtain a court order granting specific performance of a contract.

If a court accepts the recited consideration as valid, the seller had no right to revoke the offer and it remains in force, so that the buyer can accept it up to the end of the lapse date specified in the offer.

12. Unlike the offer in Example 11, this offer makes no reference to consideration for the promise to keep the offer open, so this would not be a valid option under common law. However, the necklace is goods, so the sale is governed by UCC Article 2. If the requirements of UCC §2.205 are satisfied, the seller's promise to keep the offer open is binding as a firm offer despite the lack of consideration. The section's requirements are satisfied:
    (i) The seller must be a merchant. The seller is a jeweler, and therefore satisfies the definition in §1.104(1) as a person who deals in goods of that kind. Section 2.205 requires only that the offeror is a merchant. It is not necessary that the offeree be a merchant as well.
    (ii) The offer is in a record and is signed by the seller.
    (iii) The offer gives the assurance that it will be held open for a stated time, not exceeding three months.

    The promise to keep the offer open until March 7 is therefore binding on the seller and the seller had no right to revoke it. The buyer may disregard the attempted revocation and may accept the offer until its stated lapse date.

13. Bogey had no communication with Caddy Lack until he saw the display at the tee, so no contract could have been created until that time. The display of the golf cart and the sign qualifies as an offer made by Caddy Lack to tournament participants—it proposes an exchange on clear terms, leaves nothing open for negotiation, and conveys the reasonable understanding that the offer can be accepted by performing the requested action—hitting the ball from the tee at the eighth hole. (The act of acceptance is hitting the ball, so that the acceptance takes place as soon as that happens. Achieving the hole-in-one is just a condition of winning the prize.) This is therefore a unilateral contract, which may be accepted only by the performance of hitting the ball. The offer cannot be interpreted as permitting acceptance by a promise to hit a hole-in-one.

    Caddy Lack argues that Bogey could not accept its offer because the offer was not open to him as a professional golfer. However, there is no such restriction expressed in the offer. Under the objective test, any uncommunicated reservation or qualification in the offer is not binding on the offeree. However, an offer could contain terms that are not expressed if those terms are implied into the offer by widely-accepted usage. The question of whether an unexpressed term is part of a contract is determined objectively, so if the usage exists, it does not matter that Bogey did not know about it, as long as he had reason to know of it. Caddy Lack claims that everyone knows of the restriction. It has the burden of proving that this is so.

This Example is based on *Wayment v. Schneider Automotive Group, LLC*, 438 P.3d 1005 (Utah. Ct. App. 2019), which involved similar facts relating to a Subaru parked next to a tee box by a car dealer that sponsored the tournament. Wayment, a professional golfer, hit the hole-in-one. The dealer refused to give him the car on the ground that the prize was restricted to amateur golfers. There was no indication of this restriction in the car display, but the dealer claimed that the restriction was implied in the contract by common usage. Testimony showed that there was no uniformity of opinion on this matter in the golfing community. The trial court granted summary judgment to Wayment on the ground that in the absence of an express restriction or an established custom to the contrary, Wayment was reasonable in believing that professional golfers were eligible for the prize. The court of appeals reversed, holding that the trial court should not have granted summary judgment. Because no express term of the offer dealt with this issue and there was no uniform understanding about eligibility, the matter must go to trial for the jury to decide the reasonable meaning of the parties' manifestations of assent.

There are more hole-in-one cases than one might expect. In *Harms v. Northland Ford Dealers*, 602 N.W.2d 58 (S.D. 1999), a car dealer had likewise made a unilateral offer of a car to any tournament participant who hit a hole-in-one at a particular hole. Harms, a women golfer, hit the hole-in-one from the women's tee at the stated hole, but the car dealer refused to award the car to her, claiming that the competition rules required women golfers to hit the ball from the men's tee to qualify for the prize. The problem was that no one told tournament participants of this rule, so, under the objective test, the dealer could not rely on an unexpressed qualification and was bound to give the prize to Harms.

CHAPTER 5

Standard Contracts and Contracts Through Electronic Media

§5.1 INTRODUCTION

Some contracts are individually negotiated and drafted, but many contracts are based wholly or partly on standard terms—that is, terms that have been drafted in advance of the transaction to be incorporated into many contracts of the same kind. This chapter focuses on these terms.[1] Most contracts involve commonplace repetitive transactions, so predrafted standard terms are pervasive. Standard language that is used routinely in many contracts is called "boilerplate," apparently a reference to metal plates with type in place, that were used by newspapers to print syndicated material.

The objective test and the rules of offer and acceptance predate the extensive use of standard contracts, but they are generally adaptable to take standard contracts into account and usually apply irrespective of whether the contract is individually negotiated or is on standard terms. This process of adaptation continues as technological advances give rise to changes in business practices and new opportunities for standardized contracting. Therefore, courts recognize that the assent given by a nondrafting party (nondrafter) to standardized terms may be more tenuous than assent to an

1. Chapter 6 also deals with standard terms, but in the particular context of how UCC §2-207 deals with mismatching terms in an offer and the response to it in a sale of goods. Because these discrepancies most commonly result from the exchange of standard terms, this issue is known as "the battle of the forms." Standard terms were introduced in section 4.1.4 and are also discussed in section 13.11 on unconscionability.

individually negotiated and drafted contract, so they have developed principles for evaluating whether the nondrafter's apparent agreement to the standard terms satisfied at least minimum standards to qualify as reasonable manifestation of assent.

§5.2 THE PROCESS AND TERMINOLOGY OF STANDARD CONTRACTING

Standard contract terms may be presented to the nondrafter in a number of different ways. The most common of them are illustrated in the following variations of a sale transaction in which the seller drafted a standard term presented to the buyer. In each of these situations, provided that the buyer was given reasonable notice of the term (*see* section 5.3) and it is not unconscionable (*see* section 5.4), the objective test of assent will likely bind the buyer to the standard term, whether or not the buyer actually read it.

§5.2.1 Preprinted Terms

A buyer goes to a retail store, selects a laptop computer, and takes it to the cashier. Before the buyer pays for the laptop, the cashier prints out and gives the buyer a piece of paper headed "Invoice." The invoice has a description of the computer and the price and contains the following language, printed in bold letters at the foot of the page: "Return Policy on Computers and Other Electronic Equipment: Defective electronic equipment may be returned for replacement within ten days of purchase. The buyer's remedy is confined to replacement of the defective product. The buyer is not entitled to return electronic equipment for any other reason and is not entitled to a refund of the price." The cashier has the buyer sign the invoice in a blank space provided. The parties have executed a contract that incorporates the store's standard return provision. The buyer may or may not have read the invoice before signing it, but that does not matter. The buyer had a duty to read it under the objective test of assent, and the buyer is bound by manifested assent, evidenced by the signature on the invoice.

§5.2.2 Box-top Terms

In the sale described above, the cashier does not print out an invoice. Instead, the return policy is set out in bold print on a clearly visible sticker affixed to the box containing the laptop. Standard terms brought to the attention of the nondrafter in this way are called box-top terms and bind a buyer who saw or reasonably should have seen them.

§5.2.3 Shrinkwrap Terms

There is no invoice and no sticker on the box. The sale is completed at the cashier's counter and the buyer takes the laptop home in its shrinkwrapped box. Upon opening the box, the buyer finds a piece of paper in the box that sets out the return policy. This is called a shrinkwrap term—an allusion to the thin plastic wrap that is commonly used to seal packaged products—because the term is included in the package or container and has not been seen by the buyer until it is opened, after the transaction in the store has been completed. Unless the seller has given the buyer the opportunity to reject the term and terminate the contract after reading it,[2] the shrinkwrap term may not bind the buyer because the seller did not make it known to the buyer until after the contract was made at the store. As a general rule, once a contract has been concluded, one of the parties cannot unilaterally add terms to it or change its terms. Any change in terms would have to be agreed to by both parties in a valid modification. However, this rule is not absolute. The nondrafter could be bound to a shrinkwrap term if a reasonable person would have expected that the contract was subject to standard terms and the standard term in question was of the kind likely to be included in the contract. That is, in some circumstances, the duty to read may require the nondrafter to take action to discover standard terms that were not actually presented by the drafting party (the drafter) at the time of contracting.[3]

§5.2.4 Terms in Internet-based Contracts

The illustrations in sections 5.2.1 to 5.2.3 involve in-person transactions in a store. Where the transaction takes place electronically, there are other opportunities for the drafter to make its standard terms available to the nondrafter at the time of contracting. Although these methods of incorporating standard terms into an Internet-based contract have nothing to do with wrapping, the word "shrinkwrap" inspired courts to coin a set of words ending in "wrap" to label them. There are variations of these methods, but the most common categories are clickwrap, scrollwrap, browsewrap, and a hybrid form that lies somewhere between clickwrap and browsewrap. These

2. This is called a rolling contract and is discussed in section 5.5.2.

3. This is discussed further in section 5.5.1.

different formats are described briefly here, and section 5.3.2 provides a more detailed analysis of their effectiveness.

a. Clickwrap

For example, instead of buying the laptop at a store, the buyer visits the seller's website, selects the laptop from the products shown on the website, places it in the virtual shopping cart, and proceeds to the virtual checkout. The website presents the standard terms, including the return policy, in a manner that requires the nondrafter to take affirmative action to acknowledge acceptance of the standard terms. A common form of clickwrap term presents a pop-up window on the webpage. The window allows the user to scroll through the standard terms and contains a button or box that the user must click to acknowledge having read those terms and to signify assent to them. The website does not allow the user to complete the transaction until that signification of assent has been made. Because the user cannot complete the transaction without clicking to express assent to the standard terms, provisions presented in this way have come to be called clickwrap terms. Provided that the terms themselves are clearly and coherently written, this is the most reliable way for the website host to ensure that the contract is subject to its terms. Whether or not the user actually read the terms before signifying assent to them, courts usually find that the affirmative act of clicking on the box or button is the user's clear manifestation of assent, which binds the user and cannot be overturned on the basis that the user did not actually read the terms.

b. Scrollwrap

A scrollwrap term is an enhanced form of clickwrap. Like clickwrap, the user must affirmatively acknowledge acceptance of the standard terms, such as by clicking on a box to signify assent. However, while clickwrap does not require the user to access the terms before clicking the box, scrollwrap does not allow the user to click the box until physically having scrolled through the text of the standard terms. Thus, although it cannot force the user actually to read the terms, it at least requires the user to view them before manifesting assent. A user who does not bother to read the terms cannot plausibly claim lack of notice or justifiable ignorance of them, so scrollwrap is even more effective than clickwrap in binding the user to the terms.

c. Browsewrap

Like a clickwrap term, a browsewrap term is set out on a website and is available to be read by the user of the website before submitting an order for the service or product purchased. However, a browsewrap term is different from a clickwrap term in that the user is able to complete the transaction without having to indicate assent to it by affirmative conduct, such as clicking on a button. That is, the link to the standard terms is displayed on the site, but the user can choose to ignore it and to place the order without acknowledging agreement to the terms. Even if the user has not clicked on the link and has no actual knowledge of the browsewrap terms, courts are likely to bind the user to the terms if the website gave the user reasonable notice of them. However, because the website does not require the user to signify assent to the terms to complete the transaction, the presence of the standard terms must be clearly apparent to make the user accountable for reading them.

d. Hybrid or Sign-In Wrap Terms

Not all terms fit neatly into the clickwrap, scrollwrap, or browsewrap categories. Some have features that do not qualify them as clickwrap or scrollwrap in that they do not prevent the user from proceeding with the transaction without clicking a button manifesting agreement. However, they are more reliable indicators of assent than browsewrap terms that rely on a more passive form of assent. Some courts have labelled terms presented in this way as "hybrid terms." Although a hybrid term may not be as strong an expression of assent as a clickwrap or scrollwrap process, there is conduct that more clearly signifies assent than a browsewrap process, so the user is more likely to be bound to the terms.

§5.3 NOTICE AND CONSPICUOUSNESS

§5.3.1 Actual Knowledge Distinguished from Constructive Knowledge

a. Actual Knowledge

If the nondrafter actually does read the standard terms before executing the contract, it is clear that the parties have entered into the contract on those terms. The duty to read is not implicated because the terms were actually read and the manifestation of assent was made with knowledge of those terms. For example, in *Southwest Airlines Co. v. Boardfirst, L.L.C.*, 2007 WL 4823761 (N.D. Tex. 2007), the court held that a browsewrap term on the Southwest website bound Boardfirst because it had actual knowledge of the term.

b. Constructive Knowledge (Notice)

However, people often do not read standard terms. The objective test imposes a duty to read a contract before manifesting assent to it, so failure to read is not usually a basis for denying the existence of a contract or escaping unfavorable terms. However, the duty to read is balanced against a duty owed by the drafter to present the terms in a way that makes them reasonably accessible and understandable to the nondrafter and allows the nondrafter a reasonable opportunity to read them. If the drafter does not do this, a court may excuse the nondrafter's failure to read the terms because the terms were not reasonably apparent or comprehensible. In essence, the nondrafter's duty to read presupposes that notice of the terms was fairly given in a way that would come to the attention and comprehension of a reasonable person in the nondrafter's position. If this standard is satisfied, the objective test treats the nondrafter as having knowledge of the standard terms notwithstanding the absence of actual knowledge. This is commonly referred to as constructive knowledge. (Sometimes the term used is "constructive notice," which has the same meaning.)

Where the nondrafter has no actual notice, but a reasonable person should know that the transaction is likely subject to standard terms, the duty to read may require the nondrafter to take affirmative steps to ascertain what those terms are. This is sometimes called "inquiry notice" And is discussed in section 5.3.3.

§5.3.2 The Requirement of Clarity and Conspicuousness for Constructive Knowledge

a. The General Principle of Adequate Notice of Standard Terms

A drafter that does not set out standard terms in a clear, conspicuous, and intelligible form takes the risk that a court will find that, despite the general duty to read, the insufficient notice does not provide constructive knowledge to the nondrafter and therefore does not bind that party in the absence of actual knowledge of the terms. Notice of the terms may be inadequate because they are not apparent and understandable to a reasonable person. This may occur where, for example, there is no clear and conspicuous language alerting the nondrafter to the existence of the terms, or the terms cannot be readily accessed, or they are buried in fine-print, or they are written in dense or complex language, or they can only be found by clicking on a badly placed link on a website. A court is most likely to scrutinize the adequacy of notice where the term would not reasonably be expected in a contract of that kind, or where the typical nondrafter is commercially unsophisticated. In *Oberstein v. Live Nation Entertainment, Inc.*, 60 F.4th 505 (9th Cir. 2023), the court classified the question of whether notice is adequate and conspicuous as a legal question as to the validity of the disputed terms. Therefore, if there is no factual dispute as to what a document or website contained, the judge, and not the jury, decides if the nondrafter had constructive knowledge of the terms.

These general principles apply to all standard terms, whether the contract is recorded in a tangible medium or is in electronic form. For example, in *Noble v. Samsung Electronics America, Inc.*, 682 Fed. Appx. 113 (3d Cir. 2017), Samsung set out its standard terms (including the arbitration provision at issue in the case) on page 97 of its 143-page Smartwatch user's manual, included in the box containing the watch. The court held that the arbitration provision did not bind the buyer because it was not adequately brought to the buyer's attention. It was buried deep within the user's manual, without any indication on the cover of the manual, in its table of contents, or otherwise, that the booklet contained contractual provisions. *Lewandowski v. Megabus USA, LLC*, 613 F. Supp. 3d 909 (W.D. Pa. 2020), also involved a standard arbitration provision. Lewandowski, who was wheel-chair bound, was unable to get onto a bus because its wheel chair lift did not work. When she sued Megabus for violating the Americans with Disabilities Act, Megabus sought to enforce its standard arbitration agreement. Megabus tickets could be bought either online or by phone and Lewandowski chose to buy her ticket by phone. At the time of the purchase, the ticket agent told her that the ticket was subject to applicable terms, gave her some of the terms, and said that the full terms were available on the Megabus website. The agent did not specifically mention the arbitration provision. Lewandowski did not look at the website. The court held that it was not enough that the agent referred her to the website. Reviewing the terms was not a prerequisite to completing the transaction, and Lewandowski could not be bound by a term that was only available on a separate medium.

In summary, court opinions show that if a drafter designs a clear, accessible, and comprehensible set of standard terms, there is a strong likelihood that the nondrafter will be deemed to have assented to them on the basis of constructive knowledge, even if the nondrafter did not actually read or know of them. However, courts are careful to evaluate the design and presentation of the standard terms, and will not find constructive knowledge if those terms are not fairly and clearly presented to the nondrafter.[4]

---

4. There is a link between the role that adequacy of notice plays in determining constructive knowledge and the role that it plays in deciding whether the standard term is unconscionable. This is discussed in section 5.4.

b. Clickwrap and Scrollwrap Terms

The principles of conspicuousness and notice apply to standard terms on websites. Provided that the standard terms are clearly written and understandable, the problem of adequate notice is largely alleviated where the website employs the clickwrap or scrollwrap process described in section 5.2.4a and b. This is because the terms are set out in a link or text box and the user cannot complete the transaction without clicking on (or in the case of scrollwrap, first viewing and then clicking on) an acknowledgement that the user has read the terms and agrees to them.

Feldman v. Google, Inc., 513 F. Supp. 2d 229 (E.D. Pa. 2007), illustrates the effective use of clickwrap. Google sold advertising on its site, subject to standard terms, including a forum selection clause.[5] The person purchasing the advertising online was presented with Google's standard terms in a prominent scrollable window, headed by language in boldface type, that stated, "**Carefully read the following terms and conditions.** If you agree with these terms, indicate your assent below." The window also contained a printer-friendly version of the terms, and the advertiser could not complete the order for the advertising without clicking an "I agree" button at the bottom of the webpage. The court held that the terms were clear and conspicuous and presented in a way that would alert a reasonably prudent Internet user to the existence of the terms before manifesting assent by clicking the "I agree" button. The terms therefore bound the advertiser. *Santana v. SmileDirectClub, LLC*, 292 A.3d 529 (N.J. Super. Ct. App. Div. 2023), is another example of effective clickwrap. To receive clear-aligner orthodontic treatment as an alternative to traditional braces, a potential patient had to register online and create an account with SmileDirectClub. Before creating the account, the user had to check a box next to language that stated, "I agree to SmileDirectClub's informed consent and Terms & SmilePay Conditions." The underlined text was in blue, signifying three separate hyperlinks to the full text of the terms and conditions. The "informed consent" link contained an arbitration provision. The user could not complete setting up the account unless the box had been checked. The court held that the arbitration provision was binding. By checking the box, the user was placed on inquiry notice that there were terms for which informed consent was required.

A website's use of clickwrap terms is the surest way to ensure that the user's manifestation of assent will be binding. However, clickwrap terms are not infallible and can fail to achieve the desired effect if the website is poorly designed or the terms themselves are difficult for a reasonable user to read or comprehend. For example, in *Sgouros v. TransUnion Corp.*, 2015 WL 507584 (N.D. Ill. 2015), TransUnion operated a website on which customers could buy a credit report. To complete the purchase, a customer was required to

5. Forum selection clauses are explained below.

click an "I accept" button after being presented with a scrollable window setting out the terms of the transaction. The problem was that the language immediately before the "I accept" button was confusing. It did not specifically state that the customer accepted the terms but seemed merely to authorize TransUnion to access the customer's credit information. The court held that the customer's click could not operate as a manifestation of assent to the terms.

c. Browsewrap Terms

Browsewrap terms are made available for the user to read by following a link, but, because they do not require the user to manifest assent to them before ordering the goods or services, they will not bind the user to constructive knowledge unless the website provided unequivocally clear and conspicuous notice of them, which would lead a reasonably prudent user to be aware of the existence of the terms. For example, the courts refused uphold browsewrap terms in *Savetsky v. Pre-Paid Legal Services, Inc.*, 2015 WL 604767 (N.D. Cal. 2015), and *Berman v. Freedom Financial Network, LLC*, 30 F.4th 849 (9th Cir. 2022).

In *Savetsky*, the court held that a browsewrap arbitration provision on Pre-Paid's website did not provide sufficient notice to users because the link to the terms, headed "More Plan Details," was displayed only after the user clicked the "Buy Now" button to join up for the services. In addition, even if the user followed the "More Plan Details" link, the terms were not immediately displayed but could be read only after following an additional link to the "member contract." The court concluded that the placement of the links and general setout of the site failed to put a reasonable user on notice to look into the terms of the purchase.

Berman involved a class action commenced by visitors to websites operated by Fluent, Inc., a digital marketing company, that used information gained from visitors to its sites in targeted marketing campaigns on behalf of its clients, including Freedom Financial. The plaintiffs alleged that unwanted calls and text messages sent by Fluent in a telemarketing campaign violated the Telephone Consumer Protection Act. Fluent moved to dismiss the suit and to compel arbitration in terms of its standard arbitration provision. The dominant contents of the websites (www.getsamplesonlinenow.com and www.retailproductzone.com) were brightly colored promotional graphics proclaiming "getting free stuff has never been easier." Below the graphic display, the customer was asked to confirm a prepopulated zip code, followed by a large button stating "This is correct, continue." Clicking the "continue" button brought up a screen for entering personal information to obtain free products and promotional deals. Between the zip code and the "continue" button, there were two lines of grey text, too small to be easily legible and dwarfed by the large, colorful matter, stating "I understand and agree to the Terms and Conditions, which includes mandatory arbitration and Privacy Policy" The underlined hyperlinks in the text were not in the typical blue print, but were in the same grey font as the rest of the sentence. Clicking on the link to the terms would take the customer to a page with lengthy provisions, including the arbitration provision. The court held that the browsewrap terms were not reasonably conspicuous and did not bind users of the site. The dominant colorful content of the page directed the user's attention away from barely noticeable links to the standard terms.

d. Hybrid Terms

Hybrid terms may be presented in different formats. One example is a "sign-in" term. The website contains language on the registration or sign-in page that states that the user agrees to the standard terms by registering for or signing into the account. That is, the standard terms are presented to the user at the outset of the transaction, and the user's assent to the terms is manifested by the act of setting up a new account or logging onto an existing account. This format was used in *Meyer v. Uber Technologies, Inc.*, 868 F.3d 66 (2d Cir. 2017). The case involved a challenge to an arbitration provision in Uber's standard terms. Uber employed the sign-in method of procuring the user's assent to its terms. The website stated that the user agreed to the terms of service by creating an Uber account. The court evaluated the reasonable conspicuousness of the notice from the perspective of the reasonably prudent smartphone user. It concluded that the format and placement of the notice, capitalized and readily visible on an uncluttered screen, with a clearly apparent link to the terms, gave unequivocal notice of the standard terms to the reasonable user. It did not matter that the website did not require the user to signify express consent because implied consent is inferred when the user registers or signs in to the account.[6]

Lloyd v. Retail Equation, Inc., 2022 WL 18024204 (D.N.J. 2022), exemplifies another form of a hybrid term. Lloyd was prevented from returning merchandize bought on the T.J. Maxx website because of a program set up to prevent fraudulent returns. This induced her to commence a class action against the operator of T.J. Maxx retail stores. T.J. Maxx sought dismissal of the class action on the ground that Lloyd had assented to its standard arbitration provision, which barred class actions. The website had a "place order" icon directly below a notice that stated "By placing your order, you agree to the T.J. Maxx terms of use." The underlined language was a hyperlink,

---

6. Uber was not as successful in a motion to compel arbitration in another case, *Sarchi v. Uber Technologies, Inc.*, 268 A.3d 258 (Me. 2022). Instead of using the sign-in process described in *Meyer*, its website used an ineffectively-designed browsewrap process with a confusing screen that was ambiguous as to whether the user was agreeing to the standard terms by clicking a "done" button, and did not present the link to the terms in a clear and obvious manner.

which would bring up the clearly-drafted terms if clicked, but it was not a clickwrap term because the customer was not required to signify assent to the terms by clicking the hyperlink or a separate "I agree" button. However, the court held that Lloyd was bound by the arbitration provision because the relatively uncluttered webpage, with the clear textual notice proximate to the "place order" button, made it improbable that a reasonable user would complete the purchase without observing the hyperlink.

By contrast, *McKee v. Audible, Inc.*, 2017 WL 4685039 (C.D. Cal. 2017), illustrates a sign-in screen that did not afford adequate inquiry notice of standard terms, either on a website or on a corresponding mobile app. The screen had a "start now" button that allowed the user to sign up for a free membership, but was drafted in confusing language and was set up in a way that did not alert the user that clicking on the button bound the user to standard terms (including the arbitration provision at issue in the case). The terms themselves were accessible by a link that was badly placed and not readily apparent. The confusion was exacerbated by the fact that Audible was an Amazon affiliate, and the account was associated with the user's Amazon and Alexa accounts, which had their own standard terms.

§5.3.3 Inquiry Notice: The Relevance of Reasonable Expectations

As explained in section 5.3.2, the manner in which standard terms are presented is crucial to the decision of whether the nondrafter had constructive knowledge of them. However, general knowledge of the existence and nature of standard terms has some relevance to this determination. In a market in which contracts are routinely subject to standard terms, a reasonable person is forewarned of their existence. In addition, some standard terms are so commonplace that a reasonable participant in the market would assume that such terms would be included in the contract about to be executed. This reasonable expectation may place a greater duty of inquiry on the nondrafter, which would make it harder to claim convincingly that poor presentation of the terms defeats constructive knowledge of them. Similarly, familiarity with the mode of presentation commonly used in platforms of a particular kind may itself alert a reasonable user about finding and recognizing links to standard terms. For example, in *Meyer v. Uber Technologies, Inc.*, the court remarked, with reference to a link to standard terms on a mobile app, that it is not to be presumed that the user has never before encountered a smartphone app or used it to make a contract. That is, where standard terms are reasonably expected, the duty to read may include some responsibility to take the initiative to seek out and check the content of standard terms, even if the drafting party's efforts at providing constructive knowledge of them are not as effective as they could be—the very nature of the transaction gives inquiry notice to the nondrafter. For example, a reasonable purchaser of copyrighted material such as software or recorded music would be aware that the intellectual property is subject to a license that restricts its use and dissemination, or the reasonable purchaser of an airline ticket would be aware that the ticket is subject to standard terms governing the rights and responsibilities of the parties. It could even be argued that because arbitration clauses are so pervasive, a reasonable person entering into any standard contract should not be surprised to find that the standard terms include a clause compelling the parties to arbitrate any dispute that may arise out of the transaction. In short, inquiry notice does not necessarily preclude the nondrafter's argument that the drafter failed to make the standard terms reasonably apparent and accessible, but may weaken that argument where a reasonable person would have expected standard terms and should have taken the trouble to look for them and find out what they provided.

§5.3.4 Implied Terms

The rules of offer and acceptance require that the offer set out all the terms of the contract. This does not mean that all the terms in a contract, whether individually negotiated and drafted or based on standard terms, are necessarily expressed in the offer. A contract may be subject to terms that are not actually mentioned in the offer, but are implied by law or usage. For example, a standard contract for the sale of goods may not state whether the goods are warrantied, but in the absence of any contractual provisions to the contrary, in a sale of goods by a merchant, UCC Article 2 implies a warranty that the goods are at least fit for their ordinary purpose.[7]

§5.3.5 Standard Arbitration and Forum Selection Provisions

a. Arbitration Clauses

Arbitration provisions are ubiquitous in both negotiated and standard contracts.[8] Many of the cases in which a nondrafter challenges assent to standard terms involve an arbitration provision. By agreeing to arbitrate any disputes arising out of a contract, a party forgoes the right to litigate disputes in court and must instead have the dispute resolved by arbitration. The arbitration is conducted by a private person or panel designated in

7. This is an example of a gap filler, covered more fully in sections 10.2. to 10.3.

8. The process of arbitration as a means of enforcing a contract was first introduced in section 1.2.4.

the agreement. The arbitrator's decision binds the parties and cannot be reviewed by a court except on limited grounds. Therefore, by entering an arbitration agreement, a party abandons the fundamental right to have a court resolve a dispute relating to the contract. Because arbitration provisions are so commonly found in standard contracts, there is justification for the concern that the parties who have the power and sophistication to set the terms of those contracts are routinely imposing the obligation to arbitrate on their customers.

There is a longstanding policy in favor of arbitration, based on the rationale that arbitration relieves the pressure on crowded court dockets and is speedier, less formal, and less expensive than litigation. This policy is the basis of the Federal Arbitration Act, 9 U.S.C. §§1-16 (FAA), which expressly recognizes the validity of an agreement to arbitrate unless there are grounds to invalidate it under principles of contract law. State courts follow this policy as well. Notwithstanding, arbitration does not always serve the interests of a party seeking redress.

Where the term is in a standard contract, the widespread inclusion of arbitration provisions in nonnegotiable standard contracts means that nondrafters have little choice but to agree to them in many transactions. Once a contractual dispute arises, the nondrafter may challenge the validity of the arbitration provision. To overturn the arbitration agreement, the nondrafter must show that it has some defect that makes it unenforceable or invalid as a contract. The most common grounds on which to challenge the agreement are either that the nondrafter did not assent to the standard arbitration provision because of a lack of actual or constructive knowledge of it, or because the provision is unconscionable. In many cases, the nondrafter alleges both of these grounds. There is not much chance of succeeding on either if there has been adequate notice of the term and the prescribed arbitration process is standard and not unduly burdensome.

For example, in *D'Antuono v. Service Road Corp.*, 789 F. Supp. 2d 308 (D. Conn. 2011), exotic dancers challenged an arbitration agreement in an "entertainment lease" under which the dancers performed at clubs operated by Service Road. (The contract was structured as a lease of performance space, rather than an employment contract.) The standard lease was presented to the dancers, who signed it immediately, apparently without reading it. The arbitration clause was set out on the last page of the four-page lease, just above the signatures. Most of it was in underlined capital letters. The court rejected the dancers' argument that they had not assented to the arbitration provision. They had a duty to read the standard terms, the clause was clearly apparent, and there had been no conduct by the club to dissuade them from reading it or to put them off their guard. As discussed in section 5.4, the court also held that the clause was not unconscionable. Similarly, in *Temple v. Best Rate Holdings, LLC*, 360 F. Supp. 3d 1289 (M.D. Fla. 2018), the court upheld an arbitration provision where the provision was adequately presented in a sign-in term on a website and the court found nothing in the arbitration procedure to merit a conclusion of unconscionability.

Arbitration provisions commonly include a waiver of class actions. A class action is a suit by a small group of named plaintiffs in which the named plaintiffs bring the suit for the benefit of a larger class of similarly situated persons. Members of the class are not joined in the suit but are entitled to share in any remedy that the court grants if the suit is successful. The ability to initiate a class action is important because it allows the named plaintiffs to aggregate all the claims of members of the class, which could lead to a very substantial recovery against an entity that has engaged in conduct that violates the rights of a large number of people. It is particularly beneficial where the claims of individual plaintiffs are too small to merit litigation, but the total amount of claims by the whole class is significant. For this reason, a class action presents a significant threat to the defendant, which has a strong incentive to prevent class actions. In *AT&T Mobility LLC v. Concepcion*, 563 U.S. 333 (2011), the U.S. Supreme Court held that the policy in favor of arbitration supports the validity of a class-action waiver because the speedier and less complex arbitration process is not suited to the resolution of classwide disputes.

Temple, as well as many of the cases discussed elsewhere in this chapter (for example, *Lloyd*, *Meyer*, *Oberstein*, and *Berman* in section 5.3.2 and *Engen v. Grocery Delivery E-Services USA, Inc.*, 453 F. Supp. 3d 1321 (D. Minn. 2020) (in Example 5.7) involved challenges to arbitration provisions by plaintiffs who had commenced class actions against the defendant.

b. Forum Selection Clauses

A forum selection clause is a term in a contract under which the parties agree to litigate any dispute arising out of the contract in the courts of a specified jurisdiction. That is, the parties agree in advance that the selected court will have exclusive jurisdiction to hear and resolve any controversy relating to the contract. Like arbitration clauses, forum selection clauses are commonly found in standard agreements and usually designate the jurisdiction most convenient to the drafter. When a dispute arises, a nondrafter who prefers to litigate elsewhere may challenge the clause. As with arbitration clauses, this challenge is not likely to succeed unless the nondrafter can show circumstances that excuse the duty to read or that demonstrate that the selected forum is inappropriate and unfair. For example, in *Witt v. Nation-Wide Horse Transportation, Inc.*, 197 F. Supp. 3d 1146 (S.D. Iowa 2016), Witt, the owner of a horse, entered into a contract for the transportation of the horse. Witt signed an authorization form on Nation-Wide's website without reading the standard terms that were set out at the head of the form. One of the terms was a forum selection provision requiring any disputes under the contract to be litigated in Colorado. When a dispute arose over the treatment of the horse in transit, Witt sued Nation-Wide in Iowa. The court upheld the forum selection clause. Even though Witt did not read it, it was clearly and conspicuously presented at the beginning of the form to be filled out by the customer and had language at the end of the form that alerted the customer that submission of the form signified agreement to the terms.

Once a court has determined that the forum selected is reasonable and that the forum selection term was adequately brought to the attention of the nondrafter, the term is presumptively valid. A nondrafter who cannot invalidate the clause on grounds of lack of assent may argue, in the alternative, that the clause is unconscionable. However, once the court has determined that the nondrafter had adequate notice of the term, it would be unlikely to find procedural unconscionability unless the drafter had committed some other bargaining impropriety. It would also be difficult to establish substantive unconscionability merely on the basis that the selected forum is inconvenient. The nondrafter would have to go beyond that to establish that the hardship of litigating in that forum is so extreme as to deprive the nondrafter of obtaining recourse on the claim.

§5.4 THE PROBLEM OF ADHESION AND UNCONSCIONABILITY IN STANDARD CONTRACTS

The concepts of adhesion and unconscionability are discussed in section 13.11 and are applied specifically to standard contracts in section 13.12. However, these concepts are introduced here because the nondrafter may assert unconscionability or adhesion as an alternative basis for challenging a contract or term. That is, as an alternative to claiming a lack of assent because of the absence of actual or constructive knowledge, the nondrafter may assert that the term should not be enforced because it is adhesive or unconscionable.

§5.4.1 Adhesion

The party who drafts standard terms is likely to create terms that best serve its own interests. For the most part, the drafter is entitled to favor its own interests and has no duty to be altruistic or evenhanded. However, where the drafter's terms are harsh or unfairly one-sided, and it has enough market power to make those terms nonnegotiable, a court may refuse to enforce the terms on grounds of unconscionability.

Where standard terms are proffered on a take-it-or-leave-it basis by a party with the market power to refuse to contract except on the standard terms, the resulting agreement is called a contract of adhesion—the nondrafter who wishes to enter the contract has no choice but to adhere to the nonnegotiable terms. Adhesion is even more apparent where the nondrafter has little or no alternative but to enter into the contract. This may occur, for example, where the product or service is not merely a luxury and there is no competing provider with whom to contract on different terms. Contracts with nonnegotiable standard terms are commonplace. For example, a passenger usually does not have any ability to negotiate the standard terms and conditions to which travel is subject, the purchaser of software cannot usually negotiate the standard terms of the license, and a patient cannot usually negotiate the hospital's standard conditions of admission and treatment. As a general matter, a nondrafter who assents to an adhesive contract cannot challenge its terms merely because they were nonnegotiable. The nondrafter has to go one step further and show that the drafter took unfair advantage of its dominant bargaining power to impose unfairly one-sided terms on the nondrafter. In short, adhesion in itself is not a ground for seeking avoidance of a contract, but it could be relevant to the question of whether the contract is unconscionable.

§5.4.2 Unconscionability

A contract or term of a contract is unconscionable if the contract or term is imposed on the party by unfair means (called "procedural unconscionability") and the term itself is unfair or unduly harsh or one-sided (called "substantive unconscionability"). These two elements of unconscionability are explained briefly here and are discussed in greater detail in sections 13.11 and 13.12.

The following example illustrates how a claim of unconscionability ties in with the question of whether the nondrafter received adequate notice of a standard term: Ad Here.com operates an online advertising agency that places advertisements on websites. Potential advertisers buy advertising space through a contract on Ad Here's website. Before placing the order for the advertising, the advertiser is presented with a text box containing Ad Here's standard contract terms and must click on a button at the bottom of the text box to signify assent to them. The advertiser cannot submit the order until it clicks a box that records its acceptance of the standard terms. One of the standard terms states that Ad Here is not responsible for any damages suffered by the advertiser as a result of errors in the content or placement of advertisement, resulting from any cause, including Ad Here's negligence. An advertiser sues Ad Here for damages resulting from Ad Here's negligent mangling of the content of an advertisement. The court holds that the clickwrap terms were properly presented, so that the advertiser had constructive knowledge of them and a reasonable opportunity to read them. The advertiser therefore formed a contract with Ad Here subject to the clickwrap terms.

However, although the court decided in favor of Ad Here on the formation issue, the advertiser makes the further argument that the waiver of the right to claim damages is unconscionable. To succeed in this argument, the advertiser must establish two elements: that the term resulted from improper bargaining or abuse of superior bargaining power (procedural unconscionability) and that the term is so unfair or one-sided that it shocks the conscience of the court (substantive unconscionability). Courts usually require that both of these elements must be satisfied, but not necessarily in equal strength, so that if one of the elements is strongly present, a relatively modest showing of the other could be enough. In some cases, either the procedural or the substantive unconscionability is so severe, that a court might give relief without requiring any showing of the other. In the clearest case of procedural unconscionability there is some kind of improper pressure, deception, or other disreputable bargaining conduct. However, if the contract terms are harsh, oppressive, grossly one-sided, or of a kind not reasonably expected in such a transaction, a court may accept a lesser degree of procedural unconscionability. In such a case, the mere fact of adhesion may be enough, especially if the drafter took advantage of the nondrafter's bargaining weakness or unsophistication to impose the term on a take-it-or-leave-it basis. In addition, apart from the role that it plays in determining assent to the terms, the manner in which the term is presented—its conspicuousness and clarity—is also relevant to the determination of procedural unconscionability.

There appears to be little that was procedurally improper about the way that Ad Here obtained the advertiser's manifestation of assent. The court has already decided that the terms were not concealed or obscure, and the facts do not indicate that there was any improper bargaining such as high-pressure selling techniques or exploitation of the advertiser's weakness. The question of whether a term is substantively unconscionable involves a complex set of considerations that call for an examination of the contract as a whole in its commercial context, in light of commercial practices and mores. It may well be that a provision insulating a contracting party from damages for negligence may not be substantively unfair under all the circumstances of the case.

In *D'Antuono v. Service Road Corp.*, described in section 5.3.5, the court noted the distinction between the formation issue (whether the dancers agreed to the clause) and the validity issue (whether the clause is valid and effective). The duty to read is pertinent to the formation issue, but unconscionability doctrine is concerned with the validity of what was agreed. (These issues do overlap because procedural unconscionability is also concerned with the circumstances under which the manifestation was made.) After finding that the dancers were bound by their manifestation of assent to the arbitration clause, the court went on to decide if the arbitration provision was unconscionable. Because of the general policy in favor of arbitration, it is most unlikely that a court will find an agreement to arbitrate, in itself, to be unconscionable. There must be something in both the manner that the agreement was reached and in the terms of the arbitration that is procedurally and substantively unfair. As noted in section 5.3.5, the court found no impropriety in the manner in which the standard contract was presented to the dancers. There was no attempt to conceal its content or to prevent the dancers from reading it or getting legal advice on its terms. The fact that the contract was presented on a take-it-or-leave-it basis (that it was adhesive) was not enough, on its own, to make the arbitration provision procedurally unconscionable. The dancers argued that the terms of the arbitration provision were substantively unconscionable. They based this argument on three features of the arbitration: (1) it waived the right to collective and class actions, (2) it provided for cost and fee shifting (the losing party would pay the costs of the arbitration and the attorney's fees of the prevailing party), and (3) it required claims to be made within six months (which shortened the usual statute of limitations—the time within which a claim may be brought).[9] After an extensive discussion of these features of the agreement, the court concluded that they were not sufficiently draconian to overcome the advantages of speed and informality that would be achieved by arbitration and they therefore did not render the agreement substantively unconscionable.

Davis v. USA Nutra Labs, 303 F. Supp. 3d 1183 (D.N.M. 2018), involved the validity of an arbitration provision in Groupon's standard terms of use. The court found that Davis, the plaintiff, had assented to the clickwrap arbitration provision by clicking on the box acknowledging awareness and acceptance of the standard terms. Davis also argued that the arbitration provision was procedurally unconscionable because it was adhesive, and it was substantively unconscionable because it bound Davis to arbitrate without imposing a reciprocal obligation on Groupon. The court rejected Davis's argument that the contract was procedurally unconscionable because the mere fact that a contract is adhesive is not enough to satisfy that element. It rejected Davis's substantive unconscionability argument as well. The court was not convinced that Davis was correct in interpreting the arbitration provision as inapplicable to Groupon, but held that even if the arbitration provision did not bind Groupon, Davis had received other benefits from the contract, so that a one-sided arbitration commitment was not unreasonably favorable to Groupon.

---

9. At the time of the suit, the club had waived the last two features (the cost- and fee-shifting provision and the truncated statute of limitations). However, the court analyzed the agreement for unconscionability as if all three features were present.

§5.5 DEFERRED COMMUNICATION OF TERMS AND ROLLING CONTRACTS

§5.5.1 Deferred Communication of Terms

The drafter may have drafted standard terms that are not made available to the nondrafter at the time of contracting, but are revealed only after the contract has been formed. Three examples illustrate this situation:

1. Instead of booking a hotel online, a person may call the hotel by phone to book a room. Offer and acceptance occurs during the phone call, and the hotel then sends an email to the customer confirming the booking and setting out the hotel's standard terms which were not discussed at the time of booking.
2. A person calls an insurance agent to buy an insurance policy. The parties enter into the insurance contract during the phone call, but they do not discuss the detailed terms of the policy. After the phone call, the insurer mails a written copy of the policy to the insured.
3. A customer buys a boxed product at a store. The clerk at the checkout counter does not mention any standard terms to the buyer, but on later opening the box, the buyer finds standard shrinkwrap terms printed on a piece of paper in the sealed carton.

As a general rule, once a contract has been formed, neither party can unilaterally impose terms on the other beyond those that were agreed to by the parties at the time of contracting. A party who wishes to change or add terms to the contract must therefore obtain the other party's consent to a modification of the contract. However, as explained in section 5.3.3, if contracts of that type are routinely subject to standard terms, and the terms in question are reasonably expected, the nondrafter may have had reason to know this and should have ascertained what they were. Failure to do that could impute constructive knowledge of the terms on the nondrafter, who would be bound by manifested assent.

§5.5.2 Rolling Contracts

The discussion in section 5.5.1 is based on offer and acceptance having occurred at the point of purchase of the goods or services, so that the standard terms were made available only after the contract had been formed. However, in some situations, the facts may indicate that the transaction is a rolling contract—final assent to the contract is deferred until after the nondrafter has an opportunity to read the terms. That is, no final contract was made at the point of purchase, but at delivery of the standard terms (which occurs, for example, upon delivery of an emailed confirmation of the transaction, or upon opening the box containing the product, which includes a paper copy of the printed terms). The document containing the terms is couched in the form of an offer, which the buyer is deemed to accept by not rejecting it within a reasonable time. This imposes a duty to read at the time of delivery and gives the buyer the opportunity to refuse to contract on the offeror's standard terms.

ProCD, Inc. v. Zeidenberg, 86 F.3d 1447 (7th Cir. 1996), is an influential case involving a rolling contract. Zeidenberg bought software, in the form of a boxed disk, at a retail store. The software was sold in two versions, one for commercial use and the other for personal use. The program itself was the same in both versions, but the cheaper version contained a restriction in the license that prohibited its commercial use. Zeidenberg bought the cheaper version but used it for commercial purposes. ProCD sought an injunction to enforce the restriction.[10] The issue was that the restriction on use of the software was not communicated to the customer at the time of purchase. Instead, it was contained on the disk and in a printed user's manual in the box containing the disk. The term appeared on the computer screen when the disk was inserted, and the user could not proceed to use the software without indicating assent to the terms. The license expressly gave the buyer the right to return the software for a refund if the license terms were unacceptable and treated the buyer as having accepted the terms by continuing to use the software and not returning it. The trial court held that offer and acceptance occurred at the retail store. Therefore, because the term restricting use of the software was made known to the buyer only after contracting, it was not part of the contract and did not bind the buyer. The court of appeals disagreed. Because the terms gave the buyer the right to return the software if the terms were unacceptable, the court found that ProCD made an offer by supplying the software with the license, and Zeidenberg accepted by failing to return the software and using it.

There are two facts crucial to the court's decision that offer and acceptance occurred at the time that Zeidenberg failed to reject the terms by returning the disk. First, ProCD did not sell the program to Zeidenberg. He bought it at a retail store. Therefore, there was no contract between ProCD and Zeidenberg at the point of purchase. Second, the buyer's right to reject the terms after opening the box justifies the conclusion that the buyer had a power of acceptance or rejection at that stage. In the absence of a power of rejection after being presented with the terms, it is hard to argue that the

---

10. An injunction is a court order compelling or prohibiting the defendant from taking specified action. In this case, ProCD was asking the court to prohibit Zeidenberg from using the software commercially.

contract is a rolling contract.[11] *Ballou v. Asset Marketing Services, LLC*, 46 F.4th 844 (8th Cir. 2022), emphasizes that the nondrafter's right to reject the terms and return the product after receiving the terms is a crucial feature of a rolling contract. Asset Marketing Services (AMS), doing business as GovMint.com, sold commemorative and collectible coins. Over a period of a few years, it sold huge numbers of these coins to the plaintiffs for many thousands of dollars. The plaintiffs commenced a class action against AMS, on behalf of all persons who had bought coins from AMS, alleging that AMS had engaged in consumer fraud and deceptive trade practices. AMS moved to stay the suit and compel arbitration on the basis of an arbitration provision mentioned in shipping invoices that accompanied delivery of the coins to the buyers. Many of the coins were ordered over the phone, so the shipping invoices were sent to the buyers only after the coins had been ordered. The invoices did not give the buyers the right to return the coins if they rejected the standard terms. The court held that this distinguished the phone sales from the software sale in *ProCD* because offer and acceptance occurred during the phone calls, so these were not rolling contracts. Instead, the invoices were merely written confirmations of the oral contract, with a proposal to add its standard terms. The proposed terms, including the arbitration provision, could not become part of the contract unless the buyers expressly accepted them, which they never did.[12] Because there was some confusion as to which of the many sales were concluded by phone, the court remanded the case for trial to resolve that factual question.

In *Dye v. Tamko Building Products, Inc.*, 908 F.3d 675 (11th Cir. 2018), a roofing contractor purchased roof shingles from Tamko on behalf of two homeowners who commenced a class action suit against Tamko, alleging that the shingles were defective. Tamko delivered the shingles to the site in bundles secured by wrapping. Tamko's standard terms, including a limited warranty and an arbitration provision, were printed on each bundle. On the strength of the arbitration provision, Tamko moved to dismiss the complaint and compel arbitration. The standard terms, printed on the wrapping

---

11. Although the decision in *ProCD* is based on the fact that the transaction was a rolling contract, the court indicated that it probably would have bound the buyer to the license terms even if the buyer had no right to reject the license terms by returning the software. The court observed that standard terms are widely used in many contracts and a nondrafter should be deemed to have inquiry notice of reasonably expected terms that are fair and necessary to protect the legitimate rights of the drafter. The court considered the bar on commercial use of the software to be fair because the restriction on its use was directly related to the reduced price of the software sold for private use.

12. The coins were collectibles, not valid currency, so they were not money, which is excluded from the definition of goods in §2.105. They therefore qualified as goods, so the transaction was governed by UCC Article 2 and the court applied UCC §2.207 in determining that the invoices were post-contractual written confirmations that must be accepted expressly by the buyers. This case is discussed again in section 6.4, which deals with written confirmations under §2.207.

in all capitals, warned the buyer to read the terms carefully before opening the bundle. The homeowners did not order the shingles themselves — they were ordered by the roofing contractors, and the homeowners never inspected the wrapped shingles or saw the notices on the wrapping. They alleged that they were not even aware that the bundles included contract terms, and could not reasonably have been expected to look for terms in such a place. The court rejected that argument and held that the homeowners were bound to arbitrate their disputes. The terms were not literally shrinkwrap because they were on the outside of the packaging, so were closer to box-top terms. (The court, rather facetiously, called the terms "shinglewrap.") However, the exact nomenclature was not the issue. The crucial factor was that, even though the standard terms on the packages did not expressly give the buyer the right to reject the contract after reading the terms, the court inferred that the transaction was a rolling contract. It held that Tamko made an offer by placing its standard terms on the bundles, which the homeowners accepted by their agents (the contractors') conduct in opening the bundles. Contract formation therefore did not occur when Tamko accepted the order for the shingles, but it was deferred until the homeowners, with a reasonable opportunity to reject the shingles on the terms set out, accepted the terms by opening the bundles.

The court was unpersuaded by the homeowners' argument that contract terms could not reasonably be expected on the wrapping of building materials. The court said that the terms were conspicuously emblazoned on the wrapping and that it should hardly be a surprise to modern consumers that products are sold subject to standard terms. This part of the court's opinion, emphasizing inquiry notice where standard terms are to be expected, suggests that the court would likely have reached the same conclusion, even if it had not found this to be a rolling contract.

The Court did not find it relevant that the roofing contractors, not the homeowners, ordered and unwrapped the shingles, because the court considered the contractors to have been acting as agents of the owners in buying and using the shingles, so that notice to the contractor was imputed to the owners.

Where the contract formation is set up so that the customer has the right to reject the shrinkwrap terms and terminate the transaction upon receiving them (that is, it is actually a rolling contract), the approach of *ProCD* and *Dye* is justified provided that the customer is given clear and understandable notice of the right to reject the terms by declining to keep the goods or to use the services. However, where there is no such right of rejection upon being presented with the terms, the contract was already concluded before the terms were presented. The terms included in the packaging may be treated in one of two ways. The first alternative is to treat the terms as a proposal for addition to the existing contract, which do not become part of the contract unless accepted by the customer. The second alternative is to bind the customer even though the terms were delivered only after the contract was formed. This alternative is justified only if the terms are of a kind that might reasonably be expected in the transaction, placing the customer on inquiry notice of them, and the customer had ready access to them at the time of contracting.

§5.6 POST-CONTRACTUAL MODIFICATION OF STANDARD TERMS

Many standard contracts provide for a future modification of the standard terms during the course of the relationship. For example, a credit card issuer's standard terms, or the standard terms of a service provider, may provide that the drafter has the right to modify them at its discretion at any time in the future. The term allowing for modification may further provide that the customer accepts any such modification by continuing to use the drafter's services following the modification. Like other standard terms, a provision giving the drafter the right to modify its terms is a binding part of the agreement if the customer can be held to have manifested assent to it at the time of entering the contract.

Where the term allowing for modification provides that the customer is deemed to have consented to the modification by continuing to use the services, the requirement of reasonable notification applies not only at the time of the original contract, but also at the time of the modification. That is, even if the original contract reasonably notified the customer that the drafter had the power of unilateral modification, the subsequent modification will not bind the customer if the customer is not reasonably notified of the modification and warned that continued use of the services will be acceptance of it. This is illustrated by *Douglas v. U.S. District Court for the Central District of California*, 495 F.3d 1062 (9th Cir. 2007). Douglas contracted for long distance telephone service, subject to the provider's right to make unilateral changes to the terms of service. The provider made subsequent modifications to the terms and posted them on its website but it never notified subscribers of the changes. Douglas, unaware of the changes, continued to use the provider's services. The district court held that posting of the notice on the website was sufficient, but the court of appeals disagreed. The court pointed out that the modification of a contract is itself a contract—the drafter proposes the modification, which must be accepted by the other party. It held that assent cannot be deemed to have occurred through the continued use of the services unless the subscriber had reasonable notice of the proposed modification. Because the subscriber had no obligation to visit the website or to check for changes, the mere posting of changes on the website was not enough. Even had the subscriber looked at the website, the changes would not be apparent unless the subscriber checked them against an earlier version of the terms. In short, the court concluded that a subscriber must receive clear and separate notice before assent to the changes could be attributed to the subscriber as a result of continued use of the services. By contrast, in *Sacchi v.Verizon Online, LLC*, 2015 WL 765940 (S.D.N.Y. 2015), the original agreement provided for revisions of the contract and specifically stated that the customer agreed to visit the Verizon website periodically to check for revisions. Verizon subsequently amended the agreement to include an arbitration provision, posted the change on its website, and notified customers by email and by notification on its billing statements. The court said that the customer's undertaking to visit the website to check for revisions, as well as the additional notices by email and on the billing statements, distinguished this case from *Douglas* so that the customer's continued use of the services constituted assent to the modifications.

§5.7 STATUTORY RECOGNITION OF ELECTRONIC CONTRACTING

Federal and state statutes recognize the formation of contracts through electronic means. In 1999, the Uniform Law Commission (ULC)[13] promulgated the Uniform Electronic Transactions Act (UETA), which, like the UCC, is a uniform model law that must be enacted by state legislatures to become effective. It has been enacted by almost every state. In 2000, Congress enacted the Electronic Signatures in Global and National Commerce Act (E-SIGN). These state and federal statutes are similar in scope and language, and E-SIGN defers to state law provided that the state has enacted UETA or an equivalent statute. The statutes have a narrow focus: Their goal is to ensure that general principles of contract formation and validity are applied to electronic transactions. They validate electronic signatures[14] and electronic records (the computerized equivalent of writing) and generally remove legal barriers to the recognition and enforcement of electronic commerce. The statutes do not deal with substantive principles of contract law, which are left to the common law or, in a sale of goods, to UCC Article 2. These statutes are discussed further in relation to the statute of frauds in section 11.3.

13. The ULC was formerly called the National Conference of Commissioners on Uniform State Laws (NCCUSL). The ULC is one of the two bodies that were responsible for drafting the Official Text of the UCC. *See* section 2.7.1.

14. An electronic signature is the computer equivalent of a signature on paper—some kind of recognizable symbol associated with a party and executed or adopted by the party to validate a writing or record. Signatures, in both traditional and electronic form, are discussed in section 11.3.3 in relation to the statue of frauds.

§5.8 CONTRACTING BY AUTOMATED MEANS

One or both parties may use technology designed to execute transactions automatically. For example, a seller of goods, services, or software may create a website that automatically accepts orders without the involvement of a human operator, or a buyer may use an automated system to order inventory from designated suppliers when its stock falls below a specified level. Where a party uses an automated means of making or accepting an offer, no human represents that party in the transaction at the time that the contract is concluded. However, under the objective test, the party using the automation has manifested contractual intent by setting up that contracting process. Both UETA and E-SIGN recognize this by treating the computer program as the electronic agent of the party who employs it. UETA §2(6) and E-SIGN §7006(3) define an electronic agent as "a computer program or an electronic or other automated means used independently to initiate an action or respond to electronic records or performances in whole or in part without review or action by an individual." UETA §14 and E-SIGN §7001(h) recognize that a contract can be formed by an electronic agent used by one or both parties, even if no human reviews or approves the resulting agreement.

§5.9 ONLINE AUCTIONS

Many websites (such as eBay) provide a means for users to sell goods or services by auction. The websites require users to consent to a clickwrap or browsewrap agreement that governs the use of the website's services, and likely also provides standard terms that are applicable to transactions on the website. The general rules of contract formation are applicable to online auctions and can be used to determine when an offer was made, what its terms were, and whether and when acceptance occurred.

EXAMPLES

Examples

1. Spammer's Seaside Resort sent an email to a mailing list, stating, "Take advantage of our off-season rates! Spend a week at the beach for $1,500! This is a limited-time offer, so visit our website and book now!" Annette was on the mailing list and received the email. She visited Spammer's website and filled in the appropriate boxes on the website, selecting an arrival and departure date and a seafront room for a weekly rate of $1,500. Annette then clicked on the "Book now" button. Another page appeared, where she filled out her name, address, and credit card information. Finally, she clicked on the "Submit booking" button. A message

appeared that set out the particulars of her booking and stated, "Thanks for your booking. Your confirmation number is 100889456. Please print out this page for your records." The next day Annette changed her mind and no longer wished to spend a week at Spammer's Seaside Resort. Has she committed herself to a contract?

2. Minnie lives in Minnesota. She noticed termites in her house. She called in Standard Termite Controls, Inc., a large pest control company with branches across the country. Its local representative visited her home and offered to rid the house of termites for $600. Minnie agreed, and the representative presented her with a document headed "Contract." The document was a single page, printed on both sides. The front page had blanks for the customer information and a description of the work and the price. At the foot of the front page there was a blank for the customer's signature immediately below a sentence in bold type, larger than the type used on the rest of the page, which read: "**By signing below, I acknowledge that I have read and agree to the terms of this contract, including the terms printed on the reverse side of this page**." The reverse side of the page contained 5 numbered paragraphs in normal 12-point type. Minnie signed the front page of the document without turning it around and reading the writing on the reverse. After the work was done, Minnie claimed that the chemical used by Standard Termite to kill the termites was toxic to humans and had made her ill. She sued Standard Termite for damages in a Minnesota court. Standard Termite moved to dismiss the suit on the grounds that clause 13 on the reverse side of its contract form specifies that all disputes must be resolved in the courts of California, where Standard Termite is headquartered. Is the forum selection clause enforceable against Minnie?

3. Standard Terminals, Inc. operates a parking structure. Carr Parker drove his car to the entrance of the structure, where he encountered a ticket dispenser and a boom. Carr pressed a button on the dispenser, which issued a ticket that Carr put in his pocket. The boom lifted, and Carr drove into the structure. As he was driving through the structure, looking for a parking space, another car suddenly backed out of a parking stall and smashed into the side of his car. The driver of that car was a valet employed by Standard, and he was clearly negligent in not looking for oncoming traffic before reversing out of the stall. Carr claimed the cost of repairing his car from Standard. Standard denied liability based on a disclaimer printed on the back of the parking ticket, which stated, "All cars are parked at the customer's risk. Standard Terminals, Inc. bears no responsibility for any loss or damage, whether caused by the negligence of its employees or otherwise. By entering this parking structure, the customer consents to this term." The ticket is one-and-a-half

by two-and-a-half inches in size. Carr argues that he did not read the disclaimer, had no knowledge of it, and never agreed to it. Is this a good argument?

4. Fanny Fervent was a devoted fan of the rock group Rolling Rockers, who were scheduled to perform a concert in her city on June 1. On April 1, Fanny visited the website of Ticketmaker.com to buy tickets to the concert. To buy tickets on the website, Fanny had to click on the "Look for tickets" link, printed in blue and underlined. Immediately above the link, there was a sentence in bold print that read, "**By clicking on the 'Look for tickets' link, you agree to Ticketmaker's standard terms of use**." The words "terms of use" were in blue print and underlined, indicating that they were also a link. Clicking on them would open a page containing the terms of use. One of the terms stated, in capital letters, "DATE AND TIME ARE SUBJECT TO CHANGE. TICKETS MAY BE EXCHANGED FOR A RESCHEDULED PERFORMANCE, BUT IN NO EVENT IS THE CUSTOMER ENTITLED TO A REFUND." Fanny clicked on the "Look for tickets" link and bought tickets for the concert. She did not click on the "terms of use" link, so she did not see the capitalized term precluding refunds. In late May, the Rolling Rockers canceled the performance for June 1 and rescheduled it for June 15, a date on which Fanny will be out of town on business and cannot attend. Does Fanny have the right to claim a refund from Ticketmaker?

5. Meg O'Pixel is an amateur photographer. She decided to buy a program to edit and manipulate the photographs taken on her digital camera. She visited a retail store operated by Hard Driver, Inc., a large producer of software, and selected Hard Driver's Fotofabulous program. The program was contained on a disk packaged in a box. The box was adorned by the product's name in a colorful and attractive graphic design. At the back of the box, the following language appeared in the smallest print possible: "© Hard Driver, Inc. All rights reserved. This program is sold subject to the license terms enclosed." Apart from this, there was no mention of license or contract terms on the box. They were also not mentioned by the sales clerk or on the sales receipt.

   Meg bought the program, took it home, and inserted the disk into her computer. An installation window appeared that stated: "You are about to install Fotofabulous. The use of this program is subject to license terms. By installing the program, you agree to these terms. Click here to view the terms." The "Click here" was a link to the terms. The window did not give the user any means of proceeding further with the installation without clicking on the link. Meg therefore clicked on it, and a window appeared with a page of terms, preceded by the following boldface language: **"Please read these terms carefully. By clicking on the 'Install'**

button at the bottom of this page, you indicate your acceptance of these terms and are bound by them."

Meg did not read the license terms. She just scrolled down to the "Install" button and clicked on it. One of the license terms was a forum selection clause that required all litigation concerning the contract to be before the courts of California, Hard Driver's home state. A few months after installing the software, Meg claimed that it was defective and unusable. She also claimed that Hard Driver misrepresented the features and qualities of the program and that it committed a fraud on the public by marketing the program, knowing that it would not work properly. Meg commenced a class action suit against Hard Driver in her home state of New Jersey. Hard Driver moved to dismiss the suit on the ground that Meg was obliged to commence the suit in a California court. Is Hard Driver correct?

6. Ticketmaker.com sells concert tickets online. To purchase tickets, a user must create an account. When creating the account, or when signing into an existing account, the user must click on a "Sign In" button immediately below bold text stating "**By continuing past this page, you agree to our <u>Terms of Use</u>**." The underlined text, in blue print, is a hyperlink to Ticketmaker's standard terms, including an arbitration provision and a waiver of the right to bring a class action. After signing in, the user selects tickets to a concert, fills out payment and other information, and must then click a "Place Order" button immediately below bold text stating, "**By placing your order, you agree to our <u>Terms of Use</u>**." As before, the underlined text is in blue and is a link to the same standard terms. Subsequent to buying tickets, the plaintiff commenced a class action against Ticketmaker, alleging that it had employed anticompetitive practices that enabled it to charge excessive booking fees. Ticketmaker moved to dismiss the class action on the basis that the plaintiff had agreed to arbitration and had waived the right to commence a class action. Is the plaintiff bound by the arbitration provision?

7. Amazing.com is an online retailer. To buy goods from Amazing, a customer must create an account on Amazing's website. The customer cannot create the account until checking a large, boldly colored box that affirmatively states, "**BY OPENING THIS ACCOUNT, I AGREE TO AMAZING'S <u>TERMS OF SERVICE</u>**." This sentence is in bold, capitalized font and the underlined text is a clearly demarcated link in contrasting blue print, which gives the user easy access to the coherently drafted terms of service. One of the terms states, "Amazing reserves the right to change these terms at any time. Any such changes will apply to orders placed after Amazing has sent notice of the change to the email address in the customer's profile. By placing an order following that notice, the customer assents to all such changes."

Amazing's terms of service did not include an arbitration provision when Clinton Clicker opened his account. About a year later, Amazing added an arbitration provision that barred class actions. Amazing routinely sends several emails to its customers each month, advertising new products and special offers. At the bottom of every email there is a sentence in relatively small print that reads, "Amazing may have changed its terms of service since you opened your account. Click here for the current terms of service." The sentence is in black print, except for the underlined "here," which is a blue link to the current terms.

Clinton just glanced at the promotional emails when he received them and deleted them without ever clicking on the blue link. However, he regularly continued to order goods on the website. A while after Amazing added the arbitration provision, Clinton commenced a class action against Amazing, alleging that it had sold counterfeit goods under well-known brand names. Amazing moved to dismiss the class action on the grounds that Clinton had waived the right to bring a class action by agreeing to the arbitration provision. Should Clinton be bound by the provision?

Explanations

1. The traditional rules of offer and acceptance, formulated on the assumption that the parties actually engage in active bargaining in person, are adaptable enough to be applied to standard contracting, even when part of the process is automated.

   Spammer's initial email to the mailing list cannot reasonably be interpreted as an offer even though it uses the words "limited-time offer." It proffers the accommodation and its cost in a general way, without any specific proposal that could be accepted by simple assent to its terms. Such specificity is achieved once Annette has made the selections on the website. It is therefore possible that Spammer makes an offer on its website by showing the selected room, price, and dates as available for booking on the website. If it is an offer, Annette manifests assent to it and accepts by clicking the "Submit booking" button. However, if, based on the wording of the advertisement and marketplace custom, a reasonable customer would expect Spammer to have the final say by deciding whether to accept Annette's submission, the offer would not have been made by Spammer but would instead have been made by Annette when she submitted her booking.

   If Spammer's listing of the property on its site is not an offer, Annette's clicking on the "Submit booking" button meets all the criteria of an offer to take the accommodation for the stated period at a price of $1,500. The automated booking confirmation that appeared immediately afterward does not actually state that Spammer accepts the offer, so Annette may argue that it was just a confirmation that the booking was received. However, that is not a likely interpretation because it thanks her for her booking and provides a confirmation number, without any qualification or equivocation. The more reasonable understanding is that the unqualified assent to Annette's offer is an acceptance. It does not affect the quality of acceptance that the window was generated automatically, and that Spammer had no conscious and deliberate intent to accept at the time that the response was sent. A party can set up an electronic response in a way that will allow the law to treat the automatic response as an effective acceptance. Modern law has come to recognize that a party can, in effect, create an "electronic agent" to act on its behalf by accepting an offer that the program identifies as meeting predetermined standards. It therefore appears that Annette has committed herself to a contract.

2. The Example asks whether the forum selection clause is enforceable against Minnie. This raises two issues. First, whether Minnie assented to it even though she did not know about it, and second, whether the clause may be avoided on grounds of unconscionability.

   Although Minnie did not read or know of the forum selection clause, she is bound by her manifestation of assent to it if she had constructive knowledge of it. A nondrafter has constructive knowledge of and is bound by unread terms if a reasonable person in that party's position would have ascertained them. The question of reasonable notice is decided with reference to the accessibility, conspicuousness, and comprehensibility of the terms. That is, Minnie had a duty to read terms of which Standard Termite Controls gave her reasonable notice. The reasonableness of notice and conspicuousness are factual questions, dependent on the context and nature of the transaction. The boldface large-type sentence just above the signature line seems to be adequately designed to draw the attention of a reasonably prudent customer to the terms on the reverse side of the page. The Example does not describe the layout and clarity of the five terms on the reverse side of the page, but provided that they are clear, readable and readily understandable to a lay customer, Minnie has assented to the forum selection provision.

   In addition to claiming that she did not assent to the terms, Minnie may also argue that the forum selection clause is unconscionable because it gives Standard the right to litigate in its home state, while it compels her to incur the expense and hardship of suing in a distant court. This is not enough to establish unconscionability. The facts do not indicate procedural unconscionability. There is no suggestion that Standard employed unfair bargaining tactics or placed pressure on Minnie to agree to the terms, and, as concluded above, the terms were adequately brought to her attention. The mere fact that the contract was adhesive does not, on its own, make it procedurally unconscionable. The forum selection provision is not substantively unconscionable just because it favors Standard. Courts generally uphold forum selection provisions unless the nondrafter can show extraordinary circumstances that make it particularly burdensome or unfair. Minnie does not have grounds to avoid the term as unconscionable.

3. The valet was Standard's employee and he was negligent in damaging Carr's car. An employer is vicariously liable for the negligent conduct of its employee, acting in the course and scope of employment, so Standard would be liable for Carr's loss in the absence of the disclaimer. Carr has a good argument that he did not assent to the disclaimer. A contract came into being when Carr drove his car into the structure after taking the ticket. In offer and acceptance terms, Standard, using the dispenser as its electronic agent, made an offer on the terms set out in the ticket. Carr manifested acceptance by proceeding into the garage after receiving the ticket. The issue is whether Carr's assent encompassed the standard liability disclaimer printed on the back of the ticket. Carr did not read the ticket, so he did not know that it contained the disclaimer, but he would be bound by it if he had constructive knowledge of it. A nondrafter has constructive knowledge of a standard term if the drafter has provided clear and conspicuous notice of the term, under circumstances that would alert a reasonable person to the existence of the term and allow access to and comprehension of its content. The disclaimer is printed on the back of a small ticket, so the print would have to be small to fit into the space available. In addition, the parking customer receives the ticket under circumstances that make it likely that a reasonable person would not stop to read the ticket, but would do what Carr did—put the ticket away and drive into the structure to look for a parking space. Had Standard set out the disclaimer on a large notice at the entrance to the structure, clearly visible to drivers at the time of taking the ticket, it would have had a more compelling argument of adequate notice.

   In support of its standard term, Standard could argue that disclaimers of liability are so common in car parks that a reasonable customer would anticipate that the parking contract would contain the term, even without reading the ticket. A court may be persuaded by such an argument if disclaimers of this kind are so widely used as to put the reasonable customer on inquiry notice. However, a drafter cannot be sure that summarized or truncated standard terms on a ticket or other small document will provide sufficient notice to be binding.

   Zuniga v. Major League Baseball, 196 N.E.3d 12 (Ill. App. 2021), also involved a standard term printed on a ticket. Zuniga attended a Chicago Cubs baseball game, using a paper admission ticket that her father had given to her. She was badly injured when she was hit in the face by a foul ball during the game, and she sued MLB and the Cubs for personal injury damages. The defendants filed a motion to compel arbitration on the basis that arbitration was provided for on the reverse side of Zuniga's paper admission ticket. A statement on the front of the ticket stated that it was subject to the terms on the reverse. A third of the space at the back of the ticket was taken up by an advertisement. The rest of the space contained a fine-print summary of several standard terms in four-point type. It stated that by using the ticket, the holder agreed to those terms and conditions, the full text of which was available either on the Cubs' website or at its administrative offices. It then summarized several terms, including a disclaimer of liability for injury and a requirement that claims and disputes must be resolved by binding arbitration.

Zuniga had not read the back of the ticket and had no actual knowledge of the terms. She could have argued that the terms were not conspicuous enough to give her constructive knowledge either, but she chose not to dispute contract formation and focused her argument on procedural unconscionability. The court's opinion is therefore confined to the issue of whether the arbitration provision was unconscionable. Its discussion of procedural unconscionability closely mirrors the principles and analysis that courts use in deciding whether a nondrafter had sufficient notice of a standard term to be bound by it. The court found the arbitration provision to be procedurally unconscionable because the brief, small-print reference to arbitration on the ticket did not provide adequate notice of the detailed, eight-paragraph arbitration provision which could only be accessed on the website or by getting a copy of it from the Cubs' administrative office, which a ticket holder was unlikely to be able to do in the tumult of entering a baseball stadium. One of the factors that persuaded the court to refuse enforcement of the provision was that Zuniga had not bought the ticket herself, so she had not had the opportunity to access the terms at the time of purchase. A ticket holder who had bought the ticket online may have had a less convincing argument of lack of reasonable notice. It is also possible that another court would not have been as receptive to the argument that the ticket itself did not provide adequate notice of the term. Although the font was small, and it merely summarized the terms, it did clearly and unambiguously alert the ticket holder to the essence of the terms.

4. This Example is based on *Druyan v. Jagger*, 508 F. Supp. 2d 228 (S.D.N.Y. 2007). Druyan had bought a ticket to a Rolling Stones concert in Atlantic City through the Ticketmaster website. A while before the concert, Mick Jagger contracted a sore throat, and the Rolling Stones decided to reschedule the show. Ticket holders were told of the rescheduling at 4 P.M. on the day of the concert. Ticketmaster offered to refund the price of the tickets or to exchange them for the rescheduled show, but Druyan

declined and commenced a class action[15] in which she sued Mick Jagger, the Rolling Stones, Ticketmaster, and others on a number of theories, including breach of contract. She claimed that the defendants had a duty to give her adequate notice of the cancellation and that the late notice had caused her and other members of the class to suffer damages in the form of wasted travel and hotel expenses incurred to attend the concert in Atlantic City. Unfortunately for Druyan, the Ticketmaster website was set up in much the same way as the Ticketmaker website described in the Example: It had a prominent notice that the user agrees to Ticketmaster's terms of use by clicking on the "Look for tickets" button. The notice had a link to the terms of use, which included a term that made it clear that Ticketmaster did not have an obligation to notify ticketholders of cancellations and precluded suit against Ticketmaster for damages. The court dismissed the breach of contract claim against Ticketmaster, holding that regardless of whether Druyan actually read the terms of use, she was bound by them because they were sufficiently conspicuous. (The court also dismissed all her other claims against all the defendants.)

5. Hard Driver's process for binding buyers to its license terms has some similarity to that used by ProCD (*see* section 5.5.2) in that the license terms are not readily apparent when the software is purchased, but are brought to the buyer's attention only when the software is about to be used. However, there are four important differences. First, unlike ProCD, Hard Driver is itself the seller of the software. Second, there was apparently no reference to the license terms on ProCD's box, but Hard Copy's box does mention the license, albeit in very small print that is not easily noticed. Third, ProCD gave the buyer the right to return the software if the terms were unacceptable, but Hard Driver does not. Fourth, the term in issue in ProCD related directly to the use of the software, and the restriction was justified by a lower price. The term in issue here is a forum selection clause that is unrelated to the use of the software.

   These are important factual differences and could lead to a different result from that reached in *ProCD*. As noted in section 5.5.2, the conclusion in that case is justifiable because ProCD was not the seller of the software and apparently did not have any contractual relationship with Zeidenberg at the time that the software was purchased. It was therefore deemed to make an offer by setting out its terms in the manual and the software, and Zeidenberg plausibly accepted the offer by not taking advantage of the right to return the software. The fact that ProCD had charged a lower price for the software to be used for noncommercial purposes also meant that the restriction was necessary to ensure that a

15. *See* section 5.3.5a for an explanation of class actions. In this case, the class of plaintiffs represented were the holders of tickets to the concert.

buyer did not buy the cheaper consumer package and use it for commercial purposes. Because of these differences, the better analysis is to find that Hard Driver and Meg entered into a contract at the time that Meg bought the software. As a result, Hard Driver cannot unilaterally impose the standard license terms on her after contract formation, so the terms, including the forum selection clause, are not part of the contract unless she knew of them when contracting or had reasonable notice or expectation of them, so that she is deemed to know of them. The tiny print on the box is likely insufficient to alert her to the existence of the standard terms. However, even in the absence of adequate notice of standard terms, a court may hold a nondrafter to inquiry notice of terms that must so obviously exist that a reasonable buyer would take the initiative to ascertain what they provided. This is probably true of the terms of use in a software license. Even if this is so, it does not necessarily mean that Meg would be bound by a forum selection clause, which is unrelated to the actual use of the software. It is difficult to predict how a court would resolve this issue. The rolling contract basis of *ProCD* is not applicable here, but, as explained in section 5.5.2, some courts do not treat terms expressly revealed after the formation of the contract as post-contractual proposals to modify the contract if the nondrafter had inquiry notice of the terms at the time of contracting.

6. It is likely that the plaintiff is bound by the arbitration provision and that the class action will be dismissed. This Example is based on *Oberstein v. Live Nation Entertainment, Inc.*, 60 F.4th 505 (9th Cir. 2023), in which purchasers of concert tickets commenced a class action against Ticketmaster and Live Nation, alleging anticompetitive practices that enabled them to charge excessive booking fees. The booking website was set up in the way described in the Example, with buttons both at the sign-in stage and the order stage, preceded by clear and conspicuous text stating that by signing in or creating an account and by placing the ticket order, the user agrees to the terms of use, hyperlinked in blue print. The court said that the terms were not pure clickwrap because the user was not required to click a box that specifically manifested agreement to the standard terms. Instead, the court characterized this as a hybrid process. The court noted that clickwrap is the safest means of ensuring that a user is bound by standard terms, but this hybrid method is sufficient to provide constructive knowledge of the standard terms where, as in this case, the notice of standard terms is conspicuously displayed and makes it clear that the user agrees to readily accessible terms by proceeding with the transaction.

7. When Clinton opened the Amazing account, he manifested assent to its terms of service by checking the prominent box expressing his agreement to the terms. This is a clickwrap process that likely binds Clinton to

the terms in existence at the time that he opened the account, including the commonplace term giving Amazing the right to amend its terms of service. The box and its embedded statement are prominent and the coherent terms are readily accessible via the obvious link. However, Clinton did not consent to the arbitration provision at that time, because it was added by the subsequent amendment. He would only be bound by his conduct of ordering goods after the amendment if he had actual knowledge of the new term (which he did not) or if Amazing had given him constructive knowledge of it by providing reasonable notification of the new term. The emails sent to him by Amazing should not qualify as reasonable notifications of the change in terms and should not constitute a waiver of the right to commence a class action. They were routine promotional emails, primarily focused on making sales of advertised products. The reference to changes, in relatively small and unnoticeable text at the bottom of the emails, is vague, nonspecific, and tentative. It states only that the terms "may" have changed, with no indication of what those changes might be.

This example is based on *Engen v. Grocery Delivery E-Services USA, Inc.*, cited in section 5.3.5. Grocery Delivery, trading as "HelloFresh" sold meal preparation kits to customers who ordered them online. Engen created an account with HelloFresh and accepted its standard terms by clickwrap. At the time, the terms did not include an arbitration provision, but they gave HelloFresh the right to change its terms, which would apply to orders made after the customer was notified of the change. HelloFresh subsequently added an arbitration provision and waiver of class actions to its terms. The only notice of the change in terms was included in about 50 emails over the next two years, primarily advertising special offers, but also containing a small-print hyperlink to the new version of the terms, buried at the bottom of the email where a customer was not likely to notice it or to appreciate its significance. When Engen later commenced a class action against HelloFresh, the court refused to dismiss the suit on the basis of the class action waiver, holding that the notice of the change in terms in the emails was not presented in a reasonably conspicuous manner.

CHAPTER 6

Mismatching Standard Terms

The "Battle of the Forms" Under UCC §2.207

§6.1 THE SCOPE AND PURPOSE OF UCC §2.207

§6.1.1 The Basic Purpose of §2.207

Like all provisions of Article 2, §2.207 applies only where the agreement qualifies as a sale of goods.[1] When it was originally drafted in the mid-twentieth century, §2.207 was aimed at tackling the problem of contradictory terms proposed by the parties in correspondence relating to the formation of a contract for the sale of goods, particularly where that contradiction arose from clashing standard terms used by each of the parties. The drafters considered that common law rules of offer and acceptance did not rationally resolve this problem because they were too formalistic and were inconsistent with commercial practice. The reform enacted by §2.207 has engendered interpretational difficulties because the section was not well conceived or coherently drafted. Courts have resolved some of its inelegancies over the years, but it remains awkward and its language sometimes leads to results that are no less random than that of the common law rules that the section replaced.[2]

---

1. *See* section 2.7.2 for a discussion of the scope of Article 2.
2. As part of an overall revision of Article 2 in 2003, the American Law Institute (ALI) and the Uniform Law Commission (ULC), formerly called the National Conference of Commissioners on Uniform State Laws (NCCUSL), proposed a redraft of §2.207 to simplify it and make it easier to apply. However, the proposed revision of Article 2 was not adopted by states and never became law.

§6.1.2 The Two Distinct Issues Covered by §2.207: Formation and Confirmation

Section 2.207 was enacted long before the advent of widespread electronic communications, so it is focused on the exchange of paper documents, such as purchase orders, order acknowledgments, and invoices. Today, it is applicable to the exchange of documents in electronic form as well, as explained in section 6.1.3. The key factor that brings §2.207 into force is that there is a conflict or disparity in the terms contained in the written communications used by the parties in the process of forming an agreement for the sale of goods. For example, say that Boilerplate, Inc., a boilermaker located in Alabama, sends a purchase order form to Ironclad Steelworks, Inc., a steel manufacturer in Pennsylvania, ordering two tons of steel. Boilerplate's order form contains a standard printed clause that states that all disputes arising under the transaction must be resolved by arbitration. Ironclad receives the order and sends an order acknowledgment in which it accepts the order. However, Ironclad's acknowledgment contains a standard printed forum selection clause that states that all disputes under the contract must be litigated in the courts of Pennsylvania. As a result, although the order and acknowledgment agree on the core terms of the sale itself, they have conflicting provisions relating to the resolution of any dispute that may arise in the transaction. If the parties do not bother to read each other's standard terms at the time that the forms are exchanged, they would not realize that their standard terms conflict. The purpose of §2.207 is to resolve the question of whether a contract was formed despite this disparity in the offer and response, and, if a contract was formed, which of the conflicting terms became part of the contract. The manner in which §2.207 deals with these matters is discussed in section 6.3.

Although §2.207 is principally involved with the offer and acceptance questions described in the previous paragraph, it also applies in a completely different situation in which there is no issue of offer and acceptance because it is clear that a contract has been formed (say, by oral communication). However, one or both of the parties subsequently send a written or electronically recorded confirmation of the contract that either adds to or contradicts terms that were agreed to. For example, Boilerplate orders the steel by phone, and Ironclad accepts the order during the phone call. The parties do not discuss the question of how disputes under the agreement will be resolved. Following the phone conversation, Ironclad sends a written or recorded acknowledgment of the contract to Boilerplate containing the forum selection clause. Here the purpose of §2.207 is not to decide whether a contract was formed through offer and acceptance—the formation occurred during the phone call.[3] Rather, its role is to determine whether the forum selection clause in the acknowledgment became part of the contract. This function of §2.207 is dealt with in section 6.4.

The text of §2.207(1) covers these two separate issues of formation (offer and acceptance) and written confirmation of an oral agreement. However, the section is poorly drafted, and so it does not set out this distinction clearly, but rather hints at it by referring to both an "expression of acceptance" and a "written confirmation." Sections 6.3 and 6.4 look more closely at the language relating to each of these separate aspects of §2.207.

In the illustrations used above, the conflicting terms were standard terms, drafted before the transaction in issue. Because the use of pre-drafted standard terms is common, §2.207 usually applies where there is disagreement between the standard terms set out in the parties' communications, which explains its nickname, "battle of the forms." However, there is nothing in the language of §2.207 that confines it to situations in which standard terms are used, so it could apply where the conflict or difference is in terms that have been individually drafted for this particular transaction by each party. However, this situation is much less common, and §2.207 cases typically do involve conflicting forms.

§6.1.3 The Application of §2.207 to Electronic Communications and Web-based Contracts

Although §2.207 was drafted with paper documents in mind, there is nothing in its language that precludes its application to electronic communications, such as email. Although the section uses the words "written" and "writings," it is clear in modern law that these words encompass forms of electronic recording. Therefore, had Boilerplate ordered the steel by an email message containing an arbitration clause, and Ironclad had responded by an email message containing a forum selection clause, §2.207 would be applicable to decide whether a contract had been formed, and if so, which of the conflicting terms was part of the contract.

---

3. In some cases, an oral agreement is not enforceable. As discussed in Chapter 11, a sale of goods for a price of $500 or more is subject to the statute of frauds provided for in §2.201. That is, the sales agreement must be memorialized in a record (written in a paper or electronic document) signed by the party against whom it is to be enforced. Therefore, when such a contract is made orally, it exists but cannot be enforced. However, a recorded confirmation sent by one of the parties will often satisfy the statute of frauds, at least against the sender and possibly against both parties, even if the confirmation contains a disputed term. If both parties send confirmations, those documents together might satisfy the statute of frauds. This is discussed more fully in Chapter 11.

Note, however, that §2.207 is not normally pertinent where contract formation takes place through the website of one of the parties, because the owner of the website can set up the formation process to avoid a nonconforming response. A clickwrap transaction usually requires the nondrafter to signify assent to the terms provided on the website without any opportunity to proffer its own terms during the contracting process. For example, Boilerplate visits Ironclad's website to order the steel. The website sets out Ironclad's standard terms, including the forum selection clause, and Boilerplate cannot complete its order until it has clicked an "I accept" button on the website. The contract is complete once Boilerplate has done this, and Boilerplate never has the opportunity to proffer its arbitration clause as part of its offer. It cannot effectively add the arbitration clause by sending a standard confirmation after completing its order, because contract formation has already occurred, and the effect of the subsequent communication can be nothing more than a proposal to modify the contract, which Ironclad can ignore or decline without jeopardizing contract formation. Although a browsewrap transaction does not require signification of assent to the standard terms before the order is placed, browsewrap terms do bind the party submitting the order, and therefore also become part of the contract, provided that the website is properly designed to ensure that the link to the terms is conspicuous, and provides adequate notice of the terms, which are reasonably accessible and clearly written. (*See* section 5.3.) Therefore, to the extent that web-based contracting replaces contracting by the exchange of forms, §2.207 is implicated in fewer transactions.

§6.2 THE PROBLEM TACKLED BY §2.207: THE COMMON LAW "MIRROR IMAGE" AND "LAST SHOT" RULES

Under principles of traditional common law, a response to an offer that seeks to vary the terms proposed in the offer would be treated as a counteroffer. For example, in the above transaction involving Boilerplate's steel order, Boilerplate made an offer by ordering two tons of steel, on terms that included the arbitration clause. Ironclad sought to accept the order by sending Boilerplate its standard order acknowledgment, which accorded with the order in all respects, except that it included the forum selection clause that conflicts with the arbitration clause. Assume that neither party read the other's standard terms, so they did not notice the conflict and thought that they had a contract. Had traditional common law principles applied to the transaction, no contract would have been formed by the exchange of the documents because Ironclad's nonconforming response would be treated as a counteroffer, which Boilerplate never accepted. The drafters of Article 2 considered this result wrong. They felt that the common law rule that required the acceptance to match the offer exactly (the so-called "mirror image" rule[4]) was too formalistic. The parties did in fact intend a contract, and contract formation should not be precluded simply because there was a discrepancy in the standard terms included in the offer and acceptance. To allow this preclusion simply aids the party who subsequently looks for a technicality to renege on the contract. Section 2.207 was therefore drafted to eliminate the "mirror image" rule and to allow a court to find a contract if Ironclad's response constituted a definite expression of acceptance, despite the conflicting term. Section 2.207 then contains rules on how the conflicting terms should be handled. As explained in section 6.3, except in limited circumstances, the result is usually that the conflicting term in the acceptance falls away, and the contract is on the offeror's terms.

In the example above neither party had performed under the contract before formation of the contract was challenged. However, if, after the exchange of forms, Ironclad shipped the steel and Boilerplate accepted it, there would no longer be a basis for arguing that no contract was formed. The parties' conduct proves that they both intended to contract. Because traditional common law rules treat the order as the offer and the nonconforming acknowledgment as a counteroffer, Boilerplate's acceptance of the goods becomes its acceptance of the counteroffer by conduct. As a result, a contract is formed on Ironclad's terms, so that the arbitration clause in Boilerplate's original offer falls away, and the parties are deemed to have agreed to the forum selection clause. This result is called the "last shot" rule because common law tends to find a contract on the terms of the party who sent the last communication before performance. The drafters of Article 2 considered the "last shot" rule to be random and formalistic, especially where standard terms are involved. They therefore drafted §2.207 to replace this rule by a different test for deciding whether Ironclad's or Boilerplate's terms should be part of the contract. As explained in section 6.3, §2.207 provides for two alternative resolutions of this situation: If Ironclad's response is an acceptance, the conflicting term in the acceptance enters the contract only in limited circumstances. More likely, it simply falls away, and the contract is on the offeror's terms. If it is not an acceptance, but a counteroffer, the conflicting terms in both parties' forms fall away and are replaced by a gap filler that is supplied by law.

The drafters' purpose in eliminating the "mirror image" and "last shot" rules was to treat conflicting terms in the offer and response more realistically. Although §2.207 did remove the formalistic mirror image and last

4. As explained in section 4.8, even at common law, many modern courts do not strictly apply the "mirror image" rule but treat a response as a counteroffer only if it materially varies the terms of the offer.

shot rules, the section is not well conceived. As a result, it has created interpretational problems and a different set of arbitrary rules.

§6.3 OFFER AND ACCEPTANCE UNDER §2.207

§6.3.1 Section 2.207(1): Acceptance, Rejection, and Counteroffer

The language of §2.207(1), relating to offer and acceptance, may be charted as shown in Diagram 6A.

Diagram 6A

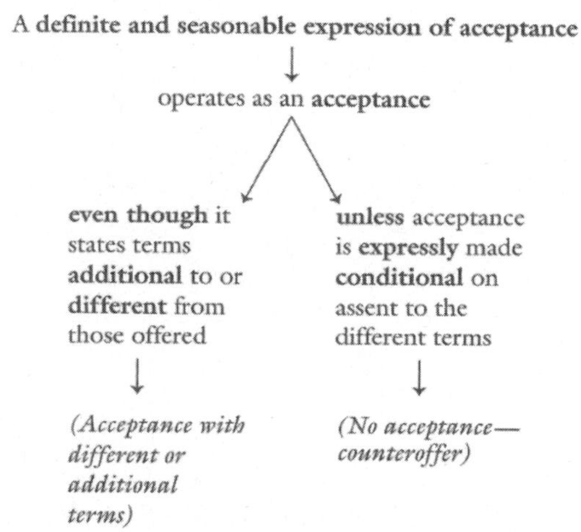

a. The Offer

Section 2.207(1) provides no guidance on whether the initial communication qualifies as an offer. This question must be resolved under the general common law principles set out in section 4.4. Once an offer is established under common law, §2.207(1) concentrates on the question of whether or not the response is an acceptance. It abolishes the "mirror image" rule, so the response to the offer need not match it exactly to be an acceptance. Instead, §2.207(1) adopts a fact-based approach to distinguish a reply that is clearly not an acceptance (so it can fairly be interpreted at best only as a counteroffer) from a reply that really is an acceptance with terms at variance with the offer. Diagram 6B illustrates this dichotomy.

Diagram 6B

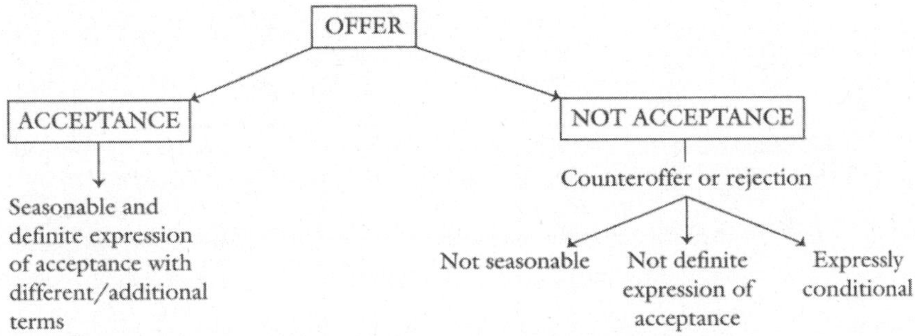

b. Replies That Are Not an Acceptance

If the response is clearly not a definite expression of acceptance or if it is sent after the offer has lapsed (that is, it is not "seasonable") or if it expressly states that acceptance is conditional on assent to its new terms, then it is a rejection or counteroffer.

i. A Response That Is Not Seasonable

"Seasonable" means that the response must be made in good time. The requirement that the response must be timely expresses the general rule that an offer must be accepted before it has lapsed. For example, On June 1, Boilerplate sent a purchase order to Ironclad in which it ordered two tons of steel at a stated price, to be delivered by July 1 and paid for on delivery. The offer had no term providing for arbitration, forum selection, or dispute resolution, and it stated that it must be accepted by June 5. If Ironclad accepted on June 7, the acceptance was not seasonable and hence ineffective.

ii. A Response That Is Not a Definite Expression of Acceptance

Even had Ironclad responded in time, its response would not be an acceptance if, based on a reasonable interpretation of its language, it did not manifest an intent to accept the offer. Because §2.207 rejects the mirror image rule, the mere fact that the response deviates from the terms of the offer is not enough to disqualify it as a definite expression of acceptance. There must be something in the response that is so fundamentally at odds with the transaction proposed in the offer, that it leads to the conclusion that it cannot qualify as an acceptance. This level of fundamental disagreement, going to the central purpose of the contract, might be demonstrated by a proposed alteration of terms that are not standard boilerplate, but are transaction-specific terms deliberately included in the offer. For example, if Ironclad's response to Boilerplate's offer changed the quantity of steel, or the price, or the delivery date specified in the offer, a court would be likely to regard this alteration of the offeror's transaction-specific term as a counteroffer rather than a definite expression of acceptance.

iii. A Response Making Acceptance Expressly Conditional on Assent to the Offeree's Terms

Whether or not the variation in the acceptance relates to a transaction-specific term, central to the performance requested in the offer, the response is not an acceptance if it specifies that acceptance is conditional on the offeror's assent to some new or altered term. For example, Ironclad would have made a counteroffer if it had returned a timely acknowledgment in accord with all Boilerplate's proposed terms, but with the following added provision: "Your order is accepted on the express condition that you agree to the following term: Any dispute or claim under this contract shall be litigated in the courts of the state of Pennsylvania. No court of any other state shall have jurisdiction over disputes or claims arising under this contract." By using clear and express language making its acceptance of the offer conditional on Boilerplate agreeing to its forum selection term, Ironclad is deemed by §2.207(1) to have rejected the offer by making a counteroffer. Courts usually require that the language in the response clearly manifests the offeree's refusal to enter the transaction unless the offeror agrees to the different or additional terms in the response. The clearest way of doing this is to include language in the response that mirrors the language used in §2.207(1), as Ironclad did in the above example. Courts have found that language that does not closely follow the formulation of §2.207(1) can achieve this purpose provided that it states directly and distinctly, not just implies, that the acceptance is expressly conditional on assent to its terms, so that it would lead a reasonable offeror to understand that it is intended as a counteroffer.

The expressly conditional assent could be contained in pre-drafted standard language. Even if it is, §2.207(1) gives effect to the form of words used in the standard term by treating the response as a counteroffer. This is ironic because the purpose of §2.207 is to underplay the effect of standard terms. As mentioned in section 6.3.2, this is not the only instance in which §2.207 can be interpreted as adopting an inconsistent approach to standard terms.

c. The Result When a Reply Is Not an Acceptance

If the response is not an acceptance, it is either a rejection or a counteroffer. As under the common law, a rejection or a counteroffer terminates the offeree's power of acceptance. However, the counteroffer is a new offer by the offeree that creates a power of acceptance in the former offeror. If the offeror elects to exercise that power, it can accept the counteroffer, creating a contract on the offeree's terms. If not, no contract comes into being merely as a consequence of the exchange of communication.

However, if the parties thereafter perform the contract, §2.207 follows the same principle as the common law and treats performance as a manifestation of acceptance of the offer, so that a contract is created. The difference between §2.207 and the common law is that §2.207 does not follow the common law "last shot" rule with regard to the question of what terms apply to the contract that has been created by performance. As noted in section 6.2, §2.207 does not apply the common law presumption that counterofferee's performance constitutes its acceptance of the terms set out in the counteroffer. Instead, §2.207(3) determines the terms of the contract by the method explained in section 6.3.3.

This may be represented as shown in Diagram 6C.

Diagram 6C

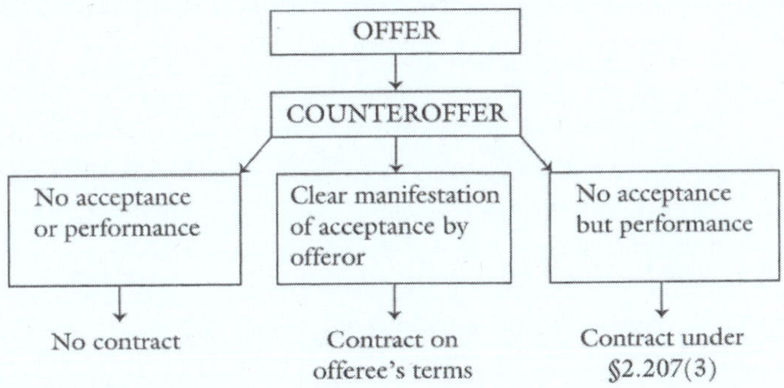

d. A Response That Is an Acceptance with Additional or Different Terms

If the response is a definite and seasonable expression of acceptance, and it is not expressly conditional on assent to any new terms, it is an acceptance even though it states terms different from or additional to those in the offer.

For example, say that Ironclad's response in the last illustration had no language making the acceptance expressly conditional on Boilerplate's assent to the forum selection clause but had simply contained pre-drafted language stating, "Any dispute or claim under this contract shall be litigated in the courts of the state of Pennsylvania. No court of any other state shall have jurisdiction over disputes or claims arising under this contract." Assume that in the absence of this term, the courts of Alabama (Boilerplate's state) would have had jurisdiction to deal with disputes under the contract. The response is likely to be an acceptance despite the new term. The fact that Ironclad expressed agreement with all the central terms of the offer and that the forum selection clause is set out in a pre-drafted standard term gives rise to the reasonable interpretation that Ironclad's primary focus was on making the sale, and its intent was to accept. A contract is therefore formed, and the question of whether the forum selection clause becomes part of it is dealt with in §2.207(2), discussed below.

Note that §2.207(1) covers both "additional" and "different" terms—a distinction that creates problems discussed in section 6.3.2c. It is not always easy to decide if a term is "additional" or "different," and this depends on the interpretation of the offer and the response. As a rough guideline, a term is different if it varies or contradicts something provided for in the offer, but it is additional if it adds new matter not covered in the offer. Although this guideline is of some help, it may not always easily resolve the ambiguity, as illustrated by the forum selection clause in the above example: Had Boilerplate's order contained an arbitration clause, it would have been quite easy to conclude that the forum selection clause is in conflict and hence "different." However, Boilerplate's order form did not have an arbitration clause and made no mention of dispute resolution or forum selection. In this case, one could characterize Ironclad's forum selection clause as additional because it seems to add a new term that is not covered in the offer. However, the absence of any dispute resolution or forum selection clause in Boilerplate's order would usually be interpreted by implication to allow suit in the courts of an appropriate state other than Pennsylvania. This would mean that the forum selection clause actually conflicts with an implied term in the purchase order and is therefore "different," rather than "additional."

§6.3.2 Section 2.207(2): The Treatment of Proposals in an Acceptance

The language of §2.207(2) may be charted as shown in Diagram 6D.

Diagram 6D

The **additional** terms are construed as **proposals** for addition to the contract.

↓

Between **merchants**
such terms become **part of the contract**

↓

unless:
(a) the **offer expressly limits** acceptance;
(b) they **materially alter** it; or
(c) notification of **objection** to them has already been given or is given within a reasonable time after notice of them is received.

a. The Scope and Basic Purpose of §2.207(2)

Section 2.207(2) only applies if the response to an offer is found to be an acceptance. It does not apply to a counteroffer, which only leads to a contract if accepted or if performance occurs as contemplated by §2.207(3). Because §2.207(1) recognizes the existence of a contract despite a variance between the terms of the offer and acceptance, §2.207(2) treats any such additional terms as proposals that do not become part of the contract unless the conditions in the subsection are satisfied.

b. The Grounds for Excluding Proposals from the Contract

Section 2.207(2) begins by stating the basic principle that additional terms in an acceptance are to be treated as proposals for addition of the contract. It then goes on to state a rule that prescribes when these additional terms will enter the contract if both parties are merchants. The rule applicable to merchant parties is discussed in section 6.3.2.c. Section 2.207(2) does not state what the rule is if both parties are not merchants, so the general principle relating to proposed modifications to a contract applies: Unless the offeror agrees to the modification proposed by the offeree, it does not become part of the contract. The offeror's agreement must be clear and deliberate, and is not inferred from conduct simply because the offeror fails to object or proceeds to perform the contract.

If both parties are merchants, §2.207(2) states that the proposed term does enter the contract unless one of three exceptions in §2.207(2)(a), (b), or (c) apply. The exceptions do not all have to be satisfied for the term to be excluded. If any one of them applies, the additional term in the acceptance does not enter the contract. Most terms of any importance are likely to be excluded by one of the exceptions, so the offeree usually does not succeed in adding terms to the contract by the acceptance.

c. The Inclusion or Exclusion of Proposals for Addition to the Contract If Both Parties Are Merchants

i. Both Parties Must Be Merchants

Section 2.7.2 introduces the concept of a merchant in Article 2, which is defined in §2.104(1) in terms that are much broader than in common usage. The definition includes not only a person who deals in goods of that kind but also one who, by following a particular occupation, has or represents having knowledge or skill concerning the goods or the practices involved in the transaction. Therefore, as Official Comment[5] 1 to §2.104 points out, even a person that does not trade in the goods could be a merchant if that

5. Section 2.7.1 introduces the role and effect of the Official Comments to the UCC. They are the drafter's explanation of the intent and purpose of code sections. They are very influential but are not part of the statute.

person is a "professional" user of the goods, as opposed to a "casual or inexperienced seller or buyer." Section 2.207(2) requires that the transaction be "between merchants." They must both be merchants, and if either of them is not a merchant, §2.207(2)(a), (b), and (c) do not apply and the proposals do not become part of the contract unless they are deliberately accepted by the offeror, as explained in section 6.3.2.b.

ii Section 2.207(2)(a): The Term Does Not Enter the Contract if the Offer Limits Acceptance to Its Terms

Even if the parties are merchants the term does not become part of the contract if there is language in the offer expressly limiting acceptance to its terms. This means that an offeror can simply eliminate the possibility of proposals entering the contract by putting appropriate standard language in the offer. For example, in *HIL Technology, Inc. v. Engineering/Remediation Resources Group, Inc.*, 2018 WL 2210428 (D. Me. 2018), the standard language in the buyer's purchase order stated, "By accepting this purchase order . . . Seller agrees to sell Buyer the goods . . . on this Order's terms. . . . Buyer hereby rejects any terms . . . in Seller's acceptance that add to, vary from, or conflict with . . . [Buyer's terms]." The court held that this language in the offer prevented a forum selection clause in the seller's invoice from becoming part of the contract under §2.207(2)(a) because the offer expressly limited acceptance to its terms.

By recognizing an advance standard rejection of the offeree's terms in the offer, §2.207(2)(a) creates the same ironic result as the recognition of expressly conditional language in §2.207(1). Both subsections give effect to standardized exclusions or conditions despite the section's avowed purpose of downplaying the impact of pre-drafted standard language.

iii. Section 2.207(2)(b): The Term Does Not Enter the Contract If It Materially Alters It

Materiality is a complex issue.[6] Simply speaking, a term is material if it provides for an important aspect of the contractual performance. That is, it is a significant element of the exchange bargained for by a party. *Bourdeau Bros., Inc. v. Boissonneault Family Farm, Inc*, 236 A.3d 1263 (Vt. 2020), expresses the usual interpretation that by stating, "between merchants such terms become part of the contract unless . . ." §2.207(2) creates the presumption that the addition becomes part of the contract. This places the burden of proving materiality on the party seeking to exclude the term.

---

6. The meaning of materiality is discussed in several sections of this book. The fullest discussion is in section 17.3 on material breach of contract.

Some terms seem to be so obviously important that a court may need little persuading that they are material, and may even find that they are *per se* material so that materiality can be decided as a matter of law. However, courts usually treat materiality as a matter of interpretation, dependent on the circumstances of each case and requiring an examination of the facts under which the contract was entered. *Bourdeau Bros.* emphasized this principle. Bourdeau sold agricultural supplies to Boissonneault under oral contracts and sent invoices to Boissonneault with each delivery. The invoices provided that Boissonneault would be liable for Bourdeau's attorneys fees if Bourdeau had to sue Boissonneault to collect unpaid bills. Both parties were merchants, so this additional term in the written confirmation would have become part of the contract under §2.207(2) unless it materially altered the oral agreement. The court reversed the trial court's holding that the attorney fees provision was a material alteration as a matter of law, and remanded the question for a factual determination of materiality.

The test for materiality prescribed in *Bourdeau Bros.* is based on Official Comment 4 to §2.207, which courts regularly apply. The Comment says that a proposed alteration in an acceptance is material and does not enter the contract if it would result in "surprise or hardship" to the other party. "Surprise" is determined with reference to reasonable expectations in light of common practice and usage. If a particular term is widely used, the party has reason to assume that it would be part of the contract, and its inclusion should be no surprise. "Hardship" means that the term imposes an unbargained burden (financial or otherwise) on, or detracts significantly from, the reasonable expectations of the other party. The concept of hardship does not do much to help resolve the question of whether an alteration is material, because it begs the question of materiality rather than helping to answer it: A material alteration causes hardship, therefore it is material.

The disjunctive "or" in Official Comment 4 is misleading because the concepts of surprise and hardship are usually both elements of materiality and, in most cases, must both be satisfied to some degree. That is, even an important alteration may not be material if its inclusion should be fully expected, and a trivial alteration should not be treated as material, even if it is unexpected. The basic point of the exclusion is this: Even if the sale is between merchants, a proposed term does not enter the contract if it has more than a minimal impact on the exchange, and it is not sufficiently common to be expected. The forum selection clause in Ironclad's response to Boilerplate's offer illustrates how tricky the question of materiality may be. Although the forum selection clause does not relate to a central aspect of the transaction, such as the nature of the goods sold, the price, payment terms, or delivery terms, the waiver of the right to sue in a court other than in Pennsylvania may or may not be material, depending on whether it is so unexpected (surprising) or so burdensome as to impose hardship on

Boilerplate. This is not a question that can be decided without reference to all the facts of the transaction and its context.

Rocheux International of New Jersey, Inc. v. U.S. Merchants Financial Group, 741 F. Supp. 2d 651 (D.N.J. 2010), deals with the concept of materiality in relation to §2.207(2). The case involved multiple disputes arising out of the sale of a large quantity of raw plastic from Rocheux to U.S. Merchants. One of the issues in the case was whether the parties' contract contained a term that obligated the buyer to pay a service charge on outstanding balances plus collection costs and attorney's fees. The seller contended that this term became part of the contract because it was included in the standard order confirmations that it sent to the buyer following each of the buyer's orders. Both parties were merchants, so the crucial issue was whether the term materially altered the contract. The court noted that the determination of materiality involves a complex inquiry including both legal and factual elements, encompassed within the "surprise or hardship" standard set out in Official Comment 4. A term is unreasonably surprising if, under all the circumstances (including such factors as the prominence of the term in the writing, industry custom, and any course of dealings between the parties) it cannot be presumed that a reasonable merchant would have expected or consented to the term. The court found that the buyer could not claim unfair surprise because the term was prominently displayed in multiple acknowledgments sent to the buyer over an extensive course of dealings and was not an uncommon provision in transactions of this kind. Although the total amount due for interest and attorney's fees would be substantial—about $3 million—this did not, in itself, impose unfair hardship on the buyer because the inclusion of the term was not an unfair surprise, and the amount of the liability was within the range of commercial practice.

Ridgelawn Cemetery Ass'n v. Granite Resources Corporation, 2017 WL 3783401 (N.D. Ind. 2017), is one of many cases that have considered whether a forum selection clause included in the response to an offer materially altered the offer. The seller alleged, but could not prove, that it actually sent the order acknowledgment with the forum selection clause to the buyer. However, the court held that even if it had been able to sustain this burden of proof, the clause would not have entered the contract under §2.207(2)(b) because it materially altered the offer. Applying the surprise and hardship test of Official Comment 4, the court held that the term was surprising because the buyer had no forewarning or expectation of it, and it would impose hardship on the buyer by compelling it to undergo the expense and inconvenience of litigation in a distant forum. The court did not explain its conclusion in any depth and there is a good argument for the opposite conclusion—forum selection clauses are so common, that a reasonable merchant should not be surprised by them, and, absent special circumstances, the inconvenience of litigating in a distant court is not severe enough to constitute a hardship.

Northwest 1 Trucking, Inc. v. Haro, 613 F. Supp. 3d 1081 (N.D. Ill. 2020),[7] also held a forum selection clause to be a material alteration. The parties had not dealt with each other before, so the court found the clause to be unreasonably surprising in the absence of a course of dealing between the parties that would have made the clause a familiar feature of their contracts. It acknowledged that materiality must be determined on the facts and circumstances of each case, but it relied heavily on judicial precedent, citing numerous cases that found forum selection clauses to be material alterations.

Because arbitration provisions are so frequently challenged, there are many cases that address the question of whether an arbitration provision is a material alteration. Some cases, for example, *Bayway Refining Co. v. Oxygenated Marketing & Trading A.G.*, 215 F.3d 219 (2d Cir 2000), have treated arbitration provisions as *per se* material. However, many courts have recognized that the materiality of an arbitration provision should not be decided as a matter of law, but must be determined under the general principle that materiality is dependent on the circumstances of each case. For example, this was the approach in *Nu-X Ventures v. SBL, LLC*, 568 F. Supp. 3d 829 (W.D. Ky. 2021). SBL made several sales of cannabinoid (CBD) gummies and capsules to Nu-X. The transactions were initiated by purchase orders sent by Nu-X. SBL responded by sending its "sales orders" to Nu-X which conformed with the purchase orders in all respects, but also included a provision stating "By making payment for your order, you acknowledge and agree to all of our terms and conditions at this link . . ." The link led to SBL's standard terms, which included an arbitration provision. When Nu-X later sued SBL, alleging breach of contract, SBL moved to compel arbitration. Both parties were merchants and the "sales order" was an acceptance with additional terms, so §2.207(2) applied and the issue was whether the arbitration provision was a material alteration under §2.207(2)(b). The court applied the test of materiality set out in Official Comment 4 and found that Nu-X had not sustained its burden of proving surprise or hardship. Nu-X had not shown that the arbitration would impose any hardship on it, and there was no surprise because Nu-X had ample opportunity to read the standard terms over the course of repeated transactions, and had not shown that arbitration deviated from industry practice.

iv. Section 2.207(2)(c): The Term Does Not Enter the Contract If the Offeror Objects

If the offer did not limit acceptance to its terms, the offeror still has an opportunity to eliminate the proposal by subsequent objection, either in anticipation of the proposal or within a reasonable time of acquiring notice of it. This appears to contemplate not only a deliberate objection

7. This case involved a written confirmation following an oral contract, so it is discussed again in section 6.4.

but also a standard objection issued by the offeror as a matter of course. This again raises the inconsistency displayed by §2.207 in its reaction to standard terms.

d. The Omission of "Different" Terms from the Text of §2.207(2)

As noted in section 6.3.1, §2.207(1) refers to "additional" and "different" terms, while §2.207(2) only mentions "additional" terms. This has created two problems. First (as stated in section 6.3.1) it is not always easy to tell if a term is "additional" or "different." Second, it is not clear if the omission of "different" terms in §2.207(2) was really intended or was just an oversight. The failure to include "different" terms in §2.207(2) has led courts to adopt divergent approaches to the treatment of terms found to be "different."

Some courts have treated the omission as inadvertent and have applied the subsection irrespective of whether the term may be classified as "additional" or "different." This approach has some support in Official Comment 3, which seems to assume that both fall within §2.207(2). (The Official Comment is not entirely clear on this point because it makes this remark in relation to confirmations, not acceptances.) It also has the obvious advantage of eliminating the problem of struggling to distinguish them.

Other courts have taken §2.207(2) literally and have held that because "different" terms are not covered in the subsection, they must simply be excluded from the contract because §2.207(2) provides no basis for a unilateral proposal for a "different" term in the acceptance to enter the contract. The fact that "different" terms are not mentioned in §2.207(2) suggests not that they be treated more favorably than "additional" terms, but that they be treated less so. In other words, the "different" term can never become part of the contract, even if it meets all the tests for inclusion in §2.207(2).

A third approach is to treat the conflicting terms as canceling each other out. Some courts have reasoned that if the purpose of §2.207 is to take standard terms less seriously, it makes no sense to prefer one party's "different" term over that of the other. Therefore, they should both fall away and be replaced by whatever term the law would supply in the absence of agreement. (This has been called the "knockout" rule.) Although this approach seems to accord with the spirit of §2.207, there is no basis for it in the express provisions of the section. It sounds a little like the solution prescribed in §2.207(3), but that provision applies only where the parties perform despite their failure to conclude a contract. Section 2.207(3) therefore does not apply to a situation in which the offeree's response is an acceptance with different terms, so courts that use the "knockout" rule to resolve conflicts between different terms in an offer and acceptance are just using the resolution of §2.207(3) by analogy.

§6.3.3 Section 2.207(3): The Effect of Mutual Performance When No Contract Is Formed by the Parties' Writings

The language of §2.207(3) may be charted as shown in Diagram 6E.

Diagram 6E

Conduct by both parties
that recognizes the existence of a contract
is **sufficient to establish a contract** for sale
↓
although
the writings of the parties do not otherwise establish a contract.
↓
In such a case
the terms of the particular contract consist of
those terms on which the **writings** of the parties **agree**
together with
any **supplementary terms** incorporated under any other provisions of
this Act

Section 2.207(3) only applies when there is no contract formed by the writings—typically because the offeree's response is not an acceptance with additional or different terms but a counteroffer that the initial offeror did not accept deliberately. As noted earlier, the common law "last shot" rule treated the original offeror's performance as an acceptance by conduct of the counteroffer, thereby imposing the risk of inadvertent assent to the counteroffer's variation in terms.

Section 2.207(3) eliminates this risk. If no contract was formed by the writings of the parties, but their conduct (typically in the form of tendering and accepting performance) shows that they intend a contract, §2.207(3) recognizes the contract as existing. However, its terms are not simply those contained in the last communication. The contract includes only those terms on which the parties' writings agree, and all conflicting terms fall away. Any gaps in the contract are filled by supplementary terms recognized by the UCC. If there is any applicable trade usage or course of dealing or performance between the parties, the missing terms can be supplied as a matter of factual implication.[8] Failing that, Article 2 itself provides a number of standard terms (known as "gap fillers") that are implied as a matter of law into all sales of goods unless excluded by the contract. For example, unless

8. Section 10.6.2 explains the role of trade usage, course of dealing, and course of performance in the interpretation of contractual intent. For the present, it is enough to understand in general terms that the context in which the parties made their contract often provides much useful information on what they must have intended their contract terms to be.

the parties agree otherwise, §2.308 states that delivery must take place at the seller's premises; §2.310 requires payment on delivery; and §2.314 provides that a merchant seller warrants that the goods are merchantable (generally, that they are fit for their ordinary purposes and are acceptable within the trade). These are just a few examples. There are many other gap fillers in Article 2 and also many default terms recognized by common law that would apply where Article 2 does not have a gap filler that covers the particular gap in question.

The transaction between Boilerplate and Ironclad can be used to illustrate the operation of §2.207(3). Boilerplate sent a purchase order to Ironclad in which it ordered two tons of steel at a stated price, to be delivered on a stated date and paid for on delivery. The offer had no term providing for dispute resolution. Ironclad returned a timely acknowledgment in accord with all Boilerplate's proposed terms, but with an additional provision stating, "Your order is accepted on condition that you agree to the following term: Any dispute or claim under this contract shall be litigated in the courts of the state of Pennsylvania. No court of any other state shall have jurisdiction over disputes or claims arising under this contract." This expressly conditional language makes the response a counteroffer, as explained in section 6.3.1b. Boilerplate never communicated assent to this condition. In fact, having not read the reply, Boilerplate was not even aware of the term. Ironclad shipped the steel and it was accepted by Boilerplate. Some time later, Boilerplate had a dispute with Ironclad over the quality of the steel, and sued Ironclad in Alabama, Boilerplate's home state. In the absence of the forum selection clause, the Alabama court would have had jurisdiction over the litigation, but Ironclad insisted that Boilerplate had agreed to sue only in Pennsylvania.

Under common law, Boilerplate's conduct in accepting the delivery would be deemed an acceptance of the terms of the counteroffer, making Ironclad's forum selection clause part of the contract. Under §2.207(3), however, a contract is recognized only on the terms on which the writings agree (description, quantity, price, delivery, and payment) and the forum selection clause falls away. The resulting gap may be filled by trade usage, if any such usage exists and is applicable. If not, it is filled by a gap filler supplied by Article 2 or, if Article 2 does not address that issue, by a general principle of common law.

Assume that there is no applicable trade usage. Article 2 does not address questions of jurisdiction, so this question must be settled by common law principles. The general principle under common law is that in the absence of a forum selection clause, suit may be brought in any court that has jurisdiction over the litigation. Therefore, in this case, the result under §2.207(3) happens to favor Boilerplate because its offer contemplated the same result as the gap filler. This was the result in *Niagara Bottling, LLC v. Rite-Hite Co.*, 2019 WL 1768875 (C.D. Cal. 2019), which also involved a forum selection clause in an expressly conditional acceptance.[9] The court held that the expressly conditional acceptance was a counteroffer under §2.207(1), so that the exchange of documents did not form a contract. However, the parties had performed, so §2.207(3) applied, knocking out the forum selection clause and permitting suit in any forum that has jurisdiction over the litigation.

§6.4 WRITTEN CONFIRMATION FOLLOWING AN ORAL OR INFORMAL CONTRACT UNDER §2.207(1) AND (2)

Section 2.207(1) is poorly drafted and obscure with regard to written confirmations. The subsection states that "a written[10] confirmation that is sent within a reasonable time operates as an acceptance even though it states terms additional to or different from those . . . agreed upon, unless acceptance is expressly made conditional on assent to the additional or different terms." Read literally, this makes no sense. The "written" (recorded) confirmation apparently follows an agreement. Although §2.207(1) does not itself articulate this, Official Comment 1 indicates that the drafters contemplated a situation in which an oral or informal agreement is followed by recorded confirmations. That is, the parties have actually made a contract already, so, the subsequent record cannot be an acceptance, conditional or otherwise. The process of offer and acceptance has already been concluded. If a contract already exists, the purpose of any confirmation is, of course, to confirm what has been agreed. This may be motivated by a need to satisfy the statute of frauds[11] or simply by a desire to create a record of the transaction.

Therefore, the references to acceptance in §2.207(1) are inappropriate in the context of confirmations and should be disregarded, leaving just a

9. The transaction involved the sale of both goods and services, so it was a hybrid transaction and the court first had to determine whether the transaction was predominantly a sale of goods to which Article 2 applied. (Section2.7.2.e explains hybrid transactions and the use of the predominance test to decide whether and to what extent Article 2 governs.) After determining that the transaction was predominantly a sale of goods, the court applied §2.207.

10. Section 2.207(1) refers to a "written" confirmation, which is understood in contemporary law to include both a tangible writing on paper and an electronic confirmation. An Official Comment to §2.207, added by the 2022 amendments to the Official Text of Article 2, clarifies this. (The 2022 amendments to the Official Text of Article 2 are referred to in several chapters of this book, and are introduced in section 2.7.2.)

11. As mentioned in footnote 3, the contract is fully enforceable in its oral form unless the price of the goods is $500 or more, in which case it does not become enforceable until reduced to writing sufficient to comply with the statute of frauds.

few snippets of disjointed statutory language to interpret. This is what the language relating to confirmations means:

1. An oral or informal contract is formed.
2. Thereafter, one or both parties send recorded confirmations.
3. One or both confirmations go beyond or vary what was agreed orally or informally.
4. Any such terms in a confirmation that add to or differ from the oral contract cannot simply become part of the contract, but must be treated as proposals in the same way as proposals in an acceptance.

Therefore, where confirming records are involved, the only issue is whether the additional or different terms in a confirmation become part of the contract. This question is decided using the same analysis, set out in section 6.3.2, as would be used if the additional or different term were contained in an acceptance. In this situation, the issue is not whether there is a clash between conflicting records (in fact, only one party may have sent a confirmation) but between one or more records and the original oral or informal agreement.

Section 2.207(3) states that it governs where conduct establishes contractual intent but "the writings [records] of the parties do not otherwise establish a contract." If mutual performance occurs after a confirmation, a literal reading of §2.207(3) suggests that it is applicable. The contract arises, not from the records but from the earlier oral agreement. This is surely not the intent. Section 2.207(3) is meant to deal with situations in which no contract would exist in the absence of performance and not where an oral contract has been concluded.[12] *Ballou v. Asset Marketing Services, LLC*, 46 F.4th 844 (8th Cir. 2022), discussed in section 5.5.2 in relation to rolling contracts,[13] illustrates the application of §2.207(1) when a recorded confirmation is sent by one of the parties after a contract has been formed. Asset Marketing Services (AMS), doing business as GovMint.com, sold a large number of commemorative and collectible coins to the plaintiffs for many thousands of dollars. Commemorative and collectible coins are not legal tender, so they are not money, which is excluded from the definition of goods in

---

12. As explained in section 6.3.2d, although §2.207(3) is not directly applicable to differences between terms in the oral or informal contract and a confirmation, some courts may adopt the "knockout" rule by analogy, as they do where an acceptance has terms "different" from the offer.

13. As explained in section 5.5.2, a rolling contract is one in which standard terms are sent by the drafter to the nondrafter after the parties have initially agreed to the transaction, and the nondrafter is given the opportunity to reject the contract after receiving the standard terms. This has the effect of delaying acceptance of the contract terms until the nondrafter fails to reject the terms in the time allowed after receiving them. The buyers in *Ballou* did not have this right, so the contracts did not qualify as rolling contracts.

§2.105, but qualify as goods. The sales were therefore governed by UCC Article 2. Two of these buyers later commenced a class action against AMS, alleging that AMS had engaged in consumer fraud and deceptive trade practices. AMS moved to stay the suit and compel arbitration on the basis of an arbitration provision stated in shipping invoices sent to the buyers when the coins were delivered. Many of the coins had been ordered over the phone, so the shipping invoices were sent to the buyers only after the buyers and AMS had made an oral agreement for the sale of the coins. Because these sales were not rolling contracts, the court held that offer and acceptance had occurred at the time of the oral phone sales. The invoices with the arbitration provision were therefore written confirmations of the oral contract under §2.207(1), with a proposal by AMS to add its standard terms. The buyers were not merchants, so §2-207(2)(a), (b), and (c) did not apply and the proposed terms, including the arbitration provision, could not become part of the contract unless the buyers expressly accepted them, which they never did.

In *Northwest 1 Trucking, Inc. v. Haro*, cited in section 6.3.2.b(iii), both parties were merchants, so §2-207(2)(b) did apply to a proposed additional term in the written confirmation of an oral contract. The term in question was a forum selection provision, included by the seller in an invoice accompanying the delivery of a bulldozer that was sold for more than $150,000 under an oral contract. Despite assurances by the seller that the bulldozer was in perfect shape and would run forever, it began to smoke and then shut down after only two hours of operation. The cost of parts alone to repair it would have been $75,000. The buyer sued the seller in Illinois, and the seller moved to dismiss the suit on the grounds that a forum selection clause in the invoice required the parties to litigate any disputes in Texas. The offer did not limit acceptance to its terms under §2-207(2)(a), and the buyer did not object to the term under §2-207(2)(c), so the term would have become part of the contract under §2-207(2) unless it materially altered it under §2-207(2)(b). The court found that the forum selection clause was not part of the contract because it was a material alteration. (See section 6.3.2.b(iii) for the court's reasoning on why the alteration was material.)

§6.5 A TRANSNATIONAL PERSPECTIVE ON THE "BATTLE OF THE FORMS"

Both the UNIDROIT Principles and the CISG contain general principles of acceptance that can be used to address conflicts between terms in an offer and acceptance.

Article 2.1.11 of the UNIDROIT Principles sets out the broad general principle relating to all forms of acceptance: A response to an offer is a counteroffer if its terms digress materially from the offer, but a response with nonmaterial alterations qualifies as an acceptance unless the offeror objects. In the absence of objection, the terms in the acceptance become part of the contract. Article 2.1.12 adopts a similar approach to additional or different terms in a confirmation, which become part of the contract unless they are material or are objected to. Where standard forms are used by the parties, Article 2.1.22 specifically addresses the "battle of the forms" and provides for a form of knockout rule: Where the parties use standard forms and reach agreement except on the standard terms, the contract consists of those terms on which the writings agree, including the standard terms that are essentially the same. One-sided standard terms fall away. However, both parties have the ability to reject the contract by notice.

The CISG does not have a provision that deals specifically with "battle of the forms" situations, so its general principles of acceptance apply where a conflict arises in the exchange of forms. CISG Article 19(1) treats a response to an offer as a counteroffer if it contains modifications of the offer, but Article 19(2) relaxes this "mirror image" approach by recognizing the response as an acceptance if the modifications are nonmaterial. They become part of the contract unless the offeror objects to them without delay. Article 19(3) contains a list of examples of material alterations, which includes price, payment, quantity, delivery, and dispute resolution terms.

Examples

EXAMPLES

1. Carr Buff's hobby is restoring vintage cars. He just completed the restoration of a 1957 Ford after working on it for many years. On December 15, he parked the car in the parking lot of a shopping mall. When he returned to it, he found a note stuck under the windshield wiper that read: "Dear owner of 1957 Ford, my name is Rod Hott. I love this car and would like to buy it from you. I offer to pay you $100,000 for it, which I will pay on delivery of the car and its title papers. If you would like to sell the car to me, please reply to me at rodhott@email.com. by no later than December 20. On your acceptance, we will arrange a date to complete this transaction before Christmas."

   After thinking about the offer for a couple of days, Carr decided to accept it. At 7:00 p.m. on December 20 he sent an email to the address in the note in which he said, "Rod, I agree to sell the Ford to you for $100,000. Please note that payment must be in cash or by cashier's check. Reply to me as soon as you get this message to arrange the time for delivery. The server hosting Rod's email account was down for maintenance during the evening of December 20, so Carr's email was not delivered to Rod's inbox until 6:00 am on December 21.

Do Rod and Carr have a contract?

2. Carr Buff is not a vintage car hobbyist, but a vintage car dealer. Carr displayed a restored 1957 Ford in his showroom. Rod Hott, a consumer, saw the car in the showroom and made a written offer to buy it for $100,000, to be delivered in one week and paid for on delivery. On the next day, Carr sent a document to Rod, headed "Order Acknowledgment." It stated, "I am pleased to accept your order for the 1957 Ford on the terms indicated in your order. The car will be ready for you in one week." There was preprinted sentence at the bottom of the order acknowledgment that read, "This order is accepted subject to your agreement that any dispute arising out of this transaction will be submitted to binding arbitration under the rules of the American Arbitration Association."
   a. Do Carr and Rod have a contract?
   b. If they do have a contract, is the arbitration provision a term of the contract?
   c. Would the answers to a or b change if, after Rod received the order acknowledgment, Carr delivered the Ford to Rodd and Rodd paid for it?

3. Ballet de la Forms, Inc., a manufacturer of dance apparel, needed to replenish its stock of fabric. It submitted a written purchase order to Material Alterations, Inc., a fabric manufacturer, in which it specified the description, quantity, and price of the fabric ordered as well as the delivery date and payment terms. Ballet's order form contained a preprinted term that stated, "Ballet de la Forms shall have the right to return unused goods to the seller within 60 days of delivery of the goods under this order. Acceptance of this offer is limited to the terms stated in this purchase order." Material Alterations received the order on the next day and immediately mailed its order acknowledgment to Ballet. Unquestionably, the response was mailed and received in good time and before the offer had lapsed. The acknowledgment expressed assent to the order and accorded in all respects with the order, except that it contained a printed term that stated, "Return Policy: Goods may be returned only if defective. No returns will be accepted for any other reason." Material Alterations has not yet shipped the goods. Do the parties have a contract? If so, what is the contract's term relating to return of the goods?

4. Tutu O'Severn decided to take up dance lessons. She needed a tutu, so she searched the web and found the website of Ballet de la Forms, Inc., a supplier of dance apparel. She selected a tutu for $150, clicked on it to place it in her virtual "shopping cart," and filled out the online order form in which she inserted her name, email address, shipment and

billing address, and credit card particulars. In the box called "delivery options," she selected "standard, 1 to 2 weeks delivery." She clicked the "submit order" button at the bottom of the screen. A couple of seconds later, an automated response headed "Order Confirmation" appeared on the screen. It set out a confirmation number, the details of the order as submitted by Tutu, and instructions on how she could track the progress of the shipment.

Two days later, Tutu received an email from Ballet, which stated, "We regret to inform you that the tutu that you ordered is no longer available for the price of $150 because the manufacturer has increased the price since you placed your order. The tutu now costs $250. If you would still like to buy the tutu at the new price, please resubmit your order." Tutu insists that she had already bought the tutu at the original price and that Ballet is obliged to deliver it to her at that price. Is she correct?

5. In addition to a tutu, Tutu needed tights for her dance lessons. She called Leo Tard, a specialist in dancing attire, and ordered three pairs of tights for a total of $350. She arranged with Leo that the tights would be delivered within a week and that $350 would be charged to her credit card on shipment of the tights. Leo immediately shipped the tights to Tutu, accompanied by his standard invoice. The invoice stated, "For sanitary reasons, we cannot accept the return of clothing delivered to a customer. All sales are final once the clothing leaves our premises." By the time that Tutu received the tights, a week later, she had changed her mind about taking dancing lessons and no longer wanted the tights. She called Leo and told him that she was returning the tights and that the $350 payment must be credited to her credit card. Leo refused, insisting that she had bought them and could not return them. Is Leo right?

6. Ballet de la Forms, Inc., a retailer of dance apparel, sent an email to Formfitting Fashion Fabricators, Inc., in which it ordered 1,000 pairs of tights. The order simply contained the quantity, price, and description of the goods and the particulars relating to payment and delivery. Formfitting responded by email on the same day, acknowledging the order and agreeing to supply the tights on the terms set out in Ballet's email. Formfitting's email contained a standard term, automatically included in all its order acknowledgments, stating that any dispute arising out of the sale would be resolved by final and binding arbitration under the rules of the American Arbitration Association and the Federal Arbitration Act. The goods were shipped and accepted, but a dispute has arisen about their quality. The parties concede that they are both merchants, that Formfitting's email was an acceptance of Ballet's offer, and that the arbitration provision is an additional term in the acceptance, to be dealt with under §2.207(2). However, they disagree on whether the

arbitration provision should fall away as a material alteration of the contract. How can you tell if it is a material alteration?

Explanations

1. a. This is a sale of goods, so §2.207 applies. Although it is nicknamed the "battle of the forms," §2.207 is not confined to transactions in which forms are used. Article 2 does not deal with the question of whether a communication qualifies as an offer, so general common law principles apply. Rod's letter appears to qualify as an offer. It set out the terms on which he proposed to buy the car, and can be reasonably understood to confer a power of acceptance on the offeree. Although Rod did not know who the owner of the car was, he addressed the offer to the owner, an identifiable person. The offer just asked for a reply by December 20, and did not actually say that it would lapse if not accepted by that date. However, this is its reasonable meaning.

   Carr intended to accept and communicated his acceptance on December 20 by the mode specified in the offer. The message was not instantly delivered to Rod because the medium of communication, the server, was not operational when Carr sent his email. It was not delivered to Rod until the next morning, after the offer had lapsed. The acceptance would have been timely if it was effective on dispatch, but not if it was effective only on receipt. The mailbox rule applies to noninstantaneous communications through the medium of a third party, so it could apply to email. (*See* section 4.11.2.) If it does, Carr's acceptance is timely (seasonable).

   Even if Carr's email was timely, §2.207(1) also requires that it must be a definite expression of acceptance. Carr's response appears not to be exactly in accord with the offer, but it actually is. His statement that the price must be paid in cash or by cashier's check does not deviate from the offer. Rod's letter is silent on the method of payment, and unless the offer provides to the contrary, payment in cash on delivery is implied in the offer. (This is specifically stated in §2.310(a), which provides that "unless otherwise agreed, payment is due at the time and place at which the buyer is to receive the goods. . . .") Carr's response is therefore a definite expression of acceptance.

2. a. Although Rod's order acknowledgment accepts the transaction-specific terms set out in the order, the preprinted arbitration provision goes beyond the order's terms. The statement at the foot of the acknowledgment declares that the order "is accepted subject to your agreement that any dispute arising out of this transaction will be submitted to . . . arbitration. . . ." This does not use the exact language of §2.207(1) by stating that Rod's acceptance is expressly conditional on Carr's assent to the arbitration provision. However, the language suggests quite

strongly that this is the intent. The words "subject to" are commonly used to express a condition, and the sentence does appear to require Carr's assent to the arbitration term as a prerequisite to moving forward with the transaction. A court might therefore find the response to be an expressly conditional acceptance. However, this conclusion is not assured because courts tend to construe the term "expressly conditional" in §2.207(1) narrowly, and require that the response must clearly indicate that the offeree will not enter the contract unless the offeror assents to the terms in the response. The printed language in the acknowledgment does not actually say that Carr must agree to this term to conclude a contract, and it does not make it clear that Rod will not enter the contract unless Carr agrees to the term. The language may not be strong enough to convey that intent. If the language does not make the acknowledgement into an expressly conditional acceptance, Rod has accepted and a contract has been formed. If the language makes the acceptance expressly conditional, §2.207(1) treats it as a counteroffer, even though the acknowledgment is otherwise in accord with the offer. As a result, Carr and Rod would not have a contract.

b. If a court does hold that the language is not strong enough to make the response into an expressly conditional acceptance, the acknowledgement would qualify as an acceptance, and the arbitration provision would merely be a proposal for a new term. A proposal for a new term in the acceptance does not normally become part of the contract, but §2.207(2) creates a narrow exception to this rule. Section 2.207(2) does not apply unless both parties are merchants. Although Carr would qualify as a merchant under §2.104(l) because he deals in goods of that kind, Rod is not. The Example describes him as a consumer and does not indicate that he bought the car for any purposes other than his personal enjoyment. Even if he bought old cars as a hobby, that would not make him a merchant. To qualify as a merchant under §2.104(1), Rod would have to deal in antique cars by buying and selling them with some regularity, or he would have to hold himself out, by virtue of his occupation, "as having knowledge or skill peculiar to the practices or goods involved in the transaction." This language is not intended to cover an occasional buyer or seller, even if that person has periodically bought or sold antique cars. Section 2.207 does not say how a new term in an acceptance should be handled if one or both of the parties are not merchants. In the absence of a provision governing this situation in §2.207, the common law rule applies, and the additional term is nothing more than a proposal for a post-formation modification, which Rod never accepted. It would therefore not be part of the contract.

c. The parties proceeded with performance of the contract, so there is no longer any question of whether a contract exists. If Carr's response was an acceptance with a proposal for an additional term, the fact that the parties have performed the exchange would not be significant. The analysis to decide if the arbitration provision became part of the contract would be the same as in Explanation b. The term would simply be treated as a proposal for addition to the contract. The subsequent performance by both parties would not be sufficient to indicate that Rod assented to the proposal. Section 2.207 does not recognize performance of the contract as consent to proposals that were never specifically agreed to. A more deliberate and unambiguous signification of assent is required. However, if Carr's response was not an acceptance but a counteroffer, the parties' subsequent performance is important because it would create a contract under §2.207(3). Section 2.207(3) applies where the conduct of both parties recognizes the existence of a contract, even though their writings do not otherwise do so. The resulting contract is on the terms on which the writings agree, supplemented by Article 2 gap fillers. The arbitration provision is the term on which the writings do not agree, so it falls away. In the absence of an arbitration agreement, the default rule is that the parties must have recourse to the courts to resolve disputes.

3. Ballet's order form was an offer. The question is therefore whether Material Alterations' acknowledgment with the conflicting term on return of the goods was an acceptance and, if it was, whether Ballet's or Material Alterations' term became part of the contract. If the common law "mirror image" rule applied, the conflicting term in the acknowledgment relating to return of the goods would make it a counteroffer, unless the conflict was nonmaterial. However, §2.207(1) would likely treat Material Alterations' acknowledgment as a definite and seasonable expression of acceptance, rather than a counteroffer, because it expresses agreement on all the transaction-specific terms and conflicts with the offer only in its standard printed terms.

   This being so, there is a contract, and the question to be resolved is which of the conflicting terms becomes part of it. Because both parties are clearly merchants, §2.207(2) should resolve this question. The problem is that it is not clear if §2.207(2) applies because Material Alterations' term directly conflicts with Ballet's term, and so it is better characterized as "different" rather than "additional." Some courts decline to apply §2.207(2) to "different" terms because the subsection refers only to "additional" terms. A court that adopts this approach will find that as there is nothing in §2.207 that allows the term to enter the contract, it simply falls away. On this analysis, the contract is on Ballet's terms.

   Other courts treat the omission of "different" from §2.207(2) as inadvertent and apply it irrespective of whether the term is "different" or "additional." On this analysis, Material Alterations' term enters the contract only if none of the barriers in §2.207(2) apply. The exclusion in §2.207(2)(a) applies. It does not allow the proposal for the term to enter the contract if the offer expressly limits acceptance to the terms of the offer. Ballet included such language in its order form, so Material Alterations' term cannot enter the contract. It is not necessary to decide whether it is material.

Although there is no statutory language authorizing it, some courts adopt a third approach to "different" terms, under which they use a knockout rule to resolve the conflict. On this approach, both terms relating to return of the goods are eliminated, and the question of whether Ballet can return unsold goods must be resolved by trade usage or, if none exists, by a gap filler. Article 2 makes no provision for the return of goods in the absence of a defect, so the neutral principles of Article 2 would favor Material Alterations in this situation.

4. The proffering of goods on a website, catalog, or advertisement might be an offer, or it might be merely a solicitation for offers from the public. To determine which it is, the language on the website must be interpreted in light of all the circumstances, including the reasonable expectations of the marketplace. If Ballet made the offer, Tutu accepted it by submitting her order, and Ballet is bound. However, if Ballet did not make an offer, then Tutu made the offer when she clicked the "submit order" button. Tutu's order was made on an electronic form supplied by Ballet, but this does not detract from the order's qualities as an offer, and it can reasonably be interpreted as such. It sets out the terms of the proposed transaction with particularity and reasonably appears to invite acceptance by shipment or promise to ship the goods. Ballet's immediate automated response might conceivably be seen as an acceptance, which can be accomplished by an electronic agent, as explained in section 5.8. However, the response may not be an acceptance at all because it has no language that signifies assent to the order. It could therefore be interpreted as nothing more than an acknowledgment that the order was received. If it is an acceptance, Ballet was bound immediately upon communication of the confirmation and it cannot unilaterally change the price of the goods thereafter. If it was not an acceptance, then Ballet's later email is a rejection of Tutu's offer and a solicitation of a new offer from Tutu. Section 2.207 has no relevance on these facts because there is no "battle of the forms." The question simply involves an analysis of offer and acceptance principles to determine if the parties made a contract through their communications. (Note, also, that the facts do not indicate that Ballet's website referred to or contained a link to any standard terms, so there is no question here of whether Tutu is bound through clickwrap or browsewrap assent to any standard terms proffered by Ballet.)

5. The facts make it clear that Tutu and Leo made an oral contract on the phone. Because an enforceable contract came into existence at the time of the telephone call,[14] there are no offer and acceptance issues implicated in Leo's response. The only question to be decided is if Leo's "no return" term was part of the contract. The garbled language of §2.207(1) muddles the very different situations that occur when the additional or different terms are in a confirmation rather than an acceptance. However, where a post-contractual confirmation is concerned, the purpose of the section is not to raise an offer and acceptance issue, but simply to provide the same rule for confirmations as applies to additional or different terms in an acceptance. That is, they only become part of the contract if both parties are merchants and none of the three other barriers to entry in §2.207(2) apply. Because Tutu is not a merchant, the answer is simple: An additional or different term in the confirmation would not become part of the contract unless she specifically agreed to modify the contract by adding it. The twist here is that Leo's term may not actually be additional or different on the facts of the case. In the absence of a term in the contract (whether express or implied through a clearly established usage in the marketplace) that gives Tutu the right to cancel the sale and return the goods if she no longer wants them, she cannot simply change her mind and refuse to accept the goods. Therefore, in the absence of such a return right expressly or impliedly included in the oral contract, Leo's confirmation does not seek to change the terms of the contract.

6. Ballet's order was silent on the means of dispute resolution, and Formfitting's acknowledgment includes a standard arbitration provision. Because the parties have conceded all other issues arising out of §§2.207(1) and (2), the only question raised by this Example is whether the additional arbitration provision in the acceptance falls away as a material alteration of the contract. The language of the contract must be interpreted in context to decide if this alteration is material. The test for materiality, set out in Official Comment 4 to §2.207, is that the term would result in "surprise or hardship" to the offeror. As explained in section 6.3.2b, despite the Official Comment's use of the word "or," these two elements must both be present and are considered in combination. Because arbitration provisions are so commonly included in standard terms, the problem of deciding the impact of such a provision in an acceptance comes up periodically. For example, in *Shaney Co. v. Crain Walnut Shelling, Inc.*, 2012 WL 1979244 (E.D. Cal. 2012), an arbitration provision was included in the seller's order confirmation relating to the

14. The price of the goods is less than $500, so the sale is not subject to the statute of frauds and the oral agreement is enforceable. Had the price been $500 or more, the oral agreement would not have been enforceable on its own, so the subsequent written confirmation would have had to be a record sufficient to satisfy the statute of frauds.

sale of walnuts. The issue was whether the arbitration provision materially altered the contract. One might think that a provision that precludes the buyer from resorting to litigation to enforce its rights under the contract would be important enough to qualify as material. However, the court held that the buyer had not made an adequate showing of surprise and hardship. Even though there was no course of dealing or discussion in negotiations that would have alerted the buyer to the presence of an arbitration provision, such provisions were sufficiently common in the industry to preclude an argument of surprise and hardship. The Example does not provide enough facts about the commercial context of the contract between Ballet and Formfitting to decide if it would point to the same conclusion, but the general prevalence of standard arbitration provisions may make it difficult for an offeror to claim the degree of reasonable surprise and hardship that would make such a term a material alteration of the contract.

CHAPTER 7

Consideration

§7.1 CONSIDERATION AS THE BASIS OF CONTRACT OBLIGATION

When the word "consideration" entered the lexicon of English law, many centuries ago, its usage by lawyers was apparently close to its lay meaning of "reflection," "contemplation," or "thinking." It was a vague concept that probably did no more than assert the general principle that a promise must be seriously contemplated and deliberately intended to be legally binding. As courts expounded on this principle over the years, they gradually embellished it so that it came to require something more than a serious and deliberate intent to be bound. It required that the promise of a party (the promisor) must be exchanged for some quid pro quo to be given or promised to the promisor by the person to whom the promise was made (the promisee).[1] In other words, a purely gratuitous promise—one that is not "paid for" in some way—cannot be enforced as a contract. This is the essence of consideration doctrine.

1. In most contracts, both parties make promises to each other, so each of the parties is both a promisor with regard to the promise made by that party, and a promisee with regard to the other party's promise. In the context of consideration doctrine, the focus is on whether the promise of one of the parties is enforceable as contractually binding, so "promisor" denotes the person whose promise is sought to be enforced, and "promisee" refers to the recipient of that promise whose return promise is challenged as insufficient to constitute consideration.

Consideration doctrine is peculiar to the common law. Civilian jurisdictions have never had a similar doctrine, and simply operate under the general principle that a contract must be founded on just cause, which is constituted by a serious and deliberate intent to be bound. The UNIDROIT Principles expressly adopt the civilian position by stating, in Article 3.2, that a contract is concluded by the mere agreement of the parties, without any further requirement. (The CISG does not directly address consideration doctrine and largely defers, in Article 4, to domestic law on issues relating to the validity of a contract.) This shows that it is possible for a legal system to operate without the doctrine and that many of the functions that it serves could be accomplished by the use of other doctrines of contract law.

Consideration doctrine could be summed up by stating a set of rules, but recitation of these rules would not present an accurate picture of the doctrine. Over time, courts have manipulated the rules by creating exceptions and legal fictions that permit the enforcement of promises that may not neatly fit into a more doctrinaire approach to consideration. In addition, the doctrines of promissory estoppel and moral obligation, discussed in Chapters 8 and 9, recognize alternative grounds for enforcing some promises that lack consideration. It is therefore not enough simply to learn the rules of consideration and to attempt to apply them mechanically to a set of facts. Consideration must be studied with an awareness of the purpose of these rules, a focus on their impact in each transaction, and an understanding of the way in which consideration doctrine fits in with the broader principles and policies of contract law.

§7.2 THE ESSENCE AND SCOPE OF CONSIDERATION

Consideration doctrine is concerned with the enforcement of a promise—a commitment to perform in the future. In essence, the doctrine does not recognize a promise as a valid and enforceable contractual commitment unless the person making the promise (the promisor) received consideration from the person to whom the promise was made (the promisee) in exchange for it. Because consideration doctrine applies only to promises, no consideration is required to validate a transfer that has already been executed. For example, Benny Fishery was in financial difficulty, so his friend, Phil Anthropist promised to give Benny a gift of $10,000 to help him. This was an outright gift with no strings attached. Phil made it clear that the money was intended as a gift, and he did not impose any conditions on it or ask Benny for anything in return. If Phil later changes his mind and refuses to pay the $10,000, Benny cannot enforce the promise because Phil merely promised a gift, without any consideration given or promised by Benny in exchange for it. However, once Phil has actually paid the $10,000 to Benny, consideration doctrine does not apply and Phil cannot demand the return of the money on the grounds that Benny did not give any consideration for it.

Consideration doctrine applies to a spectrum of cases. The two situations in which the absence or presence of consideration is obvious lie at opposite ends of the spectrum. At the one end are unquestionably gratuitous cases, in which there can be no argument that the promisee gave any consideration. These cases typically involve a promise motivated by kinship, friendship, or generosity, in which the promisor unconditionally undertakes to make a future gift and asks for and receives nothing in return. This type of promise is illustrated by the above example of Phil's purely gratuitous promise to pay $10,000 to Benny. Such promises are not legally binding. At the other end of the spectrum is the straightforward commercial exchange in which the promise is clearly exchanged for an economically equivalent price, so that there is no plausible argument that consideration was lacking. For example, Carr Buyer entered into a contract with Value Vehicles under which Carr agreed to buy a new car from Value for $30,000, its market value. In this commercial exchange, Carr's promise to pay the $30,000 is clearly consideration for Value's promise to deliver the car to him. The parties have a valid contract. Between these two poles lie the most interesting and complex cases, in which apparently commercial promises are made for an unclear or questionable exchange, and apparently gratuitous promises have strings attached to them.

§7.3 THE ELEMENTS OF CONSIDERATION: DETRIMENT, BENEFIT, AND BARGAINED-FOR EXCHANGE

As noted above, exchange is the fundamental component of consideration. For consideration to exist, each party must suffer a legal detriment, and those legal detriments must be exchanged for each other. The exchange of legal detriments leads to a corresponding legal benefit to each of the contracting parties. That is, in this exchange transaction, each party suffers a legal detriment by giving up property, money, or some legal right, and the receipt of that detriment translates into a benefit to the other party. This formulation, known as the "bargain theory" of consideration has been firmly established in the law for many years and is reflected in Restatement, Second, §71(1), which states that consideration is constituted by a bargained-for return promise or performance. Section 71(2) goes on to explain that a return promise or performance is bargained for if the promisor seeks it in exchange for the promise and it is given by the promisee in exchange for that promise. The following discussion gives more concrete form to this abstract description of the doctrine by explaining what is meant by the terms of art, "detriment," "benefit," and "bargained-for exchange."

§7.3.1 The Meaning of "Detriment"

A legal detriment is any relinquishment of a legal right. In the context of consideration doctrine, "detriment" does not mean that the person has suffered some horrible harm, loss, or injury. In fact, a detriment could even be something that benefits or advances the interests of the person who incurs the detriment. The important element is not harm but the yielding of a legal right. It could take the form of an immediate act (that is, doing or giving something), a forbearance (refraining from something), or the partial or complete abandonment of an intangible right.

Consideration may be found either in the action of incurring the detriment or in the promise to perform (to act or forbear) in the future. That is, provided that an immediate performance would be a detriment, a promise of that performance creates a future liability to perform, which is also a detriment. (Stated differently, a promise to do something in the future is an abandonment of the legal right not to do it, and is therefore consideration.) In the example of the sale of the car by Value Vehicles to Carr for $30,000, Carr's payment of $30,000 would be a detriment to him. Therefore, his promise to pay $30,000 is equally a detriment. In the same way, Value's detriment would be the delivery of the car to Carr, so its promise to do so is likewise a detriment. This a standard bilateral contract, in which the promise by each party is exchanged for and induces the promise by the other. To be a promise, and hence a detriment, the undertaking must be a genuine commitment. If it is too vague, too discretionary, or too qualified, it may not qualify as a promise. This is discussed in section 7.9.

In the above example, consideration consists of the exchange of promises to act in the future. Consideration may also be furnished by a forbearance from acting or a promise to forbear from acting in the future. For example, Carr bought a new car from Value Vehicles last year. The car turned out to be a lemon, which gave Carr the right to sue Value for damages under a consumer protection statute. Carr exercised this right by commencing suit for damages of $30,000 against Value. Value offered to settle the suit, and the parties entered into a settlement agreement under which Value agreed to deliver a new car to Carr in exchange for Carr's agreement to dismiss his suit against Value. Carr's detriment is his promise to forbear from continuing with a suit that he had the legal right to bring.

Diagram 7A illustrates the exchange of detriments in these examples.

Diagram 7A

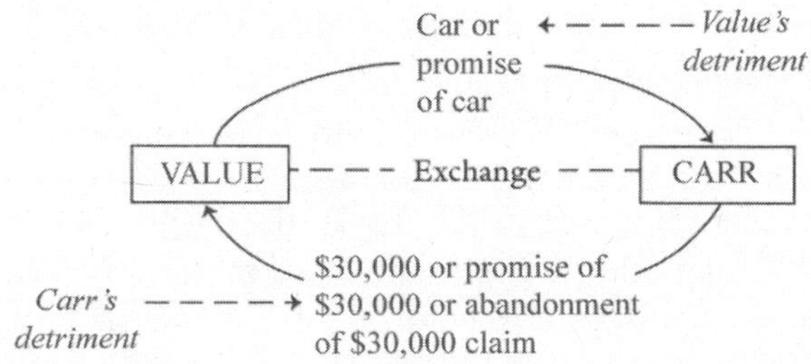

In the above transactions, it is clear that both Carr's and Value's detriments have economic value. However, as long as a party has suffered a detriment by giving up a legal right, it is not necessary that the detriment has a value that is measurable in economic terms. It is also not necessary that the detriment must have been detrimental in its usual meaning of harmful. It is important to understand that the concept of legal detriment in consideration doctrine focuses purely on the abandonment of a legal right, not on an economic loss or injury. For example, Phil Anthropist is unhappy that his friend, Benny Fishery, smokes. Phil therefore offers to pay Benny $5,000 if Benny quits smoking. In the usual sense of the word, giving up smoking is not detrimental to Benny, but is beneficial. Notwithstanding, because Benny has the legal right to smoke, his promise to refrain from doing so (forbearance) is a legal detriment and can qualify as consideration for Phil's promise of $5,000. Restatement, Second, §79(a) reflects this principle by stating that if the requirement of consideration is met, there is no additional requirement of loss or disadvantage to the promisee.

Hamer v. Sidway, 27 N.E. 256 (N.Y. 1891), is an old favorite case illustrating the meaning of detriment. Uncle William Story promised $5,000 to his nephew, William II, if the nephew refrained from drinking, using tobacco, swearing, and playing cards or billiards for money until he reached the age of 21. Young Willie complied but had not been paid by the time that his uncle died. The court enforced Willie's claim against Uncle William's estate. It rejected the estate's argument that Willie had not given consideration for his uncle's promise. The court found that Willie's abstention from the stated activities pursuant to the promise was sufficient detriment, because it was the abandonment of his legal right to engage in them. The legal benefit to Uncle William did not need to be economic. His benefit lay in having his expressed desire fulfilled.

§7.3.2 The Relationship Between Detriment to the Promisee and Benefit to the Promisor

In *Hamer*, the court used the definition of consideration articulated in an earlier English case: Consideration "may consist in either some right, interest, profit or benefit accruing to the one party, or some forbearance, detriment, loss, or responsibility given, suffered, or undertaken by the other." This definition, which can still be found in some modern cases, is inadequate and misleading because it does not articulate a crucial requirement of consideration that is universally accepted in modern law: It is not enough that each party has suffered a detriment. It is also required that these detriments are exchanged for each other. That is, the detriment suffered by each party must induce the other's detriment. Nevertheless, the decision in *Hamer* is consistent with this requirement because it is clear that the detriments suffered by the parties in *Hamer* did induce each other—Willie's detriment of abandoning his right to engage in the activities was exchanged for the Uncle William's detriment of promising to pay $5,000. Benefit is not really an element of consideration, but a consequence of it. A benefit accrues to each party because it is in the nature of an exchange transaction that the detriment suffered by each party benefits the other. Willie's benefit is easy to see because it consists of an economic reward—the promised $5,000 payment. Uncle William's benefit is less obvious because it has no apparent economic value. Nevertheless, he bargained for controlling his nephew's conduct and he benefitted by getting what he bargained for. Stated differently, under the bargain theory of consideration, benefit to a party plays only an evidentiary role. If a benefit can be identified, this is strong evidence that the detriments were bargained for in exchange for each other.

Phil's promise to pay Benny $5,000 for quitting smoking reinforces this point. Phil does not receive any tangible economic benefit from Benny's forbearance, but because the parties apparently intended to make an exchange, Phil's expected benefit was getting what he wanted—Benny's giving up smoking. The crucial point is that, in the same way that "detriment" does not require actual harm or suffering, "benefit" does not requires a tangible economic gain. Instead, benefit is determined by interpreting the transaction to decide if the parties bargained for the exchange of detriments. This is illustrated by Diagram 7B.

Diagram 7B

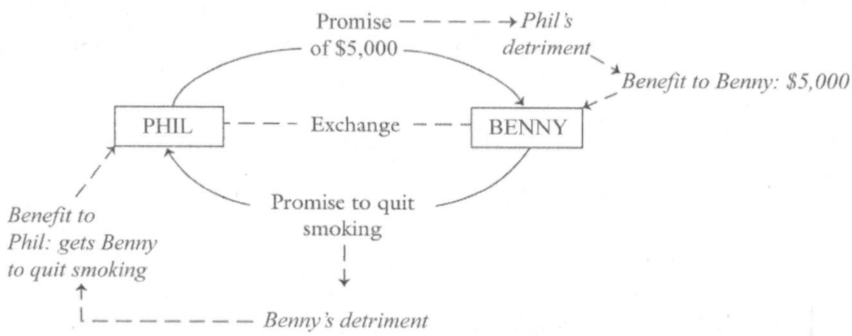

The subjective motivation that Uncle William or Phil might have had in curtailing the behavior of Willie or Benny is not dispositive. It does not matter if they were motivated by kindly concern or were just interfering and controlling busybodies. The intent to exchange the detriments (the mutual inducement) is determined objectively. If it is apparent from the terms of the transaction, reasonably interpreted in context, that the parties intended an exchange of detriments, the detriment incurred by each of the parties translates into the benefit received by the other. This does not mean that subjective motive is entirely irrelevant, because it could be evidence of intent to make the exchange. Similarly, if it is possible to identify a tangible gain or advantage to a party, this bolsters the argument that the party did in fact bargain for the detriment suffered by the other. This issue is discussed further in the next section.

§7.3.3 The Bargained-for Exchange

As stated earlier, the bargain theory is well established and is reflected in Restatement, Second, §71, which requires that a performance or return promise must be bargained for to constitute consideration. That is, based on the parties' manifestation of intent, it must reasonably appear that the performances or promises of the parties induced each other: Each party must have manifested the intent to seek the other's performance or promise, and must have manifested the intent to exchange it for the return promise or performance. Restatement, Second, §33 reinforces this by defining a bargain as an agreement (in turn defined as a manifestation of mutual assent) to exchange promises, performances, or promise for performance. The bargain theory recognizes that contracts are voluntary exchange relationships involving reciprocal promises or performances. It means nothing if a party suffers a legal detriment unless the parties agree that it is the price for the promise. The use of the word "bargain" does not suggest that the parties must dicker back and forth or negotiate at length. It means simply that each manifests agreement to render the performance stipulated by the other.

§7.3.4 The Distinction Between Bargained-for and Incidental Detriment

In the example of the sale of the car by Value Vehicles to Carr, the fact that the parties had agreed to an exchange is obvious. In most commercial transactions the existence of a bargained-for exchange is not in question. Exchange also seems to be quite clear in the case of Phil's promise of $5,000 for Benny's giving up smoking. Even though the motivation is apparently not commercial, it is possible to identify Phil's incentive to alter his friend's behavior. However, such an incentive to induce action is not always as apparent. For example, Phil Anthropist came across a box of old vinyl records when he was clearing out his attic. He did not want the records anymore and remembered that his friend, Benny Fishery, had recently bought a record player and was enthusiastically buying old records. Phil sent a text message to Benny saying "I found a box of vinyl records in my attic. They are yours if you would like them. I left the box on my porch. You can collect it from the porch sometime this week if you are interested." Under the broad concept of legal detriment, Benny's action of going to Phil's porch and picking up the box of records is a detriment because he gave up the legal right not to do that. However, this detriment is only incidental to Phil's promise. The facts provide no basis for concluding that Phil bargained for Benny's picking up the records as the price exchanged for them. It is simply the action needed to take delivery of the gift of the records. This conclusion is based, not on a probing of Phil's innermost thoughts but on the apparent purpose of his offer, based on an understanding of human motivation. There is no evidence from which one could reasonably understand that Phil was so desirous of having Benny visit his porch to collect the records that this was a bargained-for benefit that he sought to induce by the promise of the records. This is shown in Diagram 7C. However, it is worth recognizing the subtlety of the distinction between incidental and bargained-for detriment, which can be illustrated by a slight change in the perspective of this example: If Benny does not accept Phil's invitation to pick up the records, Phil will have to dispose of them in some other way. Maybe the benefit of being relieved of that burden could lead to the conclusion that this was not an incidental detriment but a bargained-for exchange.

Diagram 7C.

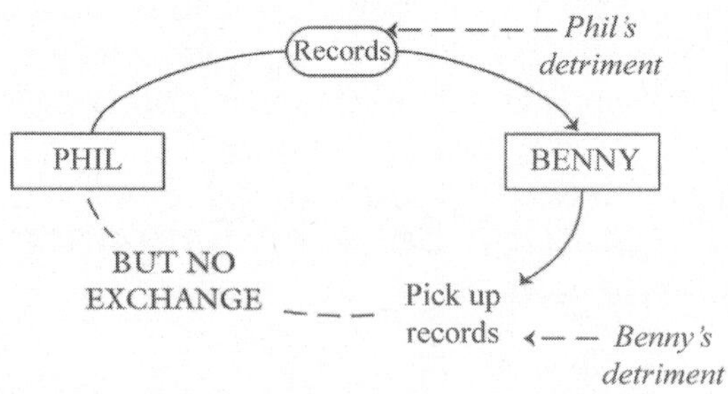

The same conclusion would follow if Uncle William had said to Willie, "I plan to give you $5,000 for your birthday. Give me the routing number for your bank account so that I can transfer the funds to you." Uncle William's apparent purpose is to give a gift to Willie. The facts of the transaction reveal no reason why Uncle William might want the routing number for any purpose other than to make the fund transfer, so the reasonable interpretation of his request is that he is not bargaining for the benefit of getting the routing number in exchange for his promise. Instead, it is just the means that he plans to use to deliver his gift. Willie's detriment in giving the routing number to Uncle William is just incidental to the proposed transfer of the gift. On the other hand, if the facts indicate some benefit that Uncle William may gain from having the routing number, Willie's revelation of the number would no longer be just an incidental detriment, but a bargained-for exchange. The dividing line between a detriment that is incidental, and one that is consideration can be indistinct. However, as explained in section 7.3.2, identifying a benefit to the promisor is probative evidence that the parties intended an exchange of detriments.

§7.3.5 The Distinction Between a Detriment and a Condition of Gift

a. A Gift with Conditions Distinguished from Detriment

When a promise of a gift is made subject to conditions, the promisee's acquiescence in those conditions may seem like a legal detriment, but may not qualify as one. The distinction between a legal detriment and a condition of gift can be subtle and elusive. This can be illustrated by varying the facts of the example in section 7.2 involving the gift from Phil Anthropist to Benny Fishery. Benny Fishery was in financial difficulty and could not pay the $10,000 owed on his credit card. His friend, Phil Anthropist, promised to give Benny a gift of $10,000 to help him. Phil made it clear that this would be a gift and that Benny did not have to repay it give him anything else in exchange for it. However, Phil did insist that Benny must use the money to pay off his credit card, and not for any other purpose. Benny promised to use the money for that purpose. If Phil later changes his mind and refuses to pay the $10,000, Benny still cannot enforce the promise because he gave Phil no consideration for the promise of $10,000. It may sound as if Benny's promise to use the money for the purpose designated by Phil is a legal detriment, but this should not qualify as consideration because Benny has not actually suffered a legal detriment. At the time that Benny made the promise, he had not yet received the money from Phil, so he had no right to spend it. Therefore, when Benny promises to use Phil's prospective payment in a specified way, he does not forbear from any legal right that he had at the time that he made the promise. On this reasoning, there is no contract. Phil has simply made a gift to Benny with a condition attached as to its use.

b. Conditional Gifts to Charitable Organizations

The same situation may occur when a donor promises a gift to a charitable organization. For example, Al Umnus promised to donate $10,000 to his alma mater and specified that the gift was to be allocated to the college's scholarship program. The college accepted the promise and agreed to use the funds as specified by Al. As a doctrinal matter, this should be treated in the same way as Phil's promise to Benny. At the time of its promise, the funds did not yet belong to the college, so it had no right to spend Al's money. It therefore did not forbear from any legal right relating to the use of the money.[2] On this reasoning, there is no contract. Al has simply made a gift to the college with a condition attached relating to the use of the gift. Although this is the logical result of applying the requirement of detriment, some courts have not applied the doctrine strictly where the donation is promised to a charitable organization, and have found consideration in the organization's promise to use the donation for the purpose stipulated.

In *Massachusetts Eye & Ear Infirmary v. Eugene B. Casey Foundation*, 417 F. Supp. 2d 192 (D. Mass. 2006), the foundation pledged to give $2 million to the infirmary to be used for a voice restoration research program. When the foundation retracted its pledge, the infirmary sued it for breach of contract. The foundation moved to dismiss the case on several grounds, one of which was that the infirmary gave no consideration to the foundation for its promise. The court refused to dismiss the case on the basis that there was a colorable argument that the infirmary gave consideration for the pledge by committing to use the funds only for the express purpose of supporting the voice restoration program and by undertaking to submit biannual reports to the foundation. The infirmary's undertakings could have been characterized as no more than conditions of the gift, but the court justified its holding on the policy rationale that the public interest in protecting and supporting charitable subscriptions calls for a different standard to decide on the existence of consideration in relation to charitable pledges.

c. Consideration Beyond a Promise to Use a Gift for Designated Purposes

Even if a court finds no consideration in the donee's promise to use the funds for the purpose designated by the donor, consideration is present if the donee has given or promised something beyond that. Say, for example, Al and the college had agreed not only that the promised funds would be used for the scholarship program, but also that the college would include

2. Apart from this, the college may have already had the legal duty to spend donated money in furtherance of its mission, so the preexisting duty rule, discussed in section 7.5, may be another ground for finding no consideration.

Al's name on a donor's list published in its alumni magazine. The college's promise to publicize the gift goes beyond the use of the money, so it can constitute a legal detriment. The detriment to the college seems small in relation to the value of the gift promised by Al, and Al may or may not have actually been induced to make the promise by the college's promise to recognize his generosity publicly. However, that does not matter. As discussed in section 7.7, consideration doctrine does not generally require courts to evaluate the adequacy of consideration.

For example, *PeaceTech Lab, Inc. v. C5 Accelerate, LLC*, 2021 WL 106718 (D.C. 2021), concerned a promise of $1.5 million by a company, Pinard S.à.r.l., to PeaceTech, a nonprofit organization with the mission of promoting peace through technology. The donation was promised for the specific purpose of creating an accelerator program for organizations developing peace-building technologies. In addition to expressly requiring PeaceTech to use the funds for the stipulated purpose, the pledge provided that the donor would have the sole naming rights for the laboratory in which the accelerator program would be operated, and it would be recognized on a plaque, a donor wall, a website, and a press release. Pinard never paid the promised donation and PeaceTech sued. Pinard sought to dismiss the case on several grounds, including that PeaceTech gave it no consideration for its promise. The court found consideration. It obliquely suggested that a promise to use a gift for the express purpose given could be consideration, but it did not have to rely on this principle, because it held that the grant of the naming and publicity rights was an additional detriment and was therefore consideration for the promise of the gift.

In *King v. Trustees of Boston University*, 420 Mass. 52 (1995), the estate of Dr. Martin Luther King Jr. sued the university to recover papers that Dr. King had deposited with the university library, alleging that Dr. King had given the university only temporary custody of his papers. At the time of handing over the papers, Dr. King had written a letter to the university reserving ownership of the papers until his death, but stating that they would become the property of the university when he died. In taking custody of the papers, the university committed to protect and index them and to make them available to researchers. The question was whether this promise to transfer ownership of the papers was merely an unenforceable gift, or a contract for which the university had given consideration. Although the university's promises could be interpreted as merely conditions relating to the use of the gift, the court upheld the jury's finding that the promises were consideration because the duties assumed by the university went beyond a mere promise to use the gift as instructed by the donor.[3]

---

3. In both *King* and *Massachusetts Eye &and Ear Infirmary*, the court also discussed the issue of whether the promise would be enforceable, even in the absence of consideration, on the grounds that the donee had acted in reliance on the promise. In such a situation, the promise could have been enforceable under the doctrine of promissory estoppel, covered in Chapter 8.

§7.4 THE PURPOSE AND FUNCTION OF CONSIDERATION DOCTRINE

§7.4.1 The Formal and Substantive Basis for the Doctrine in Relation to Gratuitous Promises

There has been much written over the years in an effort to explain why the consideration doctrine arose in the common law, and why it has survived. A plausible argument can be made that there really is no coherent and persuasive policy basis for the continued existence of the doctrine, which is nothing more than an historical relic that has survived in our law because of inertia and tradition. Indeed, the various policy justifications that have been advanced by courts and scholars over the years seem to be quite dubious and not very convincing. Whatever the rationale for the continued vitality of the doctrine, it unquestionably remains part of our law, and courts routinely assert that the presence of consideration is one of the crucial elements of a valid contract.

Probably the most influential and enduring justification of consideration doctrine is Professor Lon Fuller's 1941 article, *Consideration and Form* (41 Colum. L. Rev. 799). Fuller identified both formal and substantive bases for consideration. He identified three formal functions of consideration, which he called "evidentiary," "cautionary," and "channeling." In essence, he argued that by requiring consideration, the law gives courts some evidentiary indication that a contract was intended, allows them to distinguish between contractual commitments and mere informal or tentative expressions of intent, and makes the promisor aware of having made a serious legal commitment. Since Fuller wrote his article there has been much scholarly discussion of his identification and characterization of the formal functions of consideration. Some of the discussion reinforces his views, and some of it refutes them. Nevertheless, Fuller's analysis is still widely cited, and the comment to Restatement, Second, §72 adopts it.

Fuller recognized that the formal functions of consideration do not fully justify the doctrine's continued vitality in our law. If its role was purely formal, it could easily be dispensed with because these formal functions could be accomplished simply by having a rule that upholds written, signed promises. American law does not have such a rule.[4] In fact, as section 7.7.3

4. In this respect, modern law has moved away from older common law, which did have a formal device—the seal—that could be used to make a promise binding without consideration. The promisor could create a binding gratuitous promise by sealing the document. Originally, the seal was made by dripping sealing wax on the document and impressing the hot wax with a signet ring. In time it became acceptable simply to append the letters "L.S." (*locus sigilli*—meaning "in place of a seal") to a signature. The seal did not develop

explains, the parties cannot usually circumvent the requirement of consideration by using sham or nominal consideration purely for the purpose of validating the promise. Fuller therefore also identified a substantive (policy-based) justification for the doctrine. The doctrine's substantive function may better explain its durability.

The substantive basis of consideration lies in the policy that the law should not hold a person to a promise that was made gratuitously. The point here is that the law should be concerned only with the enforcement of exchanges, and should not hold a promisee to a promise motivated by affection, generosity, or altruism, and lacking in any return benefit. Because the promisor has received nothing in exchange for the promise, and the promisee loses nothing by nonenforcement except the prospect of a gift, the promisor should be able to recant without legal liability. This policy protects the promisor from improvidence. It also indirectly protects the promisor's heirs and creditors by ensuring that their claims against the promisor's assets will take priority over a promise to donate them.

There is a contrary policy argument, especially in relation to charitable promises. Charitable organizations serve a crucial role in society, and important public interests are served by the sustenance and support of these organizations. A strict application of consideration doctrine precludes enforcement of these promises, but flexibility in the concepts of detriment and exchange may give a court a basis for finding consideration in cases that are not clear-cut. In addition, the doctrine of promissory estoppel, discussed in Chapter 8, provides an alternative basis for enforcing promises without consideration if the promisor induced the promisee to act in justifiable reliance on the promise and enforcement of the promise is necessary to avoid injustice.

§7.4.2 Consideration Doctrine in the Commercial Context

Although consideration doctrine plays an important role in precluding the enforcement of gratuitous promises, it is not confined to promises of gifts, but can arise in commercial transactions that are not motivated by generosity, charity, or altruism. Of course, consideration is not a problem in most commercial transactions because the bargained-for exchange of detriments is commonly the obvious basis of those transactions. Nevertheless, there are situations in which consideration issues do arise in commercial

---

as an exception to consideration doctrine but predates the doctrine, which applied only to "informal" (i.e., unsealed) promises. Today, the seal has been abolished or given only residual evidentiary effect in most jurisdictions. In only a few states has the formal device of the seal been replaced by a statutory method of formally validating a gift promise.

transactions because there is some problem with the apparent consideration that is claimed to support the promise. For example, a claimed detriment may not actually qualify as a legal detriment because of a preexisting duty (*see* sections 7.5 and 7.6), or because the apparent consideration is patently inadequate (*see* section7.7), or because the detriment was suffered before the promise and therefore could not actually have been exchanged for it (*see* section 7.8), or because the apparent consideration in the form of a promise is illusory or unenforceable (*see* section 7.9). In a commercial transaction, in which there is no charitable or donative intent, the rationale relating to the nonenforcement of gifts is inapplicable. The usual justification for not enforcing the promise is that the lack of consideration shows that the parties did not have the legal intent to create a binding contractual relationship.

§7.5 DETRIMENT AND PREEXISTING DUTY

§7.5.1 The Basic Rule

If a detriment is the relinquishment of a right, it follows that a person does not suffer a detriment by doing or promising to do something that the person is already obliged to do or by forbearing to do something that the person is already not entitled to do. Therefore, the rule is often stated that the performance of, or promise to perform, a preexisting duty is not consideration. For example, say that Al Pine owns a ski lodge. He entered into a contract with Ava Lanche under which he sold the lodge to Ava for $1,000,000. Before the sale closed, Al realized that he had underpriced the lodge, which was worth at least $1,250,000. He approached Ava and asked her to agree to change the price to $1,250,000. Ava recognized that she had underpaid and felt that the lodge was still a good buy at $1,250,000. Not wishing to take advantage of Al's mistake, Ava agreed to pay the extra amount, and the parties amended their written contract. An agreement to modify an existing contract is itself a contract, and needs new consideration, separate from the consideration given under the original contract. Therefore, the agreement to modify the contract by increasing the price is not a valid contract because Al gave Ava no consideration for her promise to pay $250,000 more. Al already had a duty to transfer the lodge under the original contract, and he neither gave nor promised anything new. It cannot be a legal detriment for Al to promise what he is already obliged to do. Because Ava's second promise is not binding, she can refuse to perform it and can insist on transfer of the lodge for the original price of $1,000,000. This is shown in Diagram 7D.

Diagram 7D

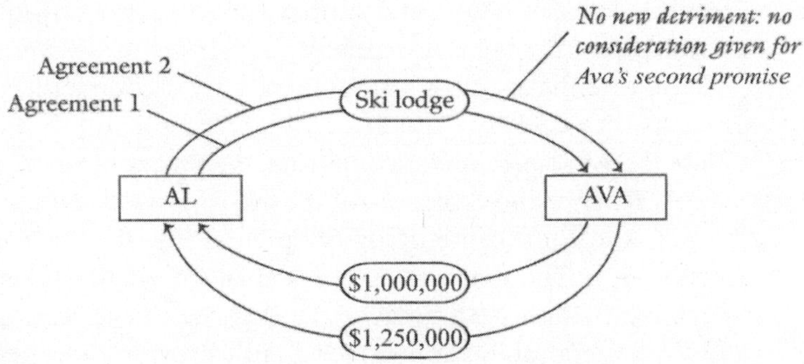

The preexisting duty rule only applies if the performance of the promisee is completely encompassed by the preexisting duty. Therefore, if Al had in any way added to his performance or obligation as an apparent incentive to Ava's agreement to pay more (for example, Al offered to include a snowplow in the sale), this new increase in his detriment would be sufficient to constitute consideration for Ava's promise of more money. It would not matter if the snow plow was worth much less than $250,000 because, as explained in section 7.7, economic equivalence is not normally required in the exchange. *See* Diagram 7E.

Diagram 7E

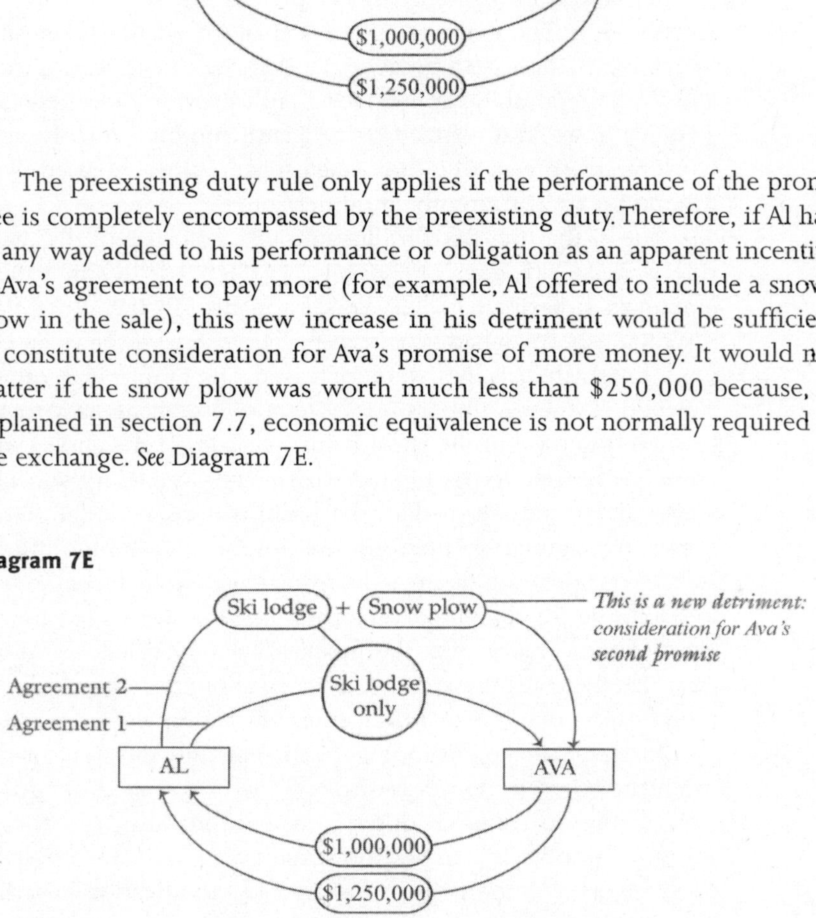

§7.5.2 The Justification for the Rule Where the Duty Is Owed to the Promisor: Coerced Modifications

It is quite easy to express the preexisting duty rule in its basic form, but application of the rule is seldom this simple. In some cases, the problem may be factual. For example, it may be unclear if a preexisting duty exists or if the detriment in the later agreement really is coextensive with this duty.

However, the bigger problem is a conceptual one. Why have the rule at all? True, it is consistent with and simply a specific application of the concept of detriment, so the rule is doctrinally justifiable. But what policy does it serve?

The rule makes most sense when, after a contract has been made, one of the parties coerces a modification by threatening to breach the contract unless the other promises to increase the payment or other return performance. When a modification of an existing contract has been coerced in this way, the court can employ the preexisting duty rule to void the unfair modification. The court does not actually need the preexisting duty rule to achieve this purpose because the doctrines of duress, unconscionability, and the general obligation of good faith provide more efficient and direct grounds to avoid a coerced or bad faith modification. (*See* section 13.9.) However, the preexisting duty rule can sometimes be used as an alternative ground for overturning the modification.

One of the best-known illustrations of this use of the preexisting duty rule is *Alaska Packers' Ass'n v. Domenico*, 117 F. 99 (9th Cir. 1902). A cannery employed fishermen to harvest salmon during the short Alaskan season. After the fishermen had been transported to Alaska, they refused to continue work unless their wages were increased. The employer acquiesced because it would have been impossible to get a replacement crew to Alaska in time to harvest salmon in the short fishing season. At the end of the season, the employer refused to pay the fishermen any more than the originally agreed wages. The fishermen sued for the additional payment, but the court refused to award judgment to them on the ground that the modification contract lacked consideration because the fishermen had incurred no new detriment in exchange for the employer's promise of a wage increase. Although the basis of the opinion was the preexisting duty rule, the opinion makes it clear that the court was more concerned about the extortionate nature of the modification than the technical rules of consideration doctrine.

As noted above, although the preexisting duty rule can be used to invalidate coerced modifications, it really is not necessary for this purpose because the doctrines of duress, unconscionability, and the general obligation of good faith. In addition, the doctrine is an unreliable means of preventing the enforcement of a coerced modification because a promisee who knows of the rule can evade it simply by agreeing to undertake some minor additional detriment. A modest new detriment would preclude invalidation under the preexisting duty rule because the courts do not generally inquire into adequacy of consideration. (*See* section 7.7.) For example, the fishermen would have made it harder for the employer to challenge the modification on grounds of lack of consideration if they had promised, in apparent exchange for the increase in wages, to sing a sea shanty every Friday before starting work.

Another problem with the application of the preexisting duty rule to modifications is that it covers all modifications, even those such as the genuinely consensual increase in the price of the ski lodge in the example of Al and Ava's modification of their contract. In these circumstances, unless the parties provide for some new detriment by the promisee, application of the rule precludes parties from making a binding agreement to modify the obligations of one of them, even when circumstances justify a modification and the promisor genuinely agreed to it without unfair pressure. The application of the rule under these circumstances allows a party to use a technicality to renege on fairly agreed commitment. (This is the common law position, which is not followed in UCC §2.209, as discussed in section 7.5.3.)

The requirement of consideration for a modification may arise where an employer requires an existing employee to agree to a change of the terms of employment. For example, the original employment agreement had no provision restricting employees from working for a competing business after leaving the employment. The employer subsequently requires the employee to sign a noncompetition agreement, under which the employee undertakes not to engage in any business in direct competition with the employer, anywhere in the state for one year after leaving the employment.[5] Had the noncompetition agreement been included in the original employment contract, there would be no consideration problem because it would have been part of the bundle of obligations undertaken by the employee in exchange for the employer's promise of employment and payment. (Both cases cited below so held.) However, where the noncompetition agreement is entered into after the employment has commenced, it is a modification of the employment agreement. The employer must therefore give the employee new consideration in exchange for the undertaking not to compete. In *Socko v. Mid-Atlantic Systems of CPA, Inc.*, 99 A.3d 928 (Pa. Super. Ct. 2014), the court held a noncompetition agreement signed by an employee during the course of employment to be invalid because there was no change in the employee's employment status or any other consideration given to the employee in exchange for it. The court also held that because the law disfavors noncompetition agreements by employees, the court must inquire into the adequacy of consideration[6] in this situation—the consideration given to

5. Noncompetition agreements are discussed in section 13.13.3. In short, a noncompetition agreement is an undertaking by a person associated with a business (such as the seller of a business, a partner in a business, or an employee of a business) that upon leaving the business the person will not work in competition with the business in a specified area for a specified time. Such agreements are carefully regulated by courts because they have the harmful effect of stifling competition and restricting the promisor's freedom to make a living. In some states a noncompetition agreement by an employee is per se invalid. Even where the agreement is not absolutely unenforceable, a court will only enforce it to the extent that it is reasonable in its scope and protects a genuine economic interest of the promisee, such as customer goodwill or confidential information.

6. Adequacy of consideration is discussed in section 7.7.

the employee must be new, real, and valuable. It may not be nominal or of disproportionally small value.

In *Socko* the employee was an at-will employee,[7] and the court said that the mere fact that the employer continued to employ him was not in itself enough to constitute consideration. However, in *Runzheimer International, Ltd. v. Friedlen*, 2015 WL 1933300 (Wis. 2015), the court reached the opposite conclusion. Friedlen had been employed by Runzheimer for 15 years as an at-will employee when Runzheimer required all employees, including him, to sign a noncompetition agreement. Runzheimer told Friedlen that if he did not sign the agreement, he would be fired. Although Friedlen was an at-will employee, it was enough for consideration purposes that Runzheimer forbore from firing him at the time in exchange for the undertaking not to compete. That is, as an at-will employee, Friedlen had no guarantee of continued employment in the future, yet the mere forbearance from firing him immediately qualified as consideration. Contrary to *Socko*, the court applied the usual rule that it would not inquire into the adequacy of Runzheimer's consideration.[8]

Sysco Philadelphia, LLC v. Silva, 525 F. Supp. 3d 582 (E.D. Pa. 2021), also involved a noncompetition agreement entered into some time after the employment began. Sysco told Silva, an at-will employee, that he would be terminated if he did not sign the noncompetition agreement. When Silva later left Sysco to work for a competitor, Sysco sought to enjoin him from violating the noncompetition agreement. The issue was whether Sysco gave Silva consideration in exchange for entering into the noncompetition agreement. Sysco argued that it had given him consideration in the form of a complex new compensation package and job security. However, on a close examination of the compensation package, the court found that Silva actually earned less under the new compensation structure that he had earned before it, and Sysco's claim of better job security was specious because he remained an at-will employee. The court pointed out that in exchange for giving up his valuable right to use his talents in the market, Silva had received nothing more than a pay cut, which could not possibly qualify as consideration.[9]

---

7. An at-will employment contract, as opposed to a contract for a stated term, permits either party to terminate the employment at any time—the employee may resign, or the employer may fire the employee at will, for any reason other than a reason (such as unlawful discrimination) prohibited by law.

8. As it happened, Runzheimer continued to employ Friedlen for 29 months after he signed the agreement.

9. As in *Socko*, the court recognized that it is appropriate to inquire into adequacy of the consideration for a noncompetition agreement. However, inadequacy of consideration was not an issue in this case because there was no consideration at all.

§7.5.3 The Abolition of the Preexisting Duty Rule in Relation to Modifications Under Article 2

Although the preexisting duty rule precluded the enforcement of Al's promise to pay more for real property (the ski lodge), the result would have been different if the contract involved a sale of goods. For example, Al and Ava contracted for the sale of Al's skis to Ava for $100, and the parties later agreed to increase the price to $150. UCC §2.209(1) states that an agreement modifying a sale of goods needs no consideration to be binding. Instead, the Official Comment to §2.209 explains that all that is required to validate the modification is that it meets Article 2's test of good faith. In essence, an extorted modification would not satisfy that test, but a modification that is fairly agreed to and justified by a legitimate business reason is valid even in the absence of consideration.

§7.5.4 Modifications in Light of Supervening Difficulty

The requirement that contract modification requires consideration is not applied where the modification was motivated by supervening difficulties that materially affect the basic assumption under which the contract was made. The underlying rationale for this exception is that a modification to take account of an unexpected burden on the promisee is less likely to be coercive. The exception can only be used where the facts support it. The promisee must be able to show that such an unforeseen difficulty did arise in the course of performance and did motivate the modification.

§7.5.5 Preexisting Duty to a Third Party

a. Duty to a Private Third Party

Some courts, and Restatement, Second, §73, confine the preexisting duty rule to a preexisting duty owed by the promisee to the promisor and do not apply it to a preexisting duty owed by the promisee to someone else. For example, Al contracted to sell his ski lodge to Ava for $1,000,000. Before the sale had closed, Ava had granted a concession for food service at the lodge to Gordon Bleu. Gordon expected the concession to be lucrative, so he was anxious to ensure that Al completed the sale of the lodge to Ava. Therefore, to give Al an additional incentive to close the sale to Ava, Gordon promised Al that he would pay him $10,000 upon the closing of the sale. Al had already contracted with Ava to sell the lodge to her, so Al had a preexisting legal duty to perform that promise. However, that preexisting duty was not owed to Gordon, so Restatement, Second, §73, Comment *d* argues that the rule should not be applicable. It offers two rationales for this approach. First, Al did in fact give consideration to Gordon for his promise of the $10,000 because Al incurred a legal detriment by forbearing from the right to negotiate with Ava for the cancellation of the contract to sell the lodge to her. Second, the preexisting duty rule is not needed in this case because it does not raise the concern about extorted contract modification. Diagram 7F illustrates these relationships.

Diagram 7F

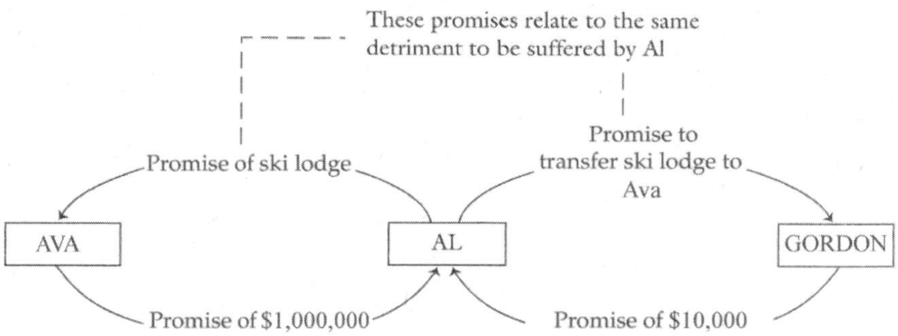

b. Public Duty

In the above example, Al owed his preexisting duty to Ava, a private party. Some duties are owed to the public by virtue of a law that imposes that duty on a person. For example, Willie got his driver's license soon after he turned 16. Willie's Uncle William wanted to give Willie an incentive to drive responsibly, so he promised to pay Willie $5,000 on his 21st birthday if Willie received no citations for traffic violations before he reached the age of 21. Willie has a preexisting legal duty not to violate traffic laws. He owes that duty to the public at large, which includes Uncle William as a member of the public. However, a court may not apply the preexisting duty rule to this duty. It is owed to Uncle William only indirectly, and the promise advances the public interest by giving Willie an incentive to obey traffic laws.

However, a court is likely to apply the preexisting duty rule if the person to whom the promise is made is a public official whose preexisting performance duty is owed to the public. For example, a police officer has a preexisting duty to apprehend criminals. Therefore, if the owner of a store promises a police officer a reward for catching the robber who robbed the store, the court is likely to invalidate this promise on the basis of the preexisting duty rule. It is not in the public interest for a court to increase the risk of corruption by permitting enforcement of a promise intended to influence the police officer's priorities in performing official duties.

The preexisting duty rule applies to a government agency which has a preexisting duty to the public. In *White v. Village of Homewood*, 628 N.E.2d 616 (Ill. App. Ct. 1993), White sued the Village of Homewood, alleging that it negligently caused her injury while she was taking a physical agility test to qualify as a firefighter for Homewood's fire department. Homewood moved to dismiss her negligence claim on the ground that she had signed an exculpatory agreement before taking the test, in which she released Homewood from liability for any injury suffered during the test. White claimed that the exculpatory agreement was invalid because Homewood gave her no consideration in exchange for signing it. Homewood argued that it did give White consideration by allowing her to take the test. The court agreed with White: Homewood had a preexisting duty under state law to administer the test to all applicants, including White, who had the right to participate in it.

§7.6 CONSIDERATION IN AN AGREEMENT TO SETTLE A DISPUTED CLAIM OR DEFENSE

The preexisting duty rule applies to an agreement between a debtor and a creditor under which the creditor agrees to accept partial payment of, or to extend the payment period of an undisputed debt. This is because the debtor already owes the undisputed debt, and a new promise by the debtor to pay in part or after due date is nothing more than a promise to pay what is already owed. For example, a borrower owed $100,000 to a lender. When the loan became due for repayment, the borrower was in severe financial difficulty and could not pay in full. The borrower approached the lender, explained its dire financial circumstances, and persuaded the lender to reduce the debt to $75,000. Clearly, the lender has suffered a detriment by forgiving a quarter of the debt. However, unless the borrower undertook some new detriment in addition to the promise to pay the reduced amount of the debt, the borrower has given no consideration to the lender for this new agreement. The lender's promise to reduce the debt is therefore not binding. *McGowan v. Homeward Residential, Inc.*, 2012 WL 6115984 (11th Cir. 2012), illustrates the same principle in relation to a lender's agreement to extend payment of a debt and forbear from foreclosure. The McGowans had mortgaged several properties to secure loans by Homeward. They subsequently entered into an agreement with Homeward under which Homeward allowed them to make lower monthly payments on their mortgages and agreed not to commence foreclosure proceedings against them provided that those payments were made. Although the McGowans made the payments, Homeward did commence foreclosure proceedings. The court held that it was entitled to do so because the McGowans had incurred no new detriment and had therefore given Homeward no consideration in exchange for the accommodations that it promised them.

The preexisting duty rule applies only where the debt is undisputed. If there is a genuine dispute over the debt, an agreement between the parties is supported by consideration because, by compromising the dispute, each of them gives up a right: In exchange for the creditor party's forbearance from asserting its full claim, the debtor party forbears from asserting its defense to the claim. For example, Sue Slider slipped on the highly polished marble floor of a hotel lobby and was injured. Sue sued the hotel for $500,000 damages for medical expenses, pain and suffering, and public humiliation, on the grounds that the hotel was negligent in having such a slippery floor in its lobby. The hotel defended the suit, denying liability on the basis that the floor was not unduly slippery, and that Sue had slipped because she was walking too fast in shoes with high heels and smooth leather soles. Just before the trial, the hotel offered to settle the suit by paying Sue $50,000 and she accepted the offer. Although the injury occurred before the settlement agreement, and the hotel may have already incurred the duty to compensate Sue for her injury, the fact and extent of liability were uncertain. Therefore, this agreement to compromise the disputed and uncertain claim is very different from the settlement of the undisputed loan debt in the previous example because each party incurs a detriment. Sue's detriment is her agreement to accept less than she claimed and to forbear from pursuing her suit against the hotel. The hotel's detriment, exchanged for Sue's, is its promise to pay Sue $50,000 and its forbearance from asserting its defense to liability. Because a jury could have found that the hotel had no liability, or lesser liability to Sue, the hotel's uncertain debt is not treated as a preexisting duty to pay Sue $50,000 or any other amount. Not only is this result in accordance with consideration principles, but it is also good public policy. There is a strong public interest in the settlement of disputes by agreement, and the law should therefore encourage and uphold honest and legitimate compromise agreements.

The words "honest and legitimate" indicate an important qualification: While the law should encourage genuine compromises, it should not be used as a means of extorting payment or evading obligations through spurious or vexatious claims or defenses. Say, for example, that Sue did not slip on the hotel floor. However, she dishonestly claimed that she did, and the hotel could not prove otherwise. Sue commenced suit against the hotel, claiming damages of $50,000 for emotional distress and pain and suffering. To avoid the cost and publicity of a trial, the hotel offered to settle the claim for $10,000 and Sue accepted. Before paying, the hotel discovered that Sue's claim was false and it refused to pay her. Sue cannot enforce the hotel's promise to pay because she gave it no consideration in exchange for that promise. She had no right to assert a false claim, and it is therefore not a legal detriment for her to forbear from doing something that she had no legal right to do.[10] The same principle applies to a vexatious defense: A party who defends a claim without having a genuine basis for disputing it cannot claim that giving up the defense is a legal detriment.

Sue's trumped-up claim is clearly spurious, but in some cases, it is harder to decide whether the claim or defense is genuine. In any claim that is litigated, one of the parties will ultimately win and the other will lose. Therefore, a party seeking to establish that a claim or defense was legitimate does not need to show that the claim or defense would have prevailed in the litigation. Rather, the test for legitimacy is based on the existence of enough doubt about the claim or defense to make the dispute genuine. Restatement, Second, §74 adopts a test that measures legitimacy on, alternatively, an objective or subjective standard. Either the claim or defense must be objectively reasonable (that it is subject to reasonable doubt because of uncertainty in fact or law), or the party asserting the claim or defense must have an honest belief in its merits (that is, the party is subjectively in good faith). Some courts are stricter and require the claim or defense to satisfy both the objective and subjective standards—that it has a colorable legal basis, and also that it is asserted in good faith. Some courts do not inquire into the objective plausibility of the claim or defense, but require only an examination of the good faith of the party asserting it. In many cases, the outcome of these tests may amount to the same thing because it may be hard for a party to make a persuasive argument of a genuine belief in the validity of a claim or defense that has no objective basis of support. However, the subjective test does allow honest ignorance to be taken into account. Whatever test is used, the legitimacy of the claim must be determined as at the date of the agreement, not in light of later events.

For an example of a case in which the court required only a good faith belief in the merits of the claim, *see Denburg v. Parker, Chapin, Flattau, & Klimpl*, 624 N.E.2d 995 (N.Y. 1993). A law firm's partnership agreement contained a clause that created financial disincentives for a partner to leave the firm and practice in competition with it. This provision was void as against public policy because, by discouraging a partner from setting up a competing practice upon leaving the firm, it inhibited the right of the clients of the partner to maintain access to the attorney of their choice. The firm sought to enforce the provision against a partner who left the firm and the partner challenged its right to do so. The parties then settled the dispute by agreement. Thereafter, the ex-partner claimed that the settlement agreement

10. In addition to challenging Sue's consideration, the hotel has grounds for avoiding the agreement for fraud. (Fraud is discussed in section 13.6.) Sue's fraud is also a criminal offense.

lacked consideration because it compromised an invalid claim. The court upheld the settlement. Although the partnership's claim was not legally tenable, the firm believed in good faith that it was viable. This was enough to validate the firm's forbearance as consideration. As mentioned earlier, the test of good faith may not be that far from the reasonableness test. It would surely have been very difficult for the law firm to establish its good faith if a reasonable lawyer in its position would have known that the provision was clearly unenforceable.

§7.7 THE MEASUREMENT OF DETRIMENT: ADEQUACY OF CONSIDERATION

§7.7.1 The General Rule: Courts Are Not Concerned with Adequacy of Consideration

In some cases, it is easy to tell if there is equivalence of value in an exchange. For example, if a used car is sold for $10,000, an item of ascertainable economic value is exchanged for a stated sum of money. In other cases, economic equivalence is difficult or impossible to evaluate. For example, in *Hamer v. Sidway*, discussed in sections 7.3.1 and 7.3.2, there is no way to tell if young Willie's forbearance from the stated activities until he reached the age of 21 was worth the $5,000 promised by Uncle William. However, this generally does not matter, because consideration doctrine does not require that the performances or promises exchanged be of equal value. As long as a legal detriment has been suffered in exchange for the promise, consideration is present, and the court will not invalidate the contract on the ground that the consideration given for a promise is inadequate in relation to the value of the promise. (Restatement, Second, §79(b).) A related principle is that there does not have to be an equivalence in the number of promises or performances provided by each party. One party can exchange a single promise or performance for multiple promises and performances by the other. This too, is illustrated by *Hamer*, in which Uncle William's single promise to pay $5,000 to Willie was exchanged for multiple forbearances by Willie.

The rule that the court will not inquire into adequacy of consideration is based on the policy of enforcing the voluntary exchange on the terms agreed by the parties. As long as consideration has been found to exist, the court should not second-guess the value placed on the exchange by the parties at the time of contracting, even if one of the parties subsequently seeks to overturn the transaction because the other received too great a bargain. The disparity in value may be the result of many and varied factors such as poor judgment, inaccurate cost calculations, bad luck in market predictions, or even deliberate underpricing. Whatever the reason, the party who fairly agreed to take less than the value of the promised performance has no basis to complain after entering the contract.

§7.7.2 Inadequacy of Consideration as the Result of Unfair Bargaining

Notwithstanding the principle that a court does not examine the adequacy of consideration, inadequate consideration is relevant under other doctrines where the disparity in the exchange results from oppressive or underhanded bargaining or justifiable mistake. Where a party is induced to enter into a contract by fraud, duress, or undue influence, or the contract is unconscionable (*see* Chapter 13) or it results from actionable mistake (*see* Chapter 15), the disadvantaged party may seek to avoid the contract or to adjust its terms to make it fairer.

§7.7.3 Sham or Nominal Consideration

The rule that a court does not inquire into adequacy of consideration may not apply where it is clear that the purported consideration is merely a sham or is so patently inadequate that it clearly was not really intended as consideration. Where the parties intend a promise to be gratuitous, they may seek to make the promise binding by creating an apparent consideration. They may do this by falsely reciting that the promisee did give consideration. For example, Phil Anthropist executed a signed writing in which he pledged to pay $100,000 to Benevolent Benefactors, a charitable organization. The pledge stated that it was given for consideration received, but this was really an unconditional gift and Benevolent did not actually give or promise any consideration to Phil. Here, the recital of consideration for the $100,000 pledge is a sham. Alternatively, the pledge may provide for Benevolent to suffer some nominal detriment in apparent exchange for the promise. For example, it might have stated that Phil's promise to pay $100,000 to Benevolent was given in consideration for Benevolent's promise of a coffee mug bearing its logo. It defies common sense to believe that Phil really bargained for a cheap coffee mug in exchange for $100,000, so the purported consideration was merely used as a device to try to make the gift into an enforceable contract.

There is a convincing policy argument that the parties should be able to use the device of recited or nominal consideration to validate a gratuitous promise, provided that the pretense at consideration is not designed to defraud a third party and the promisor has not been tricked or coerced into making the promise. However, Restatement, Second, does not take this approach. While it asserts the general rule that courts should not inquire into adequacy of consideration, it states several times that the pretense of a bargain does not satisfy the exchange element. It does not treat as sufficient consideration a false detriment that cannot reasonably be conceived as inducing the return promise. (*See* §71, Comment *b*; §72, Comment *c*; §79, Comment *d*; and §81, Comment *b*.)

Sham or nominal consideration satisfies the formal functions of consideration doctrine: The parties' effort to go through the formality of constructing apparent consideration provides evidence of their serious intent to be bound, cautions the promisor that it has made a binding commitment, and allows the court to distinguish this as such. Therefore, any justification for the Restatement, Second's position must lie in the substantive function of the doctrine: It is contrary to the public interest for courts to become involved in the enforcement of gratuitous promises. Sometimes the circumstances may suggest that the goal of protecting against generosity outweighs the policy of upholding private autonomy, but in other situations, despite what the Restatement, Second, says, the better approach may be to treat the apparent consideration as sufficient where the formal functions of consideration are fully satisfied by a clear document, there is no suggestion of advantage taking or underhanded conduct by the promisee, and no indication that the promisor acted impulsively and with immediate regret.

In some cases, courts adopt the position of the Restatement, Second, and refuse to recognize consideration when it is clearly nominal or false. In others, courts have been willing to give effect to the parties' effort to validate the promise and have upheld promises that were really gratuitous, but were supported by recited or nominal consideration. They have recognized nominal consideration on the basis of the general principle that a court will not inquire into adequacy of consideration, and they have upheld a false recital of consideration either by interpreting the recital as an implied promise to provide the stated act or forbearance at some future time, or by estopping[11] the promisor from denying receipt of recited consideration. For many courts, the decision to validate recited or nominal consideration depends on the court being satisfied that the equities do not favor protecting the promisor for ill-considered generosity or unfair imposition.

---

11. Estoppel is explained in section 8.4. In short, its impact in this context is that a promisor who participated in setting up the pretense of consideration, cannot thereafter deny that consideration was given if the promisor's earlier conduct induced the promisee reasonably to rely on the validity of the promise. If such reasonable reliance can be shown, the promisor is held accountable for that conduct and is precluded from asserting that the consideration is a sham.

§7.7.4 Nominal Consideration in Options

The discussion of offer and acceptance in section 4.13 introduced the option, which is a promise not to revoke an offer for a stated period. That section stated the general principle that, at common law, an option does not bind the offeror unless the offeree has given consideration to the offeror in exchange for that promise. (In a sale of goods, this rule is generally not applicable because UCC §2.205 dispenses with consideration for a firm offer that satisfies its requirements.[12]) The consideration required from the offeree to support the option is distinct from the consideration that the offeree would give in the underlying contract if the contracts is ultimately formed.

However, in relation to options, Restatement, Second, adopts a more lenient attitude to purely formal consideration because an offeror does not typically have gratuitous motives in promising not to revoke an offer. Therefore, there is less concern about protecting a grantor of an option from legal liability for the promise of a gift. Many courts that follow the stricter attitude toward nominal consideration in other situations are willing to follow the Restatement, Second, and adopt a more flexible approach to options. Similarly, if the consideration recited in an option is a sham, the court will more readily interpret the recital as a promise to furnish the consideration or will more easily estop the grantor from asserting that the recital was a sham.

§7.8 PAST PERFORMANCE

Exchange is the basis of consideration, so each party's detriment must induce and be induced by the other's. Therefore, if the promisee's detriment was suffered before the promisor made the promise, that detriment cannot have been induced by the promise and therefore cannot qualify as consideration for the promise. This means that there is no consideration for a promise if the promisor makes it to compensate the promisee for some benefit that the promisee conferred on the promisor before the promise was made. For example, in *Lewis v. Ikner*, 825 S.E.2d 443 (Ga. Ct. App. 2019), Lewis gave Ikner, her son, $80,000 as a down payment on a house that he was buying. At the time, Lewis signed a gift letter recording that the money was given to Ikner as an unconditional gift. About two years later, Ikner

12. *See* section 4.13.4, which explains that consideration is still required for a firm offer relating to a sale of goods if the offer does not satisfy the requirements of UCC §2.205 because, for example, the offeror is not a merchant or because the offer is held open for more than three months.

agreed to treat the payment as a loan, not a gift, and he executed a promissory note in which he promised to repay the money to Lewis. When he did not pay the note, Lewis sued on it. The court held that the note was unenforceable for lack of consideration. Lewis' prior payment to Ikner predated the promissory note and was not given in exchange for it. Even though Lewis had suffered the detriment of paying the $80,000 to Ikner and thus conferred a valuable benefit on him, it predated his promise and therefore was not induced by or exchanged for the promise. The court used the common term "past consideration" to label Lewis' previous payment. Although this term often appears in court opinions to denote a detriment suffered by a party prior to, rather than in exchange for the promise, it is a misnomer. "Past consideration" is not consideration at all and is more accurately called "past detriment."

§7.9 THE QUALITY OF A PROMISE AS CONSIDERATION: "MUTUALITY OF OBLIGATION," ILLUSORY, CONDITIONAL, AND ALTERNATIVE PROMISES

§7.9.1 Mutuality and Illusory Promises

The requirement of mutuality of obligation is sometimes expressed by the maxim, "both parties must be bound, or neither is bound." This maxim should not be taken literally because it is legally permissible to have a contract that commits only one of the parties to a future commitment. This is true of unilateral contracts, in which the offeree's act of acceptance is also the completion of that party's performance under the contract, so that upon contract formation, only the offeror's promise of future performance remains outstanding.[13] It is also true of bilateral contracts in which only one of the parties has the right to cancel the transaction. For example, a contract can validly grant to only one of the parties the right to end the relationship by giving notice of termination. Similarly, an option contract[14] paid for in advance binds only the offeror. There are also several situations, such as a party's minority, mental incapacity, or mistake, or the other party's bargaining impropriety, in which only one of the parties is bound because the other has the right to avoid the contract.[15]

13. Unilateral contracts are explained in section 4.12.

14. *See* section 4.13.

15. *See* section 14.2.1 (minority), section 14.3.3 (incapacity), section 13.3 (bargaining impropriety), and section 15.5 (mistake).

Therefore, "mutuality" does not mean that both parties must make a future commitment or, if they do, that each must be bound with the same degree of firmness. It also does not mean that the parties must have equal and coextensive obligations under the contract. Because there need not be economic equivalence in the exchange, it is permissible and common for one party to incur far more numerous, extensive, or onerous obligations than the other.[16] Instead, "mutuality" just means that where consideration consists of the exchange of mutual promises, the undertakings on both sides must be real and meaningful. If the promise of one party has qualifications or limitations so strong that they negate it, it is really no commitment at all. Because it does not bind that party, this lack of consideration voids the apparent contract, so neither party is bound. This is no more than a specific application of the general principle of consideration. In fact, it is really not necessary to use the word "mutuality" at all. It is more accurate and less confusing to simply express the principle that an illusory promise, in which the party does not actually make a binding commitment, does not qualify as consideration. Restatement, Second, §79(c) and Comment f disavow the concept of mutuality as redundant and misleading and stress that it should not be thought of as a separate or additional requirement for consideration.

An apparent promise is illusory and therefore is not consideration if it is couched in terms that allow the party to escape commitment at will. For example, a contract for the sale of packaged snacks by a supplier to a retailer provides that the supplier undertakes to deliver to the retailer "such goods as the retailer may, in its discretion, order from time to time." The retailer has such wide discretion to order or not order snacks that it really makes no commitment at all, and therefore has not given consideration to the supplier in exchange for the supplier's promise to deliver goods as ordered. In reserving such unencumbered discretion over its ordering of snacks, the retailer may believe that it has gained the advantage of binding the supplier while keeping its own options open. However, the retailer's lack of a real promise precludes the creation of a binding contract, so the supplier is not contractually bound either and has no obligation to fill any order submitted by the retailer.

In *Harris v. Blockbuster, Inc.*, 622 F. Supp. 2d 396 (N.D. Tex. 2009), Blockbuster made this miscalculation in trying to retain its freedom of action while firmly binding its customers. A subscriber to Blockbuster's online video rental program sued it, claiming that it had violated a federal statute protecting the subscriber's privacy. Blockbuster sought to invoke an arbitration provision in its standard terms, to which the subscriber had signified assent at the time of subscribing by clicking an "I agree" box on

16. If the imbalance in commitments has been caused by unfair bargaining, the doctrine of unconscionability (*see* section 13.12) may be used to address the problem of unfair imposition.

Blockbuster's website. (That is, the subscriber was bound to Blockbuster's standard terms through a clickwrap agreement, as discussed in sections 5.2 and 5.3.) Notwithstanding the subscriber's signification of assent, Blockbuster was not able to enforce the arbitration clause because the court found that it lacked consideration. In its standard terms, Blockbuster had reserved the right to modify the terms, including the arbitration clause, at its discretion. It had no duty to notify its subscribers of the modification, which would take effect immediately and which would be deemed assented to if the subscriber continued to use the service following the modification. Furthermore, modifications were not stated to be prospective, which meant that changes relating to the arbitration provision could affect disputes that had arisen prior to the modification. The court held that by retaining such broad power to change the terms, Blockbuster had in fact not committed itself to anything, so that any apparent promise that it made was illusory. *See also Hooters of America, Inc. v. Phillips*, 39 F. Supp. 2d 582 (D.S.C. 1998),[17] in which the court held that an arbitration agreement between Hooters and its employee lacked consideration because Hooters' promise was illusory. The agreement was structured to absolutely bind the employee to arbitrate but left Hooters with the discretion to terminate the agreement on notice and to change the arbitration rules and procedures without notice.

The courts in the above two cases found the promises to be illusory because Blockbuster and Hooters had reserved such broad discretion to alter their undertakings. They went too far in formulating one-sided terms. However, this does not mean that a discretionary promise or a party's retention of the power to change terms in the future will inevitably make the party's promise illusory. Sections 7.9.2 to 7.9.5 provide several examples of promises in which discretion is subject to sufficient controls and limitations to qualify the promise as a real commitment. Further, it is worth restating the point made in section 7.7.1 on adequacy of consideration that there does not have to be an equivalence in the consideration exchanged in the contract, either in terms of the number of promises or performances provided by each party, or on the relative value or extent of the exchanges. Had Blockbuster or Hooters drafted terms in a way that placed some limit on their discretion to make future changes to the standard terms, they probably would have made enough of a commitment to validate their self-serving terms. As discussed in section 5.6 on the post-contractual modification of standard terms, many standard contracts allow the drafter to make future modification of the standard terms during the course of the relationship. This does not create an illusory promise problem if the discretionary right to modify is provided for in the contract, the drafter gives reasonable notice of modifications when they are made, and the nondrafter is given a reasonable

17. The case was affirmed without discussion of the consideration question at 173 F.3d 933 (4th Cir. 1999).

opportunity to reject the modifications by ceasing to use the services provided under the contract.

§7.9.2 Interpretation and the Use of Implied Terms to Cure an Apparently Illusory Promise

It may sometimes appear that the party to a contract has such broad discretion over the decision to perform that the party has really made no commitment at all. However, in most transactions with a commercial purpose, apparently unlimited discretion is curtailed by an implied obligation to exercise that discretion reasonably or in good faith. For example, the buyer of a house for $500,000 has $100,000 in savings to pay towards the price, but needs a loan for the balance. The contract for the sale of the house therefore provides that the sale is conditional on the buyer obtaining a loan of $400,000, secured by a mortgage on the house. The seller's promise to transfer the house to the buyer is a firm commitment, but the buyer's promise to buy it is subject to the condition that the buyer obtains the loan. On the surface, it may seem that the buyer has made no real commitment because the buyer can evade any commitment under the contract by simply not applying to a bank for the loan. However, even if the contract does not say so expressly, the buyer has the implied obligation to use best efforts to secure a loan. This obligation of best efforts imposes a limit on the buyer's discretion and prevents the conditional promise from being illusory.

Wood v. Lucy, Lady Duff-Gordon, 118 N.E. 214 (N.Y. 1917), is a famous example of a court implying an obligation of best efforts to an apparently illusory promise. Lucy, a fashion maven of her time, entered into a contract appointing Wood as her exclusive agent for placing her endorsements and selling her designs. The contract provided that Wood would pay Lucy half the profits earned from these sales, but the there was no express language in the contract that committed him to do anything to make the sales that would earn those profits. When Lucy breached the exclusive agency by endorsing products on her own and keeping all the profits for herself, Wood sued for his share. Lucy argued that there was no contract: Although Wood had undertaken to pay half the profits to her, he had not actually promised to do anything to earn those profits. In light of the obviously commercial intent of the agreement, the court concluded that Lucy's grant of an exclusive agency necessarily gave rise to the implication that Wood was obliged to use best efforts in generating profits. UCC §2.306(2) follows this approach by implying an obligation of best efforts in exclusive dealing contracts involving goods.

Of course, this does not mean that courts will always interpret contracts to impose some limit on apparently overbroad discretion. As *Harris* and *Hooters* show, it is sometimes apparent that one of the parties really did reserve such broad discretion over its performance, so that the only conclusion is that the party's promise is illusory and cannot constitute consideration.

§7.9.3 "Mutuality" in Requirements and Output Contracts

a. Requirements and Output Contracts for the Sale of Goods Under UCC §2.306

Most contracts for the sale of goods involve a single item or a specified quantity of goods. In some situations, however, it may suit the parties to leave the quantity of goods open-ended on the understanding that the quantity to be supplied under the contract will be determined either by the buyer's requirements or by the seller's output. A requirements contract serves the parties' needs where the seller is confident that it can produce enough to satisfy the buyer's demands, and the buyer is unsure of its exact needs and wishes to avoid the risk of ordering a specified quantity which may turn out to be short or excessive. An output contract suits the parties when the seller wishes to dispose of its full production in one transaction, and the buyer is confident that it can use all that the seller can supply.

For example, a winery only buys grapes to supplement what it produces on its own vines. It is not sure what quantity of grapes it will need to buy next year because the quantity it needs will depend on its own crop yield. The winery therefore does not want to try to predict its needs in advance by contracting for a set quantity of grapes because this could lead to waste if its own grapes are plentiful, and a shortfall if they are scarce. The winery therefore enters into a requirements contract with a vineyard, the seller, covering a specific year or period of years, under which the winery promises to buy and the vineyard promises to supply the winery's total demand for grapes in excess of its own harvest. By contrast, an output contract better suits the parties' needs if the winery knows that it can use everything that the vineyard produces—it can never grow enough of its own grapes to satisfy its needs, and it has enough capacity to use all its own grapes plus all the grapes that the vineyard can produce. The vineyard is happy to sell its entire crop to the winery, because this saves the costs of multiple transactions with different buyers. The parties therefore enter an output contract under which the vineyard promises to sell and the winery promises to take all the grapes grown by the vineyard during a specified period.

It may seem at first glance that the flexible quantity term in an output or requirements contract could be an illusory promise because a requirements buyer could elect to have no requirements and an output seller could decide to produce no goods. However, UCC §2.306(1) overcomes this problem by recognizing that even if the contract does not say so expressly, the discretion to determine quantity is limited by an implied obligation of good faith.[18] The commitment to determine quantity in good faith, whether express or implied, is sufficient commitment to prevent the promise from being illusory. "Good faith" is defined in §1.201(20)[19] to include both the subjective standard of "honesty in fact" and the objective standard of "the observance of reasonable commercial standards of fair dealing."

Even if not expressed, the obligation of good faith imposes on the party with discretion an implied obligation of exclusive dealing with regard to the goods that are covered by the contract. The obligation of exclusive dealing need not necessarily relate to the party's entire requirements or output of the product. It is permissible to confine it to a defined portion of the requirements or output, provided that the scope of the exclusive dealing is clear and identifiable. For example, a seller of corn could agree to commit only the output from particular fields, or a buyer of office stationery could commit to take only its requirements of copier paper from the seller.

Exclusive dealing is essential for an arrangement to qualify as a requirements or output contract. The buyer's discretionary promise to buy its requirements or the seller's discretionary obligation to sell its output is meaningless if the party with the discretion could simply manipulate the extent of the requirements or output by buying or selling elsewhere. The contract does not need to state expressly that the party with the discretion promises to deal exclusively with the other party with regard to the goods to be supplied under the contract. This obligation can be inferred from the circumstances of the transaction. For example, in *Williams v. Medalist Golf, Inc.*, 910 F.3d 1041 (8th Cir. 2018), the contract provided that the seller would supply all the sod required by the buyer for construction of a golf course. The buyer repudiated the contract and the seller sued the buyer for breach. The buyer moved for summary judgment on the ground that the contract was invalid in that it did not commit the buyer to buy all the sod exclusively from the seller. The court acknowledged that the buyer's promise to buy its sod requirements for the golf course from the seller would be illusory unless the buyer committed to buy all its requirements exclusively from the seller. This contract did not expressly promise that, but the buyer should not get summary judgment because the seller had adduced contextual evidence

---

18. This section focuses on the good faith standard in relation to requirements and output contracts. However, there is also an implied general obligation of good faith and fair dealing that applies to the performance and enforcement of all contracts. This obligation is discussed in section 10.3.1.

19. "Good faith" is also defined in §2.103(1)(b) in the same way. However, the definition in §2.103 applies only to merchants. Article 2 originally had a different definition of good faith for merchants and nonmerchants—the objective standard applied only to merchants, and nonmerchants were held only to the subjective standard. This difference was eliminated by an amendment to §1.201(20) in 2001, adopted by most states. As a result, the definition in §2.103(1)(b), applicable only to merchants, is redundant in the majority of states, which apply that same standard to everyone.

from which a jury could find that the parties intended the buyer to have the obligation of exclusive dealing.

In *Williams* the contract was unclear on the buyer's obligation to buy all its sod from the seller. However, in *Brooklyn Bagel Boys, Inc. v. Earthgrains Refrigerated Dough Products, Inc.*, 212 F.3d 373 (7th Cir. 2000), the language used in the agreement precluded the interpretation that the buyer had committed to buy all its bagel requirements from the seller. The court held that the transaction did not qualify as a requirements contract. It was just an ongoing offer by the seller to sell bagels at a stated price, accepted by the buyer each time it placed an order. That is, it was no more than a series of discrete contracts that imposed no ongoing obligation on the buyer to buy bagels.

The relationship between a buyer and seller in a requirements contract is illustrated by Diagram 7G. (In an output contract, the discretionary performance would be on the seller's side of the exchange.)

Diagram 7G

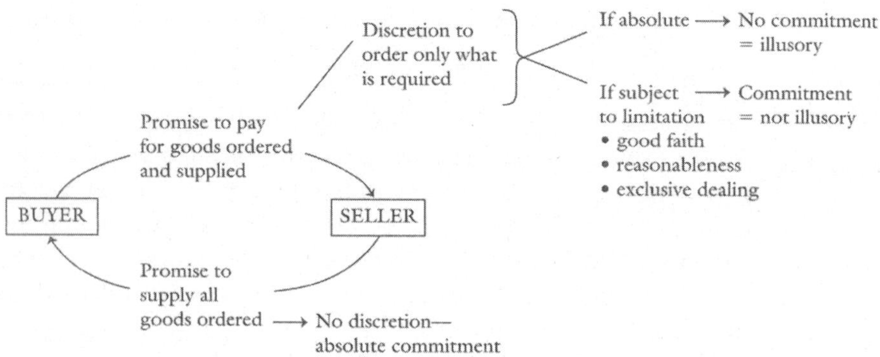

Apart from giving rise to the obligation of exclusive dealing, the good faith standard applies to any decision that has an impact on the quantity of the goods selected by the party with discretion. One of the principal problems in enforcing the obligation of good faith is that honesty and fair dealing are such elastic and relative standards. It is therefore difficult to apply those broad standards to particular conduct and to predict whether a court will find that the conduct satisfies or falls short of them. To decide whether action is honestly motivated and commercially reasonable, the court must evaluate all the circumstances under which the contract was made and the requirements or output were determined. Clearly, the very fact that the parties have made a requirements or output contract means that they must contemplate that the buyer or seller is not bound to fixed quantities, and that it may make a decision that significantly changes its requirements or output. The crucial question is therefore to determine if that decision was made in good faith. *Empire Gas Corp. v. American Bakeries Co.*, 840 F.2d 1333 (7th Cir. 1988), is one of the leading cases on this issue. The court said that it would clearly not be good faith for a buyer to reduce its requirements by buying the goods from another seller, or to reduce orders simply because it has second thoughts about the contract or because the contract is not as advantageous as it had hoped. However, a buyer may be in good faith in reducing its requirements for legitimate and compelling business reasons, such as technological advances that change fundamental needs or dramatic changes in market demand for the buyer's products. In *Wiseco, Inc. v. Johnson Controls, Inc.* 155 F. App'x 815 (6th Cir. 2005), the buyer entered into a requirements contract with the seller to buy components used by the buyer to make headrests for Jeeps. The buyer's orders for the parts dropped dramatically when Jeep changed the headrest design, making the particular components supplied under the requirements contract inappropriate. The court applied the good faith test and concluded that the buyer had legitimate business reasons for its reduced requirements. It no longer needed the parts because its customer had changed the design of the headrest. The seller bore the burden of proving that the buyer's reduction in requirements was in bad faith, and it had not sustained that burden.

In re Fieldwood Energy, LLC, 636 B.R. 463 (Bankr. S.D. Tex. 2021), concerned an output contract under which Fieldwood committed to deliver approximately 10,000 barrels of crude oil from specified fields to the buyer. This was an output contract because the 10,000 barrels was an estimate of the total output from the fields, and the contract contemplated that the quantity could be more or less, depending on the actual output of the fields. About two years later, Fieldwood temporarily shut down the specified oil fields because a fall in the market price of oil made it uneconomical to continue drawing oil from the fields. The buyer sued, claiming that this failure of delivery was a breach of the contract. Oil is goods, so the court applied §2.306, which requires the seller to operate in good faith. The court held that Fieldwood had no control over the reduction in market price, which would result in selling its oil at a loss. It therefore made a good faith and prudent economic decision to suspend production. This result is not necessarily assured and another court may have reached a different conclusion. An output seller takes the risk of normal market conditions, such as a drop in market price, and a court may require something more than that to justify failure to deliver an estimated quantity.

In addition to the good faith standard, §2.306(1) includes a reasonable expectations test that applies only to increases in quantity. It states that the quantity tendered or demanded may not be disproportionate to any estimate, or if no estimate was stated, to any normal or otherwise comparable output or requirements. The disproportionality standard is an objective measure that prevents the buyer in a requirements contract or the seller in an output contract from demanding or tendering a quantity of the goods that is disproportionate to an estimated or historic requirement or output. In essence, the purpose of this standard is to protect the output buyer or requirements seller by pegging the quantity of goods at a level approximate to what might reasonably be expected, based on an estimate or on prior dealings under the contract. The disproportionality standard does not apply in every case. It is relevant only where the parties have stated an estimate or where prior dealings under the contract have established a comparable prior quantity. Also, a number of courts have interpreted the disproportionality standard to apply only to increases in demand or output, and not where a disproportionally small quantity is demanded or tendered. In that situation, only the good faith test applies.

b. Requirements and Output Contracts for Services Under Common Law

Although requirements and output contracts typically involve goods and are governed by §2.306, it is possible to have such contracts for services. Although §2.306 does not apply, common law principles accord closely with it. *Silver Foam Distributing Co. v. Labatt Brewing Trading Co.*, 2021 WL 859043 (E.D. Mich. 2021), was concerned with a contract for services. For the purpose of selling its beers in Canada, SABMiller entered into a five-year contract with Silver Foam under which Silver Foam would pack its beers for shipment to Canada. In preparation for this contract, Silver Foam made substantial investments in equipment. About halfway through the contract period, SABMiller's parent company, Anheuser-Bush, sold the Miller Beer brand, so SABMiller lost the Canadian rights to the brand and ceased using Silver Foam's services. Silver Foam sued SABMiller for breach of the contract on the ground that it had not acted in good faith by reducing its requirements to zero. The court dismissed this breach of contract claim. The court characterized the contract as a requirements contract for services, not goods, but held, citing cases decided both before and after the enactment of the UCC, that the common law has long followed the same principles as §2.306, and has recognized that a buyer of services can reduce its requirements to zero, as long as the reduction is in good faith. The court found that SABMiller's loss of the Canadian rights to the Miller Beer brand, resulting from the sale of the brand by SABMiller's parent company, was a legitimate business reason for the reduction of its requirements to zero.

§7.9.4 Conditional Promises

A conditional promise is a promise that is subject to an uncertain event. If the event occurs, the promise must be performed, but its performance is excused if the event does not occur. For example, the buyer of a plot of land plans to build apartments on it. Apartments cannot be built on the land unless a rezoning application, submitted by the seller, is approved by the local authority. The buyer does not wish to buy the land unless it can be used for the apartment development, so the contract of sale contains a provision making the buyer's obligation to buy the land contingent on approval of the rezoning application. This conditional promise does not present consideration problems because the buyer's commitment is not illusory. The buyer is bound to the promise to proceed with the sale if the condition is satisfied and the buyer does not have control over the fulfillment of the condition, which is in the hands of the zoning authority. The example in section 7.9.2 of the sale of a house subject to the buyer getting a loan is another illustration of a valid conditional promise: The buyer of the house needed to obtain a loan of $400,000 to pay for the house, so the contract made the sale conditional on the buyer obtaining that loan, secured by a mortgage on the house. The buyer does not have to proceed with the purchase of the house if, despite best efforts, the buyer does not succeed in getting the loan. The buyer's promise is not illusory, first, because the buyer has the obligation to make those efforts, and second, because the buyer is committed to the promise to buy the house if the loan is obtained.

§7.9.5 Conditions of Satisfaction

A type of conditional promise that appears to involve very wide discretion is a condition of satisfaction. This is a condition that allows one of the parties to reject a performance by the other, and to refuse to render its own performance, on the ground that the performance is unsatisfactory.[20] For example, a sale of goods on credit provides that the sale is conditional on the seller obtaining a satisfactory credit report on the buyer. Such a condition might appear to render the seller's promise illusory because it could simply negate its promise to sell the goods to the buyer by declaring itself dissatisfied with the buyer's credit record. The contract itself may overcome the appearance of unrestrained discretion by specifying a standard or set of criteria on which to determine satisfaction. However, even if it does not, unless the only plausible interpretation of the agreement is that the parties intended to give unrestrained discretion to the party making the judgment of satisfaction, a court will imply a term that limits the discretion enough to avoid the problem of illusory promise. Therefore, even if the contract does not expressly say so, the party who determines satisfaction is obliged to exercise its judgment either in good faith or reasonably.

Unless the contract specifies either the subjective good faith standard or the objective reasonableness standard, the court decides which is appropriate based on all the circumstances of the transaction. The rule of thumb

20. Conditions of satisfaction are discussed further in section 16.8.2.

is that dissatisfaction is usually judged on a reasonableness standard unless the parties manifest the intention that it should be determined by the good faith standard. The inference that the parties intended to use a good faith standard is usually confined to contracts involving matters of personal taste. In other contracts, particularly those involving a commercial or technical performance, a court is not likely to infer that a party would expect its performance to be judged by a purely idiosyncratic standard. The evaluation of the buyer's creditworthiness is a matter of commercial judgment, so an objective approach, based on what a reasonable lender would consider satisfactory, would be more appropriate.

§7.9.6 Promises of Alternative Performances

A form of discretionary promise involves alternative performances. To illustrate, change the facts of the example in which the buyer's obligation to purchase a plot of land was conditional on the land being rezoned to allow for the construction of apartments. In that example, the buyer did not wish to buy the land unless it could be used for the apartment development, so nonfulfillment of the condition would lead to termination of the sale. However, say that the buyer wanted to buy the land whether or not the rezoning was approved, but the land would be worth considerably less without the rezoning. The contract could provide that if the rezoning is approved, the buyer would pay a stated higher price for the land, but if it was denied, the buyer would pay a stated lower price. Instead of leading to termination of the contract, the condition now keeps the contract in force, but provides for alternative promises by the buyer—to pay either the higher or the lower price. Provided that each of the promises, on its own, would be consideration, there is nothing objectionable in permitting a party to select between alternative promises. This is illustrated by Diagram 7H.

Diagram 7H

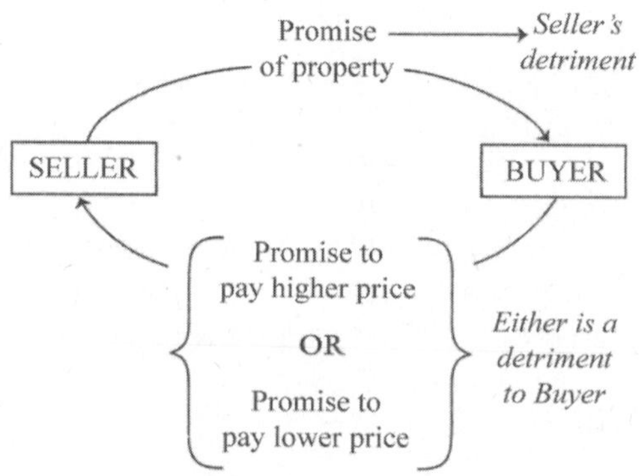

It may be more difficult to find consideration for alternative performance where one of the alternatives imposes so small a burden on the party who has the choice that this alternative would not likely have induced the promise on its own. For example, a contract for the sale of a property binds the buyer to proceed with the sale unless the buyer gives the seller notice of termination of the contract within 30 days of executing it. These are alternative performances—the buyer may either proceed with the purchase or may give the notice. Both alternative performances qualify as legal detriments—the detriment of buying the land or the detriment of giving notice. The purpose of providing for these alternatives is to allow the buyer to escape the contract if the buyer decides not to buy the land within 30 days of entering the contract. Although the obligation to give notice is a detriment, it is such a slight detriment that it would not on its own have induced the seller to promise to sell the property. Nevertheless, seen as a package with the more burdensome alternative, the seller may have been willing to take the risk of cancellation in exchange for the chance that the buyer would not exercise the discretion to cancel. A court could uphold the transaction by refusing to inquire into the adequacy of the alternative detriment of giving notice. This was the result in *Johnson Lakes Development, Inc. v. Central Nebraska Pub. Power & Irrigation District*, 576 N.W.2d 806 (Neb. 1998). The court held that an obligation to give advance notice of termination was enough to prevent a party's promise from being illusory, provided that the party was irrevocably bound until and unless the notice was given. This may seem like the exultation of form over substance when compared to an invalid purely discretionary promise, but the provision of notice gives the court a basis for validation if it deems the agreement to have been fairly bargained for.

Examples

EXAMPLES

1. Penny Less entered college two years ago at the age of 22. At the time, her Uncle Rich, concerned about reports of excessive drinking by college students, promised her that if she did not drink any alcoholic beverages in her first year of college, he would give her $5,000 at the end of that year. Penny thanked Uncle Rich, but she did not specifically say whether she would do as he had asked.

   It was easy for Penny to comply with Uncle Rich's condition because she hated the taste of alcohol and would not have drunk it anyhow. Accordingly, Penny did not consume any alcohol during her first year of college. When she reported this to Uncle Rich at the end of the year and asked for her reward, he said, "I have changed my mind about giving you the money. Don't be disappointed. Temperance is its own reward." Was Uncle Rich free to change his mind?

2. Would your answer to Example 1 change if Penny was 19 years old at the time that she made her agreement with Uncle Rich? At that time she was old enough to be a major for the purposes of contracting. However, state law prohibits a person below the age of 21 years from consuming alcohol and provides for penalties to be imposed on a minor who violates the prohibition.

3. In January, Dotty Com borrowed $500,000 from Angela Investor to finance her new startup business. The loan bore 6 percent interest and was due for repayment on June 1. In late May, Dotty told Angela that the business was struggling and she did not have the cash to repay the loan. She believed, however, that if her creditors would give her a break she could save the business, but if they refused to cooperate, she would have to liquidate it. Dotty told Angela that the business was insolvent, and if it was liquidated creditors would receive only about 50 percent of their claims. Dotty asked Angela to accept 80 percent of the debt in full settlement, and to wait six months for payment. Dotty told Angela that she planned to ask all her other creditors for the same concession. Angela agreed and the parties executed a written agreement reflecting that Dotty would pay Angela $400,000 in full settlement of the debt, with interest at 6 percent, by no later than December 1. Did Angela receive consideration for this agreement?

4. When Chevy K. Marro was 29 years old, his Aunt Charity expressed the intention of buying him a new car for his thirtieth birthday. Chevy knew that Aunt Charity always talked big but never did what she promised, so he suggested that if Charity really meant what she said, she would write out the promise and sign it. Charity agreed, and Chevy (known for his shrewd business sense) drew up the document. It stated that Charity, "in consideration for value received" from Chevy, undertook to deliver the car (which was specifically described by make, model, and year) to Chevy on his thirtieth birthday. Charity and Chevy signed the writing. True to form, Aunt Charity gave Chevy a sweater for his thirtieth birthday and did not deliver the car.
   a. Is Aunt Charity obligated by her promise of the car?
   b. Change the facts to the following extent: The writing stated that Charity undertook to deliver the car "in consideration for a cheeseburger, which Chevy has delivered to Charity upon signing this agreement." Chevy did in fact deliver the cheeseburger to Charity when they signed the agreement. Is Charity obligated by her promise of the car?
   c. When Chevy threatened to sue Aunt Charity for the value of the car, she became very annoyed. She demanded that he return the sweater that she gave him as a thirtieth birthday present on the basis that Chevy gave her no consideration for it. Does Aunt Charity have the right to reclaim it?

5. Hunter Fortune used to work as a gardener on the country estate of Buck Plentiful, a billionaire. After Hunter was discharged by the groundskeeper for incompetence, he sued Buck for $1 million, alleging that he was sexually harassed and emotionally abused by the groundskeeper while in Buck's employ. Buck believed that the claim was without substance but did not want any scandal in his household, so he offered to settle the claim out of court for $10,000. Hunter accepted, and a settlement agreement was executed. After the agreement, Buck had second thoughts and refused to pay Hunter. Does Hunter have a valid claim arising from the agreement?

6. Ivor E. Keyes is a gifted pianist. On hearing him play, his beloved Aunt Charity determined to do something to help him advance his career. Ivor told her that he needed to get some training from a really fine pianist to improve his interpretation and style. He had contacted the celebrated Maestro Molto Magnifico but had not engaged him as a teacher because he could not afford his fee of $500 an hour. Aunt Charity declared: "You shall have him as your teacher. I will send you a check for $50,000 tomorrow. That should cover 100 hours of lessons." Ivor thanked her and said, "Auntie, if I ever make it to Carnegie Hall, I will get you the best seat in the house." She replied, "Yes, that will be nice, dear. I'll hold you to it." Do Ivor and Aunt Charity have a contract?

7. Cat Advancement and Training Society (CATS) is a nonprofit organization formed to educate and train cats. One evening an articulate and persuasive fundraiser for the organization called on Kitty Kuddle to solicit a contribution. Kitty liked cats and thought that the goals of the society were admirable. She therefore decided to promise a contribution. The fundraiser gave her a preprinted pledge card, which Kitty signed after inserting her name, the amount of her contribution, and the date. The text of the completed pledge card read as follows:

    > In consideration of my love of and respect for our feline friends, and in consideration for the promise of CATS to use my contribution to advance the cause for which it was constituted, I, Kitty Kuddle, hereby pledge the sum of $500 to CATS, payable in ten equal monthly installments, beginning one week from the date of this pledge. I understand that my contribution is fully tax-deductible.

    The next day, Kitty realized that she had been irresponsible in making the pledge, which she really cannot afford. She would like to cancel her pledge. Is she bound by it?

8. Gutter Press, Inc., publishes a weekly tabloid newspaper. It plans to publish a series of articles on the sordid life of Sally Bratty, a recently-deceased celebrity. It needs a manuscript for the serialized story as soon

as possible so that the series can begin before the inevitable lapse of the public attention span.

Gutter Press engaged Tabb Lloyd, a journalist, to write the manuscript for the serial. The parties signed a written agreement, which included the following terms:

a. Tabb promised to submit a completed manuscript within four weeks.
b. Gutter Press promised to publish the manuscript in serialized form over five issues of its newspaper provided that it found it to be satisfactory.
c. If it did not find the manuscript to be satisfactory and did not publish it for that reason, Gutter Press would have no obligation to pay Tabb anything. However, if it found the manuscript to be satisfactory, it would publish it and would pay Tabb $500,000.
d. During the first week following execution of the agreement, Gutter Press had the right, for any reason, to cancel it by delivering written notice of termination to Tabb.

The day after signing the agreement, Tabb decided that he did not wish to write the manuscript. Is he contractually bound to Gutter Press?

9. Constance De Votion decided to retire after working for the Turn Coat Corporation for 40 years. After the close of business on her last day of work, Turn Coat held a retirement party for her during which the president of the company made a speech thanking her for her long and faithful service. At the end of the speech, the president held up a large photograph of a gold Rolex watch and announced that the company would be giving Constance the watch to show its appreciation for her years of service. Constance thanked him tearfully. Turn Coat never gave Constance the watch. Does she have the legal right to demand it?

10. Stifle Enterprises, Inc. hired Abel Seller as a sales representative under a two-year employment contract. A year after the employment contract was executed, Stifle offered Abel a promotion to sales manager on condition that Abel agreed to sign a noncompetition agreement, under which Abel would agree, for a period of one year after leaving the employ of Stifle, not to engage in any business in direct competition with Stifle, anywhere in the state. Abel agreed to this condition and signed the noncompetition agreement. Six months later, Abel resigned and immediately set up his own competing business in the same city. When Stifle sued Abel to enforce the noncompetition agreement, Abel challenged the validity of the agreement on the ground that it lacked consideration. Is Abel's contention correct?

11. Peters Pickled Peppers manufactures pickled peppers. Last fall it made an agreement with Hal Apeno, a farmer, under which Hal undertook to supply all the peppers Peters would need for its bottling operations next

season, and Peters agreed to buy peppers only from Hal. During negotiations preceding the agreement, Peters told Hal that its average needs in the last five years had been between seven and ten tons of peppers. Hal was satisfied that he could grow sufficient quantities to meet this range of demand. This range of expected requirements was recorded as an estimate in the written contract.

A short time later, Peters' Board met to discuss disappointing sales in the prior year. Studies showed that new and aggressive competitors had gained the lion's share of the pickled pepper market, and all indications were that next year would be even worse. The Board decided to switch from peppers to persimmons, for which there was very little competition. Peters' existing plant was suitable for the processing of persimmons, so the conversion could be achieved at small cost.

Because of this decision, Peters had no need for peppers, and it wrote to Hal telling him so. Hal sued Peters for breach of contract and Peters defended the suit and moved for summary judgment on the ground that the agreement was not a valid contract because it lacked consideration. The trial court agreed and granted summary judgment to Peters. It held that Peters' promise to buy pickles from Hal was illusory because Peters had the discretion to order no peppers at all. Is the trial court right?

12. Mutual Obligations, Inc. leased space in a building to tenants. Mutual's standard lease contained a provision that read, "The lessor reserves the right to modify, delete, or add to any of the conditions in this lease without notice and reserves the right to cancel this lease at any time with or without notice." Tenant, Inc. entered into a five-year lease with Mutual, subject to Mutual's standard terms. A month later, before Tenant had taken occupation of the premises, it decided that it no longer needed the premises, so it notified Mutual that it was cancelling the lease. Mutual asserts that Tenant had no right to cancel the lease and is liable for damages for breach of contract. Is Mutual correct?

Explanations

EXPLANATIONS

1. This Example is based on *Hamer v. Sidway*, discussed in section 7.3.1, in which a well-to-do family member promises some reward for specified behavior. It does not matter that Penny would not chose to drink alcohol anyhow, or that refraining from consuming it is probably in her best interests, and therefore not detrimental to her in the usual sense. She has the right to drink alcoholic beverages and therefore incurs a legal detriment simply by forgoing something that she is entitled to do. She exchanges this for Uncle Rich's promise of payment, providing him with a noneconomic but identifiable benefit. Therefore, Penny has given consideration to Uncle Rich. Because she performed her part of the bargain,

Uncle Rich is contractually bound to pay her the $5,000 that he promised her. (The parties have entered into a unilateral contract in which Penny gave no promise to Uncle Rich but accepted his offer by rendering the performance, which she completed at the end of her first year of college.[21])

The benefit to Uncle Rich has no commercial purpose and is apparently motivated by his concern for Penny's well-being. However, a promise made for noncommercial purposes may be bargained for if it reasonably appears intended to induce particular action desired by the promisor.

2. In Example 1, Penny had the legal right to drink alcohol, so there is no question that her forbearance from drinking it was consideration. However, on this change of facts, she is a minor and does not have that legal right because the state prohibits her from consuming alcohol. The prohibition and penalty are directed against minors who consume alcohol, not merely at an adult who provides alcohol to a minor. Therefore, her abstention is not a legal detriment because she does not give up any legal right. In fact, she has a preexisting duty to the state not to drink. Penny could disobey the law, but consideration doctrine emphasizes that detriment is the giving up of a legal right and does not recognize as a detriment forbearance from illegal activity. Therefore, there is a strong argument that Penny's forbearance from violating the law is not a legal detriment and therefore not consideration for Uncle Rich's promise.

   However, there is an argument for finding consideration: Uncle Rich apparently values Penny's obedience to the law and does bargain for it in exchange for his offer of a reward. This is not a coerced modification of an existing contract, and Uncle Rich's offer actually serves the public interest by creating an incentive for lawful conduct. Consideration doctrine confines the preexisting duty rule to a duty owed to the promisor, and Penny's duty is to the state and the community at large, not a duty owed specifically to Uncle Rich. A contract that gives an incentive to a private party to obey the law does not implicate the concern about the danger of corrupting a public official by offering the official a reward for performing a public duty that is already part of that official's responsibility.

---

21. Section 4.12 explains the acceptance of an offer for a unilateral contract. In short, if Uncle Rich's offer could be accepted only by the completion of Penny's performance (forbearing from drinking for the entire year), no contract comes into existence until completion of Penny's performance. Once the performance is complete, a unilateral contract arises in which only Uncle Rich's obligation remains outstanding. If Penny does not perform, she never accepts the offer, and Uncle Rich has no contractual right to enforce. To protect Penny from having the offer revoked after she has begun her performance in reliance on it, the law deems the offer irrevocable as soon as Penny begins her performance.

3. The principal focus of this Example is the application of the preexisting duty rule to contract modification.[22] The general rule is that a creditor's promise to accept less than the amount owing on an admitted debt or to extend the due date of the debt is not binding, because the debtor incurs no legal detriment in exchange for that promise. (*See* Restatement, Second, §73.) The debtor had a preexisting duty to pay the full debt when it fell due on June 1, and her promise to pay only 80 percent of it over time after that date adds nothing to that duty.[23] As noted in sections 7.5.2 and 7.6, if the agreement to reduce and extend the debt was fairly bargained, it is hard to justify the policy of invalidating the agreement under the preexisting duty rule. However, a strict application of doctrine will invalidate it unless the court can find that Dotty incurred some new detriment in exchange for Angela's promise to reduce and extend the debt.

   It is not easy to find any new detriment on Dotty's part. Her undertaking to pay interest at 6 percent is not a new detriment because she was already obliged to pay interest at that rate under the original contract. (The fact that she will pay the 6 percent interest over a longer period may seem like an added detriment, but the original agreement would have obliged her, expressly or impliedly, to pay that interest beyond the repayment date if her repayment was late.) Dotty's statement that she intended to approach other creditors with the same proposal could be a detriment if she made a promise to do that, but the facts suggest that this was just a statement of intent, not a commitment. Finally, a promise not to liquidate a business could be consideration provided that the business is truly in financial trouble and Dotty had the legal right to liquidate it. The liquidation must be a legitimate solution to the financial problems, and not suggested in bad faith as a form of blackmail. However, again, Dotty's vague reference to the possibility of liquidation does not seem to rise to the level of a promise.

   The common law recognizes a narrow exception to the requirement that a modification must be supported by consideration: It dispenses with the need for consideration if the modification is in response to unforeseen difficulties that have imposed an unexpected burden on the promisee. The problem with this argument is that financial adversity may have been foreseeable in a new business venture unless Dotty can establish some significant and unexpected external cause for the difficulty.

---

22. In addition to the discussion in this chapter, contract modification is dealt with in section 13.9.

23. Had the debt been disputed, an agreement to compromise the dispute would likely be supported by consideration, as discussed in section 7.6 and Example 5. However, this debt is not disputed.

4. a. Chevy has given no consideration to Aunt Charity for her promise, which is clearly intended as a gift, not an exchange. The parties have attempted to validate the transaction by reciting that an unspecified consideration has been given. Restatement, Second, §71, Comment *b*, regards such a false recital as ineffective. Some courts may be more sympathetic to this kind of effort at satisfying the formal function of consideration, but other courts will only uphold a formal recitation of consideration if a promise to furnish the recited consideration can be implied (which cannot be done when the recital does not specify what the purported consideration is), or the promisee's reliance on the promise creates grounds for estopping the promisor from denying the receipt of consideration.

   b. There is obviously a huge disparity in value between a new car and a cheeseburger. However, the cheeseburger could qualify as consideration if the court adopts the approach of refusing to inquire into the adequacy of consideration. The value difference between the cheeseburger and the new car is monumental, which leads to the reasonable conclusion that the burger is not real consideration, but just a formality, inserted into the contract in an attempt to validate Charity's promise of a gift. Some courts respect the parties' use of this formal device and decline to inquire into the adequacy of the exchange. Others refuse to employ the rule against measuring the adequacy of consideration where the consideration is so slight as to be nominal.

   c. The gift of the sweater has already been given, and there is no longer a promise to be enforced. Although the absence of consideration precludes enforcement of a promise, it is not grounds for recovering an executed gift.[24]

5. Unlike the agreement between Dotty and Angela in Example 3, this settlement agreement compromises a claim disputed on the merits and unliquidated in amount.[25] An agreement to settle a disputed claim is supported by consideration because each party forbears from persisting in the full claim and defense. However, as discussed in section 7.6, for consideration to exist the dispute must be genuine. A person has no legal right to assert a bogus claim or defense, so suffers no legal detriment in forbearing from a false claim or defense. This technical explanation accords with a more compelling public policy concern: A person should not be allowed to assert a vexatious claim or defense and then to argue that its settlement constitutes consideration. Restatement, Second, §74

24. If there are grounds for reclaiming a gift outside of contract law, they are beyond the scope of this question.

25. A claim is unliquidated where its amount is uncertain and cannot be determined by simple arithmetic means. The only way that the amount of Hunter's damages can be determined is by a trial.

applies an alternative objective or subjective test to decide if a dispute is genuine. Either the claim or defense must be reasonably tenable because of uncertainty in law or fact, or the party asserting it must have a good faith belief in its merits. Some courts require both these standards to be met, and some focus only on subjective good faith.

The Example is deliberately ambiguous on Hunter's claim. The claim appears to be based on alleged sexual harassment, the intentional infliction of emotional distress, and possibly wrongful discharge. If the wrongful acts were committed by Buck's employee, acting in the course of employment, Buck could be liable for damages. There is, doubtless, a plausible basis in law to make the claim for damages. The crucial question is whether there is a genuine dispute on the facts. If Hunter was in fact discharged for incompetence and his claim is fabricated for revenge or to extort a nuisance payment from his wealthy ex-employer, his forbearance from asserting this bogus claim cannot furnish consideration for the settlement on either a good faith or a reasonableness test.

6. Aunt Charity clearly has suffered a detriment in promising to pay $50,000 to Ivor. However, this is nothing more than a gratuitous promise, like her promise to Chevy in Example 4, unless Ivor has given consideration in exchange for it. The only undertaking that could conceivably qualify as consideration is his assertion that he will get her the best seat in the house if he ever makes it to Carnegie Hall. (His implicit undertaking to use the money for piano instruction is best treated as nothing more than a condition of the gift and should not qualify as consideration.)

   It is not clear that Ivor's statement was really a serious promise at all. The context in which it was made and its tone suggest that it may have been nothing more than an expression of gratitude and hope for spectacular success. Even if it is a real promise, it has several problems. First, it is very vague. It does not make it clear what is meant by the "best seat"; nor does it specify the concert or concerts for which it will be obtained. Second, it is contingent on a very uncertain future event. A conditional promise could qualify as consideration unless the fulfillment of the condition is entirely at the will of the promisor or the condition is a sham because it could not possibly occur. Here the condition is not impossible, so not a sham, but it is remote enough to add doubt to its validity as true consideration. Third, unless Ivor can be interpreted to have promised a large number of free concerts, the value of his apparent consideration is disproportionately small in relation to Aunt Charity's promise. (It is worth even less than the face amount of a ticket because its value must be discounted to take account of the uncertainty of the condition occurring.) Courts normally do not evaluate the adequacy of consideration, and a court may decline to do so in this case. However, sometimes (especially when there are other indications of gratuitous intent) a court could take a significant discrepancy in values into account, and may find that the transaction is really not an exchange but a gift formalized by a nominal return.

Finally, even if Ivor did make a promise and Aunt Charity accepted it by her response, it does not seem that his promise was in exchange for Aunt Charity's promise. He made it after she had already told him she would give him $50,000, so it cannot be said to have induced her promise.

The basis for holding that Ivor gave consideration for Aunt Charity's promise is therefore quite thin, and the transaction really seems to be nothing more than a promise of a gift. An argument for consideration is not inconceivable, but it is shaky.

7. The pledge suggests three forms of purported consideration, but none of them likely qualifies as consideration.

First, the pledge form recites that the pledge is in consideration for Kitty's "love of and respect for our feline friends." This may have motivated Kitty to make the pledge (and even this is suspect, given that it is a standard recitation on the pledge form), but motive must be distinguished from consideration that must consist of a legal detriment suffered by CATS in exchange for her promise.

Second, the pledge form recites as consideration CATS's promise to use the contribution to further the purpose for which it was established. Even if this commitment by CATS is a promise, given in exchange for Kitty's promise to donate money, CATS's promise may not qualify as a detriment for two reasons. One is that CATS may have a preexisting duty, under its charter as a nonprofit organization, to use donated funds to further the purpose for which it is established. This duty likely is owed not only to the state, but also to the public, including contributors. The other is that to suffer a detriment, CATS must have had the legal right not to use Kitty's contribution for the promised purpose. However, at the time of making the promise, and until Kitty actually gives the funds to CATS, it has no legal right to use them at all. Therefore, its undertaking to use them for the purpose specified by Kitty seems more in the nature of an undertaking to use a gift for the purpose designated by the donor. As noted in section 7.3.5, it can be very tricky to distinguish a promise that is a legal detriment from one that is merely a condition of gift. A court may underplay this distinction so that it can validate a charitable promise. The task of finding consideration for a rather obvious gift is made easier if the donee makes a commitment that extends even slightly beyond the mere promise to use the gift as specified. That small additional detriment could qualify as consideration, even if it is implausible that it really induced the promise. In this case, no such additional detriment is apparent.

Third, the pledge form indicates that the contribution is tax-deductible, which may suggest that Kitty receives consideration for her pledge in the form of the benefit of a tax deduction. However, a benefit to the promisor is not enough for consideration. The benefit must be linked to a detriment suffered by the promisee. The benefit of a reduction in taxes, gained from the government, does not translate into a legal detriment suffered by CATS.

It would be a stretch to find that CATS gave consideration for Kitty's pledge. If the pledge is not supported by consideration, she can cancel it without liability. Consideration doctrine has fulfilled its cautionary function by enabling the donor to escape her generous impulse.

8. Gutter Press and Tabb have exchanged promises. The issue is whether Gutter Press' discretion to escape its commitment to publish the manuscript and pay for it is so wide as to make its promise illusory. The agreement gives Gutter Press two grounds for escaping its commitment. First, it can refuse to publish the manuscript if it finds it unsatisfactory. Second, it has the absolute right to terminate the agreement in the week after execution by giving notice.

Conditions of satisfaction are explained in section 7.9.5. Unless the contract made it clear that Gutter Press would have unbridled discretion to be dissatisfied (which it does not) the satisfaction clause obliges Gutter Press to exercise its discretion either in good faith or reasonably. Even if this commitment is not expressed in the agreement, it is readily implied. The implication of either a good faith or a reasonableness standard cures the problem of unbridled discretion, so Gutter Press' promise is not illusory. These facts do not require a determination of whether the good faith or reasonableness standard applies, because Gutter Press has not rejected the manuscript. The conclusion that one or other of these standards applies is enough to qualify Gutter Press' promise as consideration. (Had Tabb written a manuscript that Gutter Press rejected as unsatisfactory, it would have been necessary to decide which standard applied. The agreement does not specify the standard, so the court would have to determine whether it is subjective or objective. The rule of thumb is that a subjective standard is used if the purpose of the contract is to serve the party's personal taste, but an objective test is used if the satisfaction clause relates to matters of technical or commercial utility. This is a commercial venture, so Tabb would not reasonably expect that the publisher could reject the manuscript on the basis for purely subjective reasons. The proper inquiry would therefore be objective—whether a reasonable publisher would find the manuscript up to the generally acceptable journalistic and literary standards expected of this kind of writing in the trade.)

Apart from the condition of satisfaction, the agreement also gives Gutter Press the right to terminate the transaction for any reason by giving written notice to Tabb within the first week after execution of the agreement. This termination right may seem to be an unbridled right to escape the contract, but courts usually uphold agreements subject to such termination provisions provided that notice of termination must be given. The provision of notice is essential and the right to terminate without notice makes the promise illusory. (Even where there is no express requirement of notice, a court may have the basis to imply a promise of reasonable notice if the implication is consistent with the express language of the agreement and supported by the context in which the agreement was made.) The giving of the notice is regarded as a detriment because it is a new duty assumed under the agreement. This may sound a little flimsy and Tabb surely would not have bargained for this as the exclusive consideration for his promise. However, the prospect of earning a significant fee for a satisfactory manuscript if the contract is not terminated in its first week could be an incentive to enter into the bargain. A court is not likely to question the adequacy of notice as consideration where it is part of a potentially lucrative commercial bargain.

In this contract, only Gutter Press has the right to terminate, and Tabb has no equivalent right. However, this does not cause a consideration problem because the parties' obligations do not have to be coextensive. "Mutuality" in that sense is not required, and as long as each party has given consideration in some form, it does not matter that one of them has greater rights under the contract.

In short, neither the satisfaction clause nor the termination provisions should invalidate the contract and Tabb cannot escape his commitment to Gutter Press.

9. The relationship between Constance and Turn Coat is commercial, and Turn Coat's promise is in recognition of valuable work. Nevertheless, the promise is donative and unsupported by consideration. Constance's services were rendered prior to the promise, and not in exchange for it. Her work preceding the promise is sometimes called "past consideration," which is a misleading term, because it is not consideration at all—more accurately, it is past detriment. She has not suffered any new detriment to support the promise, so there is no basis on these facts to find consideration for Turn Coat's promise.

10. The issue in this Example is whether Abel's undertaking not to compete with Stifle Enterprises is supported by consideration. The noncompetition agreement was not included in the original employment contract,

but was entered into after the employment has commenced, and during the two-year term of the agreement. It is therefore a modification of the employment agreement, and Stifle must give Abel new consideration in exchange for his undertaking not to compete. Stifle has given Abel new consideration because it promised Abel a promotion in exchange for his undertaking. Abel was not an at-will employee at the time of the agreement—he was in the middle of a two-year employment contract. Had Stifle not promised the promotion, continued employment would not have been consideration because Stifle had the preexisting duty to employ Abel for the contract period.

11. The trial court is wrong. The parties have entered into a requirements contract governed by UCC §2.306, which makes it clear that a contract giving the buyer discretion to determine the quantity of goods ordered is not subject to the buyer's unbridled discretion, and therefore does not create a consideration problem. Peters' requirements must be its actual requirements as may occur in good faith.

    For §2.306 to apply, the contract must in fact be intended by the parties to be a requirements contract. If the buyer does not agree to buy the requirements covered in the contract only from the seller, leaving the buyer free to buy from other parties, there is no restriction on the buyer's discretion and its promise is illusory. That is, although §2.306(1) does not say so expressly, one of the hallmarks of a requirements contract is that the buyer must commit to fill those requirements exclusively from the seller. Peters has made this commitment. The contract is therefore valid.

    The next question is whether Peters breached its obligation of good faith by deciding to eliminate its requirement for peppers. Good faith is defined in UCC §§1.201(20) to include both subjective honesty in fact and the observance of commercially reasonable standards of fair dealing. Is Peters' decision, based on a business judgment to discontinue production of pickled peppers, in good faith? Official Comment 2 to UCC §2.306 indicates that the good faith standard permits an honest discontinuance of requirements resulting from lack of demand. It draws a distinction between the justifiable shutdown of the buyer's plant for lack of orders and an impermissible shutdown merely to curtail losses. This suggests that the good faith standard may not be satisfied merely because Peters has made a sensible business judgment based on profitability. A court may find that this hardship is not serious enough to overcome Peters' duty to honor Hal's reasonable expectations. This seems to be a close case, and good faith is notoriously difficult to determine under these circumstances. While Peters' decision to cease pickled pepper production is a legitimate business decision, a court may decide that the downturn in sales because of increased competition is not so severe as to necessitate the change in product line as a matter of survival.

The contract includes a stated estimate of Peters' requirements. Section 2.306(1) provides that, in addition to the good faith standard, there is an alternative test that Peters' orders for peppers may not an unreasonably disproportionate to the stated estimate. A quantity of zero is dramatically disproportionate to the estimate, so it may seem that this test is easily satisfied and that the case can be resolved on the disproportionality test, rather than on the less certain good faith test. However, many courts interpreting §2.306 have held that it confines the disproportionality test to increases in demand, and does not apply to decreases in demand.

12. Mutual is wrong. The contract reserves broad discretion to Mutual to modify the terms of the lease as it sees fit, without notice, and even to cancel it at any time "with or without notice," which effectively does not even require notice of cancellation. This broad discretion to make unilateral changes in the lease or terminate it without notice makes Mutual's promise illusory so that it does not qualify as consideration for the promises made by Tenant.

    The contract language used in this Example is closely based on the actual language contained in a standard lease drafted by the lessor of premises in *De Angelis v. Nolan Enterprises, Inc.*, 2018 WL 4566280 (S.D. Ohio 2018). The court enunciated the principle that "mutuality of obligation" requires the contract to bind both parties, otherwise it is binding on neither. The lessor had reserved such wide discretion to modify or terminate the lease, that it could not be said to have made any binding commitment, making its promise illusory. As a result, the lessor's promise was not supported by consideration, so the agreement did not bind the tenant either. The court distinguished this contract from one that requires notice of changes or termination. Although the commitment to give notice is a rather modest detriment, it would be enough consideration to prevent the promise from being illusory.

    In some cases, it may be possible to curtail apparently unlimited discretion by implying an obligation to exercise the discretion in good faith or reasonably, as happened in *Wood v. Lucy, Lady Duff-Gordon*, discussed in section 7.9.2. However, this can only be done if the language and circumstances of the contract admit of it. In *Pharma Conference Education, Inc. v. State*, 2023 WL 2470288 (Tenn. Ct. App. 2023), the producer of continuing education programs for the pharmaceutical industry entered into an agreement with the University of Tennessee to produce programs "as is feasible." When the university terminated the agreement, Pharma sued it for breach of contract. The court granted summary judgment to the university on the grounds of lack of consideration. The court noted that courts try to avoid finding a promise illusory where it is possible to imply an obligation of good faith or reasonableness. However, the language of the agreement and the context of the transaction showed that Pharma's determination of feasibility was really intended to be entirely within its unrestricted discretion.[26]

26. The court also noted that, in addition to creating a consideration problem, a term that reserves broad discretion to a party may be unenforceable on grounds of indefiniteness (discussed in sections 10.4 and 105).

CHAPTER 8

Promissory Estoppel as the Basis for Enforcing Promises

§8.1 INTRODUCTION

As Chapter 7 shows, consideration is a prerequisite to a valid contract. A promise that has not been bargained for in exchange for some detriment cannot be enforced as a contract. Chapter 7 also shows that courts apply consideration doctrine with a degree of flexibility that enables them to stretch the concept of bargained-for exchange in some cases where the exchange or detriment may be tenuous or doubtful. But this only works up to a point. Sometimes the facts are such that there is no realistic argument that consideration was given for a promise. In many cases the resulting nonenforcement of the promise is an appropriate consequence, but this result can be unfair when the promisee incurred some loss in relying justifiably on the promise. Promissory estoppel has developed to provide relief in such cases. When all its elements are satisfied, a promisor may be held accountable for a promise without consideration, and the court may enforce it either to the same extent as if a contract was made, or to the extent necessary to remedy the unfair result of reliance on it.

Promissory estoppel was first articulated as a distinct basis of liability in §90 of the First Restatement. The original formulation, with subtle revisions, survives in §90 of Restatement, Second. Although the Restatement section does not itself call the doctrine promissory estoppel, this name is firmly established by long usage.

Several factors must be considered in deciding whether promissory estoppel relief is appropriate, as discussed shortly. However, its essential elements can be stated simply: A promise coupled with detrimental reliance on that promise.

This chapter first discusses the general principles of promissory estoppel and then looks at some specific applications of the doctrine in various contexts such as charitable pledges (section 8.8), negotiations (section 8.9), and options (section 8.10). In addition, promissory estoppel comes up again in other contexts later in the book, for example, in relation to the statute of frauds (section 11.4.3).

§8.2 THE NATURE OF PROMISSORY ESTOPPEL AS AN INDEPENDENT BASIS OF RELIEF OR AS A CONSIDERATION SUBSTITUTE

Promissory estoppel is an ancillary basis for upholding a promise that does not qualify as contractual. It is not needed where the promise is supported by consideration and there are no other problems that prevent the promise from being enforced as contractual. When analyzing a problem, it is therefore logical to first consider if a contract has been formed and to turn to promissory estoppel only if that question is answered negatively.

Courts and commentators disagree over the categorization of promissory estoppel and its relationship to contract. This debate is partly philosophical, reflecting contrasting opinions on how the law should be conceived, and partly empirical, based on different interpretations of how the courts actually treat promissory estoppel. Some courts and commentators classify promissory estoppel as a substitute for consideration. On this view, promissory estoppel is a contract-based doctrine that allows for the enforcement of a promise, even in the absence of consideration, provided that the elements of promissory estoppel are satisfied. That is, promissory estoppel is treated as an alternative basis for finding contractual liability where consideration is lacking or there is some other defect in the formation process. Comment *d* to Restatement, Second, §90 suggests that the drafters favor this approach by stating that a promise binding under §90 is a contract.

Other courts and commentators categorize promissory estoppel as an alternative and independent basis for enforcing the promise—a separate theory of obligation, based not on bargain but on accountability for conduct that induces reliance. This conception of promissory estoppel emphasizes its affinity to tort and to equitable estoppel (explained in section 8.4) and sees it more as a redress for injury suffered in reliance than as a contract-like relationship.

The characterization of promissory estoppel is not just a matter of theory, but can have significant practical consequences. As explained in sections

8.3 and 8.7, it has an impact on the remedy awarded to the promisee. Apart from the question of relief, the nature of promissory estoppel could give rise to other legal consequences. Here are three examples of practical legal consequences arising from the classification of promissory estoppel:

1. If promissory estoppel is classified as a contractual cause of action, it is likely subject to the statute of limitations[1] applicable to contract suits, which is commonly six years. However, if it is classified as a tort-based cause of action, it is likely to be subject to the statute of limitations for tort actions, which is typically much shorter.
2. The doctrine of sovereign immunity precludes a tort action against a governmental authority without its consent, but the doctrine does not bar contract claims against the government. Therefore, if promissory estoppel is classified as tort-based, a promissory estoppel suit cannot be brought against a government entity unless the entity has waived immunity. However, if promissory estoppel is contract-based, the government is not immune from the claim. In *Cornell Narberth, LLC v. Borough of Narberth*, 167 A.3d 228 (Pa. Commw. Ct. 2017), a real estate developer applied for permits to build houses in a subdivision. At the time of the application, the borough's representative incorrectly told the developer that the building code did not require the installation of automatic sprinkler systems in detached single-family residences. The borough issued building permits based on construction drawings that did not provide for sprinklers and the houses were built without them. When the houses were completed, the borough refused to issue certificates of occupancy because of the lack of sprinkler systems, so the developer had to incur the additional expense of having to install the sprinklers in the completed homes. The developer sued the borough for these additional costs on several theories, including contract and promissory estoppel. The court upheld the trial court's grant of summary judgment to the borough on both the contract and promissory estoppel claims. It found no contract cause of action on the ground that a permit was not a contract—it was not an exchange relationship with consideration because the borough had a preexisting legal duty to issue the permits, and the developer made no promise to erect the building. The developer had no promissory estoppel claim because the claim was not based on a promise, but on the negligence of the borough representative in incorrectly telling the developer that the sprinkler systems were not required. This negligence claim was based in tort and therefore fell within the borough's sovereign immunity.

1. A statute of limitations specifies the period within which a person must commence suit on a claim. If suit is not initiated within that period, it is barred.

3. *Douglas E. Barnhart, Inc. v. CMC Fabricators, Inc.*, 149 Cal. Rptr. 3d 440 (Cal. Ct. App. 2012), offers a third example: Because the plaintiff had sued to enforce a promise under the theory of promissory estoppel, not contract, the court held that the plaintiff was not entitled to attorney's fees under a statute that allowed such an award to the prevailing party "in an action on a contract."

§8.3 THE DIFFERENCE IN REMEDIAL EMPHASIS BETWEEN CONTRACT AND PROMISSORY ESTOPPEL

The way in which promissory estoppel is characterized—as a contract-based doctrine or an independent tort-like theory—has a bearing on the question of its most appropriate remedial goal. As discussed more fully in section 8.7, if promissory estoppel creates contractual liability, the normal relief for promissory estoppel should be the normal measure of expectation damages for breach of contract, and it would only be appropriate to limit relief under special circumstances. Conversely, if one focuses on the protection of reliance, the remedy should usually be confined to reimbursement of actual loss, with fuller enforcement reserved for cases when justice so demands. This could make a substantial difference in recovery: Expectation damages, the primary form of contract damages, look toward the future and aim to place the promisee in the same economic position that the promisee would have been in had the contract been honored. The goal of expectation damages is to give the promisee the benefit of the bargain by awarding the money equivalent of what the promisee would have gained as a result of the contract.[2] On the other hand, if the principal focus of promissory estoppel is merely to reimburse for loss caused by reliance, the most appropriate form of relief is an award of damages that looks toward the past and aims to award a sum of money that would restore the promisee to the economic position that the promisee was in before the promise was made. Damages that reimburse loss or expense incurred in reliance on a promise are called reliance damages. The aim of reliance damages is similar to that of tort damages, which also aim to restore the victim to the position that the victim was in before the tort was committed.

2. As mentioned in section 1.2.4 and discussed more fully in section 18.10, expectation damages are the usual form of relief for breach of contract. In some situations, it is possible for the aggrieved party to obtain the relief of specific performance—a court order compelling the breaching party to perform. However, courts do not award specific performance as a matter of course, and confine that relief to situations where the equities favor it and an award of damages would not adequately compensate for the breach.

§8.4 AN INTRODUCTION TO EQUITABLE ESTOPPEL AND ITS LINK TO PROMISSORY ESTOPPEL

As intimated above, the essential function of promissory estoppel is to provide relief for justifiable reliance on a promise given without consideration. Promissory estoppel derives from the much older principle of equitable estoppel, also known as estoppel in pais. A basic explanation of equitable estoppel is helpful to understanding promissory estoppel. Equity is introduced in section 2.5. A court of equity exercises its discretion to do justice between the parties, so it is a general principle of equity that the litigants must themselves behave equitably in seeking the court's assistance. Relief that may otherwise be available is barred by the claimant's unworthy conduct.

Equitable estoppel reflects this principle. Its basic purpose is to preclude (i.e., "estop") a person from asserting a right when, by deliberate words or conduct, that person has misled the other party into the justifiable belief that the right does not exist or would not be asserted. Like many equitable doctrines, estoppel involves a balancing of the equities between the parties and a comparative evaluation of the fault and responsibility of the parties. Therefore, it generally only bars relief when the party asserting the rights deliberately engaged in the misleading behavior with knowledge or reason to know it could be misleading and could induce reliance by the other. In addition, the other, unaware of the true facts, must have relied on the apparent facts in a way that would result in some loss or prejudice if the claimant is permitted to assert the right.

For example, the syllabus for Professor Punctilio's law school class on equitable remedies states that students will be evaluated in the class by four short written papers, to be assigned during the course of the semester. The syllabus declares, in bold print, that all assignments must be submitted by the due date and that the professor will refuse to accept a late submission and will record a failing grade for it. Di Latory struggled with the first assignment and could not finish it on time. Although it was two days late, she emailed it to Professor Punctilio and hoped for the best. The professor did not reject it and later emailed it back with comments on its substance and a B grade. Di was delayed in completing her second paper by trouble with her computer. She emailed the second paper to Professor Punctilio three days late. Again, the professor returned it a short while later with comments and an A grade. When it was time for the submission of the third paper, Di did not worry about getting it in exactly by the due date, and she submitted it two days late. Professor Punctilio returned it the next day with a note stating, "Rejected as untimely. Grade: F." When Di goes to Professor Punctilio's office to confront him over the failing grade, she should be able to persuade him, as a scholar of equitable remedies, that he is estopped from rejecting her third paper on grounds of tardiness: She suffered prejudice by submitting the third paper late in reasonable reliance on his deliberate conduct. It does not matter that Professor Punctilio did not intend his conduct to mislead Di. Estoppel is based not on deception, but on accountability for deliberate words or conduct that induced justifiable reliance and consequent detriment.

This is a case of equitable, not promissory, estoppel, because Professor Punctilio did not promise Di that he would accept her late paper. However, equitable estoppel is the doctrine from which promissory estoppel developed. Courts originally refused to apply estoppel to promises and confined it to conduct or factual speech that was not promissory in nature. However, during the nineteenth century (and possibly even before that) some courts began to recognize that reliance on a promise was just as worthy of protection as reliance on a factual assertion, and they began to apply equitable estoppel to promises. The theory of these cases was that the promisor was estopped from asserting a lack of consideration for the promise, hence consideration was deemed to be present. Therefore, early cases did treat estoppel as a consideration substitute. Not all courts followed this approach. Some refused relief despite reliance if consideration was absent, and others sought to protect reliance indirectly by bending over backward to find consideration in the most tenuous of detriments.

By the time of the drafting of the First Restatement, there was enough caselaw to support the inclusion of a new doctrine that came to be called promissory estoppel. The Restatement's formulation (in §90) did not treat the promise as estopping the denial of consideration but simply recognized detrimental reliance on the promise as a basis of enforcing it. Therefore, while the drafters of the Restatement did not necessarily conceive of promissory estoppel as a theory of liability separate from contract, they planted the seeds of this idea. Following publication of the Restatement, the judicial recognition of promissory estoppel grew, and the doctrine has become well established, even though courts differ on its scope and range. Its formulation in Restatement, Second, §90 follows that of the original Restatement quite closely but makes changes to reflect its development over the intervening years.

The derivation of promissory estoppel from equitable estoppel means that it has an equitable basis. Depending on the nature of relief sought, this could have an impact on the parties' rights at trial. For example, in *InCompass IT, Inc. v. XO Communications Services, Inc.*, 719 F.3d 891 (8th Cir. 2013), the court held that where promissory estoppel is used as the basis of claiming reliance damages, rather than as a consideration substitute seeking expectation damages, the suit is equitable in nature. As a result, the court held that the plaintiff was not entitled to a jury trial, because jury trials are available only in law and not in equity.

§8.5 THE RANGE OF PROMISSORY ESTOPPEL: GIFTS AND COMMERCIAL TRANSACTIONS

A principal function of promissory estoppel is the enforcement of a gratuitous promise, such as a family gift or charitable donation, for which no consideration was given. Promissory estoppel is not needed to overcome an absence of consideration in most commercial transactions because these are exchanges by nature, and once agreement has been reached, consideration is present. However, as Chapter 7 shows, consideration problems do sometimes arise in the commercial setting—for example, where the modification of a contract is not supported by new consideration, or where a party had a preexisting duty to incur the detriment, or where a promise is illusory. Even if there is no issue with consideration, a commercial promise may be unenforceable as a contract for other reasons. There are at least three broad types of situation in which promissory estoppel may be applicable to a commercial promise in which both parties have given consideration, but there is some other reason why the transaction cannot be enforced as a contract.

1. A promise made for good consideration is unenforceable because of noncompliance with legal formality such as the statute of frauds. Some (but not all) courts may allow the party who relied on the oral promise to use the doctrine of promissory estoppel to enforce the oral promise that would otherwise be unenforceable as a contract. Discussion of this ground is deferred to section 11.4, where it is treated in conjunction with the statute of frauds.[3]
2. Promissory estoppel may be used to hold a party to a promise made during negotiations for an abortive contract. When parties negotiate, they may make tentative commitments, not intended to bind unless and until final agreement is reached. Therefore, as a general rule, statements of intent made during negotiations are not treated as promises, and a party who incurs expense or relinquishes an opportunity on the strength of such a statement usually assumes the risk of loss if no contract comes about. Sometimes, however, a precontractual statement may reasonably be intended as a binding commitment, justifying reliance and attracting liability if not honored. The situations in which this might happen are discussed in section 8.9.

3. Although it could technically be argued that consideration is absent in such cases because an unenforceable informal promise is not a legal detriment, the real issue is whether the promise should be enforced despite the failure to comply with required formalities.

3. Promissory estoppel may afford relief for reliance on a promise that falls short of becoming contractual because of some defect or omission in the agreement formed by the parties. For example, there may be a fatal vagueness in the terms of the putative contract, or the promisee's commitment may be so discretionary as to be illusory, yet there is enough of a commitment to justify reliance.[4]

§8.6 THE ELEMENTS OF PROMISSORY ESTOPPEL

§8.6.1 Introduction and Overview of the Elements

Uncle Rich said to his niece, Penny Less, "You are my favorite niece, so I want to do something special for you on your twenty-first birthday next year. I am going to give you a birthday gift of $50,000." On the strength of this promise, Penny enrolled in college, committing herself to the payment of $50,000 tuition for her first year. Uncle Rich failed to honor his promise to Penny. On these facts there is no basis for finding that Penny gave any consideration to Uncle Rich for his promise. He simply promised her an unconditional gift and did not bargain for anything in return. Penny therefore cannot enforce the promise as a contract. However, because Uncle Rich made a promise to Penny and she apparently relied on it by incurring a debt for tuition, she may be able to enforce the promise fully or in part on grounds of promissory estoppel. Restatement, Second, §90 sets out the elements of promissory estoppel:

1. A promise was made by the promisor with the reasonable expectation that the promisee would rely on it. This focuses on the promisor's conduct and evaluates the promisor's intent objectively.
2. The promise did in fact induce the promisee's action or forbearance. Although §90 does not say so expressly, this reliance must be justified. This focuses on the promisee's reaction and evaluates the promisee's reliance largely on an objective standard.
3. The enforcement of the promise is necessary to avoid injustice. This focuses on the consequence of reliance. Although §90 does not refer expressly to the detriment—that is, harm or loss—suffered by the promisee as a result of reliance, this is a crucial factor.

4. This could also be characterized as a consideration issue because the vague or discretionary promise is not consideration. However, the real issue is whether fairness demands accountability even in the absence of a binding contract.

4. The remedy may be limited as justice requires. This focuses on the appropriate form of relief. The nature and extent of the promisee's detriment is relevant here too.

As these factors indicate, a court's decision to enforce a noncontractual promise involves an evaluation of the conduct and reasonable understanding of each party and the fairness of holding the promisor accountable for a promise that would not otherwise be binding in contract law. These four factors are expanded on below. Although each of them focuses on a separate inquiry, they flow into and affect each other. Thus, for example, if the promise is clear and express, it is easier to infer intent to induce reliance and to justify reliance, and enforcement is more likely to be needed to avert injustice. Conversely, if there is doubt about the apparent promise, it is harder to show these other elements convincingly.

§8.6.2 A Promise Must Have Been Made

A promise is a commitment to act or to refrain from acting in a specified way at a future time. Not every assertion or statement of intent qualifies as a promise. Unless clear language of commitment is used, it can be difficult to decide if a promise has been made. Words and conduct must be interpreted in all the relevant circumstances of the case to determine if the alleged promisor manifested an intent to commit to a particular performance or course of action. *Norton v. McOsker*, 407 F.3d 501 (5th Cir. 2005), illustrates some of the issues that can arise in deciding if a promise was made. A woman had been involved in a 23-year adulterous relationship with a married man. When he ended the relationship, she sued him under various theories. Her promissory estoppel claim was based on the grounds that he had frequently promised during the relationship to divorce his wife and marry her and also that, both during and at the end of the relationship, he had promised to support her for life. The court of appeals upheld the trial court's grant of summary judgment against the woman. Neither of the alleged undertakings established an enforceable promise. The man's promise to divorce his wife and marry the woman was void as against public policy and his undertaking of lifetime support was too general and nonspecific to qualify as an enforceable promise.

Cote v. Aiello, 148 A.3d 537 (R.I. 2016), is another example of a case in which undertakings about the future fell short as qualifying as promises. Cote had worked for Aiello's companies for many years and became president of one of those companies in 1997. At that time, and on several subsequent occasions, Aiello told Cote that when Aiello was ready to retire, he would sell the company to Cote and would structure a payment plan to enable him to buy it. Despite these assurances, Aiello sold the company to someone else in 2005. The court affirmed the trial judge's holdings that Cote had no claim in either contract or promissory estoppel. The parties never entered into a contract for the sale of the company because they never reached agreement on any of the specific terms of the sale. Furthermore, even though Aiello often reiterated that he would sell the company to Cote on his retirement, these vague and nonspecific statements were not clear and definite enough to constitute promises and Cote had no reasonable basis to rely on them.

Manifested, rather than actual, intent is determinative in deciding whether a promise was made. As in contract, intent for the purpose of promissory estoppel is gauged by an objective test. The question is not whether the promisor actually intended to make a promise, but whether a reasonable person in the promisee's position would have understood the utterance to be a promise, based on the promisor's words and conduct. This could not be otherwise because promissory estoppel aims to protect reliance that necessarily is based on a reasonable perception of exhibited intent rather than on the undisclosed thoughts and beliefs of the promisor. The objective evaluation of whether a promise was made could therefore trap a promisor into a promise that was not subjectively intended as a commitment.

The objective determination of intent in this context is subject to the same qualification that applies in deciding on contractual intent—the promise must have been voluntarily and deliberately made. Therefore, as in contract, doctrines such as fraud, duress, and mistake (covered in Chapters 13 and 15) may be used to go behind the objective appearance of a promise. In addition to affecting the quality of the promise, any improper conduct by the promisee would also undermine the promisee's claim of justifiable reliance.

The evidentiary, cautionary, and channeling functions served by consideration doctrine play some role in evaluating a promise for purposes of promissory estoppel. The fact that consideration was not given for the promise means that these functions are not fulfilled by any act of exchange. Therefore, a court must exercise particular care before finding a promise when there is little or no formality in its execution or the circumstances suggest that the promisor may have acted on impulse or with rash generosity.

§8.6.3 The Promisor Should Reasonably Have Expected the Promise to Induce Action or Forbearance by the Promisee

This element is so closely connected to the inquiry into promise that it is a little artificial to treat it separately. However, it is helpful to split the evaluation of promisor accountability into two issues for the purpose of building a framework for analysis. The promisor is accountable for a deliberate and voluntary promise, made with the reasonable understanding that the promisee would likely rely on it. To decide on the promisor's reasonable expectation of reliance, all the circumstances must be evaluated. The question is whether the promisor should be held accountable for creating the situation leading to reliance and the resulting loss. The promisor's intent to induce reliance is evaluated on an objective standard of reasonableness, irrespective of whether or not the promisor actually intended the promisee to rely on the promise. That is, the promisor must have known or reasonably should have realized that the promisee would likely understand that a promise had been made and would thereby be induced to take or refrain from action of the kind that occurred. Thus, not only the likelihood of reliance but also the general nature and extent of the response must have been reasonably foreseeable by the promisor.

§8.6.4 The Promise Must Have Induced Justifiable Action or Forbearance by the Promisee

This factor moves from the promisor's accountability to the promisee's reliance. In dealing with inducement, the text of §90 does not expressly require the reliance to be justifiable, but this principle is referred to in Comments *b* and *c* to §90 and is inherent in the purpose of promissory estoppel. The promisee's justifiable reliance on the promise has two components.

a. Actual Inducement

The promise must in fact have induced the promisee's action or forbearance. There must have been a cause and effect between the promise and the conduct, so there is no inducement if the promisee would have incurred the loss or expense even had the promise not been made, or incurred it before the promise was made. In *Thomas v. Archer*, 384 P.3d 791 (Alaska 2016), Thomas was admitted to the emergency room of a hospital in Ketchikan, Alaska, because of complications with her pregnancy. Archer, the attending physician, determined that she needed to be medevacked to a hospital in Seattle which was better equipped to handle her condition. Thomas told Archer that she needed preauthorization for the medevac from her medical insurer, and Archer assured her that she would take care of the preauthorization. She failed to do so, and the insurer therefore refused to pay the costs of about $100,000 for the medevac and the treatment at the Seattle hospital. Thomas sued Archer and the Ketchikan hospital for that amount in contract and promissory estoppel. The trial court awarded summary judgment to the defendants on the contract claim because Thomas gave no consideration for the promise to obtain the preauthorization. It also awarded summary judgment to the defendants on the promissory estoppel claim on the ground that Thomas had not relied on the promise. She had conceded that her priority was to save her unborn baby, so she would have taken the flight to Seattle even had she not been able to obtain preauthorization. The Supreme Court affirmed the summary judgment on the contract claim but reversed it on the promissory estoppel claim. It held that the facts alleged indicated that Archer made a clear promise with the reasonable expectation that Thomas would rely on it. Even if Thomas would have taken the flight to Seattle anyway, she should be permitted to go to trial to prove that she relied on the promise in that she would have called her insurer herself had Archer not promised to do so.

b. Justification

Actual inducement is not enough. In addition, the promisee's response must have been a justifiable reaction to the promise. Justification is evaluated under a largely objective standard with some weight given to the personal attributes and situation of the promisee. The essential question is whether a reasonable person in the promisee's position would have been induced by the promise to engage in the particular action or forbearance. The justifiability standard is an essential safeguard that protects the promisor from being held accountable for consequences caused by a promisee's unpredictable, rash, or unreasonable reaction to the noncontractual promise. A promisee who was not justified in relying on the promise should bear the risk of having made the judgment to incur loss or expense in the absence of a contract.

The inquiry into the nature and strength of the promise, the promisor's reasonable expectation of reliance on it, and the promisee's justification in relying on it tend to meld together. They are frequently just different aspects of the same overall pattern: The stronger the sense of commitment, the greater the likelihood of a reasonable expectation of inducement and, consequently, of justifiable reliance. For example, in the *Norton* case, discussed in section 8.6.2, the court found that the man had made no enforceable promise to marry or to support the woman during or at the end of their 23-year affair. The court also noted that even had his undertakings qualified as promises, the woman would not have been justified in relying on them. His promise of lifelong support was too vague to induce reliance. She could not have had any reliance on his promises to leave his wife and marry her because he had made and broken that promise countless times over the 23 years of their relationship.

Section 90(2) dispenses with proof of reliance for charitable pledges.[5] A few courts have followed this rule and have upheld promises

5. Section 90(2) also applies to marriage settlements, which are not discussed in this book.

of charitable contributions, even where reliance cannot be established. However, most courts have not adopted the Restatement, Second's position and still require charitable organizations to show justifiable reliance on the gratuitous promise. Comment f to §90 indicates that subsection (2) recognizes that courts tend to uphold promises of charitable gifts, even where consideration or reliance is doubtful or nonexistent. However, while many courts do still tend to find consideration for or reliance on charitable promises on flimsy grounds, few have followed the further step of declaring, as §90(2) does, that no proof of consideration or reliance is necessary.

§8.6.5 The Promise Is Binding If Injustice Can Be Avoided Only by Its Enforcement

This element reflects the total balance that the court must draw after evaluating the equities, so that its decision achieves a fair result in all the circumstances. This balancing reflects the equitable roots of promissory estoppel. It takes into account not only the issues of promise and reliance discussed above but also any other factors that bear on the appropriateness of enforcing the promise.

The most significant of these is the detriment or harm suffered by the promisee in relying on the promise. Because the protection of reliance is the fundamental purpose of promissory estoppel, it is not enough that the promisee had merely a generalized expectation of gain which has been disappointed. The promisee must have suffered some actual harm by relying on the promise. Therefore, "detriment" in this context is usually not used in the attenuated sense associated with consideration doctrine but describes a real economic loss such as an expenditure, a sacrificed opportunity, a commitment, or some other prejudice of a substantial kind. While some courts may accept less, especially if the other equities strongly favor enforcement, the need to avert injustice by enforcement of the promise is not very strong if there is no loss that needs redress and the only effect of nonenforcement is the failure to receive the promised benefit.

The quality of the promise, as discussed in section 8.6.2, is also a factor to be considered in the general balancing of the equities. Comment *b* to §90 stresses that the promisor needs protection from an ill-considered promise or a bogus claim of promise. The absence of consideration means that its safeguards—the channeling, cautionary, and evidentiary functions—are missing. Therefore, in the overall balancing of the equities, the court should pay particular attention to indications of whether or not the promisor carefully considered and seriously intended the promise under all the circumstances.

§8.7 THE REMEDY WHEN PROMISSORY ESTOPPEL IS APPLIED

Restatement, Second, §90 states that the remedy for breach of the promise may be limited as justice requires. Although Comment *d* to that section says that a promise binding under the section is a contract, this limitation of remedy means that the promisee is not necessarily entitled to full contractual relief. That is, the court could grant the promisee full contractual relief, which typically takes the form of expectation damages, designed to compensate for loss of gains resulting from the breach. Expectation damages aim to place the promisee in the position that the promisee would have been in had the promise been performed. However, the court has the discretion to provide a lesser remedy. Typically, this lesser remedy takes the form of reliance damages, which focus on the reimbursement of the actual loss or expense incurred in reliance on the promise.

Although §90 suggests a range of damages and makes it clear that the balance of the equities affects the extent of relief, there is some debate on the correct emphasis to be placed on the choice of remedy. If the role of promissory estoppel is to estop the promisor from denying the existence of a contract, it follows that the law should treat the promise as if it was a contract, and the remedy for breach of contract, usually expectation damages, should be the normal measure of relief. The lesser remedy, restricting relief to the reimbursement of reliance losses, would therefore be appropriate only in exceptional cases. However, if promissory estoppel is an independent tort-like theory of liability, reimbursement of actual reliance losses should be the normal relief, with full enforcement confined to cases in which the lesser remedy is clearly inadequate. It is difficult to say for sure where the primary focus is, given the spectrum of damages available to courts. It is important to recognize, however, that courts have a discretionary range of relief. Some of the factors that a court may consider in exercising this discretion are illustrated by *Tynan v. JBVBB, LLC*, 743 N.W.2d 730 (Wis. Ct. App. 2007). Tynan began working for the defendant as a consultant before the parties had settled the terms of an employment contract. The parties never reached agreement on the terms of the employment contract, and Tynan's consultancy was eventually terminated. He sued the defendant for specific performance of promises to pay various bonuses to him.[6] The jury found that the promises had been made and that Tynan had relied on them. However, the court refused to award expectation relief to him and confined his relief to reliance losses. The court acknowledged that it had the

6. An order of specific performance, discussed in section 18.10, is a form of expectation relief under which the court orders the breaching party to render the performance promised under the contract.

discretion to award expectation relief but declined to do so because it found that the promises were somewhat vague, Tynan had not been employed as a consultant for very long, and the defendant had not acted unfairly. The court then gave Tynan the opportunity to prove reliance damages. He tried to show that he had lost opportunities for employment in reliance on the promise, but he could not prove this with sufficient certainty, and ended up with no award of damages.

As a further illustration of the possible range of remedies for promissory estoppel and the distinction between full contractual damages and reliance recovery, consider Penny's enrollment in college on the strength of Uncle Rich's promise to give her $50,000 as a twenty-first birthday gift. Penny's expectation is $50,000, and full contractual enforcement would give her this amount. By contrast, reliance damages would depend on the extent of her actual loss or prejudice. Therefore, if she enrolled in college on the strength of Uncle Rich's promise and committed herself to pay $50,000 for her first year's tuition, injustice might be averted only by full enforcement of the promise. However, say that Penny received a scholarship so that her annual tuition is only $10,000 and Penny is committed for only one year's tuition. Enforcement to the extent of $10,000 may be enough to prevent injustice. Although Penny, in a sense, may have relied on having the balance of $40,000 to pay for future years' tuition, the broken promise of future funding disappoints her expectation but does not constitute an actual out-of-pocket loss. The facts become more complicated if, in addition to committing herself for $10,000 tuition, she gave up a job to attend college, because her sacrificed earnings are also a reliance loss that could be relevant in the decision on her recovery. The court's ability to award reliance damages where full enforcement of the promise would be excessive gives the court the flexibility to avoid an all-or-nothing resolution. This allows some measure of relief to a promisee who can show losses resulting from reliance but cannot justify enforcement of the promise as if it was a contract.

Conrad v. Fields, 2007 WL 2106302 (Minn. Ct. App. 2007), dealt with a situation in which a promisee was disappointed by the breach of a promise to pay tuition. Walter Fields, a wealthy man, encouraged his friend, Marjorie Conrad, to attend law school and promised to pay her tuition. Conrad enrolled in law school on the basis of this promise, giving up a job that paid her an annual salary of $45,000. Fields made a relatively small tuition payment immediately after Conrad entered law school but then claimed temporary financial difficulties and made no further payments. However, he did say that he would pay Conrad's tuition after she graduated and passed the bar. She did graduate and pass the bar, but Fields refused to pay. Conrad sued him on a theory of promissory estoppel for reimbursement of $87,314 that she had paid for her tuition. (She did not claim loss of the earnings.) The trial court found that all the elements of promissory estoppel were satisfied and awarded her the damages claimed. It concluded that Fields made the promise to Conrad intending her to rely on it. He knew that she would have to quit her job to attend law school and that she could not afford to pay for law school herself. Conrad knew that Fields was wealthy and generous, and she trusted him. On the faith of his promise, she did stop working and enroll in law school. The court of appeals affirmed. It rejected Fields' argument that Conrad was not justified in relying on his promise when she continued to incur tuition expenses after he stopped paying, because Fields had told Conrad that his financial difficulties were temporary and that he would pay her tuition after she graduated. Fields also argued that Conrad suffered no real detriment because she received a valuable law degree. The court conceded that the degree was beneficial to her, but she nevertheless suffered the detriment of incurring the debt to acquire it. The court characterized Conrad's damages of $87,314 as reliance damages because this was the actual expense that she incurred in reliance on the promise. However, on the facts of this case, these reliance damages are equivalent to Conrad's full expectation. If the situation had been different—say that Fields clearly repudiated his promise during Conrad's first year, and she sued him then—her actual reliance damages (her tuition payments up to the time of repudiation) would have been considerably less than her expectation damages. Under those circumstances, the court may have considered it appropriate to confine her recovery to that lesser amount.

§8.8 PROMISSORY ESTOPPEL IN RELATION TO GIFTS AND CHARITABLE PLEDGES

Section 7.3.5 raises the sometimes difficult and subtle distinction between an act or promise that constitutes a bargained-for exchange, and one that would merely be an incident of receiving the gift, or an undertaking to use the gift for the purposes for which it was given. Sometimes a court may resolve this ambiguity by finding that the promisee did suffer some detriment, so that the promise can be enforced as a contract. However, where there is no basis for finding consideration, the pledge or promise of a gift may still be enforced under the doctrine of promissory estoppel, provided that the donee can establish that the elements of promissory estoppel are satisfied.[7]

Allegheny College v. National Chautauqua County Bank, 159 N.E. 173 (N.Y. 1927), is a foundational case that demonstrates the interplay between consideration

7. As stated in section 8.6.4, most courts require all the elements, including justifiable reliance, to be satisfied even where the gift is a charitable gift. They have not adopted the approach of Restatement, Second, §90(2), which treats a charitable pledge as binding even in the absence of reliance.

doctrine and promissory estoppel where a donee gives undertakings in return for a pledge. Mary Yates Johnston pledged $5,000 to be paid to the college on her death. The pledge required the money to be used to educate students preparing for the ministry. It also stipulated that the fund would be known as the "Mary Yates Johnston Memorial Fund." She paid $1,000 of this amount while she was alive, and the college set it aside for a scholarship fund as stipulated but did nothing further in reliance on the pledge. The donor repudiated the pledge before her death. After she died, the college sued her estate for the balance of the pledged amount. The court found that the college had given consideration for the pledge because the college, by accepting the $1,000, impliedly promised to memorialize the donor's name. (The opinion did not rely on the college's implied promise to use the fund for the purpose stipulated, possibly because that seems too clearly to be a condition of the gift.) The court did not have to apply promissory estoppel because it found consideration for the promise. However, a dictum suggests that promissory estoppel could have been used as an alternative basis for enforcing the gift. It is clear from the opinion that the underlying motivation for the court's conclusion was its belief that the charitable pledge should be upheld as a matter of public policy. To get this result, the court strained to fit the facts into a theory of recovery, but those facts do not provide much support for either basis of relief. The legal detriment found by the court is quite flimsy, and it is difficult to see grounds for promissory estoppel. There is no indication that the donor reasonably intended to induce reliance until the money was paid out on her death, or that the college took any action in reliance on the pledge. The mere banking of the money cannot really be seen as the kind of detrimental reliance that would support a claim of promissory estoppel.

King v. Trustees of Boston University, 647 N.E.2d 1196 (Mass. 1995), also involved a transaction that could have been interpreted as a gift subject to conditions but that was enforced by the court under consideration theory and, in the alternative, under the theory of promissory estoppel. This case is discussed in connection with consideration doctrine in section 7.3.5. It is noted there that the court found that by undertaking to index and care for Dr. King's papers and to make them available to researchers, the university had given consideration for Dr. King's promise to transfer ownership of his papers. Although the court disposed of the case on consideration grounds, it also addressed the university's alternative claim based on promissory estoppel. The court stressed that despite Restatement, Second, §90(2), it did require a charitable organization to show justifiable reliance for promissory estoppel relief. However, that reliance was apparent in the actions that the university took (indexing and taking care of the papers and making them available for research) beyond just retaining custody of the papers.

By contrast, in *Congregation Kadimah Toras-Moshe v. DeLeo*, 540 N.E.2d 691 (Mass. 1989), the court adopted a purely doctrinal approach. The donor had promised $25,000 to the synagogue. The synagogue planned to use the money to convert a storage room into a library to be named for the donor. However, there was no indication that the donor had attached any conditions to his promise or that the synagogue had promised him that it would use the money for this purpose or that it would name the library for the donor. The donor died without paying, and the synagogue sued his estate. The court found no consideration because the synagogue had not made any promise or suffered any other detriment in exchange for the promise. It also found no basis for enforcing the donor's promise under the doctrine of promissory estoppel because the synagogue had not yet begun the renovation or taken any other action in reliance on the promise. It had merely allocated the fund to the library renovation in its budget, which was nothing more than an accounting entry with no prejudicial effect.

Because *Allegheny College* and *King* both found consideration, they fully enforced the promises as contracts. Had they not found consideration, but had given relief on the basis of promissory estoppel, the remedy may have been the same if the court decided that nothing short of full enforcement would prevent injustice. However, the court would have had the option of awarding the lesser relief of reimbursing reliance costs. For many courts, the lesser remedy is more appropriate unless the detriment to the promisee cannot be undone except by full enforcement. *Estate of Timco v. Oral Roberts Evangelical Ass'n*, 215 N.W.2d 750 (Mich. Ct. App. 1974), is an example of a case in which the court found full enforcement of the promise to be necessary to avert injustice. The court awarded judgment to the promisee for the balance of the price of a building where the promisor, as a member of the association's board, proposed and collaborated in the purchase and induced the association to buy the building by undertaking to pay the balance of the price.

All the above cases involved promises to charitable or nonprofit organizations. However, promissory estoppel relief is also available for gratuitous promises that are not charitable in nature. For example, in *In re Estate of Ryan*, 925 N.W.2d 336 (Neb. 2019), Ryan had entered into a written pledge to make a gift of $20 million to a private golf club to enable it to upgrade its golf course into a top-rated golf course. Ryan died before the pledge fell due for payment and the golf club petitioned the probate court to allow its claim against his estate. The probate court rejected the claim. The state supreme court agreed that the golf club had no claim against the estate in contract because the promise was a gift without consideration. However, the court held that the club had adequately stated a claim in promissory estoppel by alleging that Ryan reasonably expected it to incur expenses in preparation of the golf course upgrade and that it had incurred such expenses in justifiable reliance on the promise. The club's claim against the estate should therefore not be summarily rejected and the club must be given an opportunity to prove its assertions. The court did not expressly address the appropriate remedy if the club succeeded in proving the elements of promissory estoppel, but the tenor of the opinion indicates that the court considered the proper remedy to be reimbursement of reliance expenses, rather than full enforcement of the promise.

§8.9 PROMISSORY ESTOPPEL AS A MEANS OF ENFORCING PROMISES MADE IN NEGOTIATIONS

§8.9.1 Promissory Estoppel Distinguished from a Contract to Bargain in Good Faith

There are two separate doctrines under which a party may claim to enforce an alleged promise made while the parties are working toward the formation of a contract. The one is promissory estoppel, discussed in this section, and the other, based on a contract to bargain in good faith, is discussed in section 10.6.4.

The claim that one of the parties breached an implied contract to continue to bargain in good faith is different from, but similar is some respects to a claim that a precontractual promise should be enforced under the doctrine of promissory estoppel. Where one of the parties breaks off negotiations, the other party may claim that this termination of negotiations violates an implied agreement that the parties would continue good faith negotiations in an effort to reach agreement on a final contract. The cause of action in that case is not promissory estoppel, but breach of a preliminary contract, in which the parties committed to make good faith efforts to work with each other to form the contract that they are negotiating. Therefore, the theory of this cause of action is breach of the preliminary contract, not promissory estoppel. As the discussion in this section and section 10.6.4 shows, although these doctrines provide different theories for enforcing an alleged promise made during negotiations courts approach alleged agreements to bargain in good faith in much the same way as they do claims to enforce precontractual promises on grounds of promissory estoppel. There are several points of connection between them:

1. They are both concerned with the claim that an alleged promise was made during the course of negotiations for an ultimate contract that was never made.
2. They both implicate the question of whether the party making the alleged promise acted faithlessly in failing to enter the contract that was being negotiated.

3. Courts are very wary about giving relief under these theories. In the absence of compelling and extraordinary circumstances, courts do not readily imply an obligation to bargain in good faith and assume that the parties made no commitment during negotiations and are free to terminate them at will.
4. If relief is given, reliance damages are the most likely relief under both theories.

§8.9.2 The Application of Promissory Estoppel to Alleged Promises Made During Negotiations

It is rarely appropriate to apply promissory estoppel to any apparent promise made while the parties are working toward the formation of a contract. In most situations, negotiating parties understand or reasonably should understand that nothing said in negotiations is to be taken as a promise, and no commitment is made until a contract is formed. Even though a statement made during negotiations may sound like a promise, a reasonable party should normally realize that it is nothing more than a nonbinding expression of intention or a proposal for a term that will not become an undertaking unless the negotiations culminate in final agreement. Therefore, the usual assumption, in the absence of clear understanding to the contrary, is that each of the parties bears the cost of any action that it takes in the effort to reach agreement on an ultimate contract.

For example, a buyer and seller were negotiating the sale of a business. They had agreed on the price of $10 million, but the buyer did not have the funds to pay the price. The buyer therefore proposed a credit transaction to the seller, under which the buyer would pay the price with interest over a two-year period from profits gained from operating the business. After considering this proposal, the seller declined to give the buyer credit for the full $10 million price, but said that if the buyer could find an investor to provide half the price, the seller would agree to a credit sale for the balance. The buyer made great efforts to find an investor, incurring considerable expense in researching prospects, seeking legal advice on how to set up the investment, and preparing materials to show potential investors. While the buyer was in the process of doing this, the seller sold the business to another buyer and terminated the negotiations. The buyer has no claim against the seller for breach of the contract to buy the business because the parties had not yet concluded that contract. The buyer should not have a promissory estoppel claim either. In the negotiating phase, unless the seller had clearly committed to do so, the buyer was not justified in expecting that the seller would pay the buyer's expenses in trying to secure investors. Nor can the buyer use promissory estoppel to enforce the seller's nonbinding expression of intent to proceed with the sale if the buyer did find investors. It may have been reasonable, in a business sense, for the seller's expression of intent to motivate the buyer to incur costs in seeking financing. However, the buyer should have understood that in the absence of the seller's clear promise to bear the buyer's expenses of trying to set up a deal, those expenses are the buyer's responsibility, and the buyer bears the risk that they will be wasted if the negotiations to not lead to a contract

Although promissory estoppel is seldom applied to enforce an alleged promise made during negotiations, there are some cases in which a court has found that a party did make a promise in negotiations that merits enforcement under the doctrine of promissory estoppel. These cases typically involve a very clear promise, specific prejudicial action by the promisee linked to that promise, and a relationship between the parties that justified the promisee in placing faith in the promise. *Hoffman v. Red Owl Stores, Inc.*, 133 N.W.2d 267 (Wis. 1965), is one of the best-known cases to apply promissory estoppel to uphold a promise made in the course of negotiations. Hoffman approached Red Owl to set him up with a Red Owl grocery store franchise. After reviewing and approving his proposed financial arrangements, Red Owl encouraged Hoffman to take a series of actions to prepare to open a store. Hoffman conscientiously followed Red Owl's guidance, incurring expenses in the process. After some considerable time, negotiations eventually collapsed, primarily because Red Owl had not been entirely straight with Hoffman about the financing of the business. The parties had not yet made a contract, and Red Owl had never expressly promised Hoffman that he would receive a franchise. Nevertheless, the court awarded Hoffman his wasted reliance expenses on the basis of promissory estoppel. (The court made it clear that relief was confined to the recovery of wasted expenses, and could not include any claim for the profits that Hoffman might have made from operating a Red Owl store had the franchise been granted.) The court found that Hoffman had placed faith in Red Owl's expertise and good faith, and it had been careless of his interests. Red Owl's indifference to Hoffman's welfare outweighed his naiveté in unquestioningly following its advice. *Hoffman* is distinguishable from the usual negotiation situation because Red Owl so strongly influenced Hoffman's actions that a relationship of trust was created that is not normally present where parties approach each other as adversaries in negotiations.

Carey v. FedEx Ground Package System, Inc., 321 F. Supp. 2d 902 (S.D. Ohio 2004), and *Haig v. Dartmouth-Hitchcock Medical Center*, 2023 WL 1325511 (D. Vt. 2023), also illustrate circumstances that justified enforcing a precontractual promisee on grounds of promissory estoppel. *Carey* concerned negotiations between Carey, a truck driver, and FedEx for a delivery route. Carey initially approached FedEx in the hope of acquiring a FedEx delivery route. For a period of almost two years thereafter, FedEx led Carey on with assurances that he would receive the route. Carey was in constant contact with FedEx. He followed its many suggestions and directions to qualify as a carrier, and was repeatedly told that he would get a route when it became available. During this period, FedEx induced Carey to buy a truck (which was ultimately repossessed because Carey could not afford payments on it without the income from a delivery route). In addition, to the knowledge of FedEx, Carey's wife gave up her job in reliance on the prospective extra income that Carey would earn once he had the route. When routes did become available, FedEx gave them to other drivers, while reassuring Carey that he was in line for the next route to become available. In the end, Carey never received the route and he sued FedEx on several theories[8] including promissory estoppel. The court denied summary judgment to FedEx on these claims. As to promissory estoppel, the court said that on the facts alleged, a factfinder could find that Carey had justifiably relied on FedEx's precontractual promise that he would get a route. The court stressed that relief would be confined to reimbursement for Carey's reasonable reliance losses, and would not cover any profits he might have lost as a result of not obtaining the route. Lost profits are contractual expectation damages, which would not be appropriately awarded for reliance on promises made at the stage of negotiations.

Haig involved an alleged promise made during negotiations for a contract of employment. Haig was a doctor who specialized in rehabilitation and occupational medicine and was in practice in Vermont. Haig applied for a position in Occupational and Environmental Medicine at Dartmouth (located in New Hampshire). Interviews and negotiations for Haig's employment continued over an extended period, until it looked highly likely that Dartmouth would enter into an employment contract with him. In the interim, to the knowledge of Dartmouth, Haig had taken several actions in anticipation of taking up the position: He had begun to wind down his medical practice in Vermont, applied for a New Hampshire medical license, and began planning to move to New Hampshire. In the end, Dartmouth never employed Haig, who sued it in the alternative for breach of contract and promissory estoppel. Dartmouth moved for summary judgment. The court granted summary judgment to Dartmouth on the breach of contract claim because the parties had never finalized essential terms of

8. The allegations in the other causes of action were that FedEx had discriminated against Carey because he was African American (the facts suggested that FedEx's actions in giving other drivers routes before Carey could have been racially motivated) and fraud (FedEx may not have intended to fulfill its promise of a route, and just made the promise to induce Carey to stay on as long as possible as a temporary driver). These other causes of action suggest that FedEx had not been acting in good faith in making its promise to Carey, and reinforced the connection between the application of promissory estoppel to promises made in negotiations and the implied contract to negotiate in good faith discussed in section 10.6.4. The enforcement of a promise to prevent injustice is an important element of promissory estoppel, so a violation of good faith is a significant factor in granting promissory estoppel relief.

the employment. However, it denied Dartmouth's claim for summary judgment on the promissory estoppel claim, holding that Haig had made out a prima facie case for promissory estoppel relief, on which there were factual disputes to be resolved at trial. These factual issues related to the established elements of promissory estoppel: Did Dartmouth make a promise to employ Haig, rather than a mere expression of desire? Did Dartmouth's knowledge of Haig's preparations to move to New Hampshire establish its reasonable intent to induce his reliance? Was Haig's reliance justifiable? What losses and expenses had Haig suffered as a result of this reliance? The court noted that the issue of injustice is a question of law, but it could not be determined until the factual issues had been resolved.

The above cases reflect the special circumstances that might persuade a court to depart from the usual assumption that parties do not usually make enforceable promises prior to the formation of the contract that is being negotiated. *Read v. Profeta*, 397 F. Supp. 3d 597 (D.N.J. 2019), is an example of the more common kind of case that finds no actionable promise. Read proposed to Profeta that they work together to create a magazine focusing on local Newark content. The parties engaged in extensive negotiations over a few years, but they never reached the stage of entering into a contract and never launched the magazine. Read commenced action against Profeta claiming, among other things, that he was entitled to the reimbursement of expenses incurred in working on the venture. The court granted summary judgment to Profeta on the basis that any statements that he made were just expressions of intent, and were too vague, indefinite, and contingent to qualify as promises.

§8.9.3 The Application of Promissory Estoppel to Precontractual Promises in Negotiations for Employment

Unless an employment contract provides for employment for a definite term, or that employment cannot be terminated except for cause or following a specified period of notice,[9] the employment is deemed to be at will. This means that it is terminable by either party at any time for any reason (except for a reason, such as race or gender discrimination, that violates a statute or other law). At-will employment agreements present particular problems of both consideration and promissory estoppel where one of the parties reneges on the agreement during the period after the agreement has

9. Many employment agreements do eliminate the default rule of employment at will, either by the express terms of the contract itself, or by virtue of rules in an employee handbook published by the employer, or by collective bargaining agreements, or by implication from usage or conduct. Statutes have also made inroads into the at-will doctrine.

been made, but before the employee begins work.[10] Even if employment was offered and accepted on clear and specific terms, some courts hold that before the employment actually begins, there is no contract because consideration is absent—neither party has made any commitment because each of them has the complete discretion to terminate the employment, which they could do even before the performance of the agreement begins. For the same reason, some courts hold that the at-will nature of the prospective employment also precludes promissory estoppel relief for the reimbursement of loss for actions taken in reliance on the promise to employ. Although it is readily apparent that an employee is likely to incur some detriment in reliance on a promise of at-will employment, such as leaving an existing job, moving to the location of the new job, or forgoing other opportunities, these courts hold that the employee must bear the risk of this reliance because the employee has no assurance of job security.

However, other courts are more sympathetic to a promissory estoppel claim where the employer revokes the promise of employment before it has begun. These courts find that even if the employment can be terminated at will, the prospective employer had at least committed itself to allow the prospective employee an opportunity to begin, which induced the employee to take the detrimental action. This was the court's approach in *Haig*. It was not clear in that case whether the contract, had it been formed, would have been for at-will employment or for a specified term. However, since security of employment was one of the terms on which the parties had not yet agreed, Dominion argued that even had it made a promise of employment to Haig, he could not reasonably have relied on it because he could have been terminated immediately on becoming an employee. The court rejected this argument, distinguishing reliance on continued employment from reliance on a promise to make an offer of employment. Where a prospective employee incurs reliance losses on the strength of a promise that an offer of employment will be made, it is appropriate to use promissory estoppel to reimburse the prospective employee for those losses. *Cocchiara v. Lithia Motors*, 297 P.3d 1277 (Or. 2013), took the same approach. The court held that the mere fact that the promised job was for at-will employment does not mean that the employer would have fired the employee, so the at-will nature of the employment should not absolutely preclude promissory estoppel relief. The prospective employee should be allowed the opportunity to prove that reliance on the promise of at-will

10. Even after the employee starts work, both parties continue to have the discretion to terminate at-will employment. Some courts hold that the same principles apply after employment has begun—there is no basis for finding consideration for or justifiable reliance on an at at-will contract. Other courts hold that once employment has begun, the express or implied promises made in the course of the relationship are enough to support consideration and reliance.

employment was justifiable. The employee could do this by showing, with a reasonable degree of certainty, that dismissal would have been unlikely immediately after employment commenced.

§8.10 RELIANCE ON AN OPTION WITHOUT CONSIDERATION: THE APPLICATION OF PROMISSORY ESTOPPEL TO PROMISES OF IRREVOCABILITY

As discussed in sections 4.13.2 and 7.7.4, a promise to keep an offer open for a stated period does not qualify as a binding option unless the offeree gave separate consideration to the offeror to validate the promise not to revoke. In some narrow circumstances, the doctrine of promissory estoppel can be used to create an enforceable option, even though no consideration was given for the promise of irrevocability. Restatement, Second, §87(2) recognizes the possibility of applying promissory estoppel to validate an option without consideration. It sets forth requirements modeled on §90. It states that an offer is binding as an option to the extent necessary to avoid injustice if the offeror "should reasonably expect to induce action or forbearance of a substantial character on the part of the offeree before acceptance and which does induce such action or forbearance."

However, the principle enunciated in §87(2) is confined to a narrow range of cases because, in most situations, an offeree cannot satisfy the requirement of justifiable reliance on a promise to hold an offer open for which the offeree gave no consideration. For example, a seller's offer to sell real property to the buyer stated that the offer was firm and irrevocable for five days. The buyer gave no separate consideration to the seller in exchange for the promise to hold the offer open for five days, so this was not a valid option. On the day after receiving the offer, the buyer decided to accept it, but, on the strength of the seller's promise to hold it open for five days, the buyer did not accept it on that day. The seller revoked the offer on the second day, before the buyer had communicated acceptance of the offer. The buyer is not likely to succeed in an argument that its reliance on the promise of irrevocability should make the seller's promise irrevocable under the doctrine of promissory estoppel. The buyer may have suffered prejudice in relying on the promise, but the buyer should have known that the promise of irrevocability was not binding in the absence of consideration and was therefore not justified in relying on the promise.

However, courts have been willing to apply promissory estoppel to validate an option without consideration in cases in which the offeree can justify reliance on the promise not to revoke. Many of these cases involve subcontractor bids. Although there is some variation in the facts of these cases, this is their typical pattern: Reliant Contracting Co., a prime contractor, planned to bid on a contract to build an apartment building for City Housing Corp. Reliant needed subcontractors to perform many aspects of the project, so on June 1 it called for subcontractor bids for various parts of the work, to be submitted by June 15. One of the jobs to be subcontracted was the supply and installation of a central heating system. Several heating companies submitted bids for this aspect of the construction. One of them, Lowbid Heating Co., submitted a bid for $2.5 million on June 14. This was the lowest bid for the heating, and it was $200,000 less than the next lowest bid. On June 16, Reliant used Lowbid's bid in formulating its own bid to City Housing. On June 25, Reliant was awarded the contract to build the building. On June 26, Lowbid discovered that it had made an error in calculating its bid, which should really have been $2.9 million. On that same day, Lowbid told Reliant of the error. It withdrew its bid and refused to perform the work for less than $2.9 million. This placed Reliant in a very difficult position. It was committed to its contract price with City Housing, but it had to pay $200,000 more to the next highest bidder for the heating work. There are a few possible arguments that Reliant could make in claiming damages from Lowbid.

Breach of Contract

Reliant might argue that Lowbid's bid was an offer, which Reliant accepted by using the bid in making its own bid. The problem with this argument is that even if Lowbid's bid was an offer, Reliant did not communicate acceptance of it before Lowbid revoked it. Communication of acceptance is required unless the offeror dispensed with it either expressly or by implication. In the absence of such a waiver of communication, use of the bid on its own is not enough to constitute acceptance.

Actual Option

Reliant might argue that Lowbid impliedly promised that it would not revoke the bid until Reliant had a reasonable time to accept it after the award of the prime contract. The problem with this argument is, first, that there would need to be some factual basis to imply such a promise. Second, even if it could be implied, Reliant would have trouble showing that it gave Lowbid the consideration necessary to validate it. The best argument for consideration is that Reliant made an implied promise to accept the bid if it used it in its own bid to the owner and was awarded the contract. However, Reliant probably did not consider itself bound by use of the bid, and unless usage or other circumstances show otherwise, it would be difficult to imply such a promise.

Promissory Estoppel

The most plausible argument in this case is that although there is no contract or option, the promise to hold open the offer should be enforced under the doctrine of promissory estoppel, which, in effect, serves as a substitute for consideration in creating an enforceable option. To enforce the option under promissory estoppel, Reliant must establish that all of its elements are satisfied:

1. Lowbid must have made a promise. There is no express promise here, but if there is an expectation in the building trade that a subcontractor will hold open a bid for a reasonable time to allow the contractor to use it in its own bid to the customer, there could be an implied promise by Lowbid to keep its bid open to enable Reliant to accept it expeditiously after it is awarded the construction contract.
2. Lowbid must reasonably have expected that Reliant would rely on its promise. Reasonable expectations are based on the entire context in which the promise was made, including not only the language and apparent firmness of the promise but also the prevailing practices in the industry and any prior relationship that the parties may have had. Reliant must establish that, under all these circumstances, a reasonable person in Lowbid's position would have realized that Reliant might rely on its bid in formulating the bid to City Housing.
3. Reliant must have relied justifiably on this promise. This requirement not only examines the question of whether there were reasonable grounds for Reliant to believe that a serious promise was made and could be relied on but also requires examination of the nature and justification of the action taken in reliance. It precludes recovery if Reliant reasonably should have realized, in comparing Lowbid's bid with others, that Lowbid likely made an error.
4. Enforcement of the promise must be necessary to avoid injustice. This element is usually satisfied if all the other elements are present and the prime contractor suffers the significant detriment of being bound to the owner for a price based on the subcontractor's bid. However, it also takes other equities into account, such as whether Reliant acted in good faith in accepting the bid as soon as possible, and did not try to speculate at Lowbid's expense, say, by bid shopping (that is, using the bid to shop around for a lower bid from competing subcontractors).

If all these elements are satisfied, the remedy is the enforcement of the promise not to revoke the offer. Because the offer is treated as a valid option, Lowbid's attempt to revoke failed. Reliant is therefore still able to accept the bid, even after Lowbid's attempted revocation on June 26. However, Reliant must actually take the step of accepting the offer, and must do so within a reasonable time after June 26. It may sound pointless to accept an offer after the offeror has made it clear that it will not perform at the bid price, but the formal act of acceptance is legally required to create a contract for the performance of the work at the price bid. If Reliant does not accept within a reasonable time, its claim for damages will fail because promissory estoppel is used here only to validate the option—it does not validate the underlying contract, which must be created by acceptance of the offer. As noted above, if Reliant delays beyond a reasonable time in accepting, or if it acts in bad faith by bid shopping, it will not benefit from the option that was created by promissory estoppel.

Drennan v. Star Paving, 333 P.2d 757 (Cal. 1958), is the classic case that applied promissory estoppel doctrine to hold a subcontractor to an implied promise not to revoke its bid. The court saw the creation of an option in this situation as analogous to the legal recognition of an option to protect an offeree who begins to accept a unilateral offer by commencing a noninstantaneous performance.[11] The court held that in the commercial context, the subcontractor must have understood that the prime contractor might use its bid in calculating the bid for the prime contract. The prime contractor did rely justifiably on the bid. The discrepancy between the bid of this subcontractor and others did not alert the prime contractor to the possibility of a mistake. The court made it clear that the doctrine should be applied carefully and selectively in the precontractual context because promises are not normally made during negotiations prior to making a contract, and a party is not normally justified in acting in reliance until the contract is concluded. The court also stressed that the prime contractor must attempt to accept the bid within a reasonable time of being awarded the prime contract.

A number of more recent decisions have followed the approach in *Drennan*. In *Pavel Enterprises, Inc. v. A.S. Johnson & Co.*, 674 A.2d 521 (Md. 1996), the court accepted that where usage creates an expectation that a general contractor will rely on a subcontractor's bid in formulating its own bid, promissory estoppel can be used to validate the option without consideration. The court stressed that the general contractor must behave fairly to merit the protection of promissory estoppel. Any manipulation such as bid shopping

---

11. This is discussed in section 4.12.4. The situation relating to an offer for a unilateral contract is different from the situation discussed here and is not based on the claim that reliance on a revocable offer creates an option. Section 4.12.4 deals with an offer for a unilateral contract which requires performance as the exclusive mode of acceptance. To protect the offeree who has begun a noninstantaneous performance, the law deems an option to have been created in favor of the offeree. This option is created as a matter of law, to protect the reliance of the offeree in beginning the combined act of acceptance and performance. It arises even though the offeror did not expressly promise to keep the offer open and the offeree gave no consideration to the offeror to support keeping the offer open.

will defeat reasonable reliance. In *Deide Construction v. Monterey Mechanical Co.*, 22 Cal. Rptr. 3d 763 (Cal. App. 2005), the court of appeals found the doctrine of promissory estoppel to be applicable where the prime contractor had committed itself to the property owner on the basis of the subcontractor's bid. The trial court had held that when the prime contractor discovered the error in the subcontractor's bid, it should have asked the owner to release it from its contract. The court of appeals disagreed. It would be unjust to require the prime contractor to sacrifice its profit and reputation. However, because the variance between the bids of the subcontractor and its next lowest competitor was $425,000, the court remanded the case for a determination of whether the prime contractor was reasonable in relying on such a low bid. In *I&R Mechanical, Inc. v. Hazelton Manufacturing Co.*, 817 N.E.2d 799 (Mass. App. Ct. 2004), the court found that the elements of promissory estoppel were not satisfied. Applying offer and acceptance principles, the court found that the subcontractor's bid did not amount to an offer, but merely solicited an offer from the prime contractor. This in itself precluded the use of promissory estoppel because there was no promise. Even if promissory estoppel was applicable, the discrepancy between the subcontractor's price and other bids was so great that it should have alerted the contractor to an error. In addition, the contractor had also engaged in bid shopping, which was inequitable and indicated that it was not relying on the bid.

§8.11 A TRANSNATIONAL PERSPECTIVE ON PROMISSORY ESTOPPEL

Civilian legal systems do not require consideration for contract formation, so they have no need for a doctrine like promissory estoppel to enforce promises that lack consideration. However, there may be other reasons why a promise does not qualify as contractual, so an equivalent doctrine does have some role to play. In civilian jurisdictions, this doctrine does not derive from equitable estoppel. As explained in section 2.5, the distinction between law and equity is peculiar to the common law and has its origins in the particular historical circumstances under which English courts developed. Nevertheless, civil law recognizes a principle similar to estoppel under which a person is held accountable for conduct and cannot claim to enforce a right that is asserted in contradiction of that conduct. Under this principle, detrimental reliance on a promise can give rise to liability to honor the promise.

Although neither the CISG nor the UNIDROIT Principles articulate a general doctrine of detrimental reliance, equivalent to Restatement, Second, §90, they do contain a number of provisions that protect reliance on conduct or promise in specific situations. For example, CISG Article

16(2)(b) makes an offer irrevocable if the offeree acted in reasonable reliance on its irrevocability. Article 2.1.4(2)(b) of the UNIDROIT Principles is to the same effect. CISG Article 29 provides that where a contract has a provision requiring modifications to be in writing, a party is precluded from enforcing that provision where its conduct led the other party to reasonably rely on the effectiveness of an oral modification. Article 2.1.15 of the UNIDROIT Principles recognizes a principle similar to that articulated in *Hoffman v. Red Owl Stores* (*see* section 8.9) by providing that a party may be held liable for losses resulting from the bad faith termination of negotiations.

EXAMPLES

Examples

1. After Juan El graduated from college, he took a job as a sales representative. He earned well, but did not think of this as a permanent career. He really wanted to become a lawyer. Juan told his Aunt Jenny Rouse that he wanted to quit his job and go to law school, but he was worried about the huge debt that he would have to incur to pay tuition and living expenses for the three years. Aunt Jenny was very sympathetic and told Juan that she wanted to think about what she could do to help. About a week later, Aunt Jenny wrote a letter to Juan in which she said, "I have been thinking about your ambition to become a lawyer and would love to see you achieve what you want. I realize that you will not be able to work while studying and that the cost of a legal education is high. Therefore, if you do decide to go to law school, I will give you $20,000 toward your first-year tuition and living expenses, which I will pay to you when you begin law school."

   After receiving this letter, Juan immediately applied for admission to law school, paying the required nonrefundable $100 application fee. In April he was offered admission for the next academic year, beginning at the end of August. Juan told Aunt Jenny about the offer and said he was going to accept it. She was delighted and reaffirmed her intention to pay him $20,000 when he began school. A week later, Juan accepted the law school's offer and paid a nonrefundable $500 deposit. He planned to work until the end of July, and did not yet resign from his job. In May, Aunt Jenny died. In June, the executor of Aunt Jenny's estate told Juan that because Aunt Jenny's promise of $20,000 was gratuitous, the estate would not honor it. Notwithstanding, Juan quit his job in July and entered law school at the end of August. He then sued the estate to enforce the promise. Will he likely succeed? If so, how much is he likely to be awarded?

2. Faith Reliance owns a motorbike, which she has kept comprehensively insured. However, she recently lost her job and cannot afford to pay

the insurance premium due on August 1. On July 20, she asked her father to help her by paying the premium. He agreed and took the policy renewal notice from her, promising to pay it the next day. Sadly, it is well known in the family that Faith's father is a big talker, but he almost never does what he promises. True to form, he did not pay the premium on July 21 and Faith received a final warning from the insurer on July 25 that the policy would lapse if the premium was not paid by August 1. When she showed it to her father, he apologized for forgetting to pay it and assured her that he would mail the check to the insurer the next morning. Hearing nothing further from the insurer, Faith assumed that matters had been taken care of. A couple of weeks later, the bike was stolen. Faith then discovered that her father had never paid the premium. Can Faith recover anything from her father? If so, what is she entitled to claim?

3. Bo Vine owned a large ranch. His only daughter, Justine, was a lawyer working as an associate in a firm in a distant city. Bo's wife died some years ago, and Bo had lived alone on the ranch since then. As Bo got older, he developed health problems and found it difficult to manage the ranch, so he suggested to Justine that she give up her job as a lawyer and come to live on the ranch so that she could take over its management. Justine was reluctant to give up her interesting and well-paid job, but Bo assured her that if she came to help him with the ranch, he would pay her a monthly salary (which was much less than she was earning as a lawyer), and he would transfer ownership of the ranch to her one year after she began work at the ranch.

   As a result of this conversation, Justine resigned from the law firm and moved to the ranch. The arrangement did not work. Bo was stubborn, domineering, and constantly interfered with Justine's management of the ranch. Three months after Justine had moved to the ranch, Bo fired her. Justine returned to the city and was hired back by her law firm. A short time later Bo sold the ranch.

   Justine realized that she would probably not win a claim for expectation damages based on the value of the ranch because Bo's promise to transfer the ranch to her was oral and therefore unenforceable under the statute of frauds, which requires contracts for the transfer of real property to be recorded. However, she did sue Bo in promissory estoppel to recover the earnings that she lost during the period in which she gave up her well-paying job to work at the ranch for a lower salary. Should she succeed in this suit?

4. After graduating from Alma Mater College several years ago, Al Lumnis founded a successful business and had earned great wealth. During a recent visit to the campus, Al noticed that the student cafeteria had become very outdated and shabby. After the visit, Al wrote a letter

to the college president in which he stated, "In consideration of my desire to enhance and ennoble the quality of campus life at the Alma Mater College, I hereby pledge to the College the sum of $500,000 for the renovation and modernization of the student cafeteria. I will pay this pledge as soon as the College submits its renovation plans to me. The renovated cafeteria shall be known as the 'Al Lumnis Dining Area.'"

The president of the college wrote back, thanking Al for the pledge and undertaking to begin work immediately on planning the renovations. The president hired an architect to develop the plans and instructed the editor of the alumni magazine to publish a flattering article on Al and his gift in the next edition of the magazine. A few weeks later, Al changed his mind about funding the cafeteria renovation and withdrew his pledge. At that stage, the architect had done work on preliminary sketch plans. The article for the alumni magazine had not yet been written or published. Can the College hold Al to his pledge? If not, can it recover any other amount from him?

5. Chilly Winters lives in Rustburg, a cold and congested northern city. Sonny Climes, his college roommate, moved south a few years ago and lives in Tropicana, a balmy southwestern metropolis. Sonny had established a flourishing high-tech business and often told Chilly that if he ever decided to escape the snow and smog, a job would be waiting for him at Sonny's company. After suffering through a particularly harsh winter, Chilly decided that it was time to move south. He called Sonny and asked if a job was still available. Sonny responded, "As I have said so often, there is a job waiting for you here. Get down here as soon as you can. When you arrive, we can figure out the particulars and I will put you to work right away." Chilly told Sonny that he would give notice to his present employer, terminate his apartment lease, and would be in Tropicana in a month.

   Chilly immediately gave notice to his employer and to the lessor of his apartment and bought a one-way air ticket to Tropicana. When he called Sonny a week later to tell him his exact time of arrival, he received an unpleasant surprise. Sonny told him that he had just received an offer for the sale of his business that was too good to resist. He had accepted it and planned to retire. He was sorry, but he could no longer employ Chilly.

   Having lost his employment opportunity in Tropicana, Chilly decided to remain in Rustburg. He tried to retract his notice to his employer, but his employer had already hired a replacement. Chilly's apartment had been re-let and the only apartment that Chilly was able to rent was at a higher rental. After searching for two months, he found a new job that paid the same salary as the old one. He could not obtain a refund of his airfare, but airline policy allows him to cancel his booking and to use the ticket for travel within the United States at any time within the next year.

What recourse, if any, does Chilly have against Sonny?

6. In August, Primo Contracting Co., a building contractor, was invited by a developer to submit a bid for the construction of a new building. Primo was given until September 15 to submit the bid. To produce an accurate bid, Primo needed to know what it would have to pay plumbers, electricians, and other specialists to whom work would be subcontracted. On September 1, Primo sent the building specifications to a number of potential subcontractors and invited them to submit bids by September 13, explaining that it required the bids by that time to enable it to submit its own bid for the whole project on time.

   Lois Bidder was one of the electricians invited to bid on the electrical work. After studying the specifications, Lois calculated the amount of material and labor required and submitted a written bid to Primo for $100,000. The bid stated: "This bid is open for your acceptance within a reasonable time after you have been awarded the prime contract."

   Upon receiving the bid on September 13, Primo compared it to others received and saw that it was $20,000 cheaper than the next lowest bid. It therefore decided to use Lois for the electrical work and included her figure in the bid to the owner. Primo submitted its bid on September 14, and the owner accepted it on September 15.

   Primo immediately prepared letters to all the selected subcontractors, notifying them that their bids had been successful and that the project would proceed. On September 16, just before the letters were mailed, Primo received an email from Lois, stating that on checking her calculations after submitting her bid, she had discovered that she had mistakenly overlooked the cost of some of the materials that would be required. As a result, she had underestimated her costs by $30,000, and she could not profitably perform the work for the bid price. Lois apologized for the error, which resulted from having to get her bid ready in a rush, and regretted that she must withdraw her previous bid. She was willing, however, to perform the work for $130,000.

   On September 16, Primo replied to the email, informing Lois that it had already committed to the owner on the basis of electrical subcontracting costs of $100,000 and it considered Lois bound by her original bid. Immediately after sending the email, Primo mailed a letter of acceptance to Lois.

   Is Lois bound to Primo by her bid?

Explanations

1. Aunt Jenny undoubtedly made a promise to Juan. The promise was expressed clearly and definitely in writing after Aunt Jenny had time to think about it carefully, but Juan would be hard-pressed to argue that he entered a contract with Aunt Jenny because he gave no consideration for the promise. Quitting a job and enrolling in law school could qualify as a detriment for consideration purposes, but Juan made no promise to do this, and it was therefore not bargained for in exchange for Aunt Jenny's promise. Although Aunt Jenny's promised performance was conditional on Juan going to law school, this is more properly interpreted as a condition of the gift.

   If Aunt Jenny's promise was gratuitous, Juan's only basis for relief is promissory estoppel. Judged on an objective standard, Aunt Jenny, in making a clear promise, must reasonably have expected that it would induce Juan's reliance. This expectation is reinforced by her reaffirmation of the promise when Juan told her he had been offered admission to law school. The more difficult question is whether Juan's conduct was induced by the promise and was justifiable. The fact of inducement and the justification for inducement tend to flow together on these facts. Juan took several actions after the promise, so each is subject to the test of justifiable inducement. Some of the actions, but not others, may satisfy the test. Juan's actions before Aunt Jenny's death—his application to law school, his acceptance of the law school's offer of admission, and his payment of the nonrefundable fee and the deposit—are causally linked to the promise and are justifiable. Aunt Jenny's promise was clear, carefully considered, and reaffirmed before Juan accepted the law school's offer. The facts do not suggest that he had any reason to doubt Aunt Jenny's reliability in performing her commitment.

   Juan's further action—resigning from his job at the end of July and entering law school at the end of August—were taken after Aunt Jenny had died and her executor had made it clear that the estate would not honor her promise. If Aunt Jenny's promise was not binding because it was gratuitous, the estate had the legal right to refuse payment, thereby breaking the causal link between the promise and Juan's actions, and removing his justification for relying on the promise.

   This being so, his claim for promissory estoppel should be confined to the detriment incurred before Aunt Jenny died. At that stage, Juan had done nothing more than complete the law school application process and pay the fee and deposit. He had not yet made any commitment to the law school beyond the forfeiture of the nonrefundable fee and deposit. It is therefore possible that Juan could recover these expenses, but he may not be able to recover even this modest amount because the expenses were not wasted — Juan did ultimately enroll in law school.

Juan lost the hope and expectation of receiving help toward his tuition, but this is in the nature of an expectation interest, more properly confined to a case in which a contract is established. Given that Juan incurred only a modest financial expense and could have avoided any further economic detriment, this does not seem to be a case in which injustice can be averted only by enforcing the promise to its full extent. It is conceivable that a court that treats promissory estoppel as a consideration substitute may take a different view. That is, it could hold that Aunt Jenny became contractually bound to pay the $20,000 once Juan took action in reliance on her promise by accepting the offer of admission. On this theory, a contract was formed at that time, and the estate's subsequent action in reneging on the promise is merely a breach of that contract.

This Example is inspired by *Alden v. Presley*, 637 S.W.2d. 862 (Tenn. 1982). The Presley in this case was none other than the King himself and the plaintiff was his fiancée's mother. When the plaintiff decided to divorce her husband, Elvis undertook to pay the expenses of her divorce, to pay out her husband's share of their house, and to pay off the mortgage so she would own the house free and clear. Elvis died after the divorce proceedings had begun, but before the divorce settlement had become legally binding. Elvis' estate notified the plaintiff that it would not honor his promise to pay off the mortgage. Notwithstanding, the plaintiff committed herself to the divorce settlement that released her husband from the mortgage. The court refused to enforce the promise to pay off the mortgage. It was gratuitous, so it was not a contract. It was also not enforceable on grounds of promissory estoppel because the plaintiff was no longer justified in finalizing the settlement in reliance on the promise once she knew that the estate would not honor it.

2. Faith gave no consideration to her father in exchange for his undertaking to pay the premium. It was simply a gift promise motivated by family relationship and cannot be enforced as a contract. Promissory estoppel provides a basis for enforcing this kind of gratuitous promise, relied on by the promisee to her detriment.

   Faith's father clearly made a promise to her. His words, interpreted objectively, convey a clear commitment to pay the premium. It is also apparent that he did or reasonably should have expected Faith to rely on it. It was an unequivocal response to her need for financial assistance, made with knowledge of her circumstances and reiterated when Faith received the cancellation warning.

   Faith's problem is in showing that she actually and justifiably relied on the promise. It is not clear that the promise actually induced Faith's forbearance from paying the premium herself because she may not have had the financial ability to renew the policy. However, even if she could show actual reliance, she will have difficulty in showing that her reliance was justified. She knew that her father had a record of breaking his promises, which was reinforced by his initial failure to pay the premium. She should not have relied unquestioningly on his word without checking to see if he had made the payment. This point was made in Norton v. McOsker, mentioned in sections 8.6.2 and 8.6.4. (In Norton, the court held that even if a man had promised his longstanding lover that he would divorce his wife, marry her, and support her for the rest of her life, she would not have been justified in relying on the promise because he had made and broken promises to leave his wife many times before.)

Faith may therefore not be able to satisfy the elements of promissory estoppel, but it is worthwhile to consider what remedy would be appropriate if she could establish grounds for relief. There are no wasted out-of-pocket costs in this case, so reimbursement of reliance expenses is not a meaningful alternative. Full enforcement of the promise could mean either rather small damages based on the cost of the unpaid premium (this would be direct damages—the value of the performance itself) or a larger damage award based on the loss of the bike (this would be consequential damages—the consequent loss resulting from the failure to honor the promise).[12] Damages confined to the value of the promised premium would undercompensate Faith, so if full contract-like enforcement of the promise is to be awarded, the value of the lost bike would be the more appropriate measure. To decide if the full recovery of the value of the bike is appropriate, the court must weigh all the equities. It must consider the extent to which the elements of promissory estoppel have been established (a clear and unequivocal promise, significant detriment, but a weak reliance argument). It must also balance the harm Faith will suffer if it refuses enforcement against the hardship to her father if it enforces the promise. It is difficult to predict how a court may strike this balance, but the equities seem to tilt in Faith's favor, so the court could well hold her father liable for the value of the bike.

3. Justine decided not to sue Bo for contract damages because she correctly realized that noncompliance with the statute of frauds rendered their contract unenforceable. (This is an example of a situation in which a suit in contract is precluded for reasons other than lack of consideration.) Instead, she sued him in promissory estoppel for the earnings that she lost in reliance on his promise to transfer the ranch to her.

Justine has a good argument for promissory estoppel relief. Bo did promise to transfer the ranch to her with the apparent intention of inducing her to give up her legal career and move to the ranch. The

12. The distinction between direct and consequential damages is discussed more fully in section 18.5.

promise of the ranch must have played a significant role in inducing Justine to abandon her job as a lawyer and to take on the management of the ranch. Her reliance on Bo's promise appears to have been justifiable. Bo manifested a serious intent to transfer the ranch to Justine, his only daughter and closest living relative. The facts do not indicate any history of untrustworthy behavior that may have made Justine wary of trusting Bo's promise. Justine lost earnings by giving up her practice, so she has suffered a tangible economic detriment in reliance on the promise. Therefore, awarding her reliance damages, measured by the value of her lost income, sounds like the appropriate remedy to do justice. Sometimes lost income and other lost opportunity damages can be difficult to prove, but they seem straightforward and calculable in this case because she left her legal practice for three months and returned to it after Bo fired her. Her damages are the difference between what she would have earned as a lawyer for the three months, less what she earned working for Bo.

This Example is based on *Bouton v. Byers*, 321 P.3d 780 (Kan. Ct. App. 2014), in which Bouton, the daughter, sued Byers, her father, for earnings that she lost when she resigned from her position as a tenured law professor to move onto his ranch and help him run it. To allay Bouton's concerns about giving up a secure and well-paying job to move to the ranch, Byers told her that he would bequeath the ranch, worth more than a million dollars, to her. Bouton moved to the ranch and helped run it for a small salary, but the parties' relationship eventually broke down, and Byers fired Bouton. He thereafter sold the ranch. Bouton then sued Byers in promissory estoppel for damages based on what she would have earned as a law professor had she not resigned. The trial court granted summary judgment in favor of Byers, principally because it held that, as a law professor, Boulton should have insisted on a legally enforceable written agreement to transfer the land and was not justified in relying on an oral, informal promise to bequeath the ranch to her. The court of appeals reversed the summary judgment on the grounds that the trial court was wrong in summarily disposing of the question of justifiable reliance, which was a factual question for a factfinder to decide. Although Bouton's legal training was a relevant factor, so was the fact that this was a family transaction, in which she may have been less inclined to insist on legal formalities. The court indicated that Bouton had made out a prima facie case for promissory estoppel relief and must be allowed to proceed to trial.

4. This Example treads the uncertain line between a promise with consideration and a gift made subject to instructions for its use. The recited "consideration" is not consideration at all but merely expresses Al's purpose in giving the donation. The president replied by promising to use the fund for this purpose. Some courts have found this to be sufficient

consideration, but this is a doctrinally questionable approach. A donor's stipulation that a gift must be used for a specified purpose is more plausibly a conditional gift because the promisee had no right to the money in the absence of the gift, and hence gave up no legal right by promising to use it as designated by the donor. The publication of the flattering article in the alumni magazine could have been consideration, had it been bargained for in exchange for the promise. However, this seems to have been a unilateral decision by the president that Al did not request in exchange for his promise. The naming of the cafeteria is the best argument for consideration because Al's pledge provides for this. The naming is an action not directly related to the use of the funds and could qualify as a detriment distinct from the use of the gift.

This Example raises the different approaches to these ambiguous transactions raised in section 8.8, where *Allegheny College* and *King* found a basis of enforcement either under consideration doctrine or on grounds of promissory estoppel, while *DeLeo* did not. If a court finds consideration on these facts, the college would have the right to enforce Al's promise to pay $500,000 for the cafeteria renovation as a contractual obligation. If the court does not find consideration, the college would have to rely on promissory estoppel for relief. Al clearly did promise the $500,000 and objectively manifested the intent to induce the college's reliance by stipulating that plans must be drawn before he would pay the funds. The college did rely on the promise by hiring the architect. However, even if there was no basis to question Al's serious intent to make the payment, the college's reliance in incurring expenses may not have been justifiable because it should have realized that a court may find that Al's promise was a gift without consideration and not legally binding on him. (The college may have been justified in a business sense to incur the expense, but that is not the same as being justified in the expectation that it would be entitled to look to Al for the payment of those expenses.)

If the college can overcome the problem of justifiable reliance, the final question would be remedy. Promissory estoppel doctrine gives the court the discretion to enforce the promise to pay $500,000 in full if the court determines that justice so demands. However, a court may find it to be too generous a remedy to impose such extensive liability on a reneging donor. The lesser alternative would be to award the college reimbursement of its wasted expenses, which would consist of its liability to the architect for work done up to the time that Al revoked his promise.

5. Chilly has no basis for claiming that he entered into a contract of employment with Sonny. Although Sonny expressed the intent to hire him, and Chilly indicated the intent to work for Sonny, the parties never settled the terms of employment. The arrangement is too vague and indefinite to qualify as a contract. Therefore, the only basis on which Chilly can

claim relief is promissory estoppel, provided that Chilly can satisfy its elements.

It is not clear if Sonny merely expressed the nonbinding desire to hire Chilly, or if his words were strong enough to amount to a promise. Sonny's expression of intent was vague, but it reinforced his previous indications of interest in employing Chilly and it did assure Chilly of being put to work on arrival. It is therefore possible that there is enough commitment here to qualify as a promise for the purposes of promissory estoppel, which does not require the same level of definiteness as a contractual promise. Chilly told Sonny that he planned to give notice to his current employer and lessor and to prepare to move to Tropicana, and Sonny did nothing to dissuade him. Therefore, if Sonny did make a promise, his intent to induce reliance on it can be inferred.

Chilly did rely on the promise by taking those preparatory actions, but the difficult question is whether this reliance was justified. That is, Chilly maybe should have understood that by incurring loss or expense without any promise of a concrete job offer, he was risking that loss at his own expense and would not be able to shift it onto Sonny. This is particularly true where the potential employment contract would have been at will.[13] While it may be rational for a promisee to take detrimental action in reliance on a promise of at-will employment, this action may not be sufficient to constitute compensable justifiable reliance for promissory estoppel purposes. Some courts so hold, but others are willing to give relief, especially where the promise and intent to induce reliance are clear and there are no specific facts that would make the reliance unreasonable. These courts reason that even if the employment could be terminated at will, the prospective employer had at least committed itself to allow the prospective employee an opportunity to begin, which induced the prospective employee to take the detrimental action. *Cocchiara* and *Haig*, cited in section 8.9.3, take this approach.

However, even if the court grants relief, Chilly has no basis for claiming expectation damages in the absence of a contract or any settled contract terms. Chilly could possibly recover reliance damages consisting of the two months' lost salary, but he may not be able to recover his lost salary unless he had some security of employment at his old job. If he was an at-will employee in that job, he may not be able to show that loss with reasonable certainty. In addition, Chilly's delay in finding a replacement job would have to be reasonable. If he did not make a reasonably diligent

13. As explained in section 8.9.3, unless an employment contract provides for employment for a definite term or has some other restriction on dismissal, the employment is deemed to be at will and can be terminated. Because the terms of employment were never settled, it cannot be said if the employment would have been at will, but the default is at-will employment unless the parties specifically agree otherwise.

effort in seeking new employment, he cannot hold Sonny accountable for loss that he could have prevented. (This is the principle of mitigation of damages, discussed in section 18.6.3.) Chilly may also be able to claim any increase in rent as a result of having ended his apartment lease in reliance on the promise. Again, he would have to show that he would have had a right to retain his old apartment and that the substitute was reasonable. Chilly might have been able to claim the wasted expense of the air ticket, but because the ticket is salvageable, he has probably not suffered a loss unless he can show that it would not be possible for him to use it within the year or to sell it.

6. By soliciting bids, Primo was inviting subcontractors to make offers. The language used by Lois in her bid creates the reasonable understanding that she intended it as an offer with a promise of irrevocability for a reasonable time after the prime contract was awarded. The undertaking not to revoke is not a binding option contract because she received no consideration for it. (There could have been consideration if Primo had bound itself, expressly or impliedly, to use the lowest bid, but there is no indication of such a commitment.) Although Primo used Lois' offer in calculating its own bid, there is no evidence of circumstances that would make this an acceptance of the offer. Lois revoked the offer before Primo had the chance to communicate its acceptance, and there is no indication in the bid that Lois waived communication of acceptance.

   Because there is no consideration to validate the promise not to revoke, Primo can hold Lois to her promise of irrevocability only if it can validate that promise on grounds of promissory estoppel. The question is therefore whether the facts satisfy the elements of promissory estoppel. Lois made an express promise of irrevocability, so the element of promise is easily established. It is likely that this promise was made with the reasonable understanding that Primo would rely on it if Primo used Lois' bid. In *Drennan*, the court emphasized that the expectation of reliance is a factual question, to be decided under all the circumstances, including common practice in the industry. The Example does not provide any information about industry practice, but there would be a reasonable expectation of reliance if it is a general practice in the industry for subcontractors to protect contractors who use their bids as the basis of bidding on prime contracts. Even in the absence of such a clear practice, the language Lois used in her bid suggests a reasonable expectation of reliance—it recognizes that her bid might be used and that Primo needed time to accept after it was awarded the contract.

   There are two factors to be considered in deciding whether Primo's reliance was justified. First, was Primo reasonable in understanding that a promise was made on which it could rely? This question parallels the above analysis, now examined from the perspective of a reasonable person in Primo's position, and there is no reason to reach a different answer. Second, should Primo have suspected an error when it saw that there was a $20,000 discrepancy between Lois' price and the next lowest bid? Even if it did not know for sure that Lois must have made a mistake, it had a duty to enquire if the low price looked wrong, and it cannot just jump at the bargain. Of course, there could be many explanations for variations in price, so the question is whether, under all the circumstances, Primo was reasonable in not questioning it.

Promissory estoppel relief must be necessary to prevent injustice. This element calls on the court to weigh all the equities of the situation, including the strength of the elements discussed above. A predominant issue here is the degree of detriment that will be suffered by Primo if the promise to hold the offer open is not enforced. As in most of the bid cases, this detriment is an increase in the costs of the job and a corresponding loss of profit. The more dramatic this loss is, and the fewer the reasonable alternatives for averting it, the stronger the injustice. Other factors also enter the determination of injustice. Several of the cases discussed in section 8.10 examined the conduct of the prime contractor in the way it used the bid. An unreasonable delay in acceptance after the award of the prime contract, or any kind of manipulation such as bid shopping, could tip the balance against the grant of relief. In this case, Primo was not guilty of any such misconduct. It accepted the bid the day after being awarded the prime contract and just three days after the bid was submitted.

The appropriate remedy in a case like this is to enforce the promise to keep the bid open so that Primo's acceptance is effective, even though it was made after attempted revocation. Because the acceptance is effective, a contract was created. If Lois failed to perform it, Primo can claim damages measured by the difference between Lois' price and the higher price that Primo reasonably had to pay to another subcontractor for the work.

CHAPTER 9

Unjust Enrichment, Restitution, and "Moral Obligation"

§9.1 INTRODUCTION

Chapter 8 explains how promissory estoppel can sometimes be used to ameliorate the harsh consequences of consideration doctrine by enforcing a promise that induced justifiable reliance. Like promissory estoppel, the remedy of restitution allows for the enforcement of obligations that do not qualify as contractual. Beyond this general parallel, restitution and promissory estoppel have very different conceptual bases. Restitution is not predicated on accountability for promise. Its purpose is the restoration of an unfair gain. Its focus is on cases in which one party has obtained a benefit at the expense of another under circumstances that make it unfair for the recipient to retain the benefit without compensating the other party for it.

§9.2 UNJUST ENRICHMENT, THE BASIS FOR RESTITUTION

Restitution is the restoration of property or its value. When a court grants restitution, it adjudges that the recipient of a benefit is obliged to give back that benefit or to pay its value to the person who conferred it. The basis of this judgment is that the recipient has been unjustly enriched at the expense of grantor. That is, there is no legal justification for retention of the benefit without paying for it. In short, when the elements of the cause of action, unjust enrichment, are satisfied, the remedy of restitution is the relief awarded. (Courts and commentators do not always observe this distinction in terminology between the cause of action and the remedy, so it is quite common to find the word "restitution" used in reference to both the cause of action and the remedy.)

Unjust enrichment is not a subcategory of contract law. It is a distinct and independent basis of obligation, occupying a place alongside contract, promissory estoppel, and tort. Diagram 9A charts this relationship between different causes of action and remedies.

Diagram 9A

Cause of Action →	Contract	Prom. Estoppel	Unjust Enr.	Tort
Remedial Goal →	benefit of bargain	enforcement of promise	restoration of enrichment	redress of injury
Principal Focus of Remedy →	expectation damages—the sum of money needed to place plaintiff in the position the plaintiff would have been in had contract not been breached	reimbursement of expenses and losses unless justice requires fuller enforcement	restitution: disgorgement of the value of what was received	the sum of money needed to return plaintiff to the status quo ante—to compensate for loss or injury caused by the defendant

§9.3 THE RELATIONSHIP BETWEEN UNJUST ENRICHMENT AND CONTRACT

The cause of action based on unjust enrichment is sometimes also called "quasi-contract" or "contract implied in law," for reasons explained in section 9.4. However, as stated above, it is not a contract cause of action, but is an independent theory of liability applicable in many situations, having nothing to do with contract, in which one party is enriched at the expense of the other. For example, unjust enrichment is one of the causes of action that a victim of theft can bring against the person that stole the victim's money or property.

However, unjust enrichment intersects with contract law in two broad areas. In the first, the parties do have an actual contract which one of them breached. Although the aggrieved party[1] has the right to sue the breaching party for a remedy based on the contract (such as expectation damages),

1. The term "aggrieved party" is used to refer to the party who has suffered a breach of contract by the other party.

the aggrieved party has the option to sue instead for unjust enrichment to recover the value of any performance that it rendered prior to the breach. In the second, the parties made an agreement but for one reason or another the agreement is not enforceable as a contract or is avoidable. If one of the parties obtained some gain from the other during the course of the relationship, that gain or its value can be recovered by a suit in unjust enrichment. Diagram 9B charts the role of restitution in these two different circumstances, where it is a remedy following breach of contract, or where it applies in the absence of an enforceable contract. Sections 9.3.1 to 9.3.5 explain this more fully by identifying five situations in which unjust enrichment arises in the context of contract law.

Diagram 9B

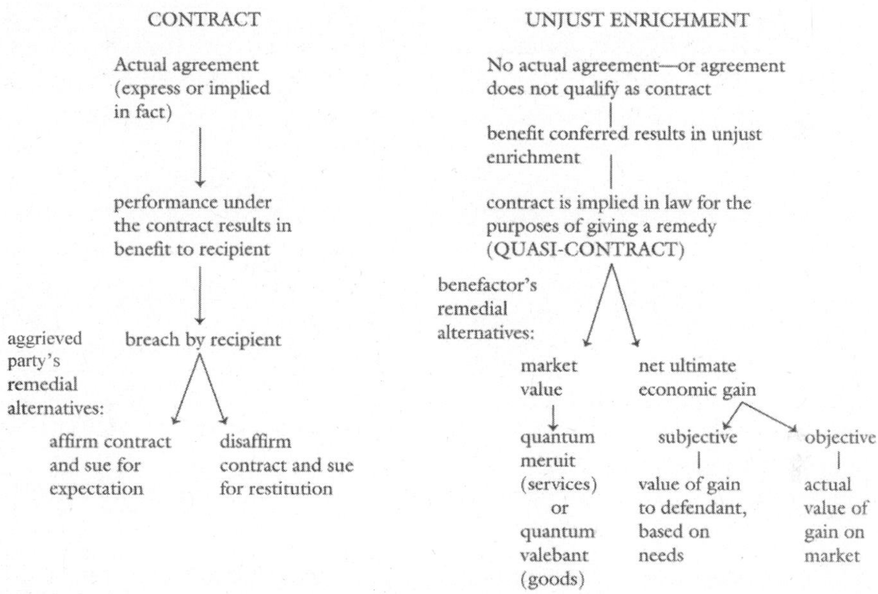

§9.3.1 Restitution as an Alternative Remedy When a Valid Contract Has Been Breached

Unjust enrichment plays an important role when a valid contract was created but has been breached or has been rescinded. In the case of breach, unjust enrichment—and its remedy of restitution—may be used as an alternative to expectation damages. One of the parties may have conferred a benefit on the other in the course of performing the contract before its breach, and restitution of that benefit may be a better option than enforcement of the contract. (In some cases, it may be the only option because contractual expectation damages cannot be proved.) Even though there is a valid contract, the plaintiff may elect to forgo contractual relief in favor of restitution.

For example, Buyer, Inc. and Seller, Inc. made a contract for the sale of Seller's building. Buyer paid a deposit of $50,000 to Seller. Seller later reneged on the contract and refused to close. Because a valid contract exists and Seller has breached it, Buyer has the right to claim expectation damages for breach of contract. Expectation damages are intended to give Buyer the benefit of its bargain by placing Buyer in the same economic position as if the contract had been performed. If the price under this contract is less than the cost of buying an equivalent building on the market, Buyer's expectation damages would typically be the difference between the contract price and the price of a substitute.[2] However, if the contract price was at or under the market value of the building, Buyer would be able to purchase an equivalent building for the same or a lower price on the market, so the breach did not result in an economic loss to Buyer, and Buyer has no expectation damages. However, Buyer has enriched Seller by the $50,000 down payment that Seller no longer has any right to keep. Seller's enrichment is unjust, and if it fails to repay, the remedy of restitution is available to Buyer to recover the down payment. Restitution is therefore an alternative remedy that the aggrieved party may choose instead of enforcing the contract by claiming expectation damages. In essence, the aggrieved party elects not to sue on the contract, but to base the claim for relief on the separate and independent cause of action for unjust enrichment.[3]

§9.3.2 Restitution When a Contract Has Been Avoided or Terminated

Where a contract has been created but is later avoided because there was a defect in the bargaining process (such as fraud, duress, mistake, or the other grounds of avoidance discussed in Chapters 13, 14, and 15), or is terminated, the remedy of restitution, based on the theory of unjust enrichment, is available to a party who rendered performance under the contract before its avoidance or termination.

For example, Buyer, Inc. and Seller, Inc. entered into a contract for the sale of a plot of land. Based on a geological survey, both parties believed that there were no valuable mineral deposits under the surface of the land. The sale was completed and Buyer paid Seller the price of the land. The parties subsequently discovered that the survey was wrong, and there are

2. The measure of expectation damages is fully discussed in section 18.3.

3. This role that restitution plays as an alternative measure of damages for breach of contract is not discussed further in this chapter, but is dealt with in connection with remedies for breach in section 18.9.

significant gold deposits under the land. Under the doctrine of mistake, discussed in Chapter 15, Seller may have grounds to avoid the contract because of the error. However, if Seller succeeds in avoiding the contract, Seller no longer has the right to keep the price of the land paid by Buyer and would be unjustly enriched by retaining it. Buyer is therefore entitled to restitution of the price paid to Seller.[4]

§9.3.3 Restitution When a Benefit Is Conferred Pursuant to an Invalid or Unenforceable Contract

Under the statute of frauds, a sale of real property must be recorded (in a tangible document or by some other means, such as electronically) and an oral agreement is unenforceable as a contract (*see* section 11.2). Therefore, if Buyer, Inc. and Seller, Inc. made an oral agreement for the sale of the building, neither party would be able to enforce it if the other breached. If Buyer had made a down payment of $50,000 to Seller at the time of making the oral agreement and Seller later reneges and refuses to transfer the house, Buyer would not be able to enforce the oral contract. But because Seller no longer has any right to keep the down payment, Buyer can obtain restitution of that payment on the theory of unjust enrichment. Although the statute of frauds precludes a claim on the contract, it does not apply to an unjust enrichment claim. In *Hoag Living Trust Dated February 4, 2013 v. Hoag*, 424 P.3d 731 (Or. Ct. App. 2018), the trust had agreed orally to transfer property to Hoag provided that he maintained the property and paid taxes and insurance on it. He did so for many years, but the trust eventually sold the property to someone else. Although the oral agreement for transfer of the property was unenforceable under the statute of frauds, the court held that unjust enrichment is a separate cause of action and the statute of frauds did not bar Hoag's unjust enrichment claim for reimbursement of his expenses for maintaining and paying taxes and insurance on the property, which benefited the trust.

Restitution is also available as a remedy where the parties reach an understanding that is too vague to qualify as a contract, but one of the parties performs under the arrangement. For example, in *Schepperley v. DePinna*, 2009 WL 765524 (Conn. Super. Ct. 2009), a mother and daughter agreed orally that the mother would pay for the construction of an "in-law apartment" in the basement of the daughter's house and, in return, would live in the apartment. The agreement was too vague to qualify as a contract because the parties had not settled crucial terms such as the exact amount

4. The role of restitution in situations involving mistake and other grounds for avoidance is taken up in Chapters 13, 14, and 15 and not discussed further in this chapter.

of the mother's contribution, the details of the construction, the term of the mother's residence in the apartment, or the extent and nature of any future obligations that she may have. The mother moved in and lived in the apartment for about six months. She then left following a disagreement with her daughter and sued her daughter and son-in-law for return of the funds that she had paid to construct the apartment. Although the court found no enforceable contract between the parties, it awarded restitution to the mother on the basis of unjust enrichment: The apartment was a capital improvement to the house, and the mother was entitled to reimbursement of what she paid for the construction.

In addition to these specific illustrations, there are many other situations in which an unjust enrichment claim allows a party to claim restoration of the value of a benefit conferred under an agreement that cannot be enforced as a contract. For example, in *Restore Construction Co. v. Board of Education of Proviso Township High School District*, 133 N.E.3d 71 (Ill. App. Ct. 2019), the school district hired Restore to do remediation work on a school building that had been damaged by fire. However, the contract was void because the board had exceeded its statutory authority in entering it. Restore sued the district to recover the value of work done under the void contract and the court upheld the claim. The court noted that even though no claim could be made on the void contract, a claim in quasi-contract is a separate cause of action, based on the fundamental principle that the district should not be unjustly enriched by failure to compensate Restore for the benefit received from it.

§9.3.4 Restitution When a Benefit Is Conferred on the Strength of a Promise Without Consideration

Owner, Inc. made a written promise to donate a building to Charity, a nonprofit organization, for use as its headquarters. Before taking transfer of the building, Charity obtained Owner's permission to make repairs and renovations to it. After Charity had done this work, Owner reneged on the promise and refused to transfer the building. Charity's enhancement of the property was intended to prepare the building for its own use and not for Owner's benefit. It was not bargained for by Owner as consideration in exchange for Owner's promise of the building. Charity cannot enforce Owner's promise as a contract because it is not supported by consideration, but Charity has improved the building that now remains Owner's property. This unjustly enriches Owner, so Charity can obtain restitution for the value of its improvements to the building.

As explained in section 9.5.2, Charity's unjust enrichment claim is founded on two basic principles: The benefit was not conferred as a gift, and it was not improperly imposed on the beneficiary without its consent.

Both these requirements are satisfied here. First, Charity made the improvements for its own use and never intended to make a gift of them to Owner. Second, Charity made the improvements with Owner's knowledge and consent. This illustration differs from the previous ones in that restitution here does not involve the restoration of a fixed sum of money but the value of an improvement to Owner's property. When the value of a benefit is not fixed and certain, the party claiming restitution must establish the value of the benefit, which is commonly determined by its market value. This is discussed in section 9.6.

It sometimes happens that the same circumstances support relief under alternative causes of action with different remedies. The claimant may pursue these causes of action in the alternative. In this illustration, the facts may allow Charity to make a promissory estoppel claim as an alternative to its unjust enrichment claim, and there is a good argument that the elements of promissory estoppel are satisfied: Owner made a promise of the building. By giving Charity permission to repair and renovate it, Owner manifested the intention of inducing Charity to rely on the promise, which it did, incurring the expense of improving Owner's building. Charity's reliance on the promise may have been justifiable because Owner made a clear promise and indicated intent to perform it by allowing Charity to make the improvements. However, this conclusion is not assured because Charity should have known that a donative promise is revocable, and may have assumed the risk of incurring the expense of making the improvements before the donation was fully executed. If all these elements are satisfied, the final element of averting injustice is probably satisfied because the improvements have enhanced Owner's property at Charity's expense. Therefore, enforcement of the promise, at least to the extent of reimbursing Charity's expenses, may be necessary to avert injustice. This relief, based on reliance loss, differs from restitutionary relief, which focuses on the restoration of the value of the benefit conferred.

§9.3.5 Restitution in Cases When No Contractual Interaction Occurred

Victim slipped on a banana peel and fell down a flight of stairs. Doctor, a stranger who happened to be walking by, administered emergency treatment to unconscious Victim. Doctor never entered into a contract with Victim, who was unconscious and could not consent to treatment. The only basis on which Doctor could recover a fee for the medical services is unjust enrichment, on the theory that Victim would have had to pay for them in the marketplace, and Victim is therefore unjustly enriched by receiving them for free. (The merits of this argument are explored in more detail in section 9.5.) Although this is not a contract case, it is historically linked to contract law through the legal fiction known as "quasi-contract."

§9.4 THE MEANING OF "QUASI-CONTRACT"

§9.4.1 Quasi-Contract—A Contract "Implied in Law"

Where a claim is not based on contract but is premised solely on the grounds of unjust enrichment, the common law tradition has created a peculiar fiction that makes the case sound as if it has something to do with contract. In early common law, courts were bound by a rigid set of writs called "forms of action."[5] To obtain relief, the plaintiff had to fit a claim into one of these recognized categories of suit. There was no writ for unjust enrichment, so courts chose to incorporate enrichment claims into the contract writ of assumpsit, and squeezed enrichment into a contractual form by creating the legal fiction that the benefit was conferred on the recipient pursuant to a contract with the grantor. Thus, in the illustration in section 9.3.5, the court would allow the Doctor who treated the unconscious patient to recover payment for the medical services under the writ of assumpsit by deeming the services to have been requested, even though they had not been. Claims for unjust enrichment based on this fictional contract were said to arise *quasi ex contractu*, and the restitutionary remedy based on this fiction has come to be called quasi-contract, or contract implied in law. It is easy to be confused by this terminology, so it is important to remember that a quasi-contract or a contract implied in law is not a real contract. Legal implication is a fiction created for remedial purposes. It must be distinguished from a contract implied in fact, which is explained in section 9.4.2.

The general principle of unjust enrichment can therefore be described in the following terms: When a benefit has been conferred on a recipient under circumstances in which it is unfair to permit the beneficiary to retain it without payment, the cause of action of unjust enrichment is available to the person who conferred the benefit. Using this cause of action, the conferrer can claim the remedy of restitution, under which the court will restore the benefit or its value to the conferrer. To fit this newly recognized cause of action into existing legal forms, early common law courts used the legal fiction that the benefit had been contracted for. That is, the court implied a contract in law, even though no contractual relationship actually existed between the conferrer and the beneficiary. Restitutionary recovery based on unjust enrichment was therefore described as "quasi ex contractu," and the

5. The derivation of forms of action is explained briefly in section 2.5.

term "quasi-contract" has come down to us as an alternative name for this form of relief.

When it comes to enforcement of the obligation, relief for unjust enrichment (quasi-contractual relief) can be very different from that for contract. For example, a Doctor who made a real contract with Victim can enforce its actual terms and can recover whatever fee was agreed on for the treatment. As no contract was made and the cause of action is quasi-contract, there cannot be an agreed fee, so recovery is based on the value of the benefit, typically determined by market value as discussed in section 9.6. Latin terms are commonly used to denote market value. Quantum meruit ("as much as deserved") is used to indicate the market value of services, and quantum valebant ("as much as they are worth") indicates the market value of goods. Sometimes there may be no difference between market value and contract price, but the difference could be significant.

§9.4.2 Quasi-Contract Distinguished from a Contract Implied in Fact

As noted in section 9.4.1, a quasi-contract (or contract implied in law) is not a contract at all but merely a legal fiction. By contrast, a contract implied in fact is an actual contract. There is no difference in the legal nature or effect of an express contract and a contract implied in fact. The only difference is in the manner and evidence of contract formation. The parties create an express contract by articulating their agreement in recorded or oral words. A contract is implied in fact where the parties do not express agreement in words, but it is apparent from a reasonable interpretation of their conduct, viewed in context, that they intended to make a contract.[6] A variation of the facts of the illustration involving Doctor rendering medical services to Victim shows the distinction between quasi-contract and contract implied in fact. Victim slipped and fell down the stairs. Although injured, Victim was fully conscious and had unimpaired mental capacity to make a contract. Victim called an ambulance and was rushed to a hospital. Victim had no discussion with the dispatcher or the paramedics in the ambulance about payment for the service. Even though no words of agreement passed between Victim and employees of the ambulance company, there is surely a contract

6. The distinction between implication in law and in fact is also made where the issue is not whether a contract was formed, but whether it contains a particular disputed term. A term might be implied into a contract in fact, based on evidence that the parties intended it to be part of the contract even though they did not express it. Sometimes, even in the absence of such evidence of agreement on the term, the court might construe a term—that is, imply the term as a matter of law—because the term should be in the contract. This is discussed in sections 10.1 and 10.2.

implied in fact under which Victim is responsible for paying a fee for the ambulance service. Given the general understanding that ambulances do not operate for free, both Victim and the ambulance company must reasonably have understood that Victim would be responsible for paying for the service. Because the parties did not discuss the fee, there is no agreed price for the service. Where parties make an actual contract (whether express or implied in fact) but do not specify the price, the contract must be interpreted in context to decide how to determine the price. A court may conclude that Victim implicitly agreed to pay the ambulance service's usual or customary fee. Alternatively, if there is no usual or customary fee, or if it is not clear if the parties intended that fee to apply, the court may determine the fee with reference to the market value of the service—that is, it may use the quantum meruit measure. Therefore, although quantum meruit is commonly associated with quasi-contract, there are circumstances in which it may be used to fix compensation for a service in an actual contract where it is the most appropriate means of determining an agreed price.

Where performance is rendered by one party to another in the absence of express agreement, it can be difficult to tell whether acceptance of the benefit of the performance created an actual contract, implied in fact, or gave rise to unjust enrichment to be remedied by the device of quasi-contract. The distinction often turns on whether there is sufficient usage and context on which to base the implication of an actual contract. In some cases, there may be no practical significance in the distinction, especially where the price under any implied-in-fact contract would have to be determined by quantum meruit. In other cases, the remedy available for an actual contract could be significantly different from that for unjust enrichment. This was intimated in the above example involving the ambulance. If there was a contract implied in fact, Victim could be bound to the ambulance service's usual or customary charge for the service, which might be higher or lower than the market price of the service.

Contractual liability, based on intent (albeit implied) to enter a contract, has a different factual basis from unjust enrichment, which is founded on the injustice of permitting the beneficiary to retain a benefit without paying for it. It is therefore possible that the facts of the case will support recovery on one theory but not the other. In the example in which the doctor renders medical services to the unconscious victim, the facts provide no basis for finding an actual contract. By contrast, the example in which the conscious victim calls an ambulance is amenable to finding a contract implied in fact and could also support an alternative basis for relief for unjust enrichment.

Contship Containerlines, Inc. v. Howard Industries, Inc., 309 F.3d 910 (6th Cir. 2002), provides an example of a situation in which the facts may not have supported recovery in contract, but did give rise to a claim in quasi-contract. Howard contracted with a Transworld Freight Forwarding to book its cargo onto a ship and paid Transworld for the entire cost of the shipping. Howard had not had any direct dealings with Contship, the shipping line on which Transworld had booked the freight for transportation. Howard delivered the cargo to the ship, and it was shipped to its destination. Transworld never transmitted payment for the freight charges to Contship, which then claimed the charges from Howard on the basis of contract implied in fact, alternatively, unjust enrichment. The court denied Contship's motion for summary judgment because there was a genuine dispute of fact on the question of whether the parties had a contract implied in fact. When Howard delivered the cargo to Contship, it knew that Contship was not performing the service for free, which could provide a basis for implying an actual contract. However, Howard had already paid Transworld for the shipping of its goods and its delivery of the goods to the ship was its only dealing with Contship, so this on its own may not have manifested the intent to make a contract with Contship. Although Howard overcame summary judgment on the contract claim, the court did grant summary judgment to Contship on the unjust enrichment claim. This may seem surprising because Howard had not actually been enriched at all—it had in fact paid the shipping costs to Transworld. The court found that this was no defense to Contship's restitution claim because Howard, by paying a third-party intermediary, assumed the risk that payment would not be transmitted to Contship. That is, the court was faced with the task of allocating the loss between two innocent parties—Howard, which had already paid someone else for the service and was not actually enriched, and Contship, which had not been paid for its service. The court allocated the risk to Howard because it had been the one to cause this problem by entrusting the funds to Transworld. Similarly, in *Restore Construction Co.*, cited in section 9.3.3, the court stressed that it could not find either an express contract or a contract implied in fact because the board did not have the legal authority to enter into an actual contract, but it was liable to Restore for restitution based on a contract implied in law.

Courts will not usually imply a contract where the parties already have an express contract, especially if the implied contract is inconsistent with the terms of the express contract. For example, in *Yarde Metals, Inc. v. New England Patriots L.P.*, 834 N.E.2d 1233 (Mass. App. Ct. 2005), the holder of a season ticket argued that the Patriots were bound by an implied contract to give it the opportunity to renew the subscription. It based this claim on the fact that over the past 20 years, the Patriots had consistently offered it the opportunity to renew the subscription. The court held that this conduct did not give rise to an implied contract because such an implication contradicted the terms printed on the ticket, which stated that the ticket was a revocable license that gave the purchaser no renewal rights for a subsequent year. The court also found that implication of a contract would be inconsistent with common practice and would confer a right on the ticket holder far more valuable than the price paid for the tickets.

§9.5 THE ELEMENTS OF UNJUST ENRICHMENT

As stated earlier, the remedy of restitution is aimed at restoring money, property, or the value of property or services when it would be unjust to permit the recipient to retain what was received without paying for it. As its name suggests, unjust enrichment is predicated on two elements: The recipient must have been enriched at the expense of the claimant, and the circumstances must be such as to make this enrichment unjust. This is represented in Diagram 9C.

Diagram 9C

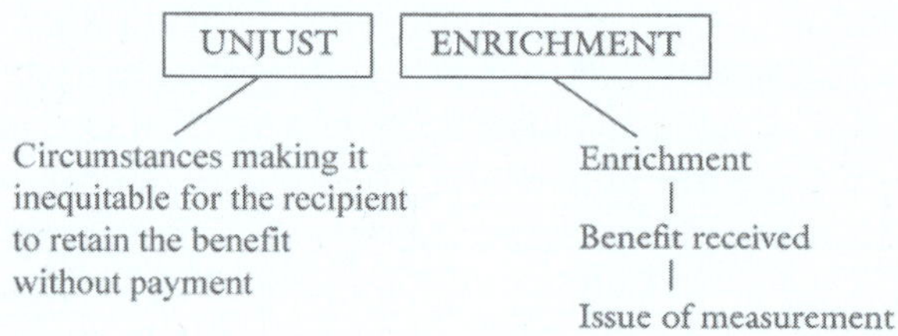

§9.5.1 Enrichment

Enrichment is an economic benefit. When a person receives and retains money or property, it is easy to see that the recipient has been enriched to the extent of the payment or the value of the property because the recipient's net worth has been increased by that amount. However, a person could also be enriched by consuming goods or receiving intangible services that result in no long-term financial advantage. A person is not obviously made wealthier by consuming a free bag of pretzels or getting a free haircut, but the person has saved the cost of buying these items in the marketplace. Naturally, the existence or absence of lasting economic advantage and its extent are factors taken into account in deciding on relief, as discussed in section 9.6. However, the general principle is that enrichment occurs whenever something of value is received, even if it is consumed so that it does not enlarge the recipient's net worth.

Usually, enrichment results only where the benefit passes directly from the benefactor to the beneficiary, but sometimes a person is indirectly enriched by a benefit conferred on a third party. For example, in *Emergency Physicians Integrated v. Salt Lake County*, 167 P.3d 1080 (Utah 2007), the physicians group sued the county for the market value of medical services rendered to county prison inmates. The county had a constitutional duty to provide medical services to the inmates and had made some payment to the physicians, based on a statutory fee schedule. However, the physicians argued that they were entitled to receive a higher rate of pay based on the market value of their services. The county countered that the benefit of the medical services went to the inmates and that it was only incidentally benefited by the services. The court rejected the county's argument. It said that it did not matter that the patients also benefited from the service. The county received the benefit of having the physicians fulfill its constitutional duty to the inmates.

Although a benefit may be conferred indirectly, the person seeking restitution must show a link between its actions and the recipient's benefit. In *Ashley County v. Pfizer, Inc.*, 552 F.3d 659 (8th Cir. 2009), the county came up with a novel but unsuccessful argument for claiming that Pfizer and other drug company defendants had been enriched at its expense and owed it restitution. The county's theory was that the drug companies had declined to cooperate in imposing controls on cold and allergy medications that could be used in the manufacture of methamphetamine. As a result, the companies had made handsome profits by selling the medications, many of which were bought for the illegal purpose of making methamphetamine. The county argued that this enrichment came at its expense in that it had to provide services to deal with the methamphetamine epidemic. The court rejected the county's argument on the basis that there was no link between the services rendered by the county and the drug companies' profits.

§9.5.2 When Is Enrichment Unjust?

To receive restitution, it is not enough that the claimant has conferred an uncompensated benefit on the recipient, because it is not always unjust for a person to receive a benefit without paying for it. Enrichment may be unjust because the recipient of the benefit has obtained the benefit by improper or dishonest conduct, or if, for some other reason, the defendant's retention of the benefit without compensating the party who conferred it would violate principles of fairness and equity. The essential issue in deciding whether enrichment is unjust is whether it would be inequitable to allow the recipient to enjoy the benefit at the expense of the party that conferred it. Courts have identified two common situations in which it is not unjust for a recipient to retain a benefit without paying for it. The first is where the party who conferred the benefit did so without the actual or implicit intent to charge for it. The second is where the party conferring the benefit imposed it on the recipient under circumstances in which it cannot be rejected or returned.

a. Actual or Implicit Intent Not to Charge for the Benefit

Enrichment is not unjust if the benefit was conferred without the actual or implicit intent to charge for it. The most obvious situation in which that occurs is where the benefit was given as a gift. It is clearly not unfair to allow the recipient of a gift to keep it without paying for it.[7] Quite the contrary, it would unfairly disrupt the donee's reasonable expectations by allowing the donor to demand payment for something originally given for free. A person who confers a benefit without intent to be paid for it is sometimes called a "volunteer." In the context of unjust enrichment, this word carries more than its common meaning. It connotes that something was done or given not only by free choice but also without the intent to seek compensation.

The party conferring the benefit may have actual subjective gratuitous intent, but even if the conferrer's actual state of mind cannot be proved, gratuitous intent may be inferred from the circumstances under which the benefit was given. That is, irrespective of the conferrer's subjective state of mind, intent can be manifested by conduct in light of all the circumstances. An objective test avoids the problem of divining the conferrer's true state of mind and protects the recipient's reasonable expectations.

Apart from situations in which the benefit is deliberately given as a gift, there are all kinds of other circumstances that raise the question of whether the conferrer had actual or apparent intent to charge for the benefit. The following two cases illustrate the diverse circumstances in which the court had to decide if a benefit was voluntarily conferred. In *Hobbs v. St. Martin*, 320 F. Supp. 3d 748 (D. Md. 2018), Hobbs and St. Martin had both participated for years in an investment scheme operated by a man named Hagen. Hagen was in fact operating a Ponzi scheme, in which he obtained money from investors with the ostensible purpose of investing it, but instead misappropriated the money. To deceive investors into believing that their investments were generating returns, Hagen used some of the funds paid by later investors to make payments to earlier investors. In a complex fraudulent scheme, Hagen induced Hobbs to pay a $500,000 debt that Hagen owed to St. Martin by representing this would enhance the value of investments that Hobbs had made in the past. The Ponzi scheme collapsed and Hagen never repaid the $500,000 to Hobbs. Hobbs sued St. Martin, claiming that St. Martin had been unjustly enriched at his expense. St. Martin moved for summary judgment on the grounds that Hobbs had paid the money to him voluntarily, so it would not be unjust to permit him to retain it. The court denied the motion—although Hobbs intentionally sent the payment to St. Martin, he did not intend to make the payment gratuitously, and a person who is induced to confer a benefit as a result of fraud (including the fraud of another person) or a mistake of fact should not be treated as a volunteer. Hobbs had the right to go to trial to establish that he was not himself guilty of inequitable conduct in doing business with Hagen.

---

7. As explained in section 7.2, there is no consideration issue once the donation has been given. Consideration doctrine applies only to the enforcement of unexecuted promises.

The court did find that the benefit was voluntarily conferred in *Devco v. T10 Meltel, LLC*, 237 F. Supp. 3d 804 (N.D. Ill. 2017). Devco, the owner of a building, had leased roof space to cellular carriers to enable the carriers to erect telecommunications equipment on the roof. Devco sold the leases to T10 Meltel. One of the terms of the sale contract required Devco to move the equipment, which was scattered all over the roof, to a single location on the roof. As an incentive to encourage Devco to get this done by a specified date, the contract allowed T10 Meltel to withhold payment of $300,000 of the sale price, to be forfeited if Devco did not complete the work by that date. Devco did not complete the work in time and T10 Meltel notified Devco that it was keeping the $300,000. Devco continued to do the work and ultimately completed it a year after the specified date. Devco sued T10 Meltel, claiming that it had been unjustly enriched by not paying for the work. The court granted summary judgment to T10 Meltel. The work may have enriched it, but the enrichment was not unjust because the parties' contract obliged Devco to do the work and provided for forfeiture of $300,000 of the sale price if it did not complete the work by the specified date. This gave T10 Meltel the right to retain the benefit without paying for it. The case stands for the principle that a party cannot circumvent a contract by claiming unjust enrichment if the benefit to the recipient is nothing more than what it was entitled to under the contract. Expressed in the language of the volunteer principle, Devco's agreement to forfeit part of the price if the work was not completed in time meant that it completed the work as a volunteer.

Sometimes a benefit is conferred under circumstances in which the conferrer was not thinking about compensation at all when taking the beneficial action. For example, a person who confers a benefit to avert harm in an emergency is probably focused on handling the crisis and not on the question of compensation. The only way that intent can be determined under these circumstances is by applying a community standard to construe what the conferrer's reasonable expectations would have been at the time of giving the benefit. One of the significant considerations in deciding whether or not the benefit was conferred with gratuitous intent is the relationship of the benefit to the trade or profession of the conferrer. For example, in the illustration in section 9.3.5 a doctor gave emergency treatment to an unconscious patient. At the time of rendering the medical services, the doctor was probably concentrating on administering emergency aid to the victim and was not thinking about compensation for the services. Nevertheless, if there is a general expectation that a doctor would charge for professional services in these circumstances, intent to charge is inferred. Some courts go so far as to say that where services are rendered by a professional, there is a presumption that they were not intended to be gratuitous. By recognizing this presumption, the court places the burden on the beneficiary to prove gratuitous intent.

By contrast, if the emergency aid was provided by a lay person, the general expectation is likely to be that there was no intent to charge. If the good Samaritan in the above example was not a medical professional, but a lay person with enough medical knowledge to render aid, the community expectation, and hence the actor's reasonable expectation, would probably be that the nonprofessional emergency intervention was public spirited, altruistic, and gratuitous. The expectation may be different if the intervention required some financial cost. For example, if the good Samaritan hailed a cab and used it to transport the victim to a hospital, the reasonable expectation may still be that the good Samaritan's services were gratuitous, but not the cost of the cab fare.

In some situations, the conferrer may have intended to charge for the benefit, but the intent may not have been to charge the recipient. If so, from the recipient's perspective, the benefit is gratuitous. For example, an apartment lease provides that the lessor is responsible for repairs to plumbing in the apartment. With the lessor's authorization, a tenant calls a plumber who handles plumbing work for the apartment building to repair a leaking pipe in the apartment. However, the plumber's reasonable expectation of payment is from the apartment building, not the tenant. Therefore, the plumber has no unjust enrichment claim against the tenant if the apartment building fails to pay for the pipe repair.

b. Imposition

If restitution was available for any benefit conferred with intent to charge, this would open the way for all kinds of imposition from busybodies and sleazy operators. For example, it would not be just to impose liability on a homeowner to pay for landscaping services rendered by a meddlesome neighbor who decided, unasked, that the homeowner's lawn needed mowing. Even if the neighbor did not intend to confer the benefit gratuitously, the neighbor was not justified in imposing a benefit on the homeowner without entering into an agreement under which the homeowner assented to the service and agreed to pay for it. Courts commonly describe a person who imposes an unrequested benefit in this way as an "officious intermeddler." The interfering neighbor meets that description completely and is not entitled to restitution of the value of the lawn mowing. The court reached the opposite conclusion in *Hobbs* with regard to the $500,000 payment that Hobbs made to St. Martin. In addition to the question of whether Hobbs was a volunteer, the court considered whether he was an officious intermeddler. The court noted that the purpose of the intermeddler rule is to prevent a person from unilaterally and unjustifiably interfering with the affairs of another. That purpose was not evident in this case, where Hobbs was fraudulently induced to make the payment in the belief that it would protect his own investment.

The interfering neighbor in the above example was clearly an officious intermeddler, but the term should not be taken literally to require the recipient of the benefit to prove that the benefit was imposed for meddlesome or officious motives. Although that would be the most obvious case for denying restitution, the focus is on protecting the recipient from unfair imposition. Therefore, there are many circumstances in which an imposed benefit precludes restitution even though the conferrer did not have the intent to meddle. *Kelly v. Cole*, 2017 WL 5462959 (Wis. Ct. App. 2017), illustrates this. The Coles owned a duplex that was in poor condition. They wished to sell it and Kelly was interested in buying it, but he needed to get a loan so he could pay the price. While the loan application was pending, the Coles permitted Kelly to do some repairs on the duplex and gave him some money for that purpose. Kelly spent considerably more on the repairs than the amount that the Coles had given him. Ultimately, Kelly was not able to obtain a loan and could not buy the duplex. He sued the Coles for the value of his repairs to the duplex in excess of the amount that the Coles had given him. The court held that Kelly had imposed the additional cost of the repairs on the Coles, so equity was not offended by allowing the Coles to retain the benefit of the repairs without paying Kelly for them. Kelly expected the repairs to be for his own benefit as prospective owner of the duplex and he exceeded the cost authorized by the Coles, knowing that he had not yet secured financing to buy it. He assumed the risk that he would fail to get financing and could not hold the Coles responsible for the consequences.

An unrequested benefit is not conferred officiously if there is a good justification for conferring it without asking first. This is illustrated by *Judge Rotenberg Educational Center v. Blass*, 679 F. App'x 71 (2d Cir. 2017). Up to her twenty-first birthday, a disabled young woman had been receiving housing, education, and legal services from the center, a foster-care provider. The county department of social services was required by law to arrange for transitioning the woman from foster care before she reached the age of 21, but it failed to do so. She had no place to go, so the center continued to provide services to her until the county arranged for the transition about 11 months after she turned 21. The county refused to pay the center for its expenses in keeping the woman after she turned 21 and the center sued. The county defended the suit on the grounds that the center was a volunteer and an officious intermeddler. The court held that it was not a volunteer because it clearly manifested the intent that the county would pay for its services. The court also held that it was not an officious intermeddler because the woman was already in its care and she had nowhere else to go—the center was the appropriate party to provide shelter to her.

As this case suggests, conferring a benefit to avert harm in an emergency can be a justification for imposing the benefit without advance consent. The justification is strongest where the emergency requires immediate action, advance assent is impracticable, and the party conferring the benefit had no reason to believe that the recipient would not wish for the action to be taken. The greater the urgency and the more at stake, the more likely that unrequested action will not be treated as intermeddling. Threats to life or health are generally regarded as giving good cause for unsolicited action. Thus, the doctor who rendered emergency care to the unconscious patient would be neither a volunteer nor an officious intermeddler. An emergency response to avert harm to property is also of value to the property owner and to society. Therefore, a person who, in response to an immediate threat, takes lawful and appropriate action to save or preserve the property, is also not likely to be treated as an officious intermeddler.

Even if an imposed benefit would be grounds for denying restitution, the equities may change in favor of restitution if the recipient accepts and uses the benefit under circumstances in which the recipient reasonably should have realized that the benefit was not conferred with gratuitous intent and it would have been possible to reject it. It is not possible to return the benefit of a completed service. In the example of the meddlesome neighbor, the homeowner cannot return the benefit of a mowed lawn by unmowing the lawn. However, if the recipient has the opportunity to refuse the benefit but keeps and takes advantage of it, the enrichment could be unjust despite the initial imposition

§9.6 MEASUREMENT OF BENEFIT

§9.6.1 The Remedial Aim of Restitution

As noted in section 9.2, the remedial focus of restitution is different from contract. Contractual damages are based on the aggrieved party's expected gains under the contract and are calculated to approximate the monetary value of the benefit that the aggrieved party would have realized had the contract not been breached. By contrast, the primary focus of restitutionary damages is not the grantor's loss of expectation, but the recipient's gain. They are calculated to approximate the monetary value of what the grantor gave to the recipient.[8] There are different means of measuring the appropriate restitutionary recovery, as set out in section 9.6.2. The selection of the most appropriate measure is within the court's discretion, exercised to achieve a result that is fair under all the circumstances. The goal is to reach a figure that neither overcompensates nor undercompensates the claimant while imposing liability on the recipient that is realistic and not excessive.

8. Chapter 18 deals with damages for breach of contract and section 18.9 discusses further the distinction between contractual expectation damages and restitution.

§9.6.2 Alternative Methods for Measuring Enrichment

The following illustration suggests the two principal ways in which enrichment can be measured.

Maggie Zine owns a newsstand in an office lobby. As she was opening the booth early one morning, she fainted and was rushed to the hospital. She spent the day there for observation and tests and was discharged that evening. Sam Aratan, Maggie's friend, happened to be in the lobby coffee bar when he heard that Maggie had been taken away in the ambulance. As he had the day off, he decided to help Maggie by keeping her booth open. He ran the booth for 10 hours, making $600 in sales, of which $200 is profit. The going wage for a kiosk clerk is $15 per hour. Assume that Sam is neither a volunteer nor an intermeddler, so that he should receive restitution for his services. There are two alternative means of calculating Maggie's enrichment:

1. The market value of Sam's service, represented by the going wage of kiosk clerks at $15 per hour, for 10 hours — $150, or
2. Maggie's net economic gain—her profit for the day, $200 (not her net sales, of course, because she had to buy $400 worth of goods to generate the $600 income).

Market value of the benefit and the recipient's ultimate net fiscal gain are the two alternative choices for measuring enrichment. Market value is the standard measure, but net gain is an appropriate alternative when the circumstances make recovery of market value either excessive or inadequate. If net gain is the basis of measurement, the gain could be valued differently depending on whether it is measured in the abstract, based on what it is reasonably worth in general (the objective value) or in light of the beneficiary's particular circumstances (the subjective value). This breakdown may be represented as shown in Diagram 9D.

Diagram 9D

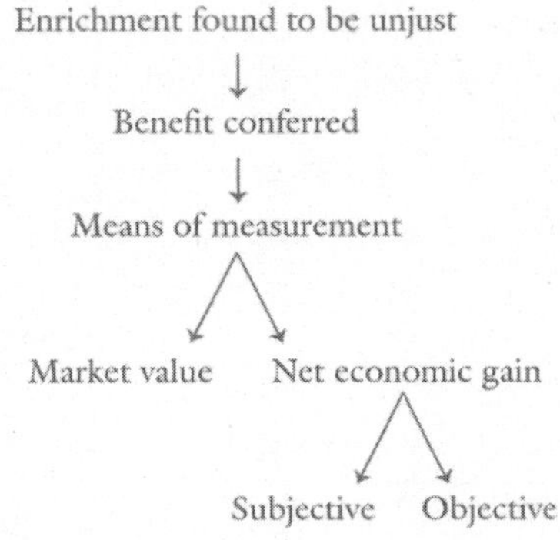

a. Market Value

When the benefit is the payment of money, value is readily apparent, but if the benefit consists of the receipt of property or services, their value must be established by evidence of their price on the market. As noted in section 9.4.1, Latin terms are commonly used to express market value. Quantum meruit expresses the market value of services, and quantum valebant expresses the market value of goods.[9] Market value is most reliably determined by testimony of an expert who is familiar with the market and can provide objective information about customary pricing. However, if such evidence is not available, the plaintiff may be able to make a prima facie showing of value by providing evidence of its own usual price. This is not the most convincing evidence, but if the defendant offers nothing to rebut it, and the plaintiff's basis for calculating it appears reasonable, it may be sufficient. If the benefit was requested (for example, if the parties did agree on a price but the agreement does not qualify as a contract), the agreed price is probative evidence of value and may be used in preference over other measures.

If there is no evidence of either the objective market value or the plaintiff's usual price, evidence of the plaintiff's costs in providing the property or services may be accepted as the best evidence of value, provided that it appears that the plaintiff acted efficiently and that costs were not higher than they should be. (Of course, the reimbursement of cost is likely to be a less attractive basis of recovery for the plaintiff, because market price usually consists of cost plus profit.)

Market value is likely to be the fairest and most balanced basis of compensating the conferrer at a rate that could reasonably be expected by the beneficiary. Also, because quantum meruit and quantum valebant approximate what the contract price would have been if the parties had made a contract for the services or property, it is conceptually most consistent with the underlying theory of quasi-contractual recovery, which is based on a fictional contract. This basis of calculation is therefore particularly appropriate when the benefit had been requested (even though there is no contract), or circumstances indicate that it likely would have been had the beneficiary had the opportunity to do so. Therefore, Sam's most appropriate recovery from Maggie would be the $150 reasonable wage, rather than the $200 profit.

Baer v. Chase, 392 F.3d 609 (3d Cir. 2004), illustrates that quantum meruit recovery can be quite modest, even if the actual benefit to the beneficiary was more significant. Baer, an ex-prosecutor and would-be screenwriter,

9. This terminology is not confined to restitution, but is also used in connection with contracts in which the parties have left the price open. In fact, the terms derive from contract law and enter the language of restitution through the fiction of quasi-contract.

assisted Chase, the creator of the hugely successful series, *The Sopranos*, by helping him with background information on the New Jersey mob and by reading and commenting on his draft script. Baer asserted that Chase had agreed orally that if the show became a success, he would "take care" of him and would reward him "in a manner commensurate with the true value" of his services. This agreement could potentially have entitled Baer to a significant payment, given the success of the show. However, the court held that was too vague to constitute a contract. (This is discussed in relation to the problem of indefiniteness in section 10.5.1.) As an alternative to his contract claim, Baer sought relief in restitution, claiming that Chase had been unjustly enriched by Baer's services. The trial court initially dismissed this claim on the ground that the statute of limitations had run. Dismissal on that ground was reversed on appeal, and the trial court ultimately awarded Baer restitutionary damages. However, because the court found the market value of Baer's services to be modest, the amount of his recovery was small. The question of whether the benefit of using those services may have contributed significantly to Chase's success in developing the show was irrelevant to the determination of the market value of Baer's work. *Baer v. Chase*, 2007 WL 1237850 (D.N.J. 2007).

b. The Recipient's Net Gain

Market value is the standard measure of benefit, and restitution based on the recipient's net gain is a less common means of measurement, used only where the equities call for it. The net actual enrichment of the recipient—that is, the actual amount by which the recipient's wealth is increased—could be the same as the market value of the services, but it could be greater or lower. For example, although the market value of hiring Sam was \$150, Maggie actually gained \$200 from his services. Conversely, had it been a slow day, her takings from the booth could have been less than \$150.

In some situations, net gain may be different if measured objectively, based on what it is worth generally, or subjectively, based on its actual worth to the particular recipient under the circumstances of the case. For example, without getting permission from the lessor, a lessee hired a builder to build a sauna room in the basement of the lessor's house. Soon after having the sauna built and before paying the builder for it, the lessee abandoned the house and absconded. The builder may try to claim payment from the lessor as owner of the house that has been enhanced by the new sauna room. There are four possible amounts that the builder could claim—the contract price of the work, its market value (quantum meruit), the lessor's objective net gain, or the lessor's subjective net gain. Assume the following facts: The contract price agreed to by the lessee was \$10,000, which is higher than the \$9,000 market value of the work. The addition of the sauna increased the market value of the house by \$1,000, if the house was to be sold. However, the lessor does not plan to sell the house, which the lessor uses as rental property. The addition of the sauna adds no value to the house as a rental property because the sauna does not increase its rental value. The builder cannot sue the lessor for the $10,000 contract price unless it can prove that the lessee was the lessor's agent. If the builder has an unjust enrichment cause of action against the lessor (which it may not have if it was either a volunteer nor an intermeddler) there are three possible ways of measuring the lessor's benefit—the $9,000 market value of the work (which would be the standard measure), the lessor's objective net gain, which is the $1,000 increase in the market value of the house, or the lessor's subjective net gain, which is zero. Given the circumstances of the case, even if the builder overcomes the hurdle of establishing that the lessor's enrichment was unjust, the builder's award may be limited to the $1,000 enhancement of the market value of the house, or the builder may get no award if the court decides that the lessor's subjective net gain is the appropriate measure of enrichment.

There are some circumstances in which using net gain as an alternative to quantum meruit is inappropriate. Consider the example of the doctor who came to the emergency aid of the unconscious victim. The reasonable market fee for the services that the doctor performed is $500. As a result of the doctor's prompt efforts, the victim was saved from death or crippling injury, so the victim's net gain, measured as the monetary value of the victim's life and health, is greatly in excess of the market value of the doctor's services. Conversely, if the victim died despite the doctor's valiant effort, the victim received no ultimate benefit and has no net gain. However, it would be absurd to base the doctor's recovery on the ultimate value gained by the victim, either grossly overcompensating the doctor and ruining the victim financially if the victim survives, or awarding nothing to the doctor if the victim dies. Quantum meruit recovery is more in keeping with the customary and reasonably expected method of compensating a medical professional for services, irrespective of ultimate outcome.

c. The Impact of a Party's Improper Conduct on the Measure of Relief

i. Restitution in Favor of a Party Who Materially Breached a Contract[10]

When a party materially breaches a contract after having partially performed, the breaching party cannot recover under the contract but can obtain restitution for what has been given. Because the breaching party is at fault for breaking the contract, restitutionary recovery is limited to the smaller of the market value of what was done or the portion of the price allocated to the performance under the contract. For example, a builder wrongfully

10. This is discussed more fully in section 17.6.

abandons work after erecting part of a building. The market value of what had been done before abandonment is $5,000, but because the builder underbid, the amount of the contract price attributable to that work is only $4,000. The builder cannot recover more than $4,000. (In addition, the builder's recovery is further reduced by offsetting any damages that the owner suffered as a result of the breach.)

ii. Dishonest or Improper Conduct by the Beneficiary

If the recipient of the benefit has been guilty of dishonest or improper conduct, the highest measure of relief is likely to be used. To illustrate, return to the example in which Maggie fainted while she was opening her newsstand and was rushed to the hospital. Her friend, Sam, kept her booth open and ran it the whole day, making $600 in sales. Instead of paying over the $600 proceeds to Maggie, Sam used the money to buy lottery tickets and won $100,000. Sam is now the recipient of enrichment by using Maggie's property without authority, and his wrongful act in misappropriating it justifies holding him liable for the full extent of his gain. That is, he is treated in law as having won the $100,000 on Maggie's behalf so that he has to disgorge the full amount of his winnings. If he won nothing in the lottery, so that he has no ultimate gain, Maggie's recovery would be the $600 that he misappropriated from her.

d. Situations in Which Conventional Measures of Benefit Cannot Be Applied

In some cases, none of the usual bases of measurement work at all, which may defeat a claim of restitution unless a court is willing to use its discretion to make an award that does not fit within the recognized elements of unjust enrichment. For example, a climber was stranded on a cliff. A passerby climbed the cliff and rescued the climber. In doing so, the rescuer fell and was injured. The rescuer acted altruistically, without the intent to charge for the service of rescuing the climber, so does not claim the value of that service. However, the rescuer incurred medical expenses as a result of the fall and claims reimbursement of these expenses from the climber on the theory that the climber would be unjustly enriched by not paying for them. Although there is some justice in requiring the climber to reimburse the rescuer, it is difficult to fit the claim into the elements of unjust enrichment. The rescuer would first have to argue that even though the rescue was altruistic, there was an implied expectation of reimbursement for any loss incurred by the rescuer as a result of the rescue. Even if a court accepts that, the medical expenses do not fit into any of the categories mentioned—they are not the market value of the service or the net enrichment of the climber, objectively or subjectively determined. It is conceivable that a court may use its discretion to create a remedy based on plaintiff's post-benefit medical expenditure. However, the court may decline to give any relief at all on the basis that, notwithstanding the unfortunate consequences to the rescuer, the case does not satisfy the elements of unjust enrichment. Section 9.7 considers whether the resolution of the case may be different if, in gratitude for the rescue, the climber made a promise after the rescue to pay the rescuer's medical expenses.

§9.7 "MORAL OBLIGATION" AND THE MATERIAL BENEFIT RULE

The doctrine commonly called "moral obligation" consists of a discrete set of exceptions to consideration doctrine that permit the enforcement of a promise for which the promisee did not give consideration. In each of the situations covered by the doctrine, the promise is made in recognition of a previous benefit conferred by the promisee on the promisor that unjustly enriched the promisor, so that the moral obligation to pay for the benefit justifies upholding the subsequent promise to pay for it. The name of the doctrine, "moral obligation," is potentially confusing because it may suggest that a moral obligation is generally sufficient to support a valid promise. This is not the usual rule. In most situations, a promise without consideration is not binding, even if the promisor had a moral obligation to perform it. In fact, when it is said that a person has a moral obligation to do something, this usually means that the person has a moral responsibility, but has no legal responsibility to do it. Despite its confusing name, the doctrine of moral obligation is very narrow and applies only in particular circumstances to a judicially recognized set of situations. These well-recognized narrow exceptions to the requirement that a promise must be exchanged for the promisee's new legal detriment all involve specific situations in which a debtor makes a promise to pay an earlier unenforceable debt. Although the later promise lacks consideration, courts treat the moral obligation to pay the preexisting unenforceable debt as sufficient justification for making the promise enforceable. The three specific situations in which the exceptions are widely recognized are a promise to pay a debt barred by the statute of limitations, a promise to pay a debt discharged in bankruptcy, and a promise to pay an avoidable debt.

A Debt Barred by the Statute of Limitations. All claims are subject to a statute of limitations which requires a plaintiff to initiate suit before the expiration of a specified period after it arises, failing which the right to sue is lost. The expiry of the limitation period does not eliminate the claim but only the right to sue on it. Therefore, if after the expiry of the limitation period, the defendant promises to pay the debt, courts treat the moral obligation to pay the debt as sufficient grounds to validate the promise, even though the plaintiff did not give the defendant new consideration for the promise.

A Debt Discharged in Bankruptcy. When a debtor becomes bankrupt, the debtor's prebankruptcy debts are paid only to the extent of funds in the estate. If the estate has no available funds, creditors receive no payment at all. If it has only enough funds to pay debts in part, creditors receive only partial payment of their claims. The balance of the debts is discharged and creditors are forbidden by law to take any steps to try to collect it. However, the doctrine of "moral obligation" validates a later promise by the debtor to pay the discharged debt.[11]

A Voidable Debt. A voidable debt is one that can be avoided by the debtor because of some defect in formation such as fraud or mistake, or lack of contractual capacity. If the party with the right of avoidance ratifies the contract by a second promise after becoming aware of the defect or after the basis for contractual incapacity has ended, the later promise is binding despite the lack of new consideration.

These narrow exceptions to consideration doctrine do not recognize a broader basis for applying the moral obligation doctrine to validate a promise made in recognition of a prior benefit that does not fit into one of these categories. They would therefore not help the rescuer in the illustration at the end of section 9.6 to enforce the climber's promise to pay medical costs, made after the rescue. As noted in the illustration, the rescuer's unjust enrichment claim is problematic, and if, after the rescue, the climber made a promise to pay the rescuer's medical expenses, consideration doctrine makes enforcement of the climber's subsequent promise problematic as well. The climber's promise made in recognition of the prior benefit conferred by the rescuer is not enforceable under consideration doctrine because the rescuer's detriment (the action of rescuing the climber) occurred before the climber's promise and so was not exchanged for the promise.[12] Therefore, neither a suit in contract or in unjust enrichment offers the rescuer a clear path to recovery. Similarly, promissory estoppel would not be a basis for remedy except to the extent that the promisee took detrimental action in reliance on the promise. *See* Diagram 9E.

The leading case of *Webb v. McGowin*, 168 So. 196 (Ala. 1935), devised a solution to this problem by expanding the moral obligation doctrine beyond its recognized categories into a general principle. Webb, working on the upper floor of a mill, was in the process of dropping a large wooden block to the ground when he noticed that McGowin was in the path of its

11. Although the common law validates the promise, the debt may still not be enforced under the federal Bankruptcy Code, which imposes restrictions and safeguards on the revival of a discharged debt.

12. As noted in section 7.8, a detriment incurred before the promise is made is sometimes inaccurately called "past consideration."

Diagram 9E

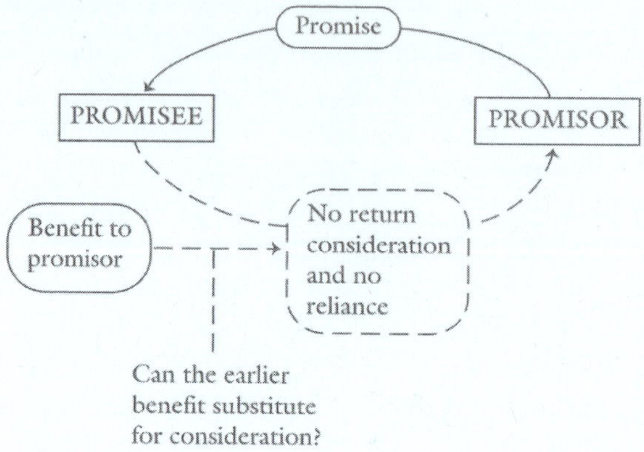

fall. To divert the block from crushing McGowin, Webb held onto it and fell with it. He thereby saved McGowin from death or severe injury at the cost of serious and disabling injury to himself. In gratitude, McGowin promised a life pension to Webb which he paid for several years until his death. His estate discontinued payment. McGowin's promise was not enforceable as a contract because Webb's detriment of falling with the block preceded and was not exchanged for the promise. However, the court recognized that the strict application of this rule would be very unjust in the circumstances, particularly because McGowin's serious intent to honor it was evidenced by his payments until his death. To overcome the consideration barrier, the court used the legal fiction of deeming the detriment to have been contemporaneous with the promise.

The court supported its decision with reference to the existing narrow exceptions to consideration doctrine that courts had developed to deal with the specific discrete situations identified above. The court extrapolated from the cases that recognized the exception in these discrete situations to create a broader doctrine of moral obligation as an exception to the "past consideration" problem. Restatement, Second, §86 adopts *Webb*'s expansion of the moral obligation doctrine, which it labels as "promise for benefit received." The doctrine is more commonly called the "material benefit rule." Section 86 does not employ the legal fiction used in *Webb*. Instead, it formulates the doctrine as a distinct cause of action under which, despite the lack of consideration for a promise to pay for a previous benefit, a court may enforce a promise made in recognition of a previous benefit that unjustly enriched the promisor and was not given with gratuitous intent. The court has the discretion to enforce the promise to the extent necessary to prevent injustice, and to the extent that the promise is proportionate to the value of the benefit.

The elements set out in §86 make it clear that although the material benefit rule provides for the enforcement of a promise, its focus is very different from contract and promissory estoppel. It does not enforce the promise to protect a contractual expectation or reliance interest, but to rectify a situation in which the promisor had been unjustly enriched and the equities call for enforcement of the promise in full or part. To evaluate the equities of the case, the court must take into account all the circumstances of the case, including the circumstances of the enrichment and of the promise. The promise is without new consideration, so the evidentiary and cautionary functions of consideration doctrine are relevant to evaluating this promise too, to ensure that it was a sober voluntary commitment, unaffected by impulsivity or manipulation.

As the discussion of unjust enrichment emphasizes, restitution is not based on any promise made by the beneficiary and is calculated on the value of the benefit conferred. Therefore, the material benefit rule is a hybrid, in that it covers situations in which the relief claimed does not fit within the usual value-based recovery, but the justification for giving that relief is bolstered by a promise made after receipt of the benefit. In other words, it blends restitutionary concepts and promise. There are very few cases in which the material benefit rule of §86 has been in issue, and the few courts that have considered it have generally not followed the lead of §86 in extending the "moral obligation" doctrine beyond the few well-recognized narrow situations involving prior unenforceable or avoidable legal obligations.

Examples

EXAMPLES

1. Consider whether the following transactions gave rise to a contract implied in fact and, if not, whether they create grounds for finding a contract implied in law by establishing grounds for relief on the basis of unjust enrichment:
   a. Sara Nade is a violinist who makes her living as a street musician. When she plays, she places a hat on the sidewalk in front of her, with a note attached to it reading, "Thanks." One afternoon, while she was playing on a street corner, Mel Odious walked up to her and stood near her, listening to her play. When she finished, he applauded and asked her to play another tune, which she did. He applauded again and then began to walk away. Sara called out to him, "Hey, you have to put some money in my hat!" He replied, "No, I don't."
   b. Change the facts of Example a: Mel was enjoying a picnic with friends in a nearby park when he heard Sara playing on the street corner. He thought that she played beautifully, but it was hard to hear her well over the traffic noise. He therefore went up to her and said, "I enjoy your playing very much. Would you come and stand near us in the park and play while we have our picnic so that we

can hear you better?" Sara agreed. She played for Mel and his friends until their picnic was over, about 30 minutes later. At the end of the picnic, as Mel was packing up and getting ready to leave, Sara said, "That will be $200."

2. Last Saturday, Benny Fishery locked up his house and left on a two-week fishing trip in the wilderness. He told his neighbor Sam Aritan that he would be away and out of communication for two weeks and asked Sam to "keep an eye on" his house. Sam said that he would. On Sunday evening a fierce wind knocked a tree onto Benny's roof and smashed a large hole in it. Realizing that the interior of the house would be exposed to the elements and damaged if the hole was left open until Benny's return, Sam went to the hardware store and bought a heavy waterproof tarpaulin. He then went to great effort, at the risk of personal injury, to climb onto Benny's roof and secure the tarpaulin over the hole. After Benny returned from his vacation, Sam claimed $1,000 from him, made up of the $200 cost of the tarpaulin and $800 for his services, including danger pay for climbing onto the roof to put the tarpaulin in place. Is Sam entitled to payment of this amount?

3. Change the facts in Example 2 as follows: When trying to secure the tarpaulin, Sam fell off the roof and injured himself. As a result, he incurred $4,000 in medical expenses and had to take three weeks unpaid sick leave, losing an additional $2,000. He has no medical or disability insurance. Apart from the financial loss, he has suffered excruciating pain.

   When Benny returned from vacation and heard what had happened to Sam in his brave attempt to protect Benny's house, he was overcome with gratitude. He visited Sam in the hospital and tearfully promised to pay Sam $200 per month for the next three years to compensate Sam for the medical expenses, loss of earnings, and pain. Sam accepted this offer. Benny paid installments for two months and then stopped paying. Is his promise enforceable?

4. Carla Clunker began hearing noises from her car when she accelerated on the freeway. She took the car to Mark Price, a mechanic, to have the trouble determined and repaired. She told Mark that he was to call her for authorization if the repair would cost more than $200. Mark neglected to communicate this instruction to his assistant, who completed an expensive repair without checking with Carla. When Mark presented Carla with a bill for $650, she refused to pay it and insisted that she was liable for no more than $200. Mark admits his mistake but argues that the repair was necessary and that $650 is a fair charge for the parts and labor. This is in fact true. Is Carla obligated to pay the $650?

5. Kwazi Contracting Co. entered into a contract with Flyby Nightwatch, Inc. under which Flyby agreed to provide nighttime security services for Kwazi's office premises for a monthly price of $60,000. Flyby had undertaken too many contracts and did not have the staff to perform all of them. It therefore made a contract with another security company, Beneficial Security, Inc. under which Beneficial provided the security officers to patrol Kwazi's offices. Beneficial charged Flyby a monthly fee of $40,000 for this service. The arrangement worked for two months, but ended when Flyby became insolvent and went out of business. Although Kwazi had paid Flyby the full $120,000 due for two months' services, Flyby had failed to make any payment to Beneficial for the work. During the two months that the services were performed, Kwazi's executives had noticed that the premises were being patrolled by security guards who wore Beneficial arm patches. They thought nothing of this and assumed that Flyby and Beneficial were associated. Because it cannot recover anything from Flyby, Beneficial claims that Kwazi owes it $80,000. Is Beneficial correct?

6. Quantum Merriment Co., Inc. was planning to build a theme park. It needed to develop some preliminary plans for the park so that its board of directors could be better informed about the cost of building the park and could determine whether the project was economically feasible. The president of Quantum approached Ben E. Factor, a designer of amusement parks, and asked him to draw some preliminary plans. Quantum's president made it clear to Ben that he would be doing the work "on spec," which meant that he would only be paid for it if the board ultimately decided to build the park. Ben drew the plans and the board reviewed them. After careful consideration, the board decided not to build the park because it was too expensive and its prospects of profitability were too uncertain. Does Ben have a contract claim against Quantum? If not, does he have a claim for unjust enrichment?

7. The wooden fence on the side of Val Unteer's property had become rotten and rickety and needed to be replaced. Val asked Justin Richmond, her neighbor on the other side of the fence, if he would share the cost of replacing the fence. He refused. Notwithstanding, Val decided that she had to replace the fence because it was in such bad condition, so she removed the existing fence and erected a new one. Val thinks that it is very unfair that she had to bear the full cost of replacing the fence because Justin also received the benefit of the new fence at the side of his property. Can Val successfully claim half the cost of the fence from Justin on the basis that he has been unjustly enriched?

Explanations

1. a. Sara and Mel made no express contract because no words of agreement were uttered or articulated. They may have entered into a contract implied in fact, under which Mel agreed to pay for Sara's services, provided that such a contract could be inferred from their conduct, reasonably interpreted in context. Mel clearly did take the benefit of Sara's playing and even asked her to play an encore. If there is a general expectation in the community that street musicians are paid for their services, an implied-in-fact contract could be inferred. Because the parties did not agree to a fee, the amount due to Sara in contract would be her customary fee or a fee based on the market value (quantum meruit) of her services. If, as is more likely, there is no reasonable expectation that a street musician is paid for her services, there is no contract and Sara provided the entertainment for free. Her hat on the sidewalk merely invited members of the public to show their appreciation by giving her a gratuity. If Sara did not have a reasonable expectation of payment, she also cannot claim restitution for unjust enrichment because she conferred the benefit on Mel as a volunteer. Alternatively, Sara likely fits the category of officious intermeddler by imposing the unrequested benefit of playing her music on anyone who happened to be in the vicinity. Just listening to her music could not constitute an acceptance of the benefit. Even Mel's action of deliberately listening and applauding should not be sufficient to infer that he accepted the benefit with the intent to compensate Sara for it.

   b. Mel has now asked Sara to come and play at his picnic and she has done so. Although the usual expectation may be that street musicians perform gratuitously, this expectation could change when Mel specifically asks Sara to come into the park and to play for him and his friends. If these circumstances do give rise to a reasonable expectation of payment, the parties may have entered into a contract implied in fact, under which Mel is liable to pay Sara for her services. As in Explanation 1a, in the absence of an agreement on the amount of the fee, the contract price would be Sara's customary fee or a fee based on the market value (quantum meruit) of her services. The $200 that she claims may or may not be the appropriate market or customary fee. An implied-in-fact contract is the most plausible conclusion, but even if there is no actual contract, quasi-contract would allow for quantum meruit recovery provided that Sara had a reasonable intent not to render the service gratuitously. She clearly is not an intermeddler because Mel asked her to play.

2. It might be tempting to try to make the argument that Sam's actions were encompassed within an actual contract with Benny, but Sam's almost

meaningless undertaking to "keep an eye on" Benny's house is too indefinite to constitute a contractual undertaking, and there is no hint of compensation for this favor in the casual conversation. Any relief awarded to Sam would have to be on the basis of unjust enrichment. Sam acted in an emergency situation to prevent harm to Benny's property. His action did confer a benefit on Benny. He knew that Benny was away and out of communication, so he could not get advance authorization to make the temporary roof repair. Sam should not be treated as an officious intermeddler. A person is generally not justified in imposing an unrequested benefit, but intervention in an emergency situation is not intermeddling if the harm of inaction would be serious, there is no opportunity to get authorization, and there is no reason to believe that the beneficiary would object. This emergency is not as dire and urgent as one in which failure to act on the spur of the moment would result in death or serious injury. Nevertheless, the potential property harm is real and serious enough to justify Sam's response, which seems to be no more extensive than the minimum required to achieve the purpose of preserving the property until Benny's return. It is not clear whether Sam had gratuitous intent when he bought the tarpaulin and installed it on the roof. He may not have thought about compensation at all until later. However, gratuitous intent is objectively determined based on Sam's reasonable expectations, and it does not matter whether he was actually thinking of compensation as took the urgent action. It is reasonable to attribute to Sam the intent to claim reimbursement for the cost of the tarpaulin because altruistic intent may reasonably not extend to the donation of out-of-pocket expenses. However, the services rendered by a neighbor to protect property are more likely to be treated as altruistic and gratuitous, even if they involve some degree of personal risk. (A person who risks injury in performing a favor for a neighbor may make the rational decision not to take the risky action but cannot claim "danger pay" if he elects to take the risk.) Therefore, Sam should be reimbursed for the cost of the tarpaulin but not for the value of his services in installing it.

3. This Example is inspired by *Webb v. McGowin*, discussed in section 9.7. This case is distinguishable from *Webb* in that Sam was injured saving Benny's property, not his person. Although rescue from personal injury or death provides the strongest equities in favor of enforcing the beneficiary's later promise, there is also moral value in upholding a promise in recognition of property preservation.

   Sam would have trouble enforcing Benny's promise as a contract because of the "past consideration" rule. Although it is conceivable that a court would award relief for Sam's medical expenses and loss of earnings on a theory of unjust enrichment, Sam's claim is an awkward fit for restitutionary recovery. As discussed in Explanation 2, Sam did not reasonably intend to receive compensation beyond the cost of the tarpaulin, so he was a volunteer in climbing on the roof. In addition, restitution focuses on the benefit to Benny, which does not bear a relationship to Sam's loss.

However, because Benny made the promise in recognition of Sam's prior service, the material benefit rule of Restatement, Second, §86 provides a much more satisfactory basis for relief. The premise of §86 is that Benny's subsequent ratifying promise shifts the equities in Sam's favor by recognizing and placing a value on the benefit and creating the presumption that it was not conferred with gratuitous intent. The disproportionality principle assures that the promise is not too generous in relation to the value of the benefit. However, where the focus is not on the value of the benefit but on the relationship between the promise and the injury, it seems fair to measure proportionality in reference to the injury, not the benefit.

A court that applies §86 must also take care that the promise was made under fair circumstances, and that it was not induced by coercion or motivated by impulsive generosity. There is no hint that Sam put any pressure on Benny to make the promise. The fact that he made it tearfully in Sam's hospital room soon after the incident could give pause. (The cautionary function of consideration doctrine plays a role here.) However, this concern is alleviated by the fact that Benny continued to make payments for some time after this emotionally charged moment.

Notwithstanding that Sam has a plausible case for recovery under the material benefit rule, he may have difficulty in recovering under the rule because few courts have been willing to adopt §86.

4. In contrast to Examples 2 and 3, there is a contract in this case under which services were requested by Carla. The problem is that Mark exceeded his authority under the contract. He may have the right to claim $200 from Carla on the basis that this was the agreed maximum price, but he has no contractual right to payment of the amount in excess of that.

   Although Carla was enriched by receiving a $650 repair for $200, Mark cannot claim the full value of the repair under principles of unjust enrichment. If asked, Carla may have authorized the repair, but she was given no opportunity to exercise this choice and had the repair imposed on her. She cannot return it because it is incorporated into her property. This imposition makes Mark an intermeddler as much as if he had made the repair without any request, so he is not entitled to restitution based on the full market value of the repair.

   In *Deck v. Jim Harris Chevrolet-Buick*, 386 N.E.2d 714 (Ind. 1979), the case on which this Example is based, the court reached this conclusion.

Although the mistake may have been honest, the repairer was in a better position than the customer to prevent it and must take responsibility for the negligence that led to the customer's enrichment. *Kelly v. Cole* cited in section 9.5.2b is based on the same principle. The Coles authorized Kelly, the prospective buyer of their duplex, to make repairs on the duplex up to a stipulated amount. He did repairs in excess of that amount without their authorization. Kelly could not raise the funds to buy the duplex, so the sale fell through. Kelly sought to recover the additional repair costs from the Coles, claiming that they had been unjustly enriched. The court held that Kelly could not obtain restitution of those costs because he had imposed the benefit on the Coles.

5. Beneficial should not be able to recover from Kwazi on grounds of either contract or unjust enrichment. The parties never dealt with each other at all and certainly never made an express contract. The facts do not support the factual implication of a contract either. A party can be held to an implied contract if it voluntarily accepts services without objection on the reasonable understanding that the services are not rendered gratuitously. However, there is nothing in these facts to indicate such assent or reasonable expectation on Kwazi's part. A contract can be implied in fact only if there is some conduct from which agreement can be inferred. Kwazi's conduct does not give rise to this inference. As far it was concerned, its contract was with Flyby. Nothing alerted it to the possibility that Beneficial might look to it for payment, and it had no involvement in any arrangements that Flyby might make to find the staff to perform its obligations under the contract.

   Beneficial's claim also does not satisfy the elements of unjust enrichment. Kwazi paid for the services, so it received no free benefit. In addition, because Beneficial provided the services under a contract with Flyby, it had no expectation of compensation directly from Kwazi and never asked Kwazi to guarantee Flyby's payment obligation. Therefore, as far as Kwazi is concerned, Beneficial is in the position of a volunteer in that it conferred the benefit without intent to receive compensation from Kwazi. It would also be an unfair imposition to allow Beneficial to hold Kwazi liable for services rendered where Beneficial could have but failed to demand a guarantee of payment before rendering the services. Like *Contship Containerlines v. Howard Industries, Inc.*, described in section 9.4.2, this case involves the allocation of loss between two innocent parties. However, unlike the carrier in *Contship Containerlines* the loss here should rest with Beneficial. The shipper in *Contship Containerlines* was saddled with the loss because it bore the risk of paying a third-party intermediary who failed to transmit the funds to the carrier. The situation here is quite different. Beneficial dealt only with Flyby and gave it credit. Flyby was not an intermediary for Kwazi, which did not even have reason to know of the transaction between Flyby and Beneficial.

6. Ben and Quantum have a contract, but the contract does not give Ben the right to payment for his services. The parties expressly agreed that Ben's services would be "on spec," which means that Quantum Merriment's obligation to pay Ben is expressly made conditional on its decision to proceed with the project and the condition of payment is not satisfied. The agreement that Ben would not be entitled to a fee unless the board decided to build the park also means that he has no claim for unjust enrichment. In the absence of fulfillment of the condition, he agreed to perform the services gratuitously.

   This Example is inspired by *Forrest Associates v. Passamaquoddy Tribe*, 760 A.2d 1041 (Me. 2000), in which the plaintiff conducted a market assessment for the tribe's possible development of a high-stakes bingo operation. The plaintiff's work was done "on spec," subject to the understanding that it would not be paid unless the tribe went ahead with the development. The tribe did not proceed with the project, and the court held that the plaintiff was not entitled to recover for the value of its work, either in contract or in unjust enrichment. *Forrest Associates* and this Example also reflect the principle articulated in *Devco v. T10 Meltel, LLC*, cited in section 9.5.2a. Devco owned a building on which roof space had been leased to cellular carriers to enable the carriers to erect telecommunications equipment. When Devco sold the leases to T10 Meltel, it agreed to clean up the roof by consolidating the equipment and agreed to forfeit $300,000 of the sale price if it did not get the work done by a stated date. Devco did not complete the work in time and T10 Meltel refused to pay it the $300,000. Devco sued, claiming that T10 Meltel had been unjustly enriched by not paying for the work. The court held that T10 Meltel had not been unjustly enriched because it had agreed to the forfeiture for late completion in its contract. The party that conferred the benefit cannot claim unjust enrichment where the recipient received no more than what it was entitled to receive under a contract.

7. Val cannot claim a contribution to the cost of the fence from Justin. He refused when she asked him to share the cost, so they certainly have no contract. True, he has benefited from the replacement of the fence, but Val imposed that benefit on him despite his advance refusal to pay for it. In *Birchwood Land Co. v. Krizan*, 115 A.3d 1009 (Vt. 2015), Birchwood installed utilities and infrastructure for the purpose of developing some land that it owned. This benefited Krizan, an adjacent landowner, who could now develop her own property that had previously been undevelopable because of lack of access and infrastructure. Birchwood had not made any contract with Krizan for a contribution to the cost of the improvements. Nevertheless, it sued her for a contribution on the grounds that

the improvements benefited her and she would be unjustly enriched as a "free rider" if she made no contribution. The court held that Birchwood was not entitled to relief because it had imposed the benefit on her without her consent. It had made the improvements for its own purposes and Krizan was merely in the fortunate position of benefitting incidentally from work done by Birchwood to further its own interests.

CHAPTER 10

Interpretation and Construction

Resolving Meaning and Dealing with Uncertainty in Agreements

§10.1 ASCERTAINING THE MEANING OF AN AGREEMENT: INTERPRETATION AND CONSTRUCTION

§10.1.1 Introduction to the Process of Interpretation and Construction

The processes of interpretation (inferring meaning from facts) and construction (inferring meaning as a matter of law) have been alluded to in earlier chapters.[1] This section more closely examines and differentiates the methods and uses of the related, but separate, functions of interpretation and construction. To begin, a broad distinction may be drawn:

Restatement, Second, §200 describes interpretation as the ascertainment of the meaning of a promise or agreement. It is an evaluation of facts (that is, evidence of what the parties said and did and the circumstances surrounding their communications) for the purpose of deciding the parties' mutual intent. The word "construction" is sometimes used interchangeably with "interpretation," but properly speaking, it does have a different meaning. Construction is the implication of a term in law. It usually occurs where

1. For example, section 7.9.2 discusses the implication of a promise to use best efforts or to exercise reasonable judgment as a means of giving content to an apparently illusory promise, and section 4.1 discusses the interpretation of objective manifestations of assent in the context of offer and acceptance. This is not a definitive list. The issue of interpretation comes up often.

it appears that the parties did not actually deal with a particular issue in their contract, and there is no factual evidence to establish how they intended that issue to be handled. That is, although it is clear that the parties did make a contract, they just did not address this particular issue. The court may therefore determine, based on what it knows of the contract and its context, how the parties would have dealt with this issue had they thought of it. Stated differently, a court will use the process of construction only when the existing evidence supports the reasonable conclusion (based on objective manifestations of assent) that the parties did intend to make a contract, but there is little or no evidence from which a factual inference can be drawn on their intent regarding a particular aspect of that contract. In seeking to effectuate the parties' intent, the court builds on what it knows of the transaction to interpolate from that a meaning that the parties probably would have agreed on, had they focused on the issue. Although courts are wary of devising an agreement that the parties did not actually make, it is sometimes preferable to do this instead of defeating contractual expectations by demanding clear proof of intent for every gap and uncertainty.

The difference between interpretation and construction can be subtle. *Wood v. Lucy, Lady Duff-Gordon*, 118 N.E. 214 (N.Y. 1917), discussed in section 7.9.2 in relation to illusory promises, may be used as an illustration. Lucy, a well-known fashion designer, appointed Wood as her exclusive agent to sell her designs and place her endorsements on the designs of others. Under their agreement, Wood was to pay Lucy half the profits generated by the sales and endorsements. However, the text of the agreement did not expressly promise that Wood would do anything to promote her designs and endorsements. Lucy endorsed products on her own and kept all the proceeds. When Wood sued her for his share of this income, she argued that they had no valid contract because Wood had given her no consideration. Even though he promised to share any profits that he generated, he made no promise to do anything to earn those profits. The court rejected that argument on the basis that it was necessarily inferable from Lucy's grant of an exclusive agency to Wood, under circumstances in which the parties clearly intended a serious commercial relationship, that Wood had obligated himself to use best efforts to earn profits. If the court's recognition of Wood's promise to use best efforts was based on evidence of intent, such as discussions in negotiations, a course of performance by the parties after the agreement had been made, or prevailing usage in the trade, the court's conclusion would be classified as a matter of interpretation. However, if there was no such evidence, the court's implication of the obligation to use best efforts would be classified as construction—the term is not based on evidence of what the parties actually did agree, but on what the parties would rationally have agreed had the question been presented to them at the time that they made the agreement. This shows that there is often a fine dividing line between interpretation and construction and it is not always easy to classify the court's conclusion as one or the other. For practical purposes, the distinction may not be significant because the meaning of the term, rather than the route the court has taken to reach it, is the determinative issue. However, the distinction is important to an understanding of the process by which courts resolve disputes over the meaning and scope of contract terms.

§10.1.2 Interpretation as a Question of Fact or Law

There is some confusion over the proper roles of the judge and jury in deciding the meaning of agreements, and cases offer conflicting views on whether the ascertainment of meaning is a matter of fact or law. Where interpretation involves the determination of meaning by the evaluation of evidence, it is most appropriately performed by the finder of fact—the jury, unless the case is being tried without one. However, if interpretation merely involves the ascertainment of the plain or ordinary meaning of words, and there is no factual dispute requiring an assessment of credibility, or where meaning must be construed based on what the parties must have intended, the determination of meaning is a legal question for the judge. This dichotomy is not always carefully observed by courts, and the fact-law distinction sometimes becomes blurred. This is particularly so where meaning is based on a combination of the grammatical meaning of words, contextual evidence, and legal implication. In such cases, it can be very difficult to unravel the proper roles of judge and jury, and concern about control over decisionmaking tends to push in the direction of the judge assuming the function of weighing the relative probity of these different elements.

Apart from the question of who decides meaning, the fact-law distinction has significance beyond the trial phase of the case. If meaning is determined as a matter of law, it can be reversed on appeal on the standard of review for legal questions: that the judge erred in the application of the law. However, if the determination is a question of fact, it can be reversed only if it satisfies a much stricter standard: The evidence must provide no reasonable basis for supporting the factfinder's conclusions. Also, a legal determination has weight as precedent, but a factual one does not.

§10.1.3 The Sources of Evidence Used in Interpretation

The process of interpretation was introduced in section 4.1 on the objective test, where it was noted that agreement is manifested by the use of outward signals: words—whether recorded in a document or spoken; actions; and, in appropriate situations, a failure to speak or act. As the parties move toward developing consensus in the process of contract formation, intent thus communicated by each party is necessarily interpreted by the other. If a dispute later arises about whether consensus was reached or about what was agreed, the communications of the parties must again be interpreted—this time in court—to determine which party's interpretation is correct. Under the objective test, meaning is based on how words and actions reasonably would be perceived by the party to whom they were manifested. The subjective understanding of the parties may have some relevance to the inquiry to the extent that it is consistent with, and may help explain, the meaning of the manifestation.

This section looks more closely at the process of interpretation and examines the type of evidence that may be available to cast light on the meaning of manifestations of apparent intent. Interpretation first focuses on the normal, accepted meaning of the words used by the parties. However, words are never spoken in a vacuum, so there is always some context in which the words were used. To the extent that this context provides information of what the words might mean, the process of interpretation goes beyond the language used by the parties to take this context into account.

Context does not always provide information that may be relevant to the meaning of a term in dispute, so neither party may be able to offer contextual evidence that bears on what the parties must have meant. Where the court has no evidence of meaning extrinsic to the bare language of the agreement, it is necessarily confined to interpreting that language to ascertain its meaning. However, where a party does seek to prove contextual evidence pertinent to meaning, that evidence should be considered and given appropriate weight. The degree to which it is persuasive often depends on the clarity of the contractual language. Where the contract expresses the disputed term in apparently clear and unambiguous language, extrinsic evidence as to its meaning is treated with caution.[2] A court may be resistant to considering extrinsic evidence if the language used in the contract is clear on its face. However, courts are generally receptive to relevant extrinsic evidence, even if the language of the contract seems clear, because they recognize that words do not have a constant and immutable meaning and can be colored by context. This is the appropriate approach because interpretation aims at ascertaining what the parties intended by using the words that they chose, and contextual evidence can be helpful in getting to the meaning that the parties intended.

2. Where the agreement is recorded, either in a tangible paper document or in electronic or other media, a party's ability to offer evidence of context is much more heavily restricted because of the parol evidence rule, discussed in Chapter 12. This chapter focuses on the sources of evidence available to interpret language in the agreement, and is not concerned with the parol evidence rule. Chapter 12 examines barriers to admissibility of contextual evidence created by the parol evidence rule.

Where contextual evidence is available and pertinent, the interpretation of a contract involves five principal areas of factual inquiry. At the center of the inquiry are the actual words used by the parties in the agreement. Even where there is contextual evidence, the language of the agreement is the starting point and the primary source of meaning. The wording of the very term in dispute is the central focus of the interpretation effort, but it cannot be read in isolation from the rest of the agreement and must be interpreted in light of the document (or oral agreement) as a whole. Beyond the language of the agreement, the inquiry spreads to its context. This context includes the discussions and conduct of the parties when they negotiated the contract, their conduct in performing the contract after it was formed (course of performance), their conduct in any prior comparable transactions between them (course of dealing), and the customs and usages of the market in which they are dealing with each other (trade usage). (*See* Diagram 10A.)

Diagram 10A

The Environment for Contractual Interpretation

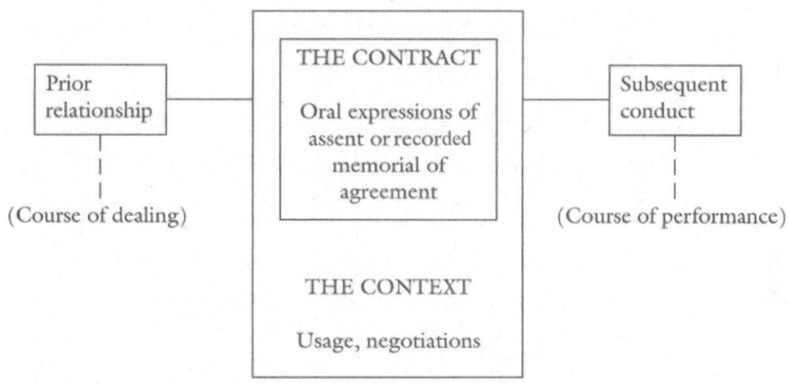

Each of these five areas is concerned with objective evidence in the form of words or conduct manifested by the parties, or verifiable facts in the contractual environment. The evidence of one party concerning what that party may have thought or believed is only marginally helpful or relevant. Not all of these components are present in every transaction. However, the more that exist in a transaction, the richer the background from which meaning can be ascertained. The conclusion about meaning is most strongly supported where all the evidence drawn from these different aspects of the context points to the same meaning. If they conflict, the general rule (reflected in UCC §§1.303(e) and 2.208(2) and in Restatement, Second, §203(b)) is to give greatest weight to the express terms used by the parties, followed in order by any course of performance, course of dealing, and usage.

In *Frigaliment Importing Co. v. B.N.S. International Sales Corp.*, 190 F. Supp. 116 (S.D.N.Y. 1960), the court tried to determine the meaning of a word in a contract by considering the terms of the contract as a whole in light of all available contextual evidence, but was not able to resolve what meaning the parties intended. The buyer, a Swiss importer, ordered a large quantity of chicken from the seller. The contract called for "U.S. fresh frozen chicken, grade A" of two different sizes. The agreement reflected a lower price per pound for the larger chickens than the smaller ones. When the seller delivered the chickens, the buyer protested that the larger, cheaper ones were not in accordance with the contract because they were stewing chickens, not suitable for frying. The buyer claimed that the word "chicken" used in the contract meant frying chicken so that all chicken delivered had to be of this quality. The seller denied that it had breached the contract by delivering stewing chickens. It contended that the word "chicken" was a generic term for both frying and stewing chickens and that the price difference in the contract made it clear that the cheaper birds would be stewing chickens.

The subsequent litigation centered on the meaning of the word "chicken" as used in the contract. The definition of "chicken" in dictionaries and U.S.D.A regulations did not exclude either party's meaning. The court's examination of the terms of the contract document as a whole was somewhat more helpful in casting light on the meaning of "chicken." The price term supported the seller's contention that two different types of chicken were contemplated because the price of the larger birds was below the market price for fryers. The court moved beyond the written agreement to explore the entire context of the transaction in an attempt to decide if "chicken" should be understood in the narrower or wider sense. Several experts testified as to the meaning of "chicken" in the trade, but the expert testimony was in conflict and did not clearly support the position of either party. Finally, the court considered evidence of the parties' course of performance to see if it cast any light on what they may have meant. The course of performance did not show a common intention because the buyer protested about the stewing chickens immediately on delivery. In the end, despite these efforts, the court was not able to establish what the parties meant by the use of the word "chicken" in the contract, so the case was resolved on the basis of the burden of proof. The buyer lost because it bore the burden of proving that the seller had breached and it had failed to prove that the word was used in the narrow sense that it alleged.

a. The Express Words Used by the Parties

The ordinary meaning of words used by the parties in formulating their rights and obligations is always the primary indicator of what they intended. Restatement, Second, §203(b) and UCC §§1.303(e) and 2.208 give greatest weight to express terms. These express terms might be oral or recorded.[3] In evaluating the meaning of express terms, the court does not narrowly confine itself to the terms in dispute, but considers the contract in its entirety because other terms in the contract may help to ascertain the meaning of the disputed terms. As noted above, clear and unambiguous express terms may be strong enough to exclude contextual evidence that is not reconcilable with the express language of the contract.

b. Discussions and Conduct of the Parties During Negotiations

Apart from the actual words spoken or recorded to express agreement, there may be a history of communication and negotiation leading up to the execution of the contract. Evidence of what was expressed by the parties during the period leading up to contract formation could be useful and relevant to establish the meaning of what was ultimately provided for in the agreement.[4]

c. Course of Performance: Conduct by the Parties in the Course of Performing Under the Agreement

If the parties have begun to perform the contract before the uncertainty to be resolved by interpretation becomes an issue, their conduct in proffering and accepting, or otherwise reacting to performance, may provide evidence of what was intended by an indefinite term. This post-formation behavior is called the "course of performance" and its relevance to interpretation is based on the assumption that the actual performance tendered and accepted without objection is a strong indicator of what must have been intended. The evidentiary value of the course of performance is recognized by UCC §§1.303(e) and 2.208, mimicked by Restatement, Second, §202(4).

For example, a lease provides that "dogs, cats, and other animals may not be kept on the premises." Lessee owns a pet duck that he thinks of as a bird, not an animal. Dictionaries offer alternative definitions of "animal." One includes all breathing creatures, and the other confines it to four-legged land creatures, excluding birds and fish. Lessee has kept the duck on the premises for several months. Lessor has seen it on several occasions

---

3. An oral agreement is legally binding and enforceable unless the statute of frauds, discussed in Chapter 11, requires it to be recorded. However, even if valid, an oral agreement presents problems of proof that are obviated or reduced by recording the agreement. If there is a dispute over the exact language used by the parties in an oral agreement, the actual words used must be proved as a fact before they can be interpreted. This can be difficult to do where the parties cannot recall precisely what was said, or they have contrary recollections of their conversation.

4. Again, if the agreement is recorded, the parol evidence rule may restrict the admission of this evidence. *See* Chapter 12.

and has never complained. The mutual conduct of the parties creates the fair inference that they were in agreement that the term "animals" does not include ducks.

Not all post-formation conduct necessarily reflects what the parties intended at the time of contracting. The conduct may simply not be pertinent to the meaning of the term in issue, or even if it is, it may reflect a subsequent change of mind or a disinclination to enforce rights under the contract. It can be difficult to distinguish a course of performance, which casts light on what the parties meant at the time of contracting, from post-formation conduct that could be nothing more than a decision not to assert rights under the contract, or a waiver of rights or a tacit modification of the contract. For example, the lessor's failure to complain about the duck could indicate that the parties did not include it in the definition. However, it could mean instead that the lessor has simply chosen not to enforce the ban on ducks, or that the parties have implicitly agreed by conduct to eliminate the restriction on animals. If it is not a course of performance but a waiver or modification, it is subject to different rules. Therefore, it is possible to draw the wrong inference from behavior that is ambiguous or does not really have a bearing on the term in issue. There are several guidelines that help avoid misconstruing conduct as a course of performance:

1. For a course of performance to be valid as a source of interpretation, it must be pertinent to the meaning of the term in controversy. For example, if the term in dispute concerned the date on which the rent payments were due, lessor's tolerance of the duck does nothing to clarify the uncertainty.
2. The conduct must show that the party performed or accepted performance without a protest or reservation of rights. Therefore, if Lessor protested that the duck was not allowed on each occasion that Lessor saw the duck, Lessor's failure to take stronger action does not support the conclusion that the parties intended "animals" not to include ducks. This is also illustrated by *Frigaliment*, in which the buyer's protest on accepting the stewing chickens meant that the buyer's taking delivery of the chickens did not constitute a course of performance casting light on the intended meaning of "chicken."
3. Conduct by only one of the parties, not known and acquiesced in by the other (for example, if Lessee kept the duck inside and Lessor never saw it or knew about it), may show what the performing party understood the agreement to be, but does not prove that the other party shared this view.
4. The more extensive or repetitious the conduct, the stronger the inference that it does reflect what was intended by the parties. By contrast, isolated or single instances of conduct are more ambiguous and could simply be a waiver of, or disinclination to enforce, rights

on a particular occasion. For example, merely because Lessor sees the duck on one occasion and does nothing about it, does not necessarily show that the parties share the same meaning of "animals."

d. Course of Dealing: Prior Dealings Between the Parties in Similar or Analogous Contractual Relationships

While "course of performance" means the parties' post-contractual relationship, the term "course of dealing" refers to any relationship they may have had in the period before the transaction in question. The parties may have dealt with each other on prior occasions, and the current transaction may be the latest in a series of similar ones that have taken place over a period of time. If so, the parties' conduct in prior dealings may provide information that helps to interpret a term that has generated a dispute in the present transaction. This is recognized by UCC §1.303(b) and Restatement, Second, §§202 and 203.

For example, Lessee previously rented premises from Lessor under a lease that had the identical clause forbidding animals. During the prior lease term, Lessor discovered the duck and told Lessee to get rid of it or face eviction. Lessee sadly obeyed. If, on expiration of the lease, the parties enter into a new lease with the same clause forbidding animals, it is reasonable to infer that they intend its wording to have the meaning established under the prior relationship. If they intend otherwise, they must make this clear in the new lease. If they do not, Lessee cannot claim that the parties intend that "animals," as used in the new lease, does not include ducks.

A course of dealing is only pertinent if the earlier relationship is comparable or analogous. The transactions must be substantially similar, the term in controversy must have been present in the earlier dealings, and past conduct must be relevant to the meaning in issue. As with course of performance, repetition strengthens the inference, so multiple transactions with consistent, pertinent behavior more clearly establish intended meaning.

e. Trade Usage, Common Usage, or Custom That Is Reasonably Applicable to the Parties' Dealings

Although the ordinary or general sense of words must be the starting point in any exercise of interpretation, UCC §1.303(c) and Restatement, Second, §§202(5) and 222 emphasize the significant impact of trade usage on the meaning of language. Parties usually deal with each other in the context of a larger community. This may be a particular market (whether international, national, or more local), or it may be a specialized trade or industry. If the market or industry has a well-accepted custom or practice that explains language or supplements an omission in an agreement, this customary usage is of value in ascertaining the parties' intent. Although UCC §1.303 and

Restatement, Second, §§202(5) and 222 use the term "usage of trade," this does not mean that custom or usage is only pertinent where the parties are members of a particular trade, industry, or profession. Rather, "usage of trade" must be understood to encompass any applicable commercial custom, whether it derives from a specific trade or from a broader market in which the parties are involved. UCC §1.303(c) and Restatement, Second, §222 recognize this by defining "usage of trade" to include any regular practice or method of dealing in a place, vocation, or trade.

Wolf v. Superior Court, 8 Cal. Rptr. 3d 649 (Cal. Ct. App. 2004), illustrates the role that evidence of trade usage could play in interpreting an agreement. The dispute in that case involved the royalties payable by Walt Disney Pictures and Television to the author of the book on which the 1988 movie *Who Framed Roger Rabbit* was based. The agreement between Disney and the author provided that the author would receive a royalty of 5 percent of "gross receipts." The dispute was whether this term meant only cash receipts, or also included the value of other consideration Disney had received from licenses granted for the use of the characters in the movie. The meaning of the term "gross receipts" had to be determined to resolve this dispute. None of the people involved in the negotiations had any recollection of ever discussing the meaning of the term. The plain meaning of the words, read in relation to other language in the recorded contract, suggested that royalties might be confined to cash receipts. However, the author sought to introduce the testimony of an expert that "gross receipts" was generally understood in the movie industry to include noncash consideration, and the court of appeals held that the trial court had erred in refusing to admit the evidence of usage. (The expert did subsequently testify on remand but apparently did not persuade the jury to interpret the term in light of the alleged usage. This case, like *Frigaliment*, shows that even if evidence of usage is offered, its probative weight is ultimately decided by the factfinder.)

Older common law did not recognize any practice as a usage unless it was so firmly established as to be notorious, universal, and ancient. The modern approach is more flexible. Official Comment 4 to UCC §1.303 and Comment *b* to Restatement, Second, §222 explicitly reject any requirement of great longevity and universality and admit the possibility of new usages.

A party who alleges that a usage explains or supplements an agreement must (1) define the trade or market with which the transaction is associated and show the parties' connection to it, (2) prove (usually by expert testimony) that the usage actually exists in the applicable trade or market, (3) show that the usage is pertinent to the dispute in that it relates to the matter on which the parties disagree, and (4) show that the usage is consistent with the express terms of the agreement and has not been excluded by them.

The initial issue of defining the trade or market and showing the relationship of the transaction to that trade or market can be crucial. The determination of the market is sometimes, but not always, straightforward. For example, say the dispute arises from a transaction between a manufacturer of television sets and one of its distributors. Is the relevant market confined to the distribution market for televisions, or is it broader—say the distribution market for home electronics, or for all electronics? Or is the appropriate market wider still, covering the electronics industry as a whole? The choice of the market could be crucial because the existence and nature of usage could be different, or relatively stronger or weaker, if the market is defined more broadly or narrowly.

One of the key factors in defining the trade or market is the parties' relationship to it. If both parties are active participants in the market or trade, usages in that market or trade are readily attributable to their contract, except to the extent that the contract clearly excludes a usage. However, if one of the parties is not involved in the market or trade, its usages should not be relevant to the contract unless the nonmember party knew or should have known of the usage and the circumstances show that the parties reasonably expected it to apply to the transaction. As usual, the objective standard is used to decide if a party should be subject to a usage. Even if the party did not actually know of the usage, it will apply if the party had reason to know of the usage and reasonably should have expected it to apply.

Nanakuli Paving & Rock Co. v. Shell Oil Co., 664 F.2d 772 (9th Cir. 1991), illustrates the inquiry into the appropriate market.[5] The case involved a contract between Shell and Nanakuli under which Shell supplied asphalt for Nanakuli's use in paving projects on the island of Oahu. The contract did not have a fixed price term, but provided that the price would be Shell's "posted price at time of delivery." Despite this, Nanakuli claimed that usage in the Oahu paving trade required Shell to "price protect" Nanakuli. That is, where Nanakuli had committed itself to the customer based on a lower posted price at the time of its bid, Shell would charge Nanakuli that price, even if the posted price at the time of delivery was higher. The court defined the scope of the paving trade broadly to include not only paving contractors but also asphalt suppliers because the suppliers had a close relationship with the pavers and had reason to know of the usage. *Nanakuli* also addressed the issue of whether the alleged usage was consistent with the express terms of the contract. This is important because usage should not be employed to interpret the contract if the parties have indicated the intention to exclude it. If the usage cannot be reconciled with the express terms of the contract, this strongly indicates that the parties did not intend to follow the usage. Because established and applicable usage is such a strong indication of intent, courts usually require the term excluding usage to be very clear and unequivocal. In *Nanakuli*, the court held the price protection usage to be

5. This case is discussed further in relation to the parol evidence rule in section 12.10.

consistent with the contract's express term that the price was to be Shell's posted price at the time of delivery. This is a very liberal approach to consistency because it is difficult to reconcile the clear language of the contract with the usage. However, the court justified its conclusion in the basis that there was no clear indication that the parties did not intend price protection to qualify the express language of the contract. On this approach, probably the only reliable way that the contract could have excluded the usage would have been to state expressly that it was inapplicable.

f. Interpretation of Contractual Language in the Absence of Contextual Evidence

In some cases, there is no contextual evidence pertinent to the interpretation of contractual language — the parties did not address the intended meaning of the disputed terms at the time of contract formation, there is no relevant course of performance or course of dealing, and no common or trade usage relating to the terms in issue. As noted in section 10.1.2 and at the beginning of this section, in the absence of contextual evidence, the language of the contract is the only basis for deciding the meaning of the disputed terms, and the court decides this meaning as a question of law. Although the language of the disputed term is at the center of the court's examination of the disputed term, the court does not look at that language in isolation, but considers it in light of the agreement as a whole—all the terms of the recorded agreement or the entire oral contract. Often terms in one part of a contract cast light on terms in another. The importance of interpreting language in the context of the whole agreement is demonstrated by *Hahn v. GEICO Choice Insurance Co.*, 420 P.3d 1160 (Alaska 2018). Hahn was sitting on his motorbike at a stoplight when he was rear-ended by a vehicle driven by GEICO's insured. The impact of the collision threw Hahn backwards onto the hood, windshield, and roof of the car, where he landed momentarily before falling onto the street. In terms of GEICO's policy, Hahn would have been entitled to higher payment if he had been an occupant of the vehicle that hit him. He argued that his brief sojourn on the front of the car qualified him as an occupant under the policy definition of "occupying" which included being "upon" the vehicle. The court disagreed. The word "upon" could not be looked at in isolation, and when read with other language in the policy, it meant someone who was in some way associated with the vehicle before the collision, such as a passenger.

Neuro-Communication Services, Inc. v. Cincinnati Insurance Co., 2022 WL 17573883 (Ohio 2022), also involved the interpretation of a term in light of the agreement as a whole. Neuro held a commercial property insurance policy issued by Cincinnati Insurance Co. The policy covered the insured for "direct loss to covered property at the premises caused by or resulting from any covered cause of loss." The policy defined "loss" as "accidental physical loss or actual physical damage." At the start of the COVID pandemic, the state required all non-essential businesses to close for a period of about six weeks. As Neuro's business did not qualify as essential, it was forced to close for this period and lost revenue. It claimed that this loss was covered by the policy. The insurer denied the claim on the grounds that the policy covered only losses caused by physical damage to property, and did not cover loss from the COVID-mandated shutdown because the suspension of business did not cause any such physical property damage. Neuro argued that the dictionary definitions of "physical" and "loss" were broad enough to encompass a loss resulting from a mandatory shut-down. The dictionary definition of "loss" covered any deprivation, and "physical" was defined in the dictionary to include something having an objective existence, as distinct from being merely imaginary. The court rejected this argument based on another term of the policy that covered the loss of business income suffered while the property was being restored. This provision made it clear that "restoration" contemplated the repair of damaged property.

§10.1.4 Some General Rules of Interpretation and Construction

When a term is omitted or its meaning is uncertain, this indefiniteness can often be resolved by having recourse to one of a variety of general principles that have been developed by courts as guidelines in the ascertainment of reasonable but unexpressed intent. These principles are usually based on commonsense inferences, but some are dictated by policy or a perception of fairness. These rules are guides to enable the court to draw the proper inferences of meaning from whatever facts may be available. Typically, they are used only when there is some uncertainty in the intent of the agreement. They should not be applied mechanically and must take into account the reasonable expectations of the parties and the underlying purpose of the agreement.

There are many rules of interpretation and construction. They are not all of equal strength, and some are more compelling than others. Obviously, they are not all relevant to every case. Although several of the common ones are included here, no attempt is made to catalog them all. These examples sufficiently illustrate the range and kind of rules covered under this category:

1. If possible, the court should try to interpret an agreement in a way that gives effect to all its terms.
2. Unless the context indicates otherwise, words used in a contract should be given their ordinary, general, or lay meaning rather than

a specialized or technical meaning. For example, in *E.M.M.I., Inc. v. Zurich American Insurance Co.*, 84 P.3d 385 (Cal. 2004), a jeweler's insurance policy excluded coverage where jewelry was stolen from a vehicle unless the jeweler's representative was "in or upon the vehicle" at the time of the theft. The jewelry was stolen from the car while the sales representative was checking the car's tailpipe. The insurer argued that the term "in or upon" was used in a technical sense to mean that the insured must actually be in the vehicle, not just next to it. The court disagreed. If the insurer intended to use a term in a technical sense, it should so indicate, say by defining the term in the policy. Because the term "upon" was ambiguous, it should be interpreted in a sense that accords with the insured's reasonable expectation that the exclusion applies only where the car is unattended. *Meridian Leasing, Inc. v. Associated Aviation Underwriters*, 409 F.3d 342 (6th Cir. 2005), followed the same approach in finding that an insurance policy on an aircraft covered damage to the engine when it caught fire upon being started. The insurance policy excluded damage caused by "wear and tear" and the insurer argued that the exclusion for "wear and tear" should be broadly understood to restrict coverage to damage from an accident and to exclude damage resulting from a mechanical problem. The court disagreed. The policy had no technical definition of "wear and tear." In ordinary usage, a fire caused by mechanical fault is not "wear and tear," which means deterioration resulting from the ongoing operation of the plane.

3. The rule *Ut res magis valeat quam pereat* means "The thing should rather have effect than be destroyed." If one interpretation would make the contract invalid and another would validate it, the court should favor the meaning that validates the contract. In the same spirit, a court should prefer an interpretation that would make a term reasonable and lawful over one that would have the opposite effect and should prefer an interpretation that positively rather than negatively affects public policy or the public interest. For example, say that a partnership agreement, entered into in New York City, contains a covenant not to compete. This covenant states that a partner will not engage in a competing business "in New York" for a period of two years after leaving the partnership. Agreements that stifle competition and restrict a person's ability to earn a living are unenforceable as against public policy unless they are reasonable in scope.[6]

6. *See* section 13.13.3 for a further discussion of the public policy concerns relating to covenants not to compete.

A partner leaves the partnership and sets up a competing business a few blocks away, claiming that the covenant is unenforceable because it is overbroad and unreasonably extends to the entire state of New York. The partnership contends that it is not unreasonable because it is intended to cover only to the city of New York. There is no extrinsic evidence from which the court can determine the intended meaning of "New York." Therefore, if the more restrictive meaning would save the covenant from invalidity, the court should favor that meaning.

4. Specific or precise provisions should be given greater weight than general provisions. For example, one clause in a lease says, "No pets may be kept on the premises." However, there is another provision in the lease that says, "Guide or service dogs shall be kept on leashes at all times in the public areas of the building." The specific provision concerning guide and service dogs makes it clear that the general rule on keeping pets on the premises does not apply to them.
5. Where an agreement consists of both standard terms and terms that were specifically agreed to by the parties in the particular transaction, any conflict between them should be resolved in favor of the specifically agreed terms.
6. The rule of *ejusdem generis* ("of the same kind") holds that when specific and general words are connected, the general words are limited by the specific ones, so that the general words are deemed to refer to things of the same kind. For example, a lease states that "skateboards, roller skates, rollerblades, and other means of locomotion are prohibited in common areas and hallways." The common denominator here is that all these items make use of wheels under the feet. On this reasoning, the general words "other means of locomotion" do not include wheelchairs or motorbikes. However, if the common denominator is taken to be wheels, these two items would be included in the general language, but a jet pack strapped to the back would not be.
7. The rule of *noscitur a sociis* ("known from its associates") is similar to *ejusdem generis* but is not confined to linked general and specific words. Whenever a series of words is used together, the meaning of each word in the series affects the meaning of others. For example, if a term in a lease provides that "no dogs, cats, or primates may be kept on the premises," the meaning of "primates" is qualified by the others. It would therefore cover only primates in the sense of apes and monkeys and would not forbid the lessee's friend, a bishop, from staying with the lessee.

8. The rule *Expressio unius est exclusio alterius* means "The expression of one thing excludes another." This is in some sense the opposite of the *ejusdem generis* rule. When a thing or list of things is specifically mentioned without being followed by a general term, the implication is that other things of the same kind are not covered by the list. For example, a term in a lease that prohibits "dogs, cats, and rabbits" impliedly does not prohibit hamsters.
9. The *contra proferentum* rule (stated in full, *omnia praesumuntur contra proferentum*) means "all things are presumed against the proponent." When one party has drafted or selected the language of an unclear provision, the meaning is preferred that favors the other party. This rule is often said to be a tie breaker, in that it should be used as a last resort when no more direct and pertinent guide to meaning is applicable. It is not always used as a last resort, however, and tends to be much favored when the proponent of the terms is a party with relatively strong bargaining power who has produced a predrafted standard contract for the other's signature. Insurance policies are prime examples of standard contracts that call for application of the *contra proferentum* rule.

   The *E.M.M.I* and *Meridian Leasing* cases in item 2 above both demonstrate this approach to the interpretation of an insurance policy, as does *Hoban v. Nova Casualty Co.*, 335 F. Supp. 3d 1192 (E.D. Cal. 2018). Trusses supporting the roof of the insured's bowling center failed. The roof did not fall in completely, but it dropped several inches, showered debris below, and required closure of the building for public safety reasons until the roof was repaired. The building was insured under a policy that included coverage for collapse, which the policy defined as "an abrupt falling down or caving in of a building or any part of a building with the result that the building or part of the building cannot be occupied for its intended purpose." The insured claimed that the failure of the roof and its sagging satisfied the policy definition of collapse, but the insurer denied coverage, arguing that the definition covered only a complete collapse in which the structure had fallen to the ground. The court found the definition to be ambiguous with regard to the question of whether complete collapse was required and there was no helpful extrinsic evidence. The parties had not discussed the scope of coverage, there was no usage on the meaning of the term, and other cases interpreting the meaning of "collapse" were not helpful because they involved policies with different language. The court did find some provisions in the policy that suggested that complete collapse was not required, but it ultimately settled the ambiguity by applying the *contra proferentum* rule and interpreting the definition in favor of the insured and against the insurer.

§10.2 GAP FILLERS USED TO EFFECTUATE THE PARTIES' REASONABLE INTENT

§10.2.1 Introduction

A gap filler is a provision legally implied into a contract to supplement or clarify its express language. As its name suggests, the principal purpose of a gap filler is to supply a logically inferable contract term when it is clear that the parties intended a contract, but have failed to provide adequately or at all for the question in issue. Of course, some apparent gaps in an express agreement could be filled by contextual evidence, so a legally implied gap filler is usually used only when no pertinent contextual evidence is available to establish the existence of a term as a matter of fact. Gap fillers are therefore standard terms supplied by law. Some have been developed by courts and others are provided by legislation. Courts and legislatures do not pick them out of the air but base them on common expectations, commercial practice, and public policy. For this reason, standard terms supplied by law are meant to reflect what the parties likely would have agreed had they discussed the issue and resolved it reasonably. As this description indicates, when a court resorts to legally implied gap fillers, it is usually engaged in construction, rather than fact-based interpretation.

For example, Buyer agrees to buy Seller's house, subject to Buyer being able to secure the necessary financing. Nothing is said in the written agreement or in the negotiations about Buyer having the duty to make a conscientious effort to obtain the financing. If Buyer does nothing to seek financing, this is likely a breach of a legally implied promise to make reasonable efforts to apply for and secure the financing. The implication of such a promise is a logical extension of the express provisions of the agreement and gives effect to the presumed intent of the parties. It recognizes that they probably did not contemplate that Buyer could slip out of the obligation to buy the house simply by not bothering to apply for a loan. In this way, the implied term constructs what the parties must have intended, had they been acting fairly and reasonably, and it gives effect to their reasonable expectations and to the underlying purpose of the agreement. Legally implied terms are derived from common expectations in the market, so they have an affinity to usage. Therefore, this same term requiring best efforts in seeking a loan might have been established by evidence of the customary practices pertaining to the sale of a home subject to the contingency of financing. However, the difference is that if a usage is so well established that it has reached the point of being recognized as a gap filler, it becomes part of the contract as a matter of law, not of fact. It is therefore not necessary to establish it by evidence.

Some gap fillers are well established and others have been recognized more recently. Additional ones will continue to develop in the future as new legal implications are drawn from changing market expectations. Of course, there cannot be standard terms for every conceivable gap, so there are some omissions that cannot be cured by legal implication. Some gap fillers supply generalized obligations that are likely to be implied in all kinds of contracts, and some are very specific, relating to particular types of term in specialized contracts. The following samples of general and specific gap fillers illustrate their range and nature.

§10.2.2 Gap Fillers That Supply General Obligations

When a contract does not clearly specify a level of performance but it is clear that the parties' purpose can be achieved only if the obligor puts some energy and dedication into the performance, the law implies an obligation to make best efforts or reasonable efforts[7] to achieve the contract's purpose. The above example of the house sale subject to financing illustrates this. Another illustration is provided by *Wood v. Lucy, Lady Duff-Gordon*, discussed in sections 10.1.1 and 7.9.2, in which the court found that an exclusive distributorship contract impliedly required the distributor to make best efforts to sell the product. This general principle is likely to apply in any type of contract under which the grantor of a license, distributorship, or dealership relies on the conscientiousness of the grantee to market a product effectively. The facts and resolution of *B. Lewis Productions, Inc. v. Angelou*, 2005 WL 1138474 (S.D.N.Y. 2005), are strikingly similar to *Wood*. The poet Maya Angelou entered into a written agreement with Lewis under which she granted him the exclusive right to represent her in placing her work in greeting cards, calendars, and other stationery items. Lewis agreed to contribute "all the capital necessary" and Angelou agreed to contribute "original literary works." The agreement did not particularize Lewis' duties, but it did provide that the parties would share the net profits of the venture after revenue had been applied to the repayment of Lewis' capital contribution and expenses. Lewis began work immediately. Just over two years after the agreement was entered, and when Lewis was close to executing a licensing agreement with Hallmark cards, the personal relationship between the parties soured, and Angelou terminated the agreement. Shortly thereafter, Angelou entered into

7. There may be a difference between "reasonable efforts," which appears strongly objective, and "best efforts," which suggests some blend of subjective and objective standards. However, the distinction is probably not substantial. Whichever term is used, the decision on what constitutes an acceptable effort should take into account both the objective market standards and the subjective honesty and particular circumstances of the party who is to exert the effort.

a licensing agreement with Hallmark on her own. Protracted litigation followed in which Lewis sued Angelou for breach of contract. The court, quoting from *Wood* at length, noted that like Wood and Duff-Gordon, Lewis and Angelou unquestionably intended to form a business relationship in which each party assumed obligations. Rather than defeat this intent by declaring the contract to be too indefinite to enforce, the court followed the approach of *Wood* and supplied an obligation of good faith and fair dealing to give content to the vaguely expressed undertakings of the parties.

The problem with the legal implication of broad, generalized obligations is that they are vague in themselves. Therefore, although they may go part of the way in curing a vagueness or omission in the agreement, they may not settle the scope and content of the obligation. That is, a concept such as "best efforts" is mushy and nonspecific, so that it is not enough simply to imply the obligation. The further step must be taken to determine with some precision what degree of effort is required by the obligation. It may be easy to find a breach when no effort is made at all, but it is more difficult to decide if some degree of effort is an adequate performance. This question has to be resolved by examining the underlying purpose of the contract and any applicable standards in the trade or market that may form the basis of the parties' reasonable expectations.

§10.2.3 Gap Fillers That Supply More Specific Rights and Duties

Both the UCC and the common law supply gap fillers that relate to specific aspects of particular kinds of contracts. Some of these are concrete and precise, but others include generalized concepts, such as reasonableness, that present interpretational problems similar to those discussed above. The following selection illustrates the kind of supplementary terms available to fill gaps left by the parties. These are merely random examples. No attempt is made to be comprehensive. Remember, they are used only if the contract has a gap or uncertainty that has not been resolved by contextual evidence.

The common law has developed many gap fillers through the process of judicial decision. Three examples, discussed elsewhere in this book, are enough to illustrate this point. First, if the parties to an employment contract do not specify its duration, it is deemed to be terminable at will—that is, either party has the right to terminate it at any time. Second, if the parties do not state that rights under a contract are personal to the obligee, the obligee may transfer (assign) those rights to another person. (*See* sections 12.9 and 19.3.3.) Third, if the contract does not provide for the sequence of performance, it is presumed that when both performances are a single instantaneous act, they must be made concurrently. But if one performance is instantaneous and the other needs time to perform, it is presumed that the longer performance must take place first. Therefore, in the sale of a house, unless otherwise stated in the contract, it is implied that transfer of title and payment occur at the same time, but in a contract to build a house, the builder must complete the construction before the owner has to pay. (*See* section 16.8.4.)

UCC Article 2 also has a number of gap fillers. Because they are set out in the statute, they are easier to find than those provided by common law. For example, unless the agreement expresses otherwise, §§2.312, 2.314, and 2.315 imply certain minimum warranties that a seller makes under defined circumstances regarding the title to and quality of the goods; if the parties do not specify the price of the goods, §2.305 infers that they agreed to a reasonable price unless the apparent intent of the agreement is otherwise; if payment terms are not expressed, §§2.307 and 2.310 assume that payment must be made upon delivery of the goods; §§2.307, 2.308, and 2.309 require that the goods be delivered in a single lot at the seller's place of business within a reasonable time; in a requirements or output contract,[8] §2.306(1) implies both a good faith and a reasonableness obligation on the party who is to determine the quantity of goods ordered or supplied; and §2.306(2) implies an obligation of best efforts on both parties when the contract imposes an obligation on one of them to deal exclusively with the other.

§10.3 TERMS CONSTRUED AS A MATTER OF POLICY

§10.3.1 The General Obligation of Good Faith and Fair Dealing: A Supplementary Term That Cannot Be Excluded by Agreement

UCC §1.304 and Restatement, Second, §205 recognize that every contract imposes on the parties a general obligation of good faith and fair dealing in the performance and enforcement of the contract. This obligation is implied in the contract as a matter of law, even if the agreement does not expressly articulate it. The obligation is so fundamental to fair dealing and so strongly demanded by public policy that it is a mandatory part of the contract irrespective of the parties' actual intent, and it cannot be effectively disclaimed by a term in the contract. Although the obligation of good faith and fair dealing is construed if not stated expressly in the contract, it is not a gap filler of the kind described in section 10.2. It does not supply a term to fill

8. *See* section 7.9.3 for an explanation of this type of contract.

a gap in the parties' express agreement. Rather, it enters the contract as a matter of law, whether or not there is a gap or uncertainty about the parties' intent. It is more a matter of regulation than of seeking what the parties reasonably must have intended — it is a limitation on contractual autonomy in the interest of public policy.

It is one thing to recognize a general obligation of good faith and fair dealing, but quite another to give specific content to these broad and abstract concepts when one of the parties claims that the other's conduct breached the obligation. This question is discussed in section 7.9.3 in relation to the obligation of good faith imposed by UCC §2.306 on buyers and sellers in output and requirements contracts. The general principle set out in that context is applicable more broadly to the inquiry into good faith in other types of contracts: Good faith is determined with reference to the reasonable expectations of the parties in the context of the transaction. It is not always easy to decide what those reasonable expectations should be.

For example, in *United Airlines, Inc. v. Good Taste, Inc.*, 982 P.2d 1259 (Alaska 1999), United entered into an in-flight catering contract with Good Taste. To perform the contract, Good Taste had to expand its capacity extensively, incurring $1 million in costs to enlarge its operation. The period of the contract was three years, but the contract provided that either party could terminate it on 90 days' notice. After about one year, United exercised its right to terminate the contract by giving the 90 days' notice. It terminated because it had decided to use another company for its in-flight catering. Good Taste claimed that United had violated its obligation of good faith by terminating the contract. It contended that it would not have spent the money to expand its operations had it not had a reasonable assurance of a three-year contract, and that United's representative had told it that United would not use the termination provision unless it stopped flying to Alaska. Because the termination provision had no qualification, the majority of the court interpreted it as allowing termination at will, without any requirement of cause. The majority recognized that this contract, like every contract, contained an implied covenant of good faith and fair dealing. However, it granted summary judgment to United because it refused to find that United had violated this obligation merely by exercising a clear and unambiguous termination right. The obligation of good faith precludes a party from opportunistic advantage-taking and actions motivated by malicious or improper motives (such as the intent to drive the party out of business). However, where the contract contains an at-will termination clause, the obligation of good faith and fair dealing does not preclude exercise of that right to terminate, even if motivated by the purpose of getting a better deal elsewhere. To so hold would convert the contract's clear at-will termination right into one that required cause for termination. A dissenting justice argued that the termination clause did not expressly state that United could terminate at will, but was silent on the question of whether United needed to show cause for cancellation. Therefore, the termination clause must be read in light of the obligation of good faith, to be determined in light of the parties' reasonable expectations. The parties understood that Good Taste would not have made a significant investment in its facilities unless it had some assurance that United would not simply terminate the contract if a better deal came along. United's termination without cause violated Good Taste's reasonable expectations, and the case should go to trial so that a jury could decide if this constituted a violation of United's obligation of good faith.

The implied general obligation of good faith and fair dealing has arisen quite frequently in the context of insurance policies, where the insured alleges that the insurer has acted in bad faith by failing to pay a claim under the policy without proper cause or with an improper motive. A claim of the insurer's breach of the obligation of good faith and fair dealing could be made as a breach of contract claim, but some courts recognize it as a tort claim too, which gives the insured the advantage of being able to claim damages for emotional distress and punitive damages.[9] An insurer breaches its obligation of good faith and fair dealing if it has an ulterior motive for denying or withholding payment of the claim, or it otherwise rejects it without a fair and proper investigation and determination of ineligibility. In *Hoban v. Nova Casualty Co.*, the case involving interpretation of the meaning of "collapse" cited in section 10.1.4, the insured also argued that the insurer's failure to compensate for the dropped roof violated the insurer's obligation of good faith and fair dealing. However, the court found that it had not done so because it had a genuine dispute with the insured over the meaning of an ambiguous term that defined the scope of coverage. Even if the insurer might ultimately be found to have breached the contract by not paying the claim, it does not have liability for breach of the obligation of good faith and fair dealing if its challenge to the claim was reasonably based on a genuine dispute.

§10.3.2 Construed Terms That Can Be Excluded Only by Express or Specific Language

Below the level of the absolute legal implication of the duty of good faith and fair dealing, there are construed terms that are important enough to be more strongly implied than other gap fillers. Although public policy does not preclude the parties from contracting out of them, it requires the intent to exclude them to be clearly expressed. Stated differently, while most gap fillers enter the contract only when necessary to resolve an uncertainty or

9. Emotional distress and punitive damages are generally not available for breach of contract, as explained in section 18.13.

omission, there are some that are so strongly implied as a matter of policy that they become part of the contract unless its express terms clearly exclude them. In some cases, even a clear exclusion is not good enough unless it complies with specified rules that may prescribe the use of particular language or format.

For example, UCC Article 2 has a policy in favor of providing warranties in certain types of sales of goods. Therefore, although §2.316(2) allows the seller to contract out of them, it recognizes a warranty disclaimer as effective only if it satisfies certain formalities. To disclaim the merchant[10] seller's warranty of merchantability (that is, that the goods meet minimum trade standards), the sales contract must mention "merchantability" and, if in writing, the disclaimer must be conspicuous. When goods are sold for a particular purpose, the seller gives an implied warranty of fitness for that purpose unless it is disclaimed conspicuously in writing. The goal of these rules is to make it more likely that the buyer notices the disclaimer, and to prevent the seller from hiding it in a mass of boilerplate.

§10.4 THE PROBLEM OF INDEFINITENESS IN AN AGREEMENT

If the terms of an agreement are expressed clearly and comprehensively, the fact of contract formation and the extent of each party's commitment can be ascertained with relative ease by the interpretation of their language in context. However, parties sometimes fail to express their assent adequately because they have left a material aspect of their agreement vague or ambiguous, or they have failed to resolve it or to provide for it at all. When the agreement suffers from this kind of uncertainty, it is said to be indefinite.

There could be many different causes of indefiniteness. For example, the parties may not discuss all aspects of the proposed relationship, they may not give enough attention to detail, they may be unclear in their thinking or articulation of what is expected, or they may avoid confronting thorny issues that threaten to collapse the deal. Sometimes it is clear that the parties genuinely intended a contract despite the indefiniteness, but in other cases the lack of resolution means that they had not yet achieved consensus.

The general rule is that no contract comes into being if a material aspect of the agreement is left indefinite by the parties and the uncertainty cannot be resolved by the process of interpretation or construction. The existence of such an irresoluble key aspect of the relationship means that the parties

10. *See* sections 2.7.2 and 6.3.2 for the definition of "merchant."

never reached sufficient consensus to conclude an enforceable contract, and the court should not try to concoct a contract for them.

This statement of the general rule suggests two central issues that must be confronted in dealing with problems of indefiniteness: First, for an apparent contract to fail for indefiniteness, there must be an incurable uncertainty about what the parties agreed to, so that their intent to enter a contract is in doubt, or the court is at a loss in establishing a basis for enforcing what was agreed. This first issue involves many considerations that form the basis of the remainder of this chapter. Second, the uncertainty must relate to a material aspect of the relationship. Although an indefinite nonmaterial term must be settled by the court if it is relevant to the dispute, the uncertainty does not preclude contract formation.

A term is material if it is an important component of the contract. It is so central to the values exchanged under the contract that it is a fundamental basis of the bargain.[11] Although materiality is sometimes obvious, the significance of some terms is less clear and must be determined by interpreting the agreement in context to uncover the reasonable expectations of the parties.

Although a court should not find a contract where indefiniteness is severe enough to indicate a lack of assent to its material terms, this does not mean that the court should refuse contractual enforcement unless every material term of the agreement has been expressed with piercing clarity. Such a rigorous standard would err in the opposite direction by failing to recognize a contract when the evidence suggests that the parties reasonably expected to be bound, did intend to enter a contract despite the indefiniteness, and had relied on the existence of a contract.

The balance between these poles results in a general principle that tolerates some degree of indefiniteness if the evidence indicates that the parties did intend a contract and there is some means of resolving the uncertainty so that a breach can be identified and a remedy provided. Both UCC §2.204(3) and Restatement, Second, §33(2) adopt this approach by emphasizing that a contract should be treated as reasonably certain if the language of agreement, interpreted in context and in light of applicable legal rules, provides enough content to establish an intent to contract, a basis for finding breach, and a means of providing a remedy.

Although remedies are not discussed until Chapter 18, it is useful to focus on the relationship between definiteness and remedy suggested by Article 2 and Restatement, Second. Definiteness is not absolute but relative, and the degree of certainty required may be different depending on the nature of the controversy and the relief claimed. For example, if the plaintiff claims

11. This broad definition of materiality is sufficient for present purposes. Materiality is also discussed in section 6.3.2 in connection with the battle of the forms and is examined in greater detail in section 17.3 in relation to breach of contract.

enforcement of a clear obligation due by the defendant, and the defendant contends that the contract is too indefinite because of vagueness in the plaintiff's obligation, the court does not have to establish the plaintiff's obligation with as much certainty as it would have to do if that was the obligation in issue. Similarly, if the plaintiff is claiming damages for the breach of an unclear obligation of the defendant, the court needs just enough information to determine the fact of breach and a monetary award. However, if the plaintiff is seeking specific performance of the obligation (that is, a court order compelling the defendant to perform the contract[12]), the court needs a greater degree of certainty to grant the order because the court must be able to define the obligation clearly if it is going to order its performance.

Although it is relatively easy to identify the general range of appropriate judicial intervention to cure indefiniteness, it is much more difficult to know if an individual case falls within that range—that is, whether the indefiniteness is properly remediable or should preclude contractual enforcement. As in so many other situations, the answer can be reached only by finding the mutual intent of the parties through the process of interpretation and construction.

§10.5 DIFFERENT CAUSES AND FORMS OF INDEFINITENESS

Indefiniteness in an agreement could be caused by vagueness, ambiguity, omission, or irresolution. These different shortcomings have much in common, but they may raise different concerns that call for separate treatment. It is therefore useful to begin by articulating this distinction.

§10.5.1 Unclear Terms: Vagueness and Ambiguity

a. Vague Terms

A term is vague (or uncertain) if it is stated so obscurely or in such general language that one cannot reasonably determine what it means. For example, Lessor agrees to let certain business premises to Lessee for one year in exchange for "a periodic rental payment based on a fair percentage of Lessee's earnings." One cannot determine on the face of this language the amount and the due date of the rent. The wording fails to convey a certain and concrete meaning. *Baer v. Chase*, 392 F.3d 609 (3d Cir. 2004), discussed in section 9.6.2 in relation to unjust enrichment, provides another illustration

12. *See* section 18.10.

of incurable vagueness. Baer, an ex-prosecutor, wished to become involved in screenwriting and in directing and producing films. He was introduced to Chase, who was working on a project that would ultimately become the celebrated series, *The Sopranos*, which centered on organized crime in New Jersey. Baer helped Chase with background information on the New Jersey mob, introduced him to various people who had stories about organized crime in New Jersey, and read and commented on his draft script. Baer asserted that Chase had agreed orally that if the show became a success, he would "take care" of him and would reward him "in a manner commensurate with the true value" of his services. The court of appeals affirmed the trial court's grant of summary judgment against Baer on the contract claim. It held that even if such a promise was made, these terms were too indefinite to enable the court to ascertain with reasonable certainty what performance was to be rendered by Chase. The court acknowledged that indefiniteness can sometimes be resolved by the implication of a term, such as a reasonable price. However, the vagueness in this undertaking was beyond cure.[13]

By contrast, the court did not find indefiniteness to be fatal in *B. Lewis Productions, Inc. v. Angelou*, discussed in section 10.2.2. Recall that Maya Angelou granted to Lewis the exclusive right to represent her in placing her work in greeting cards, calendars, and other stationery items. Lewis agreed to contribute "all the capital necessary" and Angelou agreed to contribute "original literary works." The agreement did not set out Lewis' duties, but it did provide that the parties would share the net profits of the venture. About two years later, just as Lewis was about to secure a licensing agreement with Hallmark cards, Angelou terminated the agreement. She ultimately entered into a licensing agreement with Hallmark on her own. When Lewis sued Angelou for breach of contract,[14] she moved for summary judgment on the ground that the agreement was too indefinite to be enforced as a contract. The court denied her motion. It noted that the court's role was not to make a contract for the parties, and it would not enforce an agreement whose terms are so indefinite that the parties' intentions cannot be ascertained with reasonable certainty. However, it observed that courts are reluctant to strike down contracts for indefiniteness and cautioned that courts should not turn the search for certainty into a "fetish." Some degree of indefiniteness can be found in most contracts. The court recognized that the parties

13. As an alternative to his contract claim, Baer sought relief in restitution, claiming that Chase had been unjustly enriched by Baer's services. The discussion of the case in section 9.6.2 reveals that he had only modest success on this alternative cause of action because the court awarded him restitutionary damages based on the market value of his services, which the court found to be small — a far cry from the reward he may have hoped for by contributing to the blockbuster series.

14. He also sued Hallmark for tortious interference with contract on the grounds that it induced Angelou's breach by contracting directly with her knowing that Lewis had been negotiating with Hallmark on her behalf.

did intend to form a business relationship, and it felt that all of the open-ended terms could be given adequate content by applying a standard of reasonableness and good faith to the parties' undertakings.

b. Ambiguity

A term is ambiguous if it is capable of more than one meaning. Ambiguity can lie in a word itself or in the structure of a sentence. Ambiguity in a word may be illustrated by a term in a lease that confines the use of the premises to "the purpose of conducting a bookmaking business." The word "bookmaking" could refer either to the manufacture of books or to the making and placing of bets on horses and sporting events. Ambiguity can also result from inept sentence construction. For example, although the lease makes it clear that "bookmaking" is used in the latter sense, it goes on to provide that Lessor "shall be entitled to 10 percent of Lessee's profits from all gambling activities that shall be lawfully conducted on the premises." The clumsy sentence construction may mean that Lessor is entitled to 10 percent of all profits earned by Lessee from gambling, and that Lessee is obliged to conduct only lawful activity on the premises, or it may mean that Lessor is entitled to 10 percent of the profits from lawful gambling but gets no share of illegal gambling proceeds.

Ambiguity in language must be distinguished from a dispute over the application of unambiguous language to a particular set of facts. The court made this distinction in *Psenicska v. Twentieth Century Fox Film Corp.*, 2008 WL 4185752 (S.D.N.Y. 2008), *aff'd*, 409 F. App'x 368 (2d Cir. 2008). The case involved the movie *Borat*, in which the character, a fictional Kazakh television reporter, tours America with the apparent purpose of making a documentary on American life. The movie is a comedy, and its particular brand of humor (described by the court as "childish and vulgar") is to dupe ordinary people (that is, members of the public who are not actors) into believing that they are participating in a documentary film. As the filming proceeds, it becomes apparent that the film is not a documentary at all, but a tasteless satire in which the Borat character shocks the unsuspecting movie participants by surprising, outrageous, and offensive conduct. Several of the people set up in this way sued the studio for damages for the use of their images in the movie. Each had signed an agreement consenting to appear in a "documentary-style motion picture," and the studio therefore moved to dismiss their suits on the basis of this consent. One of the issues in the case[15] involved the interpretation of the term "documentary-style motion picture." The plaintiffs argued that dismissal was not appropriate because the consent

---

15. The plaintiffs' other principal allegation was that the producers of the movie had committed fraud by disguising the fact that the movie was a parody in which the plaintiffs were going to be the hapless butts of the humor. The court dismissed the fraud claim because the consent that the plaintiffs signed included a waiver of their right to sue for misrepresentation. This aspect of the case is discussed in section 13.5.2.

was too indefinite to enforce, in that the term "documentary-style motion picture" was ambiguous. The court disagreed. The dictionary definition of the words "documentary" and "style" make it clear a "documentary-style movie" is "a work displaying the characteristics of a film that provides a factual record or report." None of the parties challenged this dictionary-based definition, and the court held that while the film was a parody, it was set up in a style that made it look like a documentary, so it was, indeed, in a documentary style. The court therefore dismissed the suits.

c. Curing Vagueness or Ambiguity with Contextual Evidence

A term that is not readily comprehensible on its face may not be incurably vague or ambiguous, because it may become clear if interpreted in context. Evidence of what the parties said or did in negotiations, correspondence, or dealings prior to the agreement or during the period following it may help clarify what they meant by the language used. In addition, clarity may be supplied by a custom or usage in the commercial environment in which the parties made the agreement, or by gap fillers recognized by law. Therefore, language that seems vague or ambiguous in isolation may become more certain if interpreted in the wider environment of the transaction. In the example in which Lessor agrees to let business premises to Lessee for one year in exchange for "a periodic rental payment based on a fair percentage of Lessee's earnings," the vague rental provision may not be as unclear as it sounds if its meaning is embellished by facts in the context. Say, for example, that these clauses are regularly used in the commercial real property market, in which "fair rental" is widely understood to be based on an index published by an association of landlords, and rent is customarily paid monthly in advance. Similarly, the word "bookmaking," in the lease of premises for that purpose is ambiguous in isolation, may become more definite if other provisions in the lease, discussions during negotiations, or other facts are available to show what the parties meant.

But contextual evidence cannot always save a vague or ambiguous term. Sometimes unclear language defies interpretation, even in context, because the circumstances of the transaction are devoid of helpful indicators of meaning. If a central component of an apparent agreement suffers from this degree of incurable indefiniteness, one can only conclude either that no contract was intended or, if it was, that the parties failed to form a clear intent or failed to communicate it well enough to create an enforceable relationship.

d. Plain Meaning or Contextual Ambiguity

While an unclear term can be clarified by contextual evidence, the opposite may also be true: A term that seems clear on its face may turn out to be ambiguous if viewed in the context of the transaction. If the plain meaning of words is clear at face value, a court may refuse to go behind that plain meaning to examine contextual evidence that may undermine the plain meaning. However, courts do not generally restrict interpretation to the plain meaning of the language where there is contextual evidence that has relevance to the possible meaning of the words used. They recognize that words do not always have a single, fixed meaning. To base interpretation of the parties' intent on nothing more than the apparent meaning of words is too rigid and may lead the court to a literal interpretation that the parties did not intend. Therefore, if extrinsic evidence is available to cast light on the meaning of language, most courts are willing to take it into account in determining what the parties intended. This is known as the contextual approach to interpretation. It does not mean that the court will ignore the plain meaning of the parties' language or that it will ultimately be persuaded to reach an interpretation contrary to the evident plain meaning of the language. The probity of contextual evidence is dependent on the clarity with which the parties have chosen to express their intentions and the degree to which the meaning suggested by the context is consistent with the language used by the parties.

Pacific Gas & Electric Co. v. G.W. Thomas Drayage & Rigging Co., 442 P.2d 641 (Cal. 1968), is a landmark in the development of the principle that the words used by the parties must be interpreted, not at face value, but within the entire context of the transaction. A provision in a contract to repair machinery provided that the repairer would "indemnify" the owner "against all loss, damage, expense, and liability resulting from . . . injury to property" arising in the performance of the contract. The repairer damaged property belonging to the owner. The owner claimed that the indemnity made the contractor liable for this damage, but the contractor argued that the provision was intended to apply only to damage to property of third parties. The trial court interpreted the language of the provision solely at its face value and concluded that its plain meaning did not restrict the repairer's liability to damage to the property of third parties. The Supreme Court reversed the trial court's decision because the trial court had refused to admit extrinsic evidence offered by the repairer (such as evidence of admissions by the owner and prior practices of the parties) that allegedly showed that the parties intended the indemnity clause to apply only to damage to the property of third parties. The court emphasized that the purpose of interpretation is to determine the intent of the parties, which cannot be done if the court refuses to look beyond the meaning of the words as the judge understands them. Words are just symbols of thought, and the context in which they are used can affect their meaning.

The court applied the principles set out in *Pacific Gas* in *Wolf v. Superior Court of Los Angeles County*, discussed in section 10.1.3, involving a dispute over royalties between Walt Disney Pictures and Television and the author of the book on which the movie *Who Framed Roger Rabbit* was based. The agreement under which Disney had bought the rights to the book provided that the author would receive a royalty of 5 percent of "gross receipts." The author claimed that "gross receipts" included the value of consideration, other than cash, that Disney had received from licenses granted for the use of the characters in the movie. The author sought to admit the testimony of an expert that trade usage in the movie industry supported the broader interpretation, but the trial court refused to admit the evidence on the ground that the term (interpreted in light of the writing as a whole) was unambiguous on its face and covered only cash receipts. On the basis of this conclusion, the trial court granted Disney's motion for summary judgment. Citing *Pacific Gas*, the court of appeals reversed the summary judgment and remanded the case for trial, holding that the trial court erred in refusing to consider extrinsic evidence that could show that the term was in fact ambiguous.[16]

Pacific Gas represents a judicial approach that is most receptive to contextual evidence to elucidate the meaning of apparently clear and unambiguous language. However, some courts are more wary of resorting to contextual evidence where there is no facial ambiguity in the language of the contract. For example, in *Wilson Arlington Co. v. Prudential Insurance Co. of America*, 912 F.2d 366 (9th Cir. 1990), the court criticized the broad definition of ambiguity in *Pacific Gas*, which it felt allowed a party too much leeway in creating ambiguity in contract language that is not reasonably understood in more than one way.

§10.5.2 Omitted Terms

A term is omitted if it should be in the agreement but the parties have failed to include it. The agreement has a gap regarding that particular aspect of the relationship. Say that Lessor and Lessee discussed and recorded most of the terms of the lease, but did not address the amount of the rent orally or in writing. This could mean that they failed to reach agreement on this crucial term, so that no lease came into being. However, it could also mean that the parties did not consider it necessary to articulate the amount of the rent, because they intended that the rent would be reasonable, based on the fair market rental for commercial property of this kind. In other words, the apparent gap in their agreement may indicate not a lack of consensus, but an intent to adhere to some "off-the-shelf" market or legal standard that they did not bother to articulate. To decide which of these two possibilities is the right one, their intent must be determined by looking at the language of the agreement as a whole in light of all the circumstances of the transaction.

16. In the end, the admission of the evidence did not help the author. On remand, the jury heard the expert evidence on usage, but nevertheless concluded that the term covered only cash receipts. *See Wolf v. Walt Disney Pictures & Television*, 76 Cal. Rptr. 3d 585 (Cal. Ct. App. 2008).

§10.5.3 Terms Left for Future Determination

a. Unresolved Terms and "Agreement to Agree"

An unresolved term differs from a vague or unarticulated term in that the parties have not yet settled it, leaving it to be resolved by agreement at some later time. Where parties deliberately postpone agreement on a material term, it cannot be said that they have yet formed a contract, even if they have reached consensus on all the other terms of their relationship. Where the parties agree in principle that they will make a contract, but they have not yet settled a material term, courts sometimes describe their understanding as an "agreement to agree," which is not yet a contract and cannot be enforced. For the incomplete agreement to be unenforceable as an "agreement to agree," the unresolved term must be material—it must go to the core of the contract. A contract will not fail on the grounds of unresolved terms if it is clear that the parties intended to be bound, but the terms on which they have deferred agreement are nonmaterial. In *Mr. Olympia, LLC v. Ultimate Nutrition, Inc.*, 2018 WL 1322201 (S.D.N.Y. 2018), the agreement set out all the essential terms of the parties' relationship and included language making it clear that the parties intended it as a binding contract. However, the agreement left for future negotiation certain supplementary and incidental benefits listed in a schedule. The court held that the deferral of agreement on those nonmaterial terms did not make the contract into a nonbinding "agreement to agree."

Conversely, in *Joseph Martin Jr. Delicatessen, Inc. v. Schumacher*, 417 N.E.2d 541 (N.Y. 1981), the court held that deferred agreement on a material term defeated contract formation and left the parties with nothing more than a nonbinding "agreement to agree." A renewal option in a lease gave the tenant the right to renew the lease for an additional five-year period at "annual rental to be agreed upon." The court found this to be an unenforceable "agreement to agree" because the parties had not agreed to the rent for the renewal period, clearly a material term, and had merely postponed agreement on that term to a future date. The court noted that the parties could have entered into an enforceable contract without fixing the actual amount of the rent, had they provided some standard or formula for determining the rent in the renewal period, or if they had agreed to base the rent on a reasonable or market standard. However, they had not done this. A dissent in the case argued that as the parties clearly intended to create a binding renewal option, the court should give effect to their intent by deeming that they agreed to renewal at a reasonable rent based on the market rent for the premises at the time of renewal. In *U Street Music Hall, LLC v. JRC Standard Properties, LLC*, 285 A.3d 1250 (D.C. 2022), the court rejected the majority's approach in *Joseph Martin* and opted for a resolution more in keeping with the dissent. A lease of real property gave U Street, the tenant, the option to renew the lease for an additional five-year term. The option stated that the annual base rent for the option term "shall be based on the fair market value rental rate applicable at the expiration of the initial term." It also provided that this annual base rent would escalate annually "at a rate agreed to by both the Landlord and Tenant." When U Street sought to exercise the option, JRC claimed that it was unenforceable because it failed to specify the rent for the renewal period, and the trial court agreed. The court of appeals reversed. It had no trouble concluding that the "fair market rental rate" was an adequate objective standard, synonymous with "reasonable rent." The court recognized that the provision leaving the annual escalation rate for future agreement might be treated by some courts as making the renewal option an unenforceable "agreement to agree." However, the court considered this to be inequitable because it would defeat U Street's reasonable expectations. The court should simply infer that the agreement on a reasonable rent should extend to the escalation rate too.

Even a court that may be inclined to a more forgiving approach cannot save a hopelessly inconclusive agreement. In *Alaska Fur Gallery, Inc. v. Tok Hwang*, 394 P.3d 511 (Alaska 2017), a sublease provided that the "lease includes an option to purchase the premises with lease amount to be applied to the negotiated purchase price." It did not state the purchase price or any method or standard for determining it. The court said that it would have filled the gap in the option had it any way to determine what the parties intended, but the sublease was devoid of any indication of how the price should be decided or of any signification of intent that the parties intended to use a market standard.[17]

b. Agreement to Settle an Open Term by an Objective Standard

No contract is yet formed if the parties have deferred agreement on a material term, but the parties may wish to leave a term open for future determination. This commonly happens where the exact content of the term is dependent on uncertain future events. A contract can validly provide for the final determination of a term at some later date, provided that the contract sets out a standard that will allow that term to be settled without the need for further negotiation and agreement. As *Joseph Martin Jr. Delicatessen* shows, the contract should clearly provide for the application of a determinative standard to settle the open term, otherwise a court may find that the parties had merely reached an "agreement to agree."

Say, for example, that Owner has completed the plan for a new commercial building and construction is about to begin. Owner has been negotiating with Lessee for a lease of space in the building upon its completion. The parties have reached agreement on the period of the lease, the location and

17. In some circumstances, even though the court finds that deferral of a term precluded contract formation, it may conclude that the parties did make a commitment to continue to bargain in good faith. This possibility is discussed in section 10.6.

size of the premises, and all other terms—except for the rent to be paid. They wish to enter the lease agreement now, even though the premises will not be ready for occupation for two years. However, neither wishes to agree to a set figure because they do not know what the rental market will be like when the building is completed. The parties are not able to bind each other to the lease now if they simply agree to resolve the question of rent closer to the time of occupation. However, they can enter into a binding contract now, even without settling the amount of the rent, if they identify some formula or external source or standard that will allow the rent to be determined by some objective criterion at the appropriate time in the future. For example, they could provide for the rent to be calculated by applying a published economic indicator to a base figure, or they could base the rent on a market standard derived from average rent charged for comparable buildings in the area at the time of occupation, or they could provide for market-rate rent to be set by an independent arbitrator. *Feldman v. Google, Inc.*, 513 F. Supp. 2d 229 (E.D. Pa. 2007),[18] illustrates a valid future pricing formula. The price term in the contract for advertising on the Google site based the price of the advertising on the number of clicks on the advertisement—the more people who clicked on the ad, the higher the rate charged to the advertiser. The court found this to be a practicable method of determining price with reasonable certainty, based on ascertainable objective data.

Of course, the formula or objective standard must itself be clear, so the parties must at least be able to agree now on what criterion should be used. One of the best examples of an incomprehensible formula can be found in *Walker v. Keith*, 382 S.W.2d 198 (Ky. 1964). The renewal option in a lease expressed the rent payable for the renewal period in the following exquisite prose: "[R]ental will be fixed in such amount as shall actually be agreed upon by the lessors and the lessee with the monthly rental fixed on the comparative basis of rental values as of the date of the renewal with rental values at this time reflected by the comparative business conditions of the two periods." Unsurprisingly, when the time for renewal arrived, the parties disagreed on the meaning of this language. The court held that the parties had not entered into a renewal contract because the incoherent language did not set out any kind of workable formula or objective standard for calculating the rent, and there was no basis to assume that the parties meant to contract for a reasonable rent.

c. Agreement to Allow One of the Parties Discretion to Decide an Open Term

The parties may decide to leave the determination of an open term to the discretion of one of them. If this is done, there is no problem with deferred

18. This case is discussed in the context of clickwrap terms in section 5.3.

agreement, because the parties have committed to this method of settling the term and will not have to try to reach agreement on it at a future time. For example, in the above illustration involving the lease of premises, the parties could have agreed that the rent would be set by the lessor in its reasonable discretion. The lessee takes a risk in deferring to the lessor's discretion, but the lessor's obligation to act reasonably provides the lessee with some measure of control over the exercise of discretion. Even if the contract did not expressly state that the lessor must use its discretion reasonably, a court will likely imply either a good faith or a reasonableness standard to restrict the lessor's discretion.[19]

The court upheld a term allowing one of the parties to set the price in *Arbitron, Inc. v. Tralyn Broadcasting, Inc.*, 400 F.3d 130 (2d Cir. 2005). Arbitron provided listener demographics data used by radio stations to attract advertisers. It entered into an agreement with Tralyn, the owner of a radio station, under which Arbitron granted a five-year license to Tralyn to use these reports. The agreement provided that if Tralyn acquired additional radio stations or assigned the license to a successor that owned additional stations, Arbitron had the right to increase the license fee. It did not specify the amount of the increase or provide a standard for determining it. About two years later, Tralyn was bought by a corporation that owned four other stations and it assigned the license to the buyer. Arbitron increased the license fee. When neither Tralyn nor its buyer paid the increased fee, Arbitron sued. The district court granted summary judgment to Tralyn on the grounds that the agreement was unenforceably vague because it contained no basis for determining the amount of the increase in the license fee. The court of appeals reversed the summary judgment. The contract was not too indefinite because it allowed Arbitron to determine the increase, which it must do in good faith. (On remand, the district court found that Arbitron had acted in good faith in determining the fee increase. 526 F. Supp. 2d 441 (S.D.N.Y. 2007), *aff'd*, 328 F. App'x 755 (2d Cir. 2009).)

§10.6 PRELIMINARY AGREEMENTS

§10.6.1 The Categorization of Preliminary Agreements

In many transactions, particularly in complex ones, the parties may negotiate at length as they move in the direction of making an agreement. It is not uncommon for parties to record preliminary understandings and

19. *See* section 7.9 for a discussion of the implication a good faith or reasonableness standard to limit the apparent wide discretion of a party.

agreements during the course of their negotiations and before they reach the stage of making a final and comprehensive contract. Common terms used by parties to label such preliminary agreements are "memorandum of understanding" (sometimes abbreviated as MOU) or "letter of intent" (sometimes abbreviated as LOI). For example, the owner of property in the central city, currently used as a parking lot, wishes to develop it into a mixed-use complex consisting of offices, apartments, and shops. The owner begins discussions with a construction contractor with a view to forming a joint venture to accomplish this development. Before construction can begin, the parties must develop plans, seek financing, obtain permits, and try to attract anchor tenants, all of which will take time. It could be years before this complex project is realized. In such a project, it is often not possible for parties to reach a comprehensive and final contract at an early stage because there are too many contingencies and uncertainties that must be resolved. They may therefore first enter into a preliminary agreement, set out in a memorandum of understanding or letter of intent, in which they set out the framework of their relationship and express the intention of working together to reach the final goal of completing the development of the property. As the project proceeds, further issues will be negotiated and as they are settled the parties might record them in successive preliminary agreements. A final and definitive agreement may not be executed until months or even years after the parties first embarked on the project.

Sometimes the parties make clear the legal effect of these preliminary agreements by specifying whether they are intended to be informal, non-binding expressions of intent or binding contracts. If the parties clearly and unambiguously state that the preliminary agreement is not yet a binding contract and imposes no legal obligations on them, this resolves the question of its legal effect. However, if they do not do this, there may later be a dispute over the legal effect of the preliminary agreement that will have to be resolved by a court through the process of interpretation. In *Teachers Insurance & Annuity Ass'n v. Tribune Co.*, 670 F. Supp. 491 (S.D.N.Y. 1987), the court formulated a categorization of preliminary agreements that has been widely used by later courts. It identified three types of preliminary agreements: A "Type I" preliminary agreement is a binding contract. Although preliminary in form, it does reflect agreement on all the major issues that need negotiation and the parties' intent to be bound by it. Even though they contemplate executing a final memorandum of agreement, they regard that step as a formality. A "Type II" preliminary agreement settles some terms of the relationship but leaves other important aspects of it to future negotiation. It therefore cannot be a final and comprehensive contract that binds the parties to their ultimate objective. However, it does commit them to continue to work with each other and to negotiate in good faith in an effort to reach a final agreement. A "Type III" preliminary agreement is merely an expression of the parties' intent to work together in the hope of being able to conclude a contract, but they do not intend it to create any binding obligation. In *Teachers Ins. & Annuity Ass'n*, the court identified several factors to be taken into account in deciding how to categorize a preliminary agreement. The most important are (1) whether the agreement indicates the parties' intent on the binding effect of the agreement, (2) whether there has been partial performance, (3) whether all the terms have been settled, and (4) whether the agreement is of the type that would usually be committed to a final and formal writing.

§10.6.2 Nonbinding Preliminary Agreements

It is easiest to deal first with Type III preliminary agreements because the usual assumption is that a preliminary agreement is most likely to fit into this category—it is no more than a tentative record of what the parties have agreed so far and it creates no obligation on them. It merely records their desire to work together in an effort to reach agreement and enter into a contract. Until that happens, neither party has any obligation to the other and can terminate negotiations at any time. For example, in *Cochran v. Norkunas*, 919 A.2d 700 (Md. 2007), the court examined the language and context of a letter of intent to sell real property and found that the parties did not intend to be bound until they had executed a formal contract. In *Janky v. Batistatos*, 559 F. Supp. 2d 923 (N.D. Ind. 2008), the parties had engaged in an email exchange during the course of trying to settle protracted litigation. One of them claimed that the emails constituted a binding settlement agreement, but the court held that they did not. It found the emails to be merely an "agreement to agree" because the parties contemplated the execution of a formal agreement, and the emails did not fully and clearly resolve all the terms that would have to be addressed in the formal contract. *Miller v. Flegenheimer*, 161 A.3d 524 (Vt. 2016), also involved an email exchange that the court found to be a nonbinding preliminary agreement. The transaction involved email negotiations between partners in a business for the proposed buy-out of the one partner's shares by the other. The transaction involved a number of complex provisions that had not been settled by the email exchange, and the emails made it clear that the parties intended the sale to be memorialized in a definitive document. The seller withdrew from the transaction before the definitive memorandum of agreement was finally drafted. The court, emphasizing the usual assumption that parties do not intend to be bound until negotiations have been completed, applied factors similar to those set out in *Teachers Ins. & Annuity Ass'n* and found the emails to be no more than nonbinding preliminary agreements. The emails did not expressly state whether the parties intended them to be binding, but the reference to a forthcoming definitive agreement suggested an intent not to be bound until it was drafted and signed; neither party had rendered any performance; not all the terms had been agreed upon; and an agreement of that complexity would normally be reduced to writing.

§10.6.3 Preliminary Agreements That Bind the Parties to Their Ultimate Objective, So That the Final Memorandum of Agreement Is a Formality

A Type I preliminary agreement is preliminary in form, but despite this form, it is clear that the parties intended to be bound by it. It is in fact a completed contract that does bind the parties to their ultimate objective. Even though it might contemplate that a final and comprehensive memorandum of agreement is still to be executed, the parties intend this to be a formality, rather than a prerequisite to contractual commitment. The crucial quality of a binding Type I agreement, which distinguishes it from a non-binding "agreement to agree," is that it must reflect agreement on all the material terms of the contract. It cannot qualify as a binding commitment to the final objective if there are still important terms to be settled.

§10.6.4 Preliminary Agreements That Bind the Parties to Negotiate in Good Faith

Where parties have not yet resolved a material term of their agreement, the most appropriate conclusion is that they have not yet made a contract. However, even if they have not yet reached final agreement and formed a contract, it is possible that they have made a Type II preliminary agreement that commits them to continue negotiating in good faith to attempt to resolve the outstanding terms.[20] It is possible that the parties expressly agreed to continue negotiation in good faith, which makes it easier to conclude that they did intend to bind themselves to do that. However, in many

---

20. Section 8.9 discusses the possibility that in a rare case, a court may apply promissory estoppel to compensate a party for reliance on a promise made in negotiations. The underlying premise of the cases discussed in section 8.9 (such as *Hoffman v. Red Owl Stores*, 133 N.W.2d 267 (Wis. 1965)) was that the promissory estoppel relief was needed to avert injustice because the promisor had violated a duty to bargain in good faith. Therefore, there is some affinity between what is discussed in section 8.9 and the discussion in this section. However, the important difference is that section 8.9 deals with situations in which there is no contract, but the doctrine of promissory estoppel may apply based on a promise by one party, relied on by the other. This section contemplates the possibility that the parties entered into a preliminary contract in which both of them committed to continue good faith negotiations. Although these situations are conceptually different, courts are reluctant in both to find a commitment to bargain in good faith in the absence of the special circumstances described here and in section 8.9.

cases, this intent is not clear and must be implied from the circumstances of the transaction. Courts are wary of implying an obligation to bargain in good faith because parties who are negotiating usually do not intend to make any promises unless and until they reach final agreement and make a contract. Up to that final stage when the bargain is struck, the usual expectation is that either party can break off negotiations at will for any reason. Neither has any duty to persist in negotiations or to pursue consensus. Both are free to lose interest, make unreasonable demands, or refuse reasonable offers. The only sanction for uncooperative behavior is the possible loss of the deal. Therefore, courts usually interpret a letter of intent or memorandum of understanding that does not qualify as a Type I binding contract as nothing more than a nonbinding expression of intent to work toward a contract. *See*, for example, *Burbach Broadcasting Co. of Delaware v. Elkins Radio Corp.*, 278 F.3d 401 (4th Cir. 2002).

However, it does sometimes happen that the facts are strong enough to imply an obligation to continue good faith negotiations. If so, a court may find that the parties entered into a preliminary contract, subsidiary to the hoped-for final contract, in which each gave consideration by forbearing to exercise the right to terminate negotiations at will and promising to negotiate in good faith in an effort to reach agreement on the principal contract.

This was the conclusion reached in *Brown v. Cara*, 420 F.3d 148 (2d Cir. 2005), the case on which the hypothetical at the beginning of section 10.6.1 is based. The owner of a parking lot in Brooklyn and a construction contractor decided to embark on the development of the lot for commercial and residential use. They entered into a memorandum of understanding in which they agreed to work together to "develop, build, market, and manage a new real estate venture" which they planned for the site. The memorandum of understanding recorded negotiations up to that stage, set out a general framework for the project, allocated responsibility for various tasks that had to be completed, and stated the parties' intent to enter into a formal contract later. One of the first tasks was to apply for rezoning of the property. This task was allocated to the contractor, which completed it successfully, spending considerable effort and resources in drafting preliminary designs, attending public meetings, and lobbying officials. However, negotiations did not proceed smoothly after this, and the owner eventually terminated the collaboration. The contractor sued the owner to enforce the memorandum of understanding. The court held that the parties had not entered into a Type I preliminary agreement. The memorandum of understanding did not bind the parties to the ultimate objective of completing the project because it had not settled all important matters that needed to be resolved in the future and it contemplated further negotiations before a final comprehensive agreement could be executed. However, the court found that the memorandum of understanding was a Type II preliminary agreement that bound the parties to continue to negotiate in good faith in an attempt to reach final agreement. The factors that most influenced the court in reaching this conclusion were that the memorandum of understanding had expressed the parties' agreement to work together toward their ultimate goal; the project was complex and was subject to many contingencies that made it impossible to settle all the terms in advance, so the parties needed to commit to a general framework in advance while leaving details open for later resolution; and the contractor had already made an extensive and valuable contribution to the project by obtaining the rezoning.

As noted at the beginning of this section, it is easier to find a Type II preliminary agreement if the agreement expresses the parties' intent to commit to good faith negotiations. In *Brown*, the memorandum of understanding did not state this in so many words, but its language strongly indicated that the parties considered themselves bound to work together in good faith towards the final agreement. This language was an important factor in finding it to be a Type II agreement. However, sometimes the parties create a confusing situation by including contradictory indications of intent in the preliminary agreement. In *Gas Natural, Inc. v. Iberdrola, S.A.*, 33 F. Supp. 3d 373 (S.D.N.Y. 2014), the parties' letter of intent stated expressly that it was nonbinding and that no obligation would arise until a definitive agreement has been executed. However, elsewhere in the letter it stated that the parties would engage in good faith negotiations over a stated period of time. The court found that the stated obligation to negotiate in good faith weighed more strongly than and qualified the statement that the letter did not create a binding obligation, making the letter a Type II preliminary agreement.

It is one thing to recognize a duty to negotiate in good faith, but quite another to determine, once negotiations have broken down, what conduct constitutes a lack of good faith and whether the failure of agreement is attributable to a breach of the duty. In some situations, it is easy to see that a party made no good faith attempt to negotiate. For example, in *Brown* the owner of the lot terminated negotiations and made no pretense of trying to work through the unresolved issues. Lack of good faith may also be clear where a party does not abandon negotiations, but behaves obstructively, for example, by raising new objections to settled terms or remaining inexplicably obstinate. Lack of good faith is much harder to establish if the party goes through the motions of negotiations with the ulterior resolve not to reach agreement.

In *Apothekernes Laboratorium for Specialpraeparater v. IMC Chemical Group, Inc.*, 873 F.2d 155 (7th Cir. 1989), the court provided some guidance on the general standard imposed by the duty to negotiate in good faith. It said that a party is not required to abandon its interests or to make undesired concessions. Rather the standard contemplates that the party makes a genuine and sincere effort to build on what has been settled and to attempt to resolve differences. In *Gas Natural*, after deciding that the letter of intent did bind the parties to negotiate in good faith, the court had to decide whether the defendant had breached the obligation of good faith by conducting negotiations with another party at the same time, and not telling the plaintiff that it was doing so. The court held that self-interested conduct is not in itself bad faith. Bad faith requires some form of deliberate conduct that is dishonest or aimed at backing out of the commitment. In the absence of a provision committing the defendant to negotiate exclusively with the plaintiff, it was not bad faith for the defendant to simultaneously negotiate with another party to explore the possibility of ultimately making a contract with the other party instead.

Even if a breach of faith can be proved, the victim may have trouble showing the fact and extent of loss. The breach of a contract to bargain in good faith would theoretically give rise to a claim for expectation damages—a monetary award designed to place the plaintiff in the economic position it would have been in had the other party not breached. The problem is that the plaintiff must prove those damages with reasonable certainty, and this is a difficult burden with regard to a contract to bargain in good faith. This is because a promise to negotiate in good faith is not a promise that agreement will be reached but merely a commitment to make honest efforts to reach agreement. The plaintiff therefore has no guarantee and will find it difficult to show with reasonable certainty that good faith negotiations would have led to a contract. Even if the plaintiff can prove that, it may not be able to show what the ultimate contract terms would have been or what gain it would have made from the contract. As a result, in many cases, the plaintiff cannot recover expectation damages because its alleged loss caused by the breach of the duty is too speculative. However, where a party to a contract cannot prove expectation damages, reliance damages are available as an alternative. (This is discussed in sections 18.7 and 18.8.) As in the case of promissory estoppel, reliance damages for breach of the contract to negotiate in good faith aim at reimbursing losses and expenses incurred in reliance on the promise. The effect of this is that damages for the breach of a contract to negotiate in good faith usually turn out to be the same as promissory estoppel damages for reliance on a promise to bargain in good faith, discussed in section 8.9.

§10.7 MISUNDERSTANDING: TOTAL AMBIGUITY

As discussed in section 10.1, interpretation is based on the objective meaning of the language of an agreement, viewed in its context. The goal is to ascertain not what each party thought or believed but what they reasonably appeared to intend. Therefore, when the parties have different understandings of their agreement, the party with the more reasonable understanding prevails.

However, it sometimes happens that while the parties have diametrically opposite understandings of a term, each of their interpretations is entirely reasonable, and there is no basis for preferring one over the other. In such cases, interpretation and construction cannot resolve the uncertainty in the apparent agreement. If the uncertainty relates to a material aspect of the agreement, the only conclusion to be reached is that no contract came into being.

Cases involving this kind of irresoluble clash of reasonable interpretations are rare. One of the few cases involving such a situation is the classic mid-nineteenth-century English case, *Raffles v. Wichelhaus*, 159 Eng. Rep. 375 (Ex. 1864). A buyer and seller agreed to the sale of cotton on board the ship *Peerless* sailing from Bombay. It so happened that there were two ships named *Peerless* due to leave Bombay with a cargo of cotton in October and December, respectively. The seller had the later ship in mind and the buyer the earlier. Neither of them knew of the existence of the second ship. The ship contemplated by the buyer arrived in England first, but the seller did not tender delivery from that ship. In fact, he apparently did not even own that cotton. When the second ship arrived and the seller tendered delivery, the buyer refused to accept the goods, contending that he had bought the cotton on the earlier ship. The seller sued for breach of contract, but the court granted judgment in favor of the buyer on the ground that the misunderstanding prevented a contract from arising.

The doctrinal basis of the opinion is obscure, so it can be (and has been) interpreted simply as an outmoded subjectivist case, in which the court refused to find a contract in the absence of an actual meeting of the parties' minds. However, the case is now widely accepted as illustrating the kind of situation in which even an objective approach cannot resolve the misunderstanding. As each party was reasonable in believing that the agreement referred to a particular ship, and neither had any reason to know of the other's contrary understanding, there is no way to decide whose meaning should be preferred. That is, there is no objective criterion for deciding which ship must have been intended, and a contract on reasonable terms cannot be established. Hence, assuming that the date of delivery is a material term, no contract came into being.

Restatement, Second, §20, in the chapter on contract formation, and §201, in the chapter on interpretation, seek to convey this principle in language so convoluted that it boggles the mind. In essence, the Restatement's rule boils down to this: A material misunderstanding precludes contract formation when the parties were equally innocent in not reasonably realizing the misunderstanding or equally guilty in realizing it but saying nothing. However, if on balancing the degree of fault of the parties, it appears that one is more accountable than the other for knowing of the misunderstanding, a contract must be found to exist on the terms understood by the more innocent party.

Konic International Corp. v. Spokane Computer Services, Inc., 708 P.2d 932 (Idaho 1985), illustrates the *Peerless* principle. A Spokane employee was instructed to investigate the purchase of a surge suppressor. After making inquiries of several sellers, in which he was quoted prices ranging from $50 to $200, he had a telephone conversation with a Konic representative, who had a product suitable for the purpose. When asked the price of the suppressor, the Konic salesman said, "Fifty-six twenty," by which he meant $5,620. However, the Spokane employee, having been used to hearing prices in the $50 to $200 range, assumed he meant $56.20. Spokane ordered and installed the suppressor before this misunderstanding was discovered. Upon realizing what had happened, Spokane tried to return the suppressor, but Konic refused to take it back. Applying *Peerless* and Restatement, Second, §20, the court held that no contract had been concluded because there had been a complete failure of communication. Each party attached a materially different but reasonable meaning to the manifestation, and neither knew or had reason to know the meaning attached by the other.

§10.8 A TRANSNATIONAL PERSPECTIVE ON INTERPRETATION

Both the UNIDROIT Principles and the CISG approach interpretation as a broad inquiry into the language and overall context of the transaction for the purpose of most accurately determining the parties' intent. Article 4.3 of the UNIDROIT Principles identifies as relevant to interpretation the parties' negotiations, their prior dealings, their conduct subsequent to contracting, and usages. Articles 8 and 9 of the CISG are to similar effect.

The CISG requires a contract to be definite, but several articles (for example, Articles 31 and 32) provide gap fillers that may be used in the absence of specific agreement on various terms. Article 55 recognizes that a reasonable price can be supplied in the absence of a stated price. The UNIDROIT Principles also include gap fillers (for example, in Articles 5.1.6 on quality of performance and 5.1.7 on price). Article 2.1.4 adopts a flexible approach to indefinite terms. It allows the court to settle indefinite terms on a reasonable basis unless it is clear that the parties did not intend a contract until they resolved the indefinite term. Article 2.1.15 of the UNIDROIT Principles generally recognizes that parties are not bound until negotiations are complete, but it does impose liability on a party who negotiates in bad faith.

Examples

1. Claire Cutter decided to remove a large oak tree in her front yard. She hired Jack Lumber, a tree remover, to cut it down. Jack has no liability insurance, so he requires his customers to sign a simple one-page written contract that includes the following standard term: "By signing this contract, the customer assumes sole responsibility for any loss, damage, or injury caused by the performance of work under this contract and indemnifies Jack Lumber for any such claims."

   Claire read and signed the contract. Jack began work a few days later. He negligently failed to take proper precautions to ensure that the tree would fall safely. As a result, it crashed down onto Claire's driveway, pulverizing Jack's truck that was parked there. Jack says that the indemnity clause in the contract makes Claire liable to him for the cost of replacing his truck. Is he right?

2. Fairest Fowls, Inc., is a poultry supplier. Gordon Bleu is a trained chef who owns and operates a restaurant. Gordon had often ordered duck and chicken from Fairest Fowls before. Although he had always ordered the cheaper quality "regular" birds, rather than the more expensive "gourmet" quality, he had always been well satisfied.

   Gordon decided to begin serving more exotic game birds at his restaurant. He found a recipe for pheasant and checked Fairest Fowls' price list to see what it cost. The list showed "regular" pheasant for $5.00 per pound, and "plump deluxe" pheasant for $12.50 per pound. Gordon ordered and received 50 pounds of the "regular" quality.[21] He prepared the birds according to his recipe. When they were cooked, he tasted them and discovered that they were tough and uneatable. He called Fairest Fowls to complain. Fairest Fowls' representative expressed surprise that Gordon did not know what was "common knowledge" in the trade—that "regular" pheasants were old, scrawny birds, sold only for making soup. The more expensive "plump deluxe" variety were intended for eating.

   After being told this, Gordon asked some other chefs and wholesale poultry suppliers (eight people in all) if they knew about the distinction between "regular" and "plump deluxe" pheasants. Five of them were fully aware of it and used the same terminology in their businesses. Two did not know the terminology, but they knew that you

21. The order was oral, but as the total price of the birds was $250, the statute of frauds is not applicable. Also, because there is no recorded memorial of agreement, the parol evidence rule does not apply to complicate matters. This same contract, in recorded form, is used in Example 4 of Chapter 12 to illustrate the impact that the parol evidence rule would have on the resolution of this interpretational issue.

could not buy eatable pheasant for $5.00 per pound. One had never heard the terminology and would have assumed that you could eat regular pheasant.

In light of this, did Fairest Fowls breach the contract by delivering uneatable birds to Gordon?

3. Beau Teek operates a clothing store in a shopping mall under a five-year lease. One of the terms of the lease gives Beau the option to renew the lease for a further period of five years "at a rental to be agreed at the time of renewal in light of the prevailing economic conditions."

   Beau properly exercised his option to renew within the time specified in the lease. Although the parties tried to agree on rent for the renewal period, they were unable to reach consensus. The lessor called on Beau to vacate the premises, but he refused to leave and commenced suit for specific performance, requesting that the court order the lessor to extend the lease for a five-year period at a rent determined by the court to be reasonable. Should the court grant the order and determine a reasonable rent?

4. Jill Loppy agreed to sell her old car to Carr Less. They wrote out the following on a piece of paper and both signed it: "Jill Loppy agrees to sell her 2015 Chev to Carr Less for 90 percent of its retail Bluebook value."

   The next day, Jill changed her mind and no longer wished to sell her car. She claims that she does not have a binding contract with Carr and points out that the piece of writing is too skimpy to be a contract because it does not fully describe the car, has an indefinite price term, and omits many essential terms. In particular, it makes no mention of the delivery and payment obligations and does not say if the car is sold with or without any warranty. Furthermore, these issues were not discussed by the parties. Is this a good argument?

5. Lacey Lingerie, is a budding fashion designer. She entered into an agreement with Deadwood Design Agency, a fashion design agent, under which Lacey granted Deadwood the exclusive right for two years to sell her fashion designs. In consideration, Deadwood promised to pay Lacey half of all profits and revenues that it earned from any such sales. Lacey delivered her extensive portfolio of designs to Deadwood.

   Hearing nothing from Deadwood for a month, Lacey called to find out how sales were going. Deadwood told her that sales were slow, but she should be patient because things would pick up soon. After waiting another month, Lacey received a check for $300 from Deadwood, her 50 percent share of earnings for the sale of two designs for small garments. In a note accompanying the check, Deadwood apologized for the small return, saying that it hoped to do better in the future.

About two weeks later Lacey ran into one of her classmates from design school. The classmate told Lacey that he had been approaching manufacturers directly and had sold over $2,000 worth of designs in the last six weeks. Lacey would like to dump Deadwood. Can she do so without breaching the contract?

6. Woody Cutter owned a sawmill. His business was failing, and he had accumulated debts of $1.5 million. He decided to sell the sawmill, which was appraised at $3.5 million. Empire Building Products Co. wished to buy a sawmill. It heard that Woody's mill was on the market, so it approached him to negotiate a sale. After several weeks of meetings, involving attorneys, accountants, and technical advisors, the parties had reached agreement on all the terms of the sale except price. They were deadlocked on this issue. Empire had refused to pay more than $2.5 million. However, Woody refused to take less than $4 million for it. The parties therefore felt that a cooling-off period would be useful, and they agreed to meet two weeks later to see if they could resolve their differences on price. They signed a joint memorandum drafted by their attorneys, setting out the terms on which they agreed so far, and recording simply that they would meet on a stated day to continue discussions on price.

   Empire's board met just before negotiations were to resume. Realizing that Woody was under pressure to sell and that he had no other prospective buyer, the board decided not to budge on the $2.5 million price. They knew that this would be a bargain because of the $3.5 million appraised value of the mill. At about this same time, Woody, reviewing his precarious financial position, decided not to hold out for his asking price but to come down as low as $3.2 million, which he realized was below the mill's true value.

   When the meeting took place as arranged, Woody made great efforts to persuade Empire to close the gap between the price proposals, but Empire refused to consider anything above $2.5 million. As a result, the negotiations terminated in failure. Unable to sell his sawmill, Woody could not pay his debts. His creditors seized his sawmill in execution and sold it at auction. Because prices at such execution sales are depressed, the sawmill sold for $1.5 million. Woody claims that had Empire negotiated with him in good faith, they would have reached agreement on the sale of the sawmill for $3.2 million, which would have been enough to pay his creditors with a significant surplus over for him. Woody has sued Empire for $1.7 million, the difference between $3.2 million and the execution sale price of $1.5 million. Is he entitled to those damages?

7. Molly Fido owned a profitable and successful restaurant. She decided to sell the business and she solicited inquiries by placing an advertisement in a trade journal. Faith Fullness responded and they met to discuss

the possible sale. At their initial meeting, Faith examined the premises, equipment, and financial records and the parties had extensive but inconclusive discussions about price. Faith expressed strong interest in buying the business and they agreed to meet again in a week. During that week, Faith visited the restaurant several times to observe the operations, service, and customer traffic. She visited her bank to discuss financing and spoke to a couple of potential investors to see if she could raise some capital. Everything looked promising, and she became enthusiastic about buying the business.

At their next meeting, Faith and Molly discussed the sale in earnest. After some hours they had reached agreement in principle on the basic terms of the sale, which Faith wrote down on a yellow legal pad: Faith would pay Molly $750,000 for the equipment, name, goodwill, lease rights, and transferrable licenses. A third of the price would be paid upon the signing of a written agreement, and the balance would be paid in installments over two years. Faith would take over the business and receive transfer of its assets as soon as possible after the agreement was signed, and Molly would remain on as an employee of the business for six months at a salary to be mutually decided. Faith would immediately instruct her attorney to draw a written contract reflecting these terms and dealing with any necessary matters of detail that the parties had not thought of. Later that day, Faith consulted her attorney and gave the attorney the pad with the notes of the meeting. The attorney promised to set to work as soon as possible on drafting the memorandum of agreement.

The next day, Molly received a call from Ruth Less who had also read the advertisement. Molly told Ruth that she had almost certainly sold the business already, but agreed to meet with Ruth anyhow. After a whole day's negotiations, during which Molly disclosed to Ruth the terms of the understanding with Faith, Ruth made a very attractive offer. She is willing to buy the business for $900,000 cash. Molly would like to accept the offer but is unsure if she has legally committed herself to Faith. Has she?

8. Kay Nine's black poodle, named "Raffles," had wandered from home and Kay could not find him. She therefore placed a homemade poster on a lamppost near her home reading, "Lost Dog—Reward $100. If anyone sees a black poodle with the name tag "Raffles" on his collar, please bring him to 1864 Bombay St. to receive this reward." Pierre Less saw the poster. The next day Pierre came across a black poodle which was scurrying about the neighborhood in a state of distress. He looked at the poodle's collar and saw that he had a name tag showing his name as "Raffles." Pierre took Raffles to the address on the poster but Kay would not accept the dog, claiming that it was not her Raffles. It turned out, by strange coincidence unknown to both parties, that another black poodle

named Raffles had wandered from his home and had become lost in the neighborhood. The poodle that Pierre found was the wrong one. Nevertheless, Pierre feels that he went to a lot of trouble on the faith of the poster and he wants his reward. Is he entitled to it?

9. An insurance policy on a commercial building excluded from coverage any damage caused by "flood, water overflow, mudslide, or mudflow." However, it did cover damage resulting from "fire or explosion." During a torrential rain, water and mud flowed down a hill behind the insured's building, colliding with it violently. The force of the fast-flowing mud smashed the building into debris, which was thrown in all directions. The insured submitted a claim for the demolished building. The insurer denied the claim on the ground that the building was destroyed by a mudslide, which was excluded from coverage under the terms of the policy. The insured disagrees, and argues that the building was destroyed by an explosion—the force of the mud hitting the building caused it to explode into pieces, which were flung by the force in all directions. The policy does not define "explosion" and there is no contextual evidence, such as discussions between the parties or trade usage, that might help in determining its meaning. It must therefore be interpreted based on its plain meaning in the context of the policy as a whole. Does the insured have a good argument that the building was destroyed by an explosion, not a mudslide, and is therefore covered by the policy?

Explanations

1. The question here is whether the indemnity clause is broad enough to impose liability on Claire for loss suffered by Jack as a result of damage he negligently inflicted on his own property in the course of his performance. It is best not to ridicule Jack's claim—he is handy with a chainsaw.

   This Example invokes *Pacific Gas and Electric Co.* (discussed in section 10.5.1), in which the court held that extrinsic evidence had to be admitted to decide whether an indemnity provision in a repair contract covered damage to machinery belonging to the owner or applied only to claims of third parties. In Jack's case, there is no similar concern about admitting extrinsic evidence of meaning because neither party offers any such evidence. Where there is no contextual evidence that bears on the meaning of contractual language, the court is necessarily confined to finding meaning on the basis of the language used in the document.

   The argument could be made that the language used in this contract is wide enough to cover damage to Jack's truck. It places on Claire the "sole responsibility for . . . damage . . . caused by the performance of work under this contract." This may suggest that she is responsible for any damage that may occur during the course of performance, whatever its kind, and whoever its victim may be. However, this interpretation is overborne by other indications of reasonable intent in the contract.

The words "indemnifies . . . Jack . . . for any such claims" suggest that the contract contemplates that Claire is responsible only to protect Jack from third-party claims. This meaning makes sense in light of the purpose of the clause: work is being done on Claire's property, and she therefore assumes responsibility for any loss suffered by a third party as a result of the work. The trial court in *Pacific Gas* did make the point that "indemnifies" is capable of a broader meaning. However, that case was concerned with damage to the owner's property, not the repairer's. Even if the language can be taken to extend beyond third-party liability, it surely cannot mean that Claire should be responsible for damage caused by Jack to his own property as a result of his own negligence. Such an interpretation seems absurd, and it is most unlikely that Claire reasonably expected a generally worded indemnity provision to impose liability on her for Jack's self-inflicted injury.

In addition to being beyond Claire's reasonable expectations, such a provision is not in the public interest. Courts usually require a very specific disclaimer of liability to exclude damage caused by a party's negligence.[22] A fortiori, a generally worded provision like this cannot give Jack the right to seek compensation from Claire for damage caused by his own negligence. This conclusion is also in accord with the interpretation principle that where the meaning of language is in doubt, a court should choose an interpretation that is reasonable and in accord with public policy. Finally, if doubt still remains over the proper interpretation of the clause, the *contra proferentum* rule may be used to resolve the doubt against Jack, the drafter of the indemnity provision.

2. This is a sale of goods under UCC Article 2, but interpretation of the agreement is based on the same principles as those applied in current common law. UCC §1.303 recognizes the primacy of express terms but also articulates the importance of trade usage and course of dealing in the ascertainment of meaning.

   This Example is loosely based on the famous chicken case, *Frigaliment Importing*, discussed in section 10.1.3. The principles set out in that case are helpful in resolving this dispute. The ordinary meaning of language is the point of departure, but "regular" has many meanings. Possibly Gordon's prior dealings would support his interpretation that a "regular" bird is eatable, but the prior contracts are not very helpful as a course

---

22. *See* section 13.3.3a for a discussion of the public policy issues relating to liability disclaimers. Such disclaimers are also the subject matter of the Examples in Chapter 3.

of dealing because they involved different birds and distinguished "regular" quality from "gourmet," not "plump deluxe." Therefore, the bare surface meaning of "regular" is not dispositive of its meaning in the contract. The entire context in which it was used must be examined, and this context indicates that Fairest Fowls' meaning should prevail.

Sometimes other terms in a contract can cast light on the meaning of the term in dispute, so courts interpret language in the context of the agreement as a whole. For example, in *Frigaliment Importing*, the contract's price term was of some help in supporting the seller's argument that "chicken" was used generically, rather than more narrowly to refer only to fryers. It reflected a different price per pound for the larger and smaller chickens, and the price of the larger chickens was below the market price of fryers. The Example does not mention any terms in this contract that could explain what the parties meant by "regular," and the price term is not as helpful because it does not reflect comparative prices for different types of pheasant.

More significantly, the preliminary information on trade usage strongly supports the meaning claimed by Fairest Fowls. (If the dispute goes to litigation, trade usage would have to be established by sworn expert testimony, but Gordon's informal survey is good enough for present purposes.) Gordon asked chefs and suppliers what they understood "regular" pheasants to mean. Although they were not unanimous in their response, there seems to be widespread recognition in the trade (defined here as the wholesale poultry market) that the word "regular" refers to pheasants that can be used only to make soup. To prove a trade usage, a party needs only establish it on the preponderance of the evidence. A severe clash of the experts could result in failure to discharge this burden, but there does not need to be unanimity to make a credible showing. As a professional chef who buys poultry from suppliers, Gordon is surely a member of this trade. Even if he did not actually know what "regular" meant, he had reason to know the usage and is bound by it.

3. The term relating to the rental for the renewal period is unquestionably vague. It suggests an "agreement to agree," but it does seek to limit the parties' discretion in negotiating by stating a standard: the economic conditions prevailing at the time of renewal. Although the rent provision in this lease is not as tortured and nonsensical as the one in *Walker v. Keith* described in section 10.5, it may not be any more workable, and a court may refuse to give effect to the renewal agreement. However, there is a plausible argument for upholding it because the rental provision does refer to what could be seen as a market-based standard, albeit poorly expressed. It is not a great leap beyond their expressed intent for a court to determine and apply a reasonable market standard if they cannot reach

agreement. In so doing it upholds an apparent serious intent to be bound and conforms to the rule of interpretation that favors an effective meaning over one that renders the term ineffective.

4. Jill does not make a good argument. This is a sale of goods, and the UCC is very clear on the question of omitted terms. Section 2.204(3) states that a contract for sale does not fail for indefiniteness, even though terms are left open, provided that the parties intended to make a contract and there is a reasonably certain basis for giving a remedy. In addition, Article 2 contains a number of gap fillers that apply to any agreement for the sale of goods in the absence of contrary provisions expressed by the parties. As a result, this skimpy-looking contract is much fuller than Jill suggests.

   The goods sold need not be fully described in the writing. Because Jill owned only one 2015 Chev, the identity of the car is not uncertain, and it can be established by oral testimony. The parties need not fix a specific price, as long as they have indicated an objective market standard or some other reasonably certain means of determining it. This agreement expresses a workable market standard. (Even had it not done so, UCC §2.305 provides the gap filler of a reasonable price unless it is apparent that the parties did not intend to contract for a reasonable price.) If any of the remaining terms had been settled orally by the parties and just not stated in the writing, oral evidence of their actual agreement would establish these terms. In the absence of any such agreement (and any applicable usage and course of dealing or performance), the UCC provides an array of supplementary terms that cover most of aspects of an ordinary agreement for the sale of goods:

   a. Jill is obliged to transfer and deliver the goods, and Carr must accept and pay for them (§2.301).
   b. Jill accomplishes tender of delivery by holding the car available for collection by Carr at Jill's home at a reasonable hour and for a reasonable period (§§2.308 and 2.503). In addition, because the state requires registration of transfer of title for motor vehicles, Jill must tender the certificate of title, endorsed to enable Carr to register the change of title to himself.
   c. Jill must tender the delivery within a reasonable time (§2.309).
   d. Carr must pay for the goods in cash on receiving them (§2.310).
   e. Jill warrants that she has good title to the goods (§2.312).[23]

23. The UCC provides for other implied warranties in §§2.314 and 2.315, but they are not applicable on the facts of this case—§2.314 applies only to merchant sellers, and §2.315 applies only where the buyer relies on the seller's expertise to furnish goods required for a particular purpose.

5. As in *Wood v. Lucy, Lady Duff-Gordon*, discussed in sections 10.1.1 and 10.2.2, the inference from the underlying commercial purpose of the contract is that Deadwood impliedly promised to make best efforts to place Lacey's designs. In *Wood*, the court did not have to decide whether Wood had satisfied the standard of best efforts because that was not in issue in the case. It was not Wood's duty to Lucy that was in question, but Lucy's duty to Wood—Lucy had sold designs herself in violation of the agreement, and Wood sued her for his share of the profits. Therefore, in *Wood*, the court just needed to imply the obligation of best efforts to reject Lucy's argument that Wood gave no consideration for her promise. However, in this Example, Deadwood's performance is in issue because Lacey asserts that Deadwood has fallen short of best efforts. It is therefore necessary to decide what level of effort would satisfy Deadwood's obligation to use best efforts.

   Unless the contract defines what constitutes best efforts, this is decided by examining both the reasonable expectation in the trade and the scope and resources of Deadwood's operation. The standard is a blend of reasonable efforts (evaluated objectively) and honest efforts (measured subjectively). The example does not give enough information to decide whether Deadwood's efforts would qualify. Deadwood apparently had very little success, and Lacey's classmate did better without representation. But that, on its own, is not enough to prove that Deadwood breached its obligation of best efforts. The test is not one of result but of endeavor.

6. The parties clearly did not have a final contract at the end of their first set of negotiations. The price term was unresolved and there is no indication that they intended to be bound unless it was settled. This is not a case in which it would be justifiable to infer that they agreed to a sale at a reasonable or market price.

   Therefore, the only basis of liability is that the parties had entered into a Type II preliminary agreement that bound Empire to continue negotiating in good faith, which it breached by standing firm and refusing to negotiate further on the price. Negotiations are normally precursors to legal commitment, and they do not in themselves usually give rise to any legal obligations. In most cases, until the parties actually reach agreement and conclude a contract, neither assumes the legal duty to keep negotiating or to try to reach consensus. This has to be the general rule otherwise it would become difficult to distinguish negotiation from agreement, and entering into negotiations would carry too high a risk of liability. As stated in section 10.6, courts are concerned about hampering negotiations by imposing a duty of good faith negotiation and are cautious about implying such an obligation except in the most compelling cases.

In this case, the parties had proceeded quite far in their negotiations and had agreed to meet further to try to resolve their differences over the purchase price. Empire knew that Woody was in trouble, he needed to sell, and his options for preserving his business were running out as time passed. It deliberately used his distress to obtain bargaining leverage. A great deal of energy had gone into negotiations already, and substantial consensus had been reached. Given Empire's apparent interest in the transaction and its willingness to meet again, these facts could support the conclusion Empire had the duty to return to the bargaining table in a spirit of honest compromise. However, this is not an easy case to make because Woody has to overcome the usual presumption, in the absence of an express commitment, that the parties do not intend to make binding commitments in negotiations. To overturn the presumption, the relationship between the parties must be close enough, and the contributions made to the transaction by one or both parties are substantial enough that the parties can reasonably be seen to have assumed an extraordinary duty of collaboration.

If an obligation to bargain in good faith is implied in this case, the next question is what Empire must have done to satisfy it. Bad faith is easy to identify in situations where a party simply refuses to negotiate, but it is much more difficult to define in close cases where there is a thin dividing line between bad faith and acceptable commercial hardball. It would not in itself have been bad faith for Empire to make a business decision to stick to its price limit. A party should not be compelled to pay more than it desires. However, when Empire's knowledge of Woody's circumstances and its motive for the refusal to budge are taken into account, its insistence on the low price looks decidedly less wholesome. This is particularly so given Woody's concessions that considerably narrowed the price gap between them.

If Empire did breach its duty to bargain in good faith, Woody's remedy is not likely to be the expectation damages that he claims, based on the difference between the $3.2 million he wished to get for the property and the $1.5 million execution sale proceeds. The problem with this claim is that it assumes that had Empire bargained in good faith, the parties would eventually have made a contract and that they would have settled on a price of $3.2 million. Woody may be able to prove this on the preponderance of the evidence, but it is more likely that he will not be able to show that good faith negotiations would have led to a contract and, if they did, what the sale price would have been. Therefore, Woody's chance of recovering expectation damages is poor. At best, he might be able to recover reliance damages based on any cost and expense that he wasted in the course of the negotiation.

7. When parties have agreed in principle to the essential terms of a contract, but they contemplate executing a formal, signed record, the legal effect

of their oral or informal[24] agreement may be unclear if they do not specifically express the intended effect of the oral or informal understanding. They may have intended no commitment whatever until the writing is signed. Conversely, they may have concluded a contract already, subject merely to the formality of writing. As a third possibility, even if they have not yet made a final commitment, they may at least have undertaken to bargain over the unresolved issues in good faith. Their purpose must be determined from all the circumstances of their interaction.

All the usual avenues should be explored for helpful indications of intent: the language of agreement itself, statements or actions during negotiations, trade usage, and course of dealings or performance. No facts are given to suggest that there is any specific trade usage, and there is no indication of prior dealing or subsequent performance, so the only source of information is the circumstances of the transaction itself, evaluated in light of usual commercial standards. *Teachers Insurance & Annuity Ass'n v. Tribune Co*, cited in section 10.6.1, identifies several factors to be taken into account in deciding how to categorize a preliminary agreement. The most important are whether the agreement indicates the parties' intent on the binding effect of the agreement; whether there has been partial performance; whether all the terms have been settled; and whether the agreement is of the type that would usually be committed to a final and formal writing. Comment *c* to Restatement, Second, §27 suggests a similar set of factors, which include considerations such as the extent of the express agreement; the nature and extent of unresolved issues; whether it is normal practice—or, stronger still, legally required—to put a contract of this kind in writing; and the value and complexity of the transaction.

There are some indications that suggest that the parties did not yet intend to be fully bound in contract. The sale of a business is a commercial exchange of a relatively complex and valuable nature, and it seems reasonable to assume that parties would normally expect to sign a full and formal recorded memorandum before being bound. This assumption is strengthened by the fact that a number of known or possible issues were left unresolved. Not only did they deliberately leave open the salary to be paid to Molly for her work in the six months following the sale, but they also anticipated further unidentified issues to emerge when Faith's attorney drafted a comprehensive record. Some of these

24. The term "oral or informal" indicates that the preliminary understanding could either be oral or in some recorded form short of a final contract. In this Example, the parties' agreement was oral, but it was noted down in an unsigned writing on a yellow pad. As discussed in section 10.7, an agreement in principle could be even more formal, and could be recorded as a signed memorandum of understanding or a letter of intent, which memorializes what has been agreed and provides a framework for further negotiation.

may be trivial, but some could be significant and contentious. These are merely indications. They are not conclusive, and an argument can be made for the opposite result. It is therefore conceivable that Molly and Faith had entered a binding contract of sale at the conclusion of negotiations. If so, Molly risks legal liability if she reneges.

If Molly and Faith did not enter a binding contract, the other alternatives are that there is simply no contract, or that the parties at least agreed to bargain in good faith on unresolved issues, promising to sign unless they encounter a genuine deal breaker. The circumstances are ambiguous and may not be strong enough to deprive Molly of her normal right to abandon these negotiations in favor of a better deal. The facts do not indicate the level of trust, commitment, or reliance discussed in section 10.6 and Example 6. Nevertheless, Faith's dealings with Molly are quite far advanced, the parties have reached substantial agreement on most apparently material terms, and Molly has at least given some implicit assurance that there are no obstacles to the completion of the transaction. It is therefore possible that a court may find that they had reached a stage that precluded Molly from walking away from the deal.

If this is so, it does not invariably mean that Faith is entitled to relief, because she has to prove economic loss. As stated in Example 6, this means that to recover expectation damages, she will have to prove both that the contract probably would have resulted but for Molly's refusal to proceed further and that following the purchase of the business, she would have been reasonably likely to have made profits in a reasonably certain amount. In the absence of this proof, she may be awarded reliance damages if any reliance loss was suffered. Even if the parties had committed to continue to negotiate in good faith, the facts do not indicate that Molly incurred any losses or expenses in reliance on that commitment. (Molly may have incurred some expenses relating to her inquiries before the second meeting, but these were not incurred in reliance on any promise and are therefore not recoverable.)

8. By placing the poster on the lamppost, Kay made an offer for a unilateral contract, which Pierre sought to accept by the act of returning a dog called Raffles to Kay.[25] The answer to this Example could be that although Pierre intended to accept, he did not in fact do so because return of the wrong dog was not performance of the act required for acceptance. However, if the offer is read literally, Pierre's act could be an acceptance because the poster simply offers the reward to anyone who "brings" to the stated address a lost black poodle with the name tag "Raffles" on his collar. Pierre performed that act exactly as specified, even though it was

25. Unilateral contracts are explained in section 4.12.

not what Kay had in mind. Kay intended to refer to her own dog, but her subjective intent is not determinative.

However, even if Pierre prevails on the offer and acceptance issue, he is not likely to get his reward. While the objective test holds Kay to the reasonable meaning of her words, it presupposes that it is possible to determine the reasonable meaning of the disputed language. If the parties have different understandings of a word and the court cannot say which of them is more reasonable, the objective test cannot resolve the dispute and the conclusion must be that the agreement is subject to a fatal and irresoluble ambiguity. On the principle of *Raffles v. Wichelhaus*, as embodied in Restatement, Second, §20 (*see* section 10.8), there can be no contract, even under the objective test, if the double meaning of the name cannot be settled by recourse to its most reasonable meaning and the parties are equally blameless for the misunderstanding. Maybe Kay can be faulted for the way that she worded her poster, but she probably cannot be held accountable for failing to anticipate the bizarre coincidence that there were two lost black poodles called Raffles in the neighborhood.

9. Unquestionably, the building was destroyed by the mudslide. However, the insured argues that the mudslide hit the building with such force that it caused the building to explode. Since there is no contextual evidence available, it's time to open the trusty dictionary to see what "explode" means. It turns out that the dictionary includes a number of definitions of "explode" that support the insured's argument, such as "break or burst forth," "resound with a sudden loud noise," "shatter with a loud report," and "change state or appearance expansively and suddenly." The problem is that all these definitions are figurative. The dictionary also includes the literal definition of "explode" which favors the insurer's interpretation: "to undergo rapid combustion with sudden release of energy in the form of heat that causes violent expansion of the gases formed and consequent production of great disruptive pressure and a loud noise" or, more simply, "to burst violently as a result of pressure within." The shortcoming of using a dictionary to ascertain plain meaning is that dictionaries commonly provide several definitions of words, which can be quite different. In this case, some definitions support the insured while others support the insurer. There are two reasons why the insurer's meaning should prevail. First, unless the context clearly appears otherwise, a contractual document is not a literary work, so it presumptively uses words literally, not figuratively. Second, an interpretation of "explosion" in the context of the contract as a whole should give effect, as far as possible, to every term of the contract. The insured's meaning of "explosion," which would cover violent destruction resulting from a mudslide, essentially negates the mudslide exclusion. This was the court's conclusion in *Paros Properties v. Colorado Casualty Insurance Co.*, 835 F.3d

1264 (10th Cir. 2016), the case on which this Example is based. The court expressed the standard rule of interpretation that the court should try to give effect to the reasonable expectations of the parties by giving words in the policy their plain and ordinary meaning in the context of the policy as a whole, and resolving remaining ambiguity against the insurer as the drafting party. On this basis, the court recognized that the word could be used in the figurative meaning advanced by the insured, but rejected that meaning because there was no basis to find that the parties meant "explosion" in its figurative sense, and such an interpretation would undermine the term that excluded coverage of damage caused by a mudslide. This resolved the ambiguity in the word, so it was not necessary to use the tiebreaker rule of construing the term against the drafter.

CHAPTER 11

The Statute of Frauds

§11.1 INTRODUCTION

As a general rule, the law gives effect to oral contracts. Although it is almost always a good idea to record a contract (whether in a physical writing or in some other retrievable form) to facilitate proof of the fact and terms of agreement, for many contracts this record is not a prerequisite to validity or enforceability. However, certain types of contract fall outside this general rule and must be recorded, either on a tangible written document or in electronic form, and signed to be enforceable. The requirement of a written record for specified types of contracts was originally enacted in an English statute, "An Act for Prevention of Fraud and Perjuries," in 1677. American jurisdictions enacted statutes modeled on the original English statute, covering much the same types of contracts.[1]

The basic rule of the statute of frauds (referred to in this chapter as "the statute") is that a contract within its scope may not be enforced unless a memorandum of it is recorded[2] and signed by the party to be charged.

1. In addition to the original statute of frauds, states have enacted statutes that impose the requirement of record on other types of contract. These are not discussed here.

2. Although the traditional statute of frauds focused on tangible writing, it is universally accepted in contemporary law that electronic records and other forms of retrievable recording satisfy the "writing" requirement of the statute. For this reason, "record" is used here instead of "writing" unless the facts of a case, a hypothetical, or an Example indicate that the document in question is a tangible paper document. In addition, as discussed in section 11.3.3, an electronic signature is also valid.

The principal function of the statute is evidentiary—to provide reliable evidence, in the form of an adequate signed record, of the contract's existence and terms, and to prevent a person from seeking to enforce an alleged obligation purely on the basis of unreliable and possibly perjured oral testimony. As noted above, this concern about the false claim of an oral contract only applies to the types of contract that are covered by the statute (or by some other law requiring recording), and does not extend to the many types of contract for which this formality is not required.

The statute does not require the entire contract to be recorded, but only a memorandum of it. The degree to which a record must set out the detail and content of the contract to qualify as a sufficient memorandum is discussed in section 11.3.2. The record need not be signed by both parties. Only the party who is to be charged, that is, against whom enforcement is sought, needs to have signed it. The question of what constitutes a signature is discussed in section 11.3.3.

Although the goal of the statute is to prevent a person from enforcing a falsely alleged contract through perjured testimony, it can be abused by the party against whom enforcement is sought to evade an oral contract that was genuinely made but not recorded in compliance with the statute. Courts recognize this and apply the statute with some degree of flexibility to reduce opportunities for abuse. This flexibility is apparent in the approach to applying the statute described in the rest of this chapter.

To determine whether problems of enforcement exist under the statute, it is useful to ask three questions in the order represented in Diagram 11A.

§11.2 THE FIRST INQUIRY: IS THE CONTRACT OF A TYPE THAT FALLS WITHIN THE STATUTE?

The original statute covered six types of contract. Although additional statutes have been enacted to require recording for some other types of contracts, these six have been remarkably durable, considering that the types of contract covered by the statute are more reflective of the commercial priorities of seventeenth-century England than of today's economy. The following subsections of this section describe the six categories of contracts that were included in the original statute and continue to be subject to the traditional statute as enacted in American states. (The categories are listed in Restatement, Second, §110 and expanded on in subsequent Restatement sections.) The first three—contracts for the sale of land or an interest in land, contracts that cannot be performed in a year, and sales of goods—cover more common types of transactions. They are the dominant categories and are more likely to be encountered. The last three—suretyships, executors'

Diagram 11A

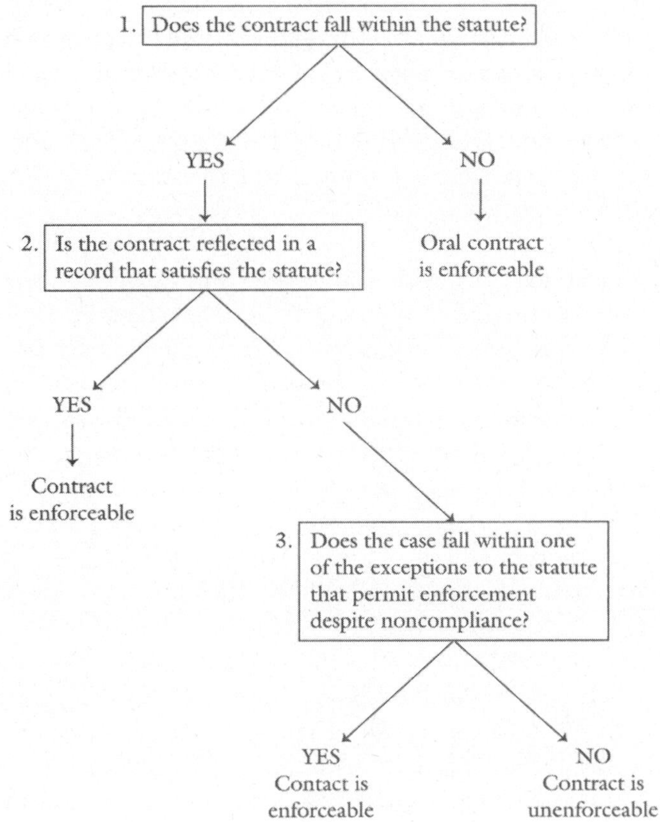

contracts to answer for a duty of the decedent, and contracts made upon consideration of marriage—relate to a narrower range of more specialized contracts and are merely described in this section, without further discussion in the rest of this chapter. Each of the six types of contract is explained below.

§11.2.1 Contracts for the Sale of Land or an Interest in Land

Like many rules derived from older English law, this rule reflects the importance of land as the principal means of wealth in English society at the time. The statute applies not only to a contract to sell land but also to any contract under which land is disposed of by other means, as well as a transfer of an interest in land short of full ownership, such as the grant or transfer of an easement or mortgage. A lease is also an interest in land. The statute of frauds usually applies to long-term leases, but commonly is not applicable to short-term leases. The statute only applies if the contract is in fact the sale of an interest in land. In *Thies v. Wheelock*, 100 N.E.3d 903 (Ohio Ct. App. 2017), Theis and Wheelock agreed orally that they would bid jointly on five parcels of real property. Wheelock would make the bids on behalf of both of them and if his bid was successful, Wheelock would take title to three of the parcels and Thies would take title to two of them. Wheelock's bid was successful, but he refused to allow title of the two parcels to be transferred to Thies and took title to all five parcels himself. Thies sued, and Wheelock raised the defense that even if they had entered into a contract, it would be a contract for the sale of land, and therefore unenforceable under the statute. The court rejected this defense on the ground that although the agreement concerned land, it was not a contract for the transfer of an interest in land—neither party owned the property at the time of the contract. The transfer of the land would only occur at a later stage between the owner and the buyer. Thies could therefore enforce Wheelock's oral agreement to transfer the two parcels to him.

§11.2.2 Contracts That Cannot Be Performed Within a Year

Any contract, irrespective of its subject matter, must comply with the statute if it cannot be performed within a year of its execution. The one-year period does not relate to the length of performance but the period between the making of the contract and the end of performance. Therefore, the rule is not confined to contracts that will take a year or more to perform, but also includes any contract that involves a short performance that is not due to be completed until a year or more from the date of execution. Therefore, if on July 2, 2024, a customer makes a contract with a popular resort to rent a room for July 3 and 4, 2025, the contract falls within the statute, even though the performance will last only two days.

The apparent rationale for the rule is that if the contractual performance cannot be completed within a year of the contract's execution, it should be recorded so that proof of it is not dependent on the parties' fading memory of the interaction that led to its alleged formation and of its terms. The one-year period is arbitrary—if the parties in the above example made their contract on July 5, 2024, the statute would not apply.

The one-year rule clearly applies where the contract commits a party to a period of performance that, by the express or implied terms of the contract, cannot be completed within a year of the execution of the contract. That is, it would be a violation of the contract for the party to cease performance before the end of the period. For example, on June 1 the owner of a building enters into a two-year contract with a property management company for the day-to-day management of the building, including such matters as rent collection, tenant services, janitorial services, and security.

By its nature, the clear purpose of this contract is that the management company will continue to perform its ongoing duties for the entire contract period. The performance is not of the kind that could be accelerated so that the management company could work extra hard to get done with its management duties in 11 months. The contract must be interpreted to determine if it is one that permits acceleration of performance. In *Holloway v. Bucher*, 2018 WL 3957097 (Ohio Ct. App. 2018), an oral loan agreement provided for repayment of the loan by monthly installments which, based on the amount to be paid each month, clearly would take more than a year to pay off. Although it seems logical to assume that the borrower could have completed performance within a year of contract formation by repaying the loan early, the court found that the contract did not permit an early payoff. It was therefore subject to the statute.

The application of the one-year rule is less certain where the contract does not require the performance to last more than a year, but by its nature, the performance is not likely to be completed within a year of contract formation. For example, the owner of a building hires a construction contractor to renovate the building. The renovation work is extensive and would normally take about 14 months to complete, so the contract provides for a completion date 14 months in the future. However, there is nothing in the contract that forbids the contractor from completing the work early, and in fact the owner would be very pleased if that happened. Therefore, the builder could theoretically work longer hours and accelerate the project to get it done in 11 months. Some courts interpret the one-year rule narrowly and hold that it does not apply to a contract in which performance is expected to extend beyond a year from formation, but it would not be a breach to complete it within a year of its execution. Other courts adopt a broader test and hold that a contract falls within the rule, either if a party would violate it by completing performance within a year of execution, or if it would be factually impossible for the party to do so.

Where a contract is of indefinite duration, courts generally do not treat it as falling within the one-year rule, provided that the contract performance could conceivably be completed within a year, or the contract allows for a party to terminate it within a year. In *Knigge v. B&L Food Stores, Inc.*, 890 N.W.2d 570 (S.D. 2017), the court held that a long-term employment contract did not fall within the one-year rule because the contract gave one of the parties the right to terminate it within the year. In *Leon v. Kelly*, 618 F.Supp.2d 1334 (D.N.M. 2008), the court held that the statute did not apply to a partnership agreement for an indefinite term because the contract was capable of being completed in a year: Even though the agreement contemplated a long-term business endeavor expected to last for several years, a partner had the right to dissociate from the partnership and dissolve it at any time. In *Browning v. Poirier*, 165 So.3d 663 (Fla. 2015), the parties were in a romantic relationship. In 1993 they agreed orally that each of them would buy lottery tickets and that they would share the proceeds of any tickets that won. Many years later, in 2007, Poirier bought a ticket that won a $1 million prize, but she refused to share the prize with Browning, who sued her for his share of the winnings. Poirier denied the existence of an oral agreement and claimed that in any event any oral agreement would be unenforceable under the one-year rule of the statute. The court noted that the agreement had been in effect for many years and that the parties had intended it to last as long as their romantic relationship continued. However, the parties never fixed a definite time for the agreement to last, and it could conceivably have been performed within a year had they won the lottery in that period or if they decided to terminate the arrangement. The court noted that the question is not whether the performance is unlikely to be completed within the year but whether it cannot be performed within the year.

However, the performance period of some contracts for an indefinite term must, by its nature, necessarily extend beyond a year, and the contract is therefore subject to the statute. For example, in *Tucker v. Roman Catholic Diocese of Lafayette-in-Indiana*, 837 N.E.2d 596 (Ind. Ct. App. 2005), the plaintiff had been sexually abused as a child by a church employee. She agreed with the church not to pursue legal recourse in exchange for the church's promise that it would strip the abuser of his duties and would ensure that he had no contact with children at the parish. The church did not honor its promise and the victim sued, claiming emotional distress damages for breach of contract. The court of appeals upheld the trial court's dismissal of the complaint. The diocese could have fired the abuser within the year, but its promise to ensure that he would not have contact with parish children was an ongoing obligation with no time limit. It therefore could not be treated as performable within a year.[3]

§11.2.3 Contracts for the Sale of Goods

Contracts for the sale of goods were included in the traditional statute but are now provided for in UCC §2.201. Section 2.201(1) requires compliance with the statute where the total price of the goods sold under the contract is $500[4] or more, so the price of all items sold under the contract

3. Apart from noncompliance with the statute, the court found other problems with the plaintiff's case. The contract was invalid for lack of consideration because the statute of limitations had already run on the plaintiff's claim at the time that of the parties' agreement, so she suffered no legal detriment in forbearing from suit. In addition, the court held that emotional distress damages are not available for breach of contract. (*See* section 18.13.)

4. Five hundred dollars is the amount that was set in the original enactment of Article 2 over 60 years ago, and it has never been increased in the Official Text to account for inflation. An attempt was made to increase the amount to $5,000 in a proposed comprehensive revision

must be added together to determine if it is subject to the statute. If the price consists of property other than cash, the property must be valued to establish the price.

The scope of Article 2 is discussed in section 2.7.2. In many cases a contract obviously is or is not a sale of goods. However, sometimes the nature of the contract is not so clear. This could be because it is not certain if the item sold qualifies as goods (as opposed to intangible rights or real property), or it is not certain that the transaction is a sale (as opposed to, say, a lease). It could also be because the transaction is a hybrid—it consists of both a sale of goods and the rendition of services related to them. As explained in section 2.7.2, a predominance test is used to decide if a hybrid transaction is subject to Article 2. Under this test, in essence, Article 2, including the statute under §2.201, applies to the transaction if the sale of goods is the predominant component of the contract.[5]

§11.2.4 Contracts to Answer for the Debt or Obligation of Another

This provision covers suretyship contracts. A surety is a person who promises the creditor to pay another person's debt, so that if the other person fails to pay the debt, the surety is obliged to pay it. (Sometimes the term "guaranty" is used synonymously with "suretyship." These two types of transactions both involve a commitment by a person to pay the debt of another, and they are very similar. The subtle differences between them are not relevant here. They both constitute contracts to answer for the debt of another and are subject to the statute.) A suretyship arises, for example, when a lender demands, as a condition of lending money to a borrower, that a third party undertakes to pay back the loan if the borrower defaults. The borrower arranges with the third party to promise the lender to pay the borrower's debt if the borrower fails to do so. The borrower is primarily liable on the loan and is called the principal debtor. The third party, as surety, is secondarily liable. The surety is, in effect, a backup debtor that assumes the duty to pay a debt that it would not otherwise owe. For the statute to apply to the

---

of Article 2 in 2003. However, the proposed revision failed and was never enacted by states. Some states have amended their version of §2.201 to increase the amount.

5. As explained in section 2.7.2, the Official Text of Article 2 was amended in 2022 to deal with hybrid transactions, and the amendment has already been enacted by a number of states. In addition to tackling hybrid transactions, the amendment enacted a set of housekeeping provisions that reinforce what courts had already determined — that the statute is satisfied by an electronic or other form of recording, and that signatures include electronic symbols, sounds, or processes. *See* the 2022 definition of "sign" in §1.201(37) and the 2022 amendment to §2.201, which substitutes the word "record" for the word "writing."

suretyship, the surety's obligation to pay must be secondary to the debtor's obligation, and the surety's duty to pay the debt must be conditional on the debtor's default. If the person undertaking to pay the debtor's debt assumes primary liability on the debt, that person is not a surety, but a joint debtor, and the statute does not apply.

There are two justifications for subjecting a suretyship agreement to the statute. First, the formality of recording serves a cautionary function by alerting the surety that it is undertaking a serious, legally enforceable commitment. Second, it serves the usual evidentiary function of the statute by preventing the assertion of a possibly bogus claim that a person agreed to pay the debt of another.

The statute relating to suretyship has several difficult qualifications and nuances. One of them is that the statute presupposes that the surety undertakes the suretyship for the primary purpose of accommodating and benefiting the principal debtor. Therefore, if the main purpose of the suretyship is to serve the surety's own financial interest—that is, the surety receives a direct economic benefit—the statute does not apply and an oral undertaking is enforceable. This principle only applies if the economic interest of the surety is the main purpose of the suretyship. It is not enough that the surety has some personal stake or self-interest in undertaking liability for the debt.

§11.2.5 Contracts of Executors or Administrators to Answer for the Duty of Their Decedents

The type of contract covered here is one in which the executor or administrator of an estate assumes personal liability to a creditor of the decedent for a debt or obligation incurred by the decedent before death. That is, the executor promises the creditor that if the estate does not have the funds to pay the debt, the executor will pay it. The statute only applies to debts that the decedent incurred, not to new debts incurred by the estate itself. This provision is analogous to the suretyship provision discussed in section 11.2.4, in that the executor undertakes to answer for the debt of the decedent if the estate cannot pay it.

§11.2.6 Contracts Upon Consideration of Marriage

This category does not cover a promise of marriage, which can be and usually is oral. Rather, it relates to a contract in consideration of marriage in which the prospective spouses agree to a marriage settlement or to financial arrangements relating to the marriage. It also covers a promise by a third person (say, a parent of one of the spouses) to settle property or money on the spouses in consideration of their marriage. The requirement that the contract is in consideration of marriage means that the statute applies only to prenuptial contracts motivated by the impending marriage.

§11.3 THE SECOND INQUIRY: IF THE STATUTE APPLIES, IS THE CONTRACT REFLECTED IN A RECORD THAT SATISFIES ITS REQUIREMENTS?

To satisfy the general statute, the recorded memorial of agreement must comply with a number of requirements. The requirements of UCC §2.201 are similar, and any significant differences are noted below. The requirements are as follows.

§11.3.1 A Recorded Memorandum

As stated in section 11.1 and 11.2.3, it is clear in contemporary law that the statute is satisfied by either a tangible document or a retrievable recording in an electronic or other medium. There is no particular formality needed for the record as long as it contains the statute's minimum required content and signature. For example, in *Lucy v. Zehmer* (the joke case discussed in connection with the objective test in section 4.1.5) the valid and enforceable contract under which the Zehmers sold their farm to Lucy was recorded by a short, handwritten scrawl on the back of a restaurant guest check. The record need not be executed with the deliberate purpose of evidencing the contract. It need not be the joint product of the parties or even delivered to the other party. It could be an internal memorandum or a document recorded for some other purpose than to satisfy the statute. It need not be recorded at the time of contracting. (The fact that it was not a purposeful contemporaneous attempt to record the agreement could affect its credibility, but this is a different issue.) Note, however, as discussed in section 11.3.3, a record signed by just one of the parties only satisfies the statute with regard to the party who signed it, and does not satisfy the statute as against the party who did not.

The record of the contract need not be in a single document, so it is possible to satisfy the statute by a series of correspondence or other linked records, including an exchange of electronic communications such as emails or text messages. It must be clear from the face of the records that they all refer to the same transaction and, taken together, they must contain all the content required by the statute, including a signature on at least one of them. Some courts require the signed record to refer to the others so that the signature can be attributed to the unsigned record without extrinsic evidence. Other courts are not as strict and require only that it is apparent from the records that they refer to the same transaction. Oral testimony can then be used to prove that the signature was intended to authenticate the content of the unsigned records. Provided that the record was made, the statute is satisfied even if it has been lost by the time of litigation. Its prior existence and its contents can be proved by oral testimony. This may sound like a strange rule, given that the principal purpose of the statute is to require a record to prevent a false allegation of contract. It could be just as difficult to detect perjured evidence of a record claimed to be lost as it is to expose a bogus claim that a contract was made. Nevertheless, when there is convincing evidence that a record did exist at one time, this is one further safety valve that prevents abuse of the statute by a party who seeks to escape a genuine contract.

§11.3.2 The Content of the Record

Evidentiary adequacy for the purpose of satisfying the statute is set quite low. All that is needed is enough in the record to show the existence of a contract. Therefore, the record does not have to contain every term of the contract and does not need to be completely clear and unambiguous in all respects. The common law and UCC have different standards for sufficiency of the record, but, as usual, the looser UCC test tends to influence courts even in common law cases. Therefore, in some jurisdictions, the difference has faded.

The common law rule requires that the record must at least identify the parties and the nature of the exchange, and it must set out the material terms of the agreement. Provided that it has this content, missing nonmaterial terms can be proved by oral evidence and any lack of clarity in the record can be resolved by the process of interpretation and construction discussed in Chapter 10. As in other contexts, materiality is determined as a matter of interpretation, and a term is material if it is an essential part of the exchange and goes to the very basis of the bargain.

UCC §2.201(1) provides for a less stringent standard. The only term that must be stated in the record is the quantity of goods sold, so that the contract is not enforceable beyond the stated quantity. If the record does not contain a quantity term at all, it does not qualify as sufficient to satisfy the statute. In *Wesdem, LLC v. Illinois Tool Works, Inc.*, 70 F.4th 285 (5th Cir. 2023), the parties entered into a requirements contract which, by its nature, is designed to have a flexible quantity term so that the buyer can order the quantity of goods that it actually requires.[6] However, the contract in this case

6. Requirements contracts are introduced and explained in section 7.9.3. In essence, the buyer undertakes to buy the quantity of goods that it requires during the course of the contract, so the exact quantity of goods to be sold is deliberately left flexible.

had no language indicating any expected or estimated quantity of goods that the buyer may require, and also did not provide that the buyer was obliged to buy all goods of that kind exclusively from the seller. The court held that the record therefore failed to provide any basis for assessing the quantity that the buyer would be entitled to demand, and so it did not meet the requirement of §2.201 that the record contain a quantity term.

Apart from the requirement that quantity be stated, §2.201 demands only that there is some record sufficient to indicate that the parties made a contract of sale. It expressly states that a record is not insufficient merely because it omits any term other than quantity, or incorrectly states any term.

Because the level of recording needed to satisfy the statute is quite minimal, it is important to recognize that a record sufficient for the purposes of the statute may not be clear and full enough to ultimately convince the fact-finder that a contract was made on the terms alleged. Compliance with the statute is a different issue from adequate proof of the contract for the purpose of relief. If the record is skimpy or uncertain, the statute may be only the first hurdle to be jumped by the party seeking enforcement. Thereafter, enforcement of the agreement is dependent on the plaintiff's ability to cure the gaps or indefiniteness in the record by interpretation, persuasive extrinsic evidence, or applicable gap fillers.

§11.3.3 Signature

a. The Basic Rule of Signature

It is not necessary that the enforcing party signed the record, because the evidentiary role of the statute is satisfied as long as the party disputing the existence of the contract has signed it in person or through an agent. A signature is any mark or symbol placed by the party on the record with the intention of authenticating it, so a full and formal signature is not needed. Initials, a logo, or even an "x" is enough. The signature does not have to be placed on the record after the terms are written down, so a party can adopt a symbol (such as a logo in an electronic document or on a printed page) by recording the terms of the contract on the written or electronic document containing the preexisting symbol. UCC §1.201(37) codifies this principle by defining "sign" to include any symbol executed or adopted with present intention to authenticate the record. Restatement, Second, §134 is to the same effect, defining "signature" to include any symbol made or adopted with the actual or apparent intent to authenticate the record as that of the signer.

When the record consists of several pieces of paper or other records (such as a series of notes, letters, or emails), it is not necessary that every piece has been signed, provided that it appears from the records themselves that they all refer to the same transaction. Some courts require that the signed record actually makes some reference to unsigned ones, but other courts require only that the records, on their face, relate to the same transaction.

b. Electronic Signatures

Where the record is not in tangible form, but is recorded in an electronic or other medium, the concept of signature has been adapted by federal and state legislation to include other means of verifying authorship and adopting the recorded information.[7] The federal statute, the Electronic Signatures in Global and National Commerce Act, 15 USC §§7001 to 7031 (called E-SIGN), applies to any transaction involving interstate or foreign commerce. States have enacted equivalent statutes, either by drafting their own statutes or by adopting a uniform statute, the Uniform Electronic Transactions Act (UETA). The principal focus of the federal and state statutes is to give legal effect to electronic signatures, and they declare that a signature or other record relating to a transaction may not be denied legal effect solely because it is in electronic form (15 USC §7001(a); UETA §7). This language indicates the limited scope of the statutes. They provide that to the extent that the law requires a signature, it may not deny effect to a signature in electronic form. The statutes do not purport to deal with the question of whether the signature could be denied effect for some other reason.

E-SIGN defines "electronic signature" as "an electronic sound, symbol, or process, attached to or logically associated with a contract or other record and executed or adopted by a person with the intent to sign the record" (15 USC §7006(5)); the definition in UETA §2(8) is almost identical. This definition recognizes as a signature both an identifying symbol that is automatically generated by a computer (such as the "from" line on an email) and a deliberate placing or adoption of a signature on the communication. While the sender's deliberate typed name on the email is quite clearly a signature, an automatically generated name (such as in the message header or in a signature block automatically added to the end of the email) is less obviously so. However, an automatically generated name qualifies as a signature if the party adopts it with intent (objectively determined) to sign the record. If the name and message are genuine, this adoption should usually occur as a matter of course, even if the sender has no specific subjective awareness of "signing" the communication. For example, in *International Casings Group, Inc. v. Premium Standard Farms, Inc.*, 358 F. Supp. 2d 863 (W.D. Mo. 2005), the court, applying UETA, found that the statute of frauds was satisfied by email correspondence. The sender of the emails did not challenge their authenticity, and there was no question that they were forged. The court held that when

7. As noted in section 11.2.3, the 2022 amendment to the Official Text of §1.201(37) brings the definition of "sign" in Article 2 into line with these statutes.

the sender hit the "send" button, it intended to adopt its name in the email header to authenticate the email, and that the header qualified as a signature. Note, however, that the mere fact that a party's name appears in an email does not automatically mean that the party has signed the email. It must be established that in generating the name, the party reasonably intended to adopt or accept the record. For example, in *Buckles Management, LLC v. Investordigs, LLC*, 728 F. Supp. 2d 1145 (D. Colo. 2010), the court held that a defendant's name in an email string did not qualify as a signature under E-SIGN, because the defendant's name was not intended as a signature. The defendant had sent an initial internal email outlining terms proposed for a contract. The email was then forwarded to various people, including the plaintiff, by a junior employee of the defendant (who had no authority to bind it). The court found that the mere fact that the defendant's name was on one of the emails in the string was not enough to constitute its signature.

With electronic signatures, as with handwritten or printed signatures on paper, a party may challenge the genuineness of its signature, claiming that it was forged or placed on the record by someone else without authority. In the field of electronic communications, technological means are usually used to resolve problems of forgery. However, the evidentiary issue of proving the signature is applicable to tangible documents as well as electronic records, and this involves a problem of proof rather than the legal question of recognizing the validity of an electronic signature. In *International Casings* the court, in accepting an email header as a signature, recognized the possibility that an email message can be fraudulently generated in the name of a person who did not send it. However, the court noted that forgery is not confined to electronic communications, and this possibility should not make an email header insufficient as a matter of law where the alleged sender does not successfully impugn its genuineness.

c. Article 2's Exception to the Signature Rule Where Both Parties Are Merchants

Section 2.201(2) recognizes one situation in which a record can be enforced against the party who did not sign it. All the following requirements must be met: Both parties are merchants; within a reasonable time of the oral contract, one of the parties sends a recorded confirmation to the other, which is signed by the sender and otherwise satisfies the statute as against the sender; the recipient has reason to know its contents; and the recipient does not give recorded notice of objection to it within ten days of receipt.

In other words, although the contract could normally be enforced only against the sender, as signatory, when both parties are merchants, the non-signing recipient is also bound if the recipient fails to protest after receiving a record that it read or should have read. *Bazak International Corp. v. Tarrant Apparel Group*, 378 F. Supp. 2d 377 (S.D.N.Y. 2005), illustrates the operation of the merchant rule where the party seeking enforcement of the contract sends the confirmation by email. The parties made an oral contract for the sale of a large number of pairs of jeans. When the seller failed to deliver the jeans, the buyer sued. The seller moved for summary judgment on the grounds that the oral contract did not comply with §2.201. The buyer successfully invoked the merchant exception in §2.201(2). The buyer had sent an email to the seller setting out the terms of the sale and containing the buyer's typed name. The parties were clearly merchants, and the buyer's email was sent within a reasonable time. The email was a written confirmation containing the essential terms of the contract, signed by and sufficient against the buyer who sent it. The focus of the opinion was whether §2.201(2) could be satisfied by an email. The court found that it could be. Although an email is an intangible form of communication, it is stored on the computer, is objectively observable, and can be rendered tangible. The court also found that the UCC definition of "signed" is broad enough to include the typed signature on the email. Finally, the court found that the buyer had shown sufficiently for the purpose of overcoming the seller's application for summary judgment that the seller had received and had reason to know of the content of the email and had not objected to it.

§11.4 THE THIRD INQUIRY: IF THE STATUTE APPLIES AND IS NOT COMPLIED WITH, DOES THE ORAL CONTRACT FALL WITHIN ANY OF ITS EXCEPTIONS?

When a contract falls within the statute and fails to comply with it, the contract is unenforceable as discussed in section 11.5. However, there are a few exceptions that permit enforcement despite the lack of a sufficient signed record. These exceptions are narrow and specific and apply only if the party seeking enforcement can establish their elements. Each of the exceptions is justified on one or both of two grounds. One is evidentiary—the circumstances recognized by the exception tend to prove that a contract was made despite the lack of a record. The other is the protection of a party who incurred a detriment in justifiable reliance on the contract.

§11.4.1 The Part Performance Exception

Following an oral contract, the parties may begin performance, which may provide reliable evidence that a contract was made. Even if the statute applies to the transaction, the performance satisfies its function, so that refusal of enforcement would be too rigid and would allow a party to renege on an established contract through a technical application of the statute. For the part performance exception to apply, the parties' performance must be unequivocally referable to the oral agreement. That is, there must be a very clear showing that the conduct does in fact refer to and demonstrate the existence of a contract. In *Knorr v. Norberg*, 844 N.W.2d 919 (N.D. 2014), the parties entered into an oral lease that gave the lessee the option to purchase the property. Because the option related to the sale of real property, it was subject to the statute. The lessees argued that the option was enforceable under the part performance exception because they performed extensively under the agreement by making rent payments, paying real estate taxes and utilities, keeping the property insured, and physically maintaining it. The court rejected this argument, holding that the performance was not consistent only with the existence of the oral purchase option. It was just as consistent with a lease without an option. Many courts impose the additional requirement that the party seeking to enforce the oral agreement suffered some degree of prejudice in rendering performance in reliance on the agreement.

The part performance exception did apply in *In re Estate of Ewing*, 993 N.W.2d 358 (N. Dak. 2023). Siblings had been left equal shares of a property in their mother's will. One of the siblings lived on the property and entered into alleged oral agreements with the rest of the siblings under which they sold their shares in the property to him. He occupied the property and made numerous substantial and permanent improvements to the property. The court held that the extent and value of the improvements were consistent only with the fact that the siblings must have sold their shares in the property to him. In *Thies v. Wheelock*, cited in section 11.2.1, the court found that the contract to bid jointly on parcels of land was not a sale of an interest in land and was therefore not subject to the statute. However, it noted that had it been a sale of land, the part performance exception would have applied. After Theis and Wheelock agreed orally that they would bid jointly on five parcels of real property and that Wheelock would make the bids on behalf of both of them, Thies withdrew his own bids. In foregoing the opportunity to bid on the property himself, he changed his position in reliance on the agreement under circumstances in which that action was consistent only with the existence of the agreement.

The part performance exception is commonly raised in relation to contracts for the sale of land. Some courts recognize the exception in relation to other contracts subject to the statute, but others do not. For example, in *Holloway v. Bucher*, cited in section 11.2.2, the court confined the exception to contracts for the sale of an interest in land and refused to apply it to an oral loan agreement that required repayment by monthly installments over a period in excess of a year. Similarly, in *Coca Cola Co. v. Bayback's International, Inc.*, 841 N.E.2d 557 (Ind. 2006), the court, stating that this reflected the majority approach, refused to apply the exception to a contract that could not be performed within a year of its making.

Because the part performance doctrine is equitable in derivation, some courts apply it only where the plaintiff seeks the equitable remedy of specific performance, and not where the claim is for the legal remedy of damages. Some courts recognize the exception only if the party seeking enforcement has fully performed. The broad point is that at common law, part performance may allow enforcement of a contract that does not satisfy the statute, but the exception can be difficult to establish, and there are restrictions on its application.

Two subsections of §2.201 give limited recognition to the part performance exception when the contract is for the sale of goods. The two exceptions are narrow and apply only in specific circumstances. The first, in §2.201(3)(a), covers cases in which the seller has begun the manufacture of goods that are specially made for the buyer and not otherwise easily saleable. The exception has its basis in the principle, recognized to some extent at common law too, that the statute should not be applied to defeat relief to a party when post-formation conduct both indicates detrimental reliance on the oral contract and provides evidence of the contract's existence. By commencing performance or procurement of goods that are specific to the buyer's needs and not readily resaleable, the seller incurs prejudice and the seller's actions demonstrate the existence of a contract.

To qualify for the exception under §2.201(3)(a), the buyer must have ordered custom-made goods from the seller, which the seller is to make specially for the buyer, and the nature of the goods must be such that if the buyer reneges on the contract, the seller would not be able to resell them to another buyer in the ordinary course of its business. In addition, the seller must have substantially begun work on making the goods or must have procured them before the buyer repudiated the contract. For example, the buyer's home has a peculiarly-shaped room with awkward angles. The seller can show that the buyer ordered custom-made furniture from the seller, designed to fit the strange shape of the room and that the seller procured materials to make the furniture and began making it before the buyer reneged on the contract. The seller can also show that the furniture is so specific to the buyer that it cannot be used anywhere except in the room for which it is designed, so that the seller cannot resell it to anyone else in the ordinary course of its business.

The second exception, in §2.201(3)(c), allows enforcement of the contract only to the extent payment for the goods has been made and accepted, or goods have been delivered and accepted. The import of §2.201(3)(c) is that if one party has performed and the other has accepted that performance, the party who performed can enforce the contract to recover the consideration due for the performance rendered. If only part performance has been made (that is, only part of the goods were received or only part of the price was paid), the contract is enforceable only with respect to what has been done but cannot be enforced with regard to the balance.

In *Power Restoration International, Inc. v. PepsiCo, Inc.*, 2015 WL 1208128 (E.D. Pa. 2015), the court held that the part performance exceptions in §2.201(3) did not apply. The goods were not specially manufactured for the buyer because the seller carried them in its inventory and they were suitable for sale in the ordinary course of the seller's business, and the goods had not been delivered to and accepted or paid for by the buyer.

§11.4.2 The Judicial Admission Exception

As the statute is intended to guard against a fraudulent assertion of contract, it would seem logical that a party who admits the contract in pleadings or testimony should not be allowed to raise the statute as a defense. Nevertheless, the common law has been resistant to such a rule because of a concern of its impact on litigation. First, it has been perceived as creating an incentive for perjury because a party may choose to deny the contract to avoid losing the defense by an admission in litigation. Second, because a party can be compelled to disclose information in litigation, the admission may not be truly voluntary. These arguments have been criticized as inadequate to overcome the obvious relevance of admissions in litigation. The UCC has not followed them, and it does recognize a limited exception for judicial admissions under certain conditions.

The exception is specific and narrow. Section 2.201(3)(b) permits enforcement of a contract against a party, despite noncompliance with the statute if that party admits in "pleading, testimony or otherwise in court" that a contract was made. The contract is enforceable only to the extent of the quantity of goods admitted. Note that the admission must be made in connection with litigation, and the exception does not extend to admissions in other circumstances. (Of course, a recorded admission outside of litigation may itself be a memorandum satisfying the statute, but an oral admission in those circumstances has no effect.)

One of the more difficult issues that has arisen in connection with this exception is what constitutes an admission. Clearly, if the party breaks down under cross-examination and concedes the contract, an admission has been made. However, it could also be taken as an admission if a party's pleadings raise a defense on the merits (such as claiming that the other party breached by failure to deliver), rather than clearly denying the existence of a contract. There are also a number of procedural complexities, not addressed here, raised by the question of whether a party can be compelled to admit or deny the contract.

§11.4.3 The Issue of Seeking Promissory Estoppel Relief to Overcome the Unenforceability of an Oral Agreement Subject to the Statute of Frauds

The doctrine of promissory estoppel is covered in Chapter 8. As explained there, where there has been justifiable reliance on a promise, the doctrine may be the basis for enforcing the promise, even though it is not enforceable as a contract. Restatement, Second, §90 is the general Restatement provision on promissory estoppel. However, §139, a modified version of §90, expands recognition of promissory estoppel as a possible alternative basis of enforcing an oral promise that is unenforceable under the statute. The elements of promissory estoppel in §139 are similar to those in §90: A promise reasonably expected to induce reliance, the inducement of justifiable reliance on the promise by the other party, and the need to enforce the promise to prevent injustice. In addition, given the evidentiary purpose of the statute, §139 provides that the court should also take into account whether the promisee's conduct in reliance or other available evidence corroborates the existence of a contract.

Notwithstanding §139, courts are generally unsympathetic to the use of promissory estoppel as an alternative means of enforcing an oral promise that is unenforceable under the statute, and it is difficult, and in some states impossible, to persuade a court to allow promissory estoppel relief in this situation. Some courts have taken the position that promissory estoppel is simply not available to provide any relief where a party seeks to enforce a contract subject to the statute. In *DK Arena, Inc. v. EB Acquisitions I, LLC*, 112 So. 3d 85 (Fla. 2013), the parties agreed orally to extend the due diligence period relating to the sale of real property. EB suffered a detriment in reliance on that oral agreement, but the court refused to allow promissory estoppel relief, stating unequivocally that it was inappropriate to use promissory estoppel to evade compliance with the statute. Similarly, in *Doe v. Roe*, 500 F. Supp. 3d 1319 (S.D. Fla. 2020), the defendant, a married man, and the plaintiff, a woman, had a nine-year sexual relationship which resulted in the birth of a child. When the relationship ended, the parties entered into an oral agreement under which the defendant agreed to pay $1 million to the plaintiff and to create a trust in favor of the child into which he would make substantial payments until it matured upon the child reaching the age of 27. In exchange, the plaintiff undertook to raise the child without involving the defendant and not to reveal that the defendant was the child's father. This oral agreement was unenforceable under the statute because it clearly could not have been performed within a year of the agreement, not only in light of the defendant's long-term obligation to make payments into the trust, but also because the plaintiff's obligation to raise the child on her own would last until the child became an adult, and her promise not to reveal the defendant's parentage would last in perpetuity. The court refused to allow the plaintiff to claim relief under the doctrine of promissory estoppel, holding that the doctrine cannot be used to bypass the statute.

Some courts that do not take such an absolute position nevertheless impose stringent restrictions on when promissory estoppel may be used to overcome the statute. For example, in the *Coca Cola* case cited in section 11.4.1, the court followed a line of cases that declined to apply promissory estoppel to enforce the oral contract itself and confined relief to substantial independent detriment. The court found that the plaintiff was seeking to enforce the very bargain that was rendered unenforceable by the statute and refused relief. Similarly, in *Brown v. Branch*, 758 N.E.2d 48 (Ind. 2001), the court refused to apply promissory estoppel to enforce an oral contract to convey land. The court said it was not enough for the plaintiff to show that breach of the oral promise resulted in a denial of her rights under the contract. She must show a substantial and independent injury for which justice demands relief. In *Shedd v. Gaylord Entertainment Co.*, 118 S.W.3d 695 (Tenn. Ct. App. 2003), Gaylord, the developer of a new record label, entered into oral multi-year employment contracts with music industry executives, which it breached when it decided not to proceed with creating the new label. The oral agreements were unenforceable under the one-year rule and the court refused to allow the plaintiffs to raise promissory estoppel as an alternative basis for relief. The court held that the doctrine can be used only in an exceptional case, where enforcement of the statute would make it "an instrument of hardship and oppression, verging on actual fraud." This case did not qualify because Gaylord merely abandoned the project, and there was no improper motive, fraud, or unconscionable advantage-taking to warrant the use of promissory estoppel.

Even where a court is amenable to allowing the use of promissory estoppel to enforce a promise that is unenforceable under the statute, it can be very difficult for the plaintiff to establish the elements set out in §139. In *Tucker v. Roman Catholic Diocese of Lafayette-in-Indiana*, discussed in relation to the one-year rule in section 11.2.2, the plaintiff sought to use promissory estoppel as an alternative basis for enforcing the promise. The court of appeals upheld the trial court's dismissal of the claim on this ground as well. Because the statute of limitations had run on the plaintiff's claim when the diocese made the promise, she could not have sued anyhow, so she suffered no detriment in forbearing from suit in reliance on the promise, and there was no need to enforce the promise to prevent injustice.

§11.5 THE IMPACT OF NONCOMPLIANCE WITH THE STATUTE

There is some variation in the statutes of different states and some confusion in the caselaw about the effect of failure to satisfy the statute. The noncompliant contract is sometimes said to be invalid or void—that is, a legal nullity, of no force or effect. Sometimes it is called unenforceable—that is, a contract that is valid but cannot be sued on and enforced in court. Some cases use these words interchangeably. It is more generally accepted that noncompliance with the statute does not void the contract, but merely makes it unenforceable. Although there are instances in which consequences follow from characterizing a contract as void rather than unenforceable, the distinction is not practically significant for most purposes. In either case, the plaintiff is unable to sue on the contract.

If the contract is unenforceable for noncompliance with the statute, the party seeking to rely on the statute as a defense cannot raise it by a general denial. It must be specifically pleaded as an affirmative defense, otherwise it is waived. If the defense is raised and succeeds, the contract cannot be enforced. If neither party has given or done anything under the contract, the practical effect of nonenforcement for most purposes is to put an end to any obligations that the parties might otherwise have had under the contract. However, sometimes a party may have rendered some performance (insufficient for the part performance exception) before the contract was declared unenforceable. Once the contract is unenforceable, the party who received the performance no longer has a right to keep it, so the other party can seek restitution of the benefit or its value under principles of unjust enrichment. If it was a money payment or the delivery of property still in the hands of the beneficiary, the money or the property itself must be restored. If it was services or property that has been consumed, restitution is usually measured based on its market value, but the court has the discretion to value it differently if fairness so dictates.[8]

§11.6 THE EFFECT OF THE STATUTE ON MODIFICATIONS OF A CONTRACT

Although neither party can unilaterally change the terms of a contract after it has been made, a contract can always be modified by agreement between

8. The measurement of restitutionary benefits is discussed more fully in section 9.6.

the parties. A modification is a contract in itself, distinct from the original contract that it changes. As a separate contract, it is subject to most of the usual requirements of contract law for formation and validity.[9] As a general rule (unless the statute of a particular state provides otherwise), this means that the statute of frauds applies to modifications. Therefore, whether or not the original contract was subject to the statute, if the contract as modified falls within the statute, the modification must be recorded sufficiently to satisfy it.[10] For example, under an original contract, entered into on July 1, 2024, a customer booked a room at a resort for July 3 and 4, 2025. As the contract cannot be performed in a year, it is subject to the statute. Two weeks after making the contract, the customer called the resort and the parties agreed to change the booking to December 25 and 26, 2024. The statute no longer applies to the modified contract. The opposite would occur if the original booking was for December 25 and 26, 2024, and was changed to August 3 and 4, 2025, dates more than a year after the modification. The statute did not apply to the original contract, but it does apply to the modification.

§11.7 A TRANSNATIONAL PERSPECTIVE ON THE STATUTE OF FRAUDS

Neither the CISG nor the UNIDROIT Principles contain a statute of frauds. This comports with the civilian tradition of not generally requiring the formality of recording for the validity or enforcement of a commercial contract. CISG Article 11 states that a contract of sale is not subject to any requirements of form, and need not be evidenced by a record. However, Article 11 is qualified by Article 12, which does allow a signatory country to opt out of Article 11 with regard to a party that has its place of business in that country. If the country exercises its power to opt out, the statute of frauds provided for in its domestic law will apply. (The United States has not exercised the power to opt out, so the Article 2 statute of frauds does not apply to a transaction governed by the CISG.) Article 1.2 of the UNIDROIT Principles follows the same approach as CISG Article 11 in not requiring any

9. As discussed in sections 7.5 and 13.9, at common law one of these requirements is that the modification must be supported by consideration. However, Article 2 dispenses with the need for consideration to support the modification of a contract for the sale of goods.

10. Even if the modification would not otherwise be subject to the statute, the contract may provide that all modifications must be recorded and signed. Such a provision can be effective as a kind of contractually created statute of frauds which prevents the enforcement of an oral modification. However, courts sometimes uphold oral modifications notwithstanding the provision. This is discussed in section 12.13.

recording or other formality to validate a contract. It is also worth noting that England, the country from which American jurisdictions derived their statutes of frauds, abolished it some years ago.

Examples

1. On May 15, Viva Voce, the president of Wright Recording, Inc. interviewed Juan Annum for the position of sales manager. The parties reached agreement on a one-year period of employment, beginning on June 1 at an annual salary of $200,000. At the end of the interview, Viva tore a piece of paper from a blank pad and wrote, "Call HR dept. to enroll Juan Annum as a sales mgr.— 1-yr contract starting 6/1. Pay $200,000 p.a." She told Juan that the purpose of the note was to remind her to call the personnel department so that they would put him on the payroll from June.

   On May 17, Juan received an email from the Human Resources department of Wright Recording, Inc., saying "Welcome to the Wright Recording family. Please click on the secure link in this email to access and complete your personal information questionnaire." A signature box at the end of the email contained the name and position of the HR employee who wrote the email as well as the company's name, address, and phone number.

   On May 23, before he had clicked on the link to access the questionnaire, Juan received a letter in the mail from Viva on the company's letterhead. It read:

   > Dear Juan,
   >
   > I was happy to be able to extend an offer of employment to you last week. I regret, however, that since then we have reevaluated our earnings for the last quarter and find them disappointing. We have therefore decided not to hire any new employees at this time. I am sorry that we cannot use your services. I am sure that a person of your talents will have no difficulty in finding a suitable position elsewhere.
   >
   > Sincerely,
   > Viva Voce
   > President

   Did Juan enter into an enforceable employment contract with Wright Recording?

2. Change the facts of Example 1 as follows: Viva did not send the letter of May 23 and Wright Recording still wished to employ Juan. However, on May 23 Juan received a better job offer and is no longer interested in working for Wright Recording. Apart from this, all the facts are the same as in Example 1. Can the company enforce the contract against him?

3. Clay Potter owns a pottery in which he manufactures ceramic ovenware and crockery. Terry Cotta sells such items in his retail store. On June 1, Terry called Clay and spoke to one of his employees who accepted his order of 1,000 ceramic mugs of various designs at $5.10 each, for immediate delivery. Later that day, Terry mailed the following printed form to Clay, with the blanks filled out by hand (the handwriting is denoted here by italics):

> TERRY'S HOUSEWARES. Terry Cotta, Proprietor.
> PURCHASE ORDER
> Date: *June 1, 2024*
> To: *Clay Potter*
> Please ship the following goods immediately: *1,000 assorted mugs as discussed by phone at $5.10 each*

On June 6, Terry received the following letter from Clay:

> Dear Mr. Cotta,
> I have received your order of June 1. I am sorry that I am out of mugs at present and cannot supply them right now. I am in the process of making a new batch and should have them in stock next month. Due to increased costs, I am going to have to raise the price to $5.50 each. If you would like me to hold your order until that time let me know. Also, tell me which designs you want. Your order refers to an assortment as discussed by phone, but no one here remembers talking to you and we have no record of your call.
>
> Yours truly,
> Clay Potter

Terry claims that he already has a contract for immediate delivery at the old price. Can he enforce it against Clay?

4. On March 1, Chip Chisel, a sculptor, entered into an oral contract with Foundry, Inc., under which Chip agreed to sculpt a life-size statue of Foundry's founder to be erected in the lobby of Foundry's head office. Chip would buy the block of marble to be used for the sculpture as well as all other needed materials, and would have the sculpture completed at his studio and ready for Foundry to collect it on August 1. Foundry would transport the sculpture to its head office and erect it there. Foundry would pay Chip the price of the sculpture, $100,000, upon taking delivery of it. On March 15, Chip bought the block of marble for the sculpture and had it delivered to his studio. Between March 15 and April 10, Chip began to work on the sculpture by chiseling its rough form on the marble block. On April 10 Foundry's president called Chip and repudiated the contract by telling Chip that Foundry was cancelling

the contract because it no longer wanted the sculpture. Does the statute preclude Chip from suing Foundry for damages for breach of contract?

5. Rollo Rolex visited the website of Big Browser Megastore.com and selected an expensive gold watch for $10,000. Rollo ordered it by clicking on various links; keying in his name, address, and credit card particulars; and finally clicking a "confirm order" button to confirm his order. After he did this, a message appeared on his screen thanking him for his order and stating that the goods would be shipped in 10 to 20 days. Assuming that a contract was formed through this process, does it satisfy the statute?

6. Sissy and Sybil Sibling are sisters. They were very close and made regular trips together to Atlantic City, where they played on the slot machines. About a year ago, they entered into an agreement under which they each promised that they would share any gambling winnings that either of them made. They recorded this agreement in a writing that read, "Sissy and Sybil Sibling hereby agree that for a period of two years from the date of this agreement, they will share any gambling winnings that either of them make in playing the slot machines in Atlantic City." Both sisters signed the writing. During the next eight months, the sisters visited Atlantic City three times. Each made modest winnings on the slot machines and they shared them. Eight months after signing the agreement, the sisters had a ferocious argument about a family matter and ceased speaking to each other. In a heated telephone call during the course of this argument, Sissy said, "As for our agreement to share our gambling winnings, you can forget that!" Sybil replied, "That's fine with me." A month later, Sissy went to Atlantic City on her own and won $20,000 on the slots. When Sybil heard about this, she sued Sissy for $10,000. Sissy contends that Sybil has no claim against her because they agreed to terminate their contract to share gambling winnings. Is this contention correct?

7. CarPets, Inc., a manufacturer of carpeting for cars, entered into an oral agreement with Auto Agents, Inc., under which Auto acted as a sales representative for CarPets in soliciting orders for its carpeting from vehicle makers. The parties agreed that Auto would receive commission of the "life of the part," which meant that once Auto had solicited an order from a customer for particular carpeting, Auto would be entitled to commissions on all subsequent orders of that carpeting received by CarPets from that customer. "Life of the part" commissions can continue for many years into the future if the customer uses the same component in its vehicles for a long period of time. Auto solicited orders for carpeting from several vehicle makers, which subsequently placed additional orders with CarPets for the same carpeting. However, CarPets

refused to pay commission to Auto on those sales. Does the statute bar Auto from enforcing CarPets' oral agreement to pay "life of the part" commissions?

Explanations

1. Although the letter of May 23 suggests that Wright Recording is revoking an unaccepted offer, it is clear that an oral contract was made between Juan and the company, represented by its president, on May 15.

The first question to answer is whether the contract is subject to the statute. It is, because the contract cannot be performed within a year of its execution—it is a one-year employment contract, performance of which will begin about two weeks after contract formation. This is a fixed-term contract, so it is not the kind of contract in which performance could be completed within a year. Neither party has the right to accelerate its performance to complete it before the end of the stated term.

The next question is whether there is a record to satisfy the statute. To comply with the statute, there must, at a minimum, be a record, signed by the party against whom enforcement is sought, identifying the parties, setting out the nature of the exchange, and containing the contract's material terms. The record need not be contained in a single document, but can be made up of a set of linked documents. Three documents are referred to in the question: Viva's note to herself, the email from the Human Resources department, and the letter from Viva. None of these documents on its own is sufficient to satisfy the statute.

Viva's note to herself could satisfy the statute even though it was intended as an internal document. The record need not be addressed or given to the other party. The note probably has enough content to show that a contract was made for a year's employment, and it seems to contain the central terms that were agreed. However, it lacks two elements needed to satisfy the statute: First, it identifies only one of the parties, Juan, and gives no indication of who the other party is—it makes no reference to Wright Recording. It is usually a requirement of the statute, in its common law version, that the record must identify the parties. Second, the note is devoid of any kind of mark or symbol that could satisfy the requirement of a signature, even under the liberal definition of signature reflected in Restatement, Second, §134, which can consist of any symbol made or adopted by the signer with the actual or apparent intention to authenticate the record as that of the signer. Had the piece of paper contained the company name or logo, or had Viva signed or initialed the note, this would have satisfied the requirement of signature, but she wrote the note on a blank piece of paper and placed no mark on it that could constitute a signature.[11] Therefore, the absence of a signature by or on behalf of Wright Recording prevents the note from being an adequate memorial of agreement.

The email from the Human Resources department was signed on behalf of the company. The electronic signature of the company's representative is contained in the signature box. Even if there had been no signature in the body of the email, the "from" line in the address section of the email would likely have constituted a signature. The email identifies Juan and suggests the existence of an employment contract. However, it is devoid of any contract terms and its vague "welcome to the Wright Recording family" is not enough.

Viva's letter of May 23 is signed, but it does not help Juan because it makes no mention of any contract terms and does not evidence a contract. On the contrary, it suggests the opposite because it is phrased like the revocation of an unaccepted offer and is an implicit denial of a contract. However, the other two documents—Viva's note and the email from the Human Resources department—appear to contain all the content needed to satisfy the statute. As discussed in section 11.3.1, a set of records in combination can satisfy the statute if, on their face, they refer to the same transaction and together they include all the required content. (Some courts insist that the signed record actually refers to the unsigned ones, but other courts find that test too rigorous and require only that it is apparent from the records that they refer to the same transaction.)

Juan should succeed in establishing compliance with the statute, making the contract enforceable and allowing him to claim any expectation damages that he suffered. It is therefore not necessary to proceed to the third stage of the inquiry on whether the contract fits into any of the recognized exceptions to the statute. If that inquiry had been necessary, the agreement would not have fitted into any exception.

2. Although Juan can enforce the contract against Wright Recording, as explained in Example 1, the company has no corresponding right. When the record has been signed by just one of the parties, the statute makes the contract enforceable against that party only. If the rule were otherwise, the statute would have little purpose because it would be too easy for one of the parties to write and sign a bogus document and to claim a contract binding on the other.[12] Juan has not signed anything, so Wright

11. Even if a handwriting expert could identify the writing as Viva's, this would not satisfy the signature requirement. The party must place or adopt an identifying symbol to authenticate the record—a requirement independent of the writing itself.

12. Although not applicable here, UCC Article 2 has a limited exception to this rule if both parties are merchants. *See* section 11.3.3c and Example 3.

Recording cannot enforce the contract against him when he decides to renege on it.[13]

3. Although the price of each item of goods is only $5.10, they are sold together in a single contract, so the price of the sale is their total price of $5,100. The contract is therefore subject to the statute in UCC §2.201. Terry is the party who seeks to enforce the contract, so the first question to ask is if Clay's letter satisfies the statute. It does not. Although Clay's letter is signed as defined in §1.201(37), it fails to satisfy §2.201(1) because it does not indicate that a contract has been made. In fact, phrased as a counteroffer, it suggests just the opposite. Terry's order form would satisfy the statute as against Terry, but it does not satisfy §2.201(1) as against Clay because it must be signed by the party against whom enforcement is sought. If this was a contract at common law, this would end the matter—Terry could not enforce the oral agreement against Clay.

   However, if all its requirements are satisfied, UCC §2.201(2) provides an exception to the rule that that contract must be signed by the party against whom it is to be enforced. If one of the parties sends a confirmation of the oral contract to the other, the statute is satisfied as against the recipient if all the following conditions are satisfied: both parties are merchants; the record is sufficient under §2.201(1) to satisfy the statute as against the sender; it was sent within a reasonable time; it was received by the other party who has reason to know its contents; and the recipient does not give recorded notice of objection to it within ten days of receipt.

   Both parties are merchants under §2.104(1) because they both deal in goods of that kind. For the record to be sufficient against Terry, the sender, it must indicate that a contract of sale has been made between the parties and must be signed by Terry. Beyond this, it need not accurately or fully state all the terms agreed, but it is not enforceable beyond the quantity stated. The order form does set out the essential terms of the contract, including the quantity of the goods. Terry's printed name at the top should qualify as his signature because it was adopted by him to authenticate the form when he filled out the blanks. The only problem is that the form is described as an order, which suggests not a contract, but an offer. It would have been clearer if the form had been headed "order confirmation." Nevertheless, this difficulty can be overcome by

13. There is no problem of "mutuality of obligation" where Juan can enforce the contract against Wright Recordings but it cannot enforce the contract against him. As discussed in section 7.9.1, provided that both parties' promises are genuine and not illusory, there is no general rule of "mutuality" that prevents one party from being bound because the other has no right of enforcement.

the reference to the telephone call that, on a reasonable interpretation, suggests a prior oral order accepted by or on behalf of Clay.

The form was sent on the same day as the telephone call, surely within a reasonable time, and Clay's response shows that it was received and its contents read. All is well for Terry so far, but Clay's letter could constitute a recorded notice of objection. To be an effective objection to the contents of the record, the response must challenge the existence of a contract. Although the letter from Clay does not say in so many words that it denies Terry's claim of a contract, its import is clearly to that effect. It treats the order as an offer and claims no knowledge of the telephone call. It is recorded and is given within ten days of receipt of Terry's form. Therefore, Clay has a plausible argument that he made an objection sufficient to prevent Terry's form from satisfying §2.201(2).

4. This is a sale of goods. Although Chip's skill and labor goes into the creation of the sculpture, the object of the contract is for the sale of the tangible, movable end product of his labor. The contract does not require Chip to perform any services relating to the transaction, such as delivery or installation of the product, so this is not a hybrid transaction. The contract is subject to the statute under §2.201 because the sale price of the sculpture is $100,000. There is no record at all, so the statute is not satisfied unless one of the exceptions in §2.201(3) applies. The only exception that has any possible relevance is the version of the part performance exception set out in §2.201(3)(a). To invoke this exception, Chip must show that the goods are to be specially manufactured for Foundry; they are not suitable for sale to others in the ordinary course of Chip's business; before receiving notice of the Foundry's repudiation, Chip made a substantial beginning on manufacture of the goods or commitments for their procurement; and the circumstances reasonably indicate that the goods are for Foundry.

   The exception is based on the fairness principle that the statute should not preclude relief to a party when post-formation conduct both shows the seller's detrimental reliance on the oral contract and provides evidence of the contract's existence.

   This sculpture is specially commissioned by and is of a subject matter that is of particular and exclusive interest to Foundry, which strongly indicates that the sculpture is for the buyer. It is unlikely that there is another buyer who would be interested in a sculpture of Foundry's founder, so Chip can probably show that he would not be able to sell the sculpture to another buyer in the ordinary course of his business.

   Chip bought the marble block and began to carve it roughly before the repudiation. Although it is difficult to draw a definite line at which the commitment of time and materials passes from insubstantial to substantial, this is likely enough to constitute a substantial beginning of manufacture.

This requirement, combined with that of difficulty of resale, is intended to confine the exception to cases in which nonenforcement would cause hardship to the seller. However, it sounds like the marble block is still largely intact and it could be used for a different sculpture, which Chip would be able to sell in the ordinary course of business, so this may weaken Chip's argument that he will suffer the detriment contemplated by §2.201(3)(a). In short, Chip's performance seems to serve the evidentiary function well, but is less compelling on the question of detriment, making it difficult to be sure that Chip will be able to invoke the exception.

5. This is a sale of goods for a price of $10,000 so it falls within §2.201 and there must be a recorded memorandum of agreement, signed by the party against whom enforcement is sought, sufficient to show that a contract has been formed.

   There is no doubt that the electronic records generated in the computers of both parties satisfy the requirement of §2.201 that there be a record sufficient to indicate a contract of sale. Rollo's order, with particulars of the parties, the goods, the price, and the quantity term, accepted by Big Browser with the delivery information, surely evidences the existence of a contract. In contemporary law, electronic records are unquestionably valid and electronic signatures are given effect by E-SIGN and UETA, provided that such electronic signatures exist and they are genuine and otherwise in conformity with the law. The facts present no question of forgery or unauthorized use of equipment, so the sole issue is whether the parties did execute or adopt a symbol associated with the contract. The facts indicate that Rollo deliberately entered his name in the appropriate space on the electronic order form. Undoubtedly this qualifies as his signature.

   Although the facts do not specify, Big Browser's name or symbol surely appears in its response. The response could have been written by a Big Browser employee, or it could have been generated automatically by an electronic agent. In either case, Big Browser is bound by the message that incorporates its electronic symbol.[14]

6. The agreement to share gambling winnings is subject to the statute because it has a definite term of two years and therefore cannot be performed within a year of execution of the contract. However, the signed written agreement to share winnings satisfies the statute, so Sissy cannot claim that the original agreement is unenforceable. Instead, she argues

14. Section 5.8 explains that a party can contract through an electronic agent—a computer program that is set up to initiate action or respond automatically to a communication. UETA recognizes this possibility in §14, and comment 1 to §14 points out that intention to enter into a transaction can be attributed to a party who sets up a machine to act as its agent. Therefore, a signature can be attributed to a party where the automatic signature is by a machine programmed to be an electronic agent.

that the agreement was rescinded by mutual consent. The sisters did enter a termination agreement through an offer by Sissy that was accepted by Sybil. The agreement is supported by consideration because each suffers the detriment of giving up her rights under the terminated contract. If that termination agreement is enforceable, Sissy has a good defense to Sybil's suit. However, the termination agreement is oral, so the question is whether it is subject to the statute. If it is, the oral termination agreement is unenforceable, and Sybil does have a cause of action under the original contract. An agreement to terminate a contract is itself a contract. Like a modification, it is subject to all the usual rules relating to formation and validity, and it must comply with the statute if it falls within the statute. The argument could be made that it is subject to the statute of frauds because the underlying contract still had more than a year to run, so the agreement to terminate rights under the contract must last just as long and cannot be performed within a year of its making. However, that is not persuasive. It is better to view the termination agreement as taking effect immediately, and being fully performed as soon as each party commits to give up her rights under the terminated contract.

This is what the court held in *Sokaitis v. Bakaysa*, 49 Conn. L. Rptr. 812 (Conn. Super. Ct. 2010), on which this Example is based. Two octogenarian sisters enjoyed gambling at a casino and buying lottery tickets. They had made a written agreement to share their gambling winnings. Their formerly close relationship ended when they had an argument over a loan that one of the sisters made to the other. During the course of an argument over the loan, there was a heated exchange in which one of the sisters said, "I don't want to be your partner anymore," and the other replied, "OK." Thereafter, one of the sisters bought a Powerball lottery ticket with her brother and they won $500,000. Upon hearing of this, the other sister sued for breach of the contract to share gambling winnings. The court noted that an agreement to rescind a contract is itself a contract. An effective agreement of rescission ends the contract and waives all rights to enforce or sue on it. The court found that the sisters had entered into a valid agreement to rescind the contract. It held further that the rescission agreement was not subject to the statute because the rescission involved an instantaneous performance under which each party's duties under the original contract were immediately discharged.

7. The oral contract to pay "life of the part" commissions is for an indefinite period, and CarPets' performance of its obligation to pay the commissions could last for many years if vehicle makers continue to order the same carpets for successive models of its vehicles. Performance of the contract could therefore continue well past a year from the date of the contract's execution, and there is a strong likelihood that it would do so. However, it is possible that vehicle manufacturers could decide to

change carpeting suppliers or, for whatever other reason, could cease to place any more orders for the carpeting for which Auto obtained the initial order. It is therefore possible that CarPets' obligation to pay "life of the part" commissions to Auto could end at any time, even during the year following contract formation. This was the court's conclusion in *Jesa Enterprises, Ltd. v. Thermoflex Corp.*, 2016 WL 4376176 (E.D. Mich. 2016), on which this Example is based. The court noted that it was fair to assume that the parties contemplated that the contract performance could extend well beyond a year, and it may well do so. However, the fact that it could terminate within the year removed the contract from the one-year rule so that it was not subject to the statute.

CHAPTER 12

The Parol Evidence Rule

§12.1 THE RELATIONSHIP BETWEEN THE PAROL EVIDENCE RULE AND INTERPRETATION

The parol evidence rule is closely intertwined with the process of interpretation, so there are many links in this chapter to the discussion of interpretation in Chapter 10. There are passing references to the parol evidence rule in Chapter 10, but that chapter was concerned purely with the rules and principles governing the interpretation or construction of contracts to determine the parties' reasonable meaning. The central point of Chapter 10 is that unless there is no evidence of context available, the meaning of language used in the contract is usually determined not purely by reference to the dictionary meaning of the words but by evaluating the meaning of the words in the entire context of the transaction. This context may include the discussions between the parties in forming the contract, their previous course of dealing in prior contracts of the same kind, trade usage, and their post-formation course of performing the contract. Where the agreement has been recorded, the parol evidence rule qualifies what was discussed in Chapter 10 by placing controls on recourse to this extrinsic evidence. In short, it restricts the extent to which some contextual evidence may be considered in deciding what the parties intended in entering the contract.

In its original form, the parol evidence rule applied to evidence outside of a written physical document. In contemporary law, as explained in Chapter 11, it applies equally to an agreement recorded by some other means, such a retrievable electronic or other record. Therefore, the words "record" and "recorded" are used here instead of "writing" or "written" unless the facts of a case or an Example indicate that a physical writing was executed. The impact of the parol evidence rule on the contextual evidence used to interpret the contract depends both on the completeness and clarity of the record of agreement and on the quality of the contextual evidence. The clearer and more comprehensive the record, the higher the barrier to the admission of extrinsic evidence. On the other hand, the more compelling the extrinsic evidence, the greater the prospect of persuading the court that it should be admitted. To decide whether the record is clear and comprehensive, the court must interpret the record itself. The effect of this is to create a circular process that can be confounding: the parol evidence rule impacts interpretation by restricting evidence extrinsic to the recorded contract, but interpretation, often in the light of that very extrinsic evidence, must be used to decide whether and to what extent the record should have the effect of excluding the extrinsic evidence. One of the most difficult tasks in understanding the parol evidence rule is to appreciate how courts navigate this circular route. They do it by trying to strike a balance between the parties' reasonable expectations arising from the language of the recorded contract and their reasonable expectations arising from the context in which that recorded contract was formed.

§12.2 A BASIC STATEMENT OF THE RATIONALE AND CONTENT OF THE RULE

The parol evidence rule applies only when the parties' agreement has been recorded in a paper document or another retrievable record in electronic or other form. The rule comes into effect where one of the parties proffers parol evidence to prove a term that is not contained in the record or to negate, qualify or expand on a term in the record. "Parol" derives from the French *parole*, meaning "a word."[1] Parol evidence consists of oral and recorded terms allegedly agreed to prior to execution of the record of the contract, but not reflected in that document. It also covers terms allegedly agreed to orally at the time of the recorded memorandum of agreement, but not reflected in that document.

The parol evidence rule is based on the principle that when the parties commit their agreement to a record, they often intend the record to be the final expression of their agreement. That is, they intend it to supersede

1. "Parol" has the same etymological root as the more familiar modern English word "parole," which means a prisoner's early release from jail subject to conditions. It is incorrect to use the final "e" in relation to the parol evidence rule.

anything that might have been proposed, discussed, or agreed to prior to execution of the record but not ultimately included in it. Accordingly, the factfinder should not hear evidence of terms that were allegedly agreed to but are not reflected in the record. This evidence is suspect, unreliable, and irrelevant, and is more likely to mislead and confuse than to inform the factfinder. (This rationale is taken up again and illustrated in section 12.3.)

Restatement, Second, §213 sets out the common law parol evidence rule, as it is applied by many contemporary courts. The UCC rule, in §2.202, is worded somewhat differently, but is largely similar in effect. In essence, both versions of the rule provide that to the extent that the parties execute a record that is and is intended to be a complete and final expression of their agreement, no parol evidence may be admitted to supplement, qualify, or contradict it. However, to the extent that the record is not a final and complete expression of agreement, consistent, but not contradictory, parol evidence may be admitted to supplement or explain those parts of it that have not been finally expressed.

§12.3 THE SCOPE OF PAROL EVIDENCE

§12.3.1 Evidence of Prior or Contemporaneous Oral Terms and Prior Recorded Terms

As stated in section 12.2, parol evidence includes evidence of oral terms allegedly agreed to prior to or contemporaneously with the recorded contract, but not incorporated into it. It also covers terms allegedly agreed to in recorded form prior to execution of the recorded memorandum of contract, but not incorporated into it. These three forms of parol evidence—prior oral and recorded agreements and contemporaneous oral agreements—are illustrated below and the range of the parol evidence rule is represented in Diagram 12A.

Example of an oral term allegedly agreed to prior to the recorded contract, but not incorporated into it. A recorded contract for the sale of an office building makes no mention of any warranty. After the sale has been concluded and the property transferred, the buyer discovers a defect in the building and sues the seller for breach of warranty, claiming that they had a conversation prior to signing the recorded agreement in which the seller warranted that the building was structurally sound. The rationale for filtering such evidence through the parol evidence rule is that an allegation of prior consensus on an oral term is suspect when the oral term is not incorporated into the record executed for the purpose of memorializing the agreement. Its absence from the record suggests either that it is a fabrication by the buyer, or even if it was initially

Diagram 12A

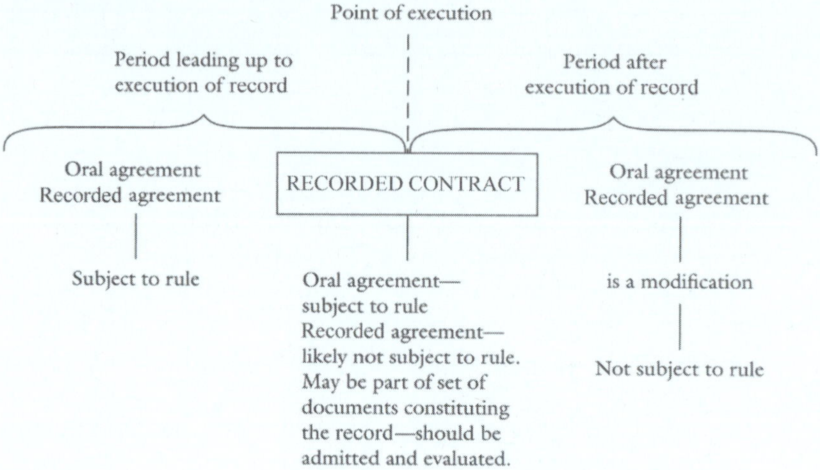

agreed to, that the parties did not agree that it would be part of the final contract. Therefore, the evidence should be evaluated with special care by the judge before it is admitted for the factfinder's consideration.

Example of an oral term allegedly agreed to contemporaneously with the recorded contract, but not incorporated into it. A recorded contract for the sale of an office building makes no mention of any warranty. As in the first example, the buyer of the office building discovers a defect in the building after the sale and sues the seller for breach of warranty. Although the recorded agreement contains no warranty, the buyer claims that at the time that the parties met to sign the recorded contract, they had a conversation in which the seller assured the buyer that the building was structurally sound. The rationale for subjecting this evidence to the rule is similar to that for evidence of alleged prior oral agreement—the claim of the parol agreement could be a fabrication, but even if it is not, the fact that it is not in the recorded contract indicates that the parties did not agree to include it in the contract.

Example of a term allegedly agreed to in a record prior to execution of the recorded contract, but not incorporated into it. As in the first example, the buyer of the office building discovers a defect in the building after the sale and sues the seller for breach of warranty. The recorded agreement contains no warranty, but the buyer seeks to offer in evidence email correspondence a week before execution of the recorded agreement, in which the seller assured the buyer that the building was free of structural defects. Their email correspondence indicates that the seller did warrant the structural soundness of the building, but their final recorded contract of sale does not contain any such warranty. The evidence of the email correspondence is parol evidence, even though it is recorded, not oral. The presence of objectively verifiable recorded evidence of prior agreement reduces concern that the buyer made up the claimed agreement, but its absence from the final writing still suggests that the parties must not have intended to include the warranty in the final contract. In *Baker DC, LLC v. Baggette Construction, Inc.*, 378 F. Supp. 3d 399 (D. Md. 2019), a subcontractor's bid for concrete work specified that the work would take 16 working weeks. The contractor accepted the bid, and the parties entered into a detailed written contract that did not specify the duration of the work, but provided that the contractor would control the work schedule. The work took considerably longer than 16 weeks to complete, and the subcontractor sued the contractor for loss resulting from the delay. The court held that the parol evidence rule precluded the subcontractor from testifying about bid's 16-week schedule because it was superseded by the scheduling provision in the final written agreement.

The parol evidence rule covers only evidence of prior recorded agreement and does not include evidence of contemporaneous recorded agreement. This is because a contract need not be contained in a single document. Where the recordings are contemporaneous, it can no longer be assumed that one of them was intended to supersede the other. They may simply be supplementary to each other. As a result, the contemporaneous record is not treated as parol evidence

§12.3.2 Evidence of Subsequent Agreement

Evidence of oral and recorded agreements claimed to have been made after the execution of the recorded contract are not parol evidence. The theory behind the parol evidence rule is that the recorded contract is likely to have subsumed prior or contemporaneous agreement, and this presumption has no relevance to an agreement entered into subsequent to the recorded contract. This is in fact a modification, which is subject to its own particular rules but it is not affected by the parol evidence rule.[2]

It is usually easy to tell if an oral agreement was made after the writing because it is separated from the writing by some distance in time. However, in some situations it may not be clear if the oral agreement is contemporaneous with or subsequent to the writing. For example, in *Kehr Packages, Inc. v. Fidelity Bank*, 710 A.2d 1169 (Pa. 1998), the bank had agreed to finance the purchase of shares in a corporation. The closing of the transaction took all day. The parties signed a written loan agreement during the course of the day. After the agreement was signed, but before the closing was over, the borrowers asked the lender to increase the amount of the loan. The borrowers claimed that the lender agreed to this increase orally, but the written

2. Modifications are dealt with in sections 7.5.2 and 13.9. The recorded memorial of agreement may itself seek to prevent future oral modifications by requiring that all modifications must be recorded and signed by the parties. The effectiveness of such a provision is discussed in section 12.13.

agreement was not changed to reflect this. The trial court admitted evidence of the oral agreement on the basis that it was subsequent to the writing and not subject to the parol evidence rule. The supreme court reversed and held that the evidence was barred by the rule. The closing was a single, continuous transaction and it was artificial to focus on the exact sequence of the signing and the alleged oral agreement. The crucial point is whether they are both within the same process of formation, and if they are, the parties (especially sophisticated parties, as in this case) should ensure that the writing is changed to include any oral understandings. Because the court found the oral agreement to be contemporaneous and irreconcilable with the writing, evidence of it was excluded.

§12.4 A CLOSER LOOK AT THE PURPOSE AND PREMISE OF THE PAROL EVIDENCE RULE

The primary purpose of the parol evidence rule is to control the jury's decision making. It allows the judge to restrict the information given to the jury, thereby shielding it from evidence the judge finds to be suspect and unreliable. A secondary justification for the rule is that it promotes efficiency in the conduct of litigation. By excluding suspect evidence at the outset (often at the stage of a motion for summary judgment or dismissal), the judge saves the time that would otherwise be wasted in presenting the evidence to the jury and cross-examining the witnesses. Finally, the existence of the rule may help promote transactional efficiency. Because it exists, parties are more likely to make an effort to record their agreement fully and accurately.

Although the parol evidence rule leads to the exclusion of evidence of the parol agreement, it is characterized as a rule of substantive contract law, not a rule of evidence. In essence, the substantive rule nullifies the offending parol agreement, so that evidence of it becomes inadmissible as irrelevant. For most purposes, this distinction makes no practical difference, and the rule operates largely in the same way as a rule of evidence.[3]

The basic concept of the parol evidence rule is quite simple and its premise is grounded in common sense. However, this basic simplicity is overwhelmed by the considerable difficulty of defining the scope of the rule and applying it to inconclusive facts. The complexity and confusion generated

3. The principal impact of characterizing the parol evidence rule as a rule of substantive law is on matters of procedure. For example, if a federal court deals with a contract case, it follows its own rules of evidence, but because the parol evidence rule is treated as a rule of substantive law, the court is obliged to follow the rule as formulated in state law. Also, if it was a rule of evidence, a party could waive it by failing to object to the evidence at trial. As a rule of substantive law, it can be raised on appeal despite the failure to object at trial.

by the rule result largely from the dilemma it presents to courts: The rule serves a useful role in permitting the exclusion of evidence that is probably unreliable or dishonest, but it also has the potential of producing injustice by preventing a party from proving what was actually agreed. A firm rule is more efficient at keeping out undesirable evidence but is also more likely to exclude legitimate evidence. A more flexible rule allows the court greater discretion in evaluating and determining the reliability of evidence, but it weakens the protection against undesirable evidence and detracts from the certainty and clarity of the law. The caselaw shows that courts usually try to balance these considerations as best they can, but the process can be difficult and the results hard to predict.

The following illustration indicates the premise of the rule: The Four Crooners is a popular troupe of tenors who sing light opera and ballads. The Four Crooners entered into a written contract with Integrated Recording Co., under which Integrated Recording would design, produce, and disseminate an album of the Four Crooners' music and distribute it through various media. The Four Crooners would receive a royalty of 15 percent of gross receipts from sales of the album. The album was made, and 150,000 units were sold in the first month. This resulted in a dispute between the parties and a suit by the Four Crooners for larger royalties. As the basis of the suit, the Four Crooners claim that before they signed the written contract they told Integrated Recording that they were willing to accept a 15 percent royalty on the first 100,000 units sold, but if sales exceeded that volume, they wanted a royalty of 18 percent on all sales beyond 100,000 units. They allege that Integrated Recording agreed to this orally. This change does not appear in the written contract and Integrated Recording denies agreeing to it.

Because the written contract does not mention this alleged term, the Four Crooners have no case unless they are allowed to testify to the oral promise. The rule of law could simply be to admit the evidence of both parties and to leave it to the factfinder (usually the jury) to decide if such an oral agreement was reached. However, the common law has not taken this approach. Instead, it has developed the parol evidence rule, which acts as a gatekeeper by allowing the judge to determine if the factfinder should be allowed to hear the evidence of the oral agreement. Where the factfinder is a jury, the judge's determination not to admit the evidence means that, if the matter then goes to trial, the jury will not hear it and will not be influenced by it. However, in a bench trial, where the judge is the factfinder, the judge already knows about the evidence because the judge was the very person who made the determination not to admit it. This means that the judge is not insulated from the alleged evidence if the matter goes to trial, but must exercise judicial objectivity in disregarding it. This is probably not as difficult as it sounds—the fact that the judge excluded it as a matter of law means that the judge did not find it very convincing to begin with.

The remainder of this chapter assumes that the factfinder is the jury, and uses the word "jury" rather than "factfinder."

How is the court likely to react to the Four Crooners' attempt to testify to the alleged oral term? It is quite easy to see why the parol evidence rule might be useful in a case like this. The parties went to the trouble of recording their contract in writing and the royalty provision seems definitive and clear. Surely, had the parties agreed to an 18 percent royalty on sales over 100,000 units, this would have been in the writing. The absence of the term in the writing suggests either that the Four Crooners are mistaken in thinking that Integrated Recording agreed to it, or they were very sloppy in not making sure that the writing reflected what was actually agreed, or worse, they are making it up. Whatever the reason, the testimony is suspect and maybe it is best that the jury never gets to hear it. Because the Four Crooners' case is entirely based on the alleged oral term, the lawsuit can be dismissed summarily.

Say that the facts of the dispute were different. The written contract is as stated above, but the Four Crooners do not claim an agreement for increased royalties. Instead, they claim that Integrated Recording made an oral promise at the time of signing the contract that it would arrange a ten-city concert tour to promote the album. It failed to do this and denies agreeing to it. The written agreement is completely silent on the question of promotional tours and concerts. If the parol evidence rule simply barred all testimony of oral agreement, it would be too blunt an instrument. Therefore, the rule is more nuanced. As this testimony does not directly contradict the writing, it may be less presumptively suspect and there may be a greater justification for admitting it. The following sections explore these nuances. Before that, it is useful to articulate some of the features of the rule that have been stated or suggested by the preceding discussion:

1. The rule only applies when a recorded agreement has been executed. The rule applies whether the record is comprehensive or incomplete. However, the more complete the recorded agreement, the more rigorous the application of the rule.
2. The record must have been adopted by both parties. It need not be signed by them as long as it is shown to be a mutual document. Naturally, the presence of signatures more strongly proves that it is a joint memorandum, but a communication written by one party and received by the other without objection qualifies. A memorandum composed by only one of the parties and not disseminated to the other does not bring the rule into effect. To invoke the parol evidence rule, a record must therefore have qualities beyond those needed to satisfy the statute of frauds. This is because the statute of

frauds is concerned with the minimal amount of content needed to establish the existence of a contract, while the parol evidence rule is concerned with the degree to which the record should be used to exclude extrinsic evidence of what was agreed.

3. The word "parol" suggests that the rule is primarily concerned with oral communications between the parties before or at the time of execution of the recorded contract. However, the rule also covers prior recorded communications.
4. The rule is not designed to bar all parol evidence, but to exclude presumptively irrelevant or concocted testimony while allowing the jury to hear honest and pertinent evidence of what was actually agreed. The rule must therefore be sufficiently fine-tuned to allow the court to make this distinction. Herein lies the greatest complexity and difficulty in devising and applying a rational rule.
5. The rule contemplates a two-stage process. When the parol evidence is proffered, the judge must make an initial finding of admissibility. If the judge finds that the evidence is admissible, it is presented to the jury, which makes the ultimate finding on credibility. The judge's initial determination is characterized as a question of law, but it is not necessarily devoid of factual evaluation. This is one of the confusing aspects of the rule. Although the jury may eventually have to decide if the evidence is believable, the judge, in making the initial decision on admissibility, is also concerned with the plausibility of the proffered evidence, a preliminary issue of credibility. This two-stage process is not confined to parol evidence, but is commonly used where a judge has to decide the admissibility of any evidence. To prevent the jury from hearing inadmissible evidence, judges routinely conduct a hearing outside the presence of the jury to decide if the evidence should be admitted. This reinforces the point made above that the parol evidence rule really does operate as a rule of evidence for most purposes, even though its characterization as a rule of substantive law has some legal consequences.

§12.5 THE DEGREE OF FINALITY OF THE RECORDED CONTRACT: TOTAL AND PARTIAL INTEGRATION

The impact of the parol evidence rule depends on the degree to which the record executed by the parties constitutes a comprehensive and final memorandum of their agreement. In short, if the record is full, complete, unambiguous, and clear, the rule excludes all parol evidence. But to the extent that the record does not fully and unequivocally cover all of the agreed terms, parol evidence is admissible to supplement it. Even here, however, the parol evidence cannot contradict what has been recorded or add to those aspects of the agreement that have been fully dealt with in the record. As discussed in section 12.6, it can be a difficult question of interpretation to determine whether and to what extent the record is comprehensive and final.

If the record is a complete, final, and certain expression of the parties' agreement (that is, it unambiguously and clearly expresses every term in the agreement, and it is intended to be the exclusive statement of everything that was agreed), it is said to be totally or completely integrated. If the record is truly a total integration, then, by definition, no terms can exist beyond those set out in it. It follows that neither party should be allowed to offer parol evidence tending to prove terms extrinsic to the record because such evidence is irrelevant or incredible.

If the record is not a complete and final expression of the agreement it is said to be partially integrated or unintegrated. The record may fully and finally express some but not all of the terms, or it may not fully and finally express any term. If so, the parol evidence rule permits parol evidence to be admitted to supplement or explain the record to the extent that it is not integrated. However, the parol evidence must be consistent with the record and cannot contradict or vary terms that are covered by the record.

§12.6 THE PROCESS OF DEALING WITH PAROL EVIDENCE

The issue of the admissibility of parol evidence could arise early in the suit if one of the parties applies for summary judgment or dismissal in response to a claim or defense based on an alleged parol term. Because the admissibility of parol evidence is a legal question, a dispute on admissibility is often appropriate for summary adjudication. If the case is not disposed of on the pleadings and it goes to trial, the admissibility of the evidence may be challenged when an attempt is made to introduce it. As noted before, the evaluation of parol evidence involves two stages. In the first, the judge decides admissibility as a legal matter. If the evidence is admitted, the jury evaluates its credibility. The following discussion looks more closely at the process involved in each of these two stages, which may be charted as shown in Diagram 12B.

Diagram 12B

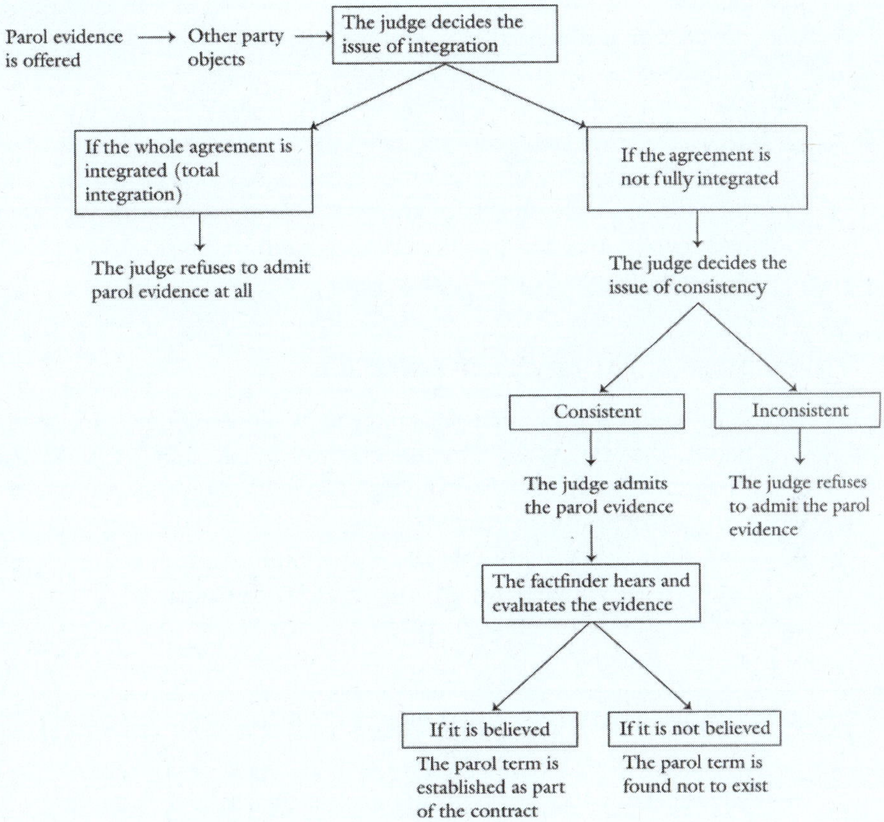

Stage 1: The judge's determination

In making the finding of admissibility, the judge conducts an inquiry that may itself be split into two sequential components:

1. Logically, the first issue to be resolved by the judge is the question of integration—whether the record is a full and final expression of the agreement as a whole (that is, a complete integration). If so, the court does not get beyond the first inquiry, because the parol evidence may not be admitted.
2. If the record is not a complete integration, consistent supplementary parol evidence is admissible. The judge's inquiry then turns to whether the proffered parol evidence is in fact consistent with and not contradictory to what has been recorded. If it contradicts the record, it may not be admitted, and it still never reaches the jury.

In some cases, it may be easy to separate the issue of integration from the issue of consistency, and it is logical that the first must be resolved before the second is reached. However, in other cases, the inquiry into integration is influenced by the question of whether the alleged parol term is consistent with the record, and these two stages often meld into one another. That is, unless the intent to integrate is so clear that there is no doubt on the matter, the extent to which the alleged parol term is reconcilable with the writing may affect the court's decision on whether an integration was reasonably intended by the parties. Therefore, courts do not always proceed in the sequence that is charted here.

Stage 2: The jury's determination

If the judge's preliminary inquiry into the evidence leads to the determination that the subject matter covered by the alleged term has not been integrated into the record and that the proffered parol evidence is consistent with what has been recorded, the judge rules the evidence admissible. It may then be presented to the jury, which is responsible for the ultimate decision on whether the parties agreed to the term.[4]

§12.7 DETERMINING THE QUESTION OF INTEGRATION

The determination of admissibility of evidence is the judge's function, so in the context of the parol evidence rule, intent to integrate is treated as a question of law. A court must interpret the record to decide if the parties intended it to be a full and final expression of their agreement. In some cases, the parties' intent to integrate is clearly apparent from the completeness of the record and its language. If so, intent to integrate may be determined under the objective test by interpreting the plain meaning of the language of the record as a whole. If a court determines intent to integrate purely on the basis of the record itself, without any recourse to extrinsic evidence of intent, it is said to reach that conclusion on the basis of the "four corners" of the document.

However, it is not always appropriate to determine integration purely on the basis of the objective appearance of the record. A strict and invariable "four corners" approach may disregard contextual evidence that is helpful in deciding intent to integrate. Even when a record appears at face value to

4. As noted in section 12.4, where the parties have agreed to a bench trial, the dichotomy between judge and factfinder is rather strained because the judge acts both as legal arbiter on admissibility and as ultimate factfinder.

be comprehensive, inquiry into the context in which it was recorded may dispel this impression. Therefore, if there is contextual evidence relevant to deciding whether the parties intended the record to be fully integrated, a court should go beyond the face value of the record to decide if the parties intended the record to be a full and final expression of their agreement. This does not mean that courts will always consider extrinsic evidence in deciding integration. Some courts are more open than others to going beyond the four corners of the document. Even courts that are generally receptive to extrinsic evidence may refuse to consider it where the intent to integrate is strongly expressed in the record, particularly where the record contains a merger clause that expresses the intent to integrate.[5] If the court does consider extrinsic evidence, the judge's evaluation of that evidence is preliminary. If the judge concludes that the evidence is admissible as a matter of law, the jury will be the final arbiter of its factual truth.

When an apparently integrated agreement does not contain the term that was allegedly agreed to, one of the key questions in determining integration under the contextual approach is to ask whether the circumstances offer an explanation of why the term may not have been included in the writing. Restatement, Second, §216(2)(b) expresses this concept by asking whether the term is such as "might naturally be omitted" from the record. UCC §2.202, Official Comment 3, suggests a similar inquiry: Would the term "certainly have been included" in the document had it been agreed to? The UCC test sounds more favorable to admission because it excludes the evidence only if it clearly would have been part of the writing if the parties had agreed to it. However, in most cases, this test would not likely give a different result than the Restatement's inquiry into whether the term might naturally have been agreed separately. Even under the contextual approach to integration, the parties' manifested intent to integrate, apparent from the record itself, is given great weight. Therefore, where the record is clear, unambiguous, and apparently complete, proffered extrinsic evidence has to be very plausible and compelling to overcome the conclusion that the record itself demonstrates an intent to integrate. The extrinsic evidence must both be reconcilable with the apparent intent and demonstrate a justification for going beyond the writing.

Masterson v. Sine, 436 P.2d 561 (Cal. 1968), is a well-known example of the contextual approach, focusing on whether a term absent from the writing might naturally be omitted from it. Masterson and his wife sold a ranch to the Sines, Masterson's sister and her husband. The written contract granted the Mastersons an option to repurchase the ranch at a price to be fixed by a formula. Masterson later became bankrupt and his trustee attempted to exercise the repurchase option to bring the property into Masterson's estate

5. Merger clauses are explained later in this section.

for the benefit of his creditors. The Sines claimed that the trustee could not exercise the option because the parties had orally agreed at the time of the sale that the option was personal to the Mastersons and could not be transferred to or exercised by anyone else. The majority found that such an agreement might naturally be made outside the written contract in a family transaction. The dissent disagreed with the majority's approach and resolution. It found the writing to be integrated on its face and criticized the "might naturally be omitted" test as too uncertain and open-ended. Even if that test was appropriate, the dissent did not find that this oral term would have satisfied it. A restriction on transfer of the option would not naturally be excluded from the writing if the parties had agreed to it. The option itself was granted in the writing, so surely any restriction on its exercise would be set out there too if it was part of their agreement. The dissent also commented on the credibility of the Sines' assertion: it was particularly suspicious because it was aimed at keeping the property out of Masterson's bankruptcy estate.

Myskina v. Conde Nast Publications, Inc., 386 F. Supp. 2d 409 (S.D.N.Y. 2005), is a good contrast to *Masterson*. Myskina, a Russian tennis champion, agreed with Conde Nast to pose semi-nude for photographs to be published in a "sports" issue of *GQ* magazine. Immediately before the photographs were taken, Myskina signed a written release in which she irrevocably and unqualifiedly consented to the use of the photographs by Conde Nast. The first photos taken during the photo shoot portrayed Myskina as Lady Godiva. She was not entirely nude in these photos, but wore flesh-colored pants and, had long hair covering her breasts. The photos taken after that were more revealing. Myskina alleged that she had expressed discomfort over posing for them but the photographer assured her that only the Lady Godiva photos would be published.[6] *GQ* magazine published the Lady Godiva photos. The photographer subsequently sold the more revealing photos, which were published in another magazine. Myskina sued Conde Nast and the photographer for damages and an injunction on the grounds that those photos were published without her authorization. Her suit did not survive summary judgment. She sought to testify to the oral undertaking to publish only the Lady Godiva photos, but the court refused to admit that evidence. The court found that the release, interpreted in its plain meaning within the context of the transaction, was an integrated document that clearly and comprehensively expressed unrestricted consent to publication. The alleged

6. Myskina did not argue (and the court did not consider) that the alleged oral agreement was not subject to the parol evidence rule because it was made subsequent to the written release. This probably would not have been a good argument. Even though the oral agreement followed the writing, which was executed at the beginning of the photo shoot, they did occur during the same period of interaction and should be viewed as contemporaneous. (*See* the *Kehr Packages* case discussed in section 12.3.)

oral term imposed a fundamental condition on that consent that would not have been omitted from the writing had it been agreed to by the parties.

Many recorded contracts contain a merger clause, so called because it signifies that all the terms of the agreement have been merged into the record. (Sometimes courts use the synonymous term "integration clause.") A merger clause states that the recorded contract is the entire agreement between the parties, and that no representations or promises have been made save for those set out in the record. Where the record appears to be complete, the inclusion of a merger clause is strong evidence of integration. *Baker DC, LLC v. Baggette Construction, Inc.*, cited in section 12.3.1, is a typical example of this. The court concluded that the final written contract was fully integrated because it was 12-pages long, detailed and apparently comprehensive, and contained a merger clause. A merger clause in a record that seems to be complete is therefore likely to be effective in disposing of the issue of integration and insulating the writing from parol evidence. However, a merger clause is not always conclusive. Sometimes courts will go behind a merger clause and admit parol evidence, where, under all the circumstances of the transaction, one of the parties makes a plausible argument that, despite appearances, the record is not really integrated, and the alleged parol term can be reconciled with it. A court may be more amenable to such an argument where the merger clause is a standard term.

The following variations of the facts of the contract between the Four Crooners and Integrated Recordings (used in section 12.4) illustrate some of the difficulties in deciding the question of integration. Assume that the parties' agreement is set out in a five-page written contract. The contract specifies the songs to be used in the album, the design, production, and dissemination of the album in various media, the production and release dates, and the 15 percent royalty to be paid on "gross receipts." It has numerous provisions setting out the duties of the Four Crooners in the development of the album as well as detailed provisions relating to the sale of the album and the accounting for and payment of royalties. It ends with a merger clause. The writing appears to be full and comprehensive. Consider the same two alternative allegations of parol agreement made by the Four Crooners in section 12.4. One was that the parties agreed orally to a royalty of 18 percent on sales over 100,000 copies. The other was that Integrated Recording undertook to arrange a ten-city concert tour to promote the album. On a strict "four corners" approach, the writing is unquestionably integrated, and no evidence would be admitted of either of these alleged parol terms. The Four Crooners are not likely to do any better on the alleged royalty increase on a contextual approach. The written contract specifies the royalty percentage, so it is not natural that the parties might agree to part of that term separately. It is hard to reconcile the parol augmentation of the royalty term with the unequivocal written term. The term relating to the concert tour is not as badly at odds with the writing, but it does not seem natural that this single term would have been omitted from an otherwise detailed written agreement. In addition, the only contextual evidence tendered is the disputed, self-serving testimony of the Four Crooners themselves about what was said at the time that the writing was signed. This shows that credibility issues cannot be entirely divorced from this legal inquiry, and the issues of integration and consistency, while doctrinally distinct, often intermingle in the decision on integration.

However, say that the written contract was not as detailed as described above. It is a simple, one-page document that sets out the songs to be included in the album, the production dates, and the release dates, and the 15 percent royalty to be paid on gross receipts. It has none of the detailed provisions relating to the parties' performance set out above and no merger clause. Parol evidence on the increase in royalties is still not likely to be admissible because the royalty clause appears to be definitive and not easily reconcilable with the alleged parol agreement. However, evidence of the undertaking of a concert tour stands a better chance of admission. The absence of details about the obligations of the parties in performing the contract and the lack of a merger clause could make it more natural that an agreement about a promotional tour might be made separately from the writing.

§12.8 AMBIGUITY OR INDEFINITENESS IN AN INTEGRATED RECORD

The discussion of integration up to now has assumed that the terms of the record are clear and unambiguous. Where that is not so, a further complication arises: no matter how firmly the parties may have intended the record to be a full and final expression of their agreement, if a term of the agreement expressed in the record is unclear or ambiguous, the record cannot be treated as an integration of that term. If extrinsic evidence is available to clarify the indefiniteness, that is the best means of ascertaining the parties' intended meaning. Parol evidence is therefore admissible to clarify the uncertainty or ambiguity. This does not mean that uncertainty or ambiguity allows for the admission of whatever parol evidence may be tendered on any aspect of the contract. The evidence must be pertinent to the meaning of the unclear term, and it must be reconcilable with what has been written.

The discussion of interpretation in Chapter 10 explains that courts are generally receptive to available contextual evidence that casts light on the meaning of the recorded language. Even if the record seems clear and unambiguous on its face, the contextual approach assumes that recorded words do not have a constant, immutable meaning, and that evidence of the context in which the words were used could color their meaning. For example, the written contract between the Four Crooners and Integrated Recording provided that the Four Crooners would receive a royalty of "15 percent of gross receipts from sales of the album." Contrary to the facts used in previous versions of this illustration, the Four Crooners do not make any allegation that the parties agreed to a higher royalty for sales over 100,000 copies. Rather, the dispute centers on the meaning of "gross receipts from sales of the album." The dispute has arisen because Integrated Recording has granted limited licenses to various online music providers which allows them to make the album available to their customers for a short time. The Four Crooners contend that the revenue from these short-term licenses are "sales of the album" that must be included in "gross receipts." Integrated Recording argues that the clear language of the written contract intends to confine the royalties to 15 percent of "sales" and short-term licenses are not sales. The Four Crooners seek to testify that the parties discussed what was meant by "sales" at the time of signing the contract, and they orally agreed that "sales" meant all income generated by the album. A literal four corners approach may focus on the ordinary meaning of "sales" and conclude that the agreement is unambiguous—a short-term license is not a sale, but just a temporary grant of the right to use the album. On that approach the agreement is not ambiguous and the parol evidence rule would apply, so that even if the agreement is not fully integrated, the evidence is deemed contradictory to the writing and is inadmissible. However, a contextual approach places less confidence in the face-value meaning of the record. Provided that the written language is reasonably susceptible of the meaning alleged by the Four Crooners, this evidence must be considered as a preliminary matter to decide the question of whether the writing is unclear. If the evidence indicates that the writing is not as clear as might seem on a literal reading, the parol evidence rule does not exclude the evidence to clarify it, even if the writing otherwise appears to be full and final. (If the court decides to admit the evidence, this does not end the matter. The Four Crooners would then have to persuade the jury that the oral agreement was made.)

§12.9 DISTINGUISHING CONSISTENCY FROM CONTRADICTION

If the judge decides that the record is a full and final expression of the parties' agreement (that is, it is totally integrated) the inquiry ends and the parol evidence is excluded. However, if the judge determines that the record is not totally integrated, parol evidence is admissible to supplement or explain the record, but not to contradict it. Stated differently, even where the agreement is not fully integrated, parol evidence cannot be admitted if it is inconsistent with, and cannot be reconciled with, what has been recorded.

It may be obvious that an alleged parol agreement contradicts the record. For example, if a recorded contract for the sale of a house states that the price is $500,000, evidence of a contemporaneous oral agreement that the parties agreed to a price of $475,000 cannot be reconciled with the record. A second example of inconsistency is the illustration in section 12.7 involving the Four Crooners' proffered testimony that the parties had agreed to an 18 percent royalty on sales over 100,000 copies. It is very hard to reconcile this with the clear term in the written contract that provides for a 15 percent royalty on gross receipts. However, in some cases, the possible inconsistency is less clear and may be trickier to decide. A conflict may go beyond an obvious clash with an express term and may arise where the alleged parol term cannot be reconciled with the legal import of the record. Both *Masterson* and *Myskina*, discussed in section 12.7, involved this more subtle question of contradiction. The alleged parol term did not directly clash with a written term, but it departed from the normal legal or factual implications of the language. That is, there was no language in the written contract in *Masterson* stating that the option was assignable, and there was no language in the release in *Myskina* that expressly authorized the publication of the nude photos. However, the absence of any stated limitations on transfer or on authority to publish created the implied understanding that they did not exist.

Maday v. Grathwohl, 805 N.W.2d 285 (Minn. Ct. App. 2011), provides another example of a nuanced contradiction. The Grathwohls, owners of a pig farm, needed a means of disposing of the manure generated by their pigs. They therefore entered into a written "manure easement agreement" with Maday, the owner of neighboring farmland, under which the Grathwohls had the right to apply manure generated on their farm on Maday's farmland. The written agreement made it clear that this arrangement was mutually beneficial to the parties—the Grathwohls would be able to get rid of their manure, and Maday would get manure to fertilize his land. The agreement did not require any other compensation to be paid by either party. The agreement also contained no language suggesting that the Grathwohls were obligated to provide manure to Maday, and it specifically stated that they made no warranty as to the quantity or quality of the manure. For several years after this contract was executed, all the manure from the Grathwohls' farm was applied to Maday's land. However, about seven years after the agreement was made, the Grathwohls began to sell some of the manure to third parties, thereby reducing the amount available for fertilizing Maday's land. Maday sued, claiming that by selling the manure, the Grathwohls had breached an oral agreement, made when the easement was granted, under which they had promised that Maday would receive all the manure generated by the pig farm. The trial court refused to admit this evidence of the alleged oral agreement and granted summary judgment to the Grathwohls. On appeal, Maday argued that the evidence should have been admitted because the oral agreement was separate from and consistent with the written easement. The court of appeals disagreed and affirmed the trial court's grant of summary judgment. It found that the written contract gave the Grathwohls the right, but not the duty, to spread the manure on Maday's land, and there was no provision in the contract that transferred ownership of the manure. Therefore, the court held that because the alleged oral agreement covered the same subject matter as the written agreement (the manure), and was part of the same transaction, it would not naturally be made as a separate agreement. In addition, the alleged oral term was inconsistent with the written agreement, which did not appear to contemplate that the Grathwohls made any commitment to give Maday manure.

Courts do not approach the issue of conflict with implied terms uniformly. A judge who is not enthusiastic about barring parol evidence will likely be reluctant to find a conflict unless there is a very clear and express inconsistency between the record and the parol evidence. A judge who is more favorably disposed to excluding parol evidence is likely to be more willing to find a conflict between the proffered parol evidence and a term that is implied into, but not expressly articulated, in the record.

It is possible, as a doctrinal matter, to separate the inquiry into integration from the question of consistency, but court opinions show that in practice these two concepts are often interrelated. That is, if the court considers the parol term to be at odds with the record, this factor may influence the court in deciding whether the record is integrated. In fact, Restatement, Second's "might naturally be omitted" test and Article 2's "would certainly have been included" test speak as much to consistency as they do to finality of the record. These two inquiries melded into each other in both the *Masterson* and *Myskina* cases. In *Masterson* the majority's conclusion that the limitation on the option might naturally be made as a separate agreement was motivated in part by its perception that the limitation did not directly contradict any express language in the written grant of the option. The dissent saw the limitation as contradictory because the usual implication of law is that an option is transferable unless the agreement clearly states otherwise. In *Myskina*, the court's conclusion that the release was integrated was based in its view that the limitation on the release would certainly have been included in the writing had the parties agreed to it. The court went on to say that, in any event, a parol term qualifying the extent of the release was inconsistent with the absolute release in the writing. *Maday* also shows that courts do not always neatly separate questions of contradiction and integration. The written contract contained a merger clause, which the court found on its face to be a clear integration of the writing. However, the court's discussion of integration comes after its determination of contradiction. If integration and contradiction were completely distinct questions, the court should have disposed of the integration issue first, because once the agreement is integrated, the question of whether the alleged term is consistent would be irrelevant.

§12.10 THE IMPACT OF THE PAROL EVIDENCE RULE ON EVIDENCE OF COURSE OF PERFORMANCE, COURSE OF DEALING, AND TRADE USAGE

In dealing with interpretation in context, section 10.1.3 explained the meaning of and the role played by course of performance, course of dealing, and trade usage. This section focuses on what impact the parol evidence rule might have on the admissibility of this type of contextual evidence. Course of performance can usually be disposed of easily because it is typically not parol evidence. Although it is conceivable that there could be a course of performance between the oral agreement and the execution of the record, in most situations any course of performance only takes place after the record has been executed. However, course of dealing is, by definition, something that occurs prior to the contract and trade usage exists prior to and contemporaneously with it. Therefore, a court could treat evidence of course of dealing or trade usage as a form of parol evidence and could exclude it if the agreement is integrated or, even if not, if it cannot be reconciled with the written terms. However, course of dealing and trade usage differ in an important respect from a party's testimony relating to the discussions that led to the alleged parol agreement—a course of dealing or trade usage can be established by more reliable objective evidence of mutual conduct or accepted custom. Courts are therefore more likely to admit evidence of course of dealing and trade usage.

Restatement, Second, §213 provides no guidance on how a court should approach this kind of contextual evidence. It refers only to parol terms that were allegedly agreed to between the parties during their interaction leading up to the execution of the record. By contrast, UCC §2.202(a) specifically permits an otherwise integrated agreement to be supplemented by evidence of course of dealing and trade usage. (Section 2.202(a) also specifically permits supplementation of the writing by evidence of course of performance, but this provision is not necessary to allow admission in most cases because, as noted above, course of performance typically does not even qualify as parol evidence.)

Where the record of the contract is not a full and complete expression of the terms of the contract, it is easy to see why a court would be receptive to course of dealing or trade usage evidence to supplement or explain the contract's terms. For example, *Grace Label, Inc. v. Kliff*, 355 F. Supp. 2d 965 (S.D. Iowa 2005), involved a contract to supply trading cards bearing the likeness of Britney Spears, to be placed in packets of snack food. Sadly, the cards smelled bad and were unfit for inclusion in food packages. The seller sought to admit evidence of a course of dealing to establish that it had not breached the contract by supplying smelly cards. The seller offered this evidence of prior transactions to establish the parties' expectation that the seller would use the same materials in printing the cards as it had used in similar prior transactions. The seller had done so, and therefore argued that it was not responsible for the problem with the cards. The court overruled the buyer's objection to the admission of this evidence, which it held merely explained and supplemented, but did not contradict the recorded contract term.

However, UCC §2.202 goes beyond merely allowing evidence of course of dealing, trade usage or course of performance where the agreement is not integrated. It makes it clear that this type of contextual evidence should be admitted even where the record is intended as a final expression of agreement.[7] That is, §2.202 presumes very strongly that the parties intend to contract in light of their own and the market's customary practices. This means that the parties could reasonably take for granted that the contract includes terms arising from these sources, and may not mention them in the record, even where that record is otherwise fully integrated. This strong recognition of course of dealing and trade usage compels parties to use very clear and specific language in the record if they truly do intend to exclude a course of dealing or a trade usage from their contract.

The strength of trade usage and the likelihood that it will be found consistent with the writing in all but the most overwhelming cases of direct conflict is illustrated by *Nanakuli Paving & Rock Co. v. Shell Oil Co.*, 664 F.2d 772 (9th Cir. 1981).[8] Shell and Nanakuli entered into a contract under which Shell supplied asphalt for Nanakuli's use in paving projects on the island of Oahu. The contract did not state a fixed price for the asphalt, but provided that the price for each order would be Shell's "posted price at time of delivery." Nanakuli claimed that despite that language, usage in the Oahu paving trade required Shell to "price protect" Nanakuli by charging it the price posted at the time that Nanakuli bid on a project, rather than the price at the time of delivery. This protected Nanakuli by charging it no more than the price on which it based its bid if the price rose between that time and the time of delivery. The court allowed the admission of evidence of the usage notwithstanding the contract provision fixing the price at the time of delivery. Although the price term was clear and seemed quite absolute, the court found no inconsistency between the price term and the price protection usage. *Nanakuli* may go further than other courts in its notion of

7. Official Comment 1(c) to §2.202 states further that the court does not need to find that the record is ambiguous as a precondition to admissibility of this type of evidence.
8. This case is also discussed in section 10.1.3 in connection with the role of trade usage in interpretation.

consistency, but it does show that, at least where a sale of goods is involved, parties should not lightly assume that trade usage or course of dealing evidence will be barred by an apparently integrated record that does not specifically negate the usage or course of dealing.

§12.11 THE COLLATERAL AGREEMENT RULE

The collateral agreement rule is sometimes referred to as an exception to the parol evidence rule, but it is not really an exception at all. Rather, it follows from an application of the general principles of the parol evidence rule. The collateral agreement rule developed as a means of softening a firm "four corners" approach to parol evidence at a time when courts were more inclined to determine integration by looking no further than the four corners of the record. A court that adopts a broader contextual approach to parol evidence and uses the Restatement, Second's "might naturally be omitted" test or Article 2's "would certainly have been included" test does not need the collateral agreement rule because those tests cover the same type of situation and are less rigorous. However, the rule still features in some modern cases.

The gist of the rule is that even where a contract is integrated, if the parol agreement is sufficiently distinct from the scope of the record, it can be seen as a different contract, related to but separate from the integrated recorded agreement. If so, evidence of this collateral agreement is not barred by the parol evidence rule. Stated differently, even if the alleged parol agreement relates to the same transaction as the record, if it is self-contained and distinct enough to be seen as a collateral agreement, the parties may not have intended it to be covered by the integrated record. Evidence of the collateral agreement may therefore be admitted. The requirement of consistency applies even where the parol agreement is found to be collateral, so evidence of a collateral agreement that contradicts the record is inadmissible. The determination of whether an agreement is collateral can be slippery, and different courts have different views on the relationship between the record and the parol agreement. A requirement that is regularly expressed is that both the subject matter of and the consideration for the parol agreement must be distinct and capable of being separately identified.

Mitchell v. Lath, 160 N.E. 646 (N.Y. 1928), is an early, well-known case on the collateral agreement rule. The seller of real property agreed orally to remove an unsightly ice house on land adjacent to the property sold to the buyer. This undertaking was not included in the written contract for the sale of the property. The written contract appeared comprehensive and included a number of other terms ancillary to the sale. The majority of the court refused to find that the agreement to remove the ice house was a collateral agreement—it was related closely enough to the sale of the property that one would expect to find it in the writing if it had been agreed to. The dissent felt that the oral undertaking was distinct enough that the parties could have made it as a separate ancillary contract, not intended to be integrated into the writing.

The collateral agreement rule was also considered in *Myskina v. Conde Nast Publications, Inc.*, discussed in sections 12.7. and 12.9. The court held that the oral agreement limiting the magazine's right to publish the nude photos was not collateral to, but an integral part of the release, and that it contradicted it. The close conceptual connection between the collateral agreement rule and the Restatement, Second, and UCC tests is apparent from the account of these cases. It is even more striking in *Maday v. Grathwohl*, the case involving the manure easement agreement, also discussed in section 12.7. The court did not mention the collateral agreement rule and discussed consistency on the basis of a test equivalent to the Restatement, Second's "might naturally be omitted" test. However, in discussing the admissibility of the evidence that the Grathwohls made an oral commitment to give all the manure to Maday, the court focused on factors associated with the collateral agreement rule: The agreements addressed the same subject matter and had the same consideration.

§12.12 EXCEPTIONS TO THE PAROL EVIDENCE RULE: EVIDENCE TO ESTABLISH GROUNDS FOR AVOIDANCE OR INVALIDITY OR TO SHOW A CONDITION PRECEDENT

§12.12.1 The Exception Relating to the Validity or Voidability of the Contract

The purpose of the parol evidence rule is to protect the integrity of a recorded contract by preventing a party from asserting alleged parol agreements that cannot be reconciled with the recorded contract. The rule is not intended to prevent a party from challenging the validity of the recorded agreement on grounds of fraud, duress, illegality, mistake, and other bases for invalidating or avoiding the contract. *Riversisland Cold Storage, Inc. v. Fresno-Madera Production Credit Ass'n*, 291 P.3d 316 (Cal. 2013), explains this rationale succinctly: The parol evidence rule is meant to protect the terms of a valid recorded contract but should not bar evidence that goes to the very validity of the agreement, even if that evidence contradicts the recorded agreement. The court took the same approach in *Golden Eye Resources, LLC v. Ganske*,

853 N.W.2d 544 (N.D. 2014), holding that contradictory parol evidence is admissible where the evidence relates to fraudulent misrepresentations made to induce the contract.

A court may allow the fraud exception even where the victim of the fraud specifically affirms in the recorded contract that it has not relied on any misrepresentations made outside the record. For example, in *America's Directories, Inc. v. Stellhorn One Hour Photo, Inc.*, 833 N.E.2d 1059 (Ind. Ct. App. 2005), the president of America's Directories, a corporation that sold advertising in a telephone directory, used persistent hard-selling techniques to persuade Stellhorn to sign three standard contracts under which it purchased three years' advertising in the directory. Stellhorn was reluctant to buy the ads, and only did so after being assured orally that it could cancel after one year. The standard contracts stated unequivocally that they could not be canceled, and they contained a merger clause excluding all verbal agreements and representations not contained in the writing. Despite that, the court admitted evidence of the oral agreement because the evidence indicated that Stellhorn had grounds to avoid the contracts on the basis that America's Directories never intended to allow Stellhorn to cancel and it made several other false representations to induce him to enter the contracts.[9]

If the evidence is admitted, the party claiming avoidance of the contract must still prove that the elements justifying avoidance are satisfied. For example, as discussed in section 13.6, one of the elements of fraud is that the victim must have been justified in relying on the false representation. The party alleging fraud may have difficulty persuading a jury of justifiable reliance on a material misrepresentation that is not contained in the record, especially if the record contains a merger clause and states that no representations have been made apart from those contained in the record. In *Riversisland*, the borrowers, who had fallen behind in their loan payments, entered into a written agreement with the lender under which the lender undertook to extend the loan for three months in exchange for additional collateral. The lender's representative told the borrowers that the agreement extended the loan for two years. The borrowers claimed that this was a fraudulent misrepresentation and sought to offer evidence of the misrepresentation. Although the court held that the evidence was admissible under the fraud exception to the parol evidence rule, it pointed out that the borrowers would still have to establish fraud to avoid the contract, and suggested that they may have trouble proving the element of justifiable reliance, given their failure to read the recorded agreement.

The fraud and other avoidance exceptions can only be used if the purpose of introducing the evidence is to avoid the contract. They cannot be

9. Fraud usually involves a misrepresentation of fact. However, a misrepresentation of intent can also constitute fraud if, at the time of entering the contract, the party making the misrepresentation intends to renege on its promise. *See* section 13.6.2.

used as a pretext for trying to enforce the parol term. In *Goens v. Blood*, 437 F. Supp. 3d 793 (S.D. Cal. 2020), a lessee of commercial premises claimed that the lessor had made an oral assurance that the lessor would not terminate the two-year lease term during the period of the lease. The lessor did terminate the lease and the lessee sued to enforce the oral undertaking, which directly contradicted a term in the recorded lease that permitted the lessor to terminate on 60-days' notice. In addition, the lease included a merger clause. The lessee argued that the lessor had committed fraud in making the oral representation, and invoked the fraud exception. The court rejected this argument — the lessee was not raising fraud to avoid the lease, but for the impermissible purpose of trying to enforce the inadmissible alleged parol agreement.

§12.12.2 The False Recital Exception

Along similar lines, parol evidence is also admissible to show that a fact recited in a record is false. For example, a recorded contract between the buyer and seller of a car may state that in consideration of $10,000 paid by the buyer, the seller agrees to transfer ownership of the car to the buyer. If the buyer did not in fact pay the $10,000, the seller would be permitted to introduce evidence that the money was never paid. The purpose of this is to prevent the buyer from using the parol evidence rule to evade payment by blocking the seller's testimony of nonpayment. That testimony would, in effect, turn the recital of payment into an implied promise to pay.[10]

§12.12.3 The Condition Precedent Exception

Another exception to the rule permits parol evidence to be admitted to show that the agreement was subject to a condition. Conditions are explained more fully in Chapter 16. In essence, the parties may reach agreement on an exchange of performances, but provide that one or both parties' performance obligation will take effect only if an uncertain event occurs or does not occur. For example, a buyer and seller enter into a contract for the sale of real property for $500,000, but the buyer has only

---

10. Section 7.7 discusses the possibility that parties may use a false recital of consideration in an attempt to validate a gift. That is, the transaction may not have been a sale of the car at all, but a donation of the car from the party designated as the seller to the party designated as the buyer. The parties may merely have recited the fact of payment to make it appear as if the donor received consideration for the promise of the gift. In this situation, although the seller's parol evidence of nonpayment is admissible, the buyer would defend the seller's suit for the price at trial by testifying that the parties never intended the buyer to pay for the car.

$100,000 in savings and needs to obtain a loan of $400,000, secured by a mortgage on the property, to pay the price. The parties therefore agree that the sale is conditional on the buyer being able to obtain a loan of $400,000 from a financial institution. The effect of the condition is that if the buyer succeeds in getting the loan, the sale proceeds, but if the buyer is unable to obtain the loan despite making best efforts to do so, the performance duties under the contract fall away. Such a condition would normally be included in the recorded contract, but a parol evidence issue is presented if the parties agreed to it orally at the time of entering into the contract and did not include it in the recorded contract of sale. If the buyer fails to proceed with the sale and the seller sues the buyer for breach of contract, the parol evidence rule would normally preclude the buyer from offering testimony of the oral condition, either because the recorded contract is integrated, or even if not, because the alleged condition contradicts the unconditional nature of the buyer's obligation to buy the property. However, the condition precedent exception to the rule may allow admission of the parol condition. The rationale for the exception is that the condition goes to the very existence of contractual obligations, so it does not add to or contradict the terms of the contract, but goes to the issue of whether there is a contractual undertaking at all. The rationale is not convincing because a contract subject to a condition precedent is a contract nevertheless. There is no reason to treat the allegation of a parol condition with any less suspicion than some other term claimed to have been left out of the record. Nevertheless, the exception has long been recognized by courts and is reflected in Restatement, Second, §217.

However, a party's ability to use the exception is restricted by the qualification that the condition precedent cannot be clearly contradictory to the express terms of the recorded contract. As explained in section 12.9, sometimes contradiction is obvious — the parol evidence is contradictory to a term expressed in the record. However, a contradiction may be more subtle — the evidence does not contradict anything expressed in the record, but is inconsistent with a term that would be implied in the absence of agreement to the contrary. The force of the condition precedent exception depends on whether the court defines contradiction narrowly or broadly for its purposes. This is demonstrated by *Torres v. D'Alesso*, 910 N.Y.S.2d 1 (App. Div. 2010). A written contract for the purchase of real estate had no financing contingency and included a merger clause. The buyer failed to proceed with the transaction and the seller sued him for damages. The buyer defended the suit on the basis that the sale was subject to an unfulfilled oral condition precedent that the buyer would be able to obtain financing. The majority of the Appellate Division affirmed the trial court's refusal to admit this testimony and its grant of summary judgment to the seller. The court acknowledged the general rule that parol evidence is admissible to prove a condition precedent to the legal effectiveness of a recorded agreement, provided that the condition does not contradict the express terms of the record. However, the court found that the parol condition did contradict the express terms of the writing, which contained a merger clause and an apparently absolute obligation to pay. A dissenting judge disagreed that the alleged condition was irreconcilable with the writing, arguing that for purposes of the exception, the contradiction must be explicit. The condition here did not contradict any express term of the contract, but merely changed an apparently absolute obligation into a conditional one.

§12.13 RESTRICTIONS ON ORAL MODIFICATION

As stated before, the parol evidence rule does not exclude testimony relating to agreements made after the record. These are not part of the environment in which the record was executed. However, the parties may wish to avoid disputes over possible future allegations of oral modification and may therefore insert a "no oral modification" clause in the record, stating that no modification will be binding unless recorded and signed by both parties. Such clauses are difficult to enforce because courts do not usually consider that the parties can effectively restrict in advance their right to modify orally. The parties' power to modify the contract must include the power to modify the "no oral modification" clause, and the fact that they made an oral modification in itself indicates that they did so. Therefore, although a "no oral modification" clause may make it more difficult for a party to succeed in asserting an oral modification, such a clause may not be a watertight exclusion. A court may be willing to admit evidence of an alleged oral modification despite the existence of the restriction in the record, and to leave it to the jury to decide whether the modification was in fact made.

UCC §2.209(2) appears to change this approach by expressly recognizing the effectiveness of "no oral modification" clauses in sales of goods. However, the recognition is half-hearted because §2.209(4) provides that even if the later oral modification is ineffective because the original contract requires recorded modification, the attempt at oral modification may still operate as a waiver of rights under the original contract. Under §2.209(5) the waiver is generally effective. It can only be retracted in relation to future performance if it has not been detrimentally relied on by the other party, and it cannot be retracted to the extent that it covers performance that has already been rendered.

§12.14 A TRANSNATIONAL PERSPECTIVE ON THE PAROL EVIDENCE RULE

As explained in section 12.4, a principal rationale for the parol evidence rule is that it keeps suspect and unreliable evidence from the jury. Civilian jurisdictions do not generally have jury trials in civil cases, so there is less need for a rule that controls potentially misleading and prejudicial evidence from the jury. Although civilian systems may recognize a presumption in favor of the accuracy of a recorded contract, and some may impose restrictions on the admission of parol evidence in some cases, the general rule is that the terms of a contract may be proved by all relevant evidence. The CISG and the UNIDROIT Principles have adopted the civilian approach and do not contain a rule restricting parol evidence. However, if the parties include a clearly drafted merger clause in the recorded contract, the clause is likely to be given effect to exclude any alleged oral agreement that was not incorporated into the record.

Examples

1. Ann Cestral owned a house on a large central city lot that had been in her family for four generations. When she decided to move to an apartment, she agreed to sell the house to her cousin, Ava Rice. They settled on the price and Ann arranged for her attorney to draw up a contract of sale. When the document was ready for signature, Ann and Ava drove together to the attorney's office. On the way Ann said to Ava, "Our family has owned this house for a long time, and I sold it to you because I want it to remain in the family. Promise me that if you ever decide to sell the house, you will give members of our family the right of first refusal to buy it before you sell it to a stranger." Ava agreed. When Ann and Ava arrived at the attorney's office, the attorney gave them a sales agreement with terms conventionally included in such agreements and they both signed it. The agreement was several pages long and had lots of details. However, it did not include a merger clause. Neither Ann nor Ava told the attorney about their discussion on the way over, so the attorney did not incorporate their agreement on the family's right of first refusal into the written contract.

   Ava took transfer of the house and moved in. Over the next couple of years, large lots in the neighborhood became very valuable because of their central location. Developers were buying houses and demolishing them so the land could be used for high-rise apartments. Two years after she bought the house from Ann, Ava accepted a developer's offer to buy the house for an extraordinarily high price. When Ann found out that Ava had sold the property to the developer, she confronted Ava angrily. In response, Ava handed their written contract to Ann and said, "Show me where this says I can't sell the property to anyone that I please!" Does Ava have a point?

2. Klaus Merger owned two adjoining quarter-acre lots. One had a house on it and the other, overgrown and neglected, had been used by Klaus as a dumping ground for assorted bits of junk, including a couple of broken-down cars. A few months ago, Klaus placed the quarter-acre with the house on the market. Perry Parol expressed interest in buying it and negotiations ensued. Perry eventually agreed to buy it for the asking price on condition that Klaus cleared up the adjacent lot and removed all the junk. Klaus agreed to do this.

   Klaus then produced a standard agreement of sale that he had downloaded and printed from the Internet. The form had the usual provisions found in transactions of this kind, with blank spaces for details such as the property description and price. One of its standard terms was a merger clause, stating, "This is the entire agreement between the parties. No agreements or representations have been made save for those stated herein." There was also a large blank space at the end of the form headed "Additional Terms." Klaus filled out all the other blanks in the form but wrote nothing in the space provided for additional terms. The form therefore did not mention the clearing of the adjacent lot. Both parties signed the form.

   Klaus never cleared the lot and denies ever agreeing to do so. What are Perry's chances of proving and enforcing the oral agreement?

3. Di Aquiri owns a tavern. Margie Rita runs a small, exclusive distillery that makes a variety of health-conscious, socially responsible, nonalcoholic versions of popular liquors. Di entered into a written contract with Margie under which Di bought 100 bottles of Margie's "fat-free, sugar-free, sodium-free, nonalcoholic, non-animal-tested, all-natural faux tequila." In addition to this description of the goods, the writing stated the names and addresses of the parties, the price of "$10 per bottle, subject to discount for cash," the payment date (30 days after delivery), and the delivery date. It also contained a merger clause stating that the writing was intended to be "the complete, exclusive, and final expression of all terms agreed to by the parties." Both parties signed the writing, and Margie delivered the liquor on the due date.

   Consider how the parol evidence rule would affect the following different disputes that arose after delivery.

   a. Upon delivery, Di gave Margie's driver a check for $900, this being the stated contract price of $1,000 less a 10 percent discount for early payment. Margie refuses to allow Di a 10 percent discount. She says that the parties discussed the amount of the discount orally, and she told Di that it was 5 percent. Di claims that they agreed to a 10 percent discount.

b. Di did not pay the driver. Five days later she sent a check for $900 in payment, less a 10 percent discount. Margie concedes that the parties did agree orally that the discount for cash would be 10 percent, but she says that Di is not entitled to the discount because she did not pay cash. Margie argues that "cash payment" means cash on delivery, so Di's payment five days after delivery does not entitle her to any discount. Di says that Margie told her orally that payment within a week of delivery qualifies as cash. Margie denies ever discussing the question.
c. After delivery Di, who is very fussy about the quality of what she serves to her customers, conducted a chemical analysis of the faux tequila. She found that it has traces of fat and sugar (about 0.5 percent of each). Di's tests also revealed that the faux tequila contains about 0.08 percent alcohol. She wishes to reject the goods as nonconforming to the contract and to get her money back. Margie claims that she is not entitled to do this for two reasons. First, Margie has sold faux liquor to Di in the past with similar small traces of fat, sugar, and alcohol, and Di has never objected before. Second, it is widely accepted in the make-believe-liquor industry that one can never completely remove the good stuff, and beverages described as free of a substance may acceptably contain up to 1 percent of it.

4. Gordon Bleu, a chef who owns and operates a restaurant, decided to begin serving game birds to his customers.[11] He found a recipe for pheasant and checked the catalog of his usual supplier, Fairest Fowls, Inc., to see what it cost. The catalog showed "regular" pheasant for $5.00 per pound, and "plump deluxe" pheasant for $12.50 per pound. Gordon decided that "regular" pheasant would be fine, and he called Fairest Fowls and placed an order for 50 birds.

   A couple of days later Fairest Fowls delivered the birds, accompanied by its written delivery invoice. The invoice contained the parties' names and addresses, the date, and the statement "Delivered as per order, 50 regular pheasants @$5.00 per pound. Cash on delivery." The invoice was signed by a representative of Fairest Fowls. Gordon signed the form as requested and paid the driver.

11. This Example is based on Example 2 of Chapter 10, which involved the interpretation of an oral contract. In the present Example, the contract is recorded in the invoice, which is a recorded memorial of agreement for parol evidence purposes. The goal of this Example is to present a parol evidence issue that was absent from Example 2 of Chapter 10. Although there are variations in the facts of these two Examples, a comparison of them highlights how interpretational issues are handled in the presence or absence of a parol evidence issue.

Gordon prepared the birds exactly in accordance with his recipe, but they were tough and uneatable. Gordon complained to Fairest Fowls, which explained that it used the word "regular" in its catalog to denote scrawny birds useful only for soup, and that the more expensive "plump deluxe" variety had to be used if the flesh was to be eaten. Fairest Fowls said that "everyone knew this about pheasants," and it was surprised that Gordon, as a trained chef, was unaware of the distinction.

Gordon insists that there is no reason why he should have understood "regular" in the sense used by Fairest Fowls and he points out that the dictionary meaning of "regular" is "usual, normal, or customary." Fairest Fowls claims that it can produce several experts in the restaurant trade who would attest to the fact that "regular" pheasants are commonly understood to be suitable only for soup.

If Gordon and Fairest Fowls cannot settle their dispute and Gordon decides to sue Fairest Fowls for the return of his money, would Fairest Fowls be able to introduce the testimony of its expert witnesses over Gordon's objection?

5. Beverly Hill, a movie producer, offered a leading role in a new movie to Holly Wood, an actor. The parties met with their lawyers and agents and spent the full morning negotiating the terms of the contract. By noon they had reached agreement. Their attorneys spent the rest of the day drafting the written agreement.

   The parties met again on the following morning and signed the agreement. It provided for Beverly to pay an advance of $2 million to Holly within a week of signing and to pay royalties to Holly when the movie was released. After signing, the lawyers and agents left. Beverly and Holly remained in Beverly's office to celebrate making the deal. As she was sipping her champagne, Holly said, "You know, I am really unhappy about that advance of $2 million that you agreed to pay me next week. I think that it should be higher, say $2.5 million. After all, I have to live until the box office receipts come in." Beverly replied, "No problem, I'll send you a check for $2.5 million instead." The parties did not amend the figure of $2 million in the written contract, and the agreement to increase the advance was not otherwise recorded. The next week, Beverly sent a check of $2 million to Holly as specified in the written agreement. She denies ever agreeing to pay more. The written agreement does not have a "no oral modification" clause.

   Holly immediately sued for the additional $500,000. Beverly applied for summary judgment on the ground that the written contract clearly calls for a payment of $2 million, and no parol evidence can be tendered by Holly to support her claim for more money. Should Beverly be granted summary judgment?

6. Buffy Beefcake is a well-known football star. He was approached by Cal Candid, who asked him if he would pose for a semi-nude photograph to be used in a "Superjocks" calendar that Cal was producing for the next year. Cal told Buffy that the calendar would feature one scantily-attired sports hero per month. Buffy would receive a modest fee of $5,000 (really just an honorarium) for posing and allowing the use of his photo, and all profits from the sales of the calendars would go to a hospital that conducted research on the prevention of sports injuries. Buffy was bashful and did not like the idea of having his revealing photograph on a calendar, but he felt that it was for a good cause, so he agreed. Cal produced a five-page standard contract, which Buffy signed without reading. Had he read it, he would have seen that it said nothing at all about the donation of the profits to the hospital. Instead, it provided that apart from the payment of the $5,000 fee, Buffy had no rights or claims whatsoever, and that all profits from the sale of the calendars would be solely the property of Cal. The writing also contained a merger clause.

   After the calendar was produced, Buffy discovered that Cal had not donated any of the calendar's proceeds to the hospital. He would like to institute action against Cal for an order compelling him to pay the profits to the hospital. Will the parol evidence rule prevent him from testifying about Cal's oral undertaking?

7. Mel Odorous operates a fish processing plant. To get rid of the detritus generated by his operation, he entered into a written contract with Pungent Puppy, Inc., a manufacturer of dog food, under which he agreed to "deliver" his entire output of fish waste to Pungent Puppy at the end of each week. The contract was for a term of two years. It recorded that the delivery of fish waste was mutually beneficial to the parties, and that neither was obliged to provide any additional consideration under the contract. Immediately after the contract was executed, the parties had a dispute. Mel says that Pungent Puppy must collect the waste from his plant, but Pungent Puppy says that it's Mel's responsibility to transport the waste to its facility. Mel claims that he has been in business for 30 years. He has always disposed of waste by giving it to fertilizer and pet food manufacturers, and the manufacturers have always collected the waste from his plant. He therefore asserts that this was a term of his contract with Pungent Puppy. Pungent Puppy says that Mel's previous arrangements with other manufacturers have nothing to do with this case, and that by using the word "deliver," the contract clearly places the duty on Mel to transport the waste to Pungent Puppy. If this dispute gets to the stage of litigation, would Mel's testimony about his prior practices be admissible?

Explanations

1. Yes, faithless Ava does have a point, because if Ann decides to sue on the basis of Ava's undertaking, she is confronted with two hurdles. She must first convince the judge to admit her evidence of the oral term that qualified the writing, and if she succeeds, she must then convince the jury that such a term was in fact agreed to. A written memorandum of agreement was executed, and Ann seeks to testify about a prior oral agreement. Ava may object to admission of the evidence under the parol evidence rule, and the judge must determine as a question of law whether the evidence is admissible. If not, it is excluded and the jury does not hear it, leaving Ann with no case. If Ann can jump this hurdle by satisfying the judge that the evidence is not barred by the rule and is admissible, she may then testify about the conversation before the jury. The next hurdle is to convince the jury that the conversation occurred. If Ava denies it, Ann will win only if the jury believes her over Ava.

   In the first stage of this process, the judge considers two questions. The first concerns the issue of integration and involves two possibilities: The one is that the writing may have been intended as the full and final expression of the parties' agreement (that is, a total or complete integration). If it is, parol evidence is inadmissible. The other is that the writing is not a total integration. If so, the judge goes to the next level of the preliminary inquiry to decide the second question — whether the proffered evidence is consistent with the writing. The parol evidence may be admitted to the extent that it is consistent with what has been recorded in the writing. Thus, the evidence may explain an ambiguity or vagueness, or it may fill a gap, but it may not contradict the writing.

   The parties' agreement is integrated if they intended the writing to fully express everything that they agreed, so that no additional undertakings were made. As usual, the parties' intent is gauged by objective evidence. Under the strict "four corners" test, the only objective evidence that the court uses is the written contract itself. On this test, it is integrated if it appears complete and unambiguous, and there is no obvious gap or inadequacy. Although the facts do not set out the terms of the contract, they were apparently detailed. Even though the written contract did not contain a merger clause, it seems, at face value, to be final and complete and would be perceived as integrated under this test.

   The contextual approach to integration, which is followed by many modern courts, goes beyond the face of the writing and evaluates contextual evidence to decide the question of integration. The only contextual evidence here apart from the parol evidence itself (Ann's testimony of the conversation) is the fact that the parties were members of the family that had owned the house for generations. This has a bearing on the question of integration. If the parties were strangers, dealing at arm's length, one would expect a term restricting the buyer's right to dispose freely of the property to be stated in the apparently complete writing. However, the trust and perceived mutual sentiment engendered by the family relationship might plausibly explain why the parties in this case would be happy to allow the writing to reflect only the routine legal formalities and to omit this more personal aspect of their agreement. The point, as expressed in Restatement, Second, §216(b) is whether the circumstances are such that the term might naturally be omitted from the writing.

In *Masterson v. Sine*, discussed in section 12.7, the parties' family relationship persuaded the majority of the court that an oral agreement prohibiting the assignment of a repurchase option might naturally be made separately from the writing that granted the option. The dissent rejected the majority's test of integration and went on to say that even if that test was used, the oral agreement did not satisfy it. An agreement directly qualifying an absolute right in the written contract would not naturally be omitted from the writing. These contrary approaches show that the resolution of the question of integration largely depends on how liberal a view the court takes on this issue. It is conceivable but not assured that a court could find that the writing executed by Ann and Ava was not intended as a complete expression of the parties' agreement.

If the judge finds that the writing is not fully integrated, Ann's evidence is admissible provided that it does not contradict the writing. The oral agreement does not directly contradict an express term, but a restriction on Ava's right to transfer her property freely does contradict the normal legal assumption that an owner has the right to dispose of her property as she sees fit. This is a subtler contradiction. A court that distrusts evidence of alleged prior oral agreement can make a good argument that this is a contradiction, but a court that is more amenable to the admission of parol evidence can make an equally good contrary argument. Again, this difference of view appears in the majority and dissenting opinions in *Masterson*. The narrower test of inconsistency would allow Ann to go to trial and to attempt to convince the jury that the oral agreement was made. A wider view would enable the court to dispose of Ann's case summarily.

2. The analysis of this problem is the same as that in Example 1, but Perry's problem is worse than Ann's. To begin with, there is a merger clause in the writing, and an unfilled blank suitable for inserting a term like this. Courts tend to be wary of standard merger clauses, because they may not have been conspicuous or understood, but this does not mean that such clauses are invariably treated as ineffective. A signatory has a duty to read the document before signing it, even if the document is a standard form, and a party who fails to exercise that duty cannot expect relief unless the

bargaining circumstances compel the conclusion of unfair imposition. (This issue is raised in sections 4.1.4 and 5.3 and is fully discussed in section 13.12.) There is nothing in the facts of this case to indicate that Perry could not be expected to read and understand the writing or that Klaus had a bargaining advantage that allowed him to impose unfairly one-sided terms.

On a "four corners" test the apparent completeness of the document, the unfilled blank space, and the merger clause will surely lead to the conclusion of integration. Even on a contextual approach, the terms of the writing, including the merger clause, are taken seriously. However, the contextual approach at least gives Perry a shot at explaining why the apparent integration was not intended as such. In other words, Perry is given the opportunity to persuade the court that despite the existence of an apparently complete and final writing, this term might naturally have been agreed to separately. On these facts, this does not seem like an easy task. One basis for making this argument might have been that a standard form was used which does not admit the addition of special terms tailored to the transaction. However, that will not work here because there was space for its insertion on the form. Family connection or some other relationship may explain an informal approach to some special term of a contract, as discussed in Example 1, but Perry had no prior connection with Klaus.

The facts of this Example are reminiscent of *Mitchell v. Lath*, cited in section 12.11 on the collateral agreement rule, which found the rule to be inapplicable to an oral promise to remove an ice house from property adjacent to the property sold. The underlying rationale of the collateral agreement rule is similar to that of the Restatement, Second, test. In fact, the tests are really just alternative formulations of the same principle. However, the collateral agreement rule is more difficult to satisfy because it requires the parol agreement to be distinct enough from the record to qualify as a separate but related agreement. To satisfy this standard, the subject matter of the oral and recorded agreements must cover different performances with identifiably separate consideration. It is hard to imagine that an oral agreement could qualify as separate if it might not naturally be agreed to separately. In addition, Perry made no promise of additional consideration for the oral promise, and there is no indication that the parties intended to allocate any portion of the property's purchase price to the clearing of the adjacent land.

3. This Example involves a sale of goods, so UCC §2.202, the Article 2 version of the parol evidence rule, applies. In general principle, it is substantially similar to the contemporary common law rule, so many courts would not answer these questions differently had this not been a sale of goods. The writing in this case is apparently intended as a complete

integration. It contains all the terms essential to a sales contract and it has a merger clause. Notwithstanding, it is not a watertight final and complete memorial of agreement, so most of the parol evidence suggested by the questions should be admissible.

a. Despite the attempt at integration, the parties did not fully express their agreement. They provided for a discount but failed to specify its amount. With regard to this term, the writing cannot be a complete and final expression of their agreement, so evidence of what they agreed orally is admissible to supplement it. Note that neither denies making an oral agreement, but they argue about what was agreed. Neither party's evidence is inconsistent with the writing, so it will all be admitted, and the jury will have to decide whose version of the discussion is correct.

b. Although the parties' testimony on the amount of the discount is admissible to fill that gap in the writing, this does not give Di license to produce parol evidence on other terms that are fully, clearly, and finally expressed in the writing. On a "four corners" test, the agreement is apparently integrated on this issue, and Di would probably prevail on the plain meaning of the word "cash." However, Official Comment 1 to §2.202 makes it clear that the "four corners" approach is not to be used in sales of goods, and that meaning must be determined in the commercial context in which the words were used. Nevertheless, the contextual evidence must point to a meaning of which the writing is reasonably susceptible—it must persuade the court that there is some basis for going beyond the apparent clarity of the writing to find an ambiguity that is not apparent in the plain language of the writing. If not, the evidence should not be admitted because the party offering it has not shown that the apparently integrated writing suffers from an ambiguity or vagueness that requires explanation. In the absence of ambiguity, the parol term is inadmissible if the writing is integrated, and even if it is not integrated, the term is probably inadmissible as contradictory to the writing.

   The only contextual evidence of the meaning of "cash" is the disputed parol evidence itself: Di's allegation about what was said during negotiations. This self-serving testimony is apparently not corroborated by more objective evidence, such as usage or course of dealing. In the absence of some indication that there is a common understanding or a practice between the parties that "cash" means credit of up to a week, it is difficult to reconcile Di's evidence with the word's normal meaning. Even under the liberal rule of the UCC, the evidence should be excluded.

c. Margie is trying to establish both a course of dealing and a trade usage to show that her faux tequila conforms to the contract even though it has traces of fat, sugar, and alcohol. Section 2.202(a) makes it clear that even if a writing appears fully integrated and has a merger clause, evidence of usage and course of dealing should always be allowed to supplement or explain it. However, they may not contradict it. The rationale for this more liberal rule is twofold. First, parties normally take it for granted that a transaction is subject to well-established custom or their own prior practices, so they are unlikely to take the trouble of spelling them out in the writing. Second, the evidence to establish these facts is objective and harder to make up than an account of what was said in negotiations. Therefore, unless the parties negate usages or prior understandings by clear wording (in which case the evidence would contradict the writing), they are assumed to apply despite the silence of an apparently complete agreement.

There is nothing in the writing to indicate that the parties deliberately excluded the usage or practice claimed by Margie, so the general merger clause does not keep out the evidence, and it is admissible unless it is inconsistent with the writing. The writing unqualifiedly describes the tequila as free of fat, sugar, and alcohol, so it could be argued that the writing is contradicted by testimony that small quantities of these substances are acceptable. This again raises the difficult question of deciding whether a qualification to an absolute undertaking is a supplementation or a contradiction. There is no sure dividing line, but courts tend to favor admission of this kind of objective evidence in cases of doubt, requiring quite strong wording of negation to exclude it. The court's decision to admit the evidence is just the first step in the process. Margie must then convince the jury that the course of dealing and trade usage did exist and that they support her position.

4. The issue here is the meaning of the word "regular." Gordon contends that its plain meaning is self-evident, but Fairest Fowls argues that it is ambiguous if understood in light of trade usage. If Fairest Fowls is right, it is not necessary to decide whether the parties expected the written invoice to be an integration. The ambiguity of the word means that, at least insofar as the quality of the pheasant is concerned, the writing did not succeed as a complete and final expression of what the parties agreed. Evidence may therefore be admitted to explain the meaning of "regular" provided that the evidence supports a meaning reconcilable with the writing.

   A court adopting a "four corners" approach may be inclined to find that there is no ambiguity about "regular" in the context of the writing as a whole, and that it can only have the meaning contended by Gordon. However, such an approach is clearly not appropriate in a sale of goods, because UCC §2.202, Official Comment I rejects it and calls for consideration of the commercial context in establishing meaning. Section 2.202

gives very strong credence to trade usage, which is presumed to enter the contract unless the parties clearly and unequivocally indicate a contrary intent or the usage cannot be reconciled with the writing. As nothing else in the writing even remotely pertains to the quality of the pheasant, the only language that must be reconciled with the proffered evidence is the word "regular" itself. If looked at from the patterns of normal speech, it is hard to think of "regular" as meaning "old and scrawny." However, from the perspective of the trade in which the parties are engaged,[12] the evidence suggests that there is no inconsistency. If trade usage supports such an esoteric meaning, the word is ambiguous and its meaning in the trade can be reconciled with the word "regular." The expert testimony should therefore not be excluded as parol evidence, and Fairest Fowls should be able to present it to persuade the jury that the word means what it contends.

5. The alleged oral term for the payment of $2.5 million directly contradicts the clear and unambiguous provision in the writing for payment of $2 million. Whether or not the agreement is fully integrated, it does definitively express the amount of the advance, and there is no way in which the written and alleged oral terms can be reconciled by interpretation. Therefore, if the oral agreement is contemporaneous with the writing, evidence of it would be barred by the parol evidence rule. However, if the oral agreement was made subsequent to the writing, the parol evidence rule does not apply, and there is no provision in the agreement barring oral modifications. This Example focuses on what is meant by a subsequent agreement for the purposes of the parol evidence rule. On a literal approach, the oral agreement was unquestionably made after the writing, and the evidence is admissible. However, such a technical distinction may lead to an absurd result that places too much emphasis on the sequence of events in a single interaction. The alleged amendment was made almost immediately after the execution of the writing, while the parties were still together following the meeting at which it was signed. If the parties really did agree to change the amount of the advance, it would have been easy and natural for them to alter the writing to reflect the change. The fact that the writing was not amended casts suspicion on the claim that the parties agreed to the change.

   A possible argument that Holly could make is that the departure of the parties' lawyers and agents terminated the stage during which the writing was executed, so that the informal agreement to increase the advance

12. Example 2 of Chapter 10 discusses the issue of defining the trade and holding Gordon accountable for the usage in that trade. That issue is not duplicated here. The facts indicate that the expert evidence covers the restaurant business, of which Gordon is a member.

should be treated as subsequent.[13] A timing issue similar to this arose in *Kehr Packages, Inc. v. Fidelity Bank*, discussed in section 12.3.2. The borrowers alleged that after the written agreement was signed, they made an oral agreement with the lender to increase the amount of the loan. The court found the alleged oral agreement to be contemporaneous with the writing because it was made in the course of the closing process during which the writing had been executed.

6. Buffy can obtain the order only if he can prove that Cal's undertaking to donate the profits to the hospital was a term of the contract. His problem is that this term was agreed orally before the writing was executed and it is absent from the writing. Buffy cannot claim that he did not realize at the time of signing the written contract that it failed to reflect the oral understanding. He had a duty to read it and is bound by its terms. (In *Myskina v. Conde Nast Publications, Inc.*, discussed in section 12.7, the court invoked the duty to read and firmly rejected Myskina's argument that she did not read the release because she was not fluent in English.) The five-page standard contract is likely compendious and fully integrated. The fact that it has a merger clause adds weight to this conclusion. Even if the agreement is found not to be integrated, a prior oral promise to donate the profits to a hospital contradicts the express term that the profits belong to Cal alone.

   Although there is not much chance that the parol agreement would be admitted under the normal operation of the parol evidence rule, the facts make out a case for application of the fraud exception. As a matter of public policy, courts do not allow a party to use the parol evidence rule to mask a fraud, so parol evidence is admissible to the extent that it is offered to establish fraud. (See *America's Directories, Inc. v. Stellhorn One Hour Photo, Inc.*, discussed in section 12.12.) Section 13.6 discusses the elements of fraud in detail. For the present, it is enough to note that a victim of fraud can avoid a contract by showing that the other party made a fraudulent misrepresentation that justifiably induced him to enter the contract. Although fraud usually involves a misrepresentation of fact, it can also arise where a person makes a contractual promise with the deliberate intention of breaking it, or where a person deliberately misrepresents the content of the document presented for signature. As section 13.6 explains, Buffy's biggest problem in establishing fraud will be to show that he was justified in relying on an oral representation that was not included in the writing.

13. Note that even if the court treats the informal agreement as a subsequent modification, the admission of this evidence may not ultimately help Holly in her claim for the extra $500,000. She apparently did not give any consideration to Beverly for the promise to increase the payment.

7. This Example may surpass *Maday v. Grathwohl* in the repulsiveness of the subject matter of the contract. Unlike that case, Mel is not claiming that the parties made a prior oral agreement that speaks to the issue in dispute. Rather, it seems that the parties did not address this question at all in any negotiations or communications, and that each had a different understanding of who would be responsible for the transport of the waste. The word "deliver," used in their written contract, is ambiguous. It could mean that Mel must physically transport the waste to Pungent Puppy, or it could mean (as it is used in UCC §2.503) that Mel must hold the waste for Pungent Puppy to collect. If the term is ambiguous, there is no bar on parol evidence to establish its meaning. Mel's past practices with other pet food manufacturers do not constitute a course of dealing because these transactions did not involve Pungent Puppy. Therefore, the exclusion of this evidence would be based on grounds of irrelevance, rather than under the parol evidence rule. Mel may seek to argue that his past arrangements with other manufacturers reflect a more widespread practice in the market that constitutes a trade usage, which would be admissible to clarify the meaning of the ambiguous term "deliver." However, Mel's dealings with other manufacturers in the past are not, on their own, sufficient to establish trade usage. Mel would have to go beyond his own transactions to show, by expert testimony, that collection of waste by manufacturers is a practice that is currently and widely observed in the market in which the parties operate.

CHAPTER 13

The Judicial Regulation of Improper Bargaining and of Contracts That Violate Law or Public Policy

§13.1 INTRODUCTION

This chapter deals with several related but distinct doctrines. The doctrines of misrepresentation, duress, undue influence, and unconscionability, discussed in sections 13.2 to 13.12, allow courts to go behind a party's objective manifestation of assent where that manifestation was induced by the improper bargaining conduct of the other party in the process of contract formation. The word "bargaining" is used here in the broad sense to mean contract formation, not in the narrow sense to mean negotiation. These doctrines apply whether or not the parties actually negotiate with each other in the process of contract formation, and they commonly apply to contracts that are not negotiated at all, but are standard contracts imposed by one party on the other without any opportunity to bargain over their terms.

Section 13.13 deals with the courts' treatment of contracts that violate the law or public policy. The focus of these doctrines is not on whether one of the parties induced the other's manifestation of assent by deceit or improper tactics, but whether the contract violates a statute, a rule of common law, or an important public policy. If it does, one of the parties to the contract may seek to avoid the contract, even though that party manifested assent to it and may have participated knowingly in contravening the law or public policy.

§13.2 THE OBJECTIVE TEST AND APPARENT ASSENT RESULTING FROM IMPROPER BARGAINING CONDUCT

The discussion of the objective test of assent in section 4.1 stressed that although contract is based on consensus, the law does not require a genuine subjective "meeting of the minds." The focus is on apparent assent, as it would reasonably be perceived by one party from the manifested words and actions of the other. This has to be the general rule, otherwise no one could ever rely on overt indications of assent, and the one party's reasonable expectation of agreement could be defeated by a showing that the other really did not mean what those indications reasonably conveyed. The principal purpose of the objective test is therefore the protection of reasonable expectations. However, a rigid adherence to objectivity could mask the fact that the apparent assent was not genuine but was obtained by deceit or improper tactics that subvert voluntary and knowing consent. The doctrines of misrepresentation, duress, undue influence, and unconscionability protect a party whose manifested assent to a contract was induced by the improper conduct of the other party in the formation of the contract. They allow the court to go behind the manifestation of intent to decide if a party's apparent agreement is based on an acceptable degree of volition. They are regulatory in that they allow the court to respond to and correct the consequences of improper bargaining behavior. The theme that connects these doctrines is the balance between the policy of protecting reliance that underlies the objective test of contract and the policy of freedom of contract that dictates not only that a person should have the freedom to enter contracts but also that a person should not be bound to a manifestation of assent that was induced by improper and unfair means. In essence, these doctrines are safety valves for the objective test, so that it cannot be used as a tool of oppression, deceit, or advantage-taking.

§13.3 GENERAL NOTE ON REMEDIES FOR IMPROPER BARGAINING: AVOIDANCE AND RESTITUTION, ADJUSTMENT OF THE CONTRACT, OR DAMAGES

The remedies available for improper bargaining are covered in the discussion of each of the separate doctrines in the following sections. This overview identifies and introduces the common remedial principles that apply to the granting of relief under the doctrines.

a. Avoidance and Restitution

A contract induced by improper bargaining is voidable. This means that it can be avoided (rescinded) by the party who is the victim of that improper conduct. A voidable contract must be distinguished from a void contract. If a contract is void (as it would be, for example, if one party failed to give consideration), it is a legal nullity, and neither party can sue to enforce it. By contrast, a voidable contract is a valid contract that remains fully effective unless the aggrieved party elects to exercise the right to terminate it. The aggrieved party therefore has a choice, either to sue to avoid the contract, or, to keep the contract, despite the other party's improper bargaining. An aggrieved party who chooses not to avoid the contract may pursue one of the alternative remedies described below. Note that only the aggrieved party has the election to avoid the contract or keep it in force. The party who engaged in improper bargaining cannot use that wrongdoing as the basis of a claim to avoid the contract. The aggrieved party may use the right of avoidance affirmatively to avoid the contract, or defensively, by raising voidability as a defense when sued on the contract. When a contract is avoided, the general rule is that both parties are entitled to restitution because it would unjustly enrich a party to retain a benefit under an avoided contract. In appropriate cases, the fact that the contract was induced by improper means may affect the equities relevant to restitutionary recovery, resulting in a reduction or elimination of the restitutionary claim of the party at fault.

b. Adjustment of the Terms of the Contract to Correct the Consequences of Improper Bargaining

If the aggrieved party decides not to avoid the contract, but the other party's improper bargaining resulted in terms that are unfair, the aggrieved party may ask the court to enforce the contract after removing its unfair aspects. Offending terms may be removed entirely or may just be altered to eliminate their unfair effect. This alternative is not available in all situations and may not be possible when the problem affects the very basis of the contract. In other cases, it may be the only remedy available because the problem is not serious enough to merit avoidance.

c. Damages

As noted above, restitutionary damages are available where a contract is avoided. However, if the aggrieved party elects not to avoid the contract, there may be the possibility of compensatory damages to remedy the effects of the improper bargaining. Compensatory damages are not available in all cases, but courts do have remedial discretion to award such relief where appropriate. This relief may be aimed at compensating the aggrieved party for a loss in consequence of the improper bargaining, or it could compensate for tortious injury where the wrongful act is a tort as well as a bargaining impropriety.

§13.4 THE NATURE AND RELATIONSHIP OF THE DOCTRINES REGULATING IMPROPER BARGAINING

The doctrines of misrepresentation, duress, undue influence, and unconscionability allow a court to go behind a party's apparent manifestation of assent, and to examine whether that apparent assent was induced by the other party's improper bargaining conduct. Courts apply these doctrines carefully so as not to intrude more than necessary in the process of contract formation. Contracting parties are expected to try to serve their own interests and to use their available information and resources to obtain the best deal possible. There is nothing inherently wrong in the resourceful use of superior information, persuasive sales techniques, and the exploitation of market advantage. Furthermore, it is to be expected that transactions routinely occur between parties having great disparity in power, sophistication and resources. This judicial regulation of bargaining aims, not at trying to make the parties equal by cutting down economic advantage, but rather at allowing the court to step in when behavior crosses the line from hard bargaining to unacceptable exploitation. In some cases, it is obvious that the line has been crossed, but in more equivocal cases opinions differ on the question of when judicial intervention is appropriate. Some courts and commentators see robust judicial regulation of bargaining practice as a crucial means of curbing abuse. Others favor court intervention for only the more extreme cases and see judicial regulation as leading to inefficiency and market interference.

Each of these doctrines have their own distinct elements, but there is also some common ground on which they intersect. Although the facts of some cases may support the invocation of only one of the doctrines, in other cases, the facts may permit alternative analyses under more than one of them. Therefore, it is quite common to find that the party seeking relief sues under different doctrines in the alternative.

§13.5 MISREPRESENTATION GENERALLY: THE MEANING OF "MISREPRESENTATION" AND THE DISTINCTION BETWEEN FRAUDULENT AND NONFRAUDULENT MISREPRESENTATIONS

§13.5.1 The Distinction Between Fraudulent, Negligent, and Innocent Misrepresentations

A "misrepresentation" is defined in Restatement, Second, §159 as an assertion not in accord with the facts. It is a factually incorrect representation made by one of the parties at the time of contracting. Misrepresentations fall into one of three categories, each of which has different rules. If the assertion is made with knowledge that it is false (that is, a deliberate lie) and with the intention of inducing the other party's agreement, it is fraudulent. The misrepresentation is nonfraudulent if it is not a deliberate lie, but the party made it either negligently or even innocently. A party's misrepresentation is negligent if the party did not know it was untrue, but nevertheless violated a duty of reasonable care by failing to check the facts on which the representation is based. The misrepresentation is innocent if the party making it is accountable for misrepresenting the facts even in the absence of intentional deceit or negligence.

The severity and consequences of a misrepresentation depend on the state of mind of the party making the assertion. A fraudulent misrepresentation is the most serious deviation from legal and ethical obligations, which not only violates the contractual obligation of fair dealing but is also tortious and could have criminal sanctions, too. In addition, a party guilty of fraud cannot be said to have justifiably relied on the other's manifestation of assent. The elements of fraudulent misrepresentation reflect the law's disapprobation of deliberate falsehood: If a fraudulent assertion is proved to have been made, a court may be comparatively lenient in finding the remaining prerequisites for relief to have been satisfied. The court may evaluate the consequent inducement on a more subjective standard and the perpetrator's accountability for purposeful deceit is much more likely to outweigh any culpability the victim may have for gullibility or carelessness. A negligent or innocent misrepresentation is not as morally reprehensible and may not entirely defeat the perpetrator's reliance interest. Therefore, the decision on whether or not to grant relief involves a closer balancing of the relative culpability of the parties, and a stronger focus on the objective importance (materiality) of the misrepresentation and the victim's duty to verify the

Diagram 13A

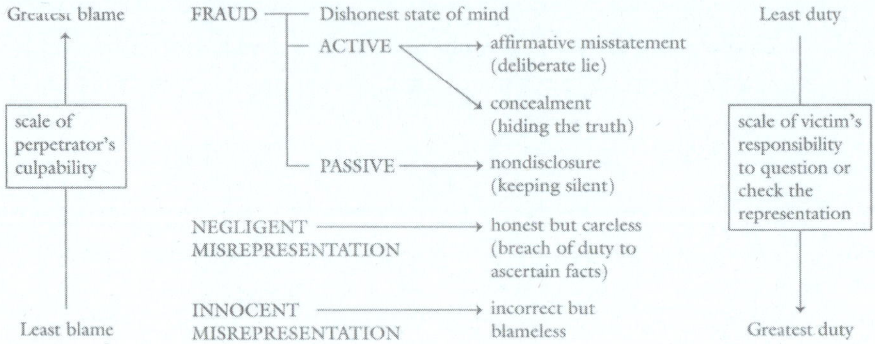

facts. A negligent misrepresentation weighs more heavily against the perpetrator than an innocent one, and negligence may give rise to tort liability, too. This is represented by Diagram 13A.

§13.5.2 The Application of the Parol Evidence Rule to Misrepresentations Made Outside a Recorded Contract

When a contract is recorded (whether in a physical or electronic document) the party claiming misrepresentation must prove the falsity of the representation by adducing evidence of facts extrinsic to the record. The parol evidence rule does not bar this extrinsic evidence because it is not parol evidence. It is offered not to prove a term allegedly agreed to outside the record but rather to prove that a fact represented in the record is wrong.

However, the parol evidence rule does apply where the misrepresentation is not included in the record but was allegedly made orally before or at the time of execution of the recorded contract, or in a record apparently superseded by the recorded contract The effect of the parol evidence rule differs depending on whether or not the misrepresentation was fraudulent.

Section 12.12.1 deals with the fraud exception to the parol evidence rule—even if a recorded agreement is fully integrated, a party may not invoke the parol evidence rule to exclude proof of a fraudulent misrepresentation. The policy of shielding the factfinder from suspect and unreliable parol evidence is usually outweighed by the policy of protecting a party from dishonesty. However, although the parol evidence may be admissible, it may not ultimately help the victim of the fraud for the reason explained in section 12.12.1: Although the court may admit the evidence of the alleged parol misrepresentation, the plaintiff may still not be able to win on the fraud claim because the omission of the misrepresentation from the record could lead to the conclusion that the plaintiff was not justified in relying on it, thereby failing to satisfy that element of fraud. (Justifiable reliance is discussed in section 13.6.6.) This is a particularly serious problem if the alleged oral misrepresentation directly contradicts an express term in the record or if the record contains a merger clause that specifically disclaims reliance on any oral representations. This issue was addressed in *Psenicska v. Twentieth Century Fox Film Corp.*, 2008 WL 4185752 (S.D.N.Y. 2008), the case involving the *Borat* movie discussed in connection with interpretation in section 10.5.1. The plaintiffs had consented to being filmed for the movie, believing it to be a documentary. They sued the studio and filmmakers when they discovered that the movie was a crude satire presented in the style of a documentary and that they had been tricked into participating in it. The issue was whether the plaintiffs' consent to be filmed was effective. As a matter of interpretation, the court held that the consent did cover the movie because the term "documentary-style film" unambiguously included a faux documentary. As an alternative argument, the plaintiffs sought to avoid the consent on the grounds that the defendants had fraudulently misrepresented the nature of the film in oral discussions. The court rejected that argument as well because the consent specifically stated that the plaintiffs waived reliance on any promises or statements made about the nature of the film or the identity of the other persons involved in it. In light of this language, the court said that the plaintiffs could not have justifiably relied on any such oral statements that may have been made.

A negligent or innocent misrepresentation is not as morally indefensible as a fraudulent one, and is not covered by the exception to the parol evidence rule. Therefore, the rule applies as usual. It bars evidence of a negligent or innocent parol misrepresentation where the recorded contract is fully integrated, and particularly if it contains not only detailed terms but also a merger clause. If the record is not fully integrated, evidence of a parol misrepresentation that contradicts the recorded terms is also inadmissible.

§13.6 FRAUDULENT MISREPRESENTATION

§13.6.1 Introduction

To qualify as fraudulent, a misrepresentation must be made with deliberate dishonest intent. The person making it must know it is false and must intend to induce the other party to enter the contract. The most common type of fraud, called fraud in the inducement, is a fraudulent misrepresentation concerning a fact that forms the basis of the contract, giving the party to whom it is made a false incentive to enter it. A less common type of fraud, fraud in the factum, is a misrepresentation relating to the nature or effect of a document to be signed (for example, persuading someone to sign an order for goods by asserting that it is merely a request for a catalog). The discussion and illustrations in this section are concerned only with the more common fraud in the inducement.

For fraudulent misrepresentation to arise, a party must have made a false representation of fact with knowledge of its falsity and with intent to induce the other party to enter the contract. The misrepresentation must have related to a material fact and the other party must have relied on it justifiably and suffered injury as a result. The rest of this section examines each of these elements of fraud.

§13.6.2 Fact, Opinion, Prediction, and Promise

a. What Is a "Fact"?

A fact is an objectively ascertainable reality. For example, the seller of a sofa clearly makes a representation of fact by saying "this sofa is made of leather" or "this sofa was made in the U.S.A." If the sofa is actually vinyl or it was made in some other country, the asserted facts are false. Fact can be distinguished from opinion ("I think this is a very beautiful sofa"), a future prediction ("this sofa will appreciate in value"), or a promise of future action ("if the sofa does not look good when you put it in your living room, you can return it"). The general rule is that only a misrepresentation of fact constitutes fraud. An opinion or a prediction should be understood as nothing more than an expression of personal belief, taste, or preference, so even if it is not honest, it should not give grounds for relief for fraud. This is particularly true if the expression of opinion or the prediction should be reasonably understood as seller's hyperbole (sometimes called "puffery"). Similarly, a promise of future action is not a representation of fact but an undertaking. If it is breached, the proper remedy is a suit for breach of contract, not an action for fraud. However, the distinction between fact, opinion, and promise is not hard and fast. In some circumstances a dishonest opinion or a false promise can constitute a fraudulent misrepresentation.

b. Opinion

Courts recognize that it is not always possible to make a clear distinction between fact and opinion because most opinions have a factual basis. This is not always true, of course. A seller's claim that a sofa's green and orange plaid fabric is a "fun color" is clearly just opinion. However, if the seller says "this sofa will appreciate with age," this suggests familiarity with facts concerning the trends in the market with regard to used furniture. The fact-based opinion constitutes a misrepresentation if the party expressing it knows that it is not supported by the facts on which it is based or makes the statement with reckless disregard of whether it is true or not. Where the opinion of one of the parties is a decisive factor in inducing the other to enter the transaction, the misrepresentation of that opinion goes to the heart of the contract. This is particularly true where the party expressing the opinion has expertise and the other party is justified in relying on that party's recommendation. For example, an attorney who believes that a prospective client has a weak case on the facts makes a fraudulent misrepresentation by expressing a contrary opinion to the prospective client with the goal of inducing the client to litigate the case.

Rodi v. Southern New England School of Law, 389 F.3d 5 (1st Cir. 2004), is a good illustration of fraudulent opinion. Rodi was a law student who claimed that he was induced to enroll in the law school on the basis of representations by the dean that the school was "highly confident" that it would receive American Bar Association (ABA) accreditation. The school knew that accreditation was important to Rodi because he could not be admitted to practice in his state of residence if his degree was not from an accredited school. After the school failed to receive the accreditation in Rodi's first year of study, Rodi sent transfer applications to ABA-accredited schools. On hearing of this, the dean (the successor to the dean who made the original representation) assured Rodi that "there was no cause for pessimism" that the school would be accredited before he graduated. It was not, and Rodi sued. The district court dismissed his claim, but the court of appeals reversed and permitted the case to go to trial on a theory of fraudulent misrepresentation. The school knew that it had substantial problems in obtaining accreditation, and Rodi had made a credible preliminary showing that the opinions expressed by school officials were not honest, given their knowledge of the ABA's criteria and the school's prospects of satisfying them.[1]

c. Prediction

A future prediction is not a misrepresentation of an existing fact but an opinion about what is expected to come to pass after the contract has been executed. It is really no different conceptually than an opinion, and should be approached in the same way. The deans' assertion in *Rodi* and the attorney's assertion about the strength of the client's case in the above illustration are opinions and predictions. If the prediction is based on facts that are known at the time of contracting, it must be an honest assessment of how

1. Although the court held that the deans' false representation of their opinions qualified as fraud, Rodi ultimately lost the case because the trial court held on remand that even though the deans had made false statements, Rodi had not reasonably relied on them—he knew that the school had accreditation problems and that there was a distinct possibility that the ABA would not accredit the school, and he did actually try unsuccessfully to transfer to other schools. The court of appeals affirmed, 532 F.3d 11 (1st Cir. 2008).

those facts will lead to the predicted result. However, if the incorrect prediction is just a guess about future events, patently not based on a projection of verifiable present facts, it is not a representation of fact and therefore not fraud. For example, *Hoffman v. L&M Arts*, 838 F.3d 568 (5th Cir. 2016), involved the private sale of a famous painting (called "the red Rothko") by Marc Rothko for $17.6 million. The seller, a well-known patron of the arts, did not want it to be publicly known that she had sold the painting, and therefore insisted that the sale must be to a private collector who would not resell it publicly. L&M acted as intermediary for the sale to an undisclosed buyer, and assured Hoffman that the buyer was a very private individual and that the painting would "disappear" into the buyer's collection. A few years later, the buyer placed the painting for sale at public auction, and Hoffman sued L&M for breach of contract and fraud. She lost on both counts. With regard to the fraud claim, the court held that L&M's assurance that the painting would disappear into a private collection and would not be sold was merely a nonactionable prediction because it was not based on present facts, but just anticipated the future action of the buyer, a third party over whom L&M had no control. (It is possible to imagine a contrary conclusion if, say, L&M had no factual basis for predicting that the buyer would not sell the painting in the future.)

d. Promise

A promise of future performance is not a representation of fact, but an expression of intent. However, it relates to the present state of mind of the party making it and if the party dishonestly represents that state of mind, the misrepresentation could qualify as fraudulent. It can be very difficult to distinguish a mere breach of contract from a fraudulent misrepresentation of intent. To assert fraud, it is not enough for the victim to show that the promise was broken. The victim must prove that at the time the contract was made, the party making the promise intended not to keep it. Fraud can be proved by circumstantial evidence, so it is not necessary to have direct evidence of the promisor's state of mind in the form of an admission. However, there must at least be compelling circumstantial evidence to show that the promisor had already decided to breach at the time of entering the contract. That evidence may be hard to find if the promisor was careful to keep its intent hidden.

American Directories, Inc. v. Stellhorn One Hour Photo, 833 N.E.2d 1059 (Ind. App. 2005), discussed in relation to the fraud exception to the parol evidence rule in section 12.12, involved a fraudulent promise. The court held that it could qualify as fraud where a seller of advertising in a phone directory made a promise that the buyer could cancel the contract after a year, intending at the time of making the promise not to honor it. *Carey v. FedEx Ground Package System, Inc.*, 321 F. Supp. 2d 902 (S.D. Ohio 2004), discussed in section 8.9 in relation to promissory estoppel, is another example. FedEx had kept Carey waiting for a delivery route for almost two years. During this period, it induced Carey to incur economic detriment by reiterating the assurance that he would receive the route while it took advantage of his services as a temporary driver. The court denied FedEx's motion for summary judgment and allowed Carey to proceed to trial on the basis of promissory estoppel. In addition, the court held that Carey had made out a cause of action for fraud. The court noted that although fraud is not usually predicated on a promise of future action, such a promise can qualify as fraudulent if it can be shown that, at the time of making the promise, the promisor had no intention of keeping it.

Sometimes it is not easy to decide if a misrepresentation related to a fact or to a promise—a representation of future intent. *Kaloti Enterprises, Inc. v. Kellogg Sales Co.*, 699 N.W.2d 205 (Wis. 2005), is a case with such an ambiguity. Kaloti and Kellogg had a longstanding arrangement under which Kaloti bought Kellogg products, which it resold to large stores. Kellogg then decided to change its marketing procedures by selling some of its products directly to the same large stores that were Kaloti's customers. As a result, Kellogg would become Kaloti's competitor in that wholesale market. After it had made this decision, Kellogg accepted an order from Kaloti without telling it that Kellogg was about to devour its market. Kaloti only discovered this upon hearing from its customers that they would be buying directly from Kellogg. Kaloti sued Kellogg when it refused Kaloti's demand for cancellation of the sale and refund of the price. The issue in the case was whether Kellogg's failure to tell Kaloti about its impending change in marketing strategy constituted a fraudulent misrepresentation. The court held that Kaloti had made a sufficient case of fraud to overcome an application for dismissal. The court treated Kellogg's decision to sell its products directly to stores as a fact. However, this is not strictly correct. The real fact in issue was Kellogg's intentions, and the question was whether Kellogg had made an implied promise not to undercut Kaloti, knowing that it was about to break that promise.[2]

§13.6.3 Types of Fraudulent Misrepresentation: Affirmative Statements, Concealment, and Nondisclosure

a. Affirmative False Statement

An affirmative false statement (such as the seller's assertion, mentioned in section 13.6.2, that a vinyl sofa is made of leather) is the most direct and easily identifiable type of fraudulent misrepresentation. *Rozen v. Greenberg*, 886

2. The case also presents the question of whether Kellogg committed fraud by failing to disclose that it had begun to sell directly to Kaloti's customers. This aspect of the case is discussed in section 13.6.3.

A.2d 924 (Md. Ct. Spec. App. 2005), illustrates fraud by affirmative misrepresentation. Greenberg was a tax preparer. She received an email from Rozen, whom she did not know, suggesting that as they were in the same business, they should enter into a cooperative arrangement. In the email Rozen represented that he had "headed" a tax preparation service for "the last few years." He referred Greenberg to his organization's "powerful" website. On visiting the website, Greenberg read that the organization had a team of account and tax professionals headed by Rozen, who was an experienced CPA. In a subsequent phone conversation, Rozen again told Greenberg that he was very experienced and had many people working for him. Greenberg then met with Rozen, who showed her an impressive office that he claimed to be his office. As a result of these representations, Greenberg agreed to sell her client list to Rozen in exchange for a share of the income that he generated from preparing her clients' returns. It turned out that at the time that he contacted Greenberg, Rozen had no business and no clients and had prepared no tax returns. He had been a CPA for only a few weeks, and the office that he showed Greenberg belonged to a tax preparation company at which he was employed. The court of appeals affirmed the trial court's decision that these misrepresentations were fraudulent.

Willen v. Hewson, 622 S.E.2d 187 (N.C. Ct. App. 2005), is another example of affirmative fraud. The seller of a large house on an estate advertised it as "peaceful" and "serene." When the buyers inspected the estate, they met the seller's niece, who mentioned that there had been problems with "kids coming onto the property after high school football games around Halloween." This caused the buyers some concern, and they called the seller to ask her if there had been trespass problems on the property. She assured them that such incidents occurred only once or twice and that her niece was prone to exaggeration. After the buyers bought and moved into the house, they found that there was a serious and constant problem with trespass and vandalism that they could not eliminate even by installing a security system and fence. The court of appeals upheld the trial court's determination that the seller was aware of the trespass problem and had made a fraudulent misrepresentation by advertising the property as "peaceful" and "serene" and by answering the buyer's inquiry dishonestly.

b. Concealment

Deliberate conduct to hide a fact is also an affirmative act. Although it may not involve any verbal lie, it is just as dishonest and morally reprehensible. *Jablonski v. Rapalje*, 14 A.D.3d 484 (N.Y. App. Div. 2005), is a good example. In contrast to *Willen*, which involved human pests, *Jablonski* was concerned with trespassing bats, which inhabited the attic of the house bought by the plaintiff. The bat infestation was serious and ongoing. Over the 36 years that the sellers had lived in the house, they had tried to get rid of the bats, but the bats always returned. During the time that the buyer inspected the house preparatory to buying it, the sellers went to considerable trouble to conceal the bat infestation by using mothballs (which bats apparently dislike) and floodlights to keep them away and by cleaning up the telltale signs of bat presence such as bat droppings and urine. (The case also involved an affirmative misrepresentation. On one occasion the sellers did not do the best job in disposing of droppings, which the buyer noticed. The sellers asserted that they were bird droppings.) The court refused the seller's motion for summary judgment and permitted the buyer to proceed to trial on the basis of fraudulent concealment. *Weintraub v. Krobatsch*, 317 A.2d 68 (N.J. 1974), is an equally repulsive case involving a cockroach infestation of nightmarish proportions. The court declined the seller's application for summary judgment and permitted the buyer of a house to proceed to trial on the theory that the seller actively concealed the presence of cockroaches by leaving all the lights on.

c. Nondisclosure (Silence)

Affirmative dishonesty, whether in the form of a false statement or active concealment of the truth, is the clearest case of fraud. However, under some circumstances, a person can commit fraud by keeping silent and failing to disclose a fact. Nondisclosure is the most difficult basis for claiming fraud because it is only fraudulent if the circumstances impose a duty on the party to disclose information. The usual assumption is that where parties contract, each is a free agent in the market, entitled to act out of self-interest. A party may use the advantage of superior information, and owes no duty to the other to reveal motivating facts that make the transaction attractive. Therefore, a buyer of property, having studied the market carefully, is not obliged to tell the seller that the property is underpriced, and the buyer of a commodity does not have to tell the seller that its research on crop yield indicates that the price will soar after the sale. Notwithstanding, a party does not have the absolute and invariable right to keep information secret. Under some circumstances honesty and fair dealing require disclosure. The difficult question is to determine when the line is crossed between facts that may fairly be kept private and those that must be revealed.

Restatement, Second, §161 and Restatement, Second of Tort §551(2) provide guidelines to answer this question. They identify several situations in which nondisclosure amounts to an assertion that a fact does not exist, such as where the party knows that disclosure of that fact is necessary to correct a previous assertion, or where it is needed to clarify a partial or ambiguous assertion, or where there is a relationship of trust between the parties, or where the party knows that disclosure is necessary to correct the other party's mistake as to a basic assumption of the contract, and nondisclosure would violate the duty of good faith and fair dealing. The last situation, involving the concept of good faith and fair dealing, is the most general and open-ended, so it depends on the circumstances of each case. Two significant factors that may be relevant are whether the information should be treated as the property of the party who possesses it (for example, because that party has incurred cost and effort in conducting research or inquiry to obtain it) and whether the information is readily available on diligent inquiry.

The following cases illustrate the duty to disclose. The court found no duty to disclose in *DePrince v. Starboard Cruise Services, Inc.*, 2018 WL 443153 (Fla. Dist. Ct. App. 2018). A jewelry shop on a cruise ship sold a 20-carat diamond to the buyers for $235,000, which was one-twentieth of its retail value. This happened because the store's sales staff were inexperienced in selling large diamonds and mistook the per-carat price of $235,000 for the total price of the diamond. The buyers realized that the price was way below the value of the diamond, but proceeded with the purchase without saying anything about the price to the store. When the store discovered the error, it sought to cancel the sale. The buyers sued to enforce the contract, and the store raised the defenses of fraud by nondisclosure and mistake.[3] The court held that the buyers' failure to disclose did not amount to fraud because the fact of the retail value of the diamond was readily discoverable by the store through due diligence. By contrast, in *Stambovsky v. Ackley*, 572 N.Y.S.2d 672 (N.Y. App. Div. 1991), the court did allow the buyer of a house to proceed to trial on grounds of nondisclosure where the seller of a house failed to disclose to the buyer that the house was reputed to be haunted. (Unlike the buyers in *Willen* and *Jablonski*, who actually encountered the trespassers and bats, the buyer here did not allege that he met the ghosts. It was the reputation of the house that bothered him.) The seller was well aware of this reputation and was largely responsible for creating it by including the house in tours of haunted homes and reporting apparitions in the local press and in the *Reader's Digest*. The majority of the court held that while the buyer would have had the duty to inspect the house for structural and physical defects, there was nothing to alert him to the possibility that the house had a reputation for being haunted, so he could not reasonably be expected to inquire into this. The seller had a duty in good faith to disclose the reputation of the house, particularly because she had been instrumental in fostering it. The dissent argued that the reputation of the house as haunted had been widely publicized and could have been ascertained by the buyer on reasonable inquiry. Therefore, he should not be able to rely on the seller's failure to disclose it. Both the majority and the dissent sought to balance the seller's

---

3. The store's alternative defense of mistake is discussed in Example 6 of Chapter 15. A subsequent en banc decision, 271 So. 3d 11 (Fla. App. 2018), resolved a question relating to the claim of mistake, but did not address or disturb the court's earlier decision on fraud.

duty to disclose facts against the buyer's duty of reasonable inquiry and reached contrary conclusions on how the balance is to be struck.

In *Kaloti Enterprises, Inc. v. Kellogg Sales Co.*, discussed in section 13.6.2, the court held that Kellogg's failure to tell Kaloti that it planned to sell products directly to Kaloti's customers made out a case for nondisclosure as an alternative to affirmative fraud. Although one party is not generally under a duty to disclose its business plans or marketing strategy to the other, commercial mores and the duty of fair dealing do sometimes require disclosure. This appeared to be such a case because Kellogg's action would undermine Kaloti's expectations under the contract, and the information was solely within Kellogg's knowledge, not accessible to Kaloti through diligent inquiry.

Even if a party does not have the duty to take the initiative of disclosing a fact and would be entitled to keep silent about it if not asked, if the other party asks a direct question relating to that fact, failure to answer it truthfully would constitute affirmative fraud. For example, in *Lerner v. DMB Realty, LLC*, 322 P.3d 909 (Ariz. Ct. App. 2014), the sellers of a house decided to sell it because a convicted sex offender lived next door. An Arizona statute provided that a seller is not obliged to disclose certain facts about the property, including that it is located in the vicinity of a sex offender. The deed of sale itself referred to this statutory provision and stated that the buyer had the duty to investigate the presence of sex offenders if a sex offender in the vicinity was material to the buyer. The buyers did not conduct this investigation and discovered the presence of the sex offender only after moving into the home. The buyers sued on several theories, including fraud. The trial court dismissed the fraud claim on the grounds that it was barred by the statute. The court of appeals reversed the dismissal. It noted that the sellers would not have had a duty to disclose the presence of the neighboring sex offender. However, when the buyers asked them why they were moving, they answered that they wanted to be closer to friends. They thereby misrepresented the true reason for their desire to move. The court said that when asked a question that fairly calls for disclosure, a person commits fraud by answering in a manner deliberately calculated to mislead. It did not matter that the question was not specifically about sex offenders; it was a specific enough question that imposed on the sellers the duty not to answer falsely.

§13.6.4 Knowledge of Falsity and Intent to Induce the Contract

A guilty state of mind—knowledge of falsity and intent to mislead—is the essence of fraud. (The word "scienter" is sometimes used to describe this guilty state of mind.) In defining knowledge of falsity, Restatement, Second, §162 covers not only an assertion made with the actual knowledge that it is not in accord with the facts but also an assertion made without confidence in its truth or without a known basis in fact. This means that there is some blurring of the line between fraudulent and negligent misrepresentation, because reckless disregard for the truth or an extreme degree of negligence in ascertaining information before making an assertion may qualify as fraud.

For example, in *Jordan v. Knafel*, 880 N.E.2d 1061 (Ill. App. Ct. 2007), Michael Jordan, the basketball star, sued for a declaratory judgment avoiding a settlement agreement that he had entered into with Karla Knafel. Knafel had become pregnant after the parties had a sexual relationship. She claimed that Jordan was certainly the father of the baby. On the strength of that assertion, Jordan and Knafel entered into the settlement agreement under which Jordan promised to pay Knafel $5 million in exchange for her not initiating paternity proceedings against him. Subsequent tests revealed that the child was not Jordan's. The court of appeals affirmed the trial court's summary judgment in favor of Jordan. Although Jordan could have been the father of the child, Knafel had made a fraudulent misrepresentation by categorically stating that he was the father, thereby impliedly representing that he was her only sexual partner during the period of conception. Although she did not know that he was not the father, she did know that he might not be. She therefore made the assertion without confidence in its truth.[4] (This case could also support a claim of fraudulent nondisclosure because Knafel failed to disclose that Jordan was not her only sexual partner at the crucial time. However, where affirmative fraud can be proved, it is a stronger cause of action than passive nondisclosure.)

§13.6.5 Materiality

A misrepresentation is material if it substantially contributes to a party's decision to enter the transaction. The test of materiality is objective. The misrepresentation must relate to a fact that is important or central enough to the bargain that it is reasonably likely to have had a significant influence on the party's decision to manifest assent to the transaction. Materiality is logically an element of fraud, because if the misrepresentation did not relate to an important aspect of the transaction, it is less likely to have induced the party to enter the transaction, and presents a less compelling case for relief. There is a clear link between the elements of materiality and justifiable

4. As explained in section 7.6, a settlement agreement that compromises a doubtful claim is valid for consideration purposes, provided that there is a good faith or reasonable basis for the dispute. Therefore, the fact that Jordan turned out not to be the father would not, in itself, have defeated the settlement agreement if the parties were unsure about the child's paternity. Knafel's problem in this case was that she concealed any doubt on this issue by categorically asserting that Jordan had to be the father, thereby inducing him to enter the settlement.

inducement. Courts commonly identify materiality as an element of fraud. (For example, this is explicitly stated in *Kellogg*, *Stambovsky*, *Hill*, *Jablonski*, *Willen*, *Jordan*, and *Rozen*.)[5]

§13.6.6 Justifiable Inducement

The element of justifiable inducement breaks down into two requirements. First, the fraud must actually have induced the victim's manifestation of assent to the contract, and second, the victim must have been justified in relying on the misrepresentation. The requirement of actual inducement means that there must be a causal link between the fraud and the contract—that is, the fraud must have motivated the victim to enter the contract or to enter it on the terms that were agreed. The fraud did not induce assent if the victim would have entered the contract on those terms anyway, even knowing truth. Even if the victim's assent was actually induced by the fraud, the victim is not entitled to relief if the victim was not justified in relying on the misrepresentation. In *Psenicska v. Twentieth Century Fox Film Corp.*, discussed in section 13.5.2, the court held that the plaintiffs' reliance on an alleged parol fraudulent misrepresentation was not justified in light of a disclaimer of reliance that they had signed. Similarly, lack of justifiable reliance was the ultimate ground for denying relief for fraud in *Rodi v. Southern New England School of Law*, discussed in section 13.6.2.

To determine if the plaintiff was justified in relying on the fraudulent misrepresentation, the court must evaluate the impact of the false fact on the victim's state of mind. The difficult question here is whether this impact should be measured objectively (was the victim reasonable in relying on the misrepresentation) or subjectively (even if a reasonable person may not have been hoodwinked, was this victim in fact induced to enter the contract). Although an objective test is used to determine assent in most situations, public policy dictates a less objective standard where fraud is involved. When a court balances the fault of the perpetrator, who has deliberately lied, against the fault of the victim, who may have been unduly gullible or even careless in believing the misrepresentation, the balance tends to weigh in favor of the victim. The result in most cases is a blend of objective and subjective considerations. That is, the court asks whether the victim's assent was in fact induced by the fraud, but also tests this inducement against the question of whether a reasonable person in the victim's position would have

5. Restatement, Second, §§162 and 164 and Comment *c* to §162 confuse the question of whether materiality must be proved as an element of fraud by requiring materiality to be proved only as an element of negligent or innocent misrepresentation, and not for fraud. However, courts do not generally take this approach and judicial decisions commonly identify materiality as an element of fraud.

been induced. Often, these inquiries point in the same direction because if a reasonable person would not have relied on the false fact, the victim may have trouble showing reliance on it in the absence of some special individual circumstances or attributes. The degree to which a court applies objective assessment is also influenced by the nature of the misrepresentation—a court is more likely to impose a tougher standard of reasonable inquiry on the victim where the fraud lies in failure to disclose facts, rather than in active statement or concealment.

The cases discussed in section 13.6.3 illustrate the element of justifiable reliance and the blend of subjective and objective considerations that go into determining justification. *Stambovsky v. Ackley* considered that the buyer could justifiably have been misled by the nondisclosure because he was not local, had no reason to know of the house's reputation, and could not have discovered the ghosts by reasonable inspection of the house. The dissent in the case considered that the court was too generous to the buyer in concluding that the house's reputation was not easily discoverable. The haunting was quite widely publicized and was featured in both national and local publications. In *Rozen v. Greenberg*, the court recognized that Greenberg was not experienced in the sale of a business and was rather gullible. However, the court focused on Greenberg's subjective attributes and rejected the argument that she reasonably could and should have investigated Rozen, should have called for references, and should have noticed that the office that she was taken to did not belong to him. In *Willen v. Hewson*, the court approached the buyers' reliance from a reasonableness perspective but rejected the seller's argument that the buyers' reliance on her assertions was unreasonable because her niece's mention of the trespassing problem should have caused them to conduct an independent investigation. The court noted that there were no visible indicia of trespass and vandalism to place the buyers on inquiry and, in any event, even if the buyers were unreasonable, the seller cannot seek to avoid the consequences of her false representation by arguing that the buyers should not have trusted her. In *Jablonski v. Rapalje*, the buyer visited the house many times and had it professionally inspected. There were several clues that should have alerted the buyer to the bat infestation—bat droppings, floodlights in the attic, the smell of mothballs and bat urine, and the repeated flushing of a toilet as the real estate agent was busy scooping up bat droppings and flushing them. The seller contended that the buyer's reliance was not justifiable because he had ample opportunity to discover the bats. Applying a reasonable diligence standard, the court rejected this argument because there was enough evidence to suggest that the sellers had thwarted the buyer's ability to discover the infestation.

These cases treat victims leniently in evaluating justifiable reliance. That is often true, but it is not always so. Courts do hold victims responsible for exercising due diligence in ascertaining the true facts. As noted above, Rodi ultimately lost his case because the court found his reliance unjustifiable.

Nigro v. Lee, 882 N.Y.S.2d 346 (N.Y. App. Div. 2009), is another example of a case in which the court found a lack of justifiable reliance—in this instance because the victim failed to seek information that would have revealed the falsity of the representations. The plaintiff bought a 1995 Mercedes on an eBay auction. The seller's advertisement described the car as "gorgeous," with three minor blemishes, and stated that it was in the condition as disclosed, to the best of the seller's knowledge. The car was located in Nevada, and the buyer resided in New York, so he did not inspect the car when he bought it. After the car was delivered, the buyer discovered that it was in very poor condition. It had been damaged in an accident, its upholstery was stained, it had areas of rust, and it required extensive and expensive mechanical repairs. The buyer sued the seller, claiming that, despite knowing about all the problems with the car, the seller had fraudulently misrepresented that the car was gorgeous and virtually unblemished. The Appellate Division affirmed the trial court's dismissal of the buyer's suit. The court pointed out that the description of the car as "gorgeous" was a generalized expression of opinion and mere puffery. The court recognized that the remaining misrepresentations were more substantial, but it refused relief to the buyer because they were all easily discoverable by obtaining a vehicle history report and a mechanical inspection. The court said it was no excuse that the car was located in Nevada—the buyer could have arranged for an inspection there.

Section 13.5.2 deals with the application of the parol evidence rule to misrepresentations, and refers back to the discussion of the fraud exception to the parol evidence rule in section 12.12.1, which generally allows the admission of parol evidence to prove a fraudulent misrepresentation, even if the recorded agreement is integrated. However, as noted in section 13.5.2, although the parol evidence may be admissible, the fact that the representation was not included in the record —or worse, is inconsistent with a term in the record—could make it difficult for the victim to satisfy the requirement of reasonable reliance. This happened in *Psenicska*, as explained in section 13.5.2. The point was made even more strongly in *Pinnock v. Kings Carlyle Club Apartments, LLC*, 819 S.E.2d 515 (Ga. Ct. App. 2018), in which the court stated that it is axiomatic that a merger clause in an integrated contract operates as a disclaimer and renders any reliance on the parol representation unjustifiable. Not all courts would take such an absolute approach, but *Pinnock* shows that it is hard to make a convincing case of justifiable reliance on a parol misrepresentation.

§13.6.7 Injury and Remedy

Courts commonly require, as a final element of fraud, that the victim must have been injured. Injury is easy to see if misrepresentation caused the victim to overpay for the contractual performance—that is, that the performance is valueless or less valuable than it would have been had the representation been true. For example, the presence of bats, bugs, or vandals very likely diminished the market value of the houses in *Jablonski*, *Weintraub v. Krobatsch*, and *Willen* or would have resulted in cost to rectify these unpleasant phenomena. In buying Kellogg products that it could not sell, Kaloti suffered loss of its anticipated profit and had to dispose of the goods at sacrifice prices. However, sometimes the precise economic injury is more difficult to ascertain. For example, say that the reputed presence of ghosts had no effect on the market price of the house in *Stambovsky* or that Rozen did a decent job on the tax returns of Greenberg's clients and generated the expected profits. The fact that there may be no measurable economic loss in these cases does not inevitably mean that there is no injury. The injury could lie simply in the fact that the victim was tricked into a contract that the victim would not have agreed to in the absence of the misrepresentation.

Fraud may be used by the victim as a cause of action to ground a suit for avoidance or damages, or it could be used defensively against the other party's claim to enforce the contract. The alternative remedies available for fraud allow a court to give relief whether or not actual economic loss resulted from the fraud. Even if there is no economic loss, a victim who does not desire the contract once becoming aware of the misrepresentation is entitled to avoid it—to claim rescission. Upon rescission, a claim for restitution arises in favor of a party who has performed in whole or in part. In the absence of a contract, there is no basis for retaining a benefit given under the contract, so principles of unjust enrichment require that benefit to be returned. Benefit is measured by the value of property, which could be different from its contract price. This principle applies whether it is the victim or the perpetrator who has been enriched. However, the law imposes limits on the restitutionary rights of the perpetrator. Any doubts on the value of the perpetrator's performance are resolved against the perpetrator, and the victim is not obliged to return property or its value to the extent that it was worthless when received or deteriorated as a result of its own defects. (*See* Restatement, Second, §§164, 376, and 385.)

As noted in section 13.3, a contract induced by fraud is voidable, not void. This means that the victim may elect either to rescind it or to keep it in force. A victim who chooses not to rescind the contract is entitled to damages to compensate for the difference between the actual value of the performance and the value that it would have had as represented. This claim for damages includes such losses as reduction in market value or the costs of bringing the property into the condition as represented.

Traditionally, the remedy of rescission and restitution derives from contract law, but the remedy of damages has its roots in tort (fraud being a tort as well as a breach of contract). This could make a difference to remedy. For example, a court that applies the traditional distinction would allow a plaintiff who sues for damages to claim punitive damages as well, because the suit is based on tort. However, the court would not allow the plaintiff to claim punitive damages in a suit for rescission because those damages are not available in contract. This does not make a lot of sense, since the defendant's wrongful act is exactly the same, whichever form of relief is sought. Also, a rigorous focus on the tort-contract distinction would mean that a plaintiff who sues for rescission cannot claim any damages, even if the tort led to economic loss. This distinction between the contract and tort derivation of the alternative remedies has faded, and many modern courts do not apply it. Rather, they simply treat the remedies as available possibilities and provide the relief called for by the harm to the victim. This means that in appropriate circumstances, a court may award rescission together with damages for proven loss beyond restitution (offset by any restitution due to the perpetrator) or that it may permit punitive damages in a rescission suit.

§13.7 NONFRAUDULENT MISREPRESENTATION

A misrepresentation made without the deliberate intent to mislead is nonfraudulent. This includes a negligent misrepresentation, made without reasonable care in ascertaining and communicating the truth. (But as explained in section 13.6.4, if the lack of care rises to the level of recklessness or gross negligence, the misrepresentation could qualify as fraudulent.) It could also include a material misrepresentation made innocently, without any fault.

Although a nonfraudulent misrepresentation does not carry the same degree of disapprobation as a deliberate lie, it does permit avoidance if it is material and has induced justifiable reliance. It must relate to a fact central to the transaction, the party making it must have known or had reason to know of its importance, and the other party must have been justified in relying on it. It is also noted in section 13.5.2 that while an exception to the parol evidence rule allows the admission of parol evidence to show fraud, parol evidence relating to a nonfraudulent misrepresentation is excluded by the parol evidence rule if the record is integrated or the term is inconsistent with a partially integrated record.

A nonfraudulent misrepresentation is akin to a contractual promise. For example, the seller of a house, having inspected it and finding no termites, honestly but erroneously informs the buyer that the house is termite-free. This misrepresentation could be a negligent misrepresentation of the seller whose error was caused by a lack of reasonable care in inspecting the house, or it could be an innocent misrepresentation of the seller who was not negligent, but the assertion is interpreted as a warranty—a contractual promise that the house does not have termites. If the absence of termites is a material fact, this could allow for avoidance of the contract and restitution on grounds of material misrepresentation, or it could alternatively give rise to the buyer's claim for breach of the warranty term in the contract and expectation damages, aimed at placing the buyer in the economic position that the buyer would have been in had the property been as represented.

§13.8 DURESS

§13.8.1 The Nature of Duress

In its earlier formulation, duress doctrine allowed avoidance of a contract on grounds of duress only in extreme circumstances. A party claiming duress had to show that the other had induced the contract by using actual force or an unlawful threat of death or bodily harm, not merely property damage. The doctrine has moved beyond these narrow confines, and it is now well established that a person's free will can be undermined by unfair pressure short of physical compulsion or a threat of death or personal injury. An illegitimate threat to proprietary or economic interests (sometimes referred to as "economic duress") is now widely accepted as a basis for relief, and is the much more common form of duress. The duress must have induced the manifestation of assent by leaving the victim with no reasonable alternative but to agree. Duress may be raised either as the basis of a suit for avoidance of the contract or as a defense to a suit for enforcement of a contract. As with fraud, the basis of avoidance is consistent with, but an exception to, the general objective test of assent. The underlying rationale is that the victim should not be held accountable for apparent assent that is not genuine, but was improperly induced by an illegitimate threat of harm. The party who made the threat does not have a compelling reliance interest that is worthy of protection. The elements of duress are set out in Restatement, Second, §§175(1): One of the parties must make a threat, the threat must be improper, and it must induce the apparent assent by leaving the victim no reasonable alternative but to agree.

§13.8.2 The Threat

A threat is fundamental to a claim of duress, and distinguishes cases in which duress can be claimed from cases in which a party was compelled to enter a contract by external circumstances that do not emanate from the other party. *Zuckerman v. The Metropolitan Museum of Art*, 307 F. Supp. 3d 305 (S.D.N.Y. 2018), draws the distinction between duress and terrible external circumstances motivating a contract. The executrix of an estate sued to recover a Picasso painting from the museum. The painting had been owned by the Leffmanns, a Jewish couple who lived in Nazi Germany, and then Fascist Italy during the period leading up to the Second World War. The Leffmanns sold the painting to a Paris art dealer at a price well below its value in 1938 to gather together enough money to flee Nazi persecution. After passing through various owners, the painting was ultimately donated to the museum in 1952. The estate claimed duress in the 1938 sale of the painting as the basis for recovering the painting from the museum, but the court rejected that claim. Although the Leffmanns sold the painting under the severest of dire circumstances, which left them no reasonable alternative but to sell the painting at a sacrifice price, those circumstances were created by the Nazi persecution, not by any wrongful threat of the buyer. The economic need to enter into the transaction, even though created by extreme and horrific circumstances, did not constitute duress.[6]

A threat is an indication of intent to do or refrain from doing something so as to inflict some harm, loss, injury, or other undesirable consequences that would have an adverse effect on the victim's person or personal or economic interests. This encompasses a wide range of behavior, including not only explicit intimidation but also subtle or even implicit threats. The presence of an implied threat is determined by interpretation in the usual way, taking into account the circumstances of the relationship between the parties. The transaction is examined in context to ascertain if the words or actions of the one party show a reasonable intent to make a threat, reasonably so understood by the other. The threat may be either to take positive action or to refrain from acting, and the harm may consist of any adverse consequences sufficient to overcome the victim's resistance to the contract.

The mere fact that one of the parties will suffer bad or undesired consequences unless the contract is made does not constitute a threat, even if the other party realizes and takes advantage of this vulnerability. For example, the owner of a failing business urgently needed funds to keep the business operating, but no mainstream bank or financial institution would approve a loan to a business in such bad financial condition. The business owner therefore entered into a contract with a lender that was willing to undertake high-risk loans for an exorbitant (but legally permissible) interest rate and a security interest in all the assets of the business, which would allow the lender to seize those assets if the loan was not repaid on the due date. The borrower did not want to enter into this contract, but the lender made it clear that the terms of the loan were nonnegotiable and it would not make the loan unless the borrower agreed to them. The borrower had no choice but to agree to the terms if the business was to have any chance of surviving because there was no alternative means of trying to save it. The lender took advantage of the borrower's plight by insisting on draconian terms.

6. The denial of relief was affirmed on other grounds (that the claim was barred by laches), 928 F.3d 186 (2d Cir. 2019), *cert. denied*, 140 S. Ct. 1269 (2020).

In a sense, it could be said that the lender threatened not to enter into the contract unless the borrower agreed to its terms. However, a threat not to contract except on nonnegotiable terms (a threat often implicit in contract negotiations) is not improper and does not qualify as a threat for duress purposes.[7]

Relief for duress is usually premised on wrongful coercion by one of the contracting parties, so that party must usually be responsible for the threat. If the threat is made by a nonparty, the victim cannot normally avoid the contract unless the other party is implicated in the threat or knowingly took advantage of it. (This is the basis of the decision in the *Zuckerman* case, above.) Outside pressure should not readily defeat the legitimate expectations of an innocent party who relied on the transaction in good faith and without knowledge of the threat. This principle is expressed in Restatement, Second, §§175(2). *Gascho v. Scheurer Hospital*, 400 F. App'x 978 (6th Cir. 2010), illustrates economic and third-party pressure that did not constitute duress. Gascho, a nurse and a longtime employee of the hospital, entered into a separation agreement with the hospital under which she would receive a year's salary and benefits in exchange for her voluntary resignation and release of any claims that she may have had against the hospital. The agreement was the culmination of a very messy, drawn-out, and unpleasant situation that arose because of a conflict that Gascho had with her husband, who was the CEO of the hospital. Gascho subsequently filed suit to rescind the agreement, claiming that she had entered into it under duress on two grounds. First, that she had no reasonable alternative but to accept the settlement to avoid economic hardship and the prospect of uncertain and lengthy litigation to vindicate her rights. The court rejected this argument: The only implicit threat that the hospital made was that she would not get the severance package and would have to litigate her claims if she did not accept its offer. The court said that this was not an improper threat, but merely the kind of adverse consequences and economic pressure that people have to contend with in deciding whether to enter a contract. Gascho's second ground of duress was that her husband had intimidated her into entering the agreement by abuse and threats. The court recognized that the alleged threats made by her husband could amount to duress, but the hospital did not make those threats, dealt fairly with Gascho in relation to the settlement, and could not be held accountable for them. (Even though the husband was the CEO of the hospital, the court treated him as acting independently of his role as CEO of the hospital and not as an agent of the hospital, so his threats were not imputed to it.)

---

7. Although the borrower did not enter this contract under duress, unconscionability doctrine may provide grounds of avoidance if the borrower can satisfy the requirements for relief discussed in section 13.11

§13.8.3 Impropriety

A threat does not constitute duress unless it is improper. Threats of criminal or tortious conduct, such as a threat of physical harm to person or property, are clearly improper, but impropriety extends past these obvious categories to include any threatened behavior that goes beyond the legitimate rights of the party applying the pressure, or that constitutes an abuse of those rights. This would include, for example, a threat to withhold a performance or property to which the victim is entitled, to disclose information that would embarrass the victim, or otherwise to engage in spiteful or vexatious conduct that would cause distress to the victim. It is, of course, not duress to threaten consequences, even dire ones, that may lawfully and properly be pursued in the absence of agreement. For example, at the time for renewal of an employment contract, an employee who has become indispensable may legitimately threaten not to renew the contract unless the employer agrees to a substantial raise. Similarly, a person with a colorable tort claim may justifiably threaten to sue unless the tortfeasor agrees to a settlement. As *Gascho* shows, it is also not improper to threaten (expressly or impliedly) to refuse to enter into a contract unless the other party accepts proffered terms.

However, a threat to file criminal charges is regarded as improper, even if prosecution is warranted, because it is against public policy for a person to use the threat of criminal prosecution as a bargaining chip. This is illustrated by *Weinberg v. Baharav*, 553 S.W.3d 131 (Tex. App. 2018), in which Weinberg alleged that he had been induced to enter into an agreement to pay investors in his real estate business by a threat from the investors that if he did not sign the agreement, they would file criminal charges against him for misappropriation of investment funds. When Weinberg ceased making the payments, the investors sued him for breach of contract and he raised the defense of duress. The court permitted Weinberg to proceed to trial on the duress defense, holding that the threat of criminal prosecution is a misuse of the criminal justice process and therefore an improper threat. Weinberg did not have to prove that he was innocent of the alleged criminal conduct because the threat is improper whether or not the party threatened was actually guilty of the alleged crime.

§13.8.4 Inducement

Courts commonly use the test of inducement articulated in Restatement, Second, §§175(1)—the improper threat must leave the victim no reasonable alternative but to agree. The reasonableness standard is clearly objective, but it also takes the subjective attributes of the victim into account, recognizing that a bully should not be able to enforce a contract merely because the victim is easily intimidated. The inquiry is whether, under all the circumstances, the duress substantially overcame the victim's free will, leaving the victim with no reasonable alternative but to acquiesce. Inducement is therefore considered not in the abstract but in light of the victim's needs, personality, and circumstances.

An alternative is only reasonable if it is a feasible and practical means of evading the consequences of the threat. If it would be unduly burdensome or risky, or would not likely avoid the threatened consequences, the victim cannot be said to have had a reasonable alternative to manifesting assent. For example, the buyer of industrial equipment owes the seller $2 million, but refuses to pay the full price of the goods on the basis of a bogus claim that they are defective. Instead, it offers to pay the seller $1.25 million in full settlement of the price. It is clear that the goods are not defective, and that the buyer's claim is just a pretext for demanding a reduction in the price. For some sellers, rejecting the buyer's offer and suing for the full price would be a reasonable alternative, but this seller is in financial difficulty and has severe cash flow problems, so cannot afford to incur substantial litigation costs and to wait for payment while the litigation proceeds. The seller therefore accepts the buyer's offer of settlement. The buyer's threat is improper because it is a threat not to perform its contractual obligations unless the seller reduces the price. If the seller later decides to avoid the settlement on grounds of duress, it would have a good argument that it had no reasonable alternative but to succumb to the buyer's unlawful threat.[8]

Merry Gentleman, LLC v. George and Leona Productions, Inc., 2013 WL 4105578 (N.D. Ill. 2013), is another illustration of lack of reasonable alternative. Merry Gentleman, LLC, a production company, engaged the actor Michael Keaton to direct the movie *Merry Gentleman*. After the filming was completed, the prestigious Sundance Film Festival selected the movie for screening. There were two cuts of the movie, one made by Keaton and the other by the company, and a dispute arose between them over which cut should be screened at the festival. One of Sundance's requirements for screening at the festival was that the director of the movie must be present at the screening. Keaton refused to attend the screening unless his cut of the movie was used. At that point the company had invested $4 million in the film and screening it at the festival was important to the success of the movie, so the company entered into a settlement with Keaton under which Keaton agreed to attend the festival in exchange for the company's agreement to screen his cut at the festival and to release any claims it may have against him. After the screening, the company sued Keaton for breach of contract. He raised the release as a defense and moved to dismiss the claim, but the company argued that

8. In addition to duress, the seller can argue that the settlement lacks consideration because forbearance from asserting a bogus, bad faith claim or defense does not qualify as a legal detriment. *See* section 7.6.

the release was invalid because it had been entered into under duress. The court held that the company had made out a sufficient case of duress to go to trial. Keaton's threat to boycott the Sundance film festival unless his cut was used was a wrongful threat—it was an opportunistic exploitation of a situation in which the production company had no meaningful option but to accede to the release. The production company's only alternative to signing the release was to sue Keaton at that stage for his breach of the contract. But given the investment that the company had made in producing the movie, the coveted opportunity to screen it at Sundance, and the need to satisfy Sundance's requirement that the director attend the screening, it had no reasonable alternative but to agree to the release.

§13.8.5 Remedy

Duress renders the contract voidable, not void, so the victim may elect either to abide by the contract despite the duress, or to avoid it. If the victim avoids the contract, both parties must restore any benefit received under the contract. The remedy of avoidance and restitution is subject to the same general principles discussed in connection with misrepresentation.

Although in most cases the victim must choose between keeping the contract, subject to all its terms, or avoiding it entirely, there are circumstances in which courts allow a middle path—retention of the contract subject to an adjustment of its terms. For example, if a party desires to keep property purchased, but can show that an excessive price was compelled by duress, the court may enforce the contract, subject to a refund to the victim of the amount in excess of fair value. This remedy is not often employed in duress cases, but it is within the courts' discretion. If the act of duress is a tort, such as a threat of physical attack, the victim may also obtain damages in tort in addition to any relief under contract law.

§13.9 DURESS IN THE MODIFICATION OF AN EXISTING CONTRACT

Section 7.5 explained that under the common law preexisting duty rule, the modification of a contract requires new and separate consideration, and is not valid without it. However, it is not difficult to avoid this problem by ensuring that some new consideration, even quite slight, is given in exchange for the modification. In addition, in a sale of goods, UCC §2.209 does not require new consideration for a contract modification. Even if there is no consideration issue, the modification of an existing contract could be compelled by duress. A party to an existing contract may use leverage that it has under that contract to extort a modification of the contract from the other party. Duress doctrine provides a remedy to the victim of that extortion.

Say that Precision Engineering Co. has a commitment to supply custom-designed, precision engines to a vehicle maker by a specified date. Precision entered into a contract with Hi-Tech Tooling for the manufacture of complex components for the engines, with a delivery date that would give Precision enough time to incorporate the components into its engines to meet the vehicle maker's deadline. Knowing of the pressure that Precision is under to deliver its engines on time, Hi-Tech threatens Precision to go slow on completing its components unless Precision agrees to a substantial increase in price. Precision protests, but Hi-Tech will not back down. Precision knows that it could not possibly find any other company to make these complex components on time, so Precision agrees to the price increase. This is an obvious case of duress, satisfying both the requirement of Hi-Tech's improper threat to breach the existing contract, leaving Precision no reasonable alternative but to agree. After it has received the components from Hi-Tech, Precision can seek avoidance of the contract modification on grounds of duress.

§13.10 UNDUE INFLUENCE

The doctrine of undue influence was developed by courts of equity to deal with situations in which duress was not present but one of the parties had a particularly strong influence over the other and abused this position of dominance to persuade the subservient party to enter a disadvantageous contract. Thus, while duress provides relief to one whose apparent assent has been induced by an unlawful threat, undue influence is concerned with cases of abuse of trust. Like duress, undue influence makes the contract voidable at the instance of the victim. In most jurisdictions, the doctrine has not been extended beyond its original confines and is not available to redress unfair persuasion in arm's-length transactions. Restatement, Second, §177 reflects this narrow scope by confining the doctrine to relationships of dependence and trust. Although it would have been possible for courts to enlarge the scope of undue influence, making it available in all cases of unfair persuasion, the expanded concept of duress and the wide recognition of unconscionability doctrine (described in section 13.11.2) provide a sufficient basis for courts to regulate unfair bargaining, eliminating the need for a broader application of undue influence. As a result, undue influence has retained its specific character in most states.

To obtain relief for undue influence, the victim must establish three elements: first, that a relationship of trust and dependency existed between the victim and the other party; second, that this relationship gave the other party dominance over the victim, imposing the duty not to act contrary to the victim's interests; and third, that the dominant party abused this position by unfairly persuading the victim to enter a contract adverse to the victim's interests.

The law does not absolutely bar contracts between a dominant and a dependent party. To avoid the contract or any of its terms on grounds of undue influence, the weaker party must show that the dominant party abused power or influence over the weaker party by unfair persuasion. Unfair persuasion is an elastic concept. When the relationship of dependency is strong and the resulting contract is clearly disadvantageous to the weaker party, unfair persuasion may be inferred from those facts alone, and it may not be necessary to point to any specific underhanded bargaining strategy. However, if the degree of dependency is not as intense or the terms of the contract are not patently unfair, evidence of improper bargaining or oppressive circumstances may be needed to bolster the claim of undue influence. Unseemly bargaining can, as usual, take many forms, including the use of high-pressure tactics, the failure to disclose information, concealment of self-interest, failure to protect the interests of the weaker party, or discouraging recourse to other advisers.

A relationship of dependence can arise in many situations including a family relationship, a friendship, and a professional relationship. Undue influence in a professional relationship may be illustrated by a contract under which a client agrees to perform services for a lawyer. A lawyer-client relationship imposes a fiduciary duty on the lawyer which extends beyond the matters in which the lawyer represents the client into all other transactions between them. For example, a lawyer is representing a builder in litigation. The lawyer's home needs remodeling, so the lawyer decides to hire the builder to do the work. The lawyer drafts a construction contract, which the parties sign. In doing this, the lawyer is not representing the builder, but is merely acting in the personal capacity of a customer who contracts for the builder's services for a price. Nevertheless, because the lawyer has an attorney-client relationship with the builder in relation to the unrelated litigation, the lawyer has an ongoing fiduciary duty to the builder which affects this relationship too, and requires the lawyer to safeguard the builder's interests. Therefore, if a dispute arises out of the building contract, any terms in the contract that are unfair to and not in the best interests of the builder would be presumed to have been the product of undue influence and would be avoidable by the builder.

The presumption of undue influence is significant because it means that once the party seeking relief establishes that the other party had a duty arising from a relationship of trust, a presumption of undue influence arises, which places the burden of proving a lack of undue influence on the other party. The impact of this is illustrated by *Moore v. Moore*, 429 P.3d 607 (Kan.

Ct. App. 2018), in which the court of appeals reversed the jury verdict and required a new trial because the trial court failed to instruct the jury correctly on the burden of proof. Steven Moore ran a family farm on behalf of his aged parents. The parents had placed the farm properties in a trust for the benefit of all their children. At a time when the father was dying and the mother was emotionally distraught, Steven manipulated his parents into entering a contract under which they transferred the farm properties to Steven's son, Jebediah, for a fraction of their value and on generous payment terms, effectively disinheriting Steven's siblings. After the father's death, the mother and the trust sued Steven and Jebediah for avoidance of the contract. The jury gave judgment for the defendants, which the court of appeals reversed on the basis that the trial court committed reversible error in failing to instruct the jury that the defendants bore the burden of proving an absence of undue influence. The court noted that a presumption of undue influence arises where parties are in a confidential relationship, and the evidence indicated that Steven held a position of trust and confidence with his parents, who were particularly vulnerable and subject to manipulation. This created a presumption that Steven had unduly influenced his parents to execute the contract that greatly benefitted Steven and Jebediah.

A case involving undue influence may also support an alternative cause of action for unconscionability because the imposition of a contract by the use of undue influence could qualify as procedural unconscionability, and the terms favoring the dominant party could qualify as substantively unconscionable. If so, the plaintiff may sue on the causes of action of undue influence and unconscionability in the alternative.

§13.11 UNCONSCIONABILITY

§13.11.1 The Role, Nature, and Origins of Unconscionability Doctrine

Some forms of unfair bargaining do not satisfy the elements of fraud, duress, or undue influence but nevertheless result in the unfair imposition of a contract or contract terms on one party by the other. The more general and flexible elements of unconscionability doctrine give courts the discretion to provide relief for unfair bargaining in these situations. The name of the doctrine, "unconscionability," refers to the conscience of the court. The idea behind it is that one of the parties so unfairly used its bargaining power to impose harsh and one-sided terms on the other that the court cannot in good conscience enforce the contract as a whole or the offending terms. A doctrine based on the conscience of the court is necessarily open-ended and discretionary, and the court's reaction to any particular set of circumstances may be difficult to predict. However, it would be a mistake to assume that a court's conscience will be offended whenever the parties are not of equal bargaining power and the stronger party has used its dominance to dictate terms that favor its interests. Courts are careful in using the doctrine and have developed standards for evaluating contracts based on the elements and considerations discussed below.

Unconscionability originated as a discretionary bar to equitable relief in a contract suit. It is the function of a court of equity[9] to do justice between the parties, and the equity court would therefore deny relief to a plaintiff who had behaved inequitably. For example, if a party to a contract sued for equitable relief (such as specific performance) under a contract that was unfairly bargained and harsh, the court would refuse to enforce it on the ground that to do so would offend its conscience. Even after the courts of law and equity were combined, many courts did not recognize unconscionability as generally available and would only consider using the doctrine when the relief sought in the case was equitable in nature. Because most contract cases involve claims for damages or other relief at law, and claims in equity (usually for specific performance or an injunction) are less common, relief for unconscionability was often unavailable.

This changed dramatically from around the time that the UCC was enacted in the mid-twentieth century because §2.302 adopted the doctrine as a general rule, applicable to all contracts for the sale of goods. As a result of the strong influence of the UCC on the common law, courts began to apply unconscionability doctrine in cases at law involving contracts other than sales of goods. This trend was recognized and bolstered by Restatement, Second, §208, which closely follows the wording of UCC §2.302. Unconscionability is now firmly established as a general doctrine of contract law, applicable whether the basis of the suit is legal or equitable.

Unconscionability is decided by the judge, not the jury. The origin of this rule is in the equitable derivation of the doctrine, because juries have never been used in cases at equity. However, even though the doctrine is now applicable in law cases as well, the rule has not changed. Both Article 2 and the Restatement, Second, specifically state that unconscionability is a matter of law, to be decided by the judge. The main reason for preserving this rule is that a determination of unconscionability has a strong discretionary content, so it is better left in the hands of the judge.

9. The distinction between law and equity is explained in section 2.5.

§13.11.2 The Elements of Unconscionability

The UCC and Restatement, Second, simply acknowledge that the court has the power to refuse enforcement of an unconscionable contract or to adjust the contract by removing or modifying the unconscionable provision. Neither section attempts to say what constitutes unconscionability, but the Official Comments to §2.302, largely echoed in the comments to §208 of Restatement, Second, provide some general guidance to the court in exercising its discretion to determine whether unconscionability exists. Official Comment 1 to UCC §2.302 states that the basic test is whether, in the context of the commercial background and transactional circumstances, the contract or term is so one-sided as to be unconscionable. It expresses the aim of the doctrine as the prevention of "oppression and unfair surprise" but not the disturbance of the "allocation of risks because of superior bargaining power." Restatement, Second, Comment *d* to §208 makes a similar observation and expands on it by noting that gross inequality of bargaining power may satisfy the requirement of unconscionability if combined with substantively unfair terms. The Restatement comment also lists some indicia of oppressive bargaining, such as some degree of deception or compulsion, or an awareness by a dominant party of infirmity, ignorance, or lack of understanding on the part of the other. In essence, the comments point to a two-part test that examines both the process of bargaining and the resulting contract terms. *Williams v. Walker Thomas Furniture Co.*, 350 F.2d 445 (D.C. Cir. 1965), is one of the earliest cases to deal with the modern approach to unconscionability. Walker Thomas sold furniture and appliances on credit to low-income buyers. As security for payment of the balance of the price, Walker Thomas structured the transaction to include a "cross-collateralization" provision in the contract. This gave it a security interest in the goods bought under the new transaction as well as in all goods that the customer had ever bought from it in the past. The effect of this was that if the customer defaulted, Walker Thomas could repossess not just the goods sold in that transaction, but all other goods bought in previous transactions. Used furniture and household items do not have much value and were probably not worth enough to settle the debt. Therefore, the real purpose of the clause was to increase the stakes of default and to put pressure on the customer not to miss payments. The court of appeals defined unconscionability as the absence of meaningful choice by the one party resulting in contract terms unreasonably favorable to the other, and remanded the case to the district court to decide whether the contracts satisfied this test.

Subsequent caselaw has crystallized these vague guidelines into a two-part test. A contract is unconscionable if it is both procedurally and substantively unconscionable. That is, the unfair conduct of one of the parties in forming the contract (procedural unconscionability) leads to a contract

Diagram 13B

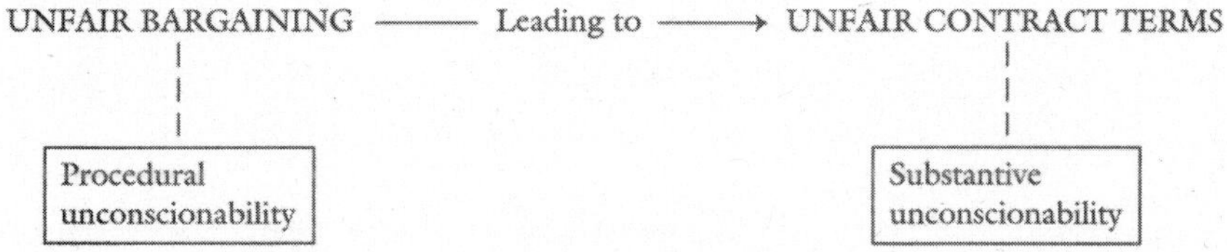

that has terms that are unduly one-sided and unfair to the other party (substantive unconscionability). As a general rule, courts require that both elements must be satisfied for a finding of unconscionability—the party seeking relief must demonstrate both improper conduct of the other party in the bargaining process and substantive unfairness in the resulting contract. However, courts have shown considerable flexibility in weighing these elements, so that if one of them is present in a significant degree, a court may find unconscionability even if the other is quite weakly shown. Courts sometimes refer to this balancing of the two elements as a "sliding scale." That is, a strong showing of one of the elements may persuade the court to find, without much concrete proof, that the other must be present as well. For example, in a situation involving disparate bargaining power, great unfairness in the terms of the contract may itself lead to the conclusion that the party who benefits from the unfair terms has engaged in procedurally unconscionable conduct by taking unfair advantage of its dominance. Some courts have even gone so far as to dispense with proof of one of the elements if the other is powerfully shown. Diagram 13B sketches the relationship between the two elements of unconscionability, examined more fully in the following sections.

§13.11.3 Procedural Unconscionability

This element focuses on the bargaining conduct of the party who is alleged to have behaved unconscionably in the formation of the contract. The doctrines of duress, fraud, and undue influence are also aimed at improper bargaining conduct, but they have specific elements. The concept of procedural unconscionability is more flexible. It allows the court to deal with pressure, deception, or unfair persuasion that does not fit into the narrower requirements of duress, fraud, or undue influence. Therefore, the principal value of unconscionability doctrine is that it expands the court's power to provide relief for unfair bargaining that would not be available under these other doctrines.

However, the flexibility of procedural unconscionability has its limits. The comments to UCC §2.302 and Restatement, Second, §208 emphasize that mere disparity of bargaining power is not enough to make a contract procedurally unconscionable. It is not the doctrine's purpose to correct an imbalance between the parties in their market advantage, sophistication, or resources. Such a broad use of the doctrine would undermine the policy of protecting reliance by allowing a party dissatisfied with a contract to request relief just because the other party was smarter, bigger, or wealthier or had better lawyers. This does not mean that the relative strength of the parties is irrelevant to the issue of unconscionability. Often it is only because of a disparity in power that a dominant party is able to behave in an unfair or oppressive manner or to insist on unfair terms. Similarly, a dominant party may take unfair advantage of the weaker party's lack of sophistication. Therefore, the key is not whether one party was more powerful, sophisticated, or knowledgeable than the other but whether it abused its power to impose its will on the other party.

Abuse of power can be quite subtle. There may be no obvious dishonesty or unfair persuasion, yet it is nevertheless clear that one of the parties used its position of dominance to impose the contract or particular contract terms on the weaker. That is, one of the parties enters the transaction with such bargaining power relative to the other, that the stronger party has enough control over the transaction to leave the weaker with no choice but to enter it on the terms proposed by the dominant party. Contracts entered into under these circumstances have come to be known as contracts of adhesion because the weaker party is seen as adhering without choice to terms dictated by the stronger. Contracts of adhesion were introduced in section 5.4 and are examined more fully in section 13.12, but it is useful to anticipate and emphasize the point made in that discussion, that a contract does not become adhesive or unconscionable merely because one of the parties has greater bargaining power. Some degree of procedural impropriety—an abuse of that power—should be present as well. Nevertheless, when substantively unfair terms are present and are attributable to the bargaining dominance of the party favored by the terms, it is relatively easy to conclude that the weaker party was deprived of free choice by a degree of dominance that, in itself, amounted to procedural unfairness.

§13.11.4 Substantive Unconscionability

There is a close relationship of cause and effect between the procedural and substantive elements: By engaging in unconscionable conduct during formation, one of the parties has been able to impose a substantively unconscionable contract or contract term on the other. It is not usually enough to show merely that the contract is disadvantageous to the complaining party or strongly favorable to the other. A court will not usually inquire into the question of whether the contractual exchange was adequate or equivalent, and will not normally invalidate or adjust a contract merely because one of the parties overpaid, underbid, or otherwise made a disadvantageous or unwanted deal.[10] Unless the unequal exchange was caused by behavior that qualifies as procedurally unconscionable, the parties should both be held to their manifested agreement. As explained in section 13.11.2, this general rule is qualified by the caveat that the substantive and procedural elements do not have to be present to an equal degree. When the contract terms are grossly oppressive, procedural unfairness may be found simply in the opportunistic use of a position of dominance.

Most commonly, a contract is substantively unconscionable when its terms are harsh, unfair, or unduly favorable to one of the parties. There are endless examples of disadvantageous terms that could be unfair and one-sided, such as an excessive price for goods or services, an exorbitant interest rate, harsh penalties in the event of default, the waiver or restriction of legal remedies, the waiver of the right to seek legal redress in a proper forum, and so on. The test suggested by Official Comment 1 to §2.302 calls on the court to decide whether, "in the light of the general commercial background and the commercial needs of the particular trade or case, the clauses involved are so one-sided as to be unconscionable under the circumstances existing at the time of the contract." This is a hopeless circumlocution, but it does at least suggest that a contract or term is unconscionable if it favors one of the parties more than should reasonably be expected, given the commercial context in which the contract was made. Official Comment 1 goes on to identify one of the goals of the doctrine as the prevention of oppression, which, while also rather vague, gives some further hint of the direction of the inquiry.

Although the conclusion that a contract is substantively unconscionable is normally based on the presence of unfair terms, it is possible for substantive unconscionability to be present even when the contract appears fair and reasonable from an objective standpoint. The unfairness could lie in the fact that the weaker party did not desire the transaction but was unfairly persuaded to enter it. For example, a seller's conduct could be procedurally unconscionable because high-pressure techniques and smooth talk are used to bamboozle a hapless buyer into buying unneeded goods or services. Even if the price of the goods or services and the other terms are reasonable, the contract as a whole may nevertheless be unconscionable, because it was unwanted by and imposed on the buyer.

---

10. Section 7.7 discusses the principle of consideration doctrine that a court will not usually inquire into adequacy of consideration.

§13.11.5 The Remedy for Unconscionability

Both UCC §2.302 and Restatement, Second, §208 articulate three possible remedies for unconscionability—avoidance of the contract as a whole, removal of the unconscionable terms, or rewriting the unconscionable terms to eliminate their unconscionable aspects. These provisions make it clear that the court has broad discretion to devise the most appropriate response to an unconscionable contract or term. In exercising its discretion, the court is influenced, but not bound, by what relief the victim requests.

If the unconscionability permeates the contract or profoundly affects the basis of the bargain, avoidance is the most appropriate remedy. In such a case, the court would refuse enforcement of the contract as a whole and require each party to restore any performance received under the contract under principles of unjust enrichment. In other cases (particularly where the victim would like to keep the contract with appropriate adjustments), the better remedy may be to enforce the basic bargain but to change its terms to eliminate its unconscionable aspects. This may involve either severing the unconscionable part of the contract (that is, eliminating the unconscionable provision entirely) or just altering the term to make it fair. For example, a standard contract for the sale of goods between a large retailer and a consumer requires all disputes to be arbitrated. The court finds that although the contract as a whole is unobjectionable, the arbitration term provides for a procedure that unduly favors the retailer. The consumer does not wish to avoid the contract as a whole but would like to avoid the arbitration term. The court could sever the arbitration term in its entirety, so that there is no longer any requirement to arbitrate and the parties must litigate their dispute before a court. Alternatively, the court could remove the unfair aspects of the arbitration term, but otherwise enforce it. This would mean that the parties are still bound to arbitrate, but the terms governing the arbitration are less one-sided. In deciding whether it is appropriate to sever or alter a term, the court considers factors such as the degree to which the term was imposed without meaningful choice, the form of relief requested by the victim of unconscionability, and the impact that the change will have on the basis of the parties' bargain. Courts usually aim to interfere as little as possible with the contract's terms, and to correct the contract without fundamentally altering its purpose. Where a term cannot be severed without doing significant harm to the basis of the bargain, alteration of the term may be less intrusive. If neither severance nor alteration can cure the unconscionability, or the change in the terms fundamentally changes the nature of the agreement, avoidance of the contract is probably the only proper remedy.

Beltran v. AuPairCare, Inc., 907 F.3d 1240 (10th Cir. 2018), demonstrates a court's evaluation of the most appropriate remedy for unconscionability. AuPairCare (APC) was an official sponsor under a U.S. Department of State program that permitted foreign nationals to be placed as au pairs with families in the United States for a one-year period. An au pair lived with the host family and earned wages by providing child care services for the family. Some of the au pairs commenced a class action against APC and several other defendants, alleging that its program violated various laws. The issue in the case was whether the plaintiffs' case should be dismissed and arbitration should be compelled under an arbitration provision in the au pair contract. The plaintiffs argued that the arbitration provision should be avoided on grounds of unconscionability. They claimed that it was procedurally unconscionable because it was adhesive, the plaintiffs were young, had no experience with contracts, and were not fully proficient in English. They argued that it was substantively unconscionable because it contained a fee-shifting provision, required all disputes to be resolved in San Francisco, which was distant from their places of residence in the United States, and gave APC the right to select an arbitrator unilaterally. The district court found the provision to be unconscionable and denied the motion to compel arbitration. The court of appeals decided that complete avoidance of the arbitration provision was too extreme. It was willing to treat adhesion on its own as creating a modest degree of procedural unconscionability, which would allow for a remedy on the "sliding scale" if significant substantive unconscionability was present as well. The court found the only substantively unconscionable aspect of the arbitration provision was APC's right to select the arbitrator unilaterally. The court therefore severed that aspect of the provision and enforced the arbitration clause without it.

Beltran is a good example of a case in which the flexibility of the remedy for unconscionability had an impact on the court's decision to find that a term is unconscionable. Had avoidance of the arbitration agreement been the only remedy, the court may not have found the agreement to be unconscionable, given the modest degree of procedural unconscionability and only a single substantively objectionable aspect of the agreement. However, the availability of the severance remedy allows the court to make a finding of unconscionability and to craft a remedy that is less drastic than a total avoidance of the entire contract.

§13.12 UNCONSCIONABILITY AND ADHESION IN STANDARD CONTRACTS

§13.12.1 The Role of Adhesion in Unconscionability Analysis

This section builds on the concept of adhesion that is alluded to briefly in section 13.11.3 and is also introduced in section 5.4 in relation to standard contracts. Adhesion is usually associated with standard contracts, and this is the focus here. However, note that an argument of adhesion could be made in any situation in which one of the parties has no choice but to accept nonnegotiable terms proffered by the other. A contract is described as a contract of adhesion where one of the parties refuses to contract except on nonnegotiable terms, and the other party has no choice but to adhere to those terms if that party wants the contract. Usually, the party that insists on the nonnegotiable terms has the market power to impose its will. It is much harder to label a contract as adhesive if the market for the desired object of the contract (such as goods, services, or employment) is competitive, and the other party is able to enter into a contract without those terms with someone else. Adhesion is more likely to be present if there is no competing provider who will contract on different terms, especially if the desired object of the contract is not a luxury.

Adhesion is not a basis of relief independent of and separate from unconscionability. Rather, it is encompassed within unconscionability doctrine. It is one of the factors that may persuade the court that the contract satisfies the elements of procedural and substantive unconscionability. That is, the fact that the dominant party had the power to insist on a contract on its own nonnegotiable terms may allow that party to take advantage of its dominance to impose an unfairly one-sided contract on the other. In effect, the abuse of the power to dictate the terms has resulted in an unfair contract. It is important to keep this perspective in mind, especially when dealing with nonnegotiable terms in standard contracts. As explained in Chapter 5, standard contracts are both widespread and necessary, whether the standard terms are in a signed paper or are presented in an electronic communication or on a website as clickwrap, browsewrap, shrinkwrap, or hybrid terms. A court would not be likely to go so far as to say that it is per se unconscionable for a party to insist on contracting on nonnegotiable standard terms that it drafted to protect its own interests. This point is illustrated by *Feldman v. Google, Inc.*, 513 F. Supp.2d 229 (E.D. Pa 2007), cited in section 5.3. The aspect of the opinion discussed in section 5.3 is whether Feldman had assented to a clickwrap forum selection clause by clicking the "I agree" button on Google's website. The court held that the clause was easily accessible and conspicuously set out on the website, so a contract was formed by Feldman's signification of assent. In addition to arguing that he did not assent to the term, Feldman claimed that the contract was adhesive and the term was unconscionable. The court disagreed. Although the term was standard and nonnegotiable, there was no procedural unconscionability because Feldman did have reasonable notice of the term, and he had not shown that a lack of alternatives in the marketplace left him with no meaningful choice. The court also held that the term was not substantively unconscionable because it was not unreasonable, unexpected, or unduly one-sided.

In addition to *Feldman*, the opinions in several other cases cited in Chapters 4 and 5 address the question of whether a standard term is unconscionable after deciding that the nondrafting party had manifested assent to it. Unsurprisingly, once a court has found that the standard term was adequately brought to the notice of the nondrafting party, this usually disposes of the procedural unconscionability question as well. *Kendall Imports, LLC v. Diaz*, 215 So. 3d 95 (Fla. Dist. Ct. App. 2017), cited in section 4.1.4 on the duty to read, involved the sale of cars from a dealer to the buyers, plaintiffs in a class action. Although the buyers could not read or speak English, they signed English purchase orders and financing agreements that included an arbitration clause. The court held that the arbitration agreement bound the buyers even though they did not read it and could not have understood it. The buyers had a duty to read and understand what they were signing. The buyers also argued that the arbitration provision was unconscionable, but lost on that ground as well. The court noted that the mere fact that the contract was adhesive does not make it unconscionable—the buyers had a full opportunity to inquire into the contract's terms and there was nothing oppressive in the seller's bargaining behavior. Having found no procedural unconscionability, the court rejected the buyer's unconscionability claim. In *Witt v. Nation-Wide Horse Transportation, Inc.*, 197 F. Supp. 3d 1146 (S.D. Iowa 2016), cited in section 5.3 on standard contracts, the term in issue was a forum selection provision in a standard contract for the transportation of a horse. The court held that Witt, the nondrafting party, was bound by the clause even though he had not read it. It was clearly and conspicuously presented at the head of an electronic form that he filled out and had to submit. The form also included language alerting the customer that by submitting the form, the customer signified agreement to its terms. On the question of unconscionability, the court found that Witt had not shown either procedural or substantive unconscionability. There was no procedural unconscionability because this was a simple clickwrap form, providing conspicuous notice, and not imposed by unfair bargaining. The clause was not substantively unconscionable because the forum selection was reasonable and Witt had not shown that litigating in that forum would be so onerous as to impose grave hardship on him or deprive him from obtaining recourse on the claim. In *Davis v. USA Nutra Labs*, 303 F. Supp. 3d 1183 (D.N.M. 2018), cited in section 5.4, the court found that Davis, the plaintiff, had assented to Groupon's clickwrap arbitration provision by clicking on the box acknowledging awareness and acceptance of the standard terms. The court also rejected Davis' argument that the contract was unconscionable. The mere fact that the contract was adhesive was not enough to make it procedurally unconscionable. Davis' claim of substantive unconscionability was based on the argument that the provision bound Davis to arbitrate without imposing a reciprocal obligation on Groupon. The court held that even if the provision could be interpreted as not binding Groupon to arbitrate, the parties' obligations do not have to be coextensive. Davis received other benefits from the contract, so a one-sided arbitration commitment was not unreasonably favorable to Groupon.

Although a standard nonnegotiable term is not adhesive or unconscionable by that fact alone, it could satisfy the elements of unconscionability if the dominant party crosses the line that separates acceptable self-serving terms from abusive imposition. For example, in *Mazur v. eBay, Inc.*, 2008 WL 618988 (N.D. Cal. 2008), the court found a clickwrap dispute resolution clause to be unconscionable. The clause was part of a standard agreement required by an auction house (HotJewelryAuctions.com) that operated on the eBay site. The clause required disputes to be resolved by a law firm that was nominated in the standard term, and waived all other forms of dispute resolution. The element of procedural unconscionability was satisfied because the contract was adhesive and the standard terms were laid out on the website in a manner that made them difficult to read. They were presented as a massive block of impenetrable text, without any paragraph, section, or heading breaks, and the text box allowed for only a few single-spaced lines to be read at a time. The court found substantive unconscionability in that the dispute resolution process provided for was not neutral and unduly favored the auction house. The court therefore avoided the provision and allowed the plaintiff to continue the lawsuit.

In summary, adhesion on its own, unaccompanied by any specific improper bargaining conduct, could satisfy the procedural element of unconscionability where it deprives the weaker party of meaningful choice and leads to the conclusion that the stronger party used its market power illegitimately. However, the absence of specific bargaining misbehavior would make this a borderline case of procedural unconscionability. Because the procedural and substantive elements should be balanced against each other, a strong degree of substantive unfairness must be present to compensate for the weak form of procedural unconscionability.

§13.12.2 Terms Made Available Only After the Contract Has Been Entered

Section 5.4 introduces adhesion in standard contracts and Section 5.5 deals with the issue of standard terms that are not disclosed to the nondrafting party until after the contract has been executed. Section 5.5.2 explains that if the contract is a rolling contract, the standard terms are not revealed only after contract formation because the contract was not formed at the time of initial purchase. Formation is deferred until the nondrafting party has had the opportunity to reject the contract after receiving adequate notice of the terms. However, Section 5.5.1 notes that if the contract is not a rolling contract, standard terms not made available to the nondrafter at the time of contracting may simply not be included in the contract at all if the lack of reasonable notice of the terms precludes actual or constructive notice of them. This conclusion is not invariable, because the terms could bind the nondrafter if they are reasonable in content and reasonably should have been expected by the nondrafter. The discussion in section 5.5 is focused primarily on whether the nondrafter implicitly assented to terms presented after contract formation. However, there is a link between that question and unconscionability doctrine, so that a nondrafter may make an argument of unconscionability as an alternative to the argument of lack of consent.

Where adhesive standard terms are made available only after the contract has been entered, a court may find that the delay in transmitting the terms is procedurally unconscionable, but if the terms are reasonably to be expected and the nondrafting party had reasonable notice that the contract was subject to standard terms, the delay in transmitting the terms may not be procedurally unconscionable. If, in addition, the terms are not unfair or unduly one-sided, there may not be substantive unconscionability either. As a result, in many cases, if the court holds that the terms became part of the contract, the same reasoning likely leads to the result that the terms are not unconscionable either.

§13.12.3 Adhesion and Unconscionability in Relation to Arbitration Provisions

Sections 4.1.4 and 5.3.5 discuss standard arbitration provisions in relation to the duty to read. They note that arbitration provisions have become increasingly common in standard contracts (including employment contracts) and that legal challenges to those provisions have become quite common. Because there is a general public policy in favor of arbitration, as reflected in the Federal Arbitration Act, 9 USC §§1-16, a court should uphold a standard arbitration agreement unless the party challenging it can show grounds to invalidate it under principles of contract law. Sections 4.1.4 and 5.3.5 explain that the duty to read precludes the argument that a party did not read or consent to the terms unless the party can show that the provision was not adequately brought to the attention of or expected by a reasonable nondrafting party.

Courts recognize that in the employment context, where a prospective employee is required to agree to an arbitration agreement (whether in a recorded document, or in some other form, such as an employee handbook) as a condition of being hired, the contract is commonly adhesive—an employee who needs the job has no choice but to agree to the nonnegotiable arbitration provision. However, this is not in itself enough to constitute procedural unconscionability if there is no indication of oppression or surprise in the bargaining context. This was noted, for example, in *Serpa v. California Surety Investigations, Inc.*, 215 Cal. App. 4th 695 (Cal. Ct. App. 2013), in which a court found that a nonnegotiable arbitration provision in an employment contract was not procedurally unconscionable merely by virtue of being adhesive. The court also held that the arbitration provision was not, as a whole, substantively unconscionable because the arbitration procedure was fair and applied to claims by both parties. The court did find, however, that a provision requiring each party to bear their own attorney's fees was unconscionable because it waived the employee's statutory right to recover attorney's fees if the employee prevailed on the claim. The court expunged this unconscionable aspect of the agreement by severing the waiver of attorney's fees. It otherwise left the arbitration agreement in force.

However, a court is likely to react to a challenge to an arbitration provision with more sympathy where the overall circumstances show overreaching by the dominant party in the imposition of an adhesive and unfairly one-sided contract. For example, in *Samaniego v. Empire Today LLC*, 140 Cal. Rptr. 3d 492 (Cal. Ct. App. 2012), the employer required employees to sign an employment agreement that contained an arbitration provision. The agreement was dense—11 pages long, single-spaced in a small font, and full of legal terminology. The arbitration provision was the penultimate of 37 sections. The agreement was in English, and the employees were Spanish-speaking with little or no facility in reading English. The employer required the employees to sign the agreement as a condition of employment and gave them little or no opportunity to seek advice. The agreement stated that the arbitration was subject to the rules of the American Arbitration Association, but those rules were not provided to employees. In addition, the terms of the arbitration agreement were strongly favorable to the employer. It shortened the statute of limitations for bringing claims against the employer; it had a unilateral fee-shifting provision that allowed the employer, but not an employee, to recover attorney's fees; and while it bound the employees to arbitrate their claims, it excluded from arbitration any claims that the employer might bring against the employee to safeguard its own interests. The court found that the adhesive manner in which the agreement was presented to employees satisfied the element of procedural unconscionability, and the one-sided nature of the arbitration provision was substantively unconscionable. The court refused to sanitize the arbitration provision by severing or amending its unconscionable aspects and upholding the arbitration provision without them. It found the entire arbitration provision to be permeated with unconscionability—the multiple defects in the agreement showed it to be a systematic effort to impose arbitration on employees as an inferior forum that worked to the employer's advantage. It therefore avoided the provision in its entirety.

§13.13 ILLEGAL CONTRACTS AND CONTRACTS THAT ARE CONTRARY TO PUBLIC POLICY

§13.13.1 Illegality, Public Policy, and Freedom of Contract

The assent and reliance policies of contract law are not the only policies that may be implicated in the enforcement of a contract. Even when the contract is a full and genuine exercise of both parties' freedom of contract, it may break the law or so offend public policy that the court refuses to enforce it. This distinguishes regulation on grounds of illegality and public policy from the other doctrines discussed in this chapter: The issue here is not that one of the parties dealt wrongly with the other or that one party's assent is deficient (even though this factor could also be present in some cases), but that the contract violates the law or damages the public good. Therefore, the goal of judicial intervention here is different from that in cases where the only issue is bargaining impropriety. The court's concern goes beyond doing justice between the parties, to the protection of the public interest.

The dividing line between illegality and violation of public policy is not sharply drawn, but there is a conceptual distinction between a contract that is illegal and one that offends public policy. A contract is illegal if it contravenes a statute or a rule of common law. A contract violates public policy, where there is no rule of law that forbids the contract, but enforcement of the contract would significantly harm the public interest. The principal difference between an illegal contract and one that violates public policy therefore lies in the degree to which a court uses its discretion to avoid the contract. There is more clarity over the illegitimacy of the contract if it violates the law, so the court's focus is to apply the law and to decide whether and to what extent the violation of the law should deprive the party suing on the contract of a remedy. If the contract does not violate the law, but is alleged to offend public policy, the illegitimacy of the contract is not as certain. Therefore, the court must weigh the public policy in favor of upholding the contract against the public policy that would be violated by enforcing the contract. This requires policymaking, a task that is better left to the legislative branch, so courts are generally careful in using their discretion to articulate public policy and usually require a strong showing of clear harm to the public interest before finding that a contract contravenes public policy.

Although the focus here is on the public interest, it is not typically some government agency or public body that challenges the contract. The claim of illegality or a violation of public policy is made by one of the parties who seeks to escape an obligation arising out of the contract. Therefore, in adjudicating an issue of illegality or public policy, a court is commonly resolving a dispute between the parties. One of them is trying to enforce the contract (or sometimes trying to obtain restitution for performance under the contract) and the other is resisting. Although balancing the equities between the parties is not as dominant a consideration as the public interest, it does have an influence on the outcome.

The end result of a determination that a contract is illegal or contravenes public policy has some similarity to the remedies for improper bargaining and is in some ways analogous. A court may decide to refuse enforcement of the improper contract in its entirety, which sounds like the equivalent to avoidance, or it may keep the contract in place and refuse enforcement of only the offending term, which approximates severance. However, because protection of the public interest is the court's principal goal in dealing with a contract that is illegal or violates public policy, the case is conceptually different from a situation of improper bargaining. This calls for a different approach to the issue of remedy. Society is the principal victim of a contract that is illegal or in violation of public policy. Therefore, where a contract directly violates a rule of law, or its harm to society is serious enough, a court is most unlikely to enforce it under any circumstances. Such a contract is more correctly characterized as void rather than voidable. The same is often true where the parties are joint perpetrators of the offense and it cannot be said that one used the illegal contract to victimize the other. On the other hand, where one of the parties is more to blame for the transaction, the other is a member of a group which the law seeks to protect, and the contract does not involve serious illegality, the contract is more accurately described as voidable. In short, the treatment of a contract that is illegal or contrary to public policy depends on the nature and gravity of the violation, the goals of the law or public policy, and the extent to which the impropriety permeates the contract. Sometimes the best way to protect the public interest is to refuse enforcement of the contract altogether, but in other cases, enforcement of the contract, with or without the adjustment of its terms, may best serve the public good. Sometimes, a contract's illegality or violation of public policy could even affect a restitutionary claim of one of the parties arising from nonenforcement of the contract.

§13.13.2 Illegal Contracts

Some illegal contracts are such a serious violation of the law that performance of the contract (or sometimes even making the contract) is a criminal act. This would be true, for example, of a contract under which one of the parties pays the other to murder someone. Such a contract is not enforceable and its making or performance would lead to criminal prosecution. However, there is a difference between illegality and criminality, and not all illegal contracts are criminal. A statute or the common law could simply forbid a type of contract or a contract term without making the violation of the law a criminal offense. Contract law is not directly concerned with whether the transaction attracts criminal penalties—this would be handled by a separate criminal prosecution. However, the seriousness of the illegality is a consideration in the court's decision on remedy, so the criminal nature of the contract has some relevance to the contract case.

a. The *In Pari Delicto* Rule

Where the parties share the guilt of having entered an illegal contract, the *in pari delicto* rule holds that the court will keep aloof from the dispute and will not intervene to help either party. The name of the rule is an abbreviation of the maxim, *in pari delicto potior est conditio defendentis.* (When the parties are in equal guilt, the defendant's position is stronger.) The *in pari delicto* rule creates an affirmative defense to a claim based on the illegal contract. That is, the party who is sued on the contract may raise the rule as a defense to the suit.

The rule is not as straightforward as it sounds. First, although it refers to equal guilt, it really means that the guilt of the party seeking relief must be equal to or greater than that of the other party. Second, although it is sometimes possible to assign greater fault to one of the parties, it is not always easy to do this. Third, and less obvious, the rule does not simply depend on an evaluation of the relative guilt of the parties. It also takes into account the seriousness of the illegality, the equities between the parties, and the impact on the public interest in giving or declining relief. This means that weighing the relative guilt of the parties is just one aspect of a broader inquiry into the circumstances of the transaction, the relationship of the parties and their motivations, the protection of the public interest, and the furtherance of the public policy served by the law.

In some situations, the court's task in deciding how to apply the *in pari delicto* rule is made easier by a provision in a statute that prescribes how these considerations should be balanced or at least offers some guidance on how the court should weigh them. For example, a statute may specifically state that a contract that violates it is void or unenforceable, thereby making it clear that the court should not enforce it, even if the equities and balance of guilt would otherwise point in the opposite direction. Or a statute that declares the contract to be unenforceable may specifically allow a party to obtain restitution of any benefit conferred under it, thereby telling the court that avoidance is required but the remedy of restitution is available.[11] Some statutes do not have such a clear prescription, but the provisions or purpose of the statute may indicate that the goal of the law is to protect persons in

11. Restitution upon the avoidance of an illegal contract is discussed below in section 13.13.2b.

the position of one of the parties. This signals to the court that a resolution favoring that party is called for.

The *in pari delicto* rule is therefore not an absolute bar to relief, even where the court finds that the party requesting relief bears equal or greater guilt. Rather, it is a starting premise from which the court may depart to the extent that it considers that the equities between the parties, the policy of the law, and the public interest so demand. The weighing of these factors is illustrated by *Parente v. Pirozzoli*, 866 A.2d 629 (Conn. App. Ct. 2005), and *Homani v. Iranzadi*, 211 Cal. App. 3d 1104 (Cal. Ct. App. 1989). In *Parente*, the defendant wished to buy a bar but would have had difficulty in taking transfer of the liquor license because he was a convicted felon. He therefore entered into an agreement with the plaintiff under which the plaintiff would apply for the license as a front man, and the parties would then run the bar as equal partners. The license was granted and the parties went into business. When the partnership was later dissolved, the defendant refused to pay the plaintiff his share of the profits and the plaintiff sued. The court refused to enforce the contract because it was based on the unlawful purpose of evading the liquor control laws. The plaintiff argued that if the court refused to award him his share of the partnership profits, the defendant, who instigated the scheme to evade the liquor control laws, would be rewarded by a windfall. Although the court recognized this, it felt that the public interest was best served by refusing enforcement. Not only should the court not sanction such a contract, but the refusal of enforcement would create a disincentive for people like the plaintiff to act as front men in the future. This decision shows the difficulty of achieving the right balance. It could just as well have been argued that allowing the defendant to keep the plaintiff's share of the profits created an incentive to use a front man to deceive the liquor control authority.

In *Homani* the court refused to enforce an agreement to pay interest on a loan in a situation in which, for the purpose of evading tax on the interest, the parties had agreed orally to the payment of interest but signed a promissory note showing the loan as interest-free. The court was unpersuaded by the lender's argument that the borrower received a windfall. The court considered that the public interest was best served by removing the lender's incentive to enter such a transaction. This result makes sense. After all, it was the lender who stood to benefit from the tax evasion, and he was most guilty of breaking the law.

b. Restitution Where an Illegal Contract Is Avoided

The effect of applying the *in pari delicto* rule in *Parente* and *Homani* is that the court refused enforcement of the contract and left the parties as it found them. Refusal of enforcement is a natural consequence of illegality because enforcement is an affirmative recognition of the contract, and a court is understandably reluctant to play any role in upholding the improper contract. However, the *in pari delicto* rule also has a less obvious impact. The court may also apply it where a party does not claim enforcement of the contract but concedes it is illegal and asks for restitution of a benefit conferred on the other party under the contract. The refusal of restitution is not as easily justified as nonenforcement because the grant of the remedy would not require recognition of the contract. Quite the opposite; it is based on the premise that no contract exists. Also, the equities usually favor the plaintiff more strongly where restitution is claimed because of the defendant's unjust enrichment. Some courts recognize this and are more sympathetic to restitutionary claims. However, the *in pari delicto* rule is broad enough to cover restitutionary claims as well as claims of enforcement and a court may decide that even recognition of a restitutionary claim is not in the public interest.

The following illustrations identify the considerations that a court weighs in deciding whether the *in pari delicto* rule should preclude the restitution of a benefit conferred under an illegal contract. In contravention of a statute forbidding the ownership of casinos by mobsters, the owner of a casino sold it to a gangster, for $10 million. Both parties knew about the prohibition. At the time of executing the agreement, the buyer made a down payment of $100,000 to the seller. A few days later the seller repudiated the contract. Clearly, the contract is unenforceable, and the buyer cannot sue for relief on the contract, whether in the form of specific performance or damages for breach. There is no obvious answer to the question of whether the buyer can get the $100,000 back. It could be argued that, as the mobster seeking to acquire the casino, the buyer is more to blame than the seller. But the contrary argument could be made that the seller, by deliberately violating the law, made possible the very harm that the statute seeks to avert. The determination of which of these alternatives best serves the public interest is also difficult to make: Is it better to allow the seller to keep a windfall profit from the deliberately wrongful transaction, or to allow the court's process to be used by a mobster to recover the down payment made in an attempt to violate the law? Unless it is demonstrated that judicial intervention is the more appropriate alternative, the thrust of the *in pari delicto* rule is to leave the parties as they are.

As a second example, a liquor store sells a case of scotch to a 20-year-old minor, violating a statute (known to both parties) that prohibits the sale of alcohol to persons under the age of 21.[12] The buyer paid for the scotch in cash, but the seller now refuses delivery. Again, the buyer clearly cannot enforce the contract, but can the buyer obtain restitution of the payment? The seller could argue that the buyer had no business trying to purchase

12. Although the general rule is that a person must be over 21 to buy liquor, in most states a person acquires contractual capacity at 18. The contract is therefore not avoidable for lack of capacity.

the liquor and deserves no help from the court in recovering the payment. However, it seems intolerable to allow the seller to keep the payment for goods that were not given to the buyer. If the reason for barring the sale of liquor to young people is that they do not have the maturity to use it responsibly, it would seem that this lack of maturity also diminishes the buyer's blame in the transaction. It is also relevant that a central purpose of the law is to protect minors, and return of the money better serves this goal.

§13.13.3 Contracts Contrary to Public Policy

If a contract is not actually illegal, but it nevertheless offends public policy, the court's decision on whether or not to enforce it involves a balancing of policy concerns and of the equities between the parties. Assuming that the contract suffers from no deficiencies in assent, the regulation of contracts on the basis of broader public interest creates a tension between the policy of enforcing contracts and the other public policy that would be frustrated by enforcement. To resolve this dissonance, the court must balance the countervailing policies. If the harm to the public interest outweighs the benefit of enforcement to the public and the parties, the court may decide that the public interest requires avoidance of the contract completely. However, a court may decide that enforcement on adjusted terms is a better solution when the equities favor the party who seeks enforcement and the harm to the public interest can be averted or minimized by eliminating the offensive aspect of the contract.

Public policy may be apparent from legislative action that does not go so far as to make the contract illegal, but is nevertheless relevant to the subject matter of the transaction, or the policy may have been enunciated in prior caselaw. To the extent that these sources do not clarify policy, the court has to identify and articulate the policy itself, based on testimony and argument. Disclaimers of liability and noncompetition provisions are two types of contract that commonly give rise to public policy analysis, and they are used here to show how courts go about conducting this analysis.

a. Disclaimers of Liability

Disclaimers of liability for injury (exculpatory clauses) feature frequently in the caselaw, and provide a good illustration of public policy analysis. A disclaimer of liability for wrongful conduct pits the policy of freedom of contract against the tort policy of holding a tortfeasor accountable for injury caused by its actions and of deterring wrongful conduct. The policy of freedom of contract calls for the enforcement of a freely bargained consensual agreement, but the tort policy of accountability for injury caused by fault disfavors an agreement that absolves a tortfeasor in advance from liability for future conduct. This means that the public policies of contract and tort pull in opposite directions and must be balanced. It is relatively easy to decide in favor of the tort policy where there is some problem with the way in which the disclaimer was entered into. The policy of freedom of contract is not well served by enforcing the contract unless the disclaimer is voluntary, fairly bargained, and expressed clearly and conspicuously. Therefore, as an initial matter, the court examines the disclaimer itself to decide if the injured person was bound by it, and if so, whether the disclaimer's language covers the injury suffered. Most exculpatory agreements are standard contracts of adhesion, so the first inquiry should be into the question of whether the exculpatory provision was adequately brought to the attention of the nondrafting party (the victim). This requires the language of the disclaimer to be explicit and to show clearly the intent to exonerate the drafting party from liability. Any unclear language is interpreted restrictively to cut down the scope of or eliminate the disclaimer. Once it is established that the victim's manifestation of assent is effective, the next task is to interpret the agreement to ascertain that it does cover the injury in question. If the disclaimer survives these inquiries, the next question is whether it is avoidable because of improper bargaining, most commonly unconscionability.

Where the provision is absolutely clear, the victim's agreement to it is not in question, and there has been no improper bargaining, the competing tort and contract policies are in the starkest opposition. To decide which policy should predominate, courts weigh all the circumstances and considerations. Courts have identified several factors that are relevant to this decision. The scope and extent of the disclaimer is important. Although it may be acceptable to exclude liability for negligence, a disclaimer will not be enforced to the extent that it exculpates gross negligence, recklessness, or intentional misconduct. Where only ordinary negligent injury is covered, the court considers the importance or necessity of the service to the public (for example, a disclaimer in a residential lease is potentially much more harmful than one in a skydiving contract); the kinds of people who are likely to execute the disclaimer (for example, whether the service is used by the public at large, or only by a specialized or qualified group); the extent to which the provider of the service has control over the person or property of the victim; and the impact of nonenforcement of the disclaimer on the public's ability to obtain the service at all or at reasonable cost. If factors such as these balance in favor of holding the service provider responsible for negligence, the court will not enforce the disclaimer, even if it is freely executed and not adhesive.

A court's approach to the determination of public policy is illustrated by the fictitious opinion, used as the basis for the Examples on judicial precedent in Chapter 3. The opinion deals with the issue of whether a parent can bind a minor child to an agreement releasing the operator of a ski area from liability for any injury that the minor may suffer while skiing.

There was no statute or rule of common law that invalidated a parent's contract waiving liability on behalf of a minor, and no statute that invalidated contractual releases of liability in general. The court therefore had to decide for itself whether to invalidate the disclaimer as a matter of public policy. A review of the fictitious opinion[13] provides some insight into the way in which a court reaches a decision based on public policy. The court begins by noting that the legal rule that a minor lacks capacity to enter into a binding contract is intended to protect minors from exploitation, improvidence, and bad judgment. The court then goes on to consider whether that policy should apply where the minor's parent enters the exculpatory agreement on behalf of the minor. It cites several opinions from the courts of other states that have allowed a minor to disaffirm such waivers. It then balances the public interest in protecting volunteer and nonprofit organizations from liability against the ill effects of creating a disincentive to care, which leaves minors unprotected from negligence. It next balances the public interest in allowing parents to make decisions for their minor children against the public interest in protecting minors from negligent injury. It concludes that the policy of protecting the minor outweighs the countervailing policies and decides that the disclaimer does not bind the minor.

In its opinion, the fictitious court expressly does not decide whether, as a general matter, it is good public policy to uphold an adult's contractual disclaimer that allows a service provider to shift the burden of injury to the other party and to escape responsibility for negligence. It concludes, in dictum, that public policy does not require the invalidation of an adult's disclaimer, which should be upheld to the extent that it appropriately balances the public interest in holding a party accountable for negligent conduct and the countervailing public interest in freedom of contract. The cases described below, *Hanks v. Power Ridge Restaurant Corp.*, 885 A.2d 734 (Conn. 2005); *Munn v. Hotchkiss School*, 933 F. Supp.2d 343 (D. Conn. 2013); *Brigance v. Vail Summit Resorts, Inc.* 883 F.3d 1243 (10th Cir. 2018); *McCune v. Myrtle Beach Indoor Shooting Range, Inc.*, 612 S.E.2d 462 (S.C. Ct. App. 2005); and *Bagley v. Mt. Bachelor, Inc.*, 340 P.3d 27 (Or. 2014) illustrate how courts reach contrary conclusions in balancing the public policy considerations relating exculpatory clauses in situations in which the protection of a minor is not in issue.

In *Hanks*, the adult plaintiff was injured while snowtubing and sued the operator of the ski resort for damages, claiming that it had been negligent in the way that it constructed and supervised the snowtube run. Prior to snowtubing, the plaintiff had signed a release that exculpated the operator from

13. Although the opinion is by a fictitious court, the issues discussed in the opinion are real and the opinion cites actual cases.

liability for negligent injury. The plaintiff had in fact read the disclaimer and had actual knowledge of it.[14] Even had he not read it, the court found that he would have had constructive knowledge of it because the disclaimer expressed the exclusion of liability in conspicuous and unmistakable language that would alert a reasonable person to its import. The agreement was very clearly written and it unmistakably emphasized that negligent conduct was covered by the disclaimer by capitalizing the word "negligence" several times. Notwithstanding this, the court avoided the disclaimer on grounds of public policy because it found that the contract was adhesive, the snowtube run was open to all members of the public who had a reasonable expectation of safety, the operator controlled the run and rented the equipment, and it would not be in the public interest to allow the operator to shift risk of liability to the customer.

The court also refused to uphold the disclaimer in *Munn*. Munn, a student of the Hotchkiss School participated in a school-organized trip to China. Prior to leaving on the trip she had executed a release of liability, in which she released the school from all claims arising during the course of the trip.[15] She contracted a serious tick-borne illness on the trip, which resulted in permanent brain damage. Munn sued the school district in tort, claiming that the school had been negligent in failing to warn students of the risk of exposure to insect-borne diseases and failing to take proper precautions against those diseases. Unlike *Hanks*, the court held that the language of the release was not broad enough to cover negligence claims. However, adopting the factors identified in *Hanks*, the court said that even had the release covered claims arising out of the school's negligence, it would be unenforceable as against public policy because the release was adhesive, the school had a duty to protect the students that it took overseas, and it had control over the students' exposure to risks of disease. In the absence of a binding release, the jury found the school liable for negligence and awarded damages of about $42 million to Munn.[16]

---

14. In light of the discussion above about protecting minors from ill-considered decisions, an ironic feature of the case was that the plaintiff's 12-year old son urged him not to sign it, but the plaintiff disregarded that advice because he did not take the disclaimer seriously or believe that it would be enforceable.

15. Munn was a 15-year-old minor and her mother assisted her in executing the exculpatory provision, but the question of whether a parent can bind a minor to such a provision was not raised as an issue in the case, so the court focused on the validity of the disclaimer in general.

16. The Hotchkiss school appealed the district court judgment on grounds unrelated to the validity and scope of the disclaimer, arguing that the school had no duty to protect students against the risk of insect-borne disease and that the damages award was excessive. The Court of Appeals for the Second Circuit affirmed the trial court judgment, *Munn v. Hotchkiss School*, 724 F. App'x 25 (2d Cir. 2018), following certification of these issues by the Connecticut Supreme Court, 165 A.3d 1167 (Conn. 2017).

Brigance involved a similar situation to *Hanks*. A skier was injured when her foot was caught in a ski lift. The court upheld the validity of an exculpatory agreement executed by the skier before she rode the ski lift. The court focused on three factors: skiing was a recreational activity, not an essential service, the disclaimer was clear and unambiguous, and it was entered into voluntarily by the plaintiff without any unfair persuasion. Contrary to *Hanks*, the court did not consider that the adhesive nature of the contract or the fact that the ski slopes were open to the public were sufficient reasons to invalidate a disclaimer relating to non-essential recreational activity.

The court also upheld the exculpatory agreement in *McCune*. The plaintiff's eye was injured while she participated in a paintball game because her mask did not fit properly. Before she began the game, she signed a release that emphasized the risks of injury, acknowledged that she assumed such risks, and absolved the defendant from all liability for injury, whether caused by negligence or otherwise. The release specifically did not cover injury resulting from gross negligence or wanton misconduct. The exculpatory provisions were printed in capital letters. The court affirmed the trial court's grant of summary judgment in favor of the defendant. The release was explicit and clear, it did not seek to exclude liability for conduct more serious than negligence, and it was a voluntary assumption of risk by the plaintiff. The court pointed out that it would not serve the public good if a business could not exclude liability by a reasonable and explicit disclaimer. The risk of liability would preclude many activities and events.

In *Bagley*, the court couched its discussion of public policy in terms of unconscionability doctrine, which shows that there can be a close connection between public policy analysis and unconscionability. The case involved the validity of a conspicuous and unambiguous provision in a snowboarding season pass that released the operator of the ski area from liability for its own negligence. In deciding that the release violated public policy, the court examined the factors taken into account to determine procedural and substantive unconscionability. It held that, despite the clarity of the release, its adhesive nature in a consumer transaction was enough to satisfy the element of procedural unconscionability. The court found the release to be substantively unconscionable because it was one-sided, imposed harsh consequences on the user of the ski area, and absolved the operator of its duty to take reasonable care to protect its customers. Although the court acknowledged that skiing and snowboarding are inherently dangerous nonessential recreational activities, and that that there is a reasonable argument that a ski operator should be able to limit its exposure to liability, it found that these considerations were not enough to outweigh the public policy against enforcing the unconscionable release.

b. Noncompetition Agreements

Noncompetition agreements (also called covenants not to compete)[17] may be invalidated completely on public policy grounds, but they could be fully valid and enforceable, or could be enforced with an adjustment to eliminate the violation of public policy.

A covenant not to compete is an undertaking by a person associated with a business that, upon leaving the business, the person will not, for a specified period and in a specified area, engage in activity that competes with the business. Such covenants may be found in employment or partnership agreements or in contracts for the sale of a business. For example, a well-established pediatrician takes a newly qualified doctor into the practice as a junior partner. The established doctor is concerned that the new partner may work in the practice just long enough to get experience and a following among the patients and will then terminate the partnership and set up practice elsewhere. To avoid this, the established pediatrician demands a provision in the partnership agreement in terms of which the junior partner undertakes, upon leaving the partnership, not to practice medicine within a ten-mile radius of the partnership premises for a period of five years.

There is a long-established public policy against agreements that stifle competition or that restrict a person's freedom to earn a livelihood by full participation in the market. Courts apply the policy when a contract unduly hampers competition or improperly restricts the ability of a party to work. Courts are more willing to uphold a noncompetition clause that bars the seller of a business from competing with it for a reasonable period and in a reasonable area. A reasonable restraint is most justifiable in this situation because the seller of the business is in a strong position to poach customers, use trade secrets, and continue trading on the goodwill of the business sold to the buyer. Noncompetition clauses in partnership agreements, such as the one involving the pediatricians, are usually more justifiable than those in employment agreements because a departing partner is more closely analogous to the seller of a business. Courts are most resistant to enforcing noncompetition agreements against employees because of the impact of the covenant on the employee's ability to earn a livelihood, and the less likely possibility that the employee takes away from the business anything more than the employee's own skills. However, unless a state has invalidated noncompetition agreements in employment contracts by statute, even a noncompetition agreement in an employment contract could be valid.

For the most part, therefore, a covenant not to compete is not per se invalid, but the court assesses its public policy implications by weighing

17. A noncompetition agreement was featured in Example 10 of Chapter 7, in which the issue was whether an employer had given consideration to an employee in exchange for a post-employment noncompetition agreement.

the legitimate interests of the party protected by the restraint against the public interest and the interests of the party who is restrained. The activity covered by the restraint and its geographical and temporal scope must all be reasonable in light of the overall circumstances. For example, in the above hypothetical concerning the pediatrics practice, the noncompetition agreement precludes the junior doctor from practicing medicine within a ten-mile radius of the practice for five years. In deciding if or to what extent this covenant should be upheld, the court would consider all the circumstances of the case, taking into account factors including the legitimate interests (such as patient goodwill) of the established doctor, the mores of the medical profession, the hardship on the junior doctor, the patients' right to use a doctor of their choice, and the fairness of the bargaining process leading to agreement on the provision. The court would consider whether, in light of these factors, the restraint is legitimate at all, and if it is, whether its extent is appropriate. In this case, a restriction on all medical practice is likely too broad because the only field in which the junior doctor would compete with the practice would be in the field of pediatrics. The ten-mile geographic scope and five-year time period may also be more than what is needed for the protection of the senior doctor's interests. If, on balance, the deleterious impact of the clause outweighs the interests of the established doctor, the court may refuse to enforce the clause altogether. Alternatively, public policy may be served by cutting down the restraint to a level that goes no further than necessary to protect the senior doctor's interests, reducing the time or geographic limit of the restraint or defining the prohibited activity more narrowly. In this case, therefore, public policy may not require complete invalidation of the restraint, but could be adequately served by adjusting the terms of the restraint.

O'Sullivan Films, Inc. v. Neaves, 352 F. Supp. 3d 617 (W.D. Va. 2018), upheld a noncompetition agreement in an employment contract as reasonable. O'Sullivan Films manufactured artificial leather film which it sold primarily to automobile manufacturers. When it employed Neaves, initially as a chemist and later as a manager of research and development, he executed a noncompetition agreement in which he undertook not to sell or assist others in selling products and services to O'Sullivan's customers in competition with O'Sullivan for a period of one year. The agreement had no geographic limitation, so it would apply worldwide. The court held that the restraints as to time and activity were narrowly drawn to protect O'Sullivan's legitimate interests in ensuring that Neaves did not exploit his relationship with O'Sullivan's customers in work that was directly in competition with O'Sullivan. The court did not find the unlimited geographic scope of the agreement too broad because the artificial leather market was a specialized niche market and O'Sullivan did compete with other manufacturers worldwide.

§13.14 A TRANSNATIONAL PERSPECTIVE ON THE CONTROL OF IMPROPER BARGAINING

Article 4 of the CISG states that the CISG is not concerned with the validity of a contract. Because the doctrines covered in this chapter affect the validity of a contract, the CISG does not provide for them. Therefore, even in a transaction governed by the CISG, the doctrines of the governing domestic law apply to the transaction.

Article 3.1 of the UNIDROIT Principles specifically refrains from addressing questions of illegality or immorality. Apart from this, the Principles include doctrines that are equivalent to those discussed in this chapter, even though there are differences in the terminology and elements. Article 3.8 allows for the avoidance of a contract for fraud, including the nondisclosure of circumstances that should have been disclosed under principles of fair dealing. Article 3.9 allows for avoidance for an "unjustified threat" that is "imminent and serious" enough to leave the party with "no reasonable alternative." A threat is unjustified if the act is wrongful in itself or is wrongful as a means of obtaining the contract. Article 3.10 has a doctrine that covers the same ground as undue influence and unconscionability. It allows avoidance of a contract or a term of the contract if the contract or term gave the other party "an excessive advantage." Article 3.16 provides for the avoidance of the specific offending terms of a contract unless it is unreasonable to uphold the contract in the absence of those terms.

EXAMPLES

Examples

1. Cookie Racha owns a house built in 1915. The house has been plagued with chronic cockroach infestation. Although Cookie fumigated it regularly, roaches reappeared in ever-increasing numbers within a few weeks of treatment. Also, the house was slowly sinking into soft ground on one side. The sinking can only be corrected by an expensive process that requires the side of the house to be jacked up while a firm concrete foundation is laid. The sinking has caused deep cracks in the living room wall. Cookie has replastered the wall a few times, but the continuing movement reopened the cracks soon afterward. Cookie had already become quite sick of the house when she recently read in the newspaper that the neighboring property had been bought by the state for use as a halfway house for paroled sex offenders. This was the final straw and she decided to sell.

   Acting on the advice of her real estate agent, Chic "The Snake" Canery, she fumigated the house, plastered the cracks, and repainted the wall just before the house was placed on the market. Each time that the house was shown, Chic ensured that all the lights were on. Not only did this present the house in a more attractive manner, but the brightness discouraged the regenerating population of roaches from venturing into full view. Chic brought Bugsy Crawley to see the house. On the very next day Bugsy made an offer to buy the house for the full asking price. Cookie accepted immediately. The terms of the contract of sale were set out in Bugsy's offer, made on a standard form provided by the real estate agent. The writing simply set out the basic terms of the transaction and made no representations concerning the property. The transaction closed a short while later, and Bugsy moved into his new home. It did not take very long before the roaches reappeared, the wall cracked, and the sex offenders moved in next door. Does Bugsy have grounds for avoiding the sale?

2. Tutu Tango is a 65-year-old retired tax lawyer. Her life had become quite dull since retirement, and she was looking for excitement. One day she was invited to accompany a friend to a free introductory dance lesson at the Fleece Foot Dance Studios. During the lesson, she fell into the clutches of Jig Aloe, a suave and unctuous dance instructor employed by Fleece Foot. Jig subjected Tutu to all the charm and flattery that he had perfected by taking Fleece Foot's super sales course. After observing Tutu's inept and clumsy cavortings on the dance floor, he pretended to be very impressed. He told her enthusiastically that she had a wonderful natural talent and ageless grace. He said that he was convinced that with proper training, she had the potential of becoming an elegant and alluring dancer. Tutu had been around the block a few times, so she didn't really believe a word of this. But Jig was cute and he would be her instructor, so she agreed to sign up for a month's worth of lessons at a cost of $250. Jig produced a form and asked her to sign it. He cleverly positioned his hand over the top of the form so Tutu could not see the top few lines. This little trick worked, because Tutu did not pay much attention to the form and signed it without trying to read it. Had she been more astute, she would have seen that Jig had given her a life membership contract form to sign, in which she irrevocably purchased a lifetime of lessons for a fee of $10,000, payable within seven days of signing.

   A few days later Tutu went to the studio for her first lesson. She discovered that Jig had been fired and replaced by a decidedly uninteresting instructor—a pot-bellied middle-aged man. Tutu went to the manager to tell him that she wanted to cancel her month's lessons. She was shocked when the manager corrected her, showing her the contract form in which she had signed up, not for a month, but a lifetime. He told her that it was studio policy never to release customers from their commitments, and pointed out that her payment was due within the next few days.

Does the common law give Tutu the right to cancel? (Answer on common law principles only. There may also be a cause of action under consumer protection legislation, which is not discussed in this book.)

3. Sweaty Shoppe, Inc., is a retailer of sports and fitness clothing. It sells a wide variety of all brands of merchandise. Brute Force, Inc. makes very expensive weightlifting equipment. Sweaty Shoppe considers these products overpriced and has steadfastly refused to carry them despite several requests by Brute Force.

   Through contact with a disloyal employee of Sweaty Shoppe, Brute Force has come into possession of some confidential internal memoranda, written by Sweaty Shoppe's management. These memoranda show that Sweaty Shoppe's buyer routinely engaged in the practice of knowingly buying inventory at bargain prices from a criminal organization that stole it by hijacking manufacturers' delivery trucks. Brute Force told Sweaty Shoppe's president that it would publish the documents unless Sweaty Shoppe agreed to stock and vigorously promote Brute Force products. Sweaty Shoppe's president realized that if the buyer's underhanded means of acquiring inventory became public, Sweaty Shoppe's business would be badly damaged and the company might even be implicated in the buyer's crime of receiving stolen property. He therefore entered into a contract with Brute Force to purchase and promote its weightlifting equipment. The contract is on ordinary market terms, and the quantity of goods, the prices, and other aspects of the contract are fair and commercially reasonable. A week after signing the contract, and before any performance had occurred, Sweaty Shoppe's board found out about the buyer's improper purchases and the president's attempt at a cover-up. The board fired the president and it decided that it would rather deal with the consequences of exposure than buy any goods from Brute Force. Does Sweaty Shoppe have grounds to avoid the contract?

4. Lunar Tech, Inc. has been engaged in a massive, hugely expensive program for the launch of a rocket to carry an innovative satellite into orbit. The project has been in development for four years and is close to completion, with a launch date a few months away. The director of the program is Dr. Stella Starburst, a highly respected and brilliant scientist, who entered into a three-year contract to lead and supervise the project. The three-year term of the contract will expire a few months after the anticipated launch date, and neither party has the right to terminate the contract before the end of the three-year term. Dr. Starburst's contract salary is $2 million per year. At about this time, a few months before the launch date, Dr. Starburst told the president of Lunar Tech that she had received a very attractive offer to head a prestigious research institute and that she planned to resign and accept that offer. The president knew that it would be impossible to replace Dr. Starburst as director of the program,

because there was no-one else with the depth of knowledge and experience needed to guide the program to its completion. The president therefore offered to pay Dr. Starburst a $3 million bonus at the end of the project if she stayed on until it was complete and agreed to take on some additional duties to ensure the successful launch. Dr. Starburst agreed and the parties signed an "addendum" to the original employment agreement setting out Dr. Starburst's additional commitment and her bonus. Dr. Starburst did remain in her position until the successful launch of the rocket a few months later. However, LunarTech refuses to pay her the $3 million bonus. Can Dr. Starburst enforce LunarTech's commitment to pay her the bonus?

5. Watertight Adhesive Co. requires all its employees to sign its standard employment contract upon being hired. Watertight's routine practice is to give a new employee a copy of the contract at the time of making an offer of employment and to require the employee to sign and return it when starting work. The standard contract is a very detailed 20-page single-spaced document, consisting of 130 numbered clauses. It is printed in 12-point type, without any headings, boldface, or other features that distinguished any of its clauses. Clause 128 reads:

    > Any claim made by the employee, arising out of this employment agreement, including claims relating to discrimination, harassment, working conditions, the payment of any amounts claimed to be due under this contract, or termination of employment shall be submitted to final and binding arbitration under the rules of the American Arbitration Association. If any such claim should arise, the employee agrees to deliver a written request for arbitration to the employer within six months of the date that the dispute arose. If the employee does not file a written request for arbitration within this time, such claim will be barred.

    Clause 128 is the only term in the contract relating to arbitration. There is no equivalent requirement of arbitration for any claims brought by Watertight against an employee. The rules of the American Arbitration Association are not appended to the contract. Watertight hired an employee, following its routine practice of giving the employee a copy of the contract at the time of making the offer. The employee signed and returned the copy on commencing work a week later. Six months after the employee began work, Watertight fired the employee who then sued it for wrongful dismissal. Watertight moved to dismiss the suit on the grounds that the employee had committed to arbitrate any dispute arising out of the contract. Should the court grant the motion to dismiss?

6. One afternoon, Hardy Ticker developed intense chest pains while digging in his garden. His neighbor, Sam Aritan, noticed his distress and came over to see if he was all right. On being told the problem, Sam put Hardy into his car and rushed him to the nearest hospital, The Sisters

of Good Conscience. The receptionist insisted that admission forms be completed before Hardy could be sent to the emergency room. Sam was concerned that Hardy needed urgent attention and begged the receptionist to admit Hardy while he completed the forms. The receptionist agreed. Sam completed as much of Hardy's biographical information as he knew and handed the form to the receptionist. She told him that he had to sign it, which he did. He noticed that the form had about half a page of printed text above the signature blank, but he did not read it. Had he done so, he would have found that he had signed a standard contract with a provision that obligated the signatory to pay all the hospital's charges for treatment administered to the patient, to the extent that those charges were not paid by the patient or the patient's medical insurance.

Sadly, Hardy died despite the efforts of the emergency room doctors. It was then discovered that he had no medical insurance and that he was insolvent and there is nothing in his estate. The hospital therefore demands payment of its fees from Sam, based on his signature on the standard contract. Must Sam pay?

7. Mary Maker, a resident of California, called her local travel agent to book a cruise. The agent booked her a seven-day cruise package from Los Angeles to Mexico on the ship S.S. Briny Binge, owned and operated by Party Lines, Inc. Party Lines has its headquarters in Miami, Florida. A week after the telephone booking, Mary received her ticket, printed on one side of a single sheet of paper. She checked to make sure that the dates and cabin booking were correct. She did not read the rest of the printed matter on the ticket, despite a warning, printed on the ticket in large red letters, that stated, "PASSENGER: THIS DOCUMENT AFFECTS YOUR LEGAL RIGHTS. READ IT!" Had she read the document beyond the cruise dates and cabin booking, she would have found the following provision:

   This ticket is issued subject to the following terms and conditions:

   1. Party Lines, Inc. shall not be responsible for loss or harm suffered by the passenger while on board the ship, whether or not caused by the negligence of Party Lines, Inc. or any of its employees or agents.
   2. In the event of any dispute between Party Lines, Inc. and the passenger arising out of this transaction, the courts of the State of Florida shall have exclusive jurisdiction to hear and resolve such dispute.

   Mary embarked on the ship. Three days into the cruise, she was injured when an inebriated entertainment director mistook her for a piñata. Upon returning home, Mary sued Party Lines in a California court, alleging that the company was liable for its employee's negligent action. She claimed medical expenses and damages for pain and suffering. Party Lines requests dismissal of the suit on the grounds that the California court has no jurisdiction in terms of the contract and that, in any event,

Mary had contractually waived any claim that she may otherwise have had. Should the court grant the motion to dismiss?

8. Hi Rate Gems, Inc., operates a retail jewelry store in a less affluent neighborhood and draws most of its customers from the local area. Its customers typically do not have the means to buy jewelry for cash; nor could they qualify for credit under the usual market standards. To make sales, Hi Rate has found it necessary to provide financing to its customers under a lenient credit policy. As a result, its losses from uncollectible debt are much higher than those of more conservative lending institutions. To compensate for this, it prices its jewelry about 20 percent higher than the prevailing market and charges interest 5 percent above the market rate. To obtain credit, a customer is obliged to sign a standard contract under which Hi Rate retains a security interest in the items purchased. This means that if the customer should default in payments, Hi Rate has the right to repossess the jewelry, to credit its value against the balance owing, and to institute collection action against the customer for any remaining deficiency.

    Rock Sparkler bought a diamond nose stud with matching earrings from Hi Rate for $2,000. Rock did not have the $2,000. His terrible credit record assured that he could not get a loan from anyone else, so he applied for credit from Hi Rate. One of the questions on the form asked if any judgments had been granted against the applicant. Rock knew of at least five such unsatisfied judgments, but he feared that disclosing them would be fatal to the application. He did not wish to lie, so he simply ignored the question and left the space blank. Luckily, the credit clerk did not look at the application very carefully before approving the financing and did not notice the omission. The sales assistant then filled out the details of the items purchased and the monthly payment rate on the standard purchase agreement, and handed it to Rock for his signature. The assistant made no attempt to explain the form's printed terms to Rock, who did not read it before signing. He then took the jewelry and left.

    A few weeks later, Hi Rate's credit manager was reviewing the applications and noticed that Rock had not answered the question about judgments. He checked the public record and discovered the unsatisfied judgments. Hi Rate wishes to rescind the contract and get the jewelry back. Has it the right to do so?

9. All the facts regarding the formation of the contract are the same as in Example 8. The only factual difference is as follows: Hi Rate's credit manager did not check the public record after the contract was executed. Hi Rate is happy with the transaction and has no desire to avoid the contract. However, a short time after the purchase, Rock had misgivings about buying the jewelry. He would like to cancel the sale and return the jewelry. May he do so?

10. Rob Graves plundered a 3,000-year-old bronze figurine from the tomb of an ancient king. He smuggled it into the United States for the purpose of selling it. He contacted Ann Teek, a well-known collector of antiquities, to see whether she would be interested in buying the figurine. Ann did not ask Rob how he acquired the figurine, but she suspected that he had stolen it and brought it into the country illegally. She also knew that it is illegal to deal in stolen antiquities. Nevertheless, her desire to own the figurine overpowered her scruples. She entered into a contract with Rob to buy it for \$50 million. In terms of the contract, Ann had to pay a deposit of \$10 million in cash to Rob on signing the written agreement and would pay the balance in cash on delivery of the figurine a few days later. Ann paid the deposit to Rob, but he never delivered the figurine. What would Ann's prospects of success be if she decided to sue Rob to enforce the contract? What would her prospects of success be if she decided not to sue Rob for enforcement but instead sued him for return of the \$10 million?

Explanations

1. There are both acts and silences that could qualify as fraudulent misrepresentations.

    The cockroaches and subsidence. Cookie did not make any statement asserting that the house was free of cockroaches or that it was stable. However, concealment of the truth by conduct is as much an affirmative misrepresentation as a verbal misstatement. Cookie knew the truth and intended by the act of concealment to hide it so as to induce the contract. Therefore, the element of knowledge of falsity and intent to mislead is satisfied. Cookie's fumigating and performing the cosmetic repairs to the wall were not simply acceptable preparations for sale but were deliberate steps to conceal serious problems that would have made the house less marketable.

    The misrepresentation must be material. Materiality is a question of interpretation, and the test is whether a reasonable person in Bugsy's position would have entered the transaction at all, or on these terms, had he known the truth. It is arguable that an infestation of pests and the sinking of the building would be significant to a reasonable buyer. The misrepresentation must have induced Bugsy to enter the contract on the agreed terms. When fraud is involved, the test for inducement is not purely objective but takes into account the persuasive impact of the falsehood on the victim. Bugsy must show that the misrepresented fact was influential to him and that, given his circumstances and personal attributes, he was justified in relying on the false words or appearance. Of course, it is easier to show inducement where the misrepresentation concerns a fact that would be regarded as material and would have been relied on by a reasonable person. The facts do not indicate Bugsy's subjective motivation in making the offer, but the concealed facts are probably important even if viewed objectively, so it should not be difficult for him to show that they influenced him to make the offer. Bugsy's justification for relying on appearances is somewhat weakened because he failed to have the house inspected for structural soundness and pests or even to ask questions. A court might find that his lack of diligence precludes relief for fraud. But courts do balance the neglect of the victim against the deliberate dishonesty of the perpetrator, and Cookie's purposeful concealment could outweigh Bugsy's failure to make proper inquiry. Finally, prejudice is obvious. Not only does the house have a chronic cockroach problem, but it requires expensive repairs.

The halfway house for sex offenders. Although Cookie knew about the plans to open the halfway house, she did not disclose this to Bugsy. Nondisclosure of known information can be fraud if the duty of fair dealing imposes an obligation to speak. It can be difficult to decide when disclosure is required, because the law recognizes that fair dealing does not compel a party to bare all information pertinent to the transaction. Furthermore, even if there was a duty to speak, the omission may not be as culpable as a positive act. As a result, the prerequisites for relief are not as heavily weighted against the perpetrator, and the victim is more readily held accountable for failure to make diligent inquiry. As a general guide, a party is only required to disclose information if four conditions are satisfied: The party knows that the other is unaware of it; the knowledge would be reasonably likely to influence the other's decision to enter the transaction; the information is not readily accessible to the other by diligent inquiry; and the information is not fairly regarded as the party's own property, having been acquired by special efforts or study.

The establishment of a residential facility for released sex offenders is likely to cause concern in a neighborhood, so it is reasonable to assume that this information would be material to a homebuyer. The information is not proprietary, so Cookie cannot claim that she had the right to keep it to herself. However, the proposed home is a public project that has already been reported in the press. The information is freely available and it would be easy enough for Bugsy to gain access to the information. On balance, if he did not know about the halfway house, his lack of inquiry could preclude relief on this ground despite Cookie's silence.

2. This example is a factual variation of a couple of infamous cases involving Arthur Murray dance studios, decided in the 1960s. In *Vokes v. Arthur Murray, Inc.*, 212 So.2d 906 (Fl. Dist. Ct. App. 1968), and *Syester v. Banta*, 133 N.W.2d 666 (Iowa 1965), Arthur Murray franchisees employed the deliberate tactic of ongoing and excessive flattery to induce untalented elderly women to sign up for astoundingly large quantities of dance

lessons at grotesque total cost. In both cases the importuning, begun at first contact, was reinforced and accelerated during a long period of continuing lessons. The courts found that the fulsome praise, unremitting sweet talk, undeserved medals and awards, and untrue claims of progress were so extreme as to pass beyond good customer relations and become outright fraud.

The fraud in these cases was not the misrepresentation of an external objective fact, but of an opinion. By pretending that they believed the victims to have talent and potential, the studio employees lied about what they thought, inducing the victims to buy copious quantities of lessons. Although false opinions do not always qualify as factual misrepresentations, a deliberate misstatement of opinion can be fraud when the party expressing it claims to have the knowledge and expertise to form a judgment and should realize that the victim is relying on an honest assessment. As the brief description of the cases suggests, the behavior of the Arthur Murray franchisees went far beyond the expression of a dishonest opinion. The transactions were thoroughly unsavory. Lonely and gullible elderly women were cruelly manipulated for a long period and induced to spend substantial amounts of their savings on extended courses of dance lessons that were unlikely to be used up in their lifetimes.

Fleece Foot's conduct was not as egregious as that of the Arthur Murray franchisees, and Tutu, being a worldly former tax lawyer, has greater business sophistication than the plaintiffs in those cases. Nevertheless, there were two instances of dishonesty by Jig, acting on behalf of Fleece Foot, that could provide an argument for fraud. First, he deliberately misrepresented his opinion. However, this may not be a good basis for establishing fraud because his misrepresentation apparently did not induce Tutu to enter the contract. Tutu was not taken in by his flattery and was motivated by deeper urges. (Although Jig turned out not to be the instructor, there is no indication that he realized that this was an inducing factor or that he knew of and failed to disclose his impending dismissal.)

Second, he concealed the true nature of the form by placing his hands over it. If this is fraud, it would be in the factum, not in the inducement, because it relates to the document being signed rather than to a motivating fact. Note also that the misrepresentation is by concealment, not affirmative assertion. Although his intent is dishonest, Tutu is probably damned by her sophistication and training. While an illiterate or naive person may be able to convince a factfinder of having been bamboozled into unwittingly signing a lifetime contract, Tutu, a trained lawyer, should have known better than to sign something without reading it. The strategically placed hand adds no force to her case. Although the writing was concealed, it was easily discoverable. (In fact, the attempt at concealment should have excited her suspicion.) While inducement takes into account the victim's subjective reaction to the misrepresentation, her attributes affect the credibility of any claim that she was actually induced to sign as a result of the clumsy deception. Having said this, it must be acknowledged that an argument of fraud is not entirely inconceivable if Tutu can show an intent to defraud. Even extreme neglect may be outweighed by clear proof of the perpetrator's dishonesty.

Fraud was the basis for relief in both *Vokes* and *Syester*, but the facts make an overwhelming case of unconscionability as well: As a result of the studios' slimy bargaining methods, their victims were induced to enter contracts for lessons well in excess of their needs at a ludicrous cost. Unconscionability doctrine is not needed when the elements of fraud are satisfied, but if there is any doubt about establishing the elements of fraud, unconscionability is an alternative theory for avoidance. Bargaining unfairness short of actual fraud may be sufficient to show procedural unconscionability, and the facts of this Example reveal a deliberate and carefully developed process to manipulate and exploit prospective customers, which surely satisfies the element of procedural unconscionability. There can be little doubt that it is substantively unconscionable to sell a $10,000 lifetime dance instruction contract to a 65-year-old retiree. Unconscionability is less potent a weapon in the hands of a well-educated and commercially proficient party, but even former tax lawyers can be caught off guard by predators in the marketplace.

3. Although this is a sale of goods, general principles of common law apply because UCC Article 2 has no provisions relating to duress. Sweaty Shoppe should be able to avoid the contract on grounds of duress because it has been induced to enter the contract by Brute Force's wrongful threat. The exposure of the criminal conduct of Sweaty Shoppe's buyer would not itself be wrongful. In fact, the revelation of such information is in the public interest. The wrongfulness arises because Brute Force's threat is made for the purpose of blackmailing Sweaty Shoppe's president into entering the contract. Even an otherwise proper act loses its legitimacy if it is used as a threat for the purpose of extorting private advantage. It adds to the wrongfulness of the threat that the information possessed by Brute Force relates to criminal activity and it is using the information as a bargaining chip to force Sweaty Shoppe's president to enter a contract to buy its products. A person harms the public interest by withholding information of a crime from the authorities in exchange for a commercial reward. For this reason, a threat to expose the crime unless Sweaty Shoppe agrees to a contract is clearly an improper threat for duress purposes.

To show inducement, Sweaty Shoppe must establish that, under all the circumstances, its management had no reasonable alternative but to acquiesce in the contract. Sweaty Shoppe's president did have an alternative—the one that its board ultimately decided to follow. However, Sweaty Shoppe can make the plausible argument that at the time that Brute Force proposed the contract, Sweaty Shoppe's president could reasonably have decided that the threatened exposure and its potentially dire impact on the company was not a reasonable alternative and that the threat undermined the president's volition in making the contract. The terms of the sale were fair and commercially reasonable, but that does not matter. Once the elements of improper threat and inducement are established, Sweaty Shoppe does not have to show that the resulting contract was substantively unfair. Because there is no substantive unfairness in the terms of the contract, duress is a better basis for avoidance than unconscionability.

Note that considerations of public policy are implicated in the determination that the threat was wrongful. If Sweaty Shoppe cannot make a convincing case of duress (say, because it cannot show that it had no reasonable alternative but to agree), it could make the argument that the contract should be avoided as illegal. On the surface, there is nothing objectionable about this contract, which is simply the sale of goods for a price. However, the contract is grounded on blackmail— the underlying purpose of the contract is for the concealment of a crime in return for financial advantage. The *in pari delicto* rule requires a balancing of the relative guilt of the parties, but goes beyond that to consider the impact of enforcement or nonenforcement on the public good. The determination of relative guilt can be difficult. Sweaty Shoppe's buyer committed the crime of buying stolen goods and its president covered up the crime. These acts of its agents are imputed to Sweaty Shoppe. However, when the guilt of the blackmailer and victim are weighed, Brute Force's guilt in extorting the contract is directly related to its procuring the contract and seems to be weightier. The conclusion that Sweaty Shoppe should be able to raise the *in pari delicto* defense to avoid the contract is reinforced by the equities between the parties and the public interest. Although the actions of its president are imputed to Sweaty Shoppe, the equities may still favor it because its innocent stakeholders, the board, and owners (stockholders), neither knew of nor approved of the illicit activity of the buyer and the president. It is also arguable that the public interest is best served by refusing enforcement because to allow enforcement would condone and provide an incentive to extortion.

4. Dr. Starburst had no right to resign under her original three-year contract of employment, so her plan to resign and accept the position at the research institute would have been a breach of contract. Lunar Tech's decision to give her an incentive not to breach is a modification of the contract. There is no consideration problem with regard to the modification, because the facts indicate that Dr. Starburst did assume some

additional duties in exchange for the bonus. The question is therefore whether Lunar Tech can avoid its promise to pay the bonus to her on the basis that was induced by duress. Had Dr. Starburst threatened to breach the employment contract, that threat would be improper. However, it is not clear if she actually made any threat at all. She just told the president that she had received a very attractive offer to head a prestigious research institute and that she planned to resign and accept that offer. She gave notice of her intention to resign, but did not demand a bonus or any other compensation in exchange for not resigning. The offer of the bonus seems to have been Lunar Tech's initiative to avert a dispute and keep the operation running smoothly. It chose to encourage her not to breach, realizing that she was indispensable and irreplaceable at this stage of the project. There may be an implied threat here, but the basis for implication is weak in the absence of anything more aggressive than her expressing the intent to leave. Lunar Tech's decision to commit to the bonus was clearly motivated by its conclusion that it had no reasonable alternative other than to give Dr. Starburst an incentive not to breach, but the requirement of improper threat does not appear to have been satisfied. This being so, Lunar Tech has not established grounds for avoiding its commitment on the basis of duress, and Dr. Starburst can enforce Lunar Tech's commitment to pay her the bonus.

5. There is a general public policy in favor of arbitration, and a party can only avoid an arbitration provision by establishing grounds for avoidance under general principles of contract law. On the facts stated, the only possible basis for avoidance is unconscionability.[18] *Samaniego v. Empire Today LLC*, discussed in section 13.12.3, found an arbitration provision in an employment contract to be unconscionable where the provision had several features in common with the one in issue here. Like the clause in *Samaniego*, the clause in this contract was in a standard contract proffered by the employer. The arbitration clause was near the end of a dense and lengthy contract and was not printed in a way that drew attention to it. The clause incorporated by reference the rules of the American Arbitration Association, but did not provide those rules. The clause imposes arbitration on employees, but not on the employer, and it shortens the limitation period for employees' claims, but not for the employer.

   This employment contract is on Watertight's standard terms and it is possibly adhesive, but that conclusion is not certain because the facts do not indicate if Watertight would have been open to negotiating different

18. Duress would not be an alternative basis for relief. Although the employee may have needed the job and may thereby have felt compelled to agree to Watertight's standard contract, economic necessity is not itself a basis for claiming duress in the absence of an improper threat.

terms had the prospective employee objected to any of the standard terms. If it is adhesive, the complexity of the contract, the inconspicuousness of the clause, and the failure to specify the rules governing the arbitration may suggest procedural unconscionability. However, there is a significant factual difference between this case and *Samaniego.* The employees in *Samaniego* were not proficient in English, and the form was presented to them on a take-it-or-leave-it basis, with little or no opportunity to seek advice. This employee was given a printed copy of the standard contract at the time of the job offer and had a week to read it, to consult an attorney and other advisors, and to ascertain the rules of the American Arbitration Association. Although the contract is dense and not well presented for clarity, the fact that the employee had the time to read and digest it and to seek legal advice weakens the argument that this contract is procedurally unconscionable, even if its terms were nonnegotiable.

Even if there is no procedural unconscionability, a court may still exercise its equitable discretion to give relief if substantive unconscionability is so strongly present that enforcement of the arbitration provision would offend the court's conscience. The provision clearly favors the interests of Watertight by obligating only the employee to arbitrate and by imposing a short claim period that limits the employee's ability to pursue the arbitration. Although mutuality of obligation (in the sense that the parties have equal and corresponding rights) is not required, where an arbitration provision imposes the obligation to arbitrate on only one of the parties and additionally limits the rights of that party to pursue the arbitration, the term could be too one-sided to enforce.

Even if the court found the clause to be unconscionable, this does not mean that it would avoid the arbitration term entirely. It could select the intermediate remedy of enforcing the clause and adjusting it to get rid of its unconscionable aspects. However, that works only where the clause can stand without the offending aspects and the severance of those aspects cures the unconscionability. Had the court found unconscionability here, this probably would not have been an appropriate case for adjusting the contract. Although the time limit on suit could be severed, the lack of bilaterally in the obligation to arbitrate cannot really be cured by an adjustment of the provision. In *Zullo v. Superior Court,* 127 Cal. Rptr. 3d 461 (Cal. Ct. App. 2011), the court refused to enforce an arbitration agreement in an employee handbook because it was adhesive and also lacked bilaterality—the contract imposed no restrictions on the employer's right to sue an employee, but the employee was obliged to arbitrate and lost even that means of recourse unless the employee gave notice of the claim to the employer almost immediately. The court refused to enforce the arbitration clause in its entirety because it found that it was permeated with unconscionability and was drafted not as a neutral means of dispute resolution but merely to maximize the employer's advantage in handling disputes

6. A similar situation occurred in *Phoenix Baptist Hospital v. Aiken*, 877 P.2d 1345 (Ariz. Ct. App. 1994). After rushing his wife to the hospital, a husband signed a standard contract obliging him to pay the hospital's charges. In the absence of this undertaking he would not have been personally liable for his wife's medical expenses. The hospital sued him and applied for summary judgment on the basis of his signature on the form. The court refused summary judgment and held that the husband was entitled to go to trial on the question of whether the contract was unconscionable. The court said that the contract appeared adhesive, signed under traumatic and hurried circumstances in which the husband had little realistic opportunity to know what he was signing. Even if he did know, the emotional stress and the need for the hospital's immediate services would likely leave him without power to bargain and give him no choice but to acquiesce to ensure that his wife received medical attention. The court considered that adhesion of this kind could make the contract procedurally unconscionable. In addition, substantive unconscionability could lie in the fact that he assumed liability for which he would not otherwise be responsible and that he could not reasonably have expected to have undertaken in the form that he signed.

   As discussed more fully in section 13.12 and Example 7, adhesion and procedural unconscionability are not present merely because the contract is a standard form drafted by the party with greater bargaining power, or because the choices of the weaker party are limited. However, when the services contracted for are desperately and urgently needed, and the party to perform the services presents a form without explanation or a reasonable opportunity to read, in circumstances in which the non-drafting party has no realistic opportunity to negotiate more favorable terms, it should not be very difficult to make a case for procedural unconscionability. It is not required that the hospital purposely used unfair bargaining methods to trick or coerce Sam into signing. The procurement of apparent assent under these circumstances should be enough. Sam's emotional stake in the rendition of the services to Hardy is not as strong as that of a spouse, but the stress and urgency of the situation are patent. Sam would not have to show that the terms were objectively unfair—for example, that the hospital charged an excessive price. The substantive unconscionability lies in the fact that Sam incurred an obligation that he would not otherwise have, for services from which he received no personal gain. In this respect, his case is stronger than that of a spouse. There is thus an adequate showing of substantive unconscionability—but even if a court may question this conclusion, the strong showing of procedural unfairness would seem to place beyond doubt the need to give Sam relief.

Although it is tempting to consider duress as an alternative cause of action, an argument of duress would be difficult to make. The threat to withhold medical services for Hardy did undermine Sam's free will and compel him to sign. However, the hospital's threat to refuse service would not be improper unless the hospital had a duty outside contract law (say, by statute) to render emergency services to any patient brought in.

7. Obviously, Mary is not seeking avoidance of the entire contract. Rather, to assert her tort claim, she must persuade the court that she is not bound by the forum selection clause and liability disclaimer.

   There are two preliminary questions to settle. The first is whether the disclaimer entered the contract at all. This does not appear to be a rolling contract because there is no indication that the parties intended that Mary would not be bound until she received and had a chance to review the tickets. That is, the contract was formed at the time that she booked, and the transmission of the tickets with the standard terms is not an offer. (*See* sections 5.5. and 13.2.) When the drafting party sends the standard terms to the other party only after the contract is formed, the terms may not be part of the contract at all. However, if the nondrafting party had reason to know that the contract was subject to standard terms and the standard terms are fair and reasonably expected, the court may find them to be part of the contract.

   The second preliminary question involves interpreting the terms. If, as a matter of interpretation, the forum selection clause and the disclaimer do not cover the claim in this suit, it is not necessary to consider whether they should be avoided or adjusted. The disclaimer's language creates some doubt about its scope. It exonerates Party Lines from "loss or harm." The provision does not expressly mention personal injury, and the juxtaposition of the words "loss" and "harm" could suggest that only economic damage is contemplated. The public policy of reading negligence disclaimers as narrowly as possible, combined with the *contra proferentum* rule, could persuade a court that the clause does not cover personal injury at all. If the court accepts this interpretation, the disclaimer is simply inapplicable and a claim of avoidance is not necessary. The forum selection clause may also be subject to interpretational challenge. Mary could argue that "any dispute . . . arising out of [the] . . . transaction" is not broad enough to cover tort claims for personal injury and should be confined to disputes relating to the performance of services promised under the contract. If the court accepts this interpretation, the California suit can proceed without any determination of whether the forum selection clause is avoidable.

If the provisions are interpreted to mean what Party Lines says they mean, they are enforceable unless they can be avoided. There is no indication of fraud or duress, so unconscionability doctrine offers Mary the best hope of eliminating the provisions. This is a contract of adhesion with standard terms that Mary did not negotiate or even read. However, that is not enough to make the terms unconscionable. To establish procedural unconscionability, Mary must produce evidence of some form of underhand dealing, which she cannot do on these facts, or must at least show that the terms were imposed on her without any meaningful choice, under circumstances that make the imposition oppressive. The terms were not made available to her at the time of booking, so this is a point in her favor. However, because cruise tickets are routinely subject to standard terms, as a reasonable consumer she should have expected them. Her failure to request and read them at the time of contracting weakens her case.

In addition, there is no indication that she tried to shop around to see if better terms were available from a competitor. Her case for procedural unconscionability is weak. She may have a better chance of showing substantive unconscionability, but this is not an easy case either. To establish substantive unconscionability, Mary must do more than show that the terms served Party Line's interests and were adverse to hers. She must establish that they were not justified by business realities and were so one-sided as to be oppressive. A forum selection clause could be fair if the forum selected is appropriate, the provision is a genuine cost-saving measure, and it is not designed to suppress suit. The liability disclaimer must be analyzed similarly. It is potentially unfair, but not per se unconscionable to disclaim liability for negligent injury. In evaluating the fairness of a disclaimer the court looks at factors such as the nature of the service, the parties who are likely to avail themselves of it, the degree to which a user of the service is subject to the control of the cruise line, the scope of the disclaimer, the conspicuousness of its disclosure, the business justification for including it, the reasonableness of the clause in light of accepted commercial practice, and whether the price of the cruise would have been higher in the absence of the exclusion of liability. In short, neither procedural nor substantive unconscionability is strongly shown on these facts, and Mary's prospects of avoiding the provisions do not look very promising.

Finally, although public policy considerations have already been raised in the discussion of unconscionability, it is worth noting that even if a provision is fairly bargained, it can still be attacked as violating public policy. Where public policy outside the area of contract is implicated, the court must balance that public policy against the policy of freedom of contract. The forum selection clause affects Mary's right to sue in a court that would otherwise have jurisdiction. It thereby impairs a strong public interest in uninhibited access to justice, which requires the justification for the clause to be scrutinized carefully.

As discussed in section 13.13.3, disclaimers of liability are also scrutinized carefully because public policy requires that a person is held accountable for tortious injury. Although a disclaimer of liability for intentional or reckless conduct is very likely against public policy, courts are more amenable to disclaimers of negligence. In deciding whether a disclaimer for negligence is consonant with public policy, courts consider factors similar to those listed above in relation to the inquiry into substantive unconscionability.

8. Rock's failure to disclose the judgments likely qualifies as a fraudulent misrepresentation. Even though he did not affirmatively lie, he deliberately omitted requested information, knowing that disclosure would imperil his credit application. In some situations, it may be difficult to decide if a party has the duty to disclose facts pertinent to the transaction, but this is not such a case. It is generally accepted that a duty of honest response does arise if the other party asks a direct question, particularly when the information sought is not of a proprietary nature.

   It is more difficult to say whether the misrepresentation induced the contract. A debtor's unreliability in other transactions is generally a crucial factor in the decision to grant credit. However, Hi Rate's cursory look at the credit application form suggests that its standard for granting credit is very low indeed. If it really cared about the applicant's credit history or was truly interested in the answers on the application, it would have taken more trouble to read the form. Furthermore, judgments are a matter of public record, easily accessible to the prospective creditor. A creditor who regards this information as crucial should not simply rely on the applicant's disclosure and should check. Normally, when fraud is involved, the serious malfeasance of the perpetrator could outweigh any lapse of care by the victim in failing to check the facts. But actual inducement must still be shown, and where the victim is sophisticated enough to know better, careless gullibility may break the chain of justified reliance.

   In addition, Hi Rate's business model—selling expensive luxury items to people who cannot afford them and padding its prices and interest rates do not make it a particularly sympathetic victim. Although this does not excuse Rock's dishonesty, Hi Rate cannot comfortably don the mantle of innocent dupe. It can fairly be expected to take care of its own interests. In short, without condoning Rock's deceitful silence, a court may be indisposed to allow Hi Rate out of the contract. As long as Rock continues to make his payments as promised, Hi Rate must live with the risk of his lack of creditworthiness.

9. There is nothing to suggest that Hi Rate made any misrepresentation to Rock, or that it applied any threat to make him enter the contract. Therefore, if Rock is to have any right of avoidance, it must be based on unconscionability.[19] Avoidance of the contract, as opposed to enforcement on adjusted terms, is within the range of relief available to Rock at the court's discretion.

   Because Hi Rate seems to have a captive market and it imposes higher prices and adverse terms on its customers under standard contracts, one may jump to the conclusion that Hi Rate is a predatory mass contractor subjecting a whole section of the community to its harsh contracts of adhesion. This conclusion is even more tempting if one perceives it as socially harmful to sell luxury items on credit to people who cannot afford them. However, one cannot conclude as a matter of law that the contract is unconscionable under these circumstances. The transaction must be evaluated to see if it satisfies the two elements of unconscionability.

   Hi Rate did not employ high-pressure selling techniques or deceptive practices that could lead to a clear-cut case of procedural unconscionability. However, *Williams v. Walker Thomas Furniture*, discussed in section 13.11.3, suggests that the contract could be procedurally unconscionable if Rock had no meaningful choice—the contract is adhesive because Hi Rate, the dominant party, had the power to dictate the terms, and Rock, the weaker party had no choice but to accept those terms. Under some circumstances, the mere fact of adhesion, without a demonstration of specific bargaining impropriety, could satisfy the procedural element of unconscionability. (This conclusion could be strengthened if the terms were not conspicuous and drawn to Rock's attention.) However, the claim of lack of meaningful choice is tenuous in relation to a sale of luxury goods. True, this may have been the only means Rock had to acquire the jewelry, but he could have chosen not to buy it at all. In addition, there is no indication that Rock tried to buy the jewelry elsewhere or that he protested over or tried to negotiate the price or other terms. In some cases the weaker party's lack of sophistication can bolster the sense of imposition, but Rock does not appear to be particularly unsophisticated—he was sly enough to practice his own bit of deception.

   Even if the basis for procedural unconscionability is shaky, a court may still find the contract to be unconscionable if the weaker party can show a strong degree of substantive unconscionability. This seems

19. As the following discussion shows, the public policy of consumer protection is inherent in unconscionability analysis in consumer transactions. This shows the close link between these doctrines, which was also highlighted in the discussion of *Bagley v. Mt. Bachelor, Inc.* in section 13.3.3.

unlikely in this case. The contract terms are adverse to Rock, but the higher price and interest rate could be based on sound business practice and could conform to reasonable commercial practice in a high-risk credit market. Hi Rate's retention of a security interest to secure the price is a widely accepted means of protecting a creditor from default, and the facts do not suggest that the security agreement has unusually harsh terms (for example, such as the cross-collateralization term in *Williams*).

10. The facts indicate that all aspects of this transaction—removing the figurine from the tomb, smuggling it, and selling it—are illegal. (In fact, these actions are surely criminal offenses as well. However, the question of whether the parties face criminal prosecution is not the concern here.) The facts also suggest that both parties were aware that they were entering into an illegal sale. Ann would have no chance of successfully suing Rob for enforcement of the contract. It is inconceivable that a court would abet a seriously illegal transaction by enforcing it, either by an order of specific performance or by the award of expectation damages to compensate for the loss of the bargain.

    The answer is less obvious if Ann does not seek to enforce the contract, but instead claims restitution of the $10 million that she paid to Rob under principles of unjust enrichment. By awarding restitution, the court does not uphold the illegal transaction, so there is a greater possibility that the court may be willing to intervene to remedy Rob's enrichment at Ann's expense. However, this outcome is not guaranteed because Ann's claim of restitution is also subject to the *in pari delicto* rule. The rule does not focus only on enforcement but declares that when the parties are in equal guilt, the court will not intervene to help either of them and will leave them as it finds them. As section 13.13.2 explains, the operation of the maxim is more complicated than its language suggests. It involves a balancing of several considerations—the relative guilt of the parties, the equities between them, and the interests of society. It is difficult to choose which of these parties is more guilty—the thief-smuggler or the buyer who knowingly buys the stolen property. It seems reasonable to conclude that the parties are in equal guilt. If this was the only consideration, Ann's restitutionary claim would be dismissed. However, the balance shifts in her favor on the other factors to be weighed. As between the parties, the equities favor Ann, who has been cheated of $10 million by Rob. The question of what best serves the public interest is also difficult to answer. Is the public best served by penalizing the buyer of stolen artifacts, thereby creating a disincentive to enter such transactions, or is it best served by forcing the thief to disgorge his ill-gotten gains from the transaction? This question is close, but allowing Rob to keep Ann's money seems to be more damaging to the public interest.

This answer assumes that there is no legislative pronouncement that might assist the court in its decision. However, if transactions are made illegal by statute, the statute may provide rules or guidance on the legal rights of a party to an illegal transaction. For example, a statute that bars the sale of stolen artifacts could state that the buyer has no recourse for recovery of any sums paid. If the legislation pronounces on these matters, the resolution is clearer and obviates the need for the court to perform the balancing itself.

CHAPTER 14

Incapacity

§14.1 THE SCOPE AND FOCUS OF THE DOCTRINES DISCUSSED IN THIS CHAPTER

The law generally assumes that all persons have the capacity to enter contracts. The two exceptions to this rule are minors and mentally incompetent adults. A minor's lack of contractual capacity is relatively easy to establish because it is largely based on the objective criterion of age. The determination that an adult lacks contractual capacity is more complex because it requires proof of mental illness or disturbance sufficiently serious to render the person incompetent. Mental incapacity is proved by objective evidence of the party's behavior observed by others, and by expert psychiatric evidence.

The underlying rationale for permitting the avoidance of a contract entered into by a person who lacks mental capacity is the protection of the incapacitated person. This suggests analogies both to improper bargaining and public policy, discussed in Chapter 13. However, there are important distinctions. Although improper bargaining may sometimes be present in an incapacity case, especially where the other party has exploited the lack of capacity, there is no requirement that any improper bargaining be proved. Where the other party has taken advantage of the incapacitated party, this obviously has an influence on the court's decision on whether to permit avoidance of the contract on grounds of incapacity. However, the fundamental basis of incapacity is the legal status of the incapacitated party. This means that incapacity can be invoked even where there was no deception or illegitimate pressure in the formation of the contract and it is on fair terms. Incapacity is based on the public policy of protecting an incapacitated person from assuming contractual duties to which the party was not truly capable of assenting. However, this public policy differs from those in issue in Chapter 13 because it does not create tension between the contract policy of freedom of contract and some other policy external to contract law. Instead, incapacity goes to the very basis of freedom of contract because the incapacitated party's lack of mental competence means that the party's manifestation of assent is illusory.

Like improper bargaining, incapacity renders the contract voidable, not void. Usually, avoidance of the contract in its entirety is the only appropriate form of relief. Severance is not a proper solution because the incapacity affects the whole contract, not just a term of it. As in other situations of avoidance, rescission of a mentally incompetent person's contract is accompanied by restitution of any benefit conferred under the contract. In the case of rescission of a minor's contract, this rule applies to any benefit conferred by the minor on the major party, but does not necessarily apply to a benefit conferred on the minor.

§14.2 MINORITY

§14.2.1 The Basis and Nature of a Minor's Contractual Incapacity

a. The Minor's Right to Disaffirm

A person attains majority at the age of 18 in most states. Before that time, the minor[1] does not have the legal capacity to be bound in contract, and the contract is voidable at the minor's instance. With some exceptions,[2] this rule applies to all contracts.

As explained in section 13.3, a voidable contract is not absolutely void, but may be avoided at the instance of the party entitled to make that election. In the context of minor's contracts, it is the minor who has this power of avoidance, commonly referred to as the minor's right to disaffirm the contract. This means that the minor may disaffirm it at any time

1. The word "infant" is sometimes used as a synonym for "minor." In this context, it refers to any person below the age of majority, and not only to babies or very young children.
2. Some exceptions to this rule are described in section 14.2.2c. In addition, a state may have enacted statutes giving minors over a specified age the capacity to enter into certain types of contract.

before reaching the age of majority, or within a reasonable time thereafter. Because a minor has no capacity to contract, it follows that the minor does not have the capacity to ratify (affirm) the contract while still a minor. This is why the right to make the election to disaffirm extends for a reasonable time past the attainment of majority. Nothing that the minor does before attaining majority, including full performance of the contract, constitutes a waiver of the right to disaffirm upon reaching majority.

In *Doffing v. Meta Platforms, Inc.*, 2022 WL 3357698 (D. Or. 2022), a 14-year-old minor created an account on Snapchat without parental permission or consent. In creating the account, the minor assented to Snapchat's terms of service through clickwrap. The terms were about 15 pages long, and included a forum selection clause requiring all disputes to be litigated in the Central District of California. The minor later sued Snapchat in her home state of Oregon, claiming that use of the site was addictive and had harmed her. Snapchat sought to transfer the case under the forum selection clause. The court refused, observing that seeking to bind a minor to a 15-page document through clickwrap was a quintessential example of overreaching. The minor's assent to the terms of service, including the forum selection provision, was contractually invalid and the minor was entitled to disaffirm the contract.

A minor who decides to disaffirm the contract must disaffirm it in its entirety. The minor cannot keep parts of it in force and seek to disaffirm others. For example, in *A.V. v. Iparadigms, L.L.C.*, 544 F. Supp. 2d 473 (E.D. Va. 2008), a school required its students to submit their class papers to a website that checked them for plagiarism. To use the website, students had to register on it. On registering, the students, who were minors, signified assent to a clickwrap agreement. One of its terms authorized the website to archive their work. The students later challenged terms of this agreement on several grounds[3] and also sought to disaffirm the contract as minors. The court refused disaffirmance because the minors did not entirely abandon the contract and still sought to retain the benefit of the services provided by the website. Similarly, in *E.K.D. v. Facebook, Inc.*, 885 F. Supp. 2d 894 (S.D. Ill. 2012), the minor continued to use Facebook's networking website while seeking to avoid a forum selection clause in Facebook's standard terms. The court held that the minor could not disaffirm only that part of the contract that does not suit him, while continuing to receive the benefit of performance under the contract. The rule that a minor cannot partially disaffirm a contract applies only to continuing benefits that the minor seeks to retain while disaffirming other parts of the contract. It does not apply to benefits that the minor received under the contract during minority and before disaffirmance. This distinction was drawn in *T.K. v. Adobe Systems, Inc.*, 2018 WL

3. One of the grounds was that they had not assented to the clickwrap term.

1812200 (N.D. Cal. 2018), in which a minor disaffirmed the renewal of a subscription to Adobe Creative Cloud after having received the benefit of that subscription for a year. The court distinguished *E.K.D* on the basis that the minor in that case continued to use Facebook while seeking to disaffirm the forum selection clause in the agreement. In this case, however, the minor's use of the Adobe subscription occurred before disaffirmance and the minor did not continue to use it afterwards. As explained in section 14.2.3, as a general rule a minor is not required to restore the value of services that were used prior to disaffirmance.

b. Ratification

A minor who has not disaffirmed the contract before reaching the age of majority may ratify it as a major. Ratification can be express, or it could be by conduct if the minor takes a benefit under the contract after majority, or it could be implied if the minor fails to disaffirm the contract within a reasonable time after becoming a major.[4] The question of whether the minor has ratified the contract upon becoming a major is dependent on whether the former minor can reasonably be expected to understand that ongoing action or inaction could constitute ratification and the loss of the right of avoidance. The degree to which the young major receives benefits from the contract, and has the experience and sophistication to understand the import of the conduct, is relevant to the question of whether ratification was deliberate or should otherwise be inferred. In *Coughenour v. Del Taco, LLC*, 271 Cal. Rptr. 3d 602 (Cal. Ct. App. 2020), the minor began working for Del Taco at the age of 16 and signed an arbitration agreement as a condition of her employment. She continued to work for Del Taco until four months after her 18th birthday. Four months after that, she sued Del Taco for sexual harassment and wage and hour claims. Del Taco moved to compel arbitration, claiming that the minor had ratified the arbitration agreement by continuing to work for the company for four months past her 18th birthday. The court rejected that argument. The minor never expressly ratified the contract, was not aware of the significance of the agreement she had signed more than two years previously, and she was never given a copy of it. She did not fully understand the legal consequences of continuing to work for the employer for a relatively short while after majority, and waiting another four months to commence suit was not an unreasonable delay under the circumstances.

---

4. However, some states may not treat conduct as implied ratification and may require an express or even a written ratification. For example, in *Foss v. Circuit City*, 477 F. Supp. 2d 230 (D. Me. 2007), the court refused to recognize ratification by conduct because a state statute required written ratification.

In some cases, deliberate ratification is easier to see. For example, in *In re The Score Board, Inc.*, 238 B.R. 585 (D.N.J. 1999), Kobe Bryant, the professional basketball player, entered into a contract at the age of 17 under which he granted rights to the use of his name and image on products. He turned 18 six weeks later. Shortly after his birthday, he deposited a check of $10,000, an initial payment under the contract, in his bank account. He continued to perform under the contract for the subsequent year and a half, and then became dissatisfied with the contract and sought to disaffirm it on the grounds that he was a minor when it was made. The court refused disaffirmance because he ratified the contract by affirmative conduct and accepting benefits under it when he deposited the check.

State v. Bishop, 240 P.3d 614 (Kan. Ct. App. 2010) illustrates a situation in which a minor lost the right to disaffirm after majority by waiting too long. In 2002, when Bishop was 16 years old, she entered into a diversion agreement with the state to avoid prosecution for the offense of driving under the influence of alcohol. Under state law, a person who avoids prosecution by entering a diversion agreement is deemed to have been convicted of the offense. Bishop became a major in 2003. She was again caught driving under the influence of alcohol in 2004 and 2007. In her sentencing for the third offense, her previous diversion agreement was treated as a prior conviction. In an attempt to avoid the more severe penalty for a third conviction, Bishop sought to avoid the diversion agreement on the grounds that she was a minor without contractual capacity when she entered it. The court held that the statute governing diversion agreements made the agreement binding on the minor,[5] but went on to state that even if the minor had not been bound to the agreement by statute, she would no longer have been able to disaffirm the agreement because she had waited about four years after majority to seek disaffirmance.

c. The Objective Nature of Minors' Incapacity

The legal incapacity of minors is based on the assumption that minors lack the maturity to make reasoned judgments in the conduct of their affairs and are vulnerable to exploitation. Some minors, especially those close to majority, may in fact be mature and sophisticated enough to enter a contract, and the other party may not have taken advantage of the minor's youth and inexperience. Nevertheless, the law places the risk of contracting with a minor on the other party, so the minor's physical appearance and apparent or actual competence does not matter. The test for a minor's contractual capacity is purely objective, and the other party cannot prevent avoidance by showing that the minor was sufficiently mature or that the contract was on fair terms.

5. *See* Section 14.2.2c on statutory provisions reducing the age of capacity for a discussion of this aspect of the case.

The purely objective test of incapacity, based on age, has the advantage of certainty and simplicity, but it has the disadvantage of inflexibility and does not take into account that some minors do have both the maturity and the need to enter into contracts. It insulates a minor from responsibility for transactions, even where the adult party has not tried to take advantage of the minor, who did in fact have enough actual competence to make a reasoned judgment about entering the contract. This is particularly true of adolescents who are not far short of the age of capacity. As a result, some courts and commentators have criticized this test as paternalistic and rigid. This bright-line test has become even more questionable in the age of the Internet because minors are now likely to be engaged in electronic commerce, sometimes from quite an early age, and in some instances, are a dominant presence in the marketplace.

d. Parental Consent

A minor might be represented by a parent in entering into a contract, or might enter the contract with express parental permission. In some situations, the parent's involvement in the contract may make it binding on the minor, but this is not assured, and a court may hold that parental representation or consent does not deprive the minor of the right to disaffirm the contract. This issue has come up in many cases involving a parent's execution of a pre-injury exculpatory agreement on behalf of a minor to enable the minor to engage in a sport or other physical activity. The fictional opinion used as the basis of the Examples in Chapter 3 (*see* section 3.5), and raised again in connection with contracts that violate public policy in section 13.13.3a, discusses this issue. It cites several cases holding that a minor who was injured while engaging in the activity may disaffirm such a pre-injury agreement executed by a parent and may sue for personal injury damages. Some courts have confined this rule to waivers of liability executed in favor of commercial entities and have not applied it to nonprofit or volunteer organizations.

Exculpatory agreements are a special class of cases because of the serious impact of the parent's waiver on the minor's ability to recover compensation for personal injury, and courts refusing enforcement emphasize the public policy of protecting a minor's recourse to any future claim for negligent injury. A court may be less likely to allow a minor to avoid a contract in other cases, involving only the minor's financial interests, where the parent executed the contract on the minor's behalf. However, some courts have extended the principle of protecting the minor from a parent's improvidence in these cases as well, and have allowed the minor to disaffirm the contract despite parental involvement in its execution. For example, in *Berg v. Traylor*, 148 Cal. App. 4th 809 (Cal. Ct. App. 2007), the court allowed a minor, a ten-year-old child actor, to disaffirm a representation agreement with an agent, even though the minor's mother represented him in entering the agreement. Although the court recognized that there are some situations recognized in the state by statute or caselaw in which a parent can bind a minor contractually (for example, a contract for medical services or a release of liability relating to participation in school activities), this was not such a situation.[6]

§14.2.2 Situations in Which a Minor May Incur Legal Liability

There are some limited situations in which a minor can incur legal liability as a result of having entered a contract. However, this liability may not be equal to the minor's full contractual commitment and may be confined to restitution for benefits received.

a. Necessaries

The most common situation in which a minor can incur liability is if the contract is for necessaries. A necessary is not the same as a necessity, and it has a broader meaning. It includes not only the bare necessities of life, such as food, clothing, shelter, education, and medical care but also whatever goods or services are needed for the minor's livelihood and well-being in accordance with reasonable standards of living, or appropriate to the minor's own circumstances and standard of living. However, it does not include luxuries. The question of what constitutes a necessary is factual and based on all the circumstances. Therefore, while some goods or services are clearly necessaries, it may be difficult to predict how a court would react to others. For example, a court may or may not see a car as a necessary if it is used by the minor to drive to work or school. If the minor lives at home or has financial support from parents, goods or services that would otherwise be required for subsistence are not likely to qualify as necessaries. For example, an apartment could be a necessary requisite to an acceptable standard of living, but it may not be if the minor has the option of living in the parents' home.

The concept of emancipation is important to the minor's liability for necessaries. The exact meaning of "emancipated" is not entirely clear. Some courts define it narrowly to include only marriage or military enlistment. Other courts adopt a broader test to include any situation in which the

6. The adult party also argued that the contract was enforceable on the grounds that the provision of representation for a child actor was a necessary, but the court rejected that argument. Contracts for necessaries are explained in section 14.2.2.

minor lives independently of parents and not supported by them. Some courts do not impose liability for necessaries on a minor unless the minor is emancipated. Other courts do not follow such a firm rule, even though they are more likely to classify goods or services as necessaries where the minor is emancipated.

Courts differ on the nature of a claim for necessaries. Some courts see a contract for necessaries as an exception to the rule that the minor can avoid the contract. They therefore simply enforce it as if it was a major's contract. Other courts avoid the contract even though it involved necessaries but hold the minor liable for restitution on the theory of unjust enrichment. This means that if the market value of the goods or services is less than the contract price, the minor is only liable for that lower value.

b. Misrepresentation of Age

A minor who makes a deliberate misrepresentation of age, claiming to be a major, may lose the ability to escape liability under the contract if the other party, acting reasonably, was misled by the misrepresentation and gave value to the minor or otherwise suffered a detriment in reasonable reliance on it. A court may fully enforce the contract by estopping the minor from asserting minority.[7] Alternatively, the court may deny enforcement of the contract but hold the minor liable for the tort of fraud. (Accountability for tortious conduct typically begins at an earlier age than contractual capacity.) The remedy in tort is different from that in contract and aims at restoring the other party's loss rather than enforcing the contract to give the major party the benefit of the bargain. To allow grounds for relief for misrepresentation, the fact misrepresented must be the minor's age. In *Foss v. Circuit City*, cited in section 14.2.1, the minor represented that he had parental consent to enter the contract by forging his mother's signature on the written agreement. The court held that this was not enough to estop the minor from asserting minority.

One of the elements of misrepresentation is actual and justifiable inducement, so that even if the minor misrepresents age, the major party has a duty to exercise due diligence in examining the representation. In *Matullo v. Sky Zone Trampoline Park*, 276 A.3d 178 (N.J. Super. Ct. App. Div. 2022), Jacob Matullo, a minor, filled out a waiver and arbitration agreement, falsely representing that he was the parent of a minor who consented to the minor's participation in the trampoline activity. He signed his name (Jacob Matullo) in the parent permission section, showing his date of birth as July 4, 1998. He then filled in the child's section with the same name and a birthdate of July 4, 2002. The information was patently and absurdly wrong, showing

7. *See* section 8.4 for an explanation of estoppel.

a 19-year-old parent purporting to waive the rights of a 15-year-old son with the same name and birthday. The court recognized the potential that a minor could lose the right of disaffirmance by fraudulently misrepresenting age, but the adult party must at least be able to show actual and justifiable reliance on the misrepresentation. Sky Zone could not remotely make such an argument here with a straight face.

c. Statutory Exceptions

Apart from any recognition of liability under these principles of common law, a state or federal statute may confer contractual capacity on a minor of a specified minimum age with regard to certain types of contract. For example, minors above a stated age are usually able to enter into insurance contracts or banking transactions, and a state may validate a minor's employment contract provided that it complies with the state's regulation of child labor.

Sometimes a statute expressly lowers the age of capacity for a particular type of contract. However, the statute may not always be that clear, so the legislature's intent to lower the age of capacity for particular types of transactions has to be determined by statutory interpretation. This issue can sometimes come up in a situation outside of the ordinary commercial context of contract law, as illustrated by *State v. Bishop*, 240 P.3d 614 (Kan. App. 2010), cited in section 14.2.1b to illustrate a minor's loss of the right to disaffirm a contract by waiting too long after reaching majority. Bishop entered into a diversion agreement with the state when she was 16 to avoid prosecution for driving under the influence of alcohol. The statute governing diversion agreements did not specifically accord minors the contractual capacity to enter such agreements, but the court concluded, as a matter of statutory interpretation, that it must necessarily have intended to cover any driver, irrespective of age, who had driven a vehicle under the influence of alcohol. The minor's agreement was therefore binding.[8]

§14.2.3 Restitution or Other Relief Following Disaffirmation

If the contract is purely executory—that is, neither party has performed—disaffirmance simply terminates it. However, if either party had given value to the other before disaffirmance, the effect of disaffirmance is more complicated. Where a contract between parties of full contractual capacity is avoided, each party must restore whatever has been received from the other under the avoided contract. When the avoidance concerns a minor's contract,

8. As noted in section 14.2.1b, even had the statute not made the agreement binding on the minor, she would have lost the right to disaffirm it by waiting too long after majority.

this general rule is not as firmly followed. The major party must always restore in full the value of anything received from the minor. However, the minor is generally only liable to return to the major party whatever is still left of the major's contract performance at the time of avoidance. As part of the goal of protecting the minor from an improvident contract, the minor is shielded from liability beyond the duty to return the present and existing economic advantage still retained by the minor at the time of avoidance. The minor does not have to pay the major the value of services or of property that has been consumed or lost. For example, say that the minor bought a car for $10,000. The minor paid $2,000 down and agreed to pay the balance in installments. A few months later, after the minor had paid an additional $1,000 in installments, the car was stolen. The minor had not bought theft insurance for it. The minor may disaffirm the contract and is entitled to restitution of the $3,000 down payment and installments. The minor no longer has the car, so cannot return it and also has no obligation to restore the value of the car to the seller. The minor is also not obliged to compensate the seller for the value of the six months' use of the car. Similarly, if the car was not stolen but damaged in an accident, the minor's only obligation on disaffirmance would be to return the damaged car to the seller. In *I.B. ex rel. Fife v. Facebook, Inc.*, 905 F. Supp. 2d 989 (N.D. Cal. 2012), a minor used his mother's credit card to purchase Facebook Credits, which were used to play a game called "Ninja Saga." The mother had authorized an initial purchase of $20 worth of credits, but Facebook stored the credit card information, so the minor was able to continue to make in-game purchases that ultimately amounted to several hundred dollars. Upon discovering this, the mother brought a class action against Facebook to disaffirm the contract on behalf of her own son and similarly situated minors. Facebook moved to dismiss the suit on several grounds, including that the minor could not disaffirm the contract because he had already received the benefit of the Facebook Credits. The court denied the motion to dismiss, holding that the minor was entitled to disaffirm and to recover all consideration paid to Facebook, without any obligation to restore to Facebook the value of the Facebook Credits used up in the game.[9] The court applied the same principle in *T.K. v. Adobe Systems, Inc.*, cited in section 14.2.1. Upon disaffirmance of a subscription to Adobe Creative Cloud, the minor had no obligation to restore to Adobe the value of services received during the period before the disaffirmance of the subscription. *See also Doe v. Epic Games, Inc.*, 435 F. Supp. 3d 1024 (N.D. Cal. 2020), in which the court likewise held that a minor's disaffirmance rights were not affected by the inability to return in-app purchases of "v-bucks" that had been used in playing the "Fortnite" game.

9. The court said that it did not matter that the payments made to Facebook came from the mother's credit card account and were not the minor's own money.

Some courts apply the rule restricting the minor's restitution absolutely, but others are concerned that it is too generous to the minor. A few courts do require the minor to restore the value received under the disaffirmed contract, even if the minor no longer has it. Others courts are willing, in limited circumstances, to impose some liability on a minor beyond the bare return of what the minor still has. For example, if the contract was fair and did not exploit the minor, and the major was not aware of the minority, a court may allow the major party to offset (deduct) the value received by the minor against what the major party is obliged to refund to the minor. (That is, if the minor has paid the major party, the restitution of that payment by the major party is reduced by the value of the benefit to the minor.) Some courts limit the value of the benefit to an offset against the major's restitution, but others have granted a judgment against the minor beyond the amount of the offset. *Dodson v. Schrader*, 824 S.W.2d 545 (Tenn. 1992), is an example of the former approach. The minor had paid cash for a truck and had then caused severe damage to its engine by neglect. The court permitted the minor to avoid the contract and to recover the cash paid for the truck, but it allowed the major party to offset against his restitutionary payment the value of the minor's use of the truck and its depreciation. In *Valencia v.White*, 654 P.2d 287 (Ariz. Ct. App. 1982), the court went beyond an offset against restitution, imposing liability on the minor for the cost of repairing a truck that the minor had used in his trucking business. Even if a court follows the traditional rule of not requiring the minor to restore anything beyond the presently held benefit, the major party may be able to recover in tort for the diminution in value of property if the minor's fault caused the deterioration in the property. For example, if a minor bought a car and then damaged it in a collision caused by the minor's negligence, the minor may still disaffirm the contract, but could be held liable in tort for negligent damage to the car.

§14.3 MENTAL INCAPACITY

§14.3.1 The Basis and Nature of Avoidance Due to Mental Incapacity

Although assent is measured objectively, on the basis of the reasonable meaning of a manifestation of assent, the objective test presupposes that the adult party manifesting assent has sufficient mental competence to form meaningful intent to contract. Mental incompetence is determined at the time of contracting. If it can be proved to have existed at that time, it is a basis for avoidance even if the condition causing the incapacity was temporary or was not present before or after the transaction. In contrast to the objective incapacity of a minor, based on the fact of age alone irrespective of the minor's actual state of mind, the mental incapacity of a major is measured by the actual state of the person's mind. The law presumes that adults are competent to contract, so a party seeking to avoid a contract on grounds of mental incapacity must rebut this presumption by proving a mental disability severe enough to preclude the formation of rational contractual intent. This is usually established by expert psychiatric testimony, corroborated by lay testimony of people who observed the party's conduct at and around the time that the contract was executed.

The purpose of permitting avoidance is the protection of the disabled person. If the disabled person no longer wishes to be bound to the contract and has sufficient capacity to sue for avoidance, the protective function of avoidance is well served. However, a person who lacks capacity to contract may also lack the capacity to sue for avoidance, so that the avoidance suit is brought by a guardian ad litem, acting on behalf of the disabled party. In such a situation, the benign motive of protection carries a risk of undermining the autonomy of a disabled party who may still desire the contract, but is overridden by others (commonly family members) who have made the decision that it should be avoided.

§14.3.2 The Test for Mental Incapacity: Cognitive and Motivational Disorders

The older-established test for mental incapacity is strict. The contract can only be avoided if, at the time of contracting, the party was unable to understand the nature and consequences of the transaction. This standard, called the cognitive test, confines avoidance to cases of profound mental disability that affects the cognitive ability of the party. Some courts still use this test as the basis of finding mental incompetence, but, as knowledge of the effects of various kinds of mental illness grew over the twentieth century, other courts came to accept that the cognitive test was too narrow and that there are many forms of mental incapacity that fall short of cognitive disability but that nevertheless affect a person's judgment, self-control, and motivation seriously enough to preclude rational assent. This led to a broader test that recognizes not only cognitive disorders but also an illness or defect that impairs the party's ability to transact in a reasonable manner. This test is commonly called the motivational test (also known as the affective, or volitional, test). Restatement, Second, §15(1) recognizes both the cognitive and motivational tests. Section 15(1)(a) sets out the cognitive test. It allows a party to avoid a contract if the party "is unable to understand in a reasonable manner the nature and consequences of the transaction." Section 15(1)(b) sets out the motivational test, under which a party may avoid the contract if the party "is unable to act in a reasonable manner in relation to the transaction." Restatement, Second, §15(1) adds to the motivational test, some protection of the other party's legitimate reliance interest by also requiring that the other party has reason to know of this condition.

Davis v. Davis, 89 P.3d 1206 (Or. Ct. App. 2004), shows why the motivational test is needed to achieve a fair result in a case in which the party seeking avoidance is not cognitively impaired. The parties entered into a divorce settlement in which the wife gave the husband full ownership of jointly owned stock options and their interest in a software company. About a month later, the wife moved to avoid the settlement on the grounds that she was not mentally competent when she made it. The couple had been married for about 17 years. The husband had physically abused the wife on numerous occasions during the marriage. A social worker who treated the wife after the dissolution testified that the wife loved and feared the husband enormously. The wife was diagnosed as suffering from depression, post-traumatic stress syndrome, and battered woman's syndrome. When the parties met to negotiate the settlement, the wife was emotionally distraught and also had hopes of reconciliation. When she expressed her desire to reconcile, the husband made it clear that he was not interested, and he also verbally abused her at one point during the course of the meeting. Near the end of this meeting, the wife told her attorney that she did not want to fight anymore and wanted to get the meeting over with. Contrary to her attorney's advice, she did not press for a half share in the stock options and interest in the software company but insisted on signing the agreement that gave the husband full ownership. The majority of the court of appeals upheld the trial court's dismissal of the wife's motion to set aside the agreement because the wife's disability did not amount to cognitive incapacity and the state supreme court had recognized only the cognitive test. A concurring judge regretfully accepted this legal conclusion but expressed the view that the motivational test is more in accord with psychological theory and reflects a better understanding of human behavior.

This description of the case shows two things. First, it demonstrates the truth of the concurring judge's view that there are many situations in which a strict cognitive test disregards what could be a real and serious impairment of the capacity to make a rational and voluntary decision. Second, it suggests the hazard of the broader test. If mental incapacity is wide enough to encompass severe emotional disturbance short of cognitive disability, the test becomes less predictable and harder to apply. At the borderline, it may be difficult to distinguish incapacity that merits avoidance from eccentric, strangely motivated, ill-advised, or irrational decisionmaking, which should not be grounds for avoidance.[10] A court that accepts the broader motivational test as a basis for avoidance can mitigate this risk by requiring

10. *See* section 14.3.4.

persuasive expert testimony to establish a clinically recognized illness, and by taking into account whether the other party knew or had reason to know of the mental condition.

It must be stressed that the basis of avoiding a contract for mental incompetence is lack of capacity, not harshness in the terms of the contract. Therefore, the party seeking avoidance need not show that the terms of the contract are unfair. Even a contract with perfectly reasonable terms can be avoided by a party who establishes mental incompetence. This does not mean that the existence of unfair or one-sided terms is irrelevant in cases of mental incompetence. As explained below, the decision to avoid the contract involves some degree of equitable balancing, and unfair terms or advantage-taking may influence the court in deciding to allow avoidance.

§14.3.3 Proving Mental Incapacity

Because adults are presumed to have contractual capacity, the party alleging incapacity has the burden of proving it. It is relatively easy to discharge this burden if the party had been declared incompetent by a court and placed under guardianship at the time of contracting. However, sustaining the burden of proof is harder if there has been no adjudication of incapacity prior to the contract. To prove incapacity, the party must demonstrate both that the condition existed at the time of contracting, and that it was in nature and extent severe enough to preclude an adequate degree of assent. This is usually shown by both expert psychiatric evidence and the testimony of people who observed the behavior of the party at the time of the transaction. In *Sparrow v. Demonico*, 960 N.E.2d 296 (Mass. 2012), the court held that psychiatric diagnosis is indispensable because a lay witness is not qualified to give an opinion on mental condition.

In *Gaddy v. Douglass*, 597 S.E.2d 12 (S.C. Ct. App. 2004), the dementia of the mentally incapacitated party, an elderly woman with advanced Alzheimer's disease, was convincingly established by the testimony of three neurologists who examined her and three lay people who observed her conduct and attested to her gradual mental deterioration, confusion, and forgetfulness. As a result of this testimony, the court avoided a power of attorney that the incapacitated woman had executed in favor of some grasping relatives who induced her to sign it after they knew that she was suffering from the disease. In some cases, the evidence relating to mental incompetence can be complex and difficult to evaluate. For example, in *In re Jack*, 390 B.R. 307 (Bankr. S.D. Tex. 2008), the bankruptcy court had to determine whether an agreement to settle a personal injury claim, executed ten years before the case by Samuel Jack, the debtor's late husband, was voidable because of his mental incapacity at that time. Prior to entering the contract, Samuel had sustained a serious head injury while working as a longshoreman.

In addition to this injury, which damaged his brain, Samuel suffered from alcoholism and had a preexisting mental disorder, known as schizoaffective disorder, which affected his judgment and reasoning ability. Around the time of entering the agreement, he was hospitalized several times, and some medical reports indicated that his thought processes were disordered and impaired. However, other expert opinion indicated that his thought processes were intact. To glean Samuel's mental capacity at the time of the contract, the court had to weigh and assess the credibility of considerable conflicting and complex evidence of medical diagnoses and observations of Samuel's conduct. It also had to take into account the nature of the contract and the degree to which a person of diminished mental capacity might be able to comprehend its purpose and effect. It ultimately determined that Samuel's wife (the debtor in bankruptcy) had not sustained the burden of proving that, at the time of contracting, Samuel was incapable of appreciating the effect of what he was doing or of understanding the nature of the transaction and the consequences of his actions.

The mere fact that a person has a serious medical condition does not lead to the conclusion that the person is mentally incompetent, but evidence of serious physical ailments that are consistent with or could contribute to mental incapacity is probative. In *Kinsel v. Lindsey*, 526 S.W.3d 411 (Tex. 2017), the court upheld the jury's finding that a 95-year-old woman was mentally incompetent at the time that she entered a contract to sell her ranch, based on evidence of her overall severe physical deterioration during the two years leading up to and including the time of the sale. Psychiatric testimony identified her worsening dementia and also drew the link between her mental state and many serious physical symptoms, including deterioration in her sight, frailness, incontinence, heart problems, and renal deficiency. Similarly, in *Estate of Matthews*, 510 S.W.3d 106 (Tex. App. 2016), the court set aside a marriage, entered into by the decedent a few months before he committed suicide, on the ground that the decedent had been mentally incompetent at the time of the marriage. The decedent had suffered from multiple sclerosis as well as depression, attention deficit disorder, and post-traumatic stress disorder. He also had a history of drug and alcohol abuse. While there was some testimony that he was able to function normally, was not delusional, and behaved coherently, expert testimony from a psychiatrist and a psychologist who reviewed his medical records after his death linked his medical condition to his mental state and concluded that he lacked the capacity to consent to marriage.

§14.3.4 Distinguishing Actionable Mental Incapacity from Nonactionable Incompetence or Infirmity

As noted in section 14.3.3, avoidance for mental incapacity is confined to psychiatrically diagnosed mental illness or incompetence. Incompetence or infirmity that falls short of psychiatrically recognized mental incapacity does not give grounds to avoid the contract. This distinction is illustrated by *In re Seminole Walls and Ceilings Corp.*, 366 B.R. 206 (Bankr. M.D. Fla. 2007),[11] and *Sparrow v. Demonico*, cited in section 14.3.3. In *Seminole Walls*, a bankruptcy court had to decide on the validity of a settlement agreement executed between a bankruptcy trustee and a photographer who claimed ownership of a collection of his photographs in the possession of the estate. The photographs were of Hollywood celebrities, including Marilyn Monroe, that had been taken by the claimant many years before and had later been acquired by the bankrupt company. The settlement agreement resolved the question of their ownership. One of the grounds raised by the claimant for avoiding the settlement agreement was that he was mentally incompetent when it was made. At the time of entering the agreement, the claimant was 87 years old and had had a mini-stroke. He was declared mentally incompetent a few months after entering the agreement. The court found that notwithstanding some degree of feebleness and considerable eccentricity at the time of contracting and the subsequent declaration of incompetence, there was insufficient evidence to show that he was incapable of entering into the settlement agreement at the time of contracting.

Sparrow involved a settlement agreement reached during mediation to resolve a family dispute over the ownership of real property. Frances Sparrow sought to enforce the settlement against her sister, Susan Demonico, and Susan's husband. The Demonicos claimed that the settlement was unenforceable because Susan had experienced a mental breakdown during the mediation and therefore lacked capacity to contract. The trial court denied enforcement of the contract on the basis of the Demonicos' testimony that Susan was very distraught and distressed at the time of the mediation. She cried most of the day, became less coherent and less in control during the course of the day, and was generally in a bad emotional state. The Supreme Court reversed. It held that the Demonicos had not sufficiently demonstrated that Susan lacked mental capacity at the time that she entered the settlement agreement. It recognized that incapacity could be present at the time of contracting, even where the party did not suffer from a permanent mental illness. However, mental incapacity cannot simply be established by lay observation of the party's emotional state but must be proved by expert psychiatric testimony that explains the nature of the party's mental incompetence and the manner in which it affected her ability to act rationally in relation to the transaction.

Even where there is expert testimony that points to incapacity, it may be insufficient to establish incapacity because it is too far removed from the time of the transaction. In *Merril Lynch, Pierce, Fenner, & Smith, Inc. v. Flanders-Borden*, 11 F.4th 12 (1st Cir. 2021), the issue was whether the deceased was mentally incompetent

---

11. The case was affirmed in part and reversed in part by the district court in relation to matters unconnected to the capacity issue: 388 B.R. 38 (M.D. Fla. 2008) and 412 B.R. 878 (M.D. Fla. 2008).

at the time that he executed a Transfer on Death (TOD) agreement, removing assets from his estate and transferring them directly to stated beneficiaries. He had been admitted to hospital four months before executing the TOD, and was considered by medical experts to be irreversibly mentally incapacitated as a result of severe substance abuse. However, at the time of his discharge from hospital he was diagnosed as having residual confusion and poor judgment, but not severe incapacity. In his estate's suit to reclaim the assets transferred under the TOD, the court held that the estate had failed to produce sufficient evidence to discharge the burden of proving the decedent's lack of mental incapacity at the time that he executed the TOD. By contrast, in *Webb v. Five Star Montebello, LLC*, 2022 WL 443837 (N.M. Ct. App. 2022), evidence of the mental condition of a resident of an assisted living facility before and after she signed an arbitration agreement on admission to the facility showed that she could not have had the capacity to enter into the agreement at that time.

§14.3.5 Avoidance and Its Consequences

Like a minor's contract, the contract of a mentally incompetent person is voidable, not void. Unlike minority, however, mental disability does not disappear on a set and certain date, after which the fact of disaffirmance or ratification can be settled. The fate of a contract by a mentally incapacitated person may therefore hang in the balance until either it is disaffirmed or the incapacity abates and the formerly incompetent party affirms it (or a guardian is ultimately appointed and does so). In the interim, there may be performance or the other party may have otherwise changed position in reliance on the contract. If the contract is on fair terms, other party did not know of the incapacity, and relied honestly on the contract, a court may take this into account in deciding if, under all the circumstances, it would be fair and equitable to permit avoidance of the contract.

If the contract is avoided, the parties must be restored to the status quo ante. Both must return money or property received under the contract, or the value of property consumed or dissipated, or of services rendered. However, the restitutionary obligation of the disabled party may be confined to actual ultimate enrichment, rather than the market value of the benefit, if the other party knew of and took advantage of the incompetence.

§14.3.6 Incapacity Induced by Alcohol or Drug Abuse

Courts recognize that if intoxication is severe enough, its impairing effect can be just as profound as mental illness. Therefore, a party is usually permitted to avoid a contract entered into under the influence of drugs or alcohol if the level of intoxication is sufficient to deprive the party of cognitive ability or of the ability to act rationally in relation to the transaction. The case for relief is even stronger if the terms of the resulting contract are unfair or unduly favorable to the other party.

Mental impairment from alcohol or drug abuse is often temporary, so that the ability to avoid the contract will be lost by ratification if the impaired party does not act within a reasonable time after regaining sobriety to disaffirm the contract. In *MGM Grand Hotel v. Long*, 2022 WL 3586442 (D. Nev. 2022), Long received about $8 million in casino credit from MGM. He claimed that he was inebriated when he bought the credits because the casino had plied him with copious amounts of free alcohol while he stayed at the hotel and encouraged him to drink continuously. The court recognized that severe intoxication could be a basis for avoiding a contract on grounds of mental incapacity, but it refused Long relief. Even assuming that he was intoxicated enough to be incapacitated, he lost the right to avoid the contract because he ratified it by repaying about $1.8 million of it some months later, after he had sobered up, and never disaffirmed the debt as a whole until he sought avoidance in this suit about three years later.

EXAMPLES

Examples

1. Major, age 19, had operated a successful part-time yard maintenance business on weekends. He was about to leave his hometown to attend college and had to give up his business. He therefore sold his lawnmower, trimmer, edger, and other garden tools to Junior, his 16-year-old neighbor, for $800. This is the market value of the equipment, and a fair price. Junior lived with his parents and was a high-school student. He bought the equipment with the intention of setting up his own yard maintenance business and hoped to take over Major's customers. Junior did not have the cash to pay the full $800 to Major, so they agreed that Junior would make a down payment of $300 and would pay the balance in installments of $50 per month, which he expected would be generated from his yard work. The parties negotiated their contract by email, so there is an electronic record of their agreement. Under the state law applicable to this transaction, a person acquires contractual capacity at the age of 18.
   a. After taking delivery of the equipment and paying Major the $300, Junior was able to take over some of Major's ex-customers and began work. He found out immediately that he hated the work and was not good at it. A couple of weeks after he began work, he lost control of the lawnmower, which ran over the trimmer, completely mangling it, and then plunged off a steep embankment and exploded. This experience convinced Junior that yard work was not for him. He wishes to cancel the sale, get his $300 back, and return all the surviving equipment to Major. May he do this?

b. Say that at the time he made the contract with Major, Junior was 17 years old and just two weeks short of his eighteenth birthday. Junior took delivery of the equipment and paid Major the $300. He used the garden equipment for five weeks and then decided that he no longer wished to do landscaping work. Contrary to question (a) above, the calamity involving the runaway lawnmower did not occur, and Junior can return the equipment to Major in much the same condition as when he bought it. Junior would like to avoid the contract, return the equipment to Major, and get his money back. Does this change in the facts affect Junior's ability to disaffirm the contract?

2. Bonna Petite, a precocious 17-year-old with an appetite for *haute cuisine*, decided to eat lunch at Trés Cher, the most elegant and expensive restaurant in town. She put on a business suit and groomed herself meticulously, succeeding in making herself look like a young executive of around 25 years of age. After eating a magnificent lunch, Bonna informed the server that she was a minor. She disaffirmed the contract and refused to pay for the lunch. The age of majority in Bonna's state is 18. Can she get away with this?

3. Gerry Atric, an 89-year-old man, had lived in his house for 45 years. He had lived alone since the death of his wife some years ago. Gerry had always been stubborn, impatient, and difficult, and this had become worse as he aged. He hated asking anyone for help, and he rarely sought or listened to advice. In recent months it had become clear to his daughter that he was no longer coping with the house, which had started to become dirty and dilapidated. In addition, he did not seem to be managing his affairs well and had become forgetful and sometimes confused. Gerry's daughter urged him to sell the house and to move to an assisted living complex. Gerry resisted at first, but finally decided to do that. Without consulting or seeking advice from his daughter or anyone else, he advertised the house for sale, intending to sell it himself to save the real estate agent's commission. Gerry was confident that he knew exactly how much the house was worth, but he was wrong. His information about the market was years out of date and he did not do any research into current prices. He therefore priced the house at about 75 percent of its market value and advertised it for sale.

   Holmes Flipper, a property speculator, visited the house in response to the advertisement and realized that it was underpriced. Holmes therefore made an immediate offer to buy the house for its full asking price, which Gerry accepted. The parties' interactions during the transaction were quite minimal, consisting of a couple of short comments. The only impression that Holmes gained about Gerry was that he was a rather unfriendly elderly man of few words.

   After the contract of sale had been signed, Gerry told his daughter about it. She was appalled because she knew that he had let the house go for a patently inadequate price. She gathered data of recent sales of comparative properties, which she showed to him, finally convincing him that he had sold too cheaply. Gerry now wishes to rescind the sale. Does he have grounds to do so?

4. Clark, age 30, suffers from bipolar disorder, a psychiatric condition that causes extreme swings in mood, ranging from periods of depression to periods of abnormally elevated energy and enthusiasm. During these periods of elation, a person with bipolar disorder may feel energetic, excitable, and hyperactive, and may experience diminution of self-control and impaired judgment. During an elevated episode, Clark visited the website of an exclusive resort and booked an exorbitantly expensive and luxurious vacation. To complete and submit his online booking, Clark signified his agreement to the resort's standard terms by clicking on an "I agree" button on the website. Clark did not read the standard terms before clicking the button. One of the terms stated, "I understand that upon submission of my booking, my credit card will be debited with the full cost of the accommodation booked. This booking cannot be changed and if I cancel it I will not be entitled to a refund of this charge." A few days after booking the vacation, Clark's elevated episode ended. He regretted booking the expensive vacation. When the resort refused to cancel the booking and refund his payment, Clark sued to avoid the contract and recover his payment. What are his prospects of success?

5. Change the facts of Example 4 to the following extent: Clark is not an adult suffering from bipolar disorder or any other psychiatric condition, but is a minor, age 17. Clark is intellectually gifted. He graduated from high school at the age of 16 and is a college student. He has his own credit card, which he used to book the vacation. (Under a state statute, a minor may validly contract for a credit card from the age of 16.) May Clark avoid the contract and recover his payment?

Explanations

1. a. This is a sale of goods subject to UCC Article 2, but the only provision of Article 2 relevant to this Example is the statute of frauds in UCC §2.201, which is probably satisfied by the exchange of emails.[12] UCC Article 2 does not deal with contractual capacity and minors' contracts are therefore governed in sales transactions by general principles of law.

   Because Junior is a minor, he may disaffirm the contract. It does not matter that he may have been fully able to understand the nature and effect of the transaction, or that he planned to use the equipment

12. *See* sections 11.2.3 and 11.3.

for a business venture. The protection from contractual commitment afforded a minor is based on the objective fact of age and does not take account of the subjective attributes of the minor. The objective criterion of minority also makes it irrelevant that Major was little over the age of minority himself, that the contract was on fair terms, or that Major did not exploit or take advantage of Junior. Junior's right to disaffirm does not depend on a showing of substantive unfairness or bargaining impropriety.

If Junior elects to disaffirm the contract, each party must restore what was received from the other. However, if Junior has lost, consumed, or damaged property obtained under the contract, the common rule is that he is responsible to restore only what he has at the time of disaffirmance and need not compensate the major for any shortfall. Under this rule, Junior is entitled to his $300 back and must return the surviving equipment to Major. Some courts have recognized that a rigid rule to this effect may not be fair in every case, and have been willing, in proper circumstances, to hold the minor liable for more than the mere return of existing enrichment. As discussed in section 14.2.3, courts following this approach have devised various means of compensating the major party beyond just return of the property that the minor still possesses. The court may require the minor to restore the value of any benefit received from the use of the property (such as its rental value for the period of use), or it may set off the major's loss against any restitution due to the minor, or it may grant a money judgment against the minor in excess of an offset of that loss against the restitution due to the minor.

Even if the court applies the common rule and does not require Junior to return anything more than the equipment in its current state, he could be liable to Major in tort if he caused the loss negligently. (Liability for tort arises at a younger age than contractual capacity.) If Junior was negligent in losing control of the mower, tort law would make Junior responsible to reimburse Major for the value of the lost mower and trimmer, in addition to returning the other equipment.

Major's prospect of recovery may be better if he can show that the mower and trimmer qualify as necessaries because Junior used them to earn money. Some courts do not allow a claim for necessaries at all unless the minor is emancipated, and Junior was not—he still lived with his parents. If the court does not follow this restriction, goods used to generate income could qualify as necessaries, but this argument is less compelling where the minor is still in school, living with and supported by his parents, and the work is not required for his sustenance. If the goods were to be classified as necessaries, some courts would treat the contract as fully enforceable, so that Junior would have no right of avoidance. Other courts would allow avoidance but would require Junior to make restitution for the value of what he received. On this basis, if the goods were held to be necessaries, Junior would, in addition to returning the other (undamaged) equipment, be liable to pay for the mower and trimmer, based on the lesser rate of the contract value or fair market value at the time of sale. In this case, fair value was apparently equivalent to the contract price, so the contract price of the destroyed mower and trimmer would be the proper measure of recovery.

b. The fact that Junior was almost 18, rather than 16, at the time of contracting does not affect Junior's right to avoid the contract. Minority is measured objectively, and the only question is whether or not Junior was a minor at the time of contracting, even if he was almost a major. However, once a minor reaches the age of majority, he may ratify the contract, thereby fully validating it and terminating the power to avoid it. Ratification may be express, or it could be implied where the minor fails to disaffirm the contract within a reasonable time of reaching majority or otherwise acts in a way that signifies an intent to ratify.

   The measurement of a reasonable time for disaffirmance is a factual question, based on all the circumstances of the case. About three weeks have passed since Junior's eighteenth birthday and he has not yet disaffirmed. His failure to act for three weeks may in itself constitute a ratification. Even if this passive delay in disaffirming is not enough on its own to constitute ratification, Junior continued to use the equipment during the three-week period. This action is inconsistent with an intent to disaffirm, and likely constitutes conduct evidencing an intent to ratify.[13]

2. As a minor, Bonna has the right to disaffirm her contract. The general rule is that she must restore any benefits that she still retains at the time of disaffirmance, but is not accountable for the value of property that has been consumed or dissipated. As she has consumed all the food, there is nothing left for her to restore.[14]

   The general rule places the burden on Trés Cher to inquire about the age of its youthful-looking customers, and it bears the risk of failing to do so, even if Bonna looked older than she was. On the other hand, Bonna has behaved very badly, and the law should not encourage this

13. As noted in section 14.2.1, if the state requires a written ratification, implied ratification may not be sufficient.

14. In a sense, Bonna is still in possession of Trés Cher's property, which she will retain until the process of digestion is complete, However, Trés Cher would probably not press too hard for the disgorgement of this benefit.

kind of thing. There are a few possibilities for holding Bonna accountable for her conduct.

Trés Cher could argue that the meal was a necessary. Food required for sustenance could qualify as a necessary, but it is harder to so classify a sumptuous meal at a fancy restaurant, especially where the minor lives with her parents and has food available at home. Alternatively, Trés Cher could argue that Bonna should be held liable in tort for fraud, which she may have committed, either by deliberately misrepresenting her age or by entering into a contract with the intention to breach it. A minor can be held responsible for tortious conduct and a finding of fraud could make Bonna liable for the loss caused by her misrepresentation. The difficulty with a fraud cause of action is that Bonna's dressing up to look older is probably not enough to constitute a misrepresentation of majority because courts usually require that the minor lies affirmatively about her age. A cause of action based on Bonna's deliberate intent, at the time of contracting, not to perform her obligations under the contract might be a promising cause of action if Trés Cher is able to prove that state of mind.[15]

In the absence of a finding of liability for a necessary or in tort, the rule that a minor is responsible to restore only the existing benefit received under the contract leaves Trés Cher with no remedy. As noted in Example 1a, some courts have moved away from that absolute rule and do recognize that the minor has some liability for restitution of the value of a consumed benefit: restoration of the value of any benefit received from the use of the property, or a setoff of the major's loss against any restitution due to the minor, or a money judgment against the minor. There is a stronger incentive for adopting this approach where, as here, the minor was willful in causing the major party's loss. Note, however, that the remedy of offsetting Trés Cher's loss against its restitutionary obligation to Bonna would not work in this case because Bonna gave nothing to the restaurant and there is no restitution owed to her against which her obligation could be offset.

As a matter of policy, a rule that confines the major party's recovery to the minor's existing benefit most strongly advances the goal of protecting the minor against improvident conduct that creates liability. However, a rule that makes a minor fully accountable for the value of the benefit, even if consumed or lost, allows the court to sanction the minor's irresponsible or antisocial conduct. A rule that makes the minor accountable for a consumed or lost benefit, but only to the extent of an

15. Fraud by misrepresentation of intent is discussed in section 13.6.2.

offset against the major party's restitutionary obligation, is a compromise solution that tries to accommodate both these goals.[16]

3. An adult person is presumed to be competent to contract. If Gerry seeks to avoid the contract on the basis of incapacity, he must prove that he was mentally incompetent at the time of entering the contract. The facts concerning Gerry's mental capacity are vague but suggestive. It appears that he has certain character traits, such as stubbornness, resistance to advice, and impatience, that are likely to place him at risk of entering into a disadvantageous contract. These flaws in his nature may indicate that he probably lacks skill in contracting, but do not, on their own, constitute the kind of mental incompetence that would give rise to a claim for avoidance. The facts hint at some possible recent deterioration of his mental capacity, but it is not clear if this had reached the level required for avoidance on the ground of incapacity. Evidence of laypersons who observed Gerry's conduct during and immediately before and after the transaction is relevant to his incapacity. Holmes apparently did not detect anything untoward in Gerry's behavior during the transaction, but Gerry's daughter has some evidence to offer about his conduct before the transaction. This anecdotal lay testimony alone is unlikely to establish a finding of incompetence without supporting expert testimony by a psychiatrist who has examined him, diagnosed his condition, and can convince the factfinder that it is serious enough to have impaired his ability to contract under the applicable test.

   It does not sound as if Gerry was so impaired as to satisfy the cognitive test—that he could not understand the nature and consequences of the transaction. However, he might satisfy the motivational standard—that his mental defect impaired his ability to transact in a reasonable manner. The motivational test is satisfied by a much less serious degree of infirmity, but the other party's reliance interest would likely be taken into account if the other party had no reason to know of the mental condition. Although Holmes did not observe any conduct that might have alerted him to Gerry's possible mental incapacity, the fact that an elderly man was selling his house at a bargain price may be sufficient to place Holmes on notice that Gerry was suffering from some mental infirmity.

   In *Heights Realty Ltd. v. Phillips*, 749 P.2d 77 (N.M. 1988), an 84-year-old woman entered into an exclusive listing agreement with a real estate agent, and then refused to sell the property when the agent found a willing and able buyer. Although there was nothing unfair or extraordinary

16. Criminal prosecution is another possibility because a minor can be held accountable for criminal conduct and Bonna appears to have obtained goods and services under false pretenses. Although criminal prosecution is aimed at punishing the offender, not compensating the victim, there is a possibility of an order of restitution in a criminal sentence.

about the contract terms, and the agent testified that the seller was "sharp as a tack" during their negotiations, the seller had been in a gradual and subtle mental decline for some years. Her deteriorating mental condition was described by a number of family members, who had noticed erratic and confused behavior, memory lapses, and mismanagement of her affairs. A psychiatrist testified that although it could not be stated conclusively that she was mentally incompetent, this could be asserted as a matter of medical probability. The psychiatrist believed that she probably realized that she was contracting for the purpose of selling her property but could not have understood the detailed terms of her contract. During the course of the suit, she was in fact adjudged incompetent and was represented by a conservator. The court, applying the stricter cognitive test followed in the jurisdiction, found that the combination of psychiatric and anecdotal evidence was sufficient to satisfy the seller's burden of establishing mental incompetence under that standard.

4. In the absence of a mental condition that impairs Clark's contractual capacity, Clark would not be able to escape this contract. He signified his assent to the standard terms by clicking the "I agree" button. As explained in section 5.3, courts commonly uphold such a manifestation of assent to standard clickwrap terms. It is unlikely that any of the doctrines discussed in Chapter 13 would provide grounds for avoidance. The facts do not suggest any basis for claiming fraud or duress. The facts also do not support a claim of unconscionability. There were no unfair bargaining tactics and the standard terms seem to be clear and accessible, so there does not appear any basis for claiming procedural unconscionability. There is also no persuasive argument for substantive unconscionability. Although the term precluding cancellation of the booking and refund is disadvantageous to the customer, nonrefundable bookings are common and such a term is therefore not likely to be unfairly surprising or unduly harsh and one-sided.

    Clark's only basis for avoidance is mental incapacity. He suffers from a well-recognized mental disorder that might have deprived him of the capacity to enter into this contract. Clark must establish the existence, symptoms, and effects of the disorder by expert psychiatric testimony, possibly bolstered by evidence of friends or family who observed his behavior during the elevated phase of the disorder. If Clark can produce this testimony, it would establish motivational incapacity, not cognitive. Although the illness impaired his judgment, motivation, and self-control, it did not disable him from understanding and appreciating the nature and consequences of his acts when entering the transaction. In *Proctor v. Classic Automotive, Inc.*, 20 So. 3d 1281 (Ala. Civ. App. 2009), the court refused to allow avoidance of a contract to lease a car, even though the lessee suffered from bipolar disorder and had behaved impulsively and irrationally when she entered the lease transaction. (She seemed to be confused about the difference between a lease and a purchase, she had gone on a spending spree just before entering the transaction, she did not test-drive the car, and she could not afford the lease payments.) The court held that despite this, the illness failed to meet the cognitive test of incapacity, which was the only test recognized in the jurisdiction, because she had enough understanding and perception to realize that she was entering into an automobile lease agreement.

A court that accepts the looser motivational test would allow Clark to avoid the booking if he can show that a mental illness or defect affected his ability to act in a reasonable manner in the transaction. Bipolar disorder likely does affect his ability to approach the transaction rationally. However, this may not end the matter because a court would likely also take into account the other party's reliance interest, and may refuse relief if the other party had no reason to know of the mental disorder. In this online transaction, the resort had no opportunity to observe behavior that may have alerted it to the possibility that Clark was suffering from a mental condition, and so it does have a legitimate reliance interest that could preclude avoidance.

5. The simpler objective test applicable to minor's contracts makes this Example much easier to answer. Clark is a minor, and he can avoid the contract. It does not matter that he is brilliant and advanced for his age. The exception relating to necessaries cannot apply here—a luxurious vacation surely cannot qualify as a necessary for a college student. Although the state has carved out a statutory exception to allow a minor to make a valid contract for a credit card, it would be a stretch, in the absence of clear statutory language, to interpret the legislation to extend to transactions in which the credit card is used.

   The traditional justification of the objective test for minority is that the other party should be placed on inquiry by the youthful appearance of the minor and assumes the risk of avoidance when contracting with someone who looks young. This rationale is not pertinent in an Internet transaction, in which the parties do not meet face to face. The resort may be able to protect itself by requiring a customer to certify majority. If a minor so certifies, the resort can argue that the minor should be estopped from seeking to avoid the contract on grounds of minority. In the absence of such a certification, the resort takes the risk that a person booking on its website could be a minor. (For some web-based traders, the risk that some transactions will be avoidable may be of minimal significance.)

CHAPTER 15

Mistake, Impracticability, and Frustration of Purpose

§15.1 THE COMMON THEMES AND THE DIFFERENCES BETWEEN MISTAKE, IMPRACTICABILITY, AND FRUSTRATION OF PURPOSE

The three doctrines considered in this chapter have common themes that make it useful to consider them together. They are each concerned with a situation in which the exchange between the parties turns out to be very different from what was expected. In the case of mistake, this is caused by a serious factual error made by one or both parties at the time of contracting, so that the contract is premised on incorrect information. By contrast, impracticability and frustration arise when there is no false premise at the time of contracting, but events change drastically enough after formation to belie the original expectations of the parties. Mistake is grounds for avoidance of the contract, whereas impracticability or frustration are grounds for excusing performance fully or in part and are commonly raised as a defense to a claim of breach.

There are two central questions common to all three doctrines:

1. *Materiality: How fundamental is the discrepancy between the expected and the actual exchange?* This question is concerned with the impact of the mistake or altered circumstances on the bargain reasonably anticipated by the parties. Relief is only available when the impact is so material that it changes the very basis of their bargain.

2. *Risk: Which party should be made to bear the consequences of this defeat of the original expectations?* The fact that original expectations have been fundamentally upset only justifies relief if the party seeking it does not bear the risk of this upset. The allocation of risk may be clear from the terms of the contract, or it may have to be established by interpretation or construction from the circumstances of the transaction. The determination of risk allocation is a crucial aspect of the judicial inquiry in all these cases.

Having identified common themes, it is important to stress the difference between mistake, on the one hand, and impracticability and frustration on the other. As noted earlier, the doctrine of mistake applies when the contract is based on an error relating to facts at the time of contracting. The error causes one or both parties to manifest assent that would not have been given had the true facts been known. When the error is later discovered the mistaken party—or one of them, if the parties shared the mistake—may have grounds to avoid (or in a special case, to claim adjustment of) the contract. The basis of mistake is that the manifestation of assent is not genuine because it was induced by error. Although one party's error may sometimes be induced by the deception of the other, improper conduct is not an element of mistake and does not have to be shown. (Of course, if there was deception, this fact strengthens the grounds for avoidance and may give rise to an alternative claim of fraud or unconscionability.) In contrast to mistake, impracticability and frustration are concerned with the impact of supervening events on the transaction. These doctrines are not based on any defect in assent at the time of contracting, but aim to provide relief when the basis of a fully consensual transaction is profoundly altered by some external event that occurs afterward. Chronology is therefore a helpful means of deciding whether a case raises an issue of impracticality or frustration rather than mistake. Impracticability and frustration should always be concerned with supervening events.

UCC Article 2 does not deal with the doctrine of mistake, so a mistake in a contract for the sale of goods is governed by principles of common law. As discussed in section 15.7.3, Article 2 does have a provision that deals with impracticability, written broadly enough to encompass frustration of purpose as well.

§15.2 THE MEANING OF MISTAKE AND THE DISTINCTION BETWEEN MUTUAL AND UNILATERAL MISTAKE

§15.2.1 The Legal Meaning of Mistake: An Error of Fact

In lay terms, "mistake" has quite a wide range of meaning. It could refer to a factual error, but it might also include a bad judgment, a rash decision, or simply a situation that did not work out well. For example, it may have been a real mistake to buy that ugly chair, to invest in a promising startup that flopped, or to waste two hours sitting through a well-reviewed but tedious movie. The legal meaning of "mistake" is much narrower. It is confined to errors of fact—that is, to errors about some thing or event, the occurrence or existence of which is ascertainable by objective evidence.

A mistake of fact must be distinguished from a mistake about the meaning of a contract term. Where the parties dispute the meaning and intention of a contract term, this is a mistake in the broad sense in that each of the parties is mistaken as to the intention of the other. However, mistake doctrine is not concerned with this type of error, which is not a mistake as to some external fact, but rather a mistake as to the meaning of a manifestation of assent. It is resolved by the process of interpretation, governed by the principles set out in Chapter 10. Extrinsic evidence of the factual context may be relevant to resolve the intended meaning of the parties' manifestations of assent, but unless one or both parties made an error as to those extrinsic facts, this is not a mistake issue, but an issue of determining the reasonable meaning of the words or conduct in context.

a. An Error in Judgment Does Not Qualify as a Mistake

A party cannot escape a disadvantageous or regrettable contract resulting from poor judgment. Say, for example, that a buyer of a plot of land purchases it in the belief that it is worth more than the asking price but then finds that this is untrue. Or a buyer of stock believes wrongly that the company is undervalued and the stock is considerably more valuable than its price. If these parties were to be allowed to avoid their obligations simply because they had judged wrongly, no transaction could be secure. Although this distinction can be drawn in principle, it is not always a simple matter to distinguish an error in judgment from a mistake of fact. Judgments are usually based on fact, and less obvious cases could require some unraveling.

A famous nineteenth-century case and a late twentieth-century one illustrate the subtle distinction between a mistake of fact and one of judgment. In *Sherwood v. Walker*, 33 N.W. 919 (Mich. 1887), a cattle breeder, believing a highly pedigreed cow to be infertile, sold it as a beef cow for a fraction of its value. Before delivery, the seller discovered the cow to be pregnant and he refused to deliver it to the buyer. The buyer sued to compel delivery but the court allowed the seller to avoid the contract for mistake. The majority and dissenting opinions differ on whether the belief that the cow was infertile should be treated as a mistake. The majority thought that it was, but the dissent felt that the cow's ability to breed was really a question of judgment. In the dissent's view, neither party knew for sure that the cow was infertile. The seller gambled that it was, and the buyer that it was not. The buyer's judgment was right and he should not be deprived of the fruits of his successful speculation.

Firestone & Parson, Inc. v. Union League of Philadelphia, 672 F. Supp. 819 (E.D. Pa. 1987), involved the sale of a painting attributed to Albert Bierstadt, the celebrated landscape painter. At the time of the sale, art experts regarded the painting as Bierstadt's and the parties had no reason to believe otherwise. As a result, it was sold for $500,000. Several years after the sale, scholarly research revealed that the painting was not by Bierstadt. As a result, it was worth only a tenth of what the buyer paid for it. The buyer sued for avoidance of the contract. The suit was dismissed because the statute of limitations had run. However, the court discussed the claim of mistake and suggested that even had the buyer sued in time, the contract would not have been avoidable. The value and authorship of a work of art, based on the decision to accept expert opinion, is more a matter of judgment than of fact.

b. An Incorrect Prediction of Future Events Is Not a Mistake

A future event may one day become a fact, but it is not a fact until it has happened. Therefore, as a rule, it is generally accurate to say that the mistake must relate to a fact in existence at the time of contracting. A party cannot claim relief for an erroneous prediction. This is often closely related to point *a* above, because most predictions at the time of contract are speculations concerning the future value of the transaction and are therefore in the nature of judgments. As with judgments, predictions are usually based on data derived from current facts, so it can be difficult to decide if an erroneous prediction should be treated as a mistake and difficult to predict how a court might characterize it. For example, based on a careful analysis of current trends and new construction projects, an investment company predicts that a run-down neighborhood is on the verge of a renaissance and buys several properties in the neighborhood. Although this prediction is based on existing facts, it is nevertheless a prediction and if it turns out to be wrong, it is not a mistake in the legal sense, but simply an erroneous prediction (or misjudgment) of profitability.

Paramount Petroleum Corporation v. Superior Court, 227 Cal. App. 4th 226 (2014), illustrates the distinction between an error of fact and an erroneous prediction—a judgment of what will happen in the future. Paramount had entered into a multiyear requirements contract with GAF, a roof tile manufacturer, to supply all GAF's requirements of asphalt used in the fabrication of the tile. The price to be paid for the asphalt was based on an index keyed to the price of crude oil in a specific market. (Asphalt is derived from crude oil.) Because of an unexpected glut of crude oil as a result of significant quantities of oil from fracking entering the market selected in the contract, there was a dramatic reduction in the price of crude oil in that market. This caused the pricing formula in the contract to become unrealistically low. After failing to get GAF to agree to a different pricing formula, Paramount terminated the contract and GAF sued it for breach. Paramount raised the defense of mistake, but the court held that the selection of the pricing formula was not a mistake but an error in judgment—Paramount made the erroneous judgment that the pricing formula would work for the period of the contract.

c. A Mistake of Law Could Qualify as a Fact

Courts differ in their approach to errors of law. Some courts are willing to treat the legal rules applicable to a transaction as facts—to see those legal rules as constituting an existing state of affairs that can be objectively ascertained. On this approach, a mistake of law could be the basis for relief. For example, in *Mattson v. Rachetto*, 591 N.W.2d 814 (S.D. 1999), the court held that a party to a sale of land could rescind the contract on grounds of mistake where both parties operated under the mistaken belief that a leaseback right provided for in the contract (that is, a provision in the contract that the buyer would lease the property to the seller following the sale) was lawful. The parties did not know that a state statute invalidated such leasebacks. Other courts, motivated by the rationale that parties are expected to know the law (embodied in the well-known maxim, "ignorance of the law is no excuse"), have refused to treat a mistake as to the law as a basis for relief under the doctrine of mistake. For example, the court adopted this approach in *Burggraff v. Baum*, 720 A.2d 1167 (Me. 1998), which involved a sale of seafront property. The buyers and seller both believed, based on the buyers' research of the applicable zoning ordinance, that the buyers would be able to build a cabin on the property 75 feet from the water. The buyers had erred in their research. After the sale, they discovered that they had overlooked another statute that required a 250-foot setback from the water. Upon discovering the error, the buyers sought rescission. The court refused relief on the grounds that the mistake related to law, not fact, and the parties are presumed to know the law.[1] In *Janusz v. Gilliam*, 947 A.2d 560 (Md. 2008), the court refused to allow avoidance of a divorce settlement agreement on the ground of mistake where the spouses had entered the agreement in the erroneous belief that federal regulations entitled the wife to a survivor's annuity under the husband's pension plan.

Even if a court does treat an error of law as a mistake of fact, the maxim "ignorance of the law is no excuse" could still have an impact on the right of avoidance. The court might deny avoidance because the party claiming

1. The opinion made an interesting distinction. The court suggested that had the parties not known that any regulation existed, this ignorance might have been a mistake of fact. But once they knew that the setback was regulated and they erred as to the law's provisions, this was a mistake of law. This suggests that the court may have treated complete ignorance of the law as grounds for mistake, but not an error in legal research.

avoidance should have known the law and therefore bore the risk of mistake. (Risk allocation is discussed in sections 15.3 and 15.4.)

§15.2.2 Mutual and Unilateral Mistake

Established doctrine draws a distinction between mutual mistake, in which the error is shared by both parties, and the unilateral mistake of only one of the parties. This sounds like a simple distinction, but it can be quite subtle and elusive. This is because a mistake is only mutual if it relates to a factual assumption shared by the parties. That is, it is a joint premise of their bargain. A mistake is unilateral, not only in the obvious case where one party knows the true facts and the other does not but also where both parties may be unaware of the truth, yet the fact in issue affects the decision of only one of the parties—although neither realizes the error, the incorrect fact is a basic assumption of only one of the parties because the other does not use it as a basis for deciding to enter the contract. This means that the distinction between mutual and unilateral mistake is not necessarily merely a matter of deciding whether one or both parties had been misinformed. The contract must be interpreted in context to decide if it was built around the mutual assumption that a particular fact was true.

The distinction between mutual and unilateral mistake is best illustrated by bidding errors, which are commonly treated as unilateral mistakes. For example, the owner of a plot of land entered into a contract with an excavator to excavate the land in preparation for a building. In determining the price charged under the contract, the excavator made an arithmetical error in calculating the number of hours required to perform the excavation and accordingly submitted a bid 25 percent lower than its actual cost of doing the work. The owner, not realizing the error, accepted the excavator's figure. This may sound like a mutual erroneous assumption that the excavator's calculations are correct because both parties did not know the true facts. However, it is better treated as a unilateral error of the excavator because the determination of the price that it will charge for its work is the responsibility of the excavator, not the owner. The owner was not privy to the data used by the builder to reach a decision on the price to be charged, played no role in determining the price, and merely accedes to it if it is acceptable. *Bert Allen Toyota, Inc. v. Grasz*, 909 So. 2d 763 (Miss. Ct. App. 2005), is another example of a unilateral mistake relating to pricing. An auto dealer's computer miscalculated the price of a pickup truck, resulting in a sale price $2,000 lower than it should have been. The dealer argued that this was a mutual mistake because both parties relied on the erroneous price calculated by the computer. The court disagreed. The buyer was interested only in what it would cost him to buy the truck and the miscalculation that led to the final price was the dealer's unilateral mistake. These examples provide some insight into the determination of whether a mistake is mutual or unilateral. However, they are not meant to enunciate a firm rule for making this distinction, which is a question of interpreting the contract to decide on the relationship of the mistaken fact to the basis of the contract.

Although it may be tricky to distinguish mutual from unilateral mistake, an incorrect classification will often not have an impact on the outcome of the case because both forms of mistake have essentially the same elements and involve the same basic inquiry: Which party should suffer the consequences of the error, in light of the factual indications of contractual intent and the surrounding equities? The principal difference between their elements is that unilateral mistake calls for a stronger focus on the reliance interest of the nonmistaken party so that the party who made the unilateral mistake must demonstrate that the unfairness of enforcing the contract outweighs the need to protect the reasonable reliance of the other party.

§15.3 THE ELEMENTS OF MUTUAL MISTAKE

According to Restatement, Second, §152 (read with §§151 and 154), a mutual mistake is avoidable by the adversely affected party if the following prerequisites are satisfied:

1. *At the time of contracting, the parties must have shared an error of fact.* As noted already, to allow for avoidance, the mistake must be an error relating to a fact. The error must be made at the time of contracting and it must relate to a state of affairs existing at the time, rather than one predicted to occur in the future.
2. *The erroneous fact was a basic assumption on which the contract was made.* The mistaken fact must be so fundamental to the shared intent and purpose of both parties that it is reasonable to conclude that they would not have made the contract at all or on the present terms had they known the truth. For example, the seller sold a lakefront lot to the buyer for $500,000. The price was that high because this is a prime waterfront location surrounded by expensive homes in a popular vacation area. The seller knew that the buyer intended to build a luxury home on the lot and both parties believed that the lot was suitable for building. Neither party knew at the time of contracting that the lot is on porous and unstable land and it cannot support a building. Given the parties' shared understanding of the purpose of the sale, the mistake is the basis of the bargain.
3. *The mistake must have a material effect on the agreed exchange of performances.* This sounds like a repetition of the prior element, because it would seem to follow that an erroneous basic assumption of the contract will

inevitably have a material effect on the exchange. This is often true, but the focus of these elements is different. The test of basic assumption examines the relationship of the incorrect fact to the underlying purpose of the contract, as understood by both parties, but materiality calls for an assessment of the mistake's impact on the balance of the exchange to see if it substantially deprived the adversely affected party of the value expected. Restatement, Second, §152, Comment c, suggests that the test is whether the error creates an overall imbalance between the parties by making the exchange less desirable to the adversely affected party and more advantageous to the other. This element thus contains a component of equitable balancing, in which the court examines the effect of the mistake on both the parties to decide the fairness of enforcing the contract despite the mistake.

Sometimes, the materiality of the effect on the exchange is obvious. For example, if the land in the above illustration is worth only \$25,000 because it cannot support a building, the contract price of \$500,000 reflects the contrary erroneous belief. The mistake not only forms the basis of the bargain but also has a material effect on the exchange. However, the interaction between the basis of the bargain and materiality could be subtler. Say that the lakefront location is so desirable that the land can be resold to a campground operator for \$500,000 despite its unsuitability for building. The evaluation of materiality is more difficult, and it could lead to a different conclusion. Although the mistake still forms the basis of the bargain, the mistake might not have a material effect on the exchange because it did not affect the market value of the property. This is not to say that the effect of the mistake is unquestionably immaterial. After all, the buyer is deprived of the benefit of using the property as contemplated. However, this illustration shows that the considerations taken into account to decide materiality are different from those relating to the parties' basic assumption and could lead to a different conclusion.

4. *The adversely affected party must not have borne the risk of the mistake.* Although this question is commonly phrased so as to focus on the assumption of risk by the adversely affected party, the issue is to allocate the risk of error to one party or the other. There is no such thing as a neutral decision on risk because a determination that one party did not bear the risk inevitably means that the other did. The allocation of risk is often the dispositive element in mistake cases. Despite everything that has been said up to now, and no matter how serious the error, if the adversely affected party bore the risk of mistake, there can be no avoidance of the contract.

The first place to turn for an answer to the question of which party assumed the risk of the mistake is the contract itself. The resolution is clearest if the contract expressly addresses the risk. In the example involving the sale of the lakefront property, allocation of risk would be clear if the contract for the sale of the lakeside lot states, "The seller acknowledges that the buyer contemplates erecting a building on the property but the seller neither represents nor warrants that the lot is suitable for building. The buyer bears the risk that the property may not be suitable for building and may not terminate this contract on the ground that it cannot be built upon." In *Gibbs v. Gilleland*, 2016 WL 792418 (Tenn. Ct. App. 2016), the buyers of land sought to avoid the contract on grounds of mistake after they discovered that the property was below the county's base flood elevation. The buyers argued that the parties entered into the contract under the mutual mistake that the land was suitable for construction of a house. The court denied relief because the contract allocated the risk of unsuitability of the property for building by stating that the buyers waived inspection and bought the property in its condition at the time of closing.

Even if the contract is not that clear, risk allocation may be inferred from the contract terms in context by the usual process of interpretation or construction. As always, factual interpretation is attempted first, but if no evidence of actual agreement can be found, the court must assign the risk in the way most reasonable under the circumstances, based on general expectations and practices in the market or community. That is, the court must resolve the question by construction, determining how the parties would reasonably have allocated the risk, had they thought of the issue.

Many different factors may come into play in the process of construing risk allocation. If a pertinent commercial practice exists, it is a strong indicator of the parties' reasonable expectation of risk. For example, it would be useful to know if buyers of land normally investigate its suitability for building. If so, this buyer's failure to investigate would be an assumption of the risk of error. Similarly, if loss or liability can be insured against in transactions of this type, it would be helpful to know which party normally takes out the policy. In some cases, there may be a legal rule that dictates or suggests risk allocation in the absence of contrary agreement. For example, the rule of *caveat emptor* (buyer beware) usually applies to a sale of real estate, so the buyer bears the risk of any defect in the property in the absence of an express warranty by the seller. The relative responsibility of the parties to ascertain the true state of affairs is also a consideration. If one of the parties had greater responsibility for investigating the facts, that party's lack of diligence in ascertaining the facts will likely influence the allocation of risk to that party.

A party might be deemed to have borne the risk of a mistake relating to a fact where the party could have found out the fact by due diligence and yet proceeded with the transaction without taking the trouble to determine it. Courts sometimes refer to this as conscious ignorance of the fact. The majority and dissent in *Eisenberg v. Hall*, 147 A.D.3d 602 (N.Y. App. Div. 2017), had different views about whether the buyer of forged antiquities may have been consciously ignorant of the fact that they were not genuine. Eisenberg, the buyer, was a dealer and self-proclaimed expert in antiquities. He bought a roman bust and Etruscan statue from Hall, another art dealer. Both parties believed that the works were genuine antiquities, but it was later discovered that they were relatively recent copies. Eisenberg sought to avoid the contract on grounds of mutual mistake and the issue was whether he assumed the risk of the mistake by relying on his own expertise instead of consulting the more highly qualified experts who later determined that the pieces were not genuine. The majority held that it was a question of fact, to be decided at trial, whether Eisenberg was justified in relying on his own expertise. However, the dissent argued that, given the expertise of both Eisenberg and Hall, and their mutual belief that the works were genuine antiquities, there was no basis for holding that Eisenberg acted out of conscious ignorance in relying on his own expertise in evaluating the authenticity of the works—he did not have reason to consider that his knowledge was limited, and did not make the conscious decision to proceed with the transaction in the face of insufficient information.

§15.4 THE ELEMENTS OF UNILATERAL MISTAKE

The elements of unilateral mistake are set out in Restatement, Second, §153. Relief for unilateral mistake has basically the same prerequisites as mutual mistake, with some variations to take account of the fact that the parties do not share the erroneous basic assumption. In addition, because the error affected the assent of only one of the parties, the protection of the reliance interest of the other party is emphasized more strongly. Therefore, unilateral mistake is grounds for relief only if the equities favoring release of the mistaken party outweigh the need to uphold the reasonable expectations of the nonmistaken party. (The presence of this element in unilateral mistake does not distinguish it from mutual mistake as significantly as one may think because the elements of mutual mistake also take into account the reliance interests of the party against whom avoidance is sought. Therefore, this express requirement of the balancing of the equities in unilateral mistake is a matter of stronger emphasis, rather than an element completely absent from mutual mistake.)

The elements for unilateral mistake are:

1. *The error concerns a fact.* This requirement is no different from mutual mistake.
2. *The fact is a basic assumption on which the mistaken party made the contract.* This corresponds to the similar element for mutual mistake, but focuses on the individual motive of only one of the parties, which has not necessarily been communicated to the other. This element is therefore more subjective than the corresponding formulation for mutual mistake, but the equitable balancing described in the fifth element protects the nonmistaken party's reliance on the mistaken party's manifestation of assent.
3. *The mistake has a material effect on the exchange, adverse to the mistaken party.* As with mutual mistake, this element concerns the mistake's objectively determinable impact on the exchange of values.
4. *The mistaken party must not bear the risk of the mistake.* The allocation of risk involves issues of interpretation and construction the same as those in mutual mistake, but any negligence of the mistaken party in causing the mistake plays an even stronger role in risk allocation because the mistaken party is most likely the party who had the responsibility to ascertain the correct facts. This does not mean that negligence invariably precludes relief if the other elements are satisfied, but the presence and degree of the mistaken party's negligence are highly relevant to the decision on whether to grant relief. For example, in *Bert Allen Toyota, Inc. v. Grasz*, cited in section 15.2.2, the court refused the dealer's claim for avoidance of the contract where its computer miscalculated the price. The court found that the dealer failed to exercise reasonable care when it did not check the computer's calculations, especially because it was aware that the computer had made errors before. The more serious the degree of negligence—such as gross negligence, recklessness, or dereliction of a duty owed to the other party—the greater the likelihood that the court will find that the risk of mistake should be borne by the party who could have avoided the error by taking greater care. Quite apart from its role in the element of risk allocation, the carelessness of the mistaken party could have an impact on the balance of the equities discussed below. That is, even if there has not been enough sloppiness or serious negligence to dispose of the case on the question of risk allocation, the mistaken party's fault could tip the balance in favor of the other party.

5. *The equities must favor relief for the mistake.* While equitable balancing takes into account factors beyond the first four elements, it obviously cannot be performed in isolation from them. In other words, the degree to which the first four elements are satisfied forms a vital component in the overall balance. Beyond this, the court also balances the impact of avoidance on the parties. It weighs the hardship that enforcement would have on the mistaken party against the hardship of avoidance on the other party. These equitable considerations are therefore quite far ranging. They take into account not only relative innocence and fault but also the economic consequences of avoidance on each of the parties.

   Therefore, the balance weighs most heavily in favor of the nonmistaken party when the mistake involved a degree of negligence by the other, the nonmistaken party had no reason to realize the mistake, and took action in reliance on the contract that has led to some commitment or expense. The protection of good faith reliance is the central issue, but the principle may be articulated in different ways—for example, it is sometimes expressed as a rule to the effect that a contract cannot be avoided for unilateral mistake unless the innocent nonmistaken party can be restored to the status quo. The balance of the equities also takes into account whether the mistaken party acted diligently and promptly in notifying the other upon becoming aware of the error, so as to ameliorate any prejudicial reliance on the mistake. At the other end of the scale, the nonmistaken party's reliance is at its weakest if the nonmistaken party caused the error or realized the error and kept quiet about it to grab a bargain. In fact, a party who knows that the other party has made a unilateral mistake and takes advantage of it could violate the duty of good faith and fair dealing, thereby committing fraud by nondisclosure.[2] Between these extremes, there are countless variations in relative fault and hardship, so that the balance may be harder to find.

   Drennan v. Star Paving, 333 P.2d 757 (Cal. 1958), discussed in section 8.10 in relation to the application of promissory estoppel to validate an option, also discussed unilateral mistake. A subcontractor made an error in its bid to the prime contractor which then used that bid in calculating its own bid to the owner. After the owner accepted the prime contractor's bid and the prime contractor was committed to the owner, the subcontractor discovered the error and attempted to revoke its own bid. The court applied the doctrine of

2. *See* section 13.6.3c.

promissory estoppel to make the subcontractor's bid irrevocable even though it did not qualify as option with consideration and the prime contractor had not accepted it before attempted revocation. Because the bid was irrevocable, acceptance by the prime contractor within a reasonable time created a contract with the subcontractor. The subcontractor raised unilateral mistake as an alternative basis for not being held to its bid, arguing that even if a contract had been created by the process of offer and acceptance, it should be avoidable because of the error in compiling the bid. The court rejected this argument and refused relief to the subcontractor for unilateral mistake. The error was caused by the subcontractor's negligence, and because there was a considerable variation in bids for the work, the prime contractor had no reason to suspect that the subcontractor's low bid was a result of error. The prime contractor had committed itself to the owner on the strength of the bid, and the equities favored leaving the loss with the subcontractor. In *Drennan*, the balance of the relative hardship on the parties was about even. However, the result could have been different if, say, the prime contractor had such a good profit margin in its contract with the owner that the extra cost of the subcontract could have been absorbed without making the prime contract unprofitable, but the subcontractor was in such perilous financial circumstances that the loss on this job might have put it out of business.

§15.5 RELIEF FOR MISTAKE

§15.5.1 Avoidance and Restitution

The principal remedy for mistake is avoidance of the contract. If the mistake is unilateral, the party seeking avoidance is the one who made the mistake. If the mistake is mutual, the party seeking avoidance is the one who is adversely affected by the mistake. Avoidance brings the contract to an end and both parties must restore any benefit (or its value) resulting from performance that was rendered prior to termination. Value is normally based on the market worth of the property or services (of which the contract value may be probative evidence). However, the court has some discretion in determining the basis of valuation, and it may use some other measure appropriate under the circumstances. For example, if the party who conferred the benefit was more to blame for the mistake, the value of consumed goods or services could be confined to the actual ultimate economic benefit enjoyed by the other party.

§15.5.2 Other Relief, Including Reformation

Although avoidance and mutual restitution is the standard and common remedy for mistake, the equitable derivation of mistake doctrine gives the court some flexibility in remedy, so that it could provide relief other than avoidance and restitution if the equities so dictate. For example, avoidance on the grounds of unilateral mistake could be ordered subject to the payment of reliance expenses designed to restore the nonmistaken party to the status quo.

In relatively rare cases, the court may keep the contract in force with an adjustment to its terms to counter the effect of the mistake. In the context of mistake, this remedy is known as reformation—that is, the court reforms the agreement to negate the effect of the mistake. As explained in section 15.6, reformation is more commonly used where the parties have not made a mistake of fact, but have made an error in recording the terms of their agreement. However, it is sometimes an appropriate exercise of the court's equitable discretion to use this remedy to alter the terms of the agreement so as to counteract a mistake of fact. Reformation is not a common remedy for mistake, and courts use it sparingly. It is not an appropriate remedy if the mistake is so fundamental that reformation would alter the entire character of the transaction or would defeat the contract's basic purpose. It is also seldom the best solution if the contract is entirely executory, and neither party performed or otherwise relied on it before the mistake was discovered. However, in some cases, if avoidance would be disruptive and the error relates to an aspect of the contract that can be adjusted (say to a price calculation), an alteration of terms may be a fair remedy. For example, the court did reform the contract's price term in *Aluminum Company of America v. Essex Group, Inc.*, 499 F. Supp. 53 (W.D. Pa. 1980).[3] The parties had made a mutual mistake in adopting a particular pricing formula, believing it to be an accurate predictor of Alcoa's costs. It turned out not to be, and the price payable under the formula fell far short of Alcoa's cost of performance. The court felt that it would be unfair to allow Alcoa to avoid the contract as a whole because this would completely deprive Essex of its bargain and would give Alcoa the windfall of full release from its contractual commitment. It therefore adjusted the price term to give Alcoa a profit that accorded with the parties' reasonable expectations.

---

3. In the *Alcoa* case, the facts were ambiguous enough to be treated either under mistake or impracticability doctrine. This is explained in section 15.7.1, which contains a fuller account of the facts of the case.

§15.6 MISTAKE IN TRANSCRIPTION

§15.6.1 Reformation to Correct Mistakes in Transcription

A mistake may relate not to a factual premise of the agreement but to the way in which the agreement is expressed in a record.[4] For example, a memorandum of agreement reflects the price of a piece of land as $280,000. The buyer contends that the parties had orally agreed to a price of $250,000, and that the recorded price is a typographical error not noticed by the parties when signing the document. If the parties later recognize that an error occurred in transcription and they act honestly, the problem can be disposed of simply by amending the record by agreement. However, the party who benefits from the error may claim (whether genuinely or disingenuously) that the record is correct. If so, the other party can seek the equity-based remedy of reformation to have the court correct the record so that it accurately reflects what was agreed. This remedy involves both a declaration by the court that the contract is on terms other than reflected in the record, and enforcement on those terms.

A mistake in transcription is completely different in nature from a mistake of fact, discussed in the prior sections. The error did not motivate the transaction but is in the record of the transaction—the problem is not that the manifestation is based on a faulty premise but that it incorrectly records the parties' agreement. Nevertheless, an error in expression has one thing in common with a mistake of underlying fact: In both cases one of the parties seeks to avoid the apparent meaning of a manifestation of assent by showing that it was induced by error. In the case of mistake as to an underlying fact, the goal is to negate assent and avoid the contract. When the mistake is in transcription, the desired relief is to have the record changed to reflect what was actually agreed. It must be stressed that the goal of reformation in this situation is to correct the record of the contract so that it reflects what was actually agreed, not to adjust or rewrite its terms. For example, in *Sikora v. Vanderploeg*, 212 S.W.3d 277 (Tenn. Ct. App. 2006), Sikora bought a chiropractic practice from Vanderploeg. Prior to the sale, the seller had a detailed financial report prepared, which included a disclosure of the earnings of the practice in the seven months prior to the sale. The buyer was given a copy of this financial report. The agreement of sale warranted the accuracy of the earnings stated in the report. However, in preparing the agreement of sale, the buyer's attorney made an error in drafting the warranty, which stated that the earnings were for a six-month period, not for seven months. After

4. In accord with the practice throughout this book, the word "record" is used instead of "writing" to reflect that a contract can be memorialized in either a tangible physical writing or an electronic record.

the buyer took over the practice, it deteriorated and its earnings declined. The buyer sued the seller, claiming that the contract misstated the presale earnings. The court held that since both parties intended the agreement to reflect the earnings in the report, and both had overlooked the error in the agreement, there was a mutual mistake in expression. The court therefore reformed the agreement, defeating the buyer's claim that the agreement falsely recited presale earnings.

A court will not reform a contract unless it is clear that both parties erroneously believed that the memorial of agreement embodied what they actually agreed. For example, in *Silsbe v. Houston Levee Industrial Park, LLC*, 165 S.W.3d 260 (Tenn. Ct. App. 2005), the last day for exercising an option turned out to be a public holiday. As a result, the option holder could not exercise it on that day, and the grantor refused to accept the exercise of the option on the following day. The option holder sought reformation of the contract on the grounds that the parties had mistakenly selected a public holiday as the deadline for exercising the option. The court refused reformation. Although the parties may not have realized that the deadline fell on a public holiday, this was the date that they intended. The option therefore correctly reflected the parties' intent and reformation would have changed the contract rather than corrected an error in expression.

Because a signed record is usually regarded as the most reliable evidence of what was agreed, a party seeking reformation has the difficult burden of showing that an error was indeed made in recording the terms agreed, as well as explaining why the error was made and then overlooked when the document was signed. Because the right to reformation cannot be shown except by recourse to evidence extrinsic to the record, the parol evidence rule does not bar the introduction of evidence for the purpose of showing a mistake in transcription. If it did, the remedy of reformation could never be used.

§15.6.2 Reformation to Rectify the Unintended Legal Effect of Language

A question of reformation could also be presented when the parties chose words in their record that do not have the legal effect intended. For example, a record of a contract for the sale of a car states that it is sold "as is." This is a legal term of art that means that it is sold without any warranties. However, the buyer contends that the parties were unaware of that meaning and did not intend it at all. The seller had added a number of accessories to the car, and the words "as is" were used merely to reflect their agreement that these accessories were to be included. This kind of error in recording the agreement is more complicated than a simple error in transcription, such as the incorrect recording of the price in the illustration in section 15.6.1, because the exact nature of the problem is less clear: If the dispute centers around what the parties meant by the term "as is," the determination of its meaning is a matter of interpretation, but if the evidence establishes that the parties had agreed on what the term meant but that they just used the wrong words to record that agreement, reformation is the more appropriate course. Also, it is difficult to distinguish this kind of erroneous expression of agreement from a mutual mistake of law. By wrongly using the phrase "as is" the parties do, in a sense, make a legal error—but that error relates not to what the law is, but to the legal meaning of the word-symbol used in the writing.

§15.7 IMPRACTICABILITY OF PERFORMANCE

§15.7.1 The Nature of Impracticability Doctrine, Contrasted with Mistake

Mistake concerns an error of fact in existence at the time of contracting, so fundamental to the premise of the contract that it precludes the formation of true assent. Impracticability applies when events following contract formation are so different from the assumptions on which the contract was based, that it would be unfair to hold the adversely affected party to its commitments. Although there are close affinities between mistake and impracticability, as demonstrated by similarities in their elements, they have an important difference in scope and purpose. A mistake causes a defect in contract formation, permitting a party to be excused from accountability for a manifestation of assent. Impracticability has nothing to do with any problem in formation and presupposes that a binding contract was made. Rather, it is concerned with whether a post-formation change of circumstances has such a serious effect on the reasonable expectations of the parties that it should be allowed to excuse performance wholly or in part.

An example illustrates this difference: The owner of a beachfront cabin makes a contract to sell it. The parties execute the contract at the owner's place of business in an inland city, many miles from the cabin. Unknown to both parties at the time of contracting, a tidal wave swept the cabin into the sea just a few hours before the contract was executed. They are mutually mistaken that the cabin exists. However, if the tidal wave hits after the contract was made, but before the seller transfers and delivers the cabin to the buyer, there was no error about its existence at the time of contracting. Instead, the issue is whether this supervening event should permit the seller to escape liability for failure to deliver the cabin as promised in the otherwise valid and enforceable contract.

Although it is usually easy to distinguish mistake from impracticability, sometimes the facts are ambiguous enough to make this unclear. The case could be resolved either on grounds of mistake or impracticability, depending on the court's perspective. For example, in *Aluminum Company of America v. Essex Group, Inc.*, cited in section 15.5.2, the parties entered into a long-term contract under which Alcoa would smelt alumina for Essex. The period of the contract was 16 years, with a five-year renewal option. The parties based their pricing formula on the Wholesale Price Index-Industrial Commodities (WPI). They used the WPI because it had reliably corresponded to Alcoa's costs of production in prior years and they assumed that it would continue to do so. However, a few years after the contract had been executed, electricity prices increased steeply because of the OPEC oil embargo and the higher cost of producing electricity in compliance with pollution regulations. As a result, the WPI ceased to be an accurate predictor of Alcoa's costs, which escalated to such an extent that its costs exceeded the contract price under the formula. Had Alcoa been obliged to perform the contract on its original terms, it would have lost about $60 million over the term of the contract. The court treated this as a case of mistake because it held that the parties erroneously assumed at the time of the contract that the WPI index was an appropriate standard for achieving the goal of measuring Alcoa's future costs. However, the court discussed impracticability as an alternative basis for relief because it recognized that the case fitted equally well into that doctrine—the oil embargo and tougher environmental regulations were supervening events that overturned a basic assumption of the contract.

The issue in an impracticability case is not whether the party can be forced to perform. Clearly, in the above example of the cabin being demolished by the tidal wave after the contract was executed, the seller cannot deliver it because it is flotsam on the ocean. The issue is whether, by failing to perform, the seller has breached the contract. If failure to perform is excused on grounds of impracticability, the seller is not in breach and is therefore not liable to pay damages for breach of contract to the buyer. On the facts of this example, impracticability would completely excuse the seller's performance. It follows, of course, that the buyer would not be required to perform either, so the effect of impracticability is to terminate the contract. In some situations, the supervening event may not affect the performance so extensively as to result in complete termination of the contract, but it could have enough of an impact to excuse performance on the exact terms of the contract. That is, performance can still be rendered, but not exactly as agreed, so that impracticability might excuse the deviation from the promised performance. In the sale of the cabin swept out to sea by the post-formation tidal wave, the complete impracticability of performance is obvious. However, say that there was no tidal wave, but an unexpected strike of county workers prevented the recording of the transfer of the cabin to take place on the date stipulated in the contract. This impracticability may not excuse the seller's performance in its entirety, but could excuse the seller's failure to transfer title on the date appointed by the contract.

The fact that impracticability is a defense to a claim of breach of contract, thereby precluding liability for damages for breach of contract, does not mean that there is no remedy where a contract is found to be impracticable. If either party has partly performed before this (say, for example, that the buyer made a down payment), the benefit of that performance must be restored under principles of unjust enrichment. This is illustrated by *Petrozzi v. City of Ocean City*, 433 N.J. Super. 290 (N.J. Super. Ct. App. Div. 2013). The city planned to perform a beach restoration project and had to get easements from beachfront property owners to access the privately-owned beach area in front of their properties. It obtained the easements under contracts with the owners in which it paid no monetary compensation for the easements, but instead undertook that it would create and maintain the dunes at a stated maximum height so as not to interfere with the owner's view of the sea. After the contracts were executed and the restoration was completed at the height required by the contracts, natural accretion caused the dunes to grow in height and width. The contract obliged the city to reduce the height of the dunes. However, its ability to do this was restricted by regulations, promulgated by the state after the contracts were executed, that required the city to obtain a state-issued permit to work on the dunes. The city applied for the permit, which was denied. The court held that the state's permit requirement and its denial of the permit were supervening events that met the required elements of impracticability (discussed below) and excused the city from performing its obligation to maintain the dunes at the height specified in the contracts. The owners therefore could not sue the city for breach of contract. However, the court recognized that because the city was excused from performing its part of the bargain, it had been unjustly enriched by not paying any compensation for the grant of the easements. The court therefore held that the owners were entitled to restitution based on what the city would have had to pay for the easements had the contracts provided for money compensation rather than maintenance of dune height.

§15.7.2 The Early Form of the Doctrine: Impossibility of Performance

In older common law, once a contract had been made, the parties were absolutely bound and remained committed even if a change in circumstances made it extremely difficult or even impossible for one of them to perform. Although the party could not actually perform the impossible, failure to perform was not excused by the supervening event and was a breach giving rise to a damages claim. By the mid-nineteenth century, the harshness of this rule was ameliorated by judicial recognition of the doctrine of impossibility of performance. In its original form, as articulated by the English case of *Taylor v. Caldwell*, 122 Eng. Rep. 309 (Queens Bench, 1863), the doctrine was quite narrow: If, when making the contract, the parties reasonably contemplated that its performance was dependent on the continued existence of a person or thing, the post-formation death of the person or destruction of the thing, not caused by the fault of the party seeking relief, would excuse performance by that party, and hence, also the return performance, resulting in termination of the contract without liability for breach.

In *Taylor*, the contract was for the hire of a music hall that burned down after the contract was made and before the time for performance. Although the obligation to provide the hall was not qualified by any express term of the contract, the court found the continuing existence of the hall to have been a basic assumption of the contract, and hence an implied term of the contract. As originally formulated, the defense of impossibility was confined to situations in which the change of circumstances made the contract objectively impossible to perform. That is, the event must have completely defeated the ability to deliver the performance, not only by this party but by a reasonable person in the party's position. Say, for example, that the fire merely damaged the music hall. If a reasonable owner could have restored it sufficiently in time for the performance, this owner's subjective inability or disinclination to do so would not support a defense of impossibility.

§15.7.3 The Contemporary Doctrine of Impracticability of Performance

During the course of the twentieth century, the doctrine of impossibility came to be perceived as too restricted. There are situations in which events do not make performance absolutely impossible, yet they place such a great and unexpected burden on the party that fairness demands relief. As a result, the scope of the doctrine has broadened and has been renamed "impracticability" in recognition of this change. Impracticability doctrine is articulated in both UCC §2.615 and Restatement, Second, §§261 to 272. There are a number of differences between UCC §2.615 and the provisions of the Restatement, Second, but the basic concepts are the same. This discussion focuses on general principles applicable to both.

If all of its elements are established, the excuse of impracticability is available to the party who is adversely affected by the change in circumstances. (In a sale of goods, UCC §2.615 assumes that it will always be the seller who claims impracticability, but this need not necessarily be so, and courts have recognized that a buyer can use the excuse in appropriate circumstances.) Although the following discussion identifies and discusses these elements separately, they are very much interwoven and that the facts affecting one are often relevant to the others. All the elements must be satisfied for the defense to be available. As in mistake, risk allocation is usually the predominant and pervasive consideration.

a. After the Contract Was Made, an Event Occurred, the Nonoccurrence of Which Was a Basic Assumption of the Contract

This concept is very much like its equivalent element in mistake doctrine, except that the basic assumption relates not to an existing but to a future state of affairs. When the parties entered the contract they expressly or impliedly made assumptions about the future course of events and these assumptions were a central motivation of the contract. Whether or not a basic assumption is articulated, it must be patent enough from the circumstances and the apparent purpose of the contract that it is reasonable to conclude that the parties must have shared it.

Having entered the contract on this basic assumption, the parties are then faced with an event so contrary to the assumption that it changes the very basis of the exchange. Official Comment 1 to UCC §2.615 describes this occurrence as an "unforeseen supervening circumstance not within the contemplation of the parties at the time of contracting." This suggests that the event must be so unexpected that the parties did not think of it at the time of contracting, or if they did, that they did not consider it to be a realistic likelihood.

The Official Comment uses the word "unforeseen," which must be distinguished from "unforeseeable." An event is unforeseen by the parties if they themselves did not contemplate it as a real likelihood. That is, although it could be imagined, the parties did not expect it to happen and contracted on the assumption that it would not. It may be a possibility, but is not treated by the parties as a probability. An event is unforeseeable if it could not have been conceived of by a reasonable person. To require unforeseeability would impose too stringent a test, making the defense of impracticability available only when the supervening event is beyond human experience. For example, it is unforeseeable that a music hall could be demolished by a rampaging dinosaur, a monstrous robot, or a fleet of alien space ships, but its destruction by fire is certainly within the range of possibility. Therefore, fire was foreseeable at the time of contracting, but it was not foreseen by the parties if, under all the circumstances, it is shown that they did not think of it at all or, even if one or both may have realized the possibility, it was not considered a strong enough likelihood to be raised and dealt with as a contingency. Of course, the fact that the event was unforeseen does not, on its own, mean that the defense of impracticability will succeed. This is only the first of the elements that must be satisfied. Often, even though the nonoccurrence of the event was a basic assumption of the contract, the risk of the occurrence may have been impliedly assumed by the party claiming impracticality. That is, if the parties foresaw the likelihood of the event, they probably allocated the risk of the event happening (expressly or impliedly) in the contract. However, even if they did not foresee it, commercial practice or other surrounding circumstances may give rise to an implication of risk assumption.

Impracticability arises from the occurrence of an event. Again, there is an analogy to mistake, in that an event is a factual situation, albeit one that arises after the contract. Most occurrences external to the contract qualify as events: war, a natural disaster, a strike, and so on. A change in the law or government regulation is also an event. Therefore, if the law changes to prohibit a performance that was lawful at the time of contracting, the change in the law defeats a basic assumption of the contract. UCC §2.615(a) and Restatement, Second, §264 expressly recognize this by providing that good faith compliance with governmental regulation excuses performance, even if the regulation is later found to be invalid. Say, for example, that the music hall did not burn down, but shortly after the contract was made, the city council strengthened its public safety regulations so that the hall no longer satisfied them and cannot be lawfully let for public performances. If the council's action was unexpected and was not publicized prior to formation of the contract, this would be an unforeseen contingency that defeats the basic assumption that the hall could be used lawfully for the purpose of the contract. This example highlights the development of the law from impossibility to impracticability. Although it would still be possible for the lessor to make the hall available and for the buyer to pay the rent, the contract is made impracticable because its basic assumption that the performance would be lawful has been overturned.[5]

A change in market conditions is generally not regarded as a contingency beyond the contemplation of the parties because the very purpose of setting a price or committing to a future delivery of goods or services is based on the possibility that prices or demand may change. Therefore, the basic assumption of most contracts is not that the market will remain constant, but that it might change. For example, in *Ferguson v. Ferguson*, 54 So. 3d 553 (Fla. Dist. Ct. App. 2011), *aff'd*, 239 So. 3d 63 (Fla. App. 2018), the parties entered into a divorce settlement agreement under which the husband kept the marital home. In exchange, he agreed to refinance it and to pay the wife $185,000. Until that payment was made, the wife and child had the right to reside in the house. Shortly after the agreement was executed, home

5. In anticipation of the discussion in section 15.8, it is also worth pointing out that these facts would support an argument that the purpose of the contract has been frustrated: Although the lessor can still deliver possession of the hall and the lessee can still pay the rent, the purpose of the hiring—the use of the hall for a public concert—has been negated by the new regulations. This illustrates the observation in section 15.8 that impracticality is broad enough to cover most, if not all, situations that would have required a separate doctrine of frustration in earlier law.

prices in Florida plunged. The husband claimed that because of this downturn in the market, he had not been able to refinance the house, and it had therefore become impracticable to make payment to the wife. He sought to evict the wife, sell the house, and give her half the net sale proceeds. The court held that the impracticability doctrine did not excuse the husband from performing his promise in the settlement agreement to pay the wife $185,000. The Florida real estate market is subject to periodic downward adjustment, and a market decline is not an unanticipated circumstance in a market-based economy.

This does not mean that a market disruption could never be grounds for claiming impracticability. The basic assumption of any particular contract is a factual question. It is therefore possible that a constant market was assumed in a contract, or even if not, that the market variation results from a disruption which causes changes way beyond reasonable expectations. This is particularly so if some unexpected calamity, such as a sudden war, embargo, or natural disaster is the cause of the market changes. This has happened a number of times, and there are cases arising from events such as the Suez crisis of the 1950s (when Egypt blocked the canal, making it impracticable for shipping companies to use it), the Vietnam War, and the OPEC oil embargo of the 1970s, in which the supplier of a commodity or service has claimed impracticability based on greatly added expense or burdens on performance caused by the crisis. Most recently, the disruption caused by the COVID pandemic has generated a significant amount of litigation, in which one of the parties claimed excuse based on impracticability (or, alternatively, frustration of purpose).

Courts have sometimes allowed relief for impracticability resulting from the COVID pandemic, but the defense often does not succeed. For example, the defense failed in *Le Fort Enterprises, Inc. v. Lantern 18, LLC*, 199 N.E.3d 1257 (Mass. 2023). Lantern bought a home cleaning franchise from Le Fort, the price to be paid by installments over a set period. About 19 months later, COVID struck and the Governor issued an executive order shutting down non-essential businesses, which included home cleaning businesses. Lantern could not operate its franchise for several months, until the order was lifted, and it continued to struggle thereafter because its business declined precipitously when many of its customers still chose not to have cleaners in their homes. As a result, it missed several payments due under the franchise agreement, and Le Fort sued it for breach of contract. Lantern raised the defense that the Governor's prohibition and the continuing decline in business afterwards created a temporary impracticability, which excused its suspension of payments. The court rejected the defense. There was no requirement in the contract that payments had to come out of franchise revenue, and Lantern had not produced any evidence from which a factfinder could rationally conclude that the pandemic made it objectively impossible for Lantern to make the payments, which could have been made from sources other than franchise revenue. Mere difficulty in performing is not enough, and Lantern bore the risk that changing market conditions might reduce the revenues from its business.

The courts were similarly unsympathetic in *Vereit Real Estate, LP v. Fitness International, LLC*, 365 So. 3d 442 (Fl. Dist. Ct. App. 2023), and *AWG Sono Partners, LLC v. Downtown Soho, LLC*, 273 A.3d 186 (Conn. 2022). *Vereit* involved a 15-year lease of premises between Vereit, the lessor, and Fitness, the lessee, under which Fitness would operate a gym on the premises. As in *Le Fort*, the Governor's executive order at the start of the COVID pandemic forced the closure of the gym. Fitness was not able to operate its gym for about three months and suspended its rent payments during that period. Fitness claimed that the suspension was justified on the basis that its performance had become impracticable as a result of the executive order. The court rejected this excuse. The lease had a force majeure clause[6] that allowed for the suspension of performance for various reasons, including restrictive laws, but the clause made it clear that this did not apply to financial inability or permit suspension of monetary payments. The court held that the force majeure clause allocated the risk of reduced revenue to Fitness, and it therefore could not claim that the forced closure of its business excused the payment of rent. *AGW Sono* also involved a commercial lease under which Downtown Soho leased restaurant premises from AGW. As in the other cases, the restaurant was forced to close as a result of a Governor's order at the start of the pandemic and Downtown suspended lease payments, claiming impracticability. The court rejected the defense on the ground that closure of the restaurant did not prevent use of the premises or make rent payment impracticable because the restaurant still had the capacity to do takeout business, and the lease placed the burden on the tenant to comply with governmental laws and regulations.

Restatement, Second, §262 states that where the existence of a particular person is necessary for the performance of a duty (that is, where the contract contemplates the personal performance of a particular person), the death or incapacity of that person is to be treated as an event, the nonoccurrence of which was a basic assumption of the contract. Comment *a* to §262 suggests that the usual assumption should be that death or incapacity will excuse personal services unless the contract makes the contrary intention clear. Obviously, a dead person cannot perform personal services, so this is a form of objective impracticability, but the issue in impracticability is not whether the party can be compelled to perform the impossible but whether nonperformance is a breach giving rise to a cause of action for damages. The possibility of death or incapacity of the party is certainly foreseeable, and

6. The purpose of a force majeure clause is to allocate the risk of identified types of events to one or the other party. This type of provision is explained in the discussion of risk allocation in section 15.7.3d.

the crucial question in such a case will be which party assumed the risk of the death or incapacity.

b. The Effect of the Event Is to Render the Party's Performance Impracticable—That Is, Unduly Burdensome

The older test of objective impossibility is more certain than the flexible requirement of impracticability, which calls for a decision on how extensively the performance must have changed to qualify as impracticable. If impracticability merely required a showing of inconvenience, lack of profitability, or the loss of a better opportunity, it would be too easy for a party to escape a contract that turns out to be disadvantageous because of a change in the market or commercial environment. Therefore, relief is only appropriate if the change is extreme or very burdensome. In a sense, this requirement is similar to the element of materiality in mistake. The event must have such a severe impact on the performance that it cannot be rendered without great loss, risk, or other hardship. A determination of whether the event satisfies this standard is based on all the facts of the case.

In the easiest case, an event that creates objective impossibility likely also renders the performance impracticable. Therefore, if the parties contemplated the rental of a specific music hall, it is relatively easy to conclude that the destruction of the hall makes performance impracticable. However, as the facts move beyond this clearer case, the determination becomes more difficult. Two examples illustrate this. First, although the hall burns down, there is another hall in the vicinity owned by a competitor of the lessor. This other hall is about the same size, is equally suitable for the performance, and it is available for the night of the concert. The lessee contends that the lessor's performance is therefore still possible, because there is nothing in the contract that makes the exact identity of the hall material, and the lessor can still provide appropriate premises by hiring the second hall and making it available to the lessee as a substitute for the destroyed hall. The problem is that the owner of the surviving hall demands an amount of rent from the lessor that greatly exceeds the rent to be earned under the contract, so the lessor will lose money by doing this. If the lessee's contention is correct and the identity of the hall was not a central term of the contract, the lessor's performance is not impossible, so the question becomes whether the loss to be incurred in finding a substitute renders it sufficiently burdensome to constitute impracticability. Second, say that the music hall did not burn down, but after the contract was made, the premium payable by the lessor for liability insurance increased tenfold because of a large number of theater fires in the region over the last year. The lessor dares not make the hall available as a concert venue without liability insurance, but if the lessor pays the increased premium, the lessor's costs will exceed the earnings from renting the hall. Both parties can still perform—the lessor can make the hall available and the lessee can pay the rent—but the increase in insurance rates has imposed a financial burden (or a massive risk of liability, if the policy is not renewed) on the lessor that may make its performance impracticable.

There is no definitive answer to the question in these cases. However, they point to the focus of the inquiry—the economic impact of the unforeseen supervening event. The magnitude and effect of the prospective loss are obviously of crucial significance, and a huge loss that threatens the party's financial survival is more likely to be seen as making the performance impracticable than a manageable smaller loss. This does not mean that the defense of impracticability can be easily invoked whenever a serious prospective loss is shown because this element is only one of several that must be satisfied, and proof of the most devastating loss is not enough to assure relief if the other elements are not also present.

c. The Party Seeking Relief Was Not at Fault in Causing the Occurrence

A party should not be able to claim impracticability caused by the party's own wrongful or negligent act. Thus, the lessor of the music hall cannot base a claim of impracticability on a fire caused by the lessor's deliberate arson or disregard of fire-safety requirements. Similarly, a party cannot be excused from liability where the failure of performance results from that party's incompetence. However, the issue of fault and its causal connection to the impracticability can be difficult to decide. In *CNA International Reinsurance Co. v. Phoenix*, 678 So. 2d 378 (Fla. Dist. Ct. App. 1996), the actor River Phoenix died from a drug overdose during the filming of two movies in which he was acting. The question was whether his estate was relieved from paying damages to the movie producers arising out of his failure to complete the movies. His estate argued that it was not liable for breach of contract because his death rendered the contracts impracticable, but the producers responded that Phoenix was at fault in creating the impracticability because he caused his own death by the drug overdose. The court rejected this argument in relation to contract for personal services because it felt it unwise for a court to assess blame for an individual's personal risk-taking, not directly related to the contract performance. The court simply applied Restatement, Second, §262 and held that the death of a party to a personal services contract makes performance objectively impracticable and therefore excuses that performance. (Note, however, that the question of fault also goes to the crucial issue of risk allocation, discussed in section d below.)

d. The Party Seeking Relief Must Not Have Borne the Risk of the Event Occurring

As with mistake, risk allocation is often the dispositive issue in impracticability cases. In many ways, the other elements foreshadow the question of risk allocation and build up to this crucial determination. In fact, the issue of risk allocation can be identified as a subtext in the above discussion of the other elements. The analysis of risk allocation is basically the same as for mistake: If the party adversely affected by the event had expressly or impliedly assumed the risk of its occurrence, the nonperformance cannot be excused even though all the other elements are satisfied.

The first place to look in determining risk allocation is the contract itself. If the parties realized that a particular future event could affect performance, the contract may have an express and specific term assigning risk. For example, a consignor of goods and a shipping company may contemplate the possibility that a war may break out along the route, requiring a diversion of the ship. If so, they may specifically state in the contract which party will bear the loss and expense of the diversion. Even if the parties do not have a particular contingency in mind, the contract may have a more general provision allocating the risk of disruptions or calamities. This is known as a force majeure clause. It may provide, for example, that the shipping company will not be responsible for any delay (or will have the right to charge for the cost of any diversion or delay) of the ship resulting from war, revolution, national disasters, governmental action, and other listed events.

Even in the absence of these more direct types of risk allocation clauses, the contract may impliedly place risk on a party by means of a provision such as a warranty, an undertaking to obtain insurance, or some other commitment from which the assumption of risk may be inferred. A term expressly allocating the risk of certain events to one party may give rise to the inference that the other assumed the risk of events not enumerated. For example, a clause states that the shipping company will not be responsible for delay caused by war, revolution, and governmental action. If the ship is seized by pirates and held hostage for ransom, this disruption is not apparently covered by the contract, so it could be inferred that the shipping company assumed this risk. It is good planning for the parties to consider potential risks and to provide for them clearly in the contract. This reduces the possibility of later disputes and litigation. Of course, as the last example suggests, no risk allocation provision is foolproof. It may fail to contemplate and provide for an event of the type that actually occurred.

If the contract terms do not settle the issue, its context, including normal commercial practices and expectations may provide some insight into where the risk should lie. For example, if *Taylor v. Caldwell* was decided today, a court may conclude, in the absence of a contract term providing otherwise, that the owner should bear the risk of the fire because property owners customarily insure their properties against fire and other damage. In *CNA International Reinsurance Co.*, the court did not discuss risk allocation, but the effect of its decision was to allocate the risk of Phoenix's death to the movie producers. It is not clear that this was the right allocation of risk because it is arguable that the risk of inability to render personal performance should fall on the individual who undertakes to render it. However, there was another factor in the case that may have influenced the court's decision—the movie producers had taken out insurance to cover their losses if Phoenix failed to complete the filming. (The insurers had compensated the producers for their loss and were the actual plaintiffs in the case, seeking reimbursement from the estate.) The fact that a party has insured against an event is a factor taken into account in allocating the risk of that event to that party.

§15.7.4 Relief for Impracticability

When impracticability fully defeats the feasibility of performance by a party, it is a complete defense to that party's failure to perform, excusing the duty of performance and liability for damages. Release of that party's performance obligation also discharges the contractual duties of the other. If any performance had been rendered by either party under the contract prior to the finding of impracticability, the benefit or its value must be returned, measured in accordance with the same restitutionary principles applicable to mistake. This is illustrated by *Petrozzi v. City of Ocean City*, discussed in section 15.7.1.

If impracticability does not go to the entire basis of the contract, the court has the discretion to award relief short of fully excusing performance. It may be more appropriate to adjust the terms of the contract to excuse a portion of the performance (with any appropriate reciprocal reduction in counterperformance), or in some cases to excuse a delay in performance resulting from the event. This is articulated in Official Comments 6 and 7 to UCC §2.615, which recognize the court's equitable discretion to excuse performance partially where the impracticability does not fundamentally affect the entire performance, and in Restatement, Second, §§269 and 270, which recognize relief short of complete excuse where the impracticability is temporary or partial.

§15.8 FRUSTRATION OF PURPOSE

The doctrine of frustration of purpose developed as an extension of the original doctrine of impossibility. It was designed to provide relief when an unexpected supervening event did not render performance impossible, yet it so destroyed its value to a party as to frustrate the contract's underlying purpose. The case responsible for this extension of the impossibility doctrine was *Krell v. Henry*, 2 K.B. 740 (1903). Krell owned a flat on the route to be taken by the coronation procession of King Edward VII. Krell placed a sign in the window stating that the flat was available to be let for viewing the procession. Henry responded to the sign and contracted to hire the flat on the two days of the coronation celebrations. The King became ill before the coronation, and it was postponed, so Henry was left with no need for the premises on the days in question, and he did not use them. Krell sued him for the balance of the agreed rental. (Henry had made a down payment but apparently did not pursue a counterclaim for a refund of the deposit.) The court resolved the case by using an adaptation of the impossibility defense of *Taylor v. Caldwell*. Although the contract did not expressly state the purpose of the rental of the flat, both parties understood that Henry's sole purpose in making the contract was to view the coronation procession. This purpose was the very foundation of the contract. The postponement of the coronation was a supervening event that had not reasonably been contemplated by the parties at the time of contracting. Although it did not make either party's performance impossible (Henry could still pay the agreed rent and Krell could give him possession of the flat), it so defeated the purpose of the contract that it should excuse Henry's performance.

Since impossibility doctrine has expanded to encompass impracticability, which is no longer confined to objective impossibility, most cases of frustration could probably be resolved by using impracticability doctrine. In fact, in several of the cases discussed in section 15.7.3 on impracticability (for example, *Le Fort Enterprises, Inc. v. Lantern 18, LLC*; *Vereit Real Estate, LP v. Fitness International, LLC*; and *AWG Sono Partners, LLC v. Downtown Soho, LLC*) the party seeking relief argued for frustration of purpose in the alternative, and the result was the same under each of the doctrines. This lessens the need for a separate doctrine of frustration of purpose, but these closely linked defenses continue to coexist and are treated by courts (and by Restatement, Second, §265)[7] as separate but allied. It is therefore necessary to understand what distinguishes them from each other. The only difference between them lies in the sometimes subtle distinction between an event that makes a party's performance unduly burdensome, and one that makes it pointless. Beyond that, the elements of the two doctrines are identical, involve the same issues, and would lead to the same result.

Like impracticability, frustration is concerned with a post-formation event, the nonoccurrence of which was a basic assumption on which the contract was made. This event must not have been caused by the fault of the party whose purpose is frustrated, and that party must not have borne the risk of its occurrence. The essential difference lies in the effect of the event. It does not directly affect the performance of the adversely affected party by making it unduly burdensome. Rather, its impact is on the benefit reasonably expected by that party in exchange for the performance.

7. UCC Article 2 has no doctrine of frustration of purpose, so cases of frustration in sales of goods must be dealt with either by resolving them as impracticability cases under §2.615 (which is broad enough to encompass frustration of purpose as well) or by applying the common law doctrine of frustration of purpose.

The event so seriously affects the value or usefulness of that benefit that it frustrates the contract's central purpose for that party. This cannot be a secret or obscure purpose, because a party's private motivation is not relevant to the contract and cannot be the basis of disappointing the other party's reliance. Therefore, the purpose must be so patent and obvious to the other party that it can reasonably be regarded as the shared basis of the contract. *Krell v. Henry* remains one of the best illustrations of a shared basic assumption. Note, however, that the court did not pay much attention to the crucial question of risk allocation. This was raised in a concurring opinion that queried whether Henry, the lessee, may have been the more appropriate party to bear the risk of the coronation's postponement. This is a fair question, and it reinforces the point that when the contract does not itself provide for risk allocation, it is not always easy to know who should suffer the loss caused by the frustration. It is by no means self-evident that the court was right in imposing it on the lessor rather than the lessee.

The purpose of most commercial contracts is to make a profit. However, although it could be said that profit is the underlying purpose of a contract, this does not mean that a party can invoke the doctrine of frustration of purpose merely because the contract is no longer profitable to that party as a result of events after contract formation. A party cannot so easily escape the performance of a contract that turns out to have been a bad deal. This distinction was made in *Karl Wendt Farm Equipment Co. v. International Harvester Co.*, 931 F.2d 1112 (6th Cir. 1991). Following losses resulting from a bad downturn in the farm equipment market, I.H. sold its farm equipment division and terminated a number of dealerships. The plaintiff, one of the terminated dealers, sued I.H. for breach of contract. I.H. raised the defense of frustration of purpose on the grounds that the loss of profit from adverse economic conditions frustrated the purpose of the contract. The court rejected the defense of frustration of purpose. It said the primary purpose of the contract was to sell farm equipment. This purpose could still be achieved, even if the desired goal of profitability could not be.[8]

8. I.H. also raised the defense of impracticability, which the court also rejected. It held that the poor market conditions were not so severe as to pass beyond the range of the normal risk that I.H. bore, and the impact of the market downturn was not grave enough to constitute undue hardship to I.H. The fact that the circumstances of the case gave rise to alternative arguments of impracticability and frustration of purpose, and that both failed, shows the close connection between the doctrines.

§15.9 A TRANSNATIONAL PERSPECTIVE ON MISTAKE, IMPRACTICABILITY, AND FRUSTRATION

The CISG does not deal with mistake. (As noted in section 13.14, Article 4 of the CISG states that it is not concerned with the validity of a contract.) Any question of mistake would therefore be resolved under domestic law in an international sale of goods. Articles 3.4 and 3.5 of the UNIDROIT Principles cover mistake. Articles 3.17 and 3.8 are general provisions that deal with the effect of avoidance on any grounds, including mistake. Although the concepts are phrased slightly differently from the common law, the basic tenor of the doctrine is largely comparable to the common law. Article 3.4 defines a mistake as an "erroneous assumption relating to facts or to law existing when the contract was concluded." Article 3.5 sets out the elements of mistake. Unlike the common law, it does not specifically distinguish mutual and unilateral mistake. Article 3.5(1)(a) generally permits avoidance if the mistake was objectively material and the other party made the same mistake or caused the mistake, or knew or should have known of the mistake. Article 3.5(1)(b) provides an alternative basis for avoiding the contract for mistake: if the mistake was objectively material and the other party has not yet acted in reliance on the contract. Article 3.5(2) precludes avoidance if the party bore the risk of the mistake or was grossly negligent in making the mistake. Under Article 3.17, mutual restitution is available upon avoidance for mistake. However, Article 3.18 allows for the possibility of a claim of compensatory damages if the nonmistaken party knew or had reason to know of the mistake.

Article 79(1) of the CISG contains a principle equivalent to impracticability, under which a party is not liable for a failure to perform obligations under a contract if it proves that the failure was due to an "impediment" that the party could not reasonably have been expected to take into account at the time of contracting, that was beyond its control, and that the party could not reasonably be expected to overcome or avoid. Article 7.1.7 of the UNIDROIT Principles excuses performance of a party as a result of "force majeure." (This term should be familiar, because it is used in common law to describe a general risk-allocation clause in a contract. *See* section 15.7.3d.) The concept of force majeure is similar to that used in Article 79(1) of the CISG: an "impediment" beyond the control of the party, which could not reasonably have been taken into account by the party at the time of contracting, and which the party could not have avoided or overcome. (In a sense, force majeure is equivalent to the common law concept of objective impossibility.) Apart from this, Article 6.2 recognizes a broader concept that is more akin to the doctrine of impracticability, but more restricted in its relief. It allows excuse for "hardship," which is not as severe as force majeure but makes performance more onerous for the party. Hardship occurs where supervening events "fundamentally alter the equilibrium of the contract," the events could not reasonably have been taken into account by the "disadvantaged party" at the time of contracting, they are beyond its control, and the disadvantaged party did not assume the risk of the events. Hardship does not necessarily result in complete excuse. It allows the disadvantaged party to request renegotiation of the contract, provided that it acts without undue delay. If the parties cannot settle the problem by negotiation, either party may ask the court to terminate or to adapt the contract to restore its equilibrium.

Examples

1. Tiffany De Canter owned an ornate silver jug. She inherited it from her grandmother who had told her that it was very valuable because it was made by Maestro Da Silva, an important nineteenth-century silversmith. Since she acquired it, Tiffany has had it examined by several experts. Although some of them thought that it might have been made by Da Silva, the prevailing view among them is that it was the product of one of his pupils. It has therefore been appraised at $10,000. Had it been authenticated as the work of Da Silva, it would be worth $1 million.

   Tiffany decided to sell the jug. She offered it to Sterling Silverman, an art collector, for $12,000. Sterling was familiar with Da Silva's work. He had a hunch that the experts may have been wrong in concluding that the jug was not made by Da Silva. He accepted Tiffany's offer to sell the jug for $12,000. The parties executed a simple written contract that set out the physical description of the jug and stated the price and delivery obligation. A few months after the sale was completed, a scholar unearthed some previously unknown notebooks and sketches by Da Silva that conclusively proved that he had made the jug.

   Can Tiffany avoid the sale to Sterling?

2. Manny Lisa recently became wealthy through the exercise of his stock options. All his newfound rich friends owned portraits of themselves painted by the celebrated society portraitist Leonardo De Fancy. Although he is clueless about art, Manny decided to get hold of the divine Leonardo and commission a portrait. He searched on the Internet for the name "De Fancy" and found the website of "Leonardo De Fancy, Portraitist." He called the number on the website and spoke to Leonardo, who agreed to paint his portrait for $250. Manny was astounded at how reasonable this was, and he accepted. The parties arranged a date for a sitting at the end of the week.

   A couple of days later, Manny discovered from a more worldly friend that the person whose website he visited is not *the* Leonardo but his father, Leonardo De Fancy the Elder, a talentless hack who ekes out a meager living by painting the children of middle-class suburbanites. Being unschooled in the ways of the art world, Manny had not known that a famous celebrity portraitist like Leonardo, the Younger, would not deign to have a website and only accepts commissions on referral. Furthermore, his charge for a portrait would be about 40 times what Manny had agreed to pay Leonardo the Elder.

Understandably, Manny no longer desires the portrait for which he contracted. Can he avoid the contract?

3. Reliabuild Contractors, Inc., was invited by the owner of property to submit a bid for the erection of a new building. Reliabuild planned to do all the work itself except for the excavation of the land. It needed to know the cost of excavation before it could complete its bid, so it sent the building plans to Bill Dozer, an earthmover whom it had used with satisfactory results on several prior projects. Bill studied the plans and calculated his own cost. Because Bill was very busy and distracted, he did not pay careful enough attention to this task and he miscalculated his cost as $500,000 instead of $800,000. He then added a 10 percent profit of $50,000 and submitted a written bid of $550,000 to Reliabuild. Reliabuild calculated its own bid on the basis of this figure and submitted it to the owner. Reliabuild's bid was about $400,000 less than the lowest competing bid, so the owner accepted it. Reliabuild then accepted Bill's bid.

   A few days before Bill was to begin his performance, he reviewed his bid and discovered his miscalculation. The error not only would deprive him of his expected profit but would result in a loss of $250,000. He could not absorb such a loss, which would put him out of business. Bill called Reliabuild immediately, explained the error, and withdrew from the contract. Reliabuild told Bill that it regarded this as a repudiation and would hold him liable for damages. Reliabuild then sought other bids and accepted the lowest one of $900,000. As a result, Reliabuild had to pay $350,000 more than it originally expected and lost about 40 percent of the profit it had anticipated on the project.

   Reliabuild claims the $350,000 from Bill as damages for breach of contract. Does Bill have a defense?

4. Change the facts of Example 3 as follows: Assume that when Bill explained the mistake, Reliabuild did not wish to drive him out of business by pressing its claim for damages. It therefore took pity on him and agreed to release him from his obligation. Reliabuild does not itself wish to assume the extra cost of employing a more expensive subcontractor, so it in turn seeks to withdraw from its contract with the owner. The owner is not so kind and threatens suit if Reliabuild does not perform as agreed. Can Reliabuild escape its contract with the owner?

5. Merlin Magnifico, Master of the Impossible, is a magician. On July 1 he entered into a contract with Showstopper Promotions, Inc., under which he agreed, for a fee of $500,000, to perform a magical extravaganza at the Pyro Palace Theater on August 30. This contract forms the basis of the separate and distinct factual variations set out in the following questions.
   a. On July 20, Merlin tried to perform the most daring escape trick ever attempted. He jumped out of a plane all trussed up like a turkey, allowing himself two minutes to free himself and pull his parachute cord. He succeeded in loosening his bonds, but in his feverish unraveling, also mistakenly untied his parachute harness. Is the estate of the late Merlin Magnifico liable to Showstopper for the substantial profits it lost as a result of having to cancel the show and refund the price of tickets sold?
   b. By July 15, all the tickets to Merlin's show had been sold, and people were clamoring to buy tickets from those who had been lucky enough to get them. Buck Fast had managed to buy a ticket for $200 when they first went on sale. His friend Fanny De Voted adored Merlin and desperately wanted to see the show. She nagged Buck to sell the ticket to her, offering an increasingly higher price each time he refused. By July 19 Fanny had increased her offer to $1,000. Buck gave in and sold the ticket to her. When Merlin was killed in the accident on July 20, Showstopper canceled the show and announced that ticketholders should return their tickets for a refund. Naturally, Showstopper will only refund the face value of the ticket, so Fanny demands that Buck repay her the excess of $800. Buck refuses. Is Fanny entitled to the return of her money?
   c. Change the facts of (a) so that Merlin did succeed in accomplishing the parachute trick. As a result, he became an instant worldwide sensation. He is now able to command a fee of $1 million for a booking. He does not wish to perform for Showstopper at the measly rate of $500,000. Can he escape the contract?
   d. Merlin did not perform the trick of July 20, so he was willing and able to perform his show on August 30. On August 15 the Pyro Palace burned down. Showstopper had sold almost all the tickets to the extravaganza and did not wish to cancel or postpone it. There is another theater in town that was available on August 30 and is suitable for staging the show. Showstopper proposed to change the show's venue to the other theater. Merlin refused to perform at the other theater. He argued that the parties intended the show to be performed at the Pyro Palace, and its destruction made the contract impracticable. Should Merlin be able to terminate the contract on this ground?
   e. Merlin did not perform the trick of July 20, so he was willing and able to perform his show on August 30. However, ticket sales for

the show were appalling. Despite intensive promotion, Showstopper had filled only 30 percent of the house by August 20. It is clear that Showstopper will incur a substantial loss if the show goes on. Showstopper takes the position that, known to Merlin, its obvious purpose in entering the contract was to make a profit. The supervening lack of interest on the part of the public has frustrated this purpose, and Showstopper is therefore entitled to cancel the contract with Merlin. Is this a good argument?

6. Jewel Bedecked enjoyed jewelry and had bought several pieces over the years. She recently bought a two-carat diamond ring from Bijou Bargains, Inc., a jewelry store. The stone in the ring was a natural mined diamond with a retail value of $40,000. However, the inexperienced store clerk misread the description of the diamond in Bijou's price list and thought that the diamond was a synthetic, laboratory-produced diamond, with a retail value of $3,000. The clerk therefore sold the ring to Jewel for $3,000. Bijou's manager realized this shortly after the sale. Bijou seeks to avoid the contract. Does it have grounds to avoid the sale?

7. Crystal Springer owns land on which a pristine spring is located. The sweet water emerges from the earth in a completely pure state. Crystal bottles her water and sells it to health food shops. Because Crystal's water is so exquisite, it is regarded as the champagne of bottled water. Although it is more expensive than other brands, it is whisked away by customers as soon as stores place it on the shelf. Holy Foods, a preeminent organic grocery store, entered into a contract with Crystal under which it bought 20,000 bottles of her water a year for five years, to be specially bottled for Holy Foods under its own "Holy Water" label. The contract provides a stated price for the water, to be adjusted at the beginning of each year in accordance with the Consumer Price Index. The contract makes no provision for changing the quantity of water supplied or terminating the contract.

   The contract was performed satisfactorily for two years. Just before the third year, Crystal's spring dried up. A hydrologist has determined that this was caused by an unusual phenomenon. A subterranean tremor had blocked the channel to the surface of the land and prevents the stream from reaching it. The problem can be rectified by an expensive excavation. Crystal can obtain a mortgage on the land to pay for the excavation, but the payments under the mortgage would be so high that Crystal could not expect to make a profit from sales of her bottled water for the next 15 years. Crystal therefore decided not to do the excavation. She notified her customers, including Holy Foods, that she would not deliver the water promised for the remaining years of their contracts.

The only source of water of a quality equivalent to Crystal's is in the foothills of the Himalayas. Holy Foods cannot economically import and bottle this water because the cost of transporting it would be so high that Holy Foods would have to charge more for it than even the most fervent "Holy Water" fans would pay. Holy Foods therefore abandoned its "Holy Water" brand. Holy Foods can prove a loss of profits as a result of termination of the brand. Is Crystal liable to Holy Foods for this loss?

8. Fifteen years ago, Commercial Development, Inc. developed a ten-acre office campus and sold lots to various buyers. The sales contemplated that the buyers would erect office buildings on the lots. Land Investments, Inc. was one of those buyers. Although all the other buyers had built on their lots since buying them, Land Investments had not developed its lot, which was the last piece of vacant land on the campus. Land Investments decided that it was time to erect a building on the lot and began planning it. One of the other lot owners heard about this and pointed out to Land Investments that a restrictive covenant on the land required the approval of any new building on the campus by Commercial Development's Architectural Review Committee, which it had established when it created the campus. The other lot owner told Land Investments that it would oppose the construction of the new building unless it had the approval of the committee. The problem was that Commercial Development had ceased business operations ten years ago and was no longer in existence, so there was no longer an Architectural Review Committee. This meant that enforcement of the restrictive covenant would place an insurmountable barrier to Land Investments being able to build on its land. Land Investments therefore sued for a declaratory judgment excusing compliance with the covenant. Do these facts indicate grounds for granting the declaratory judgment?

Explanations

1. This is a sale of goods, but mistake is not specifically dealt with in UCC Article 2, so it is governed by common law rules. Tiffany is a sophisticated seller who made her judgment without any reliance on a representation by Sterling or under any pressure from him. In the absence of deception or other improper bargaining, the only possible basis for avoidance is mistake.[9]

---

9. Under some circumstances, the sale at a grossly inadequate price could constitute substantive unconscionability. However, this is not the likely conclusion in this case where the low price did not result from any type of procedural unconscionability. These were sophisticated parties who entered into a negotiated contract. Neither of them was vulnerable and there was no wrongful bargaining conduct or an abuse of the power to impose an adhesive contract. Tiffany is most unlikely to succeed in arguing that the contract was unconscionable. *See* section 13.11.

The error in this case does not concern the actual identity of the jug itself, but of its maker. The identity of its maker is a fact, and the low price reflects an erroneous shared basic assumption (that is, a mutual mistake) about it. However, both parties were aware of the possibility of incorrect attribution, and if they were wrong, this is more a question of incorrect judgment. Tiffany gambled that she was correct in believing it to be a work of Da Silva's pupil, in which case, she obtained a good price, somewhat above its true market value. Sterling speculated that the experts might be wrong, in which case he would make a killing. When parties deal with each other in an arm's-length market transaction, their respective reliance interests are entitled to protection. One of them cannot be deprived of his bargain because it later turns out that the other made a poor judgment.

Thus, the case can be disposed of quickly by treating it as a misjudgment on Tiffany's part and not an error of fact at all. However, even if it was to be conceded that there was a mistake of fact, the analysis of risk allocation leads to the same result: Tiffany must be held responsible for her own judgment. The written contract simply describes the jug without making any representation of authorship, and there is no other term that expressly allocates the risk of error. In the absence of guidance in the contract itself, risk must be allocated to the party who should most appropriately bear it under all the circumstances of the transaction. When the parties knowingly enter a contract for the sale of a work of art of uncertain attribution, the risk must lie with the party whose judgment proves to be wrong. This is the resolution suggested in *Firestone & Parson, Inc.* and the dissent in *Sherwood v. Walker* discussed in section 15.2.1.

2. There are two possible arguments that Manny could make for avoidance, but both would be difficult to establish on these facts. He could claim that Leonardo the Elder made a fraudulent misrepresentation by creating a website under the name shared with his celebrated son and failed to make it clear on the website that he was not *the* Leonardo. This argument is tenuous. Although there is some chance of confusion, and maybe a possibility that Leonardo was consciously taking advantage of his son's name recognition, the two painters operate in different spheres. Leonardo the Elder has not misrepresented his name and he made no claim to be a society painter. In addition, the modesty of his fee suggests that he may not even have imagined that there would be any reasonable confusion. Furthermore, any duty that he may have had to alert potential customers to the fact that he was not *the* Leonardo seems to be outweighed by Manny's carelessness in not making proper enquiries to obtain easily ascertainable information, especially in light of the low price.

Manny's other possible argument is that the contract was induced by unilateral mistake. A mistake as to the identity of the other party is treated as a factual error. The mistake did relate to Manny's basic assumption in entering the contract. It is harder to say whether the error materially affected the exchange of values. Manny got what he paid for, but there could still be a material impact on the exchange because this was not the portrait that Manny bargained for. There is probably not much of a market for hack-painted portraits of the nouveau riche, so Manny does not have much chance of recouping the price by selling the painting.

However, even if these elements are satisfied, Manny is likely to lose on the allocation of risk and the equities. Manny may have been untutored in the ways of the art world, but he had ready access to information and advice and should have proceeded more carefully before committing himself to ordering a painting from the wrong artist. There do not seem to be strong equities for shifting the risk to Leonardo. There is nothing to suggest that Leonardo had reason to suspect an error and exploited it, and he has a legitimate reliance interest worthy of protection.

3. This Example does not implicate the promissory estoppel issue in *Drennan v. Star Paving*, discussed in sections 8.11 and 15.4, because the offer was accepted before Bill tried to revoke it. Therefore, the only issue is whether Bill's mistake is grounds for his avoidance of the contract.

This mistake is not mutual, but unilateral on Bill's part. In a sense, Reliabuild has also been in error over the correct price for the earthmoving, but this does not make the mistake mutual. The calculation of Bill's price is solely within his realm and forms his individual basic assumption. Reliabuild was not involved in the determination of Bill's price. It simply reacted to the end result of Bill's calculations, which it accepted without interest in knowing how Bill reached his price. Bill should not have much trouble in satisfying three of the elements of unilateral mistake: His cost in doing the work is a fact. It was a basic assumption on which he entered the contract. It materially affects the exchange, in that it causes him to undercharge so badly that his expected profit becomes an unbearable loss.

He is not likely to do as well with the issues of risk allocation and equitable balancing. His miscalculation is not simply a matter of conscientious error, but results from sloppy inattention to his work. Although negligence is not an absolute bar to relief for mistake, it is a factor that is taken into account in deciding whether a party assumed the risk of the error. Even if this does not dispose of the matter, the cause and nature of the mistake weighs against him in the balance of the equities. On the other side of the balance is the hardship he will suffer if the contract is enforced. The damages may put him out of business, but shifting the loss to Reliabuild will apparently have a less devastating effect because it has a bigger profit margin and may be able to better absorb it. When the potential impact of the mistake is so severe to the mistaken party as to threaten his livelihood, and only reduces the gains of the other party, a court may be swayed by the balance of hardship.

Nevertheless, the relative economic impact on the parties, while a relevant consideration, may not be weighty enough to be the overriding factor in the decision to foist the loss onto one of them. Relative blame and innocence are also relevant. In this case, Bill's carelessness must be weighed against Reliabuild's justifiable reliance on his contractual commitment. It could be that Reliabuild, as an experienced prime contractor, should have realized that the bid was too low. If this was so, Reliabuild would have no legitimate reliance interest, and in fact may even have been guilty of fraudulent nondisclosure in keeping silent and seizing on Bill's erroneous bid. The facts do not provide enough information to reach a conclusion on whether Reliabuild acted in bad faith in accepting a bid that it knew or should have known was incorrectly calculated. If Reliabuild had no reason to suspect the mistake and made its own commitment to the owner in reasonable reliance on Bill's manifestation of assent, the equities do not favor avoidance on the basis of Bill's mistake.

4. If Reliabuild releases Bill from his subcontract, the question becomes whether Reliabuild itself could use mistake as the basis for seeking relief under the prime contract. That is, Reliabuild could seek relief for unilateral mistake by arguing that it made an error in its own cost calculations, based on having been given incorrect information by Bill. Reliabuild should not have much trouble establishing two of the elements of unilateral mistake: Bill's charges are a fact that gave rise to Reliabuild's basic assumption in entering the prime contract, and the mistake has a material effect in the exchange of values. However, Reliabuild may have greater difficulty with risk allocation and the balance of the equities. There are no facts to suggest that the owner realized or should have realized that Reliabuild's bid was too low to be correct. (Reliabuild itself did not notice Bill's error, so it seems even less likely that the owner would have been aware that Reliabuild's bid was too low). The owner therefore has a strong reliance interest. Although enforcement of the bid would severely diminish Reliabuild's profits, nonenforcement would deprive the owner of its bargain to the same extent. In addition, it is more appropriate to allocate the risk of this error to Reliabuild than to the owner. Reliabuild, not the owner, selected and dealt with Bill as its subcontractor, and the owner had no direct contact with Bill, had no means of evaluating his bid, and had no role in releasing him.

   The error in this example is in the bid at the time of contracting, so it is best characterized as an issue of mistake. However, it could conceivably be treated under the doctrine of impracticability. Bill's withdrawal after formation of the contract could be seen as an unforeseen supervening event, the nonoccurrence of which was a basic assumption of the contract between Reliabuild and the owner. As a result, Reliabuild's performance becomes unduly burdensome. However, even if the case is analyzed under impracticability, the result should not change, because fault and risk allocation are again the dispositive considerations and they should be resolved in the same way.

5. All the factual variations in this example involve supervening events—occurrences after contract formation that may be grounds for a claim of impracticability or frustration of purpose.

   a. Even under the original doctrine of impossibility, performance was excused by the death of a party whose continued existence was necessary for the performance. Restatement, Second, §262 adopts this rule for impracticability as well. It may seem ridiculously obvious that the death of the party who has to perform the service would render the performance objectively impossible, but, as the question indicates, the issue is not whether Merlin's corpse can be made to do magic tricks but whether his estate is liable for damages. Two elements of impracticability are satisfied: As the contract was for Merlin's personal services, it was clearly dependent on his continued vitality. His death is a supervening event contrary to the contract's basic assumption. Foresight of the event is relevant to the parties' basic assumption, and it is foreseeable that Merlin could have died because he was a mortal. However, the mere possibility that an event may occur does not make it foreseen for purposes of deciding if its nonoccurrence was a basic assumption of the contract. There must have been some reason for the parties realizing it as a probability.

      The more difficult question concerns who bore the risk of his death. The contract itself does not assign the risk, so the allocation must be made in light of the parties' reasonable expectations, determined from all the circumstances surrounding the transaction. These circumstances may include a particular practice in the entertainment industry that may help determine the normal incidence of risk when an artist dies before a show. (For example, promoters may regularly insure the lives of performers who have been booked.) If not, the court must make a reasonable assignment of risk, taking into account any general community expectations and any pertinent considerations of public policy. It is difficult to be sure what result would be reached. Many contracts do not terminate as a result of the death of a party, so that performance or damages becomes an obligation of the decedent's estate. As noted above, this may not be the reasonable expectation when the contract is for personal services. In this case, however, the risk allocation is also influenced by the circumstances of Merlin's death. Impossibility or impracticability cannot be used as a defense by a party who is at fault in causing the supervening event, and it could be argued that Merlin recklessly caused his own death. This may, in itself, be grounds for withholding relief from his estate. If not, it may tip the balance in the determination of risk. Note, however, that in *CNA International Reinsurance Co. v. Phoenix*, cited in section 15.7.3, the court rejected the argument that the estate of River Phoenix, could not claim impracticability because Phoenix was at fault in creating the impracticability by causing his own death by a drug overdose. The court considered it inappropriate to deprive a party of the impracticability defense in a personal services contract where the risky behavior was not directly related to the contract performance.

b. Fanny's demand for refund of the $800 is, in effect, a claim of restitution based on the implicit contention that the cancellation of the magic show frustrated the purpose of her contract with Buck. (The situation here is analogous to *Krell v. Henry*, cited in section 15.8.) These facts show how difficult it can be to distinguish impracticality and frustration. The latter seems more appropriate here because the contractual performance—the exchange of a ticket for $1,000—has not been altered by the supervening event. Rather, the goal and purpose of the exchange have been defeated. However, it could just as plausibly be argued that the supervening event so devalued the exchange for Fanny that her performance was rendered unduly burdensome, and impracticality doctrine is applicable.

Three elements of frustration are clearly satisfied: Merlin's death and the ensuing cancellation of the show were supervening events that defeated a shared basic assumption of the parties entering the contract, and neither was at fault in causing the event. Therefore, once again, risk allocation becomes the determinative issue.

In the absence of any assignment of risk in the contract itself, the risk of the show's cancellation must be placed where the parties reasonably would have expected it. It is not clear what this reasonable expectation might be. In *Krell v. Henry* the majority of the court, without expressly addressing the issue of risk allocation, resolved the case in a way that placed the risk of the coronation's cancellation on Krell, the owner of the flat (in the same position as Buck), rather than on Henry, the party who had hired it to view the coronation procession (in the same position as Fanny). The concurring opinion in that case questioned the issue of risk allocation and it is not clear that the majority allocated the risk correctly. It could be that Fanny, as the buyer of the ticket, should take the risk that it turned out to be less valuable than she anticipated. On the other hand, the fact that the promoters of the event refunded the face value of the tickets might suggest that it is the norm for the seller of tickets to bear the risk of cancellation of the event. However, that norm may not apply to a transaction in which a ticket purchaser resells the ticket at a premium to another consumer. Although the balancing of the equities between the parties is not an express element of frustration of purpose, the equities could be taken into account in the court's determination of what risk allocation is most reasonable. Therefore, the fact that allocating the risk to Fanny leaves Buck with an $800 profit at Fanny's expense may make allocating the risk to her unpalatable. In short, it is not clear what the reasonable risk allocation should be. There are arguments both ways, but maybe *Krell v. Henry* had it right — like Krell, the flat owner, the risk should be placed on Buck, the seller.

c. The only basis on which Merlin could escape the contract is to contend that his new-found fame is a supervening event that defeats the basic assumption on which the parties contracted for his services at the relatively modest sum of $500,000. As a result, his loss of the opportunity to earn double that amount is such a burden as to make his performance impracticable. He should not get away with this because he does not show either that performance has become unduly burdensome or that Showstopper bears the risk of the change in circumstances. Impracticability should not be permitted as an excuse when the change in market conditions merely has the effect of making the performance more valuable than anticipated, especially when the harm to Merlin is nothing more than the loss of an opportunity to sell his services at greater advantage. Each party made a judgment in assenting to the price of $500,000, and neither can complain if that judgment turns out to have been wrong.
d. At last, the fiery destruction of the Pyro Palace, but with a twist on *Taylor v. Caldwell*: It is not Showstopper, the party who is obliged to supply the hall, that raises the excuse of impracticability. Rather, Showstopper tenders a substitute performance and it is Merlin who claims impracticability on the basis of the destruction of the hall. This may therefore not be a proper case for invoking the doctrine of impracticability, which is intended to provide a defense to the party who cannot perform as promised as a result of the supervening event. The language of Restatement, Second, §261 contemplates this by stating that where a party's performance has become impracticable, that party's duty to render the performance is discharged. On the facts of this Example, it is not Merlin's performance that has become impracticable but Showstopper's. It is conceivable that Merlin could argue that the destruction of the hall renders his performance impracticable as well. He could show that there was some special reason why that venue was a basic assumption of his performance—for example, that the Pyro Palace had special facilities or characteristics essential to his performance that were not available in the new venue. However, the

facts do not suggest that he is making this claim. Therefore, unless he can show that the substitute venue defeats a basic assumption of the contract, rendering his performance unduly burdensome, Merlin cannot use the change in venue as a basis for discharging the contract.[10]

e. Most commercial contracts are motivated by the prospect of profit, so if Showstopper's argument was taken seriously, no party could ever be held to a contract once it becomes apparent that its expectation of profit will be disappointed. Therefore, although profitmaking may, in a sense, be the purpose of a contract, the doctrine of frustration does not simply focus on this underlying "bottom line" purpose, but calls for a more penetrating examination of the parties' mutual objective in entering the contract. This shared objective must be determined in light of the contract's allocation of risk. The facts do not make it clear who bore the risk of poor sales. However, if the contract did not specifically allocate this risk to Merlin, and there is no usage to the contrary, the reasonable inference from the structure of the contract is that Showstopper assumed this risk. Merlin agreed to perform for a fixed fee, and Showstopper would keep whatever proceeds were generated from ticket sales. If Showstopper bore the risk of poor ticket sales, it follows that it was not the common purpose of the contract that Showstopper would make a profit. Rather, the common purpose was to stage a public entertainment. The prospect of making a profit may have strongly motivated Showstopper to undertake the venture, but that was its purpose, not Merlin's. Viewed this way, the purpose of staging the show has not been frustrated.

Showstopper based its argument on frustration of purpose. It could equally have argued that the supervening event of poor ticket sales rendered the contract impracticable. (A similar alternative argument was made and rejected in *Karl Wendt Equipment Co. v. International Harvester Co.*, discussed in section 15.8.) Because the defenses of frustration of purpose and impracticability are so closely related, the answer should be the same, whichever one is used. Again, the key to resolving an impracticability defense is to determine who bore the risk of poor ticket sales. If Showstopper bore that risk, it cannot escape the contract on grounds of impracticability.

6. This is a classic case of unilateral mistake, analogous to bidding errors discussed in section 15.2.2. Even if both parties may have been unaware

10. This Example is based on the premise that Merlin seeks to avoid the contract on the basis of impracticability, but there is another way in which the dispute could be framed. Instead of claiming impracticability, Merlin could have sought rescission of the contract on the ground that Showstopper breached the contract by failing to make the Pyro palace available for the show. If Merlin made this claim, Showstopper would raise the defense of impracticability to excuse this failure and its tender of a substitute hall instead.

of the truth, the error in identifying and pricing the ring affects only Bijou's decision on what price to ask. Jewel is concerned only with the price proposed by Bijou and was not privy to the pricing decision, which forms the basic assumption of only Bijou. The mistake clearly has a material effect on the exchange, adverse to Bijou. Nevertheless, risk allocation may defeat Bijou's claim for avoidance. There is no indication that the sales agreement addressed the risk of error in identifying and pricing the ring, so risk must be allocated on a reasonable basis, taking into account general commercial expectations. Even in the absence of negligence, it is usually reasonable to allocate the risk of underpricing to a seller (and the risk of overpricing to the buyer). This is even more appropriate where the seller is in possession of the correct facts and negligently overlooks them. The only basis that Bijou may have to reverse this result is to show that, notwithstanding its negligent error, the equities favor relief. Jewel received a great bargain in getting a mined diamond for the price of a synthetic diamond and she can be restored to the status quo by a price refund. She would lose nothing but her unexpectedly generous bargain. The facts do not reveal what Jewel knew or expected when she bought the ring. She has some experience as a jewelry buyer and may have been aware of the significant difference in value between mined and synthetic diamonds. However, it is not clear if Jewel was acting deceptively by taking advantage of Bijou's mistake in the realization that Bijou had sold her a mined diamond for the wrong price, or if she just thought that she was buying a synthetic diamond for the correct price. It is therefore not clear if, on balancing these factors, a court would allow Bijou to avoid the sale.

This example is inspired by *DePrince v. Starboard Cruise Services, Inc.*, 2018 WL 443153 (Fla. App. 2018), *aff'd en banc*, 271 So. 3d 11 (Fla. App. 2018), cited in section 13.6.3 on fraudulent nondisclosure. Inexperienced salespeople working in a jewelry shop on a cruise ship sold a 20-carat diamond to the buyers for $235,000, which was one-twentieth of its retail value. The salespeople made this error because they mistook the per-carat price of $235,000 for the total price of the diamond. The buyers realized that the price was way below the value of the diamond, but said nothing and bought the diamond for the asking price. When it realized the error, the store sought to cancel the sale on grounds of fraud and mistake. The discussion of the case in section 13.6.3 focuses on the claim of fraud by nondisclosure and the court's rejection of that claim because the store could readily have discovered the retail value of the diamond by due diligence. However, the store ultimately prevailed in avoiding the sale on the basis of unilateral mistake. The trial judge's jury instructions focused on whether the store was negligent in making the error, whether the buyers could be returned to the status quo, and whether it would be inequitable to enforce the contract. The jury found for the store. The appellate opinion focused on the propriety of the jury instruction, which it upheld.

Because a jury's rationale for its finding is not revealed, one can only guess at the jury's reasons for finding in favor of the store. However, one could surmise that, in balancing the equities, the jury probably found that the negligence of the store was overshadowed by the immensity of the error, the buyers' realization that an error had been made, and the ability to restore the buyers to the status quo by refunding the price.

7. Crystal has breached the contract and is liable for Holy Foods' damages unless she has the defense of impracticability. Bottled water satisfies the definition of "goods" under UCC article 2, so the issue of impracticability must be resolved under UCC §2.615. The analysis of impracticability under §2.615 is substantially the same as under contemporary common law.

   The blockage that diverted the stream was a supervening event. Section 2.615 requires that it must have been an event "the nonoccurrence of which was a basic assumption on which the contract was made." Official Comment 1 to §2.615 paraphrases this by stating that the contract must have become impracticable because of unforeseen supervening circumstances not within the parties' contemplation at the time of contracting. The blockage is described as an unusual phenomenon. This suggests that the parties probably did not contemplate it as a probability. There is no indication that they discussed or provided for it in the agreement.

   The supply of water is not objectively impossible because there is a means of restoring the stream. However, §2.615 (like the common law) does not require impossibility, but impracticability. Mere increase in cost, lack of profit, or even some degree of loss, is not enough to make a performance impracticable. The scale of the problem must be large enough that it makes the performance so burdensome that it cannot be rendered without devastating loss, great risk, or serious hardship. The facts here have a good chance of meeting this standard. The high cost of curing the problem is disproportionate to the value of the water. It would take Crystal 15 years of sales to pay off the cost of the work. Although the excavation may pay for itself in the very long term, it would impose a significant burden on Crystal. She would not derive any income from her business for 15 years, even if the market for her water remains strong.

   Crystal was not in any way at fault in causing the occurrence, so she is doing well so far in establishing the elements of impracticability. This leaves risk allocation as the crucial factor in deciding if she should be excused from performance. The contract makes no provision for reductions in quantity for any reason, so the parties' intent must be determined from interpretation of the contract as a whole in context. If no factual indicators of intent are available, the court must construe the parties' reasonable intent. The facts do not indicate any express terms or pertinent usage or custom, so the terms and nature of the contract are the only basis for deciding if Crystal assumed this risk. The contract establishes a formula for fixing the price of the water over the five-year period. Where parties fix the price in the contract, whether in a dollar amount or by a formula, the seller is usually assumed to undertake the risk of any increases in cost. In addition, the seller of goods should bear the risk of not being able to produce the goods promised in the contract. However, the cost increase here was so unforeseen and so great that a court could conclude that it goes well beyond the normal level of risk assumed by the pricing provision in the contract. If so, Crystal can escape the contract on grounds of impracticability.

Where parties enter into a long-term relationship, they run a greater risk of unforeseen future contingencies. Although it may be difficult to imagine all the things that could go wrong to make the contract unexpectedly burdensome to one of the parties, a generally worded clause, excusing performance in case of a force majeure could help a party like Crystal in establishing grounds for excusing performance.

8. The restrictive covenant is a contractual term. The basis for Land Investments seeking the declaratory judgment is that an event subsequent to contract formation (the demise of Commercial Development and its Architectural Review Committee) has rendered performance of the contract term impracticable. Although impracticability is most commonly used as a defense to a claim for breach of contract, it can be used proactively, as Land Investments is using it here, as the basis of a suit to eliminate the contract term in anticipation of a threatened suit to enforce it.

   This Example is based on *Dutrac Community Credit Union v. Radiology Group Real Estate, LC*, 891 N.W.2d 210 (Iowa 2017), which involved a similar situation. The developer of an office campus had established an Architectural Control Committee in the restrictive covenants. All new construction had to be approved by Committee, which consisted of two people, specifically named in the covenants. The covenants made no provision for succession if either of them ceased to serve. By the time that Dutrac, the lot owner, was ready to build on its lot, the Committee had become defunct because one of its named members had died and the other had retired and refused to act. The court found all the elements of impracticability to be satisfied: The demise of the Committee was a supervening event, the nonoccurrence of which was a basic assumption of the contract; the event made the performance of getting Committee approval objectively impossible and hence impracticable; Dutrac was not at fault in causing this situation; and it did not bear the risk of the event occurring. The court granted Dutrac's suit for a declaratory judgment excusing the term on grounds of impracticability. (The owners of the other lots on the campus argued that instead of excusing the term entirely, the court should modify it to create a successor committee. The court refused to do so because the covenant made no provision for successors to the named members and its apparent purpose was really just to give the developer control over buildings to be erected on the campus. The court declined to make up contract terms to which the parties had not agreed.)

CHAPTER 16

Conditions and Promises

§16.1 THE STRUCTURE OF A CONTRACT: AN INTRODUCTION TO PROMISES AND CONDITIONS

Most terms in a contract are promises or conditions or both. The meaning, nature, and effect of a promise was introduced at the very beginning of this book (section 1.2.3) and promises have featured throughout since then because promises are fundamental to all contractual relationships. Conditions have been there too, but the crucial role that conditions play in contracts has not been highlighted until now. This chapter focuses on the concept of conditions and examines how they function in conjunction with promises to create the structure of a contract. Some of the terminology relating to conditions has not been used before in this book, so it may be unfamiliar. However, this is mostly just a matter of labeling—introducing new words to describe how a contract is structured and how its terms interact. As is so often the case, the key to analysis is interpretation—the determination of the parties' intent, as expressed by them in their contract or as inferred from surrounding evidence and reasonable expectations.

A promise (sometimes called a covenant) is an undertaking to act or refrain from acting in a specified way at some future time. The exchange of promises (or of at least one promise for a performance) is what contracts are all about. Thus, for example, when parties make a contract for the sale of land, the buyer promises to pay the price in exchange for the seller's promise to convey title and possession of the land. Diagram 16A illustrates this in a manner similar to that used to explain the exchange element of consideration:

Diagram 16A

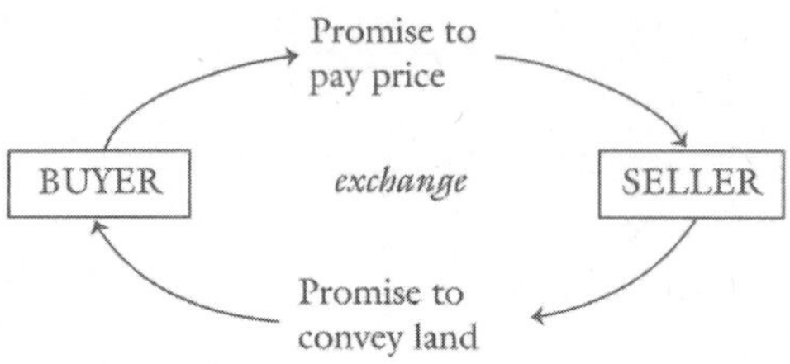

A condition is an event that is not certain to occur. A promised performance under a contract is subject to a condition if the parties agree that the performance is contingent on the occurrence of the uncertain event. That is, when making the contract, the parties agree that a particular promised performance or set of performances will not become due unless a particular uncertain event occurs. It is also possible that the parties could make the continued existence of the entire contract subject to a condition. That is, the parties can agree that the contract as a whole will not come into effect unless the stated uncertain event occurs. It is a matter of interpretation as to which of these alternatives the parties intend. As a practical matter, in most cases it does not really make a difference whether the condition relates to the performance of one of the parties or to the contract as a whole. As explained in section 16.4, if one party's performance does not become due because of nonfulfillment of a condition, the usual effect is that the other party's duty of performance falls away as well because the performances are dependent on each other. Therefore, end result is that the contract as a whole comes to an end.

Conditions commonly concern future events because, in most cases, the uncertainty no longer exists once the event has happened. However, there are situations in which a useful purpose is served by making performance conditional on a past event. Although the event in question may have occurred, the parties themselves may be uncertain about whether it took place, and it may be inconvenient or impossible for the parties to find this out at the time that they wish to execute their contract. To avoid the risk of having the agreement unravel while they delay to get the information, they could enter the contract immediately subject to the condition that their agreement—or the obligation of one of them—is contingent on the event having occurred. (This is illustrated in section 16.2.)

The following example provides a simple illustration of the way in which conditions and promises may be combined to structure a contract in a way that binds the parties, yet allows them to deal with the risk of

Diagram 16B

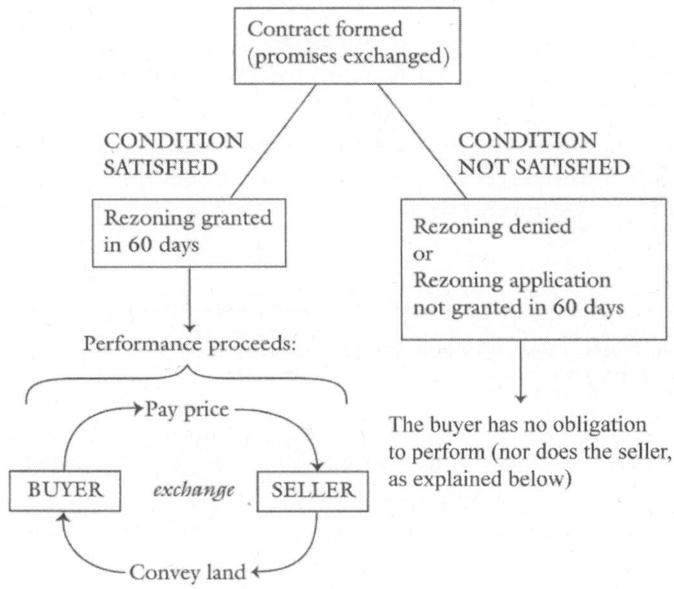

uncertainty: The buyer is interested in acquiring land to build a housing tract. At the time of negotiations, the land is zoned for agricultural use, but the seller has applied for rezoning for residential development. If the application succeeds, the land can be developed profitably. If not, it can be used only for farming. The parties do not know how the zoning authority will rule on the application, but neither wants to delay contracting until its outcome for fear that the other will lose interest in the transaction. The buyer does not wish to commit absolutely at this stage, because it does not wish to be stuck with farmland. To solve this problem, the parties can make a contract now for the sale of the land and include a provision in the contract stating, "The buyer's obligation to purchase this property is conditional on the grant of the pending rezoning application within 60 days of the date of this agreement." The success of the rezoning application within the next 60 days—a future uncertain event—is therefore a condition of the buyer's promise to pay and take transfer of the land. (Or stated differently, the buyer's promise to pay and take transfer of the land is conditional on the grant of the application.)[1] Until the condition occurs, the buyer's duty to perform is suspended. If it occurs, the duty becomes due and must be performed, but if the condition is not satisfied by the time that the 60 days has passed,

1. This variation in terminology can be confusing, but these statements mean the same thing, whether made in the active voice (rezoning is a condition of the buyer's performance) or the passive voice (the buyer's performance is conditional on the rezoning).

the buyer's obligation to perform never takes effect, and it falls away. This can be represented as shown in Diagram 16B.

The parties' purpose in structuring the transaction in this way is to allocate the risk of the denial or inaction by the zoning authority. If the buyer had simply purchased the property unconditionally, it would have taken the risk of being saddled with an unwanted farm or a costly delay in the ability to develop it. The buyer uses the condition as a means of escaping the contract to avoid assuming this risk.

§16.2 THE MEANING AND SCOPE OF "UNCERTAIN EVENT"

As noted earlier, uncertainty most commonly relates to future events, but it is possible for parties to be unsure about an event that has already happened at the time of contracting. Although a past event is not uncertain in a general sense—someone probably knows that it did or did not occur and the parties themselves can find out about it—it may nevertheless be unknown to and not readily ascertainable by them at the time they are ready to form the contract. If they wish to avoid the inconvenience or risk of suspending formation until they obtain the information, they can enter the contract immediately, but make performance conditional on the event's currently unknown outcome. For example, say that the buyer and the seller know that the zoning authority made a decision late on Friday afternoon, but it is now Saturday and the decision cannot be discovered until Monday morning. The parties would like to sign their contract immediately to bind each of them right away if the property has the desired zoning. By making the buyer's obligation to purchase conditional on the application having been granted, they can execute the contract on Saturday without subjecting the buyer to the risk of having bought farmland incapable of development. Although this condition is based on a past event, there is still some element of futurity in that the knowledge cannot be obtained until Monday. The outcome therefore does qualify as uncertain as far as the parties are concerned.

Most conditions, however, do not relate to unknown past events, but are based on something that has not happened at the time of contracting. All future events may be thought of as uncertain to some degree, so in the broadest sense, everything that has not yet occurred must be a future uncertain event. But the law regards an event as uncertain only if, in light of human experience, its occurrence is not regarded as inevitable (or, at least, that there is such a strong probability of occurrence that stating it to be a condition is factually and legally insignificant). Therefore, although a pessimist may fear otherwise, it is regarded as certain that the sun will rise tomorrow morning, or that Friday will follow Thursday, or that January 1 of next year will arrive. The passage of time is not regarded as a condition, so a provision in a contract that calls for performance upon the future occurrence of a particular date or time is not a condition at all, but merely fixes the time for performance. Conversely, the grant of the rezoning application is not a sure thing. Even if it was carefully prepared, complies with the prescribed procedures, and makes a compelling case on the merits, its success is not inevitable. It therefore qualifies as uncertain.

Although uncertainty about the happening of the event is necessary to qualify the event as a condition, this does not invariably mean that a condition is intended merely because the contract links performance to some uncertain future event. It could be that the parties do not really contemplate the event as uncertain, but that they assume that it will occur, and merely use it as a means of setting the time for performance. If, as a matter of interpretation, the parties do not intend the performance to be contingent on the event, it should not be treated as a condition. For example, say that a general contractor enters into a contract with a subcontractor under which the subcontractor is to perform electrical work on a house that the general contractor is building for the owner. The subcontract states that the general contractor's payment to the subcontractor will be due "within ten days of the contractor receiving payment for the work by the owner." This could be a condition—that is, the general contractor's obligation to pay the subcontractor is conditional on the owner paying the general contractor. However, it could also be seen merely as a term fixing the time for payment—the general contractor must pay the subcontractor ten days after the due date for the owner's payment. To resolve this question, a court would interpret the intent of the parties by examining the apparent purpose of the language in context. Because the subcontractor had no contractual relationship with the owner, did not deal with the owner directly, and did not have the opportunity to evaluate the owner's creditworthiness, it seems unlikely that the subcontractor would have assumed the risk of the owner's nonpayment in the absence of very clear language assuming this risk.

Although a condition is spoken of as an event, the contingency need not be an affirmative happening. It could also be a negative contingency—a nonhappening. In the above example, the zoning authority's approval of the application is an affirmative event. But it would just as much be a condition if the buyer's performance was subject to something not taking place: Say that the zoning authority had approved the application at the time of contracting, but irate neighbors had threatened to appeal the decision. The contract of sale could provide that the buyer's obligation to purchase is conditional on the approval not being successfully appealed.

§16.3 THE INTENT TO CREATE A CONDITION: EXPRESS, IMPLIED, AND CONSTRUED CONDITIONS

Like all terms of a contract, a condition exists because the parties have agreed to it. Similarly, like all other contractual provisions, the mutual intent to create a condition and the condition's scope and meaning are matters of interpretation. Sometimes the language used by the parties to articulate this intent is clear, express, and unambiguous, but it could just as likely be obscure and uncertain. In some contracts, the intent to create a condition is not articulated at all, but such intent may be established by evidence extrinsic to the express words used by the parties, or it may be construed by the court. These issues are resolved by applying the general principles of interpretation discussed in Chapter 10.

§16.3.1 Express Conditions

The example of a land sale contract contingent on the zoning of the land (used in section 16.1) illustrates an express condition: The contract expressly stated that the buyer's obligation to purchase the land was contingent on approval of the zoning application within 60 days of the date of the agreement. A condition is express if the language of the contract, on its face, articulates the intent to make performance contingent on the event. Commonly, conditions are expressly denoted by using conditional language such as "on condition that," "subject to," "provided that," or "if," but no special incantation is required as long as the intention of establishing a condition arises from the language itself. For a term to be an express condition, it is not enough that the term itself is expressed. Its conditional nature must also be apparent from the language used. For example, a contract for the sale of land has two provisions. One is an undertaking by the seller to transfer title and possession of the land, and the other is an undertaking by the buyer to pay the seller $500,000 for the land. These are both express promises, but neither performance is expressly conditional on the other because there is no express language to that effect. However if, in addition to these express promises, the contract also stated expressly that each party's obligation to perform is conditional on the other performing, these express promises become express conditions as well.

Sections 16.3.2 and 16.3.3 explain that even if these conditions are not expressed, a court will read them into the contract by implication or construction. An implied or construed term is just as effective and binding as an express term, so for most purposes, it makes no difference if a condition is express, implied, or construed—in all these cases the condition will be part of the contract and binding on the parties. The advantage of articulating a condition expressly is that the parties make it clear that they intend a condition. Because this intent is clear, courts enforce express conditions strictly: The condition must be fulfilled exactly as stated, and cannot be satisfied by substantial compliance. For example, a contract for the sale of property, executed on July 1, specifies that the buyer's obligation to proceed with the purchase is conditional on the seller paying all arrear property taxes on the property and getting tax liens on the property discharged by not later than July 31. The seller pays the tax arrears immediately and works diligently to get the tax liens discharged, but the county's process is slow and the liens are not discharged until August 1. Because the condition is express, it must be strictly enforced. The buyer has the right to refuse to proceed with the sale because of nonfulfillment of the condition, and the seller cannot avoid this result by claiming that discharge of the liens on August 1 was substantial satisfaction of the condition.

As technical as the result of strict compliance may be, it is important to recognize that the parties did go to the trouble of making the condition express, thereby manifesting the intent that it be taken literally. In some cases, the harsh results of this approach may be ameliorated by excusing the condition on one of the grounds discussed in section 16.10, but only if the facts fit into one of the narrow bases for excuse. It is also sometimes possible to avoid an unfair result by interpreting the condition so as to find that it was in fact satisfied, but this solution is available only if the language of the condition admits of such a meaning. It would not, for example, be easy to interpret the clearly stated date of July 31 in the above condition to mean August 1. However, say that the condition stated that the sale was contingent on the seller paying all arrear property taxes on the property and getting tax liens on the property discharged "within 30 days of this agreement." A court may be able to find that the condition was satisfied by obtaining the lien discharge on August 1 by interpreting the vaguer language "30 days of this agreement" to refer to business days, not calendar days.

§16.3.2 Conditions Implied in Fact

Even if there is no express language creating a condition, contextual evidence may support the inference that the parties intended a performance to be conditional. Like other terms in a contract, a condition can be implied in fact by interpreting the words used by the parties in light of the circumstances surrounding the formation of their contract. As with other terms, there is no difference in legal effect between an express and an implied condition. The difference lies in the nature of the evidence available to establish its existence. An express condition is apparent from the language of the contract itself—the actual words of the parties are the best evidence of what they intended. However, even where a condition is not ascertainable from the wording of the contract, it could be established by contextual evidence that shows that the parties did intend the condition to exist. For example, in *Medical Recovery Services, LLC v. Neumeier*, 415 P.3d 372 (Idaho 2018), a doctor failed to submit a bill for medical fees to the patient's insurer and ultimately sued the patient directly for recovery of the fees. The court held, based on the fact the patient had given his medical insurance information to the doctor's office, that the parties intended the doctor's right to recover the fees directly from the patient to be subject to the implied condition precedent that the doctor would first submit a claim to the medical insurer.

Courts do not rigidly apply the doctrine of strict compliance to an implied condition because the parties have not made it clear in the language of the contract that exact compliance is required. For example, the contract for the sale of property used as an illustration in section 16.3.1 simply stated that the seller undertakes to pay all arrear property taxes on the property and get the tax liens on the property discharged by not later than July 31. This is a promise in the contract, but it is not expressed as a condition of the buyer's obligation to proceed with the sale. Nevertheless, the court will interpret it to be an implied condition if the agreement in context indicates that this was the apparent intent of the parties. However, because the parties did not express this promise as a condition, the court has more flexibility in interpreting the implied condition in a way that averts a rigorous strict compliance and accepts compliance on August 1 as being substantial fulfillment of the condition.

As with all terms implied in fact, if the agreement is recorded in some way (such as in a physical written document or electronically), the parol evidence rule may preclude contextual evidence of a condition that varies an integrated term or conflicts with the writing. However, as noted in section 12.12, there is a traditionally recognized exception to the parol evidence rule when the evidence is offered to establish that the contract was subject to a condition precedent.

§16.3.3 Construed Conditions (Constructive Conditions of Exchange)

Although a condition may not be expressed or inferable from contextual evidence, it could be implied in law. The process of legal implication of conditions is the same as for any other contractual term, and is subject to the general principles discussed in Chapter 10: In essence, although there may be no evidence that the parties actually agreed to the condition, a court will imply it as a matter of law if the circumstances and nature of the contract compel the conclusion that if the parties had addressed the issue, they reasonably would have intended the condition to be part of their contract.

Construed conditions may be illustrated by returning to the example in section 16.1 involving the sale of land subject to the express condition that the rezoning application would be granted. Although the express condition of rezoning is the only one specifically articulated in the contract, the exchange of performances contemplated in the contract gives rise to the reasonable inference that there are in fact two other conditions in the contract: In promising to pay the price of the land, the buyer must reasonably have expected that its obligation to pay is conditional on the seller conveying the land, and the seller surely did not expect to transfer the land to the buyer without getting paid. Thus, each party's performance must reasonably be intended as a condition of the other's. The buyer's duty to pay is contingent on the seller's transfer and vice versa. The respective performances do qualify as uncertain events, because the honoring of a contractual commitment is not inevitable and assured.

These conditions are construed rather than implied in fact, because there is apparently no actual evidence that the parties discussed the question or expressed this intent to each other. But the dividing line between factual interpretation and legal implication is not always easily discernable, and they tend to blur into each other at the edges. In other words, the conclusion that each performance is conditional on the other could be reached as a question of fact if there is evidence (such as common commercial usage, prior dealings, or statements made during negotiations) to support it. But even in the absence of any such evidence, it may be possible to reach the same conclusion by implication of law from the nature of the exchange relationship. In an exchange transaction, unless the language of the contract or its surrounding circumstances clearly indicate a contrary intent, the parties must almost always be taken to have expected that the principal promises exchanged would be dependent on each other — that they would be what are known as constructive conditions of exchange. If they were not, this would lead to the bizarre situation in which a party could be forced to perform even when the other has failed or refused to do so.

The effect of this is that there is an initial condition that the rezoning must be approved. If it is not, the buyer has no obligation to pay and because the buyer's payment is a condition of the seller's obligation to convey, the nonfulfillment of the condition of payment releases the seller, too. If the rezoning is approved, these two construed conditions relating to the performances must be satisfied, and each party must tender performance (that is, show a readiness, willingness, and ability to perform) to be entitled to performance by the other. This can be shown by expanding Diagram 16B in the way shown in Diagram 16C.

Diagram 16C

Hogan v. Goldsmith, 533 S.W.3d 921 (Tex. App. 2017), provides another example of a construed condition. The parties entered into a lease-purchase agreement of land under which the buyer had the option to buy the land at any time during the term of the lease. The buyer exercised the option and sued the seller for specific performance when the seller failed to convey the land. Although the contract did not expressly so state, the court held that the buyer was not entitled to enforce performance of the contract because the buyer failed to satisfy a construed condition precedent. The court found that the seller's obligation to transfer the land to the buyer was subject to the construed condition precedent that the buyer tendered payment of the price to the seller in cash—that is, that the buyer provided proof, at the time of exercising the option, that he had the price available in cash and was ready, willing, and able to pay the price.

The standard of strict compliance, applicable to express conditions, does not apply to construed conditions because the parties have not clearly indicated, by express language, that they intend the condition to be strictly enforced. In addition, because construction is a search for the apparent intentions of the parties, measured in light of what would be reasonable, a court is unlikely to construe a condition so strictly that it would require exact technical compliance and admit of no flexibility. The issue of substantial compliance with a construed condition is discussed further in section 16.9.

In summary, the preceding sections have introduced the concept of conditions and have sketched the difference between promises and conditions and the role that they play in the contract. It has also introduced the way in which conditions enter a contract, either by express language in the contract, or by implication or construction. The rest of this chapter builds on these principles to show how conditions work and what purpose the parties intend to achieve by including them in the contract, either expressly or impliedly.

§16.4 A CONDITION OF ONE PARTY'S PERFORMANCE, AS DISTINCT FROM A CONDITION OF THE CONTRACT AS A WHOLE

Section 16.3 describes the success of the rezoning application as a condition of the buyer's obligation. Because the buyer's performance is, in turn, a condition of the seller's obligation, it follows that if the rezoning is denied and the buyer does not perform, the seller is also relieved of its obligation to perform. As a result, the entire contract falls away. This is shown by Diagram 16D.

Diagram 16D

Rezoning refused

↓

The buyer does not perform

The seller does not perform

This two-stage analysis is necessary because of the language used in the contract. It provides that the buyer's obligation to buy the property is conditional on the rezoning. The parties could have drafted the contract differently by stating that, not only the buyer's obligation, but the contract as a whole is conditional on the rezoning. If the contract so provided, the two-stage analysis would not be needed, and it could simply be said that the contract as a whole is conditional on the grant of the application, so that the performance obligations of both parties fall away if the condition is not fulfilled. This is shown in Diagram 16E. For example, in *Kortright Capital Partners, LP. v. Investcorp Investment Advisers, Ltd.*, 327 F. Supp. 3d 673 (S.D.N.Y. 2018), the parties entered into an agreement under which Investcorp undertook to invest in a fund managed by Kortright. The contract provided that it was conditional on the closing of another transaction under which Kortright would amalgamate its fund with another asset management company. The condition stated that if the closing did not occur by a specified date, "this agreement shall not come into effect and shall be null and void." The closing did not take place by the specified date. The court held that the language of the contract, particularly the statement that the agreement would be "null and void" clearly made the contract as a whole conditional on the closing.

Diagram 16E

Rezoning refused

↓

Contract falls away—neither party performs

These two situations sound like the same thing, with the second having one less step in the analysis, but there is a difference. If the parties made the contract as a whole conditional on rezoning approval, this would mean that if the application is denied, neither party is bound to the transaction. However, when the event is stated to be a condition of the performance of only one of the parties, the nonfulfillment of the condition affects only that party's obligation. Parties usually draft the condition in these terms to signal that the condition is intended to benefit the party with the contingent performance. In the sale of the property in which the buyer's obligation is conditional on rezoning, the purpose of the condition is to benefit the buyer by allowing the buyer to escape the contract if the rezoning is not approved. The buyer, not the seller, cares about the result of the application because it is the buyer that will develop the land after buying it. The seller will not be involved with the property after the sale and is indifferent to whether the buyer will be able to develop it. This being so, the buyer should be able to waive the condition and proceed with the purchase if the buyer decides to buy the land anyhow, despite the failure of the rezoning attempt.[2] The seller is not in any way deprived of the benefit of the expected exchange—receipt of the purchase price—and has no cause for complaint.

The determination of whether a condition is purely for the benefit of one of the parties, and therefore unilaterally waivable by that party, is a matter of interpretation. The court must determine the intent of the parties in light of the contractual language in context. For example, in *Mayfield v. Koroghli*, 184 P.3d 362 (Nev. 2008), a contract for the sale of real property was subject to the condition that the buyer could obtain rezoning of the property for commercial subdivision. The parties worked together for a number of years in attempting to obtain the rezoning. They were unsuccessful, and the seller told the buyer that he would no longer sell the property to him. The buyer responded that he wished to proceed with the sale despite the failure of the rezoning efforts. When the seller refused, the buyer sued for specific performance of the contract. The court found that the condition had been included in the contract at the buyer's request, for the purpose of allowing him to abandon the transaction if he could not subdivide the property as intended. The court therefore held that the condition relating to rezoning was purely for the buyer's benefit, so that he could waive it and insist that the sale be completed.

2. The waiver of a condition is relevant in two distinct situations. In the situation here, the condition benefits only one of the parties, the buyer, and that party decides to proceed with performance of the contract despite nonfulfillment of the condition. The other situation, covered in section 16.10.2, occurs where one of the parties acts in a manner inconsistent with the condition, and the other party claims that the conduct constitutes a waiver by that party of its right to enforce the condition.

If the parties had drafted the contract to state that performance of the contract as a whole is subject to the condition of rezoning, they would have made it clear that neither party can unilaterally waive the nonfulfillment of the condition. However, even if the parties draft the contract as in this example, providing only that the buyer's obligation is conditional, the terms or circumstances of the transaction may compel the conclusion that the parties did intend the contract to benefit both parties, so that the buyer could not waive the condition unilaterally. For example, say that the sale price of the land was fixed at a base amount of $100,000 (being its current market value as farmland) plus 10 percent of the buyer's profits upon selling off the subdivided lots. If the condition of rezoning is not satisfied, the buyer could not subdivide, and the seller would be deprived of its expected share of the profits. The seller's apparent incentive for selling the land was to share in the profit of development, and it surely would not have sold the property for $100,000 without the additional reward of a share of profits. Therefore, the condition can no longer be seen as merely for the buyer's benefit. It affects the contract's value to the seller as well. It must surely have been intended that neither the buyer nor the seller could unilaterally waive the condition and hold the other to the contract despite its nonfulfillment. This means that the condition was an event on which the duties of both parties were contingent—the entire contract was subject to the condition.

§16.5 PURE CONDITIONS AND PROMISSORY CONDITIONS

§16.5.1 The Distinction Between Pure and Promissory Conditions

As indicated in section 16.1, when the operative terms of a contract are analyzed, each can be classified as a promise, a condition, or both. Some terms may be classified as pure promises—they are not conditions at all, but merely undertakings.[3] Others may simply be conditions that contain no promise but merely describe an event that must occur for a duty of performance to arise—these can be described as pure conditions. However, some terms in a contract combine both these elements. They not only identify an event that must occur for performance to become due but also contain a promise by one of the parties that the event will take place. A term that is not only a condition, but is both a condition and a promise that the condition

3. The role and effect of pure promises is explained in sections 16.6 and 16.8.4.

will occur, is called a promissory condition. This concept sounds confusing on first exposure, but it actually describes commonplace contract terms.

The classification of a term as a pure promise, a pure condition, or a promissory condition is determined by the usual process of interpretation and construction. If the express language of the contract does not clearly settle this question, it must be resolved with reference to any factual evidence of intent or, failing that, by construing the parties' reasonable intention. The land sale subject to the express condition of successful rezoning can be used to illustrate: In agreeing to the sale of the land conditional on the success of the rezoning application, the parties apparently intend to place the fate of the transaction on an event beyond their control. The application has been made, nothing more can be done by either to influence the result, and there is no indication in the contract that either of them guarantees the outcome of the application. From this it must be inferred that they intended the rezoning to be a pure condition. By contrast, the conditions that make the performance of each party (payment of the price in exchange for transfer of the land) contingent on that of the other are promissory conditions. Each party does have control over the satisfaction of the condition that the party has undertaken to perform, and each, by committing to perform, has promised that the condition will be satisfied. The payment and conveyance of the land are not simply conditions but promises as well. This distinction is portrayed in Diagram 16F.

Diagram 16F

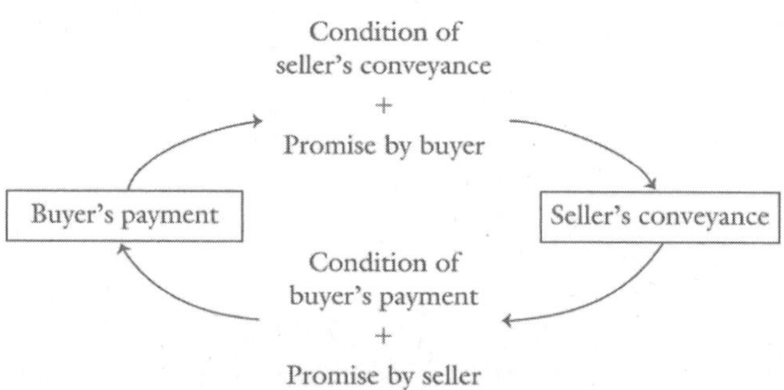

In the above example, the event constituting the condition of each party's performance is the actual performance of the other. When a party's own performance is the condition, that party has a significant amount of control over the fulfillment of the condition and can make the commitment with some confidence that the condition will be satisfied. However, if the condition is some event that is beyond the party's control, it is riskier to promise that it will occur. Therefore, in cases of doubt, it is generally assumed that a pure condition is intended when a party has no power to influence the happening of the event, but a promissory condition is intended if the party can play a role in affecting the outcome. It must be stressed that this is merely an assumption—a rough guide. It is not a firm rule. The agreement could expressly or impliedly indicate that the parties intended otherwise. If a party is willing to take the risk, there is no barrier to the party assuming responsibility for the happening of an event beyond its control. For example, instead of simply making their land sale contract conditional on approval of the rezoning application, the parties could have included a guarantee by the seller that the application would be granted. Although the disposition of the application is beyond the seller's control, the seller promises that it will succeed. If it does not, there is both a failure of the condition and a breach of the seller's contractual promise.

The significance of the distinction between a pure and a promissory condition lies in the different effect of promises and conditions. If a condition is not satisfied, the performance contingent on that condition does not become due. If it is a pure condition, the performance obligation falls away and there is no basis for claiming breach of contract. However, if a contractual promise is broken, the promisor is liable for breach of contract. It follows that if a promissory condition is not fulfilled, the party whose performance was contingent on it is entitled both to withhold counter-performance and to seek a remedy for breach. Therefore, in examining the language of a contract in context to interpret a term as a pure or promissory condition, it is helpful to ask two questions: First, did the parties intend a performance to be excused if the event does not occur? If the answer is yes, the event is a condition of that performance. If the answer to the first question is affirmative, the second question is whether the parties intended that one of them would be responsible for the event's occurrence and would be liable for breach of contract if it does not occur. If the answer is no, the event is a pure condition. If it is yes, it is a promissory condition.

§16.5.2 A Pure Condition Subject to an Ancillary Promise

Section 16.5.1 classified the rezoning contingency in the land sale contract as a pure condition, so that the buyer escapes the obligation to buy the property if the condition is not satisfied. The application has been made and is pending, so there is nothing for the buyer to do, and the buyer has no obligation to make any effort to bring about its fulfillment. However, some pure conditions do have an ancillary promise attached to them that expressly or impliedly obliges one of the parties to take steps to try and make the event happen. If so, the party is released from performance only if the condition is unfulfilled despite reasonable efforts to make it come about. This can be illustrated by changing the facts of the example. Say that at the time of sale, the application for rezoning had not yet been made. The buyer plans to submit an application, but does not wish to gamble on its success. The parties could enter a contract in which the buyer undertakes to make and conscientiously pursue the application, but is excused from proceeding with the purchase if the application is declined. In this contract, the buyer makes an initial promise to apply for and pursue the rezoning, but the success of the application is a condition precedent to the buyer's obligation to buy the land. This is not completely a promissory condition, because the buyer does not promise that the condition of rezoning will be satisfied. However, the buyer does make a promise to take all reasonable steps to try to get it fulfilled. If the buyer does this and fails, the buyer's performance under the contract does not become due and the contract comes to an end. However, if the buyer does not make a conscientious effort to get the rezoning, the seller may ask the court to excuse the condition so that the buyer loses its protection. This means that if the buyer then fails to proceed with the (now unconditional) performance under the contract, this will be a breach. This is shown in Diagram 16G.

Diagram 16G

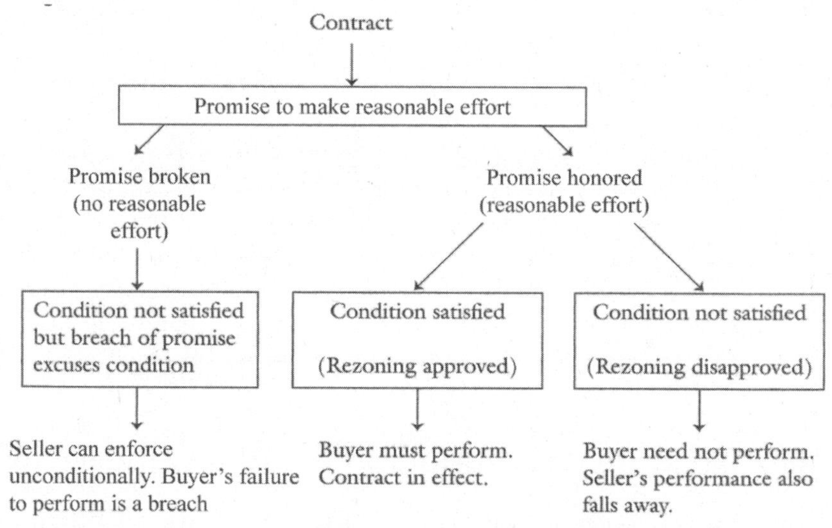

A common example of a pure condition with an ancillary promise of reasonable efforts is a contract to buy a property subject to a financing contingency. The buyer commits to buy the property subject to the condition that the buyer is able to obtain a mortgage loan. The buyer does not promise or guarantee that the loan will be approved—the grant of the loan is out of the buyer's hands because a lender must agree to make it. Therefore, the condition is not promissory. However, it would be a peculiar transaction (and likely would not be a contract at all for failure of consideration[4]) if the buyer did not promise to make reasonable efforts to secure it. This promise

4. *See* section 7.9, on illusory promises.

may be expressed in the contract, but if not, it is readily implied. If the buyer breaches this promise, the condition is excused. Where the buyer makes no effort at all to obtain the financing, the breach of the promise of reasonable efforts is obvious. However, if the buyer took some steps to get the loan, but was unsuccessful, the parties may dispute whether the buyer's efforts were sufficient, and the court will have to decide this question. For example, say that the buyer applies to only one lender, which refuses the application because the buyer has a poor credit history and insufficient income to qualify for the loan. If all other lenders use the same standard, it may be futile for the buyer to try any further, and the single application may satisfy his duty. But if other lenders have different or more lenient standards, the buyer's failure to pursue other opportunities to obtain financing would breach the buyer's obligation of reasonable efforts.

Phoenix-Talent School District v. Hamilton, 210 P.3d 908 (Or. App. 2009), provides another example of a pure condition accompanied by a promise to make reasonable efforts to try to bring the condition about. The school district entered into a contract with the owners of land to purchase land on which it intended to build a school. The land consisted of one lot and a portion of another lot, so it was necessary for the county to approve a lot line adjustment to alter the boundaries of the property. One of the express conditions in the contract was that the county would approve a lot line adjustment by a specific date. The parties made a joint application to the county, but the county would not grant the application as submitted and required further work. As a result, the adjustment was not approved by the contract deadline. Although the school district was willing to extend the deadline, the sellers were not. The school district sued for specific performance. The court refused the claim and granted summary judgment in favor of the sellers. It found that the condition of county approval by the specified date was a pure condition, because the county's decision on the application was beyond the parties' control. The court also found that the parties had made mutual promises to cooperate in good faith in making the application. However, the sellers had not breached this promise because they had cooperated fully in trying to get the application approved.

§16.6 THE TIME SEQUENCE: CONDITIONS PRECEDENT AND CONCURRENT CONDITIONS

There is a sequence of events implicit in the example of the land sale subject to the condition of rezoning. The condition of rezoning must occur before the buyer's (and consequently, the seller's) performance becomes due. Because its fulfillment must precede the performance contingent on it, it is known as a condition precedent. However, the contract does not indicate a sequence for fulfillment of the conditions of paying and conveyance of the land. If no such order of performance is expressed, it must be determined by interpreting the parties' intent in light of any contextual evidence or, in the absence of such evidence, by construing what must reasonably have been intended. When a contract provides for counterperformances in exchange for each other, and the contract does not prescribe a sequence of performances, the general presumption is that if the performances are capable of being rendered simultaneously, they are due at the same time. They are called concurrent conditions. Thus, the promissory conditions of payment and conveyance of the land, each being capable of exchange by a single act, are concurrent conditions. Each is a condition of the other and they must be performed at the same time. This means that the parties must get together at an appointed place and perform simultaneously. If this had been the sale of goods, there could have been a physical exchange of the goods and cash, but in a real estate transaction, the funds would be deposited in escrow[5] and released to the seller upon recording of the transfer. Because the performances are concurrent conditions of each other, both parties must participate in the exchange, being ready, willing, and able to tender performance. If one of them tenders performance but the other can or will not, the tendering party is excused from delivering its performance and may sue for breach. This is represented by Diagram 16H.

Diagram 16H

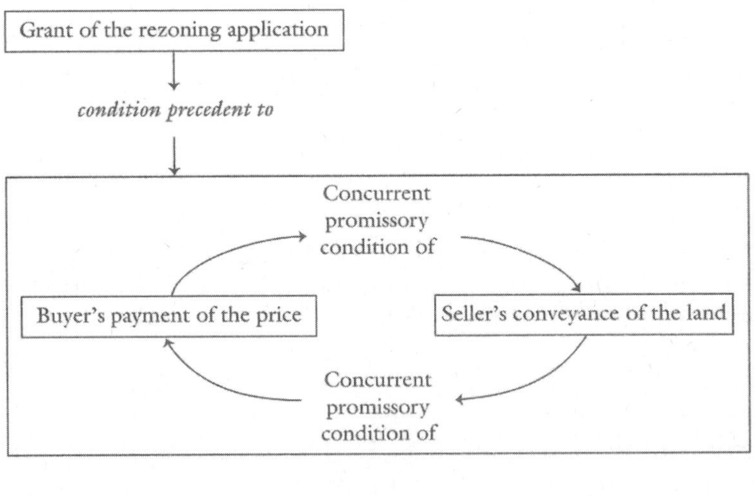

5. "Escrow" means that the parties appoint an independent third party (an escrow agent) to whom the buyer must pay the price of the property. The escrow agent holds the buyer's payment in trust until the seller has completed the documentation transferring the property to the buyer. The escrow agent then transmits the funds deposited by the buyer to the seller. This process protects both parties. The buyer does not take the risk of paying the seller before getting title to the property, and the seller does not take the risk of transferring the property to the buyer before receiving payment.

If performances are not capable of being rendered simultaneously because one of them requires a period of time to perform and the other can be rendered instantly, the general presumption, unless the contract indicates a different sequence, is that the performance that takes time must go first and must be concluded before the instantaneous one is due. That is, the completion of the longer performance is a condition precedent to the instantaneous one. For example, the owner of a building enters into a contract with a builder to renovate it. Unless the contract provides otherwise, the builder's performance, which will take time to complete, is treated as a condition precedent to the owner's obligation to pay, which is capable of being completed instantaneously. This general presumption is just a default rule, which the parties can change by providing for a different sequence of performances. For example, the contract could provide that the owner has to pay in advance, so that the owner's performance becomes a condition precedent to the builder's performance. Alternatively, the parties could break the performance into stages so that the builder's work and the owner's payment of part of the price become a series of conditions precedent. This is illustrated and explained in section 16.8.4.

When one party's performance is a condition precedent of the other's, their mutual promises are still dependent in a broad sense. They are exchanged for each other, and both parties are motivated to perform by the incentive of receiving the other's performance. However, they are not mutually dependent in the same way as concurrent promissory conditions because one of the parties must go first. Therefore, unless the parties have set up a different sequence of performances, the builder must complete its performance in full before the owner's payment obligation becomes due. This means that while the owner's promise of later performance is fully dependent on the builder's completion of its earlier performance, the builder's performance is not subject to any condition at all. It is not contingent on the happening of any prior event, but is absolute and unconditional.

The effect of this is that the builder's performance is a promissory condition precedent to the owner's payment, but the owner's payment is the final performance under the contract and no further contractual duties are contingent on it. It is therefore a pure promise in that it is not a condition of anything that must happen after it. In short, although the promises are still dependent in the exchange sense (and as explained in section 17.7.2, the builder would not have to perform if the owner repudiated its obligation in advance), the nature of the performances has the effect of making the builder's promise a promissory condition, but the owners promise is a pure promise. This is shown in Diagram 16I.

Diagram 16I

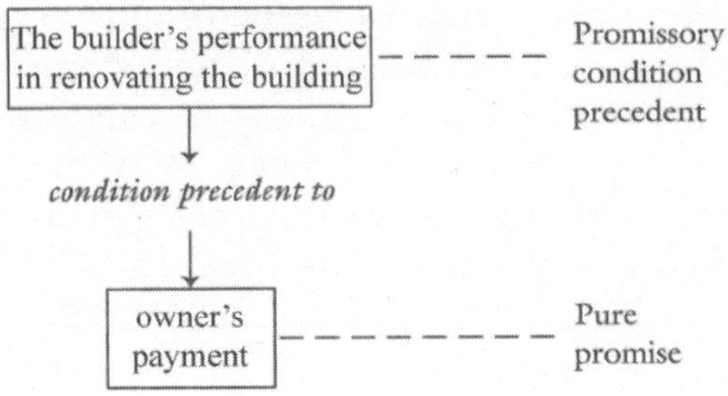

§16.7 THE CONFUSING DISTINCTION BETWEEN CONDITIONS PRECEDENT AND SUBSEQUENT

The distinction between a condition precedent and a condition subsequent is arcane and, for the most part, not particularly helpful or pertinent. It is explained in this section simply to clarify the confusion that it causes. Conditions subsequent are not referred to again in this book. First, unlike the distinction between conditions precedent and concurrent conditions, it has nothing to do with the sequence of performances. In fact, conditions precedent and subsequent have the same general effect: If the condition is not satisfied, the performance that is contingent on it does not have to be rendered. Second, the distinction is based on a semantic difference in the language used in the contract to create the condition. Third, the distinction has very little practical effect, and its principal relevance relates to burden of proof.

As explained in the land sale example in section 16.6, the rezoning must occur before the buyer's performance becomes due, so it is a condition precedent to the buyer's obligation to buy the land. The language used by the parties in the contract makes this clear by stating, "The buyer's obligation to purchase this property is conditional on the grant of the pending rezoning application within 60 days of the date of this agreement." That is, the buyer's obligation to proceed with the purchase does not become due until the condition is satisfied. However, if the language of the contract had stated, "The buyer's obligation to purchase this property will be discharged if the pending rezoning application is not granted within 60 days of the date of this agreement," this subtle change in wording would turn the term into a condition subsequent. That is, if the obligation to perform the promise is suspended until the occurrence of the condition, the condition is classified as precedent, but if the performance is discharged by nonoccurrence of the condition, the condition is classified as subsequent. Stated differently, a condition precedent is a prerequisite to the duty arising, while a condition subsequent terminates a duty that came into existence when the contract was formed. This distinction between two types of condition that have the same legal effect for most purposes does little more than create needless confusion. It is based on a very fine difference in the way in which the provision is worded, but the ultimate effect of both of these types of condition is the same—if there is no rezoning in 60 days, the buyer does not have to proceed with the purchase of the property.

Because the impact of the condition on performance is the same, whether it is precedent or subsequent, the distinction makes no difference in most situations, and can usually be disregarded. In fact, the distinction seldom comes up in modern cases, and Restatement, Second, does not even refer to "condition subsequent" in the text of any of its sections.[6] However, there is one area in which the distinction could make a difference—with regard to the incidence of the burden of proof. The fulfillment of a condition precedent is regarded as an element of the plaintiff's case in suing on the contract and must be proved by the party seeking to enforce it. Conversely, the occurrence of a condition subsequent is a defense to nonperformance and must be proved by the party whose performance obligation has allegedly been discharged. (Therefore, if the grant of the rezoning application is a condition precedent, the seller would have to prove that rezoning was granted to enforce the contract, but if the failure of the application is a condition subsequent, the buyer would have to prove refusal of the application to escape the obligation to purchase the land.) Allocation of the burden of proof could have significant results where it is difficult to prove that the condition was fulfilled, but it has little impact in most cases, where nonfulfillment is easily shown or is conceded.

§16.8 THE PURPOSE OF USING CONDITIONS IN A CONTRACT

The preceding discussion has already provided several indications of the role played in the contract by conditions. This section focuses more directly on the different purposes that conditions serve and explains what the parties seek to achieve by using them. Conditions are contractual terms, so parties

6. In defining the term "condition" in §224, the Restatement, Second, confines it to an event that must occur before a performance becomes due. Although it concedes, in Comment *e* to §224, that a contract may provide for the discharge of a duty upon the happening of a specified event, it does not consider such a term to be a condition at all. The comment indicates a preference for interpreting contractual language as creating a condition precedent and suggests that a condition subsequent should not be found merely because the contract speaks of a duty being "discharged" or "extinguished." Section 227(3) reinforces this by stating that in cases of doubt, a condition should be interpreted as precedent.

may choose to include conditions in their agreement if they desire them, or not to include them if they do not. By properly using conditions, they can provide for contingencies, allocate risks, and generally control the way in which their bargain is to be performed. To the extent that they can do this clearly and expressly, they are less likely to have disputes later on. However, even in the absence of clear provisions, unexpressed conditions may still be found by applying principles of interpretation and construction to determine what the parties had or reasonably must have intended. The following are the most common purposes achieved by conditions.

§16.8.1 The Use of a Condition as a Means of Allowing One of the Parties to Escape the Contract Fully or Partially

The land sale example introduced in section 16.1 illustrates the use of a condition as a provision allowing a party to escape the contract. The buyer did not wish to buy the farmland if it could not be developed for housing, so the parties agreed to include the term in the contract, making the buyer's obligation to proceed with the purchase of the land conditional on the grant of the pending rezoning application. That is, the condition in this contract allows the parties to enter the contract now, while permitting the buyer to escape the commitment to buy the land if the condition is not fulfilled. Because the rezoning application had already been submitted, its determination rested with the local authority and was out of the parties' hands, so, as explained in section 16.5, it was a pure condition. Section 16.5 also explains that some pure conditions have an ancillary promise of reasonable efforts attached to them. Therefore, had the rezoning application not yet been submitted, and the buyer was responsible for submitting it, the buyer would have had the obligation, either expressly or by implication, to make reasonable efforts to pursue it. In this situation, the condition still functions to allow the buyer to escape the contract, but allows the buyer the escape only after making the required efforts to get the rezoning application approved.

§16.8.2 Conditions of Satisfaction: The Use of a Condition to Permit the Exercise of Judgment by One of the Parties or a Third Party

One of the parties to a contract may wish to have some discretion in evaluating a future state of affairs (whether this relates to circumstances external to the contract or to the other party's performance) before rendering its own performance. To achieve this, the party could have a term included in the contract making its satisfaction (or its agent's satisfaction) with a specified state of affairs a condition precedent of its performance. This type of term, known as a condition of satisfaction, is useful to a party who does not wish to take the risk of performing until it is sure that circumstances are as desired or that the other party has properly done what the contract requires. The following examples illustrate conditions of this kind and show how they may be employed.

A contract under which a person commissions the painting of a portrait includes a term stating that the customer's obligation to take the portrait and to pay the artist for it is conditional on the customer being satisfied with it. This condition gives the customer a means to escape the contract if dissatisfied with the portrait, and places the risk of making the customer happy on the artist. In this illustration, the future state of affairs to be evaluated by the customer is the adequacy of the painter's performance.

A buyer contracts to purchase an old building for the purpose of restoring it and making it into shops, but is not sure if this kind of development would be successful. The buyer therefore makes the promise to buy the building conditional on the buyer's determination, following a feasibility study, that it can be profitably renovated. The risk to be managed by the condition of satisfaction in this case is not related to the adequacy of the other party's performance but to an external state of affairs—the economic environment—on which the buyer has inadequate information at the time of contracting.

In some cases, the contract may provide that the evaluation of satisfaction will not be made by the party, but by some expert third party. For example, a buyer may contract to buy a building subject to the condition that an engineer hired by the buyer finds it to be structurally sound, or the owner of a property may promise to pay a builder for construction work on condition that the owner's architect certifies the work as competent.

The discussion of illusory promises in section 7.9.4 on consideration doctrine explains that if a promisor reserves unrestrained discretion to perform, the apparent promise is illusory and cannot be consideration. Therefore, a promise conditional on the satisfaction of one of the parties could fail as consideration unless there is some limitation on that party's ability to claim dissatisfaction. The contract may itself express the standard by which to measure satisfaction, but if it does not, the appropriate standard can be determined in most cases, either as a matter of factual interpretation or legal implication. As a general rule, in the absence of the expression of a contrary intent, an objective test is used to limit discretion if, based on the underlying purpose and nature of the contract, the reason for the evaluation is to ensure that commercial or technical standards are satisfied. Under such an objective test, the question is whether the party is reasonable in being dissatisfied. In the above example of the purchase of the building on condition that it can be profitably renovated, it is a fair assumption that the market feasibility of the renovation would be determined on a reasonableness standard. Conversely, if the goal of the contract is to provide a performance that satisfies personal preference involving matters of taste or aesthetics, satisfaction could be more appropriately judged on a subjective standard: Is the party's dissatisfaction honest and genuine? The painting probably falls into this category, and the buyer may be able to show honest dissatisfaction with the portrait, even if art critics consider it to be a fine piece of work. Restatement, Second, §228 expresses a preference for use of the objective standard in case of doubt, because it is obviously fairer and more predictable. A contract should not be interpreted to impose the risk of dissatisfaction on a party's purely subjective foibles unless this is made clear in the contract or is necessarily inferred from the nature of the transaction.

A condition of satisfaction is not a promissory condition—obviously, the party does not promise to be satisfied because this would defeat the purpose of the condition. However, it is subject to an express or implied promise to act reasonably or in good faith in judging satisfaction. It is therefore similar in nature to the conditions described in section 16.5.2—a pure condition subject to an ancillary promise. This means that if a party refuses to perform on the basis of unreasonable dissatisfaction or a false claim of dissatisfaction, the condition of satisfaction is excused or deemed fulfilled, and the refusal of performance is a breach.

Two cases illustrate some of the court's considerations in deciding whether to imply a subjective or objective standard of satisfaction where the contract does not expressly state the standard to be used. In *Hutton v. Monograms Plus, Inc.*, 604 N.E.2d 200 (Ohio Ct. App. 1992), a franchise agreement permitted the franchisee to terminate the franchise and get a refund of the franchise fee if he could not obtain "financing suitable to him." The trial court held that the term "to him" signified a subjective standard. The court of appeals disagreed. The use of that language was not enough to overturn the usual assumption that the parties intend an objective standard in the evaluation of matters of commercial utility. Because it would be unusual for the parties to agree to a subjective standard in a commercial contract, much clearer language must be used to express that intent.

By contrast, in *Forman v. Benson*, 446 N.E.2d 535 (Ill. App. Ct. 1983), the court did find that the parties to a commercial contract intended satisfaction to be subjective. A contract of sale was conditional on the seller's satisfaction with the buyer's credit report. The seller rejected the report on the basis that it showed the buyer to be in shaky financial condition. The loan officer of a financial institution testified that his company would regard the buyer's credit as excellent on the basis of the report. The trial court applied an objective standard and held that the seller had been unreasonable in rejecting the report. The Appellate Court agreed that an objective test of satisfaction normally applies to matters of commercial quality and that the seller's dissatisfaction would not have met the reasonableness standard. However, it held that on the particular facts of the case, the parties intended a subjective standard. The seller was an individual, not in the business of lending money or familiar with commercial standards of evaluating credit, and the condition was included in the contract to allay his concerns about giving credit to the buyer and to induce his agreement.[7] The court need not to have applied a subjective standard. It could have accommodated the seller's individual circumstances just as well by using an objective test: His satisfaction could have been measured by the standard of a reasonable nonprofessional lender in his position, based on his level of expertise and his economic circumstances.[8]

§16.8.3 The Use of a Condition to Provide for Alternative Performances

In the example involving the sale of land subject to rezoning, the denial of the application completely released the buyer's commitment to buy the land. However, a condition need not invariably result in the total termination of a party's performance obligation. Because a condition is a contractual term, the parties can agree that some other consequence will follow its nonfulfillment. This can be illustrated by slightly changing the facts of the land sale example: As before, at the time of contracting, the seller's application for rezoning was pending. If it succeeds, the land can be used for a housing development, but if not, it can only be used for farming. The buyer wishes to have the land irrespective of the outcome, but the parties recognize that its value will be very much higher if the zoning is changed. To accommodate the uncertainty of the application's outcome, they provide in the contract that the buyer will buy the land irrespective of the outcome of the zoning application. However, the price to be paid is contingent on the outcome of the application. The buyer will pay $500,000 for it (its market value as farmland) if the rezoning application is denied, but will pay $2 million for it (its value for land that can be developed) if the application is granted. The parties have still agreed to make the buyer's performance contingent on the uncertain future event—the change in zoning. However, the condition does not operate to release the buyer from performance entirely. Instead, it commits the buyer to alternative promises. The condition is used

7. Although the court applied a subjective standard, it ultimately ruled against the seller. It found that the seller did not satisfy the standard of good faith because his dissatisfaction was not genuine. The evidence showed that he claimed dissatisfaction as a pretext for terminating the agreement because the buyer refused to renegotiate the price.
8. Although the subjective and objective standards do have a different focus, the ultimate result of using a subjective good faith standard may not be different from using an objective reasonableness standard because a party may have a credibility problem in claiming that unreasonable dissatisfaction is honest and genuine.

as a channeling device, not as a means of escaping the contract entirely. This is illustrated in Diagram 16J.

Diagram 16J

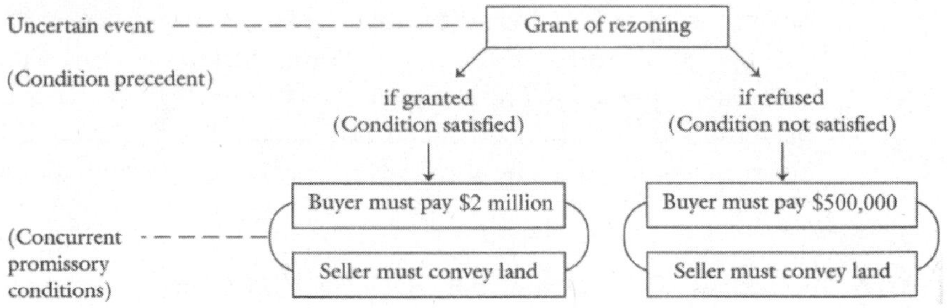

§16.8.4 The Use of a Condition to Regulate the Sequence of Performances

Conditions are routinely used to set the sequence of performances under the contract. That is, where parties structure a contract so that one performance must occur before another is due, they are, either expressly or impliedly, using conditions as a means of sequencing performances. If the parties say nothing in the contract about which performance must occur first, the default rules mentioned in section 16.6 apply: If the performances are capable of being rendered simultaneously, the presumption is that the parties intended concurrent performances. However, if one of the performances is capable of being rendered instantaneously and the other needs time to be accomplished, the completion of the longer performance is deemed to be a condition precedent of the instantaneous one. This means that the party with the longer performance must go first. These are only default rules, so the parties can change them by providing differently in their contract. They can set up any sequence of performances that they think fit, and can even split up one or both parties' performances to provide for portions of each to be rendered serially.

Where parties provide for the sequencing of performances in a contract, they are using conditions to achieve this end. They may do so expressly, by stating that an earlier performance is a condition precedent to a subsequent performance. However, even if they do not say this expressly, the fact that a sequence of performances is provided for readily leads to the implication that the parties intended an earlier performance to be a promissory condition precedent to a later one. To illustrate: A property owner contracts with a builder to build a house on it. The builder's performance—constructing the house—will take several months, while the owner's performance—payment—could be accomplished in a single instant. If the parties do not provide for a sequencing of performances in the contract, the default rule is that the builder must fully perform before the owner has to pay. Completion of construction is therefore construed as a promissory condition precedent to payment. This requires the builder to wait for payment until the house has been built and places the entire risk of the owner's nonpayment on the builder. A builder who does not want this result can negotiate a different order of performance with the owner. The owner probably would not agree to assume the whole risk of the builder's nonperformance by paying in advance. Therefore, the parties will probably agree on a sequence that allows the builder to be paid as the work progresses and that more evenly shares the risk of default. To do this, the parties use promissory conditions to break the performance into stages. For example, the contract may require the owner to pay a 10 percent deposit one week after the contract is signed; after receipt of this payment, the builder must excavate and build the foundation; on completion the owner must pay a further 10 percent of the price; the builder must then frame the house; and when that is done the owner must pay another 10 percent. This sequence of alternating performances goes on until the entire house is built and the builder has received periodic payments of 90 percent, at which time the owner must pay the final installment. Each of the incremental performances is a promise by the one party and also (whether stated so expressly or implied or construed) a condition precedent to the next stage of performance by the other. This means that if any one stage of performance is not rendered, the party entitled to that performance can refuse to render the consequent return performance and can claim breach. For instance, if the owner fails to pay after the excavation and foundation, the builder has the right to refuse to do the framing and may also sue the owner for breaching the contract.

§16.9 THE DOCTRINE OF SUBSTANTIAL COMPLIANCE WITH CONSTRUED PROMISSORY CONDITIONS

Section 16.3.1 explains that if the parties have taken the trouble to create an express condition by clear language in the contract, the court will strictly enforce the express condition and unless the express condition is exactly satisfied, the conditional duty does not become due. The justification for this doctrine of strict compliance is that the parties have clearly chosen to make performance subject to the stated event, and the court should honor this intention by upholding the beneficiary party's right to demand nothing less than exact fulfillment of the condition. Therefore, even if it seems that the condition is rather technical and apparently unimportant, or even if it has been substantially satisfied, so that the shortcoming in compliance is rather unimportant or trivial, the court should not second-guess the parties by treating the condition as having been met.

Section 16.3.3 explains that the doctrine of strict enforcement does not apply to construed conditions. This difference in approach to express and construed conditions has particular importance where one of the parties has not exactly complied with a promissory condition. This may be illustrated by looking again at the example in section 16.8.4 involving the building contract under which the owner undertook to make a 10 percent down payment a week after execution of the contract, and the builder committed to begin construction after receiving that payment. If the language of the contract clearly articulates that this is also a condition precedent to the builder's duty to commence performance (that is, the condition is express), the owner's failure to pay the full amount of the deposit exactly by due date constitutes nonfulfillment of the condition, so that the builder's obligation to perform does not arise. Because strict compliance is required, the owner will not be deemed to have satisfied the condition by paying less than the full amount of the deposit or paying it after its due date, even if the shortfall or delay is slight. However, if the promise's role as a condition is not expressly stated but is construed as a matter of reasonable intent from the way in which the contract has set out the sequence of performances, the court has more flexibility. It may employ the doctrine of substantial compliance and decide whether, despite the shortfall or delay in payment, the owner substantially complied with the condition of payment so as to constitute fulfillment of the condition.

Even if the court finds that the owner's noncompliant down payment substantially fulfills the condition, the condition is also a promise (a promissory condition). This means that even though the condition has been satisfied, the owner's shortfall or delay in payment is still a breach of the promise to pay the stipulated amount at the time specified. This leads to the question of whether the breach is serious or minor. This issue is deferred to Chapter 17, but it is useful to note at this stage that where a promissory condition is involved, the impact of the deficiency in performance must be evaluated from both perspectives. As Chapter 17 shows, there is usually a close coordination in the results of these two enquiries, so that a minor breach that qualifies as substantial performance of the promise is likely to be also a substantial compliance with the condition, and a material breach will likely be a nonfulfillment of the condition as well. The categorization of a breach as material or immaterial has a significant effect on the rights of the parties. If the owner's short or late down payment is a serious violation of the contract, the builder would be entitled to withhold performance and also to rescind the contract and claim the full extent of relief necessary to compensate for the lost expectation. However, if the shortfall or delay is trivial, substantial compliance with the condition does not discharge the builder's duty to perform, and the minor breach does not permit rescission. The builder must perform and is confined to claiming compensation, in the form of a monetary allowance, for any loss caused by the inadequacy of performance.

§16.10 THE EXCUSE OF CONDITIONS: WRONGFUL PREVENTION, WAIVER OR ESTOPPEL, AND FORFEITURE

If a performance is subject to a condition, it does not fall due unless that condition is satisfied. However, circumstances may change after the contract is entered into, making it unfair or unreasonable to require the condition to be satisfied, or the inequitable conduct of the beneficiary of the condition may preclude the beneficiary from asserting that it was not fulfilled, or the impact of the condition may otherwise be so harsh that its enforcement would be unjust. To take account of this, the law recognizes certain limited and defined situations in which the condition may be excused to prevent injustice. If grounds for excuse exist, the condition falls away and the contingent obligation becomes absolute. That is, it is no longer conditional and must be performed despite the nonoccurrence of the event originally contemplated in the contract. This section covers three of the most common and important bases for excuse.

§16.10.1 The Party Favored by the Condition Wrongfully Prevents or Hinders Its Fulfillment

Some conditions are completely beyond the control of the party whose performance is subject to the condition, so the party has no power to do anything to facilitate or to hinder the condition's occurrence. For example, if a lease provides that the lessor undertakes to install air conditioning in the premises next year if the average temperature for this August reaches 100 degrees, there is nothing that the lessor can do to manipulate the weather so as to influence the fulfillment of the condition. However, some conditions are, to a greater or lesser extent, capable of being influenced by one or both parties.

a. When a Party Has a Duty to Take Active Steps to Facilitate Occurrence of the Condition

Section 16.5.2 deals with situations in which a party does not promise that the condition will be fulfilled, but does make an ancillary promise, expressly or impliedly, to make reasonable efforts to attempt to bring it about. Section 16.5.2 used the example of a contract to buy a home, under which the buyer's obligation to proceed with the purchase is subject to the buyer being able to obtain a mortgage. Although the buyer does not promise to obtain the mortgage (so the condition is not promissory), the buyer does make a promise, either express or implied, to make reasonable efforts to secure it. If the buyer makes adequate efforts to obtain the financing, but fails, the condition is not fulfilled and the buyer has no duty to proceed with the purchase. However, if the buyer does not try to get the loan, or makes an insufficient or token attempt, the buyer has hindered or prevented fulfillment of the condition. This allows the seller to claim that the condition is excused, so that the buyer's promise to purchase the house becomes enforceable as if the condition had not existed. This means that if the buyer then refuses to proceed with the purchase on grounds of nonfulfillment of the condition, that refusal is not justified and is a breach.

b. Obstructive Conduct

Even if a party has no duty to cooperate actively in the condition's fulfillment, the obligation of fair dealing may require the party not to do anything to obstruct fulfillment of the condition. The example involving the sale of farmland subject to rezoning, used several times in prior sections, may be used again to illustrate this point. The seller had already submitted the rezoning application when the parties entered the contract, and they are awaiting disposition by the zoning authority. The buyer is therefore not required to make active efforts to try to bring about the condition's occurrence. (That is, it is a pure condition, without any promissory elements.) Nevertheless, the buyer's general obligation of fair dealing does create an implied promise not to act in bad faith to prevent its occurrence. Therefore, the condition may be excused if its nonoccurrence resulted from some wrongful action by the buyer to influence the local authority's decision negatively. (For example, the buyer persuaded a neighboring landowner to file an objection to the application, or lobbied members of the board to vote against it.)

The buyer's action is only wrongful if it is a violation of the buyer's duty of good faith and fair dealing under the contract. In the above example, the buyer's attempt to influence the local authority's action clearly violates this duty because it undermines the contract's purpose. However, not every contract imposes an implied duty to refrain from acting in a way that obstructs fulfillment of a condition. This is a matter of interpretation, dependent on the apparent intent of the parties, and some contracts may contemplate that the party whose performance is subject to the condition does have the right to try to avoid satisfaction of the condition. For example, if a buyer promises to purchase goods from the seller on condition that the buyer cannot find them cheaper elsewhere, the buyer obviously has the right to try to avoid satisfaction of the condition by seeking cheaper goods, and these efforts would not be a wrongful obstruction of the condition. *Rastek Construction & Development Corp. v. General Land Commercial Real Estate Co., LLC*, 806 S.E.2d 740 (Va. 2017), offers another illustration of the principle that a condition is excused because of a party's prevention of the condition's fulfillment only if the party's conduct is wrongful. A real estate agent sued the seller of property for its commission. The seller's duty to pay the commission was conditional on the sale of the property, which had not taken place. However, the broker claimed that the condition should be excused because the seller prevented its fulfillment by refusing to consummate the sale. The court found that the seller was acting within its rights under the agreement of sale in refusing to go ahead with the transaction, so the seller's action was not grounds for excusing the condition.

c. The Link Between Conduct and Nonfulfillment

When the promisor has wrongfully failed to make a reasonable effort to facilitate occurrence or has acted in an obstructive way, it may not be clear if that conduct was directly responsible for nonfulfillment of the condition. For example, the buyer of the house may not have obtained a mortgage, even with a genuine and conscientious effort, or the rezoning board may have refused the application even without the buyer's interference. Some courts have imposed a strict test of causation, excusing the condition only if it can be shown that the condition would have been fulfilled, but for the obstruction. A less rigorous test, favored by other courts, does not require the party seeking excuse of the condition to demonstrate as strong a causal link, but merely to show that the other party's conduct played a significant role in the condition's nonfulfillment.

§16.10.2 Estoppel or Waiver

Estoppel and waiver are distinct doctrines, but they are quite muddled in the context of excuse of conditions because conduct is often ambiguous enough to be classified as giving rise to either of them. As a result, courts sometimes do not take the trouble to differentiate them, and Restatement, Second, §§84 and 230(3) combine them into a general principle of excuse. The basic idea is that after the contract is entered into, the party whose duty is conditional indicates the intention, by words or conduct, to perform even if the condition does not occur. This indication of intent not to require compliance with the condition may take place either before the time on which the condition is to occur, or after that time has passed and the condition has not been satisfied. Although there are some differences in legal analysis depending on whether the condition is dispensed with before or after it is due to occur, they are not explored here. This discussion is confined to an explanation of the basic principles applicable in either case. Although the doctrines of estoppel and waiver are intermingled in this area, they do give rise to distinct justifications for excusing a condition, so it is useful to describe them separately and to show why they are so easily mixed up.

a. Estoppel

Estoppel, an equitable doctrine, is introduced in section 8.4. Its purpose is to prevent the unfair assertion of rights by a person who has acted inconsistently with those rights. The basic effect of the doctrine is to preclude a person from asserting a right when, by deliberate words or conduct, and with knowledge or reason to know that the words or conduct will likely be relied on by another, that person causes the other party detriment by inducing the justifiable belief that the right does not exist or that it will not be asserted. In the context of conditions, the party who is the beneficiary of the condition may be estopped from claiming its nonfulfillment if, by words or conduct, that party induces the other party to act to its detriment by causing it justifiably to believe that the condition has been satisfied or that compliance with it will not be required.[9]

The operation of estoppel doctrine can be illustrated by using the example of the land sale contract subject to the condition of rezoning. The contract provided, "The buyer's obligation to purchase this property is conditional on the grant of the pending rezoning application within 60 days of the date of this agreement." Say that fifty-eight days after execution of the contract, the zoning authority told the seller that it would not be ready to make its decision for another two weeks. The seller told the buyer of this and the buyer expressed willingness to wait an additional twelve days. On the strength of this, the seller gave up an opportunity to sell the land to someone else. If, on the 61st day, the buyer sought to escape the contract by asserting nonfulfillment of the condition, the buyer would likely be estopped from doing so, because it deliberately indicated to the seller that it would not insist on compliance with the 60-day provision and the seller, having no reason to question the buyer's sincerity in stating that it would wait, justifiably relied on that assertion to its detriment.

b. Waiver

In essence, the waiver is a party's voluntary abandonment of a contractual right. One situation in which waiver occurs is discussed in section 16.4: When the event is stated to be a condition of the performance of only one of the parties and is solely for the benefit of that party, the beneficiary party has the right to waive it. Section 16.4 used the example of the sale of the property in which the buyer's obligation is conditional on rezoning. The purpose of the condition is to benefit the buyer by allowing the buyer to escape the contract

9. If, instead of acting in a way that induces reliance, the beneficiary party promises not to require compliance with the condition, the basis for relief would be promissory estoppel rather than equitable estoppel. The doctrines have corresponding basic requirements: Action by the party benefitted by the condition, justifiable reliance by the other party, and equities favoring relief.

if the rezoning is not approved. Only the buyer is impacted by the result of the application because the buyer will develop the land after buying it and once the sale is complete and the seller has been paid, the seller has no interest in whether the buyer develops the land or not. In such a situation if the rezoning is denied, but the buyer decides to buy the land anyhow, the buyer can waive the condition for its exclusive benefit and proceed with the purchase.

The application of the waiver doctrine discussed in this section is different. Here, it is not the beneficiary of the condition who wishes to abandon it, but the other party who claims that the condition is excused because the beneficiary, by words or conduct, manifested the intent to waive it. In this situation, a waiver occurs when, after the contract has been made, the beneficiary of the condition expressly or impliedly agrees to perform even if the condition is not satisfied. A dispute over waiver under these circumstances arises if the other party seeks to have the condition excused, but the party who benefits from the condition denies having waived it. For example, a lease of premises provides expressly that the lessee's right to remain in possession of the premises is conditional on the lessee paying the rent for the premises by not later than the first day of the month. This is an express condition, requiring exact compliance. In the first eight months of the lease, the lessee pays the rent two or three days after the first of the month and, despite the express condition, the lessor accepts these late payments without complaint. When the lessee pays the rent for the ninth month two days late, the lessor terminates the lease on grounds of late payment and seeks to evict the lessee. The lessee could resist the eviction by claiming that by its action in accepting late payment over the preceding eight months, the lessor has impliedly waived the condition of strict compliance with the express condition.

A waiver must be distinguished from a contract modification. A waiver is one-sided—one of the parties unilaterally gives up a contractual right without asking for or receiving anything in exchange. However, a modification is a contract in itself—a mutual agreement under which one party agrees to relinquish rights in return for consideration given by the other. Because consideration is required for a valid modification, the general rule is that if the right to be given up is an important part of the exchange under the contract (that is, it is a material right) it cannot be validly relinquished by a unilateral waiver. Its abandonment must be exchanged for consideration in a full-fledged contractual modification.[10] However, if the

10. Note that the rule invalidating the waiver of a material condition only applies where the party entitled to the conditional performance claims that the beneficiary of the condition waived it. The rule is not relevant in the situation discussed in section 16.4, where the beneficiary of the condition elects to abandon its right to a condition included in the contract solely for its benefit. A party's abandonment of its own right for its own purpose does not qualify as a bargained-for exchange requiring consideration. Note also that the requirement of a modification with consideration does not apply to a sale of goods because UCC §2.209 does not require consideration for a modification. (*See* section 13.9.3.)

right relinquished is nonmaterial—ancillary, and not a central part of the contractual exchange—consideration is not required and it can be validly waived. To decide if the grant of the rezoning application was a material part of the exchange and therefore not validly waivable without consideration, the role of the condition and its significance in the exchange must be determined by the usual process of interpretation.

c. Distinguishing Waiver from Estoppel

As noted earlier, it can be difficult to distinguish waiver from estoppel. The estoppel example given above can be used to show just how ambiguous the distinction can be. That example concluded that the buyer's agreement to wait an additional 12 days for the rezoning decision estopped the buyer from asserting nonfulfillment of the condition on the 61st day. It could just as well be said that the buyer waived its right to have the condition fulfilled within 60 days. If the time for approval is not a central component of the exchange (which it appears not to be, but that is a question of interpretation), the waiver without consideration is valid and binding. Thus, in some situations, conduct by the party benefitted by the condition could equally well support an estoppel or waiver argument, so they should generally be regarded as alternative bases for excuse. However, the facts of the case could preclude use of one of the bases of avoidance. Waiver would not work if the condition of rezoning within 60 days is a material part of the exchange, and estoppel would not work if the seller took no action in reliance on the buyer's manifestation of willingness to wait the additional 12 days.

d. Retraction of a Waiver

Because a waiver is a unilateral abandonment of right without consideration, the party waiving it can retract the waiver by notice unless the other party acted in reliance on the waiver before receiving notice of retraction. A waiver is also treated as final and irrevocable if it was made after the condition's nonfulfillment. When a party waives a condition after it has become clear that the condition failed to occur, this is treated as binding election to proceed with the transaction despite nonoccurrence of the condition.

§16.10.3 Unfair Forfeiture

The doctrine of unfair forfeiture is a general principle under which the court may exercise its discretion to decline the full enforcement of one party's legal rights where doing so would have a disproportionately harsh impact on the other party. Courts use the doctrine sparingly, and only under circumstances that strongly demand the exercise of this discretion. To claim unfair forfeiture, it is not enough for a party to point to a loss or disadvantage resulting from nonfulfillment of the condition—the failure of a condition commonly leads to some forfeiture of a benefit under the contract. Therefore, the doctrine of unfair forfeiture is confined to situations in which enforcement of the condition would result in an inequitable windfall or benefit to one of the parties at the expense of a disproportionate and harsh consequence to the other. Thus, in deciding forfeiture, the court balances the relative hardships between the parties. It weighs the burden on the party who would suffer if the condition was enforced against the harm that excuse would do to the beneficiary of the condition.

This ground for excusing a condition is really a safety valve that ameliorates the harsh results that may follow from the rule of strict compliance with express conditions. It is therefore most useful when the condition is express and unambiguous, and is not needed when the court has flexibility in construing the terms and scope of the condition, or when ambiguous language can be interpreted in a way that avoids an unfair result. (In setting out standards of interpretation, Restatement, Second, §227 expresses a general preference in favor of interpretation that will avoid forfeiture in cases when there is doubt about the existence, scope, or nature of a condition.)

The principal purpose of the forfeiture doctrine, set out in Restatement, Second, §229, is to allow the court to disregard an express condition of a technical or procedural nature where the strict enforcement of the condition would have the unfair impact described above. It should therefore not be used if the occurrence of the condition is a material part of the exchange. A condition of notice in an insurance contract is a good illustration of the unfair forfeiture rule. A court is more likely to apply the unfair forfeiture doctrine to claim submission requirements in an insurance policy because courts are particularly wary of an insurer that accepts premiums from the insured over a period of time—maybe even for years—and then raises the technicality of late submission of the claim to avoid paying it. Typically, an insurance policy is likely to have at least three conditions precedent to payment of a claim: the insured's payment of the premium, the insured suffering the loss or expense covered by the policy, and the insured submitting the claim with supporting documentation within a specified period of the loss. Clearly the first two conditions—payment of the premium and loss—are material. The premium is the total consideration that the insurer bargains for in exchange for its undertaking to indemnify the insured, and no reasonable person would expect to be able to claim on an insurance policy in the absence of an insured loss. However, the condition of timely claim submission may or may not be material. Its purpose is to give the insurer early notice and proof of loss so that it can investigate and verify the claim. A delay in giving notice could cause prejudice to the insurer, but it may not. The court applied the unfair forfeiture doctrine against an insurer in *Estate of Gleason v. Central United Life Insurance Co.*, 350 P.3d 349 (Mont.

2015). Ms. Gleason purchased a cancer benefit insurance policy in 1990. In 2002 she was diagnosed with breast cancer, from which she died in 2010. During the entire time that the policy was in force, she paid all the premiums, but she never made any claim on the policy. After she died, her estate submitted a claim to the insurer for the cost of her cancer treatments. The policy provided that claims must be filed within one year and 90 days after the expense was incurred. The insurer paid the estate the most recent claims that arose within the one-year and 90-day period but refused to pay older claims. The court found that enforcing the condition would result in severe forfeiture for the estate, which would lose the right to reimbursement of most of Ms. Gleason's medical expenses. Balanced against this, the only negative consequence for the insurer was that it would have to pay out on the policy. It had not suffered any actual prejudice as a result of not getting timely notice. The court therefore concluded that the condition of notice should be excused because the estate's unfair forfeiture outweighed the principle of strict enforcement of an express condition.[11]

§16.11 A TRANSNATIONAL PERSPECTIVE ON CONDITIONS AND PROMISES

The common law's terminology relating to conditions and promises and its mode of analyzing the distinction developed through the judicial interpretation of contractual intent. Civilian systems do not use the same analytical framework, but general principles of interpretation usually lead to similar results. Like UCC Article 2, the CISG does not set out general rules relating to conditions and promises, which are governed by general principles of applicable law. (Article 7(2) makes general principles of law applicable in areas not specifically covered by the provisions of the CISG.) The CISG does contain some more specific provisions that comport with the common law's understanding of the distinction between conditions and promises, even though the language of the provisions is quite general and is not couched in terms of condition or promise. For example, Article 58 contains a default rule similar to UCC Article 2 that requires payment and delivery to be concurrent.

11. In the field of insurance law there is a parallel principle called the "notice-prejudice rule," which holds that late submission of a claim can only be used by an insurer to resist payment of the claim if the insurer can show that it suffered prejudice as a result of the late notice. This rule has been enacted by statute in some states and recognized at common law in others. The court referred to this rule, noting that it accords with the unfair forfeiture rule of general contract law.

The UNIDROIT Principles likewise do not address the distinction between conditions and promises expressly or in the detail in which they have been analyzed in this chapter. However, the outcome of issues discussed in this chapter would commonly be the same in many situations because Article 4.1(1) calls for interpretation to ascertain the intent of the parties. There are a few provisions of the Principles that are somewhat more specific. For example, Article 6.1.4 deals with order of performance and contains a default rule that unless otherwise agreed, instantaneous performances are to be rendered simultaneously, but a performance that is to take time should be rendered before an instantaneous performance. Article 7.1.3 allows a party to withhold performance until it receives a performance that is to be rendered previously or simultaneously, and Article 7.3.1 allows a party to terminate performance in response to "fundamental nonperformance."

Examples

EXAMPLES

1. This Example is an exercise in classification. Identify the promises, conditions, and promissory conditions in the following contracts. Having identified the conditions, consider whether they are express or construed and precedent or concurrent, and also identify the purpose that the condition serves in the contract.
   a. A lessor and a lessee entered into a lease of real property for a two-year term at a rent of $12,000 a month, payable in advance by the first day of each month. The lease gave the lessee the right to renew the lease for a further two years provided that it delivered written notice of renewal to the lessor not later than 30 days prior to the end of the second year of the lease. The rent for the renewal period would be $15,000 per month, but if the lessee satisfactorily repainted the premises in the first month of the renewal period, the rent would be $14,500 per month.
   b. The insured took out an insurance policy to insure a building against loss by fire. The insured paid the premium at the time that the policy was issued. The insurance policy stated that in consideration for the premium, the insurer would reimburse the insured for any loss caused by fire occurring on the insured premises, provided that the insured furnished satisfactory proof of loss to the insurer within 30 days of the loss.
   c. On June 1, the owner of land granted an option to purchase the land. The prospective buyer had until June 30 to exercise the option. On June 10, a second buyer expressed interest in purchasing the land, and the owner entered into a contract with the second buyer under which the owner agreed to sell the land to the second buyer if the grantee of the option failed to exercise it by its expiration on June 30.

d. Following discussions on the possible sale of a car, the owner of the car wrote to the prospective buyer, stating, "I will sell you my car for $5,000 on condition that you communicate your acceptance to me within five days of the date of this letter."

2. Byron Buyer entered into a contract with Stella Seller for the purchase of Stella's house for $400,000. The written contract provided that Byron would pay $100,000 in cash on closing and would pay the balance of the price in installments over 15 years. To secure payment of the balance, Stella would take a first mortgage in the property, to be recorded at the time of transfer. The contract also provided, "This contract is contingent on seller's approval of buyer's credit report."

   Shortly after the contract was signed, Stella obtained a credit report on Byron. It showed that Byron had gone on a credit-card spending binge five years ago and had to file a voluntary bankruptcy petition to discharge unmanageable debt. The report also showed that since obtaining his bankruptcy discharge, Byron apparently no longer used credit cards and had not defaulted on any other debts. Stella considers bankruptcy to be shameful and thinks it immoral for a person to go on a spending spree and then file bankruptcy to get out of the full payment of those debts. Stella therefore no longer wishes to deal with someone as unworthy as Byron, and certainly does not trust him enough to give him credit. Stella therefore disapproved the credit report and declared the sale to be terminated.

   Byron objected and said that Stella had no basis to reject the credit report. Byron can show that Stella's attitude is tougher than that prevailing among financial institutions in the consumer credit industry, which would be likely to approve Byron's credit under these circumstances. The reasoning in the industry is that a five-year-old abuse of credit and bankruptcy filing should not be held against a borrower who has behaved responsibly since then, particularly when the loan applied for is fully secured by a mortgage on real property. Did Stella have the right to disapprove the report and cancel the sale?

3. As in the contract in Example 2, the contract between Byron and Stella provided for the sale of the home to Byron for $400,000, of which $100,000 would be paid in cash on closing, and the balance would be paid to Stella over 15 years, secured by Stella's mortgage on the property. Unlike the contract in Example 2, this contract had no condition concerning a credit report. Instead, it provided, "This contract is subject to the buyer's sale of his present home for not less than $350,000 within 30 days of the execution of this contract."

   The reason for including this term was that at the time of the contract Byron already owned a smaller house that he needed to sell, so that he could use the proceeds of his equity in the house to pay the $100,000 cash due on closing. Byron's old home was subject to a mortgage of $200,000, so he had to sell it for at least $350,000 to pay the mortgage, broker's fees, and other costs and expenses, leaving at least $100,000 clear for the cash payment to Stella.

Consider the following separate and distinct factual variations:

a. After signing the contract, Byron decided that he would save having to pay real estate agent's commission by marketing the house himself. He erected a "for sale" sign on the property and advertised the house in various media. Although several prospective buyers responded to Byron's advertising, Byron is pushy and insensitive, so he scared all of them away with his overbearing and aggressive sales technique. As a result, he had not managed to sell his house by the end of the 30-day period. Byron therefore claims that he is no longer obliged to buy Stella's house. Is he correct?

b. After signing the contract with Stella, Byron decided that he would not sell his existing house as planned but would keep it as rental property. Instead, to raise the down payment, Byron borrowed the $100,000 from his sister. Byron immediately called Stella, explained this, and told Stella that he waived the condition. Does Stella have any grounds for objection?

4. Consider another variation of the contract between Byron and Stella. As in Example 3, the contract provided for the sale of the house to Byron for $400,000, of which $100,000 was to be paid in cash on closing. However, the contract in this variation did not provide for Stella herself to extend credit for balance of the price on the security of a mortgage. Instead, Byron was to seek his own financing to pay the $300,000. Therefore, the contract was not contingent on a satisfactory credit report. Also, Byron did not currently own a home, so the contract was also not conditional on the sale of his existing house. Instead, it contained the following provision:

> This sale is subject to the buyer obtaining a loan from a bank or other lending institution, secured by a first mortgage on the property purchased hereunder, in an amount of not less than $300,000, extending for a term of at least 15 years, and at a rate of interest not exceeding 5 percent per annum. If, after the exercise of due diligence, the buyer is unable to obtain financing on these terms, this contract shall terminate, and neither party shall have any liability to the other.

Immediately after Byron signed the agreement, he consulted a mortgage broker. Upon reviewing Byron's truthful and accurate financial statement, the broker told Byron that no bank or financial institution would lend him $300,000 because his income was too low and his indebtedness was too high. This made Byron realize that he had bought a house beyond his means, and he was relieved that the financing contingency had been included in the agreement of sale. Byron promptly notified

Stella of termination of the sale on the ground that the condition had not been satisfied. On hearing that Byron had given up after a single interview with a broker and had done nothing more to seek financing, Stella claimed that Byron had not exercised due diligence in trying to satisfy the condition. Is she correct?

5. Primo Contracting Co. is a general contractor. It was engaged in the renovation of an office building under a contract with the owner of the property. Primo entered into a subcontract with Cool Conditions, Inc. (CC) for the supply and installation of a new air conditioning unit for the building. The subcontract between Primo and CC required the unit to be installed by July 1, and further stated: "The price due to CC under this contract shall not be payable until the air conditioning unit has been properly installed in working order and Primo has received payment for this work from the owner."

   CC competently installed a fully operational air conditioning unit by June 15. On June 17 the owner of the property filed for bankruptcy. The office building is subject to preexisting mortgages, so the owner has no equity in the building.[12] Furthermore, the owner's estate is hopelessly insolvent so no funds will be available to pay any of the debts arising from the construction. The project was abandoned and Primo has not been paid for any recent work, including the air conditioning.

   CC demanded payment from Primo, but Primo refused on the ground that a condition precedent to its obligation to pay CC—the owner's payment to Primo—had not been fulfilled. Is this a good argument?

6. President Property, Inc. owned an old vacant office building in a bad part of town. Because the building was unoccupied, President did not see the point of paying for burglary insurance, but it did buy an insurance policy from Equity & Fidelity Indemnity Co., Inc. (E&F) to cover damage or destruction resulting from other causes. The relevant terms of the policy stated:
   a. In consideration for the premium paid, Insurer undertakes to reimburse Insured for any loss resulting from damage to or destruction of the above-described premises caused by fire, storm, explosion, nuclear accident, civil commotion, or vandalism.
   b. For the purposes of this policy, "vandalism" is restricted to and includes only willful and malicious physical injury to the premises and excludes any loss by pilferage, theft, or burglary.

12. Unpaid contractors and subcontractors are entitled to a statutory lien (called a construction lien or a mechanic's lien) for unpaid labor or materials used to improve real property. This lien attaches to the real property and it arises in favor of a subcontractor even though the subcontractor had no contract with the owner. However, preexisting mortgages on the property take priority over the lien, so the lien would not have any practical value to CC in this case because the property is fully encumbered by preexisting mortgages.

c. No claim shall be paid under this policy unless Insured notifies Insurer of loss within seven days thereof, and submits proof of loss within a further 14 days.

The plumbing in the building was copper pipe that has some value as scrap. A few months after the policy was issued, someone broke into the building and removed all the copper pipe. To extract the pipe, the thief ripped open walls and floorboards, causing extensive damage to the building.

President employees did not visit the building regularly because it was vacant. Therefore, President did not find out about the break-in until one of its employees went to check on the building eight days later. When President notified E&F of the loss, it told the E&F representative that the break-in had occurred eight days previously. The E&F representative did not comment on this. E&F sent out a loss adjuster the next day. After inspecting the premises, the adjuster said to President's property manager, "Get estimates for fixing this damage, and get them to me as soon as you can. I must warn you, however, that this looks like burglary, not vandalism, and I don't think it is covered by your policy." President's property manager protested that it looked like vandalism of the worst kind, but the adjuster said that there was no point in their arguing about it. The claims department would make the decision, so President should submit the estimates and see what happens. President submitted the estimates a couple of days later. Shortly afterward, it received a letter from E&F rejecting its claim on the basis that the loss resulted from burglary and was excluded from coverage. President sued E&F for reimbursement of the loss. E&F defended the suit on two grounds—first, that the loss was not covered by the policy and, second, that President had not notified it of the loss within the time prescribed by the policy. Should these defenses succeed?

7. Sue Burbanite owned a piece of land in a fast-growing suburb. Sprawling Malls, Inc., a developer of shopping malls, was interested in building a mall on Sue's land, but it could not do that without raising funds from investors. In January Sprawling Malls entered into a contract with Sue under which Sprawling Malls agreed to buy the land from Sue for $1.5 million on condition that it succeeded in raising 80 percent of the price from investors by not later than August 1 and delivered notice to Sue in writing by that date of its intention to complete the purchase. After the contract was signed, Sprawling Malls sought investors and had raised the required capital by July 15. On July 30 Sprawling Malls mailed written notice of intention to complete the purchase to Sue. It sent the letter by ordinary mail and Sue did not receive it until August 2.

   Sue wanted to escape her contract with Sprawling Malls because the value of the property had increased since January, and she would now be able to sell it for more than $1.5 million. She therefore rejected the notice on the basis that it was received after August 1. Does Sprawling Malls have a basis for challenging this?

EXPLANATIONS

Explanations

1. a. The lessee's payment of rent and the lessor's obligation to give the lessee use and occupation of the premises are dependent promises. That is, each party's performance is a promissory condition of the other's. Even if the conditional nature of the promises is not expressly stated in the lease, it is easily construed as being what the parties reasonably must have intended. The parties have structured the lease so that the performance of each is broken into monthly segments. The lessee's payment of the month's rent is a condition precedent to that month's tenancy, and the lessor's making the premises available for that month is in turn a condition precedent to the next rent payment. (So, if either party breaches its obligation, the other can withhold the next performance in the sequence in addition to suing for damages for breach of the lease.)

    With regard to the lessee's renewal option, the lessee's delivery of notice of renewal within the prescribed time is an express condition precedent to the extension of the lease for another two years. (Its conditional nature is expressed in the language of the lease by use of the term "provided that.") It is not a promissory condition, or even a condition subject to an implied promise to use reasonable efforts in good faith, because the lessee has no obligation to renew the lease. However, if the lessee decides to extend the lease, it must comply exactly with the terms of the condition. As an express condition, it will be strictly enforced.

    If the lessee does exercise the renewal option, the same set of promissory conditions—payment of rent and occupation of the premises—continue through the renewal period. In addition, the lease contains another condition intended to give the lessee a choice of alternative performances: If the lessee paints the premises in the first month of the renewal period, the rent is reduced by $500 per month. Although this condition does not use clear language of condition such as "on condition that" or "provided that," its conditional nature is clear enough to qualify it as express. It is not a promissory condition, in that the lessee has no obligation to paint the premises and may choose to pay the higher rent instead. The condition is therefore one that provides for alternative performances.

    Finally, if the lessee does elect to paint the premises, it implicitly promises to do so in a workmanlike manner. The rent reduction is contingent on the paint job being satisfactory to the lessor. This condition of satisfaction is subject to a promise (implied in law, if not expressed) that the lessor will act reasonably or in good faith in assessing whether the painting is satisfactory. The preference is for the objective reasonableness standard to measure satisfaction, particularly if the work is commercial or technical in nature. This standard is more appropriate here. A subjective good faith standard would be more appropriate if it is clear from the wording of the contract or from the nature of the performance that the parties intended satisfaction to be measured by the individual taste of the party who is to make the judgment.

b. In an insurance contract, the insured's payment of the premium is usually a condition precedent to the insurer's obligation to indemnify the insured for the loss. However, this question is not in issue here because the insured paid the premium when the policy was issued. There are three other terms of the policy that are conditions precedent to payment of the claim. The first is that a loss by fire on the premises occurs, the second is that the insured gives proof of loss within the time specified, and the third is that the insurer is satisfied with the proof.

The condition of loss does not use expressly conditional terminology, but there can be no doubt that loss must be a condition precedent to indemnity. This is so obvious that the implication of a condition is inevitable. It is also obvious that this cannot be a promissory condition. It would be a bizarre policy indeed, under which the insured committed to suffer a loss.

The condition of notice is express. It is also a pure condition because the insured has no obligation to submit the proof if it does not wish to claim under the policy. That is, the insurer would have no claim for breach if the insured failed to notify of loss. It would simply have no duty to indemnify. This condition is included in the policy to benefit the insurer, and its purpose is to ensure that the insurer will have no obligation to pay a claim that is not properly established within a short time of the loss.

The condition of satisfactory proof is likewise designed to protect the insurer by requiring probative proof of loss. Like the condition of satisfaction in Example 1(a), it is subject to an implied promise that limits the insurer's discretion to be dissatisfied. Unquestionably, satisfaction must be measured here on an objective reasonableness standard.

c. The owner's obligation to sell the land to the second buyer is subject to an express condition precedent that the option-holder does not exercise the option by June 30. This is not a promissory condition, because the seller makes no promise that the option will not be exercised. The purpose of the condition is to allow the parties to execute the sale agreement immediately but to protect the seller from committing to sell the property to two separate buyers. The condition enables the seller to escape the second contract if the grantee of the option (the first offeree) binds the seller by exercising the option. If the grantee of the option does not exercise it, the seller's obligation to convey the property to the second buyer becomes due, and accordingly, so does the second buyer's obligation to pay for it. Even in the absence of expressly conditional language, these mutual promises of performances are construed as conditions of each other. Unless a different sequence is prescribed by the contract, they are deemed to be concurrent conditions because both are capable of instantaneous performance.

d. This may sound like a condition because the offer says that the creation of the contract is conditional on acceptance within the time prescribed. However, despite the use of the word "condition" in the letter, the acceptance within five days is not a condition at all, in the sense used in this chapter. It is simply the time specified for acceptance. If the offer is accepted in time, a contract will be formed, under which the car is exchanged for $5,000. At that point, conditions in the contract will come into effect. The seller's promise to deliver the car and the buyer's promise to pay for it are dependent promises. Even if not expressly stated to be conditions of each other, they are construed promissory conditions. As in Example 1(c), they can be performed at the same time and are therefore deemed concurrent unless the contract specifies an order of performance.

2. This Example builds on *Forman v. Benson*, discussed in section 16.8.2. The provision concerning the credit report is a condition of satisfaction. It is an express condition precedent to Stella's obligation to sell the property to Byron on credit. The purpose of the condition is obvious: It is intended to protect Stella from having to extend credit to Byron if he proves to be uncreditworthy. Of course, Stella could have checked Byron's credit before making the contract, but this would have delayed execution of the contract and risked loss of the deal. Stella avoided this risk by entering the contract immediately, subject to a satisfactory credit report.

   A condition of satisfaction is not fully a promissory condition because Stella does not promise that she will be satisfied. However, this does not mean that Stella has unfettered discretion in deciding whether to be satisfied. Even if nothing is expressed in the contract to restrict Stella's discretion, the law imposes the restriction that Stella must exercise judgment honestly or reasonably. Unless the contract indicates differently, the objective standard is more appropriate in the commercial context, where the judgment involves matters of technical or commercial quality. Creditworthiness is quintessentially a matter of commercial utility, capable of being judged by market standards. The subjective standard of good faith should be confined to contracts in which it is clearly contemplated that the performance must appeal to the party's aesthetic sense or personal taste. A buyer who submits to a credit check is not likely to have assumed the risk of making performance of the contract subject to the seller's idiosyncrasies. Therefore, the fact that Stella has atypically strong moral qualms about bankruptcy is probably not good enough a basis for his dissatisfaction. She must judge Byron's credit history purely on the basis of whether a person with Byron's credit history presents a risk of default beyond a reasonably acceptable level.

Having decided that an objective reasonableness standard applies, the next task is to identify and apply that standard. If the industry standard applies, Stella dissatisfaction seems to fail the test of reasonableness. However, the industry standard is probably not the correct one to apply because Stella is not a member of the consumer financing establishment but a homeowner who is selling her home on credit. A large and wealthy institution, which can distribute risks of default among many customers, is likely to be less risk-averse than a private seller. For this reason, the question is not what would constitute a reasonable credit report for the consumer credit industry but what would be an acceptable report for a reasonable self-financing private seller. That is, even though the objective test applies, the standard of reasonableness should be based on a lender in Stella's position, not on a professional lender.[13]

3. a. Byron cannot afford to buy Stella's property without first selling his existing home, so he sensibly made his obligation to Stella contingent on selling it. He thereby averted the risk of being committed to Stella if he cannot raise the $100,000 for the down payment. Byron's sale of his existing home within 30 days is an express condition precedent. Although this is not a fully promissory condition, in that Byron does not absolutely promise that the house will be sold, it is subject to the implied promise that Byron will make a diligent effort to try to fulfill the condition. Diligence is not to be judged entirely subjectively, because Stella cannot be taken to have assumed the risk of idiosyncratic or irrational behavior.

   Therefore, the test is whether Byron made an honest and genuine effort, as may reasonably be expected from a person in his position. Byron may have tried hard to sell his house, but that does not seem good enough. Quite apart from Byron's unfortunate personality, he is not an experienced dealer in real estate and it was arguably not

13. As noted in section 16.8.2, *Foreman v. Benson* applied a subjective standard, which seems counter to the approach of most courts. An objective test, based on a reasonable person in Stella's position, is a more appropriate measure but, as pointed out in section 16.8.2, would probably lead to the same result in most cases.

reasonable for him to have attempted to sell the house without the help of an agent. It seems that the parties had the expectation that Byron would hire an agent because the contract takes broker's commission into account in fixing the minimum price to be realized in the sale of his house.

If Byron did not satisfy his implied obligation to use best efforts, this would be a ground for excusing the condition, so that the condition is deemed fulfilled. Stella can insist on Byron's performance and if he fails to render it, he is in breach and Stella can sue for appropriate relief.

b. Although Byron could have abandoned this condition had it been solely for his benefit, the condition was not necessarily intended for his protection alone, so he should not be able to waive it unilaterally. In addition to allowing Byron an escape if he cannot sell his house, the condition ensures that upon buying Stella's house, Byron will have discharged the mortgage debt on his prior home. Stella has agreed to finance Byron's purchase of the house, so she has a stake in the level of Byron's debt and may reasonably have been influenced by this in agreeing to extend credit to him for the balance of the price. If Byron keeps his existing house and borrows money for the down payment, he increases his debt load, which may heighten the risk that he will default on his mortgage payments to Stella. Although Byron's debt to Stella will be secured by a mortgage, this does not eliminate Stella's interest in Byron's financial security because foreclosure is inconvenient and costly, and there is always a danger that the proceeds of a foreclosure sale will not fully cover the balance of the mortgage.

4. Like the conditions in Examples 2 and 3, the financing contingency is not fully a promissory condition, but the beneficiary party (Byron) does commit to make best efforts to attempt its satisfaction. As long as he diligently applied for financing, he can escape the contract without liability for breach if he fails to obtain it. In this Example, Byron's promise of due diligence need not be construed because it is expressed in the contract. The sole issue is whether his single discouraging interview with a mortgage broker was enough of an effort to qualify as due diligence.

The question of whether a buyer used best efforts to try to satisfy a financing contingency is factual, to be decided under all the circumstances. If Byron was reliably assured, on the strength of what the broker told him, that all further efforts to secure financing would be futile, his approach to a single broker may be sufficient. He should not be required to go through the motions of making doomed applications. However, he takes a risk in abandoning efforts to get financing in reliance on the opinion of a single broker. Unless he can show that the broker was clearly correct, so that loan applications would be a pointless waste of time, he should have made applications notwithstanding the uncertain prospects of success. Byron's desire to buy the house cooled once he realized that the house was too expensive for him, which suggests that his lack of effort may have been motivated by a desire to back out of the contract.

5. The contract expressly makes payment conditional on the air conditioning unit having been properly installed in working order. This condition has been satisfied and Primo does not contend otherwise. Primo's argument that its receipt of the owner's payment for the air conditioning is also a condition precedent to its obligation to pay CC is not persuasive. In deciding if the contract actually made the owner's payment a condition of Primo's obligation to pay CC, the parties' intent on this matter must be interpreted. If there is extrinsic evidence that casts light on the meaning of the clause (such as evidence of trade usage or of discussions between the parties), this would help determine the intent of the language. If no such evidence is available, the reasonable meaning of the wording of the contract must be sought in light of the purpose of the contract as a whole. The facts do not indicate any usage or other contextual evidence, so interpretation to determine if the owner's payment to Primo is a condition precedent to Primo's obligation to pay CC is based solely on the language used in the contract.

   At first sight, the language seems relatively clear. Payment from the owner does sound like an express condition precedent. It follows the condition of proper completion of the work in the same sentence. This suggests that both of these events must occur before Primo's payment obligation falls due. However, courts interpreting payment provisions like this one tend to be skeptical of the argument that they are intended to be conditions. Unless the language (read in light of any contextual evidence that might be available) makes it very clear that the owner's payment was intended as a condition precedent, the assumption is that a term like this is more likely to have been intended as merely fixing a time for payment. Therefore, even if the owner does not pay the contractor, the contractor must pay the subcontractor within a reasonable time. *Koch v. Construction Technology, Inc.*, 924 S.W.2d 68 (Tenn. 1996), explains the reasoning behind this interpretation: Unless the parties express such an intention unequivocally, they cannot be taken to have placed the risk of the owner's nonpayment on the subcontractor, who has no contractual relationship with the owner but is employed by the prime contractor. Risk is more rationally left with the prime contractor, who has dealt with the owner and had the opportunity to evaluate its creditworthiness. Therefore, although the language in the contract does admit of the interpretation that the owner's payment is a condition, it is not strong enough to overturn the usual assumption that the parties could not have intended to shift the risk of the owner's default to CC.

6. In addition to the condition (implied if not express) that President must pay the premium, which appears not to be in issue, there are two express conditions precedent implicated in this dispute. The first is that a loss must occur of a kind covered by the policy. The second is that the insured must follow the prescribed claim procedure.

The condition that the loss must fall within the policy's coverage. The policy covers loss by vandalism, which it defines as willful and malicious damage to the premises. However, it specifically excludes coverage for pilferage, theft, or burglary. The language of the policy must be interpreted to determine if the losses are encompassed within the risk that is insured. Because this is a standard insurance policy drafted by the insurer, the contra proferentum rule is particularly applicable. Any doubt in the meaning of a provision in it will be resolved against the insurer.

There are two separate items of loss caused by the removal of the pipe: The loss of the pipe itself and the damage caused to walls and floors in removing it. The question is whether either of these losses results from vandalism. Vandalism is commonly thought of as the deliberate harming or defacement of property, purely for its own sake. However, the concept could be broad enough to include purposeful damage motivated by economic gain. It is beyond doubt that the thief acted willfully (deliberately) and maliciously (with intent to violate the law and President's rights) in causing the loss. This applies not only to the taking of the pipe but also to the concomitant destruction. The problem is that the policy draws a distinction between loss from vandalism and that from burglary, so when a wrongful act gives rise to injury of both kinds, the apparent conflict in terms must be reconciled. If "vandalism" is interpreted to include any malicious damage to the building even if motivated by burglary, the loss is covered by the policy. If it is interpreted more narrowly to include only malicious damage, without burglary, the loss is not covered. The former interpretation may be too generous to President because the policy does distinguish burglary from vandalism, and once property is removed, this fits better into the excluded loss from burglary.

The condition of notice. Even if the loss is covered by the policy, satisfying the first condition precedent, E&F is still not obliged to indemnify President for the loss unless the second condition—notice within seven days of loss and proof of loss 14 days thereafter—is also fulfilled. Because the condition is express, strict compliance is required. President's late notice failed to satisfy the condition exactly. This would preclude recovery under the policy unless there is a basis for excusing strict compliance.

President was about a day late in giving notice of its claim. However, E&F may have tacitly waived the condition of seven-day notice by not raising the delay during the phone call reporting the loss, and by sending an adjuster out to investigate the claim, knowing that the loss had occurred eight days before. In addition, both the adjuster and the letter rejecting the claim based the rejection on the coverage, not on the late notice. E&F did not make an argument of waiver until after President sued on the policy and E&F raised waiver as an alternative defense. A waiver does not have to be by express words. It can be inferred from conduct if the party knows or has reason to know of noncompliance with a condition and yet acts as if the condition is satisfied. (Such conduct could also give rise to an estoppel, but waiver is a better theory because President has taken no detrimental action in reliance on the representation.) A waiver of rights without consideration is effective provided that the condition is ancillary and technical, rather than a material component of the exchange. Although prompt notice is important to an insurer, which needs the opportunity to investigate a claim while it is fresh, a relatively short delay in notice is likely to be interpreted as a waivable ancillary matter.

7. Sprawling Malls' purchase of the land from Sue is subject to two express conditions precedent—its ability to raise the investment capital and notice to Sue by not later than August 1. Sprawling Malls did raise the capital, so that condition is satisfied and not in issue. The problem is that Sprawling Malls' notice was received a day late. Because the delivery of notice by August 1 is an express condition, it must be complied with strictly. If Sprawling Malls wanted the land, it had to deliver its notice to Sue within the time stated. Although the notice was mailed before August 1, the contract specified delivery—that is, receipt—by that date, and delivery occurred a day after the deadline. A day's delay may be a small deviation from the terms of the condition, but this is not relevant under the rule that requires strict compliance with express conditions. The rationale is that once the parties have taken the trouble to articulate and define the condition, the court should not tamper with their expressed intention. (Had the language of the condition been unclear, the court may have had some flexibility in interpreting what the condition required, but the language of this condition concerning the manner and time of notice is unambiguous and provides no basis for an interpretation favorable to Sprawling Malls.) Therefore, unless there is some ground for excusing exact compliance with the condition, the day's delay in delivery results in nonfulfillment of the condition, and Sprawling Malls has lost its right to buy the land.

   The only possible ground for excuse presented by these facts is unfair forfeiture. Courts have the discretion to excuse exact compliance with a condition (or to excuse the condition altogether, if appropriate) when strict enforcement of the condition would result in a disproportionate and unfair forfeiture by one of the parties and a windfall gain by the other. The policy of preventing unfair forfeiture acts as a counterweight to the rule of strict compliance, allowing courts some flexibility in averting particularly harsh and unfair results where there has been a minor or technical noncompliance with a condition. This does not mean that courts routinely excuse express conditions on the basis of unfair forfeiture. Courts are wary about applying the doctrine too readily because its overuse would eliminate the rule of strict compliance. In fact, cases in which courts apply the doctrine are quite rare. For unfair forfeiture to apply as a ground for excuse, the strict enforcement of the condition must result in undue hardship to the party seeking excuse and inappropriately extensive gain to the beneficiary of the condition. The balance of hardship against unfair gain must be evaluated in light of the relationship of the condition to the exchange as a whole.

In this case, the short delay in delivery of the notice certainly results in hardship to Sprawling Malls because it loses its right to buy the land and to enjoy the fruits of its efforts in securing financing for the project. However, apart from that, it has not suffered a significant forfeiture, and it was sloppy in just mailing the notice by regular mail, rather than using a method that would ensure timely delivery. Given the reluctance of courts to excuse express conditions, except in the most serious cases of forfeiture, there is probably not enough here for Sprawling Malls to get relief.

CHAPTER 17

Breach and Repudiation

§17.1 THE SCOPE OF THIS CHAPTER: NONFULFILLMENT OF A PROMISE

Chapter 16 draws the distinction between the nonfulfillment of a condition, which excuses the conditional performance, and the failure to honor a promise, which results in liability for breach of contract. If a term is a promissory condition—that is, one of the parties undertook that it would be satisfied—a material and total breach[1] of the promissory condition has the combined effect of entitling the other party both to withhold the performance that was subject to the condition and to seek a remedy for breach. Chapter 16 concentrates on the effect of conditions and their nonfulfillment. This chapter considers the impact and consequences of the breach of a promise.

This concept is illustrated by the following simple lease of a warehouse, entered into on July 1, to commence on August 1. The lease contained the following terms:

1. The lessee will pay a security deposit to the lessor by 5 P.M. on July 15.

1. The term "material and total breach" is explained in section 17.3.

2. The lessee will pay the rent for August by not later than 5 P.M. on July 31, and will thereafter pay the monthly rent for the premises by not later than 5 P.M. on the last day of the preceding month.
3. The lessor will clear, clean, and repair the premises before the lessee takes occupation and will make the premises available for the lessee's occupation by 9 A.M. on August 1. During the period of the lease, the lessor will assure the lessee's undisturbed possession of the premises.

Although no express language of condition has been used, it is easily inferable from the sequence set out in the contract that the parties intend the lessee's payment of the security deposit on July 15 and its payment of the August rent on July 31 to be promissory conditions precedent—the payments are not only expressly promised but also impliedly a condition precedent to the lessor's performance. The lessor's commitment to deliver the premises to the lessee by 9 A.M. on August 1 is also a promissory condition precedent—it is both an express promise and a construed condition of the lessee's rent payment for September. Thereafter there is an ongoing sequence of promissory conditions by each party—the lessee's payment of rent by the last day of each preceding month is a promissory condition precedent to the lessor's obligation to allow the lessee to remain in possession of the premises for the month after, which is in turn a promissory condition precedent to the lessee's obligation to pay the next month's rent, and so on until the end of the lease period.

If both parties perform as undertaken, the promises are honored, the conditions are fulfilled, and the transaction ends happily. As Restatement, Second, §235(1) says (maybe somewhat self-evidently), a contractual duty is discharged by full performance. However, all kinds of things could go wrong: At some point before performance is to commence on July 15, one of the parties may renege or indicate an intention to breach the contract; or the lessee may not make the security deposit or the advance rent payment at all, or in full, or on time; or the lessor may not clean and clear the premises, or give the lessee possession of the premises on time or at all. The purpose of this chapter is to discuss the legal effect of breaches like this relating both to pure promises and to promissory conditions. Sections 17.2 to 17.6 deal with breach proper (that is, the breach of a promise that occurs at or after performance is due) and section 17.7 examines the particular issues that arise when a party repudiates the contract in advance of the time of its performance. The importance and extent of the breach are crucial considerations throughout this chapter, which begins by distinguishing breaches of different degrees of gravity.

§17.2 THE NATURE OF BREACH

As intimated above, a party breaches a contract by failing, for whatever reason, to honor a promise of performance when that performance falls due. Four questions need to be resolved to establish that a breach of contract has occurred.

1. Determine the existence and content of the contractual undertaking to ascertain the exact nature and extent of the promise that was made. This involves interpreting the contract through the process discussed in Chapter 10.

2. Establish the date that the promised performance fell due. Although a party can repudiate a contract before its performance is due (as discussed in section 17.1), a breach by failure to perform or improper performance cannot occur until the time arises for the party's duty to render it. If the contract does not clearly and expressly state the due date for the party's performance, this must be determined by interpretation or construction. Also, if the performance is subject to a condition precedent, it is not due until the condition is satisfied.

3. Decide if the performance complied with the promise. Any shortfall from the promised performance is a breach. If the party has not performed at all, noncompliance is easy to see. However, where a party has rendered a performance that is alleged to be inadequate or deficient, the question of whether it satisfies the contractual duty can be difficult to resolve.

4. Having determined that a breach did occur, decide on the severity of the breach and on the aggrieved party's[2] rights in reacting to the breach. Some breaches are serious and fundamental enough to entitle the aggrieved party to withhold any return performance, terminate the contract, and sue for whatever damages that were suffered as a result of the breach. Commonly, those damages are for expectation relief, aimed at placing the aggrieved party in the financial position it would have been in had the contract not been breached. A breach of this kind is described as total and material. However, a breach is not total and material if it can be rectified (cured) or if it does not go to the fundamental basis of the contract. If the breach can be cured, the breaching party is entitled to an opportunity to cure it. If the beach is not material, the response of terminating the contract is too extreme. The aggrieved party must perform the contract and is confined to damages to compensate for the shortfall in performance. These issues are explored in the following sections.

2. The term "aggrieved party" is used in this chapter to mean the party against whom the breach has been committed.

§17.3 THE SIGNIFICANCE OF A BREACH: MATERIAL BREACH OR SUBSTANTIAL PERFORMANCE, AND TOTAL OR PARTIAL BREACH

§17.3.1 Introduction to the Distinction

Any performance that falls short of that promised is a breach. However, some breaches are relatively trivial and others are serious, and not all breaches should be treated in the same way. This section introduces the nature and consequences of breaches of different degrees of severity. Each of these types of breach are expanded on in the following sections.

a. Total and Material Breach

When a breach is profound enough to qualify as material and total, the aggrieved party's expectations under the contract have been completely dashed, and it should therefore have the right to terminate the contract—that is, to end the transaction and to sue the breaching party for whatever relief is necessary to compensate the aggrieved party for the breach. In most cases, these damages are based on the aggrieved party's contractual expectations and the goal of the remedy is to award a sum of money to place the aggrieved party in the financial position it would have been in had no breach occurred.[3] Because most promises exchanged in a contract are dependent, as explained in section 16.3.3, each party's performance is an express, implied, or construed condition of the other's duty to perform. Therefore, if one party materially breaches its performance obligation, this is not only a breach of the promise but also the nonfulfillment of the condition to any performance that may not yet have been rendered by the other party. For this reason, a total and material breach gives the aggrieved party the right not only to claim damages but also to refuse to render any part of its own performance that is still outstanding and to terminate the contract.

b. A Material Breach That Is Not Yet Total—Partial Breach and Cure

A breach that would qualify as material may be capable of rectification by the breaching party. If, under the circumstances, the breaching party has the ability to correct the nonconforming performance—to cure the

3. The nature and extent of damages for breach are considered in Chapter 18. Expectation damages could include the extra cost of a substitute transaction, loss of profits, and reimbursement of costs or other losses arising as a consequence of the breach.

breach—the breach does not become material and total unless the breaching party fails to cure it. A material breach that is capable of cure is classified as a partial breach, rather than a total breach, because there is a possibility that the deficiency in performance could be rectified or ameliorated by cure. When a breach is curable, the aggrieved party does not yet have the right to terminate the contract, but must give the breaching party an opportunity to cure the breach. The conditional nature of the breached material promise allows the aggrieved party to suspend its own performance until the breaching party does effect a cure. In some cases, cure may completely eliminate the breach, but even if it does not, the cure may reduce the gravity of the breach so that it is no longer material and becomes substantial performance. However, if there is no cure, the material breach becomes total, giving rise to all the rights and remedies identified in (a) above. The concepts of partial breach and cure are expanded on in section 17.3.6.

c. Nonmaterial Breach (Substantial Performance)

The term "partial breach" is also used to describe a situation in which a party's performance falls short of what was promised, but is not so severely deficient to constitute a material breach. A partial breach of this degree is called "substantial performance" to denote that even though it is a breach, it is not so serious as to defeat the aggrieved party's reasonable expectations under the contract. Where the breaching party's performance is substantially in compliance with what was promised, it would be unfairly harsh to allow the aggrieved party to terminate, thereby depriving the breaching party of all benefit of the bargain and making it liable for the whole range of damages. Therefore, the substantial performance is treated as substantial compliance with the condition, so that the aggrieved party cannot treat the condition of its performance as unfulfilled. The aggrieved party is obliged to stick to the contract and perform its side of the bargain. However, it is entitled to monetary compensation for the deficiency in the performance received from the breaching party. This measure of damages is usually based on the cost of rectifying the deficiency, or possibly on the actual loss in the value of the performance, as discussed in section 17.3.4. Such damages could be substantially less than what would be awarded for a total and material breach.

§17.3.2 What Makes a Breach Material?

The gravity and extent of a breach are a matter of interpretation that can only be resolved by examining the language of the contract in context and evaluating the shortfall in performance in light of the reasonable expectations of the parties. The concept of materiality has arisen many times before in relation to other doctrines.[4] The test for deciding whether a breach is material corresponds to that for deciding whether a term is material for other purposes. A breach is material if the failure or deficiency in performance is so central to the contract that it substantially impairs its value and deeply disappoints the reasonable expectations of the aggrieved party. The determination of whether the breach satisfies this test is based on interpretation of the contract. Although some breaches are obviously material because it is self-evident that they go to the heart of the contract, the importance of other breaches is less clear, and they must be evaluated under all the circumstances of the case. In essence, in situations where the severity of the breach is not obvious, materiality must be determined by considering the entirety of the exchange contemplated in the contract and deciding if the defective or absent performance forms a significant part of the consideration bargained for by the aggrieved party. The crucial question is whether the breach will deprive the aggrieved party of its reasonably expected benefit of the bargain. Restatement, Second, §241 articulates this test and includes a list of other factors that a court may consider, such as the extent to which the aggrieved party can be adequately compensated for the breach, the likelihood that the breaching party will cure the breach, and the extent to which the behavior of the breaching party comports with standards of good faith and fair dealing. These other factors do not speak directly to the core of materiality, but are equitable considerations that a court may weigh in deciding on the impact of the breach. They indicate that the equities between the parties have some relevance to the determination of the seriousness of the breach, and that a court may look not only at the deprivation suffered by the aggrieved party as a result of the breach but also at the degree of hardship (that is, forfeiture) that would be suffered by the breaching party if termination was allowed. A breach does not need to be deliberate or willful to be material, and its importance is not diminished merely because it was unintended or undesired by the breaching party. However, §241 indicates that in balancing the equities, courts may give some weight to the question of whether the breach was willful or innocent, or a violation of standards of fair dealing. The significance of the breach is also affected by the stage of performance at which the breach occurs. A breach at the outset of performance that affects the value of the entire exchange is likely to be more material than one occurring near the end of the performance and having an impact on only a small aspect of what was promised.

As noted above, the importance of some breaches is so obvious that the resolution of their materiality requires no effort at probing contractual intent. In the warehouse lease, it would not require deep analysis to conclude that it would be a material breach if the lessee failed to make the

4. *See, for example,* sections 6.3.2 (battle of the forms), 10.1 (indefiniteness), 13.6.5 (misrepresentation), and 15.3 (mistake).

payment of rent at all or if the lessor failed to give occupation of the premises to the lessee. In each case, the party has broken a promise that goes to the very heart of the exchange. However, the issue of materiality would be less obvious if the lessee failed to pay the security deposit on July 15, but tendered its payment at 10 A.M. on July 16. The decision on whether that short delay in payment is a material breach is based on the apparent intent of the parties: Are the lessor's contractual rights (including the security it is entitled to expect from advance payment) seriously affected by receiving payment the next morning? If the contract expressly states that failure to pay the security deposit exactly on time will be a material breach, the court will likely give effect to the parties' express intent and will not second-guess their decision to treat late payment as a material breach. However, in the absence of such a clear expression of intent, the court must examine the nature and purpose of the contract in context to decide if the short delay in payment is material. The apparent purpose of the provision is to ensure the lessor's receipt of the security purpose ahead of the commencement date of the lease. There is no obvious reason why a delay of about 17 hours past the due time fundamentally impairs the lessor's benefit of its bargain and should be treated as material.

A couple of cases illustrate a court's assessment of whether a breach was material. *Raymond Weil, S.A. v. Theron*, 585 F.Supp.2d 473 (S.D.N.Y. 2008), involved a contract between the actor Charlize Theron and Raymond Weil, S.A. (RW), a watchmaker, under which RW agreed to pay Theron $3 million in exchange for the use of her image in a worldwide advertising campaign. The contract committed Theron to represent RW exclusively during its 15-month term, and she promised not to wear any watches by other manufacturers during the period of the contract. Theron committed two breaches of the contract. One of them[5] was wearing a Dior watch for about an hour during a panel discussion in which she participated at a film festival. Theron argued that the wearing of the watch for such a short time within a 15-month contract period did not amount to a material breach. This may have been a plausible argument but for the fact that many photographs were taken of her during the panel discussion, and these photographs, showing the Dior watch, were widely distributed on the Internet. Some were sold to a prominent retailer of Dior watches, which used them for advertising purposes. The court held that the breach, however fleeting, had a material effect on Theron's promise to endorse RW products exclusively. The court considered it irrelevant that Theron was not responsible for the wide dissemination of the photographs and pointed out that, as a famous actor, she should have foreseen the likelihood that the photographs would be distributed and sold to a competitor of RW.

---

5. Theron's other breach is discussed in section 17.3.6.

Al Hirschfeld Foundation v. Margo Feiden Galleries, Ltd., 296 F. Supp. 3d 627 (S.D.N.Y. 2017), concerned the breach of a contract under which the gallery represented the renowned cartoonist, Al Hirschfeld. (The foundation succeeded to Hirschfeld's rights and obligations under the contract after his death in 2003.) The gallery's principal obligations under the representation agreement were to take care of Hirschfeld's original works in its custody and to sell those works. In 2016, the foundation terminated the contract on the ground that the gallery had breached it in several respects. One of the most significant allegations of breach was that the gallery had, without authorization, produced and sold giclee prints[6] of some of Hirschfeld's original cartoons. The court held that this was a material breach, entitling the foundation to terminate the contract. The court reasoned that the unauthorized reproduction and sale of the cartoons went to the root of the parties' agreement, which was a fiduciary-like relationship under which the gallery had a duty to treat the cartoons as trust property, and to deal with them only as authorized. By reproducing cartoons for sale, largely for its own benefit, it diluted the market for Hirschfeld's work and undercut the essential purpose of the contract.

§17.3.3 Relief for Material Breach

As noted earlier, if the breach is material, it so badly defeats the aggrieved party's expectations that it is entitled to terminate the contract and sue for whatever relief is necessary to compensate for the breach. The usual measure of those damages aims at compensating the aggrieved party for the loss of its bargain by placing it in the financial position it would have been in had the contract not been breached. These are called expectation damages.[7] For example, in the lease of the warehouse, if, during the course of the lease, the lessee completely fails to pay the rent, thereby breaching materially, the lessor has the right to terminate the lease, eject the lessee, and sue the lessee for expectation damages, calculated by the difference between the unpaid rent due for the total period of the lease, less any rent earned by re-letting the premises to another tenant during that period. Conversely, if the lessee did pay the rent but the lessor materially breached by wrongfully barring the lessee's access to the premises, the lessee could terminate the lease, withhold all future rent payments, and sue for expectation damages, in the simplest case, calculated as the difference between any higher rent that the lessee has to pay for substitute premises for the period of this lease and the rent that would have been payable for that period under this lease. If, in addition, the

6. A giclee print is a high-quality reproduction of original artwork by means of a high-resolution inkjet printer.

7. Expectation damages are discussed more fully in sections 18.1 to 18.6.

lessee had suffered further losses, such as lost revenue because of the disruption of its business, the lessee would be able to claim those losses as well.

Although an aggrieved party is most likely to seek expectation damages following termination for material breach, there are other alternatives available to the aggrieved party if, for one reason or another, the aggrieved party has not suffered or cannot prove expectation damages.[8] For example, in *Forbes v. Prime General Contractors, Inc.*, 255 So. 3d 448 (Fla. Dist. Ct. App. 2018), a building contractor demanded that the property owners pay it substantially more than it was due under the contract to renovate a house. When the owners refused, the contractor abandoned the job, thereby materially breaching the contract. Instead of claiming expectation damages, the owners sued the contractor for all losses and expenses that they had incurred in reliance on the contract. These damages, which included monies paid to the contractor under the contract and the wasted cost of drawing plans for the renovation, are called reliance damages.[9] Unlike expectation damages, which aim to place the aggrieved party in the position it would have been in had the contract been performed, these damages aim to restore the aggrieved party to the position it had been in prior to the contract. The court held that the owners were entitled to elect to claim reliance damages instead of expectation damages and awarded them the damages claimed.

§17.3.4 Substantial Performance

Substantial performance is a breach because it falls short of the performance required by the contract. To decide if a breach is nonmaterial and therefore qualifies as substantial performance the contract must be interpreted to examine the relationship of the breach to the overall exchange in values. Consider again the situation in which the lessee failed to pay the security deposit by July 15, but tendered payment of it on the morning of July 16. Unless payment on July 15 is material, the slight delay in payment would be substantial performance. If so, the lessor has no basis for terminating the lease and must accept the delay in payment with whatever monetary adjustment is needed to compensate for the delay. On these facts, this may be nothing or, at most, a few hours interest on the amount of the deposit.

Jacob & Youngs v. Kent, 129 N.E. 889 (N.Y. 1921), is a foundational case involving substantial performance. A builder had completed the construction of a grand country home for a total price of $77,000, a considerable sum when the house was built in 1914. The owner refused to pay the balance

8. The alternative bases for damages are discussed more fully in sections 18.7 to 18.9.

9. Reliance damages are explained and more fully discussed in relation to breach of contract in sections 18.7 and 18.8. They are also discussed in relation to the doctrine of promissory estoppel in section 8.7.

of the contract price (about $3,500) to the builder on the grounds that the builder had breached the contract by installing plumbing pipe of the wrong brand in the house. The builder had overlooked a specification in the contract that called for the pipe to be of Reading brand. As a result, more than half the pipe was made by other manufacturers. There was no difference in quality between the Reading pipe and the other brands that had been installed. However, the owner refused to pay the balance of the contract price on the grounds that the cost of remedying the breach far exceeded this amount. Because the pipe was already encased within the walls, the cost of removing and replacing the wrong pipe would have involved the demolition and rebuilding of a significant portion of the house. The majority of the court found the breach to be both inadvertent[10] and trivial. Although the specification of the brand was an express promise in the contract, there was nothing in the contract to indicate that the parties considered the actual brand to be a significant term. They were more concerned about the quality of the pipe, and as the other brands were of equal quality, the breach was not material. The dissent disagreed that the breach should be treated as trivial. The owner had specified that Reading pipe be used, and the court should not deprive him of his bargain by assuming that the pipe brand was unimportant to him.

The disagreement between the majority and dissent in *Jacob & Youngs* shows that it can be difficult to decide if a breach is material. Some other examples illustrate how courts try to ascertain the underlying purpose of the contract in resolving this question. In *Lyon v. Belosky Construction*, 247 A.D.2d 730 (N.Y. App. Div. 1998), the court found that a builder did commit a material breach by centering the roof of a house incorrectly. Although this did not affect the structural utility or soundness of the roof, it changed the aesthetic appearance of the house. The aberration in the roof was an important breach of the owners' expectations under the contract because the house had been custom-designed to reflect the aesthetic appearance desired by the owners.. In *21st Century North American Insurance Co. v. Perez*, 173 A.3d 64 (Conn. App. Ct. 2017), an insured paid part of the premium due under a vehicle insurance policy by due date, but did not pay the balance of the premium until about two weeks after the due date. Both the policy and a notice of cancellation sent to the insured made it clear that the policy would lapse if the premium was not paid in full by the due date. About ten days after the insured had paid the balance, the insured vehicle was involved in a collision in which the passenger in the other vehicle was killed. The insurer refused to defend or indemnify the injured on the ground that the policy had lapsed before the collision. The trial court held that the policy had not lapsed because the

10. The majority opinion emphasizes the inadvertence of the breach and indicates that this was an important factor in the court's ultimate decision on the appropriate measure of relief. (The remedial aspect of the case is discussed in section 17.3.5.) The dissent disagreed with the majority's finding that the breach was not deliberate.

insured's payment of the balance of the premium two weeks later was substantial performance. The court of appeals reversed—the late payment was a material breach because timely payment of the premium was a material term of the policy. It went to the root and essence of the contract, and to allow an insured to pay late would create chaos in the insurance industry and fundamentally undermine an insurer's ability to control its exposure to liability. This case is also a good illustration of the connection between material breach and the doctrine of strict compliance with an express condition, discussed in sections 16.3.1 and 16.9.

§17.3.5 Relief for Substantial Performance and Adjustment to Avoid Unfair Forfeiture

As explained above, where a breach qualifies as substantial performance, the aggrieved party cannot withhold performance or terminate the contract, but is entitled to claim any damages suffered as a result of the breach. These damages may be offset against any payment still due to the breaching party or, if no such return performance is outstanding, they form the basis of a money judgment against the breaching party. The usual measure of damages is the cost to place the aggrieved party in the position it would have been in had the performance been in full compliance with the contract. In most cases, this is represented by an award of the amount of money necessary to correct the shortfall in performance. For example, if work was improperly done or property supplied was defective, compensation is measured by the cost to the aggrieved party of fixing the defect in the performance. If the breach lies in a failure to complete performance, the completion cost is the proper measure. If the breach involves a delay in performance, compensation is appropriately measured by determining the loss caused by the delay.

In some cases, the cost of rectifying the performance may be disproportionate to any realistic loss actually suffered by the aggrieved party. If the court feels that damages measured by the cost of rectification are not an accurate measure of actual harm, but would provide a windfall to the aggrieved party and impose an unfair forfeiture on the breaching party, the court may adjust the damages to better represent the true harm to the aggrieved party.[11] This measure of damages is based on the difference in value between what

11. Sometimes a disproportionate award of this kind is described as economically wasteful because it would be a waste of money for the aggrieved party to spend a disproportionate amount of money to fix a nonmaterial defect. However, that is not an accurate characterization. The aggrieved party has no obligation to use the damages to fix the defect in performance, and it could just bank the damages or spend them for some other purpose. Therefore, the basis for not awarding the cost of rectifying the defect is best described not as economic waste, but as the prevention of unfair forfeiture.

was promised and what was performed. Because a determination of unfair forfeiture is not simply a matter of arithmetic, and also balances the equities between the parties,[12] a court is more likely to make this adjustment if the noncompliance was inadvertent and is less likely to do so if the failure to perform in accordance with the contract was deliberate. *Jacob & Youngs* applied the unfair forfeiture principle. The majority of the court held that the contract had been substantially performed because it found the use of the wrong pipe, equal in quality to Reading pipe, to be a trivial breach. The court recognized that the cost of rectifying the defect by replacing the nonconforming pipe would be the usual measure of damages. However, it considered that damages based on the cost of replacing the pipe, which would be the cost of substantial demolition and rebuilding, would be grossly out of proportion to the actual loss suffered by the owner as a result of the minor breach and would be unduly harsh on the builder. The court therefore limited the owner's damages to the difference in market value between a house fitted only with Reading pipe and a house fitted with pipe of the same quality made by different manufacturers. This market difference was zero. (The court stressed that the breach was inadvertent and indicated that it would have been less solicitous of the builder had the breach been willful.)

Khiterer v. Bell, 2005 WL 192354 (N.Y. City Civ. Ct. 2005), followed the approach of *Jacob & Youngs*. A patient sued her dentist for fitting porcelain crowns instead of crowns made of porcelain on gold. The court accepted that this was a breach of contract. However, the dentist testified that all-porcelain crowns were no less expensive and were therapeutically superior. It was also apparent that the dentist's breach was inadvertent and not deliberate. The court held that the cost of replacement would be unfairly disproportionate and confined the patient to loss in value. As the patient could show no actual injury, she was awarded nominal damages.

§17.3.6 Partial Breach and Cure

Some breaches have such an immediate, irreparable, and significant impact on the aggrieved party's rights that they are unavoidably material as soon as they occur, and there is nothing that the promisor can do to rectify them. Other breaches are by nature so trivial that they could never result in a total breach of the contract, even if no attempt was made to remedy them. However, between these poles, there are breaches that would be material if left unrectified, but the circumstances are such that it is still possible for the breaching party to take steps to cure the defect in performance. A curable

12. The concept of balancing the equities in the context of forfeiture is discussed in sections 16.10.3 and 18.6.6.

Diagram 17A

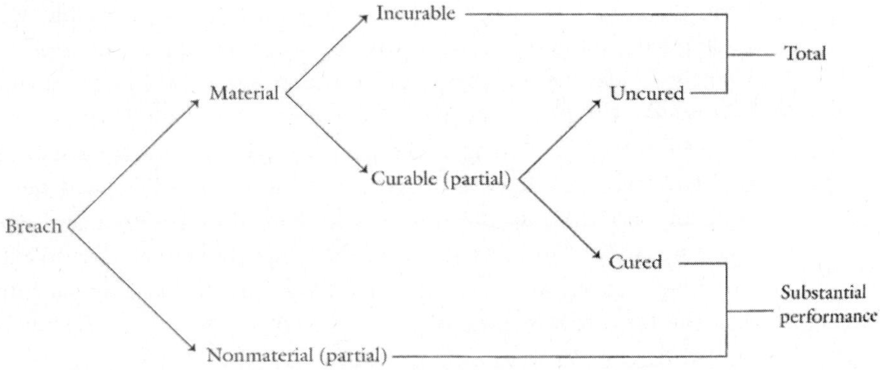

material breach is treated as partial because the breaching party can prevent total breach by taking remedial action within a reasonable time. This is shown in Diagram 17A.

To illustrate, consider the warehouse lease again. The lease included the lessor's promise to clean, clear, and repair the premises before the August 1 occupation date. This was an important provision to the lessee because the prior tenant had damaged the premises and left piles of junk in the warehouse, making it unusable for the lessee's purposes. Assume that the lessor's failure to remove the junk and to clean and repair the premises would be a material breach. If the lessor had not completed this work by the August 1 occupation date, but got it done a few days later, this might constitute a sufficient cure of the breach, converting the material breach into the substantial performance of slightly late delivery of the premises in good condition. An effective cure could eliminate the breach entirely, but where, as in this example, the cure does not completely remove the breach, it can convert a material breach into a partial breach. Even where the breaching party is willing to cure the breach, there may be a dispute about whether the cure would be adequate and timely. The effectiveness of a tendered cure in averting material breach, and converting it into substantial performance is decided, as usual, with reference to the aggrieved party's reasonable expectations under the contract.

The question of cure arose in the *Raymond Weil* case, discussed in section 17.3.2. In addition to wearing the Dior watch during the panel discussion, on another occasion Theron allowed herself to be photographed with a Montblanc necklace draped over her forearm. Montblanc used the photograph as an advertising poster. This was also a violation of the exclusivity agreement because, apart from the promise not to wear other watches in public, Theron undertook not to endorse the jewelry of other manufacturers. She therefore breached the contract by lending her image to Montblanc for the poster. A couple of days after the poster was displayed, RW complained to Montblanc, which withdrew it. RW argued that the breach was incurable, despite the withdrawal of the poster, because people who saw the poster during the time that it was displayed could not "un-see" it. This argument may have worked because the damage resulting from display of the poster, like the public display of Theron wearing the Dior watch, could not be undone by removing the poster after it had been seen by many people. However, in the case of the poster, Raymond Weil had demanded that Montblanc withdraw the poster, which it did and Raymond Weil accepted the cure at the time. As a result, the court held that the breach had been effectively cured and Raymond Weil was precluded from arguing in court that the breach was not adequately cured. [13]

§17.4 A SUMMARY OF THE RELATIONSHIP BETWEEN THE MATERIALITY OF BREACH AND THE NONFULFILLMENT OF A CONDITION

The previous sections identify the relationship between material breach and the nonfulfillment of a condition. This summary encapsulates and reinforces what has been said about this relationship.

1. Where a term of a contract is both a promise and a condition (a promissory condition), a material and total breach of the promise is also the nonfulfillment of the condition. This is why the aggrieved party is entitled to withhold its own performance, which is contingent on the promissory condition, as well as suing for damages.
2. If the breach is material, but not total because it can be cured, the aggrieved party cannot immediately terminate the contract and sue for damages for breach. However, the conditional nature of the breached promise allows the aggrieved party to suspend its own performance until such time as the condition is fulfilled by cure.
3. If the breach is not material so that the promissory condition is substantially performed, the doctrine of substantial compliance with the condition also applies. This means that the aggrieved party cannot sue for total breach and cannot suspend its own contingent performance but must perform and seek recourse for the breach through compensation for the shortfall in performance. In *Jacob & Youngs*, the court

13. The contract provided for the right to cure. It required the party claiming breach to give notice of the breach to the other party, which had five days to cure the breach. Montblanc removed the poster within five days of Raymond Weil's demand. Even if the contract had not contained the provision, Montblanc's removal of the poster following demand and Raymond Weil's apparent acceptance of this cure at the time would have led to the same conclusion.

couched its discussion of substantial performance in the language of conditions. Because the court found that the failure to use Reading pipe was a trivial breach, it described the brand specification as an "independent promise." By this it meant that although promises in a contract are normally dependent (that is, promissory conditions of each other) a nonmaterial breach of one of those promises should not be treated as a complete failure of the condition. Therefore, the aggrieved party's remaining obligation of performance must not be treated as conditional on exact fulfillment of the breached promissory condition. As a result, the aggrieved party cannot claim total breach and withhold its return performance, but remains bound to perform, subject to the offset of any damages caused by the breach. If the breached promise is an express condition, the doctrine of substantial compliance does not apply, and failure to perform exactly as promised must be treated as a material breach.

§17.5 UCC ARTICLE 2: PERFECT TENDER, SUBSTANTIAL PERFORMANCE, AND CURE

§17.5.1 Perfect Tender on Delivery of Goods and Substantial Performance on Revocation of Acceptance

a. Perfect Tender

Following the execution of a contract for the sale of goods, the seller is obliged to deliver the goods to the buyer at the time and place specified in the contract. Upon tender of delivery, the buyer has the right to inspect the goods to see if they conform to the contract, and if they do not, the buyer may reject them. Both the inspection and rejection must be within a reasonable time. This book does not deal with Article 2's detailed rules concerning the tender and acceptance or rejection of goods, but focuses on the UCC's treatment of substantial performance and cure, which is notably different from the common law.

The rule was established, long before the enactment of the UCC, that the doctrine of substantial performance is not applicable to a sale of goods. The buyer is entitled to "perfect tender" of the goods ordered and has the right to reject goods that fail to conform exactly to what was called for by the contract. This rule has been retained in §2.601, which permits the buyer to reject goods that "fail in any respect to conform to the contract." This is reinforced by §2.106(2), which defines "conforming" as meaning "in accordance with the obligations under the contract." The question of whether goods conform to the contract is factual, based on an interpretation of what was called for under the contract and an evaluation of the character of what was performed. Nonconformity may lie in the quality, quantity, or attributes of the goods themselves, or in the manner in which they are provided, such as the way in which they are packaged or delivered. It is not always easy to resolve a dispute concerning the fact and extent of an alleged nonconformity with the contract.

Albrecht v. Fettig, 932 N.W.2d 331 (Neb. Ct. App. 2019), is a clear case of nonconformity. The parties entered into a contract for the sale of 150 head of cattle, 80 percent of which were required to be Red Angus and 20 percent Black Angus. When the seller delivered the steers only about 55 percent were red steers, about 43 percent were black steers, and the remainder were neither. The buyer rejected the steers. The court applied the perfect tender rule and held that the buyer was entitled to reject the entire delivery. The seller argued that the perfect tender rule had eroded, so that a buyer may only reject a delivery that is substantially nonconforming. The court rejected that argument, holding that the perfect tender rule still applied with full force. In addition, even if the seller's legal argument had been correct, the delivery of significantly different quantities of black and red steers would not be in substantial conformity with the contract.

Although the perfect tender rule provides little room for a court to recognize substantial performance, there is some scope for avoiding the rule under the right circumstances. For example, where the buyer's rejection of goods is clearly pretextual—that is, the buyer rejects them on the basis of some minor nonconformity as a means of escaping an undesirable contract—a court may apply the general obligation of good faith and fair dealing to preclude rejection on a technicality.

Also, the rules relating to acceptance and rejection of goods sometimes give the court an opportunity to prevent a rejection of goods on trivial grounds. Without going into the intricacies of rejection, it can be noted generally that the buyer must act promptly and follow the proper procedure to effectively reject goods. If the buyer delays beyond a reasonable time or slips up procedurally in rejecting, the rejection is ineffective and the buyer is deemed to have accepted the goods.

b. Revocation of Acceptance and Substantial Performance

A buyer that has accepted the goods is able to revoke acceptance under UCC §2.608 provided that it meets specified requirements, which include, in essence, the requirement that the nonconformity was difficult to discover at the time of acceptance of the goods, that revocation occurs within a reasonable time, and that the nonconformity substantially impairs the value of the goods to the buyer. The requirement that the nonconformity substantially impairs the value of the goods recognizes the principle of substantial performance where the buyer seeks to revoke its acceptance of goods. That is, although the perfect tender rule applies at the time that the buyer rejects the goods, it does not apply where the buyer accepts the goods and subsequently revokes that acceptance. At that stage, Article 2 does recognize the principle of substantial performance, so that the buyer cannot revoke acceptance if the goods substantially comply with the contract. The application of the substantial performance doctrine at the stage of revocation of acceptance of the goods is illustrated by *Kettering Adventist Healthcare v. Jade Designs, LLC*, 677 F. Supp. 3d 735 (S.D. Ohio 2023). At the outbreak of the COVID-19 pandemic, medical facilities were required by government regulation to obtain N95 masks certified by the National Institute for Occupational Safety and Health (NIOSH). Kettering ordered 300,000 3M-made N95 masks from Jade for the price of $1,185,000. The masks were delivered and accepted by Kettering. It subsequently turned out that the masks were not manufactured by 3M, but were counterfeit. Kettering revoked its acceptance. The revocation was timely and otherwise in accordance with UCC §2.608, but Jade argued that the counterfeit masks worked just as well as those made by 3M, so it had substantially performed. The court rejected this argument. Even if it was true that the masks were of the same quality as the 3M masks, as counterfeits they were not NIOSH certified and were therefore useless to Kettering because government regulations did not permit their use.

If the goods have been accepted and the acceptance cannot be revoked the buyer is confined by UCC §2.714 to damages based on the loss in value as a result of the nonconformity. The interaction between the perfect tender rule and the buyer's failure to reject the goods is illustrated by *Khiterer v. Bell*, discussed in section 17.3.5, in which a dentist fitted crowns made of porcelain instead of gold and porcelain. The court held that the dental services predominated over the sale aspect of the contract, so the common law rule of substantial performance applied. However, it went on to point out that even if this had been predominantly a sale of goods, the perfect tender rule would not have applied because the patient had accepted the crowns by not having them removed for two years after they were fitted. She could thereafter only revoke her acceptance if the nonconformity substantially impaired their value, which it did not.

§17.5.2 Cure Under UCC Article 2

Under prescribed circumstances, UCC §2.508 permits the seller to avoid final rejection of nonconforming goods by curing the deficient tender. Where cure is possible, §2.508 mitigates the harsh effect of the perfect tender rule. The strength of the seller's right to cure depends on whether the seller would have time to complete the cure before the date due for the delivery of the goods under the contract. If the seller tenders delivery before due date, so that the buyer's rejection occurs before that date, the seller has a much greater right to cure than if the goods were delivered on or after due date. The reason for this is the perfect tender rule. Unlike the common law, which treats late performance as a material breach only if the date of performance is material, the perfect tender rule gives the buyer the right to reject late delivery even if time of delivery is not a material term. Section 2.508 takes this into account by imposing more stringent limitations on the seller's right to cure after the contractual delivery date. Section 2.508 operates as follows.

When the goods are delivered, the buyer has the right to inspect them within a reasonable time. If they are nonconforming, the buyer has the right, within a further reasonable time, to reject them. If the seller delivered the goods in good time before the time required for delivery in the contract, the delivery date may still not have passed by the time that the buyer (having acted with the required reasonable promptness) exercises the right of rejection. If so, §2.508(1) gives the seller an unconditional right to notify the buyer seasonably of intent to cure and to affect the cure by substituting a conforming delivery before that time expires.

If the contractual delivery date has passed, this unrestricted ability to cure is no longer available, but a qualified right to cure still exists for a reasonable time. Section 2.508(2) permits the seller to notify the buyer seasonably of intent to cure and to effect the cure within a reasonable time, provided that "the seller had reasonable grounds to believe [that the tender of delivery] would be acceptable with or without money allowance." This means that if the seller had no reason to know that the goods were nonconforming, or realized that they were, but reasonably believed that the buyer would nevertheless take them if an appropriate price adjustment was made, the seller may be able to rectify the nonconformity even after the date for delivery had passed. However, the cure must be within a reasonable time, and the issue of what is reasonable depends on the nature and purpose of the sale. When delivery on the exact date specified is a material term of the contract (that is, it is clear from the contract that any delay in delivery would be a serious breach), there may be no reasonable time for cure. In other cases, the time for substituting a conforming delivery could range from a few hours to days, depending on the circumstances of the contract.

In light of the perfect tender rule, the cure must actually eliminate the breach. An offer of cure that does not do that is not an effective cure. In *Albrecht v. Fettig*, cited in section 17.5.1, the buyer rejected the seller's delivery of cattle because it failed to conform to the contract. The cattle consisted of only 55 percent Red Angus, instead of 80 percent required by the contract and 43 percent of Black Angus, instead of 20 percent required by the contract. The seller offered to cure by taking back as many of the black steers as necessary to get the proportions of 80 percent of red to 20 percent of black steers. The court pointed out the rather obvious reason why this would not be an adequate cure: even if the proportions were thereby corrected, the seller would have breached the obligation to deliver 150 steers.

In other cases, it may be more difficult to know whether a proffered cure would be sufficient to remove the nonconformity. For example, say that a consumer buys a new dining room table from a furniture store. When it arrives on the date scheduled for delivery, the buyer notices a large scratch across the top and rejects the table. The seller concedes that this is a nonconformity and gives the buyer a couple of options: The buyer can keep the scratched table at a discount of 10 percent off the price, or the seller will take the table back, refinish it, and redeliver it in a week. The buyer refuses to accept either option and demands delivery of another table on the same day, failing which the buyer threatens to terminate the sale, purchase a substitute elsewhere, and hold the seller liable for any additional cost. The buyer's objection to the proposed cure is that the contract called for a new table, not a discounted scratched table or a refinished one delivered a week late. This dispute relates to the sufficiency of the seller's offer to cure. The buyer adopts the position that nothing short of the immediate delivery of a new table would be an adequate cure, but the seller considers it appropriate to offer a monetary allowance or the delivery of a repaired table in a week.

Both parties take the risk of breaching the contract by insisting on their positions. If the buyer is not justified in rejecting the seller's offer of cure, the buyer's termination of the contract would be based on partial breach, which the seller was not given a reasonable opportunity to cure. This would make the buyer the breaching party. If the seller is wrong, it loses the chance to rectify the breach by an effective cure within the time for delivery and converts its partial breach into a total one. To decide who is right, the judgments called for by §2.508 must be made: Was the seller justified in believing that the tender was conforming or otherwise acceptable? Is delivery by the date specified in the contract of the essence, and if not, is a week's delay reasonable? Will the table, as refinished, conform to the contract? The answers to these questions lie in an interpretation of the contract to determine the parties' reasonable expectations.

In the above example, the contract involves a single delivery of one item. When the contract calls for the delivery of a quantity of goods in installments, the perfect tender rule is further qualified. This issue is deferred until after the discussion of repudiation and is covered in section 17.7.8.

§17.6 THE BREACHING PARTY'S RECOVERY FOLLOWING MATERIAL BREACH AND THE CONCEPT OF DIVISIBILITY

§17.6.1 The Forfeiture of Contractual Rights by a Party Who Breaches Materially

As stated in sections 17.3.4 and 17.4, a party who substantially performs is entitled to return performance under the contract, subject to an offset for damages caused by the partial breach. This means that if the aggrieved party fails to render the return performance, the breaching party may sue for enforcement of the contract despite the partial breach. However, if the breach is material and total, the breaching party has no right to sue for enforcement of the contract. A material breach operates as a renunciation of the contract by the breaching party, who thereby forfeits all rights under it and has no contractual claim to enforce. This follows naturally from the principle that a material and total breach terminates the aggrieved party's obligation to render return performance.

§17.6.2 Restitution in Favor of a Party Who Has Breached Materially

The above rule is concerned with suit on the contract and does not cover the breaching party's right to claim restitution on the theory of unjust enrichment if the breaching party has given some benefit to the aggrieved party by performing part of its obligation before breaching materially. Once the contract has been terminated following material breach, the aggrieved party no longer has the right to retain the benefit of that performance without accounting to the breaching party for the value conferred.

For example, say that the lessee of the warehouse premises paid the security deposit to the lessor on July 15. When the time came for the lessee to pay the first month's rental on July 31, the lessee refused to pay it and told the lessor that it no longer intended to lease the warehouse. The lessee thereby materially breached the lease, giving the lessor the right to terminate the lease, withhold its own performance, and claim damages from the lessee. However, the lessee has already paid the security deposit and since the lessor rescinded the contract, it has no contractual right to retain the security deposit. Under principles of unjust enrichment, the lessor must restore the payment to the lessee. This does not mean that the lessee will get the cash back, because the restitutionary recovery of a party who has committed the material breach is offset against any claim the aggrieved party has for damages. This principle is adopted by Restatement, Second, §374, which recognizes a right of restitution in favor of a party who has breached materially to the extent that the benefit conferred on the aggrieved party exceeds its claim for damages.[14] *See* Diagram 17B.

14. The Restatement's position is widely recognized by courts, but some courts, particularly in older cases, may refuse to allow any remedy at all to a party that has breached materially, particularly if the breach was deliberate. This punitive stance withholds even restitutionary recovery to the breaching party and can have very unfair results because it disproportionally punishes a party who has rendered considerable performance before breaching. That is, the greater the value of what was performed before the breach, the greater the forfeiture.

Diagram 17B

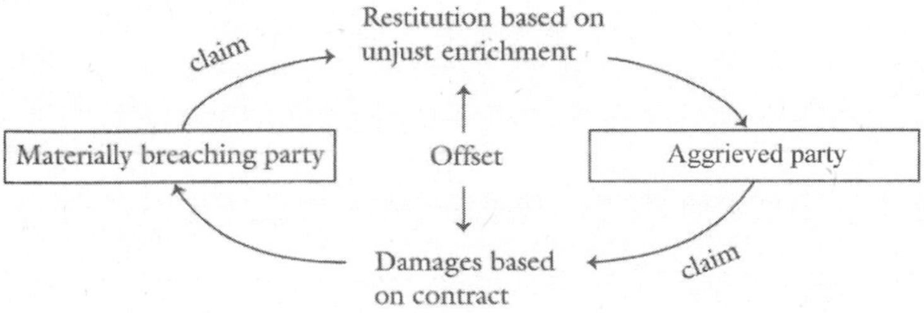

UCC Article 2 follows an approach similar to that of Restatement, Second, in that it permits restitution in favor of a breaching party, whether or not the breach was willful, but it imposes a modest penalty on a breaching buyer. Section 2.718(2)(b) allows a defaulting buyer to obtain restitution of payments made to the seller to the extent that they exceed any amount of validly agreed damages,[15] or the smaller of $500 or 20 percent of the price. Apart from this penalty, any restitutionary recovery under §2.718(2) is offset under §2.718(3) by any damages to which the seller is entitled under Article 2.

The example involving the payment of the security deposit by the lessee that later committed a material breach involved restoration of a money payment. It therefore did not present any issue of valuation of the benefit. However, if the breaching party's performance was not the payment of money, but the rendition of a service, the value of the benefit could be a matter of dispute. The general approach, reflected in Restatement, Second, §371 and §374, Comment *b*, is to give the breaching party the lesser of the market value (quantum meruit) of the service or the aggrieved party's ultimate economic enrichment (the actual increase in its economic wealth). Although the contract price may be used as evidence of value, it is not dispositive. The same principle applies if the benefit was property and it is not possible to restore the property to the breaching party.

§17.6.3 The Enforcement Rights of a Party That Breaches Materially When the Contract Is Divisible

Divisibility is a concept of limited application, only relevant when there is some reason to break a contract into discrete units, and the contract is capable of being divided up into a set of self-standing components. Most contracts are not divisible because they contemplate the exchange of each party's complete performance and cannot be fragmented into a collection of independent, self-contained exchanges. However, some contracts are

15. Agreed damages are explained in section 18.11.

structured in a way that allows them to be broken up into sets of matching performances, each of which can be treated as a self-sufficient contractual component within the larger contractual relationship. The determination of whether a contract is divisible is a matter of interpretation, and a court should not find a contract to be capable of division unless it is clear that this does not conflict with the apparent intent of the parties or damage the value of a performance reasonably expected by either of them.

Menorah Chapels at Millburn v. Needle, 899 A.2d 316 (N.J. Super. A.D. 2006), is a good illustration of the analysis used to determine divisibility. Needle contracted with Menorah, a funeral home, for the provision of funeral services for his father-in-law. The contract specified that the funeral services would comply with orthodox Jewish ritual. One of the requirements of orthodox ritual is that the body must be attended at all times prior to burial by watchers or *shomers* who take shifts in maintaining a constant vigil over it. Menorah's price list specifically included the provision of watchers on request and it was undisputed that Needle made such a request. In breach of this provision, Menorah provided a watcher for only three of the six shifts during the period prior to the burial. When Needle refused to pay Menorah, it sued for the contract price less a deduction of $390 for the three missed shifts. Menorah argued that the contract was divisible because each of its services was separately priced and could be ordered or declined by the customer. The trial court found the contract to be divisible, but the appellate court disagreed. The crucial question is whether it was the basis of the parties' bargain that the contract be performed in its entirety. The mere fact that the services were separately priced was not enough to make the contract divisible, especially in this case where itemization was required by state consumer protection laws. The underlying purpose of the contract was to provide a complete orthodox funeral, and Menorah could not simply fail to provide one of the services and sue under the contract for the price of what it did perform. The court remanded the case to the trial court to determine if the breach was material, and, if so, to determine what value, if any, Menorah gave to Needle.

As *Menorah Chapels* shows, division of a contract may be useful when there has been a breach or some other problem, such as illegality or impracticability, that affects only a portion of the contract, but does not taint the contract as a whole. In the context of material breach, if a contract is capable of division, splitting it into a set of autonomous subparts may enable a party who has materially breached one part to isolate the breach and confine it to the affected part, so that the remainder of the contract is not sullied by the breach. This will enable the breaching party to treat the unaffected portion of the contract as if no breach had occurred and to enforce rights that have accrued in that portion. That is, if a contract is divisible, a material breach relating to only part of it is confined to that part, and the breaching party can enforce the remainder without being subject to the general rule precluding action on the contract by the party who has materially breached it.

Carrig v. Gilbert Varker Corp., 50 N.E.2d 59 (Mass. 1943), is one of the best illustrations of divisibility. Under a contract between a developer and a builder, the builder agreed to construct 35 houses for the developer. The builder repudiated the contract after completing 20 houses. Although the repudiation was material, the court allowed the builder to sue on the contract for the contract price of the 20 houses that had been completed. The court found the contract to be severable because the contract set out the price and specifications for each house individually, and each house was a self-contained economic unit. The builder's claim for the price of the completed houses was offset against the developer's claim for expectation damages—the additional cost of having the remaining 15 houses built by another contractor.

No section of UCC Article 2 speaks directly to the question of severability, so the above principles of common law are applicable. To the extent that Article 2 deals indirectly with severability, its approach is consistent with these principles. There are several provisions that recognize the concept of divisibility where the language and purpose of the contract, viewed in its commercial context, indicate that division of the goods into separate units would not impair the value of performance. Section 2.601 suggests that contracts for the sale of goods are normally divisible if the goods can be broken down into "commercial units." It contemplates that a buyer has the right to accept a commercial unit of goods that complies and to reject the rest. To constitute a commercial unit, an item or collection of goods must be regarded by commercial usage as a unit and must be capable of being traded as a unit without any impairment of value on the market. (*See* §2.105(6).) This approach is also reflected in the general remedy provisions in §§2.702 and 2.711 and in some of the more specific remedial provisions. For example, §2.709 allows the seller to recover the price of goods that have been accepted, even if others have been rejected, and Comment 2 to §2.612 makes it clear that when the parties apparently intended delivery in installments, a commercially reasonable fact-based interpretation must be used to break the contract into a set of self-standing exchanges, with the price apportioned among the deliveries.

§17.7 ANTICIPATORY REPUDIATION

§17.7.1 The Distinction Between Breach and Repudiation

Section 17.2 states that a breach, properly speaking, can only occur when the promised performance falls due. However, it is possible for a party to breach in advance of performance—to repudiate its obligation in anticipation—if, before the time for performance, the party makes it clear by words or actions that it will breach when performance falls due. A repudiation may occur between the time that the contract is made and the time due for its first performance—that is, one of the parties repudiates before either party has begun performance under the contract. It may also occur after performance under the contract has begun, but before the due date of the repudiated performance.

To illustrate, in the example of the lease of industrial premises, the lease was executed on July 1, the lessee did not have to pay the security deposit until July 15, and the lessor did not have to give the lessee occupation of the premises until August 1. It stands to reason that the lessee cannot be in breach for not paying the security deposit before payment falls due on July 15 and the lessor cannot be in breach by failing to give occupation of the premises to the lessee before August 1. However, if before the time due for performance, a party manifests the intent in advance that it will not perform when that date arrives, it repudiates the contract. For example, the lessee would repudiate the contract if it notified the lessor on July 2 that it no longer intended to lease the premises. Here, the lessee has repudiated the lease in the period before performance was due by either party. Even after performance of the contract is underway, a party might repudiate a performance due by it in the future. For example, in mid-August, after the lessee has paid the security deposit and the August rent and the lessor has given occupation of the premises to the lessee, the lessee notifies the lessor that it will be abandoning the lease and vacating the premises at the end of August. Despite the fact that performance has begun, this qualifies as a repudiation rather than a breach because the September rent payment is not due until August 31.

§17.7.2 The Purpose and Value of the Doctrine of Anticipatory Repudiation

Older common law did not recognize the concept of anticipatory repudiation. If one of the parties ("the promisor") repudiated the contract in advance of the due time of its performance, the other party ("the promisee") had to wait until that performance fell due to see if breach would in fact occur. In the interim, the promisee had to hold itself available to tender its return performance and had no right to suspend any performance that became due before the promisor's. During the nineteenth century, courts came to recognize that this approach was both unfair to the promisee and inefficient. The English case of *Hochster v. De La Tour*, 118 Eng. Rep. 922 (Q.B. 1853), is generally regarded as the preeminent judicial pronouncement that when one of the parties clearly repudiates a material promise in advance, the other may treat this as a breach immediately and may seek relief for breach without delay. That is, a clear, unequivocal, and voluntary repudiation by one of the parties is recognized as the equivalent of a material breach, provided that the threatened action or failure to act would be a material breach if it happened at the time due for performance. The doctrine of anticipatory repudiation is now well established in common law and under the UCC. Although the UCC does not define what constitutes a repudiation (thus leaving this issue to the common law, even in sales of goods), it does codify and make some refinements to the doctrine in UCC §§2.609-2.612. As in other areas, the changes brought about by the UCC have been influential in developing common law rules, and their spirit is reflected in the treatment of repudiation in Restatement, Second, §§243 and 250 to 257.

§17.7.3 The Elements of Repudiation

As stated already, for a prospective nonperformance to constitute a material repudiation of the contract, the promisor must clearly, unequivocally, and voluntarily communicate an intention not to render the promised performance when it falls due. This intention could be communicated by words or conduct. This definition indicates that words or conduct must satisfy the following prerequisites to qualify as a repudiation.

a. Material Repudiation

An advance repudiation by one of the parties does not allow the other to terminate the contract and claim damages unless the threatened deviation from what was promised would constitute a material breach if it occurred at the time performance falls due. As with breach at the time of performance, the severity of the repudiation is determined by interpreting the contract in context. A repudiation is material if the promisor manifests the intent of not performing at all, or of rendering a performance that deviates in a significant way from what the contract requires.

b. Clear and Unequivocal Intent to Breach

The promisor's statement or conduct must clearly and unequivocally indicate that the promisor intends to commit a material breach when the time for performance arrives. The promisor's intent is interpreted objectively from the perspective of a reasonable person in the promisee's position. A verbal expression of intent can be difficult to interpret. It may not be clear if the promisor is saying that it will not perform, or is merely expressing a lack of confidence in its ability to perform, or is just complaining about the terms of the contract. It could be even trickier to determine intent from conduct. To constitute a repudiation by conduct, the promisor's action must be so inconsistent with an intent to perform as promised that the only reasonable conclusion is that it has deliberately abandoned the contract. Some courts require that the conduct must make it impossible for the promisor to perform the contract.

c. Voluntary Statement or Conduct

To constitute a repudiation, the promisor's statement or conduct must be voluntary and deliberate, rather than inadvertent or beyond its control. Voluntariness is not usually an issue where repudiation is in the form of a statement of intent not to perform. However, where the alleged repudiation is by conduct, it is possible that the actions of the promisor were not deliberately intended to be a repudiation, but were compelled by circumstances beyond the promisor's control. For example, in the case of the warehouse lease, a few days before the lessee's payment of the security deposit fell due, the lessor received reliable information that the lessee's business was struggling, it had defaulted in paying several of its debts, and some of its creditors had obtained judgments against it. This calls into question whether the lessee will be able to fulfill its payment obligations under the lease. However, this financial adversity is neither a voluntary statement of intent not to perform nor voluntary conduct indicating such intent, so it cannot be treated as a repudiation. (These circumstances may give the lessor grounds to seek an assurance of performance, as discussed in section 17.7.5.)

§17.7.4 The Response to a Repudiation

When a material repudiation has occurred, the promisee has a choice between two alternatives. One of its options is to treat the repudiation as an immediate breach. This entitles the promisee to refuse to render its own performance, to terminate the contract, and to sue for relief for total breach. The promisee's other alternative is to delay responding to the repudiation to give the promisor the opportunity to reconsider its repudiation and to retract it.

a. Treating the Repudiation as an Immediate Breach

If it is clear that the promisor has committed a material repudiation, the promisee may react by suspending its own performance, terminating the contract, and immediately claiming damages for breach. However, the elements set out in section 17.7.3 make it clear that the advance manifestation of intent not to perform must be clear and serious enough to constitute a material repudiation. These elements impose an appropriate restraint on the promisor's ability to declare breach in advance, and prevent a premature claim of prospective breach merely because some uncertainty arises about the promisor's future performance.

In some cases there could be doubt about whether these elements are satisfied. Where it is unclear whether a party's words or conduct constitute a material repudiation, neither party can be sure, until the matter is settled by litigation, if a court would agree that the promisor did in fact commit a material repudiation. This imposes a risk on both parties. If the court finds that there has been a material repudiation, the promisor will lose the benefit of the contract and will be liable for damages. If the court finds otherwise, the promisee will not have been justified in declaring a repudiation and will itself be in breach of the contract. In the example of the warehouse lease, the lessee was obliged to pay the security deposit on July 15 and the August rent on July 31, and the lessor was obliged to give the lessee occupation of the cleaned, cleared, and repaired premises on August 1. Say that on July 10, the lessor notified the lessee that it would not perform any of that work on the premises, and it would be up to the lessee to get them into a fit state for use. If the lessor's duty to deliver the premises in a clean, clear, and repaired state is a material term of the lease, the lessor's repudiation of this duty would entitle the lessee to declare a breach on July 10, to refuse payment of the security deposit and rent, and to terminate the contract and claim damages. However, if the term is not material, the lessee would itself be the repudiating party if it so reacted to the lessor's repudiation of a nonmaterial term of the contract. Instead, it would have to make its payments on due date, take occupation of the premises, and claim the restoration costs from the lessor. Until a court rules on the question of materiality, neither party can be sure if the lessor's repudiation was material, so each of them risks being the repudiator.

b. Encouraging Retraction of the Repudiation

Retraction of a repudiation has some conceptual similarity to the cure of a breach—after repudiating the contract, the promisor can repair its advance breach by recanting its repudiation and recommitting to perform as promised. Because a repudiation occurs before the due date of performance, no harm is done if the promisor reverses its repudiation before the due date of its performance, provided that the promisee has not accepted or acted upon the repudiation. The promisee may decide not to accept the repudiation when it occurs and may even give the promisor a reasonable opportunity to retract the repudiation. However, the promisor's ability to retract the repudiation ends when the promisee notifies the promisor that it has accepted the repudiation, or (even without notice to the promisor) when the promisee takes some substantial action in reliance on it.

A promisee's decision not to act immediately on the repudiation, and even to urge the promisor to retract it, offers the hope of salvaging the transaction. However, it does carry some risk to the promisee. If the promisee waits beyond a reasonable time in the hope of a retraction, the promisee may incur losses that could have been avoided by an earlier acceptance of the repudiation and may not be able to recover the aggravated damages. For example, in the case of the warehouse lease, say that the lessor clearly and unequivocally repudiated the lease on July 5. At the time of the repudiation, rents on industrial property were rising daily because of a shortage of industrial space. In the hope that the lessor would retract the repudiation, the lessee waited three weeks before renting substitute premises. Had the lessee not waited so long, it could have found substitute premises at a lower rent. The lessee's damages may be confined to the lower amount of additional rent that it would have paid had it not waited so long to accept the repudiation and enter a substitute transaction.[16]

§17.7.5 Prospective Nonperformance and Assurance of Performance

The promisee's statement or conduct may not be clear and unequivocal enough to constitute a repudiation, but its words or actions, or a change in circumstances, may cast doubt on its willingness or ability to perform when its performance becomes due. Although the promisor does not have grounds to declare a repudiation, it may be entitled to react to the possible prospect of breach by demanding an assurance of performance. In a sale of goods, the right to demand an assurance is statutorily conferred by UCC §2.609. In contracts at common law, the right is generally recognized by courts as available under the circumstances outlined by Restatement, Second, §251.

UCC §2.609 provides that if a party has reasonable grounds for insecurity regarding the other's performance, it may make a recorded[17] demand for an adequate assurance of due performance. Until that assurance is received, the party requesting it may, if commercially reasonable, suspend any of its own performance for which it has not already received the agreed return. The party receiving a justified demand for assurance must provide an adequate assurance within a reasonable time, not exceeding 30 days. If it

16. This is an application of the general principle that an aggrieved party must take reasonable steps to mitigate damages, discussed in section 18.6.3.

17. As part of the overall substitution of "record" for "writing" in the 2022 amendments to the Official Text of Article 2, the Official Comments to §2.609 were amended to make it clear that "recorded" should be used rather than "written."

fails to do so, it has repudiated the contract. Restatement, Second, §251 is formulated slightly differently, but is largely to similar effect.

Although UCC §2.609 and Restatement §251 set out the broad rules under which a party who feels insecure about the prospect of receiving performance may demand an assurance of adequate and due performance, they leave many questions to the judgment of both the party demanding the assurance and the party responding to the demand. An error in judgment by either party could lead to serious consequences for that party. To begin with, the party requesting the assurance must be satisfied that there are reasonable grounds for insecurity. In making the demand, that party must decide what assurance would solve the insecurity and whether it is reasonable to ask for it. When the party seeking the assurance receives the response, it must decide whether it cures the problem. If the demanding party misjudged and asked for too little, the assurance may be meaningless. If the misjudgment was to make a demand that was unjustified or went beyond the demanding party's rights, it would commit a breach by insisting on the assurance and in suspending its own performance.

This can be illustrated by reusing the example relating to the warehouse lease, used in section 17.7.3c: A few days before the due date of lessee's payment of the security, the lessor heard reliably that the lessee's business was struggling, it had defaulted on several debts, and some of its creditors had obtained judgments against it. Section 17.7.3c pointed out that this information creates uncertainty over the lessee's capacity to fulfill its payment obligations under the lease, but it is not a repudiation. The lessee has not made a voluntary statement of intent not to perform nor engaged in voluntary conduct indicating such intent. However, these circumstances may give the lessor reasonable grounds to believe that the lessee will breach when its performance falls due, and entitle the lessor to demand an adequate assurance of performance from the lessee. The lessee must respond satisfactorily within a reasonable time. While the lessor is waiting for the lessee's response, it may suspend any performance that would otherwise be due, and if it does not get an adequate assurance in time, it may treat the contract as repudiated.

Each one of these steps could involve serious dispute and uncertainty. For example, do these facts about the lessee's financial trouble give the lessor reasonable grounds for feeling insecure? If not, any suspension of performance would itself be a repudiation or a breach. If the lessor is justified in demanding assurance, what should it ask for? Merely asking the lessee to reaffirm that it will pay is not very helpful, because the assurance is nothing more than just another promise by a financially distressed debtor, without anything to back it up. A stronger demand (for example, that the lessee's shareholders provide personal guarantees of the lessee's performance) may provide more substantive assurance, but it could go beyond what the lessor is entitled to demand under the contract and therefore could itself be a repudiation by the lessor. Maybe a demand for a verified financial statement, showing the availability of funds, would be a workable alternative to these two extremes. Once the lessor makes its demand, the lessee must decide how to respond. If the lessee concludes that the lessor is not justified in feeling insecure, it could refuse to give any assurance. If the lessee accepts that the lessor is justified in making the demand but it considers the demand to be excessive, it could offer a more modest assurance. However, if the court ultimately finds the lessor's demand to have been justified and the lessee's response to be inadequate, the lessee's refusal to comply with the demand crystallizes the uncertainty into a repudiation.

There are no easy answers to these fact-based questions, but this example highlights the kinds of concerns that may arise when a prospective breach is perceived. In some situations the ability to demand assurances can clarify the uncertainty of future performance either by removing doubt that the performance will be rendered or by establishing a repudiation. In other cases, the process can be very uncertain. *Smargon v. Grand Lodge Partners, LLC*, 288 P.3d 1063 (Utah Ct. App. 2012), illustrates how tricky in can be to navigate these issues. The Smargons bought a condominium unit from Grand Lodge Partners (GLP). The condominium was located next to a mechanical room containing the climate control unit for the complex. Prior to the closing the Smargons noticed that the equipment in the mechanical room was noisy and caused vibrations in the unit that they had bought. GLP acknowledged the problem. The closing was postponed, and GLP initially gave the Smargons specific assurances of what it was going to do to remedy the problem. However, it apparently did not take those actions, and its assurances thereafter became vaguer and more equivocal. GLP also began to underplay the problem and suggested that the Smargons' concerns were exaggerated. The tone of the communications from GLP became more aggressive, asserting that GLP had performed its obligations under the contract, that it had made significant efforts to resolve the Smargons' concerns, that the condominium unit met or exceeded applicable industry standards, and that the Smargons had breached the contract by failing to close. Because the noise and vibration issue was not resolved, the sale collapsed. The Smargons sued GLP for breach of contract, and GLP counterclaimed, asserting that it was the Smargons who had breached. The court found that it was a term of the contract that GLP would mitigate the noise and vibration from the mechanical room. The Smargons had made a reasonable demand for assurances that this would be accomplished. In response, GLP had given some assurances to them that it would do this, but the assurances were too noncommittal and were accompanied by other statements that blamed the Smargons for the failure to close the sale and called into doubt that GLP really accepted responsibility for fixing the problem. Because the assurances were inadequate, the court found GLP to be the repudiating party.

§17.7.6 Transactions Involving Installments

Issues of repudiation and total breach are highlighted in contracts that call for performance in installments. When a breach occurs in the performance of an earlier installment, it can be difficult to know if the breach affects only the defective installment or is so serious as to undermine the contract in its entirety, operating as a repudiation of all remaining installments.

For example, a manufacturer of machinery, contracts to sell three of its machines to the buyer for use in the buyer's factory. Under the contract, the seller agrees to deliver the machines a month apart from each other. Because the buyer is depending on prompt delivery to avoid disruption of its business, the contract requires delivery of the machines on the exact dates specified. The first machine is delivered on time and is installed. After two days of operation it breaks down as a result of a defect that cannot be repaired without removal of the machine. Timely delivery of the machines is an important element of the contract, so the defect in the first machine is likely to be a material and total breach of the seller's performance obligation with respect to the first installment. However, even if this is so, it may not be a material repudiation of the future installments, entitling the buyer to terminate the whole contract. That is, the crucial question is whether the delivery of a defective first installment so seriously impairs the buyer's expectations concerning the remaining machines that it is a repudiation of the seller's promise of future performance. If so, the buyer may use the present breach as the basis for terminating the entire contract. If not, the breach does not impact future performance, so that the buyer remains obliged to accept and pay for the later two machines, and is confined to a remedy for breach of the current installment.

As this is a sale of goods, the principles governing these questions are set out in UCC §2.612, which qualifies the perfect tender rule of §2.601 in contracts providing for delivery in installments. Section 2.612(2) states that a nonconformity in an installment permits the buyer to reject that installment only if the nonconformity substantially impairs the value of the installment, and the nonconformity cannot be cured. For the nonconformity to impair not just that installment but the contract as a whole, §2.612(3) requires that the deficiency in the installment "substantially impairs the value of the whole" contract. This means that when a breach occurs in an earlier installment, it must be determined whether this is a breach so fundamental to the whole contract as to constitute not merely a partial breach but a total and material breach of the contract as a whole. If it does, the breach operates not only as a breach of the current installment but also as an advance breach (that is, repudiation) of the performance obligations due in the future. The question is whether it is pervasive and irreparable enough to make it clear that the promisor is incapable of rendering, or unwilling to render, substantially compliant performance in the future.

An express rule governing installment sales is particularly necessary when a sale of goods is involved because the perfect tender rule does not permit application of the doctrine of substantial performance. At common law there is less need for having a special rule for installment contracts because the result of §2.612 can be achieved by applying the general principles of substantial performance, under which the breach relating to one installment will be a material and total breach of the entire contract only if it results in an incurable material violation of the contract as a whole. This is reflected in Restatement, Second, §243(4), which, in dealing generally with total breach (and not with specific reference to installment transactions), adopts language similar to that used in UCC §2.612.

§17.8 A TRANSNATIONAL PERSPECTIVE ON BREACH AND REPUDIATION

Fundamental breach is the civilian concept equivalent to the common law concept of total and material breach. Unlike UCC Article 2, the CISG does not have a perfect tender rule, but requires a fundamental breach as grounds for terminating a contract for the sale of goods. Articles 49 and 64 of the CISG allow a buyer or seller, respectively, to terminate a contract for fundamental breach, which is defined in Article 25 as a breach that is so detrimental to the other party "as substantially to deprive him of what he is entitled to expect under the contract." Article 25 qualifies this by stating that a breach is not fundamental if the breaching party "did not foresee and a reasonable party of the same kind in the same circumstances would not have foreseen such a result." Chapter 18 deals with the concept of foreseeability in relation to damages, but it is interesting to note that the CISG connects foreseeability to the question of whether a breach is fundamental. Articles 47(1), 49, 63(1), and 64 recognize an exception to the rule that only a fundamental breach is grounds for termination: They adopt a procedure from German law known as the *Nachfrist* exception, under which a party can make a delay in performance into a fundamental breach by giving notice to the other party fixing a reasonable additional time for performance.

Article 7.3.1 of the UNIDROIT Principles also allows an aggrieved party who has suffered a fundamental breach to terminate the contract. It sets out factors to be considered in deciding whether a breach is fundamental. These factors are quite similar to the guidelines set out in Restatement, Second, §241 to decide whether a breach is material. They include the extent to which nonperformance substantially deprives the aggrieved party of its entitlement under the contract, whether strict compliance with the terms of the contract was of the essence, whether nonperformance was intentional or reckless, whether the nonperformance reasonably undermines the aggrieved party's reliance on the breaching party's future performance, and whether the breaching party will suffer disproportionate loss if the contract is terminated. Like the CISG, Article 7.3.1 raises the concept of foreseeability in its definition of material breach by providing that a breach should not be treated as material if the breaching party did not and could not reasonably foresee that the breach would substantially deprive the aggrieved party of what it was entitled to expect under the contract. Where performance is delayed, Article 7.3.1 allows the aggrieved party to terminate the contract if the delay is fundamental. If the delay is not fundamental, Article 7.3.1 adopts the same *Nachfrist* exception as the CISG, allowing a party to make delay fundamental by giving the other party notice of a reasonable extension of the time of performance. If the delay is not fundamental, Article 7.1.3 allows the aggrieved party to withhold performance until the other party performs or tenders performance.

The CISG and UNIDROIT Principles recognize the concept of repudiation and prospective inability to perform. Article 72 of the CISG allows a party ("the promisee") to terminate a contract if it is clear that the other party ("the promisor") will commit a fundamental breach. However, unless the promisor has declared that it will not perform, the promisee should give it the opportunity to provide a reasonable assurance of performance if time allows. Article 71 deals with prospective inability to perform. It allows the promisee to suspend performance if it appears that the promisor party will not perform a substantial part of its obligations as a result of a "serious deficiency" in the promisor's ability to perform or of the promisor's conduct in preparing to perform or in performing the contract. The promisee must give immediate notice to the promisor and must cease the suspension if the promisor gives an adequate assurance of performance. The UNIDROIT Principles set out provisions very similar to those in the CISG, but in language that is even closer to the formulations of American law: Article 7.3.3 allows a party to terminate a contract where it is clear that there will be fundamental nonperformance. Under Article 7.3.4 a party who reasonably believes that there will be a fundamental nonperformance may demand adequate assurance of due performance, and if adequate assurance is not provided within a reasonable time, may terminate the contract.

Examples

EXAMPLES

1. Standard Home Construction, Inc., entered into a contract with Lofty Long to build a house on a lot owned by Lofty. One of the specifications in the contract and in the plans was that the ceiling height must be 9 feet. Lofty included this specification in the contract because he is 7 feet tall, and feels claustrophobic if he does not have plenty of clearance between the top of his head and the ceiling. Standard began work

and building proceeded on schedule. It was not until the house was fully framed and work had begun on building the roof that Lofty first noticed that the ceilings were only 8 feet high. Standard conceded that this was not in accordance with the contract—it had overlooked the contract specification and had assumed that the house would have the more common 8-foot ceiling height. The only way to correct the error is to demolish and rebuild a significant part of the existing work. This would entail considerable additional labor and the destruction and waste of materials, which would increase Standard's cost of building the house. Nevertheless, Standard accepted responsibility for fixing its mistake and was willing to incur the cost. There was enough time left before the date specified in the contract for completion of the house, so the demolition and rebuilding would not have delayed completion beyond that date. However, Lofty was upset by Standard's error and had lost faith in its ability to build the house competently. He therefore refused to allow Standard to correct the error or to proceed with the construction. He terminated the contract and hired another contractor do the demolition and to complete the house. He then sued Standard for damages based on his additional cost. Was Lofty entitled to fire Standard and hold it liable for the extra cost?

2. As in Example 1, Standard overlooked the contract specification and failed to make the ceilings 9 feet high. However, Standard's reaction to this error was quite different. Although it conceded the mistake, it refused to dismantle the completed work and to rebuild it in conformity with the contract. It argued that this would be an economic waste because 8 feet was a standard ceiling height and the error would have no impact on the value of the house. Lofty refused to accept this argument and demanded that Standard correct the error. When Standard refused to do so, Lofty terminated the contract and hired another contractor to do the demolition and complete the house. He then sued Standard for damages based on his additional cost. Assume that Standard was correct in saying that the lower ceilings would not diminish the value of the house. Was Lofty entitled to fire Standard and hold it liable for the extra cost?

3. Sandy Shaw owns a small motel (called "Sandy Shaw's Motel"), a few blocks off the main strip of a seaside town. Sandy entered into a contract with Bill Board, a signwriter, under which Bill undertook to make a sign advertising the motel, which Sandy planned to erect overlooking the road at the entrance to the town. The contract stipulated that the sign was to measure 12 feet long and 6 feet high. Bill delivered the sign to Sandy on time. On inspecting it, Sandy found that it was only 10 feet long and 5 feet high. Sandy rejected the sign and refused to pay for it. Was she justified in doing that?

4. As in Example 3, Sandy Shore and Bill Board entered into a contract under which Bill agreed to make a sign advertising Sandy's motel. Bill made the sign satisfactorily and delivered it to Sandy, who paid for it. Sandy then realized that she needed to get a permit from the town to erect the sign. She therefore entered into a second contract with Bill under which he undertook to get the permit and erect the sign within one month of execution of the contract. Two days after the parties made the contract, Sandy read in the local newspaper that Bill's business license had been revoked by the municipality because of repeated violations of the town's signage ordinances. Sandy wrote an email to Bill, immediately, saying, "I read in the paper that your business license has been revoked. This means that you will not be able to secure a permit for the sign or to erect it. Unless you can assure me by responding today that the newspaper report is wrong, and that you will be able to perform our contract on time, I will treat our contract as at an end and will hire someone else to get the permit and erect the sign." Bill sent an email in reply about an hour later, saying, "Do not believe everything that you read in the newspaper. Do not worry. I will get your permit and install the sign on time." Sandy is not satisfied with Bill's response. She would like to terminate their contract and hire someone else. Is she entitled to do so?

5. On May 1, Sandy Shaw entered into a contract with Peter Pater under which Peter booked all 20 rooms in the motel for a family reunion on the nights of June 15 and 16. Sandy gave Peter a special group rate on the understanding that the booking was firm and could not be canceled. On May 10, Sandy received an email from Peter that stated, "My family has decided that it would prefer to have its reunion in Las Vegas. I am therefore cancelling our booking and plan to find a place there. Go ahead and rent our rooms to someone else." Sandy responded by email immediately, "I received your email today. Remember that when you made this booking, we agreed that you could not cancel it. You will therefore be obliged to pay for the rooms, even if you do not use them. Think about that before you decide to change your reunion plans." On May 13, Peter sent an email in response saying, "OK, you are right. Besides, Las Vegas turns out to be too expensive. We'll stick to the original plan. See you on June 15." On May 12, the day before Peter had sent this response, Sandy received an offer from a tour group to take all 20 of her rooms at full price for a week, beginning June 13. Sandy had not yet accepted this offer when she received Peter's email of May 13, but she would like to let the rooms to the tour group instead of Peter. Does she have the right to do so?

6. In May, Cleaver Carnage, a famous chef, entered into a contract with Televicious, Inc., the owner and operator of a television network, to

produce and star in a weekly cooking show, to be called "Cleaver's Critter Cookout." The show was to run for a trial season from September 1 to October 30. Each weekly installment was to begin with live video footage showing Cleaver hunting and slaughtering various woodland creatures. The scene would then change to Cleaver's well-equipped studio kitchen, in which he would prepare a delectable dish from the day's catch.

In July, Televicious came under great pressure from various consumer groups and government agencies to reduce the level of violence in its broadcasts. In attempting to respond to community concerns, it reviewed its fall programming and decided to cancel several shows that seemed unnecessarily gruesome. Cleaver's cooking show was one of them. Televicious proposed to replace it with a program titled *Longevity with Legumes*, to be hosted by Lena Lofatt, a widely published author of health-conscious recipe books. Televicious wrote to Cleaver on July 30, informing him that his services were no longer required. Cleaver responded immediately by writing a letter to Televicious, pointing out correctly that the contract did not giveTelevicious the right to cancel unilaterally and notifying it that he continued to hold it to the contract.

By August 10, Cleaver had heard nothing more from Televicious. On that day he received an offer to work during September as camp chef for a culinary safari of central Africa. Although he was quite attracted by the invitation, he decided that it was not nearly as beneficial to his career as a television program would be. He still hoped that Televicious would repent if given some time, so he declined the offer of the safari and waited for Televicious to respond to his letter. His optimism was in vain. A week later, he received a terse note from Televicious, stating that the decision was final. By now, it is too late for Cleaver to find anything else to replace his aborted television venture. What are his rights?

7. Hunk De Lectable is a famous actor. He entered into a contract with Matt Arial & Co., an advertising agency, under which Hunk agreed to star in a series of six interconnected TV commercials advertising hair products manufactured by one of Matt Arial's clients. The commercials were designed as a set that required the same actor to maintain and build on the narrative of the messages throughout the series. Under the contract, Hunk was to be paid $1 million for each commercial. The commercials were to be shot over a two-week period, and Hunk would be paid the total contract price of $6 million at the end of that period. Hunk performed well in the filming of the first two commercials. When he arrived to film the third commercial he was drunk. He slurred, threw up on a producer, and eventually passed out. Matt Arial fired Hunk immediately afterward. Hunk concedes that Matt Arial was justified in firing him, and he accepts that the contract is at an end. Matt Arial has abandoned the commercials featuring Hunk, and it has found another actor to do them.

Because the commercials are a set, Matt Arial cannot use the first two in which Hunk appeared, and it must therefore redo those commercials with the new actor. Matt Arial has decided to absorb the wasted costs itself and it does not seek damages from Hunk. However, it did not pay Hunk for the two commercials that he completed, and he claims that because he performed as required in those commercials, he is entitled to be paid the full contract price of $1 million each for them. Matt Arial denies that he is entitled to any payment for the two commercials. What, if anything, should Hunk be able to recover?

Explanations

1. Standard breached the contract by failing to comply with the specifications. If the breach was material and total, Lofty had the right to respond by terminating the contract and claiming any expectation damages that he suffered.[18]

   Standard conceded the breach and offered to cure by demolishing and rebuilding those parts of the structure necessary to correct the work. The only issue is whether Lofty had the right to terminate immediately without giving Standard the opportunity to perform the tendered cure. Standard proposed to give Lofty his exact contractual expectations, and could have completed the house on time despite the demolition and rebuilding. Lofty rejected this offer of cure because he was upset and had lost faith in Standard.

   When the contract involves a sale of goods, the right to cure a defective performance has a clear statutory basis under UCC §2.508. This is not a sale of goods, but the common law concept of partial breach also envisages the possibility of cure when the breach is not so immediately and irrevocably material as to be incapable of reversal, and the breaching party shows a desire to remedy the defective performance within a reasonable time. The efforts at cure must produce a performance in compliance (or at least substantial compliance) with the contract. If the finished product remains significantly deficient, the failure to cure adequately will itself be a material breach. Lofty refused to give Standard an opportunity to cure. His reasons for doing so may be understandable, but they are not legally justifiable unless Lofty can show that Standard's error constitutes such incompetence as to lead to the reasonable conclusion that it would be incapable of properly completing performance in accordance with the contract. If cure is feasible and the will to cure

18. This Example deals only with the breach issue and defers detailed discussion of damages for total breach to Chapter 18. As a general matter, the basic measurement of damages would be the difference between the contract price and the reasonable cost of having another contractor complete the house as specified in the contract. This would include the cost of demolishing the nonconforming work and completing the house.

is apparent, Lofty takes a risk that a court may later disagree with his prediction of inadequate performance, and may find him to have acted unreasonably in preventing rectification of the breach. If so, he would himself be the repudiator. Not only would he be denied damages, but he would be liable for any damages that Standard suffered.

2. Lofty did not immediately terminate the contract but treated the breach as partial and offered Standard an opportunity to cure it by rectifying the construction to bring the house into conformity with the contract. Standard refused, claiming, in essence, that construction of a house with 8-foot-high ceilings would be substantial performance of its contract obligations. If Standard was wrong, Lofty had the right to declare total breach. If Standard was correct, Lofty had no right to terminate the contract and would have been obliged to accept the defective performance. He would then have had a claim for damages to compensate for the breach. On Standard's theory, these damages would not be the cost of rectifying the breach, but merely a reduction in the value of the house, which would be zero.

   The question of whether the construction of lower ceilings was a material breach of Standard's contract obligations is answered by interpreting the contract to determine the parties' reasonable expectations. The term must have been so central to the bargain that its breach deprived Lofty of the value that he reasonably anticipated. The construction of a house with 8-foot-high ceilings might possibly have been substantial performance if the lower ceilings did not affect the value or salability of the house, and Lofty did not intend to live in the house but was merely building it on speculation for immediate resale. However, even here this conclusion would not be assured.[19] By contrast, in this case, Lofty was building the house for his own use and he had a particular reason for including the specification in the contract. The fact that the lower ceilings would not affect the market price should not be a significant consideration.

   The facts of Lofty's case invoke *Jacob & Youngs v. Kent* and *Lyon v. Belosky Construction*, discussed in section 17.3.4. As those cases show, the court's task in deciding on the materiality of a breach is to differentiate those deviations that go to the heart of the contract from those that do not. This distinction is made by measuring the gravity of the breach in light of the contract's language, circumstances, and purpose. The circumstances of this case make the breach akin to the material breach found in *Lyon* and

19. It is not a foregone conclusion that the breach would have been immaterial merely because the house was being built on speculation to be sold. A court that takes the same view as the dissent in *Jacob & Youngs* could hold that once the parties go to the trouble of specifying a term in clear and express language, the court should be slow to second-guess them and to declare the term immaterial merely because it seems unimportant to the court.

distinguish it from the minor breach found in *Jacob & Youngs*. Lofty is therefore entitled to declare total breach, terminate the contract, and claim damages from Standard based on the difference between the contract price and the cost of completing the house to contract specifications.

3. Bill's undertaking to make the sign is not a contract to perform a service for Sandy, but a sale of goods. The transaction involves the exchange of an end product—the completed sign—for money.[20] As this is a sale of goods, the doctrine of substantial performance does not apply. Under §2.601, the buyer may reject the goods if they fail in any respect to conform to the contract.[21] This right of rejection is mitigated by the seller's right to cure under §2.508. The facts of the example do not indicate if Bill has tendered a cure, or provide enough information to determine if an effective and timely cure would be possible.

   The perfect tender rule therefore takes a very different direction from the common law. Had the common law applied to this contract, the significance of the breach—whether the exact size of the sign was a material term of the contract—would be decided by interpreting the contract to ascertain if the dimensions of the sign went to the very basis of the bargain. The only information on this question is that Sandy planned to erect the sign overlooking the road at the town's entrance, so the apparent purpose of the sign was to advertise the motel to people driving past the sign. The visibility and readability of the sign to passing motorists is obviously important to the sign's effectiveness, so too small a sign would defeat the benefit that Sandy reasonably expected from the contract. However, it is less clear, and would have to be established factually, whether the smaller dimensions of the sign that Bill delivered would substantially impair this purpose, making his breach material. If it was, the common law would justify Sandy's rejection of the sign and her refusal to pay for it. However, if the delivery of the smaller sign is not material, the otherwise competent performance may qualify as substantial. The common law would preclude Sandy from rejecting the performance and would confine her to whatever damages she incurred as a result of the nonconformity.

4. Unlike the contract in Example 3, this is not a sale of goods but a contract for the performance of services. It is therefore subject to the common law, not UCC Article 2. However, this would not likely make a difference

20. Most goods are fabricated and the sale of the manufactured product is a sale of goods, even where the goods are custom made.

21. As noted in section 17.5.1, the circumstances may allow the court some flexibility if the buyer did not reject properly or in time or there are clear grounds for finding that the buyer acted in bad faith in rejecting the goods, but no circumstances of this kind are present here.

to the analysis or result, because the applicable legal rules in UCC §2.609, and Restatement, Second, §251 are very similar.

The revocation of Bill's license is not a repudiation because this is the action of a third party. Bill himself has neither made an unequivocal statement nor taken clear voluntary action to indicate an intention not to perform this contract when the time for performance becomes due. Notwithstanding, the revocation of his license does justify Sandy in feeling insecure about Bill's ability to perform his contract obligations. She is therefore entitled to make a demand for an adequate assurance of performance, and if she does not receive it, to treat the contract as having been repudiated. The problem is that her demand is weak. It seems to ask for nothing more than an assurance that the newspaper report is false and asks Bill for an assurance that Bill will perform on time. Bill's response seems evasive and does not offer any concrete assurance, apart from the vague statement that he will perform as promised. Sandy is right in not feeling much reassured, but she may be trapped by her inept demand, which really did not call for much more than Bill gave her. True, he did not assure her that the report was wrong, probably because it was not. However, Bill reaffirmed his commitment to perform, and given her inept demand, Sandy will likely have difficulty in arguing that his failure to provide a more substantive assurance is a repudiation. Sandy would have gained greater security had she demanded a more substantive assurance, but the problem there is that if she demands too much and threatens to withhold her performance in the absence of a satisfactory response, she could end up being the repudiator herself.

5. Peter's email of May 10 seems to be a clear repudiation of the entire contract. It is not simply an exploration of the possibility of cancellation but states unequivocally that he is canceling the booking, which he had no right to do. Sandy did not accept his repudiation but instead wrote an email to him encouraging him to retract it, which he did on May 13. Because a repudiation is a prospective breach, Peter is able to repent and retract it before the time for performance is due and before Sandy has accepted it or taken substantial action in reliance on it. (Action in reliance on the repudiation is enough to end Peter's power to retract, even if Sandy has not communicated acceptance of the repudiation.) Sandy did not accept the offer from the tour group on May 12, so she had not yet acted in reliance on the repudiation before Peter retracted. Peter's retraction reversed his repudiation and the contract is restored to full effect. Sandy is bound to it and would breach it herself if she terminated it.

6. On July 30, Televicious unequivocally repudiated the contract. This gave Cleaver the option either of accepting the repudiation and immediately pursuing his remedy for total breach or of declining to act on the

repudiation and giving Televicious the opportunity to repent within a reasonable time. He chose the latter course. After about ten days had passed without any sign of retraction from Televicious, Cleaver was given the chance to recoup some of his potential loss by agreeing to join the African safari during September. Despite his initial decision, Cleaver has the right to change his mind and accept the repudiation at any time before a retraction is communicated to him. He therefore could have accepted the offer to be a chef on the safari. He would have had no obligation to notify Televicious of this, because the repudiation cannot be retracted once Cleaver has made another commitment on the strength of it. Having accepted the repudiation, Cleaver would no longer have had to hold himself available to perform for Televicious and could have sued immediately for damages based on his economic loss resulting from termination of the Televicious contract, offset by what he earned from the substitute employment.

However, Cleaver decided to pass up the opportunity in the hope that Televicious would have a change of heart. When he was eventually left with nothing to do in September, his decision to wait may be held against him. If, when he ultimately sues Televicious for damages, he is found to have acted unreasonably in continuing to await a retraction, his recovery from Televicious will be reduced to the extent that he should have acted to avoid the loss. That is, if his decision to wait aggravated his loss, the principle of mitigation of damages prevents him from holding Televicious liable for the amount that he could have recouped had he resigned himself to the repudiation and gone on the safari.

The crucial question is therefore whether Cleaver was reasonable in continuing to hold out hope for a retraction on August 10. Reasonableness is always a factual issue, to be decided in light of the nature and clarity of the repudiation and the likelihood of repentance under all the circumstances of the case. Televicious clearly and unconditionally expressed its intention to breach and completely ignored Cleaver's invitation to reconsider. He was given no reason to believe that Televicious would change its mind and was unduly optimistic in waiting further. He did not even attempt another communication before refusing the substitute employment. Under these circumstances, he would have quite a difficult task in convincing a court that he acted reasonably to cut down his loss.

7. Hunk concedes that he materially breached the contract and he does not resist Matt Arial's termination. Matt Arial does not claim damages for Hunk's breach. Therefore the only issue in this Example is whether Hunk is entitled to be paid the contract price, or any other amount, for the two commercials that he completed. A party who materially breaches a contract cannot sue under the contract for any performance that he would have been entitled to in the absence of breach. He is confined to a claim

of restitution, to the extent that the other party has been enriched.[22] Because a party who commits a material breach is at fault, enrichment is limited by the lower of the market value of the breaching party's services and the aggrieved party's net economic gain. The commercials were designed as a set, requiring the same actor to perform in all of them, so Matt Arial could not use the first two commercials and had to redo them with another actor. Matt Arial therefore did not gain any economic benefit from Hunk's performance, so Hunk is not entitled to any restitution.

If Hunk could have shown that the contract is divisible, he would have been able to enforce those portions of the contract that he had fully performed and would have been entitled to the payment of $2 million for the two commercials that he completed. Divisibility is a question of the parties' intent, to be decided by interpreting the contract in context. The contract is not divisible if the parties intended the exchange as an integrated whole, so that the injured party's reasonable expectations are defeated if any portion of it is eliminated. However, the contract is divisible if it can be separated into component parts, each with a distinct consideration, and the value of the components that were performed is not diminished by removing those that were not performed. This contract called for six interconnected commercials featuring the same actor, as part of an overall campaign. The fact that the contract identified a separate fee for each commercial could, under the right circumstances, support an argument of divisibility. However, that argument cannot be made here because each of the separate commercials was not a self-contained and economically viable exchange.

22. As noted in section 17.6.2, some courts refuse to allow the breaching party any recovery, even for unjust enrichment. However, most modern courts have moved away from this punitive approach.

CHAPTER 18

Remedies for Breach of Contract

§18.1 THE SCOPE OF THIS CHAPTER

A contract creates obligations enforceable in law, so its breach by one of the parties entitles the other to commence action to enforce it. This action may be a suit in court or, where parties have so agreed, may be by some form of alternative dispute resolution, such as arbitration. This does not mean, of course, that the aggrieved party[1] will inevitably take enforcement action. Litigation or arbitration to enforce the contract is usually the last resort, after it becomes clear that the breach cannot be resolved by less formal means, such as a demand to rectify the breach or by negotiation. Even where informal resolution fails, the aggrieved party may decide not to seek enforcement of the contract for any of a number of reasons. For example, this may damage an important relationship between the parties, or the amount at stake may be too small to justify the expense of litigation or arbitration, or it may be too difficult to prove economic injury, or the breaching party may have no funds or other assets available to pay any judgment or award that may be obtained. Although these considerations should always be borne in mind, they are not addressed here. It is the concern of this chapter to set out the policies, general principles, and rules that govern the choice of remedy for breach and the measurement of compensation. It therefore focuses on the judicial enforcement of the contract following its breach.

1. The term "aggrieved party" is used in this chapter to mean the party against whom the breach has been committed.

This chapter examines the remedies available for a material and total breach of contract.[2] It does not deal with formation, validity, and breach issues, which have been covered in earlier chapters,[3] and it presupposes that a valid and enforceable contract has been entered into and that one of the parties has breached it materially and totally. There are four distinct but interrelated questions to be answered in dealing with remedies:

1. What is the nature and extent of the aggrieved party's compensable loss—that is, what is the economic harm that the aggrieved party has suffered?
2. What legal remedy or remedies are available to redress the harm?
3. If there is more than one means of remedying the loss, which of the available remedies most efficiently and comprehensively compensates for it?
4. What policies or principles may limit the breaching party's liability for the loss.

§18.2 THE BASIC GOAL OF REMEDIES FOR BREACH: ENFORCEMENT OF THE EXPECTATION INTEREST

§18.2.1 The Nature of the Expectation Interest

A valid and enforceable contract justifies a future expectation by each of the parties. They are both entitled to expect that the other will honor the contractual promise made and will perform as undertaken. If one of the parties fails to do so, thereby breaching the contract, the expectations of the other have been disappointed. Therefore, the fundamental goal of the remedy for breach is to compensate the aggrieved party for that disappointed expectation by providing the equivalent of what was promised and justifiably expected under the contract, usually in the form of a monetary award that approximates its value. This starkly contrasts contract damages from those for tort: While tort damages seek to compensate for something lost—to restore the tort victim to the pre-injury position—contract damages aim

2. Remedies for nonmaterial breach are discussed in Chapter 17. Some of the principles discussed here, such as mitigation of damages and reasonable certainty of damages, are applicable to nonmaterial breach as well.

3. Some contracts courses cover remedies at or near the beginning, before dealing with principles of formation, validity, performance, and breach. Because the focus of this chapter is on remedies for breach, and it presupposes that the aggrieved party is entitled to a remedy, it is written to be comprehensible to someone who has not yet studied formation, validity, performance and breach.

at compensating for something that was not gained—what the aggrieved party should have had. This goal of enforcing contractual expectations is the beacon that guides contract remedies. The principle underlying expectation damages is described in a number of alternative ways, all of which have essentially the same meaning: Sometimes it is said that the goal is to protect the aggrieved party's expectation interest; sometimes it is described as giving the aggrieved party the benefit of its bargain; and sometimes it is said that the purpose of contract remedies is to place the aggrieved party in the position that it would have been in had no breach occurred. This goal of expectation damages applies both at the common law and under the UCC, which codifies it in §1.305.[4]

A party's expectation interest is the value of the performance to that party, based on the purpose of the contract, as gleaned from its wording and the circumstances surrounding the contract's formation. However, even though the expectation interest is based on the contractual expectations of the particular party aggrieved by the breach, it is not determined on the purely subjective criterion of the aggrieved party's privately held, subjective belief about what it would derive from the contract. Contracts are interpreted objectively, and compensation for breach is determined on the basis of objective evidence of loss. Therefore, a party's compensable expectations must be in accordance with what a reasonable person in the party's position would have expected as the benefit of the transaction, given the language used by the parties to express their agreement, and the circumstances surrounding it.

§18.2.2 An Introduction to the Means of Enforcement: The Primacy of Monetary Compensation over Specific Relief

The most direct and accurate way of enforcing the aggrieved party's reasonable expectations under the contract would be for the court to grant an order of specific performance of the contract. This is an order to the breaching party requiring it to perform as promised. For example, Harpo C. Cord owns the only extant piano known to have been used by Chopin. He entered into a contract with Nick L. Odeon under which he agreed to sell it to Nick for $25 million. Harpo breached the contract by refusing to go through with the sale. Nick's expectation is to gain the piano in exchange for depleting his bank account by $25 million, so the most accurate means for the court to ensure that he achieves that expectation is to issue an order of specific performance that compels Harpo to deliver the instrument against

4. Section 1.305 is a general rule in UCC Article 1 that applies to all Articles of the UCC, including Article 2.

payment of its price. This seems like the most obvious solution, and on these facts—because the piano is unique—the court may see this as the most effective and desirable resolution. However, specific performance is not the norm. It is reserved for unusual cases where damages are shown to be incapable of adequately compensating the aggrieved party.[5] More commonly, the aggrieved party's disappointed expectations are compensated for by an award of money.

The law's preference for a money equivalent of expectation over the real thing lies partly in considerations of practicality and policy, and partly in the traditional dichotomy between law and equity. The practical and policy issues may be illustrated by the following example: Sara Nade, an aspiring singer, had entered a singing competition in the hope of winning first prize, the chance to sing the national anthem at an important sports event. To give herself the best chance of winning, she contracted with Harmony R. Peggio, a voice coach, to receive an intensive period of voice training in the week before the competition. Under their contract Harmony undertook, for a fee of $1,500, to give Sara four hours of coaching every day in that week. A few days before the course of instruction was to begin, Harmony notified Sara that she would be leaving town for two weeks, so she could not give the lessons as promised. Harmony thereby repudiated the contract. Sara's expectation interest is to have the lessons for $1,500, and therefore the most accurate way of ensuring that Sara gets exactly what she expected would be for a court to compel Harmony to cancel her travel plans and to give the promised lessons. However, in this situation the remedy of specific performance presents a number of problems: It would be difficult for the court to ensure that Harmony puts her best efforts into a job that she is forced to do; the compulsion takes on the aspect of involuntary servitude; and the solution is not very efficient if another teacher could be found instead. For these reasons, it makes sense to allow Harmony to go on her trip, but if her breach results in a loss to Sara, to hold her liable to compensate for that loss.

In addition to being based on concerns of practicality and efficiency, the preference for monetary relief also derives from the common law tradition that emphasizes damages as the standard remedy for breach of contract and disfavors specific relief in all but the most compelling circumstances. This is because the award of money damages was a remedy that could be granted by courts of law, whereas specific performance was granted only by a court of equity. (The distinction between law and equity is explained in section 2.5 and is discussed further in section 18.10.1.) Courts of equity were intended to intervene only when the available remedies at law were inadequate, and therefore an aggrieved party who sought the equitable relief of specific performance was required to show that the nature of its expectation

---

5. *See* section 18.10.

interest was such that the only means of achieving adequate relief was by the specific enforcement of the contract. Although courts of law and equity were merged some time ago, this ancient distinction is still followed. As a result, even if it is practicable to give the aggrieved party its precise expectation through an order compelling that performance, a money substitute is used in the great majority of cases: The aggrieved party is awarded a sum of money that aims, as closely as possible, to put the aggrieved party into the economic position that it would have been in had the contract been performed.

The basic principle on which this monetary award is calculated can be illustrated by adding some facts to the case of Harmony's breach of the voice-training contract: After Harmony's breach, Sara was able to find another voice coach who was available to give her equivalent lessons for the same amount of time, but who charged $1,800 for the course. By hiring the new coach, Sara got the lessons that she expected but had to pay $300 more for them. So, to place her in her expected position, damages of $300 must be awarded against Harmony. Of course, this is not exactly Sara's expectation, because the teacher was different. However, it is seldom possible to achieve the aggrieved party's exact position by a monetary award. The aim is to get as close as possible. It should also be apparent that the concern here is only with economic loss, so if Sara could obtain the equivalent lessons at exactly the same price as Harmony charged under the contract, she has suffered no financial loss at all and is entitled to no damages for the breach, even though she may have suffered inconvenience, stress, and aggravation by having to find a new coach at the last minute.

§18.2.3 Fundamental Principles of Expectation Relief

The above examples suggest a number of important basic principles.

a. The Achievement of the Aggrieved Party's Expectation Is an Approximation

Contractual remedies aim to place the aggrieved party in the position it would have been in had there been no breach, but because specific performance is available in only limited circumstances, the precise attainment of that expectation is seldom achieved. The best a court can do, in most cases, is to try to determine, as closely as possible, what monetary award will approximate that result.

This is already clear from the discussion of Sara's employment of a substitute voice coach. The monetary award provides her with the compensation of getting the same hours of instruction for the same price, but it does not give her the less tangible benefit of being instructed by the teacher that she bargained for. The facts of the example are deliberately simple, deferring for later discussion some of the additional difficulties that may get in the way of an accurate measure of the value of the expectation. In cases involving more complex facts and less certain consequences of breach, it is harder to be sure of the amount of damages necessary to approximate the aggrieved party's rightful position. Sometimes the amount awarded may undercompensate, and sometimes may overcompensate the aggrieved party. The burden of proving damages is on the aggrieved party, who bears the ultimate risk of failing to persuade the factfinder about the fact or extent of loss. This burden is alleviated in some situations by evidentiary presumptions or inferences.

b. Contract Damages Compensate for Economic Loss, Not Emotional Distress

Contract law strongly emphasizes monetary compensation for the financial consequences of breach. The discussion of Harmony's breach noted that Sara's damages award would not include compensation for any aggravation, inconvenience, or emotional distress that she may have suffered in trying to cope with this last-minute letdown and in finding a replacement for Harmony. Unlike tort law, which does permit compensation for emotional trauma in some situations, contract law is dry-eyed and coldly commercial. It does not, except in the most unusual cases, take any account of noneconomic injury. The principle that contract law compensates only for economic injury means that a party usually incurs no legal sanction for a breach that causes no economic loss. There are limited exceptions to this rule when the breach is also tortious or the contract is especially aimed at giving the aggrieved party a noneconomic benefit.[6] Outside of this narrow area, an aggrieved party has no suit for damages if the breach did not result in economic loss.[7]

c. Contract Damages Are Meant to Compensate for Loss, Not to Punish Breach

It follows naturally from the rule that damages are based purely on the aggrieved party's economic loss that the extent of the damages award does not take into account whether the breach was inadvertent and unintended

6. *See* section 18.13.

7. In some situations the remedy of specific performance may be available to an aggrieved party who has suffered no economic loss. An order of specific performance, which compels a breaching party to perform as promised in the contract, does not necessarily require the aggrieved party to prove economic loss. However, as discussed in section 18.10, the remedy of specific performance is available only in the limited situations in which the aggrieved party can satisfy the prerequisites for this form of relief.

or was deliberate and purposeful. Because the focus is on rectifying harm and not on sanctioning improper conduct, punitive damages—damages aimed at punishing the breaching party—are not available for a breach of contract, even when the violation of the contractual duty was deliberate.[8] However, there are some rules of contract law that have particular or stricter application where a breach is willful or has an immoral dimension. In addition, there are various ways in which the court's or jury's disapprobation of the breaching party's conduct might be more subtly reflected in the disposition of the case. For example, a court may use flexible rules to shift the burden of proof or otherwise give an aggrieved party some advantage where the breach was purposeful, and a jury usually has enough leeway to be more generous to the aggrieved party in awarding damages against a defendant whose breach was calculated and unethical.

d. The Concept of Efficient Breach

A breach of contract is said to be efficient if the breaching party's cost to perform would exceed the benefit that performance would give to both parties. Where this is so, the breaching party makes enough gains by breaching to enable it to pay compensatory damages to the aggrieved party and still come out ahead. Provided that one looks only at the economic impact of the breach, one can say in such a case that the breach does not harm the aggrieved party, who receives the financial benefit of its bargain, and yet it improves the breaching party's position. In this sense, it satisfies the criterion of economic efficiency in that it makes the breaching party better off without making the aggrieved party worse off. If this is true, it could be argued that a rational contracting party with full information may have a greater incentive to breach where circumstances make the breach efficient. This leads to the argument that the law should not discourage this because a legal rule that permits efficient breach—such as the rule that an aggrieved party is entitled only to damages for economic loss—is itself efficient and thus best serves the interests of society.

Although analysis of this type is of some help in understanding and justifying the approach to contract damages, it has many limitations. The most significant is that it does not take into account either important non-economic values (such as reliability, fair dealing, or faithfulness) or those consequences of breach that are not measurable in economic terms (such as inconvenience, disappointment, or frustration). As a result, a conclusion that a breach imposes no harm on the aggrieved party or on society may be misguided if based purely on quantifiable financial considerations.

---

8. There are some narrow exceptions to this rule in unusually egregious cases, as explained in section 18.13.2.

Furthermore, economically efficient decisionmaking can only be achieved if all the conditions are right: The market must be competitive and stable, so that the relative costs and benefits of performing and breaching can be gauged. The party contemplating breach must be capable of acting voluntarily and rationally, and must have sufficiently full and reliable information to enable it to make a prediction of likely losses and gains. In addition, the transaction costs (including possibly significant legal fees) involved in terminating this contract and making substitutes must be small enough so as not to eliminate any advantage achieved by the breach.[9] Such ideal conditions are seldom likely to exist, which means that it will often be difficult to know at the time of breach whether it will turn out to have been economically efficient. Even if the party predicts an advantageous outcome at the time of the breach, economic conditions and subsequent circumstances may render it otherwise. To the extent that a theory of efficient breach is predicated on an unrealistic assumption of rational, voluntary, and informed behavior in a perfect market, with negligible transaction costs, it is likely to be unreliable and more an academic model than a reflection of reality.

§18.2.4 The Enforcement of a Damage Award

A court's award of damages is just a judgment that the breaching party owes the stated amount of money to the aggrieved party. The aggrieved party must then collect payment of the award from the breaching party. A detailed discussion of the means of collecting payment on a judgment is beyond the scope of this book, but it is useful to describe it briefly to provide an overall picture of the enforcement process. After the judgment is obtained (or if appealed, once it is affirmed on appeal), the breaching party may pay it voluntarily, thereby ending the matter. If there is no voluntary payment, the aggrieved party's means of enforcing the judgment is to have a writ of execution issued by the clerk of the court to the sheriff (or equivalent official), calling on that official to find, seize, and sell property owned by the breaching party to satisfy the judgment. The sheriff tries to execute the writ by finding property sufficient to satisfy the amount of the judgment, taking custody of it (levying upon it), and selling it at public auction. The proceeds of the sale are then paid to the aggrieved party, less the costs of execution. (There are variations of this procedure that need not be covered here.)

The point is that a judgment itself is merely a finding of liability. It does not guarantee that the aggrieved party will get paid. If the breaching party fails to satisfy it, and the sheriff cannot find any assets to seize in execution,

9. The total transaction costs incurred as a result of the breach include those costs incurred by the breaching party in entering into the more attractive transaction and the costs incurred by the aggrieved party in dealing with the breach and making any substitute transaction.

the aggrieved party may recover nothing on the judgment. This sobering reality must be taken into account by anyone who decides to initiate litigation, and it means that being able to establish breach and damages are only part of the problem of enforcement. A judgment in law for damages is said to be *in rem*—it is enforceable only against the property of the breaching party, and if the breaching party has no property that can be seized and sold, the aggrieved party loses in the end, having incurred substantial legal costs in the process.

§18.3 THE CALCULATION OF EXPECTATION DAMAGES

As stated in section 18.2.3, the aim of expectation damages is to simulate as closely as possible the aggrieved party's economic situation in the absence of breach. To determine the amount of money needed to approximate that position, a comparison must be made between what the aggrieved party had the right to expect and what it actually got. Although the facts needed to calculate these two points of comparison can be very complicated and sometimes immensely difficult to prove, the basic concept of the comparison is straightforward and should be used as a yardstick to check that any calculation of damages is correct.

Different formulations have been devised for use in making the comparison. These are really just checklists of the factors to be taken into account, and they are only helpful to the extent that they reliably cover every component of the calculation and signal clearly what figures go into each of them. A particular formulation may be specific to certain kinds of cases and may not work well in others. In general, there are two essential elements to any formulation, no matter how it structures the calculation: One part of it will count up the aggrieved party's losses caused by the breach, and the other will calculate any savings, gains, or recoupments that the aggrieved party has made as a result of termination of the contract. Damages consist of the losses less the savings, gains, and recoupments. Restatement, Second, §347 suggests the following general formula:

Damages =
Aggrieved party's loss in value caused by the breaching party's nonperformance
(This is determined by deducting the contractual value of what the aggrieved party received from what it was promised)
Plus
Any **other loss**
(This includes consequential and incidental damages)
Less
Any **cost or loss** the aggrieved party **avoided** by not having to perform

The principles and method of calculation are best explained by some concrete illustrations that describe some different types of situations and the various considerations under each of them. Note that the actual ingredients of the calculation shift in accordance with the nature of the contract in question, but that the basic inquiry is always the same—the determination of damages always revolves around a comparison between the aggrieved party's rightful position under the contract and its actual situation as a result of the breach.

a. Damages Based on a Substitute Transaction

Section 18.2.2 shows that in the simple contract for the purchase of voice training services, Sara's damages could be calculated by measuring the difference between what it would have cost her to receive the services under the contract, and what it ultimately cost her to obtain equivalent services elsewhere. That is, had the contract not been breached by Harmony, Sara would have had 28 hours of voice training for $1,500. As a result of the breach, she had 28 hours of training for $1,800, so damages of $300 puts her in the position she would have been in had the contract been performed. This is represented in Diagram 18A.

Diagram 18A

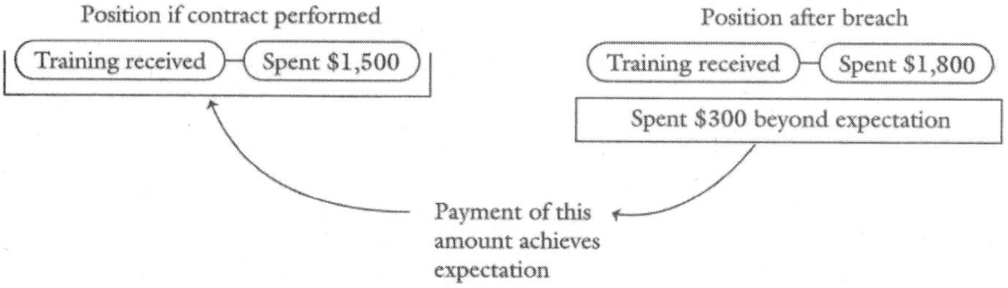

Exactly the same calculation and result would occur if, instead of purchasing lessons for $1,500, Sara had bought a car from Harmony for that price, Harmony breached by refusing to deliver, and Sara managed to find an equivalent substitute on the market for $1,800. UCC §2.712 codifies this by expressing the buyer's damages as the difference between the cover (i.e., repurchase) price and the contract price.

Change the facts: It is Sara who breached by canceling the lessons, and Harmony entered a substitute transaction by taking on a new student to fill the slot left open by Sara's breach. The same principle applies, but because the aggrieved party is the provider of services, damage results only if the gains from the substitute transaction are less than those expected from the breached contract. For example, assume that Harmony could not find a replacement student at Sara's advanced level, and so she accepted a more junior student at the lower rate of $700 for the 28 hours. Harmony would be entitled to damages of $800, calculated by deducting the $700 earnings under the substitute contract from the $1,500 she expected to earn under her contract with Harmony. Similarly, a seller of goods who reasonably resells the goods at a lower price following the buyer's breach is entitled under UCC §2.706 to the difference between the contract price and the lower resale price.

b. Damages Based on the Market Value of the Promised Performance

Under both the common law and the UCC, an aggrieved party who did not enter into a substitute transaction is entitled to sue for loss based on a hypothetical substitute, valued at the market rate, which would have to be established by testimony, typically of an expert witness. Therefore, if, after Harmony's breach, Sara decided not to find a replacement teacher, and if the market value of the lessons is higher than what Harmony charged her, she could still sue Harmony for the difference between the market value of 28 hours of equivalent instruction and the contract price. Even though she is not actually going to pay more, because she will not have any lessons, she has nevertheless lost the benefit of a transaction below the market value, and can be compensated for this loss of benefit. The same principle applies under the UCC. Section 2.713 allows the buyer the difference between the higher market price of the goods and the contract price and §2.708(1) provides for seller's damages measured by the difference between the contract price and the lower market price of the goods.

The market price may also be used as the basis for calculating damages when the aggrieved party did enter a substitute transaction, but the principle of mitigation, discussed in section 18.6.3, makes it inappropriate to award damages based on the actual cost of the substitute because the cost of the substitute transaction was higher than it needed to have been. This may happen when the market was rising and the aggrieved party waited too long before making the substitute contract, or it chose an unreasonably expensive substitute. For example, following Harmony's breach, Sara hired a substitute teacher for $1,800, but that teacher charges more than the market rate of $1,600. If Sara could reasonably have found a teacher at the market rate, her damages will be confined to $100. This principle applies under the UCC as well and is reflected in UCC §§2.706 and 2.712, which require resale or cover to be without unreasonable delay and on reasonable terms.

When market value is used as the basis of determining damages, it must be decided at which place and time the value must be determined. If the parties reside in the same place and the performance was to occur in that place, there is no problem in deciding on the locality of the market, but if more than one location is connected to the contract, it must be decided which one should be used to measure market value. In addition, a market may fluctuate, so it is necessary to decide the date on which value is to be measured. There are different views on the most appropriate choice of market, and some inconsistency on this issue between the common law, the treatment of the seller under UCC §2.708, and the treatment of the buyer under UCC §2.713. Without getting into that complexity, it may simply be observed that the most sensible approach is to use the time and place that most closely approximates the market that the aggrieved party would reasonably have entered to obtain the substitute.

c. Loss of Income in a Contract for Services

Sometimes it may not be possible for the aggrieved party to find a substitute transaction. If the contract is for services, such as an employment contract in which the employee's only performance is the provision of labor, and if the employee cannot find another job, a breach by the employer results in the loss of the employee's entire expectation under the contract. In such circumstances, the only way to compensate for the employee's disappointed expectation is to award damages equivalent to the full consideration due under the contract. For example, a few days before the voice training lessons are to begin, Sara reneges on her contract with Harmony because she decides that she does not need voice training. At this late date, Harmony cannot find another pupil to substitute for Sara, so she loses 28 hours of gainful employment. Sara would have come to Harmony's home for the lessons, and Harmony would not have incurred any costs in performing the service. That is, the full $1,500 would have been profit to her. Had the contract been performed she would have spent nothing and gained $1,500; now she still spends nothing, but gains nothing. Therefore, a payment of $1,500 is needed to give her the benefit of her bargain. Of course, this award really puts her in a better position than the contract would have done, because she does not have to work for it. But this is not taken into account when her only gain—not having to work for her fee—has no monetary significance. *See* Diagram 18B.

Diagram 18B

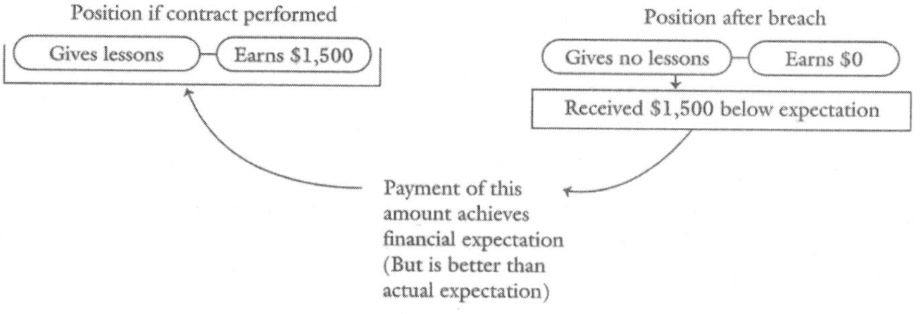

d. Savings Resulting from the Breach Must Be Offset Against Loss

The result in the above example would be different if Harmony would have had to incur costs to perform. Say that she would have needed to hire an accompanist for $600 to play the piano during the lessons and she is able to avoid doing so as a result of the breach. This cost, which is incurred solely in the process of and for the purpose of performing her contractual obligation to Sara, is known as a direct or variable cost. It must be distinguished from fixed cost or overhead, such as Harmony's rent or utilities, which would have to be paid whether or not she performed this contract, and is hence not saved by the breach. Because direct costs would have reduced her expected profit had the contract been performed, it stands to reason that if they are actually saved as a result of the breach (or would have been saved had the aggrieved party acted reasonably), they must be deducted from expected gains to achieve true expectation. This concept is represented by Diagram 18C.

Diagram 18C

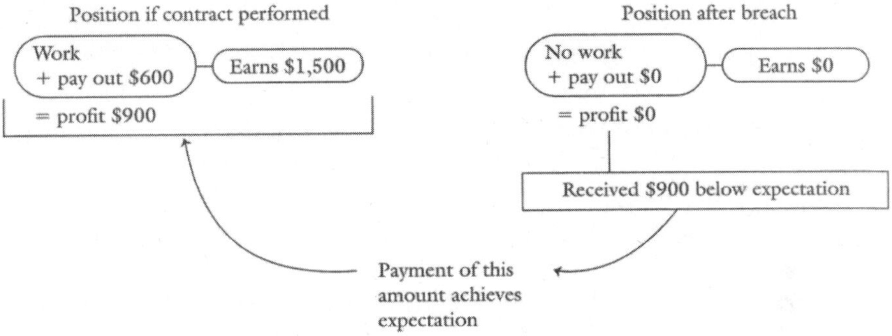

Of course, Harmony must have been able to save the costs by reasonable action. The above example assumed that Harmony had the right to cancel her contract with the accompanist, thereby avoiding that direct cost. However, if she could not cancel without incurring liability to him for his fee (that is, she had made an irrevocable contractual commitment to him) she would not save these costs as a result of Sara's breach, and they would not be deducted. This is represented by Diagram 18D.

Diagram 18D

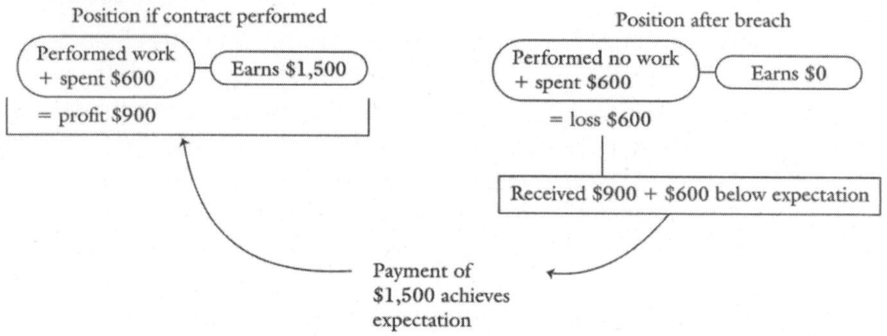

The same result would be reached if, instead of a contract for the provision of services, the contract is a sale of goods to be manufactured by the seller. If the buyer breached before the fabrication has begun, so that the seller avoids the direct costs of making the goods, the seller's damages are its lost profits on the sale, calculated by deducting the costs saved from the contract price.

As noted earlier, fixed costs (overhead expenses) are not saved by the breach and are not therefore deducted from damages. The above calculations therefore do not include costs such as the rent that Harmony paid for her studio or any other expenses that she had to incur in the course of her business, whether or not she taught Sara. The recovery of profit in a case like this means gross, not net, profit.

In the first of the above illustrations, Harmony could avoid the direct cost of hiring the accompanist, so her damages are pure profit. But in the second, because she could not save this direct cost, her recovery includes both her expected profit and the reimbursement of the wasted expenditure that she incurred (or was committed to pay) in reliance on the contract. In a situation like this, when the aggrieved party has incurred the expense of partial performance before the breach, a convenient formulation for calculating expectation damages is as shown in Diagram 18E.

Diagram 18E

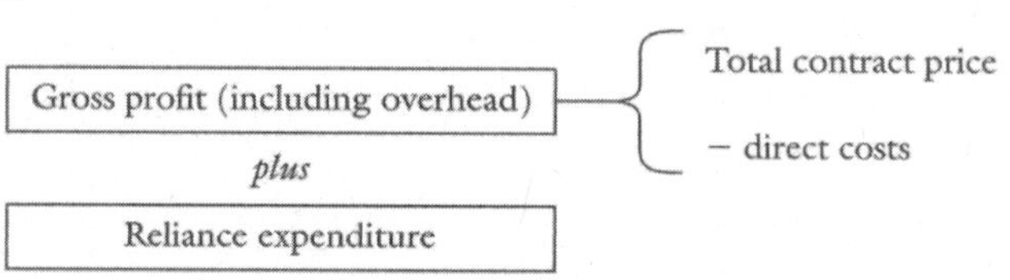

e. Offsets for Part Payment and Salvage

Any payment that the aggrieved party received under the contract, as well as any loss that may be salvageable, is treated in the same way as costs saved—these amounts must be offset against the aggrieved party's recovery. For example, some months before the singing competition, and in anticipation of winning it and becoming an internationally renowned star, Sara decided to build a fully equipped recording studio onto the back of her house. She had the plans drawn, and entered into a contract with Ken Tractor to construct it for a total price of $75,000. The contract required Sara to make a down payment of $5,000 and to pay the remainder of the price in installments as the construction proceeded. Sara made the down payment, and Ken began work about two weeks before the competition. On the eve of the competition, he had reached the stage of completing the foundation and the framing of the new studio. Sara did not win the competition, and she immediately terminated the contract for construction of the studio. She had no right to do this, so she has breached. At that point, Ken had received only his initial payment of $5,000. His costs in material, laborer's wages, and subcontractor charges to date were $10,000. He can show that had he completed the studio, his total direct cost would have been $60,000. The above formulation leads us to a damage recovery of $20,000:

Gross profit	Contract price	$75,000
	– total direct cost	$60,000
	=	$15,000
Plus reliance expenditure	+	$10,000
Total (profit + reliance)	=	$25,000
Less payments received	–	$5,000
Recovery	=	$20,000

A comparison between Ken's expected position and his position following breach shows that the payment of $20,000 achieves his expectation: Had he performed the contract in full and been paid for his work, he would have made a profit of $75,000 – $60,000 = $15,000. The award of $20,000 damages reimburses him for the $10,000 that he actually spent, less the $5,000 that he was paid (i.e., $5,000 net expenditures) and gives him the profit of $15,000 that he expected.

Consider a different case: Sara decided to have a special evening gown made for her appearance at the competition. She contracted with Cadenza La Scala, a dressmaker, for the manufacture of the dress for $1,500. Sara paid a deposit of $150 to Cadenza. After Cadenza had begun work, Sara decided that she had been profligate in ordering such an expensive outfit and decided to use an old prom dress instead. She immediately told Cadenza to stop work, thereby breaching the contract. At that stage, Cadenza had spent $200 on fabric that she had cut according to the pattern designed for Sara. In its present form, the cut fabric could be sold as scrap for $5. If Cadenza completes the dress, she will have to spend a further $50 on materials, but it would be very hard to sell the completed product because it was cut to fit Sara and it reflects her peculiar and rather eccentric fashion sense. This contract is a sale of goods, and UCC §2.708(2) codifies the formulation set out above. Under §2.708(2). Her recovery would be:

Gross profit	Contract price	$1,500
	− total direct cost	$250
	=	$1,250
Plus reliance expenditure	+	$200
Total (profit + reliance)	=	$1,450
Less payments made ($150) and salvage ($5)	−	$155
Recovery	=	$1,295

Sara's down payment is an offset, as it was in the prior example, but the salvage must also be included in the deduction because it is, in a sense, a substitute transaction. Cadenza gains the $5 because she was able to sell the fabric—something she would not have been entitled to do in the absence of breach. A comparison between Cadenza's expected position and her position following breach shows that the payment of $1,295 achieves her expectation: Had she performed the contract in full and been paid for her work, she would have made a profit of $1,500 − $250 = $1,250. The award of $1,295 damages reimburses her for the $200 that she actually spent, less the $150 and the $5 scrap value of the fabric (i.e., $45 in net expenditure) and gives her the profit of $1,250 that she expected.

Cadenza scrapped the dress and claimed her damages on that basis. However, as a manufacturer of the goods, Cadenza had the option under §2.704(2) of not scrapping the dress and deciding instead to complete it and sell it to someone else. In making this choice, she must exercise commercially reasonable judgment. She would be justified in completing and attempting to resell the dress if she reasonably believed that by doing so, she could recoup all or most of the profit lost by Sara's breach, thereby reducing or eliminating her damages. In this case, there is unlikely to be a ready market for such an idiosyncratic piece of clothing, so the more reasonable judgment would be to scrap it and to seek damages to recover lost profits and wasted expenses.

f. The Addition of Incidental and Consequential Damages

Consequential damages are more fully discussed in section 18.5 and incidental damages in section 18.12. However, it is helpful at this stage to show how they fit into the above formulations. In short, incidental damages are expenses that the aggrieved party incurs in handling the breach—the cost of taking whatever reasonable action is needed to protect and enforce the aggrieved party's rights under the contract. They may include such expenses as the transaction costs of taking action to mitigate the effects of the breach and of entering into a substitute transaction. Consequential damages compensate the aggrieved party for loss or injury suffered in other transactions that were dependent on this contract, or for loss or injury otherwise caused by the breach. For example, Cadenza La Scala, the dressmaker, becomes very busy during the period of the singing competition because so many of the competitors order dresses from her. To cope with the increase in demand she enters into a contract with Tex Tile, under which Tex agrees to work as her assistant for a month. Tex reneges at the last moment. Cadenza spends money advertising for another assistant, but she cannot find another person with the requisite skills, so she does not hire an assistant. As a result, Cadenza cannot make as many dresses as she had expected and has to turn away several customers. The cost of trying to find a substitute is incidental damages, and the profit that she lost as a result of turning away the customers is consequential damages. The formulation suggested by Restatement, Second, §347 and set out at the beginning of this section includes incidental and consequential damages in the "any other loss" category. That is:

Aggrieved party's loss in value (direct damages)
+ any other loss (including incidental and consequential damages)
− any cost or loss avoided

Incidental and consequential damages must be distinguished from direct damages,[10] which are represented in that formula as "aggrieved party's loss in value." On the facts of this illustration, Cadenza did not suffer any direct damages because she was unable to hire a substitute for Tex and had she done so, the amount paid for the substitute would not have been more than she would have paid Tex. Her claim is solely for incidental and consequential damages.

10. The term "direct damages" is explained in section 18.5. In essence, they are the damages awarded to compensate the aggrieved party for the loss of expectation under the contract itself, rather than as a result of the impact of the breach on other rights of the aggrieved party or other transactions that are affected by the breach.

§18.4 AN OVERVIEW OF EXPECTATION DAMAGES UNDER UCC ARTICLE 2

§18.4.1 The Basic Principles

The discussion of expectation damages in section 18.3 covers both the common law and UCC Article 2, and includes illustrations concerning sales of goods. However, it is helpful to review the Article 2 provisions on expectation damages as a whole to show their organization, the symmetry between buyer's and seller's remedies, and their basis in common law principles.

The concept of expectation relief under Article 2 is essentially the same as that under the common law. Like the common law, UCC §§2.709 and 2.716 reserve the remedy of specific performance for special cases and treats damages as the primary remedy for breach. The award of damages is meant to achieve, as closely as possible, the economic position the aggrieved party would have been in had there been no breach. This principle is strongly articulated in §1.305, which declares that UCC remedies "shall be liberally administered to the end that the aggrieved party may be put in as good a position as if the other party had fully performed." Article 2 provides statutory formulations for calculating compensation. It organizes them into seller's remedies for the buyer's breach (§§2.703-2.710) and buyer's remedies for the seller's breach (§§2.711-2.717). Although there is necessarily some variation between these two sets of remedies, they are largely mirror images of each other, providing approximately equivalent rights to buyers and sellers, with variations based on the somewhat different remedial needs of each.

§18.4.2 The Seller's Remedies

Sections 2.706, 2.708, and 2.709 contain the core of the seller's expectation remedies. Section 2.709 is the seller's specific performance remedy for payment of the price of the goods. Like the common law, Article 2 sees specific enforcement of the contract as a limited and secondary remedy, available only when damages are inappropriate. Section 2.709 therefore allows the seller to claim the price of the goods only when the goods have been accepted by the buyer or they are incapable of being resold because they have been lost or damaged or are just not resalable.

The other two sections contain the primary remedies of the seller's expectation damages where the buyer breaches by failing to accept conforming goods tendered by the seller. Section 2.706 permits an aggrieved seller to enter a substitute transaction by reselling the goods and, provided that the resale is made in good faith and in a commercially reasonable manner, to recover the shortfall between the contract price and the resale price. Section 2.708(1) recognizes that damages may be based on a hypothetical resale as an alternative to actual resale. It allows the seller to calculate damages based on the difference between the contract price and the market price of the goods at the time and place at which delivery was to have been tendered under the contract. This may be used, for example, when the seller elects not to resell, or when the resale was not conducted reasonably, resulting in too low a resale price. Some, but not all, courts even allow it as an alternative when the seller has resold above the market price, so that the contract-market difference provides a more advantageous recovery.

When the remedy of contract-market damages does not give an adequate recovery so that it is inappropriate to use the contract-market difference as a basis for measuring damages (such as cases in which the seller decides not to manufacture the goods following breach, or suffers a loss in volume of sales as explained in section 18.6.3), §2.708(2) permits recovery of the seller's gross profit plus reliance expenses, less allowance for payments or salvage received.

Nowhere in §2.706, 2.708, or 2.709 is any provision made for the seller to receive consequential damages. (Damages which would compensate the seller for loss or injury suffered in other transactions dependent on this contract, or for loss or injury otherwise caused as a consequence of the breach.)[11] The reason for not mentioning consequential damages in these sections is unclear. Some courts have held that even though Article 2 does not mention seller's consequential damages, it does not expressly disallow them, so they can be awarded if proved. Other courts have refused to award consequential damages to a seller on the grounds that their omission from the seller's remedy sections evinces legislative intent not to allow them.

§18.4.3 The Buyer's Remedies

The buyer's specific performance remedy is set out in §2.716. Like the seller's remedy for the price under §2.709, it is also a secondary remedy. It is available only when damages cannot adequately compensate because the goods are fairly regarded as unique under the circumstances of the case. In other situations in which the buyer has rejected nonconforming goods or the seller has failed to deliver any goods at all, the buyer is confined to substitutionary damages, based on an actual good faith and reasonable repurchase of the goods (cover) under §2.712 or a hypothetical repurchase under 2.713, calculated as the difference between the market price at the

11. *See* sections 18.3.f and 18.5.

time the buyer learned of the breach and the contract price. The language identifying the buyer's hypothetical market is different from that set out for the seller in §2.708(1). Briefly stated, the seller's market price is measured in §2.708(1) at the time and place of tender, whereas §2.713 requires the buyer's damages to be measured at the place of tender, or in some cases, at the place to which goods are to be shipped. The time for measuring the buyer's damages is the time that the buyer learned of the breach. This has led to some differences in interpreting the proper time and place for determining market price where the buyer claims market-contract damages. This complication is not addressed in this book.

Article 2 prefers the cover-contract difference as the more realistic measure, but the buyer is permitted not to cover, and instead use the market price of the goods as a basis of recovery. The market standard is also used if the buyer did not act reasonably in covering, so that the cover price is excessive. As in the case of sellers, there is some controversy over whether a buyer who has covered at a price lower than the market may nevertheless elect to sue for damages based on the more advantageous market-contract difference.

In some cases, a buyer may not be able to make a substitute transaction and may suffer consequential damages as a result of the breach. If so, §§2.714 and 2.715 permit their recovery. (The nature of consequential damages and the prerequisites for their recovery is discussed in section 18.5.) Finally, when the seller has breached by delivering goods that are defective or not in conformity with what was promised under the contract, but the goods have been accepted by the buyer, damages based on an actual or hypothetical repurchase are not appropriate. Section 2.714 therefore measures damages for accepted goods based on the loss suffered by the buyer as a result of the deficiency in the goods. This principle ties in with the discussion of partial breach in Chapter 17.

§18.5 THE DISTINCTION BETWEEN DIRECT AND CONSEQUENTIAL DAMAGES

Direct damages are damages to compensate for the loss of value that the aggrieved party would have gained from the contract itself. They are a direct result of the breach, can be readily and easily attributed to the breach, and are designed to compensate for the very performance that has been promised. Thus, for example, after Harmony breached her promise to coach Sara, Sara's cost of hiring a substitute trainer does no more than substitute for the performance of the contract itself. The same is true when Ken Tractor or Cadenza La Scala seek their outlay and expected profit in their construction or manufacturing contracts. These cases are all characterized by the fact that the award of damages goes no further than the confines of the contract itself to compensate for the breach. The payment of money is designed to give nothing more than the benefit of performance, whether in the form of the costs of a substitute or the lost gains under the contract. The payment of damages thus acts as a direct equivalent for the expected performance and thereby fully cures the disappointed expectation. This is why the compensation paid is called direct damages.

In some cases, however, it is not enough to award only these direct damages, because the breach has had more far-ranging consequences. Quite apart from any direct damages to compensate for disappointed expectations under the contract, the breach has caused further losses in other transactions or endeavors that were dependent on the contract or has resulted in some other injury, whether physical or economic. For example, recall that in the illustration of expectation damages in section 18.2.2, Harmony had undertaken, for a price of $1,500, to give Sara four hours of voice training lessons each day during the week before the competition. Harmony reneged on the contract a few days before the lessons were to begin, but Sara was able to find another voice coach to provide an equivalent course of lessons for $1,800. By entering into the substitute transaction, Sara was able to confine her loss to direct damages, calculated by deducting the contract price from the price of the substitute, and was able to avoid any adverse impact that the breach might have had on other transactions that she had planned. However, the impact of the breach could have been quite different if no other teacher was available, so that Sara could not obtain the training. As a result of being deprived of coaching in the crucial period before the competition, she was not adequately prepared for it. A whole horde of voice experts are available to testify, based on meticulous scientific tests, that Sara has talent of almost superhuman dimensions, and she would have been able to sing circles around the other competitors had she received the week's intensive training. If this can indeed be shown, a mere award of any difference between the contract price and the higher market price of a substitute would not be enough to compensate her for the loss of her contractual expectations. Her loss consequent on the breach is far more serious and must take account of all the opportunities for fame and fortune that would have flowed from her success in the competition. These losses, consequent on the breach, are called consequential damages.

This example graphically portrays the difference between direct and consequential damages, but it also suggests some of the particular problems that an aggrieved party must deal with to obtain consequential damages. Even if she has a bevy of experts to attest to her genius and the certainty of victory that would have followed proper training, Harmony may be able to summon an equivalent phalanx of experts who will conclude differently. Even if Sara succeeds in convincing the factfinder of the important role that training would have played in her success, she must also establish the probability that Harmony's breach was the only reason why she did not win, that Harmony should reasonably have understood that this consequence was likely, and that Sara could not herself have taken some reasonable action to prevent it. Finally, Sara would also have to make a credible showing of the actual harm she suffered—that is, the opportunities that she lost—and she would have to be able to place a plausible money value on her injury. All these considerations could be barriers to or limitations on her recovery, and they are discussed more fully in the next section.

In the above example, Sara's consequential damage (if it can be proved) results from the loss of the opportunity of making gains in transactions that are dependent on the contract. However, sometimes consequential damages arise from some physical or economic injury suffered as a result of the breach. For example, a homeowner contracts with a furnace repairer to fix a gas furnace. The repairer does an incompetent job, and the furnace explodes, injuring the homeowner and destroying part of the house. Direct damages (the cost of having the job done properly, or the cost of repairing or replacing the destroyed furnace) would not be adequate compensation to the homeowner. Consequential damages to compensate for the personal injury and destruction to the home would be needed to fully compensate the homeowner for the repairer's breach of contract.

The above illustrations involve common law contracts. As indicated in section 18.4.3, the buyer of goods may also suffer consequential damages as a result of the seller's breach. Sections 2.712, 2.713, and 2.714 all recognize that a buyer may suffer consequential damages apart from the direct damages covered by those sections, and §2.715(2) describes consequential damages as including "any loss resulting from general or particular requirements and needs of which the seller at the time of contracting had reason to know and which could not reasonably have been prevented by cover or otherwise." For example, say that the buyer operates a store that sells gift wrap, cards, and other such items. In July, the buyer orders its annual stock of Christmas paper, boxes, ornaments, and cards from the seller, for delivery on November 1. On October 30, the seller repudiates that contract by notifying the buyer that it will not deliver the goods. The buyer tries to order substitute goods from other suppliers, but at that time all seasonal products have been sold to other stores so the buyer cannot cover. Direct damages, in the form of the difference between the cover price and the contract price, are therefore not available. The other form of direct damages—the market-contract difference—does not adequately compensate the buyer, who has lost profits as a result of the seller's breach. These lost profits are consequential damages that the buyer can claim under §2.715.[12] Like Sara, the buyer must establish the amount of these damages and must also prove that the seller reasonably should have contemplated that the buyer would incur a loss of this kind as a result of the breach and that the buyer was unable to prevent the loss.

Although Article 2 expressly provides for a buyer's consequential damages, none of the seller's remedy provisions include them as part of the seller's recovery for the buyer's breach. In addition, §1.305(a) states that consequential damages are not available unless provided for in the UCC or another rule of law. It is possible that the drafters of the UCC did not mention sellers' consequential damages simply because they did not think that a seller would ever be likely to have consequential damages. Although sellers do not commonly suffer consequential damages, there have been cases in which a seller has been able to show that it suffered damages as a consequence of a buyer's breach. However, some courts have declined to allow those damages on the basis that a seller is not entitled to them under Article 2. *Dietec Co., Ltd. v. Osirius Group, LLC*, 2017 WL 6039557 (E.D. Mich. 2017), illustrates a situation in which a seller of goods did allegedly suffer consequential damages, but was precluded from recovering them under Article 2.[13] Osirius (the buyer) manufactured auto parts. It bought dies for the fabrication of those parts from Dietec (the seller), a die maker. Osirius failed to pay for the dies on time, creating severe financial difficulties for Dietec. Dietec claimed that because of this financial insecurity, it had been unable to get jobs from other potential customers. Dietec sued Osirius for substantial lost profits caused by the loss of this work. The court identified these lost profits as consequential damages and held that they were not claimable by a seller because they are not provided for in the seller's remedy provisions and §1.305(a) does not permit consequential damages except as specifically provided in the UCC.

---

12. This shows that in some circumstances lost profits are direct damages, but in other circumstances they are consequential damages. They are direct damages when they compensate for the profit that the party would have made under the contract itself (see sections 18.3.c and d). However, in this example they are consequential damages—profits lost in another transaction as a consequence of the breach.

13. One of the issues in the case was whether the contract was for the sale of goods (the dies) or for services (designing and making the dies). The court held that although some services were involved in the contract, the ultimate goal of the parties was the sale of the dies, so UCC Article 2 applied. This highlights the point made in section 2.7.2, that the determination of scope can have significant effects. Had the court found the contract to be for services, the common law would have applied and there would have been no bar on Dietec claiming consequential damages.

§18.6 LIMITATIONS ON EXPECTATION RECOVERY

§18.6.1 The Nature and Goals of the Limitations

There are several principles, sometimes called limitations on expectation damages, that may limit or eliminate the aggrieved party's claim for expectation damages. The requirement of foreseeability ensures that the extent and scope of damages are consistent with what was reasonably contemplated by the parties at the time of contracting. The requirement of mitigation protects the breaching party from the unreasonable failure of the aggrieved party to control or curtail the harm resulting from the breach. The requirement of causation restricts the damages to losses that can be causally linked to the breach. The requirement of reasonable certainty places the burden on the aggrieved party to prove, on the preponderance of the evidence, both the fact and the extent of loss. Finally, the doctrine of unfair forfeiture allows the court to exercise discretion to temper an award of damages that would otherwise be available on a strict application of the rules, if the award would unfairly harm the breaching party and result in a windfall to the aggrieved party.

§18.6.2 Foreseeability

a. The Concept of Foreseeability

An event or consequence is foreseeable when a reasonable person would realize the likelihood of its occurrence. Foreseeability is thus an objective concept, concerned not with what a particular person actually did foresee, but what that person should have foreseen if reasonably contemplating the course of likely future events. Applied in the context of liability for breach of contract, damages are foreseeable when, at the time of making the contract, the party who ultimately breached reasonably should have realized that those damages would be a likely consequence of the breach.

The reasonable foresight of probable consequences depends on the extent of information available to the breaching party that would alert that party, at the time of contracting, to the probable results of the breach that ultimately occurred. The fundamental rationale of the foreseeability principle is that a breaching party should not be held liable for a loss that it could not reasonably have anticipated as a consequence of breach when it entered the contract. The time of contracting, and not the time of breach, must necessarily be the point at which foreseeability is gauged.

The foreseeability principle is regarded as having been firmly established in the common law by the English case, *Hadley v. Baxendale*, 156 Eng.

Rep. 145 (Exchequer 1864). The owners of a mill delivered a broken mill-shaft to a carrier for shipment to the manufacturer so that it could be used as a model for a new one. There was a delay in the shipment. This was the mill's only shaft, so the delay idled the mill for longer than necessary. The owners sued the carrier for damages based on the profit that they lost when the mill could not operate during the period of delay. Although the court acknowledged that the delay did in fact directly result in the loss of profits, it declined to award those lost profits as damages. The court found the carrier not to be accountable for that loss because it was not told that this was the mill's only shaft and had no way of knowing that a delay would cause the mill to lie idle.[14] The court enunciated the rule of foreseeability that is still current today and is reflected in modern formulations in language that deviates little from that used in the case: It held that damages for breach may only be recoverable if one of two conditions is satisfied: Either the loss must be one that may fairly and reasonably be considered to arise naturally—in the ordinary course of things—from the breach, or it must be one that may reasonably be supposed to have been contemplated by the parties at the time of contract as a reasonable consequence of breach. (Although *Hadley* refers to the parties' contemplation, the focus is really on the reasonable contemplation of the party who breached.) In essence, the rule in *Hadley*, adopted in both Restatement, Second, §351 and UCC §2.715, treats damages as foreseeable in two situations:

1. In light of ordinary and common experience, it should have been apparent to the breaching party that such damages would likely be suffered, so that the breaching party should reasonably have expected those damages to be a likely consequence of breach, or
2. If, outside the ordinary course of events, the breaching party had information from which it had reason to know of special circumstances that could reasonably give rise to such damages.

Thus, reasonable contemplation of liability for loss is satisfied if it is established that the breaching party could reasonably expect the probable consequences of breach, either because they would arise in the ordinary course, or because the breaching party had reason to know of special circumstances that could give rise to them.[15] The concept of foreseeability does not require

---

14. The headnote in *Hadley* states that the carrier's clerk was told that the mill was stopped. This contradicts the assertion in the opinion that the carrier was not told and did not know that the millers had only one shaft and that the mill would be idle until the new shaft was delivered. Commentators have suggested that the headnote (written by the reporter, not the court) does not accurately reflect the facts or that even if there was communication to the clerk, this was not sufficient to bind the carrier.

15. A more stringent test, known as the "tacit agreement" test, articulated in *Globe Refining Co. v. Landa Cotton Oil Co.*, 190 U.S. 540 (1903), had some influence in the early twentieth century.

that the breaching party had to foresee the amount or exact nature of the loss or the precise way in which it would occur. It is only necessary that the breaching party must reasonably have foreseen losses of the kind and scale that would likely result from the breach. For example, the seller of fabric to a clothing factory need not know the exact nature of the transactions dependent on the materials to be supplied. It is sufficient that the supplier knew or had reason to know that the buyer would be using the materials for making clothing, which the buyer would sell in the ordinary course to its customers.

b. Foreseeability in Relation to Direct Damages

Foreseeability is not usually an issue in a claim for direct damages. A party entering a contract understands or should understand that if it breaches, the other party will suffer the loss of whatever benefit it promised under the contract, whether that benefit is a profit or the acquisition of services or property on advantageous terms. As stated above, the breaching party need not have foreseen the amount or exact nature of the loss, as long as the breaching party reasonably should have understood that its breach would result in the aggrieved party's loss of whatever value was reasonably expected.

c. Foreseeability in Relation to Consequential Damages

As discussed in section 18.5, a breach of contract could result in consequential damages if it causes losses beyond the actual deprivation of the contractual performance. This is the focus of the principle of foreseeability. It confines liability for consequential damages to those losses that a party reasonably should have contemplated as a probable result of its breach, based on information to which that party had access at the time of contracting. Restatement, Second, §351 and UCC §2.715 break consequential damages into two categories: General damages are those that are foreseeable as a probable result of the breach in the ordinary course of events. Special damages are those arising out of special circumstances that the breaching party would not have reason to know unless informed of them.

This stricter test of foreseeability required not merely that the probable consequences of the breach were reasonably foreseeable by the breaching party but that the circumstances of the contract led to the conclusion that the breaching party tacitly assumed the risk of liability for those damages. The tacit agreement test is generally regarded as too restrictive by modern courts, and it is expressly rejected by Restatement, Second, §351, Comment *a* and UCC §2.715, Official Comment 2. Therefore, for most modern courts, the focus of reasonable contemplation is simply on the relationship between the information available to the breaching party and the loss.

i. General Consequential Damages

Damages that arise naturally, in the ordinary course, are called "general damages." They include not only all easily imaginable direct damages but also those consequential damages that should be obvious to the breaching party without any special or particular knowledge of the other party's circumstances or affairs, because such a loss would be a normal and well-accepted likelihood of the breach of a contract of this kind. What is generally understood as a likely consequence of breach is decided not in the abstract but in light of the circumstances of the case and the contracting environment.

For example, a falling branch falls on the roof of a building, leaving a gaping hole. The owner of the building enters into a contract with a roofing contractor to make an emergency repair on the roof on the very day of the damage. The owner makes it clear to the roofer that the repair is urgent and must be performed on that day, and the roofer expressly agrees to come to the building within three hours to do the repair. Three hours later, the roofer calls the owner and reneges on the contract, stating that it is too busy and cannot do the roof repair until the next week. This is a breach of the contract. The roofer must surely contemplate the probability of direct damages—that the owner will hire a substitute contractor and will suffer direct damages if the cost of the substitute is higher than the contract price. However, the breaching roofer must also reasonably realize that the owner may not be able to get someone else out immediately and that if it rains, there could be water damage to the interior of the building in the vicinity of the hole in the broken roof. Any damage to the interior is consequential—it is not a cost of achieving the promised performance but a loss resulting as a consequence of the breach. This consequential damage would fall into the first category identified in *Hadley* because the possibility of rain damage is something that may reasonably be considered as arising naturally in the normal course of human experience. One needs no special information about the owner's affairs or the nature of the building to recognize this risk of breach.

ii. Special Consequential Damages

The second category, called "special damages," can be illustrated by embellishing the facts of the last example. Say that the area beneath the broken roof happened to contain an extremely expensive and sensitive piece of electronic equipment that is used daily and is crucial to the conduct of the business. The equipment is affixed to the floor and cannot be moved or otherwise protected. Unless, at the time that it made the contract, the roofer was told or otherwise had reason to know that this vital and immobile equipment was located under the damaged section of the roof, it would not be fair to hold the roofer liable for damage to the equipment or to the consequent disruption of the owner's business. The roofer had no basis for expecting this loss, and had it known of these circumstances, the roofer may well have declined the contract or agreed to undertake the work only if the owner paid a higher price to compensate for the assumption of greater risk of liability. By not giving the roofer the information, the owner deprives it of the means to make a rational decision on risk or to take additional steps to minimize the chance of breach. The owner therefore should not be able to hold the roofer accountable for the unusual loss. Not only does the rule protect the roofer from surprise liability, but the fact that the rule exists is likely to be an incentive to a party in the owner's position to provide adequate information, which is likely to increase the efficiency of transacting and may even lessen the chance of breach. The foreseeability principle can therefore be justified as economically efficient as well as fair.

Reasonable contemplation does not require that a reasonable person in the breaching party's position would have foreseen the exact loss with great precision and specificity. All that is required is that a loss of that nature and approximate extent could be conceived of as a probability. In requiring the contemplated loss to be probable, rather than just possible, the law does not cover every possibly imagined serendipitous or outlandish consequence, but it does cover more than those outcomes that are obvious inevitabilities. This means that it can be a subtle exercise to decide on the strength of the link between the information available to the breaching party and its reasonable accountability for the ultimate consequences of its breach.

iii. The Relationship Between the Nature of the Exchange Under the Contract and the Loss

Where the consequential damages arising from a breach are very large and the consideration earned by the breaching party under the contract is small, there could be a question of whether the breaching party should be liable for consequential damages so disproportionate to what it earned under the contract. This can be illustrated by facts based on *Hadley*. Say that the carrier charged $100 for transporting the broken mill shaft to the manufacturer for repair. The miller did inform the carrier that the mill could not operate until the shaft was repaired, so that the carrier did foresee the probability of loss of profits if it breached the contract. As a result of its breach, the mill was idle for several days, resulting in lost profits of $100,000. The carrier argues that because its charge under the contract was only $100, it could not possibly have assumed the risk of liability for $100,000. However, this is not a strong argument because a party could be held to have reasonably contemplated great liability despite the modest value of what it was to gain from the contract.[16] In these circumstances a court may elect to use its equitable power, recognized by Restatement, Second, §351(3), to limit foreseeable damages that are disproportionate to the compensation earned by the breaching party. The parties themselves have a more reliable way of protecting against damages disproportionate to earnings under the contract by including in the contract a term limiting or excluding liability for consequential damages. (Damage limitation provisions are discussed in section 18.11.3.)

§18.6.3 Mitigation

a. The Purpose and Policy of Mitigation

A rational party, faced with a breach by the other, will usually take whatever action is necessary to avoid or minimize loss. This is a matter of sensible self-interest, because the prudent aggrieved party would rather avoid or reduce the harm of breach than aggravate it in the uncertain hope of ultimately recovering damages from the breaching party. This means that it seldom happens that an aggrieved party deliberately and maliciously sets out to incur extra damages for the purpose of increasing the amount of its claim against the breaching party. More commonly, the breaching party's allegation that the aggrieved party failed to mitigate is likely to turn on the question of whether the aggrieved party's response to the breach was an unreasonable or poor judgment that aggravated damages.

The basic principle of mitigation is that if the aggrieved party, through bad faith or unreasonable action or inaction has failed to prevent or has aggravated its damages, the breaching party is not held responsible for the increase in loss caused by the aggrieved party. If the aggrieved party fails to take reasonable action to safeguard its own economic welfare, fairness dictates that it must be left with the added loss and cannot hold the breaching party accountable for it. The failure to mitigate damages does not deprive the aggrieved party of all relief but affects recovery only to the extent that the damages were increased as a result of the aggrieved party's conduct. The aggrieved party is therefore still entitled to recover those damages that it could not have avoided by good faith or reasonable conduct.

In evaluating whether the aggrieved party took reasonable steps to mitigate damages, the question is not whether the aggrieved party's response to the breach turned out, with hindsight, to be a wrong judgment that

---

16. This argument would have more weight under the old "tacit agreement" test, described in footnote 15 in section 18.6.2a, because the value of the consideration earned by the breaching party is relevant to the question of whether the breacher tacitly agreed to assume liability.

failed to contain or worsened the harm, or that a different response would have been preferable. All that is required of the aggrieved party is reasonable action, judged from the perspective of the aggrieved party at the time of the breach. As the wronged party, the aggrieved party is not expected to take unduly burdensome or risky action to keep damages at a minimum, or to explore every conceivable possibility of avoiding loss, or to try methods that reasonably appear to be futile. There must be some element of fault on the aggrieved party's part. It must be apparent that the aggrieved party's behavior in reacting to the breach deviated from rationality or fairness. The law recognizes that the breaching party has breached the contract, leaving the aggrieved party in the unhappy position of having to salvage the benefit of its bargain. Therefore, the aggrieved party should be given some leeway when its response is judged. It must be clear, under all the circumstances, that the aggrieved party's reaction to the breach is improper enough to relieve the breaching party from bearing the increased loss. Restatement, Second, §350 expresses this approach by stating that losses are not recoverable if the aggrieved party could have avoided them without "undue risk, burden or humiliation," but the aggrieved party should not be precluded from recovery to the extent that it made "reasonable but unsuccessful efforts to avoid harm."

The general principles of mitigation recognized in common law are applicable to UCC Article 2 and are reflected throughout its remedies provisions. Sections 2.706 and 2.712 require an aggrieved seller or buyer to act reasonably, in good faith, and within a reasonable time when making a substitute transaction; §2.715 bars a buyer from obtaining consequential damages that could have been prevented by cover or otherwise; §2.704(2) reflects the seller's duty to mitigate in deciding whether to complete the manufacture of specially ordered goods; and §2.709 requires the seller to make reasonable attempts at resale before claiming the price of the goods from the buyer.

The principle of mitigation makes perfect sense on its own merits because the breaching party should not be accountable to the extent that the consequences of breach are exaggerated by the aggrieved party's fault, and because a rule that encourages the aggrieved party to control loss is efficient and sensible. In addition, however, it is congruent with two other limitation principles: A loss caused by the aggrieved party's improper actions should not qualify as reasonably foreseeable, and the aggrieved party's conduct breaks the chain of causation between the breach and the aggravated loss.

b. The Reasonableness Test for Determining Whether the Aggrieved Party Violated the Duty to Mitigate

As stated earlier, unless bad faith is evident, the aggrieved party's accountability for aggravated loss depends on the reasonableness of its response to breach. As always, reasonableness is a factual matter. The aggrieved party's action or failure to act must be evaluated by an objective standard under all the circumstances of the case: Was it reasonable for a person in the aggrieved party's position to have responded to the breach as it did at the time that the breach occurred? This inquiry encompasses a whole range of factual questions such as what the aggrieved party did or did not do; what choices were available to it; what risks, hardships, or inconveniences were involved in each choice; what its motivation was in making those choices; how much time it had available to respond; and how quickly it took action. This evaluation is inclined sympathetically to the aggrieved party, who was compelled by the breach to take action to safeguard its interests. Courts are inclined to respect a judgment that had an honest and rational basis, even if the breaching party can point to a different response that may have been more effective in fully or partially preventing the loss.

Although the aggrieved party has the burden of proving its damages, once it has established loss, the breaching party has the burden of proving that the aggrieved party failed to mitigate that loss. This is because the breaching party's assertion that the aggrieved party failed to mitigate damages is treated as an affirmative defense relating to the extent of liability. The breaching party must show what reasonable actions the aggrieved party should have taken to curtail its loss, and that those actions would have reduced damages by a specific amount. Once it is established that the aggrieved party's reaction to the breach unjustifiably increased its loss, the next task is to calculate what the damages would have been had the proper response been made. This is also a factual issue, involving an inquiry into the causal link between the aggrieved party's conduct and the loss.[17]

c. The Substitute Transaction as Mitigation

The most obvious form of mitigation is a substitute transaction, such as Sara's hire of another voice coach when Harmony repudiated their contract a few days before the voice training was to begin. Sara paid the new voice coach $1,800 and was entitled to expectation damages of $300, the difference between that amount and the $1,500 price under her contract with Harmony. The decision to hire another coach is an act of mitigation in that it prevented any consequential loss that Sara may have suffered by entering the competition without the training. (The fact that such a consequential loss may have been speculative and very difficult to prove increases Sara's incentive to avoid it.)

---

17. *See also* section 17.7.4, in which the issue of mitigation is discussed in relation to the decision by the victim of a repudiation on whether to accept and act on the repudiation immediately or to await the possibility of retraction.

Although the hiring of the substitute coach prevented more serious consequential losses, the choice of the new coach is still subject to a standard of reasonableness. Sara must make reasonable and good faith efforts to find an equivalent coach at the most economic price. This does not mean that she has to use the cheapest substitute, or that she has to make exhaustive enquiries to find the best bargain available. However, she will not recover the full cost of the substitute if, by the exercise of reasonable diligence, she would have been able to find an adequate substitute at a lower price. Sometimes, even with conscientious effort, the only substitute an aggrieved party can find is superior to what was promised under the breached contract. If this is the closest reasonable replacement for the performance, the court may nevertheless award the extra cost to the aggrieved party, even though that may exceed the aggrieved party's expectation under the contract. This may be the fairest resolution given that the breaching party caused the problem and the aggrieved party had no choice but to take the more valuable substitute to approximate the performance promised by the breaching party. For example, in *Handicapped Children's Education Board v. Lukaszewski*, 332 N.W.2d 774 (Wis. 1983), Lukaszewski, a speech and language therapist, breached her employment contract by resigning. The Board sought to replace her. The only applicant for the position was more senior and had to be paid a higher salary in accordance with union rates. The Board hired that applicant and sued Lukaszewski for the difference between what it would have paid her under the contract and what it had to pay her replacement. Lukaszewski argued that she should not be liable for this additional cost because the Board received the benefit of a more experienced therapist for the higher salary. The court rejected this argument. The Board did not need or desire a more experienced therapist, but Lukaszewski's breach left it with no choice but to take the only available substitute.

In *Lukaszewski*, the issue of whether the substitute was reasonable came up in connection with the Board's claim for damages for its added cost. However, the issue also arises when the breach releases an aggrieved party from performance, so that a substitute transaction becomes available to reduce the aggrieved party's loss. For example, say that a few days before the voice training lessons were to begin, Sara repudiated the contract. Harmony now finds that she has 28 hours of free time in which she will not be gainfully employed. If she does nothing about this, she will lose her full profit from the transaction—the contract price of $1,500 less any costs. However, if she is able to take another student or otherwise use this time to generate income, she will reduce or possibly eliminate completely her loss from Sara's breach. It therefore stands to reason that if Harmony sues Sara for her lost profit, she will have to deduct whatever she earned in the time freed by Sara's breach. If she failed to use the time gainfully at all, Sara may be able to reduce her liability for Harmony's loss by showing that Harmony failed to mitigate her damages by productively redeploying this time.

Assume that as soon as Sara repudiated, Harmony put up notices at local schools and colleges advertising her availability, and she also called all the people she knew who may have referrals. However, no one expressed interest in lessons for the week in question. Harmony also saw an advertisement seeking temporary, part-time help as a sales assistant in a music store. She did not pursue this possible opportunity of part-time employment. When she sues Sara for her full profit under the contract, two issues could be raised: First, were her efforts in seeking other students reasonable under the circumstances? It sounds as if she did everything reasonably possible considering the short time available to fill the slot left empty by Sara's breach. Second, should she have made an effort to recoup at least some of her loss by seeking the advertised temporary job at the music store? This is a harder question, because working in a music store is only tangentially related to her career as a voice coach, and it sounds like inferior employment that does not advance her career and could even damage her standing as a teacher. An aggrieved party is allowed reasonable discretion in declining to pursue unsuitable alternatives, and it is arguably reasonable for Harmony to decide not to take this opportunity of generating some income to offset her loss. (As noted at the end of this section, if she did take the job at the music store, and worked there during the times that had been allocated to coaching Sara, she would have to deduct those earnings from her claim for damages.)

Parker v. Twentieth Century-Fox Film Corp., 474 P.2d 689 (Cal. 1970), is an old favorite that involved the issue of whether the actor Shirley MacLaine (Parker) acted reasonably in refusing to mitigate her loss by entering into an available substitute transaction. Parker entered into a contract with the studio to star in a musical called *Bloomer Girl* for a fee of $750,000. The studio canceled the production, thereby breaching the contract. As a substitute, the studio offered Parker the leading role in another movie, a western to be filmed in Australia. Parker rejected the substitute and sued for the full amount of the fee for *Bloomer Girl*. The studio argued that she was not entitled to any damages because she could have avoided all loss by taking the other role offered. The court disagreed and granted summary judgment to Parker for her full fee. The court found that the role in the western was both different from and inferior to the lead in *Bloomer Girl* because it was a poorer vehicle for Parker's talents and the substitute contract eliminated her rights to approve personnel and screenplay. Although the aggrieved party must take reasonable steps to mitigate her loss, she is not required to suffer undue burden or prejudice. In the employment context, the court must be particularly solicitous of the impact that the offered substitute might have on the aggrieved party's career goals, professional development, and dignity. (A dissenting justice was not persuaded that the role in the western was inferior and felt that the case should go to trial.) By contrast, in *Fair v. Red Lion Inn*, 943 P.2d 431 (Colo. 1997), an employee refused her ex-employer's offer to reinstate her after she had been wrongfully dismissed. The employee sued for damages for breach of the employment contract and claimed that she was not obliged to mitigate her loss by accepting reinstatement because she feared that the employer was not sincere and would just terminate her again later. The court conceded that it was natural for her to mistrust the employer, but she could not offer any evidence to support her concerns. She therefore could not claim damages that would have been avoided had she accepted the employer's offer of mitigation. In both these cases, the aggrieved party's best prospect of mitigation was to enter into a substitute transaction with the breaching party. As *Fair* suggests, the victim may find it quite unpalatable to accept mitigation from the very person who breached the contract, but this on its own is not grounds enough to refuse the substitute transaction.

Although the aggrieved party is not required to mitigate by entering into a substitute contract that is unduly burdensome, humiliating, or harmful to the victim's long-term interests, if the victim does in fact take the substitute, the victim's damages must be reduced by earnings from the substitute contract. For example, in *Marshall School District v. Hill*, 939 S.W.2d 319 (Ark. App. 1997), the school district wrongfully dismissed Hill, a teacher and football coach. He found work in a shirt factory for a while before he secured employment as a teacher in another school district. The court held that because his earnings from his factory work were from a substitute transaction that he actually entered following his dismissal, they should be offset against his damages. Similarly, in *Cheathem v. Los Angeles Unified School District*, 2017 WL 3498917 (Cal. App. 2017), the school district improperly dismissed Cheathem from her employment as an assistant general counsel. After her dismissal, she obtained work with a law firm as a contract attorney and later as an associate, handling workers compensation matters. The work did not require a law license, paid a lower salary and benefits, and involved more driving. The court held that although the substitute work was not as desirable as Cheathem's job as assistant general counsel, that did not make it different and inferior in the sense used in *Parker*, but even if it had been, she took the job. Her earnings from it must be offset against her damages to avoid overcompensating her for her economic loss.

d. Post-breach Transactions That Are Not Appropriately Treated as Substitutes: The "Lost Volume" Situation

In the last example, Sara repudiated the contract for voice training a few days before the lessons were to begin, but Harmony was unable, after reasonable effort, to find a substitute student. Had Harmony been able to find a new student to fill Sara's place, the new student would be a substitute for Sara provided that Harmony was fully booked and could not have taken on the new student had Sara not terminated the contract. However, if Harmony was not fully booked, and she could have accepted this student even if Sara had not breached, the new student is not a substitute for Sara. Therefore, one should not automatically assume that a similar transaction after the breach must be a substitute for the broken contract. It should only be so treated if it is clear that the aggrieved party would not or could not have entered it in the absence of breach. Failure to maintain this distinction carefully could lead to an unfair and unwarranted reduction of the aggrieved party's recovery by offsetting the proceeds of an entirely independent transaction.

The above example applies the lost volume principle to a contract at common law. The principle also applies in a sale of goods and is provided for in UCC §2.208(2). For example, a homeowner sells a used fridge for $200, but the buyer breaches the contract by failing to take delivery and pay for it. The seller then sells it to someone else for the same price. Obviously, the second sale is a substitute because the seller had only that one fridge to sell. However, if the seller was not a homeowner trying to sell a single fridge, but a huge appliance store with a whole warehouse of fridges of this exact make and model, the resale of the fridge to the second buyer is not so clearly a substitute transaction. A seller with a stock of identical products would have been able to sell another fridge to the second buyer had the first buyer not breached. It could therefore have sold two fridges instead of one, and the breach has the effect of reducing its volume of sales. If the seller can establish such a lost volume situation, the second sale is not a substitute, its proceeds should not be treated as reducing the loss from the breach, and the seller is entitled to recover its full profit expected under the breached transaction. In a sale of goods, §2.708(2) caters for lost volume. It provides in essence that when the usual measure of damages—the difference between the contract price and the market price on resale—is inadequate to fully compensate the seller, the seller's lost profit on the sale is the appropriate measure.

Rodriguez v. Learjet, Inc., 946 P.2d 1010 (Kan. Ct. App. 1997), illustrates the application of §2.708(2). After the buyer repudiated a contract for the purchase of a jet the seller sold it to someone else. The court identified three elements that a seller must establish to be treated as a lost-volume seller and found that the seller had satisfied all three: It had shown that its plant was operating at 60 percent capacity, so it could have made and sold more planes; it proved that the additional sale would have been profitable; and it established that it probably would have made the subsequent sale even if the buyer had not breached the contract. One of the elements specified in *Rodriguez* is that the seller can show that the additional sale would have been profitable. Some commentators have argued that this should be a crucial element because additional sales may not continue to generate profits equivalent to the profit on the sale in issue. Factors such as increases in the seller's marginal costs and competition in the market from used goods may reduce and ultimately eliminate profits from successive sales. Notwithstanding, many courts do not place such a rigorous burden on the seller, who is, after all, the injured party, and who is only required to prove loss on a preponderance of the evidence. In *National Controls, Inc. v. Commodore Business Machines, Inc.*, 163 Cal. App. 3d 688 (Cal. Ct. App. 1985), the court noted that profits might diminish as more sales are made. However, it observed that most courts do not require the seller to produce economic analysis to refute this possibility. It held that the seller had made out a sufficient case by showing merely that it had unused capacity and could have produced more units than it was able to sell.

The language of §2.708(2) is confusing because it provides that in calculating damages for lost profit, "due credit" must be given for "proceeds of resale." Taken literally, this language would eliminate the possibility of ever claiming lost profits if the seller resells the goods, even where the seller can show that the breach reduced its volume of sales. *National Controls*, adopting the approach of most courts, held that this part of the formula does not apply in a lost volume situation where the resale of the goods should not be seen as a substitute transaction and proceeds of the sale should not therefore be credited.

§18.6.4 Causation

The concept of causation is not as prominent in contract law as it is in tort because it is usually more self-evident and its function can largely be accommodated within the principles of foreseeability, mitigation, and certainty. It is therefore not given much separate attention by courts and commentators. Nevertheless, it is worth articulating as a distinct limitation on relief. A breaching party cannot be accountable for loss that was not caused by its breach. There must be a link between the breach and the loss. Causation is not usually an issue when direct damages are concerned. Unless the aggrieved party has broken the chain of causation by aggravating damages, there is invariably a clear causal link between the breach and the loss of the contractual bargain. However, consequential damages are by definition more remotely connected to the breach, and when they are claimed, it must be established that they were indeed a consequence of the breach.

This can be illustrated by one of the variations of the example concerning Harmony's breach of her contract to give voice training lessons to Sara: Harmony reneged on the contract just before the lessons were to begin, and Sara could not find a replacement teacher. She therefore had no choice but to sing in the competition without having had any coaching in the prior week. She lost the competition and sued Harmony for a huge amount of damages to compensate her for the loss of a career as a singing star. The theory of her suit was that Harmony's breach prevented her from winning and deprived her of the career opportunities that would have resulted. It does not take much imagination to realize that she would have great difficulty in establishing a cause and effect between the breach and her alleged loss. She may not be able to show a probable link between her failure to win and the lack of coaching because there are too many variables that could have intervened: She may not have been as talented as her competitors, she may have had a bad night, or the judges may have been wrong. Even if she could show a strong likelihood of success in the competition, there are too many unknowns that could affect her successful exploitation of the opportunities that it might present.

This example highlights the links between causation and other barriers to the recovery of damages. Some of the problems that Sara faces in proving her case may be described in terms of mitigation (whether she made reasonable efforts to prevent or reduce the negative consequences of the breach), or foreseeability (whether Harmony could have reasonably contemplated these losses), or reasonable certainty (whether Sara can establish the fact and extent of her alleged loss). Nevertheless, the question of causation is also present in the inquiry, and it is a useful adjunct to the other limitations in analyzing the issue of liability and justifying the result.

§18.6.5 Reasonable Certainty

As the party seeking to enforce the contract, the aggrieved party bears the burden of proving its loss. An aggrieved party that cannot show the fact and extent of its loss on the preponderance of the evidence cannot recover damages. The limitation of reasonable certainty is really nothing more than the embodiment of this principle—the evidence must be sufficient to persuade the factfinder that the loss is more likely to have occurred than not, and must give the factfinder enough basis for calculating a monetary award. As this suggests, reasonable certainty involves two inquiries: The threshold question is whether the aggrieved party has proved injury. If injury is shown, the next question is whether the aggrieved party has provided sufficient evidence to enable the factfinder to determine the amount of the loss.

As a general rule, if the aggrieved party can show the first element (the fact that some injury was suffered), the factfinder (court or jury) should try, insofar as possible, to come up with a figure to compensate for the loss. The aggrieved party cannot get damages if it can present no plausible and relevant evidence of the amount of its loss, but if some helpful evidence is available, the factfinder should do the best it can to fix damages in some justifiable amount. This approach is reflected in Restatement, Second, §352, Comment *a*, which notes that although damages cannot be recovered for loss beyond the amount established with reasonable certainty, the policy of holding the breaching party accountable for the breach requires that doubts should generally be resolved in favor of the aggrieved party once it is established that a significant injury has occurred. Therefore, the determination of damages is an approximation, not an exercise in mathematical precision. UCC §1.305, Official Comment 1, expresses a similar sentiment.

Because the injured party has the burden of proving both the fact and extent of loss, problems of certainty may affect damages of all kinds, whether direct or consequential. However, consequential damages usually present the greatest difficulties in proof. The following discussion first address reasonable certainty in relation to direct damages, and then in relation to consequential damages. Finally, it examines the particular problem of reasonable certainty where the aggrieved party's loss arises from a new business or venture.

a. Direct Damages

Direct damages may be difficult to prove, for example, when the aggrieved party seeks its expected profit from the contract, but cannot prove what that profit would have been. Say that an engineering firm enters a contract with a paper mill to design and manufacture an innovative system for the safe disposal of chemical wastes. The contract price for the system is $20 million. Before work begins, the mill reneges on the contract. The engineering firm's direct damages are its lost profits on the job, which must be established by deducting its expected costs from the contract price. However, the system would have been so revolutionary that the engineering firm has no reliable evidence of what its costs would have been. If it cannot establish those prospective costs with reasonable certainty, it will not be able to show that it expected a profit from the contract and will not recover any direct damages. However, had the engineering firm done careful planning before quoting a price for the work, its cost projections, if reasonably accurate and reliable, may be sufficient evidence to establish loss on the preponderance of the evidence. *Benchmark Health Care Center, Inc. v. Cain*, 912 So. 2d 175 (Miss. Ct. App. 2005), illustrates a common judicial approach to the proof of direct lost profit damages. Benchmark wrongfully terminated a contract under which Cain was to provide rehabilitation therapy services for Benchmark for one year. Cain sued Benchmark for unpaid amounts due for services that had been rendered prior to termination and also claimed the profit that it would have made for the remainder of the term of the contract had Benchmark not canceled it. Benchmark challenged the jury's award of lost profit damages on the grounds that Cain had not proved lost profits on the preponderance of the evidence. The court upheld the jury award, noting that once the fact of loss has been shown, the aggrieved party need not prove the amount of loss exactly or accurately. It is enough that the evidence allows the factfinder to make a fair and reasonable estimate of loss. The amount of probable lost profits over the remainder of the contract term was estimated by Cain's accountant, based on a projection from profits that Cain had made in the months prior to termination. The court said that while a future estimate necessarily involves some degree of speculation, the accountant documented and explained the methodology used and developed a realistic estimate.

b. Consequential Damages

Consequential damages can present difficult, and sometimes insurmountable problems of reasonable certainty. Sara's alleged loss of career opportunities, raised in the context of causation, is an extreme example of this. In addition to the trouble she would have in showing a causal link between Harmony's breach of the voice training contract and her alleged loss of career opportunities (the fact of loss), she would have great difficulty in placing a realistic value on that loss. Two cases further illustrate the problem of lack of reasonable certainty where consequential damages are claimed. In *ESPN v. Office of the Commissioner of Baseball*, 76 F. Supp. 2d 416 (S.D.N.Y. 1999), the court dismissed the damages claim of the Commissioner as too speculative. ESPN breached its contract with major league baseball when it preempted games scheduled for Sunday night broadcast in favor of NFL games. The baseball commissioner claimed that as a result of this breach, the league had suffered the loss of television exposure and the associated prestige as well as opportunities for promotions and sponsorships. The problem was that the commissioner could not offer any evidence of how much the league lost. The court said that where it is clear that an aggrieved party has suffered damages, the court will do what it can to make an award. However, it must have some foundation for making a reasonable estimate of the loss and cannot construct a figure out of the air to compensate for speculative or intangible loss. In *Central America Health Sciences University v. Norouzian*, 236 S.W.3d 69 (Mo. Ct. App. 2007), *aff'd* 249 S.W.3d 255 (Mo. Ct. App. 2008), the court overturned the trial court's award of consequential damages to a medical student. The student had completed his medical studies at the medical school, but the school refused to grant him a diploma on the grounds that he had not fully paid his tuition. The amount of tuition was in dispute, and the student established at trial that the university was not justified in its claim and that its withholding of the diploma was a breach of contract. Because the student did not have the diploma, the start of his career as a doctor was delayed by about three years, and he claimed loss of income as a result. The trial court awarded him damages of about $400,000, but this award was overturned on appeal as too speculative—the student could not show that had he been given his diploma on time, he would have passed the medical boards and been hired by a hospital as a resident. The court said that his anticipated salary was subject to contingencies that made his claim too uncertain.

Many cases do not present such insurmountable difficulties of proof, and the aggrieved party is able to provide enough evidence of the fact and quantum of loss to enable the trier of fact to make a consequential damages award. For example, in *Marvin Lumber and Cedar Co. v. PPG Industries, Inc.*, 401 F.3d 901 (8th Cir. 2005), PPG, a seller of wood preservative, breached its contract with Marvin by delivering preservative that did not work properly. As a result of the defective preservative, Marvin's products rotted, causing it problems with its customers and damaging its business. Marvin sued PPG for damages, including lost profits, and the jury awarded damages for lost profits. The court of appeals upheld the award. The court stated the general principle that although purely speculative and conjectural damages will not be awarded, the aggrieved party does not have to prove loss with exactitude. The evidence of lost profits in this case was the testimony of Marvin executives, based on its financial records, which showed that its profits had suffered since the problems with the wood preservative and that they would likely remain flat. The court held that this was sufficient evidence to support the jury award. Marvin had also claimed damages for loss of goodwill, which relates to the diminished value of the business and is distinct from lost profits. The court overturned the jury award of these damages because it found that the evidence of lost goodwill was conjectural and the loss was incapable of being quantified. In *Bollea v. World Championship Wrestling, Inc.*, 610 S.E.2d 92 (Ga. Ct. App. 2005), Bollea, professionally known as Hulk Hogan, sued WCW for damages for breach of contract. He claimed that WCW violated the terms of their contract by not making him the featured wrestler at a pay-per-view event entitled "Bash at the Beach." He alleged that as a result he had suffered significant consequential damages arising from lost bookings and reduced income from merchandising and promotions. WCW applied for summary judgment, denying that it breached the contract and arguing that any lost profits were too speculative. The court refused summary judgment and allowed Bollea to proceed to trial. It noted that he was an established wrestler with a long history of past earnings and profits. He therefore could succeed in showing lost profits with sufficient certainty to permit a jury to calculate his damages.

c. New Businesses or Ventures

Both *Marvin* and *Bollea* involved plaintiffs with established businesses and a track record of past earnings that would allow them to make projections of loss as a result of the breach. Where the breach precludes the aggrieved party from making expected profits from a new business, this track record is absent and the aggrieved party's prospect of proving lost profit is weaker. Some courts (particularly in older cases) are hostile to a claim of lost profits where a business is new and untested, and treat evidence of potential profit as too speculative. However, the better view, more commonly found in modern cases, is to evaluate each claim on its facts to decide if there is enough information to provide a reasonable basis for determining the fact and extent of likely loss.

Blinds To Go (U.S.), Inc. v. Times Plaza Development, L.P., 931 N.Y.S.2d 105 (N.Y. App. Div. 2011), illustrates how difficult it can be for a new venture to establish lost profits with reasonable certainty. Blinds To Go was not a completely new business. It was a chain with four existing stores in the New York area that sold custom-made window blinds. It planned to open a fifth store in Brooklyn and entered into a lease of retail premises. Before it opened the store, the lessor breached the lease by terminating it without justification. Blinds To Go sued the lessor for damages, including lost profits. At trial, it sought to prove those lost profits by expert evidence of the profits at its three existing stores. The jury awarded Blinds To Go about $3.75 million in lost profits. The Appellate Division overturned the jury award on the grounds that the weight of the evidence did not support it. Although Blinds To Go was not a startup business, the court treated the Brooklyn store as a new venture because it was an attempt to break into a new market. The court found that Blinds To Go had not proved with reasonable certainty that the stores in other areas were comparable—they were more suburban in nature, the customer demographics and median income were different, and parking was available at the other stores, but it was difficult to park at the Brooklyn store. The court ordered a new trial on the issue of damages, and hinted that the lost profits might be proved with a more adequate degree of certainty by expert testimony on the profitability of comparable stores in Brooklyn. This does not mean that Blinds To Go would have an easy time proving lost profits by producing evidence of the profitability of comparable stores. For many new businesses, a mere showing of the profitability of comparative businesses in the area will not likely be enough to establish with reasonable certainty that the new entrant into the market would achieve profits at that level. In addition, the aggrieved party would have to address many variables, such as the impact of a new business on the market, likely changes in the economic environment, the degree of expertise and experience of the management, the viability of the business plan, and the plausibility of income and expense projections.

§18.6.6 Unfair Forfeiture

The principle of unfair forfeiture is discussed in section 17.3.5 in relation to damages for substantial performance. That section stated the general principle, as reflected in *Jacob & Youngs v. Kent*, 129 N.E. 889 (N.Y. 1921), that when a contract has been substantially performed and the cost of rectifying the immaterial and nonwillful breach is disproportionately large in relation to the value of the benefit that full performance will confer on the aggrieved party, diminution of the ultimate value of the performance may be a more appropriate measure of damages. However, *Jacob & Youngs* confined this principle to situations in which there had been substantial performance. Where the breach is material, there is seldom a justification to limit damages merely because the amount needed to achieve the aggrieved party's contractual expectations exceeds the enhancement of the ultimate objective market value of the promised performance.

This was the approach in *American Standard, Inc. v. Schectman*, 80 A.D.2d 318 (1981). The owner of an industrial site sold the buildings and other movable property in exchange for $275,000 plus a promise to grade the property and to remove foundations and other structures from the property to a foot below grade level, leaving the vacant site in a reasonably attractive condition for resale. The buyer removed the property it had bought but did none of the grading and restoration work. The seller sued the buyer for $110,000, the cost of doing the work. The buyer sought to prove that its failure to restore the land reduced its market value by only $3,000, but the court refused to admit this evidence on the ground that the restoration of the land was a significant part of the consideration exchanged for the property sold and the parties intended the restoration of the property to be a material term of the contract. (In addition to this, *American Standard* is distinguishable from *Jacob & Youngs* because the breach was deliberate, not inadvertent.)

The decision of whether it is appropriate to confine damages to a diminution in market value is dependent on a determination that the breach is not material. As discussed in section 17.3, in cases in which the breach is not obviously material, the determination of materiality requires a careful interpretation of the contract in context. *Peevyhouse v. Garland Coal & Mining Co.*, 382 P.2d 109 (Okla. 1963), created considerable controversy at the time that it was decided because the court's determination that the breach was immaterial seemed to be based on a questionable interpretation of the contract. The court refused to award the cost of restoring strip-mined land to the owner on the ground that the cost of restoration was greatly disproportionate to the amount by which the restoration would increase the land's market value. The court justified its decision by finding that the restoration of the land was not a central obligation of the contract, but merely incidental to the contract's purpose of extracting coal for mutual profit. However, it was likely that the restoration of the land after it had been devastated by strip mining was a material part of the consideration reasonably expected by the owner, even if the value of the restored land was low in relation to the cost.

§18.7 RELIANCE AND RESTITUTION AS ALTERNATIVES TO EXPECTATION

Although expectation damages are the primary remedy for breach of contract, they can only be recovered to the extent that the aggrieved party can prove that the breach deprived it of an economic gain that would have resulted from the performance promised by the breaching party in the contract. The aggrieved party must be able to show that it received less than its entitlement under the contract or was otherwise precluded from realizing an expected gain. It can happen that a breach causes no economic loss because, say, a substitute transaction can be found at the same or a lower cost, or because the contract was not profitable. If no loss can be shown, the aggrieved party has no recourse for the breaching party's wrongful act because there is no need for monetary compensation and contract remedies are not aimed at penalizing breaches. For example, if the seller of a building breaches the contract, but the buyer can purchase an equivalent building for the same or less money, the buyer has not suffered an economic loss in expectation and has no recourse for expectation damages against the seller.

However, the aggrieved party's inability to prove expectation damages does not always end the matter of relief, because it may be able to show that it has suffered losses other than its defeated expectation. For example, it is possible that the aggrieved party incurred transaction costs in dealing with the breach and entering the substitute transaction. If so, this loss is claimable as incidental damages, as explained in section 18.2. Quite apart from incidental damages, the victim of the breach may have incurred expenditures or losses by partly or fully performing under, or relying on, the contract before its breach. For example, in the above illustration involving the seller's breach of the contract to sell the building, the buyer may have partly performed before the breach by paying a deposit to the seller. The buyer may also have incurred expenses in anticipation of receiving the benefits of the contract, such as by paying an architect to plan an alteration to the building. Damages of this kind may be recoverable under one or both of the alternative remedies of reliance and restitution.

The basic difference between reliance and restitution is that reliance, like expectation, is a remedy based on affirmation of the contract—it is an enforcement of the contract, but restitution is premised on the theory of disaffirmance—it treats the breach as having caused the contract to fall away. This distinction, which will be made clearer as the remedies are discussed below, affects their aim and focus. While the goal of expectation damages is to place the aggrieved party in the position it would have been in had the contract been performed, reliance and restitutionary damages have more limited goals. Reliance damages aim to refund expenses wasted or other losses incurred by the aggrieved party in reliance on the contract, thereby restoring the aggrieved party to the status quo ante—the position it would have been in had no contract been entered. Restitution seeks to return to the aggrieved party the value of any benefit conferred on the breaching party under the breached contract. It focuses not on the aggrieved party's expectation or expenditure, but on the extent of the breaching party's enrichment at the aggrieved party's expense.

The above description shows that there is a close similarity between the reliance or restitutionary damages described here in connection with damages for breach of contract and the equivalent remedies discussed in relation to promissory estoppel (section 8.7) and unjust enrichment (section 9.6). Although the remedies are the same, the cause of action that creates them is different. In the present context they are possible bases of recovery for breach of contract. When these remedies were discussed in the context of unjust enrichment and promissory estoppel, they were presented as grounds of recovery in the absence of contract.

An embellishment of the above example of the sale of the building illustrates the availability of and distinction between expectation, restitution, and reliance damages following a breach of contract. The seller contracted to sell the building to the buyer for $1.5 million. After the contract was signed, the buyer paid $150,000 to the seller as a deposit. It also hired an architect to draw a plan to renovate the building and paid the architect a fee of $100,000. If, after the seller breaches, the buyer finds a reasonable replacement building for $1.7 million, it would be entitled to expectation damages in the total amount of $450,000 because this is what the buyer must receive to be in the position of having a building for $1.5 million. The buyer gets not only the $200,000 extra cost of a substitute but also reimbursement of its costs of $250,000 expended in reliance on the contract. Part of that reliance is the $150,000 actually paid to the seller—called "essential" (or sometimes "direct") reliance, and part is the $100,000 wasted in having plans drawn that are now useless to the buyer—called "incidental" (or sometimes "consequential") reliance.[18]

However, assume that the buyer is able to purchase a replacement building for the same or less than the contract price, so it suffered no loss in expectation. The buyer would still be able to obtain reliance damages of $250,000 that would restore it to the status quo ante. The buyer would have the choice, instead, to recover restitutionary damages, but the benefit conferred on the seller is only $150,000. The buyer could not recover the costs of the plans in restitution because the seller is not enriched by those

18. These terms are expanded on below.

plans—it did not ask for them to be drawn and presumably does not even have them. The buyer has no incentive to choose restitution in preference over reliance because restitutionary damages would be less than reliance damages.

Notice that some items of damage are recoverable no matter which form of relief is sought. In this case the $150,000 deposit is both a reliance expense (and consequently also part of expectation damages) and a benefit subject to restitution. Others may be consistent with only two (here, the wasted architect's fee is counted in both expectation and reliance) or available only under one (the cost of a substitute is claimable only under expectation). Naturally, the aggrieved party will select as its first choice whichever of the alternative remedies provides the widest relief. The basic distinction can be represented as shown in Diagram 18F.

Diagram 18F

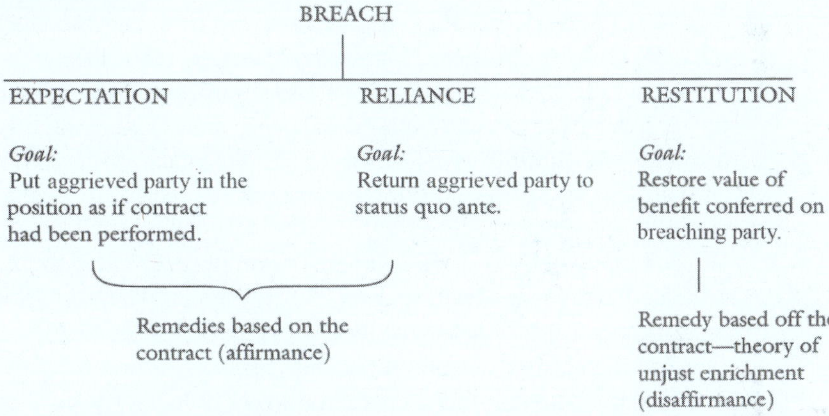

The following sections provide a more detailed examination of reliance and restitution as alternatives to expectation and to each other.

§18.8 RELIANCE DAMAGES

§18.8.1 The Distinction Between Essential and Incidental Reliance

As noted in section 18.7, when a loss or expense is incurred in performing an obligation under the contract, the reliance motivating it is called "direct" or "essential" because it is directly based on the contract and essential to fulfilling the party's contractual commitment. However, if a loss or expense is incurred as a consequence of and incidentally to the contract, for the purpose of enjoying or taking advantage of the benefit expected from the contract, it is called "consequential" or "incidental."[19]

Sometimes the distinction between essential and incidental reliance is easy to draw, as in the above example, where the deposit paid to the owner is essential reliance, and the payment for the architect's plan is incidental reliance. However, in less obvious cases, the question of whether something is essential or incidental to a party's contractual performances requires an interpretation of the party's obligations under the contract. For example, the owner of a store hires a signmaker to execute a large neon sign and to install it on the front façade of the building. In the contract, the signmaker guarantees that it will obtain approval for the sign from the city. The owner spends money in reinforcing the front of the building so that it can bear the sign, but the signwriter is unable to obtain approval for the sign. Because the signmaker promised to do this, it has breached the contract. If the owner's reinforcement of the building is interpreted as necessary to enable the signmaker to perform, the expense incurred in doing the work is essential reliance. However, if the reinforcement is interpreted merely as a means for the owner to obtain the benefit of the signmaker's performance, the costs of reinforcement are incidental reliance. In some cases, the distinction may not have any significant effect on the result, but as discussed below, different rules apply to these different types of reliance, and the characterization could be significant.

No matter how reliance expenses are classified, the basis of awarding reliance damages is waste or loss. The aggrieved party must be prejudiced in that something of value has been wasted or lost and cannot be salvaged. Thus, in the above example, if the only function of reinforcing the building was to accommodate the sign, the building owner's purpose in reinforcing the building was defeated when the signmaker could not get city approval of the sign and the expense was wasted. However, if the reinforcement has other benefits—for example, it improves the structural soundness of the building, the expense may not be a waste.

§18.8.2 Essential Reliance Damages

Section 18.3 shows that in many types of contracts (especially when the aggrieved party's performance consisted of the supply of work or work and materials), expectation damages are made up of expected profit on the whole contract plus expenditure already incurred in reliance on the

19. Incidental reliance damages are not the same as incidental damages, discussed in section 18.12. The only similarity between those two types of damages is that they share the word "incidental." They are not related and are completely different, as explained in this section and section 18.12.

contract. In cases like this, essential reliance expenses are therefore a component of expectation recovery. For example, a builder contracts to build a building for $2 million. After the builder has performed work at a cost of $1 million, the property owner breaches by terminating the project. The builder can prove that its total cost to build the building would have been $1.5 million. The builder's expectation damages are $1.5 million, consisting of its lost profit of $500,000 as well as the reimbursement of the expenses of $1 million already incurred. Both these components must be included to give the builder the benefit of its bargain—a net gain of the $500,000 profit.

On the above facts, the builder could prove that its total cost would have been less than the contract price, so the builder can show that it expected a profit. However, this is not always the case. An aggrieved party may have no reliable evidence from which to project its total expected costs, or it may have underbid so that projected total cost exceeds the contract price. If the aggrieved party cannot prove that it would have made a profit on the contract had it been fully performed, it cannot claim a loss of profit. The builder is nevertheless still entitled to recover the essential reliance component of its damages—the $1 million actually spent in performing. (As these examples show, an aggrieved party that can prove profit has no reason to confine its claim to reliance damages.)

When the aggrieved party would have made a loss in full performance of the contract—that is, it had a negative expectation—the other party's breach gave it a lucky break because it allows the aggrieved party to cease performance of the losing contract and curtail its loss. This means that if the aggrieved party is awarded full reliance damages, it actually does better than it expected. For example, say that the builder agreed to build the building for $2 million, but the builder underbid significantly, so its total cost to complete the building would have been $2.5 million. Therefore, the builder's expectation is a loss of $500,000 had its performance of the contract been completed. The owner breaches during the course of construction. At that point the builder has incurred costs of $1 million in performing the work. If the builder is given the full $1 million, it recovers all its costs. Yet had the builder completed its contract performance, it would have recovered only four-fifths of its cost. This leads to the question of whether the builder's reliance damages should be reduced to take account of the builder's negative expectation. That is, since the builder would have recovered only four-fifths of its cost had the contract been completed, it would exceed the builder's expectation and overcompensate it to award the builder its full reliance damages. Following this logic, some courts consider it appropriate to take negative expectation into account when reliance damages are claimed, and to reduce the recovery proportionately. The most appropriate way to reduce the recovery is to make a proportionate reduction in the damages. That is, to prorate the loss and to reduce the recovery of expenses by a percentage of the total loss equal to the ratio of expenses incurred to total expenses.

However, courts that apply this rule qualify it by shifting the burden of proving negative expectation to the breaching party. The allocation of this burden of proof to the breaching party recognizes that it was in the wrong for breaching the contract. Therefore, an aggrieved party seeking recovery of reliance damages need only prove its expenditure and need not show that it would have recovered all its costs had it fully performed the contract. If the breaching party seeks to reduce the award, it must show that the aggrieved party would have lost money had the contract been performed. This means that when projected costs are uncertain and the fact of loss unclear, the breaching party's failure to sustain the burden of proof will result in the aggrieved party obtaining full reimbursement of expenses. While shifting the burden to the breaching party will allow full recovery in many cases where it cannot sustain its burden, a court may be inclined to adopt an approach that is even more sympathetic to the aggrieved party by simply declining to follow the rule that reliance damages should be reduced where the builder would not have recovered all its expenses had the contract been fully performed. The appeal of this approach is that the breaching party was at fault in breaking the contract and should not be allowed to seek any reduction in its liability for the expenses actually incurred by the aggrieved party in performing the contract up to the time of breach.

§18.8.3 Incidental Reliance Damages

Incidental reliance expenditure or loss is incurred in consequence of having made the contract and for the purpose of using or enjoying the benefits expected under it. Incidental reliance damages are premised on the aggrieved party's having incurred the expenses in reliance on the contract, so they must necessarily have been incurred after the contract was entered into. A loss or expense incurred in anticipation of the contract, but before it is actually formed, is therefore not included in incidental reliance damages.[20]

The following example illustrates incidental reliance and distinguishes it from essential reliance. Jim Nast entered into a lease of premises for the purposes of opening a gym. Jim has not run a business before, and this will be a new venture for him. At the time of signing the lease, Jim paid a deposit of $5,000 to the lessor as required under the contract. In addition, a short time before the business was due to open Jim spent $1,000 on advertising

20. Although expenses incurred in anticipation of a contract are not recoverable as reliance damages for breach of contract, they may be recoverable under the separate theory of promissory estoppel, provided that its elements are satisfied. However, as explained in section 8.9, it is difficult to establish justifiable reliance on a precontractual promise in most situations.

to promote his new gym. A few days after he had incurred this expense, the lessor breached the lease by letting the premises to someone else. Jim could find no other suitable premises, so he decided abandon his attempt to open the gym. Jim does not have credible evidence to claim lost profits as expectation damages because this is a new business and Jim does not have the data to show what the anticipated profits might have been, so he decides to confine his claim to reliance damages. He has suffered both essential reliance damages—the deposit paid to the lessor as required by the contract, and incidental reliance damages—the wasted expense of the useless advertising. The former expense qualifies as essential reliance because it was incurred as part of his performance obligation. However, he had no contractual duty to advertise the gym. He did this solely for his own purpose of attracting business. Even so, the expense was incurred in reliance on the contract, and the breach has defeated that reliance and made the expenditure useless. It therefore qualifies as incidental reliance.

Most commonly, incidental reliance takes the form illustrated above—an expenditure or outlay that is wasted as a result of the breach. But sometimes it is in the nature of a lost opportunity or other gain sacrificed. For example, after executing the lease of the premises, Jim had given up his job so that he could operate his new gym, or he had declined an offer of other premises on the strength of this lease. Lost gains and opportunities are, usually harder to prove and quantify than wasted expenditure, but they are recoverable if properly established, subject to the qualifications discussed below.

Because incidental reliance is ancillary to the contract, there must be a limit on it to protect the breaching party from liability for expenses that it could not fairly have expected, or that were not incurred reasonably. Therefore, incidental reliance is only recoverable if the breaching party foresaw or reasonably should have foreseen the possibility of the loss or expenditure being incurred, and both the amount and nature of the loss or expenditure were reasonable. The mitigation principle applies here too, so the aggrieved party must take whatever action is reasonable to recoup expenses that are salvageable. As with all other types of damage, the loss or expense must be proved with reasonable certainty.

Where the contract relates to a money-making enterprise, the aggrieved party's costs, including incidental reliance costs, would be deducted from prospective earnings to determine profit. Therefore, if the breaching party can prove that the aggrieved party would not have made a profit from the enterprise, it is arguably appropriate to apply the prorating principle discussed in relation to essential reliance in section 18.8.2 to reduce the incidental reliance damages. For example, the cost of Jim's advertising would be a business expense to be deducted from the gym's earnings to determine profit, so if the lessor can show that the gym would have made a loss, it seems appropriate to reduce the cost of the flyers proportionately. However, if it is clear from the terms or nature of the contract that the aggrieved party's purpose in entering the contract was not profit, incidental reliance damages should not be subject to the rule of proportionate reduction. For example, a homeowner incurs expenses in preparing the home for a lavish birthday party. Shortly before the date of the party, the caterer hired by the homeowner repudiates the catering contract and the homeowner cancels the party. The homeowner's reliance claim against the caterer for the expenses wasted in preparing for the party should not be subject to reduction because the party was not intended to generate a profit for the owner.

§18.9 RESTITUTIONARY DAMAGES

Chapter 9 identifies restitution as the remedy for unjust enrichment and section 9.6 discusses the remedy in some detail. Chapter 9 focuses on unjust enrichment as a cause of action distinct from contract, available in situations in which no contract was formed. To obtain the remedy of restitution on the basis of unjust enrichment, the plaintiff must show that it conferred a benefit on the defendant and that it would be unjust for the defendant to retain that benefit without compensating the plaintiff for its value. Although restitution is available as a remedy in situations that do not involve a valid contract, it is also an alternative remedy for the breach of a contract. As an alternative to suing on the contract for expectation or reliance damages, the aggrieved party has the option of disaffirming the contract (treating it as if it does not exist) and suing on the theory of unjust enrichment to obtain restitution of the value of benefits conferred on the breaching party by the aggrieved party under the now-defunct contract.[21]

Stated differently, after the breaching party commits a material breach, the aggrieved party will, when possible, usually seek full enforcement of the contract to recover the value of its expectation. However, if the aggrieved party cannot recover expectation damages either because it has not suffered any expectation loss, or it cannot prove expectation damages, or because it has a negative expectation (that is, it would have lost money on the contract), the aggrieved party has the choice of claiming either reliance damages or restitution. A claim of reliance damages is a suit on the contract because, as explained above, reliance expense is a component of expectation damages. However, a claim of restitution proceeds on the theory that the breach ended

21. This section discusses only restitution in favor of the aggrieved party. It does not consider restitution in favor of a breaching party, which is discussed in section 17.6.2. That section explains that, as a general rule, when a contract is rescinded for breach, the breaching party is entitled to the restitution of any benefits that it conferred on the other party prior to the breach. However, the breaching party's restitution is subject to limitations and is offset by any damages due to the aggrieved party.

the life of the contract, so that the breaching party is no longer justified in retaining the benefit of any performance that the aggrieved party rendered under it, and is unjustly enriched by the value of that performance.

The different goals of reliance damages and restitution, identified in section 18.7, explain why restitution often provides a different measure of recovery from reliance. Reliance is aimed at the recovery of wasted expenses, while restitution is designed to restore the value of a benefit that the breaching party has unjustly retained. Sometimes the aggrieved party's expenditure may be exactly equal to the breaching party's enrichment, so it would make no difference which basis of recovery was used. This is true, for example, when the only loss suffered by the aggrieved party in reliance on the contract is the payment of money to the breaching party. Therefore, if the seller of a house breaches the contract of sale after the buyer has paid a deposit of $5,000, the value of the benefit conferred is precisely equivalent to the aggrieved party's expenditure (and interest on the money would be claimable in both restitution and reliance). However, in other situations the aggrieved party's outlay could be considerably different from the value that it conferred on the breaching party. Say that a painter entered into a contract to paint a house. After the painter had done considerable work in stripping and priming the walls, and had spent $400 on materials, the owner breached by unjustifiably firing the painter. The painter's reliance damages are the expenses of $400. However, restitution based on the value of what has been done for the owner—commonly measured by the market value (quantum meruit) of the service—is likely to be more than what was actually spent. This is because it includes not only the cost of materials but also the value of the aggrieved party's labor, including a reasonable profit. Conversely, restitution could be lower than reliance where the expenditure, although justifiable and reasonable, does not result in a benefit to the owner. This is particularly likely when the reliance is incidental so that nothing is actually given to the breaching party.

Market value is the standard measure of value. However, if the market value of the benefit exceeds the value placed on it in the contract (that is, its contract price), some courts apply a limitation on damages analogous to the proportionate reduction of reliance recovery in a losing contract,[22] and treat the contract price as an upper limit on recovery. For example, in the above contract to paint a house, say that the portion of the contract price attributable to stripping and priming the walls is $1,000, but the painter underbid and this price is lower than the market value of the work, which is $1,200. The argument against making the contract price the upper limit on recovery is that restitution, by its very nature, is based on the theory that the contract no longer exists as a result of the breach. It unduly benefits the breaching

22. *See* section 18.8.2.

party to use the price in the contract to limit its restitutionary liability. The argument in favor of limiting recovery to the contract price is that because the aggrieved party's expectation of loss is taken into account for reliance damages, consistency demands that the aggrieved party's expectation should limit restitutionary recovery as well.

§18.10 EQUITABLE REMEDIES: SPECIFIC PERFORMANCE AND INJUNCTIONS

§18.10.1 Specific Performance

Section 18.2.2 notes that the remedy of specific performance—a court order commanding the breaching party to perform the contract as promised—would seem to be the most precise means of achieving the aggrieved party's expectation. Yet, for a number of reasons, some historical and some based on practicality and principle, damages are the primary form of relief for breach of contract, and specific performance is reserved as an extraordinary remedy. The historical basis for the primacy of the damages remedy lies in the dichotomy between law and equity. As it was originally formed, the court of equity was a court of special resort, presided over by the Lord Chancellor, acting under the sovereign's prerogative power. The Lord Chancellor would exercise the crown's discretion to do justice only where the overall equities of the case called for this intervention and the regular courts of law had no power to provide an adequate remedy to the aggrieved party.[23] Although courts of law and equity have long been combined, and the same court decides on the alternative remedies of damages and specific performance, the requirement of establishing equitable grounds for the special relief of specific performance still exists in American law. These grounds are set out below.

Where a court orders specific performance, it compels the breaching party to render the performance that it promised under the contract. Unlike an award of damages, which operates *in rem*—it is a money judgment enforceable against the breaching party's property[24]—an order of specific performance operates *in personam*. This means that it is a command of the court directed at the breaching party. The breaching party can be sanctioned for contempt of court and jailed or fined for disobeying the order. The potential of punishment for disobedience is one of the considerations that may give a court pause in deciding if the remedy is apposite.

---

23. *See* section 2.5 for a fuller explanation of the distinction between law and equity.
24. *See* section 18.2.4 for an explanation of the enforcement of a damages award.

When an order is granted and obeyed, the breaching party honors its contractual obligations. Therefore, the aggrieved party must do so as well. If the aggrieved party has not fully performed its part of the bargain, it must render the return performance promised to the breaching party, and the court may grant its order conditional on the aggrieved party doing so.

Where the order for specific performance gives the aggrieved party its complete expectation, there is no occasion to award damages to the aggrieved party as well. However, when the breach has caused a loss that will not be completely averted or recouped by specific performance, it is appropriate for the court to award damages to compensate for that irretrievable loss in addition to granting specific performance. For example, if the breaching party refuses to convey business premises purchased by the aggrieved party, the court could decree specific performance and also award the aggrieved party whatever loss in profits the aggrieved party suffered for the period of delay between the date for delivery under the contract and the date on which the order is finally complied with.

a. Inadequate Remedy at Law

The court of equity intervenes to give a remedy only where the legal remedy of damages is inadequate, so the aggrieved party seeking specific performance must show that the normal legal remedy of damages would not provide adequate relief. This might occur, for example, where the contract is for the sale of unique property that cannot be substituted for on the market, or where damages would be very difficult to prove with reasonable certainty. Although it is founded on the traditional dichotomy between law and equity, the requirement that the aggrieved party shows that damages would be an inadequate remedy has survived the consolidation of courts of law and equity, and is reflected in Restatement, Second, §359; UCC §2.709 (the seller's action for the price); and UCC §2.716 (the buyer's remedy for specific performance). The continuing vitality of the rule is not based solely on tradition, but can also be justified on grounds of efficiency. If damages are an adequate remedy, a monetary award is often a simpler, fairer, and less intrusive means of providing relief to the aggrieved party.

The determination of whether damages are an inadequate remedy requires an evaluation of the purpose of the contract and the nature of the harm that will be suffered by the aggrieved party as a result of its breach. Where the contract involves the sale of real property, courts tend to grant a decree of specific performance quite readily. This is because of a long-established view that real property is unique, so that monetary compensation for the cost of a substitute is not an adequate remedy. This approach may be justified where the real property has qualities that cannot be replicated by a substitute. However, it is less supportable where there is nothing special about the property and the market price of a substitute is readily calculable.

(For example, it is questionable to find the legal remedy to be inadequate where the subject of the sale is a home of standard design in a tract development in which similar homes are available.) Nevertheless, courts tend to award specific performance quite routinely in sales of real property.

In situations other than sales of real property, courts evaluate the claimed inadequacy of damages more critically. In *Lemberg Found., Inc. v. Shuttlesworth Artists, Ltd.*, 182 N.Y.S.3d 489 (N.Y. App. Div. 2022), the court did grant the remedy of specific performance upon finding that damages were not an adequate remedy. A lease of premises provided that the lessee could not install any additions to the roof of the building without the lessor's written consent, which the lessor agreed not to withhold unreasonably. The lessee sought to install heating, ventilation and air conditioning (HVAC) equipment on the roof because the current location of this equipment violated regulations, but the lessor repeatedly refused to approve all the lessee's proposals for the installation without providing any reason for the ongoing refusal. The court granted an order of specific performance to the lessee, compelling the lessor to approve the lessee's proposal. Damages would not adequately compensate the lessee because it was required by regulation to relocate the HVAC equipment, and the lessor had been unreasonably obstructive in refusing consent. (The court also awarded the lessee damages to compensate for expenses it had incurred in its multiple unsuccessful attempts to get the lessor to consent to the project.) By contrast, in *Van Wagner Advertising Corp. v. S&M Enterprises*, 492 N.E.2d 756 (N.Y. 1986), the lessee of space on the exterior of a building was unable to persuade the court that the legal remedy of damages was inadequate. The owner of a building leased space on the building's exterior wall to an advertising agency for a term of several years. The wall faced the Manhattan exit ramp of the Midtown Tunnel and was therefore visible to traffic using the ramp. The lessor breached the contract by terminating the lease, and the advertising agency sued for specific performance on the grounds that the exposure of the wall to the busy exit ramp made it unique. The trial court refused summary judgment and awarded damages to the agency. The court of appeals affirmed. Although it accepted that the building wall offered advertising exposure that was, in a sense, unique, the court said that this was not enough to support the remedy of specific performance. Uniqueness must be judged in light of the difficulty or ease of measuring the cost of a substitute having the special qualities of the leased property. There is a much stronger argument for awarding specific performance if the information available to assess the financial loss resulting from the breach is scanty or unreliable, leading to a high risk of the inaccurate measure of compensation. However, in this case, the agency's loss could be calculated quite reliably because it had subleased the space for part of the time and its loss on that lease was reliably quantifiable. As to the remainder of the lease term, there was a well-established market for commercial billboard space from which the value lost by the agency could be readily calculated.

Where goods are sold, the assumption is contrary to that usually applied to sales of real property—except in special circumstances, goods are not considered unique. UCC §2.716 therefore relegates the buyer to a claim for damages, and it cannot get an order compelling the seller to perform unless it can show that the goods are unique or that the circumstances otherwise justify the order. Official Comment 2 to that section explains that to be unique, an item does not necessarily have to be the only one of its kind in existence. The concept is broader than that and could also apply in any situation in which it is not commercially feasible to obtain a substitute.

b. The Balance of the Equities and Hardship to the Breaching Party

As in any equitable remedy, the court considers the impact on the parties of granting or denying the remedy. That is, one of the factors that it takes into account is the balance of the equities and hardships between the parties. For example, in *Kilarjian v. Vastola*, 877 A.2d 372 (N.J. Super. 2004), the Kilarjians bought the Vastolas' house. The Vastolas breached the contract by refusing to proceed with the transfer and the Kilarjians sued for specific performance. The court noted that under ordinary circumstances, specific performance would be an appropriate remedy because real property is presumed to be unique. However, the reason why the Vastolas breached was because Mrs. Vastola was suffering from a serious, progressive neurological condition that disabled her and made it very difficult for the Vastolas to move. The court recognized that this was a hard case because the Kilarjians were entitled to the benefit of their bargain. However, it exercised its equitable discretion and refused specific performance on the grounds that it would be heartless and unjust to evict a severely ill and disabled woman from her home. Instead, the court remanded the case to the trial court to determine the Kilarjians' damages.

In *Kilarjian*, the hardship to the breaching party was profound and tragic. However, it is not always necessary to show hardship of this degree to avert an order of specific performance. In deciding whether it is appropriate to decree specific performance, a court is aware of the potential sanction for contempt of court if a breaching party should disobey the order, and is likely to be sensitive to the question of the intrusiveness of the order and any difficulty a breaching party may have in performing as promised. Hardship to the breaching party is taken particularly seriously where the performance involves personal services. The courts' concern over forcing the performance of personal services (which is often equated to involuntary servitude) makes it most unlikely that a court will ever specifically enforce such an obligation. There is also a strong efficiency and practicality of enforcement argument against compelling the performance of personal services because of the possibility that the service would be performed grudgingly and would require careful court supervision.

c. Practicality of Enforcement

In considering whether to grant an order of specific performance, the court takes some account of the ease or difficulty in enforcing the order, and the extent to which the court will be required to supervise the performance and deal with disputes over whether performance is in accord with the contract. Some orders of performance are easy to enforce. For example, if the court orders specific performance of a contract to sell real property, the sheriff can enforce this by evicting the breaching party and executing the documents transferring title to the aggrieved party. However, other cases may involve a more complex performance that requires judicial monitoring to ensure that a reluctant breaching party does not provide a grudging performance that falls below the reasonable standards required under the contract. This does not mean that a court will refuse an order of specific performance just because it needs supervision. But the ease or complexity of enforcement is a factor that goes into the balance. If the court concludes that specific performance is necessary to do justice, it will undertake the required supervision and may appoint a special master or some other person accountable to the court, who will evaluate performance and possibly mediate any disputes that might arise in the course of carrying it out.

d. Indefiniteness

It is a general principle of equity that a court will not make a vague order. Its command must clearly tell the breaching party what it must do to obey and avoid sanctions for contempt. This principle, combined with the courts' reluctance to invent contract terms for the parties, leads to the rule that specific performance will not be decreed unless the contract is definite enough to form the basis of a clear order. Sections 10.4 and 10.5 discuss the principle that if an agreement is too vague or indefinite, it may fail to qualify as a contract at all. However, even if the uncertainty is not so severe as to defeat a claim that a contract was made, it could render the contract too unclear to support an order of specific performance.

e. Public Interest and the Interests of Innocent Third Parties

As with all equitable remedies, one of the factors that the court weighs is the impact of an order of specific performance on the public interest. Because specific performance involves the enforcement of a private contractual arrangement between the parties, concerns about the general public good will not always be implicated. However, the public interest is included in the balance where an order compelling performance, or the refusal of such an order, does have some impact on that interest. For example, the public interest dimension is apparent in the reference, in section 18.10.1b, to concerns about involuntary servitude in the compulsion of a personal services contract.

The harm that an order of specific performance may have on the rights and interests of innocent third parties may also have an impact on the court's decision on whether to grant the order. For example, the seller of a house breached a contract to sell it to the buyer by selling it to someone else. The second buyer entered the transaction in good faith and without knowledge that the sale was in breach of the seller's contract with the first buyer. If the court awards specific performance to the first buyer, this would force the seller into breaching the contract with the second buyer. A court may decide that the harm caused by the order to the second buyer outweighs the equities in favor of granting specific performance to the first buyer.

§18.10.2 Injunctions

An injunction is an equitable remedy under which a court grants an order that either compels the breaching party to perform a specified act—called a mandatory injunction—or prohibits the breaching party from performing a specified act—called a prohibitory injunction. An order for specific performance is really just a form of injunction, and the standards described in section 18.10.1 for the grant of an order for specific performance apply to injunctions generally, whether mandatory or prohibitory: A court will not issue an injunction to compel or enjoin the breaching party's conduct unless the aggrieved party can show that the less intrusive legal remedy of damages is inadequate and that the need to protect the aggrieved party's rights under the contract outweighs any hardship that the injunction might impose on the breaching party, any problems of supervising the order, and any harm to the rights of innocent third parties or the public interest.

In most cases, an order of specific performance is in the form of a mandatory injunction—a court order compelling the breaching party to render the performance promised in the contract. However, in some situations, where a contract forbids certain conduct, an order of specific performance takes the form of a prohibitory injunction. That is, the order directs the breaching party not to take action that violates the terms of the contract. For example, in *Walgreen Co. v. Sara Creek Property Co.*, 966 F.2d 273 (7th Cir. 1992), Walgreen had a long-term lease of premises in a shopping mall owned by Sara Creek. The lease provided that Sara Creek would not lease premises in the mall to another pharmacy. Sara Creek breached this term by entering into a lease with a discount store that had a pharmacy department. Walgreen sued Sara Creek, seeking an injunction prohibiting it from letting the premises to Walgreen's competitor. This injunction is really just a prohibitory form of specific performance—an order compelling Sara Creek to honor the terms of the contract. The court of appeals affirmed the trial court's grant of the injunction. The court noted that damages are the norm in a breach of contract case, and are usually the most efficient remedy. Therefore, the court will not grant an injunction unless the aggrieved party can justify it by showing extraordinary circumstances and a balance of the equities in favor of granting it. Walgreen had demonstrated that an injunction was the most appropriate remedy in this case because the lease term was for many years and Walgreen would have great difficulty in accurately proving its loss of profits and goodwill over the term of the lease. The injunction was a simple prohibition and would not require court supervision, and neither Sara Creek nor the competing pharmacy would be unduly harmed by it.

A prohibitory injunction may also be helpful to an aggrieved party where it is not aimed directly at conduct in violation of the contract, but instead strikes at the breaching party's motivation to breach. That is, if the breaching party's purpose in wrongfully terminating a contract was to enter into a more advantageous contract with someone else, an injunction prohibiting the breaching party from performing the other contract could eliminate the advantage of breaching and encourage the breaching party to relent. For example, say that a singer contracted with a concert promoter to perform a concert. The singer thereafter received an offer from a different promoter to perform at a much more prestigious venue on the same night. The singer accepted this offer and repudiated the first contract. The court would not grant an order of specific performance to compel the singer to perform this personal service for the first promoter, but it may be willing to enjoin the singer from performing for the second promoter, thereby removing the singer's motive for breaching and encouraging retraction of the repudiation.

§18.11 LIQUIDATED (AGREED) DAMAGES

§18.11.1 The Test for Enforcing a Liquidated Damages Provision

A liquidated damages (also called "agreed damages") provision is a term in a contract under which the parties agree that if one of them breaches the contract, it will pay damages in a specified sum or in accordance with a prescribed formula. If such a clause is valid, it has the effect of settling in advance what damages will be due by that party in the event of a breach and binds the breaching party to pay damages in that amount irrespective of whatever actual damages might be. The contract could have a liquidated damages provision that specifies the damages due by each of the parties in the event of breach by that party, or it could liquidate damages for only one of them. (If the liquidated damages clause covers breach by only one party, a breach by the other will require proof of damages in the usual way.) Unless the provision makes it clear that the liquidated damages are the aggrieved party's exclusive remedy, Restatement, Second, §361 assumes that it does not prevent the aggrieved party from electing to claim specific performance instead of damages.

There are a number of reasons why the parties may agree to commit themselves in advance to a set amount of damages in the event of breach: The principal one is that if damages are stipulated in the contract, it is easier and more efficient to obtain relief if a breach occurs, particularly if the transaction involves a venture that is speculative. The aggrieved party avoids the problem of establishing foreseeability, mitigation, and certainty, and the breaching party has a predetermined liability which makes it easier to predict the cost of breaching. In fact, if one of the parties is particularly concerned about protecting itself from the problem of establishing damages in the event of breach, the ability to stipulate damages in the contract may be a significant incentive to entering the contract.

However, liquidated damages have an obvious negative aspect. They are nothing more than a forecast of probable loss. Even if the parties try hard to make as precise and thoughtful a prognostication as possible, they can never prophesy exactly what the actual losses will be. If the outcome of the transaction is uncertain or speculative, a reasonably accurate prediction of the impact of breach is even less likely. The problem of unreliable prediction increases to the extent that the parties are less careful in their projections. It may therefore turn out that the forecast of damage is very different from the loss that ultimately results from a breach, and that the agreed damages greatly overcompensate or undercompensate the aggrieved party.

Two policies of contract law are in tension when a court is called on to enforce a fairly bargained liquidated damages provision. The policy of freedom of contract points in the direction of enforcing what the parties agreed, but the compensation policy (confining contractual relief to economic compensation) points in the direction of not enforcing a provision that goes beyond compensation to impose a penalty for breach of contract. Courts tend to give greater weight to the compensation policy. Therefore, if a party challenges a liquidated damages provision, the court will evaluate it to determine if it was a genuine attempt by the parties to settle damages in advance. If it was not, the court will characterize it as a penalty—a provision having the purpose or effect of punishing or deterring breach by imposing liability beyond reasonably anticipated loss—and will refuse to enforce it. If the court refuses to enforce the provision as a penalty, the aggrieved party must prove the actual damages that it suffered in the usual way. Note that the issue of whether to enforce a liquidated damages provision is independent of questions of bargaining unfairness, such as duress, fraud, or unconscionability. If assent to a liquidated damages clause is obtained by one of these improper means, that would in itself provide grounds for invalidating it, even if the provision is not a penalty.

In *Barrie School v. Patch*, 933 A.2d 382 (Md. App. 2007), and *National Service Industries, Inc. v. Here To Serve Restaurants, Inc.*, 695 S.E.2d 669 (Ga. App. 2010), the courts noted that because the parties agreed to the liquidated damages provision when they entered the contract, there is a presumption in favor of its validity, so the party seeking to overturn the provision bears the burden of showing that it is a penalty. However, in *National Service Industries* the court also observed that in a doubtful case, the clause should be construed as a penalty. (The facts of both of these cases are discussed in section 18.11.2.)

The distinction between enforceable liquidated damages provisions and unenforceable penalties is difficult to draw because of the uncertainty inherent in any prediction of probable loss. The mere fact that the contract stipulates that the liquidated damages are a genuine pre-estimate of harm is not in itself dispositive. In fact, it must be regarded with some skepticism because the parties, knowing that penalties are unenforceable, are not likely to call it a penalty in the contract. Therefore, the purpose of the clause must be gleaned by interpretation in context to determine its true intent and effect. Some courts look only at the circumstances existing at the time of contracting and ask only whether the liquidated damages are reasonable in light of the anticipated harm. Restatement, Second, §356 and UCC §2.718, in almost identical language, adopt a broader, two-point test that asks whether the amount fixed as damages is reasonable in light of the anticipated or actual harm caused by the breach. This formulation provides an alternative two-point test that validates the provision if it either was a reasonable forecast of harm at the time of contracting, or turned out to be reasonable in light of the actual damages suffered.

This two-point test works as follows: The court should focus first on the question of whether the parties made a reasonable forecast of harm at the time of contracting. If they did, the court should defer to their genuine effort to settle damages in advance and uphold the clause, even if the actual damages suffered turn out to be higher or lower than predicted. However, even if the provision was not a very careful effort to predict damages and would fail the test of reasonable forecast, if the amount of liquidated damages ends up being reasonably close to the actual damages suffered, the provision should be upheld. (If actual damages can be proved, and they are about equal to the liquidated damages, there is not much benefit in having the liquidated damages provision, but it could still have some utility by making it easier for the party to establish the amount of loss.) Notwithstanding that the test is formulated in the alternative, a court may decline to enforce a liquidated damages clause, even though it was a genuine effort to fix damages in advance, where it is shown that the prediction of likely damages was very wrong. That is, even if the forecast of harm was reasonable at the time of contracting, a court may balk at enforcing it if it turns out that actual harm is much less than anticipated. It is also worth noting that the two-point test cannot be applied in all cases because the comparison with actual damages is possible only in cases where actual damages can be shown with reasonable certainty. If they are too difficult to prove, there will be no information on which to base this comparison, so the court will have to focus on the test applicable to the time of contracting.

The balancing of the considerations to be weighed in deciding on the validity of a liquidated damages provision is represented in Diagram 18G.

Diagram 18G

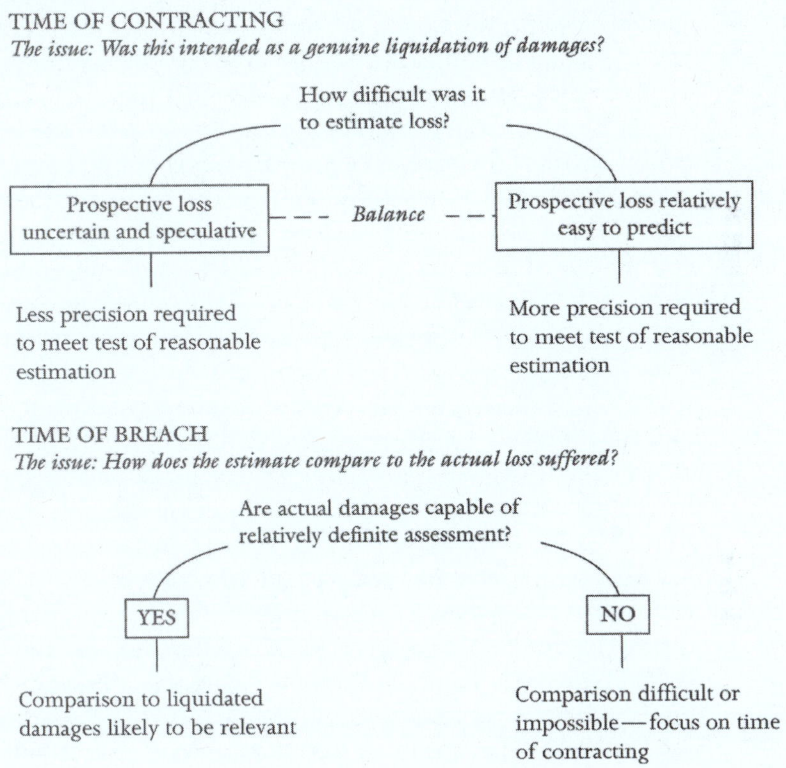

§18.11.2 The Evaluation of the Parties' Forecast of Harm

To decide the reasonableness of the anticipation of harm, the court must consider two factors: the expected difficulty of proving loss and the degree to which the estimate of harm was a reasonable advance estimate of that loss—a principled and genuine attempt to predict likely loss. On their face, these two factors appear contradictory because the more difficult it is to prove loss, the harder it must be to make any kind of reasonable pre-estimate of damages. However, the factors are not treated as rigid co-equal requirements, but as flexible considerations to be balanced against each other. Therefore, the more uncertain and speculative the damages, the less rigorous the court's examination of the reliability of the pre-estimate. However, if anticipated damages would be relatively mechanical and routine, the parties are held to a stricter standard in trying to estimate them. For example, if the contract relates to an innovative new business venture, it will likely be difficult to prove damages for breach with reasonable certainty, so the court should give more deference to the parties' reasonable effort to fix a plausible amount of agreed damages based on the best estimations that they can make in light of the uncertainty. However, if the contract involves the sale of property for which there is an active market, substitutionary damages are usually quite easy to prove, so the parties' means of determining the amount of agreed damages must be more rigorously examined.

Two cases illustrate how courts may go about balancing the factors of reasonable forecast and difficulty of proof. In *Barrie School v. Patch*, cited in section 18.11.1, the parents of a student agreed, upon enrolling their child in the school, that if they withdrew her after a certain date, they would be liable to the school for the full year's tuition. When they withdrew the child after the stated date and refused to pay the year's tuition, the school sued them for the unpaid portion. The court held that the undertaking to pay the full year's tuition was a valid liquidated damages provision because it was a reasonable pre-estimate of the likely harm that would be suffered by the school as a result of the withdrawal of a student, and that, given the school's budgeting process based on student count, it would be very difficult to estimate the loss of tuition in advance. The parents also argued that because the school eventually filled their daughter's place, the earnings from the substitute transaction should be deducted from damages. The court rejected this argument. It held that because the forecast of harm at the time of contracting was reasonable, it did not matter that the actual damages turned out to be less than the parties predicted. Therefore, because the valid liquidated damages provision fixed the amount of damages, the school had no duty to mitigate and the earnings need not be deducted. A dissenting judge in this case criticized the majority for declining to take into account that the school ultimately suffered little or no damages because it admitted a student to take the place of the child who had been withdrawn. The dissent emphasized the compensation principle of contract law, and considered that it was wrong to enforce the liquidated damages provision where it manifestly overcompensated the school.

The court refused to enforce a liquidated damages provision in *Greyhawk Homes, Inc. v. Addison*, 845 S.E.2d 356 (Ga. Ct. App. 2020). Addison was employed by Greyhawk as a construction superintendent. The contract of employment contained a provision forbidding Addison from working in competition with Greyhawk after leaving its employ, as well as a confidentiality agreement and an agreement not to solicit Greyhawk's customers. The contract included a liquidated damages clause that provided that if Addison breached these provisions, he would be liable to Greyhawk for damages of $100,000 plus $50,000 for each year that he had been employed by Greyhawk. When Addison left the employ of Greyhawk and began work for a competitor, Greyhawk sued him for the liquidated damages. The court refused to enforce the provision because it was not a reasonable pre-estimate of probable loss. Greyhawk's president testified that the figures were a broad estimate of the damage that it could suffer from a violation of the provisions, but offered no explanation of how that figure was calculated. In addition, Greyhawk used the same amount as a standard term in all its employment contracts, even though the damages that might be suffered from breaches by different employees could be quite disparate. (Although the provision was invalid as a penalty, the court noted that Greyhawk was still entitled to sue for any actual damages that it could prove at trial.)

The court also found the liquidated damages provision to be unenforceable in *National Service Industries, Inc. v. Here To Serve Restaurants, Inc.*, cited in section 18.11.1, Here To Serve Restaurants (HTS) entered onto a contract with National Service Industries (NSI) under which HTS rented linens for its restaurants from NSI. HTS breached, and NSI sought damages under a liquidated damages provision in the contract. The provision stated that if HTS breached the contract, it would pay liquidated damages to NSI "in an amount equal to forty percent (40%) of the average weekly fees charged for service prior to the date of breach . . . times the number of weeks remaining in the unexpired term." Despite the fact that the provision expressly stated that it was not a penalty, but rather a reasonable estimate of difficult-to-prove loss, the court found it to be a penalty. NSI's chief financial officer had testified that the 40 percent formula reflected its anticipated lost profits, calculated by deducting its actual historical direct costs from the contract price. However, the formula was an historical average of all NSI's contracts (and used in all its contracts), even though there were variations in the actual profitability of particular transactions. In addition, there was no evidence that NSI would be unable to secure a replacement contract to offset the profits lost as a result of the breach of this one.

§18.11.3 Damage Limitation Provisions

A term limiting damages must be distinguished from an agreed damages provision. The purpose of a damage limitation is not to forecast harm and settle the amount of the loss in advance, but to place a limit on the relief that a party may claim in the event of breach. A common example of a damage limitation is a term stating that a party will not be liable for any consequential damages arising from the breach. This provision does not anticipate the amount of damages, but rather precludes a claim for any consequential damages and confines liability to direct damages.

A provision in a contract that fixes agreed damages in an unreasonably small amount is, strictly speaking, a liquidation of damages rather than a damage limitation. It would therefore be rational to assume that it should be analyzed as described in sections 18.11.1 and 18.11.2. However both Restatement, Second, §356 and UCC §2.718 focus on the penal nature of unreasonably large liquidated damages and do not seem to encompass unreasonably small liquidated damages. (In fact, Comment *d* to §356 states that the section is not applicable to a term that fixes damages in an unreasonably small amount.)

If a term is classified as a damage limitation, it is treated differently from a liquidated damages provision and it is not subject to the tests discussed above. Instead, Restatement, Second, §356, Comment *a*, UCC §2.718, Official Comment 1, and UCC §2.719 indicate that damage limitation provisions are enforceable unless they are unconscionable. A limitation of remedy that grossly undercompensates the aggrieved party and deprives it of meaningful relief could be substantively unconscionable. However, as the discussion of unconscionability in section 13.11 explains, a finding of unconscionability requires more than a harsh result. There must also be some evidence that the unfair term resulted from procedural unconscionability—that it was imposed on the aggrieved party by improper bargaining. In addition to avoidance on grounds of unconscionability, §2.719 permits the nonenforcement of a limitation of damages where circumstances have caused the limited remedy to fail of its essential purpose. Therefore, even if the elements of unconscionability are not satisfied, §2.719 permits disregard of a damage limitation that badly undercompensates the aggrieved party or provides for a remedy that is valueless.

The plaintiff was not able to overturn a damage limitation on grounds of §2.719 in *Far East Aluminum Works Co. Ltd. v. Viracon, Inc.*, 27 F.4th 1361 (8th Cir. 2022). Far East bought specially coated color-changing windows from Viracon for use in the construction of a resort. The contract stated that Viracon would not be liable "under any circumstances for indirect, incidental, consequential, special or punitive damages" and that the buyer's remedy for defective windows was confined to replacement windows or a refund. The windows failed and Far East suffered over $8 million in consequential damages when its general contractor demanded this amount as additional compensation for replacing the windows. In suing for these consequential damages, Far East argued that the remedy provided in the contract was so disproportionate to the actual loss, that it failed as a remedy. The court acknowledged that §2.719 permits nonenforcement of a damage limitation when it causes the limited remedy to fail of its essential purpose or where the exclusion is unconscionable. However, the court held that §2.719 should not apply in a contract for highly complex and technologically advanced goods, entered into by sophisticated parties.

§18.12 INCIDENTAL DAMAGES, ATTORNEY'S FEES, AND INTEREST

In addition to the principal remedies discussed above, there are ancillary monetary awards that are often needed to fully compensate the aggrieved party for a breach of contract. They are noted briefly here.

§18.12.1 Interest

When a contract itself provides for the payment of interest on an amount due by a party, the claim of interest is simply part of the aggrieved party's damage recovery and is included in the claim. For example, if a lender makes a loan and the borrower breaches the contract by failing to repay it, the lender is entitled to sue for both the principal and for the full amount of accumulated interest at the rate provided in the contract. Interest continues to accrue until the debt is paid.

Even when the contract does not provide for the payment of interest, the general rule is that an aggrieved party may recover interest on a performance with a fixed or ascertainable money value from the time that the performance became due to the time that payment is ultimately made. Even when damages are uncertain until finally fixed in the judgment, interest is commonly awarded to the aggrieved party from the time between the judgment was rendered and its ultimate payment.

§18.12.2 Incidental Damages

Incidental damages are those expenses reasonably incurred by the aggrieved party after the breach in attempting to deal with the breach. They are essentially the administrative costs of coping with the breach and taking whatever action is necessary to protect and enforce the aggrieved party's rights under the contract or to mitigate the impact of the breach.[25] They include such items as the costs incurred in making arrangements to obtain substitute performance and to mitigate damages. For example, say that the buyer of goods breaches the contract by refusing to accept the goods when the seller tenders delivery. As a result, the seller has to transport them back to a warehouse, store them, and negotiate for their resale. All the additional costs of

25. As explained in section 18.8.3, incidental damages, as described in this section, are different from and bear no relationship to incidental reliance damages.

transport, storage, and negotiation are incidental damages and may be recovered by the seller, provided that they were incurred reasonably. This example involves a sale of goods, so the seller's incidental damages are defined and permitted in UCC §2.710 and the buyer's in §2.715. However, incidental damages are also available to the aggrieved party under common law.

Although incidental damages do, in a sense, follow as a consequence of the breach, they are distinguishable from and should not be confused with consequential damages: They do not arise as a result of the impact of the breach on some other transaction or activity dependent on the contract, but are expenses directly related to the aggrieved party's attempt to manage the effects of the breach. The distinction between incidental and consequential damages, and the potential importance of the characterization, is illustrated by *Dietec Co., Ltd. v. Osirius Group,* cited in section 18.5 in relation to the bar on a seller claiming consequential damages under Article 2. In that context, the court held Article 2 did not allow the seller (Dietec) to claim consequential damages (profits lost in other transactions) as a result of the buyer's (Osirius's) breach in failing to pay for the goods on time. However, the case also involved another claim. As a result of the late payments, Dietec suffered severe cash-flow problems which required it to incur the expense of having to obtain high-interest financing and to make other arrangements to keep its business in operation. The court held that the costs incurred in taking these actions qualified as incidental damages because they were commercially reasonable costs incurred in avoiding loss and coping with the breach. As incidental damages, they were claimable by the seller under Article 2. Had they been classified as consequential damages, they would not have been.

§18.12.3 Attorney's Fees

Based on the above definition of incidental damages, one might assume that the aggrieved party should be able to recover its attorney's fees incurred in suing to enforce the contract after breach. They are, after all, expenses that the aggrieved party was forced to undertake in dealing with the breach and seeking to enforce its rights under the contract. Despite this, attorney's fees are not recoverable by the winner of a lawsuit unless the contract specifically allows them, they are authorized by statute, or the case falls within one of a few narrow categories of exception recognized at common law. The common law exceptions apply to bad faith and vexatious litigation and to other specific situations that are not covered here. There is no statute that generally provides for the recovery of attorney's fees in contract cases.[26] Therefore, the

26. There may be a statutory basis for the recovery of attorney's fees with regard to breaches of specific types of contract.

general rule is that attorney's fees are not recoverable by the winner of a suit on contract unless the contract itself makes provision for this.

The approach to attorney's fees in the United States differs from that in many other countries, in which the prevailing party in litigation is routinely entitled to recover attorney's fees from the loser. The debate over the merits of these different approaches is complex and beyond the scope of this book. It is important to recognize, however, that because the victorious aggrieved party's judgment does not include reimbursement for the considerable expenses of litigation, it does not really achieve its goal of placing the aggrieved party in the position it would have been in had the contract been performed.

In tort cases, where a jury has a fairly wide discretion in deciding on the amount of noneconomic damages (such as those awarded for mental distress or pain and suffering), it has some ability to increase the aggrieved party's compensatory damages to take account of attorney's fees. If the case merits punitive damages, overcompensation may go far beyond this. By contrast, because contract damages are focused on provable economic loss, the jury has much less flexibility to inflate the award to cover the aggrieved party's attorney's fees. This difference in approach between contract and tort can be justified on the basis that, unlike a tort victim, a contracting party is capable of providing in the contract for the award of attorney's fees (provided that it has the bargaining power to do so).

§18.13 NONECONOMIC AND PUNITIVE DAMAGES

§18.13.1 Mental Distress and Other Noneconomic Loss

Contract damages compensate only for economic loss. Except in rare cases, the aggrieved party is not awarded damages for any mental distress, inconvenience, humiliation, or other noneconomic harm caused by the breach. This principle is applied firmly, whether the aggrieved party is a corporation without heart or soul, or some poor individual who really is traumatized and distressed by the breach. For example, in *Chrum v. Charles Heating & Cooling, Inc.*, 327 N.W.2d 568 (Mich. Ct. App. 1982), a furnace bought from the breaching party caught fire and destroyed the aggrieved party's home. The court refused to award damages for mental distress because the contract was simply a commercial transaction, the breach of which led to property loss. *Valentine v. General American Credit*, 362 N.W.2d 628 (Mich. 1984), took the same approach where an employee claimed mental distress damages for wrongful discharge. The court recognized that the breach of an employment contract would likely cause the employee emotional distress, but an employment contract is commercial in nature, and compensation must be confined to any provable economic loss.[27] Similarly, in *Gregory & Swapp, PLLC v. Kranendonk*, 424 P.3d 897 (Utah 2018), a lawyer failed to file a personal injury claim on behalf of a client before the statute of limitations had run. The lawyer then waited for ten months to tell the client that her claim was time-barred. The client sued the lawyer for malpractice (failure to file suit in time) and breach of fiduciary duty (concealing this fact from the client for ten months). The jury awarded $750,000 damages to the client to compensate for the loss of recovery against the tortfeasors. This award included emotional distress damages that would have been claimable from the tortfeasors as a result of the personal injury. The jury also awarded her $2.7 million for emotional distress caused by the lawyer's malpractice. The court overturned this additional award of emotional distress damages against the lawyer. The client was entitled to judgment against the lawyer for the emotional distress damages claimable against the tortfeasor in the underlying suit because these were part of the client's tort damages that were lost because of the lawyer's negligence. However, the client could not recover the additional emotional distress damages against the lawyer for the lawyer's breach of contract because the malpractice claim was simply aimed at recouping the client's pecuniary loss, and did not support a claim for emotional distress.[28]

Courts have recognized exceptions to this rule in two situations. First, if the breach of contract is also a tort, the tortious nature of the breach permits compensation for whatever noneconomic damages would be available to the aggrieved party under tort law. However, this is not really much of an exception at all, because a tort was committed, and the noneconomic damages are linked to the tort. Courts usually require that the tort be an independent tort—that is, the breach of the contractual obligation must be one that would give rise to liability for the breach of a duty recognized as actionable under tort law. Therefore, a breach of contract, even if negligent or intentional, is not the basis for noneconomic damages unless the aggrieved party can show that the conduct of the breaching party is also the violation of a duty under tort law. For example, if a surgeon negligently performs an operation, thereby both breaching a contractual duty of competent performance and committing the tort of battery, the patient can recover not only any economic losses but also damages for pain and suffering and emotional harm. The court recognized this in *Chrum*. After concluding that

27. Had the employee been wrongfully discharged in violation of a statute that, say, protects employees from discrimination, the statute itself may allow for both compensatory and noncompensatory damages.

28. Unlike a breach of contract claim, a cause of action based on a breach of fiduciary duty could support an award of emotional distress damages. However, on the facts of this case, the court found that the client's emotional distress was caused by the malpractice leading to loss of the tort claim, and the client had not proven that it resulted from the lawyer's breach of fiduciary duty in concealing the lapse of the claim from her.

the contract did not involve the kind of personal interests that merited mental distress damages, the court said that the plaintiff would be able to sue in tort for mental distress if the defendant had negligently breached its duty of care in installing the furnace. It remanded the case to allow the plaintiff to pursue a tort claim.

The second exception concerns a contract that is clearly not aimed at achieving an economic or commercial goal of the aggrieved party, but was deliberately aimed at giving the aggrieved party an emotional, sentimental, or psychic benefit. It is the nature of the contract, not the nature of the breach, that is crucial. Courts that recognize this exception usually apply it very narrowly to contracts that deeply involve matters of personal concern to the aggrieved party, in which the noneconomic purpose of the contract is clear, and the breaching party reasonably should have realized that a breach would likely inflict serious emotional distress on the victim.

Foreseeability of the emotional harm is a significant factor in deciding whether to award mental distress damages, but the foreseeability of likely mental distress is not enough. The sentimental or emotional character of the contract performance is crucial. In *Valentine*, the court recognized that an employer can readily foresee that wrongful dismissal will cause an employee mental distress. However, because an employment contract is commercial in nature, that foresight is not enough to entitle the employee to mental distress damages. This point is also emphasized in *Gregory & Swapp*. The court recognized that a lawyer who fails to commence suit before the statute of limitations has run must reasonably foresee that the client will be emotionally distressed by the loss of the right to sue on the claim. However, this is not enough to constitute the kind of unusual circumstances that would justify emotional distress damages. They should only be awarded where the contract is of a kind in which the parties clearly contemplate that more than the typical mental anguish would result from a breach—the contract must be specifically directed towards matters of mental solicitude.

Examples of the kinds of contract that would meet this requirement were cited in *Chrum*—a nursing home's breach of a caregiving contract by failure to notify the plaintiff of her mother's pending death, and a funeral home's breach of a burial contract by mutilating the body of the plaintiff's daughter. Breaches of contracts for funeral services feature quite regularly as the basis for awarding mental distress damages. For example, in *Menorah Chapels at Millburn v. Needle*, 899 A.2d 316 (N.J. Super. A.D. 2006) (discussed in section 17.6.3 in relation to divisibility), the court held that the son of the deceased was entitled to mental distress damages where the funeral home breached the contract to perform funeral services for the deceased by failing to ensure a proper vigil over the body in accordance with orthodox Jewish ritual. The court pointed out that because a contract for funeral services is designed to bring comfort to the bereaved, the case was one in which the chapel had the requisite foresight that its breach would cause emotional distress.

Breaches of contracts for wedding services are sometimes treated as the kind of contracts that merit an award of mental distress damages. In *Dietsch v. Music Co.*, 453 N.E.2d 1302 (Ohio 1983), a band that failed to show up for a wedding was held liable for emotional distress damages. However, other courts have not allowed recovery of damages for the emotional trauma caused by a botched wedding. In *Zumwalt v. Kevin Lee Collections, Inc.* 2008 WL 5159127 (Cal. App. 2008), a wedding planner promised the plaintiffs (the bride and her mother) that he would provide a wedding that would be a "first-class dream event" and would have "elegance with a chic Hollywood vibe." The wedding, which cost $97,000, fell far short of promised expectations. Among other things, the planner did not show up to supervise the event, the food was poor and badly served, and the planner did not provide a chocolate fountain or Veuve Cliquot champagne, as promised. The court of appeals reversed the trial court's award of emotional distress damages. Although it acknowledged that a wedding has a strong emotional focus for the couple being married, it found the production of a wedding to be nothing more than a commercial contract for catering, and associated services. The court said that it is more closely analogous to the construction of a home than to the provision of funeral services.

In *Ward v. McGarry*, 511 P.3d 1213 (Utah. Ct. App. 2022), the court recognized the possibility that emotional distress damages could be claimable where they were foreseeable as a result of the breach, were specifically within the contemplation of the parties at the time of contracting, and were actually provided for by specific language of the contract itself. Ward and McGarry had a sexual relationship, during which Ward sent nude photographs of herself to McGarry. The relationship resulted in the birth of a child and when the parties separated, they fought over the custody of the child. In settling the custody dispute, McGarry undertook to delete the photographs. Some years later, Ward discovered that McGarry had not deleted the photographs and sued him for breach of contract as well as for the torts of intentional and negligent infliction of emotional distress. The court refused to award the damages. Although emotional distress was surely foreseeable as a result of the breach, and emotional distress damages were likely the only kind of damages that would be available for the breach of a promise that resulted in no economic loss, there was no provision in the agreement that specifically provided for emotional distress damages. In addition, Ward could not claim emotional distress damages under tort law because the breach was purely based on contract, and Ward had failed to make the argument at trial that there was an independent duty in tort law that would allow recovery in tort. (There may or may not have been such a duty, but Ward failed to take the opportunity at trial to try to make that case and was precluded from raising that argument on appeal.)

§18.13.2 Punitive Damages

The purpose of punitive damages is to punish particularly egregious conduct and to deter the actor from engaging in that conduct in the future. Punitive damages are also sometimes called exemplary damages because the punishment of the actor sets an example to others, who might thereby be deterred from similar conduct. Punitive damages are principally available in tort law, where they are confined to cases in which the tortfeasor deliberately and maliciously injured the victim, or acted in callous and conscious disregard of the victim's rights. Although punitive damages are aimed at punishing the actor, they are not a fine payable to the public treasury but are awarded to the victim in addition to compensatory damages.[29]

Punitive damages are not generally available in contracts cases, because contract law is oriented towards compensating the aggrieved party's economic loss, not to the punishment and deterrence of breach. As a result, it is well established that punitive damages are not recoverable for breach of contract, even if the breach was deliberate and faithless. Restatement, Second, §355 reflects this attitude by taking the position that punitive damages are not recoverable for a breach of contract unless the breach consists of tortious conduct for which punitive damages would be available under tort law. Courts generally follow this approach and where punitive damages are awarded for breach of contract, it is almost always because the breaching party's conduct constitutes both a breach of contract and a deliberate, independent tort. This is illustrated by *America's Directories, Inc. v. Stellhorn One-Hour Photo, Inc.*, 833 N.E.2d 1059 (Ind. App. 2006), a fraud case discussed in sections 12.12 (the fraud exception to the parol evidence rule) and 13.6.2 (fraudulent promise). The seller of advertising in a phone directory made a fraudulent promise that it would permit the buyer to cancel the advertising after the first year of the three-year contract. The court upheld the jury's award to the buyer of both compensatory damages (for work and time lost in trying to deal with the fraud) and punitive damages. The court noted that in addition to violating the aggrieved party's contract rights, fraud is independently recognized as a tort, and there was sufficient evidence for the jury to conclude that the seller committed the tort willfully and wantonly by intentionally misleading the buyer.

In a narrow range of cases, particularly involving an insurer's willful breach by unjustifiably failing to indemnify the insured promptly, adequately, or at all for loss covered by the policy, courts have been willing

29. Punitive damages therefore compensate the victim beyond the harm suffered and, where the victim's lawyer is handling the matter for a contingent fee, they significantly increase the fee earned by the lawyer. If the jury award of punitive damages is too high, the court has the discretion to reduce it.

to award punitive damages even though tort law has not traditionally recognized the breach as an independent tort. (Some courts have overcome this barrier by creating a new tort, so that an egregious violation of the duty of good faith and fair dealing is recognized as a tort in itself.) If an unscrupulous insurer deliberately and unjustifiably resists paying the insured's claim, either to evade payment, or to put pressure on the insured to settle for a lesser payment, the ultimate award of nothing more than compensatory damages is not likely to be much of a deterrent to future conduct of this kind. Therefore, punitive damages serve the purpose of increasing the risk of such behavior and may better dissuade the insurer from trying to evade its obligations. Although there are other types of contracts in which it may be appropriate to award punitive damages for bad faith breach, courts have not readily expanded this doctrine beyond the field of insurance.

§18.14 A TRANSNATIONAL PERSPECTIVE ON REMEDIES

The CISG sets out the buyer's rights generally in Articles 45 to 46 and the seller's rights generally in Articles 53 to 59. It provides for damages in Articles 74 to 77. The UNIDROIT Principles cover remedies in Articles 7.2.1 to 7.4.13. It is beyond the scope on this short note on perspective to examine in detail the remedial provisions of the CISG and the UNIDROIT Principles. In general, although there are differences, many of their remedial concepts are equivalent to those set out in this chapter. For example, they expressly or impliedly recognize that the principal purpose of damages is to give the aggrieved party the benefit of the bargain, commonly measured by the difference between the contract price and the cost of a substitute transaction or the market value of the performance. They also recognize that lost profits may be the appropriate measure of damages in some cases. They require that damages be proved with reasonable certainty, be reasonably foreseeable, and be reasonably mitigated.

There are some notable differences from the common law. Neither the CISG nor the UNIDROIT Principles follow the common law's firm preference for damages over specific performance, which derives from the distinction between legal and equitable relief that is peculiar to the common law. However, Article 7.2.2 of the UNIDROIT Principles does exclude the remedy where it would be unfair or impractical—for example, where it is unreasonably burdensome or the performance is of an exclusively personal character. Article 7.4.2 of the UNIDROIT Principles deviates from the common law by allowing nonpecuniary damages for breach of contract, including damages for emotional distress. Although the CISG does not address agreed damages, Article 7.4.13 of the UNIDROIT Principles adopts a more liberal approach to agreed damages than the common law and generally upholds them irrespective of the actual damages suffered.

Examples

EXAMPLES

1. Cliff Blaster owned a piece of land on which he planned a residential development. Cliff needed to demolish a large rock outcrop on the land that was an obstacle to developing it. He entered onto a contract with Dinah Mite under which Dinah agreed to demolish the outcrop for a price of $500,000, to be paid after completion of the demolition. Shortly after the contract was executed, Dinah bought explosives at a cost of $100,000 to perform the work and she began to rig the rocks for demolition.

   On the day before Dinah was due to detonate the explosives, Cliff discovered that zoning regulations precluded any development of the property. He therefore contacted Dinah and terminated their contract. Cliff had no right to do this, so his termination was a material repudiation of the contract.[30] Dinah told Cliff that he had no legal right to back out of the contract, and she refused to accept the termination. On the next day she proceeded with the detonation and successfully demolished the outcrop. She then claimed the contract price of $500,000 from Cliff. Had Dinah accepted Cliff's repudiation, she would have been able to return the explosives to the seller or to use them in future jobs. She had already incurred other expenses of $20,000 in preparing for the demolition up to the time of Cliff's repudiation, but would have avoided additional costs of $5,000 involved in the process of demolition. Can Dinah claim the contract price from Cliff? If not, what, if anything is she entitled to claim?

2. Buddy Beautiful, a handsome young actor, better known for his good looks than his acting ability, had played minor roles in a few movies. After he had gained some fame in those roles, his agent managed to secure a contract for him with Mogul Media, Inc., an important movie producer, under which Buddy would be paid $10 million for taking the lead role in a new, big-budget superhero movie. Production of the movie was to begin two months after the contract was signed, and would last for six months.

   About a month after entering the contract, Mogul decided not to produce the film. It wrote to Buddy, informing him of the film's cancellation

30. Cliff cannot claim avoidance of the contract for mistake because he assumed the risk of mistake by failing to check the zoning regulations before entering the contract. His performance also cannot be excused as impracticable because the zoning regulations were in existence at the time of contracting.

and offering him the leading role in a new film version of Shakespeare's *Hamlet* that would be produced instead during the same period. Mogul assured Buddy that this film would do his career far more good than the superhero movie. However, on reading the script, Buddy was unconvinced. He did not enjoy the complex language, he hated the plot, and the film did not seem likely to advance his path to stardom by appealing to a young audience. Furthermore, Mogul proposed to pay Buddy only $5 million for *Hamlet* because its box office draw was anticipated to be much smaller than that of a blockbuster action movie.

Despite his misgivings, Buddy decided that *Hamlet* was better than nothing, so he accepted the offer. Does he have any claim for damages against Mogul? If so, how much?

3. Change the facts of Example 2 as follows: Buddy did not feel that Hamlet was a suitable role, so he declined Mogul's offer and insisted that it make the original movie as promised. Mogul refused and their relationship broke down. Buddy put his agent to work seeking other opportunities for a starring role in a movie. Despite a year's conscientious and persistent effort, the agent was unable to secure any film roles for Buddy. In the interim, Buddy declined several offers of small parts in television series because he felt that he should hold himself available to perform whatever new film contract his agent could find. What damages, if any, should Buddy receive?

4. As in Example 3, Buddy declined Mogul's offer to star in *Hamlet*. Although Buddy's agent worked hard to find him another starring role, nothing had come up four months after Mogul's repudiation. At that time, Buddy was presented with the opportunity to do some fashion modeling. He decided to accept it, since no offers of movie roles had surfaced. Buddy entered into a contract with Dee Ziner, a designer of men's fashions, to model her new line of summer clothing. Buddy's performance under the modeling contract began immediately after execution of the contract and lasted one month. Buddy earned a fee of $1 million. What damages, if any, should Buddy receive?

5. As in Examples 3 and 4, Buddy declined Mogul's offer to star in *Hamlet* and Buddy's agent could not find another starring movie role for him. A year after Mogul's repudiation, Buddy's agent dropped him as a client and Buddy finally accepted that his hopes for a movie career had ended in failure. Buddy is convinced that had he made the superhero movie for Mogul, he would have established himself as a star and enjoyed unlimited opportunities for further movies. He has now sued Mogul for the $10 million payable under their contract, as well as $200 million in damages for the destruction of his movie career. Should he be awarded these damages?

6. Harpo C. Chord is a young and ambitious pianist. After struggling for many months to find work, he finally received an offer to play dinner music at Trés Trendi, a fancy restaurant. This was not quite what he had in mind as a career opportunity, but his financial reserves were much depleted and he was becoming desperate. He also realized that because the restaurant was close to the city's performing arts center, many of its patrons were influential in the arts, so there was a good chance that someone important might notice his talent and offer him something better. He therefore accepted the offer and on January 15 he entered into a contract with Trés Trendi under which he would play the piano during dinner from 8 P.M. to midnight every night for a month. His performances would begin on February 1, and he would be paid "the going rate" for his services. Because neither party knew at the time of contracting what the current market rate was for a dinner pianist, Trés Trendi said that it would make inquiries and tell Harpo as soon as it found out.

   Having heard nothing from Trés Trendi for a week, Harpo called the manager to find out what rate of compensation had been established by the promised market survey. He was stunned when the manager told him that inquiries had shown that the market rate for a pianist was much higher than she had anticipated, so she had decided to scrap the idea of having live music in the restaurant. This was a clear repudiation of the contract, and despite Harpo's fervent pleas, the manager refused to relent.

   Having just gone through the agonizing process of looking for work, Harpo realizes that he has little chance of finding other employment for February. Besides, he wants to work for Trés Trendi so that he can showcase his talents to any useful diners that may be present. What recourse does he have?

7. Barney owns an acre of land in the suburbs, which is vacant except for an old barn. When Barney retired last year, he decided to move from his home in the city to his suburban acre. He had plans drawn for a new house to be constructed on the eastern portion of his lot. The existing barn was on the western side of the lot, so it did not interfere with his building plans, but it was quite an unsightly structure and would occupy space that Barney planned to use as a garden. The barn was in reasonably good condition and was easily removable, so he decided to sell it instead of demolishing it. He advertised it for sale and ultimately sold it to Penny Pincher for $5,000. In terms of the contract, Penny agreed to pay all the costs of removing the barn and also to break up its concrete foundation and remove the debris.

   A few weeks later, Penny removed the barn. She was going to hire someone to break up and remove the concrete foundation, but when she discovered that the cheapest quote for the job was $7,000, she decided that it was a waste of money and refused to do it. The concrete slab will spoil Barney's landscaping plans and leave him with a useless and ugly concrete surface in his backyard. However, because suburban land is scarce and of prime value, the presence of the slab would apparently not dissuade a typical buyer from purchasing the property at its full worth. As a result, the removal of the slab would not enhance the property's market value. What damages, if any, can Barney recover for Penny's breach?

8. To satisfy the demand for its required course on professional ethics, a law school offers a summer school ethics course every year. The course is usually in great demand and attracts about 50 students each summer. Last November, the law school contracted with Bill A. Billhours, a prominent local attorney, to teach the summer ethics course for a fee of $10,000. The contract obliged him to teach four evenings a week for five weeks, beginning on June 1. On May 15, Bill was given the opportunity of advising a new client in connection with a huge international transaction. Participation in the proposed transaction promised to be both stimulating and lucrative, so Bill grabbed the chance of working on it. Unfortunately, the work required him to be out of the country for much of June and July, so it was no longer possible for him to teach. He called the dean of the law school on May 17 and told her that he could not teach summer school as planned.
   a. Not wishing to disappoint the students who were relying on taking the course that summer, the dean immediately set to work finding a replacement. After making several unsuccessful calls, she was finally put in touch with Professor Wise, a world-famous expert on legal ethics and the author of several definitive books on the subject. Professor Wise had just retired, so he had no plans for the summer, but he was unwilling to teach for less than $15,000, plus his traveling and living expenses, which amount to a further $4,000. Desperate, the dean agreed to his terms. Can the law school recover all or any of the $19,000 from Bill?
   b. Assume that the dean was unable to find anyone to teach the course because it is too late to find a teacher on such short notice. The dean cannot bear to let down all those students who are relying on taking the course during the summer. Is there anything she can do to force Bill into teaching?
   c. Assume that the dean could neither find a substitute teacher nor compel Bill to teach. As a result, the summer ethics course had to be canceled. Based on enrollment before cancellation, the law school can show that it would have earned $75,000 in tuition revenue from the course. In addition, the law school was sued by one of the students who had enrolled in the course. The student had been relying on the

course to complete his requirements for graduation in the summer so that he could graduate in August. He had a job beginning in August, but now he cannot begin work until after he graduates at the end of December. He therefore claimed three months' salary from the law school. To avoid adverse publicity and a negative impact on alumni relations, the law school paid the student's claim. What recourse, if any, does the school have against Bill?

9. Nat Atorium hired La Goon Pool Co. to build a swimming pool in his backyard. As the yard was small, the pool had to be placed not more than five feet from the rear wall of the house. La Goon brought its excavating equipment into the yard and one of its workers began to dig the hole. After spending some hours on the job and having excavated to a depth of about six feet, the operator started to become weary and careless. As a result, he dug too close to the house, undermining its foundation and causing the rear of the house to collapse. At the time, Nat was in one of the rear rooms and he could have been severely injured or killed had he not had the presence of mind to dive out of a door just as the room began to cave in. Although he escaped physical injury, he was badly traumatized by the close call and the destruction of half his house.

   This experience has removed Nat's desire for a swimming pool. La Goon concedes that it is liable for the cost of repairing Nat's house, the fair market value of all personal property lost in the collapse, and the cost of filling in the hole and restoring the yard. However, Nat says this is not enough. He demands in addition:

   a. Compensation of $150,000 for the shock and distress that he suffered as a result of La Goon's incompetence.
   b. Compensation of $50,000 for the loss of irreplaceable family records and photographs that were among the personal property destroyed. Although they have no economic worth, they were of immense sentimental value to Nat.
   c. Punitive damages of $1 million.

   Is Nat likely to succeed on any of these further claims?

10. Chic Canery has managed to train a troupe of chickens to perform amazing tricks. She has appeared on several TV shows with them and has attracted a lot of public attention. AC9 Productions, Inc., a show promoter, decided the market was ready for a live show featuring Chic and her chickens. It approached Chic with a proposal to produce such a show. Following negotiations, in January Chic and AC9 entered into a contract for the production of a show on July 4. The show was to be staged in a sports stadium with a capacity of 100,000 seats. AC9 would make all arrangements for the show and would be entitled to all proceeds from the event, save for a fee of $1 million to be paid to Chic. An

advance of $100,000 on this fee would be paid to Chic on the signing of the contract, and the balance would be paid a week before the show.

Immediately after the contract was signed, AC9 paid the $100,000 to Chic and it began preparations for the show. It booked the stadium, hired special staff to work exclusively on publicity and sales, and committed itself to the purchase of television advertising. On March 1, Chic changed her mind about doing the show and she repudiated the contract. After trying unsuccessfully to convince her to recant, AC9 had no choice but to accept the fact that Chic would not perform. As the theme and concept of the entire show were built on Chic's unique chicken act, it was too late to begin afresh by changing the theme and trying to find a new starring attraction. AC9 stopped all further work on the show and laid off its special staff. It exercised its cancellation right under the contract with the stadium and terminated its booking, forfeiting a $50,000 deposit. It had no right to cancel the television advertising slots. At the time of Chic's repudiation, AC9 had incurred the following expenses and commitments:

a. Before making a final decision to enter the contract with Chic, it had spent $30,000 on a market analysis and profit projection for the show.
b. It paid the $100,000 advance to Chic.
c. It paid $25,000 in salary and severance pay to its special staff.
d. It forfeited its $50,000 deposit on the stadium.
e. It committed itself to pay $500,000 for television advertising.

According to the market analysis and projections made by AC9 before it entered the contract with Chic, it expected the show tickets to be sold out, generating income of $10 million. It expected further earnings of $3.5 million from the sale of T-shirts, souvenirs, and food. Its projected costs, including Chic's fee, were $5.5 million, so it expected a profit of $8 million. What damages is it likely to recover from Chic?

11. Benny Fishery Co. entered into a contract with Reliant Renovations, Inc. under which Reliant agreed to build an addition to Benny Fishery's seafood processing plant. The contract required Reliant to excavate the site, build a foundation, and erect an aluminum structure on it. The total price for the project was $230,000. Reliant began work and encountered trouble immediately because the ground was much rockier than expected. As a result, it had to hire a subcontractor to blast the rock and had to use much heavier equipment than anticipated. This greatly increased its costs of excavation from an expected $50,000 to $100,000, and its total projected cost from $200,000 to $250,000. This meant that it now projected a loss of $20,000 on the contract. However, Reliant greatly values its reputation for keeping its commitments, so it did not try to renegotiate the price or to claim relief for

mistake. Instead, it decided to bear the loss and complete the job for the contract price.

Soon after the excavation had been completed and before Reliant could proceed any further, Benny Fishery decided that it no longer needed the addition to its plant. It terminated the contract. As it had no right to do this, the termination was a total breach. The excavation work constitutes exactly one-quarter of Reliant's performance under the contract, and Benny Fishery has therefore offered to pay Reliant $57,500, which is exactly one-quarter of the contract price. Should Reliant accept this payment or demand more?

12. Gracie Spooner owns a busy hamburger joint. She recently decided to replace her grungy ketchup pumps with little plastic sachets of ketchup. To ensure a ready and stable supply of this vital condiment, she entered into a one-year contract with Sauce Source, Inc., a wholesaler. Under the contract, Gracie committed herself to buy a minimum of ten boxes of sachets a month, at a price of $25 a box. The contract contained the following provision:

> The parties record that the pricing of the product sold under this contract is based on Buyer's commitment to take the minimum quantities specified above. Therefore if Buyer should breach this contract by failing to take the prescribed minimum quantity, Seller shall be entitled to damages based on the difference between the total amount actually bought and paid for by Buyer during the contract period and the total minimum price payable for the contract period. The parties expressly agree that this provision does not constitute a penalty, but is a genuine attempt to estimate damages and to avoid the uncertainty and difficulties of proof.

Gracie bought and paid for the minimum quantities required by the contract for seven months, but she found that she had grossly overestimated the amount of ketchup that she needed. Unopened boxes of sachets were beginning to pile up in her small storeroom, and it was clear to her that she already had enough ketchup to last her for more than a couple of years. She therefore declined to order or accept delivery of any more ketchup from Sauce Source. When the yearlong contract period ended, Sauce Source sent an invoice to Gracie for $1,250, based on the price of the minimum quantity that she had failed to take during the last five months of the contract. Gracie protested to the manager of Sauce Source. Gracie pointed out that ketchup had gone up in price since they made their contract, and she suggested that Sauce Source simply sell the remaining boxes at a better price to someone else. The manager told her that they had enough ketchup to keep all their customers supplied, with plenty over, so her breach actually reduced their volume of sales for the year. In any event, he reminded her that she did agree to this payment in the contract. Gracie feels that the invoice is ridiculous. Should she pay it?

Explanations

1. Cliff had no right to terminate the contract, so his termination was a material repudiation that would entitle Dinah to claim expectation damages from him. Had Dinah fully performed before Cliff repudiated his obligations under the contract, she would have been entitled to the full unpaid balance of the contract price. She expected to receive that price, and there would have been no deduction from it because she would not have saved any costs as a result of the repudiation. Her contractual expectation would have been achieved by reimbursing the costs she expended (her reliance loss) plus her expected profit, which amounts to the contract price. However, because the repudiation occurred before Dinah had fully performed, she is not entitled to receive the full contract price. At the time of repudiation, Dinah had incurred costs of $20,000 in performing, but had not yet detonated the $100,000 worth of explosives or incurred the $5,000 costs of the detonation itself. Therefore, at the time of breach, Dinah's expectation damages would have been $395,000, made up of her reliance expenses of $20,000 plus her lost profit of $375,000 (the price of $500,000 less the total expected costs of $125,000). By disregarding Cliff's repudiation and proceeding with the demolition, Dinah aggravated her damages by using up the explosives and incurring the additional costs of demolition. Although the aggrieved party has the option of declining to accept a repudiation and to give the repudiator an opportunity to recant, the mitigation principle requires this option to be chosen reasonably. Where, on the day before her performance, Cliff unequivocally informed Dinah that he repudiated the contract, and Dinah was capable of suspending her performance, her decision to perform was not reasonable. The mitigation principle precludes her from holding Cliff liable for her obstinate persistence in performance after Cliff's repudiation. She must therefore be confined to her expectation before she increased her damages.

   This Example is inspired by *Rockingham County v. Luten Bridge Co.*, 35 F.2d 301 (4th Cir. 1929), an old case that remains one of the best examples of obstinate damage aggravation. The county breached its contract for the construction of a bridge by terminating the project and telling the contractor to stop work. The contractor disregarded the instruction and continued to build the bridge. The court held that it was entitled to recover its anticipated profit as well as those losses incurred up to the date of breach, but denied it any compensation for expenditures made after the breach.

   Dinah would not have had better prospects of recovery had she sued in restitution for the value of her services in blasting the outcrop. By continuing work after Cliff withdrew his authorization, she became an officious intermeddler. In addition, Cliff received no useful benefit from her services because the demolition of the outcrop has no value to him.

2. Buddy's acceptance of the offer to star in *Hamlet* could be seen as a modification of the contract. If it was, there is no issue of breach or damages—the parties have simply changed their terms. However, when one party seeks to substitute a performance different from that originally agreed, the circumstances are also consistent with breach combined with an offer of mitigation. It is important to distinguish an agreed modification from a breach, followed by acceptance of a mitigating contract. If the parties have agreed to modify the contract, there is no claim for damages. However, if one of the parties breaches, and then offers the other a substitute contract which the aggrieved party accepts, the aggrieved party has a claim for damages to compensate for the difference in value of the original and substitute contracts.

   In Buddy's case, the facts indicate that Mogul breached and then offered a substitute in mitigation—it made the unilateral decision to cancel the superhero movie, and informed Buddy of this, rather than offering him any opportunity to negotiate the change. Since Mogul terminated the contract before performance was due, this is an unequivocal and material anticipatory repudiation.[31] Upon Mogul's repudiation, Buddy is entitled to sue for his lost profit under the contract, less any amount recovered in mitigation. In an employment contract, lost profits could be equal to the full salary if the employee merely provides labor and does not have to incur costs to perform. However, any earnings from substitute employment must be deducted from damages as mitigation.

   Hamlet is surely a substitute contract, because Buddy would not have been able to do both films, which have the same production dates. (In fact, Mogul's decision to produce the second was apparently based on its decision to cancel the first.) When, as a result of the breach, the aggrieved party is released from his performance so that he can undertake other work that could not have been done in the absence of breach, any earnings from that other work must be treated as a gain from the breach and offset against damages. Therefore, his earnings from *Hamlet* ($5 million) must be deducted from his lost profit damages for the breach of the initial contract ($10 million).

3. Buddy has rejected the opportunity to reduce his damages by starring in *Hamlet* for $5 million. He has been idle for a year because he could find no other substitute contract for a leading movie role. The question be decided is whether Buddy's refusal of Mogul's offer and his failure to perform other work was a violation of his duty to mitigate, resulting in aggravated loss for which Mogul should not be held accountable. If so, the earnings that he should reasonably have made during the six-month production period under the contract must be offset against his

31. *See* section 17.7.2 for a discussion of repudiation.

damages. This offset would be the $5 million that he could have earned from *Hamlet*, or alternatively, what he could have earned by finding other work in the six months that would have been occupied by filming the superhero movie.

Buddy may have failed to mitigate by refusing the *Hamlet* role. It may seem outrageous to expect the victim of a breach to accept mitigation by dealing with the very person who breached the contract and caused the loss. However courts generally take the attitude that mitigation opportunities offered by the breaching party should be evaluated under the same standards as other available means to reduce damages: If this means of mitigation is not unduly risky, burdensome, or humiliating, it does not call on the victim to waive any right to relief under the breached contract, and it provides the most reasonable means of reducing the loss, the victim must pursue it, or risk losing the right to claim any damages that could have been prevented by taking it. Because Mogul has already shown itself to be untrustworthy, Buddy may have justifiable concerns about whether it will prove similarly unreliable in the substitute contract. However, Buddy needs to show more than a general apprehension that Mogul might again renege.

Notwithstanding, there is a different consideration that may justify Buddy in declining the *Hamlet* role. If he had the reasonable prospect of finding a more suitable movie, his decision to refuse the role and to hold himself available for a better opportunity may have been a rational judgment. The fact that no better offer came along does not defeat this argument. The injured party's judgment with regard to mitigation need only be reasonable, even if it later appears that it was wrong, or that a different decision would have been better.

Parker v. Twentieth Century-Fox Film Corp., discussed in section 18.6.3, held that Parker's duty of reasonable mitigation did not require her to accept work that was different and inferior to that provided for in the contract. Mogul's offer of the role in *Hamlet* is clearly very different from that promised to Buddy under the contract, but is it inferior? Although *Hamlet* may be a finer piece of work than the superhero movie, the role of Hamlet could be inferior for Buddy's purposes. It does not have the same potential to showcase his talents, to reach his targeted audience, or to further his career goals. (Note that inferiority is judged on the basis of the quality of the substitute work, and not by the mere fact that Buddy would be paid less for playing Hamlet. The difference in earnings can be compensated for by a damages award.)

If Buddy's refusal of the role in Hamlet violated his duty to mitigate, he aggravated his damages by $5 million and his damages must be reduced accordingly. However, even if he was justified in refusing the role, his other actions may have aggravated his damages. He did make considerable efforts to find another starring movie role, but he may not have been reasonable in refusing to seek or consider small television parts. Although these minor television roles are very different from a major role in a movie, this work is not necessarily inferior because it is within the field and there is nothing to indicate that taking these small parts would have a negative effect on his career goals. Buddy may have been reasonable in his decision to decline these smaller roles so as to hold himself available for a more significant movie part. However, if Mogul can show that Buddy did not act reasonably in declining the television parts in the vain hope of another movie contract, his damages should be reduced by what he reasonably could have earned during the six-month period that became free as a result of the film's cancellation.

4. If Buddy should have accepted the Hamlet role, the answer does not change—the full $5 million that he should have earned, not just $1 million he actually earned, must be deducted from his damages. However, if his refusal of *Hamlet* was justified, the fee earned from the modeling job must be offset against the $10 million loss. The performance of the modeling job took place during the period reserved for the filming, and Buddy could not have accepted it and earned the modeling fee had Mogul not breached the movie contract. It is therefore a substitute transaction and the $1 million fee is a gain that would not have been made but for the breach. (If Buddy incurred any direct costs to perform for Dee, those would be subtracted before his earnings are offset. But in the typical employment contract it is the employee's time and labor that are being contracted for, and the employee does not usually have to spend much in rendering that performance. As a result, the employee's direct costs are likely to be small or even nonexistent.)

   Therefore, provided that Buddy's refusal of the *Hamlet* role was justified, he can claim damages for breach in the amount of $9 million—his full contract salary of $10 million less the $1 million earned in mitigation. This has the effect of overcompensating him because he receives his full contract fee even though he worked only for a month. However, Mogul cannot complain because the benefit of not having to work so hard for his money does not reduce Buddy's financial loss. As in Example 2, the issue of whether the modeling job is different or inferior does not come up where Buddy accepted the substitute work. It is only relevant if he declines a substitute transaction.

5. Buddy's claim for consequential damages is based on the theory that by losing his opportunity to star in the superhero movie, he was deprived of a successful movie career and lost $200 million. The mitigation issue would arise here again, because his failure to accept the Hamlet role may have precluded an opportunity to prevent this consequence. However, Buddy may argue that this consequential loss would have

occurred whether or not he had accepted the Hamlet role, because *Hamlet* would not have advanced his career at all and may even have ruined it.

It is arguable that a movie producer should reasonably foresee that its failure to produce an actor's first major film—especially if it is planned as an expensive blockbuster—could have an adverse impact on his career and deprive him of future opportunities. However, even if this is so, the overwhelming barrier to recovery is the highly speculative nature of the claim. It is unlikely that Buddy could prove with any degree of plausibility that the proposed movie would have been successful and would have advanced his career. There are just too many imponderables: Would he have performed well? Would good judgments have been made about publicity and promotion? Would the public have been attracted to the film and to him? Would it have made enough money to make him desirable to other producers? More uncertainties could be listed, but the point is made. Even if he could overcome this burden of showing a probability that opportunities would have been created, there is a further level of uncertainty about whether he would have been lucky and clever enough to use them to advantage. In short, he cannot even prove what would have happened had the film been made, let alone establish a monetary value of the loss. The consequential damages claim must fail under the principles of certainty and causation.

The difficulty in establishing quantifiable loss when the breach results in a lost opportunity for publicity and its consequent career advancement is shown by another case springing from the entertainment industry: *Ericson v. Playgirl, Inc.*, 140 Cal. Rptr. 921 (Cal. Ct. App. 1977). *Playgirl* (a general-interest magazine that also featured photographs of nude male models) contracted with Ericson, one of its centerfold models and an aspiring actor, to rerun his photos in its *Best of Playgirl* annual and to include him as one of the models on the annual's cover. When *Playgirl* failed to include Ericson on the cover, he sued it for consequential damages for breach of contract. He produced witnesses who testified generally on the benefits of publicity to an acting career and on the economic value of appearing on a magazine cover. The court found that *Playgirl* had breached the contract, but it awarded Ericson only nominal damages. The court accepted that as an abstract matter, exposure (forgive the double entendre) is valuable to an actor, but his evidence of loss was too generalized and nonspecific. Any economically adverse consequences of the breach were pure conjecture.

6. Although Harpo's remuneration has not been settled, this should not affect the validity of the contract because the parties have agreed on a market standard for determining it. A contract for a reasonable fee, to be based on an objectively ascertainable standard, is sufficiently definite

for enforcement.[32] If Harpo was not reasonably able to mitigate his loss by finding appropriate substitute employment, he will at a minimum be able to sue for what he would have earned under the contract (less direct costs saved, if any). To establish what this amount would have been, he would have to produce evidence of the market rate paid to a pianist of his experience for equivalent work in a restaurant of similar standing. Such evidence is apparently available. However, Harpo was expecting more than a mere month's employment. He was hoping to make contacts and to open opportunities by playing in the restaurant. *Ericson*, discussed in Example 5, shows that it is difficult to establish measurable injury as a result of the loss of publicity. Therefore, an award of money damages would most likely cover only his direct damages and would fail to compensate him for speculative consequential damages.

When an aggrieved party can show that a monetary award cannot adequately achieve his expectation, he establishes one of the essential grounds for the remedy of specific performance.[33] To get the order, Harpo must satisfy the court, in addition to showing the inadequacy of the damages remedy, that the court's burden of supervision is outweighed by the need for the remedy and that the balance of the equities favor granting the order. In addition, when there is some indefiniteness in the contract terms, even if the indefiniteness is not serious enough to invalidate the contract, the court may confine the aggrieved party to damages unless the terms can be clearly established to support a precise and comprehensible order.

The indefiniteness in the fee to be paid to Harpo should not be a bar to relief because the court can establish the fee by reference to the market. There may also be some lack of detail with regard to Harpo's working conditions, which would have to be resolved, possibly also by reference to customary or reasonable standards. The primary focus of the definiteness principle in this context is to ensure that the order specifies Trés Trendi's duties precisely so that it knows what it must do to comply with the order to avoid contempt of court. By fixing the payment due to Harpo and detailing his working conditions, the court should be able to formulate a clear order. An order compelling Harpo's employment by a possibly begrudging employer does entail some burden of supervision to ensure that he is paid and that he is not mistreated or subjected to harassment. However, this supervisory task is not particularly onerous or exceptional. The court could appoint an official to oversee the

32. This issue is discussed in section 10.5.

33. Had Harpo breached, Trés Trendi would not have been able to obtain an order of specific performance to compel his personal services because of the strong policy against forcing an individual to work against his will. However, this policy is not implicated where the employee sues the employer for specific performance.

employment, but the court need not do this. It could just leave it up to Harpo to bring any alleged violation of the order to the court's attention by moving for an order calling on Trés Trendi to show cause why it should not be held in contempt of court. The court would then conduct a hearing to determine if Trés Trendi violated the order and to impose a sanction if it did.

The equities of granting relief favor Harpo, not only because a damages award cannot adequately compensate him for his uncertain consequential damages but also because Trés Trendi committed a willful breach and it suffers no undue hardship by allowing Harpo to play the piano in its restaurant for a fee that it would have to pay in any event as direct damages.

7. It is easy to identify the measure of damages required to place Barney in the position he would have been in had Penny not breached. It is the reasonable cost of demolishing the slab and removing the concrete debris, apparently $7,000. However, the facts show that although damages of $7,000 would give Barney the equivalent of performance in compliance with the contract, the breach did not actually cause him economic harm if his loss is instead measured by the diminution in the value of the property on which the work was to have been done. This raises the issue of whether the proper basis for recovery is the cost of giving him what was promised (which is $7,000) or the actual reduction in his wealth (which is zero). Stated differently, when the cost of giving the aggrieved party his contractual expectation exceeds his actual ultimate financial loss, should his damages be limited by that ultimate loss?

   As discussed in sections 17.3.5 and 18.6.6, Barney is normally entitled to the full measure of his expectation damages. However, if Penny's breach was not material or willful and the cost of giving Barney his contractual expectation would be an unfair forfeiture, the court may confine relief to Barney's ultimate economic loss, measured by the diminution in market value resulting from the breach. Penny's breach was deliberate, and that on its own is enough to preclude application of the unfair forfeiture doctrine. In addition, the breach was likely material. Materiality is a question of interpretation, to be decided by assessing the importance of the breach in light of the purpose of the contract, determined by its terms and context. Had Barney intended to resell the property immediately, Penny's failure to remove the slab may have been immaterial because it had no impact on the market value of the property. (Even under these circumstances, this outcome is not assured because the parties did stipulate for the slab's removal as part of the consideration for the barn.) However, Barney plans to live on the property, and it therefore cannot be said that the removal of the slab was merely incidental to the sale. Barney should be entitled to receive the full $7,000 damages based on the cost of rectifying the breach.

8. a. When, following a total repudiation, the aggrieved party obtains a reasonable substitute performance, expectation damages are the difference between what the aggrieved party had to pay for the substitute and what it would have had to pay under the contract for the equivalent performance. When the substitute not only is more expensive in itself but also involves the aggrieved party in the extra expense of having to go outside the local market, the additional cost of the substitute's travel and living expenses is also included in determining the replacement cost. Therefore if Professor Wise is a reasonable substitute for Bill, the law school will be able to recover substitutionary damages from Bill. These damages are not the full $19,000 paid to Wise, but rather the $9,000 difference between what it paid to Wise, $19,000, and what it would have paid Bill, $10,000.

   Although it is seldom likely that a substitute performance will exactly match that promised under the contract, both the compensation and the mitigation principle require that the replacement be as close as possible. If the aggrieved party is awarded the added cost of a more valuable or better-quality replacement, it is overcompensated, and its damages must be reduced to reflect the lower cost of a nearer substitute. However, this principle is not rigidly and invariably applied to deprive the aggrieved party of reimbursement of the full cost of a superior replacement. The breach placed the law school in the position of having to find a substitute to counter the ill effects of the breach within a very short time. When the only reasonable option open to the aggrieved party under all the circumstances is to select a replacement of superior quality, it may be appropriate to hold the breaching party accountable for the full cost, even if this means that the aggrieved party profits somewhat by a performance that is better than or more valuable than that expected.

   Although Professor Wise is a more expensive instructor, it is not clear that he is actually a superior substitute from the law school's perspective. He may be more experienced and have greater prestige, and may possibly be a better teacher. However, he does not provide the law school with any apparent economic gain, and will perform the same function of teaching the summer school class as Bill. The situation is analogous to that of the school district in *Handicapped Children's Education Board v. Lukaszewski*, cited in section 18.6.3c, in which the court found that the more experienced and more expensive speech and language therapist hired as a substitute gave it no advantage over that expected from Lukaszewski under the breached contract.

In this case, Bill breached about two weeks before classes were to begin, and the dean had little time to find a substitute. She did make immediate efforts and only hired Professor Wise when it was apparent that she would be unlikely to find anyone else. She has no duty of exhaustive inquiry, but need only make such good faith and reasonable efforts called for by the circumstances. Even if Professor Wise is a superior substitute, the facts show him to be the most reasonable substitute.

b. A court will not decree specific performance of personal services. Quite apart from the obvious difficulty in supervising the performance of teaching duties, the compulsion of personal services is rather too much like involuntary servitude. Therefore, even though the aggrieved party may have no adequate remedy at law, the considerations disfavoring specific enforcement outweigh the aggrieved party's interest in performance.

If specific performance is not available, a court may be willing to grant the aggrieved party a prohibitory injunction, restraining the breaching party from entering into the transaction that motivated the breach. The concerns about involuntary servitude and difficulty of supervision are not present in such a negative order. Preventing Bill from participating in the international transaction does not, in itself, achieve the school's expectation, but the idea is that by removing the motivation for the breach, the order will induce Bill to perform as promised. However, even when a prohibitory injunction is sought, courts are very wary about using their power of compulsion to prevent an individual from pursuing important career opportunities or otherwise working to earn a livelihood. It is therefore in only the most compelling cases that a court will issue such an order.

Like specific performance, an injunction is an equitable remedy, subject to the same general prerequisites: The aggrieved party must show that the legal remedy of damages is inadequate, and that the balance of equities favors the grant of the order. In this case, given the fact that no substitute is available, the possibility of substitutionary damages does not exist. This would lead to lost profits and consequential damages that could be very speculative and difficult to prove, as Explanation 8(c) discusses. Furthermore, no monetary award can compensate for the immeasurable harm caused by the disruption of the law school's program, its inability to provide planned educational services, and the disappointment or even hostility of its students. Overall, a good argument can be made that the school has no adequate remedy at law. If this is so, the equities of trying to protect the law school's expectation weigh heavily in the balance. They are given further weight by the fact that

Bill's breach is deliberate and motivated by ambition and financial reward. Nevertheless, Bill's primary professional pursuit is legal practice and the service of his clients' needs. It may simply be too harsh on Bill to restrain him. Also, there is a strong public interest in allowing a client access to an attorney of its choice, so an injunction may improperly interfere with the attorney-client relationship. This would be particularly so if Bill has already agreed to represent the client and had begun to work on the matter. In short, although this could be a case in which an injunction would be appropriate, a court may conclude that the public interest against granting an injunction outweighs the equities in favor of it.

c. Because the law school is unable, after reasonable effort, to replace Bill and avert the loss resulting from cancellation of the class, its net loss is claimable as direct damages. It cannot claim the full lost earnings of $75,000. First, it must establish that its forecast of revenue income is reasonably reliable. Thereafter, it must deduct its savings from the breach and any recoupment of that loss. The most obvious saving is Bill's salary of $10,000. Although the facts do not indicate them, there may be some other variable (direct) costs that are saved. Overhead expenses such as maintaining the buildings and paying support staff, which are not reduced at all by the breach, are not deducted as costs saved. In addition, there may be some recoupment of the lost earnings if some of the students decide to switch to another summer school class instead, or if the law school's fee structure is such that the students end up paying more tuition in the semester for having to take the ethics course then. Once all these savings and recoupments are calculated, the law school is entitled to claim its lost profit—expected earnings less savings and recoupment—from Bill.

The payment to the student who sued for lost salary is a consequential loss. When a breach of contract causes the aggrieved party to breach a dependent contract with a third person, the aggrieved party's liability to the third person could be recoverable provided that the requirements of causation, reasonable certainty, foreseeability, and mitigation are satisfied. It is not clear that the law school was legally liable to the student for the loss of salary because the school may have had the right to cancel the course, either by express stipulation or by common usage. If so, its payment could have been purely ex gratia, and under principles of causation and mitigation, the law school is not likely to be able to hold Bill accountable for this loss. However, the law school may have committed not to cancel the course, so that Bill's repudiation forced it into a breach of its contract with the student. Even if this is so, Bill would not be liable for this loss unless he reasonably could have foreseen it. Bill will be taken to have foreseen this damage either if the school told him of its commitment to students, or if, in normal practice, this kind of commitment was common enough that Bill should have been aware of it as a practitioner and former student. Assuming that the loss was reasonably foreseeable to Bill, the school must still satisfy the requirements of mitigation and reasonable certainty. It decided to pay the student's claim in full, rather than contesting it. However, failure to challenge the student's claim would not be an aggravation of loss if the student clearly established his claim, so that litigation over it would have been costly, pointless, and damaging to the school's reputation. Although reasonable certainty can be an issue in claims for lost future earnings, it seems that in this case the student did have a job and can establish his loss for the defined three-month period. (Maybe the student's employment was also contingent on his passing the bar, which would make his loss of earnings more speculative, but the facts do not indicate that this was an issue.)

9. a./b. These Examples raise the question of whether LaGoon must compensate Nat for shock, distress, and sentimental loss. The focus of contract damages is on economic loss, so the general rule is that no compensation is claimable for emotional distress or sentimental loss resulting from the breach. In some cases, losses of this nature could be excluded simply on the basis that they were not reasonably foreseeable. But even when there may have been some basis for contemplating them as a probable consequence of breach, in most cases the policy of confining contract damages to economic loss usually precludes the award of any compensation for emotional distress. There are, however, two situations in which courts have been willing to countenance a claim for emotional or sentimental damages:

The first occurs where the purpose of the contract is clearly and purely to enhance the aggrieved party's emotional well-being. It may seem, at first thought, that the construction of a swimming pool in Nat's backyard, for his own personal use and enjoyment, is such a contract. However, courts constrict this exception more narrowly. As explained in section 18.13.1, the very basis and nature of the contract must be to provide sentimental or emotional benefit to the aggrieved party. It is not enough, to remove the contract from the commercial realm, that the aggrieved party's desire for the performance was motivated by personal pleasure rather than profit. The reason for this rather cold-hearted approach is probably quite obvious: If the exception were extended to cases like this, it could cover almost every consumer transaction in which it is clear that the primary motivation is the use of the property or services purchased to enhance quality or enjoyment of life.

The second situation in which a court may grant the aggrieved party emotional distress damages is where the breach of contract is also a tort that is recognized in tort law as giving rise to a claim for emotional distress damages. This is not so much an exception to the rule barring emotional distress damages in contract as a recognition that some breaches of contract may involve conduct that is also a violation of duty under the law of torts. The noneconomic damages are therefore not really awarded for the breach of contract, but are based on the independent tort cause of action. The damage to Nat's house was apparently caused by negligent operation of the earthmoving equipment. If this is so, the negligent performance is likely to constitute not only a breach of contract but also a breach of the tort duty of reasonable care. Nat may therefore claim emotional distress damages if tort law recognizes a claim for emotional distress damages under these circumstances. (Tort law may not allow these damages for destruction of property, but may allow them for Nat's distress caused by the threat of severe injury from the collapse of his house.)

c. The issue in this Example is whether Nat can claim punitive damages. The compensation principle also precludes punitive damages in most contract suits unless the breach is also a tort for which such damages are appropriate. Punitive damages are not generally available in tort law unless the injury was deliberate and malicious, or was at least the result of reckless and callous disregard for the aggrieved party's rights. Therefore, even if LaGoon's employee did commit a tort by damaging Nat's house, this sounds more like a case of common negligence than the kind of conduct that warrants punitive relief.

10. If AC9's projections are credible, its expectation damages are its anticipated profit of $8 million plus the reliance expenses that it has already spent or committed for which it would have been reimbursed out of its earnings under the contract. (These expenses are discussed below.) It is not clear how convincing these projections may be. To recover lost profits, an aggrieved party must be able to prove the fact and amount of those profits with reasonable certainty. AC9's projections may have been made by people with great expertise and experience and based on careful and thorough research. However, it is generally very difficult to establish prospective lost profits from a canceled entertainment event. Public taste can be unpredictable and often surprises even the most seasoned promoter. The prospect of profit is even less certain when the show centers on something as odd as a performing chicken act. Given the substantial projected costs of mounting the show, AC9 would have to do remarkably well in selling both its tickets and its associated

knick-knacks. Its prediction that it could sell out a stadium of 100,000 seats shows laudable, but possibly misplaced, faith in the artistic sensibilities of the American public. Had ticket sales begun before Chic repudiated, AC9 would have had some data on which to project its prospects of filling the stadium, but she reneged before any promotion of the show had begun.

If AC9 cannot prove lost profits, what other alternatives does it have? Restitutionary relief would be available to reclaim Chic's unjust enrichment, but that would cover only the $100,000 down payment. None of the other expenditure enriched Chic in any way. However, an aggrieved party who cannot prove lost profit may nevertheless still recover as reliance damages the expense component of its expectation claim. A claim of reliance damages would permit the recovery of not only the $100,000 down payment, which qualifies as essential reliance, but also some of the other losses incurred in reliance on the contract. Provided that they were reasonably necessary to AC9's performance under the contract and were not profligate, the forfeited stadium deposit and the staff salaries are recoverable in reliance. (They are probably best classified as essential reliance, in that they were expended in furtherance of AC9's contractual obligation to arrange and promote the show.)

The debt for television advertising would also fall into this category, but only to the extent that the expenditure is wasted and not salvageable. Although the advertising slots cannot be canceled, they may be assignable or diverted to use for other purposes. Therefore, to the extent that AC9 can recoup its expenditure by selling the slots or using them for another show, it is not claimable as a reliance loss.

The cost of the market survey and profit projection were incurred before the contract was entered into, so even though these expenses were a waste in the end, they cannot, by definition, be treated as having been incurred in reliance on the contract. This is the general approach to precontractual expenses, notwithstanding that the breach cut off any prospect of earning income that may have reimbursed them.[34]

As noted above, AC9 would claim reliance only if it could not prove its larger claim of lost profit. The aggrieved party does not have to prove that the contract would have made a profit to recover reliance damages. However, when the purpose of the contract was profit, and

34. There have been some situations in which courts have been willing to include precontractual expenses in reliance recovery. For example, if the breaching party knew that the aggrieved party was incurring the expenses in anticipation of the contract and had strongly indicated an intention to enter the contract, promissory estoppel relief may be available for the precontractual expenses. Also, the expenses could qualify as lost opportunity reliance if the aggrieved party could have recouped them by entering a similar contract with a third party but gave up that chance by entering the contract with the breaching party.

the breaching party is able to prove that the aggrieved party would have made a loss in the event of complete performance, the court may reduce the reliance recovery to take account of this expectation of loss. (As stated in section 18.8.2 and Explanation 11, a pro rata reduction should be applied.) In a case like this one, where profit is highly speculative, the risk of uncertainty therefore falls on the breaching party. Chic probably has about as much chance of proving loss as AC9 has of proving profit, so she probably cannot satisfy her burden, and AC9's reliance recovery is therefore not likely to be subject to reduction.

Wartzman v. Hightower Productions, Ltd., 456 A.2d 82 (Md. Ct. Spec. App. 1983), involved an entertainment event almost as culturally significant as Chic's. A group of bright entrepreneurs embarked on an elaborate venture designed to make money out of breaking the world flagpole-sitting record. They planned to lodge an entertainer in a specially constructed perch atop a hydraulic lift mounted on a flatbed trailer, and to exhibit him around the country for about nine months, culminating in his descent from the perch in Times Square on New Year's Eve. They needed capital for this, so they contracted with an attorney to form a corporation that could solicit investments. The attorney did not act competently and failed to create an entity in compliance with securities law. This was discovered only after the promoters had incurred expenses in setting up the project. They could not proceed further without engaging in a complex and expensive procedure to remedy the violation of the securities law. The promoters could not afford the expense or the delay of correcting the problem and the venture collapsed. The corporation was unable to prove that it would have made a profit from the venture, but the court awarded it reliance damages to compensate for the wasted expenditures incurred in reliance on the attorney's contractual commitment to incorporate the enterprise properly.

11. Reliant is entitled to claim more than the $57,500 offered by Benny Fishery. Had Reliant's cost been as it had estimated, it would have had a reasonable expectation of profit. Benny Fishery's material breach would have entitled it to full expectation damages, calculated by adding its reliance expenditure, which would have been $50,000, to its anticipated profit of $30,000. However, Reliant's miscalculation of its cost has defeated its expectation of profit and its claim for expectation damages. Its only reasonable expectation from full performance is a loss of $20,000. As a result, its claim is confined to reliance or restitutionary damages.

    Its reliance damages are its cost of $100,000, but they may be even less than this if Benny Fishery can make a case for reducing them. If Benny Fishery can prove that Reliant's reasonable expectation under the contract was to lose money, the reliance recovery may be reduced to adjust it for that expectation of loss. The burden of proving the losing expectation is placed on Benny Fishery, and Reliant's reliance recovery is unaffected if Benny Fishery cannot sustain the burden. Even if Benny Fishery can show that Reliant would have lost money had it performed the contract, Reliant would be unfairly undercompensated if the full amount of the expected loss was deducted from a reliance recovery that constitutes only a portion of its performance. The deduction should therefore be prorated so that it is no more than a share of the loss proportionate to the performance rendered. The most rational way of allocating the loss to completed performance is to determine its proportion of the total contractual performance based on the relationship of the cost incurred to the total cost of performance. In the present case, Reliant had incurred costs of $100,000 out of a total anticipated cost of $250,000—that is, two-fifths of the total. Therefore (provided that Benny Fishery can prove this anticipated loss), the $100,000 reliance expenses must be reduced by two-fifths of the total expected loss of $20,000, which is $8,000, leaving a recovery of $92,000.

Reliant's alternative to seeking reliance damages is to claim restitution. Restitution is measured by the market value of the work performed (quantum meruit). Unless Reliant performed inefficiently, incurring costs in excess of what would be normal on the market, the value of its performance is likely to be higher than its cost, because it would include a reasonable profit. For the sake of illustration, if the costs are indeed efficient and the industry norm is to have a 10 percent profit margin on excavation work, the market value of the performance is $110,000. Because restitution would provide a larger recovery, it would make sense for reliance to choose this basis for relief. However, some courts, uncomfortable with the anomaly of achieving different results in reliance and restitution for exactly the same breach, have applied a version of the prorating principle to restitution by confining the aggrieved party to the contract value of the performance where that is less than the quantum meruit measure. In the present case, as two-fifths in value of the work was done, a court following this rule would confine Reliant to two-fifths of the contract price of $230,000. This works out to a recovery of $92,000—the same as the prorated recovery for reliance. Other courts have not extended the prorating principle to restitution because the aggrieved party claiming restitution is proceeding on the basis of unjust enrichment, not contract, and those courts do not see it as appropriate to reduce the aggrieved party's recovery by the price of the performance set by the breached and disaffirmed contract.

12. Sauce Source is attempting to enforce an agreed damages provision.[35] The principal basis[36] for Gracie to challenge the provision is that it imposes a penalty for breach, which is unenforceable as a violation of the compensation principle. The compensation principle requires that an agreed damages provision must be a genuine attempt to liquidate damages. If it is not, the court will refuse to enforce it. This is a sale of goods, so the validity of the provision is tested under UCC §2.718(1), which employs a two-point test. (Restatement, Second, §356 adopts the same two-point test, so the case should be resolved in the same way under common law.) The agreed damages are examined in light of both the anticipated harm at the time of contracting, and the actual loss following breach. (Both UCC §2.718 and Restatement, Second, §356 uphold the liquidated damages provision if the liquidated damages are reasonable in light of either "anticipated or actual" loss.) The test of anticipated loss requires that the liquidation of damages must be a genuine attempt to reasonably estimate loss at the time of contracting. The more difficult the prospect of proving loss appeared at that time, the greater leeway the parties should be given in coming up with a figure. However, if the basis of determining loss would have been reasonably straightforward at the time of contracting, the parties are held to a higher standard in calculating a figure that approximates expected loss. When actual loss can be determined following breach, the measurement against actual loss allows the court to uphold the award if it has a reasonable relationship to actual loss, even if it was not originally a reasonable estimate of loss.

The Example does not state how the agreed damages were calculated. However, it is clear from the effect of the provision that the clause cannot be justified as being a realistic prognostication of harm. In most sales of goods, the seller's damages are relatively easy to predict and calculate. If the seller resells the goods after breach, the difference between

---

35. When a party promises to take a specified quantity of goods or to pay for that quantity even if it is not taken, the term is sometimes interpreted not as an attempt to liquidate damages but as a "take or pay" provision, which is not subject to regulation as agreed damages. "Take or pay" clauses are typically found in long-term supply contracts where the supplier incurs the bulk of its costs at the outset. The buyer's commitment to pay for a minimum quantity is justified because it is needed to enable the supplier to recoup that cost. Such facts are not present in this case. The clause is both described in the contract as, and functions as, a liquidation of damages.

36. Although this is the principal basis for challenging the provision, unconscionability doctrine could be an alternative basis for avoiding it. However, to succeed in a claim of unconscionability, Gracie would have to show not only that the provision was substantively unconscionable (which it might be) but also that it was procedurally unconscionable. The fact that the provision is in a standard contract drafted by Sauce Source may support an argument that it is adhesive, which may be enough to establish procedural unconscionability if the substantive unconscionability is severe enough. *See* sections 13.11 and 13.12.

the contract and resale price is quite easily ascertainable. If the seller does not resell the goods or the resale is at an unreasonably low price, the contract-market difference can be established. If neither of these bases for calculating damages is workable (for example, because the seller loses volume of sales, as alleged by Sauce Source in this case), the seller's lost profit can be proved without too much difficulty. Finally, if the goods are perishable and cannot be resold, the seller is able to sue the buyer for their price. Although there could be uncertainties and disagreement on a number of issues, such as the reasonableness of resale, the market price, or the issue of lost volume, these difficulties are not comparable to, say, the problems of proving lost profits for a speculative venture. There is enough predictability to require Sauce Source to show a sensible basis for coming up with an estimate that bears some relationship to reality. Instead, Sauce Source has used a formula that assures it of full recovery of the sale price, no matter how much it actually delivers to Gracie. If there ever was a term designed as a disincentive to breach— that is, a penalty—this is it.

Furthermore, the amount of damages is quite random in its relationship to loss and ensures that Sauce Source is always overcompensated. To demonstrate, consider the following calculations based on arbitrarily selected, but generous, actual damage figures: Gracie breached after taking her minimum requirements for seven months, so she is liable for agreed damages of 5 × \$250 = \$1,250, representing her failure to take 50 boxes of sachets.

If the ketchup can be readily resold at full price, the damages may overcompensate Sauce Source by a full \$1,250 (less any incidental damages). But even if it resells at a huge loss, say at \$5 a box, its actual damages would still be considerably less than what was agreed: They would be \$1,000, the difference between the contract price of the 50 boxes (\$1,250) and their resale price of \$250.

Even if Sauce Source can show that Gracie's breach resulted in a reduction in its volume of sales because it has more ketchup than it can sell, the agreed damages would still exceed its lost profit, no matter how big its profit margin may be. To illustrate, say that its total cost of buying the sachets at wholesale and selling them is only \$2 per box, so that makes a generous profit of \$23 per box. Its lost profit is still only 50 × 23 = \$1,150—\$100 below the agreed damages.

This set of calculations is based on Gracie's breach in the seventh month of the contract. Had she breached earlier, the discrepancy between the damages fixed and the reasonably likely harm would be even greater—the earlier she breached, the higher the discrepancy. However, at no point, not even in the last month, does this disproportion entirely disappear. The only two situations in which Sauce Source's loss would be equal to the damages provided are both highly unlikely.

First, if its costs are zero and it has suffered loss of volume, its lost profit would be equal to the agreed damages. Second, if it could not resell at all and the ketchup would spoil and have to be discarded, it would lose the entire contract price. Although this could occur where perishables are sold, ketchup in sealed packages probably has a distant expiry date, which would give Sauce Source much more opportunity to sell it before it spoils.

The agreed damages therefore fail the first step of the test—they were not a reasonable forecast of harm at the time of the contract. These calculations also show that they fail the second step—a comparison between the amount of the liquidated damages and the actual damages shows that the amount of liquidated damages is invariably higher than any actual damages suffered by Sauce Source.

If an agreed damages provision is invalidated, the aggrieved party does not lose all remedy. It may still recover whatever actual damages it suffered. If Gracie is correct in saying that the market value of ketchup rose since the contract was entered into, Sauce Source would not be able to claim damages based on the difference between the higher market price and the contract price. Similarly, if it entered a substitute transaction by reselling in a commercially reasonable way, it probably sold at the higher price and cannot claim damages based on resale. However, Sauce Source argues that even if it did make a subsequent sale, this was not a substitute because it has enough ketchup in stock to satisfy all demand. As discussed in section 18.6.3d, if Sauce Source can show that the breach caused a reduction in its volume of sales and that it had unused capacity to supply all of the demand for ketchup, it should be able to claim its lost profit under §2.708(2). Despite the language in §2.708(2) that "due credit" must be given for "proceeds of resale," most courts accept that this does not apply in a lost volume situation.

CHAPTER 19

Assignment, Delegation, and Third-Party Beneficiaries

§19.1 INTRODUCTION

As noted many times before, contract is a consensual relationship created by agreement between the parties. In the great majority of cases, contractual rights and duties arise only between the parties and the power of enforcement resides only in each against the other—a person who is not a party to a contract cannot be bound by it and acquires no rights under it. However, this chapter deals with two situations in which this rule is qualified. Although these situations have in common the fact that a nonparty to the contract obtains the right to enforce a promise under it, they are otherwise quite distinct and are based on very different premises.

In the first situation, discussed in section 19.2, the parties to the contract expressly or impliedly agree, at the time of making it, that the performance of one of them will be rendered to or for the benefit of a person who is not a party to the contract, and that the nonparty will have the right to enforce that commitment. The creation of the third-party rights is contemplated by the parties and occurs at the time of contract formation.

In the second situation, discussed in section 19.3, there is no conferral of rights on a nonparty at the time of contracting. Rather, after the contract is formed, one of the parties transfers its contractual rights or obligations, or both, to a third party. The transfer of contractual rights is called an assignment, and the transfer of duties is called a delegation. The right to assign contractual rights is based on the concept that a party's right to performance under the contract is an asset belonging to that party. As a property interest, it is generally capable (with exceptions to be noted later) of being transferred (assigned) by sale, donation, or other means of disposition. When a party assigns rights under a contract (thereby becoming the assignor), ownership of those rights passes to the recipient (assignee) who is substituted for the assignor as the person entitled to performance. Unlike assignment, the delegation of contractual duties is not based on any concept of ownership—a duty is not owned. Nevertheless, it is also generally permissible provided that it does not impair the reasonable expectations of the party to whom the performance is due.

§19.2 THIRD-PARTY BENEFICIARIES

§19.2.1 The Distinction Between Intended and Incidental Beneficiaries

Contracts routinely benefit people who are not parties. For example, a contract for landscape services between a property owner and a landscaper confers the benefit on neighbors of an aesthetically pleasing well-groomed yard in their neighborhood; a contract between a property owner and a developer to erect a new convention center benefits nearby hotels and businesses; a county's contract with a construction company to improve a road benefits all the people who use the road. In fact, in a complex interactive economy, vast numbers of contracts between strangers allow people to enjoy facilities and services that would not otherwise be available. However, even though these bystanders may derive some advantage from the contract, and even have an important stake in its performance, they have no legal rights under the contract. Therefore, if the landscaper, developer, or construction company breaches its contract by failing to perform, the people who anticipated benefitting from it have no cause of action to enforce the contract or to claim damages. They are known as incidental beneficiaries—the benefit they anticipated was an incidental result of a transaction between others. The contracting parties may have been pleased, indifferent, or resentful to see someone else derive benefits from their contract, but they did not make the contract for the purpose of conferring on a beneficiary the right to sue for performance under the contract.

However, in contrast to these more commonplace situations in which the positive effects of the contract on a third party occur incidentally, a contract may be entered for the deliberate purpose of bestowing a benefit as well as the power to enforce that benefit—on a third party. That is, a contract is properly described as for the benefit of a third party only if it manifests the parties' intent to give a benefit to a third party, directly enforceable by that third party against the contracting party who undertakes to perform it. It is the creation of this directly enforceable right that is the hallmark of a contract for the benefit of a third party. For example, Debtor owes $200,000 to Creditor. Debtor enters into a contract with Buyer under which Debtor sells a plot of land to Buyer for $200,000, and the contract stipulates that Buyer will pay the $200,000 to Creditor. Debtor's purpose, of course, is to have the proceeds of the property transmitted directly to Creditor to settle the debt. In this case, the payment to Creditor does not occur as a fortuitous result of the contract but is specifically called for by it. Creditor's benefit is not merely incidental, but is clearly contemplated and deliberately conferred. If it is expressed or can be reasonably inferred that the parties, in contracting for the performance to be rendered to Creditor, also intended to give Creditor the right to enforce Buyer's promise of performance directly and independently of Debtor, Creditor acquires the status of intended beneficiary.

When a contract is intended to confer a benefit on and create enforcement rights in a third-party beneficiary, the contracting party who is to render the performance to the beneficiary (in the example above, Buyer) is usually referred to as the promisor, and the contracting party whose right to performance has been conferred on the beneficiary (in the above example, Debtor) is usually called the promisee. This nomenclature could be confusing because in a bilateral contract the terms "promisor" and "promisee" are relative—each party is both a promisor with regard to its own performance and a promisee with regard to the performance promised by the other. However, from the perspective of the third-party beneficiary, "promisor" means the party who has committed to perform in favor of the beneficiary. Diagram 19A illustrates the basic relationship and the terminology.

Diagram 19A

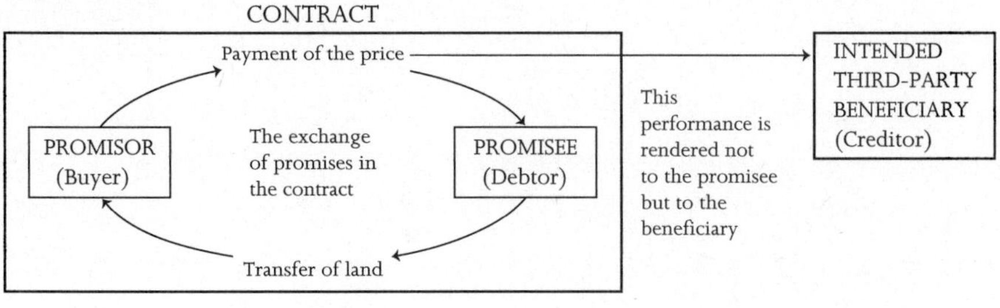

If the parties intend to confer the status of intended beneficiary on someone, that person is likely to be specifically named or identified in the contract. If this is not so, the strong inference is that the benefit is merely incidental. However, this conclusion is not inevitable. Intent to benefit is a matter of interpretation. Provided that the beneficiary will be identifiable when the time for performance falls due, it could be apparent that the parties did intend to create rights in favor of that beneficiary, despite the lack of specific identification at the time of contracting.

§19.2.2 The Essence of Intended Beneficiary Status: The Right of Independent Enforcement

As indicated above, when a contract confers the status of intended beneficiary on a third party, this does not mean only that performance must be rendered to or for the third party's benefit. It also means, as Restatement, Second, §304 provides, that the contract manifests the intent to grant the beneficiary an independent cause of action to enforce the promise. The grant of this enforcement right in the beneficiary is the central point of the third-party beneficiary doctrine and the distinguishing feature of a contract for the benefit of a third party. The beneficiary's direct cause of action against the promisor can be of great importance in making the benefit meaningful. The beneficiary can pursue the right to performance on its own and does not have to depend on the promisee to take enforcement action. This is the crucial requirement to give the third-party beneficiary standing to sue on the contract. In many opinions, such as in *Estate of Agnew v. Ross*, 152 A.3d 247 (Pa. 2017), the court identifies the parties' intent to confer a direct right of enforcement on the beneficiary as a standing requirement.[1]

In the above example, if Creditor had no independent right of enforcement, it would not be able to sue Buyer, the promisor, if Buyer failed to perform in Creditor's favor as promised. Debtor, the promisee, would be the only person who could sue Buyer for the payment, and Creditor's only claim would be against Debtor under the loan contract. However, as an intended beneficiary, Creditor can sue Buyer directly if it fails to pay. Creditor has this right of direct enforcement in addition to its right to sue Debtor under the loan contract, so it has two parties against whom it can seek recourse for the unpaid loan. (Creditor he can obtain only a single satisfaction of its claim, so one of them is released from liability to Creditor to the extent that the other pays.) This is represented in Diagram 19B.

1. This case is discussed further, and its facts are summarized, in section 19.2.10.

Diagram 19B

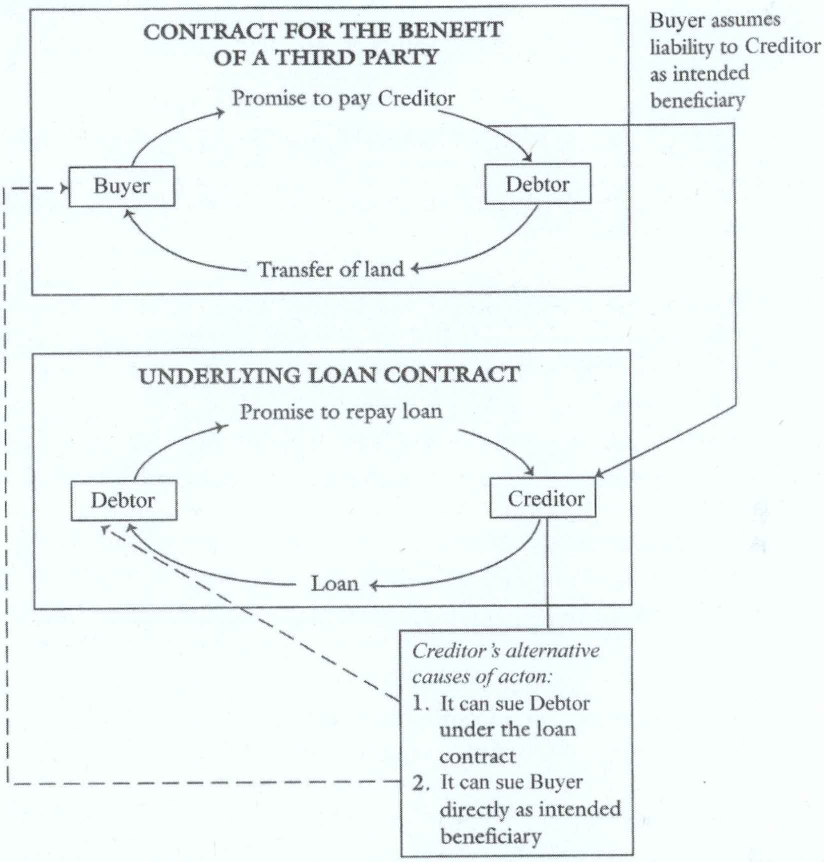

English common law did not recognize such a direct cause of action in the beneficiary unless the beneficiary could establish either that the promisee was acting as its agent or that the contract created a trust. However, in the mid-nineteenth century, the concept of direct enforcement by the beneficiary developed in American law. *Lawrence v. Fox*, 20 N.Y. 268 (1859), is recognized as the groundbreaking case. A man named Holly lent $300 to Fox. Holly was indebted to Lawrence for the same amount, and so Holly and Fox agreed that Fox would repay the loan amount to Lawrence. When Fox failed to pay, Lawrence sued him. Fox defended the suit on the basis that Lawrence had no standing to sue because he was not a party to the contract—there was no privity between them. The court rejected this defense and articulated the principle that even where no agency or trust is established, the parties to a contract do have the power to create rights enforceable by a person who is not a party to a contract, and that person can sue the promisor to enforce the performance undertaken to the promisee for its benefit.

§19.2.3 The Intent to Confer an Independent Right of Enforcement

The recognition of enforcement rights in a nonparty may seem like a radical departure from the general concept of contract as a private consensual arrangement that creates rights only between those who have bound themselves to each other. However, the third-party beneficiary doctrine is consistent with that concept because the third party only acquires the right to enforce the benefit if it is apparent that the parties intended to give it that right—they have elected to create the beneficiary status as part of their agreement. As stressed already, it is not enough that the contracting parties expect or intend to benefit the third party, or even that the contract calls for performance to be rendered to the third party. It must also manifest the intention to give the third party the right to enforce the performance if it is not rendered. This is reflected in Restatement, Second, §302(1), which recognizes a "right to performance" (which means the right to enforce the performance) in the beneficiary only when it is appropriate to effectuate the intention of the parties.

Like all other contract terms, the intent to establish third-party enforcement rights is a matter of interpretation. If the contract expressly articulates the intent to confer or not to confer enforcement rights on a third party, the resolution of this question is relatively easy. If, as commonly happens, the contract does not clearly articulate the parties' intent, it must be gleaned by the normal process of interpreting the factual evidence of intent, and if that is inconclusive, by construing what the parties must reasonably have intended. As usual, an objective test is used, and it is the mutual intent of the parties that is relevant, not the uncommunicated subjective intent of just one of them. The promisee is usually the party that desires to confer the benefit on the third party, but it is not enough that the promisee has this subjective intent. The promisor must have reasonably understood this desire and have manifested agreement to assume an obligation to the beneficiary.

A few cases illustrate the process of interpretation where the contract does not expressly designate a third party as an intended beneficiary. *Martis v. Grinnell Mutual Reinsurance Company*, 905 N.E.2d 920 (Ill. App. Ct. 2009), involved a contract between Grinnell, an insurance company, and an employer whose workers were insured against injury. The policy stated that the insurer was "directly and primarily liable to any person entitled to benefits payable by this insurance." The plaintiff, a chiropractor who had provided medical services to one of the insured employees, sued Grinnell, claiming that it had breached its contract with the employer by improperly applying a discount to the payments made to medical providers. He asserted standing to sue Grinnell on the basis that medical providers were intended beneficiaries of the insurance contract between Grinnell and the employer.

The court disagreed and held that the plaintiff had not discharged the burden of showing that medical providers were intended beneficiaries of the policy. The policy language, "any person entitled to benefits," referred to the employees of the insured employer, and showed no intent to confer an independent right of action on providers, who were merely incidental beneficiaries. *Farm Bureau Insurance Co. v. TNT Equipment, Inc.* 2019 WL 2552588 (Mich. App. 2019), is another case involving an insurance policy. The issue was whether parties whose property was stored in a storage facility had a direct cause of action for their losses against the insurer under an insurance policy between the insurer and the storage facility. The court held that even though the policy indemnified the storage facility for damage to the property of others stored in the facility, the owners of that property were not intended beneficiaries of the policy. Nothing in the policy indicated that the parties intended to confer direct enforcement rights on those property owners.

In *Taylor v. Honda Motorcars, Inc.*, 2019 WL 2152585 (Ohio Ct. App. 2019), Eric and Marcia Taylor leased a car from Honda Motorcars, a car dealer. Although both of them participated in the selection of the vehicle and they told the dealer that they were leasing the car for Marcia's use, she was not a party to the lease, which was executed only by Eric. At some time after the Taylors took delivery of the car, Marcia was driving their daughter to school when she was stopped by the police on suspicion of driving a stolen vehicle and both she and her daughter were detained. It turned out that a different car had been stolen from the dealer at about the same time as the lease was executed and the dealer had erroneously used the same temporary license plate for both vehicles. The matter was resolved, but Marcia and her daughter were traumatized by the incident. The issue in the case was whether Marcia and her daughter were third party beneficiaries of the contract between Eric and the dealer, giving them an independent cause of action against the dealer for emotional distress damages. The court held that they had no such cause of action because they were merely incidental beneficiaries of the contract. The fact that the Taylors told the dealer that the car was being leased for Marcia's use and that she participated in the car's selection was not enough to make her an intended beneficiary in the absence of any language or circumstances that evidenced an intent to give her an independent right to enforce the contract. [2]

In *Jackson v. American Plaza Corp.*, 2009 WL 1158829 (S.D.N.Y. 2009), the plaintiffs, who advertised room rentals on Craigslist, sued the defendant, a

2. The court also noted that even if Marcia and her daughter were intended beneficiaries, the contract was purely a commercial transaction, and not the exceptional type of contract in which emotional distress was a particularly likely result of breach. Emotional distress damages would therefore not be recoverable. *See* section 18.13.1 for a discussion of mental distress damages.

competitor who also advertised on the list, claiming that the defendant had violated the standard terms of use in its clickwrap agreement with Craigslist by making multiple postings of repetitive advertisements. The plaintiffs claimed that the multiple postings harmed their business, and they sought to enjoin this practice on the theory that they were intended beneficiaries of the terms of use. The court held that they were not. The terms of use did not expressly confer rights of enforcement on other list users. They made it clear that the consequence of making repetitive postings would be that Craigslist would block the postings, and that the only recourse available to a dissatisfied user was to discontinue use of the list. The court found that, interpreted as a whole, the sole purpose of the prohibition on repetitive advertisements was to prevent the overburdening of Craigslist's infrastructure.

The court did allow the plaintiff to pursue a claim as an intended beneficiary in *Cianciotto v. Hospice Care Network*, 32 Misc. 3d 916 (N.Y. Dist. 2011). The plaintiff's terminally ill father had entered into a contract with the hospice under which the hospice would provide care for him for six months. The hospice ended the services after only a few weeks. After the father died, the plaintiff sued the hospice for breach of contract, claiming mental distress damages. The hospice sought summary judgment on the basis that it had no contract with the plaintiff. The court refused to grant the motion because it found that the plaintiff had a viable claim as an intended beneficiary of the contract between the hospice and her father. The contract recognized her by name as her father's primary caregiver and contemplated that the hospice care would relieve her of the responsibility to care for him in his declining condition.[3]

§19.2.4 The Relevance of the Relationship Between the Promisee and the Beneficiary: Creditor and Donee Beneficiaries

As just mentioned, Restatement, Second, §302(1) sets forth a broad standard to guide the determination of whether a nonparty to the contract should be treated as an intended beneficiary: The recognition of the beneficiary's right to enforce performance must be appropriate to give effect to the parties' intent. The intent to confer the benefit is the central criterion and the focus of the inquiry. This is possibly all that needed to be said. However, motivated by a long tradition that it wishes neither to follow nor to abandon, §302(1) goes on to suggest what appears to be a second requirement: There must

3. In contrast to *Taylor*, the court recognized that this may be a type of contract in which mental distress damages are recoverable, because its purpose was to relieve the plaintiff of mental anguish.

also be some relationship between the promisee and the beneficiary from which it can be inferred that the parties had the beneficiary's interests in mind when entering the contract. Although this seems to be set out as a prerequisite in addition to intent, it is really just a subset of the general inquiry into what the parties intended. A relationship between the promisee and beneficiary reinforces the conclusion of intent to benefit by explaining the motivation for conferring the benefit.

Earlier caselaw broke the relationship between the promisee and the beneficiary into two categories, and a beneficiary had to fit into one of these categories to qualify as an intended, rather than an incidental, beneficiary: Either The beneficiary must have been a creditor of the promisee, or the promisee must have intended to make a gift of the benefit to the beneficiary. The status of creditor beneficiary is illustrated by both *Lawrence v. Fox* and the example involving Debtor, who made a contract with Buyer under which Buyer would render performance to Creditor. This set of relationships is represented in Diagram 19C.

Diagram 19C

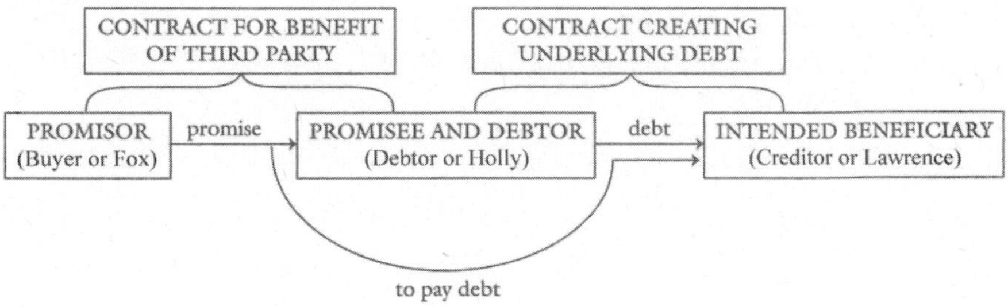

By contrast, if the promisee owes no debt to the third party, but intends to make a gift of the performance, the third party is a donee beneficiary. Although *Lawrence v. Fox* expressly dealt only with a creditor beneficiary, its basic principle was broad enough to be extended to cases in which the promisee was not indebted to the beneficiary. As a result, later cases recognized that a person could qualify as an intended beneficiary when the purpose of conferring the benefit was not to pay any debt, but to give a gift. *Seaver v. Ransom*, 120 N.E. 639 (N.Y. 1918), is the leading early case that recognized this principle. A dying woman intended to bequeath a house to her niece. Upon being presented with a will that omitted this bequest, she agreed to sign on the strength of a promise by her husband, the residual legatee, that he would cure the omission by making provision in his own will for a bequest to the niece of equivalent value. When the husband eventually died, it was discovered that he had not made the bequest as he had promised his late wife. The niece sued his estate. The trial court gave judgment in favor of the niece on the theory that her uncle had held the house from his wife in constructive trust. Although it affirmed the judgment in favor of the niece, the court of appeals rejected the trust theory. Instead, basing its decision on *Lawrence* and subsequent cases, it found that there was no reason in principle to confine the third-party beneficiary doctrine to cases involving creditor beneficiaries. The uncle and aunt had made a contract under which the niece was an intended beneficiary, and she could enforce the promise against the uncle's estate.

As another illustration, say that Donor entered into a contract with Buyer under which Donor sold a plot of land to Buyer for $200,000. Donor's purpose in selling the land was not to pay a debt, as in *Lawrence v. Fox* and the example illustrating a creditor beneficiary, but to realize funds to be donated to Charity, a nonprofit organization. Donor therefore stipulates in the contract with Buyer that the sale price be paid directly to Charity. Although the fact that Charity gave no consideration to Donor for the benefit would preclude it from enforcing the promise against Donor, the lack of consideration from Charity does not bar its suit against Buyer. The contract being enforced by Charity (assuming that it qualifies an intended beneficiary) is that between Donor and Buyer, and consideration was exchanged between the parties to that contract. This set of relationships is shown in Diagram 19D.

Diagram 19D

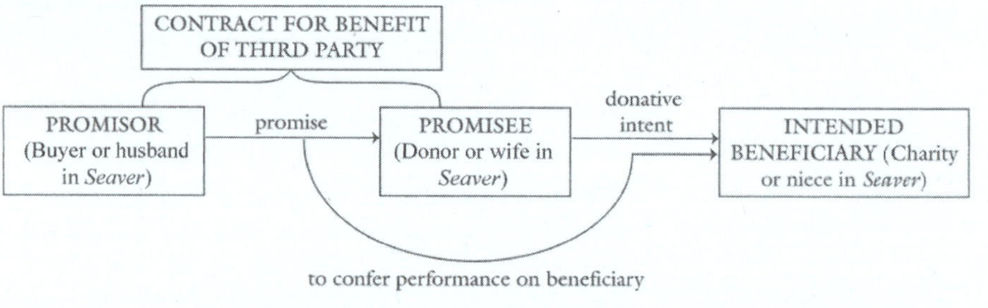

Section 302(1) attempts to move away from the creditor-donee dichotomy, which it finds too rigid and restrictive. However, it recognizes that the distinction is well ingrained in the caselaw and cannot be ignored. It therefore acknowledges the distinction but alters it to make it more flexible. Many courts have followed its lead. Section 302(1) identifies two types of situations in which it recognizes a relationship sufficient to bolster the conclusion that the beneficiary was intended: The first, set out in §302(1)(a), approximates the concept of creditor beneficiary by covering cases in which performance of the promise will satisfy a monetary obligation due by the promisee to the beneficiary. This is somewhat narrower than the original category, which included not only monetary obligations but also situations in which performance of the promise would satisfy an actual, supposed, or asserted duty of the promisee to the beneficiary. The narrowing of this category is more than compensated for by the widening of the second.

The second, set out in §302(1)(b) is based on, but more expansive than, the older category of donee beneficiaries. It encompasses not only situations in which gratuitous motives are apparent but any case in which the circumstances indicate that the promisee intends to give the benefit of performance to the beneficiary. This formulation is intentionally open-ended to be wide enough to include cases in which there is some supposed or asserted duty that is not clear enough to fall into §302(1)(a) as an actual liquidated monetary obligation. The idea is to let courts decide case by case, with a strong focus on the parties' intent, as bolstered by some relationship between the promisee and the beneficiary that plausibly points to a motive for conferring the benefit.

§19.2.5 Vesting of the Benefit and the Parties' Power to Modify or Terminate It

In the same way as parties have the power to make a contract, they have the power to modify or terminate it by subsequent agreement. The alteration or discharge of a contract, like its creation, is dependent on the parties' assent.[4] It follows from this principle that as the parties to the contract have created the beneficiary's rights, they could agree to change them or take them away entirely. However, if they had the unrestricted power to do this, the status of intended beneficiary would be very uncertain and unreliable. To protect the beneficiary's actual or potential reliance on the contract, the benefit vests in the beneficiary at some point after the contract is made—it becomes irrevocably settled on the beneficiary so that it cannot be changed or withdrawn by the contracting parties without the beneficiary's consent. If the parties do agree to modify or discharge the contract after the benefit has vested, this agreement binds the parties between themselves, but it binds only them. It does not affect the rights of the beneficiary, who can enforce the performance as it vested under the original agreement. It is therefore possible that the promisee could agree to give up its own rights of enforcement or to change them so that they are less extensive than those that have vested in the beneficiary.

Courts have adopted various approaches to the question of when the benefit vests. Some have treated it as vesting immediately upon formation of the contract, but others have required some manifestation of acceptance or some act of reliance on it by the beneficiary. Restatement, Second, §311(3) provides that the benefit vests when the beneficiary manifests assent to it at the request of one of the parties, or sues on it, or materially changes

4. The modification of a contract is itself a contract which generally requires consideration too, as discussed in sections 7.5.2 and 13.9.

position by acting in justifiable reliance on it. This formulation clearly shows the analogy between vesting and the formation of other promissory obligations. Its basis is quite akin to that for offer and acceptance or promissory estoppel: The right vests either when the beneficiary "accepts" it by manifesting assent to it, or when the beneficiary has detrimentally relied on it. Once that has occurred, the contracting parties are committed to the conferral of rights, and the beneficiary's independent cause of action on the promise is secure.

This rule is subject to a qualification: As creators of the benefit, the contracting parties can confer it subject to whatever limitations and conditions they see fit. By so stipulating in the contract, they can retain the power to modify it or take it away even after it has vested in the beneficiary. These limitations will inhere in the right created in favor of the beneficiary, and it will vest subject to them. However, the parties must clearly reserve the power to alter the rights after vesting. If they do not, their power to alter the rights, as against the beneficiary, terminates as soon as the benefit vests.

§19.2.6 The Promisee's Parallel Rights of Enforcement Against the Promisor

Notwithstanding the conferral and vesting of rights in the beneficiary, the promisee continues to be a party to the contract. As such, except to the extent that the beneficiary has enforced and obtained satisfaction of the performance, the promisee has the right to enforce the promise just as it would have had in an ordinary bilateral contract. Restatement, Second, §305(1) reflects this by stating that the promisor has a duty of performance to the promisee as well as a similar duty to the beneficiary. This does not mean that the promisor has to perform the obligation twice. The promisee's right against the promisor is discharged to the extent that the promisor performs in favor of the beneficiary. If full performance is not rendered to the beneficiary, the promisee may enforce the obligation to perform any remaining balance.

The nature of the relief available to the promisee depends on the circumstances. When a claim for damages is not an adequate remedy, the promisee may request specific performance—an order compelling the promisor to render the performance to the beneficiary. Alternatively, the promisee may have a claim for damages based on its contractual expectation. This will at least consist of the promisee's direct damages, measured by the loss in value of the promised performance. In addition, if the failure to perform results in a foreseeable and unavoidable increase in the promisee's liability to the beneficiary or other consequential loss, the promisee may claim consequential damages.

§19.2.7 The Promisor's Ability to Raise Defenses Against the Beneficiary

The beneficiary's rights derive from the contract, so it stands to reason that they are limited by any defense arising out of the contract. Therefore, the basic rule, as reflected in Restatement, Second, §309, is that unless the contract makes it clear that it confers rights on the beneficiary free of defenses, the beneficiary's rights are subject to any limitations inherent in the contract. The promisor may raise against the beneficiary any defense that would have been available against the promisee, arising out of a defect in the formation of the contract, such as invalidity due to lack of consideration, voidability on grounds of fraud, duress or some other bargaining defect, or unenforceability for failure to comply with the statute of frauds; or based on the promisee's breach of contract; or arising out of post-formation occurrences that affect the very basis of the contract, such as supervening impracticability and the nonoccurrence of a condition. (The beneficiary's position is very much like that of an assignee, discussed in section 19.3.3.)

Although a wrongful act of the promisee (such as breach or fraud) can be raised by the promisor as a defense against the beneficiary, it does not impose any liability on the beneficiary. By accepting the benefit, the beneficiary does not assume responsibility for any wrongful conduct or breach by the promisee. The promisor must pursue any recourse for the conduct or breach against the promisee.

Unless the contract expresses a contrary intent, the promisor cannot raise against the beneficiary any defense that is purely personal against the promisee, such as a defense that the promisee owes money to the promisor in another transaction. Similarly, as explained in section 19.2.5, if the promisee and promisor make an agreement to modify or discharge the performance after vesting, this agreement would be a defense to enforcement by the promisee, but it would not avail against the beneficiary.

§19.2.8 The Beneficiary's Rights Against the Promisee in the Event of the Promisor's Nonperformance

As stated in section 19.2.5, upon vesting of the benefit, the beneficiary has a direct claim against the promisor and may proceed to enforce it if the promisor fails to perform. However, it may occur that the beneficiary is unsuccessful in obtaining satisfaction of this claim against the promisor, for example, because the promisor has no money or assets to satisfy the claim. When that happens, the beneficiary's right to proceed against the promisee depends on whether or not the conferring of the benefit was based on some duty or obligation owed by the promisee to the beneficiary. That is (using the traditional terminology), whether the beneficiary is a creditor beneficiary rather than a donee beneficiary. If the promisor does not perform, a beneficiary who has not given consideration to the promisee for the benefit has no enforceable claim against the promisee, but a creditor beneficiary has the right to proceed against the promisee to enforce the promisee's debt.

Some courts have not allowed the creditor beneficiary to sue the promisee after unsuccessfully trying to enforce rights against the promisor. They have held that once the beneficiary elects to proceed against the promisor, the right of action against the promisor is substituted for and eliminates the cause of action on the original debt due by the promisee. (This is called novation.) However, the more common contemporary view, as expressed in Restatement, Second, §310, is that the beneficiary surrenders no rights against the promisee by seeking to enforce the benefit against the promisor. Instead, the promisee becomes a surety for the promisor, so that to the extent that the promisor fails to perform, the promisee remains liable for the outstanding amount of its undischarged debt to the beneficiary. (And, of course, the promisee may then attempt to recover from the promisor, based on the promisor's breach of its contract with the promisee.) This is shown in Diagram 19E.

Diagram 19E

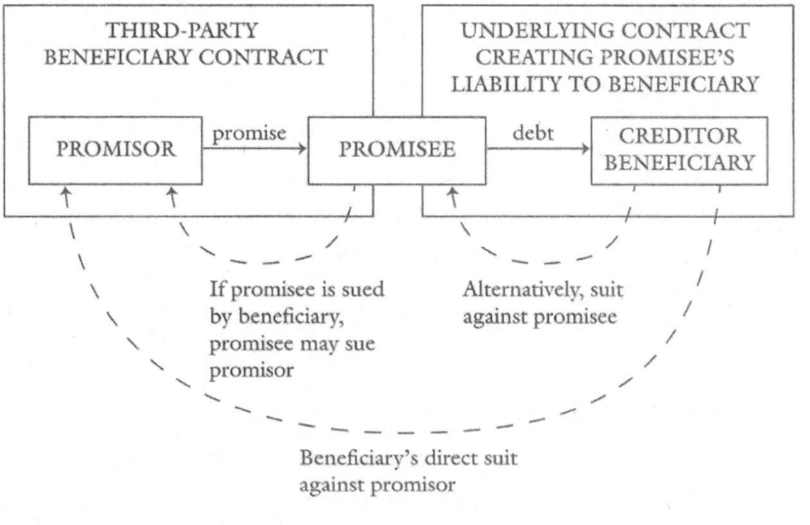

§19.2.9 Citizens' Claims as Intended Beneficiaries of Government Contracts

The government represents the public. In a broad sense, it can therefore be said that whenever the government enters a contract, it has the intention of conferring a benefit on the citizenry at large, or on a group of citizens whose interests are furthered by the contract. However, this does not mean that an individual citizen can sue the promisee to enforce the performance it promised to the government. As with other contracts that result in a benefit to a nonparty, the crucial question is not simply whether there was an intent to provide the benefit, but whether there was an intent to create an independent right of enforcement in the nonparty. Therefore, as Restatement, Second, §313(1) makes clear, government contracts are to be treated the same as contracts by private parties in deciding whether a third party was an intended beneficiary: The terms of the contract must be interpreted in context to determine if it manifests the intent to confer a direct cause of action on the beneficiary. In the case of government contracts, the context includes any statute, regulation, or ordinance that authorizes the transaction and that may provide for or preclude a citizen's right of enforcement.

Although a government contract is generally subject to the same analysis as a private contract to determine intent to confer a right of enforcement on beneficiaries, there is a presumption that the government does not usually intend to confer a private right of enforcement on citizens, who are usually just incidental beneficiaries of government contracts. Courts distinguish between an intent to confer a benefit on the public, which is the broad underlying purpose of most government contracts, and the intent to allow members of the public to take private action to enforce the benefits provided in the contract, which would be quite an unusual situation. Therefore, to overcome the presumption that a private citizen is an incidental beneficiary, the citizen must demonstrate clear intent in the contract or in any legislation that authorizes the contract to grant a right of enforcement to the class of citizens of which the private citizen is a member. Comment *a* to §313 reflects this approach by suggesting that in cases of doubt, the contract should be interpreted as not making citizens intended beneficiaries.

For example, in *Klamath Water Users Protective Assn. v. Patterson*, 204 F.3d 1206 (9th Cir. 1999), irrigators claimed that they were the intended beneficiaries of a government agency's contract with a power company for the management of a dam. They argued that they therefore had the independent right to enforce the power company's obligation to maintain flow levels required by the contract. Although the court recognized that one of the goals of the contract was to satisfy the government's duty to water users, it had other aims as well, and there was nothing in the contract to rebut the usual presumption that citizens who benefit from a government contract are incidental beneficiaries with no private enforcement rights. In *Edwards v. Aurora Loan Services, LLC*, 791 F.Supp.2d 144 (D.C. 2011), the court stressed the strong general presumption that citizens are merely incidental beneficiaries of government contracts. To rebut that presumption, the language of the contract must demonstrate a clear intent to confer enforcement rights on citizens who benefit by the contract. The court held that the plaintiffs had not discharged this burden in relation to a contract entered into between the U.S. Treasury (through the agency of Fannie Mae) and loan servicers, under which the loan servicers were obliged to modify the mortgages of homeowners in danger of foreclosure. In *Cooper v. Charter Communication Entertainments I, LLC*, 760 F.3d 103 (1st Cir. 2014), customers of Charter, a cable provider, sued it for failing to provide credits to customers for a period during which service was disrupted by a severe snowstorm. The plaintiffs based their suit on the theory that they were intended third-party beneficiaries of a licensing agreement between the city and Charter that required Charter to grant the credits and to pay the credited amount directly to customers. The court acknowledged that the contract was intended to benefit consumers of the cable service. However, the contract set out an enforcement process that provided only for enforcement by the city. This made it clear that the parties did not intend to confer a private right of enforcement on customers.

Cases in which the court found a citizen to be an intended beneficiary of a government contract are much rarer. *Zigas v. Superior Court*, 174 Cal. Rptr. 806 (Cal. App. 1981), is an example. The owner of an apartment building violated its contract with the U.S. Department of Housing and Urban Development (HUD) to keep rentals within prescribed limits. The court decided that the sole purpose of both the contract and its authorizing legislation was to benefit tenants by keeping rents at a reasonable level and that the parties must reasonably have intended to give tenants an independent cause of action to enforce the rent limitation. The court reached this conclusion because the tenants, not the government, lost as a result of the breach, the statute provided no other procedure for tenants to seek redress, the tenants' suit did not interfere with any remedial or administrative proceedings prescribed by the statute, and there was nothing in the contract that indicated that the parties expected that the owner would be shielded from tenant suits. In *Oliverio v. Transdev Services, Inc.* 2017 WL 6546338 (Cal. App. 2017), the court distinguished *Zigas* in holding that a member of the public was not an intended beneficiary of a contract between the city of San Francisco and Transdev, a company hired by the city to provide transportation services for persons with disabilities. Under the contract, Transdev hired subcontractors, such as cab companies, to perform the transport services, and undertook to properly supervise them and to ensure that they carried adequate liability insurance. Oliverio, a pedestrian (not a recipient of transport services) was injured when he was struck by a cab as he was crossing the street. The cab company, a Transdev subcontractor, did not carry adequate insurance, so Oliverio sued Transdev for damages resulting from his injury on the theory that, as a member of the public, he was an intended beneficiary of Transdev's contract with the city. The court held that he was not. The purpose of the contract was to provide transport for persons with disabilities and to protect those persons in the event of injury. Unlike *Zigas*, in which the contract term was created specifically for the benefit of the plaintiffs, there was nothing in this contract that suggested an intent to confer on members of the general public an independent right to sue Transdev for a breach of the contract. (The court did not address whether a person being transported under the program would be an intended beneficiary of the contract, but it is arguable that such a person would be in a position equivalent to the tenants in *Zigas*.)

§19.2.10 A Nonclient's Claim as an Intended Beneficiary of an Attorney-Client Contract

If an attorney acts incompetently in doing legal work for a client, the client has a cause of action against the attorney for malpractice. This claim could be based either in tort for negligence or in contract, for breach of the attorney's contractual duty to the client to perform the work in accordance with reasonable professional standards. In some situations, the attorney's incompetent performance could harm some third party who is not a client. If that happens, it raises the question of whether the nonclient has any cause of action against the attorney.

As a general rule, a nonclient who is harmed by the attorney's negligence cannot sue the attorney in tort unless the nonclient can show that the attorney expressly or impliedly assumed a duty of care toward that nonclient, such as by making some commitment to the nonclient, falsely certifying untrue information, making a misrepresentation, or failing to disclose information that the attorney had a duty to disclose. In estate planning matters, some courts, such as the court in *Blair v. Ing*, 21 P.3d 452 (Haw. 2001), have been willing to allow a nonclient testamentary beneficiary a negligence cause of action in tort against an attorney who acted incompletely in an estate planning matter, thereby causing loss to the beneficiary. However, in the absence of special circumstances, courts usually hold that an attorney's duty to act with reasonable competence runs only to the client, and gives no tort cause of action for malpractice to a nonclient who suffered economic loss as a result of the attorney's negligence in handling the client's affairs. This is based on the policy, as explained in *Guy v. Liederbach*, 459 A.2d 744 (Pa. 1983), and *Noble v. Bruce*, 709 A.2d 1264 (Md. Ct. App. 1998), that potential malpractice liability to a nonclient could distract an attorney from focusing on the client's best interests, could undermine the attorney's loyalty to the client, and could create a conflict of interest as the attorney tries to balance duty to the client against the need to safeguard the nonclient's interests.

In some cases, nonclients have sued attorneys for malpractice, not on a tort theory but on the grounds that the nonclient was an intended beneficiary of the contract between the attorney and client. A nonclient could acquire a cause of action against an attorney as an intended beneficiary of the contract between the attorney and client, provided that it is clear that the attorney and client intended to confer an independent right of enforcement on the nonclient. For example, in *Hale v. Groce*, 744 P.2d 1289 (Or. 1987), an attorney breached his contract with his client by failing to draw the client's will as instructed. As a result, a legatee was deprived of a legacy that the client had intended for him. The court found that the legatee was an intended beneficiary of the contract between the client and the attorney and therefore had an independent cause of action against the attorney for the breach. Similarly, in *Guy*, the attorney had the named beneficiary of a will sign it as a witness, thereby voiding her legacy. Although the court noted that a legatee does not become a third-party beneficiary merely because she is named in the will, it found that she was an intended beneficiary of the attorney-client contract because unless she was given a right to enforce it, there would be no one to hold the attorney accountable for his breach. The testator was dead and the estate had no incentive to sue.

Noble took a less sympathetic approach to testamentary beneficiaries. It found no express or implied intent in the contract between the testators and their attorney to confer a direct right of enforcement on the beneficiaries, and would not imply such a right merely because they were the only persons with an incentive to enforce the contract. The court's reluctance to find a right of independent enforcement was motivated by its concern that ready recognition of third-party-beneficiary rights is just as harmful to the attorney-client relationship and raises the same policy concerns as allowing a nonclient to sue the attorney in tort for malpractice. This policy issue was emphasized in *Macht v. Estate of Dobkin*, 19 Mass. L. Rptr. 318 (Mass. Super. 2005), in which the client died before the attorney had complied with her instructions to draft a new will that left her estate to the plaintiff. The court emphasized the need not to compromise the attorney's duty of undivided loyalty to the client, and cautioned that recognition of an independent right of enforcement in a nonclient could make it difficult for an attorney to focus on the client's interests while trying to avoid possible liability to the nonclient. In *Estate of Agnew v. Ross*, cited in section 19.2.2, the lawyer did not ensure that the testator signed a trust amendment drafted by the lawyer. The court held that beneficiaries of an unsigned testamentary document cannot be treated as intended third party beneficiaries of the attorney-client contract. It distinguished its earlier decision in *Guy*, in which the invalid will had been signed by the testator and held that the unexecuted trust amendment was insufficient to establish the testator's intent to confer an enforceable benefit on the heirs. The court reiterated the policy concerns expressed above and emphasized that recognition of intended beneficiary status must be narrow to avoid compromising a lawyer's duty to the client and to protect the integrity of testamentary dispositions from fraudulent claims.

§19.3 ASSIGNMENT AND DELEGATION

§19.3.1 The Basic Concept and Terminology

Section 19.2 is concerned with cases in which the parties to a contract intend, at the time of entering it, to confer an enforceable benefit on someone who is not a party to the contract. Although assignment and delegation also involve the introduction of a third party into the contract, the circumstances under which that happens and the legal relationship that arises is very different from that of a third-party beneficiary. Assignment and delegation are not concerned with a contract in which, at the time of contracting, the parties intend to confer rights on a third party. Rather, one of the parties decides, after the contract has been entered, to transfer its rights, duties, or both to a third party. Assignment and delegation are only possible once a contract has been made and those rights and obligations have come into existence.[5] The well-established general rule, reflected in Restatement, Second, §317(2) and UCC §2.210(2), is that unless a contract specifically prohibits a party from transferring rights acquired and duties assumed under it, or the nature of the contract is such that the transfer would impair the other party's reasonable expectations or would offend public policy, a party has the power to transfer contractual rights and obligations.

It is useful to begin with the terminology used to describe such a transfer and its participants: The transfer of rights is called an assignment, and the transfer of duties is a delegation. The person who assigns a contractual right is the obligee under the contract and becomes the assignor. The person to whom it is assigned is the assignee. The other party to the contract, whose duty is transferred to the assignee by the assignment, is referred to as the obligor. A person who delegates a contractual duty is the obligor under the contract and becomes the delegator of the duty. The person who assumes the duty is called the delegate. The other party to the contract, whose right to performance has been delegated, is called the obligee. The relationships are shown in Diagram 19F, in which Party 2 is the person who decides to assign its obligations or delegate its duties.

---

5. The assignment of rights under an executed contract must be distinguished from the rule that applies in the precontract period. As noted in section 4.7, the power to accept an offer is personal to the offeree and cannot be transferred unless the offer so authorizes. This rule does not apply to a valid option—a promise exchanged for consideration not to revoke the offer. As explained in section 4.13.3, the option is a contract in itself and the right to accept the offer in the option period is a binding contractual right. It can therefore be assigned unless assignment is restricted as discussed in section 19.3.3.

Diagram 19F

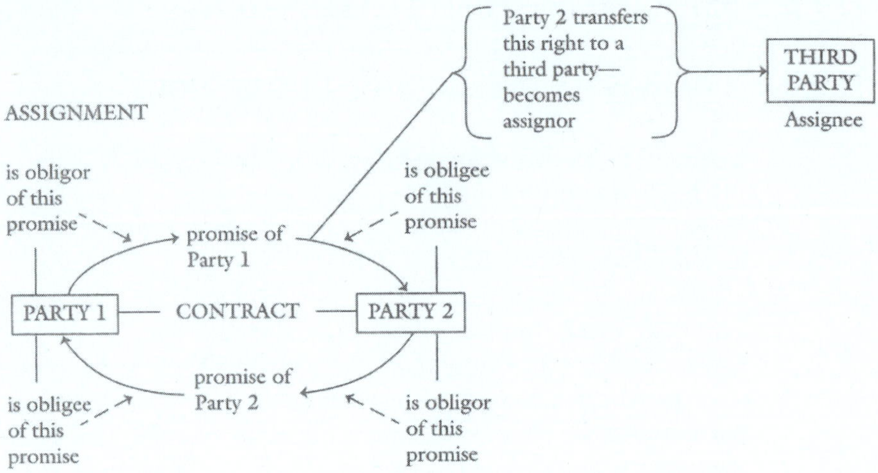

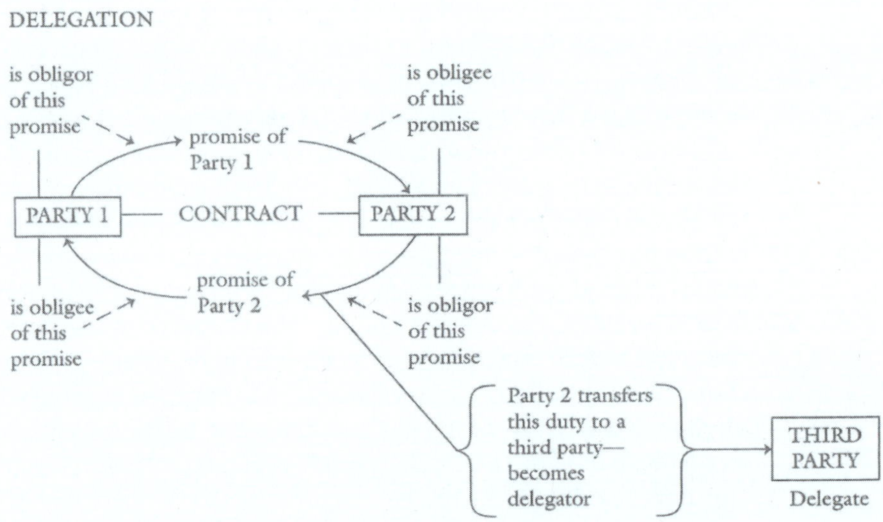

An obligee's ability to assign a contractual right is based on the recognition that the right is an asset of the obligee—an item of property with some value. Therefore, subject to some qualifications stated in section 19.3.3, the owner of a contractual right can transfer it like any other property—sell it, donate it, or use it as collateral. The law generally presumes that contract rights can be transferred, except where the contract or public policy precludes it. By contrast, contractual obligations are not property rights of the obligor, so the ability to delegate is not grounded in the right to transfer property. Therefore, the presumption of transferability is not as strong as it is with contractual rights. In addition, the transfer of contractual duties could have a more significant impact on the rights of the obligee than the transfer of the right to performance. For these reasons, the delegation of contract duties, although usually possible, is subject to greater restrictions than the assignment of rights. These restrictions are set out in sections 19.3.6 and 19.3.7.

§19.3.2 The Nature of an Assignment

Although a right can be transferred without the consent of the rightholder (for example, where a judgment creditor executes on the right by the process of garnishment, or the rightholder becomes bankrupt and the right passes to the trustee of its estate), this discussion is concerned only with the voluntary assignment of rights—a voluntary manifestation of intention by the holder of an existing right to make an immediate transfer of that right to another person. This definition of assignment breaks down into three essential components: First, the assignor must voluntarily manifest intent to assign the right; second, the right must be in existence at the time of assignment; and third, its transfer must take effect immediately.

In most cases, assignment is affected through a contract between the assignor and the assignee, but the transaction does not have to qualify as a contract. For example, a right may be transferred gratuitously so that the transfer is a gift rather than under a contract with consideration. The obligor need not be involved in the assignment unless the contract creating the right forbids its assignment without the obligor's assent. As a general matter,[6] there are no particular formalities needed for an assignment of ordinary contract rights unless the transaction is subject to the statute of frauds.

As section 19.3.4 explains, the effect of an assignment is to extinguish the assignor's right to performance from the obligee and to transfer it to the assignee. For such a complete transfer to occur, the right must be in existence and transferred immediately. Furthermore, the transfer must be a complete relinquishment of the right by the assignor in favor of the assignee, so that the assignor retains no control over it and no power to revoke it. This absolute and unequivocal transfer is necessary for the protection of the obligor, who must be able to rely on the fact that performance in favor of the assignee will discharge its obligation.

---

6. There are some specialized types of assignment involving rights evidenced by commercial paper (such as negotiable instruments or documents) for which prescribed formalities must be satisfied. This discussion of assignment and delegation is concerned with rights other than those incorporated into negotiable instruments and documents. Some of the other rules discussed in the rest of this section may also be different in relation to the transfer of negotiable instruments and documents, but these transactions are beyond the scope of this chapter and are not again mentioned in this discussion.

A right comes into existence and can be assigned as soon as the contract creating it has been formed. The right can be conditional or not yet due at the time of assignment as long as it has been created already. For example, *Speelman v. Pascal*, 10 N.Y.2d 313 (1961), involved the assignment of rights to a percentage of profits from the hit musical *My Fair Lady*. In 1952, Pascal acquired the rights from the estate of the late George Bernard Shaw to produce a musical based on his play *Pygmalion*. Before he even wrote the musical, he assigned a share of his profits to his secretary. He died soon thereafter, and the musical was not produced and staged until after his death. The court held the assignment to be effective. Although the musical was not yet in existence at the time of the assignment, the rights to future profits did exist and could be assigned. The assignee is bound by any conditions of performance and cannot enforce the right until such conditions have been satisfied and the maturity date of the right has arrived.

The assignment of a conditional or unmatured right must be distinguished from the transfer of a right that has not yet been created, but is expected to arise in the future. The transfer of a future right does not qualify as an assignment. It may be a valid contract between the transferor and transferee, but it lacks the hallmark of an assignment—enforceability against the obligor. Similarly, a promise to assign an existing right in the future does not constitute an assignment. To constitute an assignment effective against the obligor, the transfer of the right must actually be accomplished, so that the transferee acquires it immediately.

§19.3.3 Restrictions on Assignment

As noted in section 19.3.1, the general approach of the law is that contract rights should be freely assignable because the obligee's right to performance under the contract is the obligee's property. It is property of a nature different from, say, a car or a house, in that it has no tangible physical existence. (It is called a "chose in action.") Nevertheless, it is the obligee's property all the same, and the obligee should be able to dispose of it. However, this right of disposition is subject to a qualification that arises from the nature of this particular kind of property. Unlike a car or house, a contract right represents a relationship with the obligor, who also has rights under it. Therefore, the obligee's power to deal with this property is tempered by the need to assure the obligor of its contractual expectation. Accordingly, the right cannot be assigned if doing so would violate the terms of the contract or otherwise materially impair the obligor's rights under it.

a. Contractual Restrictions on Assignment

An assignment cannot be validly made if the contract prohibits it. The contractual bar must be clearly expressed to overcome the law's presumption that rights can be assigned. Restatement, Second, §322 and UCC §2.210(3) call for a restrictive interpretation of contract provisions that appear to preclude assignment. Any doubt or ambiguity should be resolved in favor of transferability, and a clause that prohibits "assignment of the contract" should, if possible, be taken to forbid only the delegation of duties. *Titan Exteriors, Inc. v. Certain Underwriters at Lloyd's, London*, 297 F.Supp.3d 628 (N.D. Miss. 2018), is an example of restrictive interpretation of an anti-assignment clause. An insurance policy forbad the insured, the owner of a shopping center, from assigning its rights and duties under the policy without the written consent of the insurer. After the shopping center was damaged in a storm, the owner of the shopping center assigned its insurance claim to a contractor that it hired to repair the damage. The insurer challenged the validity of the assignment, but the court upheld it. The court interpreted the anti-assignment provision restrictively to conclude that the assignment was not subject to it. The court held that the provision applied only to an assignment that was made before the loss occurred, and did not cover the assignment of a post-loss claim. The court reasoned that the purpose of the anti-assignment provision was to prevent a possible increase in risks to the insurer by a substitution of insured parties. However, that purpose fell away once the loss had been suffered. At that point, there is no danger that the insurer will be subject to additional risk, and all that was left is a monetary claim—a chose in action. A chose in action is property, and public policy disfavors a restraint on its alienation.

Even if the contract does clearly prohibit assignment, this does not necessarily mean that the assignment would be invalid. Unless the language clearly deprives the obligee of the power to assign (for example, by stating that an assignment will be void), the assignment may be a breach of the contract (giving the obligor grounds for seeking a remedy for breach), but the transfer of rights is itself effective.

Instead of absolutely forbidding assignment, a contract may prohibit it without the consent of the party whose obligations are being assigned (for example, as provided in the anti-assignment clause in *Titan Exteriors*). The general approach to a provision that requires permission to assign is reflected in *Julian v. Christopher*, 575 A.2d 735 (Md. 1990). Unless the contract makes it clear that the obligor has complete discretion to refuse permission, the obligor must act reasonably in refusing it. This usually means, in effect, that the obligor cannot legitimately refuse permission unless it can show that the assignment would be unduly burdensome or risky to it or would materially affect its contract rights.

b. Restrictions on Assignment Resulting from the Nature of the Contract

Even if the contract does not, by its terms, forbid or restrict assignment, the obligee may not assign rights under the contract, in the absence of specific authorization in the contract, if assignment would materially change the obligor's duty, increase the burden or risk imposed on the obligor by the contract, impair the obligor's prospects of getting return performance, or otherwise substantially reduce the contract's value to the obligor. This is recognized by Restatement, Second, §317(2) and UCC §2.210(2). Every assignment is likely to have some effect on the obligor's duty, even if that is nothing more than having to make a payment to someone other than the obligee. The requirement of material impact prevents the obligor from resisting an assignment on the basis of some trivial change in its performance obligation.

The contract must be interpreted in context to decide whether an assignment may have any of these materially adverse consequences. In many cases, especially when the performance in question is nothing more than the payment of money or the delivery of property, an assignment of rights is unlikely to have any negative impact on the obligor. It is a matter of indifference to the obligor whether it pays or delivers to the obligee or to someone else designated by the obligee. However, in some contracts, the identity of the party who is to receive performance is important, and the obligor does have a stake in performing only for the obligee. This may be true, for example, when performance is subject to a condition of satisfaction involving personal taste, or when the obligor reasonably expected to get some special advantage or credit by being associated with the obligee. (Cases like this may alternatively be viewed not as pure assignments, but as also involving a delegation of duty, on the ground that the obligee has a contractual duty to evaluate performance in good faith or to receive performance personally.)

c. Restrictions Based on Statute or Public Policy

Apart from any contractual barrier to assignment, the transfer of certain types of contract rights are contrary to the public interest, and therefore prohibited by statute or public policy. A common example is the statutory prohibition on the assignment of a claim for wages, intended to protect workers from disposing of earnings in advance of receiving them. Another example is a claim against an attorney for malpractice. Many courts have held the assignment of a legal malpractice claim to be contrary to public policy because of the uniquely personal nature of the attorney-client relationship, which implicates confidentiality, loyalty, and trust. Some courts consider that public policy absolutely bars assignment of a malpractice claim, while others, such as *Gurski v. Rosenblum & Filan LLC*, 885 A.2d 163 (Conn. 2005), adopt a case-by-case approach that considers the nature of the breach and the circumstances of the assignment. In *Gurski*, the court held the assignment to be invalid because the assignee was the adversary of the client in the very action in which the malpractice was committed. That is, to settle the action in which the attorney had committed the malpractice, the client assigned his malpractice claim to the other party to the suit.

The assignment of claims that do not arise from contract is beyond the scope of this discussion. However, it is worth noting that public policy forbids the assignment of certain kinds of noncontractual claims. For example, a tort claim for personal injury cannot be assigned because the trafficking in claims harms the public interest by enabling a litigious person to purchase and aggressively prosecute personal injury claims and by encouraging a tort victim to give up a potentially more valuable claim for advance payment.[7]

§19.3.4 The Effect of Assignment

The following simple example illustrates the basic effect and purpose of an assignment: Lender lends $10,000 to Borrower, who undertakes to repay the loan with interest in six months. After the loan is advanced, Lender no longer wishes to wait six months to get its money back. Lender therefore sells its contractual right of repayment to Finance Co. In this case, Lender is simply treating its contract right as a saleable asset and seeks to realize its economic worth.[8] Unless there is a term in the contract that forbids assignment, the transfer will surely be permissible, because it is not likely to have any materially adverse effect on Borrower's contractual burdens or expectations. Borrower has already received the performance of Lender's promise (advance of the loan funds) and its remaining duty is clear and not subject to any discretion or cooperation by the obligee. Borrower must simply pay a specified sum of money on a stated date. Lender falls out of the transaction and Finance Co. is substituted as the obligee. When the time for repayment comes, Borrower will pay Finance Co. Borrower must be notified of the assignment so that it knows (or reasonably should know) this. If Borrower is not notified, its payment to Lender will discharge its duty. This transaction is represented in Diagram 19G.

---

7. This prohibition against the assignment of tort claims for personal injury has ties to the age-old common law policy against maintenance and champerty—the promotion of litigation for profit by persons who finance it in exchange for receiving part of the proceeds.
8. The right to payment is an intangible right, the value of which is dependent on Borrower's creditworthiness. Finance Co. will therefore not be likely to buy it at its face value, but will pay a discounted price to take account of the risk of default. This discount, together with the prospect of earning the interest payable by Borrower under the contract, may make this an attractive purchase for a buyer like Finance Co. that is willing to take the risk of default in the hope of gaining more than it paid.

Diagram 19G

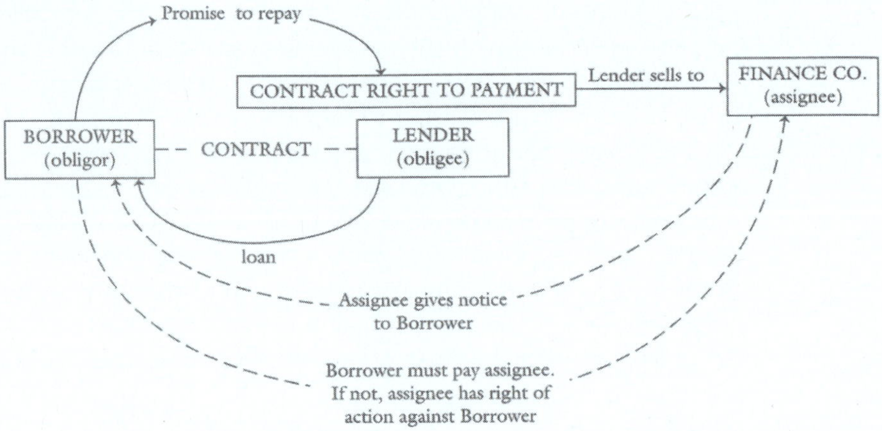

In this example, Lender assigned its contract right by sale, but sale is not the only reason for transferring rights. They may also be transferred for security—that is, used as collateral to secure a loan,[9] used to settle a preexisting debt or simply donated as a gift. Also, Lender assigned its entire right in the example, but it could have assigned just a portion of the performance, provided that a partial assignment would not materially burden Borrower.

After a valid assignment is made, the assignee substitutes for the assignor as the person to whom performance must be rendered. It therefore follows that although the obligor need not be a party to or assent to the assignment to make it effective, the obligor must be notified of the assignment so that it knows the person to whom performance is now due. There is no particular formality required for the notice, provided that it coherently indicates what right has been assigned, and to whom. The notice must be received by the obligor—that is, it must either come to the obligor's attention or be delivered so that the obligor reasonably should be aware of it. Either the assignor or the assignee may give the notice, but if it comes from the assignee, the obligor is entitled to adequate proof of the assignment.

If the obligor performs in favor of the assignor before receiving this notification, its obligation is discharged and it has no responsibility to

9. Assignments are commonly used for the purpose of securing a loan. While an important aspect of commercial transacting, the transfer of intangible rights as security is subject to complex and detailed rules that are beyond the scope of this discussion. However, a brief description of the basic structure of one form of such a transaction may be helpful: The owner of the contract right does not sell it outright, but instead borrows money from a lender and transfers the right to the lender as security for its promise to repay the money. In such a case, the transfer is not absolute. The secured creditor retains an interest in the contract right until such time as the loan is repaid but has the right to foreclose on the security and collect payment of the contract performance in the event that its debtor defaults.

the assignee. However, after receiving clear and adequate notification, the obligor, in effect, holds the performance in trust for the assignee and is obliged to ensure that the assignee receives it. An obligor who disregards the assignment and performs for the assignor incurs personal liability to the assignee and will be obliged either to perform again or pay damages. An obligor who pays the assignor after notice of assignment cannot defend against liability to the assignee merely on the ground that the assignor unilaterally countermanded its prior instruction to pay the assignee. For example, in *Herzog v. Irace*, 594 A.2d 1106 (Me. 1991), a client instructed his attorney to make payment of settlement proceeds to a creditor of the client—a doctor to whom the client owed fees for medical treatment. The client later changed his mind and told the attorney to pay the settlement to him, which the attorney did. When the doctor sued the attorney, the attorney argued that he had an ethical obligation to honor his client's instructions. The court disagreed. The attorney was aware that the client had assigned his payment right to the doctor, so the client no longer had a right to the settlement proceeds and could not validly revoke his instruction to pay the doctor.

§19.3.5 Defenses Against the Assignee

As a general rule, when rights are assigned, the assignee can get no greater right against the obligor than the assignor had. This is in accordance with the rule that a person cannot validly transfer more than it owns. This means that the assignee takes the rights subject to any conditions and defenses that the obligor may have against the assignor arising out of the contract. For example, if the contract is avoidable by the obligor or unenforceable because of a defect in formation of the contract, or the obligor's duty is subject to an unsatisfied condition, or the assignor breached the contract, or the obligor's performance has become impracticable, these defenses can be raised against the assignee in the same way as they could have been against the assignor.

As in the case of a third-party beneficiary, the obligor may only use the assignor's breach defensively against the assignee. That is, the assignor's breach operates as a defense to the assignee's claim, and damages due to the obligor by the assignor may be offset against the assignee's claim. However, the assignee has no liability for the obligor's damages to the extent that they exceed the amount of the offset.

Unless the assignment indicates an intent to the contrary, the assignor impliedly warrants to the assignee that the rights assigned are valid and not subject to any defenses. Therefore, if the obligor successfully raises a defense against the assignee, the assignee usually has a cause of action against the assignor for breach of this warranty.

§19.3.6 Delegation

Restatement, Second, §318 and UCC §2.210(1) set out the basic principles of delegation: An obligor is entitled to delegate its contractual duties unless this violates the contract or public policy. As this suggests, the law's general approach to delegation is that a party should have the freedom to engage someone else to perform its contractual duties unless the contract prohibits this or the delegation otherwise impairs the obligee's reasonable expectations. However, delegation is not a transfer of a right, so it does not invoke the policy that protects a person's interest in dealing with its own property. In addition, while a mere assignment of rights often makes little difference to the other party's contractual expectations, a delegation of duty could quite likely have a direct impact on them. This is particularly true if the contract is founded on the personal attributes or skills of the obligor. For these reasons, delegation is subject to greater restriction than assignment.

Irrespective of whether the performance involves special skill or attributes, if the contract makes it clear that delegation is forbidden, a court will give effect to this expressed intent. A party is entitled, by so stipulating in the contract, to absolutely preclude the delegation of any duty owed to it. In the absence of a clear prohibition, delegation is allowed unless the obligee has a substantial interest in having the obligor itself perform or control the duty. This would be the case where the contract contemplates personal performance by the obligor or the obligor was chosen because of some particular attribute, skill, or talent relevant to performance. An impermissible delegation may in itself be a repudiation of the contract by the delegator, which may allow the obligee to declare advance breach and claim damages. If the obligee gives the delegator an opportunity to retract the delegation and it fails to do so in time and to render personal performance, this becomes a breach.

The effect of a permissible and effective delegation is that the delegator commits no breach of the contract by having its duty performed by the delegate, and the delegate's conforming performance discharges the delegator's contractual obligation. If a performance is properly delegated but the obligee refuses to accept it, this will be a breach by the obligee in the same way as it would have been to refuse the delegator's own performance.

Unlike assignment, delegation does not result in a complete substitution of the delegate for the delegator. Unless the obligee agrees (either in the contract or subsequently) to release the delegator from any further responsibility, the delegator remains obligated under the contract. The delegator cannot unilaterally release itself from its commitment to the obligee. Therefore, if the delegate fails to perform or renders a defective performance, this is as much a breach by the delegator as its own deficient performance would have been. *Bakke v. Magi-Touch Carpet One Floor & Home, Inc.*, 920 N.W.2d 726 (N.D. 2018), illustrates this principle. Bakke entered into a contract with Magi-Touch for renovations to her bathroom. Magi-Touch subcontracted some of that work and the subcontractor failed to do the work properly. Magi-Touch refused to compensate Bakke for the defective work, claiming that it could not be held liable for the improper performance of an independent subcontractor. The court acknowledged that there was nothing in the contract to preclude Magi-Touch from delegating performance to a subcontractor, but it could not thereby escape its responsibilities under the contract. It was liable to Bakke for defective work rendered by the subcontractor.

The delegate's nonperformance or defective performance could also render the delegate liable to the obligee but this is not inevitably so. It depends on whether the delegate has assumed the duty to the obligee by promising to perform it. Such a promise could be made directly to the obligee, or it could arise where the delegate has promised the delegator to perform, and this can be interpreted as a contract for the benefit of the obligee, as an intended third-party beneficiary. It is possible, therefore, that both the delegator and the delegate will be liable to the obligee in the event of the delegate's breach.

The following example illustrates how delegation may operate: Owner enters into a contract with Painter under which Painter undertakes to repaint the exterior of Owner's building for $25,000. Just before the work is due to begin, Painter finds that it is too busy to do the painting itself, so Painter hires Subcontractor to do it. The delegation is established by a separate contract between Painter and Subcontractor under which Painter engages Subcontractor to do the job. (There is no assignment of right here because Painter does not transfer its right to receive payment from Owner to Subcontractor, but undertakes in this separate agreement to pay Subcontractor for the work.) Unless Owner's contract with Painter expressly prohibits delegation or contemplates that Painter must do the work itself, Painter's delegation of the performance is likely to be permissible. However, if an artist had been engaged to paint a mural on the side of the building, there would be a strong argument that the contract is based on the artists' particular craft and skill, so that its performance may not be delegated. Delegation is shown in Diagram 19H.

Diagram 19H

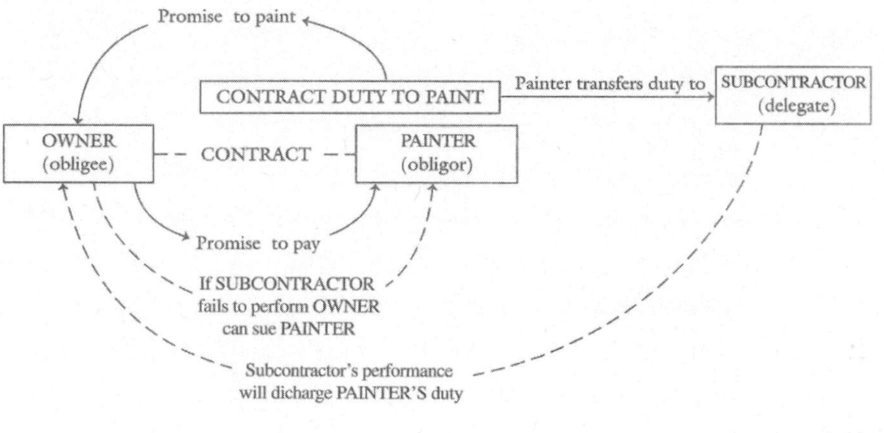

§19.3.7 "Assignment" of the Contract: The Assignment of Rights and Delegation of Duties

In the immediately preceding example involving the painting contract, Painter did not assign its rights against Owner. Painter retained its right to Owner's contractual obligation to pay $25,000 for the work and made a separate arrangement to remunerate Subcontractor. However, Painter could have decided to transfer its entire package of rights and duties under the contract. This is sometimes referred to loosely as an assignment of the contract. Restatement, Second, §328(1) more properly characterizes it as both an assignment of the party's rights under the contract and a delegation of its duties. UCC §2.210(4) provides similarly for the assignment of a contract for the sale of goods. Painter is an obligor that delegates and an obligee that assigns. Subcontractor is the assignee of Painter's rights and the delegate of its duties, and Owner is both the obligee as regards the delegated duty and the obligor as regards the assigned rights.

The transaction is subject to the rules governing both assignment and delegation. Where a contract is assigned as a whole, the assignment of rights may be unobjectionable, but the delegation of duties may reduce the value of the return performance reasonably expected by the original party. If so, the contract may not be assigned. This occurred in *Sally Beauty Co., Inc. v. Nexxus Products Co., Inc.*, 801 F.2d 1001 (7th Cir. 1986). Best Barber and Beauty Supply Co. was an exclusive distributor of Nexxus products. It sought to assign the exclusive distributorship to Sally which was owned by a competitor of Nexxus. Nexxus objected to the assignment of the contract on the grounds that the contract was for personal services and was based on a relationship of trust and confidence between the officers of Nexxus and Best. The court found the assignment of the contract was not permissible. There was no problem with the assignment of Best's rights because this had no negative impact on Nexxus. The alleged relationship of confidence and trust between the management of Nexxus and Best did not change this conclusion because, even in the absence of assignment, corporate officers can change and neither party had the guarantee that they would be able to deal with the same officers throughout the term of the contract. However, the delegation of Best's duties under the distributorship deprived Nexxus of the benefit of its bargain because the distribution of its products would be in the hands of its competitor. (The dissent did not consider this to be a good reason to preclude delegation because Sally would be obliged to use best efforts in selling Nexxus products.)

§19.3.8 Grounds for Insecurity Following Assignment or Delegation

When the assignment of a right or the delegation of a duty does not clearly impair the obligee's expectation of performance, but it gives the obligee reasonable grounds for insecurity, Restatement, Second, §317, Comment *d*, and UCC §2.210(5) recognize the obligee's right to demand adequate assurances of performance. In an assignment, the assignor could be called on to assure the obligor that the transfer of rights will not impair the obligor's prospect of return performance. In a delegation, the obligee may demand the assurance of proper performance, as appropriate, either from the delegator or the delegate. This process is equivalent to the demand for assurances discussed in section 17.7.5, when a promisee is concerned about the possibility of repudiation. Following a justifiable demand, the person to whom the demand is addressed resolves the reasonable concern about impairment if it gives an adequate assurance that the performance will be rendered in accordance with the contract. If it does not provide an adequate assurance, the party seeking the assurance may object to the assignment or delegation. In some circumstances, the lack of assurance of performance may go beyond precluding effective transfer. It could amount to a repudiation by the assignor or delegator, permitting the other party to seek relief for anticipatory breach.

§19.4 A TRANSNATIONAL PERSPECTIVE ON THIRD-PARTY BENEFICIARIES, ASSIGNMENT, AND DELEGATION

The CISG does not deal with third-party rights. Therefore, in a sale of goods subject to the CISG, the question of whether a nonparty can enforce the contract as a third-party beneficiary, or whether contractual rights or duties can be assigned or delegated, must be determined by governing domestic law. The UNIDROIT Principles do cover both these areas. Third-party beneficiaries are covered by Articles 5.2.1 to 5.2.6, and assignment and delegation are covered by Articles 9.1.1 to 9.3.7.

Articles 5.2.1 to 5.2.6 of the UNIDROIT Principles are short and quite general. They recognize that the parties to a contract may expressly or impliedly confer rights on an identifiable third party, and that the beneficiary's rights are determined by the agreement of the parties. The beneficiary's rights are subject to any defense that the promisor could assert against the promisee, and the parties to the contract may not modify the rights conferred on the beneficiary after it has accepted or acted in reliance on them. Beyond this, the UNIDROIT Principles provide no detailed principles to govern the enforcement rights of the beneficiary.

Articles 9.1.2 and 9.1.3 of the UNIDROIT Principles permit either the partial or full assignment of a monetary obligation. A nonmonetary obligation may be fully assigned (or it may be assigned in part only if it is divisible) if the assignment does not render the obligation more burdensome. Under Article 9.1.7, assignment is accomplished by simple agreement between the assignor and assignee, without the obligor's consent. However, Article 9.1.10 states that until the obligor receives notice of the assignment, its duty under the contract is discharged by performing in favor of the assignor. Under Article 9.1.13, the obligor may raise against the assignee all defenses that it could have asserted against the assignor and may exercise against the assignee any setoff right that arose before notice of the assignment.

Articles 9.2.1 to 9.2.8 of the UNIDROIT Principles deal with the "transfer of obligations," which is approximately equivalent to delegation. (Articles 9.3.1 to 9.3.7 cover assignment of the contract as a whole—they essentially combine the principles relating to assignment and transfer of obligations.) Articles 9.2.1 and 9.2.3 of the UNIDROIT Principles provide for the transfer of obligations with the consent of the obligee. Unless discharged by the obligee, the original obligor remains liable for the performance. Transfer of obligations without the obligee's consent is possible under Article 9.2.6 unless the performance is essentially personal in character. The transfer does not free the original obligor from its contractual duties. Under Article 9.2.7, the new obligor acquires all the defenses that could have been asserted by the original obligor.

Examples

EXAMPLES

1. Tess Tatrix decided to leave her entire estate to Benny Fishery, her lifelong friend. She consulted Mel Practice, an attorney, for the purpose of making a will and instructed Mel to make Benny her heir. Mel drafted the will and Tess signed it. Tess died about a year later. It was then discovered that Mel had drafted the will so incompetently that it was invalid. As a result, Tess was declared to have died intestate. Benny inherited nothing from her estate, which was distributed to Tess's distant relatives. Does Benny have any cause of action against Mel?

2. Every year, Fair City holds a weeklong celebration to commemorate its founding. This year it decided to set up a funfair in one of the city parks. It contracted with Merry Makers, Inc. to erect and operate the funfair for the week. Carr Parker owns a plot of vacant land a couple of blocks away from the park. When he heard that the fair was to be held so close to his property, he realized that parking would be at a premium in the area and

that he could make a considerable amount of money by using his land as a parking lot. A month before the fair was due to open, he cleared the weeds and debris off the lot and leveled it so that cars could drive onto it. He painted signs and built a little booth at the entrance.

Two weeks before the fair was to begin, Merry Makers repudiated its contract with Fair City. It was too late for the city to be able to make alternative arrangements, so it canceled the funfair. Carr has suffered losses as a result of Merry Makers repudiation of its contract with Fair City. Does he have a cause of action for damages against Merry Makers?

3. After Rock Sparkler and Di Amond had been dating for about a year, they decided to become engaged. They visited the showrooms of Belle Bijoux, a jewelry dealer, to pick out a ring. They selected a diamond ring priced at $4,500. Rock purchased the ring, took delivery of it, and placed it on Di's finger.

   About six months later, Di discovered that Rock had been cheating on her and broke off the engagement. Di kept the ring, which she decided to sell. She took it to an appraiser to get an accurate assessment of its value. On examining the stone, the appraiser told her that it was not a diamond at all but merely a piece of cut glass. Di and Rock are estranged, so Di does not want to ask for his help in making a claim against Belle. Does Di have any basis for proceeding directly against Belle?

4. Claire Client sold her business for $100,000. She was represented in the transaction by Lex Lawful, a lawyer. Under the terms of the sale, the buyer of the business paid the $100,000 to Lex, to be retained in his trust account and paid out to Claire when the transaction closed and the assets of the business were transferred to the buyer. Claire needed some cash right away and could not wait until the closing. She therefore negotiated a loan of $50,000 from Finance Co., Inc. The written loan agreement provided that Finance Co. would advance the $50,000 to Claire immediately, and that she would repay the loan amount with interest as soon as she received the proceeds of the sale of her business. The agreement stated that Claire authorized her attorney, Lex Lawful, to pay $50,000 plus accumulated interest to Finance Co. out of the proceeds of the sale of her business. Claire gave a copy of the contract to Lex with instructions to transmit payment to Finance Co. when the funds were released from the trust account.

   The sale of the business closed about a month later. By that time, Lex had forgotten about the letter and Claire's instructions to pay Finance Co. $50,000 and interest from the proceeds, so he paid the full $100,000 to Claire. Claire accepted the money and did not remind Lex of his commitment to pay the loan from the proceeds. Claire immediately squandered the full $100,000 and she has no resources to repay the loan. Does Finance Co. have grounds to recover the debt from Lex?

5. Gator Deli sells kosher food to the local orthodox Jewish community. For many years it had bought all its sausages from Frumme Mentsch, a devout member of the congregation and a strictly observant kosher butcher. Frumme decided to retire and sold her business to Chazzer Food Corp., a large corporation that supplies food to the general market. As part of the sale of her business, Frumme assigned to Chazzer her two-year contract to supply sausages to Gator. Chazzer makes all its sausages in a huge plant in which it processes meat from a variety of animals. Neither the plant itself nor the meat used by Chazzer to make sausages is kosher. The contract says nothing about assignment. Can Gator object to the assignment of the contract?

6. Manny Quinn sells high-quality leather products. His store is well known for its exquisite alligator-skin purses. He buys the cured skins and gives them to his old friend Dell E. Gator, who makes them into the purses of his own design. Dell is a talented designer and is obsessively exacting in his craftsmanship. Manny has had a warm friendship with Dell for years and has relied on him for a long time to produce exceptionally fine purses. Last year, Manny and Dell entered into a five-year contract under which Dell undertook to make a stated quantity of purses for Manny each year.

   A year after the contract was executed, Dell decided to retire to his cabin in the Everglades. He sold his business to Ann Phibian, his sulky and sullen apprentice. As part of the sale, Dell assigned Manny's contract to Ann. Ann has been well trained by Dell. Her designs are not as imaginative as Dell's but her craftsmanship is impeccable. However, Ann has an unpleasant nature and Manny finds her intimidating. He cannot face the thought of dealing with her over the next four years. He would prefer to terminate the contract and find someone else to make the purses. May he do so?

7. Bravo Bellissimo is an up-and-coming tenor who has sung in several opera productions in smaller cities. His opportunity to break into the big time came in July of this year, when he was offered a leading role in an opera to be performed on October 1 at the Megalopolitan Opera House, a famed world-class venue in a major city. On July 10, Bravo and Megalopolitan entered into a contract under which Bravo agreed to sing in Megalopolitan's October 1 opera performance for a fee of $100,000. At the end of July, Molto Magnifico, a celebrated tenor, suddenly became available to sing the lead role in Megalopolitan's October 1 opera performance. Megalopolitan decided that it could not pass up this opportunity so it hired Molto for the part. As a result, Megalopolitan no longer had any use for Bravo's services, so it sold his contract to the Upstate Opera Company, which operates in a smaller city and was, coincidentally, planning a performance of the same opera on the same night.

Upstate wrote to Bravo, notifying him that it had bought the right to his performance for October 1. Bravo objected, denying that Megalopolitan had the right to sell his performance, refusing to perform for Upstate, and demanding that Megalopolitan honor its obligation to cast him in the opera performance specified in the contract. Megalopolitan rejected this demand and warned Bravo that his failure to perform for Upstate would be a breach of contract. Was Megalopolitan entitled to sell Bravo's contract to Upstate, and is it correct in claiming that Bravo would be in breach of contract if he fails to perform for Upstate?

8. A lessee entered into a five-year lease of premises. The lease had a clause that provided, "The lessee may not assign this lease or any rights or interest in it without the express written permission of the lessor. Any such unauthorized assignment shall be void and shall give the lessor the right to terminate this lease immediately." A year after entering the lease, the lessee wishes to sublet the premises, but the lessor refuses to give permission. Is there anything that the lessee can do?

Explanations

1. Tess was not indebted to Benny, so he has no claim against the estate as a creditor and the invalid will left him with no basis for claiming testamentary rights. If Benny has any recourse at all for the loss of his inheritance, it will be against Mel. Mel's incompetence in drafting the will sounds like a clear case of malpractice, which would have given Tess, his client, a cause of action against him. However, Tess is dead, and her estate has no interest in pursuing a malpractice claim against Mel, because the intestate heirs will now benefit from the will's invalidity and will inherit all the property in the estate. It is Benny who has been injured by Mel's incompetence. Benny might have a tort-based malpractice claim against Mel if he can show that Mel had assumed a duty of care toward him. While this is a possibility, it is a difficult case to make. Courts do not lightly find that an attorney assumed a duty of care toward a nonclient unless the attorney actually communicated with the nonclient and gave the nonclient some undertaking, or made some misrepresentation to the nonclient, and the nonclient relied on that undertaking or misrepresentation to its detriment.

   Even if Benny has no tort-based malpractice claim against Mel, he may be able to assert a cause of action against Mel as an intended beneficiary of Mel's contract with Tess. Benny would have to show that Mel and Tess intended to confer an independent right of enforcement on him. Had the contract between Tess and Mel made their intentions clear, this would have been an easier case. However, in the absence of clearly expressed intent, the court has to determine intent as a matter of interpretation or construction. Some courts have been willing to recognize such an intent in situations involving incompetently drawn testamentary dispositions on the basis that the client is now deceased, the estate has no interest in pursuing the claim against the attorney, and the disappointed heir is the only party to hold the attorney accountable for the breach of duty. Other courts are resistant to finding intended beneficiary status in the nonclient because of the impact that this could have on the attorney-client relationship: Allowing an independent cause of action to the nonclient would compromise the attorney's duty of undivided loyalty to the client by making it difficult for the attorney to focus on the client's interests while trying to avoid possible liability to the nonclient.

2. Carr has no contract to provide parking for the fair, either with Fair City or with Merry Makers. His only basis for recovering damages from Merry Makers is as an intended beneficiary of its contract with Fair City. Unquestionably, Fair City's intent in organizing the fair was to benefit the public generally as well as the local economy, including nearby entrepreneurs like Carr who were in a position to reap profits from the event. Actions by government bodies are usually intended to benefit citizens, but that does not mean that they are intended to confer a private right on any individual citizen to enforce the contract. In fact, the usual assumption is that a private enforcement right was not intended unless the contract or any legislation authorizing it indicates otherwise or the public interest requires recognition of private enforcement rights to give effect to the governmental purpose. In the absence of such circumstances, it is solely up to the government body to decide whether to enforce its contracts. Too ready a recognition of private enforcement rights would harm the public interest by increasing the volume of litigation and making it difficult for government to function. In Carr's case there is nothing to show that the contract, its authorizing statute, or public policy conferred the right on Carr to sue Merry Makers. The city had given him no commitment to hold the fair, there is no evidence that the contract contemplated any benefit to him specifically, and there is no strong public interest at stake that can only be protected by allowing Carr a right of action.

3. If Belle knew that the diamond was fake, she is guilty of fraud. Even if she honestly believed the diamond to be genuine, the delivery of a piece of cut glass was nevertheless a breach of her warranty that it was a diamond—whether such a warranty was given in so many words or arose by necessary inference from the price and description of the ring.[10] There is no doubt that Rock would have a cause of action against Belle for

10. UCC §2.313(1)(b) provides that a description of the goods that is made part of the basis of the bargain creates an express warranty that the goods conform to the description.

breach of warranty, but the issue is whether Di can proceed against her directly without relying on Rock to assert the claim. Although Di visited the showroom with Rock and participated in selecting the ring, she was not a party to the contract for its sale. Her only basis for a direct claim against Belle (in the absence of some consumer protection statute that may extend rights to her) is as an intended beneficiary of Belle's contract with Rock. Although this is a sale of goods, UCC Article 2 has no provisions dealing with third-party beneficiary rights, which are therefore governed by common law.

It is clear that Rock intended Di to have the ring. This was obviously apparent to Belle at the time of contracting because she knew that Rock was buying an engagement ring and that Di was involved in choosing it. However, this is not enough on its own, because there must also have been an understanding between Rock and Belle that Di would acquire an independent right to enforce Belle's contractual warranty. Although it is unlikely that the parties would have discussed this, or even thought of it at the time, intent to confer a right of action on the beneficiary need not be articulated if, under all the circumstances, it is, in the words of Restatement, Second, §302(1), "appropriate to effectuate the intention of the parties." In this case, Di's close involvement in the selection of the ring and the fact that she was to receive and own it can make a plausible argument that the recognition of her right to enforce Belle's warranty is consistent with the parties' intent.

The facts of this example are adapted from those in *Warren v. Monahan Beaches Jewelry Center, Inc.*, 548 So. 2d 870 (Fla. 1989). In that case, the plaintiff did not participate in the selection of the ring and was not known to the seller at the time of its purchase. However, the seller did know that its customer, the plaintiff's fiancé, was buying it as an engagement ring. After her fiancé gave her the ring, the plaintiff noticed a chip in it and took it back to the seller, which undertook to replace it as soon as new inventory came in. The plaintiff kept the ring while she was waiting for the new stock and decided to have it appraised. The appraisal revealed that the diamond was not genuine, but was cubic zirconia. The plaintiff then sued the seller directly. The seller moved to dismiss her complaint on the basis that it did not allege sufficient facts to show that the plaintiff was an intended beneficiary of the seller's contract with her fiancé. The appellate court found that the complaint did set out a cause of action. By alleging both the seller's precontractual discussions with the plaintiff's fiancé and its post-contractual dealings with the plaintiff herself, it adequately pleaded an intent to confer an enforceable benefit on the plaintiff. (The post-contractual dealings in *Warren* were useful bolstering evidence because they helped to establish that the contracting parties intended to confer a right of enforcement on the beneficiary. Although no such evidence exists in Di's case, her evidence of the precontractual dealings is stronger than in *Warren*, and should be enough, on its own, to establish intent.)

4. Finance Co. is clearly not an intended beneficiary of the contract in which Lex agreed to represent Claire because it was not contemplated as a beneficiary at the time that the contract was made. Also, Claire's mere sending of the letter to Lex does not give rise to a contract between Finance Co. and Lex, and Finance Co. has no promissory estoppel claim against Lex because it did not take action in reliance on any promise by Lex to pay Claire's debt out of the proceeds of the business sale. Although Lex was negligent in forgetting about the letter and instructions, Finance Co. is not his client and the facts do not indicate that Lex gave finance Co. any undertaking or even that Lex ever communicated with Finance Co. at all. To protect the attorney-client relationship, courts are reluctant to allow a nonclient to sue an attorney for negligence unless the attorney has assumed a duty of care to the nonclient. In the absence of any communication with Finance Co., there is no basis for finding a duty of care.

   Therefore, Finance Co.'s only basis for recovering from Lex is as an assignee of Claire's claim against Lex for payment of the funds held in the trust account. The right to the funds held by Lex is a contract right, arising out of the representation agreement between Lex and Claire.[11] An assignment is a voluntary manifestation of intent by the owner of the right to transfer it immediately and irrevocably to another. The assignment does not need to comply with any formalities, nor does it need to use any particular form of words, provided that intent to assign is apparent. Claire's letter acknowledges her debt to Finance Co. and authorizes payment to it from the fund. Its reasonable import is that Claire intends irrevocably to assign her right to the funds to the extent stated. There is nothing in Claire's contract with Lex, or in the nature of the transaction, or as a matter of policy, that would rebut the usual presumption in favor of the free assignability of Claire's contract right.

   This is the assignment of a present right because the fund is already in existence and deposited in Lex's trust account and the contract giving rise to Claire's claim against Lex has been executed. Claire has assigned only part of her right, $50,000 and accumulated interest, out of a payment right of $100,000. The partial assignment of a right is permissible provided that the splitting of the right does not impose a substantial risk or burden on the obligor. Where the right simply involves payment from a fund, the partial assignment does not impose any impermissible burden or risk on Lex.

---

11. Although a lawyer's obligation to preserve trust funds and to pay them to the client is also a fiduciary obligation and an obligation imposed by rules of professional responsibility, the lawyer's retention of client funds is created by the contract between the lawyer and the client.

A valid assignment is binding on Lex, the obligor, as soon as he receives notice of it. (If he so requested, Lex would have been entitled to receive adequate proof of it, but Lex made no such request.) At that point, Finance Co., the assignee, is substituted for Claire, the assignor, as the party entitled to performance. Lex can only discharge his contractual duty by rendering performance to Finance Co. Lex's payment to Claire of the amount payable to Finance Co. was improper and does not discharge Lex's obligation to pay Finance Co.

5. Upon selling her business to Chazzer Food Corp., Frumme assigned to it her entire contract with Gator Deli—she both assigned her right to payment and delegated her duty to supply sausages. Because the contract for the supply of sausages is a sale of goods, the rules governing the assignment of rights and the delegation of duties are set out in UCC §2.210. The contract does not have any express terms permitting or forbidding its assignment, so §2.210 allows Gator to resist the assignment and delegation only if it would materially affect its rights and obligations under the contract, or the contract gives it a substantial interest in having Frumme personally render or control the performance. Frumme is a strictly kosher butcher, and had the contract been assigned to another strictly kosher butcher, Gator would have less grounds to complain unless Frumme's skills and attributes makes it crucial that she personally performs under the contract. However, the contract was assigned to a corporation that supplies food to the general market with a centralized butchery that neither uses kosher meat nor processes it in accordance with Jewish law. It is surely a material term of the contract that the sausages are kosher, and the delegation of the duty to supply them fundamentally affects Gator's rights under the contract.

   However, this does not mean that Gator has the immediate right to refuse the delegation and to declare Frumme to be in breach. The law's presumption in favor of assignability seeks to balance the rights of Frumme to sell her assets against Gator's right to achieve its contractual expectations. Therefore, as Chazzer has not stated that it will not comply with Frumme's contractual obligation to supply sausages that are kosher, Gator has to give it the opportunity to declare its intentions with regard to performance. Under §2.210(5) Gator should treat the delegation as creating reasonable grounds for insecurity, and should clarify Chazzer's intentions by demanding an adequate assurance of performance. If Chazzer fails to provide an adequate assurance of performance, Gator has the right to refuse the delegation. In addition, because Frumme would have repudiated the contract if she improperly delegated her duties, Gator can declare a material breach and can claim damages from her for any loss that it suffers. However, if Chazzer responds by giving the assurance that the sausages to be supplied under the contract will be processed separately from nonkosher meat in a plant and under a process that complies with Jewish law, Gator must accept the assignment and remains bound by the contract. Even if the delegation is effective, it does not release Frumme from her obligations, and she remains responsible if Chazzer fails to perform properly.

6. Manny gives Dell the materials for the leather products, so this contract appears to be only for Dell's services in making the products, and not a sale of goods. It is therefore subject to the common law. However, the common law principles are no different from those set out for a sale of goods in Example 5. Like the contract for the sale of sausages, this contract is assigned in its entirety and constitutes both an assignment of Dell's right to payment and his duty to make the purses. The contract is silent on assignment, so the rights are presumed to be assignable and the duties delegable unless this would violate public policy (which is not implicated here) or the nature and purpose of the contract is such that assignment would place an undue burden on Manny, would impair his prospects of return performance, or would defeat his substantial interest in having the obligor render or control the performance.

   Manny's contract with Dell is highly personal in two respects. First, it is based on Dell's exceptional talent in design and craftsmanship. Second, it is grounded in a long and congenial relationship. The quality of Ann's work is equivalent to Dell's but she does not quite have his design flair. Dell's identity is clearly a significant factor in the contract, as would be true of any artist. This could be an important enough a feature of the contract to make Dell's personal performance the basis of the bargain. However, this cannot be determined for sure without more knowledge of the extent of the differences between Dell's and Ann's work. The significance of the personal relationship is even more difficult to evaluate. Manny may not have entered into a long-term contract with someone with whom he did not have a good personal relationship. However, this is a commercial contract for the purpose of producing marketable products. Provided that purses of suitable quality can be produced, the parties do not have to be buddies, and their happy personal relationship may be incidental to the central purpose of the contract.[12]

   In short, there is a chance that Manny could resist assignment of the contract, but this result is not assured. When the court balances Manny's

12. Section 19.3.7 notes that a contracting party cannot reasonably expect that corporate officers with whom the party has a special relationship will not change even in the absence of assignment. This expectation may be more reasonable where the contracting parties are individuals, but the personal relationship of the parties might still be incidental, even in a contract between individuals.

reasonable contractual expectations against Dell's right to profit from the sale of his business, it could well find that Manny has not met the burden of showing this contract to be nonassignable.

7. Megalopolitan has assigned the entire contract to Upstate—both its right to Bravo's performance and its obligations to Bravo. If Bravo's only reasonable expectation under the contract was to earn the $100,000 and he had no interest in where his performance would be rendered, the assignment of the contract would likely be permissible: It would not matter where he sang, and his payment of the fee is assured, either from Upstate or from Megalopolitan, which remains liable for the performance that it promised in the contract.

   However, the context of the contract makes it clear that Bravo did not bargain only for the fee. The performance at Megalopolitan's famous, world-class opera house would have given him an unparalleled opportunity of opera stardom which he cannot achieve by performing for yet another regional company. Therefore, the sale of Bravo's performance delegates not only Megalopolitan's duty to pay him, but also its duty to provide him with the opportunity of significant career advancement. This latter duty cannot be delegated to an opera company that does not have the capacity to achieve this end.

   This being so, Megalopolitan's assignment of the contract was a repudiation, and when Megalopolitan refused to retract it before the due date for performance, Megalopolitan materially breached its contractual promise. This gave Bravo the right to withhold his own performance by refusing to sing for Upstate, so his failure to render that performance would not be a breach of contract. In addition, Bravo would have a claim against Megalopolitan for whatever damages he can prove that he suffered.

   By contrast to Bravo's case, a right to the performance of personal services was held to be assignable in *Evening News Assn. v. Peterson*, 477 F. Supp. 77 (D.D.C. 1979). Peterson was employed as a news anchor at a television station. When the television station was sold, the seller assigned Peterson's employment contract to the buyer. Peterson objected to the assignment, but the court upheld it. The assignment of the contract did not materially alter his working conditions, increase his burden of performance, or endanger his prospects of return performance.

8. Because the law has a general preference in favor of the assignability of rights and the delegation of duties, courts interpret clauses prohibiting or restricting assignment as narrowly as possible. The provision in the lease is clearly worded and it specifically states that any unauthorized assignment will be null and void. The effect of this language is that the lessee's attempt to make an unauthorized assignment would not only be a breach of contract, but would also be legally ineffective.

As the lessee cannot effectively transfer the lease without the lessor's permission, the next question is whether the lessee can do anything to compel the lessor to give its permission or to override its refusal. Unless the lease makes it clear that the lessor reserves absolute discretion to refuse permission, the law implies an obligation on the lessor to act reasonably in refusing it. This accords with the normal marketplace expectation of commercially reasonable conduct and is consistent with the law's general policy of requiring parties to deal with each other fairly and in good faith. Therefore, to legitimately refuse permission to sublet, the lessor must show that it has reasonable grounds for objecting to the subtenant—for example, that it is financially unstable, would use the premises improperly, or would otherwise be an unsuitable occupant.

Glossary

This glossary defines words and phrases that relate specifically to contract law, but also includes some common legal terms that are used more widely. Most of the terms defined here are explained more fully in the book. The relevant book sections can be found in the index.

Accord and satisfaction. A settlement of an existing claim under which the parties agree that one of them (the debtor) will give, and the other (the creditor) will accept a lesser performance than that originally claimed by the creditor. The agreement of settlement is the accord, and its execution by rendition of the settled performance is the satisfaction. Until the settlement is satisfied by performance, it is known as an executory accord.

Actions of assumpsit and covenant. *See* Assumpsit; Covenant.

Action of debt. A form of action under early common law that lay for recovery of a sum certain in money arising out of a contract under which money had been lent to or goods or services had been delivered to the defendant. *See also* Debt.

Adhesion. A contract is adhesive where the party who drafts the terms of the contract has the market power to insist that the contract may be only on the terms that it proposes, and the nondrafting party has no choice but to agree to those terms in order to enter the contract. The name "adhesion" derives from the fact that the nondrafting party cannot enter the contract without adhering the drafter's nonnegotiable terms.

Aggrieved party. As used in this book, a party who has suffered a breach of contract.

Agreed damages. *See* Liquidated damages.

Agreement to agree. Negotiating parties may have reached agreement in principle, but may not have settled all the terms of their proposed contract. They may decide to postpone resolution of those terms for later, agreeing to address them at a future date. This situation is sometimes described as an "agreement to agree." If the unresolved terms are material, no contract can come into existence until they are settled, so the term "agreement to agree" means that the parties have not yet reached the stage of entering into a binding contract.

Anticipatory repudiation. A contract cannot be breached before the time of performance falls due. However, if, before a party's performance is due, the party makes it clear by unequivocal words or unambiguous voluntary conduct that it will not perform its obligations under the contract at all, or that it will materially breach the contract when the time for performance arrives, the party repudiates in anticipation of performance. The other party may give the repudiator an opportunity to retract the repudiation, or may react to the repudiation immediately by pursuing relief for breach. *See also* Prospective nonperformance/adequate assurance of performance.

Arbitration. The parties may provide in the contract itself, or in a self-standing separate agreement, that any disputes relating to their contract will be resolved by a neutral third party (an arbitrator). By agreeing to arbitrate disputes, the parties forgo the right to litigate, and they bind themselves to the arbitrator's disposition.

Assignment and delegation. Assignment is the transfer of a contractual right, and delegation is the transfer of a contractual duty. Sometimes "assignment" is used more loosely to mean the transfer of a contract in its entirety, which involves the transfer of both rights and duties under the contract.

Assumpsit. (Latin: "He undertook.") One of the common law forms of action under which suit was brought for damages for the breach of a contractual promise. Assumpsit, an extension of the tort action of trespass, was originally only available where the defendant performed improperly, causing harm to the plaintiff (misfeasance). It was later extended to cover situations in which the defendant broke its promise by failing to perform at all (nonfeasance). As assumpsit developed, it became the most flexible, efficient, and comprehensive form of action for contract. It eventually overtook the other contractual writs of covenant and debt, emerging as the forebear of modern contract law.

Assurance of performance. *See* Prospective nonperformance/adequate assurance of performance.

Avoidable contract and avoidance. An avoidable contract has some defect (typically resulting from improper bargaining, illegality, or incapacity) that allows one of the parties to rescind or disaffirm the contract. If that party does not elect to rescind, the contract is fully in effect and enforceable. An avoidable contract must be distinguished from a void contract, which is a nullity and cannot be enforced by either party. *See also* Disaffirmance; Rescission; Void/voidable.

Balance of the equities. *See* Equitable balancing.

Bargain theory. *See* Consideration.

Battle of the forms. A nickname given to the situation in which the buyer and seller of goods attempt to form a contract by exchanging documents (whether printed in tangible form or in electronic form) with mismatching terms. Often these terms are predrafted standard provisions, designed to protect the interests of the sender.

Bilateral contract. All contracts have two or more parties, so every contract is at least bilateral (or, if not, multilateral) in that sense. However, in contract law, the word "bilateral" is a term of art, meaning that at the instant of contract formation, there are promises outstanding by both parties. This is in contrast to a unilateral contract, under which the offeree's act of acceptance is also the offeree's act of performance, so that at the instant of formation, the offeree has already performed, and only the offeror's promise is outstanding. Most contractual relationships involve an exchange of promises, so most contracts are bilateral. Unilateral contracts are less common. *See also* Unilateral contract.

Boilerplate. Predrafted standard provisions that are commonly used in contracts generally or in contracts of a particular kind. *See also* standard terms/standard contract.

Box-top terms. Standard contract terms set out or referenced on a box or other container that includes a product such as goods or software.

Breach of contract. *See* Materiality; Partial breach; Substantial performance; Total breach.

Browsewrap. Standard contract terms set out on a website or other electronic medium and available to be read by the user, commonly by clicking a link to the terms, before submitting an order for the product or services purchased. Browsewrap differs from clickwrap in that it does not require the user to signify assent to the terms before completing the transaction. *Compare* Clickwrap.

Chancery. The Chancellor's Court. That is, the court of Equity. *See also* Equity.

CISG. Abbreviation for the United Nations Convention on Contracts for the International Sale of Goods. The CISG governs international sales of goods by parties whose places of business are located in signatory states. The CISG does not apply to consumer transactions or to transactions in which the parties have excluded it by agreement.

Civil law. A general term used to describe the legal system of countries that derive their legal heritage from Roman law. Within the American legal system, the term may be used in a different sense, to describe the law governing private rights and relationships, as opposed to criminal law.

Class action. Where a large group of people all have the same claim against a defendant, a small group of named plaintiffs may commence a suit against the defendant in which they represent not only their own interests but those of the entire class.

Classical contract law. The name used to describe the law of contracts as it existed in the period running from the late nineteenth to early twentieth century, in which modern contract law was developed and systematized.

Clickwrap. Standard contract terms contained in a website or other electronic medium, set up in a way that makes the terms available for the user to read and does not allow the user to complete the transaction without signifying assent to the terms by action such as clicking an "I agree" button. The word "scrollwrap" might be used if the "I agree" button is not activated until the website user has scrolled through the terms. *Compare* Browsewrap.

Common law. A term with three related but distinct meanings. It denotes:

1. The basic legal system of countries whose law derives from the common law of England.
2. The judge-made (as opposed to statutory) component of a common law system.
3. The process of legal analysis in a common law system under which judges interpret, develop, and embellish rules of law.

Comparative law. The comparative study of the laws or legal systems of two or more nations.

Concurrent conditions. Where mutual performances under a contract are dependent on each other and the contract does not expressly or impliedly set out a sequence for performance, they must be rendered at the same time, and each performance is deemed in law to be a condition of the other. Therefore, if one of the parties fails to perform, the other is excused from doing so.

Condition. An event, not certain to occur, that must occur for the performance of a party to become due. If the parties agree that a particular performance under the contract (or the entire contract) is to be contingent on the happening of an uncertain event, the performance (or the contract as a whole) is conditional. A condition is express if it is articulated in the agreement; implied in fact if it is inferable from interpreting the agreement in context; or construed (or implied in law) if the court concludes, as a matter of legal implication, that the parties reasonably intended it. Conditions are also categorized as pure or promissory. A pure condition is simply an event specified as a contingency on which performance is dependent, and nothing more. If the event fails to occur, the performance dependent on it need not be rendered, and neither party incurs any liability for the nonoccurrence. However, a promissory condition is both a condition and a promise. That is, one of the parties promises expressly or impliedly that the condition will occur, and becomes liable for breach of contract if it does not. *See also* Express; Implied in fact; Implied-in-law term.

Conditions precedent or subsequent. A condition precedent is one that must be fulfilled before a duty to perform comes into effect. A condition subsequent is one that discharges a duty of performance. That is, the duty to perform arises immediately upon formation of the contract, but if the condition occurs, it falls away. A condition subsequent differs from a condition precedent in that it extinguishes an existing duty, while a condition precedent is a precondition to a duty arising. The distinction is arcane, irrelevant in most situations, and seldom comes up in modern cases.

Consequential damages. Losses or injuries suffered by the victim of a breach going beyond the mere loss in value of the promised performance (direct damages) and resulting from the impact of the breach on other rights, transactions, or endeavors affected by the contract. *Compare* Direct damages.

Consideration. In its earliest formulation, "consideration" probably meant no more than that the contract was deliberately considered—that it was seriously contemplated and intended to be binding. As it has developed, consideration has come to mean that something of legal value (but not necessarily economic value) must be given by each party in exchange for what was promised or given by the other. Under the bargain theory, which prevails in modern law, a promise or performance qualifies as consideration only if it has been given in exchange for and induced the return promise or performance.

Construction/construed term. *See* Implied-in-law term.

Constructive conditions of exchange. Unless the contract expressly or impliedly indicates a different intent, the law generally presumes that the performances of the parties are interdependent—that they are dependent promises. That is, each party's duty to perform is conditional on the other performing. *See also* Condition.

Contract of adhesion. *See* Adhesion.

Contra proferentum rule. A default rule of interpretation that where the meaning of language is unclear and cannot be resolved by contextual evidence, an interpretation is preferred that goes against the interests of the drafter, and in favor of the nondrafting party.

Course of dealing/performance. Where contracting parties have entered into a number of successive transactions of a similar kind, the transactions that occurred before the contract in question are referred to as a course of dealing. Where there is some uncertainty in the meaning of a term in the current contract, evidence of the parties' course of dealing can be helpful in resolving it. The conduct of the parties in performing a contract after its execution is called a course of performance. Evidence of how the parties actually performed following the formation of the contract can likewise be useful in interpreting what they must have intended.

Covenant. In general terms, a covenant is simply an agreement, but it may also be used as a synonym for "promise." At early common law, Covenant was a form of action available to recover damages for breach of a promise under seal. Under the formalistic system of pleading in early common law, the action was not available for a contract that was not executed under seal.

Cure. A breaching party's rectification of the deficiency in performance.

Damages. A monetary award to compensate for loss or harm. *See* Consequential damages; Direct damages; Expectation damages; General damages; Incidental damages; Liquidated damages; Punitive/exemplary damages; Reliance damages; Special damages.

Debt. An obligation to pay money. (Sometimes "debt" is used even more broadly—and somewhat inaccurately—to denote any obligation of performance.) *See also* Action of debt.

Delegation. *See* Assignment and delegation.

Dependent promises. *See* Condition; Constructive conditions of exchange.

Deposited acceptance rule. *See* Mailbox rule.

Detriment. In law, "detriment" is sometimes used in its ordinary sense, to mean actual harm, prejudice, or injury. (For example, many courts require detriment in this sense before giving relief for promissory estoppel.) However, in consideration doctrine, "detriment" is used as a legal term of art to denote the giving up of a legal right. A party suffers a legal detriment by doing or promising to do something that the party is not obliged to do, or by refraining from something that the party is entitled to do. For consideration purposes, a detriment does not have to be harmful or injurious to the party that incurs it.

Direct costs. *See* Fixed and variable costs.

Direct damages. Losses incurred by the victim of a breach in acquiring the equivalent of the performance promised under the contract, so as to substitute for the performance that should have been rendered by the breacher.

Direct reliance. *See* Reliance damages.

Disaffirmance. Upon breach, the victim may either sue on the contract for expectation or reliance damages, or may elect to act as if no contract exists, and to sue for restitution under a theory of unjust enrichment. Disaffirmance is the plaintiff's formal abandonment of the contract to ground the unjust enrichment claim. Disaffirmance is also sometimes used as a synonym for the avoidance of a voidable contract. *See also* Avoidable Contract

Divisibility. A contract is divisible if the mutual performances promised by the parties can be split up into a number of smaller, self-sufficient exchanges. That is, the contract can be divided into independent and self-contained sets of matching performances. *See also* Severability.

Duty to read. Under the objective test of intent, a party is bound by the reasonable meaning of its manifestation of intent. Therefore, a party is usually deemed to have agreed to recorded terms by manifesting assent to them, even though the party failed to read or comprehend them.

Economic waste. If damages for rectifying a breach are disproportionate to the victim's true loss, the court has the discretion to adjust them downward to more accurately reflect the actual loss. It is sometimes said that the basis for this adjustment is that it would be economically wasteful to spend a large sum on curing a relatively less valuable breach, but as the plaintiff would not be obliged to waste the damages award on rectifying the breach, the true basis for the rule is that it would be an unfair forfeiture to compel the breacher to pay damages disproportionate to actual loss. *See also* Unfair forfeiture.

Efficient breach. A breach is efficient if it makes the defendant better off without making the plaintiff worse off. The theory of efficient breach is that if the defendant's cost to perform the contract (including the cost of lost opportunity for a more lucrative transaction) would exceed the benefit that performance would give both parties, the defendant may save (or earn) enough money by breaching to pay expectation damages to the plaintiff and still come out ahead. In purely economic terms, a breach in such circumstances does not harm the plaintiff, who is compensated by the payment of damages, while it increases the defendant's wealth. A breach can only be efficient if the transaction costs of each party in making substitute transactions and of settling or litigating the plaintiff's claim do not exceed the gains to be made from the breach. These transaction costs may be difficult to predict and calculate. *See also* Transaction costs.

Ejusdem generis. (Latin: "of the same kind.") A rule of interpretation under which specific words limit the meaning of general words with which they are associated.

Electronic agent. A computer program or another automated means used by a party to initiate or respond to communications in the formation of a contract and intended to allow for contract formation without the intervention of a human operator.

Enforcement. A general word that denotes judicial recognition of a right. When it is said that a court enforces a contract, this means that the court will render judgment for relief upon breach of the contract. Enforcement does not necessarily take the form of a court order compelling the breaching party to perform its obligations under the contract—in fact such an order of specific performance is the exception rather than the rule. In most cases, the enforcement of a contract takes the form of a money judgment for damages. If the breacher fails to pay the damages voluntarily, the means of compelling payment is by execution. *See also* Execution; Specific performance.

Equitable balancing. In judicial decisionmaking, the process under which the court takes into account the likely impact of countervailing resolutions, and attempts to reach a fair and balanced result by weighing the potential hardship to each party as well as their respective rights and the relative justice of their positions.

Equity. Apart from meaning "fairness" in a general sense, this word has a more technical meaning in the common law. It refers to the jurisdiction originally exercised by the Lord Chancellor, representing the monarch, for the purpose of granting discretionary relief when that relief was beyond the more rigid remedial powers of the law courts. A crucial requirement of seeking equitable relief was, and still is, that the available legal remedy would be inadequate. Courts of law and equity have been combined for some time, so the firm separation of law and equity has broken down considerably. However, the distinction between suits of equitable and legal origin still exists.

Escrow. Money or other property delivered by a contracting party to an independent third party (the escrow agent) with instructions to deliver the money or property to the other contracting party upon the fulfillment of stated conditions. By using an escrow agent, the party with the duty to deliver the money or property ensures that it is kept in trust and transferred to the other party only upon fulfillment of the condition. In many cases, the condition in question is the recipient party's performance of its obligations under the contract.

E-SIGN. The Electronic Signatures in Global and National Commerce Act, a federal statute enacted in 2000, to validate electronic signatures and records. *See also* UETA.

Essential reliance. *See* Reliance damages.

Estoppel. (Also called equitable estoppel or estoppel in pais.) A doctrine derived from equity under which a person is precluded from asserting a right where that person has, by deliberate words or conduct, misled the party against whom the rights are asserted into the justifiable belief that the right does not exist or will not be asserted.

Execution. The process of enforcing a money judgment, such as a judgment of contract damages, against the judgment debtor (the party against whom the judgment has been rendered.) The judgment creditor (the party in whose favor judgment was granted) has a writ issued and delivered to the appropriate official (usually called the sheriff), who then attempts to find property belonging to the judgment debtor. If such property is found, the sheriff levies on it—that is, takes legal custody of it, and after advertising it, sells it at public auction. The proceeds of the sale are then paid over to the judgment creditor.

Executory/executed. Until a contract has been fully performed, it is executory. Once it has been fully performed on both sides, it is executed. In the case of a gift, where the gift is merely promised, but not yet given, it is executory (and hence unenforceable under consideration doctrine), but once the gift has been transferred to the donee, it is executed, and no longer subject to invalidation under consideration doctrine.

Executory accord. *See* Accord and satisfaction.

Exemplary damages. *See* Punitive/exemplary damages.

Expectation damages. The standard measure of damages for breach of contract—a monetary award designed to compensate the victim of breach for its reasonable contractual expectations lost as a result of the breach. The damages are intended to place the victim in the economic position that it would have been in had the contract not been breached.

Express. Articulated or stated in words, rather than inferred from indirect language or circumstances.

Expressio unius est exclusio alterius. (Latin: "the expression of one thing excludes another.") A rule of interpretation under which the listing of a string of specific things, not followed by a general term, is taken to exclude unlisted things of the same kind.

Extrinsic evidence. Evidence of the context in which a document was executed. These facts outside the document, such as evidence of discussions, negotiations, or prior dealings between the parties or trade usage, may help cast light on what the parties meant by the language used in the document. *Compare* Four corners (of a document).

Fiction. *See* Legal fiction.

Firm offer/option. An offer that the offeror undertakes not to revoke for a stated or reasonable time. At common law, such an undertaking is not binding on the offeror unless the offer qualifies as a valid option, but under UCC Article 2, a firm offer is binding under defined circumstances.

Fixed and variable costs. In the context of contract damages, fixed costs (overhead) are costs that a party is committed to incur in conducting business and cannot save by ceasing performance of the contract following the other party's breach. These overhead costs are distinguished from variable (direct) costs, which are costs incurred solely in the process of performance. When a material breach occurs, the breach victim must cease its performance and is therefore saved the expenditure of direct costs that had not yet been incurred at the time of the breach. Therefore, if the breach victim claims profit lost as a result of the breach, fixed costs, not being saved, are included in the breach victim's recovery, but saved variable costs are not.

F.O.B. (Free on board.) A term in a sale of goods that identifies the seller's delivery commitment and risk of loss. The initials F.O.B. are followed by a specified place (for example, F.O.B. New York). The seller is responsible for the cost and risk of getting the goods to that place, and the buyer must accept delivery there. Upon taking delivery, the buyer assumes responsibility for the freight and risk of loss from that point.

Force majeure. (French: "superior force.") A force beyond the control of the parties, such as a natural disaster or war. A force majeure clause in a contract expresses whether, and under what circumstances, a party will be released from performance if that performance is rendered impracticable as a result of such an uncontrollable event.

Foreseen/foreseeable. An event is foreseen if the party in question recognizes the possibility of its occurrence and contemplates it as a real likelihood. However, foreseeability is based on a more objective standard: Whether or not the party in question does actually foresee the event, it is foreseeable if it can be conceived of as a realistic likelihood by a reasonable person in the position of the party.

Forfeiture. *See* Unfair forfeiture.

Form of action. In older common law, different actions (for example, the contract actions of assumpsit, covenant, or debt, or the tort action of trespass) each covered a specific type of transaction or set of facts and had a particular form that had distinct features in its pleadings and in the manner in which evidence was presented and evaluated. This formalistic system no longer applies in modern law.

Forum selection clause. A term in a contract in which the parties stipulate that any litigation relating to the transaction will be commenced only in a specified court or jurisdiction.

Four corners (of a document). The face of a recorded document, examined on its text alone, without any recourse to evidence extrinsic to the document. If a court confines itself to ascertaining the meaning and intent of the document on the sole basis of the document itself, it is said to make that determination on the four corners of the document. The term is commonly used to describe a court's exclusive reliance on the text of the recorded memorial of contract to make its decision on whether parol evidence should be admitted to supplement the document. *See also* Extrinsic evidence; Integration: total or partial.

Fraud in the factum. A fraudulent misrepresentation by one of the parties of the nature and effect of a document to be executed by the other. The party making the misrepresentation must intend to deceive the other about its nature and legal effect, and the victim must have been justified in relying on the misrepresentation.

Fraud in the inducement. The most common form of fraud, in which one of the parties misrepresents something that underlies and induces the contract. The misrepresentation usually relates to a fact, but under some circumstances it could also be a false assertion of opinion, prediction, or intention. To constitute fraud, the party making the misrepresentation must have known of its falsity and have intended to mislead the other party, thereby justifiably inducing the other party to enter the contract. *See also* Misrepresentation.

Frustration of purpose. A contract's purpose is frustrated where, after it is made, an unforeseen event occurs, which so changes the circumstances surrounding it, that the contract's underlying purpose—as reasonably understood by both parties—is defeated. Although it is still possible to perform as originally intended, the point of the contract has disappeared. Under proper circumstances, the frustration of a contract's purpose is a defense to breach of the contract and could result in termination of the contract.

Gap filler. A default term implied by law into a contract where the parties have not agreed expressly to a term covering that aspect of their contract. For example, if parties to a contract for the sale of goods do not specifically agree when payment must be made for the goods, the law supplies a gap filler that the price is to be paid on delivery.

Garnishment. A form of execution under which a writ is delivered to a person who holds property of the judgment debtor or owes money or another obligation to the judgment debtor, ordering that person to turn over the property or money to the court in satisfaction of the judgment. *See also* Execution; Writ.

General damages. In contract, damages that arise in the normal course of breach, including readily foreseeable direct damages, as well as those consequential damages that were reasonably foreseeable by the breaching party at the time of contracting as a natural and probable consequence of the breach. (If the breaching party could not reasonably have foreseen the damages without special information or knowledge of the other party's particular circumstances, the damages are special.)

Good faith. Actual honesty and fair dealing, with an absence of intent to act wrongfully. Despite the prevalence of an objective reasonableness standard in contract law, there are many situations in which the honesty of a party, measured subjectively by attempting to ascertain the party's actual state of mind, is relevant to the case.

Illusory promise. An apparent promise that is so qualified, or in respect of which such wide discretion is reserved, that the apparent promisor actually makes no binding commitment at all.

Implied in fact. A contract, term, or promise is implied in fact if it is not expressly stated, but it can be deduced as a matter of factual conclusion from other language used by the parties, or from conduct or the circumstances surrounding the transaction.

Implied-in-law contract/quasi-contract. A contract implied in law, also known as quasi contract, is not a contract at all, but a legal fiction originally created for procedural reasons—to allow the formalistic common law courts of a bygone era to use the contractual form of action as a basis for giving relief for unjust enrichment. In modern law, these formalistic forms of action have long disappeared, but the terms "quasi-contract" or "contract implied in law" have survived and are now merely alternative names for the action for unjust enrichment.

Implied-in-law/construed term. A term is implied in law or construed where the court finds that it exists in a contract, even though the language of the contract does not state it, and it cannot be inferred as a matter of fact from contextual evidence. Legal implication is based on a policy judgment by the court (or by a statute or common law rule) that the term should be in the contract, even though the parties may not actually have agreed to it. The importation of the term into the contract is typically justified on the basis that the parties reasonably would have intended the term to apply had they thought about the issue.

Impracticability/impossibility. Under the older, narrower doctrine of impossibility, performance under a contract may be excused as impossible if the contract contemplated that performance to be dependent on the continued existence of a person or thing, and, without fault of the person claiming excuse, the person died or thing was destroyed after the contract's execution. The doctrine of impracticability is a modern expansion of the older impossibility doctrine. A party may be excused from performance if an unforeseen supervening event, occurring after formation of the contract, and not caused by the fault of the party claiming excuse, defeats a basic assumption on which the contract was made. To establish excuse on the basis of impracticability, the party must also show that the unforeseen event imposes a significant burden on it, beyond any risk that it expressly or impliedly assumed.

Incidental/intended beneficiary. *See* Third-party beneficiary.

Incidental damages. Costs and expenses incurred by the breach victim in attempting to deal with it and in taking action to seek a substitute transaction or to curtail losses.

Incidental reliance. *See* Reliance damages.

Indebitatus assumpsit. *See* Assumpsit.

Indefiniteness. Vagueness, ambiguity, or other uncertainty in an agreement.

Infancy, infant. A word sometimes used in contract law to mean minority—that is, to describe any person below the age of contractual capacity (typically 18).

Injunction. An order of court compelling the performance of a specified act (called a mandatory injunction) or prohibiting specific action (called a prohibitory injunction).

In pari delicto rule. (Latin: In pari delicto potior est conditio defendantis—"where the parties are in equal guilt, the defendant's position is the stronger.") This maxim applies to contracts that are illegal. If one of the parties seeks to enforce such a contract, or even to obtain restitution of performance rendered under it, the court may refuse to intervene. In making the decision on whether or not to allow relief, the court weighs the relative guilt of the parties, but also takes into account other considerations, the most important of which are the equities between the parties and the public interest.

In personam/in rem. An in personam order is a command of the court directed at the defendant and compelling the defendant to do or refrain from doing something. A defendant who disobeys the order is in contempt of court. By contrast, a judgment of the court that the defendant owes monetary damages is in rem. It is not directed against the person of the defendant, but at the defendant's property. If the defendant fails to pay the judgment, it can only be enforced to the extent that the sheriff can find property of the defendant on which to levy execution.

Integration: total or partial. A recorded memorandum of agreement is said to be totally integrated if it clearly and unambiguously expresses all the terms agreed to by the parties, and is intended by them to be a complete and final expression of their entire contract. If the record does not fully and finally incorporate all of the agreed terms, but it does set out some of them completely, clearly, and unambiguously, it is said to be partially integrated. That is, the record is a final expression of agreement with regard to those terms that are fully set out.

Interpretation. The process of inferring meaning of language, based on the words used by the parties in the contract, and on other available factual evidence of the context in which the language was used.

Judgment creditor/debtor. *See* Execution.

Knockout rule. A rule applied under some circumstances to resolve the "battle of the forms" under UCC §2.207. The rule provides that conflicting terms in the parties' correspondence cancel each other out, leaving an open term to be filled by the gap fillers provided by the UCC.

Last shot rule. Where the final communication in the process of offer and acceptance contains new or different terms, the recipient is deemed to have accepted those terms by conduct if the recipient performs without objecting to them. The rule may be followed under common law, but it does not apply in the "battle of the forms" under UCC §2.207.

Legal detriment. *See* Detriment.

Legal fiction. A factual assumption, deemed to be true in law, even though the assumed fact is not established by evidence to be true, or, in some cases, even if the assumption is contrary to the actual facts. A legal fiction may be used where necessary to effectuate a public policy or to achieve a just result.

Legal realism. A philosophy of law that rejects the concept of law as a set of certain, neutral legal rules, and views it in a multidisciplinary context, in which legal doctrine is part of a larger process of decisionmaking and policymaking. It examines the operation of legal rules in the broader context of the legal process, society, and social policy. *See also* Positivism.

Levy. *See* Execution.

Liquidated damages. To avoid disputes and uncertainty over damages if a breach should occur in the future, the parties may include a term in the contract that fixes in advance the amount of damages to be paid if a breach occurs. A fairly bargained liquidated damages provision is enforceable provided that, at the time of contracting, it reasonably appeared to the parties that actual damages would be difficult to prove, and the parties made a genuine attempt to forecast probable loss. As an alternative to examining the parties' attempt to forecast probable loss at the time of contracting, many courts also evaluate the relationship of the liquidated damages to the actual loss ultimately suffered, and uphold the clause if the liquidated damages are reasonably equivalent to actual loss. If a liquidated damages provision does not meet these standards, it is treated as a penalty and is unenforceable. *See also* Penalty.

Liquidated debt. A debt is liquidated when its monetary value is certain and fixed. In the context of damages for breach of contract, damages normally become liquidated once the breach has occurred, provided that the damages can be calculated by arithmetical means. If the determination of damages cannot be made purely by arithmetical calculation (for example, because there are factual issues relating to the extent of damages), the damages only become liquidated once the factfinder (commonly the jury) has assessed them.

Lost volume. If a seller of goods or services has the capacity to supply the full demand for those goods or services, a breach by one buyer is not substituted for by a subsequent sale of the goods or services to another customer who would have bought the goods or services in any event. The breach has caused a loss in the volume of the seller's sales and can only be compensated for by an award of lost profits.

Mailbox rule. (Also known as the "deposited acceptance rule.") Where an offer expressly or impliedly authorizes acceptance through the mail or an analogous noninstantaneous means of communication, and does not specify that acceptance takes effect only on receipt, the acceptance takes effect as soon as it is properly dispatched and cannot be recalled by the offeree.

Manifested intent. The apparent state of mind of a party, as demonstrated by the party's observable conduct or spoken or recorded words. *See also* Objective/objective test.

Material benefit/moral obligation rule. A doctrine that permits enforcement of a promise without present consideration where the promise is made in recognition of a substantial benefit previously conferred on the promisor by the promisee, and enforcement is needed to prevent injustice. Because this doctrine is grounded in the idea that the promisor is morally obliged to honor a promise to pay for the prior benefit, it is sometimes called "moral obligation." This is an ambiguous term, and can easily be confused with the different usage of "moral obligation," which means simply that the obligation in question is binding only in conscience and is not capable of being legally enforced.

Materiality/material term/material breach. A term of a contract is material if it is an important component of the contract, so central to the values exchanged that it is a fundamental basis of the bargain between the parties. A material breach is a violation of a party's obligations under the contract, so serious that it defeats the other party's reasonable expectations under the contract by substantially depriving that party of the value of the transaction. Materiality is sometimes obvious, but in less clear-cut cases, it must be determined by interpreting the contract.

Merchantable. Goods are merchantable if they meet minimum acceptable trade standards, and would be regarded as of adequate quality by a reasonable member of the trade.

Merger clause. A provision in a recorded agreement declaring that the writing contains all the terms agreed on by the parties, and that no terms, other than those expressed in the writing have been agreed to. Such a provision is called a "merger clause" because its purpose is to merge all the agreed terms into the writing, so that the writing becomes the full and complete record of what was agreed. A merger clause is a strong barrier to either party later alleging that terms exist beyond those expressed in the writing.

Mirror image rule. (Also known as ribbon matching rule.) A rule that requires an acceptance to match the offer exactly, with no alteration or qualification. Under this rule, if the acceptance deviates from the offer in any way it does not qualify as an acceptance. Many courts no longer apply the mirror image rule rigorously, but adopt a more flexible approach under which the response to an offer may qualify as an acceptance if its divergence from the offer is not material. In sales of goods, the rule is clearly abrogated by UCC §2.207.

Misrepresentation. An assertion not in accordance with the truth. If the misrepresentation is made with scienter—knowledge of its falsity and intent to mislead—it is fraudulent. If it is made without scienter, it may be either negligent (the party making it would have known of its falsity by taking reasonable care in ascertaining the truth) or innocent (the party did not breach a duty of care by failing to ascertain the truth, but is nevertheless liable for the misrepresentation by virtue of an express or implied contractual promise). *See also* Fraud in the inducement.

Mistake. An error concerning a fact existing at the time of contracting. If the mistake relates to a common, shared assumption of the parties it is mutual, but if the error concerns a fact that is a basic assumption of only one of the parties, it is unilateral. A mistake is grounds for avoiding a contract if it satisfies the requirements of relief.

Mitigation of damages. Following the breach of contract by a party, the other party's action to avoid or reduce the loss resulting from the breach.

Moral obligation. *See* Material benefit/moral obligation rule.

Mutual mistake. *See* Mistake.

Mutuality of obligation. When consideration consists of the exchange of promises, the commitment on both sides must be real and meaningful. If the apparent promise of one of the parties is illusory—so qualified or discretionary as to be no commitment at all—that party is not bound by the apparent promise. This means that the party's promise was not consideration, so that no valid contract was formed. Courts sometimes express this principle by saying that the contract lacked mutuality of obligation—if one party is not bound (because that party gave no consideration), neither is bound (because that lack of consideration voids the contract).

Noscitur a sociis. (Latin: "known from its associates.") A rule of interpretation under which the meaning of each individual word in a series is affected by and affects the meaning of the other words in that series.

Novation. A contract under which an existing contractual duty is discharged and a completely new one is substituted. The new contract may add a party who was not a party to the original contract.

Objective/objective test. Something is objective if it is presented to the consciousness, rather than subjective—within the consciousness itself. That is, it is external to the mind rather than within it. In contract law, the word is most commonly applied to describe the legal standard for gauging the state of mind—the intent or understanding—of a party. Therefore, the objective test determines intent on the basis of the reasonable meaning of the observable, external evidence of the party's words or conduct, rather than on the basis of what the party thought or believed. *See also* Reasonableness/reasonable person standard; Subjective standard.

Objective value. *See* Subjective/objective value.

Obligor/obligee. An obligor is a person who owes an obligation or debt, and an obligee is a person to whom it is owed. In a bilateral contract, each party is an obligor with regard to the performance that it promised, and an obligee with regard to the performance that is due to it.

Officious intermeddler. In the context of unjust enrichment, a person who imposes an unsolicited benefit on another in the absence of emergency circumstances that would have justified the conferral of an unrequested benefit.

Option. An offeror's legally binding promise to keep an offer open for a period of time. A valid option eliminates the offeror's usual power to revoke the offer during the duration of the option.

Output contract. *See* Requirements/output contracts.

Overhead. *See* Fixed and variable costs.

Pacta sunt servanda. (Latin: "agreements must be kept.") This phrase asserts the moral imperative that the law should enforce contractual promises.

Parol evidence. Evidence of alleged terms not included in the recorded memorandum of agreement, but claimed by one of the parties to have been agreed to orally before or at the time of execution of the record, or in a prior recorded communication.

Partial breach. A breach that is not, or has not yet become, significant enough to qualify as a total and material breach. A party who has substantially performed commits a partial breach, but even where performance is not substantial and the breach is potentially material, it is a partial breach if the breaching party is able to avert it by an effective cure.

Partial integration. *See* Integration: total or partial.

Penalty. A provision in a contract that is designed to impose, or has the effect of imposing, a burden or punishment on a party for breaching, beyond any actual or expected loss that may be suffered by the victim of the breach.

Positivism. A legal philosophy that stresses the primacy of legal rules and considers the courts' principal role as the application of settled rules to the facts of individual cases.

Precedent. *See* Stare decisis.

Preexisting duty rule. A rule of consideration doctrine that performance of or promise to perform an existing duty already owed to the other party cannot qualify as consideration. Consideration consists of an exchange of legal detriments—each party must relinquish a legal right in exchange for the promise or performance received from the other. Therefore, if a party already has a legal duty to do or refrain from doing something, that party's promise to do or refrain from that very act is no relinquishment of a right and cannot be a detriment.

Primary/secondary authority. Primary authority consists of authorities, such as statutes and binding judicial precedents, which must be followed by a court. Secondary authority consists of non-binding judicial decisions and commentary on the law, such as Restatement provisions, law review articles, and textbooks, that the court is not required to follow, but may have persuasive weight.

Promise. An undertaking to act or refrain from acting in a specified way at some future time.

Promisor/promisee. A promisor is a person who makes a promise, and a promisee is a person to whom a promise is made. In a bilateral contract, each party is both a promisor of the performance it has promised to the other party, and a promisee of the return performance promised to it by the other party. When consideration is in issue, the person whose promise is sought to be enforced (and whose consideration is not in doubt) is referred to as the promisor, and the promisee is the party whose consideration is in question. In the context of a contract for the benefit of a third party, the promisor is the party who is to perform in favor of the beneficiary, and the promisee is the other party to the contract who has called for the performance to be rendered to the beneficiary.

Promissory condition. *See* Condition.

Promissory estoppel. A doctrine, derived from equitable estoppel, under which a court has the discretion to enforce a noncontractual promise made with the intention of inducing reliance, and justifiably and detrimentally relied on by the promisee. Depending on the needs of justice, the promise may be enforced fully, or only to the extent necessary to reimburse wasted costs and expenses.

Prospectivenonperformance/adequateassuranceofperformance. Words or conduct by a party prior to the due date of performance, or other circumstances arising before that due date, may indicate the likelihood or possibility of breach when the time for performance arrives. Although the signs of possible future breach are not clear and strong enough to be a repudiation, they may suggest the prospect of material breach, and may give the other party reasonable grounds for feeling insecure about receiving the promised performance. If such insecurity is justified, the insecure party may demand an adequate assurance of performance, and if none is given, may treat the failure to furnish adequate assurance as a repudiation. *See also* Anticipatory Repudiation.

Punitive/exemplary damages. Damages awarded to a plaintiff that go beyond the amount needed to compensate for loss and are designed to punish the defendant for particularly egregious intentional or reckless behavior. Punitive damages are sometimes called exemplary damages because they make an example of the defendant, thereby creating a disincentive to others to engage in that conduct in the future.

Pure condition. *See* Condition.

Quantum meruit/quantum valebant. Quantum meruit (Latin: "as much as deserved") is the term used to denote the market value of services. Quantum valebant ("as much as they are worth") signifies the market value of goods. Market value is the common means of measuring the value of goods or services either in restitutionary claims or where a contract is based on a reasonable, rather than a specified price.

Quasi. A Latin word meaning "as if." This word, when used to qualify another (such as "quasi-contract") signifies that the word or concept so qualified ("contract") is seemingly like, but is not actually like the real word or concept (an actual contract). For example, a quasi-judicial act is not one by an actual judge, but one by an administrative agency performing an adjudicative function. In some situations, the denomination "quasi" is used to signal that a legal fiction is being used. For example, "quasi-contract" is used to describe a cause of action for unjust enrichment, which is not based on a real contract. This is the legacy of a legal fiction developed in early common law to allow a claim of unjust enrichment to be fitted into the form of action for contract.

Quasi-contract (quasi ex contractu). *See* Implied-in-law contract.

Realism. *See* Legal realism.

Reasonable expectations. A party's expectations about the performance and benefit of a contract, evaluated not on the basis of what the party claims to have actually expected, but on the basis of what the party should have expected as a reasonable person. *See also* Reasonableness/ reasonable person standard.

Reasonableness/reasonable person standard. A widely used standard in many areas of law. In contract law, this standard holds a party accountable for the reasonable import of the party's words and actions. The meaning of a party's words, or its intention, understanding, or conduct is evaluated on the basis of what a reasonable person in the party's position would have meant, understood, or done. The reasonable person is a hypothetical construct, based on a community standard, typically represented by the jury. *See also* Objective/objective test.

Record/Recorded. A contract or other document contained in a retrievable record, either in the form of a tangible writing or an electronic or other record.

Reformation. Where, as a result of mistake or error in transcription, a recorded contract does not correctly reflect the parties' true agreement, the court may grant the equitable remedy of reformation to correct the recorded memorandum of agreement so that it reflects the actual agreement between the parties.

Reliance damages. Those costs and expenses incurred in reliance on the contract (or, in promissory estoppel, in reliance on the promise) and wasted or not recouped once the contract (or promise) is breached. If the cost or expense is incurred in performing duties required by the contract, it is direct or essential reliance. If the cost or expense is incurred for the purpose of enjoying or using a benefit reasonably expected from the contract, it is incidental reliance.

Repudiation. *See* Anticipatory repudiation.

Requirements/output contracts. A requirements contract is flexible as to the quantity of goods or the extent of services to be supplied, which is based on the buyer's requirements for the goods or services during the contract period. That is, the buyer agrees to buy all its requirements for the goods or services from the seller during the term of the contract, and the seller agrees to supply whatever the buyer orders. The buyer's discretion to fix quantity is limited by an obligation to act reasonably and in good faith and may also be limited by a stated or customary range of demand. An output contract is similar, but the flexible quantity is based on the seller's production rather than the buyer's requirements. That is, the seller agrees to sell and the buyer agrees to buy the seller's entire output of goods or services during the contract period. Again, the seller's discretion to fix production levels is limited by an obligation to act reasonably and in good faith and may also be limited by a stated or customary range of demand.

Rescission. Broadly speaking, rescission is the cancellation of a contract, but its exact meaning depends on the context. It could mean the cancellation of a contract by mutual consent. It is also commonly used to mean the avoidance of a contract by one party on grounds such as fraud or mistake. "Rescission" is also used as a synonym for "termination" where the victim of a material and total breach ends the contractual relationship, withholds further performance, and sues for damages.

Restitution. A judicial remedy under which the court grants judgment for the restoration of property (specific restitution) or its value (monetary restitution) to a party from whom the property was unjustly taken or has been unjustly retained.

Ribbon matching rule. *See* Mirror image rule.

Rolling contract. A contract that is not concluded at the point of purchase but becomes binding only at some later stage, after the nondrafting party has had the opportunity to review and signify assent to standard terms drafted by the drafting party.

Scienter. A central element of fraud, consisting of knowledge of the falsity of an assertion combined with an intent to mislead.

Scrollwrap. *See* Clickwrap.

Seal. A wax impression or other insignia placed on paper by a person for the purpose of authenticating the document. In earlier law, a contract executed under seal did not require consideration, but this formal means of dispensing with the need for consideration has fallen away in most jurisdictions.

Secondary authority. *See* Primary/secondary authority.

Security interest. An interest in property (such as a mortgage), granted by a debtor to a creditor to secure payment of the debt. If the debtor defaults in payment, the creditor is entitled to foreclose on the property and sell it to satisfy the debt.

Security of transactions. The concept that the enforcement of individual contracts—and hence the protection of reliance on individual transactions—creates a broad sense of reliance throughout the economy, which facilitates market activity by promoting general confidence in the reliability of contractual undertakings.

Severability. A term in a contract is said to be severable if it can be removed from the contract or adjusted without significantly impairing the basis and purpose of the contract. *Compare* Divisibility.

Sheriff. *See* Execution.

Shrinkwrap. Standard contract terms set out in a document included in the packaging of a product or in software. Because the terms are included with the packaged product or software, they are not likely to come to the attention of the purchaser until after the container is opened or the software is downloaded.

Signature. A mark or symbol, or an electronic means of identification, executed or adopted by a party with the intention of authenticating a record.

Special damages. In contract law, special damages are consequential losses that are not reasonably foreseeable by the breaching party as an obvious and natural consequence of the breach because they result from the special circumstances of the aggrieved party. Therefore, the aggrieved party cannot claim them unless the breaching party knew or had reason to know of those special circumstances at the time of contracting. *See also* Foreseen/foreseeable.

Specific performance. An order by the court directing the breaching party to render the contractual performance as promised. Specific performance is an equitable remedy, and is available only where damages are not an adequate remedy and the equities favor it.

Stare decisis. (Latin: "The decision stands.") The doctrine of precedent, under which a court must follow the legal rule established in a previous case by a court senior enough in the judicial hierarchy to bind the court deciding the subsequent case.

Standard terms/standard contract. Standard contract terms are drafted in advance of contracting and are used in many transactions of the same kind. They may be set out in a recorded contract, a website, an invoice, ticket, or in some other form. *See also* Boilerplate

Subjective standard. A test of intent based on what a party actually understood or meant, rather than on the party's objectively manifested intent, as reasonably interpreted. The subjective standard is not used as a general test of intent, which is determined objectively. However, subjective intent is sometimes relevant, for example, when a party's good faith is in issue. *See also* Objective/objective test.

Subjective/objective value. The subjective value of property or services to the recipient is the value to that particular recipient, based on the recipient's situation. Objective value, the more common means of valuing property or services, is measured by the market value of the property or services.

Substantial performance. A performance under a contract that, while not fully in compliance with the contract (and therefore a breach), is nevertheless not deficient in a material way. Because the breach is not material, the aggrieved party may not use it as a ground for rescinding the contract, but is confined to claiming monetary compensation for the shortfall in performance.

Surety. A person who, at the request of a debtor, enters into an undertaking with the creditor to pay the debtor's debt, or otherwise perform the debtor's obligations, if the debtor fails to pay or perform.

Take-or-pay provision. A term in a contract under which the buyer of goods or services commits to take a specified minimum quantity, and promises to pay for that minimum quantity whether or not the buyer actually orders it. A take-or-pay provision may be interpreted as a penalty and could be unenforceable on that ground. *See* Penalty.

Tender. An offer of payment or performance by a party who is ready, willing, and able to render it.

Termination of contract. A general term for the cancellation or rescission of a contract, which could be by mutual consent, or by one of the parties exercising a termination right provided for in the contract, or where one of the parties has grounds to rescind the contract. *See also* Rescission.

Third-party beneficiary. A person who is not a party to a contract but on whom the parties intend to confer the benefit of performance together with an independent right to enforce that performance. A party on whom this independent right of enforcement is conferred is called an intended beneficiary. A non-party who fortuitously acquires an incidental benefit from the contract, without any intent of the parties to confer an enforcement right on that non-party is merely an incidental beneficiary and has no right to sue on the contract.

"Time is of the essence." A phrase that means that performance within the time specified is a material term of the contract, and that any delay will be a total and material breach of contract.

Total breach. A breach of contract that is both material and incurable, entitling the aggrieved party to rescind the contract and claim full expectation relief.

Trade usage. *See* Usage.

Transaction costs. The costs incurred in entering a transaction. When a contract has been breached, the transaction costs resulting from the breach include expenses such as the aggrieved party's costs in finding a substitute, the breaching party's costs in entering the other transaction perceived as more desirable, and the costs to both parties in negotiating a settlement of the plaintiff's claim or in litigating it. To decide if the breach is efficient, these costs must be deducted from the potential gains flowing from the breach. *See also* Efficient breach.

UETA. The Uniform Electronic Transactions Act, a uniform model law, promulgated in 1999, and subsequently adopted by most states, to validate electronic signatures and records. *See also* E-SIGN.

Unconscionable. A concept, derived from equity, but now also applicable in suits at law, under which a court may use its discretion to refuse enforcement of a term or contract that shocks its conscience. In its modern formulation, unconscionability normally consists of both a procedural element (unfair bargaining) and a substantive element (resulting unfair terms).

Unenforceable. A contract or term is unenforceable if it contains some defect that precludes its enforcement by a court. (For example, a contract that is subject to the statute of frauds, but does not comply with it.) An unenforceable contract or term is distinguishable from a void contract in that it is not a legal nullity. However, this distinction is not practically significant in most cases because the end result is that the party relying on the unenforceable contract or term cannot obtain a remedy for its breach. *Compare* Void/voidable.

Unfair forfeiture. A general principle of justice under which the court has the discretion to temper the enforcement of the injured party's legal rights to avoid a disproportionately harsh impact on the party against whom enforcement is sought.

Unforeseeable/unforeseen. *See* Foreseen/foreseeable.

Unilateral contract. "Unilateral" does not mean a one-sided promise by one person to another without any promise or performance exchanged in return. This would not qualify as a contract because it lacks consideration. Rather, a unilateral contract is one in which only one of the parties has a promise outstanding at the time that the contract is formed. It is distinct from a bilateral contract, in which there are promises due by both parties at the instant of formation. A unilateral contract is created where an offer prescribes or permits the act of acceptance to be the offeree's rendition of the very performance that will constitute the offeree's consideration under the contract. When the offeree renders the performance called for by the contract, it simultaneously accepts the offer and completes its performance—acceptance is signified by the act of performance. The effect of this is that at the instance of acceptance, the offeree has completed the performance of its side of the transaction, and the only thing remaining is the offeror's promise of return performance. *See also* Bilateral contract.

UNIDROIT Principles of International Commercial Contracts. A compilation of general rules and common principles of contract law that are recommended as applicable to transnational commercial contracts.

Unilateral mistake. *See* Mistake.

United Nations Convention on Contracts for the International Sale of Goods. *See* CISG.

Usage. The customs and established practices in a particular trade, industry, or market.

Ut res magis valeat quam pereat. (Latin: "The thing should rather have effect than be destroyed.") A rule of interpretation under which a court resolves uncertainty in favor of a meaning that is lawful, reasonable, and congruent with public policy.

Variable costs. *See* Fixed and variable costs.

Vesting. The irrevocable settling of rights on a person.

Void/voidable. A contract or term is void if it has no legal effect. It is a legal nullity and cannot be enforced by either party. A void contract must be distinguished from a voidable (or avoidable) contract, in which one of the parties has the election either to enforce the contract, or to rescind it. *See also* Avoidable Contract.

Volunteer. In the context of unjust enrichment, a person who confers a benefit with gratuitous intent.

Waiver. A voluntary abandonment of a legal right.

Windfall. An unexpected and undeserved benefit. In the context of damages, an amount that exceeds what the plaintiff needs to be fully compensated for the loss resulting from the breach.

Writ. An order by a court, requiring or authorizing an act to be performed. A writ of execution or garnishment is an order to the sheriff or equivalent official, requiring the seizure of property of the judgment debtor. *See also* Execution.

Table of Cases

Table of Cases

Table of Statutes

Miscellaneous Statutes

Index

References are to sections. References to Examples and Explanations are designated by the letter "E" followed by the chapter number and the Example number (e.g., "E1-2" refers to Chapter 1, Example 2).

Index

Index